A Grammar of Abkhaz

Tamio Yanagisawa

A Grammar of Abkhaz

Hituzi Syobo Publishing

First published 2013

Author: Tamio Yanagisawa

Hituzi Syobo Publishing
Yamato bldg. 2F, 2-1-2 Sengoku Bunkyo-ku Tokyo, Japan
112-0011

phone +81-3-5319-4916 fax +81-3-5319-4917
e-mail: toiawase@hituzi.co.jp
http://www.hituzi.co.jp/
postal transfer 00120-8-142852

ISBN 978-4-89476-635-8
Printed in Japan

Dedicated to the memory of
Anna Tsvinaria (1933–2008)

Аўаҩы дыпђс́ойт, ах̬а азºа пђс́ом.
‘People die, but words do not.’

Preface

I wish to offer special thanks to the Japan Society for the Promotion of Science, as this grammar has been published with the help of a Grant-in-Aid for Publication of Scientific Research Results (No. 245071).

This is a descriptive grammar of the Abkhaz language, one of the Northwest Caucasian languages, which is spoken by about 100,000 people in the Autonomous Republic of Abkhazia. It covers phonology, morphology, and syntax. Since Abkhaz is a polysynthetic language, efforts were made to comprehensively describe verbal morphology in particular, including accent shifts. In addition, an outline of the Bzyp dialect, a dialect in the northern area, as well as folk texts, have also been added to this volume.

The present book has the same plan as the author's *Analytic Dictionary of Abkhaz* (2010). It is an exhaustive description of the Abkhaz verbal complexes based on data from the author's own field notes. The author collected some data on Abkhaz from 1997 in Georgia, and worked intensively on the language from 2000 to 2006. The morphology portion of the present book is based on material mainly collected from my consultant Anna Tsvinaria. In particular, all of the word-stresses presented in this book have been marked based on criteria provided by her.

This book is not written in any set theoretical framework. I wanted to write this grammar based on the principles of the traditional work like Sanskrit and Greek grammars. However, I have adopted some of the time-tested results of Dixon's 'basic linguistic theory'—the theory of linguistics as a natural science, because Abkhaz has fairly different linguistic structures from the Indo-European languages. Also, I adopted the traditional grammatical categories used by Abkhazian and Georgian specialists of Abkhaz.

I wish to thank my Abkhaz teacher and consultant, the late Anna Tsvinaria-Abramishvili. She was born in the village of K'ut'ol in the Ochamchira district, and died in 2008 in Tbilisi. She was a native speaker of the Abzhywa dialect of Abkhaz. I also owe a debt of gratitude to Sh. Xj. Salaq'aja and S. Zyxwba, editors of the following folktale collections/anthologies: *Аҧсуа жәлар рҿаҧыцҭә рҿиамҭа. Ахрестоматиа.* Аҟуа: Қарҭ and *Аҧсуа лакуқуа*. Аҟуа: Алашара.

For their invaluable assistance in the publishing of this book, I owe a great debt to a number of people. Mr. Isao Matumoto, the president of Hituzi Syobo Publishing, supported me in the publishing of this book, and Miss Shiori Bando, an editor at Hituzi Syobo, patiently edited the manuscript. Miss Maria Kolko and Miss Astghik Movsisyan offered me much practical assistance and helpful comments.

Finally, knowledgeable colleagues have generously contributed comments on topics in this book, especially Professor B. George Hewitt of London University and his wife Mrs. Zaira Khiba Hewitt, who is from the town of Ochamchira, and Dr. Viacheslav A. Chirikba.

Tamio Yanagisawa
Nagoya University
December 2012

Contents

Abbreviations and Symbols

A = the subject of a transitive verb (in Dixon's terminology)

AAD = (Abkhaz-Abkhaz Dictionary) = Шакрыл, К. С., Конджария, В. Х. 1986. & Шакрыл, К. С., Конджария, В. Х. Чкадуа, Л. П. 1987. *Словарь абхазского языка. (Аҧсуа бызшәа ажәа).*

Abs = absolutive

Abkhaz text = (1) Зыхуба, С. (ed.) 1997. *Аҧсуа лакуқуа*. (2) Салаҟаиа, Ш. Хь. (ed.) 1975. *Аҧсуа жәлар рҿаҧыцтә рҿиамҭа. Ахрестоматиа.*

Abzh. = Abzhywa dialect

ACST = Hewitt, B. G. (2010) *Abkhaz: a Comprehensive Self-Tutor.*

AF = Hewitt, B. G. 2005a. *Abkhazian Folktales.*

AFL = (Abkhaz as a Foreign Language) Ашуба, Н. К., Ажиба, А. Ш. 1997. *Аҧсуа бызшәа тәым бызшәак еиҧш (апрограммеи арҵагеи).*

ANR = Hewitt, B. G., Khiba, Z. 1998a. *Abkhaz Newspaper Reader.*

Aor = aorist

AP = accent paradigm

ARD = (Abkhaz-Russian Dictionary) = Касландзия, В. А. (ed.) 2005. *Абхазско-русский словарь.*

bz. = bzyp dialect

C = column

C1 = the first column

C2 = the second column

C3 = the third column

Caus = causative

Cond.I = conditional I

Cond.II = conditional II

dial. = dialect

DO = direct object

Dyn = dynamic

Emph = emphasis

Evid = evidential

F = feminine

Fin = finite

Fut = future

Fut.I = future I

Fut.II = future II

GAL = (A Grammar of the Abkhaz Language) = Аристава, Ш. К. и др. 1968. *Грамматика абхазского языка: фонетика и морфология.*

Genko = Генко, А. Н. 1998. *Абхазско-русский словарь.*

Hum = human

IC = (Intensive Course in the Abkhaz Language) Шинкуба, А. Ш. 2003. *Интенсивный курс абхазского языка.*

Imp = imperative

Impf = imperfect

Ind = indefinite

Instr = instrumental
intr. = intransitive
IO = indirect object
LA = suffix lak’^{j}
Loc = locative
M = masculine
Masd /masd. = masdar
Neg = negative
NF = non-finite
Non-Hum = non-human
Nonvol = non-volitional
NS = numeral suffix
O = the object of a transitive verb
Opt = optative
OV = objective version
Par = prefixal particle
Past.Ind = past indefinite
Perf = perfect
Pl = plural
Plupf = pluperfect
Poss = possessive
Pot = potential
Pres = present
Prev = preverb
Proh = prohibition
Purp = purpose
Qu = interrogative suffix
R = root
RAD = (Russian-Abkhaz Dictionary) = Бгажба, Х. С. (ed.) 1964. *Русско-абхазский словарь.*
Rec = reciprocal
Rel = relative
S = (1) the subject of an intransitive verb. (2) subject (a universal grouping of A and S)
SA = standard Abkhaz
Self = reflexive
Sg = singular
SP = speech-particle
Stat = stative
Subj = subjunctive
SV = subjective version
tr. = transitive
Vers = version
1 = 1st person
2 = 2nd person
3 = 3rd person
* = 1) ungrammaticality, 2) unattested
< = comes from

→ = becomes
ϕ = zero (morpheme)

Part I : A Grammar of Abkhaz

0. Introduction

0.1. Abkhazians and the Abkhaz language

0.1.1. Abkhazians and Abkhazia

The Northwest Caucasian ethnic group is comprised of Circassians, Ubykhs, Abkhazians and Abazians. Prior to the conquest of the North Caucasus by Russia in 1864, they lived in the area stretching from the Kuban River in the north to the Ingur River to the south along the coast of the Black Sea; however, after the complete Russian subjugation of the Caucasus in 1864, the majority of the Northwest Caucasians escaped to the Ottoman Empire. This led to a loss of sixty per cent of the population of Abkhazia by the end of the 19th century.[1] Abkhazia was incorporated into the Soviet Union after the Russian Revolution of 1917 and its submission to Georgia was promoted under the name of the Autonomous Republic of Abkhazia. The use of Abkhaz was conspicuously suppressed during the Stalin period when Georgian was imposed as the official language. In addition, the Georgian ethnic group was encouraged to migrate to Abkhazia. Tensions mounted between the Abkhazian and Georgian ethnic groups amidst this background. With the collapse of the Soviet Union at the end of the 20th century, the Georgian-Abkhaz War between the newly independent Republic of Georgia and Abkhazia erupted in 1992–93 in a push for Abkhazian independence. During this period many Abkhazians left their homeland and migrated to Russia and other countries. In addition, many Georgians in Abkhazia escaped to Georgia. A ceasefire agreement was concluded between Abkhazia and Georgia in 1994 and at the present time a UN peacekeeping force is monitoring the truce. At present, Abkhazia has achieved independence in practice as the Autonomous Republic of Abkhazia; however, it remains an internationally unrecognised country, with only a few nations including Russia acknowledging it. According to a 1989 census, the population of Abkhazians was 102,938 with 93,267 people living in Abkhazia.

0.1.2. Abkhaz among the Northwest Caucasian languages

The languages affiliated with the Northwest Caucasian languages are: Abkhaz, Abaza, Adyghe, Kabardian and Ubykh. Of these, Abkhaz and Abaza constitute the Abkhaz-Abaza language group, while Adyghe and Kabardian form the kindred Circassian group. Ubykh is positioned in the middle of both groups.[2]

---

1. See Chirikba (2003a: 6).
2. The Ubykhs migrated to Turkey after Russia subjugated the Northern Caucasus in 1864. As a result of this,

0. Introduction

It has been posited that the Proto-Northwest Caucasian first split from the Proto-Circassian and Proto-Ubykh-Abkhaz which later divided further into Ubykh and Abkhaz.[3]

Abkhaz and Abaza form a single language unit in the strictest linguistic sense; however, they are currently treated as two languages. First of all, Abkhaz is divided into the two subdialects of South-eastern Abkhaz and South-western Abkhaz. The Abzhywa (the dialect which spread southward from Sukhum), Bzyp (which expanded northward from Sukhum) and Ahchypsy dialects are related to the South-eastern Abkhaz. The Sadz dialect which exists in the Republic of Turkey is affiliated with the South-western Abkhaz dialect. Among these, the dialect which formed the base for the Abkhaz literary language was the Abzhywa dialect, and materials procured from consultants from Abkhaz-speaking areas were used in this book.[4] On the other side, Abaza branches into the Tapanta and Ashkharywa dialects.

Circassian is divided into two languages: Western Circassian (Adyghe) and Eastern Circassian (Kabardian). Among these, Adyghe is the product of four dialects. More precisely, it is drawn from the Bzhedugh and Shapsug(h) dialects affiliated with the western dialect and the Abadzekh (or Abzakh) and Temirgoi dialects akin to the eastern dialect. The Adyghe literary language was created based upon the Temirgoi dialect. The Shapsug(h) dialect is that which is spoken in the environs of Düzce town located between Istanbul and Ankara in the Republic of Turkey. Although these Northwest Caucasian languages are mutually genetically related, the genetic relationships between these languages and the other Caucasian languages (i.e. the Kartvelian languages and Nakh-Daghestanian languages) are unclear.[5]

---

their native Ubykh language became rapidly assimilated into the Turkish tongue and at present it is believed that there are no surviving speakers of Ubykh. Esenç Tevfik, who was said to be the last speaker of Ubykh and who cooperated with Georges Dumézil, passed away in 1992. [Comrie, B., S. Matthews, M. Polinsky. *The Atlas of Languages*. 1996. p.51.; John Colarusso. How Many Consonants does Ubykh Have? p.145. In: (ed.) G. Hewitt. 1992. *Caucasian Perspectives*. Lincom Europa.]

3. See Chirikba (2003a: 11).

4. It must be borne in mind that although our consultant is from an area where the Abzhywa dialect is spoken, it cannot be assumed that all of the language characteristics of the consultant are those of the dialect. The consultant has been strongly influenced by the standard Abkhaz language through opportunities for communication such as publications and broadcasts as well as the effects of education, and in particular, the importance of written Abkhaz in the case of our consultant, who is an intellectual person. The consultant always placed phonetic or grammatical criteria in the Abkhaz literary language with regard to our language survey.

5. See Klimov (1986: 109–141). In addition, T.V. Gamkrelidze stated the following with regard to the kinship relationship between the Kartvelian languages and the North Caucasian languages: 'if one were to trace the correspondence of the regular character (i.e., the correspondence that is not the results of matches due to accidence or borrowed terms) in the substance of significant components, that is, of roots and affixal morphemes, between the Kartvelian languages and the North Caucasian languages, the existence of regular sound(phoneme)-correspondences between the Kartvelian languages and the North Caucasian languages would be evident without fail. However, since such phoneme-correspondences have not yet appeared between the individual groups of the Caucasian languages (between both Kartvelian, on the one hand, and Abkhaz-Adyghe languages and Nakh-Daghestanian languages, on the other), it is far too early to speculate that there is 'a material correspondence of morphemes' between them.' (Гамкрелидзе, Т.В. 1971. Соверменная диахроническая лингвистика и картвельские языки. II. In: *ВЯ*. No.3. pp. 43–44.)

0.1.3. The Changes in Abkhaz Characters and the Research History of the Abkhaz Language

0.1.3.1. Although there are fragmentary materials with mention of the Northwest Caucasian languages (including those thought to be the Sadz dialect of Abkhaz) by travellers prior to the 19th century, the Abkhaz language was one without written characters until the middle of the 19th century. The first scholarly account of Abkhaz was done by the Russian Baron Petr Karlovich Uslar (1816–1875) who also created the letters for the language.[6] Uslar was stationed on military duty in the Caucasus in 1837 after completing Central Engineering School. He temporarily left the Caucasus in 1840 and entered an army college after which he worked on the statistical records of guberniya Tver and guberniya Vologod. He returned to the Caucasus in 1850 to work on the statistical records of guberniya Erivan. The Tsar issued a royal command to Uslar in 1858 to create a historical compendium of the Caucasus; however, he set about researching the Caucasian languages, rationalizing that 'the actual study of ethnic groups cannot be undertaken without an understanding of their languages'. He had already earlier voiced his ideas on an alphabet for the Caucasus languages which lacked sufficient characters in 1861, and had knowledge of Mingrelian, Svan, Chechen, Ubykh and Avar. He published his research on Abkhaz in May 1862 and that on Chechen the following year. The Abkhaz research appeared in 1862 as a lithographic printing, and was published posthumously as the 'Ethnography of Caucasia. Linguistics. Abkhaz' in 1887.[7] Uslar used Russian characters as a base and referenced them with Latin and Georgian, adding original symbols used as letters to describe the Bzyp dialect of Abkhaz. There are 67 consonants in Bzyp; however, in Uslar's 'Abkhaz' only 55 characters are used in total including those for the vowels. Although Uslar was unable to accurately classify the sounds of Bzyp in this way, his Abkhaz research has been valuable to this day not only for the description of its grammar, but also for its precise details of accents. In addition, the Abkhaz characters he invented also greatly influenced the Abkhaz characters which came later. Let us examine an example in Uslar's description that illustrates his accuracy still for the present day. For example, Uslar points out that even though a verb may possess the meaning of a transitive verb in translation, it must be considered as an intransitive verb depending upon the position of the verb affixation as follows:

> càçyejт (root aç) would probably be translated as, *бью* ['I hit']; however, it originally meant *колочу* ['I strike/batter'], and in this case as well, it would not be *колочу кого-нибудь* ('I strike someone (tr.)'), but *колочу по комъ-нибудь* ['I strike on/at someone (intr.)'].[8]

---

6. Apart from Abkhaz, Uslar also described Chechen, Avar, Lak, Dargwa, Lezgian and Tabasaran, publishing them in the form of 'Ethnography of the Caucasus' (Tabasaran has been recently published in rough draft form): Услар, Петр Карлович. 1887. *Этнография Кавказа. Языкознание 1. Абхазский язык.* Тифлис. [Reprint. Sukhum. 2002]; Услар, П.К. 1888. *Этнография Кавказа. Языкознание 2. Чеченский язык.* Тифлис.; Услар, П.К. 1989. *Этнография Кавказа. Языкознание 3. Аварский язык.* Тифлис.; Услар, П.К. 1890. *Этнография Кавказа. Языкознание 4. Лакский язык.* Тифлис.; Услар, П.К. 1892. *Этнография Кавказа. Языкознание 5. Хюркилинский язык.* Тифлис.; Услар, П.К. 1896. *Этнография Кавказа. Языкознание 6. Кюриский язык.* Тифлис.; Услар, П.К. 1979. *Этнография Кавказа. Языкознание 7. Табасаранский язык.* Тифлис.

7. Усларъ, П.К. 1887. *Этнографія Кавказа. Языкознаніе. Абхазскій языкъ.* Тифлисъ. [Reprint. Sukhum. 2002]

8. ibid. p. 58.

The grammatical analysis by Uslar and the position of the accent completely matches the verb form of the modern-day Abzhywa considered in this document. It can be notated and analysed in standard Abkhaz as follows: сáсуеит /s-á-s-wa-jt'/ (I-it-hit-Dyn-Fin) 'I hit it'. This form is an intransitive verb, as Uslar mentioned. (Cf. §3.2.5.)

The literary language of Abkhaz saw its birth from the 19th through the early 20th century following in the steps of Uslar's monumental Abkhaz research and translations of primary school readers, folk tales and religious books began to be published in it (the Abkhaz used during this period was based on Bzyp). Education in Abkhaz was introduced in 1892 and initially the 51 character notational system of D.I. Gulia and K. Mach'avariani was used in teaching,[9] later progressing to the 55 character notational convention developed by the Abkhazian Andrej Ch'och'ua during the years from 1909 to 1926.[10] However, the real establishment of the Abkhaz literary language and its character reforms came about under the Soviet administration. The Soviet regime needed to entrench the Abkhaz literary language, and the character revisions which accompanied it, for propaganda purposes. The founder of Abkhaz literature, D.I. Gulia, as well as other authors, educators and social activists played an active part during this period, and the majority of them were from Abzhywa areas with the simpler phonemic system of Abzhywa as compared to Bzyp. This is one of the main reasons why the Abkhaz literary language was based upon Abzhywa. It was during this period that the Abkhaz characters were revised. Nikolaj Jakovlevich Marr (1864/5–1934) was the first to devise a unique Abkhaz character system within the latinization of 'Young Written Languages' during the early Soviet administration. Marr used a decidedly complicated 75 character Abkhaz letter set for the so-called 'analytic alphabet' he created based on Latin characters for his 'Abkhaz-Russian Dictionary' that was published in 1926.[11] For example, the Uslar verb form mentioned earlier is listed in Marr's dictionary as follows:

sáș̦wejt // sáswejt *бью его* (*нераз.*) 'I hit it'

Marr describes Abkhaz based on the Bzyp dialect, which is the reason why the consonant in the verbal root in the example above, ș̦ 'hit' and the pronominal prefix *s* 'I', use different consonants in this dialect (for details of the Bzyp dialect, see §6.2.2). In Standard Abkhaz, these two consonants are the same, and there is no distinction between the two (с-á-с-уеит /s-á-s-wa-jt'/ [I-it-hit-Dyn-Fin]). In this manner, Marr accurately describes the Bzyb dialect, including the accents.

However, the number of alphabetic characters devised by Marr was too large when compared to the number of phonemes in Abkhaz and did not reflect the actual Abkhaz phonemes.[12] Compare the

9. George Hewitt (ed.) 1998. *The Abkhazians: A Handbook*. St. Martin's Press. p. 172.

10. George Hewitt. 2004. *Introduction to the Study of the Languages of the Caucasus*. Lincom Europa. München. p. 259.

11. Марр, Н. 1926. *Абхазско-русский словарь. Пособие к лекциям и в исследовательской работе.* Ленинград: Издание академии абхазского языка и литературы.

12. Note the following statement by N. F. Jakovlev: 'There are three basic vowels in Abkhaz: *ə*, *a*, and ā. These have been verified by this author and clearly differ from the large number of vowels counted by Academy member Marr.' Яковлев, Н.Ф. 1928. Математическая формула построения алфавита. Культура И письменность Востока, кн. I. Москва. [In: Реформатский А.А. 1970. *Из истории отечественной*

number of Abkhaz alphabetic characters conceived by Marr (75) to the number of phonemes in the Bzyp dialect (69 or 70). It was due to this that it was not adopted as the official Abkhaz character notational system.

The 'standardized Abkhaz alphabet' devised by Nikolaj Feofanovich Jakovlev (1892–1974) based on Latin character notation was introduced in 1928.[13] In addition to being a theoretician, Jakovlev was a Caucasus scholar with extensive knowledge who greatly contributed to the establishment of the Moscow Phonological School and who conducted an analysis of phonemes and detailed phonetic descriptions of Kabardian in 1923.[14] In 1928, Jakovlev presented his treatise 'Mathematical Formula

---

фонологии. Очерк. Хрестоматия. Наука, Москва. стр. 143.]

13. Jakovlev was a disciple of N.J. Marr, and was involved in the tasks of creating an orthography of an alphabet for 'Young Written Languages' and for the ethnic groups lacking written alphabets that had come under Soviet administrative influence after the Russian Revolution. In addition, Jakovlev also wrote many excellent descriptive grammars for the Northern Caucasian languages. Examples are: 'Grammar of the literary Adyghe language' (Яковлев, Н.Ф., Ашхамаф, Д. 1941. *Грамматика адыгейского литературного языка.* Москва-Ленинград); 'A Grammar of the literary Kabardian-Circassian language' (Яковлев, Н.Ф. 1948. *Грамматика литературного кабардино-черкесского языка.* Москва-Ленинград.); 'Syntax of the literary Chechen (Vejnakh) language' (Яковлев, Н.Ф. 1940. *Синтаксис чеченского (вейнахского) литературного языка.* Москва-Ленинград); and the 'Morphology of Chechen' (Яковлев, Н.Ф. 1960. *Морфология чеченского языка.* Грозный). Although the writing of the 'Morphology of Chechen' was completed in 1939, it was not published until 1960. Moreover, even though Jakovlev had finished writing an Abkhaz grammar, reportedly 'the Marrism trend' delayed its publication for a long time. It was only recently that it was finally published in the Abkhazian metropolis of Sukhum. Яковлев, Н.Ф. 2006. *Грамматика абхазского литературного языка.* Сухум. (Grammar of the literary Abkhaz language). Also see. G. Hewitt. 2004. *Introduction to the Study of the Languages of the Caucasus.* p. 15.

[In his most recent published book, V.M. Alpatov (2012: 150) states the following about the reasons why Jakovlev's Abkhaz grammar was not published: "In the 1930s, Jakovlev wrote basic grammars for five Caucasian languages, which was a major contribution to Caucasian Studies in the world. At the time, only two grammars could be completely published, and one grammar was partially published: the Adyghe Grammar (1941), which he co-authored with his Adygheian student D.A. Ashkhamaf, Kabardian Grammar (1938), which initially appeared in an abridged form and then in a complete form after the war (1946), and one volume of his two-volume Chechen Grammar (1938). The second volume of Chechen Grammar and Ingush Grammar were not published, initially due to the war, and later due to the tragedy between the Chechen and Ingush peoples in 1944. Abkhaz Grammar was unlucky for different reasons. By 1935, it had already been sent out for typesetting, but the director of the Abkhazian Science Research Institute was Marr's pupil A.K. Khashba (1902–1937), who intervened and wrote a critical review which resulted in the cancellation of publication. Khashba's criticism (without Jakovlev's manuscript!) was sent to I.I. Meshchaninov (who was on the side of his Abkhazian colleague (i.e. Khashba)) at the arbitration tribunal in Leningrad. Meshchanivov's reply indicates the Nikolaj Feofanovich's (Jakovlev's) greatest sin was attempting to argue with Marr, who was already dead: 'A.K. Khashaba's criticisms of Prof. Jakovlev's misconceptions on paleontological methods are entirely correct. Prof. Jakovlev's position which attempts to restrict Academician Marr's research on the Abkhaz language to the creation of an alphabet is inappropriate and entirely wrong'. Abkhaz Grammar was not published." (Алпатов, В.М. 2012. *Языковеды, Востоковеды, Историки.* Москва: Языки славянских культур).]

14. Яковлев Н.Ф. 1923. Таблицы фонетики кабардинского языка. In: *Труды подразряда исследования северокавказских языков при Институте Востоковедения в Москве. I.* Москва.

for the Construction of Alphabets'[15] wherein he logically investigated the problems in 'Young Written Languages', or more specifically, those applying to the creation of alphabets for languages without notational systems based on structural phonology. In his treatise, Jakovlev criticizes Marr's alphabet as follows:

> The alphabet [Marr's], while being a truly phonetic notation proposed for actual use within the populace, was devised by an eminent Abkhaz scholar and initially intended purely for research. Even the results caused by the many faults in honest transcriptions of this alphabet leads to the question of why it would actually be used. Moreover, in actuality, experience in the use of the alphabet in Abkhazian schools has indicated that it is more than what children or adults can handle even when simply considered from the point of the large volume of individual characters involved.[16]

The Abkhaz alphabet was at long last streamlined from a phonological point of view in this manner through Jakovlev's standardized Abkhaz alphabet.

Jakovlev's standardized Abkhaz alphabet is an alphabet system based upon Latin characters. The establishment of the Stalin autocracy and the abandonment of internationalism which accompanied it spurred the shift to the Cyrillic alphabet for 'Young Written Languages' which had been created based on Latin characters. The entire text of 'Young Written Languages' was converted to the Cyrillic alphabet between 1936 and 1938; however, Georgia, which was the hometown of Stalin, proved to be an exception.[17] Abkhazia, which was being influenced by Georgia under the name of the Autonomous Republic of Abkhazia, together with South Ossetia, was also one of the exceptions. A new Abkhaz alphabet based on Georgian letters was established in 1938. From that time up until the period of Stalin's death in 1953, Abkhazian culture was greatly repressed by the Georgian influence, and the publication of materials written in Abkhaz was greatly reduced or almost completely prohibited. According to B.G. Hewitt, all of the Abkhaz schools had been closed in 1945–46 and had been replaced by Georgian schools. It was said that children caught speaking Abkhaz in the schools were subjected to disciplinary action.[18] This author has a copy of 'The Knight in the Panther's Skin' by Shota Rustaveli (1172–1216) that was translated from Georgian into Abkhaz and published in 1941[19]; however, it is written completely in Abkhaz based on Georgian letters. Moreover, the 'Abkhaz-

---

15. Яковлев Н.Ф. 1928. Математическая формула построения алфавита. Культура и письменность Востока, кн. I. Москва. стр. 41–64. [In: Реформатский А. А. 1970. *Из истории отечественной фонологии. Очерк. Хрестоматия.* Наука, Москва. стр. 123–148.]

16. ibid. [In: Реформатский А. А. 1970. *Из истории отечественной фонологии. Очерк. Хрестоматия.* Наука, Москва. стр. 142.]

17. In 1938 the alphabet based on Cyrillic characters was used for Abaza. The writing system for Adyghe was changed from one based on Arabic to Latin in 1928 and then to one established on Cyrillic characters in 1938. For example, 'the Grammar of the Adyghe Literary Language' (Moscow-Leningrad, 1941) by N. Jakovlev and D. Ashkhamaf (Н.Ф. Яковлев, Д. Ашхамаф. 1941. *Грамматика адыгейского литературного языка.* Издательство академии наук СССР. Москва-Ленинград), which was published in 1941, used an alphabet that was created based upon Cyrillic characters.

18. George Hewitt (ed.) 1998. *The Abkhazians: A Handbook*. St. Martin's Press. p. 171.

19. შოთა რუსთაველი. 1940. აბჟას-კოა ზშოუ. სოხუმი.

Georgian Dictionary'[20] issued in 1954 was written in the alphabet based on Georgian letters in spite of the Abkhaz change to Cyrillic characters in 1954. According to the preface in the dictionary, editing began in 1937 and had basically been completed in 1938. The reason for the publication of the dictionary being delayed until 1954 may probably be ascribed to the conditions mentioned earlier together with the deregulation of the publication of books in Abkhaz in 1954 and the conversion to Cyrillic characters.[21]

The suppression of Abkhazia ended after the deaths of Stalin and L.P. Beria in 1953, and education and publication in Abkhaz were revived.[22] The letter system for Abkhaz based on Cyrillic characters was established in 1954 and it continues to be used today after having had small changes made to its details. However, the Abkhaz alphabet lacks coherence as a notational system when compared to the Abaza alphabet created in 1938 and harbours many problems in addition to being complex. For example, in Abaza the symbol used to express an ejective is formed by adding an 'I' sign after the consonant letter; however, in Abkhaz it is depicted by using the Cyrillic consonant as is (what follows is ordered in Abaza: Abkhaz): пI : п [p'], тI : т [t'], кI : к [k'], кIь : кь [k'ʲ], кIв: кә (ку) [k'ʷ]. However, for affricates in the Abkhaz language, a special symbol is affixed to the Russian letters: цI : ҵ [ts']. On the other hand, in contrast to the simple stops which use the Russian letter consonant as it is in Abaza, a special symbol is placed under the letter in Abkhaz: п : ҧ [pʰ], т : ҭ [tʰ], к : ҟ [kʰ], кь : ҟь [kʲʰ], кв : ҟә (ҟу) [kʷʰ]. However, there are cases when the symbols under the Abkhaz letters represent an ejective: шI : ҿ [tʂ'] (cf. тш : ҽ [tʂ]), чI : ҷ [tʃ'] (cf. ч : ч [tʃʰ]). In addition, until recently the letter *у* or *ә* was attached to the consonant letter to express labials in Abkhaz: гу [gʷ], ҕу [ɣʷ], ку [k'ʷ], ҟу [kʷʰ], ҟу [q'ʷ], ху [χʷ]; ҳә [ħʷ], шә [ʃʷ], цә [tɕʷ], ҵә [tɕ'ʷ], дә [dʷ, db], жә [ʒʷ], ӡә [dʒʷ], тә [t'ʷ], ҭә [tʷʰ, tpʰ]. In Abaza, only a *в* was used to represent labials: гв [gʷ], гъв [ɣʷ], хIв [ħʷ], etc. In order to fix this inconsistency, only a *ә* has been used to express labials since 1993 even in Abkhaz: гә [gʷ], ҕә [ɣʷ], кә [k'ʷ], ҟә [kʷʰ], ҟә [q'ʷ], хә [χʷ]. Even with such improvements, the Abkhaz letter notation system still suffers from many problems and it cannot be denied that there is the possibility of changes hereafter in letter notation that may coincide with the political flux of the Caucasus. For example, Professor Hewitt recently proposed Roman-based alphabet notational systems for Pan-North-Caucasian languages.[23]

0.1.3.2. Since 1954, there has been a significant amount of research conducted in the former Soviet Union and in Europe and the United States on Abkhaz, coupled with the publication of grammars and

---

20. B. Dzhanashia. 1954. *Apxazur-kartuli leksik'oni*. Tbilisi. viii + 468.

21. The dictionary in itself is compact and the content can be considered reliable. For example, a look at the caption for 'hit' in the dictionary shows: ა-სრა (დისიტ) გარტყმა (გაარტყა). The ა-სრა [á-sra] 'to hit' item also gives the aorist form in დისიტ [d-í-s-it'] [he/she-him-hit-(Aor)-Fin] '(s)he hit him' and the Georgian translation. The aorist form in the conjugation of verbs is basic and a dictionary that lists this is very valuable.

22. It was reported that there were 91 Abkhaz schools in Abkhazia in 1966 (the total number of schools was 365 in 1980). See George Hewitt (ed.) 1998. ibid. p. 173.

23. Brian George Hewitt. 1999. Roman-based alphabets as a life-line for endangered languages. In: (ed.) E.B. Рахилина, Я.Г. Тестелец. *Типология и теория языка: от описания к объяснению. К 60-летию А.Е. Кибрика.* Языки русской культуры. стр. 613–621.

dictionaries. First and foremost would probably be the research central to Abkhaz in Tbilisi in Georgia conducted by Ketevan Vissarionovna Lomtatidze (1911–2007) who focused her studies on Abkhaz grammar and dialects from the 1930s through the 1980s. It would not be an overstatement to say that she laid the scientific groundwork for Abkhaz-Abaza research in her brilliant works (her published thesis on transitivity in Abkhaz,[24] and her monograph on the Abaza and the Ashkharywa dialect shine as examples).[25] An outline of her thesis on Abkhaz can be read in 'The Abkhaz Language': an article in 'Languages of the Peoples of USSR: IV. The Iberian-Caucasian Languages' published in Moscow in 1967.[26] Another work worthy of mention is the 'Abkhaz Grammar: Phonetics and Morphology' by Sh.K. Aristava, et al., which was published in Sukhum in 1968.[27] This is the standard grammar for Abkhaz in Russian, and it incorporates the exemplary research results reported by Lomtatidze and others. In addition, there is also the Abkhaz Byzp grammatical research by X.S. Bgazhba (the text of which is included herein),[28] the studies on dialects and on Abkhaz word order by M. Tsikolia, 'Studies on Abkhaz Syntax: Synchronic-Diachronic Description' by I.O. Gecadze,[29] the examination of tense and mood by L.P. Chkadua and other research studies.[30] With regard to dictionaries, X.S. Bgazhba published the 'Russian-Abkhaz Dictionary' in Sukhum in 1964.[31] It is a full-fledged dictionary with 16,000 words and its Russian lexis contains Abkhaz translations with simple example sentences. For example,

> бить *несов.* 1. *кого* апҟара; 2. *чем, во что, по кому-чему* асра; *бить палкой* лабала асра; *он бьет в барабан* адаул дасуеит; … .

The consummate Abkhaz dictionary is the 'Abkhaz Dictionary' published in 2 volumes by Shʲaq'ryl, et al. in 1986–87.[32] The dictionary lists only the caption words with accents and gives the corresponding simple Russian translation and example sentences in Abkhaz. With regard to verbs, it only offers the difference between transitive-intransitive and the aorist form. For example,

---

24. Ломтатидзе К.В. 1942. Категория переходности в абхазском языке. In: *Известия Института языка, истории и материальной культуры Академии наук Грузинской ССР.* т. XII.

25. Ломтатидзе К.В. 1954. *Ашхарский диалект и его место среди других абхазско-абазинских диалектов с текстами.* Тбилиси: Издательство академии наук грузинской ССР.

26. Ломтатидзе К.В. 1967. Абхазский язык. In: *Языки народов СССР. IV. Иберийско-кавказские языки.* Москва. стр. 101–122.

27. Аристава Ш.К., Бгажба Х.С., Циколия М. М., Чкадуа Л. П., Шакрыл К.С. 1968. *Грамматика абхазского языка: фонетика и морфология.* Сухуми. Алашара. 204.

28. Бгажба Х.С. 1964. *Бзыбский диалект абхазского языка (исследование и тексты).* Тбилиси.

29. Гецадзе И.О. 1979. *Очерки по синтаксису абхазского языка: синхронно-диахронная характеристика.* Наука. Ленинград.

30. Чкадуа Л.П. 1970. *Система времен и основных модальных образований в абхазско-абазинских диалектах.* Мецниереба. Тбилиси.

31. Бгажба Х.С. 1964. *Русско-абхазский словарь.* Академия наук грузинской ССР. Сухуми.

32. Шьаҟрыл К.С., Конџьариа В.Ҳ. 1986. Аҧсуа бызшәа ажәар. 1. А–О. Аҟуа.; Шьаҟрыл К.С., Конџьариа В.Ҳ. Ҷкадуа, Л.П. 1987. Аҧсуа бызшәа ажәар. 2. П–Џь. Аҟуа.

á-сра (дасит, еиҭац) *стучать* [to knock], *бить* [to beat; to strike, to hit], *ударять* [to strike].

The 'дасит' ['(s)he hit it'] contained within the parentheses is the aorist form, and the 'еиҭац' means that the verb is transitive. Although the authors of this dictionary list this verb meaning 'to strike, to hit' as a 'transitive verb', if the transitivity of the Abkhaz verb is considered systematically, the verb would have to be seen as being intransitive rather than transitive (indicated by the §3.2.5 in the verb below). In spite of faults such as those mentioned, the literary texts from which it draws examples, and its substantial vocabulary together with its other features, make it notably valuable. In addition, the 2-volume 'Abkhaz-Russian Dictionary' (2005. Sukhum) arranged by V. A. Kaslandzia (ed.) was recently published.[33] The grammar explanations for the captions are the same as those found in the Shʲaq'ryl, et al. dictionary; however, the word translations and example sentences are refined with the translations appearing in Russian. For example,

á-сра *неперех. гл.* (ди́сит) 1. *ударить, бить, постучать, стучать*: ҟамчыла аҽы дашит, *он ударил лошадь камчой, он огрел лошадь камчой*; ...

Here, the verb 'to strike, to hit' is correctly described in Russian as an intransitive verb: *неперех. гл.* In addition, the aorist form has been given an accent symbol which is helpful. Moreover, the 'Abkhaz-Russian Dictionary' (1998, Sukhum) was compiled based upon the 1930s writings of the Caucasus scholar A.N. Genko (1896–1941).[34] A major feature of this dictionary is that the Abzhywa dialect (абж.) and the Bzyp dialect (бз.) are both listed with many verb conjugations, not to mention with the vowel schwa ы̱ [ə] notated at the и̱ and у̱ positions. For example,

àсра абж. асрà бз. 1) *бить,* ... п. ўас, аор. сасыйт.

As can be seen from this example, Genko notates the difference between the Abzhywa and the Bzyp, expressing the imperative form (ўас 'hit it!') and the aorist (сасыйт 'I hit it').[35] These descriptive characteristics for dialects, which grew out of a push for accuracy in description by the outstanding Caucasus scholar Genko, are not found in other dictionaries, and thus make this dictionary especially valuable.[36]

0.1.3.3. The European and American Abkhaz research which needs to be mentioned next is undoubtedly that dealing with the Northwest Caucasian languages conducted by the eminent French Caucasus scholar and mythologist Georges Dumézil (1898–1986). Although Dumézil's research subjects spanned a range that is amazing even when limited to the Northwest Caucasian languages,

---

33. Касландзия В.А. 2005. *Абхазско-русский словарь.* Том I А-Н, Том II Н-Ць. Академия наук абхазии. Абхазский институт гуманитарных исследований им. Д.И. Гулиа. Сухум.

34. Генко А.Н. 1998. *Абхазско-русский словарь.* Алашара. Сухум.

35. The position of the accent àсра абж. асрà бз. shows that the Shʲaq'ryl and Kaslandzia dictionaries mentioned above are dictionaries based on Abzhywa (or more precisely, for the Abkhaz literary language).

36. A. N. Genko also wrote on the grammar of the Tapanta dialect of Abaza: Генко А. Н. 1955. *Абазинский язык: грамматический очерк наречия тапанта.* Москва.

his research in the field centres on describing and analysing the language of the Ubykhs living in Turkey, collecting texts and translating them while conducting comparative studies of the language concerning the other Northwest Caucasian languages (focussing on phonology and morphology). Ubykh had been described by Uslar and Julius von Mészáros prior to Dumézil.[37] However, it was Dumézil who truly raised the level of Ubykh studies to new scholastic heights, and research in other Northwest Caucasian languages is deeply indebted to his analytic methods. Considering Dumézil's investigations from the standpoint of Abkhaz studies, his most valuable research would probably be *Le Verbe Oubykh: Études descriptives et comparatives* that was published in 1975.[38] In this research work (especially in the sections after Chapter 5) Dumézil presents comparative analyses of the verb morphology of Abkhaz and East-West Circassian (Kabardian and Adyghe) centred on Ubykh. For example, he created classes A to H to group the verb conjugation in classes and used them as a basis to compare the verbs of the Northwest Caucasian languages. Although Dumézil's verb classification was already evident in his 1932 publication on 'Comparative Studies on the Northwest Caucasian Languages',[39] his 1975 work suggests the perfection of his description of the morphology of the Northwest Caucasian languages. Among the other writings related to Abkhaz which were authored by Dumézil, there are the *Études Abkhaz* in 1967, which were published as the 5th volume in the series *Documents anatoliens sur les langues et les traditions du Caucase*.[40] It includes an overview of Abkhaz grammar (pp. 9–43) and Abkhaz text (including text from the Ubykh and Circassian editions) together with annotated translations (pp. 45–195).

The German Caucasus scholar, Gerhard Deeters (1892–1961), failed to leave an Abkhaz monograph; however, a short essay on the 'linguistic structure of Abkhaz' (*Der abchasische Sprachbau*),[41] which summarizes his lecture at a linguistics colloquium in Göttingen, accurately puts together an outline of Abkhaz. In addition, 'Die kaukasischen Sprachen' (pp.1–79) in the posthumously published 'Armenian and Caucasian languages',[42] compares the phonology, vocabulary and grammar of the Caucasian languages, making it a valuable general overview of the Caucasian languages.[43]

---

37. Услар, Петр Карлович. 1887. *Этнография Кавказа. Языкознание 1. Абхазский язык.* Тифлис. [Reprint. Sukhum. 2002] pp. 75–102. Uslar surveyed the Ubykh of the Ubykhs in their homeland before they escaped en masse to Turkey. Julius von Mészáros. 1934. *Die Päkhy-Sprache*. Studies in Ancient Oriental Civilization, 9. Chicago: The University of Chicago Press.

38. Dumézil, Georges avec la collaboration de Tevfik Esenç. 1975. *Le Verbe Oubykh: Études descriptives et comparatives.* Paris: Librairie C. Klincksieck.

39. Dumézil, Georges. 1932. *Études Comparatives sur les Langues Caucasiennes du Nord-Ouest. (Morphologie).* Adrien-Maisonneuve. Paris. See pp. 156–172.

40. Dumézil, Georges. 1967. *Documents anatoliens sur les langues et les traditions du Caucase. V. Études Abkhaz.* Paris: Librairie Adrien-Maisonneuve.

41. Deeters, Gerhard. 1931. Der abchasische Sprachbau. Nachrichten von der Gesellschaft der Wissenschaften zu Göttingen. Weidmannsche Buchhandlung, Berlin. pp. 289–303.

42. Deeters, Gerhard, et al. 1963. *Armenisch und Kaukasische Sprachen.* Handbuch der Orientalistik. Erste Abteilung: Der Nahe und der Mittlere Osten. Leiden/Köln.

43. A similar general information text on the Caucasian languages is the writing of the eminent Caucasianist-typologist, G.A. Klimov (1928–1997): Климов, Г.А. 1986. *Введение в кавказское языкознание.* Москва. In addition, there is the translation with detailed annotations: Klimov, G.A. 1994. *Einführung in die kaukasische*

Furthermore, the late Professor Aert H. Kuipers of the University of Leiden and his students were tireless in conducting research on the Northwest Caucasian languages. Professor Kuipers had himself studied American Indian languages and Circassian,[44] however; it was he and C. Ebling of Amsterdam University who together provided guidance for those who came later as the chief editors of the Caucasian languages research journal, *Studia Caucasica* (1–7, 1963–1987. Peeters - Leuven). Within the field of Northwest Caucasian languages research, the University of Leiden has also produced: Rieks Smeets, who described Circassian Shapsug(h)[45]; Arie Spruit, Wim Lucassen and Albert Starreveld in the area of Abkhaz studies; and Viacheslav A. Chirikba, who is from Abkhazia and who earned his degree with a reconstruction of the Western Caucasian protolanguage. A. Spruit has also published his *Abkhaz Studies* (1986. Leiden. Private Doctor Publication) dissertation; however, this author has regrettably not yet read it. However, it is possible to learn about the content of his dissertation in *Studia Caucasica.* The focus of Spruit's research is on Abkhaz morphology and accent studies[46]. The latter in particular was research which changed the accent rules which were known as the 'Dybo's Rule of Abkhaz accent' attributed to the Russian Balto-Slavic accent scholar, Vladimir Antonovich Dybo (1931–)[47], and was of great value as such. W. Lucassen was said to be working on editing an Abkhaz-English dictionary together with A. Starreveld in the 70s; however, the work on it has ceased at present[48]. In addition to having authored a dissertation on the reconstruction of Proto-Northwest Caucasian[49], Chirikba has also written a synchronic Abkhaz outline text (Chirikba, V.A. 2003. *Abkhaz.* Languages of the World/Materials 119. Muenchen: Lincom Europa). This general informative text summarizes Abkhaz grammar very concisely and is invaluable in advancing it

---

Sprachwissenschaft. Aus dem Russischen übersetzt und bearbeitet von Jost Gippert. Hamburg: Buske.

44. Kuipers published *Phoneme and Morpheme in Kabardian* in 1960 (Kuipers, A.H. 1960. *Phoneme and Morpheme in Kabardian (Eastern Adyghe).* 'S-Gravenhage: Mouton). In it, Kuipers claimed an absence of consonant-vowel opposition in the phonemic system of Kabardian (see ibid. pp.104–107). His hypothesis drew much criticism thereafter from many researchers (O. Szemerényi, M. Halle, M.A. Kumakhov). However, his hypothesis should be revisited and considered anew, while taking into account Northwest Caucasian languages such as Abkhax-Abaza, wherein there are extremely few vowel phonemes. The following should also be consulted with regard to this: Allen, W.S. 1965. On one-vowel systems. In: *Lingua 13*, no. 2. pp. 111–124; Kuipers, A.H. 1976. Typologically Salient Features of Some Northwest Caucasian Languages. In: *Studia Caucasica 3.* pp. 101–127.

45. Smeets, Rieks. 1984. *Studies in West Circassian Phonology and Morphology.* Leiden: The Hakuchi Press.

46. Spruit, Arie. 1983. Abkhaz Verbs of Local Reference. In: *Studia Caucasica 5.* pp. 55–75; Spruit, Arie. 1985. Stress in Abkhaz. In: *Studia Caucasica 6.* pp. 31–81; Spruit, Arie. 1987. Abkhaz Verbs Morphology. In: *Studia Caucasica 7.* pp. 9–60.

47. Дыбо В.А. 2000. *Морфонологизованные парадигматические акцентные системы: типология и генезис. Том I.* Языки русской культуры. Москва. стр. 5–14, 660–734.

48. W. Lucassen recently passed away, and Hewitt and Chirikba are planning to continue the editing work based on their dictionary editing materials (according to Dr. Chirikba). Dissertations related to Abkhaz by Lucassen are: (a) Lucassen, W. 1992. Clusters in Abkhaz. In: Paris Catherine (ed.) *Caucasologie et Mythologie Comparée.* Peeters. Paris. pp. 275–287. (b) Lucassen, W. 1992. Reflexes of salient Proto-North-West-Caucasian labial-initial complexes. In: George Hewitt (ed.) *Caucasian Perspectives.* München: Lincom Europe. pp.157–171.

49. Chirikba, Viacheslav A. 1996. *Common West Caucasian. The Reconstruction of its Phonological System and Parts of its Lexicon and Morphology.* Leiden: Research School CNWS.

towards the Hewitt works described below.

At present, the most renowned figure in Abkhaz research is probably B. George Hewitt (1949–) of London University SOAS who is conducting intensive research into the Northwest Caucasian languages and the Kartvelian languages. Hewitt worked in collaboration with Zaira K. Khiba to publish *Abkhaz* in 1979 (Hewitt, B.G. In collaboration with Z.K. Khiba. 1979. *Abkhaz. Lingua Descriptive Studies* 2. Amsterdam: North Holland. [1989. Reprinted by Croom Helm and Routledge]). The author placed heavy emphasis on Abkhaz syntax, of which it is a comprehensive description. Here he conducted several grammar analyses which differed from the traditional Abkhaz analyses by Lomtatidze and others (for example, he did not recognize the grammatical category of 'version'); however, his content and analysis descriptions are more exhaustive than those of other Abkhazian and Georgian scholars (for example, all of the verb conjugations are morphologically analysed and supplemented with a gloss, accents have been provided for all terms, etc.), making it a refined outstanding work. Since then, he has presented numerous writings and papers on the Northwest Caucasian languages and Abkhaz. Among his works are his 'Abkhazian Folktales' with glosses and translations of Abkhazian story texts (Hewitt, George. 2005. *Abkhazian Folktales (with grammatical introduction, translation, notes, and vocabulary)*. Languages of the World/Text Collections 22. München: Lincom Europa) and *Introduction to the Study of the Languages of the Caucasus* (Hewitt, George. 2004. München: Lincom Europa).[50] Furthermore, he recently published an Abkhaz tutorial: Hewitt, G. 2010. *Abkhaz: A Comprehensive Self-Tutor.* Muenchen: Lincom Europa. It is an extremely remarkable entry text for Abkhaz which will provide the learner of Abkhaz with innumerable benefits.

Lastly, there are a few publications of T. Yanagisawa dealing with Abkhaz: 1) Yanagisawa, T. 2005. Schwa in Abkhaz. In: *Japanese Slavic and East European Studies*. Vol. 26. pp. 23–36; 2) Yanagisawa, T. 2010. *Analytic Dictionary of Abkhaz.* Tokyo: Hituzi Syobo. The last dictionary was an 'Abkhaz-English (-Russian) dictionary' produced with the cooperation of the Abkhazian consultant, Anna Tsvinaria-Abramishvili. All of the terms in it have been broken down into morphemes and accents provided for each word entry.

---

50. Other writings regarding Abkhaz include the following: Hewitt, Brian G. 1987. *The Typology of Subordination in Georgian and Abkhaz.* Empirical Approaches to Language Typology 5. Berlin-New York-Amsterdam: Mouton de Gruyter; Hewitt, George. 1989. Abkhaz. In: Hewitt, G. (ed.) *The Indigenous Languages of the Caucasus. Volume 2: The North West Caucasian Languages.* Delmar, New York: Caravan Books. pp. 37–88; Hewitt, George and Khiba, Zaira. 1998. *Abkhaz Newspaper Reader (with supplements).* Dunwoody Press. Kensington. This is composed of Abkhaz newspaper articles and their English translations, and it also contains a sketch of Abkhaz grammar with elementary texts and an accompanying glossary. In addition, there are also the following among his research papers: Hewitt, B.G. 1979a. Aspects of Verbal Affixation in Abkhaz (Abzhui dialect). In: *Transactions of the Philological Society. 1979.* pp. 211–238.; Hewitt, B.G. 1979b. The Relative Clause in Abkhaz. In: *Lingua.* vol. 47. pp. 151–188; Hewitt, B.G. 1982. Anti-passive and labile constructions in North Caucasian. In: *General Linguistics 22.* pp. 158–171, and Hewitt, B.G. 1999. Morphology revisited: some irregularities of the Abkhaz verb. In: Helma van den Berg (ed.) *Studies in Caucasian Linguistics: Selected Papers of the English Caucasian Colloquium.* CNWS. Universiteit Leiden. pp. 197–208.

0.1.4. Abkhaz letters

0.1.4.1. As was mentioned earlier, one of the major features of Abkhaz letters is that there are cases when a single phoneme is expressed with two letters. For example, labialization is a preeminent characteristic for Abkhaz consonants, with a dental series of sounds and an alveolar receiving a 'ə' notation and velars and postvelars followed by a 'y' notation after the Cyrillic letter (cf. the characters in parentheses in Table 1). However, since 1993 'ə' has come to be used as the labialization notation even in cases of the latter sounds (the 'ʷ' notation has been added to consonants in all cases in the transcription of this book). Furthermore, in order to express palatals, 'ь' has been added to the appropriate consonant, just as for Russian (the 'ʲ' notation has been used after the appropriate consonant in all cases in the transcription of this book).

The two vowel phonemes /a/ and /ə/ are recognized in Abkhaz; however, as a result of the contraction of /j/ and /w/ with the schwa /ə/ and the vowel colouring of /a/ before /j/, [o, e, u, i] are phonetically attained (see the letters о, е, у, и). Moreover, these phonetic sounds are used in expressing loan word sounds. That is, 'и' in the Abkhaz alphabet expresses /j/, /jə/, /əj/ and 'y' is used for /w/, /wə/, /əw/. In order to express Abkhaz vowels and semivowels phonologically, it is preferable to use the Latin alphabet notation used by Abkhaz researchers (such as Hewitt, Spruit and Chirikba) in the US and Europe rather than using the Abkhaz notation used by researchers in the former Soviet Union. However, the Abkhaz letter notation has been used by the Abkhazians, and most of their literature and publications have been printed using this notational method. Although this notational system has its problems, ignoring the literary language which has become a part of their tradition and imposing a phonemic orthography considered to be scientific by researchers could be expected to cause immense confusion.[51] It follows that using Cyrillic letter notation would conform to the norm; however, the main subject 'Phonology' in Part I 'Abkhaz Grammar' of this book is transcribed using only transcription, while on the other hand, 'Morphology, Morphosyntax and Syntax' have been notated using Abkhaz letter notation and transcription in part. Meanwhile, Part II 'Abkhaz Texts' is a compilation with Abkhaz letter notation and transcription.

Alphabet sequences vary slightly depending on the dictionary or grammar; however, for the most part they tend to be modelled on the order of the Russian alphabet. This document has been written using the most prevalent order present in recent dictionaries and grammars.[52]

Table 1

1 Upper-case	2 Lower-case	3 Name	4 Transcription	5 IPA
А	а	a	a	a
Б	б	bə	b	b
В	в	və	v	v

51. An example of this would be the reported resistance of many writers and literature scholars when the y letter was changed to the ə to express labialization during the letter reform in 1993.

52. Accordingly, the names of the letters are as described in Aristava et al. (1968: 8–9). Slight revisions have been made to the transcription method of Chirikba (2003a: 18). The IPA is according to Hewitt (2004: 260–262). In 1 and 2 of the table 1 above, ə is the notation for labialization while ь is that used for palatalization.

Г	г	gə	g	g
Гь	гь	g^{j}ə	g^{j}	g^{j}
Гә (Гу)	гә (гу)	g^{w}ə	g^{w}	g^{w}
Ҕ	ҕ	ɣa	ɣ	ʁ
Ҕь	ҕь	ɣ^{j}ə	ɣ^{j}	ʁ^{j}
Ҕә (Ҕу)	ҕә (ҕу)	ɣ^{w}ə	ɣ^{w}	ʁ^{w}
Д	д	də	d	d
Дә	дә	d^{w}ə	d^{w}	d^{w}, db
Е	е	e	e	e
Ж	ж	ʐə	ž	ʐ
Жь	жь	ʒə	ž^{j}	ʒ
Жә	жә	ʒ^{w}ə	ž^{w}	ʒ^{w}
З	з	zə	z	z
Ӡ	ӡ	dzə	ʒ	dz
Ӡә	ӡә	dʑ^{w}ə	ʒ^{w}	dʑ^{w}
И	и	i, j	j	j
К	к	k’ə	k’	k’
Кь	кь	k^{j}’ə	k’^{j}	k’^{j}
Кә (Ку)	кә (ку)	k^{w}’ə	k’^{w}	k’^{w}
Қ	қ	kə	k	k^{h}
Қь	қь	k^{j}ə	k^{j}	k^{jh}
Қә (Қу)	қә (қу)	k^{w}ə	k^{w}	k^{wh}
Ҟ	ҟ	q’ə	q’	q’
Ҟь	ҟь	q^{j}’ə	q’^{j}	q’^{j}
Ҟә (Ҟу)	ҟә (ҟу)	q^{w}’ə	q’^{w}	q’^{w}
Л	л	lə	l	l
М	м	mə	m	m
Н	н	nə	n	n
О	о	o	o	o
П	п	p’ə	p’	p’
Ԥ	ԥ	pə	p	p^{h}
Р	р	rə	r	r
С	с	sə	s	s
Т	т	t’ə	t’	t’
Тә	тә	t^{w}’ə	t’^{w}	t’^{w}, tp’
Ҭ	ҭ	tə	t	t^{h}
Ҭә	ҭә	t^{w}ə	t^{w}	t^{wh}, tp^{h}
У	у	w, u	w	w
Ф	ф	fə	f	f
Х	х	χə	x	χ
Хь	хь	χ^{j}ə	x^{j}	χ^{j}

Xə (Xу)	xə (xу)	χ^{w}ə	x^{w}	χ^{w}
Ҳ	ҳ	ħa	ħ	ħ
Ҳə	ҳə	ħ^{w}ə	ħ^{w}	ħ^{w}
Ц	ц	tsə	c	ts^{h}
Цə	цə	ts^{w}ə	c^{w}	ts^{wh}
Ҵ	ҵ	ts’ə	c’	ts’
Ҵə	ҵə	ts^{w}’ə	c’^{w}	ts’^{w}
Ч	ч	tʃə	č^{j}	tʃ^{h}
Ҷ	ҷ	tʃ’ə	č’^{j}	tʃ’
Ҽ	ҽ	ʈʂə	č	ʈʂ
Ҿ	ҿ	ʈʂ’ə	č’	ʈʂ’
Ш	ш	ʂə	š	ʂ
Шь	шь	ʃə	š^{j}	ʃ
Шə	шə	ʃ^{w}	š^{w}	ʃ^{w}
Ҩ	ҩ	ɥə	j^{w}	ɥ
Џ	џ	ɖʐə	ǯ	ɖʐ
Џь	џь	dʒə	ǯ^{j}	dʒ
Ы	ы	ə	ə	ə

1. Phonology

1.1. Phonological system of Abkhaz

1.1.1. Vowels

The Northwest Caucasian languages are well-known for their characteristic of having a large number of consonants in contrast to a small number of vowels. The great variety of consonants and their complexity tends to induce people to look at their diversity. However, with regard to Abkhaz itself, the complexity of its consonants does not present much of a problem. On the contrary, what shows the greatest need for problem resolution is the small number of vowels and the determination of their phonemes.

Various discussions have been held to date regarding the vowel phonemes in the Northwest Caucasian languages. As was mentioned earlier in footnote 44, Kuipers (1960) presented his hypothesis on the 'absence of consonant-vowel opposition' in the Kabardian phonological system. In addition, Allen (1965) posited that Abaza, which has a dialectal relationship to Abkhaz, is monovocalic, and has only the single vowel /a/ as a phoneme. However, today the majority of Abkhaz researchers (e.g., Lomtatidze, Hewitt, Chirikba) recognize the two phonemes /a/, /ə/ as the vowel phonemes in Abkhaz. This vowel system is unrelated to the position of the front or the back of the tongue and is the linear vowel system which is related only to the height of the tongue or the degrees of aperture:

high/close	/ə/
low/open	/a/

With regard to this Jakovlev (1928) recognized /ə, a, ā/ as vowel phonemes (see fn. 12). The long ā will be considered later, and the /a/, /ə/ which are recognized as phonemes by most researchers will be examined first.

1.1.1.1. Schwa ə

The schwa ə appears in Abkhaz in accordance with consonant sequences and accent positions.[53] The research by Yanagisawa (2005) meticulously investigated the environment in which the ə appeared in words, and here, the rules making the prediction of conditions of the appearance of the non-accented schwa possible are those given below (ibid. 33–34):

53. 'In our opinion, the frequently encountered unaccented vowel *ы* [ə] has not been directly taken from the vowel *a* but was vowelized to meet the needs of syllable formation in the cases of contiguous consonants.' Аршба, Нели. 1992. Некоторые вопросы акцентологии абхазского языка. In: (ed.) Hewitt, G. *Caucasian Perspectives*. Lincom Europa. pp. 236–239.

(1) Rule I (cf. Kuipers (1960: 41))
A schwa cannot appear before *C* (*C* is any consonant) followed by both *a* and ə.

(2) Rule II
If Rule I does not apply in a two-consonant sequence C_1C_2, and the sonority of C_1 is lower than that of C_2, or the sonority of C_1 is the same as that of C_2, then a schwa can appear between C_1 and C_2 : e.g., áapən 'spring', áaxəs 'from', ádəd 'thunder'. In contrast, if the sonority of C_1 is higher than that of C_2, a schwa cannot appear between C_1 and C_2: e.g., amc 'fly', ans 'so'.

(3) If Rule I does not apply in a three-consonant sequence $C_1C_2C_3$, then a schwa can appear either between C_1 and C_2 or between C_2 and C_3 according to Rule II: e.g., ámp'əl 'ball', áǯʲəmšʲ 'eyebrow'.

(4) Rule III (cf. Spruit 1985: 77)
If in a three-consonant sequence -$C_1C_2C_3$- a schwa does not appear before C_3, then it can appear between C_1 and C_2 : áʒənra 'winter', aáməšʲtaxʲ 'after'.

(5) Presumably, in a construction such as -*R*C_1C_2*V*-, Rule II which operates between C_1 of Series I and C_2 of Series II (or III) may take precedence over Rule I (for Series I, II, III, see Notes below). On the other hand, in a construction such as -*T*C_1C_2*V*-, Rule II which operates between both C_1 and C_2 may be subordinate to Rule I. In constructions such as -*TRTTV*- and -*TTTRV*- Rule I takes precedence.

(6) Rule IV (cf. Trigo 1992: 200–201)
If there is a derivational boundary after a root consisting of *C* or *CC* in a verbal complex, then *C* following this root is not taken into account when considering the occurrence of a schwa.

(7) If Rule IV applies in a three-consonant sequence, Rule III must also apply.

(8) If Rule I operates on the last C_4 of the four-consonant sequence -$C_1C_2C_3C_4V$, then Rule II is in effect among the first three consonants ($C_1C_2C_3$). Therefore, a schwa can appear either between C_1 and C_2 or between C_2 and C_3 in keeping with Rule II: áʒaxərsta 'seam', árpəzba 'young man'.

(9) If Rule IV operates in the four-consonant sequence -$C_1C_2C_3$#C_4V, then a schwa can appear between C_1 and C_2 according to Rule III: səbš#-wájt' 'you kill me'.

(10) In a four-consonant sequence -$C_1C_2C_3C_4V$#- (or -$C_1C_2C_3C_4VCV$#-) involving a verbal root, a schwa can appear between C_2 and C_3 according to Rule I and Rule III: bsəmbá#-jt' 'I did not see you', dləmk'ʷabá#-jt' 'she did not wash him/her'.

(11) Rule V
If there is word-initial consonants *j*- and *w*-, they can have a schwa regardless of Rule I: e.g. jə-

sa-wá 'the one who is going'.

[Notes:
C = any consonant, V = Vowels, T = Stops, Affricates and Fricatives, R = Resonants and Semivowels. I classify all consonants into the following three series from the point of view of sonority:
Series I: stops: labials. b-p-p', dentals. d-t-t', dʷ-tʷ-t'ʷ , velars. g-k-k', gʷ-kʷ-k'ʷ, gʲ-kʲ-k'ʲ, uvulars. q', q'ʷ, q'ʲ; affricates: dentals. ʒ-c-c', ʒʷ-cʷ-c'ʷ, alveolars. ǯ-č-č', ǯʲ-čʲ-č'ʲ; fricatives: dentolabial. v-f, dental. z-s, alveolars. ž-š, žʷ-šʷ, žʲ- šʲ, uvulars. ɣ-x, ɣʷ-xʷ, ɣʲ-xʲ, pharyngeal. h, hʷ , jʷ
Series II: resonants: n, m, r, l
Series III: semivowels: j, w]

On the other hand, the following has been said of the schwa with an accent (ibid. 24):

> Before discussing the occurrence of schwa, I should clarify the relation between schwa and stress in Abkhaz. To describe the placement of stress in Abkhaz words, Spruit (1985: 31) postulates that each word should be considered as 'consisting of a string of elements *C*(ə) or *Ca* (where *C* is any consonant)' which is subsumed under the generic symbol '*C*(*a*)'. According to Spruit, 'a stressed element *C*(á) is realized as *Cá* or, in the absence of *a*, as *Cə́*' (e.g., á-ʒ 'the-flea', á-ʒ-kʷa 'the-flea-Pl' versus a-ʒə́ 'the-water', a-ʒ-kʷá 'the-water-Pl'). Therefore, a schwa bearing stress can be viewed as a realization of stress on the preceding consonant. I will call this consonant *a potentially stressed consonant*.[54] Moreover, the schwa disappears before *a* (e.g., də-s-k'-wá-jt' 'I catch him/her' versus d-a-k'-wá-jt' 'it catches him/her').

Here, the term of '*a potentially stressed consonant*' refers to syllables that can be stressed under Spruit's Rule for Abkhaz accents, which will be discussed further later in §1.2.4. In other words, if there is stress according to Spruit's Rule on *the potentially stressed consonant C*, a schwa appears after the consonant *C*: Cə́. Using the example above to explain, among the oppositions of á-ʒ D'R 'the-flea', á-ʒ-kʷa D'RD 'the-flea-Pl' versus a-ʒə́ DD' 'the-water', a-ʒ-kʷá DDD' 'the-water-Pl' (' = stress, D = Dominant element, R = Recessive element), a-ʒə́ DD' 'the-water' may be understood as (C)a-C' > (C)a-Cə́, with the accented schwa appearing after the consonant.

If consideration is given to these conditions, the theory wherein the schwa is not recognized as a phoneme also gains some ground. However, Chirikba (2003a: 20) advocates the two-vowel theory in response to this as follows:

> Despite some claims in the special literature (cf. Allen 1965[55]) about the monovocalic, or even vowel-less character of Abkhaz (-Abaza), minimal pairs like the following prove the relevance of the phonemic contrast /*a*/ vs. /ə/ : /*a*#/ ~ /ə́#/ a-c'ʷá 'apple' vs. a-c'ʷə́ 'little stick'; /ø#/ ~

54. Also cf. Kuipers (1976: 108): 'Lomtatidze's statement that the Abkhaz *schwa* is usually stressed reflects the fact that an Abkhaz unit /p/ will always have its variant [pə] in stressed position.'

55. Allen, W.S. 1965. On One-Vowel Systems. In : *Lingua. 13*, no. 2. 111–124.

/*a*#/ ~ /ə́#/ as 'thus' vs. á-sa 'sword' vs. a-sə́ 'snow'; /*ϕ*#/ ~ /*a*#/ ~/á#/ ~ /ə́#/ ax 'wine sediment' vs. áxa 'stick used to support plants' vs. axá 'but' vs. a-xə́ 'head'.

A glance at these examples makes it appear that the minimal pair mentioned by Chirikba is being formed. However, if the examples are viewed from the standpoint of their relationships with accents, it does not seem as if there is evidence of the formation of the minimal pair. More specifically, in the first example, it is possible to recognize a-c'ʷá 'apple' vs. *a-c'ʷϕ 'little stick' which is *a-c'ʷϕ DD' > a-c'ʷə́. The second example may be recognized as ás 'thus' vs. á-sa 'sword' vs. *a-sϕ DD' > a-sə́ 'snow'. The third example may be considered as áx 'wine sediment' vs. áxa 'stick used to support plants' vs. axá 'but' vs. *a-xϕ DD' > a-xə́ 'head'. It is possible to note the appearance of the schwa in places which have the oxytone accent. For example, as regards the opposition axá 'but' vs. a-xə́ 'head' mentioned by Chirikba, since a-xə́ 'head' can be regarded as *a-xϕ DD', the oppositional member of a-xə́ 'head' is ax D'R 'wine sediment', where it is possible to recognize the accent opposition: *a-xϕ DD' 'head' vs. áx D'R 'wine sediment'. It follows that insofar as may be seen from these examples, there is no need to recognize the schwa as a phoneme.[56]

The above example shows the need for actual samples that would indicate the opposition to the unaccented /ə#/ ~ /ϕ#/ in order for the schwa to be recognized as a phoneme. There are no real examples amongst the nouns; however, they do exist in the derived forms of verbs. This can be seen in the opposition between the Absolutive -nə and the Past Indefinite -n: jə-sə́-cha-nə 'it having bitten me' vs. jə-sə́-cha-n 'it bit me and ...'. In all probability, the unaccented /ə#/ ~ /ϕ#/ opposition appears only in the opposition of these forms in Abkhaz. Furthermore, there is a fairly high frequency in both types of these forms in texts, and by considering the heavy functional load, it is probably possible to recognize the schwa as a phoneme.

1.1.1.2. Lomtatidze (1967: 103) in her description of the vowel *a* considers the *a* as a low vowel being relatively close; while on the other hand, the vowel *ə* is treated as a high vowel closer than the vowel *a*. The vowel *a* appears in all positions in words. On the other hand, *ə* does not appear at the beginning of words. However, in the verb prefix jə́- of accented third-person singulars and plurals, in cases when the cross-referencing noun comes immediately before, it becomes jə́- > ə́- with an accent at the beginning of the word. On the other hand, the vowel *a* appears in both accented and unaccented syllables: á-l 'alder' : á-la 'eye' : a-lá 'dog'. As may be seen in this example, zero and the *a* are in opposition with regard to the unaccented position. In addition, á-ləm 'lion' illustrates that *ə* > *a* as a result of the consonant *l* cannot occur, so it is possible to consider the vowel *a* as a phoneme. The vowel phoneme /a/ is realized as [e] in the position before /j/: jə-l-taa-wá-jt' [jəlta:wéjt'] (it/them-she-harvest-Dyn-Fin) 'she harvests it/them'. In addition, the vowel phoneme /a/ combined with /wa/, /w/ becomes the contracted [o:], [o:(w)].

1.1.1.3. Whether to regard the long vowel [ā] as an independent vowel phoneme or to consider it as a combination of the vowel /a/ and /a/ has long been a subject of debate in Abkhaz linguistics. However,

56. The same notation as that of Chirikba can also be seen in Hewitt (2005: 8). 'Open /a/ contrasts with mid /ə/ (/a.sá/ 'slice' vs. /a.sə́/ 'snow').'

there is no unified conclusion among scholars at the present time. For example, Hewitt (2004: 46) regarded the long vowel as an unsolved problem and had yet to conclude whether or not to consider the long vowel as a phoneme: 'I have always treated it ([a:] — T.Y.) simply as a long vowel, but is it phonemic?' (ibid.). On the other hand, Chirikba (2003a: 20) does not recognize the long vowel [ā] as an independent vowel phoneme; breaking it into the following three cases; respectively seeking combinations between the short vowel /a/, /ə/, and the pharyngeal /ħ/. In other words, considering them as: (1) [áa] reflecting the combination of phonemes /á/ə́ + ħ/ ('The sequence [áa] reflects the underlying combination /á/ə́ħ/'); (2) [aá] showing the combination of /ħ + á/ə́/ ([aá] — the sequence /ħá/ə́/); or (3) [ā] reflecting the combination of the unaccented syllable /a/ə+ħ/ or /ħ+a/ə/ ([ā] — the underlying unstressed syllables /a/əħ/ or /ħa/ə/]). Although Chirikba's theory may seem odd at first glance, he references the a < ʕ < ħ sound change garnered from a comparative study with Abaza and synchronically postulates an archiphoneme.[57] His theory is extremely logical, and the intent to reduce the vowel phonemes in Abkhaz to two vowels is evident. In relation to this, an even more realistic attempt had already been made by Jakovlev (1928 [1970: 143]) in recognizing /ā/ as an independent phoneme as was mentioned above (cf. fn. 12).

1.1.1.4. The long vowel [ā] is expressed as the reduplicated *aa* in Abkhaz orthography. Our consultant pronounced the *aa* as [a:] rather than as [aʔa].

The positions where this long vowel appears in Abkhaz are as follows:

(1) When the transitive root begins with a voiced consonant, the *aa* appears in the first-person plural pronominal prefix expressing the agent immediately preceding it: d-aa-ba-wá-jt' (him/her-we-see-Dyn-Fin) 'we see him/her'. This form appears to be in opposition with the third-person/non-human pronominal prefix form of d-a-ba-wá-jt' (him/her-it-see-Dyn-Fin) 'it sees him/her'. More specifically, it seems to be an /ā/ : /a/ opposition. However, d-aa-ba-wá-jt' may be presented as the underlying form of /də-ħ-ba-wá-jt'/. This is because the following form is seen in the pattern paralleling the paradigm of this verbal complex: cf. də-z-ba-wá-jt' (him/her-I-see-Dyn-Fin) 'I see him/her'. The process from the underlying form to the surface form may be thought of as follows: /də-ħ-ba-wá-jt'/ > da-ʕ-ba-wá-jt' > da-a-ba-wá-jt' > [da:bó:jt']. It follows that here the long vowel [ā] can be considered as a reflection of /əħ/. This is in the case of Chirikba's (3) mentioned above.

(2) This long vowel appears in the preverb and verbal particle of the verb (cf. §3.1.2.1 and §5.11): j-aa-z/s-ga-wá-jt' (it/them-Prev('hither')-I-take-Dyn-Fin) 'I bring it/them'.

(3) This long vowel occurs in the verb stem: á-taa-ra 'to harvest' (cf. á-ta-ra 'to give'). When the long vowel in this verb is immediately followed by the dynamic suffix *-wa-*, there is no phonetic contraction of the long vowel and *-wa-* (however, the short vowel *a* will contract with *-wa-* to become [o:]): jə-l-taa-wá-jt' [jəlta:wé:t'] (it/them-she-harvest-Dyn-Fin) 'she harvests it/them', cf. b-rə́-s-ta-wa-jt' [brésto:jt'] (you.F-them-I-give-Dyn-Fin) 'I give you to them'.

In the *a* + *a* joining of the short vowel *a* with another short vowel *a* in Abkhaz, there are no instances in which it becomes the long vowel [ā]. For example, the result of joining the possessive

57. See the examples of Abaza wherein the voiced pharyngeal /ʕ/ appears where pharyngeal /ħ/ > a is referenced in Abkhaz: Abaza (Genko 1955: 98): wə-ʕ-bə́jd 'we see you' (cf. Abkhaz /də-ħ-ba-wá-jt'/ > *da-ʕ-ba-wá-jt' > [da-a-ba-wá-jt']), Abaza aʕbá 'eight' (Abkhaz aabá 'eight'), Abaza aʕájra 'to come' (Abkhaz aájra 'to come').

prefix *a-* of the third-person singular/non-human class and the *a-* word initial of the postpositive ax^j 'to' is not the long [ā], but rather, the short [a]: á-$\check{z}^w j^w$an a-ax^j > á-$\check{z}^w j^w$an ax^j 'to the sky'. This makes it more rational to phonologically interpret the long vowel [ā] in Abkhaz not as a combination of /a + a/, but as a combination of /a/ and /ħ/ as Chirikba did.

1.1.1.5. Vowel Colouring

The Abkhaz vowels *a* and *ə* combine with the pharyngeal ħ and semivowels *w*, *j* to generate vowel colouring such as that which follows:

1) /ħ + ə/ or /ə + ħ/ → /ħa/ or /aħ/ > [ħa] or [aħ]
   ex. ҳалбе́ит [ħalbé:t'] < ħə-l-bá-jt' 'she saw us'
   дахбе́ит [daħbé:t'] < də-ħ-bá-jt' 'we saw him/her'
   Cf. бызбе́ит [bəzbé:t'] < bə-z-bá-jt' 'I saw you'
2) /a + j/ → [e:] (However, /ħa + j/ → [ħaj], /aa + j/ > [aaj])
   ex. сылбе́ит [səlbé:t'] < sə-l-bá-jt' 'she saw me'
   Cf. сбаха́ит [sbaħájt'] < s-b-a-ħá-jt' 'you heard me'
   саа́ит [saájt'] < s-aá-jt' 'I came here'
3) /ə + j/ → [i:(j)]
   ex. бибе́ит [bi:bé:t'] < bə-j-bé-jt' 'he saw you'
4) /j + ə/ → [jɨ] (However, /j + əħ/ > [jaħ])
   ex. и́лбаз [jɨlbaz] < jə́-l-ba-z 'the one which she saw'
5) /a + w/ → [o:]
   ex. бсы́моуп [bsə́mo:p'] < b-sə́-ma-wp' 'I have you'
6) /a + wa/ → [ɔ] (However, /ħa + wa/ > [ħawa])
   ex. бызбо́ит [bəzbɔ́:jt'] < bə-z-ba-wá-jt' 'I am seeing you'
   Cf. сбахауа́м [sbaħawám] < s-b-a-ħa-wá-m 'you don't hear me'
7) /ə + w/ → [u:]
   ex. субе́ит [su:bé:t'] < sə-w-bá-jt' 'you saw me'
8) /a + g^j/ → [eg^j]
   ex. зегь [zeg^j] 'all', егьы́рҭ [eg^jə́rt] 'other'

1.1.2. Consonants

1.1.2.1. The Abkhaz consonant system is as follows:

Table 2

		Stops		Affricates	Fricatives		Resonants	Semivowels
Labials								
bilabial	b	p[p^h]	p'				m	w
dentolabial			(f')		v	f		

Dentals											
simple	d	t[t^h]	t’	ʒ[dz]	c[ts]	c’[ts’]	z	s	n	r	
labialised	d^w[db]	t^w[tp^h]	t’^{w}[tp’]	ʒ^w[dẓ^w]	c^w[tɕ^w]	c’^{w}[tɕ’^{w}]					
Alveolars											
simple [retroflex]				ǯ[ɖʐ]	č[ʈʂ]	č’[ʈʂ’]	ž[ʐ]	š[ʂ]			
labialised							ž^w[ʒ^w]	š^w[ʃ^w]			
palatalised [palato-alveolar]				ǯ^j[dʒ]	č^j[tʃ^h]	č’^{j}[tʃ’]	ž^j[ʒ]	š^j[ʃ]			
Palatals											
simple											j
labialised											j^w[ɥ]
Laterals											
simple									l		
Velars											
simple	g	k	k’								
labialised	g^w	k^w	k’^{w}								
palatalised	g^j	k^j	k’^{j}								
Uvulars											
simple			q’				ɣ[ʁ]	x[χ]			
labialised			q’^{w}				ɣ^w[ʁ^w]	x^w[χ^w]			
palatalised			q’^{j}				ɣ^j[ʁ^j]	x^j[χ^j]			
Pharyngeals											
simple								ħ			
labialised								ħ^w			

1.1.2.2. Abkhaz (the literary language based on the Abzhywa dialect) has 58 consonants.[58] One of the major features of the Abkhaz consonant system is that there is ‘voiced : voiceless : ejective’ opposition with regard to stops and affricates.[59] For example, labials occur as [b], [p^h], and [p’] phonetically:

Table 3

---

58. V.A. Chirikba (personal communication) points out that the glottal stop [ʔ] is heard in the word <u>ʔoħ</u> ‘oh’, which is written as <u>q’oħ</u> in the original Abkhaz text. And according to Chirikba (1996: 15), Abkhaz has, at least in the periphery of the system, such minimal pairs as <u>ʔaj</u> ‘no’ : <u>aj</u> ‘yes’, <u>ʔaj</u> ‘no’ : <u>ħaj</u> ‘oh’, <u>ʔaj-ʔaj</u> ‘no’ : <u>ħaj-ħaj</u> ‘interjection of encouragement’, <u>ʔaj-ʔaj</u> ‘no’ : <u>aj-aj</u> [ajej] ‘yes’, <u>ʔaħ</u> ‘no’ : <u>aħ</u> ‘oh’, <u>ʔaħ</u> ‘no’ : <u>ħaħ</u> ‘our prince’. Chirikba’s keen observation raises the possibility that the glottal stop is a phoneme in Abkhaz. See also Hewitt (2010: 11).

59. There are gaps in uvulars and there are no voiced or unvoiced series.

	b	p^{h}	p’
Syllabicity	-	-	-
Stopness	+	+	+
Voicing	+	-	(-)
Glottalization	(-)	-	+
Labialization	+	+	+
Dentality	(-)	(-)	(-)
Velarity	(-)	(-)	(-)
Aspiration	-	+	(-)

As the aspiration of the voiceless aspirate [p^{h}] is a redundant feature among the three, it is possible to recognize this stop in opposition to /b/ ~ /p/ ~ /p’/ phonologically. This also applies to dentals and velars in the same way:

Table 4

	d	t^{h}	t’	g	k^{h}	k’
Syllabicity	-	-	-	-	-	-
Stopness	+	+	+	+	+	+
Voicing	+	-	(-)	+	-	(-)
Glottalization	(-)	-	+	(-)	-	+
Labialization	(-)	(-)	(-)	(-)	(-)	(-)
Dentality	+	+	+	(-)	(-)	(-)
Velarity	(-)	(-)	(-)	+	+	+
Aspiration	-	+	(-)	-	+	(-)

Affricatives also have ‘voiced : voiceless : ejective’ opposition. For example:

Table 5

	ʒ|dz|	c|ts|	c’|ts’]	ʒ^{w}|dʑ^{w}|	c^{w}|tɕ^{w}|	c’^{w}|tɕ’^{w}|
Syllabicity	-	-	-	-	-	-
Affricateness	+	+	+	+	+	+
Voicing	+	-	(-)	+	-	(-)
Glottalization	(-)	-	+	(-)	-	+
Labialization	(-)	(-)	(-)	+	+	+
Dentality	+	+	+	+	+	+
Velarity	(-)	(-)	(-)	(-)	(-)	(-)
Aspiration	-	-	(-)	-	-	(-)

The second feature is that the majority of obstruents are in opposition to sounds which have the features of palatalisation and labialisation. For example, in the series of stop velars, /g/ ~ /g^{w}/ ~ /g^{j}/, /k/ ~ /k^{w}/ ~ /k^{j}/ and /k’/ ~ /k’^{w}/ ~ /k’^{j}/ are in opposition (^{w} represents the labialised sound and ^{j} expresses the palatalised):

Table 6

	g	g^w	g^j	k^h	k^{hw}	k^{hj}	k’	$k’^w$	$k’^j$
Syllabicity	-	-	-	-	-	-	-	-	-
Stopness	+	+	+	+	+	+	+	+	+
Voicing	+	+	+	-	-	-	(-)	(-)	(-)
Glottalization	(-)	(-)	(-)	-	-	-	+	+	+
Labialization	-	+	(-)	-	+	(-)	-	+	(-)
Dentality	(-)	(-)	(-)	(-)	(-)	(-)	(-)	(-)	(-)
Velarity	+	+	+	+	+	+	+	+	+
Aspiration	(-)	(-)	(-)	+	+	+	(-)	(-)	(-)
Palatalization	-	-	+	-	-	+	-	-	+

The postvelar (uvular) stops create gaps in the system: there are no uvular voiced phoneme /G/ and uvular unglottalized phoneme /q/.[60]

Table 7

b	p	p’
d	t	t’
g	k	k’
-	-	q’

The palatalized stops create gaps in the labial and dental orders [61]:

Table 8

-	-	-
-	-	-
g^j	k^j	$k’^j$
-	-	$q’^j$

The labialized dentals are notated as $/d^w/$, $/t^w/$, $/t’^w/$ in this text; however, the pronunciation of those sounds by our informant is accompanied by a strong labial vibration of double articulation [d͡b], [t͡p], and [t͡p’] sounds. The labial order lacks labialized labials [62]:

---

60. Abaza (Tapanta) has the uvular unglottalized phonemes /q/ and $/q^w/$, with a gap in place of the voiced postvelar stop /G/.

61. The Abkhaz palatalized stop system finds a typological parallel in Indo-European:

b	p	bh	ph
d	t	dh	th
g^j	k^j	g^jh	k^jh
g	k	gh	kh
g^w	k^w	g^wh	k^wh

(Szemerényi, O. 1996. *Introduction to Indo-European Linguistics.* Oxford: Clarendon Press. p. 69.)

62. For examples of languages with an opposition of a labialized labial order to an unlabialized labial order, see Chomsky and Halle 1968. *The Sound Pattern of English.* New York: Harper & Row.: ‘In Nupe round

Table 9

-	-	-
d^w	t^w	t'^w
g^w	k^w	k'^w
		q'^w

Moreover, labialisation in opposition to the semivowel /j/ exists with the sound [ɥ]. This is notated as /j^w/ in this text. The fricative uvulars are pronounced [ʁ], [$ʁ^j$], and [$ʁ^w$] and should respectively be written phonologically as /ʁ/, /$ʁ^j$/, and /$ʁ^w$/[63]; however, they are described as /ɣ/, /$ɣ^j$/, /$ɣ^w$/ herein in keeping with tradition.[64]

Table 10

	ʁ	$ʁ^w$	$ʁ^j$	χ	$χ^w$	$χ^j$
Stopness	-	-	-	-	-	-
Fricativeness	+	+	+	+	+	+
Voicing	+	+	+	-	-	-
Velarity	+	+	+	+	+	+
Palatalozation	-	-	+	-	-	+
Labialization	-	+	-	-	+	-

1.1.2.3. The Frequency of consonants

The frequency in which consonants appear in Abkhaz can be summarized in the following table. The data is based on five Abkhaz folklore texts. There are 19,536 phonemes all together, and 7,923 (40.53%) of them are vowel phonemes, and 11,613 (59.46%) of them are consonant phonemes.[65]

Table 11

j	1,594	13.71%	ħ	149	1.28%	c'^w	59	0.50%	ǯ	0	0%
n	992	8.53%	g^j	148	1.27%	$ǯ^j$	50	0.43%			
r	792	6.81%	x^j	147	1.26%	č	46	0.39%			
w	714	6.14%	š	145	1.24%	$ž^j$	46	0.39%			
z	552	4.75%	p'	140	1.20%	$ɣ^j$	30	0.25%			
l	505	4.34%	q'	135	1.16%	k	28	0.24%			
s	477	4.10%	j^w	134	1.15%	ɣ	24	0.20%			

(labialized) labials are distinguished from nonround labials; e.g., [p^w] is distinct from [p].' (311).

63. Cf. the notation by Hewitt (2010: 10)

64. Cf. the notation by Hewitt (1979c: 258) and Chirikba (2003a: 18).

65. Among the vowels, 5,694 of them were *a*, and 228 were *aa* (5,922 in total). There were 645 unaccented *ə*, and there were 1,356 accented *ə́* (2,001 in total).

d	423	3.63%	ʒ	124	1.06%	q'ʷ	22	0.18%
t'	402	3.45%	g	122	1.04%	q'ʲ	21	0.18%
ħʷ	356	3.06%	cʷ	120	1.03%	k'ʲ	18	0.15%
b	339	2.91%	šʷ	107	0.92%	tʷ	18	0.15%
m	335	2.88%	xʷ	105	0.90%	kʲ	16	0.13%
x	314	2.70%	č'ʲ	102	0.87%	ʒʷ	13	0.11%
t	280	2.40%	č'	101	0.86%	čʲ	13	0.11%
p	218	1.87%	c	97	0.83%	dʷ	12	0.10%
k'	199	1.71%	kʷ	95	0.81%	ɣʷ	10	0.08%
c'	175	1.50%	t'ʷ	87	0.74%	f	10	0.08%
šʲ	154	1.32%	žʷ	73	0.62%	v	5	0.04%
k'ʷ	151	1.29%	gʷ	64	0.55%	ž	5	0.04%

1.1.2.3.1. Table 12 presents the frequency of stops (the number in parenthesis represents the percentage of the relevant consonant to the total number of consonants).[66]

Table 12

Series	I	II	III
	p' (1.20)	b (2.91)	p (1.87)
	t' (3.45)	d (3.63)	t (2.40)

66. The frequency a phoneme occurs within the phonological system is related to the phonemes markedness. Gamkrelidze (1978: 11) describes this below: "The relation of marking is connected by Greenberg with the frequency indices of linguistic units. The unmarked member of the relation, which is functionally more normal and widespread, has a greater frequency of occurrence in a text compared to the marked member, which is a more complex and textually more restricted unit. In positions of internally conditioned neutralization the unmarked member of a phonological opposition appears."

Gamkrelidze (1978) used statistical data and studied the world's languages through the markedness of stops and fricatives, and elicited a series of universal features on markedness. For example, Gamkrelidze (ibid.: 13) states the following on the universality of I Series consonants: "In the series of glottalized consonants (marked), as opposed to the unglottalized consonants (unmarked), the labial glottalized phoneme /p'/ is distinguished by the least frequency of occurrence in a text; in a number of languages in which a series of glottalized stops is represented, /p'/ is absent, creating an empty slot (gap) in the system."

Our textual data indicates a lower frequency for /p'/ compared to other unglottalized consonants /b/, /p/, but does not indicate an extremely low occurrence frequency. This is related to the fairly high functional load /p'/ has in Abkhaz. In other words, this is due to the appearance of *-wp'*, which indicates the finite forms of stative verbs in Abkhaz texts. For example, the distribution frequency of entries beginning with *p'*, *b*, *p* in Genko's (1998) dictionary is 6.8% for *p'*, 38.9% for *b*, and 54.2% for *p* (total number of lexical items: 924, p': 63 words, b: 360 words, p: 501 words), and compared to the frequency in Table 12 above, /p'/ is conspicuously frequent in the texts.

t’^{w} (0.74)	d^{w} (0.10)	t^{w} (0.15)
k’ (1.71)	g (1.04)	k (0.24)
k’^{w} (1.29)	g^{w} (0.55)	k^{w} (0.81)
k’^{j} (0.15)	g^{j} (1.27)	k^{j} (0.13)
q’ (1.16)		
q’^{w} (0.18)		
q’^{j} (0.18)		

1.1.2.3.2. Table 13 presents the frequency of affricates (the number in parenthesis represents the percentage of the relevant consonant to the total number of consonants):

Table 13

Series	I	II	III
	c’[ts’] (1.50)	ʒ[dz] (1.06)	c[ts] (0.83)
	c’^{w}[tɕ’^{w}] (0.50)	ʒ^{w}[dʑ^{w}] (0.11)	c^{w}[tɕ^{w}] (1.03)
	č’[ʈʂ’] (0.86)	ǯ[ɖʐ] (0)	č[ʈʂ] (0.39)
	č’^{j}[tʃ’] (0.87)	ǯ^{j}[dʒ] (0.43)	č^{j}[tʃ^{h}] (0.11)

1.1.2.3.3. Table 14 presents the frequency of fricatives (the number in parenthesis represents the percentage of the relevant consonant to the total number of consonants):

Table 14

Series	II	III
	v (0.04)	f (0.08)
	z (4.75)	s (4.10)
	ž[ʐ] (0.04)	š[ʂ] (1.24)
	ž^{w}[ʒ^{w}] (0.62)	š^{w}[ʃ^{w}] (0.92)
	ž^{j}[ʒ] (0.39)	š^{j}[ʃ] (1.32)
	ɣ[ʁ] (0.20)	x[χ] (2.70)
	ɣ^{w}[ʁ^{w}] (0.08)	x^{w}[χ^{w}] (0.90)
	ɣ^{j}[ʁ^{j}] (0.25)	x^{j}[χ^{j}] (1.26)
		ħ (1.28)
		ħ^{w} (3.06)

1.2. Accent

1.2.1. Accent features of Abkhaz

The accent in Abkhaz is a stress accent and it changes in position depending on the word form. For example, in a-lá 'the dog' (the ´ expresses the stress accent), the accent is moved to the plural marker -kʷa in the plural: a-la-kʷá 'the dogs'. On the other hand, in á-bla 'the eye', the accent does not move even in the case of the plural: á-bla-kʷa 'the eyes'. There are cases where the accent of verbs is moved in a similar fashion in accordance with their inflectional changes. For example, the aorist forms of á-fa-ra 'to eat' are jə-c-fá-jt' 'I ate it/them' and j-á-fa-jt' 'it ate it/them' wherein the accent is placed on the root *fa* and on the 3rd non-human singular pronominal prefix *a*. Since the position of the Abkhaz accent changes with the word form, attempts have been made to regularize the accent movement conditions under unified principles. These are the accent rules by Dybo and Spruit in §1.2.3 and §1.2.4 covered below. For the moment, an outline of the patterns of the Abkhaz accent will be laid out and the details left for later discussion.

1.2.2. The Abkhaz accent can be divided into the noun accent type and the verb accent type, and classified into three accent types for each.

1.2.2.1. Noun accent types

There are the following three accent types for Abkhaz nouns.

(a) Fixed accent type: the type where the accent position does not change in the word form. We call this 'accent type a'. For example, a-saát 'hour', a-saát-kʷa 'hours', saát-k' 'one hour'.

(b) Final-position accent type: the accent is placed on the final position of the root or on a part of a derived suffix. We call this 'accent type b'. Examples are: a-gʷə́ 'heart', l-gʷə́ 'her heart', and rə-gʷ-kʷá 'their hearts'.

(c) Mobile accent type: the accent position changes in the word form. We call this 'accent type c'. For example, á-mjʷa 'road', á-mjʷa-kʷa 'roads', mjʷá-k'/mjʷa-k'ə́ 'one road', mjʷa-kʷá-k' 'some roads'.

1.2.2.2. Verb accent types

The verb in Abkhaz takes various affixes to form a complicated verbal complex. When it does so, frequent changes of the accent position occur according to the various affixes gained in the verb complex. It follows that it is impossible to determine the accent type in the strictest sense; however, herein it is possible to classify the accent type of the aorist finite form (or the present finite form), which does not have a preverb. This allows the classification of the verb into three accent types:

(a) Root-fixed accent type: the accent position does not change with the inflection in the aorist and present forms and the accent is placed within the root. For example, a-gə́la-ra 'to stand up': s-gə́la-jt' 'I stood up', sə-m-gə́la-jt' 'I did not stand up'; s-gə́la-wa-jt' 'I am standing up'. Other examples are: a-báħa-ra 'to dig', a-xʷə́c-ra 'to think', a-c'áa-ra 'to freeze', á-xʷmar-ra 'to play': də-xʷmárə-jt' '(s)he played', a-k'ʷák'ʷ-ra 'to loosen'. a-k'ʲə́j-ra 'to mew', a-k'ak'áč'ʲ-ra 'to bloom', a-ɣʷə́x-ra 'to destroy', a-ɣʷə́r-ra 'to grunt'. a-ɣʲə́čʲ-ra 'to steal', a-ɣalát'-ra 'to betray', and a-gʷə́ɣ-ra 'to hope'.

(b) Prefix-position accent type: the accent is placed on the pronominal prefix (or the negative marker) in the aorist form. For example, á-ma-zaa-ra 'to have': s-bə́-ma-wp' 'you have me'. á-jʷ-ra 'to run': də́-jʷə-jt' '(s)he ran', d-mə́-jʷə-jt' '(s)he did not run', sə́-jʷ-wa-jt' 'I am running'. Other examples are: á-ʒ-ra 'to disappear', á-pa-ra 'to jump', á-xʷa-ra 'to help': s-bə́-xʷa-jt' 'I helped you', sə-b-mə́-xʷa-jt' 'I did not help you', s-bə́-xʷa-wa-jt' 'I am helping you'. Further examples: á-gʷa-ra 'to push', á-s-ra 'to hit', á-pxʲa-ra 'to read, to call', á-cħa-ra 'to bite', á-xʲ-ra 'to hurt; to happen to'.

(c) Final-position accent type: the accent is placed at the stem-final position in the aorist/present form. For example, a-taxə́-zaa-ra 'to want': jə-s-taxə́-wp' 'I want it/them'. a-ca-rá 'to go': d-cá-jt' '(s)he went', də-m-cá-jt' '(s)he did not go', d-ca-wá-jt' '(s)he is going'. á-ʒsa-ra 'to swim': də-ʒsá-jt' '(s)he swam', d-mə-ʒsá-jt' '(s)he did not swim', də-ʒsa-wá-jt' '(s)he is swimming'.

The (c) type above can be further classified into the following three types according to the position of the accent for the third-person non-human agent prefix *a*.

(i) a-ga-rá (агара́) type: the accent is placed on the prefix in this type only for the prefix *a* of the third-person singular non-human agent of the aorist-negative form.
Ex. a-ga-rá 'to take': bə-z-gá-jt' 'I took you', b-a-gá-jt' 'it took you', b-sə-m-gá-jt' 'I did not take you', *b-á-m-ga-jt'* 'it did not take you', bə-z-ga-wá-jt' 'I am taking you', b-a-ga-wá-jt' 'it is not taking you'. Other examples: a-ba-rá 'to see', a-k'-rá 'to catch', a-žʷ-rá 'to boil', a-šʲ-rá 'to kill', a-sa-rá 'to shave', a-q'ʲa-rá 'to wave', a-pa-rá 'to knit', a-x-rá 'to sharpen', a-cʷa-rá 'to suck', a-xʷ-rá 'to injure', a-k'ʷa-rá 'to shape a stone', a-ʒa-rá 'to hide', a-za-rá 'to measure'.

(ii) á-fa-ra (а́фара) type: in this type, the accent is placed on the prefix for forms of the third-person singular non-human agent having the prefix *a*.
Ex. á-fa-ra 'to eat': jə-s-fá-jt' 'I ate it/them', *j-á-fa-jt'* 'it ate it/them', j-sə-m-fá-jt' 'I did not eat it/them', *j-á-m-fa-jt'* 'it did not eat it/them', jə-s-fa-wá-jt' 'I am eating it/them', *j-á-fa-wa-jt'* 'it is eating it/them'. Other examples are: á-žʷ-ra 'to drink', a-ž-rá 'to dig', a-ʒ-rá 'to roast', a-šʷ-rá 'to dye', á-təj-ra 'to sell', á-q'aq'a-ra 'to chew', a-ǯʲ-rá 'to roast', á-xʲčʲa-ra 'to guard', á-ʒ(ə)b-ra 'to decide', a-ʒjʷa-rá 'to dilute'.

(iii) a-ša-rá (ашара́) type: the accent is placed at the stem-finals in all cases for the aorist form for this type.
Ex. a-ša-rá 'to divide': jə-s-šá-jt' 'I divided it/them', j-a-šá-jt' 'it divided it/them', j-a-m-šá-jt' 'it did not divide it/them'. Further examples: a-šʷa-rá 'to measure', a-ħʷa-rá 'to comb', a-ħa-rá 'to plait'.

1.2.3. Dybo's Rule of Abkhaz Accent

The Russian scholar of Slavic comparative-historical accentuation, V.A. Dybo (1981: 260–261), described the following accent principles for Slavonic accentuation.

> All of the morphemes in Proto-Slavic can be separated into two morphophonological prosodic classes in relation to their ictuses. I. The 'dominant morphemes (доминирующие морфемы)' class (morphemes affiliated with the ictus) and II. the 'recessive morphemes (рецессивные морфемы)' class (morphemes unaffiliated with the ictus). We have proposed calling the morphophonological prosodic characteristics of these classes accentuational 'valency (валентности)': with the I class being that of high valency and the II class that of low valency. We introduced special notations for these morphemes; using the '+' for high valency morphemes

and '−' for those of low valency. The ictus of sequences of morphemes made up of these notations become as follows (only a few examples are listed here — T.Y.):

(1) vy'-dĕl-a-ti (+' + + +) 'to manufacture'
(2) lĕ'n-ost-ь (−' − −) 'laziness'
(3) lĕn-ost-ь-jǫ' (− − − +') Instr.Sg. 'laziness'
(4) sta'r-ost-ь-jǫ (+' − − +) Instr.Sg. 'old age'
(5) sto'l-ič-ьn-o-jǫ (+' + − − +) Instr.Sg.fem. 'capital, urban'

(1) and (2) show the sequence of the morpheme with the same valency with the ictus being received on the initial morpheme. (3) and (4) show the sequence of the morpheme with differing valences with the ictus being received on the first dominant morpheme. Taking (5) into consideration, the general *contour rule* (контурное правило) regulating the setting of the ictus with regard to all types of Balto-Slavonic language morpheme sequences can be formulated as below: the ictus is placed at the beginning of the first sequence of the highest valency morpheme. (...) The comparative-historical analysis of an accent system such as this indicates the following: that this type of accent system is normally generated by the phonologization of the accent curve joining the tones which occurred (either partially or entirely) due to the loss of distinction between tones.

Dybo applied this principle of the 'morphophonological rank of accent valency' for Slavic to the accents in Abkhaz, which led him to produce an accent rule such as that which follows: 'The accent in Abkhaz is always placed at the tail end of the first sequence of the morpheme with the highest valency' (Dybo 1998: 132; Dybo 2000: 663). For example, if a morpheme (corresponding to the 'I class high valency' in the Slavic accent theory) with the ability to attract the accent is indicated by a '+' and a morpheme lacking the ability (corresponding to the 'II class low valency' in the Slavic accent theory) is indicated with a '−', the ictus accent becomes as follows (' ' ' expresses stress):

wasá (+) 'sheep': a-wasá (+ +') 'the-sheep', a-wasa-kʷá (+ + +') 'the-sheep-Pl'
blá (−) 'eye': á-bla (+' −) 'the-eye', á-bla-kʷa (+' − +) 'the-eye-Pl'

Furthermore, in the case where the valency is only made of the '−', Dybo states in his mention of the North West Caucasian languages other than Adyghe, that the accent in Abkhaz-Ubykh is either on the last syllable in the first sequence of the high-tonal syllable or simply placed on the last syllable in the case of phonetic words that lack the high-tonal syllable (Dybo 2000: 7).

1.2.4. Spruit's Rule of Abkhaz Accent

A. Spruit (1985) added some modifications to Dybo's Rule. The first modification made by Spruit was the changing of the 'morphemes' postulated by Dybo as the units of 'valency' given to accents to 'elements'. Spruit defines these elements as follows (Spruit 1985: 31):

To describe the place of the stress in Abkhaz words it is convenient to consider each word as consisting of a string of elements C(ə) or Ca (where C is any consonant); in addition, there are elements *a* and *aa* (*a* being counted a separate element in morpheme-initial position).

Elements C(ə), Ca (and also the instances of *a*, *aa* just mentioned) are combinedly referred to as

'C(a)'. In the absence of *a*, the occurrence of *ə* is to be a very large extent predictable. A stressed element C(á) is realized as Cá or, in the absence of *a*, as Cə́.

Spruit considered each of these 'element' units from the accent viewpoint of two classes; namely, separating them into the dominant (notated as 'D') class and the recessive (notated as 'R') class just as Dybo had postulated.[67] This allows the supposition that the words in Abkhaz are made up of 'a string of D's and/or R's' from the accent standpoint, and allows the statement of the rule for the Abkhaz accent as follows (Spruit, ibid.: 32):

> The general rule for the stress is that it falls on the first D in the word not followed by another D (hence on the first D followed by R or by #). Examples (D' is the stressed element): D', D'R, RD', DD', RD'R, RRD', RDD', DDD', RD'RR, RD'RD, RDD'R, DDDD', D'RDD, etc.

In addition, the second modification made by Spruit is one that covers words made up solely with the 'recessive class' R. He differs from Dybo's supposition, saying that the position where the accent is to be placed for such words is unpredictable (Spruit, ibid.: 32):

> The rule does not predict the position of the stress in words with element R only; for such words, the position of the stress has to be stated for each particular morphological type.

Words such as those are underlined as RR' / R'R by Spruit. First, nouns having an article and a single syllable root become as follows:

DD' : a-lá 'the dog', a-ʒə́ 'the water'
D'R : á-la 'the eye', á-ʒ 'the flea'
In addition, nouns having *z*- 'whose' and a single syllable root become as follows:
R'D : z-lá 'whose dog', z-ʒə́ 'whose water'
RR' / R'R : z-lá / zə́-la 'whose eye', z-ʒə́ / zə́-ʒ 'whose flea'
Moreover, Spruit presents the following examples to show that the accent rule can be applied identically to words of two or more syllables:
DDD' : a-ʒ-ɣʲə́ 'swift water'
DD'R : a-čə́-z 'sorrel horse'
D'RD : á-ǯʲ-jʷa 'dry oak'
D'RR : á-šʷə-žʷ 'old door'
RR'R/RRR' : šʷ-žʷə́-k' / šʷə-žʷ-k'ə́ 'old door'

Spruit also states that there are cases in which the accentual classes of the elements of plurisyllabic words cannot be determined. For example, in cases such as D'RX, the accent class of the last element X is indeterminate. Spruit expresses such an X using the I (Indeterminate) notation.

1.2.5. What are the implications of Spruit's Rule regarding Abkhaz accents?

The effectiveness of Spruit's Rule for Abkhaz is examined in §2.1.8 and §2.4.5. The conclusion drawn

67. We will refer to the D and R notation as the 'accent unit' in this text.

there is that Spruit's Rule is generally effective in describing the Abkhaz accents even though there are exceptions. Although this rule seems to be an abstract one at first glance, it elicits the question of what types of past linguistic phenomena are reflected within it.

It causes one to wonder if there are analogous phenomena stemming from typological accentuation. As was mentioned earlier, Dybo reconstructed principles similar to these for the Proto-Slavic accent system. In addition, he explained the accent characteristics as follows: 'This type of accent system is normally generated by the phonologization of the accent curve joining the tones which occurred (either partially or entirely) due to the loss of distinction between tones.' (Dybo 1981: 260–261) (underscoring added by this author).

As is generally known, there were three Accent Paradigms (abbreviated hereafter as 'AP') linking three tones during the late stage of Slavic. These were discovered by Chr. S. Stang (1957) and were respectively named AP a, AP b and AP c.[68] These accent paradigms each have the following characteristics. AP a is a fixed-stem Accent Paradigm with an acute. AP b is an Accent Paradigm which has a neo-acute for stems for certain case forms and a grave for word-ending syllables that directly follow them for other case forms. AP c is an Accent Paradigm where the accent moves between the word initial and the end of a word with a circumflex for the word initial syllable of certain case forms, and with the other accents at the end of words for other case forms. In other words, during the late stage of Slavic, the three tones mentioned above were in opposition for word initial syllables, and since the circumflex tone was eliminated for the word-medial syllable, the remaining two tones opposed each other. The Accent Paradigms and links with tones were characteristic of this period. However, in conjunction with the split of Common Slavic, each of the Slavic language family groups underwent a diversity of prosodical innovation. The quantitative opposition with tones was lost in Russian and the accent changed to a stress accent while keeping a free accent. The change in the accent system from Slavic to Russian is a resource that exemplifies the change towards a stress accent language from a tonal language. If the principles of accent formulated for Abkhaz under Dybo's Rule and Spruit's Rule and the analogous accent principles postulated for Proto-Slavic by Dybo (1981) are considered, it is possible to hypothesize the existence of a similar tonal system for Proto-Slavic in the Abkhaz protolanguage (referred to as 'Proto-Ubykh-Abkhaz' by Dybo).

Starostin and Chirikba's (1996: 35–37) assertion of the existence of a tonal system in Tapanta Abaza provides interesting collateral evidence on this. According to Starostin's examination, 'Tapanta, which possesses a system of paradigmatic accent which is on the whole identical to that of South Abkhaz, has in the stressed syllable a distinction between two tones: high and low.' (Chirikba: ibid.: 35) In addition, Chirikba himself found in his field study of Abaza that his informant had a system of three syllabic tones: high (H), low (L) and mid (M), mentioning that 'every syllable in a word, regardless of the position of stress, bears a tone'. Although Chirikba's survey material was extremely limited, he wrote the following based on it: 'The examination of the Tapanta tonal system shows a remarkable parallelism with the results of the accentological works by Dybo and Spruit. In many cases the dominant morphemes/elements described by these authors have a high tone in Tapanta, while the recessive elements have a low tone. But the actual picture of correlation between tone and stress in Abkhaz and Tapanta is not always as straightforward'. (Chirikba, ibid.: 37)

There is almost no mention of the accent system for the Tapanta dialect by Chirikba due to a lack of

68. Christian S. Stang. 1957. *Slavonic accentuation.* Oslo: Universitetsforlaget.

resources. Due to this, the comparative-historical accentology of Abkhaz and the Tapanta dialect will remain a topic for the future and there will probably be no major developments in hypotheses regarding the tonal origins of Abkhaz accent in the immediate future.

1.2.5.1. In giving consideration to these points, we compared the accent characteristics of Abkhaz with the Tokyo dialect tone system in contemporary Japanese from the standpoint of typological accentology; and found that the 'accent fall' position with regard to the tone system in this dialect is analogous to the position of the stress accent seen in Abkhaz under Spruit's Rule. According to H. Kindaichi (1967: 211–215),[69] the Tokyo dialect accent is composed of the following characteristics:

(1) It is made up of two tonemes: high 'H' and low 'L', with no other tonemes existing.

(2) A single mora is made up of one toneme. For example, there are no compound 'High' and 'Low' moras.

(3) The type of toneme always differs between the first mora and the second mora.

(4) There are no cases in which a 'High' toneme opposes a 'High' toneme with a 'Low' toneme in-between. As such, there are LHL types, there are no HLH types.

(5) There are two types where the ending is high, such as the H-type, LH-type, LHH-type and LHHH-type. When another word follows and is pronounced as one word, the next word is either followed as low or high. For example, *hana* 'flower' and *hana* 'nose' both are of the LH type; however, adding the HL-type word *made* 'as far as' results in the LHLL type for *hana-made* 'as far as flowers', while *hana-made* 'as far as a nose' becomes the LHHL type. Here, a word such as 'flower' which demands a low following word is notated as the LH↓-type.

(6) The position where 'High' descends to 'Low' is an attribute which should be especially noted. For example, a three mora word can be of an HLL, LHL or LHH type; however, Tokyo people differentiate this in the following ways:

(a) The first mora needs only to be made higher than the second mora in order to be heard as the HLL type. The height of the third mora is completely arbitrary.

(b) In order for it to be heard as the LHL type, the second mora needs to be higher than the third mora and the second mora cannot be lower than the first mora. The second mora does not always have to be higher than the first mora.

(c) In order for it to be heard as the LHH type, the third mora cannot be lower than the second mora and the second mora cannot be lower than the first mora. When these conditions are met, there is no problem even if the third mora is higher than the second, or the second mora and the first mora are the same.

Considering (a), (b) and (c) mentioned above together, it may be said that the point at which the initial drop is done is important for the Tokyo accent, and that if care is taken to pronounce that point, all of the other points do not matter.[70] The position of the initial drop is called the 'accent fall'. If the accent

69. Kindaichi, Haruhiko. *Nihongo onin-no kenkyu.* (Studies on Japanese Phonemes), Tokyodo Pub., 1967.

70. In words of four or more moras there must not be a rising-falling at some point in-between for types where three or more moras are successively 'Low'. More specifically, in types such as the HLLL type, the HLLL

fall positions of each type in the Tokyo dialect are notated using the ↓ symbol, they become as shown in Table 15.

Table 15

H↓ hi 'fire'	H↓L ame 'rain'	H↓LL kabuto 'helmet'	H↓LLL tamasii 'soul, sprit'
H ha 'leaf'	LH↓ yama 'mount'	LH↓L kokoro 'heart'	LH↓LL uguisu 'bush warbler'
	LH mizu 'water'	LHH↓ otoko 'man'	LHH↓L karakasa 'umbrella'
		LHH sakura 'cherry'	LHHH↓ otooto 'younger brother'
			LHHH niwatori 'fowl'

The tones and positions of the accent falls for the Tokyo dialect in Table 15 bear a noticeable resemblance to Spruit's Rule for Abkhaz in many points. (Hereinafter the accent fall of the Tokyo dialect will be expressed by ' ' ')
The analogous points are as follows:

(a) Both the Tokyo dialect and Abkhaz are respectively comprised of two types of oppositional units: H and L; and D and R.

(b) A single mora in the Tokyo dialect can have either an H or L. On the other hand, the Abkhaz element C(a) can have either a D or R. In both languages, there are no cases where a single mora or an element is compounded with HL or DR.

(c) An accent fall appears when a H is followed by a L in the Tokyo dialect, and in Abkhaz an accent is placed on the D when a D is succeeded with R. H'L : D'R, H'LL : D'RR, LH'L : RD'R.

(d) In the Tokyo dialect when a H appears in succession and there is an accent fall, the accent fall is after the last H and never appears after the interim H: LHH', LHHH'. In Abkhaz when Ds occur consecutively (in the first successive sequence), the accent is placed on the last D: RDD', RDDD'.

(e) In the Tokyo dialect, if there is no accent fall when H appears in succession and a HL word follows to be pronounced as a single word, the accent fall appears on the H in the following word: LH-H'L. In the case of a consecutive D in Abkhaz where the next word with a D or morpheme follows and is to be pronounced as a single word, the accent is moved to the D which follows: DD-D'.

(f) In the Tokyo dialect, the first mora only needs to be made higher than the second mora in order to be heard as the HLL type. The height of the third mora is completely arbitrary. On the other hand, in the D'RD in Abkhaz, where the accent cannot be placed on the third D, the type of the third accent unit is arbitrary with relation to the rules. The position of the accent is the same as for D'RR.

However, there are differences between the Tokyo dialect and Abkhaz.

(g) In the Tokyo dialect there is the final H which has an accent fall and the H which does not; however, there is no such distinction with the Abkhaz D. For example, in probably all words when DD' is joined to DR the accent shifts to the third position: DDD'R (ex. laba-k^{w}á-k' DD-D'R

---

tune and the HLLH tune are permitted; however the HLHL tune is not.

'some sticks'). Thus, in all probability, there are no words wherein an accent such as DD'DR cannot be shifted to the third position.

(h) With regard to the Tokyo dialect, the toneme type of the first mora and the second mora always differ; however, there is no similar restriction for the first element and second element in Abkhaz.

(i) In the Tokyo dialect, there are no cases in which a 'High' toneme opposes a 'High' toneme with a 'Low' toneme in-between; however there is no such restriction in Abkhaz. For example, DRD (ex. á-la-kʷa 'the eyes').

1.2.5.2. The position of the 'accent fall' in the Tokyo dialect is of the utmost importance. What this means is that the accent fall in the word determines the accent type for the word. For example, four accent types exist for a three-mora word with the position of the accent fall in the word automatically determining which of the four accent types appear in the word. Similarly, in Abkhaz the most important function of the accent is to determine the accent type with which a word is affiliated. The accent types are associated with tonal arrays in languages with a tonal system.[71] Therefore, if we regard prehistorical Abkhaz as a language with a tonal system, it is possible to posit that the accent system was close to the following: i.e., that Abkhaz in the past had 'High' and 'Low' tonemes similar to the Tokyo dialect. Moreover, the accent type was determined by the initial falling position from 'High (H)' to 'Low (L)'. The development of the three accent types for nouns may be postulated as follows (examples in parentheses are contemporary Abkhaz):

final-position accent type: HH > DD' (cf. a-lá 'dog'), HHH > DDD' (cf. a-la-kʷá 'dogs')
mobile-accent type: HL > D'R (cf. á-la 'eye'), LHL > RD'R (cf. la-kʷá-la 'with eyes')
fixed accent type: HHL > DD'R (cf. a-lába 'male dog'), HHLH > DD'RD (cf. a-lába-kʷa 'male dogs').

With regard to the stages before the advent of Abkhaz history, as the accent system changed from a tone accent system to a stress accent system, the ictus was placed on the 'High' syllable which had been the initial drop position from 'High' to 'Low' in the past. Alternatively, the ictus was placed on the final 'High' syllable in cases where the end was 'High' with no subsequent 'Low'.[72]

---

71. The connection between the tone arrays and the accent types is continued even in languages (such as Russian) wherein tones have become extinct and which have a free stress accent. As was mentioned earlier, there was a close relationship between the three tones: acute, neo-acute and circumflex; and the three accent types: AP a, AP b and AP c in the late stages of Slavic. These three accent types continue to this day in contemporary Russian (cf. Russian: AP a. koróva 'cow', acc. sg. koróvu, AP b. bloxá 'flea', acc. sg. bloxú, AP c. golová 'head', acc. sg. gólovu).

72. The final 'High' mora positioned where there is a 'fall' from 'High' to 'Low' is pronounced more forcefully to some degree even in the contemporary Tokyo dialect. For example, the third syllable *ka* in *karakasa* 'umbrella' (LHH'L) is pronounced somewhat stronger than the others.

2. Morphology:

Nouns, Pronouns, Demonstratives, Adjectives, Adverbs, Numerals, Postpositions

2.1. Nouns

2.1.1. Nominal Declension

Unlike other Northwest Caucasian languages, in Abkhaz there is no case inflection in the noun, adjective, or pronoun that is a core argument. In other words, the morphology of the noun phrase lacks a function to show the relationship between the subject and object of a sentence. That function is expressed by the morphology of the verbal predicate. For peripheral arguments, Abkhaz has the predicative or adverbial marker -с /s/ 'as' (or -ны /nə/), and the instrumental marker -ла /la/ 'with, by'. For example:

(1) Уи́ рҵаҩы́с дыҟоуп.
/wəj rc'aj^{w}ə́-s dә́-q'a-wp'/
he teacher-as he-be-Stat.Pres.Fin
'He is a teacher.'

(2) Сара́ лаба́ла ала́ са́сит.
/sará labá-la a-lá s-á-sə-jt'/
I stick-with the-dog I-it-hit-(Aor)-Fin
'I hit the dog with a stick.'

Furthermore, There are elements such as -н /n/ 'in, at, on', -ҟны /-q'nə/ 'in, at' with a locative meaning that are attached to nouns, as the following examples show.

(3) Сгы́лан а́мҩан.
/s-gə́la-n á-mj^{w}a-n/
I-stand-Stat.Past.Fin the-road-on
'I was standing on the road.'

(4) Аӡа́ӡа а́мраҟны ицырцы́руеит.
/a-ʒáʒa á-mra-[a-]q'nə jə-cərcə́r-wa-jt'/
the-dew the-sun-its-in it(C1)-glitter-Dyn-Fin
'The dew is glittering in the sun.'

We regard these elements as postpositions rather than as case markers. This is because we cannot confirm a case marker in the peripheral argument, even though there is no case marker in the core argument.

2.1.2. Nominal Number

Nouns can be classified as countable nouns and uncountable nouns.

2.1.2.1. Examples of uncountable nouns:

а-ҵəаҕуáга 'instrument for plowing', а-чáи 'tea', а-шáхмат 'chess', (а)-ҵьанáҭ 'heaven, paradise', бжьрабы́жьҵəа 'the nether world, a hell', áиҧшра 'likeness', аиҭáр 'the god of domestic animals', а-какáл 'breakfast', а-ҟəы́дчаҧа 'haricot bean', а-лабҿабá 'reality', а-ны́шə 'soil, earth', áр(ра) 'army', а-тəы́мҵьара 'a foreign country/land', а-ҭəá 'pus', а-фы́ 'thunder, lightning', á-ҳəара 'request', а-ҩáша 'Tuesday'.

2.1.2.2. Plural Forms

Countable nouns have singular and plural forms. The plural form of human class nouns can be formed by adding -ҵəа /cʷa/ and that of non-human class nouns by adding -қəа /kʷa/ (for nominal classes, see §2.1.3). For example:

Human class:

á-чкəын /á-č'k'ʷən/ 'a boy' : á-чкəын-ҵəа /á-č'k'ʷən-cʷa/ 'boys'

á-саби /á-sabəj/ 'a baby' : á-саби-ҵəа /á-sabəj-cʷa/ 'babies'

á-ҵəаҕəаҩ /á-cʷaɣʷajʷ/ 'a peasant' : á-ҵəаҕəаҩ-ҵəа /á-cʷaɣʷajʷ-cʷa/ 'peasants'

Non-Human class:

а-лабá /a-labá/ 'a stick' : а-лаба-қəá /a-laba-kʷá/ 'sticks'

á-ӡ /á-ʒ/ 'a louse/flea' : á-ӡ-қəа /á-ʒ-kʷa/ 'lice/fleas'

á-бга /á-bga/ 'a fox' : á-бга-қəа /á-bga-kʷa/ 'foxes'

-ӡы́ /ʒə́/ 'water' : а-ӡ-қəá /a-ʒ-kʷa/ 'waters'

Either plural marker can be used with nouns that indicate a specific ethnic group or person.

а-қы́рҭ-ҵəа/-қəа /a-kə́rt-cʷa/-kʷa/ 'Georgians' (cf. á-қырҭуа /á-kərtwa/ 'a Georgian')

á-урыс-ҵəа/-қəа /á-wrəs-cʷa/-kʷa/ 'Russians' (cf. á-урыс 'a Russian')

абáза-ҵəа/-қəа /abáza-cʷa/kʷa/ 'Abazians' (cf. абáза 'an Abazian')

á-шəан-ҵəа/-қəа /á-šʷan-cʷa/-kʷa/ 'Svans' (cf. á-шəаныуа /á-šʷanəwa/ 'a Svan')

а-дáгəа-ҵəа/-қəа /a-dágʷa-cʷa/-kʷa/ 'mutes' (cf. а-дáгəа 'a mute')

а-ҳəарҭлáҕь-ҵəа/-қəа /a-xʷartláɣʲ-cʷa/-kʷa/ 'witches' (cf. а-ҳəарҭлáҕь 'a witch')

The suffixes -аа /aa/ and -уаа /waa/ 'people' (cf. sg. ауаҩы́ /a-wa-jʷə́/ 'a person', pl. ауаá /a-w[a]-aá/ 'people') are attached to nouns that indicate persons. In the latter case, the singular suffix -уаҩ /wajʷ/ is removed and -уаа /waa/ is added.

Examples of adding -аа /aa/:

áҟəаа /áq'ʷ-aa/ 'Sukhumites' (cf. Aҟəа /áq'ʷa/ 'Sukhum')

алéмсаа /a-lémsaa/ 'Germans' (cf. а-лéмса 'a German')

áбхəараа /ábxʷaraa/ 'parents and close relatives of my wife/husband'

Examples of adding -уаа /waa/:

ақы́ҭауаа /a-kə́ta-waa/ 'villagers' (cf. а-қы́ҭа-уаҩ 'a villager', а-қы́ҭа 'a village')

аиапóнуаа /a-jap'ón-waa/ 'Japanese' (cf. а-иапóн-уаҩ(ы) 'a Japanese', Иапóниа 'Japan')

агермáнуаа /a-germán-waa/ 'Germans' (cf. а-гермáн-уаҩ(ы) 'a German')

америкáнуаа (америкáн-ҵəа) /amerəjk'án-waa/ 'Americans' (cf. америкáн-уаҩ(ы) 'an American')

2.1.2.3. When forming the plural form for deverbative nouns with the suffix -ҩ(ы) /jʷ(ə)/ that indicates an agent in the singular, there is a tendency to not infrequently drop that suffix in the plural. Examples of the suffix being dropped:
а-гәрага-ҩы́ /a-gʷraga-jʷə́/ 'a believer' : а-гәрага-цәа́ /a-gʷraga-cʷá/ 'believers'
а-ҕала́т-ҩы /a-ɣalát'-jʷə/ 'a betrayer' : а-ҕала́т-цәа /a-ɣalát'-cʷa/
а́-ӡба-ҩ /á-ʒba-jʷ/ 'a judge' : а́-ӡб-цәа /á-ʒb-cʷa/
а́-ӡырҩ-ҩы /á-ʒərjʷ-jʷə/ 'a listener' : а́-ӡырҩ-цәа /á-ʒərjʷ-cʷa/
а́ибашь-ҩы /ájbašʲ-jʷə/ 'a warrior, a fighter' : а́ибашь-цәа /ájbašʲ-cʷa/
а́иҭага-ҩ /ájtaga-jʷ/ 'a translator' : а́иҭага-цәа /ájtaga-cʷa/
а́-кәаша-ҩ /á-k'ʷaša-jʷ/ 'a dancer' : а́-кәаша-цәа /á-k'ʷaša-cʷa/
а-матҵу-ҩы́ /a-mac'əw-jʷə́/ 'a servant' : а-матҵу-цәа́ /a-mac'əw-cʷá/
а́-мҩас-ҩы /á-mjʷas-jʷə/ 'a passer-by' : а́-мҩас-цәа /á-mjʷas-cʷa/
а-рҳә-ҩы́ /a-rħʷ-jʷə́/ 'a robber' : а-рҳә-цәа́ /a-rħʷ-cʷá/
а́-хәаԥш-ҩы /á-xʷapš-jʷə/ 'a spectator' : а́-хәаԥш-цәа /á-xʷapš-cʷa/

Examples of the suffix not being dropped:
а-кәы́лаҩ /a-kʷə́lajʷ/ 'an invader' : а-кәы́лаҩ-цәа /a-kʷə́lajʷ-cʷa/
а́-жьҭааҩы /á-žʲtaajʷə/ 'a grape harvester' : а́-жьҭааҩ-цәа /á-žʲtaajʷ-cʷa/
а-ӡахҩы́ /a-ʒaxjʷə́/ 'a tailor' : а-ӡахҩ-цәа́ /a-ʒaxjʷ-cʷá/
а́-ӡбаҩ /á-ʒbajʷ/ 'a judge' : а́-ӡбаҩ-цәа /á-ʒbajʷ-cʷa/
а-нхаҩы́ /a-nxajʷə́/ 'a peasant' : а-нха(ҩ)-цәа́ /a-nxa(jʷ)-cʷá/
а-рҵаҩы́ /a-rc'ajʷə́/ 'a teacher': а-рҵаҩ-цәа́ /a-rc'ajʷ-cʷá/
а-ҵаҩы́ /a-c'ajʷə́/ 'a pupil' : а-ҵаҩ-цәа́ /a-c'ajʷ-cʷá/

2.1.2.4. A few nouns have the same form in the singular and the plural. For example:
а́-ҵан /á-c'an/ 'Ts'an ((a) mythological aboriginal inhabitant(s) of Abkhazia)'

2.1.2.5. Examples of nouns with a collective meaning that have the suffix -р(а) /r(a)/:
а-ӡа́р /a-ʒár/ 'kids' (pl. а-ӡа́р-кәа /a-ʒár-kʷa/ is also possible, cf. а-ӡы́с /a-ʒə́s/ 'a kid'), а-ҵа́р /a-c'ár/ 'a flock of birds' (cf. а-ҵа́ра-кәа /a-c'ára-kʷa/, а-ҵы́с /a-c'ə́s/ 'birds'), а-жра́цәара /a-žrácʷara/ 'blood relatives', а́-жәлар /á-žʷlar/ 'people', а-са́р(а) /a-sár(a)/ 'lambs' (cf. а-сы́-с /a-sə́-s/ 'a lamb', а-са́р(а)-кәа /a-sár(a)-kʷa/ '(individual) lambs').
Examples of nouns with a collective meaning:
а-хәы́ /a-xʷə́/ 'hair', а́-шәарах /á-šʷarax/ 'wild animals', а́-жәла /á-žʷla/ 'seed', а́илаџь /ajlaǯʲ/ 'ailadzh (a kind of Abkhaz dish)', а́-матәа-ҩыҭәа /á-matʷa-jʷətʷa/ 'belongings, household goods', а-са́ба /a-sába/ 'dust' (cf. а-са́ба-кәа), а-уаа́тәыҩса /a-waát'ʷəjʷsa/ 'humanity', а́-фатә=а-жәтә /á-fat'ʷ-a-žʷt'ʷ/ 'food and drink', а-бҕьы́ /a-bɣʲə́/ 'leaves, a leaf'.

2.1.2.6. There are some nouns where the stem changes in the singular and the plural. For example:
а-ԥҳәы́с /a-pħʷə́s/ 'a woman' : а́-ҳәса(кәа) /á-ħʷsa(kʷa)/ 'women'
а-ха́ҵа /a-xác'a/ 'a man' : а-ха́цәа /a-xá-cʷa/ 'men'
аб /a-[a]b/ 'a father' : а́бацәа /á-[a]ba-cʷa/ 'fathers'
ан /a-[a]n/ 'a mother' : а́нацәа /á-[a]na-cʷa/ 'mothers'

2.1.3. Nominal Classes

2.1.3.1. Abkhaz nouns can be split into two grammatical classes. One is the human class and the other is the non-human class, used to indicate animals and other non-human things. The human class is further subdivided into masculine and feminine groups.

As discussed in §2.1.2.2, in terms of nominal form human class and non-human class nouns are distinguished morphologically in the plural form. -цәа /cʷa/ (using -аа /aa/ or -уаа /waa/ 'people' in the case of groups of people) is used with the human class, and -қәа /kʷa/ is used with the non-human class. For examples, see §2.1.2.2.

Furthermore, the plural form of some nouns is formed by using -қәа /kʷa/ even if they are human class:
á-хәса-қәа /á-ħʷsa-kʷa/ 'women' (cf. pl. á-хәса /á-ħʷsa/ 'women', sg. а-ҧҳәы́с /a-pħʷə́s/ 'woman')
а-хәыч-қәá /a-xʷəč'ʲ-kʷá/ 'children' (cf. а-хәычы́ /a-xʷəč'ʲə́/ 'a child')
á-иаҭым-қәа /á-jatəm-kʷa/ 'orphans' (cf. á-иаҭым /á-jatəm/ 'an orphan')
а-ҧелуа́н-қәа /a-pelwán-kʷa/ 'heros' (cf. а-ҧелуа́н /a-pelwán/ 'hero, a powerful person')

2.1.3.2. The class of a noun is also reflected in the person and class prefixes of verbs. With verbs, the noun class is reflected in the 3rd person singular (in the plural, no differences arise between human and non-human classes); a distinction is made between human class (д- /d/) and singular non-human class (и- /jə/) for S (i.e. the subject of an intransitive verb) and DO (i.e. the direct object of a transitive verb). For A (i.e. the subject of a transitive verb), a further distinction is made in the human class between masculine and feminine, respectively и- /j(ə)/ and л(ы)- /l(ə)/; non-human class has the prefix а-/на- /a/na/ (For details see §3.1.6). Differences between the human and non-human classes are also apparent among possessive prefixes in the form of the 3rd person singular. Here, the human class is further subdivided into masculine and feminine. The possessive prefix takes the same form as the prefix in A (i.e. the subject of the transitive verb) noted above (non-human class takes а-). (For details see §2.2.2.)

First, we investigate whether the noun that means 'god' in Abkhaz а-нцәа́ /a-ncʷá/ belongs to the human or non-human class. First, the plural form of this noun is а-нцәа-қәа́ /a-ncʷa-kʷá/, which has a non-human class plural marker. However, since this plural marker can also be used with the human class (see §2.1.3.1), we cannot yet say which class it belongs to. Next, the prefixes of the verbs that cross-reference this noun are as follows:

(5) Анцәа́ дха́стоит.
/a-ncʷá d-xá-s-c'a-wa-jt'/
the-god *him*-Prev-I-believe in-Dyn-Fin
'I believe in God.'

(6) Анцәа́ длйҭом.
/a-ncʷá d-lə́-j-ta-wa-m/
the-god him-her-*he*-give-Dyn-Neg
'God does not give him/her to her.'

In (5), 'god' cross-references with the д- /d/ indicating the object of a transitive verb. Also, in (6), 'god' cross-references with и- /j/, showing the subject of the transitive verb to be masculine. That is, it shows that the prefix of the verb that cross-references to 'god' is human class. Furthermore, the possessive prefix of this noun takes the plural marker p- /r/ 'their' as follows:

(7) анцәá ráшәа
/a-ncʷá r-ášʷa/
the-god their-sing
lit. 'their song of the god', 'the song of prayer'

This results in an exception; the class to which this noun belongs cannot be identified from its possessive prefix.[73]

Based on the above, we rely on the following rule to determine whether a noun is of the human or non-human class: the class of a noun is determined not by the plural form of the noun, but rather by the class of the pronominal prefix that cross-references to the noun.

2.1.4. Article and Nominal Definite and Indefinite

2.1.4.1. Abkhaz has the article a- /a/. The article is attached to the first part of nouns, adjectives, and the verbal noun known as *masdar*. The article always accompanies the form used for dictionaries entries. In noun clauses modified by adjectives, the article is attached only to the head noun. For example:
а-ҵаҩы́ /a-c'ajʷə́/ 'pupil'
а-бзи́а /a-bzə́ja/ 'good'
а-ҵа́ҩ бзи́а /ac'ájʷ bzə́ja/ 'a/the good pupil'
а-бара́ /a-bará/ 'seeing'

The article attaches only to the head noun even when two or more adjectives modify a noun:
а́-ԥшӡа /á-pšʒa/ 'beautiful'
а-ҵаҩы́ ԥшӡа́ бзи́а /a-c'ajʷə́ pšʒá bzə́ja/ 'a/the beautiful, good pupil'

Normally, in noun phrases the plural marker is attached to the adjective (plural markers can also be attached to both the noun and the adjective):
а́-шьха ԥшӡа-қәа́ /á-šʲxa pšʒa-kʷá/ 'the beautiful mountains'

As the examples of а́-ԥшӡа /á-pšʒa/ and ԥшӡа-қәа́ /pšʒa-kʷá/ show, if there is an accent on the article and the word then loses that article, the accent is placed on the vowel at the end of the word. On the other hand, when the accent is in the middle of a word (а-бзи́а /a-bzə́ja/), the accent does not move (бзи́а /bzə́ja/) even if the word loses the article.

2.1.4.2. The article a- has a generic meaning and a definite meaning. Let us examine this in a text. First, an example of generic meaning:

(8) Аԥша́цәгьа а́суамызт.
/a-pšá-cʷgʲa ø-á-s-wa-mə-zt'/
a-wind-strong [it]-Dummy-blow-Dyn-Neg-Impf
'There was no strong wind.' lit. 'A strong wind used not to hit it[Dummy].'

73. Perhaps this is because а-нцәа́ /a-ncʷá/ is etymologically formed from ан 'mother' + цәа́. (See Hewitt, AF: 105).

An example of definite meaning:

(9) Урҭ еицны ишнеиуаз хуаҵьак даарыкушәеит. — Шәабацои? — ҳәа дрызтцааит ахуаҵьа.
/wə́rt ajc-nə́ jə-š-ná-j-wa-z xʷáǯʲa-k' d-aa-rə́-kʷšʷa-jt'.
they together-Adv they-how-Prev-go thither-Dyn-Impf.NF Muslim-one he-Par-them-come across-(Aor)-Fin
— šʷ-abá-ca-wa-j? ħʷa d-rə-z-c'áa-jt' a-xʷáǯʲa.
you.PL-wher-go-Pres.NF-Qu SP he-them-Prev-ask-(Aor)-Fin *the*-Muslim

'As they were travelling on together, they came across a Muslim. — "Where are you going?" *the* Muslim asked them.'

2.1.4.3. To indicate the indefinite sense—that is, to say 'a X, one X, some Xs'—, the suffix -к /k'/ is added to the noun.[74] The noun to which it is attached does not carry the article а-. When that noun is in the plural form, the suffix -к is added to the end of the plural marker. For example:

шәҟәы́-к /šʷq'ʷə́-k'/ (book-one) 'one book' (cf. а-шәҟәы́ /a-šʷq'ʷə́/ 'the book')

шәҟә-қәа́-к /šʷq'ʷ-kʷá-k'/ (book-Pl-one) 'some books'

The accent is placed either in front of the suffix -к /k'/ or on the stem. If the accent would fall on the article or the word-final vowel, it is placed in front the suffix. Accents in the middle of the stem, however, will not move even with this suffix attached. For example:

а́-даҕь /á-daɣʲ/ 'a/the frog' : даҕьы́-к /daɣʲə́-k'/ 'one frog'

а́-даҕь-қәа /á-daɣʲ-kʷa/ 'frogs' : даҕь-қәа́-к /daɣʲ-kʷá-k'/ 'some frogs'

а-лаба́ /labá/ 'a/the stick' : лаба́-к /labá-k'/ 'one stick'

а-ҧсы́ӡ /a-psə́ʒ/ 'a fish' : ҧсы́ӡ-к / psə́ʒ-k'/ 'one fish'

An example in a text:

(10) Ҳәынҭқа́рк ды́ҟан.
/ħʷəntkár-k' də́-q'a-n/
king-one he-be-Stat.Past.Fin
'There lives a king.' lit. 'One king was.'

2.1.5. Derivational Suffixes

The suffixes that form Abkhaz nouns are as follows.

2.1.5.1. The suffix -ҩ(ы) /jʷ(ə)/ attaches to a verb stem and indicates an occupation or agent:

а-ҵа-ҩы́ /a-c'a-jʷə́/ 'a schoolchild, a pupil' (cf. а-ҵа-ра́ /a-c'a-rá/ 'to study')

а-рҵа-ҩы́ /a-rc'a-jʷə́/ 'a teacher' (cf. а-рҵа-ра́ /a-rc'a-rá/ 'to teach')

а-нха-ҩы́ /a-nxa-jʷə́/ 'a peasant' (cf. а-нха-ра́ /a-nxa-rá/ 'to farm; to live')

а́-ӡырҩ-ҩы /á-ʒərjʷ-jʷə/ 'a listener' (cf. а́-ӡырҩ-ра /á-ʒərjʷ-ra/ 'to listen')

а́-ӡба-ҩ /á-ʒba-jʷ/ 'a judge' (cf. а́-ӡба-ра /á-ʒba-ra/ 'to judge')

а́иҭага-ҩ /ájtaga-jʷ/ 'a translator' (cf. а́иҭага-ра /ájtaga-ra/ 'to translate')

а́-кәашa-ҩ /á-k'ʷaša-jʷ/ 'a dancer' (cf. а́-кәаша-ра /á-k'ʷaša-ra/ 'to dance')

а-гәрагаҩы́ /a-gʷraga-jʷə́/ 'a believer' (cf. а-гәрага-ра́ /a-gʷraga-rá/ 'to believe')

а-ҕала́т-ҩы /a-ɣalát'-jʷə/ 'a betrayer' (cf. а-ҕала́т-ра /a-ɣalát'-ra/ 'to betray')

74. The suffix is derived from the numeral акы́ /ak'ə́/ 'one'.

á-ӡса-ҩ(ы) /á-ʒsa-jʷ(ə)/ 'a swimmer' (cf. á-ӡса-ра /á-ʒsa-ra/ 'to swim')
á-мҩас-ҩы /á-mjʷas-jʷə/ 'a passer-by' (cf. á-мҩас-ра /á-mjʷas-ra/ 'to pass')
а-рхə-ҩы́ /a-rħʷ-jʷə́/ 'a robber' (cf. а-рхə-рá /a-rħʷ-rá/ 'to rob')
á-хəаԥш-ҩы /á-xʷapš-jʷə/ 'a spectator' (cf. á-хəаԥш-ра /á-xʷapš-ra/ 'to watch')
а-кры́фа-ҩ /a-k'rə́fa-jʷ/ 'an eater' (cf. а-кры́фа-ра /a-k'rə́fa-ra/ 'to eat')
á-қəԥа-ҩы /á-kʷpa-jʷə́/ 'a fighter' (cf. á-қəԥа-ра /á-kʷpa-ra/ 'to fight')

Note also those instances in which they are derived from 'noun+verb stem' with the suffix -ҩ(ы) /jʷ(ə)/ attached:

а-шəҟəы́-ҩ-ҩы /a-šʷq'ʷə́-jʷ-jʷə/ 'a writer' (cf. а-шəҟəы́ /a-šʷq'ʷə́/ 'book', а-ҩ-рá /a-jʷ-rá/ 'to write')
а-ýс-у-ҩ(ы) /a-wə́sə-w-jʷ(ə)/ 'a worker' (cf. а-ýс /a-wə́s/ 'work', а-у-рá /a-w-rá/ 'to do')

2.1.5.2. -уаҩ(ы) /wajʷ(ə)/ 'person' (pl. -уаа /waa/ 'people') attaches to the nominal stem and indicates a person or the name of an ethnic group. Although it is the second element in a compound word formed from a noun and a noun, functionally it is close to a suffix. That is because the plural form of certain nouns that use it do not take the -уаа /waa/ used for the plural form of those nouns, but rather take -цəа /cʷa/ (see а-ҽы́-уаҩы). For example:

а-кы́ҭа-уаҩ /a-kə́ta-wajʷ/ 'a villager' (pl. а-кы́ҭа-уаа /a-kə́ta-waa/, cf. а-кы́ҭа /a-kə́ta/ 'a village')
áр-уаҩы /ár-wajʷə/ 'a soldier' (pl. áр-уаа /ár-waa/, cf. ар /ar/ 'an army')
а-ҵарá-уаҩ(ы) /a-c'ará-wajʷ(ə)/ 'a scholar' (pl. а-ҵарá-уаа /a-c'ará-waa/, cf. а-ҵарá /a-c'ará/ 'study')
а-ҽы́-уаҩы /a-čə́-wajʷə/ 'a horseman, a knight' (pl. а-ҽ-цəá /a-č-cʷá/ , cf. а-ҽы́ /a-čə́/ 'a horse')
а-ҵьы́нџь-уаҩ /a-ǯʲə́nǯʲ-wajʷ/ 'an aborigine' (pl. а-ҵьы́нџь-уаа /a-ǯʲə́nǯʲ-waa/)
а-герман-уаҩ(ы) 'a German' (pl. а-герман-уаа)
америкáн-уаҩ(ы) 'an American' (pl. америкáн-цəа/-уаа)

2.1.5.3. The suffix -га /ga/ attaches to the verb stem and indicates the instrument that carries out the action of the verb:

ááнкыла-га /áank'əla-ga/ 'a brake' (cf. ááнкыла-ра /áank'əla-ra/ 'to stop')
аáхəа-га /aáxʷa-ga/ 'money' (cf. аáхəа-ра /aáxʷa-ra/ 'to buy')
а-ды́р-га /a-də́r-ga/ 'sign' (cf. а-ды́р-ра /a-də́r-ra/ 'to know')
а-рҵá-га /a-rcá-ga/ 'a textbook' (cf. а-рҵа-рá /a-rc'a-rá/ 'to teach')
а-жы́-га /a-žə́-ga/ 'a shovel' (cf. а-ж-рá /a-ž-rá/ 'to dig')
á-ӡəӡəа-га /á-ʒʷʒʷa-ga/ 'a washing machine' (cf. á-ӡəӡəа-ра /á-ʒʷʒʷa-ra/ 'to wash')
а-кьы́ԥхь-га (машьы́на) /a-k'ʲə́pxʲ-ga (mašʲə́na)/ 'a printer' (cf. а-кьы́ԥхь-ра /a-k'ʲə́pxʲ-ra/ 'to print')
а-ны́ҟəа-га /a-nə́q'ʷa-ga/ 'means of transport' (cf. а-ны́ҟəа-ра /a-nə́q'ʷa-ra/ 'to travel/go')
а-ԥсы́ӡкы́-га /a-psə́ʒk'ə́-ga/ 'fishing tackle' (cf. а-ԥсы́ӡк-ра /a-psə́ʒk'-ra/ 'to catch a fish')
а-ры́цкьа-га /a-rə́ckʲa-ga/ 'a (black) board rubber' (cf. а-ры́цкьа-ра /a-rə́ckʲa-ra/ 'to clean')
а-сá-га /a-sá-ga/ 'a razor' (cf. а-сá-ра /a-sá-ra/ 'to shave')
а-хаԥы́цры́цкьа-га /a-xapə́crə́ckʲa-ga/ 'a toothbrush' (cf. а-хаԥы́ц 'a tooth'+а-ры́цкьа-ра 'to clean')
á-хəмар-га /á-xʷmar-ga/ 'a toy' (cf. á-хəмар-ра /á-xʷmar-ra/ 'to play')
а-хəынаԥкы́-га /a-ħʷənapk'ə́-ga/ 'a mousetrap' (cf. а-хəы́наԥ 'a mouse' + а-к-рá 'to catch')
а-цəаҕəá-га /a-cʷaɣʷá-ga/ 'instrument for plowing' (cf. á-цəаҕəа-ра /á-cʷaɣʷa-ra/ 'to plow')

а-ҽа́-га /a-čá-ga/ 'a hoe' (cf. а-ҽа́-ра /a-čá-ra/ 'to hoe')
а-ҽбы́-га /a-čbə́-ga/ 'a scythe'
а-ҽы́кәаба-га /a-čə́k'ʷaba-ga/ 'a swimsuit' (cf. а-ҽы́кәаба-ра /a-čə́k'ʷaba-ra/ 'to bathe')
а-шәа́-га /a-šʷá-ga/ 'a measure' (cf. а-шәа́-ра /a-šʷá-ra/ 'to measure')
а-ҩы́-га /a-jʷə́-ga/ 'an instrument for writing' (cf. а-ҩ-ра́ /a-jʷ-rá/ 'to write')

The suffix in the foregoing examples does not take an accent. When a word is derived from a verb, if the word-ending -ра /ra/ of the masdar has an accent, the accent on the derived noun is placed immediately in front of the suffix -га /ga/.

2.1.5.4. The suffix -рҭа /rta/ has a locative meaning. It attaches to the verb stem and a small number of nominal stems:

а́аҩбала-рҭа /áajʷbala-rta/ 'entrance hall' (cf. ааҩна́ла-ра 'to enter')
а-ба́-рҭа /a-bá-rta/ 'place to see' (cf. а-ба-ра́ 'to see')
а́-дкыла-рҭа /á-dk'əla-rta/ 'a reception room' (cf. а́-дкыла-ра 'to welcome')
а-ӡа́лала-рҭа /a-ʒálala-rta/ 'an estuary' (cf. а-ӡы́ 'water/river', а́-лала-ра 'to flow into')
а́-ӡахы-рҭа /á-ʒaxə-rta/ 'a sewing shop' (cf. а́-ӡах-ра 'to sew')
а́-ӡба-рҭа /á-ʒba-rta/ 'a (law) court' (cf. а́-ӡба-ра 'to judge')
а-иа́-рҭа /a-já-rta/ 'a bed' (cf. а-иа-ра́ 'to lie')
а-кахуа́жәы-рҭа /a-k'aħwážʷə-rta/ 'a cafe' (cf. а-кахуа́ 'coffee', а́-жә-ра 'to drink')
а-кнаха́-рҭа /a-k'naħá-rta/ 'a cloakroom' (cf. а-кна́ха-ра 'to hang')
а-кры́фа-рҭа /a-k'rə́fa-rta/ 'a dining room' (cf. а-кры́фа-ра 'to eat')
а́-кәаша-рҭа /á-k'ʷaša-rta/ 'a dance floor' (cf. а́-кәаша-ра 'to dance')
а́-лбаа-рҭа /á-lbaa-rta/ 'a landing place' (cf. а́-лбаа-ра 'to descend')
а-матцу́-рҭа /a-mac'wə́-rta/ 'a kitchen' (cf. а-матц-у-ра́ 'to serve')
а-мраҭашәа́-рҭа /a-mratašʷá-rta/ 'west' (cf. а́-мра 'sun', а-ҭашәара́ 'to set')
а-нха́-рҭа /a-nxá-rta/ 'a dwelling place' (cf. а-нха-ра́ 'to live')
а-ҧатцаса́-рҭа /a-pac'asá-rta/ 'a barbershop' (cf. а-ҧатца́ 'beard', а-са-ра́ 'to shave')
а-ҧсшьа́-рҭа /a-psšʲá-rta/ 'a place for a rest' (cf. а-ҧсшьа́-ра 'to take a rest')
а-ҧсы́-рҭа /a-psə́-rta/ 'a place of death' (cf. а-ҧс-ра́ 'to die')
а́-ҧхьа-рҭа /á-pxʲa-rta/ 'a reading room' (cf. а́-ҧхьа-ра 'to read')
а́-ҧшы-рҭа /á-pšə-rta/ 'a maizefield' (cf. а́-ҧш 'maize')
а-ҧшы́-рҭа /a-pšə́-rta/ 'an observation post' (cf. а-ҧш-ра́ 'to watch')
а-сасаа́и-рҭа /a-sasaáj-rta/ 'a hotel' (cf. а́-сас 'a guest', аа́и-ра 'to come')
а-тәа́-рҭа /a-t'ʷá-rta/ 'a seat' (cf. а-тәа-ра́ 'to sit')
а-ҭа́ла-рҭа /a-tála-rta/ 'an entrance' (cf. а-ҭа́ла-ра 'to enter')
а́-ҭи-рҭа /á-təj-rta/ 'a counter' (cf. а́-ҭи-ра 'to sell')
а-ҭы́жьы-рҭа /a-tə́žʲə-rta/ 'a publishing house' (cf. а-ҭы́жь-ра 'to publish')
а-у́су-рҭа /a-wə́swə-rta/ 'a place of work' (cf. а-у́с 'work', а-у-ра́ 'to do')
а́-фатәҟатца-рҭа /á-fat'ʷq'ac'a-rta/ 'a kitchen' (cf. а́-фатә 'food', а́-ҟатца-ра 'to make')
а-хцәы́ҟатца-рҭа /a-xcʷə́q'ac'a-rta/ 'a barbershop' (cf. а-хцәы́ 'hair', а́-ҟатца-ра 'to make')
а-хшьы́-рҭа /a-xšʲə́-rta/ 'a [clothes] hanger' (cf. а-хшь-ра́ 'to hang on')
а-хәшәтәы́-рҭа /a-xʷšʷt'ʷə́-rta/ 'a hospital' (cf. а́-хәшәтә-ра 'to cure')
а-ҳәы́-рҭа /a-ħʷə́-rta/ 'a pasture' (cf. а-ҳә-ра́ 'to graze')

а-цá-рҭа /a-cá-rta/ 'a passage' (cf. а-ца-рá 'to go')
á-цәа-рҭа /á-cʷa-rta/ 'a bed(room)' (cf. á-цәа-ра 'to sleep')
а-ҵарайу-рҭа /a-c'arajə́w-rta/ 'education establishment' (cf. а-ҵарá 'learning', аиу́-ра 'to receive')
á-ҵҵы-рҭа /á-c'c'ə-rta/ 'a spring, source' (cf. á-ҵыҵ-ра 'come out from under')
а-чáи-рҭа /a-čʲáj-rta/ 'a tea plantation' (cf. а-чáи 'tea')
а-ҽы́кәаба-рҭа /a-čə́k'ʷaba-rta/ 'a bath-house' (cf. а-ҽы́кәаба-ра 'to bathe')
а-ҽы́хәшәтәы́-рҭа /a-čə́xʷšʷt'ʷə́-rta/ 'a hospital' (cf. а-ҽы́хәшәтә-ра 'to be given treatment')
а-шәá-рҭа /a-šʷá-rta/ 'danger' (cf. а-шәа-рá 'to feel fear')
áшәахәа-рҭа /ášʷaħʷa-rta/ 'the place for the performance of songs' (cf. áшәахәа-ра 'to sing a song')
а-шәы́рҭи-рҭа /a-šʷə́rtəj-rta/ 'a fruit market' (cf. а-шәы́р 'fruits', á-ҭи-ра 'to sell')

This suffix does not take accents. If there is an accent on the suffix -ра /ra/ of the masdar of the verb from which the word is derived, the accent on the derived noun is placed immediately in front of the suffix -рҭа /rta/.

The suffix -ҭа /ta/ also has a locative meaning. For example:
а-гә-ҭá /a-gʷ-tá/ 'centre' (cf. а-гәы́ 'heart')
а-гәáр-ҭа /a-gʷár-ta/ 'a fence for cattle' (cf. а-гәáра 'fence')
Бзы́ԥ-ҭа /bzə́p-ta/ 'place name' (cf. Бзы́ԥ 'river name')

2.1.5.5. The suffix -ра /ra/ attaches to a verb stem to form a verbal noun. For example: а-ҭаты́нахара /a-tatə́naxa-ra/ 'smoking' (cf. а-ҭаты́н /a-tatə́n/ 'tobacco', á-хара /á-xa-ra/ 'to smoke/pull'). In Abkhaz this is called the *masdar* (abbreviated hereafter as 'Masd'). A masdar has an article and is also used as the dictionary entry for verbs. In this book, when citing verbs we shall usually present the masdar form and use the infinitive form for their English translation. For example, let us consider an example in which the masdar has the role of complement:

(11) Ахра áкәашара бзи́а ибóит.

/áxra	á-k'ʷaša-ra	bzə́ja	jə-j-ba-wá-jt'/
Akhra	the-dance-Masd	well	it-he-see-Dyn-Fin

'Akhra loves to dance.'

Here, the masdar á-кәашара /á-k'ʷaša-ra/ 'to dance' refers to the и- /jə/ 'it' that is the direct object of the verb ба /ba/ 'see'. A literal translation would read, 'Akhra is seeing the dancing well.' In Abkhaz, 'see well' is equivalent to 'love'.

2.1.5.6. The suffix -ра /ra/ also attaches to the stems of adjectives, verbs, or nouns to form abstract nouns (or common nouns). Some examples:
а-баракьáҭ-ра /a-barakʲát-ra/ 'abundance' (cf. а-баракьáҭ /a-barakʲát/ 'abundant')
áаԥса-ра /áapsa-ra/ 'tiredness' (cf. áаԥса-ра 'to become tired')
áаԥын-ра /áapən-ra/ 'springtime' (cf. áаԥын 'spring')
а-бéиа-ра /a-bája-ra/ 'wealth' (cf. а-бéиа 'wealthy')
а-бзáза-ра /a-bzáza-ra/ 'life' (cf. а-бзáзаа-ра 'to be alive')
а-бзи́аба-ра /a-bzə́jaba-ra/ 'love' (cf. бзи́а а-ба-рá 'to love')
а-бзи́а-ра /a-bzə́ja-ra/ 'goodness' (cf. а-бзи́а 'good')
á-бна-ра /á-bna-ra/ 'forest tract' (cf. á-бна 'forest')

а-гәа́ҩа-ра /a-gʷájʷa-ra/ 'a hollow' (cf. а-гәа́ҩа 'empty, deep')
а-гәы́ла-ра /a-gʷə́la-ra/ 'neighbourhood' (cf. а-гәы́ла 'a neighbour')
а-гәы́мшәа-ра /a-gʷə́mšʷa-ra/ 'courage' (cf. а-гәы́мшәа 'courageous')
а-ды́рраҭа-ра /a-də́rrata-ra/ 'information' (cf. а-ды́рраҭа-ра 'to inform')
а́-ж-ра /á-ž-ra/ 'a hole' (cf. а-ж-ра́ 'to dig')
а́-ӡын-ра /á-ʒən-ra/ 'wintertime' (cf. а́-ӡын 'winter')
аиа́аи-ра /ajáaj-ra/ 'victory' (cf. а-иа́аи-ра 'to defeat')
а́иашьа-ра /ájašʲa-ra/ 'brotherhood' (а́иашьа 'brother')
а-ҟьа́ҟьа-ра /a-q'ʲáq'ʲa-ra/ 'flatness' (cf. а-ҟьа́ҟьа 'flat')
а-ҟәа́нда-ра /a-q'ʷánda-ra/ 'warmth' (cf. а-ҟәа́нда 'warm')
а-лша́-ра /a-lšá-ra/ 'possibility' (cf. а́-лша-ра 'to be able')
а́-мдыр-ра /á-mdər-ra/ 'ignorance' (cf. м- 'not', а-ды́р-ра 'to know')
а́н-ра /án-ra/ 'motherhood' (cf. ан 'mother')
а́-ԥхашьа-ра /á-pxašʲa-ra/ 'shame' (cf. а́-ԥхашьа 'shy')
а́-ԥшӡа-ра /á-pšʒa-ra/ 'beauty' (cf. а́-ԥшӡа 'beautiful')
а-ры́цҳа-ра /a-rə́cħa-ra/ 'misfortune' (cf. а-ры́цҳа 'unfortunate')
а-та́та-ра /a-t'át'a-ra/ 'softness' (cf. а-та́та 'soft')
а-ҭа́ӡа-ра /a-táʒa-ra/ 'capacity' (cf. а-ҭаӡа-ра́ 'to fit into')
а-ҭа́ҳа-ра /a-táħa-ra/ 'a hollow, a dip' (cf. а-ҭа́ҳа-ра 'to fall in')
а́-ҭбаа-ра /á-tbaa-ra/ 'width' (cf. а́-ҭбаа 'wide')
а-ҭы́нч-ра /a-tə́nčʲ-ra/ 'peace' (cf. а-ҭы́нч 'calm')
а́-уадаҩ-ра /á-wadajʷ-ra/ 'difficulty' (cf. а́-уадаҩ 'difficult')
а́у-ра /áw-ra/ 'height' (cf. а́у 'high')
а-фырха́ҵа-ра /a-fərxác'a-ra/ 'heroism' (cf. а-фырха́ҵа 'a hero')
а́-хаа-ра /á-xaa-ra/ 'sweetness' (cf. а́-хаа 'sweet')
а-ха́ҵа-ра /a-xác'a-ra/ 'fortitude' (cf. а-ха́ҵа 'a man')
а-хка́а-ра /a-xk'áa-ra/ 'a stock farm' (cf. а-хкаа-ра́ 'to fence off')
а-хша́[а]-ра /a-xšá[a]-ra/ 'a baby' (cf. а-хша[а]-ра́ 'to give birth to')
а́-хьанҭа-ра /á-xʲanta-ra/ 'weight' (cf. а́-хьанҭа 'heavy')
а́-хә-ра /á-xʷ-ra/ 'a wound' (cf. а-хә-ра́ 'to injure')
а́-ҳаракы́-ра /á-ħarak'ə́-ra/ 'height' (cf. а́-ҳарак(ы) 'high, tall')
а-ҳәынҭка́р-ра /a-ħʷəntkár-ra/ 'nation, reign' (cf. а-ҳәынҭка́р 'a king')
а-цәаакы́-ра /a-cʷaak'ə́-ra/ 'humidity' (cf. а́-цәаак 'humid')
а́-цәгьа-ра /á-cʷgʲa-ra/ 'misfortune' (cf. а́-цәгьа 'bad; hard')
а́-ҵәаа-ра /á-c'ʷaa-ra/ 'a shout' (cf. а́-ҵәаа-ра 'to shout')
а́-шаҳаҭ-ра /á-šaħat-ra/ 'evidence' (cf. а́-шаҳаҭ 'a witness')
а́-шьха-ра /á-šʲxa-ra/ 'a mountainous area' (cf. а́-шьха 'a mountain')
а-шәшьы́-ра /a-šʷšʲə́-ra/ 'shade' (cf. а-шәшьы́ 'a storm cloud', а-шәшь-ра́ 'to be concealed by clouds')
а-ҩы́-ра /a-jʷə́-ra/ 'script' (cf. а-ҩ-ра́ 'to write')

The suffix -ра /ra/ that forms abstract nouns (or common nouns) does not take accents. Also, when the accent in the masdar is such that it will be moved to its suffix, care should be taken to not put the accent on the suffix that forms an abstract noun (or common noun): а-хка́а-ра /a-xk'áa-ra/ 'a livestock farm', cf. masdar а-хкаа-рá /a-xk'aa-rá/ 'to fence off'.

2.1.5.7. Compound suffix -дара /dara/
This compound suffix is formed by joining the suffix -да /da/ 'without' indicating a lack with the aforementioned suffix -ра /ra/ used to form an abstract noun (or common noun). This suffix attaches to the nominal stem. For example:
á-ламыс-дара /á-laməs-dara/ 'dishonesty' (cf. á-ламыс 'conscience', á-ламысда 'dishonest')
á-мҩа-дара /á-mjʷa-dara/ 'a bad road, lack of roads' (cf. á-мҩа 'a road')
а-хшы́ҩ-дара /a-xšə́jʷ-dara/ 'madness' (cf. а-хшы́ҩ 'mind')
а-шәáрҭа-дара /a-šʷárta-dara/ 'safety' (cf. а-шәáрҭа 'danger')
á-насыԥ-дара /á-nasəp-dara/ 'unhappiness' (cf. á-насыԥ 'happiness')
а-ԥáра-дара /a-pára-dara/ 'lack of money' (cf. а-ԥáра 'money')
а-уаҩы́-дара /a-wajʷə́-dara/ 'uninhabitedness' (cf. а-уаҩы́ 'a person')
The compound suffix -дара does not take accents.

2.1.5.8. Suffix -ц /c/
This suffix attaches to nouns that have a collective meaning (or the singular form of nouns normally used in their plural form) and indicates a discrete, single thing.[75] For example:
а-бҕьы́-ц /a-bɣʲə́-c/ 'a leaf, a sheet' (cf. а-бҕьы́ /a-bɣʲə́/ 'leaf')
а-быбы́-ц /a-bəbə́-c/ 'a speck of dust' (cf. á-быб /á-bəb/ 'dust')
а-ҭәы́ц/а-ҭәы́ц /a-tʷə́jc/a-tʷə́c/ 'a speck of dust, a speck (in the eye)'
а-хәы́-ц /a-xʷə́-c/ 'a hair' (cf. а-хәы́ /a-xʷə́/ 'hair, wool')
а-шьхá-ц /a-šʲxá-c/ 'one (honey) bee' (cf. а-шьхá /a-šʲxá/ '(honey) bee')
á-шәҭы-ц /á-šʷtə-c/ 'single flower' (cf. á-шәҭ /á-šʷt/ 'flower')

2.1.5.9. Suffix -уа /wa/
This suffix indicates the singular form of the name of an ethnic group. In addition to ethnic group names, it is also used to indicate persons. The origins of this suffix can be found in the word а-уаҩы́ /a-wajʷə́/ 'person'. For example:
á-қырҭ-уа /á-kərt-wa/ 'a Georgian' (cf. Pl. а-қы́рҭ-цәа/-қәа /a-kə́rt-cʷa/-kʷa/ 'Georgians')
á-гыр-уа /á-gər-wa/ 'a Mingrelian' (cf. Pl. á-гыр-цәа/-қәа /á-gər-cʷa/kʷa/)
á-шәаны-уа /á-šʷanə-wa/ 'a Svan' (cf. Pl. á-шәан-цәа/-қәа /á-šʷan-cʷa/kʷa/)
á-шьхаруа /á-šʲxarwa/ 'a mountain-dweller' (cf. Pl. á-шьхаруаа /á-šʲxarwaa/)

2.1.5.10. The suffix -шьа /šʲa/ normally attaches to the verb stem and indicates the manner in which an action is undertaken or a distinguishing feature. This suffix does not take an accent. For example:
аá-шьа /aá-šʲa/ 'manner of coming' (cf. аа-рá 'to come here')
а-гы́ла-шьа /a-gə́la-šʲa/ 'the manner in which one stands' (cf. а-гы́ла-ра 'to stand up')
á-ҙахы-шьа /á-ʒaxə-šʲa/ 'manner of sewing' (cf. á-ҙах-ра 'to sew')
á-ҙса-шьа /á-ʒsa-šʲa/ 'swimming, sailing' (cf. á-ҙса-ра 'to swim')

---

75. Etymologically, the suffix may have come from the word á-ц /á-c/ 'a tooth'.

á-ҟаз-шьа /á-q'az-šʲa/ 'character' (cf. á-ҟаза(а)-ра 'to exist, to be')
а-лабá-шьа /a-labá-šʲa/ '(of a stick) a crook' (cf. а-лабá 'a stick')
а-нагӡá-шьа /a-nagʒá-šʲa/ 'manner of performance' (cf. á-нагӡа-ра 'to perform')
а-ны́ҟәа-шьа /a-nə́q'ʷa-šʲa/ 'manner of walking' (cf. а-ны́ҟәа-ра 'to walk')
а-ҭагылазáа-шьа /a-tagəlazáa-šʲa/ 'position, situation' (cf. а-ҭагы́ла-ра 'to stand in')
á-хәмар-шьа /á-xʷmar-šʲa/ 'playing, game' (cf. á-хәмар-ра 'to play')
а-ҳәá-шьа /a-ħʷá-šʲa/ 'pronunciation' (cf. а-ҳәа-рá 'to say')
а-цәáжәа-шьа /a-cʷážʷa-šʲa/ 'one's manner of speaking' (cf. а-цәáжәа-ра 'to speak')

2.1.5.11. The suffix <u>-мҭа</u> /mta/ attaches to the verb stem and indicates the results produced by carrying out that verb action. This suffix does not take an accent. For example:
а-ҭашәá-мҭа /a-tašʷá-mta/ 'sunset' (cf. а-ҭашәа-рá /a-tašʷa-rá/ 'to set')
á-лга-мҭа /á-lga-mta/ 'end' (cf. á-лга-ра 'to finish')
а-напҩы́-мҭа /a-nap'jʷə́-mta/ 'handwriting' (cf. а-напы́ 'hand', а-ҩ-рá 'to write')
а-нҵá-мҭа /a-nc'á-mta/ 'record(ing)' (cf. а-н-ҵа-рá 'to record')
а-нҵәá-мҭа /a-nc'ʷá-mta/ 'end' (cf. а-нҵәа-рá 'to end')
а-рҿиá-мҭа /a-rč'já-mta/ 'a product, production' (cf. а-рҿиа-рá 'to create')
а-ҭы́хы-мҭа /a-tə́xə-mta/ 'a drawing' (cf. а-ҭы́х-ра 'to draw')
а-у́су-мҭа /a-wə́swə-mta/ '(scholarly) works' (cf. а-у́су-рá 'to work')
а-хы́сы-мҭа /a-xə́sə-mta/ 'a shot' (cf. а-хы́с-ра 'to shoot')
а-ҩы́-мҭа /a-jʷə́-mta/ 'composition' (cf. а-ҩ-рá 'to write')
áа-мҭа /áa-mta/ 'date, time' (cf. аа-рá 'to come')

2.1.5.12. The suffix <u>-тә(ы)</u> /t'ʷ(ə)/ attaches to the verb stem and indicates the object of that verb action. For example:
а-бааӡа-тәы́ /a-baaʒa-t'ʷə́/ 'liquid, fluid' (cf. а-бааӡа-рá 'to get soaked')
а-зҵаа-тәы́ /a-zc'aa-t'ʷə́/ 'a question' (cf. а-зҵаа-рá 'to ask')
á-жә-тә /á-žʷ-t'ʷ/ 'a drink' (cf. á-жә-ра 'to drink')
а-ры́жә-тә /a-rə́žʷ-t'ʷ/ 'a drink'
á-фа-тә /á-fa-t'ʷ/ 'food' (cf. á-фа-ра 'to eat')
á-ҳасаб-тә /á-ħasab-t'ʷ/ 'a problem' (cf. á-ҳасаб-ра 'to solve')
á-џьашьа-тә /á-ǯʲašʲa-t'ʷ/ 'something surprising, a miracle' (cf. а-џьашьа-рá 'to be amazed')

2.1.5.13. The suffix <u>-ҕь</u> /ɣʲ/ is used to indicate a male animal or bird:
á-ба-ҕь /á-ba-ɣʲ/ 'a (male) goat'
á-цә-ҕь /á-cʷa-ɣʲ/ 'a bull'
áрба-ҕь /árba-ɣʲ/ 'a cock'
а-ты́-ҕь /a-t'ə́-ɣʲ/ 'a ram'
á-да-ҕь /á-da-ɣʲ/ 'a frog'

2.1.5.14. The suffix <u>-хь</u> /xʲ/ indicates an illness:
á-мгәа-хь /á-mgʷa-xʲ/ 'a disease of the stomach' (cf. á-мгәа 'stomach')
а-хы́-хь /a-xə́-xʲ/ 'headache' (cf. а-хы́ 'head')

а-гәатцәы́хь /a-gʷac'ʷə́xʲ/ 'pneumonia'
а-гәы́-хь /a-gʷə́-xʲ/ 'heart disease' (cf. а-гәы́ 'heart')

2.1.6. Noun Word Formation

Abkhaz nouns are constructed as follows:

Article–root–(root)–derivational suffix–plural suffix–indefinite suffix–postposition

The derivational suffix refers to the suffix used to indicate an agent or location, or one of the other items discussed in §2.1.5. 'Plural suffix' refers to -цәа /cʷa/ and -кәа /kʷa/, which indicate plurality as discussed in §2.1.2.2. The 'indefinite suffix' is к- /k'/, which indicates the indefinite as discussed in §2.1.4.3. Finally, the 'postposition' is a suffix that indicates -гьы /gʲə/ 'and/too,' -и /jə/ 'and', and so forth (this also includes the predicative (adverbial) marker -с /s/ or -ны /nə/ 'as'). For example, words are constructed using the simple root as follows:
а-шәҟә-кәа-гьы́ /a-šʷq'ʷ-kʷa-gʲə́/ (the-book-Pl-and) 'the books and'
шәҟә-кәа́-к /šʷq'ʷ-kʷá-k'/ (book-Pl-one) 'some books'
шәҟәы́-к-гьы /šʷq'ʷə́-k'-gʲə/ (book-one-and) 'one book and'

Words are constructed from two roots as follows:
а-шәҟәы́-ҩ-ҩ-цәа /a-šʷq'ʷə́-jʷ-jʷ-cʷa/ (the-book-write-Person-Pl) 'the writers'
шәҟә-ҩ-ҩы́-с /šʷq'ʷ-jʷ-jʷə́-s/ (book-write-Person-as) 'as a writer'
а-кахуа́-жәы-рҭа-кәа /a-k'aħwá-žʷə-rta-kʷa/ (the-coffee-drink-Place-Pl) 'the cafes'
а-хәынаԥ-кы́-га /a-ħʷənap-k'ə́-ga/ (the-mouse-catch-Instrument) 'a mousetrap'
а-чé-икәатцәа /a-čʲá-jkʷac'ʷa/ (< а-ча́ е́икәатцәа) the-bread-black) 'the black bread'

As these examples make clear, in compound words formed from two roots the verb root is placed after the nominal root that is its object.

Words can also be constucted as 'article—stem—postposition—stem'. For example:
а-шьапы́лампыл /a-šʲap'ə́lamp'əl/ (< а-шьапы́ 'foot' + ла 'with' + а́-мпыл 'ball') 'football'

2.1.7. Compound Words from Nouns

Compound words are formed using two or more stems; their constituent elements include 'nominal stem—nominal stem', 'nominal stem—adjectival stem', 'nominal stem—verb stem', or 'numeral—noun'.

2.1.7.1. In compound words comprising 'nominal stem—nominal stem', the first element is the modifier of the second. The following are examples:

а́ншьа /[á-]anšʲa/ (< ан /[a-]an/ 'mother' + а́иашьа /ájašʲa/ 'brother', cf. с-ашьа́ /s-ašʲá/ 'my brother') 'uncle through the mother'
а́-бласаркьа /á-blasark'ʲa/ (< а́-бла 'eye' + а-са́ркьа 'glass/mirror') 'glasses'
а-ԥса́дгьыл /a-psádgʲəl/ (< а-ԥсы́ 'soul' + а́(-)дгьыл 'land') 'homeland'
а-ҽы́бӷа /a-čə́bɣa/ (< а-ҽы́ 'horse' + а́-бӷа 'back') 'horse back'
а-ҽы́рҩра /a-čə́rjʷra/ (< а-ҽы́ 'horse' + а́-рҩра 'make run') 'horse racing'
аихáмҩа /ajxámjʷa/ (< аиха́ 'iron' + а́-мҩа 'way') 'railway'
а́-мцабз /á-mcabz/ (< а́-мца 'fire' + а́-бз 'tongue') 'flame'
а-мшы́нӡ /a-mšə́nʒ/ (< а-мшы́н 'sea' + а-ӡы́ 'water') 'seawater'

а-ҧсы́жра /a-psə́žra/ (< а-ҧсы́ 'corpse' + а-жра́ 'digging') 'burial'
а-фы́мца /a-fə́mca/ (< а-фы́ 'thunder' + а́-мца 'fire') 'electricity'
а-ҳәажьы́ /a-ħʷažʲə́/ (< а-ҳәа́ 'pig' + а-жьы́ 'meat') 'pork'
а-ҿы́тца /a-č'ə́c'a/ (< а-ҿы́ 'mouth' + а́-тца 'bottom') 'palate'
а́-жәжьы /á-žʷžʲə/ (< а́-жә 'cow' + а-жьы́ 'meat') 'beef'
а-ҟарматцы́с /a-q'armac'ə́s/ (< а-ҟарма́ 'hop' + а-тцы́с 'bird') 'nightingale'
а́-цьмажьы /á-ǯʲmažʲə/ (< а́-цьма 'goat' + а-жьы́ 'meat') 'goat meat'
а-бнакәты́ /a-bnak'ʷt'ə́/ (< а́-бна 'forest' + а-кәты́ 'hen') 'pheasant'
а-кла́ссҕәы /a-k'lássɣʷə/ (< а-кла́сс 'class' + а-ҕәы́ 'board') 'blackboard'
а́-лацәа /á-lacʷa/ (< а́-ла 'eye' + а-цәа́ 'skin, cover') 'eyelid'
а-мҿлы́х /a-mč'lə́x/ (< а-мҿы́ 'wood' + а-лы́х 'material') 'wooden ware'
Cf. а́-жәаҧҟа /á-žʷapq'a/ (< а́-жәа 'word' + а-ҧҟара́ 'cut') 'proverb'
а-гәабзи́ара /a-gʷabzə́jara/ (< а-гәы́ 'heart' + а-бзи́ара 'good') 'health'
а́-саламшәҟәы /á-salamšʷq'ʷə/ (< а́-салам 'greeting' + а-шәҟәы́ 'book/letter') 'letter'
а́-хьатцла /á-xʲac'la/ (< а́-хьа 'chestnut' + а́-тцла 'tree') 'chestnut tree'
аҳәшьаҧа́ /aħʷšʲapá/ (< аҳәшьа́ < а́иаҳәшьа 'sister' + а-ҧа́ 'son') 'a son of a sister'
а-шьапы́матәа /a-šʲap'ə́matʷa/ (< а-шьапы́ 'foot' + а́-матәа 'clothes') 'shoes'
а-шьапҧы́нтца /a-šʲap'pə́nc'a/ (< а-шьапы́ 'foot' + а-ҧы́нтца 'nose') 'toe'
а-ҩны́матәа /a-jʷnə́matʷa/ (< а-ҩны́ 'house' + а́-матәа 'clothes/thing') 'furniture'
а́-дыдмацәыс /á-dədmacʷəs/ (< а́-дыд 'thunder' + а́-мацәыс 'lightning') '(thunder)storm'
а́-гыршәа /á-gəršʷa/ (< а́-гыр-уа 'a Mingrelian' + а-бызшәа́ 'language') 'the Mingrelian language'
а-ҩра́ҧхьара /a-jʷrápxʲara/ (< а-ҩра́ 'writing' + а́-ҧхьара 'reading') 'reading and writing'

2.1.7.2. Compound words in which и /j(ə)/ 'and' is inserted to indicate a connection between two nominal stems:
а-цәе́ижь /a-cʷájžʲ/ (< а-цәа́ 'skin' + и 'and' + а-жьы́ 'flesh') 'body'
а-че́ицьыка /a-čʲájǯʲək'a/ (< а-ча́ 'the bread' + и 'and' + а-цьы́ка 'salt') 'bread and salt'

2.1.7.3. In compound words formed by 'nominal stem—adjectival stem', the second element modifies the first:
анду́ /andə́w/ (< ан 'mother' + ду 'big') 'grandmother'
а-бгаду́ /a-bgadə́w/ (< а́-бга 'fox' + ду 'big') 'wolf'
а́имхәаду /ájmħʷadəw/ (< а́имхәа 'cough' + ду 'big') 'tuberculosis'
а-бҕьы́жә /a-bɣʲə́žʷ/ (< а-бҕьы́ 'leaf' + ажә 'old') 'fallen leaf'
а́-матаҧшь /á-matapšʲ/ (< а́-мат 'snake' + аҧшь 'a red-haired') 'red snake'
а́-мшцәгьа /á-mšcʷgʲa/ (< а́-мш 'weather' + а́-цәгьа 'bad') 'bad weather'
а-че́икәатцәа /a-čʲájkʷac'ʷa/ (а-ча́ 'bread' + а́икәатцәа 'black') 'black bread'
а-ҽе́икәа /a-čájkʷa/ (< а-ҽы́ 'horse' + е́икәа 'black') 'black horse'

2.1.7.4. In 'nominal stem—verb stem' compound words, the first element, i.e., the nominal stem, is the object or subject of the second element, i.e., the verb stem. First, examples where the first element is the object of the second:
а-таты́нахара /a-tatə́naxara/ (< а-таты́н 'tobacco' + а́-ха-ра 'to smoke') 'smoking'

а́жәаҳәаҩы /ážʷaħʷajʷə/ (< а́жәа 'word' + а-ҳәа-ра́ 'to say' + ҩы 'person') 'orator'
а-каҳуа́жәырҭа /a-k'aħwážʷərta/ (а-каҳуа́ 'coffee' + а́-жә-ра 'to drink' + рҭа 'place') 'cafe'
а́-мцҳәаҩ /á-mcħʷajʷ/ (< а́-мц 'lie' + а-ҳәа-ра́ 'to say' + ҩы 'person') 'liar'
а-ҧаҵаса́рҭа /a-pac'asárta/ (< а-ҧаҵа́ 'beard' + а-са-ра́ 'to shave' + рҭа 'place') 'barbershop'
а-ҧсы́ӡкра /a-psə́ʒk'ra/ (< а-ҧсы́ӡ 'fish' + а-к-ра́ 'to catch') 'fishing'
а-телехәаҧшҩы́ /a-t'elexʷapšjʷə́/ (< а-телеви́зор 'television' + а́-хәаҧш-ра 'to watch' + ҩы 'person') 'TV viewer'
а-ҭоуры́хды́рҩы /a-tawrə́xdə́rjʷə/ (< а-ҭоуры́х 'history' + а-ды́р-ра 'to know' + ҩы 'person') 'historian'
а́шәаҳәаҩ /ášʷaħʷajʷ/ (< а́шәа 'song' + а-ҳәа-ра́ 'to say' + ҩ 'person') 'singer'
а-шәҟәыҩҩы́ /a-šʷq'ʷəjʷjʷə́/ (< а-шәҟәы́ 'book' + а-ҩ-ра́ 'to write' + ҩы 'person') 'writer'
а-ҩныргы́лаҩ /a-jʷnərgə́lajʷ/ (< а-ҩны́ 'house' + а-ргы́ла-ра 'to build' + ҩ 'person') 'house-builder'

Next, examples where the nominal stem will be the subject of the verb stem:
а-ӡа́лаларҭа /a-ʒálalarta/ (а-ӡы́ 'water/river' + а́-лала-ра 'to flow into' + рҭа 'place') 'an estuary'
а-ӡе́йбафара /a-ʒájbafara/ (< а-ӡы́ 'water' + а́йбафа-ра 'to gnaw each other') 'whirlpool'
а-лҩаца́рҭа /a-ljʷacárta/ (< а́-лҩа 'smoke' + а-ца-ра́ 'to go' + рҭа 'place') 'chimney'
а-мрагы́лара /a-mragə́lara/ (< а́-мра 'sun' + а-гы́ла-ра 'to rise') 'east'
а-мраҭашәа́ра /a-mratašʷára/ (< а́-мра 'sun' + а-ҭашәа-ра́ 'to set') 'west'
а́-дгьылҵысра /á-dgʲəlc'əsra/ (< а́-дгьыл 'earth' + а-ҵыс-ра́ 'to shake') 'earthquake'
а-сасаа́ирҭа /a-sasaájrta/ (< а́-сас 'guest' + аа́и-ра 'to come' + рҭа 'place') 'hotel'

2.1.7.5. 'Numeral—nominal stem' compound words:
а-ҩы́маа /a-jʷə́maa/ (< а-ҩ-ба '2' + а́-маа 'handle') 'harp'
а-шәы́шықәса /a-šʷə́šəkʷsa/ (< шә-кы́ '100' + а́-шықәса 'year') 'century'
бжь-ра-бы́жь-ҵәа /bžʲrabəžʲc'ʷa/ (< бжь- '7' + а-ра 'cubit' + быжь-ба́ '7' + а-ҵәы́ 'measure of length') 'the nether world, a hell'

2.1.7.6. Compound words formed from three stems:
а́шәаҳәабжь /ášʷaħʷabžʲ/ (< а́шәа 'song' + а-ҳәа-ра́ 'say' + а-бжьы́ 'voice') 'a singing voice'
а-бызкаҭа́ҳа /a-bəzk'atáħa/ (< а́-быз 'tongue' + а́-каҭ 'net' + а-ҳа-ра́ 'plait') 'spider'
а-ҽуа́пҵа́ршә /a-čwáp'c'áršʷ/ (< а-ҽы́ 'horse' + а-уа́па 'felt cloak' + а́-ҵаршә-ра 'lay (down) underneath') 'saddle-cloth'
а-ҽы́ҩчкәын /a-čə́jʷč'ʲk'ʷən/ (< а-ҽы́ 'horse' + а́-ҩ-ра 'run' + а́-чкәын 'boy') 'jockey'

2.1.8. Noun Accents

2.1.8.1. Accent Rules in Abkhaz

I have already presented an overview of Abkhaz accents in §1.2. Here, I will describe accents for nouns using the accent rules proposed by Spruit (1985).

2.1.8.2. Accent Units for Plural Markers

Based on а-ӡ-қәа́ /a-ʒ-kʷá/ 'waters' DDD', а-тә-цәа́ /a-t'ʷ-cʷá/ 'slaves' DDD' (cf. а-тәы́ /a-t'ʷə́/ 'a slave' DD'), we see that both have D as the accent units for plural markers. See the following examples:

[D']RID : áх-цәа /áħ-cʷa/ (< á-ах-цәа) 'kings' (cf. áх /áħ/ (< á-ах) 'king' [D']RI, ахы́-к/ахá-к/ха-к /aħə́-k'/aħá-k'/ħa-k'/ 'one king' RI'R)

DDD' : а-ла-қәá /a-la-kʷá/ 'the dogs', а-ӡ-қәá /a-ʒ-kʷá/ 'the waters'

D'RD : á-ла-қәа /á-la-kʷa/ 'the eyes', á-ӡ-қәа /á-ʒ-kʷa/ 'the lice'

DDDD' : а-лаба-қәá /a-laba-kʷá/ 'sticks' (cf. а-лабá /a-labá/ 'stick')

DD'RD : а-лáба-қәа /a-lába-kʷa/ 'male dogs' (cf. а-лáба /a-lába/ 'male dog')

DDDDD': а-гәрага-цәá /a-gʷraga-cʷá/ 'believers' (cf. DDDDD' а-гәрагаҩы́ /a-gʷragajʷə́/ 'believer')

DDD'RD : а-ҕалáт-цәа /a-ɣalát'-cʷa/ 'betrayers' (cf. DDD'RD : а-ҕалáтҩы /a-ɣalát'jʷə/ 'betrayer')

Spruit's accent rule works well in the foregoing examples, but it does not work for the following:
а-хáҵа /a-xác'a/ 'man' DD'R : а-хá-цәа /a-xá-cʷa/ 'men' DD'D (?)

2.1.8.3. Accents on Nouns Indicating the Indefinite

The accent unit for the indefinite marker -к /k'/ 'one' is R, as in лá-к 'one dog' D'R. When the stem's accent unit is R, the accent is moveable, as in RR'/R'R (see §1.2.4). Let us look here at some examples obtained from our informant:

D'R : ӡы́-к/*ӡ-кы́ /ʒə́-k'/*ʒ-k'ə́/ 'water-one' (cf. а-ӡы́ /a-ʒə́/ 'water' DD') (* indicates a pattern our informant did not confirm)

RR'/R'R : ӡ-кы́ /ӡы́-к /ʒ-k'ə́/ʒə́-k'/ 'one louse' (cf. á-ӡ /á-ʒ/ 'louse' D'R); жәы́-к/жә-кы́ /žʷə́-k'/žʷ-k'ə́/ 'one cow (cf. á-жә /á-žʷ/ 'cow' D'R)

D'RR : қы́ҭа-к /kə́ta-k'/ 'one village' (cf. а-қы́ҭа /a-kə́ta/ 'village' DD'R)

DD'R : шәҟәы́-к /šʷq'ʷə́-k'/ 'one book' (cf. а-шәҟәы́ /a-šʷq'ʷə́/ 'book' DDD'); кәты́-к /k'ʷt'ə́-k'/ 'one hen' (cf. а-кәты́ /a-k'ʷt'ə́/ 'hen' DDD', а-кәт-қәá /a-k'ʷt'-kʷá/ 'hens' DDDD')

RR'R/RRR' : ҕбá-к/ҕба-кы́ /ɣbá-k'/ɣba-k'ə́/ 'one ship' (cf. á-ҕба /á-ɣba/ 'ship' D'RR, á-ҕба-қәа /á-ɣba-kʷa/ 'ships' D'RRD); аны́-к/ан-кы́ /anə́-k'/an-k'ə́/ 'one mother' (cf. [á-]ан /[á-]an/ 'mother' [D']RR); (а)жәá-к /(a)žʷá-k'/ 'one word' (cf. [á-]ажәа /[á-]ažʷa/ 'word')

R'RR : қәы́цә-к /kʷə́cʷ-k'/ 'one top' (cf. á-қәцә /á-kʷcʷ/ 'top' D'RR)

RI'R : даҕьы́-к /daɣʲə́-k'/ 'one frog' (cf. á-даҕь /á-daɣʲ/ 'frog' D'RI)

RID'R : даҕь-қәá-к /daɣʲ-kʷá-k'/ 'some frogs' (cf. á-даҕь-қәа /á-daɣʲ-kʷa/ 'frogs' D'RID)

D'RIR : ӡы́гьажь-к /ʒə́gʲažʲ-k'/ 'one lake' (cf. а-ӡы́гьажь /a-ʒə́gʲažʲ/ 'lake' DD'RI)

DD'RR : ҧсы́ӡ-к /psə́ʒ-k'/ 'one fish' (cf. а-ҧсы́ӡ /a-psə́ʒ/ 'fish' DDD'R)

DDD'R : шәҟә-қәá-к /šʷq'ʷ-kʷá-k'/ 'some books'

RD'RR : ӡәӡәáга-к /ʒʷʒʷága-k'/ 'one washing machine' (cf. á-ӡәӡәага /á-ʒʷʒʷaga/ 'washing machine' D'RDR)

RRD'R : ана-цәá-к /ana-cʷá-k'/ 'some mothers' (cf. [á-]ана-цәа /[á-]ana-cʷa/ 'mothers' [D']RRD)

Spruit's rule applies quite well to the indefinite forms above. Accent position is moveable in words that have three or more Rs, as in R'RR-/RR'R-. The following is an example:

қáлақь-к /kálakʲ-k'/ 'one city' R'RRR (cf. калáқь-қәа-к /kalákʲ-kʷa-k'/ 'some cities' RR'RDR, á-калақь /á-kalakʲ/ 'city' D'RRR)

In some cases the rule does not apply:

á-ҕа /á-ɣa/ 'bellows' D'R : ҕá-к /ɣá-k'/ R'R : ҕá-қәа-к /ɣá-kʷa-k'/ R'DR (?)

2.1.8.4. Accents on Nouns with a Derivational Suffix

The accent units for derivational suffixes are D and R. D can be -ҩ(ы), -тә(ы), and the masdar -ра. R can be -уаҩ(ы), -га, -рҭа, -шьа, -мҭа, -ц, -дара, -ҕь, -хь, and the -ра that forms abstract nouns. Examples of derivational suffixes with D:

-ҩ(ы) /jʷ(ə)/ D:

аҵаҩы́ /a-c'a-jʷə́/ DDD' 'pupil' (cf. аҵацәа́ /a-c'a-cʷá/ DDD' 'pupils')

а́кәашаҩ /á-k'ʷaša-jʷ/ D'RID 'dancer' (cf. а́кәашара /á-k'ʷaša-ra/ D'RID 'to dance')

-тә(ы) /t'ʷ(ə)/ D:

азҵаатәы́ /a-zc'aa-t'ʷə́/ DDDD' 'a question' (cf. азҵаара́ /a-zc'aa-rá/ DDDD' 'to ask')

а́жәтә /á-žʷ-t'ʷ/ D'RD 'a drink' (cf. а́жәра /á-žʷ-ra/ D'RD 'to drink')

Examples of derivational suffixes with R:

-уаҩ(ы) /wajʷ(ə)/ RI:

аҵара́уаҩ(ы) /a-c'ará-wajʷ(ə)/ DDD'RI 'a scholar' (cf. аҵара́ /a-c'ará/ DDD' 'study')

акы́ҭауаҩ /a-kə́ta-wajʷ/ DD'RRI 'a villager' (cf. акы́ҭа /a-kə́ta/ DD'R 'a village')

-га /ga/ R:

аҩы́га /a-jʷə́-ga/ DD'R 'an instrument for writing' (cf. аҩра́ /a-jʷ-rá/ DDD' 'to write')

ажы́га /a-žə́-ga/ DD'R 'a shovel' (cf. ажра́ /a-ž-rá/ DDD' 'to dig')

а́ӡәӡәага /á-ʒʷʒʷa-ga/ D'RIR 'a washing machine' (cf. а́ӡәӡәара /á-ʒʷʒʷa-ra/ D'RID 'to wash')

Exceptions:

аса́га /a-sá-ga/ DD'R 'a razor' (cf. аса́ра /a-sá-ra/ DD'D (?) 'to shave')

аҵәаҕәа́га /a-cʷaɣʷá-ga/ DDD'R (?) 'instrument for plowing' (cf. а́ҵәаҕәара /á-cʷaɣʷa-ra/ D'RID (?) 'to plow')

-рҭа /rta/ RI:

атәа́рҭа /a-t'ʷá-rta/ DD'RI 'a seat' (cf. атәара́ /a-t'ʷa-rá/ DDD' 'to sit')

а́ҵәарҭа /á-cʷa-rta/ D'RRI 'a bed(room)' (cf. а́ҵәара /á-cʷa-ra/ D'RD 'to sleep')

аҭы́жьырҭа /a-tə́žʲə-rta/ DD'RRI 'a publishing house' (cf. аҭы́жьра /a-tə́žʲ-ra/ DD'RD 'to publish')

-шьа /šʲa/ R:

аҳәа́шьа /a-ħʷá-šʲa/ DD'R 'pronunciation' (cf. аҳәара́ /a-ħʷa-rá/ DDD' 'to say')

а́ӡахышьа /á-ʒaxə-šʲa/ D'RIR 'manner of sewing' (cf. а́ӡахра /á-ʒax-ra/ D'RID 'to sew')

аҵәа́жәашьа /a-cʷážʷa-šʲa/ DD'RR 'one's manner of speaking' (cf. аҵәа́жәара /a-cʷážʷa-ra/ DD'RD 'to speak')

Exceptions:

анагӡа́шьа /a-nagʒá-šʲa/ DDD'R (?) 'manner of performance' (cf. а́нагӡара /á-nagʒa-ra/ D'RID (?) 'to perform')

-мҭа /mta/ R:

аҭашәа́мҭа /a-tašʷá-mta/ DDD'R 'sunset' (cf. аҭашәара́ /a-tašʷa-rá/ DDDD' 'to set')

а́лгамҭа /á-lga-mta/ D'RIR 'end' (cf. а́лгара /á-lga-ra/ D'RID 'to finish')

ахы́сымҭа /a-xə́sə-mta/ DD'RR 'shot' (cf. ахы́сра /a-xə́s-ra/ DD'RD 'to shoot')

-ц /c/ R:

ахәы́ц /a-xʷə́-c/ DD'R 'a hair' (cf. ахәы́ /a-xʷə́/ DD' 'hair, wool') а́шәтыц /á-šʷtə-c/ D'RIR ‘single flower’ (cf. а́шәт /á-šʷt/ D'RI ‘a flower’)

-дара /dara/ RI
ауаҩы́дара /a-wajʷə́-dara/ DDD'RI ‘uninhabitedness’ (cf. ауаҩы́ /a-wajʷə́/ DDD' ‘a person’)
а́мҩадара /á-mjʷa-dara/ D'RRRI ‘a bad road, lack of roads’ (cf. а́мҩа /á-mjʷa/ D'RR ‘a road’)

-ӷь /ɣʲ/ R, -хь /xʲ/ R:
аты́-ӷь /a-t’ə́-ɣʲ/ DD'R ‘a ram’
ахы́хь /a-xə́-xʲ/ DD'R ‘headache’ (cf. ахы́ /a-xə́/ DD' ‘head’)

The abstract noun suffix -ра /ra/ R:
аҩы́ра /a-jʷə́-ra/ DD'R ‘script’ (cf. аҩра́ /a-jʷ-rá/ DDD' ‘to write’)
ахка́ара /a-xk’áa-ra/ DDD'R ‘a livestock farm’ (cf. ахкаа-ра́ /a-xk’aa-rá/ DDDD' ‘to fence off’)
ахша́[а]ра /a-xšá[a]-ra/ DDD'R ‘a baby’ (cf. ахша[а]ра́ /a-xša[a]-rá/ DDDD' ‘to give birth to’)
However, there are also exceptions:
а́жра /á-ž-ra/ D'RR(?) ‘a hole’ (cf. ажра́ /a-ž-rá/ DDD'(?) ‘to dig’)
а́хәра /á-xʷ-ra/ D'RR(?) ‘a wound’ (cf. ахәра́ /a-xʷ-rá/ DDD'(?) ‘to injure’)

2.1.8.5. Accents on Compound Words

2.1.8.5.1. Spruit’s rule works without exception for accents on compound words formed by ‘nominal stem—nominal stem’. For example:

а́жәжьы /á-žʷ-žʲə/ D'RD ‘beef’ (< а́жә /á-žʷ/ D'R ‘cow’ + ажьы́ /a-žʲə́/ DD' ‘meat’); cf. жәык/жәкы R'R/RR' /žʷə́-k’/žʷ-k’ə́/ ‘one cow’

а́мцабз /á-mca-bz/ D'RRRR ‘flame’ (< а́мца /á-mca/ D'RR ‘fire’ + а́бз /á-bz/ D'RR ‘tongue’), мцабзы́к /mca-bzə́-k’/ RRRR'R ‘one flame’, cf. а́мца /á-mca/ D'RR: мца́к /mcá-k’/ RR'R ‘one fire’, а́-бз /á-bz/ D'RR: бзы́к/бы́зк /bzə́-k’/bə́z-k’/ RR'R/R'RR ‘one tongue’

а́лацәа /á-la-cʷa/ D'RD ‘eyelid’ (< а́ла /á-la/ D'R ‘eye’ + ацәа́ /a-cʷá/ DD' ‘skin, cover’); cf. ацәақәа́ /a-cʷa-kʷá/ DDD' ‘skins’, цәа́к /cʷá-k’/ D'R ‘one skin’

а́бласаркьа /á-bla-sark’ʲa/ D'RIDII ‘glasses’ (< а́бла /á-bla/ D'RI ‘eye’ + аса́ркьа /a-sárk’ʲa/ DD'II ‘glass/mirror’)

аҽы́бӷа /a-čə́-bɣa/ DD'RI ‘horse back’ (< аҽы́ /a-čə́/ DD' ‘horse’ + а́бӷа /á-bɣa/ D'RI ‘back’)

аҳәажьы́ /a-ħʷa-žʲə́/ DDD' ‘pork’ (< аҳәа́ /a-ħʷá/ DD' ‘pig’ + ажьы́ /a-žʲə́/ DD' ‘meat’), cf. аҳәа́ /a-ħʷá/ DD': аҳәақәа́ /a-ħʷa-kʷá/ DDD', ҳәа́к /ħʷá-k’/ D'R; а-жьы́ /a-žʲə́/ DD': ажьқәа́ /a-žʲ-kʷá/ DDD', жьы́к /žʲə́-k’/ D'R; аҳәажьқәа́ /a-ħʷažʲ-kʷá/ DDDD'

аҟарматцы́с /a-q’arma-c’ə́s/ DDDDD'R ‘nightingale’ (< аҟарма́ /a-q’armá/ DDDD' ‘hop’ + атцы́с /a-c’ə́s/ DD'R ‘bird’), cf. аҟармақәа́ /a-q’arma-kʷá/ DDDDD' ‘hops’, аҟарматцы́скәа /a-q’armac’ə́s-kʷa/ ‘nightingales’, тцы́ск /c’ə́s-k’/ D'RR ‘one bird’

амҿлы́х /a-mč’-lə́x/ DDDD'R ‘wooden ware’ (< амҿы́ /a-mč’ə́/ DDD' ‘wood’ + алы́х /a-lə́x/ DD'R ‘material’), cf. амҿқәа́ /a-mč’-kʷá/ DDDD' ‘trees’

аиха́мҩа /[a-]ajxá-mjʷa/ [D]DD'RR ‘railway’(< аиха́ /[a-]ajxá/ [D]DD' ‘iron’ + а́мҩа /á-mjʷa/ D'RR ‘way’), cf. аихақәа́ /[a-]ajxa-kʷá/ [D]DDD' ‘axes’, мҩак/мҩакы́ /mjʷá-k’/mjʷa-k’ə́/ RR'R/RRR' ‘one road’

ашьапӷы́нтца /a-šʲap’-pə́nc’a/ DDDD'RI ‘toe’ (< ашьапы́ /a-šʲap’ə́/ DDD' ‘foot’ + аӷы́нтца /a-pə́nc’a/ DD'RI ‘nose’), cf. ашьапкәа́ /a-šʲap’-kʷá/ DDDD' ‘feet’, ӷы́нтцак / pə́nc’a-k’/ D'RIR ‘one nose’

2.1.8.5.2. Regarding accents on compound words in which и /jə/ 'and' is inserted to indicate a connection between nominal stem and nominal stem, Spruit's rule works well if the accent unit for и is treated as R:

аҧəе́ижь /a-cʷá-j-žʲ/ DD'RD 'body' (< аҧəа́ /a-cʷá/ DD' 'skin' + и /jə/ R 'and' + ажьы́ /a-žʲə́/ DD' 'flesh')

ачéицьыка /a-čʲá-j-ǯʲək'a/ DD'RDR 'bread and salt' (< ачá /a-čʲá/ DD' 'bread' + и R 'and' + аџьы́ка /a-ǯʲə́k'a/ DD'R 'salt'); cf. ачакəа́ DDD' /a-čʲa-kʷá/ 'bread-Pl'

2.1.8.5.3. Spruit's rule works for accents in compound words formed by 'nominal stem—adjectival stem', but there are exceptions. For example:

áмшцəгьа /á-mš-cʷgʲa/ D'RRRI 'bad weather' (< áмш /á-mš/ D'RR 'weather' + áцəгьа /á-cʷgʲa/ D'RI 'bad'), cf. мшы́к/мышкы́ /mšə́-k'/məš-k'ə́/ RR'R/RRR' 'one day/weather', цəгьáк /cʷgʲá-k'/ RI'R 'bad-one'

áматаҧшь /á-mat-apšʲ/ D'RIDRI 'red snake' (< áмат /á-mat/ D'RI 'snake' + аҧшь /a-pšʲ/ D'RI 'a red-haired'), cf. маты́к /matə́-k'/ RIR 'one snake', ауаҩáҧшь /awajʷápšʲ/ DDDD'RI 'a red-haired person', ауаҩы́ /a-wajʷə́/ DDD' 'person'

Exceptions:

абгаду́ /a-bga-də́w/ DRID'R(?) 'wolf' (< áбга /á-bga/ D'RI 'fox' + ду /də́w/ D'R 'big'), cf. áбгакəа /á-bga-kʷa/ 'foxes', абгадукəа́ /a-bgadəw-kʷá/ 'wolves', аду́кəа /a-də́w-kʷa/ DD'RD 'big-Pl'

анду́ /andə́w/ [D]RRD'R(?) 'grandmother' (< ан /[a-]an/ [D']RR 'mother' + ду /dəw/ D'R 'big'), анду́цəа /[a-]andə́w-cʷa/ [D]RRD'RD 'grandmothers'

2.1.8.5.4. Accents in 'nominal stem—verb stem—derivational suffix' compound words:

First, Spruit's rule works well for accents in compound words where the first element is the object of the second. For example:

ашəҟəыҩҩы́ /a-šʷq'ʷə-jʷ-jʷə́/ DDDDD' 'writer' (< ашəҟəы́ /a-šʷq'ʷə́/ DDD' 'book' + аҩрá /a-jʷ-rá/ DDD' 'write' + ҩы /jʷə/ D 'person')

аҧатцасáрта /a-pac'a-sá-rta/ DDDD'R 'barbershop' (< аҧатцá /a-pac'á/ DDD' 'beard' + асарá /a-sa-rá/ DDD' 'shave' + рта /rta/ RI 'place'); cf. а-ҧатца-кəа́ /a-pac'a-kʷá/ 'beards'

акахуáжəырта /a-k'aħwá-žʷə-rta/ DDDD'RR 'cafe' (акахуá /a-k'aħwá/ DDDD' 'coffee' + áжəра /á-žʷ-ra/ D'RD 'drink' + рта /rta/ RI 'place')

аҩнызгы́лаҩ /a-jʷnə-rgə́la-jʷ/ DDDDD'RD 'house-builder' (< аҩны́ /a-jʷnə́/ DDD' 'house' + аргы́лара /a-rgə́la-ra/ DDD'RD 'build' + ҩ /jʷ/ D 'person'), cf. аҩнкəа́ /a-jʷn-kʷá/ DDDD' 'houses'

áмцхəаҩ /á-mc-ħʷa-jʷ/ D'RIDD 'liar' (< áмц /á-mc/ D'RI 'lie' + ахəарá /a-ħʷa-rá/ DDD' 'say' + ҩы /jʷə/ D 'person')

Next, for accents in compound words where a nominal stem (first element) is the subject of a verb stem (second element), Spruit's rule does not work in those cases where the first element has the accent unit R. For example:

амрагы́лара /a-mra-gə́la-ra/ DRID'RR(?) 'east' (< áмра /á-mra/ D'RI 'sun' + агы́лара /a-gə́la-ra/ DD'RD 'rise')

алҩацáрта /a-ljʷa-cá-rta/ DRID'R(?) (< áлҩа /á-ljʷa/ D'RI 'smoke' + ацарá /a-ca-rá/ DDD' 'go' + рта

/rta/ RI ‘place’) ‘chimney’

However, in some cases Spruit’s rule does work:

áдгьылҵысра /á-dgʲəl-c’əsra/ D'RIIDDR ‘earthquake’ (< áдгьыл /á-dgʲəl/ D'RII ‘earth’ + аҵысрá /a-c’əs-rá/ DDDD' ‘shake’)

2.1.8.5.5. Accents in ‘numeral—nominal stem’ compound words can be explained by Spruit’s rule:

аҩы́маа /a-jʷə́-maa/ DD'RR ‘harp’ (< ҩбá /jʷ-bá/ DD' ‘2’ + áмаа /á-maa/ D'RR ‘handle’); cf. маáк /maá-k’/ ‘one handle’

ашәы́шықәса /a-šʷə́-šəkʷsa/ DD'RRI ‘century’ (< шәкы́ /šʷ-k’ə́/ DD' ‘100’+ áшықәса /á-šəkʷsa/ D'RRI ‘year’); cf. шықәсы́к /šəkʷsə́-k’/ RRI'R ‘one year’

2.1.8.5.6. Accents in compound words formed by three stems:

аҽы́ҩҷкәын /a-čə́-jʷ-č’ʲk’ʷən/ DD'RRDR ‘jockey’ (< аҽы́ /a-čə́/ DD' ‘horse’ + áҩра /á-jʷ-ra/ D'RD ‘run’ + áҷкәын /á-č’ʲk’ʷən/ D'RDR ‘boy’, cf. ҷкәы́н(а)к /č’ʲk’ʷə́n(a)-k’/ RDRR ‘one boy’)

áшәаҳәабжь /[á-]ašʷa-ħʷa-bžʲ/ [D']RIDDD ‘a singing voice’ (< áшәа /[á-]ašʷa/ [D']RI ‘song’ + аҳәарá /a-ħʷa-rá/ DDD' ‘say’ + абжьы́ /a-bžʲə́/ DDD' ‘voice’, cf. ашәáк/шәáк /ašʷá-k’/šʷá-k’ RI'R/I'R ‘one song’)

Exceptions: абызкаҭáха /a-bəzk’atáħa/ DRRRI'D(?) ‘spider’(< áбыз /á-bəz/ D'RR ‘tongue’ + áкаҭ /á-k’at/ D'RI ‘net’ + аҳарá /a-ħa-rá/ DDD' ‘plait’)

2.2. Pronouns

2.2.1. Personal Pronouns

2.2.1.1. The Abkhaz personal pronoun system is as follows:

	Sg.		Pl.	
1st person	сарá	/sará/	ҳарá	/ħará/
2nd person (M)	уарá	/wará/ [76]	шәарá	/šʷará/
2nd person (F)	барá	/bará/	шәарá	
3rd person (Human M)	иарá	/jará/	дарá	/dará/ [77]
3rd person (Human F)	ларá	/lará/	дарá	
3rd person (Non-Human)	иарá		дарá	

Pronouns in the 2nd person singular are divided by class into masculine and feminine. Pronouns in the 3rd person singular are divided into human and non-human, and the former further divided into masculine and feminine. There are no distinctions by class like this with plurals. The 2nd person

---

76. уарá /wará/ is also used for addressing a child, an animal, and a thing.

77. дарá /dará/ can probably be seen as going back to рарá /rará/. The change of д < р was produced through dissimilation. Cf. the change of the 3rd person plural prefix р- to д- before the causative marker р-.

plural form шəара́ /š^wará/ is used as a mode of address for multiple persons, and also to express politeness when used as a mode of address for one person.[78]

2.2.1.2. Contracted forms, in which the -ра /ra/ is dropped from the foregoing personal pronouns, are used in the spoken language (forms given in brackets are rarely used):

	Sg.		Pl.	
1st person	са	/sa/	ха	/ħa/
2nd person (M)	уа	/wa/	шəа	/š^wa/
2nd person (F)	ба	/ba/	шəа	
3rd person (Human M)	[иа]	[/ja/]	[да]	[/da/]
3rd person (Human F)	ла	/la/	[да]	
3rd person (Non-Human)	[иа]		[да]	

2.2.1.3. The 1st person plural and 2nd person plural each have their own form, respectively харҭ /ħart/ and шəарҭ /š^wart/. The relationship between these forms and the хара́ /ħará/ and шəара́ /š^wará/ forms discussed in §2.2.1.1 has been described in a grammar text as contrastive, the former being exclusive and the latter being inclusive.[79] That is, харҭ /ħart/ means "we' excluding the addressee' in contrast with хара́ /ħará/ "we' including the addressee'. Furthermore, шəарҭ /š^wart/ means "you' without the speaker,' while шəара́ /š^wará/ means "you' plus the speaker'. However, according to our informant, this inclusive-exclusive distinction does not exist in modern Abkhaz. хара́ and шəара́ are used most often.

2.2.2. Possessive Prefixes

In Abkhaz, possession is expressed by attaching the possessive prefix for the person, number, or class that refers to the possessor to the possessed noun. The possessor is placed before the possessed noun. When the possessor is a personal pronoun, that pronoun is normally omitted when it is not being stressed. The possessive prefix system is as follows:

	Sg.		Pl.	
1st person	с(ы)-	/s(ə)/	х(а)-	/ħ(a)/
2nd person (M)	у-	/w(ə)/	шə(ы)-	/š^w(ə)/
2nd person (F)	б(ы)-	/b(ə)/	шə(ы)-	
3rd person (Human.M)	и-	/j(ə)/	р(ы)-	/r(ə)/
3rd person (Human.F)	л(ы)-	/l(ə)/	р(ы)-	
3rd person (Non-Human)	а-	/a/	р(ы)-	

78. This is due to the influence of Russian. Note *вы* in Russian.

79. See *Грамматика абхазского языка: фонетика и морфология.* 1968, стр.35. [Sh.K. Aristava, et al. *Abkhaz Grammar: Phonetics and Morphology.* Sukhumi. p.35.]

Note that unlike personal pronouns in §2.2.1.1, the human and non-human of these possessive prefixes differ from one another in the 3rd person singular.

2.2.2.1. Examples of attaching possessive prefixes to nouns:
(сара́) сҽы́ /s-čə́/ 'my horse' DD', (сара́) сҽқәа́ /s-č-kʷá/ 'my horses' DDD';
(сара́) сы́ла /sə́-la/ 'my eye' D'R, (сара́) сы́лакәа /sə́-la-kʷa/ 'my eyes' D'RD (cf. а́-ла 'eye')
(уара́) ула́ /w-lá/ 'your-M (i.e. your [masculine]) dog' DD' (cf. а-ла́ 'dog'); (уара́) уԥхәы́с /wə-pħʷə́s/ 'your-M wife' DDD'R; у́ускәа /wə-wə́s-kʷa/ 'your-M jobs';
(бара́) бха́тца /b-xác'a/ 'your-F (i.e. your [feminine]) husband' DD'R; (бара́) бхәычқәа́ /b-xʷəč'ʲ-kʷá/ 'your-F children' DDDD'; бы́мҩа /bə́-mjʷa/ 'your road' D'RR;
(иара́) ихы́лԥа /jə-xə́lpa/ 'his cap' DD'RI; (иара́) илы́мҳақәа /jə-lə́mħa-kʷa/ 'his ears' DD'RID;
(лара́) лыртҵаҩы́ /lə-rc'ajʷə́/ 'her teacher' DD'R; лнапқәа́ /l-nap'-kʷá/ 'her hands' DDDD';
(иара́) амтҵәы́жәҩақәа /a-mc'ʷə́žʷjʷa-kʷa/ 'its (e.g. the dove's) wings' DDD'RID;
(хара́) хаҩны́ /ħa-jʷnə́/ 'our house' DDD'; х-Аԥсны́ /ħ-apsnə́/ 'our Abkhazia' DDDDD';
(шәара́) шәқы́ҭа /šʷ-kə́ta/ 'your-Pl (i.e. your [plural]) village' DD'R; (шәара́) шәы́блақәа /šʷə́-bla-kʷa/ 'your-Pl eyes' D'RRD;
(дара́) рбыҕқәа́ /r-bəɣʲ-kʷá/ 'their (e.g. trees') leaves' DDDD'; (урҭ) рқы́ҭа /r-kə́ta/ 'their village' DD'R

Expressions with two possessive cases such as 'my friend's book' are rendered as (сара́) сҩы́за ишәҟәы́ /(sará) s-jʷə́za jə-šʷq'ʷə́/ '(I) my-friend his-book.' Similarly, 'his horse's hair' would be expressed as (иара́) иҽы́ ахәы́цқәа /(jará) jə-čə́ a-xʷə́c-kʷa/ 'his-horse its-hair-Pl'. Also, in cases like а́ни а́би /ánə-j ábə-j/ 'parents' (lit. 'mother-and father-and') where two words linked by the postpositional connector '-и -и' have possession, a possessive prefix is attached to both elements: са́ни са́би /s-ánə-j s-ábə-j/ 'my parents' (lit. my-mother-and my-father-and). Furthermore, when the pattern involves attaching a possessive prefix as in а́иашьа /ájašʲa/ 'brother' and а́иахәшьа /ájaħʷšʲa/ 'sister', the element аи- /aj/ is removed from both words and a possessive prefix is attached: сашьа́ /s-ašʲá/ 'my brother', сахәшьа́ /s-aħʷšʲá/ 'my sister'.

2.2.2.2. Examples of attaching a possessive prefix to a postposition:
Examples where a possessive prefix is attached to a postposition that indicates location, instrument, time, or predicative adverb as discussed in §2.7:
-ла /la/ 'with, concerning, by': са сы́ла /sa sə́-la/ 'by me', ақьырмы́т а́ла /a-kʲərmə́t' á-la/ 'with the brick', хәы-шықәса́ ры́ла /xʷə-šək'ʷsá rə́-la/ 'by five years'
-да /da/ 'without, apart from': уа у́да /wa wə́-da/ 'without you', амҽы́ша а́да /a-mčə́ša á-da/ 'except Sunday'
-а́ԥхьа /ápxʲa/ 'in front of, before, ago': са́ԥхьа /s-ápxʲa/ 'in front of me', аҩны́ а́ԥхьа /a-jʷnə́ [a-]ápxʲa/ 'in front of the house', ҩы-саа́ҭк ра́ԥхьа /jʷə-saát-k' r-ápxʲa/ 'two hours ago'
-ҿы /č'/ 'in, at': хара́ хҿы́ /ħará ħ-č'ə́/ 'at our place', ауаҭа́х аҿы́ /a-watáx a-č'ə́/ 'in the room'
-ахь /axʲ/ 'to': ахакьы́м иа́хь /a-ħakʲə́m j-áxʲ/ 'to the doctor'
-ҟны́ /q'nə́/ 'in, at, to': авокза́л аҟны́ /a-vok'zál a-q'nə́/ 'at the station', ла́б иҟны́ /l-áb jə-q'nə́/ 'to her father'
-а́хьтә /áxʲt'ʷ/ 'from': а́чкәынцәа ра́хьтә ҩы́џьа /á-č'ʲk'ʷən-cʷa r-áxʲt'ʷ jʷə́ǯʲa/ 'two of the boys'

-зы /zə/ 'for, at': сара́ сзы /sará s-zə́/ 'for me', асаа́т аабá рзы́ /a-saát aabá r-zə́/ 'at 8 o'clock'
-бжьа́ра /bžʲára/ 'between': ҩы-тцлáк рыбжьáра /jʷə-c'lá-k' rə-bžʲára/ 'between the two trees'
-áҟара /áq'ara/ 'about': ҩ-саа́тк рáҟара /jʷ-saát-k' r-áq'ara/ 'about two hours'
-ҟы́нӡа /q'ə́nʒa/ 'as far as, by': амшы́н аҟы́нӡа /a-mšə́n a-q'ə́nʒa/ 'as far as the sea', асаа́т хҧа рҟы́нӡа /a-saát xpa r-q'ə́nʒa/ 'by three o'clock'
-ҟы́нтә(и) /q'ə́nt'ʷ(əj)/ 'from': хара́ хҟы́нтәи /ħará ħ-q'ə́nt'ʷəj/ 'from us'

2.2.3. Possessive Pronouns

2.2.3.1. Possessive pronouns in Abkhaz are formed by attaching a possessive prefix to -тәы /t'ʷə/ 'ownership' (cf. а-тәы́-заара 'to belong to'):

	Sg.		Pl.	
1st person	с-тәы 'mine'	/s-t'ʷə/	х-тәы 'ours'	/ħ-t'ʷə/
2nd person (M)	у-тәы́ 'yours'	/wə-t'ʷə́/	шә-тәы 'yours'	/šʷ-t'ʷə/
2nd person (F)	б-тәы 'yours'	/s-t'ʷə/	шә-тәы 'yours'	
3rd person (Human M)	и-тәы 'his'	/jə-t'ʷə́/	р-тәы 'theirs'	/r-t'ʷə/
3rd person (Human F)	л-тәы 'hers'	/l-t'ʷə/	р-тәы 'theirs'	

For example:

(12) иара́ и-тәы́ ҟе-и-тцó-ит
/jará jə-t'ʷə́ ∅-q'a-j-c'a-wá-jt'/
he his-ownership [it-]Prev-he-do-Dyn-Fin
'He is doing his own thing.'

(13) Ҳара́ х-тә-қәá а-дáча-хьтә и-аá-ит.
/ħará ħ-t'ʷ-kʷá a-dáčʲa-xʲt'ʷ j-aá-jt'/
we our-ownership-Pl the-dacha-from he-come-(Aor)-Fin
'Our people came from the dacha.'

2.2.3.2. Attaching a possessive prefix to хатәы́ /xat'ʷə́/ produces an adjective that means 'one's own':

	Sg.		Pl	
1st person	с-хатәы́	/s-xat'ʷə́/	х-хатәы́	/ħ-xat'ʷə́/
2nd person (M)	у-хатәы́	/wə-xat'ʷə́/	шә-хатәы́	/šʷ-xat'ʷə́/
2nd person (F)	б-хатәы́	/b-xat'ʷə́/	шә-хатәы́	
3rd person (Human M)	и-хатәы́	/jə-xat'ʷə́/	р-хатәы́	/r-xat'ʷə́/
3rd person (Human F)	л-хатәы́	/l-xat'ʷə́/	р-хатәы́	

For example:

(14) (сара́) схатәы́ ҩны
/(sará) s-xat'ʷə́ jʷnə/

I my-own house
'my own house'

(15) Уи́ и́хатә машьы́на и́моуп.
/wə́j jə́-xat'ʷ mašʲə́na ø-jə́-ma-wp'/
he his-own car [it-]he-have-Stat.Pres.Fin
'He has his own car.'

2.2.4. Reflexive Pronouns

2.2.4.1. Reflexive pronouns in Abkhaz are formed by attaching хаҭа́ /xatá/ to a possessive prefix[80]:

	Sg.		Pl.	
1st person	с-хаҭа́	/s-xatá/	х-хаҭа́	/ħ-xatá/
2nd person (M)	у-хаҭа́	/wə-xatá/	шә-хаҭа́	/šʷ-xatá/
2nd person (F)	б-хаҭа́	/b-xatá/	шә-хаҭа́	
3rd person (Human M)	и-хаҭа́	/jə-xatá/	р-хаҭа́	/r-xatá/
3rd person (Human F)	л-хаҭа́	/l-xatá/	р-хаҭа́	
3rd person (Non-Human)	а-хаҭа́	/a-xatá/	р-хаҭа́	

For example:

(16) (сара́) с-хаҭа́ /(sará) s-xatá/ 'I myself', (лара́) л-хаҭа́ /(lará) l-xatá/ 'she herself', (дара́) р-хаҭа́ /(dará) r-xatá/ 'they themselves', а́-маҭәа а-хаҭа́ /á-matʷa a-xatá/ 'clothing itself'.

(17) Сара́ с-хаҭа́ а-кы́ҭа с-а́-л-ҵ-ит.
/sará s-xatá a-kə́ta s-a-l-c'ə-jt'/
I my-self the-village I-it-Prev-come out from-(Aor)-Fin
'I myself came out from the village.'

2.2.5. Interrogative Pronouns

2.2.5.1. Interrogative pronouns include да́рбан /dárban/ 'who', indicating the category of humans, and иа́рбан /járban/ 'what', indicating the category of non-humans. There is no form where the case changes for ergative, absolutive, and the like. Interrogative sentences in Abkhaz are expressed through interrogative pronouns; they can also be expressed through verbal complexes (expressing interrogative sentences through verbal complexes will be discussed in §4.7). The verbal predicate of interrogative sentences formed using interrogative pronouns uses the non-finite (for the non-finite, see §3.1.4).

Examples of да́рбан /dárban/ 'who':

(18) Ара́ и́ҟоу да́рбан?
/ará jə́-q'a-w dárban/
here Rel-be-Stat.Pers.NF who

80. Attaching the instrumental suffix -ла /la/ to the reduplicated form of хаҭа́ produces хахаҭа-хаҭа́ла /xaxata-xatála/ 'by oneself, on one's own'.

'Who is here?'

(19) Ари́ ҟазтцóз дáрбан?
/arə́j ϕ-q'a-z-c'a-wá-z dárban/
this [it-]Prev-Rel-do-Dyn-Impf who
'Who was doing this?'[81]

(20) Иналышьҭуа дáрбан?
/jə-na-lə-š^j^t-wa dárban/
Rel-Prev-she-send-Dyn.NF who
'Who is she letting go?'

Examples of иáрбан /járban/ 'what':

(21) Иáрбан игы́лоу?
/járban jə-gə́la-w/
what Rel-stand-Stat.Pres.NF
'What is standing?'

(22) Иáрбан и́ҟалтца?
/járban jə́-q'a-l-c'a/
what Rel-Prev-she-do.Aor.NF
'What did she do?'[82]

2.2.5.2. The interrogative pronoun иáрбан /járban/ 'what' also functions in a way that, when translated into English, resembles the interrogative adjective in that language. For example:

(23) Иáрбан калáкьу барá бахьынхó?
/járban kalák^j^ə-w bará b-ax^j^ə-n-xa-wá/
what city-Stat.Pres.NF you.F you-where-Prev-live-Dyn.NF
'What city do you-F live in?' (lit. 'What is the city where you-F live?')

2.2.6. Demonstrative Pronouns

The demonstrative in Abkhaz possesses three contrasting deictic elements, expressing the following three relationships based on the distance from the speaker to the object and whether or not the object can be seen:

(α) The object is close to the speaker and can be seen by the speaker.
(β) The object is far from the speaker and can be seen by the speaker.
(γ) The object is far from the speaker and cannot be seen by the speaker, or was previously discussed.

---

81. It is also possible to produce an interrogative sentence with the same meaning by using only a verbal complex and not using дáрбан: Ари́ ҟазтцóдаз? /arə́j ϕ-q'a-z-c'a-wá-da-z/ [it-Prev-Rel-do-Dyn-Qu-Dyn.II]. The interrogative marker да- /da/ expressing the category of humans is inserted here.

82. It is possible to produce an interrogative sentence with the same meaning only by using a verbal complex and not using иáрбан: и́-ҟа-л-це-и? /jə́-q'a-l-c'a-j/ [Rel-Prev-she-do-(Aor)-Qu]. The interrogative marker -и that indicates a non-human category is placed at the end here.

Each has a singular and a plural form. The plural forms are formed by attaching <u>-ҭ</u> /t/. The demonstrative pronoun system is as follows (there is a variant system; both are shown here):

	Sg.		Pl.	
(α)	ари́/абри́	/arə́j/abrə́j/	арҭ/аба́рҭ	/art/abárt/
(β)	ани́/абни́	/anə́j/abnə́j/	анҭ/аба́нҭ	/ant/abánt/
(γ)	уи́/убри́	/wə́j/wəbrə́j/	урҭ/уба́рҭ	/wərt/wbárt/

For example:

(24) Ари́ закәы́и / закәы́зеи?
/arə́j ɸ-z-ak’ʷə́-j / ɸ-z-ak’ʷə́-zaj/
this [it-]Rel-be-what
‘What is this?’

(25) амни (= абни́) ҳайӡ́ыԥшып, даайр акы ҳайц́нацҳап. (Bzyp dialect)
/amnəj (= abnəj) ħa-j-ʑ́ə-pšə-p’ d-aaj-r ak’ə ħ-ajć-na-cħa-p’/
that/he we-him-Prev-wait-Fut.I he-come-if something we-together-Prev-have a snack-Fut.I
‘we shall wait for him; when he come here, we shall have a snack together’ (Bgazhba 1964a: 100)

(26) амни (= абни́) йаайў̆а с°ныԥԥылшь (Bzyp dialect)
/amnəj j-aaj-wa sʷ-nə-l-pəl-šʲ/
that Rel-come-Dyn.NF you.Pl-Par-her-meet.Imp-really
‘meet that person who is coming here!’

(27) Убри́ а́шьҭахь шьыжьхьа́ сфо́ит. (AFL)
/wəbréj á-šʲtaxʲ šʲəžʲxʲá ɸ-s-fa-wá-jt’/
that its-after breakfast [it-]I-eat-Dyn-Fin
‘I am having breakfast after that.’

(Cf. Авто́бус <u>абна́</u> игы́лоуп.
/[a-]avt’óbəws abná jə-gə́la-wp’/
[the-]bus there it-stand-Stat.Pres.Fin
‘The bus is standing <u>there</u>.’)

Also, the demonstrative pronoun in (γ) is also used as a 3rd person pronoun: уи́/убри́ ‘he/she’, у́рҭ/уба́рҭ ‘they’. For example:

(28) Уи сара́ сы́чҟәын иа́кәӡам.
/wəj sará sə́-č’ʲk’ʷən j-ák’ʷ-ʒa-m/
he I my-son he-be-Emph-Neg
‘He is not my son.’

(29) Урҭ а́шьха инхо́н.
/wərt á-šʲxa jə-n-xa-wá-n/
they the-mountain they-Prev-live-Dyn-Impf
‘They lived in the mountains.’

(30) у́рт ра́бацәа /wə́rt r-ába-cʷa ‘their fathers’ (lit. ‘they their-father-Pl’)

2.2.7. Indefinite Pronouns

2.2.7.1. Indefinite pronouns include аӡəы́ /aʒʷə́/ 'someone' (cf. Russian 'кто-то') that indicates the category of humans and акы́ /ak'ə́/ 'something' (cf. Russian 'что-то') that indicates the category of non-humans.[83] For example:

(31) Аӡəы́ лаа́ит.
/aʒʷə́ d-aá-jt'/
someone he/she-come-(Aor)-Fin
'Someone came.'

(32) Акы́ ифо́ит.
/ak'ə́ ∅-j-fa-wá-jt'/
something [it-]he-Dyn-Fin
'He is eating something.'

(33) Акы́ уацəы́мшəан!
/ak'ə́ w-a-cʷə́-m-šʷa-n/
something you.M-it-Prev-Neg-be afraid-Proh
'Don't be afraid of anything!'

The form here entails attaching -р /r/ to the indefinite pronoun, as in аӡəы́р /aʒʷə́r/ 'anyone' (cf. Russian 'кто-либо'), акы́р /ak'ə́r/ 'anything' (cf. Russian 'что-либо'). For example:

(34) Аӡəы́р лаа́ма?
/aʒʷə́r d-aá-ma/
anyone he/she-come-(Aor)-Qu
'Did anybody come?'

(35) Акы́р утахума?
/ak'ə́r ∅-wə-taxə-w-ma/
anything [it-]you-want-Stat.Pres.NF-Qu
'Do you want anything?'

(36) Ауаҩы́ ари́ ашəҟəы́ да́пҳхьар, акы́р еилы́икаауеит.
/a-wajʷə́ arə́j a-šʷq'ʷə́ d-á-pxʲa-r ak'ə́r ∅-ajlə́-j-k'aa-wa-jt'/
the-person this the-book he-it-read-if anything [it-]Prev-he-learn-Dyn-Fin
'If one reads this book, one will learn something.'

The difference between these forms and the above pattern without the -р /r/ is properly expressed by the differences in their Russian translations. In short, existence is uncertain for the form with the -р attached, and it is certain for the form without the -р.

Also, да́рбанзаалак(ь) /dárbanzaalak'(ʲ)/ 'anyone, someone; everyone':

(37) Ари́ да́рбанзаалак иуе́ихəоит.
/arə́j dárbanzaalak' jə-w-á-j-ħʷa-wa-jt'/

83. These forms indicate 'one' of those respective numerals: аӡəы́ /aʒʷə́/ 'one (human)', акы́ /ak'ə́/ 'one (non-human)'.

this everyone it-you.M-to-he-say-Dyn-Fin
'Everyone will talk to you about this.'

2.2.7.2. Other indefinite pronouns include пъытк /pətk'/ 'some (non-human)' and пъытҩы́к /pətjʷə́k'/ 'some (human)'. These are placed after the noun and used like adjectives. For example:

(38) Кака́н пъытк сы́т.
/k'ak'án pətk' ø-sə́-t/
nut some [it-]me-give.Imp
'Give me some nuts!'

(39) Сара́ абызшәақәа́ пъытк здырыуеит.
/sará a-bəzšʷa-kʷá pətk' ø-z-də́r-wa-jt'/
I the-language-Pl some [them-]I-know-Dyn-Fin
'I know some languages.'

(40) Асасцәа пъытҩы́к аа́ит.
/á-sas-cʷa pətjʷə́k' ø-aá-jt'/
the-guest-Pl some [they-]come-(Aor)-Fin
'Some guests came.'

2.2.7.3. According to '*Abkhaz Grammar: Phonetics and Morphology*' by Sh. K. Aristava, et al. (*Грамматика абхазского языка: фонетика и морфология*. 1968, стр. 42), there are no negative pronouns in Abkhaz. The functions of the negative pronoun are instead performed by attaching the connector -гьы /gʲə/ 'too, and' to the indefinite pronoun аӡәы́, акы́, resulting in аӡәгьы́ /aʒʷgʲə́/ '(not) anyone', акгьы́/акагьы́ /ak'gʲə́/ak'agʲə́/ '(not) anything'. In this case, the verb always takes the negative form (for the negative marker -м- /m/ of the verb form see §3.1.5.2. Note 4). For example:

(41) Акгьы́ сы́маӡам.
/ak'gʲə́ ø-sə́-ma-ʒa-m/
anything [it-]I-have-Emph-Neg
'I have nothing.'

(42) Аӡәгьы́ дмаа́ит.
/aʒʷgʲə́ d-m-aá-jt'/
anyone he/she-Neg-come-(Aor)-Fin
'Nobody came.'

Words that have a similar meaning include the following:
акы́мзарак:

(43) Акы́мзарак сахаӡо́м.
/ak'ə́mzarak' ø-s-a-ħa-ʒa-wá-m/
anything [it-]me-to-hear-Emph-Dyn-Fin
'I hear nothing.'

2.2.8. Other Pronouns

(i) даҽаӡәы́ /dačaʒʷə́/ 'another person':

Даҽазәы́ д-аа́-ит. /dačaʒʷә́ d-aájt'/ 'Another person came.'
Similar pronouns: даҽакы́ /dačak'ә́/ 'another thing, anything else', азәы́ ..., даҽазәы́ ... /aʒʷә́ dačaʒʷә́/ 'one ... the other ...'

(ii) ха́уа /ħáwa/ 'who among us':

Ҳа́уа иия́шада?
/ħáwa jә-jáša-da/
among us Rel-right-Qu(who)
'Who among us is right?'

(iii) руа́зәк /rwáʒʷk'/ 'one (person) of them':

Руа́зәк ара́ даанхе́ит.
/rwáʒʷk' ará d-aan-xá-jt'/
one of them here he/she-Prev-stay-(Aor)-Fin
'One of them stayed here.'

руа́к (руакы́) /rwák'(rwak'ә́)/ 'one (thing) of them'

(iv) -цыҧхьаӡа /cәpxʲaʒa/ 'every, each':

Ры́цыҧхьаӡа шәҟәы́к-шәҟәы́к аа́рхәеит.
/rә́-cәpxʲaʒa šʷq'ʷә́-k'-šʷq'ʷә́-k' ø-aá-r-xʷa-jt'/
their-each book-one-book-one [them-]Prev-they-buy-(Aor)-Fin
'Each of them bought one book.'

(v) дасу́/доусы́ /dasә́w/dawsә́/ 'everyone':

Дасу́ хатәа́хатәа́ла ау́с жәула́.
/dasә́w xatá-xatá-la a-wә́s ø-žʷ-w-lá/
everyone oneself-oneself-by the-work [it-]you.Pl-do-Hortative
'Everyone, work by himself!'

Доусы́ ргәы́ итәа́з рхәе́ит.
/dawsә́ r-gʷә́ jә-ø-tá-z ø-r-ħʷá-jt'/
everyone their-heart Rel-[it-]be in-Stat.Past.NF [it-]-they-say-(Aor)-Fin
'Each of them said what he was thinking about.'

(vi) зегь(ы́) /zagʲ/ 'all':

Ҳара́ зегьы́ бзи́а иаабо́ит Аҟәа.
/ħará zagʲә́ bzә́ja j-aa-ba-wá-jt' aq'ʷa/
we all well it-we-see-Dyn-Fin Sukhum
'We all love Sukhum.'

Another usage is to combine it with possessive pronouns such as ха́-зегьы /ħá-zagʲә/ 'all of us'.
Similar pronouns: ры́ззагь /rә́zzagʲ/ 'all, entirely everything'
Others: у́рҭкәа /wә́rtkʷa/ 'all this', егьаҩы́ /agʲajʷә́/ 'many (human)', ака́ка /ak'ák'a/ 'something', ама́ҷыҩ /amáč'ʲәjʷ/ 'few (human)', агьы́рт /agʲә́rt'/ 'others'

2.2.9. Pronominal Adjectives

Pronominal adjectives are placed in front of the noun they modify.

(i) аҽа́/даҽа́ /ačá/dačá/ 'other, another':

Аҽа́ ҩны́к дыҩна́лт.
/ačá jʷnə́-k' də-jʷná-l[a-j]t'/
other house-one he/she-Prev-go in-(Aor)-Fin
'He/She went into the other house.'

(ii) егьи́/агьи́ /agʲə́j/ 'other, another':

Агьи́ ашәҟәы́ сы́ҭ!
/agʲə́j a-šʷq'ʷə́ ø-sə́-t/
another the-book [it-]me-give.Imp
'Give me another book!'

2.2.10. Pronominal Adverbs

-аба́нтәи /abánt'ʷəj/ 'from where?':

Баба́нтәи ааи?
/b-abánt'ʷəj aa-j
you.F-from where come-(Aor)-Qu
'Where did you (sg.F) come from?'

2.3. Demonstratives

2.3.1. Demonstrative Pronouns

On this, see §2.2.6.

2.3.2. Demonstrative Adjectives

Demonstrative adjectives have the same form as the demonstrative pronouns in §2.3.1, and agree with the singular and plural of the nouns they modify.[84] For example:

а(б)ри́ а-ҵкы́ ҩе́ижь /a(b)rə́j a-c'k'ə́ jʷájžʲ/ 'this yellow dress', lit. 'this the-dress yellow'
арҭ а-ҩн-қәа́ /art a-jʷn-kʷá/ 'these houses', lit. 'these the-house-Pl'
ани́ ахәынҭқа́р /anə́j a-ħʷəntkár/ 'that king'
анҭ а́хәсақәа /ant á-ħʷsa-kʷa/ 'those women'
уи ашәҟәы́ /wəj a-šʷq'ʷə́/ 'that book'
урҭ а́ӡӷабцәа /wərt á-ʒɣab-cʷa/ 'those girls'

2.3.3. Demonstrative Adverbs

Demonstrative adverbs form the three contrasts noted above: (α), (β), and (γ) (see §2.2.6):

---

84. However, there are also cases in which the word being modified and the demonstrative adjective are not in numerical agreement: Абри́ атҵаҩцәа́ бзи́ақәоуп. /abrə́j a-c'ajʷ-cʷá bzə́ja-kʷa-wp'/ 'These pupils are good'. (Cf. Абри́ атҵаҩы́ дыбзи́оуп. /abrə́j a-c'ajʷə́ də-bzə́ja-wp'/ 'This pupil is good'.)

(α) ара́/абра́ /a(b)rá/ 'here' ара́хь/абра́хь /a(b)ráx^j/ 'here, hither'

(β) ана́/а́бна /aná/ábna/ 'there' ана́хь/абна́хь /a(b)náx^j/ 'there, thither'

(γ) уа/убра́ /wa/wəbrá/ 'there' уа́хь/убра́хь /wáx^j/wəbráx^j/ 'there, thither' (cf. -ахь 'to, towards')

For example:

(44) Иҟоузеи ара́?
/jə́-q'a-w-zaj ará/
what-be-Stat.Pres.NF-Qu here
'What is happening here?'

(45) Миха ара́(хь) уаа́и.
/mixa ará(x^j) w-aáj/
Mikha here you.M(C1)-com.Imp
'Mikha, come here!'

(46) Авто́бус а́бна игы́лоуп.
/[a-]avt'óbəws ábna jə-gə́la-wp'/
the-bus there it(C1)-stand-Stat.Pres.Fin
'The bus is standing there.'

(47) Мура́т иҩы́за аҧте́кахь дце́ит, уа́ а́хәшәкәа аа́ихәеит.
/məwrát jə-j^wə́za [a-]apték'a-[a]x^j d-cá-jt' wá á-x^wš^w-k^wa ø-aá-j-x^wa-jt'/
Murat his-friend the-drugstore-to he(C1)-go-(Aor)-Fin there the-medicine-Pl them(C1)-Prev-he(C3)-buy-(Aor)-Fin
'Murat's friend went to the drugstore and bought the medicine there.'

2.4. Adjectives

2.4.1. Abkhaz adjectives can be divided into (a) non-derived adjectives that are not derived by means of the suffix -тә/-тәи /t'^w/t'^wəj/ and (b) derived adjectives that are derived by means of the suffix -тә/-тәи.

Non-derived adjectives are adjectives that are not derived from other parts of speech, and are mainly descriptive adjectives. Derived adjectives, on the other hand, are adjectives produced by attaching the suffix -тә/-тәи to common nouns, proper nouns, and adverbs; they are material adjectives or proper adjectives, and certain descriptive adjectives are also included here.

2.4.2. Non-Derived Adjectives

Non-derived adjectives cannot be differentiated morphologically from nouns, but can be differentiated from nouns syntactically and semantically. Examples of non-derived adjectives:

а́аигәа 'intimate', а́ашьа 'lazy', а-баа́ 'rotten', а-бааҧсы́ 'bad', а-бжьы́с 'decayed', а-бзи́аӡа 'beautiful', а-бы́рг 'old, middle-aged', а-гәы́мшәа 'bold', а-ҕа́р 'poor', а́-ҕра 'motley', а́-ҕәҕәа 'strong', а-ду́ 'big', а-елы́гьа 'Circassian', ажә 'old', а́-жәпа 'thick', а́-замана 'fine', а́-затҵә 'sole, only', а́-зла 'sweet', а́-ӡа 'damp', а́-иатҵәа 'green', а-иа́ша 'straight, just, right', а́икәа 'black', а́икәатҵәа 'black', а́илҟьа 'nimble', аихабы́ 'elder', аитҵбы́ 'younger', аиҵәа́ 'worse', а-кьа́кьа 'hard', а-кьа́ҿ 'short', а-қарҭве́л 'Kartvelian', а-қы́рҭ 'Georgian', а́-қырҭуа 'Georgian', а-қəы́ҧш 'young', а́-ҟаҧшь 'red', а-ҟьа́ҟьа 'flat', а-ҟьа́ш 'bare', а́-ҟьашь 'dirty', а-ҟəа́з 'big', а-ҟəа́нда 'warm', а-ҟəа́ш 'white', а-ҟəы́ҕа 'clever', а́-лаҟə 'low', а́-лас 'light, not heavy, quick', а́-лаша 'light, bright', а́-лашьца 'dark', а́-лашə 'blind', а-лы́г/а-лы́га 'stupid', а-маншəа́ла 'convenient', а́-мариа 'easy', а́-наа 'crooked', а-па́ 'thin, delicate', а-ҧа́гьа 'proud', а́ҧсуа 'Abkhazian', а-ҧха́ 'warm', а-ҧха́рра 'warm', а́-ҧхашьа 'shy', а́-ҧшӡа 'beautiful', а́-ҧшка 'tender', а-ҧшьа́ 'holy', а́-раз 'kind', а́рҕьа 'right', а́рма 'left', а́-сса 'fine, small', а-та́та 'soft', а-тəы́м 'foreign, strange', а-ҭацəы́ 'empty', а́-ҭбаа 'wide', а-ҭшəа́ 'narrow', а-ҭы́нч 'calm', а-ҭəы́ 'full', а́у 'tall, long', а́-уадаҩ 'difficult', а́-хаа 'tasty', а́-хара 'far', а́-хьанҭа 'heavy', а-хьтəы́ 'golden', а́-хьшəашəа 'cold', а́-хəхəа 'long', а́-хəымга 'mean', а-хəыҷы́ 'ittle', а-хала́л 'kind', а́-ҳарак(ы) 'tall', а-ца́ 'hot', а́-цкьа 'pure', а́-щак 'fast', а́-цəгьа 'bad, difficult, expensive', а-ҵаҕа́ 'thin', а́-ҵар 'sharp; swift', а-ҵау́ла 'deep', а-ҵəыҵəы́ 'sour', а-ҷкəы́на 'young', а-ҽеи́ 'good', а-ҿа́ 'young', а-ҿы́ц 'new; latest', а́ша 'bitter', а́-шкəакəа 'white', а́-шла 'gray', а-шы́ 'hot', а-шьа́хə 'splendid', а́-шəан 'Svan', а́-шəпа 'fat', а́-шəуа 'Abazin', а-ҩа́ 'dry', а-ҩе́жь/а-ҩе́ижь 'yellow', а́-џьбара 'strong'

An article, postpositions, and the indefinite and plural markers can be attached to these adjectives just like nouns. For example:

аду́кəа/-цəа /a-dә́w-kʷa/cʷa/ 'the-big-Pl.non-humna/human'

ду́к /dә́w-k'/ 'big-one'

ду́ла /dә́w-la/ 'big-with'

2.4.2.1. Non-derived adjectives have attributive uses and predicative uses. The attributive use is when the adjective modifies a noun. The predicative use is when the adjective is within a verbal complex and is used as a predicate.

2.4.2.2. Attributive Use of Non-derived Adjectives

The word order of the adjective and the noun it modifies normally runs 'noun—adjective'; the article a- is not attached to the adjective. Plural markers and indefinite markers are attached to the adjective, not the noun. The postposition is also attached to the adjective. For example:

аҩы́н ду /a-jʷә́n dәw/ (lit. the-house big) 'the big house'

ҳҳəынҭқа́р ры́цҳа /ħ-ħʷәntkár rә́cħa/ (our-king poor) 'our poor King'

а́шьха ду́кəа /á-šʲxa dә́w-kʷa/ (the-mountain big-Pl) 'the big mountains'

бжьы́ ду́ла /bžʲә́ dә́w-la/ (voice big-with) 'loudly'

ха́цəа ҕəҕəақəа́ки иаре́и /xá-cʷa ɣʷɣʷa-kʷá-k'ә-j jará-j/ (man-Pl.Human strong-Pl.Non-human-one-and he-and) 'some strong men and he'

However, the plural marker can also be attached in other ways. According to our informant, when the noun being modified by the adjective is human class, it is grammatically desirable for the plural marker to be attached in the following (a) > (b) > (c) order:

(a) аҵаҩы́ бзи́акəа /a-c'ajʷә́ bzә́ja-kʷa/ (the-pupil good-Pl.Non-Human) 'the good pupils'

(b) аҵаҩцəа́ бзи́акəа /a-c'ajʷ-cʷá bzә́ja-kʷa/ (the-pupil-Pl.Human good-Pl.Non-Human) '*ditto*'

(c) аҵаҩы́ бзи́ацəа /a-c'ajʷә́ bzә́ja-cʷa/ (the-pupil good-Pl.Human) '*ditto*'

Also, when proper adjectives and non-derived adjectives that mean 'left' or 'right' modify a noun, the word order runs 'adjective—noun'. Additionally, articles are not attached to nouns. For example:

áшәан /á-šʷan/ 'Svan': áшәан бызшәá /á-šʷan bəzšʷá/ 'the Svan language'
áҧсуа /ápswa/ 'Abkhazian': áҧсуа маҭәá /ápswa matʷá/ 'Abkhazian clothes'
аедыі́гьа /a-edə́gʲa/ 'Circassian': а-едыі́гьа бызшәá /a-edə́gʲa bəzšʷá/ 'the Circassian language'
акартвéл /a-kartvél/ 'Kartvelian': а-картвéл бызшәа-кәá /a-kartvél bəzšʷa-kʷá/ 'the Kartvelian languages'
акы́рт /a-kə́rt/ 'Georgian': акы́рт бызшәá /a-kə́rt bəzšʷá/ 'the Georgian language'
áкыртуа /á-kərtwa/ 'Georgian': áкыртуа ӡҕáб /á-kərtwa ʒɣáb/ 'the Georgian girl'
áшәуа /á-šʷwa/ 'Abazin': áшәуа кы́ҭа /á-šʷwa kə́ta/ 'an Abazinian village'
áрҕьа /árɣʲa/ 'right': áрҕьа шьапы́ /árɣʲa šʲap'ə́/ 'right foot'
áрма /árma/ 'left': áрма напы́ /árma nap'ə́/ 'left hand'
атәы́м /a-t'ʷə́m/ 'foreign': атәы́м бызшәакәá /a-t'ʷə́m bəzšʷa-kʷá/ 'foreign languages'

2.4.2.3. In phrases formed by 'noun—non-derived adjective', the article is attached to the noun and not the adjective. The possessive prefix, too, is attached only to nouns:

ашәҟәы́ жәпá /a-šʷq'ʷə́ žʷp'á/ (the-book thick) 'the thick book'
сахәшьá еихабы́ /s-aħʷšʲá ajhabə́/ (my-sister elder) 'my elder sister'

Indefinite and plural markers are attached to the final adjective when there are two or more adjectives:

ҵыс иаҵәá хәычы́к /c'əs jac'ʷá xʷəč'ʲə́-k'/ (bird blue small-one) 'a small blue bird'
áшьха ҧшӡа дýкәа /á-šʲxa pšʒa də́w-kʷa/ (the-mountain beautiful big-Pl) 'the big beautiful mountains'

The word order when there are two or more adjectives is determined by the type of adjective. For example, for the word order of the adjectives for the phrase 'the beautiful, good pupil', the only possibility is аҵаҩы́ ҧшӡá бзи́а /a-c'ajʷə́ pšʒá bzə́ja/ (the-pupil beautiful good); *аҵаҩы́ бзи́а ҧшӡá (the-pupil good beautiful) would not be allowed. The only possible word order for 'the big, beautiful, green mountain' is áшьха иаҵәá ҧшӡá дý /á-šʲxa jac'ʷá pšʒá də́w/ (the-mountain green beautiful big); neither *á-шьха дý иаҵәá ҧшӡá nor *áшьха ҧшӡá дý иаҵәá would be allowed.

2.4.2.4. Relativized Adjectives

In addition to the above-mentioned methods of adjectives directly modifying nouns, in Abkhaz a construction with a relative clause derived from the adjective can also modify a noun (for relatives see §5.4.5). For example, it is possible to form an adjective clause that resembles the above-mentioned attributive use by predicativizing the adjective азҩы́да /a-zjʷə́da/ 'clean' (in other words, by stative verbalizing it) and putting it in a form that includes the marker и- /jə/, which plays the role of the relative pronoun, and the non-finite present ending -у /w/ of the stative verb—in short изҩы́доу /jə-zjʷə́da-w/ (lit. 'which is clean'). For example:

(48) изҩы́доу ацәéижь
/jə-zjʷə́da-w a-cʷájžʲ/
Rel-clean-Stat.Pres.NF the-body
'a healthy body' (cf. а-хáуа зҩы́да /a-ħáwa zjʷə́da/ 'clean air')

Similarly, there is also a form that has the non-finite negative ending -м /m/ of the stative verb:

(49) иҧӣам аобие́кт
/jə-pə́ja-m a-objékt'/
Rel-direct-Neg the-object
'an indirect object' (cf. и-ҧӣо-у а-обие́кт /jə-pə́ja-w a-objékt'/ 'a direct object')

In phrases using adjectives turned into relativized adjectives like this, the word order runs 'adjective—noun' with the article attached to the noun.

Adjectives turned into relativized adjectives like this can also be derived from verbs. For example, one can use the stative verb а-ҭахы́-заа-ра /a-taxə́-zaa-ra/ 'to want' in a similar way to form и-а-ҭах-у́ /j-a-taxə́-w/ (lit. 'which it wants') 'necessary'. An example: и-а-ҭах-кәо́-у а-шәҟә-кәа́ /j-a-tax-kʷá-w a-šʷq'ʷ-kʷá/ 'the necessary books'. Here, the plural marker -кәа /kʷa/ that cross-references the noun is inserted into the relativized adjective. Relativized adjectives can also be derived from dynamic verbs. For example, аа́и-ра /aáj-ra/ 'to come' can be used with the relative pronoun marker и- /jə/ and the non-finite present tense ending -уа /wa/ of a dynamic verb to form the form и-аа́и-уа /j-aáj-wa/ (lit. 'which is coming') 'next'. An example: иаа́иуа а-шы́кәс а-зы́ /jaájwa a-šʷə́kʷs a-zə́/ (lit. next the-year its-in) 'in the coming year'.

2.4.2.5. Predicative Use of Non-derived Adjectives

In Abkhaz, the suffix -уп /wp'/ of the stative verb can be attached to an adjective (or noun or adverb) to form a predicate that indicates state. In this case, the pronominal prefix cross-referencing the subject is attached to the beginning of the predicate. The pronominal prefix и- /jə/ is used for the 3rd person singular non-human, д- /d/ for the 3rd person singular human, and и- for the 3rd person plural (regardless of human or non-human class). Furthermore, if the referent cross-referencing the pronominal prefix и- is placed directly in front of the prefix of this predicate, then the prefix и- is dropped. For example, see the following:

(50) Асы́ шкуа́куоуп, иҧшзо́уп.
/a-sə́ ø-šk'ʷák'ʷa-wp' jə-pšʒá-wp'/
the-snow [it-]white-Stat.Pres.Fin it-beautiful-Stat.Pres.Fin
'Snow is white and beautiful.'

Cf. Ҳара́ хкы́ҭа да́ара икы́ҭа ду́уп.
/ħará ħ-kə́ta dáara jə-kə́ta ø-də́w-wp'/
we our-village very it-village [it-]big-Stat.Pres.Fin
'Our village is a very big village.'

The pronominal prefix д- also appears in all cases for the 3rd person singular human. For example:

(51) Абри́ атҵаҩы́ дыбзи́оуп.
/abrə́j a-c'ajʷə́ də-bzə́ja-wp'/
this the-pupil he/she-good-Stat.Pres.Fin
'This pupil is good.'

If the predicate is a noun phrase in which the adjective modifies the noun, the pronominal prefix indicating person is attached to the head of the noun phrase and the adjective is stative verbalized. For example:

(52) Сара́ сыртцаҩ бзи́оуп.
/sará sə-rc’ajʷ bzə́ja-wp’/
I I-teacher good-Stat.Pres.Fin
‘I am a good teacher.’

When the subject is plural, the plural marker -кәа/-цәа /kʷa/cʷa/ appears in the predicate. Take note that even when the subject is of human class it is possible for the non-human class marker -кәа /kʷa/ to be used as the plural marker of this predicate (see §2.4.2.2). See the following examples:

(53) Санду́и сабду́и бы́ргцәоуп. (AFL)
/s-andə́wə-j s-abdə́wə-j ∅-bə́rg-cʷa-wp’/
my-grandmother-and my-grandfather-and [they-]elderly-Pl.Hum-Stat.Pres.Fin
‘My grandmother and my grandfather are elderly.’

(54) Ҳара́ хартцаҩцәа́ бзи́акәоуп.
/ħará ħa-rc’ajʷ-cʷá bzə́ja-kʷa-wp’/
we we-teacher-Pl.Hum good-Pl.Non.Hum-Stat.Pres.Fin
‘We are good teachers.’

2.4.3. Adjectives Derived Using the Suffixes -тә and -тәи

These adjectives are derived by attaching the suffixes -тә(ы) /t’ʷ(ə)/ or -тәи /t’ʷəj/ to a noun or an adverb. The process of derivation is different for these suffixes:

(i) The adjective produced by means of -тә is derived only from nouns:

а-бжьа́ратә /a-bžʲára-t’ʷ/ ‘middle’ (cf. а-бжьа́ра /a-bžʲára/ ‘an interval; between’), а-бна́тә ‘wild’ (cf. а́-бна ‘forest’), а-бота́никатә ‘botanical’ (cf. а-бота́ника ‘botany’), а-грамма́тикатә ‘grammatical’ (cf. а-грамма́тика ‘grammar’), а-гәы́рҕьаратә ‘joyful’ (cf. а-гәы́рҕьара ‘joy’), а́-зынтә ‘wintry’ (cf. а́-зын ‘winter’), а-кьы́шәтә ‘labial’ (cf. а-кьы́шә ‘lip’), а-ҟацарба́тә ‘verbal’ (cf. а-ҟацарба́ ‘verb’), а́-лагартатә ‘elementary’ (cf. а́-лагарта ‘beginning’), а-литерату́ратә ‘literary’ (cf. а-литерату́ра ‘literature’), а́-лкааратә ‘distinctive’ (cf. а́-л-каа-ра ‘to distinguish, to pick out’), а-ма́пкратә ‘negative’ (cf. а́-мапкра ‘negation’), амила́ттә ‘national, popular’ (cf. а-мила́т ‘people; nationality’), а-мраташәа́ратә ‘western’ (cf. а-мраташәа́ра ‘west’), а-ҧсы́ӡтә ‘of fish’ (cf. а-ҧсы́ӡ ‘fish’), а́-ҧхьартатә ‘reading’ (cf. а́-ҧхьарта ‘reading room’), а-рҵа́гатә ‘of teaching; educational’ (cf. а-рҵа́га ‘textbook’), а-тоуры́хтә ‘historical’ (cf. а-тоуры́х ‘history’), а́-уаажәларратә ‘social’ (cf. а́-уаажәлар ‘society’), а́-урыстә ‘Russian’ (cf. а́-урыс ‘a Russian’), а-филоло́гиатә ‘philological’ (cf. а-филоло́гиа ‘philology’), а-ха́хәтә ‘stony’ (а-ха́хә ‘stone’), а-хьтәы́ ‘golden’ (cf. а-хьы́ ‘gold’), а-хәынтка́рратә ‘state’ (а-хәынтка́рра ‘a state, nation’), а-цхы́раагӡатә ‘auxiliary’ (cf. а-цхы́раагӡа ‘aid’), а-цәатәы́ ‘of an apple (tree)’ (cf. а-цәа́ ‘apple’), а-ҩна́тә ‘domestic’ (cf. а-ҩны́ ‘house’)

(ii) The adjective produced by means of -тәи is derived from nouns (particularly proper nouns such as place or country names) or from adverbs:

а-дәны́ҟатәи /a-dʷnə́q’a-t’ʷəj/ ‘outer, foreign’ (cf. адәны́ҟа /a-dʷnə́q’a/ ‘outside’), Евро́патәи ‘European’ (cf. Евро́па ‘Europe’), жәажәа́латәи ‘literal’ (cf. жәажәа́ла ‘literally’), а-жәы́тәӡатәи ‘most ancient’ (cf. а-жәы́тәӡа ‘antiquity, in ancient times’), а-жәы́тәтәи ‘ancient’ (cf. ажәы́тә ‘in olden times’), иахьатәи́ ‘today’s’ (cf. иахьа́ ‘today’), кавка́зтәи ‘Caucasian’ (cf. Кавка́з

'Caucasus'), а-калáкьтәи 'urban' (cf. á-калакь 'city'), á-ҟәатәи 'of Sukhum' (cf. Аҟәа 'Sukhum'), а-мрагы́ларатәи 'eastern' (cf. а-мрагы́лара 'east'), á-мчыбжьтәи 'weekly' (cf. á-мчыбжь(а) 'week'), а-ҧáсатәи 'previous' (cf. ҧáса 'before'), Аҧсны́тәи 'Abkhazian' (cf. Аҧсны́ 'Abkhazia'), а-ҧы́хьатәи 'old, past' (cf. ҧы́хьа 'before'), ҭагáлантәи 'autumnal' (cf. ҭагáлан 'autumn'), а-ҭы́ҧантәи 'local' (cf. ҭы́ҧан 'in place of'), Ҭыркәтәы́латәи 'Turkish' (cf. Ҭыркәтәы́ла 'Turkey'), уаáнӡатәи 'former' (cf. уáанӡа 'until that time'), уахы́нлатәи 'nocturnal' (cf. уахы́нла 'by night, at night'), Урыстәы́латәи 'Russian' (cf. Урыстәы́ла 'Russia'), харáтәи 'distant' (cf. харá 'far'), á-шьҭахьтәи 'rear, hind' (cf. á-шьҭахь 'after'), а-шәы́шыкәсатәи 'of one hundred years, centurial' (cf. а-шәы́шыкәса 'century'), Џыгьáрдатәи 'of Dzhgjarda' (cf. Џыгьáрда 'Dzhgjarda')

2.4.3.1. Adjectives with a <u>-тә</u> /t'ʷ/ or <u>-тәи</u> /t'ʷəj/ have only an attributive use. The adjective must be placed in front of the noun it modifies.

2.4.3.2. Nouns modified by adjectives with <u>-тә</u> /t'ʷ/ do not have an article:

а-бжьáратә шкóл /a-bžʲárat'ʷ šk'ól/ 'a middle school'
а-бнáтә ҧстә-кәá /a-bnát'ʷ pst'ʷ-kʷá/ 'wild animals'
á-лагарҭатә школ /á-lagartat'ʷ šk'ól/ 'an elementary/a primary school'
а-ботáникатә бáхча /a-bot'ánik'at'ʷ báħčʲa/ 'botanical gardens'
а-дрáматә теáтр /a-drámat'ʷ t'eát'r/ 'a theater'
а-дәы́ӷбатә стáнциа /a-dʷə́ɣbat'ʷ st'ancəja/ 'a railway station'
а-кьы́шәтә цыбжьы́ҟа-кәа /a-kʲə́šʷt'ʷ cəbžʲə́q'a-kʷa/ 'labial consonants'
а-ҟатцарбáтә ҧынгы́ла /a-q'ac'arbát'ʷ pəngə́la/ 'a verbal prefix'
а-литератýратә бызшәа-кәá /a-lit'erat'úrat'ʷ bəzšʷa-kʷá/ 'literary languages'
á-лкааратә чы́дара-кәа /á-lk'aarat'ʷ č'ʲə́dara-kʷa/ 'distinguishing features'
мáпкратә хәҭáч /máp'k'rat'ʷ xʷtáč'ʲ/ 'negative particle'
а-мраҭашәáратә ҧша /a-mratašʷárat'ʷ pša/ 'a west wind'
а-ҧсы́ӡтә шша /a-psə́ʒt'ʷ šša/ 'fish oil'
á-ҧхьарҭатә зал /á-pxʲartat'ʷ zal/ 'a reading room'
а-рцáгатә цхы́раагӡа-кәа /a-rc'ágat'ʷ cxə́raagʒa-kʷa/ 'the school textbooks'
а-тоуры́хтә ромáн /a-tawrə́xt'ʷ román/ 'a historical novel'
á-уаажәларратә џарады́рра-кәа /á-waažʷlarrat'ʷ c'aradə́rra-kʷa/ 'social sciences'
áҧсуа-áурыстә жәар /ápswa-áwrəst'ʷ žʷar/ 'an Abkhaz-Russian dictionary'
а-филолóгиатә факультéт /a-filológiat'ʷ fak'ulʲt'ét'/ 'the philological department'
а-хáҳәтә шәы́шыкәса /a-xáħʷt'ʷ šʷə́šəkʷsa/ 'the Stone Age'
а-хьтәы́ лахáнка /a-xʲt'ʷə́ laxánk'a/ 'a golden washtub'
а-ҳәынҭкáрратә бызшәá /a-ħʷəntkárrat'ʷ bəzšʷá/ 'a state language'
а-цхы́раагӡатә ҟатцарба-кәá /a-cxə́raagʒat'ʷ q'ac'arba-kʷá/ 'auxiliary verbs'
а-ҩнáтә ҧстә-кәá /a-jʷnát'ʷ pst'ʷ-kʷá/ 'domestic animals'

The possessive prefix attaches to nouns:

а-жәы́тә с-ҩы́за /a-žʷə́t'ʷ s-jʷə́za/ (lit. the-old my-friend) 'my old friends'

The postposition is attached after nouns:

Ҩна́тə ҧсаа́тəс шəара́ и́жəдыруазеи?
/jʷnát'ʷ psaát'ʷ-s šʷará jə́-žʷ-dər-wa-zaj/
domestic bird-as you.Pl Rel-you.Pl-know-Dyn-Qu(what)
'What domestic bird do you know?'

2.4.3.3. Nouns (or noun phrases) modified by adjectives with -тəи /t'ʷəj/ have an article:

а-дəныҟатəи а́-хəаахəтра /a-dʷnə́q'at'ʷəj á-xʷaaxʷtra/ 'foreign trade'
а-жəы́тəтəи а-ҭоуры́х /a-žʷə́t'ʷt'ʷəj a-tawrə́x/ 'ancient history'
кавка́зтəи а-бызшəа-кəа́ /k'avk'ázt'ʷəj a-bəzšʷa-kʷá/ 'the Caucasian languages'
а́-ҟəатəи а-у́су-цəа /á-q'ʷat'ʷəj a-wə́səw-cʷa/ 'the workers of Sukhum'
ҭага́лантəи а́-мза-кəа /tagálant'ʷəj á-mza-kʷa/ 'autumnal months'
хара́тəи А-мрагы́лара /xarát'ʷəj a-mragə́lara/ 'the Far East'
а-ҽы́ а́-шьҭахьтəи а-шьап-кəа́ /a-čə́ á-šʲtaxʲt'ʷəj a-šʲap'-kʷá/ 'the horse's hind legs'
Аҧсны́тəи а-ҳəынҭка́рратə университе́т /apsnə́t'ʷəj a-ħʷəntkárrat'ʷ universit'ét'/ 'Abkhazian State University'
Урыстəы́латəи А-федера́циатə хəынҭка́рра /wərəst'ʷə́lat'ʷəj a-federáciat'ʷ ħʷəntkárra/ 'Russian Federation'
Џыгьа́рдатəи а-бжьа́ратə шко́л /ǯʲgʲárdat'ʷəj a-bžʲárat'ʷ šk'ól/ 'the middle school of Dzhgjarda'

The possessive prefix attaches to nouns:

иахьатəи́ х-а́изара /jaxʲat'ʷə́j ħ-ájzara/ 'our meeting today'

2.4.3.4. Ordinal numbers also have the adjectival suffix -тəи. Ordinal numbers are derived by attaching the suffix -тəи to a cardinal number that belongs to the non-human class. (For details of ordinal numbers see §2.6.2.1) For example:

а́ктəи [< а́-ак-тəи] /ák't'ʷəj/ 'first' (cf. акы́ /ak'ə́/ 'one'); а́ҧхьатəи /ápxʲat'ʷəj/ 'first-(Human)'
а́-ҩбатəи /á-jʷbat'ʷəj/ 'second' (cf. ҩба /jʷba/ 'two')
а́-хҧатəи /á-xpat'ʷəj/ 'third' (cf. хҧа /xpa/ 'three')
а́-ҧшьбатəи /á-pšʲbat'ʷəj/ 'fourth' (cf. ҧшьба́ /pšʲbá/ 'four')
а́-хəбатəи /á-xʷbat'ʷəj/ 'fifth' (cf. хəба /xʷba/ 'five')
а́-фбатəи /á-fbat'ʷəj/ 'sixth' (cf. фба /fba/ 'six')
а́-быжьбатəи /á-bəžʲbat'ʷəj/ 'seventh' (cf. быжьба́ /bəžʲbá/ 'seven')
а́абатəи [< а́-ааба-тəи] /áabat'ʷəj/ 'eighth' (cf. ааба́ /aabá/ 'eight')
а́-жəбатəи /á-žʷbat'ʷəj/ 'ninth' (cf. жəба /žʷba/ 'nine')
а́-жəабатəи /á-zʷabat'ʷəj/ 'tenth' (cf. жəаба́ /žʷabá/ 'ten')

Just as adjectives that have -тəи, nouns modified by an ordinal number have an article:

а́ктəи а-шьаҿа́ /ák't'ʷəj a-šʲač'á/ 'the first step'
а́ктəи а-хшáраура /ák't'ʷəj a-xšárawra/ 'the first childbirth'
а́ктəи а-кла́сс а-ҿы́ //ák't'ʷəj a-k'láss a-č'ə́/ 'in the first class'
а́ҩбатəи а-ета́ж /ájʷbat'ʷəj a-et'áž/ 'the second floor'
а́хҧатəи а-да́ҟьа /áxpat'ʷəj a-dáq'ʲa/ 'the third page'
а́ҩажəатəи а-шəы́шықəса /ájʷažʷat'ʷəj a-šʷə́šəkʷsa/ 'the twentieth century'

Possessive prefixes attach to nouns:

а́ҧхьатəи у-ҧҳəы́с /ápxʲat'ʷəj wə-pħʷə́s/ 'your first wife'

The postposition is attached after nouns:
áктәи а-програ́мма-ла /ák'tʼʷәj a-p'rográmma-la/ 'according to the first program'

2.4.4. Comparison in Adjectives

2.4.4.1. Comparative Degree

There is no special form for comparative degree in adjectives when a standard of comparison (i.e. 'than X' in English) is present. These adjectives will either have predicative use or be relativized adjectives. The standard of comparison is expressed by the postposition -áасҭа/-éиҳа/-áҭцк(ь)ыс /áasta/ájħa/ác'k'(ʲ)әs/ 'than', which has a possessive prefix cross-referencing the standard of comparison. For example:

(55) Абри́ аҧҳәы́с бара́ бéиҳа дыҧшӡóуп.
/abrә́j a-pħʷә́s bará b-ájħa dә-pšʒá-wp'/
this the-woman you.F your.F-than she(C1)-beautiful-Stat.Pres.Fin
'This woman is more beautiful than you.'

(56) Саҳәшьа́ хәышыкәса́, сара́ са́асҭа деиҳабу́п.
/s-aħʷšʲá xʷә-šәk'ʷsá sará s-áasta d-ajħabә́-wp'/
my-sister 5-year I my-than she(C1)-older-Stat.Pres.Fin
'My sister is 5 years older than I am.'

(57) Уара́ уа́ҭцкыс сара́ сеиҳабу́п.
/wará w-ác'k'әs sará s-ajħabә́-wp'/
you.M you.M-than I I(C1)-older-Stat.Pres.Fin
'I am older than you.'

(58) уи [а-]а́ҭцкыс и́маншәалоу даҽакы́
/wәj [a-]ac'k'әs jә́-manšʷala-w dačak'ә́/
that its-than which-convenient-Stat.Pres.NF another thing
'another which is more convenient than that'

When there is no standard of comparison, the adverb еиҳа́/иаҳа́ /ajħá/jaħá/ 'more' is added to the adjective[85]:

(59) еиҳа́ иҧшӡóуп
/ajħá jә-pšʒá-wp'/
more it/they(C1)-beautiful-Stat.Pres.Fin
'it is/they are more beautiful'

(60) еиҳа́ и́ҧшӡоу
/ajħá jә́-pšʒa-w/
more which-beautiful-Stat.Pres.NF

85. Cf. Сара́ а́ҧхын а́асҭа а́ӡынра иаҳа́ иéиӷьасшьоит.
/sará á-pxәn [a-]aasta á-ʒәnra jaħá j-ájɣʲa-s-šʲa-wa-jt'/
I the-summer [its-]than the-winter more it(C1)-Prev-I(C3)-prefer-Dyn-Fin
'I like winter better than summer'.

'more beautiful', lit. 'which is more beautiful'

2.4.4.2. Superlative Degree

The superlative degree of the adjective is expressed by зегь (/зегьы́) /zagʲ (/zagʲə́)/ 'all' and the postposition -е́иха /ájħa/ (-а́аста /áasta/, -а́тцк(ь)ыс /ác'k'(ʲ)əs/) 'than', the latter element having a possessive prefix р- /r/ 'their' that cross-references the former. The adjective will either have a predicative use or be a relativized adjective. For example:

(61) Уи зегьы́ ре́иха иԥшӡо́уп.
/wəj zagʲə́ r-ájħa jə-pšʒá-wp'/
that all their-than it(C1)-beautiful-Stat.Pres.Fin
'That is the most beautiful.'

(62) (зегь) реиха́ иманшәа́лоу а́мҩа
/zagʲ r-ajħá jə-manšʷála-w á-mjʷa/
all their-than which-comfortable-Stat.Pres.NF the-way
'the most comfortable way'

(63) Аԥсны́ зегьы́ ре́иха и́ԥшӡоу атәы́лақәа ируа́куп.
/apsnə́ zagʲə́ r-ájħa jə́-pšʒa-w a-t'ʷə́la-kʷa jə-rwák'ə-wp'/
Abkhazia all their-than which-beautiful-Stat.Pres.NF the-land-Pl it(C1)-one of them-Stat.Pres.Fin
'Abkhazia is one of the most beautiful countries.'

(64) Сара́ сзы́ зегь ре́иха идуу, зегь ре́иха ибзи́оу, зегь ре́иха и́ԥшӡоу, сы́калакь Аҟәоуп.
/sará s-zə́ zagʲ r-ájħa jə-déw-w zagʲ r-ájħa jə-bzə́ja-w zagʲ r-ájħa jə́-pšʒa-w sə́-kalakʲ ∅-aq'ʷa-wp'/
I my-for all their-than which-big-Stat.Pres.NF all their-than which-good-Stat.Pres.NF all their-than which-beauty-Stat.Pres.NF my-city it(C1)-Sukhun-Stat.Pres.Fin
'For me, the biggest, best, and most beautiful city is Sukhum.' (AFL)

2.4.5. Adjective Accents

2.4.5.1. Spruit's rule applies for accents on adjectives as it did for accents on nouns (see §2.1.8). For example, accents on non-derived adjectives are as follows:

а́-шкәакәа /á-šk'ʷak'ʷa/ D'RDR 'white' (cf. а́-шкәакәа-кәа /á-šk'ʷak'ʷa-kʷa/ D'RDRD 'white-Pl', шкәа́кәа-к /šk'ʷák'ʷa-k'/ RD'RR 'white-one', и́-шкәакәо-у /jə́-šk'ʷak'ʷa-w/ D'RDRI 'which-white-Stat.Pres.NF')

а́-шла /á-šla/ D'RD 'gray' (cf. а́-шла-кәа/-цәа /á-šla-kʷa/cʷa/ D'RDD 'gray-Pl', шла-кәа́-к /šla-kʷá-k'/ RDD'R 'gray-one', шла́-к /šká-k'/ RD'R 'gray-one', и́-шло-у /jə́-šla-w/ D'RDI 'which-gray-Stat.Pres.NF')

а-бзи́а /a-bzə́ja/ DDD'R 'good' (cf. а-бзи́а-кәа /a-bzə́ja-kʷa/ DDD'RD 'good-Pl', бзи́а-к /bzə́ja-k'/ DD'RR 'good-one', а-бзи́а-ӡа /a-bzə́ja-ʒa/ DDD'RD 'good-Emph/best')

а-гҿаха́ /a-gč'axá/ DDDD' 'remote' (cf. гҿаха-кәа́ /gč'axa-kʷá/ DDDD' 'remote-Pl')

а-ԥа́р /a-ɣár/ DD'R 'poor' (cf. а-ԥа́р-цәа /a-ɣár-cʷa/ DD'RD 'poor-Pl', ԥа́р-к /ɣár-k'/ D'RR 'poor-one', ԥа́р-цәа-к /ɣár-cʷa-k'/ D'RDR 'poor-Pl-one', и-ԥа́р-у /jə-ɣárə-w/ DD'RI 'which-poor-Stat.Pres.NF')

а́иқәа (< а́-аиқәа) /[á-]ajkʷa/ [D'-]RID 'black' (cf. А-мшы́н еиқәа́ (< аиқәа́) /ajkʷá/ RID' 'the Black

Sea', еиқəá-к /ajkʷá-k'/ RID'R 'black-one', áиқəа-цəа (< á-аиқəа-цəа) /[á-]ajkʷa-cʷa/ D'RIDD 'black-Emph', а-чá еиқəа-цəá (< аиқəа-цəá) /ajkʷa-c'ʷá/ RIDD' 'black bread')

áу (< á-ау) /[á-]aw/ [D'-]RD 'tall, long' (cf. áу-қəа < á-ау-қəа /[á-]aw-kʷa/ [D'-]RDD 'tall-Pl', ауы́-к /awə́-k'/ RD'R 'tall-one')

á-ҳарак /á-ħarak'/ D'RRR 'high, tall' (cf. á-ҳарак-цəа/-қəа /á-ħarak'-cʷa/kʷa/ D'RRRD 'high-Pl', ҳаракы́-к /ħarak'ə́-k'/ RRR'R 'high-one', а-ҳəадá ҳарáк /ħarák'/ RR'R 'the high hillock')

Exceptions:

аиҳабы́ (< а-аиҳабы́) /[a-]ajħabə́/ [D-]RIID'(?) 'elder' (cf. аиҳаб-қəá/-цəá (< а-аиҳаб-қəá/-цəá) /[a-]ajħab-kʷá/cʷá/ [D-]RIIDD'(?) 'elder-Pl', еиҳабы́-к /ajħabə́-k'/ RIID'R 'elder-one', áиашьа еиҳабы́ /ajħabə́/ RIID' 'an elder brother')

2.4.5.2. Spruit's rule also applies for accents on adjectives derived from the suffix -тə and -тəи. The accent unit for this suffix -тə is R:

á-ӡынтə /á-ʒənt'ʷ/ D'RRR 'wintry' (cf. á-ӡын /á-ʒən/ D'RR 'winter', ӡны́-к/ӡын-кы́ /ʒnə́-k'/ʒən-k'ə́/ RR'R/RRR' 'winter-one')

а-ҟəацарбáтə /a-q'ac'arbát'ʷ/ DDDDD'R 'verbal' (cf. а-ҟацарбá /a-q'ac'arbá/ DDDDD' 'verb', а-ҟацарба-қəá /a-q'ac'arba-kʷá/ DDDDDD' 'verbs')

а-ҩнáтə /a-jʷnát'ʷ/ DDD'R 'domestic' (cf. а-ҩны́ /a-jʷnə́/ DDD' 'house', а-ҩн-қəá /a-jʷn-kʷá/ DDDD' 'houses')

Exceptions:

а-бнáтə /a-bnát'ʷ/ DRI'R (?) 'wild' (cf. á-бна /á-bna/ D'RI 'forest', бнá-к /bná-k'/ RI'R 'forest-one')

2.4.5.3. The accent unit for the suffix -тəи is DR:

иаҳьатəи́ /jaxʲat'ʷə́j/ DDD'R 'today's' (cf. иаҳьá DD' /jaxʲá/ 'today', иаҳьа-гьы́ /jaxʲa-gʲə́/ DDD' 'today-even')

ажəы́тəтəи /ažʷə́t'ʷt'ʷəj/ DD'RDR 'ancient' (cf. ажəы́тə /ažʷə́t'ʷ/ DD'R 'in olden times')

áктəи (< á-ак-тəи) /[á-]ak't'ʷəj/ D'RIDR 'first' (cf. акы́ /ak'ə́/ RI' 'one')

(á)-шə(ы)ктəи́ /(á)-šʷ(ə)k't'ʷə́j/ (D')RRD'R 'hundredth' (cf. шəкы́ /šʷk'ə́/ RR' 'hundred')

(а)-жəáҩатəи /(a)-žʷájʷat'ʷəj/ (D)D'RDR 'twelfth' (cf. жəáҩа /žʷájʷa/ D'R 'twelve', жəа-бá /žʷa-bá/ DD' 'ten', ҩ-бá /jʷ-bá/ RD' 'two')

(á)-ҩажəатəи́ /(á)-jʷažʷat'ʷə́j/ (D')RDD'R 'twentieth' (cf. ҩажəá /jʷažʷá/ RD' 'twenty')

However, there are exceptions:

а-калáқьтəи /a-kalákʲt'ʷəj/ DRR'RDR(?) 'urban' (cf. á-калақь /á-kalakʲ/ D'RRR 'city', á-калақь-қəа /á-kalakʲ-kʷa/ D'RRRD 'cities', кáлакь-к /kálakʲ-k'/ R'RRR 'city-one', калáкь-қəа-к /kalákʲ-kʷa-k'/ RR'RDR(?) 'city-Pl-one')

Аԥсны́тəи /apsnə́t'ʷəj/ DDDD'DR(?) 'Abkhazian' (cf. Аԥсны́ /apsnə́/ DDDD' 'Abkhazia')

харáтəи /xarát'ʷəj/ RD'DR(?) 'distant' (cf. харá /xará/ RD' 'far', á-хара /á-xara/ D'RD 'distant')

2.4.6. Affixes Attached to Adjectives

When attached to adjectives, the following affixes strengthen or weaken the meaning of the adjective.

2.4.6.1. Suffixes to indicate emphasis:

-ӡа /ʒa/: а-бзи́а-ӡа /a-bzə́ja-ʒa/ 'very good' (cf. а-бзи́а /a-bzə́ja/ 'good'), á-сса-ӡа /á-ssa-ʒa/ 'very

small' (cf. á-сса /á-ssa/ 'small')
-ʒʒа /ʒʒa/: а-дý-ʒʒа /a-dә́w-ʒʒa/ 'very big, giant' (cf. а-дý /a-dә́w/ 'big')
-тцәа /c'ʷa/: áикәа-тцәа /ájkʷa-c'ʷa/ 'black, dark' (cf. áикәа /ájkʷa/ 'black')
-цәа /cʷa/: á-харак-цәа /á-ħarak'-cʷa/ 'too tall' (cf. á-харак /á-ħarak'/ 'tall'), А-бжьы́ дý-цәо-уп. /a-bžʲә́ ø-dә́w-cʷa-wp'/ 'The sound is too loud.'

2.4.6.2. Prefixes that mean 'fairly, approximately':
цә(ы)- /cʷ(ә)/: а-цә-ҟәáнда /a-cʷ-q'ʷánda/ 'warmish' (cf. а-ҟәáнда /a-q'ʷánda/ 'warm'), а-цә-и́кәатцәа /a-cʷ-jә́kʷac'ʷa/ 'blackish' (cf. áикәа-тцәа /ájkʷa-c'ʷa/ 'black, dark'), а-цә-ҩéжь /a-cʷ-jʷéžʲ/ 'yellowish' (< а-ҩéжь /a-jʷéžʲ/ 'yellow')

(65) Ицәыуадáҩ(ы)уп изанаáҭ áԥсахра.
/jә-cʷә-wadájʷә-wp' jә-zanaát á-psaxra/ (cf. á-уадаҩ 'difficult')
it-little-difficult-Stat.Pres.Fin his-profession its-changing
'It is a little difficult to change his profession.'

аазы- /aazә/: и-аазы́-ҟапшь-у /j-aazә́-q'apšʲә-w/ 'reddish' (Chirikba: 30) (< а-ҟáпшь /a-q'ápšʲ/ 'red')

2.5. Adverbs

2.5.1. Adverbs can be divided into simple adverbs and interrogative adverbs based on their usage.

2.5.1.1. Simple Adverbs

Simple adverbs express the following meanings:

(i) Temporal Adverbs: уажәы́ /wažʷә́/ 'now', уажәшьҭá /wažʷšʲtá/ 'already; now', уашьҭá /wašʲtá/ 'now', иахьá/ехьá /jaxʲá/ 'today, now', иацы́/исцы́/ецы́ /jacә́/ 'yesterday', уатцәы́ /wac'ʷә́/ 'tomorrow', иахá /jaxá/ 'last night', убáсҟан/убы́сҟан/ýсҟан 'then, at such a moment', анáҩс /anájʷs/ 'then', уашьҭáн 'afterwards', лассы́ 'soon, quickly', ԥáса/ԥы́хьа 'before', тцыԥхцәá 'the year before last', шагыу 'before', ааигәá 'recently, lately', жәахá 'recently', жәац(ы́) 'the day before yesterday', аԥы́жәап 'three days ago, two days before yesterday', а-шáмҭа 'before dawn', áаилахәламҭазы 'toward/by evening', уатцәáшьҭахь 'the day after tomorrow', а-жәы́тә-за 'in ancient times, in antiquity', á-шьыжь 'in the morning', шьыжьымҭáн 'in the morning', ааигәá 'recently', уáанза 'until then', цьарá-цьарá 'sometimes', еснáгь/ескьы́нагь 'always', есԥхынрá 'every summer', есымзá 'every month', есымшá/есы́ҽны 'every day' (cf. а-мш 'день' < *á-мша), есымшáаира 'day by day', есы́уаха 'every night', есы́шыкәса [< есы́-шыкәс] 'every year', наҟ-нáҟ 'in the future, henceforth', а-кы́раамҭа/акраáмҭа 'for a long time', акы́рынтә 'many times', ԥы́ҭрак 'a little while', убри́-нахыс 'since then', ýинахыс 'thereafter, after that', шьáрда 'for a long time', шáанза 'very early in the morning', зáа/цәы́кьа 'early', áаԥын in spring', á-ԥхын 'in summer', ҭагáлан 'in autumn', á-зын 'in winter', etc.

(ii) Adverbs Expressing Frequency: зны́ /znә́/ (cf. з- < за 'one', -ны) 'once', зны́к 'one day, once', ҩы́нтә 'twice', ласс-ласс 'often', иагáрааны 'many times, very often', зны́-зы́нла 'sometimes', цьарá-цьарá 'sometimes, here and there', дырҩéгь(ых) 'again', ҩаԥхьá 'again', еиҭá 'once again', еитáх 'once more', etc.

(iii) Locative Adverbs: арá/абрá 'here',[86] анá/áбна '(over) there', уа/убрá '(over) there', арáхь/абрáхь 'hither, here', арáнтә/арáнтәи/арсынтә́и 'from here', анáхь 'there, over there (by you)', анáхь-арáхь 'thither and hither', нахьхьи́ 'in the distance over there', нак̑ 'there, thither', нак̑-аáк̑ 'here and there', уахь/убрáхь 'thither, there', ааигәá 'near', ааигәáра 'near (to), beside, next to' [Ҭамéл сарá с-áаигәара ды-н-хó-ит. *Tamel lives next to me. Тамел живет недалеко от меня.*], ааигәá=сигәа 'here-abouts', а-зáаигәара 'near', á-мҧан/á-мҧын 'near, close', харá 'far', харaӡá 'very far', харáнтә/харантәы́ 'from afar, from a distance', а-ҩны́ 'at home', а-ҩны́к̑а 'home, homeward(s)', џьарá 'somewhere', зехьы́нџьара 'everywhere', иахьабалáк(ь) [< и-ахь-а-ба-лáк(ь) 'it/them-where-it-see-LA'] 'everywhere', џьарáкыр 'anywhere', џьарá-џьарá 'here and there', џьаргьы́ 'nowhere', адәны́ 'out of doors, outside', адәны́к̑а/адәахьы́ 'outside', нахы́с 'beyond', áҩада 'upward', á-лада 'down, downwards', хлантцы́ 'down', ҵак̑á 'down', á-ҵан 'down', а-ханы́ 'above', а-хыхь 'above; up', лбаá 'below', ҧхьак̑á 'forward, ahead', áҧхьа-нӡа 'in front of', etc.

(iv) Quantity and Degree Adverbs: ҕәҕәá 'much; many; strongly', дáара 'very', дáараӡа 'very much', дук 'a little; not much', дунеихаáн 'never', еилáкь 'many, much', зынӡá 'quite, completely, fully; very', зынӡáк/зынӡáск 'completely', каамéҭ 'a great deal; very much', кыр 'much, many', акы́р 'enough', -мáчымкәа 'much, many', мыцхәы́/á-мцхәы 'very, too much', ҧыҭк 'a little, not much', рацәа 'very, very much', -рацәаӡаны́ 'a great many', -рацәаны́ '(*of things*) many', рацәаҩны́ '(*of people*) many', убаск̑áк/уск̑áк/убырск̑áк 'so many, so much', убаск̑аҩы́к/уск̑аҩы́к/убырск̑аҩы́к '(*of people*) as many', убриáк̑ара 'so much', уиáк̑ара 'so much, so', шьáрда 'much, many', аáрлахәа 'with difficulty, barely, hardly', мáчк/хәычы́к 'a little, slightly', -мáчны 'little, few', etc.

(v) Manner Adverbs: ас/абáс 'so, thus', áсеиҧш 'so, like this', убáс 'so, thus', ус 'thus, so, like that, as follows', бзи́аны [< а-бзи́а+ны] 'well, nicely', -бзи́ахәӡа 'very well', и-ҕәҕәаны́ 'well', еиҟәшәа-ны́ 'harmoniously, well, smoothly', цкьа 'well; exactly, clearly', ҕәҕәá 'hard, strongly, firmly, soundly', -гәы́рҕьахәха(ны) 'happily, merrily, gaily', насы́ҧда 'unhappily', и́-рласны 'quickly, fast', -кәк̑ьа 'fast', лассы́ 'quickly, fast', áҧхьаӡатәи 'very fast', -ццакны́ 'quickly, hurriedly', á-шырхәа 'rapidly, quickly, fast', -пьҭк̑ьаны́ 'fast', -ны́гәнысуа 'very slowly', апшьшьы́хәа 'quietly, gently, slowly', аҕьéҩхәа 'quickly, boldly, energetically', цәгьалá 'cruelly, severely', -ҧҧы́хәаны 'with enthusiasm', -ҿазҵәы́лхны 'with effort', ҿéишәа 'well, all right', мачмáч 'gradually', etc.

(vi) Other Adverbs: нас 'then', áаи/аéи/аиéи 'yes, of course', мамóу/мап/маумóу 'no', хы́мҧада 'surely, certainly', -заргьы 'probably', издырỳада/áкәхап/и-к̑алáп 'probably', убáсгьы 'moreover, also, furthermore', бзантцы́(к) 'never', etc.

2.5.1.2. Interrogative Adverbs

The following are interrogative adverbs:
зак̑á /zaq'á/ 'how, how much, how many', шак̑á /šaq'á/ 'how many; how much', ианбá /janbá/ 'when', ианбáнӡа /janbánʒa/ 'until when', иабá /jabá/ '(to) where', иззы́ /jəzzə́/ 'for what reason', ишҧá /jəšpá/ 'how', избáн /jəzbán/ [< и-збан 'it-why'] 'why'.
For example:

86. See §2.3.3.

(66) Шаҟá цәа ýмои?[87]
/šaq'á c'ʷa ϕ-wə́-ma-wə-j/
how many apple [it/them(C1)-]you.M(C2)-have-Stat.Pres.NF-Qu
'How many apples do you have?'

(67) Шаҟá иаԥсóи ашәҟәы́?
/šaq'á j-a-psá-wə-j a-šʷq'ʷə́/
how much it(= the book, C1)-it(C2)-cost-Stat.Pres.NF-Qu the-book
'How much does the book cost?'

(68) Заҟá (/Шаҟá) иԥшӡóузеи асасаáирта ахы́бра!
/zaq'á (šaq'á) jə-pšʒá-w-zaj a-sasaájrta a-xə́bra/
how it(C1)-beautiful-Pres.Stat.NF-Qu the-hotel its-building
'How beautiful the building of the hotel is!'

(69) Ашықәс заҟá мзá áмоу?
/á-šəkʷs zaq'á mzá ϕ-á-ma-w/
the-year how many month [it(C1)-]it(C2)-have-Stat.Pres.NF
lit. 'how many months does a year have?'
'How many months are there in a year?'

(70) Ишԥá ҟалéи?
/jə-špá ϕ-q'a-lá-j/
it-how [it(C1)-]Prev-happen-(Aor)-Qu
'How did this happen?'

(71) Ишԥá ухәéи?
/jə-špá ϕ-w-ħʷá-j/
it-how [it(C1)-]you.M(C3)-say-(Aor)-Qu
'How did you say?'

(72) Избáн, ус зáа узгы́ло?
/jə-zbán wəs záa wə-z-gə́la-wa/
it-why so early you.M(C1)-why-get up-Dyn.Pres.NF
'Why do you get up so early?'

2.5.2. Adverb Formation

Adverbs can be divided into non-derived adverbs and derived adverbs depending on the manner in which they are produced. Below, we shall examine the manner in which derived adverbs are produced. The methods for deriving adverbs are adding a suffix and reduplication of the root.

---

87. If the noun 'apples' comes before шаҟá /šaq'á/ 'how many', an article and plural marker is attached to this noun:
Ацәакәá шаҟá ýмои?
/a-c'ʷa-kʷá šaq'á ϕ-wə́-ma-wə-j/
the-apple-Pl how many [it/them(C1)-]you.M(C2)-NF.Pres-Qu
'How many apples do you have?'

2.5.2.1. Derivation of Adverbs with a Suffix

The most frequently seen adverb formation method is to add a suffix to a nominal, adjectival, or an adverbial stem, etc. For example:

(i) -ла /la/: аамҭáла ‘for a while, for a time’ (cf. áамҭа ‘time’), аамҭа=аамҭáла ‘at times, now and then’, баапҙсы́ла ‘badly, terribly’ (cf. абаапҙсы́ ‘bad’), абáсла (= абáс áла) ‘in this way’ (cf. абáс ‘so’), гәапҙхары́ла ‘gladly, willingly’ (cf. агәапҙхарá ‘love’, гәҽаны́заарыла ‘carefully; cautiously’ (cf. агәҽаны́заара ‘to be cautious’), ӡәӡәáла ‘strongly’ (cf. áӡәӡәа ‘strong’), даҽакáла ‘in a different way’ (cf. даҽакы́ ‘another thing’), ажәáкала ‘in a word, in short’ (cf. áжәа ‘word’, ажәá-к ‘one word’), зны́зы́нла ‘sometimes’ (cf. зны́ ‘once’), ҟаимáҭла ‘excellently’ (cf. аҟаимáҭ ‘fine’), лымкáала ‘particularly, especially’ (cf. áлымкаа ‘except’), машәы́рла ‘by accident, unfortunately’ (cf. áмашәыр ‘accident, misfortune’), мчы́ла ‘by force, forcibly’ (cf. áмч ‘power, force’), апҙсы́шәала ‘in Abkhaz’ (cf. áпҙсшәа ‘Abkhaz’), арыцҳары́ла ‘sadly’ (cf. ары́цҳара ‘misfortune’), хаáла ‘politely’ (cf. áхаа ‘tasty, nice’), хаҭахаҭáла ‘by oneself’ (cf. ахаҭá ‘oneself’), хьыӡҳәáла ‘by name’ (cf. áхьыӡ ‘name’), áхәылбыҽхала ‘in the evening’ (áхәылбыҽха ‘evening’), хәылпҙазы́ла ‘in the evenings’ (cf. áхәылпҙаз ‘in the evening’), ҷы́дала ‘particularly, especially’ (cf. аҷы́дара ‘specific character, peculiarity’), ҽы́ла ‘on horseback’ (cf. аҽы́ ‘horse’), ҽы́нла ‘in the daytime’ (cf. а-ҽны́ ‘on that day’), шьапы́ла ‘on foot’ (cf. ашьапы́ ‘foot’), шьаҿáла ‘at a walking pace’ (cf. ашьаҿá ‘step’), маӡалá ‘secretly’ (cf. áмаӡа ‘secret’), цәгьалá ‘narrowly, barely, severely’ (cf. áцәгьа ‘difficult; hard’), шьҭахьлá ‘backward(s)’ (cf. áшьҭахь ‘behind, after’), шьыжьлá ‘in the morning’ (cf. áшьыжь ‘morning’), etc.

The suffix -ла /la/ is originally an instrumental marker and has an instrumental meaning when attached to a noun (see §2.1.1). In addition to nouns, this is attached even to adjectives and forms an adverb. In this case, the article a- is dropped. The following are example sentences with adverbs with -ла:

(73) Шьапы́ла уцá!
/šʲap’ə́-la wə-cá/
foot-with you.M(C1)-go.Imp
‘Go on foot!’

(74) Зны́=зы́нлагьы́ ны́ҟәара áкалакь áхь сцóн. (AFL)
/znə́-zə́n-la-gʲə́ nə́q’ʷa-ra á-kalakʲ [a-]axʲ s-ca-wá-n/
once-once-with-also walk-Masd the-town [its-]to I(C1)-go-Dyn-Impf
‘Sometimes I went to town to take a walk.’

(75) Шьыжьлá слеиҩéиуеит.
/šʲəžʲ-lá s-lajjʷáj-wa-jt’/
morning-with I(C1)-take a walk-Dyn-Fin
‘I take a walk in the mornings.’

(ii) -ахь/-рахь /axʲ/raxʲ/: анáхь ‘there, over there’ (cf. анá ‘(over) there’), арáхь/абрáхь ‘hither, here’ (cf. а(б)рá ‘here’), уáхь/убрáхь ‘thither, there’ (cf. уа/убрá ‘there, on the spot’); агьы́-рахь ‘on the other side’ (cf. агьи́ ‘other’), егьи́-рахь ‘from the other side’ (cf. егьи́ ‘other’), ани́-рахь ‘to the other side’ (cf. ани́ ‘that’), áрӡьарахь ‘to the right’ (cf. áрӡьа ‘right’), áрмарахь ‘to the left’ (cf. áрма ‘left’).

An adverb of direction is produced by adding the postposition -ахь /axʲ/ ‘to, towards’. The following are example sentences which use this:

(76) Ана́хь уца́.
/anáxʲ wə-cá/
there you.M(C1)-go.Imp
'Go there!'

(77) Сара́ а́рӷьарахь сцо́ит, уара́ а́рмарахь уца́!
/sará árɣʲaraxʲ s-ca-wá-jt' wará ármaraxʲ wə-cá/
I to the right I(C1)-go-Dyn-Fin you.M to the left you.M(C1)-go.Imp
'I am going to the right, while you, go to the left!'

(iii) -ны /nə/: аа́лӄьаны/иа́алырӄьаны 'suddenly' (cf. аа́лӄьара 'to rush out of'), -бзиа́ӡаны 'very well, perfectly well' (cf. абзи́аӡа 'beautiful, best'), -бзи́аны 'well, nicely' (cf. абзи́а 'good'), -гәы́рӷьаны 'joyfully' (cf. агәы́рӷьара 'to rejoice'), еизáаигәаны 'closely; thickly', еикәшәаны́ 'harmoniously, fine' (cf. аикәшәа-ра 'to harmonize'), иааркьа́ҿны 'briefly, in brief' (cf. а́аркьаҿ-ра 'to shorten'), иа́шаны 'in truth; really, indeed', ииа́шаны '(*of time*) exactly; correctly' (cf. а-иа́ша 'truth, straight'), аиӄараны 'equally' (cf. а́иӄара 'equal'), иманшәа́ланы 'successfully' (cf. а-маншәа́ла 'convenient'), -марианы́ 'easily, cheaply' (cf. а́-мариа 'easy; cheap'), и́рласны 'quickly, fast' (cf. а́-рлас-ра 'to hurry, to hasten'), и́рԥшӡаны 'beautifully' (cf. а́-ԥшӡа 'beautiful'), -ӄәы́шны 'intelligently' (cf. а-ӄәы́ш 'intelligent'), -маншәа́ланы 'conveniently', (cf. а-маншәа́ла 'convenient'), -ма́чны 'little, few' (cf. а-ма́ч 'little, few'), -ма́чыҩны '(*of people*) few' (cf. ама́чыҩ '(*of people*) few'), машәы́рны 'accidentally, by accident' (cf. а́-машәыр 'misfortune, accident'), -насы́ԥны 'luckily, fortunately' (cf. а́-насыԥ 'happiness, good luck'), ԥа́саны 'early' (cf. а-ԥа́са 'early'), -тры́сны (и-тры́с-ны а-ца-ра́ 'to rush') (cf. а-тры́с-ра 'to break away from a place'), -цклаԥшны 'zealously, diligently' (cf. а́-цклаԥш-ра 'to pay attention to'), -шкәакәаны 'whitely' (cf. а́-шкәакәа 'white'), а-гәтаны́ 'in the middle of' (cf. а-гәта́ 'the center, the middle'), ӷәӷәаӡаны́ 'very strongly; with violence' (cf. а́-ӷәӷәа 'strong'), адәны́ 'out of doors, outside' (cf. а-дәы́ 'field'), еибга-ны́ 'safely' (cf. а́ибга 'safe'), зны́ 'once; one day' (cf. з- < за 'one'), иӷәӷәаны́ 'well' (cf. а́-ӷәӷәа 'strong'), иласны́ [adv.] quickly' (cf. а́-лас 'quick, agile'), и́марианы́ 'easily, cheaply' (cf. а́-мариа 'easy, cheap'), инагӡаны́ 'completely; fully' (cf. а́нагӡара 'to complete'), инаркны́ 'from the moment of' (< и-на-р-к-ны́ 'it-it-Caus-hold-Abs'), -ԥа́хны [adv.] firmly; strongly' (cf. аԥа́хра 'to tie firmly'), иԥшӡаны́ 'beautifully' (cf. а́ԥшӡа 'beautiful'), (и)рацәаны́ '(*of things*) many', (и)рацәаҩны́ '(*of people*) many', -рацәаӡаны́ 'a great many' (cf. рацәа́ 'very much, plural'), ихаракны́ 'highly' (cf. а́-харак(ы) 'tall'), -рмарианы́ 'easily' (cf. а́рмариара 'to simplify'), сасыртаны́ 'as a guest' (cf. а́сас 'guest'), -хааны́ '(*of taste*) nicely, tastily' (cf. а́хаа 'tasty, nice, sweet'), аханы́ 'above; at the bedside' (cf. -ха- [preverb] 'above, on'), -харакны́ 'high' (cf. а́харак(ы) 'tall'), -ццакны́ 'quickly; hurriedly' (cf. а́ццак 'rapid, quick, fast', а́ццакра 'to hurry'), ҩбаны́ 'in two' (cf. ҩба́ 'two'), etc.

Adverbs with the suffix -ны /nə/ are productive and are derived from adjectives and verbs. Derivations from verbs originate from the Past Absolutive form (see §5.8.2). For example, the origin of the adverb -ццакны́ /ccak'-nə́/ 'quickly, hurriedly' can be traced to the Past Absolutive form of the intransitive verb а́ццакра /á-ccak'-ra/ 'to hurry' (it is probably also possible to regard it as the adjective а́ццак /á-ccak'/ 'rapid, quick, fast' with an adverbial suffix -ны attached to it). In Abkhaz, Column I pronominal prefix markers are attached to adverbs with this -ны, like the Past Absolutive.

(78) дыццакны́ дны́ҟәоит
/də-ccak’-nə́ d-nə́q’ʷa-wa-jt’/
he/she(C1)-hurry/fast-Abs he/she(C1)-walk/go-Dyn-Fin
'He/She is walking fast.'

Furthermore, look at the example of дԥáхны /d-páx-nə/, which is derived from а-ԥáх-ра /a-páx-ra/ 'to tie firmly':

(79) дԥáхны дҿáрхәеит (AAD)
/d-páx-nə d-č’á-r-ħʷa-jt’/
him/her(C1)-tie firmly-Abs him/her(C1)-Prev-they(C3)-tie-(Aor)-Fin
'They tied him/her firmly.'

Examples (78) and (79) above still retain the shape of the Past Absolutive, and it appears to have the characteristics of both an adverb and the Past Absolutive. In contrast, in the case of и́-рласны /jə́-rlasnə/ 'quickly, fast', which is derived from á-рласра /á-rlas-ra/ 'to hurry, to hasten', it can no longer be considered a derived form from the Past Absolutive.

(80) Ирласны бца!
/jə́-rlas-nə b-cá/
it-quickly-Adv you.F(C1)-go.Imp
'Go fast!'[88]

This is because the и- /jə/ at the beginning of the word in (80) above is not cross-referenced with anything. In addition, the following is a clear example of the adverb not having any reference with the subject of the intransitive verb:

(81) иаáлырҟьан(ы) дычмазаҩхéит (AAD)
/j-aálərq’ʲa-n(ə) də-čʲmazajʷ-xá-jt’/
it-suddenly.Adv he/she(C1)-ill-become-(Aor)-Fin
'He/She suddenly fell ill.'

From the analysis above, it appears that adverbs ending in -ны are independent adverbs due to the addition of и- at the beginning of the adverb.

We shall now examine adverbs derived from adjectives using this suffix -ны. For example, the adverb и-бзи́а-ны /jə-bzə́ja-nə/ 'well', which is derived from the adjective а-бзи́а /a-bzə́ja/ 'good', has и- at the beginning of the word:

(82) Аҟы́з аӡаҿы́ ибзи́аны иӡсóит. (AFL)
/a-q’ə́z a-ʒ-a-čə́ jə-bzə́ja-nə jə-ʒsa-wá-jt’/
the-goose the-water-its-in it-good-Adv it(C1)-swim-Dyn-Fin
'A goose swims well in water.'

88. Cf. Аамҭа и́рласны ицóит.
/áamta jə́-rlas-nə jə-ca-wá-jt’/
time it-hasten-Abs(?) it(C1)-go-Dyn-Fin
'Time races quickly'.
Here, the initial и- /jə/ does not cross-reference áамҭа 'time' immediately preceding it. (If it did cross-reference, this и- should not appear). Therefore, it is difficult to regard this -ны /nə/ as an absolutive marker.

However, when a noun cross-referenced with the prefix и- in Column I of a verb is directly before the adverb, the и- at the beginning of the adverb is dropped. For example:

(83) Ауа́да бзи́аны ирхио́уп.
/a-wáda bzə́ja-nə jə-rxjá-wp'/
the-room good-Adv it(C1)-be furnished-Stat.Pres.Fin
'The room is well furnished.'

(84) Амҿы́ бзи́аны ибылуе́ит. (RAD)
/a-mč'ə́ bzə́ja-nə jə-bəl-wá-jt'/
the-firewood good-Adv it(C1)-burn-Dyn-Fin
'The firewood burns well.' Дрова хорошо горят.

(85) Сара́ са́нгьы са́бгьы а́шәа бзи́аны ирҳәо́ит. (AFL)
/sará s-án-g^{j}ə s-áb-g^{j}ə á-$š^{w}$a bzə́ja-nə jə-r-$ħ^{w}$a-wá-jt'/
I my-mother-and my-father-and the-song good-Adv it(C1)-they(C3)-say-Dyn-Fin
'My mother and my father sing well.'

However, there are cases where и- appears at the beginning of an adverb regardless of the same conditions being present:

(86) Ахьацамҿы ибзи́аны ибылуе́ит. (AAD)
/a-x^{j}aca-mč'ə́ jə-bzə́ja-nə jə-bəl-wá-jt'/
the-wood of hornbeam it-good-Adv it(C1)-burn-Dyn-Fin
'Дерево граба хорошо горит.' 'The wood of the hornbeam burns well.'

(87) Анцәа́ иаҳҧы́хьаиршәаз, куты́к ҳа́ургьы, иеиҟараны́ илеиҩа́ҳшоит, капе́к ҳа́ургьы еиҟараны́ иааиҟуҳарчча́роуп. (Abkhaz text)
/a-nc^{w}á j-aħ-pə́x^{j}a-jə-r-$š^{w}$a-z, k'^{w}t'ə́-k' ∅-ħ-áw-r-g^{j}ə,
the-god Rel-us-Prev-he-Caus-come.into-Past.Ind.NF hen-one [it-]we-receive-if-even
j-ajq'ara-nə́ jə-l-ajj^{w}-áħ-ša-wa-jt', k'ap'ék' ∅-ħ-áw-r-g^{j}ə
it-equally-Adv it-Par-Prev-we-divide-Dyn-Fin kopeck [it-]we-receive-if-even
ajq'ara-nə́ j-a[a]-ajq'^{w}-ħa-r-č'č'á-r-a-wp'/
equally-Adv it-Par-Prev-we-Caus-split-must-be-Stat.Pres.Fin
'Whatever God may choose to give us, even if he gives us a hen, we will share it equally. If he gives us one kopeck, we have to share it equally.'

Also, in the adverb -ҳаракны́ /ħarak'-nə́/ 'high', which is derived from á-ҳарак(ы) /á-ħarak'(ə)/ 'tall', there are cases where the и- at the beginning of the word is dropped and cases where it is not dropped:

(88) Амра иҳаракны́ а́жәҩан икы́дуп. (RAD)
/á-mra jə-ħarak'-nə́ á-$ž^{w}j^{w}$an jə-k'ə́də-wp'/
the-sun it-high-Adv the-sky it(C1)-be on-Stat.Pres.Fin
'The sun is high in the sky.'

(89) Аҳаирпла́н ҳаракны́ ипыруе́ит.
/a-ħajrp'lán ħarak'-nə́ jə-pər-wá-jt'/
the-airplane high-Adv it-fly-Dyn-Fin
'An airplane is flying high.'

(iv) -мкәа /m-k'ʷa/: и-ҭахы́мкәа /jə-taxə́-mk'ʷa/ 'unwillingly' (cf. аҭахы́-заа-ра /a-taxə́-zaa-ra/ 'to want, to desire'), и-хәа́рҭа-мкәа 'badly, poorly' (cf. а-хәарҭа-заа-ра́ 'to be useful'), -ааҟәы́-м-ҵӡа-кәа 'incessantly, continually' (cf. а-ҟәы́-ҵ-ра 'to stop, to cease'), -маншәа́ла-мкәа 'uncomfortably, inconveniently' (cf. -маншәа́ла-ны 'conveniently, comfortably'), -ма́чы-мкәа 'much; many; a lot of; not a little' (cf. а-ма́ч 'little, few'), зны́кы-мкәа-ҩы́нтәы-мкәа 'repeatedly, more than once' (cf. зны́к 'once', ҩы́нтә 'twice'), ирахәы́мкәа 'poorly, badly', игәиҽанӡа́мкәа 'accidentally', хәараҭахы́мкәа 'of course', etc.

Adverbs with the suffix -мкәа are originally from the negative form of the Past Absolutive (see §5.8.2). This suffix has come to be used not just for verbal derivation, but also to derive adverbs from parts of speech other than verbs. For example:

(90) Уи́ ихәа́рҭамкәа атҵара́ итҵо́ит.
/wə́j jə-xʷárta-m-k'ʷa a-c'ará ϕ-jə-c'a-wá-jt'/
he it-useful-Neg-Adv the-learning [it-]he-study-Dyn-Fin
'He studies poorly.'

(91) Акьа́бзкәа (атҵа́скәа) има́чымкәа ажәы́тәӡа а́ахыс иааууе́ит.
/a-kʲábz-kʷa (/a-c'ás-kʷa) jə-máč'ʲə-m-k'ʷa a-žʷə́t'ʷ-ʒa áaxəs j-aa-wá-jt'/
the-custom-Pl they-little-Neg-Adv in antiquity-Emph since they-go back-Dyn-Fin
'Many customs date to deep antiquity.'

(v) -ӡа /ʒa/: -бзи́ахә-ӡа /-bzə́jaxʷ-ʒa/ 'very well, excellently' (cf. а-бзи́ахә /a-bzə́jaxʷ/ 'beautiful, excellent'), да́ара-ӡа 'very much' (cf. да́ара 'very'), -ҟьа́ҟьа-ӡа 'wide, wide open' (cf. а-ҟьа́ҟьа 'flat; wide'), а́ԥхьа-ӡа 'for the first time' (cf. аԥхьа́ 'before, at first'), ра́ԥхьа-ӡа 'for the first time' 'cf. ра́ԥхьа [< р-а́ԥхьа 'them-before'] 'at first, first'), ха́а-ӡа 'pleasantly' (cf. а́-хаа 'tasty, nice'), хара-ӡа́ 'very far' (cf. а́-хара 'far, distant'), цәгьа-ӡа́ 'violently, strongly' (cf. а́-цәгьа 'difficult; hard, bad'), etc.

(vi) -х̧әа /ħʷa/: аа́рла-х̧әа /aárla-ħʷa/ 'hardly', а́бӷьаах̧әа 'quickly', аӷьара́х̧әа 'excellently', аӷьы́ҩ-х̧әа 'quickly, boldly' (cf. а-ӷьа́ҩ/а-ӷьы́ҩ 'bold, brave'), ажәжәа́х̧әа 'in a rush, quickly', акьыжьы́х̧әа а-тҵәы́уа-ра 'to sob' (cf. а-тҵәы́уа-ра 'to cry'), ака́ҩх̧әа 'shrilly', аԥҟа́ҩх̧әа 'instantly', а́ртҵәаах̧әа 'in a shrill voice', а-хәхәа́х̧әа 'pleasantly, quietly, noisily', ца́сх̧әа 'purposely', атҵыҟьх̧әа '(of a thunder, the sound of gunfire, etc.) loudly', а-шышьы́-хеа 'slowly', а́-фыр-хәа 'quickly', etc.

The suffix -хәа originated as a speech-particle (see §5.5). The adverbs formed from this indicate the mode of action, in other words, how an action is performed. Furthermore, -хәа can attach to onomatopoetic words and form adverbs. For example:

ҟәаҿ-ҟәа́ҿ-хәа 'in a croaking voice', а́-гәара-х̧әа 'with a bang', 'with a heavy thud', пыввы́-х̧әа 'with a buzz', агәгәа́-хәа 'roaring', а́тыгә=тыгә-хәа 'with a clippety-clop sound', ахәа́ԥ-хәа 'with a plop', а́-чыӡә-чыӡәх̧әа 'with yaps', ахырхы́р-хәа 'wheezingly', а-ҟәа́к-хәа 'with a bump', ахьхьа́-хәа 'with a rustle', etc.

2.5.2.2. Derivation of Adverbs by Reduplication

Adverbs change their meaning by reduplication. For example, when лассы́ /lassə́/ 'quickly, fast' is reduplicated as лассы-лассы́ /lassə́-lassə́/, its meaning changes to 'often'. Other examples:

а́арла-а́арла 'with extreme difficulty', еиха́-еиха́ (= иаха́-иаха́) 'more and more', уажәы́-уажәы́ 'hourly' (cf. уажəы́ 'now'), мачма́ч 'gradually' (cf. ма́чк 'a little, slightly'), наҟ-на́ҟ 'in the future' (cf. наҟ 'there, thither'), ҧа́ла-ҧа́ла '(*of snowfall*) softly, gently', хəычы́-хəычы́ 'little by little, gradually', ҵьара́-ҵьара́ 'sometimes, here and there' (cf. ҵьара́ 'somewhere'), etc.

Also, suffixes of the adverbs examined above can be added to reduplicated stems. For example:

аамҭа=аамҭа́-ла 'at times, now and then' (cf. а́амҭа 'time', аамҭа́-ла 'for a while'), зны́-зы́н-ла 'sometimes' (cf. зны́ 'once'), жəа-жəа́-ла (= а́жəа-жəа́-ла) 'literally, word for word' (cf. а́жəа 'word'), а́ки-а́ки '(*of non-human being*) each other, one another', а́-кəша=мы́кəша 'around', -ҟьа́ҟьа-ӡа 'wide', хаҭа-хаҭа́-ла 'by oneself, on one's own', etc.

2.6. Numerals

Numerals include cardinal numbers, ordinal numbers, and multiplicative numbers.

2.6.1. Cardinal Numbers

Cardinal numbers in Abkhaz can be divided into the non-human class and the human class. For the non-human class, -ба/-ҧа /ba/pa/ is added to the end of the numeric root for 2 through 10. On the other hand, in the human class, -ҩы(к) /j^{w}ə(k')/ is added to the end of numeric roots (or non-human class numbers) starting from 3. For example, 3 in the non-human class becomes х-ҧа /x-pa/ and in the human class becomes х-ҩык /x-j^{w}ək'/. In the non-human class 11 is rendered as жəе́иза /ž^{w}ájza/ and in the human class as жəе́иза-ҩык /ž^{w}ájza-j^{w}ək'/.

Cardinal numbers in Abkhaz are based on the decimal system from 1 to 19, and on the vigesimal system for 20 to 99. The vigesimal system in Abkhaz uses the same method of multiples and adding numbers as the vigesimal system in French. For example, 80 is ҧшьы́-н-ҩажəа /pš^{j}ə́-n-j^{w}až^{w}a/ (4×20) (cf. French: *quatre-vingts*), 82 is ҧшьы́-н-ҩажə-и ҩба /pš^{j}ə́-n-j^{w}až^{w}ə-j j^{w}ba/ (4×20+2) (cf. French: *quatre-vingt-deux*), and 90 is ҧшьы́-н-ҩажə-и жəаба́ /pš^{j}ə́-n-j^{w}až^{w}ə-j ž^{w}abá/ (4×20+10) (cf. French: *quatre-vingt-dix*). The element н /n/ inserted between ҧшьы́ /pš^{j}ə́/ '4' and ҩажəа /j^{w}až^{w}a/ '20' is the multiplicative affix (cf. ҩынтə /j^{w}ənt'^{w}/ 'twice'). Composite numbers like 82 and 90 are expressed by adding и 'and' to the end of 80 (here, the ending vowel а is dropped) to produce '4×20 and 2' and '4 ×20 and 10'.

2.6.1.1. Cardinal Number System

	Non-human class	Human class
1	акы́	аӡəы́
2	ҩ-ба	ҩы́-ҵьа
3	х-ҧа	х-ҩы(к)
4	ҧшь-ба	ҧшь-ҩы(к)
5	хə-ба	хə-ҩы(к)
6	ф-ба	ф-ҩы(к)
7	б(ы)жь-ба́	бжь-ҩы(к)
8	аа-ба́	аа-ҩы́(к)
9	жə-ба	жə-ҩы(к)

10	жәа-бá	жәа-ҩы́(к)
11	жәéиза (< жәá-и-за)	жәéиза-ҩы(к)
12	жәáҩа	жәáҩа-ҩы(к)
13	жәáха	жәáха-ҩы(к)
14	жәи́ҧшь	жәи́ҧшь-ҩы(к)
15	жәóхә	жәóхә-ҩы(к)
16	жәаф	жәáф-ҩы(к)
17	жәибжь	жәи́бжь-ҩы(к)
18	жәáа	жәáа-ҩы(к)
19	зéижә	зéижә-ҩы(к)
20	ҩажәá	ҩажәа-ҩы́(к)
21	ҩажә(é)и́ акы́	ҩажә(é)и́ аӡәы́
22	ҩажә(é)и́ ҩ-ба	ҩажә(é)и́ ҩы́-цьа
30	ҩажә(é)и́ жәа-бá (20+10)	ҩажәи́ жәа-ҩы́(к)
31	ҩажә(é)и́ жәéиза (20+11)	ҩажә(é)и́ жәéиза-ҩы(к)
32	ҩажә(é)и́ жәáҩа (20+12)	ҩажә(é)и́ жәáҩа-ҩы(к)
40	ҩы́нҩажәа (< ҩы́-н-ҩажәа 2×20)	ҩынҩажәа-ҩы(к)
50	ҩы́нҩажәи жәа-бá (2×20+10)	ҩы́нҩажәи жәа-ҩы́(к)
60	хы́нҩажәа (< хы́-н-ҩажәа 3×20)	хынҩажәа-ҩы́(к)
70	хынҩажәи́ жәа-бá (3×20+10)	хынҩажәи́ жәа-ҩы́(к)
80	ҧшьы́нҩажәа (< ҧшьы́-н-ҩажәа 4×20)	ҧшьы́нҩажәа-ҩы(к)
90	ҧшьы́нҩажәи жәабá (4×20+10)	ҧшьы́нҩажәи жәа-ҩы́(к)
93	ҧшьы́нҩажәи жәáха (4×20+13)	ҧшьы́нҩажәи жәáха-ҩы(к)
100	шә-кы	шә-ҩы́(к)
101	шәи́ акы́ (100+1)	шәи́ аӡәы́
126	шәи ҩажәи́ фба (100+20+6)	шәи ҩажәи́ ф-ҩы(к)
200	ҩышә	ҩы́шә-ҩы(к)
300	хышә	хы́шә-ҩы(к)
400	ҧшьышә	ҧшьышә-ҩы(к)
500	хәышә	хәышә-ҩы(к)
600	фышә	фы́шә-ҩы(к)
700	быжышәы́ / бжьы́шә	быжышә-ҩы́(к)
800	аашәы́	аашә-ҩы́(к)
900	жәшәы	жәшә-ҩы́(к)
1,000	зқьы	зқьы-ҩы́(к)
2,000	ҩны́зқь (< ҩ-ны-зқь 2×1,000)	ҩны́зқь-ҩы(к)
3,000	хны́зқь	хны́зқь-ҩы(к)
4,000	ҧшьны́зқь	ҧшьны́зқь-ҩы(к)
5,000	хәны́зқь	хәны́зқь-ҩы(к)
6,000	фны́зқь	фны́зқь-ҩы(к)
7,000	бжьны́зқь	бжьны́зқь-ҩы(к)

8,000	ааны́зқь	ааны́зқь-ҩы(к)
9,000	жәны́зқь	жәны́зқь-ҩы(к)
10,000	жәааны́зқь (< жәа-ны́-зқь 10×1,000)	жәааны́зқь-ҩы(к)
1,000,000	миллио́н-к	миллио́н-ҩы(к)
365	хы́шәи хы́нҩажәи хәба	
1,950	зқьи́ жәшәи́ ҩы́нҩажәи жәаба́	
1,993	зқьи́ жәшәи́ ҧшьы́нҩажәи жәа́ха	
2,188	ҩны́зқьи шәи ҧшьы́нҩажәи ааба́	

2.6.1.2. Methods for Joining Cardinal Numbers and Nouns

2.6.1.2.1. When combining '1' with a noun, -к /k'/ (< ақы́ /ak'ə́/ 'one') is attached to the noun like the indefinite suffix. Addition is handled like an indefinite suffix (see §2.1.4.3). Noun class is irrelevant in this case. For example: саа́ҭк /saát-k'/ 'one hour', ҩны́к /jʷnə́-k'/ 'one house', ҩы́зак /jʷə́za-k'/ 'one friend'. When -к is attached to 'noun+adjective', it goes only on the adjective: бӷа́б ду́к /bɣáb də́w-k'/ 'one huge ibex'. Example with possessive prefix: иахәшьа́к /j-aħʷšʲá-k'/ 'one of his sisters'. Also, when indicating one part of a pair, the suffix -к /k'/ is used together with the infix -з- /z/. For example: сы́знапык /sə́-z-nap'ə-k'/ 'my one hand', лы́злак /lə́-z-la-k'/ 'her one eye', сызлы́мҳак /sə-z-lə́mħa-k'/ 'my one ear', сызшьапы́к /sə-z-šʲap'ə́-k'/ 'my one leg', адива́н а́зшьапык /a-diván á-z-šʲap'ə-k'/ 'one leg of the divan'.

Aside from their uses in counting or for counts, the numerals ақы́ and аӡәы́ are used with the meaning of 'one (thing)' and 'one (person)' respectively. For example:

илы́мҳақәа ақы́ /jə-lə́mħa-kʷa ak'ə́/ [his-ear-Pl one] 'one of his ears'

Аӡәы́ ла́гуп. /aʒʷə́ d-á-gə-wp'/ [one person he-it-be lacking in-Stat.Pres.Fin] 'One person is not.'

2.6.1.2.2. There are two methods for joining numbers higher than '2' with nouns.
(i) One approach entails putting the completed form of the numerals (i.e. forms that have -ба, -ҩы(к), -кы) together with but kept separate from the noun. The other (ii) method involves attaching to the noun either the root of the number (forms like ҩ- '2', х- '3', etc., without the -ба) or numbers that are not composite numbers (numbers like жәе́иза '11', ҩажәа́ '20', etc.) like a prefix.

2.6.1.2.3. In (i), in general when the noun is non-human class, the two parts will be placed in the sequence of 'noun—numeral'. For example:

а́амҭақәа ҧшьба́ /áamta-kʷa pšʲbá/ [[the-]season-Pl 4] 'four seasons'
аҵәақәа́ ҩыба́ /a-c'ʷa-kʷá jʷəbá/ [the-apple-Pl 2] 'two apples' (= ҩы-ҵәа́-к)
аҵәақәа́ ҧшьы́нҩажәи ҩба /a-c'ʷa-kʷá pšʲə́njʷažʷəj jʷba/ [the-apple-Pl 82] 'eighty-two apples'
а́мшқәа быжьба́ /á-mš-kʷa bəžʲbá/ [the-day-Pl 7] 'seven days' (= бжьы-мшы́)
схәы́цқәа ҩба /s-xʷə́c-kʷa jʷba/ [my-hair-Pl 2] 'two of my hairs'
уаса́ шәк /wasá šʷk'/ [sheep 100] 'a hundred sheep' (note: plural markers do not appear with nouns)
асаа́ҭ хҧа /a-saát xpa/ [the-o'clock 3] 'three o'clock'
(Cf. хы́нҩажәа мину́т /xə́njʷažʷa minút/ 'sixty minutes', хы́нҩажәа секу́нд /xə́njʷažʷa sek'únd/ 'sixty seconds')

2.6.1.2.4. If the noun in (i) is human-class, the two parts will be placed in a sequence that runs either ‘numeral—noun’ or ‘noun—numeral’. The noun in either case will be in the plural form. For example:

ҩы́џьа áҳәса /jʷə́ǯʲa á-ħʷsa/ [2 the-women] ‘two women’
ҩы́џьа áҷкәынцәа /jʷə́ǯʲa á-č’ʲk’ʷən-cʷa/ [2 the-boy-Pl] ‘two boys’
ҩы́џьа аԥацәá /jʷə́ǯʲa a-pa-cʷá/ [2 the-son-Pl] ‘two sons’
сáшьцәа ҩы́џьа /s-ášʲ-cʷa jʷə́ǯʲa/ [my-brother-Pl 2] ‘my two brothers’
иҩы́зцәа хҩы́к /jə-jʷə́z-cʷa xjʷə́k’/ [his-friend-Pl 3] ‘his three friends’
хҩы́к аԥацәá /xjʷə́k’ a-pa-cʷá/ [3 the-son-Pl] ‘three sons’
хҩык Куыҭо́лаа /xjʷək’ k’wətólaa/ [3 Kitolians] ‘three Kitolians’
ԥшьҩы́к áӡӷабцәа /pšʲjʷə́k’ á-ʒɣab-cʷa/ [4 the-girl-Pl] ‘four girls’
жәаҩы́к áԥхацәа /žʷajʷə́k’ á-pħa-cʷa/ [10 the-daughter-Pl] ‘ten daughters’
зқьыҩы́к ауаá /zkʲəjʷə́k’ a-waá/ [1,000 the-people] ‘a thousand people’

2.6.1.2.5. In (ii), the noun does not take a plural marker. When the number is from 1 to 10, -к /k’/, which we shall call ‘a numeral suffix’ (abbreviated hereafter as ‘NS’), is added to the end of the noun. When the number is from 20 to 99, the noun does not take a -к. For numbers from 11 to 19, in some instances the -к is added and in some instances it is not. (See Hewitt 2010: 35–36). For example: (‘-’ shows the insertion of a hyphen)

ҩы-ҵәáк /jʷə-c’ʷá-k’/ [2-apple-NS] ‘two apples’ (= аҵәақәá ҩыбá)
ҩ-шәҟәы́к /jʷ-šʷq’ʷə́-k’/ [2-book-NS] ‘two books’
ҩы-ҵлáк /jʷə-c’lá-k’/ [2-tree-NS] ‘(the) two trees’
ҩ-бызшәáк /jʷ-bəzšʷá-k’/ [2-language-NS] ‘two languages’
ҩ-кьы́лак /jʷ-k’ʲə́la-k’/ [2-kilogram-NS] ‘two kilograms’
ҩ-шко́лк /jʷ-šk’ól-k’/ [2-school-NS] ‘two schools’
ҩ-саáҭк /jʷ-saát-k’/ [2-hour-NS] ‘two hours’
ҩ-ԥаҭлы́как /jʷ-patlə́k’a-k’/ [2-bottle-NS] ‘two bottles’
ҩ-ӡысы́к /jʷ-ʒəsə́-k’/ [2-kid-NS] ‘two kids’
ҩ-океáнк /jʷ-ok’eán-k’/ [2-ocean-NS] ‘the two oceans’
х-уáдак /x-wáda-k’/ [3-room-NS] ‘three rooms’
хә-мину́ҭк /xʷ-minút-k’/ [5-minute-NS] ‘five minutes’ (cf. жәо́хә мину́ҭ ‘fifteen minutes’)
хә-кило́метрк /xʷ-k’ilómet’r-k’/ [5-kilometer-NS] ‘five kilometers’
хә-ли́трак аҩы́ /xʷ-lít’ra-k’ a-jʷə́/ [5-liter-NS the-wine] ‘five liters of wine’
жәа-мáаҭк /žʷa-máat-k’/ [10-ruble-NS] ‘ten rubles’
жәа-мину́ҭк /žʷa-minút-k’/ [10-minute-NS] ‘ten minutes’
ҩажәá-сааҭ /jʷažʷá-saat/ [20-hour] ‘twenty hours’
шә-маáҭк /šʷ-maát-k’/ ‘a hundred rubles’ (cf. хәышә маáҭ /xʷəšʷ maát/ ‘500 rubles’)
сы́-шә-мааҭк /sə́-šʷ-maat-k’/ ‘my 100 rubles’
сáн лы-хә-шәҟәы(к) /s-án lə-xʷ-šʷq’ʷə(k’)/ ‘five books of my mother’

The suffix -к /k’/ is not added when the noun indicates a time like ‘year’, ‘month’, ‘week’, ‘season’, or ‘day’, even if the number is from 1 to 10:

ҩы́-шықәса /jʷə́-šəkʷsa/ ‘two years’

ҩмыз/ҩымз /jʷməz/*or* /jʷəmz/ 'two months'
ҩы́-мчыбжьа /jʷə́-mčʲəbžʲa/ 'two weeks'
ҩы́-мш /jʷə́-mš/ 'two days'
ҩ-а́ха /jʷ-áxa/ 'two nights'
ҩ-а́ха=ҩы́-мш /jʷ-áxa-jʷə́-mš/ 'two days and nights'
ҧшьы́-шықәса /pšʲə́-šəkʷsa/ 'four years'
хәы-шықәса́ /xʷə-šəkʷsá/ 'five years'
а́-шықәстәи ҧшь-а́амҭа /á-šəkʷst'ʷəj pšʲ-áamta/ [the-year's 4-season] 'four seasons'
фы́-шықәса /fə́-šəkʷsa/ 'six years'
бжьы-мшы́ /bžʲə-mšə́/ 'seven days' (= а́мшқәа быжьба́ /á-mš-kʷa bəžʲbá/)
жәа-мш /žʷa-mš/ 'ten days'
жәа-шықәса́ /žʷa-šəkʷsá/ 'ten years'

Examples where the number and noun are written separately:
хы́шә шы́қәса /xə́šʷ šə́kʷsa/ 'three hundred years'
жәа́ҩа шықәса́ /žʷájʷa šəkʷsá/ 'twelve years'
ҩажәа́ шықәса́ /jʷažʷá šəkʷsá/ '20 years'
ҧшьны́зкь мааҭ /pšʲnə́zkʲ maát/ '4,000 rubles'
жәа́ҩа мза́ /žʷájʷa mzá/ 'twelve months'

2.6.1.3. Expressions Using Cardinal Numbers

(i) Times:

(92) асаа́ҭ жәаба́ /a-saát žʷabá/ 'ten o'clock'
асаа́ҭ ааба́ рзы́ /a-saát aabá r-zə́/ 'at eight o'clock'

(93) асаа́ҭ ааба́ ры́бжазы
/a-saát aabá rə́-bža-zə/
o'clock eight their-half-at
'at half past seven', cf. Russ. *в половине восьмого*.

(94) акахьы́ жәа-мину́тк
/ak'-axʲə́ žʷa-minút-k'/
one-towards ten-minute-NS
'ten minutes past twelve o'clock', cf. Russ. *десять минут первого.*

(95) Жәо́хә мину́ҭ аўс аухьеит ҩба́ рахь.
/žʷóxʷ minút a-wə́s ø-a-w-xʲá-jt' jʷbá r-axʲ/
15 minute the-work [it(C1)-]it(C3)-do-Perf-Fin two their-toward
lit. '15 minutes have worked towards two.'
'It is a quarter past one.'

(ii) Months and years:
Хәажәкы́ра 21(ҩажәи акы́) азы́ /xʷažʷk'ə́ra jʷažʷəj ak'ə́/ 'on the 21st of March'
зкьы́ ҧшьы́шәи ҧшьы́нҩажәи жәа́ҩа шықәса-зы́ (ANR) 'in 1492'

(iii) Age:
(96) Сара́ исхы́ҵуеит ҩажәа́ шықәса́.

/sará jə-s-xə́c'-wa-jt' jʷažʷá šəkʷsá/
I it(C1)-me(C2)-become years old-Dyn-Fin 20 year
'I am 20 years old.'

(iv) Fractions:

жәба рыбжа /žʷba rə-bža/ '9/2' (cf. а́бжа /á-bža/ 'half')

Fractions are indicated by attaching the suffix -рак /rak'/ to a cardinal number (the full form with -ба). This suffix is used when the numerator is '1':

хԥа́рак /xpá-rak'/ 'one-third'
хәбара́к /xʷba-rák'/ 'one-fifth'
фбарак /fba-rak'/ 'one-sixth'
бжьбара́к /bžʲba-rák'/ 'one-seventh'

When the numerator is other than 1, its cardinal number (the form that does not have -ба) is added as a prefix: хәы-фбарак /xʷə-fbarak'/ 'five-sixths', 'пять шестых' (Genko: Abkhaz-Russian Dictionary)

2.6.2. Ordinal Numbers

Ordinal numbers have already been discussed in §2.4.3.4. Since ordinal numbers are derived by adding to a cardinal number (the form with a -ба) belonging to the non-human class the suffix -тәи, they can morphologically be regarded as adjectives that have the -тәи. Syntactically, ordinal numbers work the same way as adjectives with the -тәи. However, in the present book they will be categorized as numerals.

2.6.2.1. The system for ordinal numbers will be discussed below together with cardinal numbers (non-human class):

	Cardinal numbers (non-human class)	Ordinal numbers
1	акы́	а́ктәи (< а́-ак-тәи) / [а-]а́ԥхьатәи
2	ҩ-ба	а́-ҩбатәи
3	х-ԥа	а́-хԥатәи
4	ԥшь-ба	а́-ԥшьбатәи
5	хә-ба	а́-хәбатәи
6	ф-ба	а́-фбатәи
7	б(ы)жь-ба́	а́-быжьбатәи
8	аа-ба́	а́абатәи (< а́-ааба-тәи)
9	жә-ба	а́-жәбатәи
10	жәа-ба́	а́-жәабатәи
11	жәе́иза	(а)-жәе́изатәи
12	жәа́ҩа	(а)-жәа́ҩатәи
13	жәа́ха	(а)-жәа́хатәи
14	жәи́ԥшь	(а)-жәи́ԥшьтәи
15	жәо́хә	(а)-жәо́хәтәи
16	жәаф	(а)-жәа́фтәи

17	жәибжь	(а)-жәи́бжьтәи
18	жәа́а	(а)-жәа́атәи
19	зе́ижә	(а)-зе́ижәтәи
20	ҩажәа́	(а́)-ҩажәатәи́
21	ҩажә(е́)и́ акы́	(а́)-ҩажәи́ а́ктәи
22	ҩажә(е́)и́ ҩ-ба	(а́)-ҩажәи́ ҩбатәи
30	ҩажә(е́)и́ жәа-ба́	(а́)-ҩажәи́ жәабатәи
31	ҩажә(е́)и́ жәе́иза (20+11)	(а́)-ҩажәи́ жәеизатәи
32	ҩажә(е́)и́ жәа́ҩа (20+12)	(а́)-ҩажәи́ жәаҩатәи
40	ҩы́нҩажәа (< ҩы́-н-ҩажәа 2×20)	(а)-ҩы́нҩажәатәи
50	ҩы́нҩажәи жәа-ба́ (2×20+10)	(а)-ҩы́нҩажәи жәабатәи
60	хы́нҩажәа (< хы́-н-ҩажәа 3×20)	(а)-хы́нҩажәатәи
70	хынҩажәи́ жәа-ба́ (3×20+10)	(а)-хы́нҩажәи жәабатәи
80	ҧшьы́нҩажәа (< ҧшьы́-н-ҩажәа 4×20)	(а)-ҧшьы́нҩажәатәи
90	ҧшьы́нҩажәи жәаба́ (4×20+10)	(а)-ҧшьы́нҩажәи жәабатәи
93	ҧшьы́нҩажәи жәа́ха (4×20+13)	(а)-ҧшьы́нҩажәи жәа́хатәи
100	шә-кы	а́-шәктәи / шәыктәи́
101	шәи́ акы́ (100+1)	(а)-шәи́ а́ктәи
126	шәи ҩажәи́ фба (100+20+6)	(а)-шәи ҩажәи́ фбатәи
200	ҩышә	(а)-ҩы́шәтәи
300	хышә	(а)-хы́шәтәи
400	ҧшьышә	(а)-ҧшьы́шәтәи
500	хәышә	(а)-хәы́шәтәи
600	фышә	(а)-фы́шәтәи
700	быжьшәы́ / бжьы́шә	(а́)-быжьшәтәи́
800	аашәы́	([а])-аашәтәи́
900	жәшәы	(а́)-жәышәтәи́
1,000	зқьы	(а́)-з(ы)қьтәи́
2,000	ҩны́зқь (< ҩ-ны-зқь 2×1,000)	(а)-ҩны́зқьтәи
3,000	хны́зқь	(а́)-хны́зқьтәи
4,000	ҧшьны́зқь	(а)-ҧшьны́зқьтәи
5,000	хәны́зқь	(а)-хәны́зқьтәи
6,000	фны́зқь	(а)-фны́зқьтәи
7,000	бжьны́зқь	(а)-бжьны́зқьтәи
8,000	ааны́зқь	([а])-ааны́зқьтәи
9,000	жәны́зқь	(а́)-жәны́зқьтәи
10,000	жәаны́зқь	(а́)-жәаны́зқьтәи
1,000,000	миллио́н-к	(а)-миллио́нктәи
365	хы́шәи хы́нҩажәи хәба	(а)-хы́шәи хы́нҩажәи хәбатәи
1,950	зқьи́ жәшәи́ ҩы́нҩажәи жәаба́	(а)-зқьи́ жәшәи́ ҩы́нҩажәи жәабатәи
1,993	зқьи́ жәшәи́ ҧшьы́нҩажәи жәа́ха	(а)-зқьи́ жәшәи́ ҧшьы́нҩажәи жәа́хатәи

2,188 ҩны́зқьи шәи ҧшьы́нҩажәи аабá (а)-ҩны́зқьи шәи ҧшьы́нҩажәи áабатәи

Notes:

1. In Abkhaz, cardinal numbers rather than ordinal numbers are used with years. For example:
зқьи жәшәи ҧшьы́нҩажәи жәáха шықәсазы́ 'in 1993'
Уи 1950 (зқьи жәшәи ҩы́нҩажәи жәабá) шықәсá рзы диит. 'He was born in 1950.'

2. The difference between áктәи and [а-]áҧхьатәи is that the former modifies non-human class elements, while the latter modifies human class (and non-human class) elements:
áктәи а-етáж 'the first [ground] floor'
áҧхьатәи у-ҧхәы́с 'your first wife'

2.6.3. Approximate Numbers

Approximate numbers in Abkhaz are formed by adding the suffix -ҟа /q'a/ 'about' to the cardinal number (the form that has a -ба). When used with nouns, a noun without a plural marker follows the approximate number. For example:

ҩажәа-ҟá /jʷažʷa-q'a/ 'about 20'
ҩба-ҟá саáҭ /jʷba-q'á saát/ 'about two hours'
ҩба-ҟá áжәа /jʷba-q'á ážʷa/ 'about two words'
50(ҩы́нҩажәи жәабá)-ҟá мéтра /jʷánjʷažʷəj žʷabá-q'á mét'ra/ 'about 50 meters'
ҩба-ҟá=хҧа-ҟá шьаҿá /jʷba-q'á-xpa-q'á šʲač'á/ 'two or three steps'

Or add -ҟа /q'a/ 'about' to a form that combines the number with the noun:
хы́-мш-ҟа 'about three days'

Approximate numbers can also be expressed by placing the postposition -áҟара /áq'ara/ after a combined word comprised of the number and the noun as discussed in §2.6.1.2.4. For example:
ҩ-саáҭ-к р-áҟара /jʷ-saát-k' r-áq'ara/ (= ҩба-ҟá саáт /jʷba-q'á saát/) 'about two hours'
мчыбжьы́-к [а-]áҟара /mčʲəbžʲá-k' [a-]áq'ara/ 'about a week'
киломéтра-к [а-]áҟара /k'əjlomét'ra-k' [a-]áq'ara/ 'about one kilometer'
Cf. ҩы́нтә р-áҟара /jʷánt'ʷ r-áq'ara/ 'about twice'.

2.6.4. Multiplicative Numbers

Multiplicative numbers are expressed by adding the suffix -нтә /nt'ʷ/ 'times' to the root of a cardinal number:

ҩы́-нтә /jʷá-nt'ʷ/ 'two times'
хы́-нтә /xá-nt'ʷ/ 'three times' (cf. хы́нтә=хынтә /xánt'ʷ-xənt'ʷ/ 'three times each')
ҧшьы́-нтә /pšʲá-nt'ʷ/ 'four times'
хәы́-нтә /xʷá-nt'ʷ/ 'five times'
Хәы́нтә хәба — ҩажәéи хәбá. /xʷánt'ʷ xʷba — jʷažʷáj xʷbá/ 'Five times five is twenty-five.'
мыш-кы́ шәынтә /məš-k'á šʷənt'ʷ/ 'frequently, often' (lit. 'a hundred times a day')

2.7. Postpositions

2.7.1. Postpositions Attached to a Noun Phrase

As discussed in §2.1.1, the case as a core argument does not exist in Abkhaz, but the language does have postpositions that indicate location, instrument, time, and predicative adverbs. The locative and instrumental functions are expressed in noun phrases, though they can also be expressed in a verbal complex as well. Postpositions can be categorized into various types depending on how they attach to nouns. The accent unit is indicated within parentheses.

2.7.1.1. Attaching the Postposition Directly to a Noun:

-ҟа /q'a/ 'toward, to (a town, a country, a village, a house, etc.)' (R): Қа́рҭҟа /kárt-q'a/ 'to Tbilisi', Аҧсны́ҟа /apsnə́-q'a/ 'to Abkhazia', Аҟəаҟа /aq'ʷa-q'a/ 'to Sukhum', Кавка́зҟа /k'avk'áz-q'a/ 'to the Caucasus', Ҭыркəтəы́ла-ҟа 'to Turkey', То́кио-ҟа 'to Tokyo', Ри́ҵа-ҟа 'to Rits'a', а́-шьха-ҟа 'to the mountain'. Example:

(97) Сыра́ху сы́ма На́аҟа сцо́ит. (GAL)
/sə-ráxʷ ø-sə́-ma Náa-q'a s-ca-wá-jt'/
my-cattle [it(C1)-]I(C2)-have.Abs Naa-to I(C1)-go-Dyn-Fin
'I am going to Naa with my cattle.'

-н(ы) /n(ə)/ 'in, at, on' (used with nouns such as road, field, village, country)' (D): а́мҩан /á-mjʷa-n/ 'on the road', адəны́ /a-dʷ-nə́/ 'in the field; outside', акы́ҭан /a-kə́ta-n/ 'in the village', Қырҭтəы́лан /kərtt'ʷə́la-n/ 'in Georgia', Ҭыркəтəы́лан /tərkʷt'ʷə́la-n/ 'in Turkey', Урыстəы́лан /wərəst'ʷə́la-n/ 'in Russia'. Example:

(98) Сара́ Қырҭтəы́лан сынхо́ит.
/sará Kərtt'ʷə́la-n sə-n-xa-wá-jt'/
I Georgia-in I(C1)-Prev-live-Dyn-Fin
'I live in Georgia.'

-нӡа /nʒa/ 'until, as far as, up to' (R): аҩны́нӡа /a-jʷnə́-nʒa/ 'up to the house', акы́ҭанӡа /a-kə́ta-nʒa/ 'up to the village', Москва́нӡа /mosk'vá-nʒa/ 'as far as Moscow', абри́ а́-шықəс а́-лгамҭа-нӡа /abrə́j á-šəkʷs á-lgamta-nʒa/ [this the-year its-end-until] 'until the end of this year', а-саа́т а́аба-нӡа /a-saát áaba-nʒa/ [the-o'clock 8-until] 'until eight o'clock'. Example:

(99) Ҳаҩны́нӡа шəаала́!
/ħa-jʷnə́-nʒa šʷ-aa-lá/
our-house-up to you.Pl-come.Imp-often
'Come up to our house!'

-нтə /nt'ʷ/ 'from (a city, a village, a country, etc.)' (R): аҩны́нтə /a-jʷnə́-nt'ʷ/ 'out of the house', а́шьхантə /á-šʲxa-nt'ʷ/ 'from the mountain', Москва́-нтə 'from Moscow', Ҭыркəтəы́ла-нтə 'from Turkey', Куыҭо́лы-нтə 'from Kitol'. Example:

(100) Ҭага́лан а́рахə а́шьхантə илбаауе́ит. (AFL)
/Tagálan á-raxʷ á-šʲxa-nt'ʷ jə-lbaa-wá-jt'/
in autumn the-cattle the-mountain-from it(C1)-come down-Dyn-Fin
'The cattle come down from the mountain in autumn.'

-нтəи /nt'ʷəj/ 'from' (R): аҩны́нтəи /a-jʷnə́-nt'ʷəj/ 'from the house', Аҟəантəи /aq'ʷa-nt'ʷəj/ 'from

Sukhum', акы́ҭантәи ашко́л 'a village school'. Example:

(101) Атәы́ла ҧха́рракәа ра́хь Аҧсны́нтәи ицо́ит аҵа́ракәа. (AFL)
/a-t'ʷə́la pxárra-kʷa r-áxʲ apsnə́-nt'ʷəj jə-ca-wá-jt' ac'ára-kʷa/
the-country warm-Pl their-to Abkhazia-from they(C1)-go-Dyn-Fin bird-Pl
'Birds fly away from Abkhazia to warm countries.'

-ны /nə/ 'as' (D): еихабны́ /ajħab-nə́/ 'as leader'. Example:

(102) Аруаҩны́ (*or* Аруаҩы́с) Берли́н сы́ҟан.
/arwajʷ-nə́ (arwajʷə́-s) berlə́jn sə́-q'a-n/
soldier-as Berlin I-be-Stat.Past.Fin
'I was in Berlin as a soldier.'

-ны́рцә /nə́rcʷ/ 'beyond' (DRI): аӡны́рцә /a-ʒ-nə́rcʷ/ 'beyond the river'.

-с /s/ 'as' (R) (noun drops the article): нџьны́рс /nǯʲnə́r-s/ 'as an engineer', рҵаҩы́с /rc'ajʷə́-s/ 'as a teacher', уаҩы́с /wajʷə́-s/ 'as a man', аруаҩы́с /arwajʷə́-s/ (*or* а́руаҩ-ны /árwajʷ-nə/) 'as a soldier', аҳы́с /aħə́-s/ (*or* аҳны́ /aħ-nə́/) 'as a king'. Examples:

(103) Аҧҳәы́с рҵаҩы́с ды́ҟоуп.
/a-pħʷə́s rc'ajʷə́-s də́-q'a-wp'/
the-woman teacher-as she(C1)-be-Stat.Pres.Fin
'The woman is a teacher.'

(104) Агәы́л ҧштәы́с иа́моузеи? (AFL)
/a-gʷə́jl pšt'ʷə́-s j-á-ma-w-zaj/
the-rose color-as what-it(C2)-have-Pres.Non-Fin-Qu
'What color is the rose?' lit. 'What does the rose have as color?'

(105) Аӡын мзакәа́с и́жәдыруеи? (AFL)
/áʒən mza-kʷá-s jə́-žʷ-dər-wa-j/
winter month-Pl-as what-you.Pl-know-Dyn-Qu
'Do you know what are the months of winter?' lit. 'What do you know as (the) winter months?'

а́-шьҭахьнӡа /á-šʲtaxʲnʒa/ 'behind': аҩна́шьҭахь(ынӡа) /a-jʷn-á-šʲtaxʲ(ə-nʒa)/ 'behind the house'

2.7.1.2. (i) Attaching a postposition directly to a noun, or (ii) attaching a possessive prefix that refers to the noun (or pronoun) to the postposition (this latter method is used when the noun is in plural form):

-ла /la/ 'by, with, concerning, during, in' (R) (when attached directly to the noun, the noun drops the article):
(i) зана́аҭла /zanáat-la/ 'by profession', авто́бусла /avt'óbus-la/ 'by bus', лаба́ла /labá-la/ 'with a stick', еиҵәа́ бҕьы́ла /ajc'ʷá bɣʲə́-la/ [green foliage-with] 'with green foliage', тролле́йбус-ла 'by trolley'. Example:

(106) Сара́ лаба́ла ала́ са́сит.
/sará labá-la a-lá s-á-sə-jt'/
I stick-with the-dog I(C1)-it(C2)-hit-(Aor)-Fin
'I hit the dog with a stick.'

(ii) акьырмы́т а́ла /a-kʲərmə́t' á-la/ 'with the brick', акьырмы́ткәа ры́ла /a-kʲərmə́t'-kʷa rə́-la/ [the-brick-Pl their-with] 'with the bricks', хәышыкәса́ ры́ла /xʷə-šəkʷsá rə-lá/ [5-year their-by] 'by five years', ҩсаа́тк ры́ла /jʷ-saát-k' ré-la/ [2-hour-NS their-in] 'in two hours'. Examples:

(107) Са́б зана́атла дынџьны́руп. (AFL)
/s-áb zanáat-la də-nǯʲnə́rə-wp'/
my-father profession-by he(C1)-engineer-Stat.Pres.Fin
'My father is an engineer by profession.'

(108) Астуде́нт ари́ а́ҳасабтә ҩса́атк ры́ла илхаса́бит.
/a-st'əwdént' arə́j á-ħasabtʷ jʷ-sáat-k' rə́-la jə-l-ħasábə-jt'/
the-student this the-problem 2-hour-NS their-in it(C1)-she(C3)-solve-(Aor)-Fin
'The (female) student solved this problem in two hours.'

(109) Сахәшьа́ хәышықәса́ рыла́ дсеиҳабу́п.
/s-aħʷšʲá xʷə-šək'ʷsá rə-lá d-s-ajħabə́-wp'/
my-sister 5-year their-by she(C1)-me(C2)-older-Stat.Pres.Fin
'My sister is older than I by five years.'

-да /da/ 'without, except' (R):

(i) ҩы́зада /jʷə́za-da/ 'without a friend', жьахәа́-да 'without using the hammer'. Example:

(110) Ачҟәын хы́лапшрада зынӡа́с дыбжьы́сит. (RAD)
/a-čʲ'k'ʷən xə́lapšra-da zənʒás də-bžʲə́-sə-jt'/
the-boy supervision-without completely he(C1)-Prev-go bad-(Aor)-Fin
'Without supervision, the boy went completely bad.'

(ii) амҽы́ша а́да /a-mčə́ša á-da/ 'except Sunday', бара́ бы́-да 'without you (sg.F)'. Example:

(111) Зны́к а́да уимы́сын! (Abkhaz text)
/znək' á-da wə-j-mə́-sə-n/
one time its-without you.M(C1)-him(C2)-Neg-hit-Proh
'Don't hit him more than one time!'

-зы /zə/ 'at; for' (D):

(i) аҩа́шазы /a-jʷáša-zə/ 'on Tuesday', асаа́ҭ аабá ры́бжазы /a-saát aabá rə́-bža-zə/ [the-o'clock 8 their-half-at] 'at half past seven', шә-бара-зы́ 'for seeing you'. Example:

(112) Сҩы́за дырҵаҩны́ дҟалаpaзы́ дта́леит аинститу́т.
/s-jʷə́za də-rc'ajʷ-nə́ d-q'a-la-ra-zə́ d-∅-tá-la-jt' a-jənst'əjt'ə́wt'/
my-friend he-teacher-as he-Prev-become-Masd-for he(C1)-[it(C2)-]Prev-enter-(Aor)-Fin the-institute
'My friend entered an institute in order to become a teacher.'

(ii) а-саа́ҭ аабá р-зы́ 'at 8 o'clock', жәабá ры́-бжа р-зы́ 'at half past nine'; сара́ с-зы 'for me', а-ҩы́за бзи́а и-зы́ 'for the good friend', ҩы́џьа р-зы а-уаҭа́х 'a room for two people'. Example:

(113) Сара́ сзы́ иҟасҵе́ит.
/sará s-zə́ jə-q'a-s-c'á-jt'/
I my-for it/them(C1)-Prev-I(C3)-do-(Aor)-Fin
'I did it/them for myself.'

-хазы /xazə/ 'for': дара́ рхазы́ /dará r-xazə́/ 'for them(selves)'.

-а́ҧхьа /ápxʲa/ 'in front of, before' (DRI):

(i) аҩна́ҧхьа /a-jʷn-ápxʲa/ 'in front of the house'.

(ii) са́ҧхьа /s-ápxʲa/ 'in front of me', аҩны́ а́ҧхьа /a-jʷnә́ [a-]ápxʲa/ 'in front of the house', ҩы-саа́ҭ-к р-а́ҧхьа 'two hours ago'. Examples:

(114) Ҳаҩны́ а́ҧхьа адәқьа́н гы́лоуп.
/ħa-jʷnә́ [a-]apxʲa a-dʷkʲán ø-gә́la-wp'/
our-house [its-]in front of the-store [it(C1)-]stand-Stat.Pres.Fin
'A store stands in front of our house.'

(115) Иара́ иа́ҧхьа сара́ саа́ит.
/jará j-ápxʲa sará s-aá-jt'/
he his-before I I(C1)-come here-(Aor)-Fin
'I came here earlier than he.'

-шьҭахь /šʲtaxʲ/ 'after' (ii) саа́ҭк а́шьҭахь /saát-k' á-šʲtaxʲ/ 'after an hour', ҩ-саа́ҭ-к ры́-шьҭахь 'after two hours', хы́-мш-ҟа ры́-шьҭахь 'after about three days', уаххьа́ а́-шьҭахь 'after supper'. Example:

(116) Мызк а́шьҭахь усы́дтцаал! (ARD)
/mәz-k' á-šʲtaxʲ wә-sә́-d-c'aal/
month-one its-after you.M(C1)-me(C2)-Prev-call on.Imp
'Call on me in a month!'

2.7.1.3. (iii) Method by which a possessive prefix that refers to the noun is inserted between the noun and the postposition:

-ҟны/-ҟын /q'nә/q'әn/ 'in, at' (DD/DR):

(iii) аҩнаҟны́ /a-jʷn-a-q'nә́/ 'in the house' (cf. аҩны́ /a-jʷnә́/ 'house'), аӡаҟны́ /a-ʒ-a-q'nә́/ 'in the river' (cf. аӡы́ /a-ʒә́/ 'water, river'), а́мҩаҟны /á-mjʷa-[a-]q'nә/ 'on the road' (cf. а́мҩа /á-mjʷa/ 'road'). Example:

(117) Ахәычқәа́ аӡаҟны́ аҧсы́ӡ ркуе́ит. (AFL)
/a-xʷәč'ʲ-kʷá a-ʒ-a-q'nә́ a-psә́ʒ ø-r-k'-wá-jt'/
the-chil-Pl the-river-its-in the-fish [it(C1)-]they(C3)-catch-Dyn-Fin
'The children is fishing in the river.'

(ii) аӡи́ас аҟны́ /a-ʒә́jas a-q'nә́/ 'at the river', а-вокза́л а-ҟны́/а-ҟы́н 'at the station', а-зауа́д а-ҟны́ (*or* а-ҿы́) 'in the factory', жәа-кла́сск а-ҟны́ 'in the tenth grade'. Example:

(118) Адәқьа́н аҟны́ хара́ иа́аххәе-ит. (AFL)
/a-dʷkʲán a-q'nә́ ħará j-áa-ħ-xʷa-jt'/
the-shop its-in we it/them(C1)-Prev-we(C3)-buy-(Aor)-Fin
'We bought it/them in the shop.'

-ахь /axʲ/ 'to, towards':

(iii) амшы́нахь /a-mšә́n-[a-]axʲ/ 'to the sea', ақы́ҭахь /a-kә́ta-[a-a]xʲ/ 'to the village', а-база́р-[а-]ахь 'to the bazaar', а-шко́л-[а-]ахь 'to the school', а-магази́н-ахь 'to the store'. Example:

(119) Уаре́и саре́и ашко́лахь хца́п.
/wará-j sará-j a-šk'ól-[a-]axʲ ħ-cá-p'/

you.M-and I-and the-school-[its-]to we(C1)-go-Fut.I.Fin
'You and I will go to the school.'

(ii) амшы́н ахь /a-mšə́n [a-]axʲ/ 'to the sea', аҩнкәа́ рахь /a-jʷn-kʷá r-axʲ/ 'to the houses', а-хақьы́м и-а́хь 'to the doctor'. Example:

(120) жәо́хә мину́ҭ ау́с аухье́ит ҩба́ рахь. (AFL)
/žʷóxʷ məjnə́wt a-wə́s ∅-a-w-xʲá-jt' jʷbá r-axʲ/
15 minute the-work [it(C1)-]it(C3)-do-Perf-Fin 2 their-to
'15 minutes past one' lit. '15 minutes have worked to 2 (o'clock)'

-а́хьтә /áxʲt'ʷ/ 'from, among' (DRI):

(iii) ада́чахьтә /a-dáčʲa-[a-a]xʲt'ʷ/ 'from the dacha'

(ii) а́урысшәа [a-]а́хьтә 'from Russian', а́-чкәын-цәа р-а́хьтә (*or* р-ҟы́нтә) ҩы́-џьа 'two of the boys'. Example:

(121) Урҭ зе́гь ра́хьтә бзи́а и́убозеи?
/wərt zégʲ r-áxʲt'ʷ bzə́ja jə́-w-ba-wa-zaj/
those all their-among well what-you.M-see-Dyn-Qu
'What do you love out of all this?'

-ҿы /č'ə/ 'in, at' (used to express a point within an area or a place) (D):

(iii) амхаҿы́ /a-mx-a-č'ə́/ 'in the field', а-ҩн-а-ҿы́ 'in the house', а-лә-а-ҿы́ 'in the yard', хара́ х-хәынҭқа́рра-[а-]ҿ 'in our state', х-кы́ҭа-[а-]ҿы 'in our village', however, there is also а-сто́л-ҿы 'in the table'. Example:

(122) Аԥсшәа ҵараҿы́ ари́ ахәычы́ зегьы́ дре́иӷьуп.
/ápsšʷa c'ara[-a]-č'ə́ arə́j a-xʷəčʲ'ə́ zagʲə́ d-r-ájɣʲə-wp'/
Abkhaz study-its-in this the-boy all he(C1)-them(C2)-be better-Stat.Pres.Fin
'In the study of the Abkhaz language, this boy is the best of all.'

(ii) амшы́н аҿы́ /a-mšə́n a-č'ə́/ 'in the sea', а́-қалақь а-ҿы́ 'in the city', а-вокза́л а-ҿы́ 'at the station', а-уаҭа́х а-ҿы́ 'in the room', а-теа́тр а-ҿы́ 'in the theater', лара́ л-ҿы́ 'at her place'. Example:

(123) Ҳара́ хҿы́ а́ԥхын шо́уроуп.
/ħará ħ-č'ə́ á-pxən ∅-šáwra-wp'/
we our-in in the summer [it(C1)-]hot-Stat.Pres.Fin
'It is hot at our place in the summer.'

(124) а́шьха хара́к аҿы́
/á-šʲxa ħarák' a-č'ə́/
the-mountain tall its-in
'on the tall mountain'

3. Morphology:

Verbs

3.1. Introduction: Abkhaz as a Polysynthetic Language

3.1.1. Structure of Verbs with a Simple Root

Abkhaz is a polysynthetic language that includes morphemes with various functions in its verbal complexes. As in other Northwest Caucasian languages, in Abkhaz very large verbal complexes can be produced by affixing within a verb not only personal prefixes that indicate the subject or object, but also morphemes that express, for example, the reflexive, relative, conjunctive, locative, negative, causative, version, potential, non-volitional, and so forth. These morphemes are expressed by the prefixes in front of verb roots. Comparatively few morphemes—such as those that indicate the root extension, dynamic, tense-aspect, emphasis, plural, negative, finite, or interrogative—are placed after the verb root (a negative marker is positioned before the root for certain tense-aspect patterns). Thus, Abkhaz is a slot-type language where many affixes are placed before the root. In the present work, a person-class prefix inserted in the slot before the root will be called a 'pronominal prefix'. Pronominal prefixes can be split up into three types based on class positioned in the slot. We shall call the slots themselves filled by pronominal prefixes 'columns' (abbreviated hereafter as 'C').[89] Also pronominal prefixes of this sort will be called 'columns'. These columns heve Column I (abbreviated hereafter as 'C1'), Column II (abbreviated hereafter as 'C2'), and Column III (abbreviated hereafter as 'C3'). Column I pronominal prefixes indicate S (i.e. the subject of an intransitive verb)[90] or O (or DO) (i.e. the direct object of a transitive verb); column III pronominal prefixes indicate A (i.e. the subject of a transitive verb); and column II pronominal prefixes indicate IO (i.e. the indirect object of a verb). These pronominal prefixes are inserted into the verb slots in the sequence of C1-C2-(C2-C2)-C3-Root, with prefixes that have various grammatical functions as noted above inserted among them. The following four types of verb structure are possible for verb forms with simple structures:

(i) C1-Root	(intransitive: C1 = S)
(ii) C1-C2-Root	(intransitive: C1 = S, C2 = IO)
(iii) C1-C3-Root	(transitive: C1 = O, C3 = A)
(iv) C1-C2-C3-Root	(transitive: C1 = O, C2 = IO, C3 = A)

C1 in (i) and (ii) above is a pronominal prefix that indicates the subject of intransitive verb. C2 in (ii) is a pronominal prefix that indicates the indirect object of an intransitive verb. C1 in (iii) and (iv) is a pronominal prefix that indicates the direct object of a transitive verb, while C3 is its subject. C2 in (iv)

89. The nomenclature 'column' derives from Hewitt (1979c).

90. Here we adopt Dixon's (1994: 6–7) symbolism of S, A, and O.

is the indirect object of a transitive verb. The prefixes indicating S and O are handled like Column I prefixes, while the prefix that indicates A is handled like a Column III one. This is the same pattern seen in ergative-type languages. As was already noted regarding the declension of nouns in §2.1.1, while declension does not occur with nouns and pronouns, the pronominal prefixes of verbs follow an ergative pattern: S=O vs. A. Hence, we can call a Column I pronominal prefix an absolutive prefix and a Column III pronominal prefix an ergative one. Furthermore, as was already noted, in terms of position the Column III prefix appears directly before the verb root and the Column I prefix appears at the beginning of the word before that. Prefixes are positioned in a verb in a strict order; the order of positions does not change based on person as we see in certain other languages.[91] Pronominal prefixes are thus positioned systematically, and agree with noun phrases outside of verbs. Pronominal prefixes are explicitly marked within verbal complexes, but there are exceptions: the Column I pronominal prefix и- /jə/ (indicating the third-person plural and the non-human class of the third-person singular) does not appear when a noun that agrees with it is directly before a verbal complex.

Examples of simple verb constructions of the four types noted above are as follows:

(125) Какáшьа дцéит.
/k’ak’ašʲa d-cá-jt’/
K’ak’asha(F) she(C1)-go-(Aor)-Fin
‘K’ak’asha went.’

(125a) Ахәакәá цéит.
/a-ħʷa-kʷá ɸ-cá-jt’/
the-pig-Pl [they(C1)-]go-(Aor)-Fin
‘The pigs went.’

(126) Сарá алá сáсит.
/sará a-lá s-á-sə-jt’/
I the-dog I(C1)-it(C2)-hit-(Aor)-Fin
‘I hit the dog.’

(127) Какáшьа Ҭарáс дылбéит.
/k’ak’ašʲa Tarás də-l-bá-jt’/
K’ak’asha Taras(M) him(C1)-she(C3)-see-(Aor)-Fin
‘K’ak’asha saw Taras.’

(127a) Какáшьа алá лбéит.
/k’ak’ašʲa a-lá ɸ-l-bá-jt’/
K’ak’asha the-dog [it(C1)-]she(C3)-see-(Aor)-Fin
‘K’ak’asha saw the dog.’

(128) Сарá Зи́на илы́сҭеит ашәҟәы́.
/sará zə́jna jə-lə́-s-ta-jt’ a-šʷq’ʷə́/
I Zina(F) it(C1)-her(C2)-I(C3)-give-(Aor)-Fin the-book
‘I gave Zina a book.’

The finite suffix/ending (abbreviated hereafter as ‘Fin’) -ит /jt’/ is attached to the verb root -ца- /ca/

91. See Forley, W.A. (1991) *The Yimas Language of New Guinea*. Stanford: Stanford University Press. §5.1.

'go', -с- /s/ 'hit', -ба- /ba/ 'see', -ҭа- /ta/ 'give' in the above examples (for details, see §3.1.4). The direct attachment of the finite suffix to the verb root like this indicates the Aorist tense (abbreviated hereafter as 'Aor'). In (125), Кака́шьа 'K'ak'asha' agrees with д- /d/ (third-person singular, human-class prefix in Column I). In (125a), the Column I, third-person plural prefix и- /jə/ that agrees with the subject ахәакәа́ /a-ħʷa-kʷá/ 'the pigs' does not appear because the subject appears immediately before the verb. In (126), сара́ /sará/ and с- /s/ (Column I, first-person singular prefix) agree with one another, as do а-ла́ /a-lá/ 'the dog' and а- /a/ (Column II, third-person singular, non-human class prefix). In Abkhaz, 'hit' is an intransitive verb. In (127), Кака́шьа 'K'ak'asha' agrees with л- /l/ (third-person singular, feminine-class prefix of Column III), and Ҭара́с 'Taras' refers to д(ы)- /d(ə)/. In (127a), the third-person singular, non-human prefix и- /jə/ that agrees with the object ала́ /a-lá/ 'the dog' does not appear because the object appears immediately before the verb. In (128), сара́ /sará/ agrees with с- /s/ (first-person singular prefix of Column III), Зи́на 'Zina' agrees with л(ы)- /l(ə)/ (third-person singular, feminine-class prefix of Column II), and ашәҟәы́ /a-šʷq'ʷə́/ 'the book' agrees with и- /jə/ 'it'. If ашәҟәы́ 'the book' is moved immediately before a verb, the Column I prefix и- /jə/ does not appear and the verbal complex becomes лы́сҭеит /lə́-s-ta-jt'/.

3.1.2. Structure of Verbs with a Preverb

All of the verbs examined above have simple roots. However, in Abkhaz there are verbs where an element called the *preverb* (abbreviated hereafter as 'Prev') is added to the root to form a stem. For example, there is a word хәаԥш /xʷa-pš/ 'watch, look at' formed by adding the preverb -хәа- /xʷa/ to the root -ԥш- /pš/ 'look'. While the verb ԥш /pš/ is a one-place intransitive verb that cannot take anything except a subject, хәаԥш /xʷa-pš/ is a two-place intransitive verb that can take both a subject and an indirect object. For example:

(129) Уи а́жәҩан ахь дыԥшуа́н.
/wəj á-žʷjʷan [a-]axʲ də-pš-wá-n/
(s)he the-sky its-to (s)he(C1)-look-Dyn-Impf.Fin
'He/She was looking at the sky.'

(130) Ателеви́зор ха́хәаԥшуеит.
/a-t'elevə́jzor ħ-á-xʷa-pš-wa-jt'/
the-television we(C1)-it(C2)-Prev(at)-look-Dyn-Fin
'We are watching television.'

In (129) above, а́-жәҩан /á-žʷjʷan/ 'the sky'—an object that can be viewed—is positioned outside the verb, while the third-person singular, non-human possessive prefix а- /a/ that agrees with it (see §2.2.2) is attached to the postposition ахь /axʲ/ 'to'. In contrast, the third-person singular, non-human prefix а- /a/ that agrees with 'television' in (130) is placed before the preverb within the verb. Furthermore, the уа- /wa/ that appears after the verb root is a suffix that indicates a dynamic action (abbreviated hereafter as 'Dyn'); taken together in (129) with the н- /n-/ that indicates the past (definite) of a word ending, it indicates the imperfect tense (abbreviated hereafter as 'Impf'). In (130), уе- (< уа- /wa/), together with the word-ending finite suffix -ит /jt'/, indicates the present tense.

Preverbs can also be attached to transitive verbs in the same way. For example, there is the word нашьҭ /na-šʲt/ 'send there' where the preverb на- /na/ 'there' that indicates direction is attached to the root of the two-place transitive verb шьҭ /šʲt/ 'send'. шьҭ is a verb root of the 'C1-C3-Root type' noted above. Preverbs are placed before C3 when they are put into transitive verbs. Accordingly, the column positions in нашьҭ /na-š^j^t/ are C1-Prev-C3-Root (compare with the column positions C1-C2-Prev-Root of the two-place intransitive verb хәапҳш /x^w^a-pš/ that has the above preverb). The following are examples of this:

(131) Сарá ателеграмма сышьҭуéит.
/sará a-t'elegrámma ϕ-sə-š^j^t-wá-jt'/
I the-telegram [it(C1)-]I(C3)-send-Dyn-Fin
'I shall send a telegram.'

(132) Ан лпҳа ашкóлахь днальíшьҭит.
/[a-]an l-pa a-šk'ól-ax^j^ d-na-lə́-š^j^tə-jt'/
the-mother her-son the-school-to him(C1)-Prev(there)-she(C3)-send-(Aor)-Fin
'The mother sent her son to the school.'

While -уе-ит /wa-jt'/ (Dyn-Fin) in (131) indicates present tense, it can also indicate 'a definite future' (Hewitt 1979c: 176).

Both (131) and (132) above are two-place transitive verbs; the verb valence number will not change even if a preverb is added. However, there are verbs whose valence is increased by attaching preverbs. For example, the verb кә-ҩ /k^w^-j^w^/ 'inscribe *sth* on *sth*' made by adding the preverb кә- /k^w^/ 'on' to the two-place transitive verb ҩ /j^w^/ 'write *sth*' is a three-place transitive verb:

(133) Иарá аконвéрт иáдрес áкәиҩит.
/jará a-k'onvért' j-ádres ϕ-á-k^w^-jə-j^w^ə-jt'/
he the-envelop his-address [it(C1)-]it(C2)-Prev(on)-he(C3)-write-(Aor)-Fin
'He added his address on the envelope.'

The first pronominal prefix in a verbal complex (though it does not actually appear) agrees with the иáдрес /j-ádres/ 'his address' directly before it, while the second pronominal prefix -а- agrees with аконвéрт /a-k'onvért'/ 'the envelope'. The preverb governs this Column II pronominal prefix.

3.1.2.1. Preverb

3.1.2.1.1. The preverb is placed before the verb root and gives the verb an adverbial meaning. According to A. Spruit (1983: 55),

> The preverb-slot can be filled with three types of mutually exclusive elements: 1 the relational preverbs a-, ay-[according to our notation, aj-], x^w^a-, which are used with a limited number of roots ('say to', 'bark at', 'look at', etc.), 2 the directional preverbs aa- 'hither', na- 'thither', la- 'downwards', j^w^a- 'upwards' and 3 a very large group of preverbs, which with minor exceptions are of a local nature.

Spruit (ibid.: 61) further divides the local preverbs in this final group (3) into the following three classes:

> type A must be combined with a personal prefix, type B may be combined with one, type C cannot be combined with a personal prefix. Moreover, type A takes prefixes of any person, whereas type B allows only 3 sg. irrational, 3 pl., and the relative personal prefix; the 3 sg. irr.

pers. prefix for type A is a-, for type B ø-. Eight Ps (P = the local preverb) allow forms of A as well as B. In the following chart the 1 sg. pers. prefix represents all pers. prefixes other than 3 sg. irr., 3 pl. and relative:

	A	B	C
1 sg.	s-	-	-
3 sg. irr.	a-	(ø-)	-
3 pl.	r-	(r-)	-
rel.	z-	(z-)	-

Concrete examples based on this chart can be seen in §§3.1.2.3–3.1.2.4 below.

3.1.2.1.2. We can define the preverb semantically and morphologically. For example, the principal preverbs added to the root ҧш /pš/ 'look' include the following: áаҧшра /áa-pš-ra/ 'to look here, to awake', áвтцҧшра /á-vc'-pš-ra/ 'to be visible from under', агәы́лаҧшра /a-gʷə́la-pš-ra/ 'to look inside *sth*', адәы́лҧшра /a-dʷə́l-pš-ra/ 'to look out of *sth*', азҧшрá /a-z-pš-rá/ 'to wait for', аӡáаҧшра /a-ʒáa-pš-ra/ 'to look in the water', акы́лҧшра /a-k'ə́l-pš-ra/ 'to gaze through', áкәҧшра /á-kʷ-pš-ra/ 'to look at the surface of *sth*', áлаҧшра /á-la-pš-ra/ 'to look closely, to peer into', áлбааҧшра /á-lbaa-pš-ra/ 'to look down from a height', áнаҧшра /á-na-pš-ra/ 'to look there', анаҧш=ааҧшра /a-na-pš-aá-pš-ra/ 'to look here and there', аны́ҧшра /a-nə́-pš-ra/ 'to be reflected in', аҭаҧшрá /a-ta-pš-rá/ 'to look from above down into', ахаҧшрá /a-xa-pš-rá/ 'to look at from above', ахы́лаҧшра /a-xə́la-pš-ra/ 'to look after', ахьáҧшра /a-xʲá-pš-ra/ 'to look around/back', áхәаҧшра /á-xʷa-pš-ra/ 'to watch, to look at', á-цкла-ҧш-ра /á-ck'la-pš-ra/ 'to pay attention to', áтцаҧшра /á-c'a-pš-ra/ 'to look up(wards) from below'. The general meaning of each preverb can be surmised based on this. Furthermore, to a certain extent we can establish what preverbs mean by observing which verbs take which individual preverbs. For example, the meaning of the preverb аа- /aa/ becomes somewhat clearer when we see that the following verbs take it: аагарá /aa-ga-rá/ 'to fetch' (cf. агарá /a-ga-rá/ 'to take, to carry'), áадгылара /áa-d-gəla-ra/ 'to approach' (cf. д- /d/ [preverb] 'next to, against' (Spruit 1983), агы́лара /a-gə́la-ra/ 'to stand'), аáира /aá-j-ra/ 'to come' (cf. анéира /a-ná-j-ra/ 'to go there'), аáҧхьара /aá-pxʲa-ra/ 'to invite' (cf. áҧхьара /á-pxʲa-ra/ 'to call'), áаҭалара /áa-ta-la-ra/ 'to come into' (cf. ҭа- /ta/ [preverb] 'into, in', ла- /la/ 'go into', аҭáлара /a-tá-la-ra/ 'to go into'), áашьтра /áa-šʲt-ra/ 'to send here' (cf. áшьтра /á-šʲt-ra/ 'to send'), ááҩра /áa-jʷ-ra/ '(of voice) to carry in this direction' (cf. анáҩра /a-ná-jʷ-ra/ 'to reach there', áҩра /á-jʷ-ra/ 'to run'). In short, аа- /aa/ is a directional preverb directed toward a speaker that adds a sense of 'here, hither' to the verb root.

Preverbs can also be defined morphologically. In transitive verbs that have a preverb, the pronominal prefix that indicates the agent is placed between the preverb and the root. This makes it possible to separate the preverb from the root. This is demonstrated by the conjugations for the aforementioned аа-га-рá /aa-ga-rá/ 'to fetch': ииаз/сгóит /j-aa-z/s-ga-wá-jt'/ [it/them(C1)-Prev-I(C3)-bring-Dyn-Fin] 'I fetch it/them'. Here, a Column III prefix з/с- /z/s/ comes in between the preverb аа- and the root га- /ga/, separating the stem.

The preverb and root cannot be separated by the prefix that indicates the subject in intransitive verbs as above, but in many cases the negative marker -м- /m/ is useful for separating the preverb and root in the aorist form. The aorist negative form of the above instransitive verb а́адгылара /áa-d-gəla-ra/ 'to approach' demonstrates this: даасы́дымгылеит /d-aa-sə́-də-m-gəla-jt'/ [he/she(C1)-Prev-me(C2)-Prev-Neg-stand-(Aor)-Fin] 'he/she did not approach me'. However, this does not necessarily occur with all preverbs. The preverb аа- is an example of this; the negative marker -м- /m/ does not separate the preverb from the root: the aorist negative form of а́аҩра /áa-jʷ-ra/ is има́аҩит /jə-m-áa-jʷə-jt'/ [it/they(C1)-Neg-Prev(here)-run-(Aor)-Fin] 'it/they was/were not heard.'

Furthermore, ана́ҩра /a-ná-jʷ-ra/ is possible in either case: ина́мҩит /jə-ná-m-jʷə-jt'/ [it/they (C1)-Prev(there)-Neg-run-(Aor)-Fin] or имна́ҩит /jə-m-ná-jʷə-jt'/ 'it/they did not reach there'. However, with most preverbs the negative marker м- /m/ separates the root and the preverb in the aorist form. For example, consider the aorist negative form of verbs that have as their stem the aforementioned ҧш /pš/ 'look': иа́вцымҧшит /j-á-vc'ə-m-pšə-jt'/ 'it/they were not visible from under it', дагәы́ламҧшит /d-a-gʷə́la-m-pšə-jt'/ 'he/she did not look inside it', ддәы́лымҧшит /d-dʷə́lə-m-pšə-jt'/ 'he/she did not look out', сыбзы́мҧшит /sə-b-zə́-m-pšə-jt'/ 'I did not wait for you-F', дӡа́амҧшит /d-ʒáa-m-pšə-jt'/ 'he/she did not look in the water', скы́лымҧшит /s-k'ə́lə-m-pšə-jt'/ *or* сымкы́лҧшит /sə-m-k'ə́l-pšə-jt'/ 'I did not gaze through (it)', ды́ҟәымҧшит /də́-kʷə-m-pšə-jt'/ 'he/she did not look at (it)', да́ламҧшит /d-á-la-m-pšə-jt'/ 'he/she did not peer into it', дылба́амҧшит /də-lbáa-m-pšə-jt'/ 'he/she did not look down', дымнаҧш=а́аҧшит /də-m-na-pš-áa-pšə-jt'/ 'he/she did not look here and there', дҭа́мҧшит /d-tá-m-pšə-jt'/ 'he/she did not look down into (it)', даҳха́мҧшит /d-aħ-xá-m-pšə-jt'/ 'he/she did not look down at us', сылхы́ламыҧшит /sə-l-xə́la-mə-pšə-jt'/ 'I did not look after her', дхьа́мҧшит /d-xʲá-m-pšə-jt'/ *or* дымхьа́ҧшит /də-m-xʲá-pšə-jt'/ 'he/she did not look back', сбы́хәамҧшит /s-bə́-xʷa-m-pšə-jt'/ 'I did not watch you-F', да́цкламҧшит /d-á-ck'la-m-pšə-jt'/ 'he/she did not pay attention to it', да́цамҧшит /d-á-c'a-m-pšə-jt'/ 'he/she did not look up at it'.

Using these semantic and morphological methods, we can extract the preverb from the verb. Morphological methods of analysis must be resorted to when we cannot divide a verb stem semantically into the preverb and the root. For example, the verb аа́хәара 'to buy' probably cannot be broken down semantically into the preverb аа- and root хәа /xʷa/.[92] Morphologically, however, we can separate it completely into two elements: иаа́сымхәеит /j-aá-sə-m-xʷa-jt'/ [it/them(C1)-Prev-I(C1)-Neg-buy-(Aor)-Fin] 'I did not buy it/them'.

Some verbs have two or more preverbs. The verb а́адгылара /áa-d-gəla-ra/ 'to approach' (cf. д- /d/ [preverb] 'next to, against' (Spruit 1983), агы́лара /a-gəla-ra/ 'to stand') observed earlier is one such example. As we discovered earlier, a pronominal prefix is inserted between the preverb аа- and the preverb д- in this verb: даасы́дымгылеит /d-aa-sə́-də-m-gəla-jt'/ 'he/she did not approach me'. Accordingly, while separation is easier with preverbs, in some cases it cannot be done with such prefixes. For example, no pronominal prefixes are inserted between the preverb кә(ы)- /kʷ(ə)/ and the preverb н- /n/ in а́ҟәынхара /á-kʷə-n-xa-ra/ 'to live on': сы́ҟәнымхеит /sə́-kʷ-nə-m-xa-jt'/ [I(C1)-Prev(on)-Prev-Neg-live-(Aor)-Fin] 'I did not live on it', ирыҟәнхеит /jə-rə́-kʷ-n-xa-jt'/ [they(C1)-them(C2)-Prev(on)-Prev-live-(Aor)-Fin] 'they lived on them'. However, the two preverbs can be separated based on most examples that have кә(ы)- 'on' as a preverb (ex. а́ҟәзаара /á-kʷ-zaa-ra/ 'to be on') and on анхара́ /a-n-xa-rá/ 'to live' (Aorist: сны́мхеит /s-nə́-m-xa-jt'/ 'I did not live').

92. The preverb аа- may be related to the directional preverb аа- 'hither' from above, but the relationship with the root is unclear.

Nonetheless, there are cases in which multiple preverbs are joined together where separation is synchronically difficult.

3.1.2.2. Preverbs in Verbal Complexes

The distribution of the preverb and the pronominal prefix in a verbal complex differ for transitive and intransitive verbs. In intransitive verbs, the preverb is positioned before the verb root and no pronominal prefixes of any sort are inserted in between the preverb and the verb root. The Column I pronominal prefix that is the intransitive verb subject (S) is placed at the beginning of the word; if an indirect object is required, a Column II pronominal prefix that indicates the indirect object is placed after that. We can diagram the distribution of preverbs and pronominal prefixes in an intransitive verb as follows:

(i) S(C1) + [IO(C2)] + Prev + Root + (Tense-Aspect suffix + Finite suffix)

The negative marker м- /m/ (abbreviated hereafter as 'Neg') in the aorist negative form is placed either between the preverb and the root as noted above, or before the preverb.

For transitive verbs, however, the Column III pronominal prefix that indicates the subject of the transitive verb (A) is without exception inserted between the preverb and the root. The direct object is placed at the beginning of the word just like the subject of the intransitive verb. If there is an indirect object, the Column II pronominal prefix that indicates such is placed before the preverb. We can diagram the distribution of preverbs and pronominal prefixes in a transitive verb as follows:

(ii) DO(C1) + [IO(C2)] + Prev + A(C3) + Root + (Tense-Aspect suffix + Finite suffix)

The negative marker м- in the aorist negative form is inserted between the root and the pronominal prefix of the A.

3.1.2.3. Preverb Government

In addition to its adverbial function, the preverb in Abkhaz has the same function as the preposition in Indo-European languages; it governs Column II pronominal prefixes placed immediately before the preverb. See, for example, the case of the local preverb кə- /k^w/ 'on':

(134) Ахəкəá ирыкəнхеит.
/a-x^w-k^{w}á jə-rə́-k^w-n-xa-jt'/
the-hill-Pl they(C1)-them(= the hills, C2)-Prev(on)-Prev-live-(Aor)-Fin
'They settled on the hills.'

Here, the preverb кə- /k^w/ 'on' governs the pronominal prefix р(ы)- /r(ə)/ 'them (i.e. the hills)' immediately before it. When the preverb -кə governs a prefix that indicates third-person singular non-human, that prefix does not appear:

(135) Ахəы́ ды́кəнхеит.
/a-x^{w}ə́ də́-ø-k^w-n-xa-jt'/
the-hill he/she(C1)-it(C2)-Prev(on)-Prev-live-(Aor)-Fin
'He/She settled on the hill.'

There also are preverbs, however, where the prefix that indicates third-person singular non-human appears. See, for example, the case of á-важьзаара /á-va-ž^{j}-zaa-ra/ 'to be lying near', which has the preverb ва /va/ 'next to':

(136) Амҽы́ аҩны́ иа́важьуп.
/a-mč'ə́ a-j^{w}nə́ j-á-va-ž^{j}ə-wp'/
the-firewood the-house it(C1)-it(= the house, C2)-Prev-lie-Stat.Pres.Fin
'A piece of firewood is lying near the house.'

Also the prefix that indicates third-person singular non-human does or does not appear depending on the sentence's meaning (for details on this point, see §5.6).

3.1.2.4. Preverbs with the vocalic alternation -a vs. -ø

Some preverbs have paired forms with the vocalic alternation -a vs. -ø. In this case, those preverbs with the vowel -a mean 'introvert' and those with the vowel -ø mean 'extrovert'. For example, -ҭа- /ta/ vs. -ҭ(ы)- /t(ə)/ indicates movement in the opposite directions 'into' or 'out of' depending on vocalic alternation:[93]

(137) дҭа́сцалеит
/d-ø-tá-s-ca-la-jt'/
him/her(C1)-[it(C2)-]Prev-I(C3)-drive-Extension-(Aor)-Fin[94]
'I drove him/her into it.'

vs.

---

93. The preverbs explored here are examples that have the vocalic alternation pair -a : -ø, but we can see a tendency even with preverbs that lack that sort of pairing where the vowel -ø appears with most preverbs that combine with a certain verb roots. For example, almost all of the preverbs that combine with the verb root -х- 'take out of' that has a sense of 'extrovert' have the vowel -ø: а́имыхра /ájmə-x-ra/ 'to take apart, to dismantle', а́-мхра /á-m-x-ra/ 'to take away (from)', а-гәа́рхра /a-g^{w}ár-x-ra/ 'to tend (cattle)' (cf. а-гәа́рҵра /a-g^{w}ár-c'-ra/ 'to go out to pasture'), а́идыхра /áj-də-x-ra/ '(of a rope, thread) to unravel', а́илыхра /áj-lə-x-ra/ 'to undress' (cf. а́илалара /áj-la-la-ra/ 'to join each other'), а-ны́хра /a-nə́-x-ra/ 'to take *sth* from, to to wipe off', а-ҽы́хра /a-č'ə́-x-ra/ '(of fruits, berries) to pick'. Similarly, almost all of the preverbs that combine with the verb root -ҵ- /c'/ 'go out of' that has a sense of 'extrovert' have the vowel -ø: а́-дҵра /á-d-c'-ra/ 'to move away from', а-кы́дҵра /a-k'ə́d-c'-ra/ 'to fall out, to go down', а-ҽыжәҵра́ /a-čəž^{w}-c'-rá/ 'to get off a horse', а́-кәҵра /á-k^{w}-c'-ra/ 'to leave/abandon the previous residence', а-дәы́лҵра /a-d^{w}ə́l-c'-ra/ 'to go out of', а-хы́лҵра /a-xə́l-c'-ra/ 'to give birth to, to be born, to (emit) smoke', а-гәа́рҵра /a-g^{w}ár-c'-ra/ 'to go out to pasturage', а-ԥы́рҵра /a-pə́r-c'-ra/ 'to move away from', а-ны́ҵра /a-nə́-c'-ra/ 'to come from', а-ҵры́ҵра /a-crə́-c'-ra/ 'to diverge', а́-нҭыҵра /á-ntə-c'-ra/ 'to go out', а-ҩхы́ҵра /a-j^{w}xə́-c'-ra/ 'to pass across'. In contrast the verb root -ҵа- /c'a/ 'put/move into' that has a sense of 'introvert' combines with preverbs that have the -a or -ø vowel: а-ӡа́аҵара /a-ʒáa-c'a-ra/ 'to put in the water', а́-ҟаҵара /á-q'a-c'a-ra/ 'to make, to do', lit. 'to move X into existence' (Hewitt 2010: 113), а-зхаҵара́ /a-zxa-c'a-rá/ 'to recognize', а-ԥхаҵара́ /a-pxa-c'a-rá/ 'to drive off', а́иҵаҵара /ájc'a-c'a-ra/ 'to load (a gun)', а́-дҵара /á-d-c'a-ra/ 'to give, to set, to entrust', а-гәы́дҵара /a-g^{w}ə́d-c'a-ra/ 'to throw *sth* at/to *sb*', а-кы́дҵара /a-k'ə́d-c'a-ra/ 'to hang (on *sth*)', а́-жәҵара /á-ž^{w}-c'a-ra/ 'to set *sb* on *sb*', а́-кәҵара /á-k^{w}-c'a-ra/ 'to lay/put *sth* on a surface', а-нҵара́ /a-n-c'a-rá/ 'to make a note of, to record'.

94. The suffix -ла- /la/ is an extension that attaches to the verb root. Together with the preverb, it gives a sense of 'introvert'.

(138) дҭы́рцеит
/d-ø-tə́-r-ca-jt'/
him/her(C1)-[it(C2)-]Prev-they(C3)-expel-(Aor)-Fin
'They expelled him/her from it.'

(139) дҭа́ҧалеит
/d-ø-tá-pa-la-jt'/
he/she(C1)-[it(C2)-]Prev-jump-Introvert-(Aor)-Fin
'He/She jumped into it.'

vs.

(140) дҭы́ҧеит
/d-ø-tə́-pa-jt'/
he/she(C1)-[it(C2)-]Prev-leap-(Aor)-Fin
'He/She leaped out of it.'

The following preverbs have pairs in which vocalic alternation of this sort takes place:

-ва- /va/ 'next to, alongside' vs. -в(ы)- /v(ə)/ 'by, from behind':

Аҩны́ да́ватәоуп.
/a-jʷnə́ d-á-va-t'ʷa-wp'/
the-house he/she(C1)-it(C2)-Prev(next to)-sit-Stat.Pres.Fin
'He/She is sitting beside/behind the house.'
vs.
Аагы́ларҭа са́всит.
/[a-]aagə́larta s-á-v-sə-jt'/
the-stop I(C1)-it(C2)-Prev(by)-go-(Aor)-Fin
'I went by the stop.'

Акәтқәа́ аҩны́ иа́вицеит. (ARD) 'He drove the hens away from behind the house.'

-гәыла- /gʷəla/ 'into, inside' vs. -гәыл- /gʷəl/ 'out of':

Ашә абы́сҭа иагәы́лалҵеит. (ARD)
/a-šʷ a-bə́sta j-a-gʷə́la-l-c'a-jt'/
the-cheese the-polenta it(= cheese, C1)-it(= the polenta, C2)-Prev(in)-she(C3)-put-(Aor)-Fin
'She put the cheese in the polenta.'
vs.
Апатре́ҭкәа альбо́м иагәы́лылхит. (ARD)
/a-p'at'rét-kʷa [a-]alʲbóm j-a-gʷə́lə-l-xə-jt'/
the-photograph-Pl the-albim them(C1)-it(C2)-Prev(out of)-she(C3)-take-(Aor)-Fin
'She took the photographs out of the album.'

-ҕра- /ɣra/ 'into' vs. -ҕр(ы)- /ɣr(ə)/ 'from':

Адокуме́нтқәа ақьаа́дҭра иаҕре́итцеит. (ARD)
/a-dok'umént'-kʷa a-kʲaádtra j-a-ɣrá-j-c'a-it'/
the-document-Pl the-folder them(C1)-it(C2)-Prev(into)-he(C3)-put-(Aor)-Fin
'He inserted the documents into the folder.'
vs.

Акьаа́дтра адокуме́нткәа аӷри́хит. (ARD)
/a-kʲaádtra a-dok’umént’-kʷa ø-a-ɣrə́-j-xə-jt’/
the-folder the-document-Pl [them(C3)-]it(C2)-Prev(from)-he(C3)-take-(Aor)-Fin
‘He pulled the documents out of the folder.’

-кна- /k’na/ ‘(hang) on/up’ vs. -кн(ы)- /k’n(ə)/ ‘(take) off:

Атӡа́мцқәа рҿы́ аса́хьақәа кна́сҳаит.
/a-tʒámc-kʷa r-č’ə́ a-sáxʲa-kʷa ø-k’ná-s-ħa-jt’/
the-wall-Pl their-on the-picture-Pl [them(C1)-]Prev-I(C3)-hang-(Aor)-Fin
‘I hung the pictures on the walls.’

vs.

Апатре́ҭ кны́лхит.
/a-p’at’ét ø-ø?-k’nə́-l-xə-jt’/
the-portait [it(C1)-it(C2)?-]she(C3)-take-(Aor)-Fin
‘She took the portrait down.’

-кҿа- /k’č’a/ ‘in the corner’ vs. -кҿ(ы)- /k’č’(ə)/ ‘out of the corner’:

Аҽы́ кҿаца́ланы иркит. (ARD)
/a-čə́ ø-k’č’a-calá-nə jə-r-k’ə́-jt’/
the-horse [it(C1)-]Prev-drive into the corner-Abs it(C1)-they(C3)-catch-(Aor)-Fin
‘They drove the horse into a dead end and caught it.’

vs.

дыкҿы́тцит
/də-k’č’ə́-c’ə-jt’/
he/she(C1)-Prev-go out of the corner-(Aor)-Fin
‘He/She went/came out of the corner.’

-кы́ла- /k’əla/ ‘in (a narrow place)’ vs. -кы́л- /k’ə́l/ ‘out of’:

Абаҩ и́хәда икылахеит. (ARD)
/á-bajʷ jə́-xʷda jə-ø-k’ə́la-xa-jt’/
the-bone his-throat it(C1)-[it(C2)-]Prev(in)-get stuck-(Aor)-Fin
‘A bone was stuck in his throat.’

vs.

Аҽы́шькыл ишьапы́ кы́лихит. (ARD)
/a-čə́šʲk’əl jə-šʲap’ə́ ø-ø-k’ə́lə-j-xə-jt’/
the-stirrup his-foot [it(C1)-it(C2)-]Prev(out of)-he(C3)-take-(Aor)-Fin
‘He took his foot out of the stirrup.’

-ла- /la/ ‘into’ vs. -л(ы)- /l(ə)/ ‘out of’[95]:

Абна ды́ларгалеит.
/á-bna də́-ø-la-r-ga-la-jt’/
the-forest him/her(C1)-[it(C2)-]Prev(into)-they(C3)-take-Introvert-(Aor)-Fin

95. Cf. а́-лагара /á-la-ga-ra/ ‘to begin’ vs. а́-лгара /á-l-ga-ra/ ‘to finish’.

'They took him/her into the forest.'

vs.

Апа́ртиа са́лцит.
/a-p'árt'ja s-á-l-c'ə-jt'/
the-party I(C1)-it(C2)-Prev(out of)-go-(Aor)-Fin
'I left the party.'

аила- /ajla/ vs. аил(ы)- /ajl(ə)/ :

Лхэычы́ деила́лхэеит.
/l-xʷəčʲ'ə́ d-ajlá-l-ħʷa-jt'/
her-child him/her(C1)-Prev-she(C3)-dress-(Aor)-Fin
'She dressed her child.'

vs.

Аҧшка деилы́схит.
/á-pška d-ajlə́-s-xə-jt'/
the-baby him/her(C1)-Prev-I(C3)-undress-(Aor)-Fin
'I undressed the baby.'

-мҕа- /mɣa/ '(put *sth*) on (one's finger, waist)' vs. -мҕы- /mɣə/ '(take one's ring, belt) off':

Сара́ смацэа́зқэа сы́мҕастцоит. (GAL)
/sará s-macʷáz-kʷa ø-sə́-mɣa-s-c'a-wa-jt'/
I my-ring-Pl [them(C1)-]me(C2/Poss)-Prev/SV(on)-I(C3)-put-Dyn-Fin
'I am putting on my rings.'

vs.

Сара́ смацэа́з сы́мҕысхуеит.
/sará s-macʷáz ø-sə́-mɣə-s-x-wa-jt'/
I my-ring [it(C1)-]me(C2/Poss)-Prev/SV(off)-I(C3)-take-Dyn-Fin
'I will take my ring off.'

-мца- /mc'a/ 'under; in front of' vs. -мц- /mc'/ 'from in front of':

Асасцэа акэа́ц ры́мцартцеит. (AAD)
/á-sas-cʷa a-k'ʷác ø-rə́-mc'a-r-c'a-jt'/
the-guest-Pl the-meat [it(C1)-]them(C2)-Prev(in front of)-they(C3)-put-(Aor)-Fin
'They put the meat in front of the guests.'

vs.

Асасцэа а́цэца ду́қэа ры́мтцх! (ARD)
/á-sas-cʷa á-c'ʷca də́w-kʷa ø-rə́-mc'-x/
the-guest-Pl the-glass big-Pl [them(C1)-]them(C2)-Prev(form in front of)-take.Imp
'Take the big glasses from in front of the guests!'

-ха- /xa/ '(be) in headgear / (put) on (headgear)' vs. -х(ы)- /x(ə)/ '(take headgear) off':

Ахы́лҧа сха́стцеит.
/a-xə́lpa ø-s-xá-s-c'a-jt'/
the-cap [it(C1)-]my(Poss)-SV-I(C3)-put-(Aor)-Fin
'I put on a cap.'

vs.

Ухҭырԥа́ ухы́х!

/wə-xtərpá ø-wə-xə́-x/

your-hood [it(C1)-]your(Poss)-SV-you(C3)-take.Imp

'Take your hood off!'

-тца- /c'a/ 'under' vs. -тц(ы)- /c'(ə)/ 'from under':

Лара́ ачуа́н а́мца а́тцалтцеит.

/lará a-čʲwán á-mca ø-á-c'a-l-c'a-jt'/

she the-cauldron the-fire [it(C1)-]it(C2)-Prev(under)-she(C3)-put-(Aor)-Fin

'She put a fire under the cauldron.'

vs.

Ацгәы́ астол и́тцытцит.

/a-cgʷə́ a-st'ól jə́-ø-c'ə-c'ə-jt'/

the-cat the-table it(= the cat, C1)-[it(= the table, C2)-]Prev(from under)-go out-(Aor)-Fin

'The cat came out from under the table.'

-втца- /vc'a/ 'in/behind (a narrow space)' vs. -втц(ы)- /vc'(ə)/ 'from behind, from under':

Ашә да́втцагылеит.

/á-šʷ d-á-vc'a-gəla-jt'/

the-door he/she(C1)-it(C2)-Prev(behind)-stand-(Aor)-Fin

'He/She stood behind the door.'

vs.

Амра а́ԥҭакәа ирывтцԥшуеит. (ARD)

/á-mra á-pta-kʷa jə-rə́-vc'-pš-wa-jt'/

the-sun the-cloud-Pl it(C1)-them(C2)-Prev(from behind)-become visible-Dyn-Fin

'The sun is emerging from behind the clouds.'

-шьа- /šʲa/ '(be shod) in' vs. -шь(ы)- /šʲ(ə)/ '(take footwear) off'[96]:

Ан ахәычы́ е́имаа и́шьалтцеит. (ARD)

/[a-]an a-xʷəč'ʲə́ [a-]ajmaa ø-jə́-šʲa-l-c'a-jt'/

the-mother the-child the-shoe(s) [it(C1)-]him(C2)-Prev-she(C3)-put-(Aor)-Fin

'The mother put the shoes on the child.'

vs.

Сара́ се́имаакәа сы́шьысхуеит.

/sará s-ájmaa-kʷa ø-sə́-šʲə-s-x-wa-jt'/

I my-shoe-Pl [them(C1)-]my(Poss)-SV-I(C3)-take-Dyn-Fin

'I am taking off the shoes.'

-шьҭа- /šʲta/ 'down on (the ground)' vs. -шьҭы- /šʲtə/ 'from (the ground); up':

Аидара а́дгьыл аҿы́ ишьҭа́стцеит.

/[á-]ajdara á-dgʲəl a-č'ə́ jə-šʲtá-s-c'a-jt'/

96. These preverbs are also used as subjective version markers. For the subjective version see §4.3.6.

the-burden the-ground its-to it(C1)-Prev-I(C3)-put-(Aor)-Fin
'I lowered the burden to the ground.'
vs.
Ахáхә ду шьҭи́жәеит.
/a-xáħ[w] dәw ø-š[j]t-jә́-ž[w]a-jt'/
the-stone big [it(C1)-]Prev-he(C3)-snatch-(Aor)-Fin
'He snatched up the large rock.'

Аҧсаáтә шьҭыҧраáит.[97]
/a-psaát'[w] ø-š[j]tә-pr-aá-jt'/
the-bird [it(C1)-]Prev-fly-Extension-(Aor)-Fin
'The bird took to the air.' (cf. á-ҧыр-ра 'to fly')

-ҿа- /č'a/ 'into the mouth' vs. -ҿ(ы)- /č'(ә)/ 'out of the mouth' (cf. аҿы́ /a-č'ә́/ 'mouth'):
Ахәы́ц иҿашәéит. (ARD)
/a-x[w]ә́c ø-jә-č'a-š[w]á-jt'/
the-hair [it(C1)-]him(C2)-Prev-get into the mouth-(Aor)-Fin
'A hair got into his mouth.'
vs.
Унацәá уҿы́х!
/wә-nac[w]á ø-wә-č'ә́-x/
your-finger [it(C1)-]you(C2)-Prev(out of the mouth)-take.Imp
'Take your finger out of your mouth!'

-ҩна- /j[w]na/ 'into (a house/room, etc.)' vs. -ҩн(ы)- /j[w]n(ә)/ 'from (a house/room, etc.)':
Наáла аҩны́ дыҩнáлеит.
/naála a-j[w]nә́ dә-ø-j[w]ná-la-jt'/
Naala the-house she(C1)-[it(C2)-]Prev-go into-(Aor)-Fin
'Naala went into the house.'
vs.
Ауáда дыҩны́сит.
/a-wáda dә-ø-j[w]nә́-sә-jt'/
the-room he/she(C1)-[it(C2)-]Prev-go through-(Aor)-Fin
'He/She went through the room.'

Furthermore, there are verbs where the relationship between 'introvert' vs. 'extrovert' may not be clear but with which the vocalic alternation *a*- vs. ø- in the preverb produces opposites in the meaning of the verbs:

-бжьа- /bž[j]a/ 'between' vs. -бжь(ы)- /bž[j](ә)/:
Ҳарá áиқәшаҳатра хабжьáхтцеит. (GAL)
/ħará [á-]ajk[w]šaħatra ø-ħa-bž[j]á-ħ-c'a-jt'/
we the-treaty [it(C1)-]us(C2)-Prev(between)-we(C3)-put-(Aor)-Fin

97. The suffix -aa- is an extension added to a verb root. Together with the preverb, it gives a sense of 'extrovert'.

'We concluded the treaty.'
vs.
Ахатәгәабзи́ара бжьы́схит.
/a-xat'ʷ-gʷabzə́jara ɸ-bžʲə́-s-xə-jt'/
the-own-health [it(C1)-]Prev-I(C3)-spoil-(Aor)-Fin
'I ruined my health.'

3.1.3. Structure of Polysynthetic Verbs with Various Morphemes

As noted above, we can insert morphemes with various grammatical functions in Abkhaz verbal complexes. For example, using the verb шьҭ /šʲt/ 'send' from (131) in §3.1.2 above, we must insert the version (abbreviated hereafter as 'Vers') marker з(ы)- /z(ə)/ 'for' along with the prominal prefix governed by it into the verbal complex to express the idea of 'send *sth* to *sb*'. For example:

(141) Сан дыбзы́сышьҭит.
/s-an də-b-zə́-sə-šʲtə-jt'/
my-mother her(C1)-you.F(C2)-Vers(for)-I(C3)-send-(Aor)-Fin
'I sent my mother to you-F.'

The original meaning of this version is 'for,' but its meaning changes depending on the verb used; here, together with the Column II pronominal prefix that precedes it, it has the dative meaning of 'to you'.

The transitivity of the verb did not change in the above example, but there are morphemes that can change an intransitive verb into a transitive one, and others that can do the reverse of changing a transitive verb into an intransitive one. The morpheme р- /r-/ that indicates the causative (abbreviated hereafter as 'Caus') is an example of the former, while the morpheme з(ы)- /z(ə)-/ that indicates the potential (abbreviated hereafter as 'Pot') is an example of the latter. See (142) below for an example of the intransitive verb с /s/ 'hit' used above in (126) in §3.1.1 being causativized, and (143) for the transitive verb нашьҭ /na-šʲt/ 'send there' used above in (132) in §3.1.2 being potentialized:

(142) сыблы́рсит
/sə-b-lə́-r-sə-jt'/
I(C1)-you.F(C2)-she(C3)-Caus-hit-(Aor)-Fin
'She made me hit you-F.'

(143) Ан лԥа ашко́лахь дылзы́нашьҭуам.
/[a-]an l-pa a-šk'ól-axʲ də-l-zə́-na-šʲt-wa-m/
the-mother her-son the-school-to he(C1)-her(C2)-Pot-Prev(there)-send-Dyn-Neg
'The mother cannot send her son to the school.'

The causative marker р- /r/ in (142) is always placed directly in front of the verb root, and the Column III pronominal prefix that is its causer is placed in front of that. In (143), the Column II pronominal prefix governed by potential is placed after the Column I pronominal prefix. Given that the potential is normally used in negative forms, the marker м- /m/ for the negative is also here.

Thus, it is possible in Abkhaz to produce something that amounts to a very complex simple sentence with a single verbal complex. Verbal complexes more complicated than this can be found in actual texts. The following example has been taken from a text of Abkhaz folk stories:[98]

(144) ишәзеимакыроузеи?

/jə-šʷ-z-áj-ma-k'ə́-r-a-w-zaj/

what(C1)-you.Pl(C2)-Pot-each other-Prev-argue-must-copula-Stat.Pres.NF-Qu

'What is it that you-Pl have to quarrel about?'

Here, the и- /jə/ at the head of the word and -зеи /zaj/ at the end indicate 'what?'. The potential marker з /z/ (used here in the interrogative form) that governs the Column II prefix is incorporated into the verb stem еимак /áj-ma-k'/ 'argue with each other about', and роу /r-a-w/ 'have to' is attached to this.

3.1.4. Finite Forms and Non-Finite Forms

All of the examples examined above were simple sentences. Revisiting examples of Abkhaz simple sentences, we see that sentences end with the suffix -ит /jt'/ with aorist and present tenses in the affirmative form. Meanwhile, present tense sentences like the example in (143) above in the negative form end with the negative marker м- /m/. In the aorist negative form, the negative marker is placed before the verb root and the word ends with -ит. The following examples using the verb ца /ca/ 'go' illustrate this:

(145) дцо́ит	/d-ca-wá-jt'/	he/she(C1)-go-Dyn-Fin	'(s)he is going'
(146) дцо́м	/d-ca-wá-m/	he/she(C1)-go-Dyn-Neg	'(s)he is not going'
(147) дце́ит	/d-cá-jt'/	he/she(C1)-go-(Aor)-Fin	'(s)he went'
(148) дымце́ит	/də-m-cá-jt'/	he/she(C1)-Neg-go-(Aor)-Fin	'(s)he did not go'

The verb forms in (145) through (148) can form complete sentences on their own. In other words, this verb form by itself can be used as a simple sentence. In contrast, there are forms where a sentence cannot be completed by verb form alone. One example is the form that indicates a relative clause. The relative clauses (relative prefixes will be referred to here as 'Rel') that correspond to the respective forms in (145) to (148) are as follows:

(145a) ицо́	/jə-ca-wá/	Rel(C1)-go-Dyn	'the one who goes'
(146a) и́мцо	/jə́-m-ca-wa/	Rel(C1)-Neg-go-Dyn	'the one who does not go'
(147a) ица́	/jə-cá/	Rel(C1)-go-(Aor)	'the one who went'
(148a) и́мца	/jə́-m-ca/	Rel(C1)-Neg-go-(Aor)	'the one who did not go'

The relative clauses above do not have -ит or the negative marker at the end; rather, they end with the /wa/ that indicates dynamic action or with the zero ø (this can be regarded as the form where the zero affix that indicates the aorist is attached). Based on this, we can surmise that the role -ит /jt'/ and -м /m/ play in (145) through (148) is to terminate the sentences. The verb forms in (145)–(148) are

98. Abkhaz text: 'The man who carried out good deeds for the dead man' (No. 55).

traditionally called the 'finite (abbreviated hereafter as 'Fin') form', and those in (145a)–(148a) are called the 'non-finite (abbreviated hereafter as 'NF') form'.[99] For all tenses other than those here, verbs have finite and non-finite forms. Other suffixes also have the function of terminating a sentence. Interrogative sentences provide one example of this. In the following example, the suffix -ма /ma/ that indicates a yes-no question is added to the end of a verbal complex and terminates it:

(149) сылды́руама?
　/sə-l-də́r-wa-ma/
　me(C1)-she(C3)-know-Dyn-Qu
　'Does she know me?'

Thus, Abkhaz verbs can terminate a sentence with a suffix like -ит, or with a suffix indicating the negative or the interrogative. However, the 'non-finite form' cannot terminate a sentence with the verb form itself; this form that indicates complementary actions or states depends on the 'finite form'. Abkhaz—which lacks the conjunctions and relatives that link sentences as in the Indo-European languages—expresses these functions by inserting affixes that indicate time, reason, place, cause, condition, relationship, and so forth; these function as subordinate clauses to the main clause. Accordingly, complex sentences are composed with a succession of non-finite and finite forms. The non-finite form depends on the finite form, and the finite form terminates the entire sentence. This is not to say that the finite form suffix should be seen as something that attaches only to a verb form itself; rather, it encompass an entire sentence, including the non-finite and finite forms, and serves to terminate it. Based on this, we can regard Abkhaz sentences as being composed of only a single finite form. One of the distinguishing features of Abkhaz sentence structure is its difference from the structure in Indo-European languages, which use multiple finite forms even in complex sentences (cf. 'I *know* [finite] that the boy *ate* [finite] the apple'). Abkhaz resembles languages in which the 'finite' and 'non-finite' forms produce the grounds for verbal conjugation like we see in Japanese and the Altaic languages. For example, in the following sentence, the non-finite form forms a subordinate clause and the finite form terminates the sentence:

(150)	[Сара́ ашәҟәы́ сана́ҧхьо]SC	[са́н	дуанҭо́ит.]MC
	[sará a-šʷq'ʷə́ s-an-á-pxʲa-wa]SC	[s-án	d-wanta-wá-jt']MC
	I the-book I(C1)-when-it(C2)-read-Dyn.NF	my-mother	she(C1)-iron-Dyn-Fin

　'While I am reading the book, my mother is ironing.'

In the sentence in (150), the subordinate clause (SC) depends on the main clause (MC). Abkhaz word order normally follows the 'subordinate clause—main clause' pattern seen here; the finite form of the main clause frequently comes at the end of the sentence. Here, the -ит /jt'/ that indicates the finite form of the main clause can be regarded as serving to complete not just the main clause section but the entire sentence; for that reason, we should see this sentence as having the following multilayer structure:

(150a) [[[Сара́ ашәҟәы́ сана́ҧхьо]SC　са́н]　　дуанҭо́]MC -ит.

Non-finite forms that use the markers и- /jə/ and з(ы)- /z(ə)/ and function as relative clauses (RC) also form structures like those above:

99. For example, see Hewitt (1979c), Chirikba (2003a: 41).

(151) [[[Уи аԥхәы́с и́лҩыз]RC ашәҟәы́]CC сы́рҭе]MC -ит.
[[[wəj a-pħʷə́s jə́-l-jʷə-z]RC a-šʷq'ʷə́]CC ø-sə́-r-ta]MC -jt'
that the-woman Rel(C1)-she(C3)-write-Past.Ind.NF the-letter it(C1)-me(C2)-they(C3)-give-(Aor)-Fin
'They gave me the letter which that woman had written (lit. wrote).' [CC = complement clause]

Here, the relative clause is the non-finite form of the past indefinite tense; modifying ашәҟәы́ /a-šʷq'ʷə́/ 'letter', the resulting word is the direct object of the main clause. The main clause uses the finite form to terminate the entire sentence. The relative clause marker и- /jə/ here is in the position of the direct object of the verb root ҩ /jʷ/ 'write', that is to say, in the same position as a Column I pronominal prefix. The prefix з(ы)- /z(ə)/ is used when the relative clause marker is put in the position of a Column II or Column III pronominal prefix. The sentence in (152) below is an example of the relative clause marker put in the position of a Column II pronominal prefix, while (153) shows it in the position of a Column III pronominal prefix:

(152) [[Ашәҟәы́ зылҭа́з]RC астуде́нт]S да́ԥхьоит.
[[a-šʷq'ʷə́ ø-zə-l-tá-z]RC a-st'əwdént']S d-á-pxʲa-wa-jt'
the-book [it(C1)-]Rel(C2)-she(C3)-give-Past.Ind.NF the-student he(C1)-it(C2)-read-Dyn-Fin
'The student to whom she gave the book is reading it.'

(153) [[Ашәҟәы́ сы́зҭаз]RC а́чкәын]CC дызды́руеит.
[[a-šʷq'ʷə́ ø-sə́-z-ta-z]RC á-č'ʲk'ʷən]CC də-z-də́r-wa-jt'/
the-book [it(C1)-]me(C2)-Rel(C3)-give-Past.Ind.NF the-boy him(C1)-I(C3)-know-Dyn-Fin
'I know the boy who gave me the book.'

Thus, verbal complexes in the non-finite form cannot terminate sentences; they are a part of the subordinate clause. On the other hand, the finite form obligatorily appears in a sentence itself and terminates it.

3.1.5. Stative and Dynamic Verbs

Abkhaz verbs are divided into stative and dynamic verbs based on their meaning and morphology. Stative verbs indicate a state expressed by a verb or the results of an action. Stative verbs in Abkhaz can be divided into three types based on how they are derived: (i) inherently stative verbs: for example, а́-ҟазаара /á-q'a-zaa-ra/ 'exist, be', а-ԥсра́ /a-ps-rá/ 'be dead', а-тәара́ /a-t'ʷa-rá/ 'sit', а́-цәара /á-cʷa-ra/ 'sleep'. (ii) Stative verbs derived from adjectives and nouns: for example, иҟа́ԥшьуп /jə-q'ápšʲə-wp'/ 'it is red' is derived from the adjective а́-ҟаԥшь /á-q'apšʲ/ 'red'. (iii) Stative verbs derived from an underlying dynamic verb: for example, ишьу́п /jə-šʲə́-wp'/ 'it is dead/they are dead' is derived from а-шьра́ /a-šʲ-rá/ 'kill'. Tensewise, stative verbs have present and past tenses. Dynamic verbs indicate active actions. One of the clearest differences morphologically between dynamic and stative verbs is that the former have an abundance of tense-aspects and moods compared to the latter. Dynamic verbs can be broken up based on the morphology of their non-finite form into group I verbs that do not end with -з /z/ and group II verbs that do.

The tense systems for stative and dynamic verbs are as follows:

3.1.5.1. Stative Verbs

агы́лазаара /a-gə́la-zaa-ra/ 'to stand'[100]

	Affirmative	Negative
Finite forms		
Present	с-гы́ло-уп /s-gə́la-wp'/	с-гы́ла-м /s-gə́la-m/
Past	с-гы́ла-н /s-gə́la-n/	с-гы́ла-мы-зт /s-gə́la-mə-zt'/
Non-Finite forms		
Present	и-гы́ло-у /jə-gə́la-w/	и-гы́ла-м /jə-gə́la-м/
Past	и-гы́ла-з /jə-gə́la-z/	и-гы́ла-мы-з /jə-gə́la-mə-z/

Notes:

1. The с(ы)- /s(ə)/ at the beginning of words in the finite form is the first-person singular prefix 'I'. It is the subject of an intransitive verb, making it a Column I pronominal prefix. The suffix -уп /-wp'/ can be further split into *-w-* and *-p'* (cf. non-finite suffix *-w* in игы́лоу /jə-gə́la-w/). Accordingly, we can regard -п /p'/ as the finite suffix of a stative verb. Furthermore, the -т /t'/ at the end of the finite negative form сгы́ламызт /s-gə́la-mə-zt'/ can be regarded as a finite suffix.

2. The и- /j(ə)/ at the beginning of non-finite forms is a Column I relative prefix marker; it functions as the subject (this prefix will be rendered as Rel(C1) in this work). игы́лоу /jə-gə́la-w/ means '(the one) who is standing'.

3. Future tense forms of stative verbs are derived from stative verbs with the suffix -заа /zaa/ by addition of the suffixes of dynamic verbs:[101]

атәара́ /a-t'ʷa-rá/ 'to be sitting':

	Affirmative	Negative
Finite forms		
Future	д-тә́а-заа-уе-ит /d-t'ʷá-zaa-wa-jt'/ he/she(C1)-sit-Suffix-Dyn-Fin 'He/She will be sitting'	д-тә́а-заа-уа-м /d-t'ʷá-zaa-wa-m/
[Future I	д-тә́а-заа-п[102]	д-тә́а-заа-ры-м]
Future II[103]	д-тә́а-заа-ш-т	д-тә́а-заа-ша-м
Non-Finite forms		
Future	и-тә́а-заа-уа	и-тә́а-м-заа-уа
Future I	и-тә́а-заа-ра	и-тә́а-м-заа-ра
Future II	и-тә́а-заа-ша	и-тә́а-м-заа-ша

Examples:

(154) дтә́азаауам

100. The root /gəla/ is also used as the root of a dynamic verb: сгы́лоит /s-gə́la-wa-jt'/ 'I am standing up'.

101. For future tenses of stative verbs, see Hewitt (1979c: 176, 204) and Chirikba (2003a: 45).

102. Cf. the evidential mood element -заап /zaap'/, §4.2.6.

103. Cf. jə-sə́-ma-zaa-š-t' 'I'll probably have' (Hewitt 1979c: 176).

/d-t'ʷá-zaa-wa-m/
he/she(C1)-be sitting-Stative.Suffix-Dyn-Neg
'He/She will not be sitting.'

(155) Шəарá абри́ асасаáирҭа шəыҩнáзааүеит.
/šʷará abrə́j a-sasaájrta šʷə-jʷná-zaa-wa-jt'/
you.Pl this the-hotel you.Pl(C1)-stay in-Stative.Suffix-Dyn-Fin
'You-Pl will stay in this hotel.'

(156) Ҳарá абри́ асасаáирҭа ҳаҩназаауáма?
/ħará abrə́j a-sasaájrta ħa-jʷna-zaa-wá-ma/
we this the-hotel we(C1)-stay in-Stative.Suffix-Dyn.NF-Qu
'Shall we stay in this hotel?'

3.1.5.2. Dynamic Verbs

áҩра /á-jʷ-ra/ 'to run'

	Affirmative	Negative
Finite forms		
Dynamic Group I		
Present	сы́-ҩ-уе-ит /sə́-jʷ-wa-jt'/ I(C1)-run-Dyn-Fin 'I run'	сы́-ҩ-уа-м /sə́-jʷ-wa-m/ I(C1)-run-Dyn-Neg
Aorist	сы́-ҩ-ит /sə́-jʷə-jt'/	с-мы́-ҩ-ит /s-mə́-jʷə-jt'/
Future I	сы́-ҩ-п	сы́-ҩ-ры-м
Future II	сы́-ҩ-ш-т	сы́-ҩ-ша-м
Perfect	сы́-ҩ-хье-ит	с-мы́-ҩ-ц(-т)
Dynamic Group II		
Imperfect	сы́-ҩ-уа-н	сы́-ҩ-уа-мы-з(т)
Past Indefinite	сы́-ҩы-н	с-мы́-ҩы-зт
Conditional I	сы́-ҩ-ры-н	сы́-ҩ-ры-мы-зт
Conditiona II	сы́-ҩ-ш-н	сы́-ҩ-ша-мы-зт
Pluperfect	сы́-ҩ-хьа-н	с-мы́-ҩ-цы-зт

Non-Finite forms

	Affirmative	Negative
Dynamic Group I		
Present	и-ҩ-уá	и́-мы-ҩ-уа
Aorist	и-ҩы́	и́-мы-ҩ
Future I	и-ҩ-рá	и́-м-ҩ-ра
Future II	и-ҩы́-ша	и́-м-ҩы-ша
Perfect	и-ҩ-хьо́-у (-хьá-(ц))	и́-мы-ҩ-хьо-у (-хьа(-ц))

Dynamic Group II		
Imperfect	и-ҩ-уа́-з	и́-мы-ҩ-уа-з
Past Indefinite	и-ҩы́-з	и́-м-ҩы-з
Conditional I	и́-ҩ-ры-з	и́-мы-ҩ-ры-з
Conditional II	и-ҩы́-ша-з	и́-м-ҩы-ша-з
Pluperfect	и-ҩ-хьа́-з	и́-мы-ҩ-хьа-з

Notes:

1. The с(ы)- /s(ə)/ at the beginning of words in the finite form is the first-person singular pronominal prefix 'I'. Because the verb ҩ /jʷ/ 'run' is a one-place transitive verb, the pronominal prefix is a Column I prefix. Accordingly, сы́ҩуеит /sə́-jʷ-wa-jt'/ means 'I am running'.

2. The и- /jə/ at the beginning of non-finite forms is a Column I relative prefix marker; it functions as the subject. Accordingly, иҩуа́ /jə-jʷ-wá/ means '(the one) who is running'.

3. The suffix ӡа /ʒa/ indicating emphasis (abbreviated hereafter as 'Emph') is often placed after the root in the negative form. For example, сы́ҩӡом /sə́-jʷ-ʒa-wa-m/, смы́ҩӡеит /s-mə́-jʷ-ʒa-jt'/ (see §1.1.1.5 regarding contractions with the vowels *a+wa* and *a+j*). However, in modern Abkhaz this suffix has lost much of its original sense of emphasis and now constitutes a simple negative form variant.

4. The negative marker м- /m/ is placed before the verb root in the aorist, perfect, past indefinite, and pluperfect tenses of finite forms, as well as the non-finite forms of all tenses. The marker is put at the end of the word for all other tenses. There is great value for Abkhaz verbal morphology in describing this negative marker. For example, in the aorist form, this negative marker is used to segment a verb stem with a preverb into the preverb and the root (see §3.1.2.2). For that reason, in the verbal morphology described below, we will always note conjugations of both the affirmative and negative forms.

5. Ending the verb root with -а produces a contraction comprised of the root vowel and the dynamic marker -уа /wa/: сцо́ит (< /s-ca-wá-jt'/) 'I am going'.

3.1.6. Pronominal Prefixes

The pronominal prefixes for verbs are as follows (M = masculine, F = feminine):

Person		Singular		Plural	
Column I (DO, S)					
1		с(ы)-	/s(ə)/	х(а)-	/ħ(a)/
2	(M)	у-	/wə/	шә(ы)-	/ʃ̃ʷ(ə)/
2	(F)	б(ы)-	/b(ə)/	шә(ы)-	
3	(Human)	д(ы)-	/d(ə)/	и-/ɸ-	/jə/ø/
3	(Non-Human)	и-/ɸ-	/jə/	и-/ɸ-	
Column II (IO)					
1		с(ы)-	/s(ə)/	ха-/ах-	/ħa/aħ/

2	(M)	у-	/w(ə)/	шә(ы)-	/ŝʷ(ə)/
2	(F)	б(ы)-	/b(ə)/	шә(ы)-	
3	(Human M)	и-	/jə/	р(ы)-/д(ы)-	/r(ə)/d(ə)/
3	(Human F)	л(ы)-	/l(ə)/	р(ы)-/д(ы)-	
3	(Non-Human)	а-/ø-	/a/	р(ы)-/д(ы)-	

Column III (A)

1		с(ы)-/з-	/s(ə)/ʒ/	ха-/аҳ-/аа-	/ħa/aħ/aa/
2	(M)	у-	/w(ə)/	шә(ы)-/жә-	/ŝʷ(ə)/žʷ/
2	(F)	б(ы)-	/b(ə)/	шә(ы)-/жә-	
3	(Human M)	и-	/jə/	р(ы)-/д(ы)-	/r(ə)/d(ə)/
3	(Human F)	л(ы)-	/l(ə)/	р(ы)-/д(ы)-	
3	(Non-Human)	а-/на-	/a/na/	р(ы)-/д(ы)-	

Notes:

1. See §1.1.1.1 regarding the appearance of the schwa ы in parentheses.

2. The third-person singular can be divided into human and non-human for Column I; for Columns II and III the human can be further divided into masculine and feminine. No such divisions occur in the third-person plural.

3. Turning to the zero prefix ø- in the third-person singular non-human and the third-person plural in Column I, as noted in §3.1.1 this zero prefix appears when the referent that agrees with it appears immediately before the verbal complex. In this situation, the schwa appears in the slot of this prefix if the prefix has an accent. For example, Ажәы́тә а́тцан ҳәа цьоукы́ ы́-ҟа-н. /ažʷə́t'ʷ á-c'an ħʷa ǯʲawk'ə́ ə́-q'a-n/ 'In the olden times, there lived a people called the Tsan'.

4. See §5.6 regarding the zero prefix for the third-person singular non-human for Column II.

5. The voiced variant з /z/, аа (< *aʕ < *aħ), жә /žʷ/ of the Column III first-person singular and second-person plural appear when the root begins with a voiced consonant (see §3.2.6 for further details). See, for example, the first-person singular бызбе́ит /bə-z-bá-jt'/ 'I saw you-F' for the root ба /ba/ 'see'. Since this variant appears only in a Column III pronominal prefix, it shows that the root this variant produces is transitive. Note also, however, that this phenomenon does not occur with certain transitive verbs. For example, игәны́сгеит /jə-gʷnə́-s-ga-jt'/ 'I endured it/them'. Both voiced and unvoiced variants are also possible in some cases: for example, ис/згәаҕьи́т /jə-s/z-gʷaɣʲə́-jt'/ 'I ventured it/them'.

6. The Column II and Column III third-person plural variant д(ы)- /d(ə)/ appears before the causative marker р(ы)- /r(ə)/ (or before the stem from which the causative is derived). For example, дды́рыҩуеит /d-də́-rə-jʷ-wa-jt'/ [him/her(C1)-they(C3)-Caus-run-Dyn-Fin] 'they are making him/her run'.

7. The Column III third-person singular, non-human variant на- /na/ appears in Class D-type verbs (three-place transitive verbs), Class G-type verbs (two-place transitive verbs with a preverb), and Class H-type verbs (three-place transitive verbs with a preverb). A Class H-type verb example: иса́наҳәеит /jə-s-á-na-ħʷa-jt'/ [it/them(C1)-me(C2)-to-it(C3)-say-(Aor)-Fin] 'it said it/them to me'.

8. The first-person plural variant x(a)- /ħ(a)/, ax- /aħ/ parallels the appearance of the schwa in other persons. In those circumstances where the schwa of other persons appears, an a will appear in place of the schwa in locations next to the x /ħ/. For example, xáҩуеит /ħá-jʷ-wa-jt'/ 'we run', cf. сы́ҩуеит /sә́-jʷ-wa-jt'/ 'I run'; дахшьи́т /da-ħ-šʲә́-jt'/ 'we killed him/her', cf. дысшьи́т /dә-s-šʲә́-jt'/ 'I killed him/her' (because дахшьи́т is parallel to ды-с-шь-и́т, it should be broken down as да-х-шь-и́т; however, it will be recorded as д-ах-шь-и́т in this work[104]).

9. Second-person, singular, masculine у- /wә/ can indicate a general meaning, as in English, in other words it is used to refer to any person in general: Алы́хәҭала́ аӡы́ хара́ иузго́м. /a-lә́xʷta-lá a-ʒә́ xará jә-wә-z-ga-wá-m/ [the-sieve-with the-water far it(C1)-you.M(C2)-Pot-take-Dyn-Fin] 'You will not be able to take the water away far with a sieve'. 'Ситом воду далеко не унесешь'.

10. The third person, plural р- /r/ can perform the same function as the Russian functional equivalent of a passive which uses the third-person plural form of a verb:

Ауаҩы иа́жәала дырдры́руеит, аҽада́ — алы́мхала.

/a-wajʷә́	j-áẑʷa-la	dә-r-dә́r-wa-jt'	a-čadá	—	a-lә́mħa-la/
a-man	his-word-by	him(C1)-they(C3)-know-Dyn-Fin	a-donkey		its-ear-by

'Человека узнают по его речи, осла — по ушам.'

'Men can be told by their words, and donkeys can be told by their ears.' lit. 'they know a man by his word, a donkey by its ear.'

3.1.7. Tense and Aspect

Here we will summarize the tense-aspect system in Abkhaz.

In terms of **aspect**, Abkhaz verbs can be divided up into Stative and Dynamic verbs. Dynamic verbs can be further divided up into the following three systems:

Dynamic Verbs:

(i) Aorist: Aorist and Past Indefinite

(ii) Imperfective: Present and Imperfect

(iii) Perfective: Perfect and Pluperfect

In terms of **tense**, stative verbs can be divided up into Past and Present (for Future tense see §3.1.5.1 Note 3. Stative future forms morphologically belong to dynamic verbs.). Dynamic verbs can be divided up in the following way:

Dynamic Verbs:

(iv) Past: Aorist, Past Indefinite, Imperfect, Pluperfect, Conditional I, and Conditional II

(v) Present: Present and Perfect

(vi) Future: Future I and Future II

3.1.7.1. Stative Verbs: Present and Past

104. Regarding my approach to transliteration, Chirikba suggested that I render this as да-х-шь-и́т /da-ħ-šʲә́-jt'/, but here I have used the traditional method.

Stative verbs have two tenses: present and past. Actions expressed using stative verbs from the perspective of aspect indicate either state or a static relationship. For example:

(157) с-гы́ло-уп /s-gə́la-wp'/ 'I am standing.'

(158) Саргьы <u>сныҟәаҩуп</u>.
sar-gʲə́ s-nə́q'ʷajʷə-wp'
I-also I-traveller-Stat.Pres.Fin
'I am a traveller as well.'

(159) Анцәагьы <u>дрымамызт</u>.
a-ncʷa-gʲə́ d-rə́-ma-mə-zt
the-God-even him-they-have-Neg-Stat.Past.Fin
'They did not even have a God.'

3.1.7.2. Dynamic Verbs: Aorist vs. Imperfect and Present

3.1.7.2.1. Aorist

Dynamic verbs have many tenses. The most basic of these is the aorist tense. The aorist refers to an action as a single past event. In terms of aspect, the aorist indicates an action as an event that occurred only once without reference to length of time, just like in classical Greek. In concrete terms, when a speaker is telling a tale, the speaker will make comments as he or she situates events on a plot line. The plot for a series of events will be expressed using the aorist tense (in discourse analysis, this is called the 'foreground'), while the features of characters and depictions of landscapes will be expressed using verbs (for example, the present or imperfect) in the imperfective aspect (in discourse analysis, this is called the 'background'). Our informant uses the perfective past in Russian when she translates the Abkhaz aorist into that language. That is because the perfective in Russian performs a function of that sort.[105] This is normally translated in English in the simple past, that is to say, as 'X -ed'. For example:

(160) Иҧхәыс <u>даныҧсы</u> ашьҭахь акыр аамҭа <u>дџьабеит</u>, <u>дгурҩеит</u> егьит, аха атцыхутәан аӡә дааимгар ҟамлазт, даҽа ҧхәыск <u>дааигеит</u>. (Abkhaz text)
Jə-phʷə́s d-anə-psə́ á-šʲtaxʲ ak'ə́r áamta d-ǯʲabá-jt',
his-wife she-when-die-(Aor.NF) it-after a long time he mourn-(Aor)-Fin
d-gʷərjʷá-jt' agʲə́jt', axá ac'əxʷt'ʷán áʒʷ
he-grieve-(Aor)-Fin and so on but after all someone
d-aa-jə-m-gá-r ϕ-q'a-m-lá-zt',
her-Prev-he-Neg-bring-Cond. [it]-Prev-Neg-be possible-Past.Ind.Fin

105. See the remarks in J. Forsyth (1970: 9–10) [Forsyth, J. 1970. *A Grammar of Aspect: Usage and Meaning in the Russian Verb.* Cambridge: Cambridge University Press.] on aspect in Russian: 'So far, the functions of perfective verbs have been discussed only in isolated sentences. Many of the meanings of one or other aspect, however, arise only from the interplay of verbs in a continuous context. (...) Each perfective verb denotes an action which is a new event, bringing about, or at least marking the transition to, a new state of affairs, and thus carrying the narrative forward. The imperfective verbs, on the other hand, do not present dynamic changes, but rather facts relating to the background (...). In contrast with the perfective verbs, the imperfectives tend to hold up the narrative of events rather than carry it forward.'

dačá phʷə́s-k’ d-aa-j-gá-jt’.
other wife-one her-Prev-he-bring-(Aor)-Fin
‘After his wife’s death [After his wife died], for a long time the man mourned her and grieved for her, but finally he had to bring along another wife, so he brought along another wife.’

The aorist verbs in the above examples are underlined. These verbs describe the events that have taken place in a story in line with the plot along with the passage of time: ‘his wife died, and he mourned, grieved, and brought along a new wife’.

3.1.7.2.2. Imperfect

The first use of the imperfect (abbreviated hereafter as ‘Impf’) is to describe a continuous past action (that is, to indicate an action’s process) or a repeated past action (that is, a habitual past action). The imperfect is translated as the imperfective past in Russian. It can be translated in English as either the past progressive, or like ‘X used to DO’, ‘X would DO’. Examples of repeated past actions:

(161) Ари цәкы иман, ахучы игуарихлон, игуараитцалон, акраҿеитцон, акраиржәуан.
Arə́j cʷ-k’ə́ jə́-ma-n, a-xʷəč’ʲə́ j-gʷárə-j-x-la-wa-n,
he bull-one [it]-he-have-Stat.Past.Fin the-child it-Prev-he-pasture-iterative-Dyn-Impf.Fin
j-gʷára-j-c’a-la-wa-n, ak’r-a-č’á-j-c’a-wa-n
it-Prev-he-drive into the farmyard-iterative-Dyn-Impf.Fin something-it-Prev-he-feed-Dyn.Impf.Fin
ak’r-a-jə́-r-žʷ-wa-n.
something-it-he-Caus-drink-Dyn-Impf.Fin
‘He had a bull. His child would often take the bull grazing, driving it into the farm, feeding it and giving it water to drink’.

Examples of continuous past actions:

(162) Ачкун атцла дахьыкутәаз ари иҟалтцоз длаҧшны ибон.
A-č’ʲk’ʷən á-c’la d-axʲə́-kʷ-t’ʷa-z arə́j jə́-q’a-l-c’a-wa-z
the-boy the-tree he-where-Prev-sit on-Past.NF this Rel-Prev-she-do-Dyn-Impf.NF
d-la-pš-nə́ jə-[j-]ba-wá-n.
he-Prev-look below-Abs it-he-see-Dyn-Impf.Fin
‘The boy was watching what she was doing from where he was sitting atop the tree.’

Another use of the imperfect is as the tense in the apodosis of a contrary-to-fact condition (see §5.4.2.2). For example:

(163) Иацы́ а́мш бзи́азар, а́калакь а́хь сцо́н.
/jacə́ á-mš ø-bzə́ja-zar, á-kalakʲ [a-]axʲ s-ca-wá-n/
yesterday the-weather [it(C1)-]good-if the-town [its-]to I(C1)-go-Dyn-Impf
‘If the weather had been good yesterday, I would have gone to town.’

3.1.7.2.3. Present

The present is used to describe an action that is continuous at the time of speaking (in short, a present progressive action in English), a repetitive action taking place even as it is being spoken about, a habitual action, or a statement of truth. The present is also used when speaking of a definite future action in the sense of ‘(if you do this) it will definitely happen’. The Abkhaz present is translated in

Russian as the imperfective present. It can be translated in English as 'X is doing', 'X does', 'X will do'. Some examples indicating present progressive actions:

(164) убри азоуп сахәызба зысх'уа
/wəbrə́j a-z-á-wp' s-áhʷəzba ø-zə́-s-x-wa/
it it-for-be-Stat.Pres.Fin my-knife [it]-why-I-sharpen-Pres.NF
'That's why I am sharpening the knife'

(165) Уабацои?
w-abá-ca-wa-j?
you.M-where-go-Pres.NF-Qu
'Where are you going?'

An example indicating a repetitive, habitual action:

(166) Сусура амш аҽены сара асаат 7 (бжьба) рзы сгылоит.
/s-wə́səwra a-mš a-čnə́ sará a-saát bžʲbá r-zə s-gə́la-wa-jt'/
my-work the-day on that day I the-o'clock 7 their-at I(C1)-get up-Dyn-Fin
'I get up at seven on weekdays.'

An example expressing a truth:

(167) Аапын ашьтахь иаауеит аԥхын.
/áapən á-šʲtaxʲ j-aa-wá-jt' ápxən/
spring its-after it(C1)-come-Dyn-Fin summer
'Summer comes after spring.'

Examples indicating definite futures:

(168) ... абаржәы аԥха даныбмоу, ибоу[у]а аԥхагьы баргьы шәысшьуеит.
/abaržʷə́ a-pħá d-anə-b-má-w, j-b-áw-[w]a
now the-daughter her-when-you.F-have-Stat.NF Rel(C1)-you.F(C2)-receive-Dyn.NF
a-pħa-gʲə́ bar-gʲə́ šʷə-s-šʲ-wá-jt'/
the-daughter-and you.F-and you.Pl(C1)-I(C3)-kill-Dyn-Fin
'... this time when you give birth to a daughter, I will kill you and the daughter you have given birth to.' (Abkhaz text)

(169) ... санутахххо схуцкуа ҩба ааихьушьыр, уара уҿы сааиуеит. (Abkhaz text)
/s-anə́-w-tax-xa-wa s-xʷə́c-kʷa jʷ-ba ø-aa-[a]j-xʲə́-w-šʲə-r,
I-when-you.M-want-become-Dyn.NF my-hair-Pl 2-non.Hum [them]-Par-Rec-Prev-you.M-rub-if,
wará w-č'ə s-áa-j-wa-jt'/
you.M you.M-at I-Prev-come hither-Dyn-Fin
'When you-M need me, if you rub these two hairs together, I will come to your side.'

In addition, the present can express the continuation of an action from a point of time in the past to the present. For example:

(170) Кама ашкол далгеижьтеи кыр аацуеит.
/K'áma a-šk'ól d-á-l-ga-jžʲtaj k'ə́r ø-aa-c'-wá-jt'/
name.F the-school she(C1)-it(C2)-Prev-finish.(Aor)-since a lot [it(C1)-]Prev-pass-Dyn-Fin
'A lot of time has passed [lit. passes] since Kama finished school.'

Cf. Russian: *Я живу здесь уже давно.* 'I have lived here a long time.' Lat.: *jam diu hic habito.*

3.1.7.3. Future I and Future II

The Future I (abbreviated hereafter as 'Fut.I') expresses a future action related to another action, as in 'When/If . . ., X will do'. For example:

(171) Шәаныбзйахалак (/Шәыбзйахар), аҭаҭы́н шәа́халап, ары́жәтә жәжәла́п. (IC)
/šʷ-anə-bzə́ja-xa-lak' (/šʷə-bzə́ja-xa-r) a-tatə́n
you.Pl-when-good-become-LA (/you.Pl-good-become-if) the-tobacco
šʷ-á-xa-la-p' a-rə́žʷt'ʷ ø-žʷ-žʷ-lá-p'/
you.Pl(C1)-it(C2)-smoke-Iterative-Fut.I the-drink it(C1)-you.Pl(C3)-drink-Iterative-Fut.I
'When you recover, you will always smoke and drink (spirits).'

Future I also expresses a suggestion together with a first-person plural subject or agent. For example:

(172) Макьа́на хааҧшы́п.
/mak'ʲána ħ-aa-pšə́-p'/
for a while we(C1)-Prev-wait-Fut.I
'Let's wait a moment!'

(173) Ҳапэ хшьып, акуац хфап, ... (Abkhaz text)
/ħá-cʷ ø-ħ-šʲə́-p', a-k'ʷác ø-ħ-fá-p'/
our-bull [it]-we-kill-Fut.I the-meat [it]-we-eat-Fut.I
'Let's kill our bull and eat the meat ...'

Future II (abbreviated hereafter as 'Fut.II') describes the indefinite future. For example:

(174) Адаукуа́ угуа́рҭар, иқ́а́ашт ихәхәа́шт ... (Abkhaz text)
a-daw-kʷá w-gʷá-r-ta-r jə-q'áa-št' jə-ħʷħʷá-št'
the-ogre-Pl you.M-Prev-they-notice-if they-cry out-Fut.II.Fin they-bawl-Fut.II.Fin
'If the ogres notice you, they will probably scream and wail ...'

3.1.7.4. Perfect and Pluperfect

The perfect (abbreviated hereafter as 'Perf') expresses the results of an event that occurred in the past that persist into the present. For example:

(175) Уара́ абзйара хәа акагьы́ сзу́мущшәа убо́ит, ахá да́ара ирацәангьы́ абзйара ду сзу́ухьеит. (Abkhaz text)
/wará a-bzə́jara ħʷa ak'agʲə́ ø-s-zə́-wə-m-wə-c-šʷa ø-wə-ba-wá-jt'
you the-good deed SP nothing [it]-me-for-you-Neg-do-Perf-as if [it]-you-see-Dyn-Fin
axá dáara jə-racʷan-gʲə́ a-bzə́jara dəw ø-s-zə́-wə-w-xʲa-jt'/
but very it-mamy-also the-good deed big [it]-me-for-you-do-Perf-Fin
'You think that you have done nothing good for me, but you have done many great, good things for me.'

(176) Иагараааны исхәахьазаргьы иагараан исычхахьазаргьы ... (Abkhaz text)
'I have told you many times and I have have been patient many times, ...'

The pluperfect (abbreviated hereafter as 'Plupf') describes an event that was completed before a specific point of past time. For example:

(177) Сарá аҩны́ҟа санхынҳәы́ сандý дыԥсхьáн.
/sará a-jʷnə́-q'a s-an-xən-ħʷə́ s-andə́w də-ps-xʲá-n/
I the-home-to I(C1)-when-Prev-return.Aor.NF my-grandmother she(C1)-die-Plupf-Fin
'When I returned home, my grandmother had already died.'

(178) Ҳарá хҟны́ иахьá уажәрáанӡа, ишы́жәдыруа éиԥш, аԥшá амы́сцызт, уажәы́ ари́ áбаӷь аԥацá зырцысуá аԥшóуп. (Abkhaz text)
/ħará ħ-q'nə́ jaxʲá waẑʷráanʒa jə-šə́-ẑʷ-dər-wa ø-ájpš
we us-at today till now it-how-you.Pl-know-Dyn.NF [it]-like
a-pšá ø-a-mə́-s-cəzt' waẑʷə́ arə́j á-baɣʲ a-pac'á
the-wind [it(C1)]-Dummy(C2)-Neg-blow/hit-Plupf.Fin now this the-billy goat its-beard
ø-zə-r-c'əs-wá ø-a-pšá-wp'/
[it]-Rel-Caus-swing-Dyn.NF [it]-the-wind-Stat.Pres.Fin
'As you-Pl all know, in our place, until today, the wind had never blown.[106] Now, that wind is moving the billy goat's beard.'

3.1.7.5. Past Indefinite

The past indefinite (abbreviated hereafter as 'Past.Ind') is used to mean the 'Aorist + and'. Accordingly, the past indefinite cannot form simple sentences with a past indefinite verb alone; after it there must be a verb that ends in the finite form. For example:

(179) Амра наскьáн ихышәáшәеит. (AFL)
/á-mra ø-na-sk'ʲá-n jə-xʲšʷášʷa-jt'/
the-sun it(C1)-Prev(thither)-move-Past.Ind.Fin Dummy/it(C1)-become cold-(Aor)-Fin
'The sun went down and it became cold.'

(180) Сарá сашьá ашәҟәы́ изы́зҩын апóчтахь сцéит.
/sará s-ašʲá a-šʷq'ʷə́ ø-jə-zə́-z-jʷə-n a-póčʲta-[a-]xʲ s-cá-jt'/
I my-brother the-letter [it(C1)-]him(C2)-for-I(C3)-write-Past.Ind.Fin the-post office-to I-go-(Aor)-Fin

106. Lit. 'The wind had not hit it [Dummy]'.
The 3rd person singular non-human pronominal prefix is used in weather-expressions. We shall call this prefix a 'dummy' prefix. Other examples:
(1) ихьтóуп /jə-xʲtá-wp'/ [it(Dummy, C1)-cold-Stat.Pres.Fin] 'it is cold' (хьтóуп /xʲtá-wp'/ is also possible.)
(2) ихәлóит /jə-xʷla-wá-jt'/ [it(Dummy, C1)-become evening-Dyn-Fin] 'it is becoming evening'
(3) асы́ ауéит
/a-sə́ ø-a-w-[w]á-jt'/
the-snow [it(snow, C1)-]it(Dummy, C2)-fall-Dyn-Fin) 'it is snowing'
In (3) above the verb аурá /a-w-rá/ meaning 'to fall, to rain/snow' may appear to be cognate with the transitive verb аурá /a-w-rá/ meaning 'to do/make'. If so, a-sə́ ø-a-w-[w]á-jt' is interpretable as 'it (Heaven?) is doing/making snow' (the-snow [it(= snow, C1)-]it(= Dummy, C3)-do/make-Dyn-Fin). For the verb see Hewitt (2005a: 117, fn. 2). Also, for the dummy prefix -k'rə- (e.g., a-k'rə-s-fá-p' [the+Dummy(C1)-I(C3)-eat-Fut.I.Fin] 'I'll have a meal'), see Hewitt (1979c: 220–221).

'I wrote a letter to my brother and went to the post office.'

(181) Амха́ԥ а́тцылшьын абы́стa лу́ит.
/a-mħáp ø-á-c'ə-l-šʲə-n a-bə́sta ø-l-wə́-jt'/
the-spoon for mush [it(C1)-]it(C2)-Prev-she(C3)-mix-Past.Ind.Fin the-polenta [it-]she(C3)-make-(Aor)-Fin
'She mixed the mush with a spoon and made polenta.' (Abkhaz text)

The non-finite form of the past indefinite is used in the subordinate clause when a simple sentence in the aorist tense (182) below is made into a (183) subordinate clause:

(182) Ишԥа́ҟабтцеи?
/jə-špá-q'a-b-c'a-j/
it/them(C1)-how-Prev-you.F-do-(Aor)-Qu
'How did you-F do it/them?'

(183) Ишы́ҟабтцаз сыздьíруам.
/jə-šə́-q'a-b-c'a-z ø-sə-z-də́r-wa-m/
it/them(C1)-how-Prev-you.F(C3)-do-Past.Ind.NF [it(C1)-]me(C2)-Pot-know-Dyn-Neg
'I do not know how you-F did it/them.'

The past indefinite is used this way quite frequently. An example from a text:

(184) Убасҟан амни иҟаутцаз са сыԥсы еилнакаан, сыԥсы абра иааин, сынаур абра игылан, уара абас узнауит. (Abkhaz text)
'My own spirit understood what you did at that time and my phantom came here and stood here. And so the phantom did what it did for you in this way.'

3.1.7.6. Conditional I and Conditional II

Conditional I (abbreviated hereafter as 'Cond.I') is used in an apodosis for contrary-to-fact conditions:

(185) Уатцəы́ акəа́ а́мур, хаанеиөе́ирын.
/wac'ʷə́ a-kʷá ø-á-m-wə-r ħ-aa-naj-jʷáj-rən/
tomorrow the-rain [it(C1)-]it-Neg-fall(Aor.NF)-if we(C1)-Par-Prev-take a walk-Cond.I
'If it were not to rain tomorrow, we could take a walk.'

Conditional II (abbreviated hereafter as 'Cond.II') is used as the non-finite form. The tense of conditional II is that which appears in the future form of a subordinate clause when the main clause is in the past, just like the 'would' in the subordinate clause of the English sentence, 'He said he would be here at nine o'clock'. Observe these examples from Abkhaz texts:

(186) ари анхаөы рыцха ичкун дызлаишьышаз ахəызба ахра далагеит. (Abkhaz text)
arə́j a-nxajʷə́ rə́cħa jə́-č'ʲk'ʷən də-z-lá-j-šʲə-šaz á-ħʷəzba
this the-peasant poor his-boy him-Rel-Instr.-he-kill-Cond.II.NF the-knife
a-x-rá d-á-la-ga-jt'.
the-sharpen-masd. he-it-Prev-begin-(Aor)-Fin
'Then the poor peasant started sharpening the knife that he was going to use to kill his son.'

(187) Иҟаитцашаз ианахəеит. (Abkhaz text)
/jə́-q'a-j-c'a-šaz ø-j-á-na-ħʷa-jt'/

Rel-Prev-he-do-Cond.II.NF [it]-him-to-it-say-(Aor)-Fin
it (= the horse) told him what he should do next.

(188) хакузхышаз дҳааӡеит. (Abkhaz text)
/ħa-kʷə-z-xə́-šaz d-ħ-aaʒá-jt'/
us-Prev-Rel-exterminate-Cond.II.NF him-we-bring up-(Aor)-Fin
'We have brought up the one being who will destroy us.'

According to Hewitt (2010: 167–170), Conditional I and Conditional II are interchangeable.

3.2. Conjugation Types of Abkhaz Verbs

3.2.1. Abkhaz verbs can be divided into transitive and intransitive verbs. Stative verbs and certain dynamic verbs are intransitive verbs, while the remaining dynamic verbs are transitive verbs. Abkhaz has three types of prefixes that indicate person and class, as noted in §3.1.1. We can label these the Column I pronominal prefix (C1), Column II pronominal prefix (C2), and Column III (C3) pronominal prefix, in order of how far they are positioned relative to the verb root. The Column I pronominal prefix indicates subject (S) of an intransitive verb and the direct object (DO) of a transitive verb; the Column II pronominal prefix indicates the indirect object (IO) of a two-place intransitive and three-place transitive verb; and the Column III pronominal prefix indicates subject (A) of a transitive verb. We can classify the conjugation types of the Abkhaz verbs as follows based on the valency of the verb, transitive or intransitive status, and the presence or absence of preverbs:[107]

	without a Preveb	with a Preverb
one-place intr.	Class A	Class E
two-place intr.	Class B	Class F
two-place tr.	Class C	Class G
three-place tr.	Class D	Class H

Class A and Class B can be further divided into their respective stative and dynamic verbs (stative verbs being classified as A-1 or B-1 and dynamic verbs as A-2 or B-2, respectively). The types and distribution of the columns for each class are as follows (R = root):

Class A-1 (intr. stative)	S+R	C1+R
Class A-2 (intr. dynamic)	S+R	C1+R
Class B-1 (intr. stative)	S+IO+R	C1+C2+R
Class B-2 (intr. dynamic)	S+IO+R	C1+C2+R

107. The verbs have been classified in this way based on the work of G. Dumézil. The classifications have been changed slightly here. See Dumézil, G. 1932. *Études Comparatives sur Langues Caucasiennes du Nord-Ouest (Morphologie)*. Paris: Adrien-Maisonneuve. 156–172.; Dumézil, G. 1967. *Documents anatoliens sur les langues et les traditions du Caucase. V. Études Abkhaz.* Paris: Librairie Adrien-Maisonneuve. 29–34.; Dumézil, G. avec la collaboration de Tecfik Esenç. 1975. *Le verbe oubykh. Études descriptives et comparatives.* Paris: Librairie C. Klincksieck. 85–102.

Class C (tr. dynamic)	DO+A+R	C1+C3+R
Class D (tr. dynamic)	DO+IO+A+R	C1+C2+C3+R
Class E (intr.)	S+Prev+R	C1+Prev+R
Class F (intr.)	S+IO+Prev+R	C1+C2+Prev+R
Class G (tr.)	DO+Prev+A+R	C1+Prev+C3+R
Class H (tr.)	DO+IO+Prev+A+R	C1+C2+Prev+C3+R

We will describe below the finite and non-finite forms of verbs based on conjugation type. In some cases, the position of the accent is moved when verbs are conjugated in Abkhaz. Accordingly, in this work when describing verb conjugation types we will attempt to classify them based on the accentuation approaches discussed in §1.2.2.2. The three types of accent paradigm are AP a, AP b, and AP c:

(i) Root-fixed accent type: The position of the accent does not change in conjugation of the aorist and present tenses for this type. The accent is placed within the root. This type is termed AP a.

(ii) Prefix-position accent type: In the conjugation of the aorist and present tenses, the accent is placed on the pronominal prefix (or the negative marker in the aorist negative form). This type is termed AP b.

(iii) Final-position accent type: In the conjugation of the aorist and present tenses, the accent is placed on the stem-final position. This type is termed AP c.

3.2.2. Class A-1

This class is the stative verb class with a single subject (S) argument. The subject takes a Column I pronominal prefix (see §3.1.6). As discussed in §3.1.5, the stative verb in Abkhaz can be produced simply from adjectives, nouns and adverbs. It can also be derived from dynamic verbs. Accordingly, stative verbs need to be broken up into the following three types when they are being described:

(α) inherently stative verbs (for example, атәара́ /a-t'ʷa-rá/ 'to sit')

(β) stative verbs derived from adjectives, nouns, or adverbs (for example, илу́уп /jə-də́w-wp'/ 'it/they is/are big')

(γ) secondary stative verbs derived from underlying dynamic verbs (for example, и-шь-у́п 'it/they is/are dead', cf. ашьра́ /a-šʲ-rá/ 'to kill')

As for this latter group of secondary stative verbs, the conjugated form илшьи́т /jə-l-šʲə́-jt'/ [it/them(C1)-she(C3)-kill-(Aor)-Fin] 'she killed it/them' of the dynamic/transitive verb ашьра́ /a-šʲ-rá/ 'to kill' is transformed into a stative verb form, as in the following: ишьу́п /jə-šʲə́-wp'/ [it/they(C1)-be killed-Stat.Pres.Fin] 'it/they is/are dead'. Stative verb forms of this sort will not be discussed here since they are derived secondarily. However, we should note this system for distinguishing them is not absolute; the borders between types (α) and (β) or (α) and (γ) are not necessarily clear.

Bearing this in mind, the following sorts of verbs can be regarded as inherently Class A-1 type that belong to (α): а-га́-заа-ра '(of a road) to lead', а-гы́ла-заа-ра 'to be standing', а-иа-ра́ 'to be lying', á-ꝁа-заа-ра 'to exist, to be',[108] а-ҧс-рá 'to be dead', а-ҧш-рá 'to be waiting', а-тәа-рá 'to be sitting', а-ха-рá 'to be headed', а-хиа-рá 'to be ready; to be covered', á-цәа-ра 'to be sleeping', а-шьҭá-заа-ра 'to be lying'[109] (-заа- /zaa/ is suffix that appears in the masdar of the stative verb; it does not appear when conjugating).

Stative verbs belonging to group (β) are extremely productive. For example, а-бзá-заа-ра 'to be alive' (cf. а-бзá 'alive'), а-бзи́а-заа-ра 'to be good' (cf. а-бзи́а 'good'), а-ҕáр-заа-ра 'to be poor' (cf. а-ҕáр 'poor'), á-ҕәҕәа-заа-ра 'to be strong' (cf. á-ҕәҕәа 'strong'), áиꝁара-заа-ра 'to be equal' (cf. áиꝁара), áиц-заа-ра 'to be together' (cf. аиц 'together'), а-тáта-заа-ра 'to be soft' (cf. а-тáта 'soft'), á-ҭбаа-заа-ра 'to be wide' (cf. á-ҭбаа 'wide'), а-ҭшәа-заа-рá 'to be narrow' (cf. а-ҭшәá 'narrow'), а-ҭы́нч-заа-ра 'to be calm/quiet' (cf. а-ҭы́нч 'quiet, calm'), а-ҭәы́-заа-ра 'to be full' (cf. а-ҭәы́ 'full'), á-хара-ра 'to exist in the distance' (cf. á-хара-ра 'distance'), á-цқьа-заа-ра 'to be clean' (cf. á-цқьа 'clean'), á-чмазаҩ-заа-ра 'to be ill' (cf. а-чы́мазаҩ 'sick person'), etc.

The plural marker -кәа/-цәа must be added to the root for stative verbs derived from nouns depending on the number of subjects. For example, the verb сҧбуп /s-pá-wp'/ 'I am a son' derived from the noun аҧá /a-pá/ 'son' is conjugated as follows:

[pres.] с-ҧб́-уп, у-ҧб́-уп д-ҧб́-уп, х-ҧа-цәб́-уп, шә-ҧа-цәб́-уп, и-ҧа-цәб́-уп

[past] с-ҧá-н, у-ҧá-н д-ҧá-н, х-ҧа-цәá-н, шә-ҧа-цәá-н, и-ҧа-цәá-н

The stative verbs derived from adjectives or nouns that belong to group (β) can be considered as having a zero-copula root. Accordingly, хҧацәбуп /ħ-pa-cʷá-wp'/ can be analyzed as ħ-pa-cʷa-ǿ-wp' [we-son-Pl.Human-be-Stat.Pres.Fin] 'we are sons'.

3.2.2.1. Inflection of AP a

а-гы́лазаара /a-gə́la-zaa-ra/ 'to be standing'

Finite forms

		Affirmative	Negative
Present			
Sg	1	с-гы́ло-уп /s-gə́la-wp'/ 'I am standing'	с-гы́ла-м
	2.M	у-гы́ло-уп	у-гы́ла-м
	2.F	б-гы́ло-уп	б-гы́ла-м
	3.Human	д-гы́ло-уп	д-гы́ла-м
	3.Non-Human	и-гы́ло-уп	и-гы́ла-м
Pl	1	х-гы́ло-уп	х-гы́ла-м
	2	шә-гы́ло-уп	шә-гы́ла-м
	3	и-гы́ло-уп	и-гы́ла-м

108. One may also regard the root ꝁа /q'a/ in á-ꝁазаара /á-q'a-zaa-ra/ as a preverb and ø as the root. On this point, see §5.2.1.

109. а-шьҭáзаара /a-šʲtá-zaa-ra/ can also be regarded as a stative verb derived from á-шьҭа /á-šʲta/ 'trail, track'.

Past			
Sg	1	с-гы́ла-н	с-гы́ла-мы-зт
	2.M	у-гы́ла-н	у-гы́ла-мы-зт
	2.F	б-гы́ла-н	б-гы́ла-мы-зт
	3.Human	д-гы́ла-н	д-гы́ла-мы-зт
	3.Non-Human	и-гы́ла-н	и-гы́ла-мы-зт
Pl	1	х-гы́ла-н	х-гы́ла-мы-зт
	2	шә-гы́ла-н	шә-гы́ла-мы-зт
	3	и-гы́ла-н	и-гы́ла-мы-зт

Non-Finite forms		
Column I		
Present	и-гы́ло-у /jə-gə́la-w/ '(the one) who/which is standing'	и-гы́ла-м
Past	и-гы́ла-з	и-гы́ла-мы-з

When there is an accent on the masdar stem, it will remain attached to the stem through all inflections. Other examples:

а-ҕа́рзаара /a-ɣár-zaa-ra/ 'to be poor': Fin. [pres.] д-ҕа́р-уп / д-ҕа́ры-м, [past] д-ҕа́ры-н / д-ҕа́р-мызт; Non-fin. (C1) [pres.] и-ҕа́р-у / и-ҕа́ры-м, [past] и-ҕа́ры-з / и-ҕа́р-мы-з. а-ҭы́нч-заа-ра 'to be calm/quiet': Fin. [pres.] д-ҭы́нч-уп / д-ҭы́нчы-м, [past] д-ҭы́нчы-н / д-ҭы́нчы-мызт; Non-fin. [pres.] (C1) и-ҭы́нч-у / и-ҭы́нчы-м. а-бзи́а-заа-ра 'to be good': Fin. [pres.] ды-бзи́о-уп / ды-бзи́а-м.

3.2.2.2. Inflection of AP b

á-цәара /á-cʷa-ra/ 'to be sleeping'

Finite forms

		Affirmative	Negative
Present			
Sg	1	сы́-цәо-уп /sə́-cʷa-wp'/ 'I am sleeping'	сы́-цәа-м
	2.M	у́-цәо-уп	у́-цәа-м
	2.F	бы́-цәо-уп	бы́-цәа-м
	3.Human	ды́-цәо-уп	ды́-цәа-м
	3.Non-Human	и́-цәо-уп	и́-цәа-м
Pl	1	ха́-цәо-уп	ха́-цәа-м
	2	шәы́-цәо-уп	шәы́-цәа-м
	3	и́-цәо-уп	и́-цәа-м

Past			
Sg	1	сы́-цәа-н	сы́-цәа-мы-зт
	2.M	у́-цәа-н	у́-цәа-мы-зт
	2.F	бы́-цәа-н	бы́-цәа-мы-зт
	3.Human	ды́-цәа-н	ды́-цәа-мы-зт
	3.Non-Human	и́-цәа-н	и́-цәа-мы-зт
Pl	1	ха́-цәа-н	ха́-цәа-мы-зт
	2	шәы́-цәа-н	шәы́-цәа-мы-зт
	3	и́-цәа-н	и́-цәа-мы-зт

Non-Finite forms

Column I

Present	и́-цәо-у /jə́-cʷa-w/ '(the one) who is sleeping'	и́-цәа-м
Past	и́-цәа-з	и́-цәа-мы-з

With a masdar, the accent goes on the a- at the beginning of the word. For all conjugations, the accent is placed on the pronominal prefix (or the relative prefix).

Other examples: á-ҟазаара /á-q'a-zaa-ra/ 'to exist, to be': Fin. [pres.] ды́-ҟо-уп, и́-ҟо-уп, и́-ҟо-уп, ха́-ҟо-уп / ды́-ҟа-м (ды́-ҟа-ӡа-м), [past] ды́-ҟа-н / ды́-ҟа-мызт; Non-fin. [pres.] (C1) и́-ҟо-у / и́-ҟа-м, [past] (C1) и́-ҟа-з / и́-ҟа-мыз.

3.2.2.3. Inflection of AP c

а-тәара́ /a-t'ʷa-rá/ 'to be sitting'

Finite forms

		Affirmative	Negative
Present			
Sg	1	с-тәо́-уп /s-t'ʷá-wp'/ 'I am sitting'	с-тәа́-м
	2.M	у-тәо́-уп	у-тәа́-м
	2.F	б-тәо́-уп	б-тәа́-м
	3.Human	д-тәо́-уп	д-тәа́-м
	3.Non-Human	и-тәо́-уп	и-тәа́-м
Pl	1	х-тәо́-уп	х-тәа́-м
	2	шә-тәо́-уп	шә-тәа́-м
	3	и-тәо́-уп	и-тәа́-м
Past			
Sg	1	с-тәа́-н	с-тәа́-мы-зт
	2.M	у-тәа́-н	у-тәа́-мы-зт
	2.F	б-тәа́-н	б-тәа́-мы-зт

	3.Human	д-тәá-н	д-тәá-мы-зт
	3.Non-Human	и-тәá-н	и-тәá-мы-зт
Pl	1	х-тәá-н	х-тәá-мы-зт
	2	шә-тәá-н	шә-тәá-мы-зт
	3	и-тәá-н	и-тәá-мы-зт

Non-Finite forms		
Column I		
Present	и-тәó-у /jə-t'ʷá-w/ 'who is sitting'	и-тәá-м
Past	и-тәá-з	и-тәá-мы-з

Notes:

1. The accent goes on the masdar suffix -ра /ra/ (or directly before the -заа /zaa/) for class (ɑ) inherently stative verbs. The accent goes on the root ending through all conjugations.

2. The conjugations of the stative verb derived from the adjective ду́ /a-dә́w/ 'big' are as follows:

Fin. [pres.] и-ду́-уп / и-дýу-м

Non-fin. [pres.] и-ду-ý / и-дуý-м, [past] и-дуý-з / и-дуý-мы-з

Other examples:

(1) а-ҧс-рá 'to be dead': Fin. [pres.] ды-ҧс-ýп / ды-ҧсы́-м, [past] ды-ҧсы́-н / ды-ҧсы́-мы-зт; Non-fin. [pres.] (C1) и-ҧс-ý / и-ҧсы́-м, [past] и-ҧсы́-з / и-ҧсы́-мы-з. а-гá-заа-ра '(*of a road*) to lead': Fin. [pres.] и-гó-уп / и-гó-м, [past] и-гá-н / и-гá-мы-зт; Non-fin. (C1) [pres.] и-гó-у / и-гá-м, [past] и-гá-з / и-гá-мы-з. а-иа-рá 'to be lying': Fin. [pres.] д-иó-уп / д-иá-м, [past] д-иá-н / д-иá-мы-зт; Non-fin. [pres.] (C1) и-иó-у / и-иá-м, [past] (C1) и-иá-з / и-иá-мы-з. а-ҧш-рá 'to be waiting': Fin. [pres.] ды-ҧш-ýп / [past] ды-ҧшы́-н; Non-fin. (C1) [pres.] и-ҧш-ý / и-ҧшы́-м, [past] и-ҧшы́-з / и-ҧшы́-мы-з. а-ха-рá 'to be headed': Fin. [pres.] и-хó-уп / и-хá-м (и-ха-ӡá-м), [past] и-хá-н / и-хá-мызт (-ха-ӡá-мызт); Non-fin. [pres.] (C1) и-хó-у / и-хá-м, [past] (C1) и-хá-з / и-хá-мыз. а-хиа-рá 'to be ready; to be covered': Fin. [pres.] и-хиó-уп / и-хиá-м, [past] и-хиá-н / и-хиá-мызт; Non-fin. [pres.] (C1) и-хиó-у / и-хиá-м, [past] (C1) и-хиá-з / и-хиá-мыз. а-шьҭá-заа-ра 'to be lying': Fin. [pres.] ды-шьҭó-уп / ды-шьҭá-м (-шьҭа-ӡá-м), [past] ды-шьҭá-н / ды-шьҭá-мызт; Non-fin. [pres.] (C1) и-шьҭó-у / и-шьҭá-м, [past] и-шьҭá-з / и-шьҭá-мыз.

(2) а-ҭәы́-заа-ра 'to be full': Fin. [pres.] и-ҭә-ýп / и-ҭәы́-м, [past] и-ҭәы́-н / и-ҭәы́-мызт; Fin. [pres.] (C1) и-ҭәы́-у / и-ҭәы́-м, [past] (C1) и-ҭәы́-з / и-ҭәы́-мы-з. á-ҕәҕәа-заа-ра 'to be strong': **Fin.** [pres.] ды-ҕәҕәó-уп / ды-ҕәҕәá-м, [past] ды-ҕәҕәá-н / ды-ҕәҕәá-мызт; Non-fin. (C1) [pres.] и-ҕәҕәó-у / и-ҕәҕәá-м, [past] и-ҕәҕәá-з / и-ҕәҕәá-мыз. á-цқьа-заа-ра 'to be clean': Fin. [pres.] сы-цқьó-уп / сы-цқьá-м, [past] сы-цқьá-н / сы-цқьá-мызт; Non-fin. (C1) [pres.] и-цқьó-у / и-цқьá-м, [past] и-цқьá-з / и-цқьá-мыз.

3.2.3. Class A-2

This class is the dynamic verb class with a single subject (S) argument. The subject takes the Column I pronominal prefix just like Class A-1. Certain stative verbs belonging to (α) of Class A-1 (see §3.2.2) are also used as dynamic verbs. For example, а-гы́лара /a-gə́la-ra/ 'to stand up', аиара́ /a-ja-rá/ 'to lie down', а-ҧсра́ /a-ps-rá/ 'to die', а-ҧшра́ /a-pš-rá/ 'to wait', а-тәара́ /a-t'ʷa-rá/ 'to sit down', а́-цәара /á-cʷa-ra/ 'to fall asleep, to sleep', etc. In Abkhaz there also are 'labile verbs' that have the same stem and are used as both transitive and intransitive verbs. For example, а-ба́ҳара /a-báħa-ra/ 'to dig' is used as both the intranstive verb дба́ҳауеит /d-báħa-wa-jt'/ '(s)he is digging' and the transitive verb ис/зба́ҳауеит /jə-s/z-báħa-wa-jt'/ 'I am digging it/them'. This intransitive verb form belongs to Class A-2. Labile verbs are discussed in §4.5.

Dynamic verbs have the following morphological characteristics:

(i) The finite forms of present and aorist end with the finite suffix -ит /jt'/.

(ii) The present and imperfect have the dynamic suffix -уа- /wa/.

(iii) The negative marker м- /m/ is placed before the root for the finite forms of aorist, perfect, past indefinite, and pluperfect, as well as for all non-finite forms. The negative marker is placed after the root for all other forms.

(iv) Dynamic Group II of the non-finite forms have -з /z/ at the end.

In keeping with the accent paradigm, this class of verbs can also be split up into AP a, AP b, and AP c.

3.2.3.1. Inflection of AP a

а-гы́лара /a-gə́la-ra/ 'to stand up'

Finite forms

		Affirmative	Negative
Dynamic Group I			
Present			
Sg	1	с-гы́ло-ит /s-gə́la-wa-jt'/ 'I stand up'	с-гы́ло-м /s-gə́la-wa-m/
	2.M	у-гы́ло-ит	у-гы́ло-м
	2.F	б-гы́ло-ит	б-гы́ло-м
	3.Human	д-гы́ло-ит	д-гы́ло-м
	3.Non-Human	и-гы́ло-ит	и-гы́ло-м
Pl	1	х-гы́ло-ит	х-гы́ло-м
	2	шә-гы́ло-ит	шә-гы́ло-м
	3	и-гы́ло-ит	и-гы́ло-м
Aorist			
Sg	1	с-гы́ле-ит /s-gə́la-jt'/	сы-м-гы́ле-ит /sə-m-gə́la-jt'/
	2.M	у-гы́ле-ит	у-м-гы́ле-ит
	2.F	б-гы́ле-ит	бы-м-гы́ле-ит
	3.Human	д-гы́ле-ит	ды-м-гы́ле-ит

	3.Non-Human	и-гы́ле-ит	и-м-гы́ле-ит
Pl	1	х-гы́ле-ит	ха-м-гы́ле-ит
	2	шә-гы́ле-ит	шәы-м-гы́ле-ит
	3	и-гы́ле-ит	и-м-гы́ле-ит
Future I			
Sg	1	с-гы́ла-п	с-гы́ла-ры-м
Future II			
Sg	1	с-гы́ла-шт	с-гы́ла-ша-м
Perfect			
Sg	1	с-гы́ла-хье-ит	сы-м-гы́ла-ц(т)
Dynamic Group II			
Imperfect			
Sg	1	с-гы́ло-н	с-гы́ло-мы-зт
Past Indefinite			
Sg	1	с-гы́ла-н	сы-м-гы́ла-зт
Conditional I			
Sg	1	с-гы́ла-ры-н	с-гыла-ры́-мы-зт
Conditional II			
Sg	1	с-гы́ла-ша-н	с-гыла-ша́-мы-зт
Pluperfect			
Sg	1	с-гы́ла-хьа-н	сы-м-гы́ла-цы-зт

Non-Finite forms		
Dynamic Group I		
Present	и-гы́ло /jə-gə́la-wa/ '(the) one who stands up'	и́-м-гыло
Aorist	и-гы́ла	и́-м-гыла
Future I	и-гы́ла-ра	и́-м-гыла-ра
Future II	и-гы́ла-ша	и́-м-гыла-ша
Perfect	и-гы́ла-хьо-у (-хьа-(ц))	и́-м-гыла-хьо-у (-хьа-(ц))
Dynamic Group II		
Imperfect	и-гы́ло-з	и́-м-гыло-з
Past Indefinite	и-гы́ла-з	и́-м-гыла-з
Conditional I	и-гы́ла-ры-з	и́-м-гыла-ры-з
Conditional II	и-гы́ла-ша-з	и́-м-гыла-ша-з
Pluperfect	и-гы́ла-хьа-з	и́-м-гыла-хьа-з

Notes:

1. Many stems for AP a are -CVCV(C)-, CVC-. In the finite form, there is a strong tendency for the accent to be fixed at the stem excepting in certain tenses. Turning to the non-finite forms, the stem is accented in the affirmative form, while with the negative form the accent is sometimes placed directly before the negative marker and sometimes in the verb stem.

2. The accentuation of this type often occurs with verbs derived from nouns. For example:

а-кака́ҷ-ра 'to bloom': Fin. [pres.] и-кака́ҷ-уе-ит / и-кака́ҷ-уа-м (-ӡо-м), [aor.] и-кака́ҷ-ит / и-м-кака́ҷ-ит (-ӡе-ит); Non-fin. [pres.] (C1) и-кака́ҷ-уа / и-м-кака́ҷ-уа, [aor.] (C1) и-кака́ҷ / и-м-кака́ҷ, [impf.] (C1) и-кака́ҷ-уа-з / и-м-кака́ҷ-уа-з, [past Indef.] (C1) и-кака́ҷы-з / и-м-кака́ҷы-з. (cf. а-кака́ч 'a wild flower')

а-ӡы́шa-ра 'to feel thirsty': Fin. [pres.] д-ӡы́шо-ит / д-ӡы́шо-м (*or* д-ӡы́шa-ӡо-м), [aor.] д-ӡы́ше-ит / ды-м-ӡы́ше-ит (ды-м-ӡы́шa-ӡе-ит); Non-fin. [pres.] (C1) и-ӡы́шо / и-м-ӡы́шо, [aor.] (C1) и-ӡы́шa / и-м-ӡы́шa. (cf. а-ӡы́шa 'thirst')

Other examples:

а-ба́ҳа-ра 'to dig': Fin. [pres.] д-ба́ҳа-уе-ит / д-ба́ҳа-уа-м (-ба́ҳа-ӡо-м), [aor.] д-ба́ҳа-ит / ды-м-ба́ҳа-ит (-ба́ҳа-ӡе-ит); Non-fin. [pres.] (C1) и-ба́ҳа-уа / и-м-ба́ҳа-уа, [aor.] и-ба́ҳа / и-м-ба́ҳа, [impf.] и-ба́ҳа-уа-з / и-м-ба́ҳа-уа-з, [past indef.] и-ба́ҳа-з / и-м-ба́ҳа-з.

а-гәа́ҟ-ра 'to worry': Fin. [pres.] д-гәа́ҟ-уе-ит / д-гәа́ҟ-уа-м, [aor.] д-гәа́ҟ-ит / ды-м-гәа́ҟ-ит; Non-fin. [pres.] (C1) и-гәа́ҟ-уа / и-м-гәа́ҟ-уа, [aor.] (C1) и-гәа́ҟ / и-м-гәа́ҟ, [impf.] (C1) и-гәа́ҟ-уа-з / и-м-гәа́ҟ-уа-з, [past indef.] (C1) и-гәа́ҟы-з / и-м-гәа́ҟы-з.

а-ды́с-ра 'to go numb': Fin. [pres.] и-ды́с-уе-ит / и-ды́с-уа-м, [aor.] и-ды́с-ит, д-ды́с-ит / и-м-ды́с-ит, ды-м-ды́с-ит; Non-fin. [pres.] (C1) и-ды́с-уа / и-м-ды́с-уа.

а-кьа́ҭа-ра 'to go out, to be extinguished': Fin. [pres.] и-кьа́ҭо-ит / и-кьа́ҭо-м, [aor.] и-кьа́ҭе-ит / и-м-кьа́ҭе-ит; Non-fin. [pres.] (C1) и-кьа́ҭо / и-м-кьа́ҭо.

а-кьи́-ра 'to mew': Fin. [pres.] и-кьи́-уе-ит / и-кьи́-уа-м, [aor.] и-кьи́-ит / и-м-кьи́-ит; Non-fin. (C1) [pres.] и-кьи́-уа / и́-м-кьи-уа.

а-леиҩе́и-ра 'to take a walk': Fin. [pres.] д-леиҩе́и-уе-ит / д-леиҩе́и-уа-м (-ӡо-м), [aor.] д-леиҩе́и-ит / ды-м-леиҩе́и-ит (-ӡе-ит); Non-fin. (C1) [pres.] и́-леиҩе́и-уа / и́-м-леиҩе́и-уа, [aor.] и́-леиҩе́и / и́-м-леиҩе́и, [impf.] и́-леиҩе́и-уа-з / и́-м-леиҩе́и-уа-з, [past indef.] и́-леиҩе́и-з / и́-м-леиҩе́и-з.

а-ны́ҟәа-ра 'to go': Fin. [pres.] д-ны́ҟәо-ит / д-ны́ҟәо-м (-ны́ҟәа-ӡо-м), [aor.] д-ны́ҟәе-ит / ды-м-ны́ҟәе-ит; Non-fin. (C1) [pres.] и-ны́ҟәо / и́-м-ныҟәо, [aor.] и-ны́ҟәа / и́-м-ныҟәа, [fut.1] и-ны́ҟәа-ра / и́-м-ныҟәа-ра, [fut.2] и-ны́ҟәа-ша / и́-м-ныҟәа-ша, [perf.] и-ны́ҟәа-хьоу (-хьа(ц)) / и́-м-ныҟәа-хьоу (-хьа(ц)), [impf.] и-ны́ҟәо-з / и́-м-ныҟәо-з, [past indef.] и-ны́ҟәа-з / и́-м-ныҟәа-з, [cond.1] и-ны́ҟәа-ры-з / и́-м-ныҟәа-ры-з, [cond.2] и-ны́ҟәа-ша-з / и́-м-ныҟәа-ша-з, [plupf.] и-ны́ҟәа-хьа-з / и́-м-ныҟәа-хьа-з.

а-ха́ха-ра 'to be engaged in spinning': Fin. [pres.] д-ха́хо-ит / д-ха́хо-м (-ха́ха-ӡо-м), [aor.] д-ха́хе-ит / ды-м-ха́хе-ит (-ха́ха-ӡе-ит); Non-fin. (C1) [pres.] и-ха́хо / и́-м-хахо, [aor.] и-ха́ха / и́-м-хаха, [impf.] и-ха́хо-з / и́-м-хахо-з, [past indef.] и-ха́ха-з / и́-м-хаха-з.

а́-хәмар-ра 'to play': Fin. [pres.] ды-хәма́р-уе-ит / ды-хәма́р-уа-м (-хәма́р-ӡо-м), [aor.] ды-хәма́р-ит / д-мы-хәма́р-ит; Non-fin. (C1) [pres.] и-хәма́р-уа / и́-мы-хәмар-уа, [aor.] и-хәма́р / и́-мы-хәмар, [impf.] и-хәма́р-уа-з / и́-мы-хәмар-уа-з, [past indef.] и-хәма́ры-з / и́-мы-хәмары-з.

а-хәы́ц-ра 'to think': Fin. [pres.] д-хәы́ц-уе-ит / д-хәы́ц-уа-м (-хәы́ц-ӡо-м), [aor.] д-хәы́ц-ит / ды-м-хәы́ц-ит (-хәы́ц-ӡе-ит); Non-fin. [pres.] (C1) и-хәы́ц-уа / и-м-хәы́ц-уа, [aor.] (C1) и-хәы́ц / и-м-хәы́ц.

а́-ҳасаб-ра 'to solve': Fin. [pres.] д-ҳаса́б-уе-ит /д-ҳаса́б-уа-м, [aor.] д-ҳаса́б-ит / ды-м-ҳаса́б-ит; Non-fin. [pres.] (C1) и-ҳаса́б-уа / и-м-ҳаса́б-уа.

а-цәа́жәа-ра 'to speak': Fin. [pres.] х-цәа́жәо-ит / х-цәа́жәо-м, [aor.] х-цәа́жәе-ит / ха-м-цәа́жәе-ит; Non-fin. [pres.] (C1) и-цәа́жәо / и-м-цәа́жәо.

а-ҵа́а-ра 'to freeze': Fin. [pres.] и-ҵа́а-уе-ит / и-ҵа́а-уа-м, [aor.] и-ҵа́а-ит / и-м-ҵа́а-ит (-ҵа́а-ӡе-ит); Non-fin. (C1) [pres.] и-ҵа́а-уа / и-м-ҵа́а-уа, [aor.] и-ҵа́а / и-м-ҵа́а, [impf.] и-ҵа́а-уа-з / и-м-ҵа́а-уа-з, [past indef.] и-ҵа́а-з / и-м-ҵа́а-з.

а-ҵәы́уа-ра 'to cry': Fin. [pres.] д-ҵәы́уо-ит / д-ҵәы́уо-м, [aor.] д-ҵәы́уе-ит / ды-м-ҵәы́уе-ит; Non-fin. (C1) [pres.] и-ҵәы́уо / и́-м-ҵәыуо, [aor.] и-ҵәы́уа / и́-м-ҵәыуа, [impf.] и-ҵәы́уо-з / и́-м-ҵәыуо-з, [past indef.] и-ҵәы́уа-з / и́-м-ҵәыуа-з.

3.2.3.2. Inflection of AP b

а́-ҧара /á-pa-ra/ 'to jump'

Finite forms

		Affirmative	Negative
Dynamic Group I			
Present			
Sg	1	сы́-ҧо-ит /sə́-pa-wa-jt'/ 'I jump'	сы́-ҧо-м /sə́-pa-wa-m/
	2.M	у́-ҧо-ит	у́-ҧо-м
	2.F	бы́-ҧо-ит	бы́-ҧо-м
	3.Human	ды́-ҧо-ит	ды́-ҧо-м
	3.Non-Human	и́-ҧо-ит	и́-ҧо-м
Pl	1	ха́-ҧо-ит	ха́-ҧо-м
	2	шәы́-ҧо-ит	шәы́-ҧо-м
	3	и́-ҧо-ит	и́-ҧо-м
Aorist			
Sg	1	сы́-ҧе-ит /sə́-pa-jt'/	с-мы́-ҧе-ит /s-mə́-pa-jt'/
	2.M	у́-ҧе-ит	у-мы́-ҧе-ит
	2.F	бы́-ҧе-ит	б-мы́-ҧе-ит
	3.Human	ды́-ҧе-ит	д-мы́-ҧе-ит
	3.Non-Human	и́-ҧе-ит	и-мы́-ҧе-ит
Pl	1	ха́-ҧе-ит	х-мы́-ҧе-ит
	2	шәы́-ҧе-ит	шә-мы́-ҧе-ит
	3	и́-ҧе-ит	и-мы́-ҧе-ит

Future I		
Sg 1	сы́-ҧа-п	сы́-ҧа-ры-м
Future II		
Sg 1	сы́-ҧа-шт	сы́-ҧа-ша-м
Perfect		
Sg 1	сы́-ҧа-хье-ит	с-мы́-ҧа-ӡа-ц(т)
Dynamic Group II		
Imperfect		
Sg 1	сы́-ҧо-н	сы́-ҧо-мы-зт
Past Indefinite		
Sg 1	сы́-ҧа-н	с-мы́-ҧа-зт
Conditional I		
Sg 1	сы́-ҧа-ры-н	сы́-ҧа-ры-мы-зт
Conditional II		
Sg 1	сы́-ҧа-ша-н	сы́-ҧа-ша-мы-зт
Pluperfect		
Sg 1	сы́-ҧа-хьа-н	с-мы́-ҧа-цы-зт
Non-Finite forms		
Dynamic Group I		
Present	и́-ҧо ‘who jumps’	и-мы́-ҧо
Aorist	и́-ҧа	и-мы́-ҧа
Future I	и́-ҧа-ра	и-мы́-ҧа-ра
Future II	и́-ҧа-ша	и-мы́-ҧа-ша
Perfect	и́-ҧа-хьо-у (-хьа-(п))	и-мы́-ҧа-хьо-у (-хьа-(п))
Dynamic Group II		
Imperfect	и́-ҧо-з	и-мы́-ҧо-з
Past Indefinite	и́-ҧа-з	и-мы́-ҧа-з
Conditional I	и́-ҧа-ры-з	и-мы́-ҧа-ры-з
Conditional II	и́-ҧа-ша-з	и-мы́-ҧа-ша-з
Pluperfect	и́-ҧа-хьа-з	и-мы́-ҧа-хьа-з

Notes:

1. The accent in finite forms is placed on the prefix immediately before the root. It is placed on the article for the masdar (this is not to say that because there is an accent on the masdar article that all are counted as AP b).

2. Very few verbs are of this type.

Other examples:

á-ҩ-ра ‘to run’: Fin. [pres.] сы́-ҩ-уе-ит, ды́-ҩ-уе-ит, ҳá-ҩ-уе-ит, и́-ҩ-уе-ит / сы́-ҩ-уа-м (-ҩ-ӡо-м), [aor.] ды́-ҩ-ит, ҳá-ҩ-ит / д-мы́-ҩ-ит, ҳ-мы́-ҩ-ит, [fut.1] сы́-ҩ-п / сы́-ҩ-рым, [fut.2] сы́-ҩ-шт / сы́-

ҩ-шам, [perf.] сы́-ҩ-хьеит / с-мы́-ҩ-ц(т), [impf.] сы́-ҩ-уа-н / сы́-ҩ-уа-мызт, [past indef.] сы́-ҩы-н / с-мы́-ҩы-зт, [cond.1] сы́-ҩ-рын / сы́-ҩ-рымызт, [cond.2] сы́-ҩ-шан / сы́-ҩ-шамызт, [plupf.] сы́-ҩ-хьан / с-мы́-ҩ-цызт; Non-fin. (C1) [pres.] и-ҩ-уа́ / и́-мы-ҩ-уа, [aor.] и-ҩы́ / и́-мы-ҩ, [fut.1] и-ҩ-ра́ / и́-мы-ҩ-ра, [fut.2] и-ҩы́-ша / и́-м-ҩы-ша, [perf.] и-ҩ-хьо́у (-хьа́(ц)) / и́-мы-ҩ-хьоу (-хьа(ц)), [impf.] и-ҩ-уа́-з / и́-мы-ҩ-уа-з, [past indef.] и-ҩы́-з / и́-м-ҩы-з, [cond.1] и́-ҩ-ры-з / и́-мы-ҩ-ры-з, [cond.2] и-ҩы́-ша-з / и́-м-ҩы-ша-з, [plupf.] и-ҩ-хьа́-з / и́-мы-ҩ-хьа-з.

а́-ӡ-ра 'to disappear': Fin. [pres.] ды́-ӡ-уе-ит, ха́-ӡ-уе-ит, [aor.] ды́-ӡ-ит / д-мы́-ӡ-ит, ха́-ӡ-ит / х-мы́-ӡ-ит, [fut.1] ды́-ӡ-р, [fut.2] ды́-ӡ-шт, [perf.] ды́-ӡ-хьеит, [impf.] ды́-ӡ-уан, [past indef.] ды́-ӡы-н, [cond.1] ды́-ӡ-рын, [cond.2] ды́-ӡ-шан, [plupf.] ды́-ӡ-хьан; Non-fin. (C1) [pres.] и́-ӡ-уа / и-мы́-ӡ-уа, [aor.] и́-ӡ / и-мы́-ӡ, [fut.1] и́-ӡ-ра / и-мы́-ӡ-ра, [fut.2] и́-ӡ-ша / и-мы́-ӡ-ша, [perf.] и́-ӡ-хьоу (-хьа(ц)) / и-мы́-ӡ-хьоу (-хьа(ц)), [impf.] и́-ӡ-уа-з / и-мы́-ӡ-уа-з, [past indef.] и́-ӡы-з / и-мы́-ӡы-з, [cond.1] и́-ӡ-ры-з / и-мы́-ӡ-ры-з, [cond.2] и́-ӡ-ша-з / и-мы́-ӡ-ша-з, [plupf.] и́-ӡ-хьа-з / и-мы́-ӡ-хьа-з.

а́-цәа-ра 'to fall asleep; to sleep': Fin. [pres.] ды́-цәо-ит, с-цәо́-ит / ды́-цәо-м, [aor.] ды́-цәе-ит, и́-цәе-ит / д-мы́-цәе-ит; Non-fin. (C1) [pres.] и́-цәо / и-мы́-цәо, [aor.] и́-цәа / и-мы́-цәа, [fut.1] и́-цәа-ра / и-мы́-цәа-ра, [fut.2] и́-цәа-ша / и-мы́-цәа-ша, [perf.] и́-цәа-хьоу (-хьа(ц)) / и-мы́-цәа-хьоу (-хьа(ц)), [impf.] и́-цәо-з / и-мы́-цәо-з, [past indef.] и́-цәа-з / и-мы́-цәа-з, [cond.1] и́-цәа-ры-з / и-мы́-цәа-ры-з, [cond.2] и́-цәа-ша-з / и-мы́-цәа-ша-з, [plupf.] и́-цәа-хьа-з / и-мы́-цәа-хьа-з.

3.2.3.3. Inflection of AP c

а-кьра́ /a-kʲ-rá/ 'to sigh'

Finite forms

		Affirmative	Negative
Dynamic Group I			
Present			
Sg	1	с-кь-уе́-ит /s-kʲ-wá-jt'/ 'I sigh'	с-кь-уа́-м /s-kʲ-wá-m/
	2.M	у-кь-уе́-ит	у-кь-уа́-м
	2.F	бы-кь-уе́-ит	бы-кь-уа́-м
	3.Human	ды-кь-уе́-ит	ды-кь-уа́-м
	3.Non-Human	и-кь-уе́-ит	и-кь-уа́-м
Pl	1	ҳа-кь-уе́-ит	ҳа-кь-уа́-м
	2	шәы-кь-уе́-ит	шәы-кь-уа́-м
	3	и-кь-уе́-ит	и-кь-уа́-м
Aorist			
Sg	1	с-кь-и́т /s-kʲə́-jt'/	сы-м-кь-и́т /sə-m-kʲə́-jt'/
	2.M	у-кь-и́т	у-м-кь-и́т
	2.F	б-кь-и́т	бы-м-кь-и́т

	3.Human	д-кь-и́т	ды-м-кь-и́т
	3.Non-Human	и-кь-и́т	и-м-кь-и́т
Pl	1	ҳ-кь-и́т	ҳа-м-кь-и́т
	2	шә-кь-и́т	шәы-м-кь-и́т
	3	и-кь-и́т	и-м-кь-и́т

Future I

Sg	1	с-ҟьы́-п	с-кь-ры́-м
	2.F	б-ҟьы́-п	бы-кь-ры́-м
	3.Human	д-ҟьы́-п	ды-кь-ры́-м
	3.Non-Human	и-ҟьы́-п	и-кь-ры́-м
Pl	1	ҳ-ҟьы́-п	ҳа-кь-ры́-м
	2	шә-ҟьы́-п	шәы-кь-ры́-м
	3.	и-ҟьы́-п	и-кь-ры́-м

Future II

Sg	1	с-ҟьы́-шт	с-ҟьы́-ша-м
	2.M	у-ҟьы́-шт	у-ҟьы́-ша-м
	2.F	б-ҟьы́-шт	б-ҟьы́-ша-м
	3.Human	д-ҟьы́-шт	д-ҟьы́-ша-м
	3.Non-Human	и-ҟьы́-шт	и-ҟьы́-ша-м
Pl	1	ҳ-ҟьы́-шт	ҳ-ҟьы́-ша-м
	2	шә-ҟьы́-шт	шә-ҟьы́-ша-м
	3	и-ҟьы́-шт	и-ҟьы́-ша-м

Perfect

Sg	1	сы-кь-хьé-ит	сы-м-ҟьы́-ц(т)
	2.M	у-кь-хьé-ит	у-м-ҟьы́-ц(т)
	2.F	бы-кь-хьé-ит	бы-м-ҟьы́-ц(т)
	3.Human	ды-кь-хьé-ит	ды-м-ҟьы́-ц(т)
	3.Non-Human	и-кь-хьé-ит	и-м-ҟьы́-ц(т)
Pl	1	ҳа-кь-хьé-ит	ҳа-м-ҟьы́-ц(т)
	2	шәы-кь-хьé-ит	шәы-м-ҟьы́-ц(т)
	3	и-кь-хьé-ит	и-м-ҟьы́-ц(т)

Dynamic Group II

Imperfect

Sg	1	сы-кь-уа́-н	с-кь-уа́-мы-зт
	2.F	бы-кь-уа́-н	бы-кь-уа́-мы-зт
	3.Human	ды-кь-уа́-н	ды-кь-уа́-мы-зт
	3.Non-Human	и-кь-уа́-н	и-кь-уа́-мы-зт
Pl	1	ҳа-кь-уа́-н	ҳа-кь-уа́-мы-зт
	2	шәы-кь-уа́-н	шәы-кь-уа́-мы-зт
	3	и-кь-уа́-н	и-кь-уа́-мы-зт

Past Indefinite			
Sg	1	с-қьы́-н	сы-м-қьы́-зт
	2.F	б-қьы́-н	бы-м-қьы́-зт
	3.Human	д-қьы́-н	ды-м-қьы́-зт
Pl	1	ҳ-қьы́-н	ҳа-м-қьы́-зт
	2	шә-қьы́-н	шәы-м-қьы́-зт
Conditional I			
Sg	1	сы-қь-ры́-н	с-қь-ры́-мы-зт
	2.F	бы-қь-ры́-н	б-қь-ры́-мы-зт
	3.Human	ды-қь-ры́-н	д-қь-ры́-мы-зт
Pl	1	ҳа-қь-ры́-н	ҳа-қь-ры́-мы-зт
	2	шәы-қь-ры́-н	шәы-қь-ры́-мы-зт
Conditional II			
Sg	1	с-қьы́-ша-н	с-қьы́-ша-мы-зт
	2.F	б-қьы́-ша-н	б-қьы́-ша-мы-зт
	3.Human	д-қьы́-ша-н	д-қьы́-ша-мы-зт
Pl	1	ҳ-қьы́-ша-н	ҳ-қьы́-ша-мы-зт
	2	шә-қьы́-ша-н	шә-қьы́-ша-мы-зт
Pluperfect			
Sg	1	сы-қь-хьа́-н	сы-м-қьы́-цы-зт
	2.F	бы-қь-хьа́-н	бы-м-қьы́-цы-зт
	3.Human	ды-қь-хьа́-н	ды-м-қьы́-цы-зт
	3.Non-Human	и-қь-хьа́-н	и-м-қьы́-цы-зт
Pl	1	ҳа-қь-хьа́-н	ҳа-м-қьы́-цы-зт
	2	шәы-қь-хьа́-н	шәы-м-қьы́-цы-зт
Non-Finite forms			
Dynamic Group I			
Present		и-қь-уа́ 'who sighs'	и́-м-қь-уа
Aorist		и-қьы́	и́-м-қь
Future I		и-қь-ра́	и́-м-қь-ра
Future II		и-қьы́-ша	и́-м-қьы-ша
Perfect		и-қь-хьо́у (-хьа́(ц))	и́-м-қь-хьоу (-хьа(ц))
Dynamic Group II			
Imperfect		и-қь-уа́-з	и́-м-қь-уа-з
Past Indefinite		и-қьы́-з	и́-м-қьы-з
Conditional I		и-қь-ры́-з	и́-м-қь-ры-з
Conditional II		и-қьы́-ша-з	и́-м-қьы-ша-з
Pluperfect		и-қь-хьа́-з	и́-м-қь-хьа-з

Notes:

1. According to our informant, the schwa may appear after the pronominal prefixes in the first-person plural, as well as both the singular and the plural in the second- and third-persons, but it does not appear in the first-person singular. See, for example, the finite form-present sg. 1. сқьуе́ит /s-kʲ-wá-jt'/, cf. sg. 2. бықьуе́ит /bə-kʲ-wá-jt'/, pl. 1. ҳақьуе́ит /ħə-kʲ-wá-jt'/. See §1.1.1.1 regarding the conditions of the presence or absence of a schwa.

2. For the masdar, in some cases (i) the accent is on the masdar suffix -ра /ra/ at the end, and in some cases (ii) it is on the article. The elements on which the accent in finite forms goes are the dynamic marker -уа /wa/, the future I marker -ры(м) /rə(m)/, the perfect marker -хьа- /xʲá/, and the conditional I marker -ры- /rə/. A schwa with an accent appears at the end of the root in those cases where there is no marker and the root ends in a consonant. When the root ends in a vowel, excepting the aforementioned markers the accent goes on the root-ending vowel.

Other examples:

(i) Words where the masdar accent is on the suffix -ра:

а-ӡҭ-ра́ 'to melt': Fin. [pres.] и-ӡт-уе́-ит / и-ӡҭ-уа́-м, д-ӡыт-уе́-ит / д-ӡыҭ-уа́-м, [aor.] и-ӡт-и́т / и-м-ӡт-и́т, д-ӡыт-и́т / ды-м-ӡыҭ-и́т; Non-fin. (C1) [pres.] и-ӡт-уа́ / и-м-ӡҭ-уа́, [aor.] и-ӡҭы́ / и-м-ӡты́, [impf.] и-ӡҭ-уа́-з / и́-м-ӡҭ-уа-з, [past indef.] и-ӡҭы́-з / и́-м-ӡҭы-з.

а-и-ра́ 'to be born': Fin. [pres.] с-и-уе́-ит, д-и-уе́-ит / д-и-уа́-м, [aor.] с-и-и́т /s-jə́-jt'/, д-и-и́т / ды-м-и́-т, [fut.1] д-и́-п / д-и-ры́м, [fut.2] д-и́-шт / д-и́-шам, [perf.] д-и-хье́-ит / ды-м-и́-ц(т), [impf.] д-и-уа́н / д-и-уа́мызт, [past indef.] д-и́-н / ды-м-и́-зт, [cond.1] д-и-ры́н / д-и-ры́мызт, [cond.2] д-и́-шан / д-и́-шаммызт, [plupf.] д-и-хьа́н / ды-м-и́-цызт; Non-fin. (C1) [pres.] и-и-уа́ / и́-м-и-уа, [aor.] и-и́ / и́-м-и, [fut.1] и-и-ра́ / и́-м-и-ра, [fut.2] и-и́-ша / и́-м-и-ша, [perf.] и-и-хьо́у (-хьа́(ц)) / и́-м-и-хьоу (-хьа(ц)), [impf.] и-и-уа́-з / и́-м-и-уа-з, [past indef.] и-и́-з / и́-м-и-з, [cond.1] и-и-ры́-з / и́-м-и-ры-з, [cond.2] и-и́-ша-з / и́-м-и-ша-з, [plupf.] и-и-хьа́-з / и́-м-и-хьа-з.

а-қә-ра́ 'to swear': Fin. [pres.] д-қә-уе́-ит / д-қә-уа́-м, [aor.] д-қә-и́т / ды-м-қә-и́т; Non-fin. [pres.] (C1) и-қә-уа́ / и́-м-қә-уа, [aor.] и-қәы́ / и-м-қәы́.

а-ҧс-ра́ 'to die': Fin. [pres.] ды-ҧс-уе́-ит, ҳа-ҧс-уе́-ит / ды-ҧс-уа́-м, [aor.] ды-ҧс-и́т / ды-м-ҧс-и́т, [fut.1] ды-ҧсы́-п / ды-ҧс-ры́м, [fut.2] ды-ҧсы́-шт / ды-ҧсы́-шам, [perf.] ды-ҧс-хье́ит / ды-м-ҧсы́-ц(т), [impf.] ды-ҧс-уа́-н / ды-ҧс-уа́-мызт, [past indef.] ды-ҧсы́-н / ды-м-ҧсы́-зт, [cond.1] ды-ҧс-ры́н / ды-ҧс-ры́мызт, [cond.2] ды-ҧсы́-шан / ды-ҧсы́-шамызт, [plupf.] ды-ҧс-хьа́н / ды-м-ҧсы́-цызт; Non-fin. (C1) [pres.] и-ҧс-уа́ / и́-м-ҧс-уа, [aor.] и-ҧсы́ / и́-м-ҧс, [fut.1] и-ҧс-ра́ / и́-м-ҧс-ра, [fut.2] и-ҧсы́-ша / и́-м-ҧс-ша, [perf.] и-ҧс-хьо́у (-хьа́(ц)) / и́-м-ҧс-хьоу (-хьа(ц)), [impf.] и-ҧс-уа́-з / и́-м-ҧс-уа-з, [past indef.] и-ҧсы́-з / и́-м-ҧсы-з, [cond.1] и-ҧс-ры́-з / и́-м-ҧс-ры-з, [cond.2] и-ҧсы́-ша-з / и́-м-ҧсы-ша-з, [plupf.] и-ҧс-хьа́-з / и́-м-ҧс-хьа-з.

а-ҧха-ра́ 'to shine': Fin. [pres.] ды-ҧхо́-ит / ды-ҧхо́-м, [aor.] ды-ҧхе́-ит / ды-м-ҧхе́-ит, [fut.1] ды-ҧха́-п / ды-ҧха-ры́м, [fut.2] ды-ҧха́-шт / ды-ҧха́-шам, [perf.] ды-ҧха-хье́ит / ды-м-ҧха́-ц(т), [impf.] ды-ҧхо́-н / ды-ҧхо́-мызт, [past indef.] ды-ҧха́-н / ды-м-ҧха́-зт, [cond.1] ды-ҧха-ры́н / ды-ҧха-ры́мызт, [cond.2] ды-ҧха́-шан / ды-ҧха́-шамызт, [plupf.] ды-ҧха-хьа́н / ды-м-ҧха́-цызт; Non-fin. (C1) [pres.] и́-ҧхо / и́-м-ҧхо, [aor.] и-ҧха́ / и́-м-ҧха, [fut.1] и-ҧха-ра́ / и́-м-ҧха-ра, [fut.2] и-ҧха́-ша / и́-м-ҧха-ша, [perf.] и-ҧха-хьо́у (-хьа́(ц)) / и́-м-ҧха-хьоу (-хьа(ц)), [impf.] и-ҧхо́-з / и́-м-ҧхо-з, [past indef.] и-ҧха́-з / и́-м-ҧха-з, [cond.1] и-ҧха-ры́-з / и́-м-ҧха-ры-з, [cond.2] и-ҧха́-ша-з / и́-м-ҧха-ша-з, [plupf.] и-ҧха-хьа́-з / и́-м-ҧха-хьа-з.

а-ҧш-ра́ 'to look': Fin. [pres.] ды-ҧш-уе́-ит / ды-ҧш-уа́-м, [aor.] ды-ҧш-и́т / ды́-м-ҧш-ит; Non-fin. (C1) [pres.] и-ҧш-уа́ / и́-м-ҧш-уа, [aor.] и-ҧшы́ / и́-м-ҧш, [fut.1] и-ҧш-ра́ / и́-м-ҧш-ра, [fut.2] и-ҧшы́-ша / и́-м-ҧшы-ша, [perf.] и-ҧш-хьо́у (-хьа́(ц)) / и́-м-ҧш-хьоу (-хьа(ц)), [impf.] и-ҧш-уа́-з / и́-м-ҧш-уа-з, [past indef.] и-ҧшы́-з / и́-м-ҧшы-з, [cond.1] и-ҧш-ры́-з / и́-м-ҧш-ры-з, [cond.2] и-ҧшы́-ша-з / и́-м-ҧшы-ша-з, [plupf.] и-ҧш-хьа́-з / и́-м-ҧш-хьа-з.

а́-ҧыр-ра 'to fly': Fin. [pres.] с-ҧыр-уе́-ит, и-ҧыр-уе́-ит / с-ҧыр-уа́-м, [aor.] сы-ҧр-и́т / сы-м-ҧр-и́т, [fut.1] сы-ҧры́-п / с-ҧыр-ры́м, [fut.2] сы-ҧы́р-шт / сы-ҧры́-шам, [perf.] с-ҧыр-хье́ит / сы-м-ҧры́-ц(т), [impf.] с-ҧыр-уа́н / с-ҧыр-уа́мызт, [past indef.] сы-ҧры́-н / сы-ҧры́-зт, [cond.1] с-ҧыр-ры́н / с-ҧыр-ры́мызт, [cond.2] сы-ҧры́-шан / сы-ҧры́-шамызт, [plupf.] с-ҧыр-хьа́н / сы-м-ҧры́-цызт; Non-fin. (C1) [pres.] и-ҧр-уа́ / и́-м-ҧ(ы)р-уа, [aor.] и-ҧры́ / и́-м-ҧ(ы)р, [fut.1] и-ҧр-ра́ / и́-м-ҧ(ы)р-ра, [fut.2] и-ҧры́-ша / и́-м-ҧры-ша, [perf.] и́-ҧр-хьоу (-хьа(ц)) / и́-м-ҧ(ы)р-хьоу (-хьа(ц)), [impf.] и-ҧр-уа́-з / и́-м-ҧ(ы)р-уа-з, [past indef.] и-ҧры́-з / и́-м-ҧры-з, [cond.1] и-ҧр-ры́-з / и́-м-ҧ(ы)р-ры-з, [cond.2] и-ҧры́-ша-з / и́-м-ҧры-ша-з, [plupf.] и́-ҧр-хьа-з / и́-м-ҧ(ы)р-хьа-з.

а-с-ра́ 'to weave': Fin. [pres.] сы-с-уе́-ит / сы-с-уа́-м, [aor.] с-с-и́т / сы-м-с-и́т, [fut.1] с-сы́-п / сы-с-ры́м, [fut.2] с-сы́-шт / с-сы́-шам, [perf.] сы-с-хье́-ит / сы-м-сы́-ц(т), [impf.] с(ы)-с-уа́-н / с(ы)-с-уа́-мызт, [past indef.] с-сы́-н, [cond.1] сы-с-ры́н / сы-с-ры́мызт, [cond.2] с-сы-ша́н / с-сы-ша́мызт, [plupf.] сы-с-хьа́-н / сы-м-сы́-цызт; Non-fin. (C1) [pres.] и-с-уа́ / и́-м-с-уа, [aor.] и-сы́ / и́-м-с, [fut.1] и-с-ра́ / и́-м-с-ра, [fut.2] и-сы́-ша / и́-м-сы-ша, [perf.] и-с-хьо́-у (-хьа́(ц)) / и́-м-с-хьоу (-хьа(ц)), [impf.] и-с-уа́-з / и́-м-с-уа-з, [past indef.] и-сы́-з / и́-м-сы-з, [cond.1] и-с-ры́-з / и́-м-с-ры-з, [cond.2] и-сы́-ша-з / и́-м-сы-ша-з, [plupf.] и-с-хьа́-з / и́-м-с-хьа-з.

а-тәа-ра́ 'to sit down': Fin. [pres.] д-тәо́-ит / д-тәо́-м (-тәа-ӡо́-м), [aor.] д-тәе́-ит / ды-м-тәе́-ит.

а-ҭәа-ра́ 'to melt': Fin. [pres.] и-ҭәо́-ит / и-ҭәо́-м (-ҭәа-ӡо́-м), [aor.] и-ҭәе́-ит / и-м-ҭәе́-ит (-ҭәа-ӡе́-ит); Non-fin. [pres.] (C1) и-ҭәо́ / и-м-ҭәо́, [aor.] (C1) и-ҭәа́ / и-м-ҭәа́.

а-ҭә-ра́ 'to be filled': Fin. [pres.] и-ҭә-уе́-ит / и-ҭә-уа́-м (-ӡо́-м), [aor.] и-ҭә-и́т / и-м-ҭә-и́т (-ӡе́-ит); Non-fin. [pres.] (C1) и-ҭә-уа́ / и-м-ҭә-уа́, [aor.] (C1) и-ҭәы́ / и-м-ҭәы́.

а-ш-ра́ 'to bark': Fin. [pres.] и-ш-уе́-ит / и-ш-уа́-м (-ш-ӡо́-м), [aor.] и-ш-и́т / и-м-ш-и́т (-ш-ӡе́-ит); Non-fin. (C1) [pres.] и-ш-уа́ / и́-м-ш-уа, [aor.] и-шы́ / и́-м-ш, [impf.] и-ш-уа́-з / и́-м-ш-уа-з, [past indef.] и-шы́-з / и́-м-шы-з.

а-баа-ра́ 'to go bad': Fin. [pres.] д-баа-уе́-ит, и-баа-уе́-ит / и-баа-уа́-м (-баа-ӡо́-м), [aor.] и-баа́-ит / и-м-баа́-ит, [fut.1] и-баа́-п / и-баа-ры́м, [fut.2] и-баа́-шт / и-баа́-шам, [perf.] и-баа-хье́ит / и-м-баа́-ц(т), [impf.] и-баа-уа́-н / и-баа-уа́-мызт, [past indef.] и-баа́-н / и-баа́-зт, [cond.1] и-баа-ры́н / и-баа-ры́мызт, [cond.2] и-баа́-шан / и-баа́-шамызт, [plupf.] и-баа-хьа́н / и-м-баа́-цызт; Non-fin. (C1) [pres.] и-баа-уа́ / и́-м-баа-уа, [aor.] и-баа́ / и́-м-баа, [fut.1] и-баа-ра́ / и́-м-баа-ра, [fut.2] и-баа́-ша / и́-м-баа-ша, [perf.] и-баа́-хьоу (-хьа(ц)) / и́-м-баа-хьоу (-хьа(ц)), [impf.] и-баа-уа́-з / и́-м-баа-уа-з, [past indef.] и-баа́-з / и́-м-баа-з, [cond.1] и-баа́-ры-з / и́-м-баа-ры-з, [cond.2] и-баа́-ша-з / и́-м-баа-ша-з, [plupf.] и-баа́-хьа-з / и́-м-баа-хьа-з.

а-хә-ра́ ' to graze': Fin. [pres.] и-хә-уе́-ит / и-хә-уа́-м (-хә-ӡо́-м), [aor.] и-хә-и́т / и-м-хә-и́т (-хәʒé-ит); Non-fin. [pres.] (C1) и-хə-уá / и-м-хə-уá, [aor.] (C1) и-хəы́ / и-м-хəы́.

а-ҵаа-рá 'to ask; to tell fortunes': Fin. [pres.] д-ҵаа-уé-ит / д-ҵаа-уá-м, [aor.] д-ҵаá-ит / ды-м-ҵаá-ит; Non-fin. [pres.] (C1) и-ҵаа-уá / и-м-ҵаа-уá, [aor.] и-ҵаá / и-м-ҵаá.

а-ҵа-рá 'to lay eggs': Fin. [pres.] и-ҵó-ит / и-ҵó-м (-ҵа-ʒó-м), [aor.] и-ҵé-ит, с-ҵé-ит / и-м-ҵé-ит (-ҵа-ʒé-ит), сы-м-ҵé-ит; Non-fin. [pres.] (C1) и-ҵó / и-м-ҵó, [aor.] (C1) и-ҵá / и-м-ҵá, [impf.] (C1) и-ҵó-з / и-м-ҵó-з, [past indef.] (C1) и-ҵá-з / и-м-ҵá-з.

а-ҵ-рá 'to pass with time': Fin. [pres.] и-ҵ-уé-ит / и-ҵ-уá-м, [aor.] и-ҵ-и́т / и-м-ҵ-и́т; Non-fin. [pres.] (C1) и-ҵ-уá / и-м-ҵ-уá, [aor.] (C1) и-ҵы́ / и-м-ҵы́, [past indef.] (C1) и-ҵы́-з / и-м-ҵы́-з.

а-ч-рá 'to swell': Fin. [pres.] и-ч-уé-ит, ды-ч-уé-ит / и-ч-уá-м, ды-ч-уá-м, [aor.] и-ч-и́т, ды-ч-и́т / и-м-ч-и́т, ды-м-ч-и́т; Non-fin. [pres.] (C1) и-ч-уá / и́-м-ч-уа.

а-чча-рá 'to crack': Fin. [pres.] и-ччó-ит / и-ччó-м (-чча-ʒó-м), [aor.] и-ччé-ит / и-мы-ччé-ит (-чча-ʒé-ит); Non-fin. [pres.] (C1) и-ччó / и-мы-ччó, [aor.] (C1) и-ччá / и-мы-ччá.

а-шə-рá 'to get ripe': Fin. [pres.] и-шə-уé-ит / и-шə-уá-м (-шə-ʒó-м), [aor.] и-шə-и́т / и-м-шə-и́т (-шə-ʒé-ит); Non-fin. [pres.] (C1) и-шə-уá / и-м-шə-уá, [aor.] и-шəы́ / и-м-шəы́.

(ii) Words where the masdar accent is on the article <u>а-</u>:

á-ʒса-ра 'to swim': Fin. [pres.] сы-ʒсó-ит, ды-ʒсó-ит / ды-ʒсó-м, [aor.] ды-ʒсé-ит / д-мы-ʒсé-ит, [fut.1] ды-ʒсá-п / ды-ʒса-ры́м, [fut.2] ды-ʒсá-шт / ды-ʒсá-шам, [perf.] ды-ʒса-хьéит / д-мы-ʒсá-ц(т), [impf.] ды-ʒсó-н / ды-ʒсó-мызт, [past indef.] ды-ʒсá-н / д-мы-ʒсá-зт, [cond.1] ды-ʒса-ры́н / ды-ʒса-ры́мызт, [cond.2] ды-ʒсá-шан / ды-ʒсá-шамызт, [plupf.] ды-ʒса-хьáн / д-мы-ʒсá-цызт; Non-fin. (C1) [pres.] и́-ʒсо / и́-м-ʒсо, [aor.] и́-ʒса / и́-м-ʒса, [fut.1] и́-ʒса-ра / и́-м-ʒса-ра, [fut.2] и́-ʒса-ша / и́-м-ʒса-ша, [perf.] и́-ʒса-хьоу (-хьа(ц)) / и́-м-ʒса-хьоу (-хьа(ц)), [impf.] и́-ʒсо-з / и́-м-ʒсо-з, [past indef.] и́-ʒса-з / и́-м-ʒса-з, [cond.1] и́-ʒса-ры-з / и́-м-ʒса-ры-з, [cond.2] и́-ʒса-ша-з / и́-м-ʒса-ша-з, [plupf.] и́-ʒса-хьа-з / и́-м-ʒса-хьа-з.

á-кша-ра 'to beat, to hit': Fin. [pres.] ды-кшó-ит / ды-кшó-м, [aor.] ды-кшé-ит / ды-м-кшé-ит; Non-fin. [pres.] (C1) и́-кшо / и́-м-кшо, [aor.] (C1) и-кшá / и́-м-кша.

á-кəаша-ра 'to dance': Fin. [pres.] д-кəашó-ит / д-кəашó-м, [aor.] д-кəашé-ит / ды-м-кəашé-ит, [fut.1] д-кəашá-п / д-кəаша-ры́м, [fut.2] д-кəашá-шт / д-кəашá-шам, [perf.] д-кəаша-хьéит / ды-м-кəашá-ц(т), [impf.] д-кəашó-н / д-кəашó-мызт, [past indef.] д-кəашá-н / ды-м-кəашá-зт, [cond.1] д-кəаша-ры́н / д-кəаша-ры́мызт, [cond.2] д-кəашá-шан / д-кəаша-шáмызт, [plupf.] д-кəаша-хьáн / ды-м-кəашá-цызт; Non-fin. (C1) [pres.] и́-кəашо / и́-м-кəашо, [aor.] и́-кəаша / и́-м-кəаша, [fut.1] и́-кəаша-ра / и́-м-кəаша-ра, [fut.2] и́-кəаша-ша / и́-м-кəаша-ша, [perf.] и́-кəаша-хьоу (-хьа(ц)) / и́-м-кəаша-хьоу (-хьа(ц)), [impf.] и́-кəашо-з / и́-м-кəашо-з, [past indef.] и́-кəаша-з / и́-м-кəаша-з, [cond.1] и́-кəаша-ры-з / и́-м-кəаша-ры-з, [cond.2] и́-кəаша-ша-з / и́-м-кəаша-ша-з, [plupf.] и́-кəаша-хьа-з / и́-м-кəаша-хьа-з.

á-лаша-ра 'to shine': Fin. [pres.] и-лашó-ит / и-лашó-м (-лаша-ʒó-м), [aor.] и-лашé-ит / и-м-лашé-ит (-лаша-ʒé-ит), [imper.] б-лашá! / бы-м-лашá-н!, шə-лашá! / шəы-м-лашá-н!; Non-fin. (C1) [pres.] и́-лашо / и́-м-лашо, [aor.] и́-лаша / и́-м-лаша, [impf.] и́-лашо-з / и́-м-лашо-з, [past indef.] и́-лаша-з / и́-м-лаша-з. (cf. á-лаша 'light')

á-лашьца-ра 'to become dark': Fin. [pres.] и-лашьцó-ит / и-лашьцó-м (-лашьца-ʒó-м), [aor.] илашьце́-ит / и-м-лашьце́-ит (-лашьца-ӡе́-ит); Non-fin. (C1) [pres.] и́-лашьцо / и́-м-лашьцо, [aor.] и́-лашьца / и́-м-лашьца, [impf.] и́-лашьцо-з / и́-м-лашьцо-з, [past indef.] и́-лашьца-з / и́-м-лашьца-з. (cf. а́-лашьца 'dark')

а́-наа-ра 'to stoop, to bend': Fin. [pres.] и-наа-уе́-ит / и-наа-уа́-м, [aor.] и-наа́-ит / и-м-наа́-ит; Non-fin. [pres.] (C1) и-наа́-уа / и-м-наа́-уа, [aor.] (C1) и-наа́ / и-м-наа́.

а́-рашәа-ра 'to weed': Fin. [pres.] д-рашәо́-ит / д-рашәо́-м, [aor.] д-рашәе́-ит / ды-м-рашәе́-ит; Non-fin. (C1) [pres.] и́-рашәо / и́-м-рашәо, [aor.] и́-рашәа / и́-м-рашәа, [impf.] и́-рашәо-з / и́-м-рашәо-з, [past indef.] и́-рашәа-з / и́-м-рашәа-з.

а́-сас-ра 'to stay': Fin. [pres.] д-сас-уе́-ит / д-сас-уа́-м (-ӡо́-м), [aor.] д-сас-и́т / ды-м-сас-и́т (-ӡе́-ит), [imper.] б-сасы́! / бы-м-сасы́-н!, шә-сасы́! / шәы-м-сасы́-н!; Non-fin. [pres.] (C1) и-сас-уа́ / и-м-сас-уа́, [aor.] (C1) и-сасы́ / и-м-сасы́. (cf. а́-сас 'guest')

а́-ццак-ра 'to hurry': Fin. [pres.] ды-ццак-уе́-ит / ды-ццак-уа́-м (-ццак-ӡо́-м), [aor.] ды-ццак-и́т / д-мы-ццак-и́т (-ццак-ӡе́-ит); Non-fin. (C1) [pres.] и́-ццак-уа / и́-мы-ццак-уа, [aor.] и́-ццак / и́-мы-ццак, [impf.] и́-ццак-уа-з / и́-мы-ццак-уа-з, [past indef.] и́-ццакы-з / и́-мы-ццакы-з.

а́-чча-ра 'to laugh': Fin. [pres.] ды-ччо́-ит / ды-ччо́-м (-чча-ӡо́-м), [aor.] ды-чче́-ит / ды-м-чче́-ит (-чча-ӡе́-ит) *or* д-мы-чче́-ит (-чча-ӡе́-ит); Non-fin. [pres.] (C1) и́-ччо / и́-м(ы)-ччо, [aor.] (C1) и́-чча / и́-м(ы)-чча, [impf.] (C1) и́-ччо-з / и́-м(ы)-ччо-з, [past indef.] (C1) и́-чча-з / и́-м(ы)-чча-з.

а́-шәҭ-ра 'to bloom': Fin. [pres.] и-шәҭ-уе́-ит / и-шәҭ-уа́-м, [aor.] и-шәҭ-и́т / и-м-шәҭ-и́т; Non-fin. (C1) [pres.] и-шәҭ-уа́ / и́-м-шәҭ-уа, [aor.] и-шәҭы́ / и́-м-шәт, [impf.] и-шәт-уа́-з / и́-м-шәҭ-уа-з, [past indef.] и-шәҭы́-з / и́-м-шәҭы-з. (cf. а́-шәт 'flower')

а́-ҵьаба-ра 'to mourn': Fin. [pres.] д-ҵьабо́-ит / д-ҵьабо́-м, [aor.] д-ҵьабе́-ит / ды-м-ҵьабе́-ит; Non-fin. [pres.] (C1) и́-ҵьабо́ / и́-м-ҵьабо́, [aor.] (C1) и́-ҵьаба́ / и́-м-ҵьаба́.

3.2.4. Class B-1

Verbs of this class are two-place stative verbs with a subject (S) in Column I and indirect object (IO) in Column II. Verbs in this class include stative verbs believed to have originally been derived from nouns. For example, агра́ /a-g-rá/ is a noun that means 'shortage'. The verb form исы́гуԥ /jə-sə́-gə-wp'/ 'I lack it/them' can be thought of as having been turned into a stative verb that takes the subject и- /jə/ 'it/they' by adding the possessive prefix сы- /sə/ 'my' to the nominal root г /g/ (cf. the construction of дсы́сасуԥ /d-sə́-sasə-wp'/ '(s)he is my guest' where the stem сы-сас- /sə-sas/ 'my guest' has been made by adding the possessive prefix to a noun). We can surmise the changes in grammatical analysis as follows: исы́гуԥ /jə-sə́-gə-wp'/ [it/they(S)-my(Poss)-shortage-Stat.Pres.Fin] 'it/they is/are my shortage' → [it/they(C1)-me(C2)-lack-Stat.Pres.Fin] lit. 'it/they is/are short for me' → 'I am short of it/them'. A similar example is offered by атәы́ӡаара 'to belong to'. P.K. Uslar and I.I. Meshchaninov have already made this observation.[110] The verb root тәы /t'ʷə/ means 'slave,

110. Услар, П.К. *Этнография Кавказа. Языкознание 1. Абхазский язык.* Тифлис. 1887. с. 73. Мещанинов, И.И. *Члены предложения и части речи.* Москва-Ленинград. 1945. с. 230.

possession' (cf. стәы /s-t'ʷə/ 'mine'). This verbal inflectional form истәу́п /jə-s-t'ʷə́-wp'/ is 'it/they-my-possession-Stat.Pres.Fin', and thus we can surmise it as meaning, 'it/they belong(s) to me'. This assumption may be considered to be speculative. However, that is not to say that there is a clear division between noun and verb roots in Abkhaz. Accordingly, the conjecture of Meshchaninov and other Russian typologists that stative verbs of this type all come from nouns is not necessarily wrong.

Verbs of this class can be separated into the following two types:

(α) inherently stative verbs (for example, а́-ма-заа-ра /á-ma-zaa-ra/ 'to have')

(β) stative verbs derived from nouns, adjectives, and preverbs (for example, иа́дуп /j-á-də-wp'/ 'it is/they are near it', даҩы́зоуп /d-a-jʷə́za-wp'/ '(s)he is like it')

The accent paradigm of the verbs in (α) for the most part applies to AP b (the type that has an accent on the Column II prefix in finite forms) and AP c (the type that has an accent on the root ending in finite forms); it does not apply to AP a (the type that has an accent in the stem and where an accent does not move). The accent paradigm of the verbs in (β), on the other hand, operates basically the same as accents for nouns and adjectives, and can apply to AP a, AP b, and AP c (see §2.1.8 for noun accentuation).

3.2.4.1. Inflection of AP a

а-гәы́лазаара /a-gʷə́la-zaa-ra/ 'to be inside' (cf. гәы́ла /gʷə́la/ [preverb] 'into')

Finite forms

	Affirmative	Negative
Present		
C1-C2		
Sg.3.Non-Hum/Pl.3-3.Non-Hum	и-а-гәы́ло-уп /j-a-gʷə́la-wp'/ 'it is/they are inside it'	и-а-гәы́ла-м
Past		
C1-C2		
Sg.3.Non-Hum/Pl.3-3.Non-Hum	и-а-гәы́ла-н	и-а-гәы́ла-мы-зт

Non-Finite forms

Present		
C1-C2		
Rel-3.Non-Hum	и-а-гәы́ло-у 'which is inside it'	и-а-гәы́ла-м
Sg.3.Non-Hum/Pl.3-Rel	и-з-гәы́ло-у 'which it is/they are inside'	и-з-гәы́ла-м
Past		
C1-C2		
Rel-3.Non-Hum	и-а-гәы́ла-з	и-а-гәы́ла-мы-з
Sg.3.Non-Hum/Pl.3-Rel	и-з-гәы́ла-з	и-з-гәы́ла-мы-з

Note: Stative verbs of this type can be seen in forms derived from nouns, adjectives, and adverbs.

Other examples:

а-зе́иҧш-заа-ра 'to be common': Fin. [pres.] и-ах-зе́иҧш-уп / и-ах-зе́иҧшы-м, [past] и-ах-зе́иҧшы-н / и-ах-зе́иҧш-мызт (cf. а-зе́иҧш 'common').

а-зы́раз-ра 'to be agreement with': Fin. [pres.] сы-л-зы́раз-уп / сы-л-зы́разы-м, [past] сы-л-зы́разы-н / сы-л-зы́разы-мызт; Non-fin. [pres.] (C1) и-л-зы́раз-у / и-л-зы́разы-м, (C2) сы-з-зы́раз-у / сы-з-зы́разы-м, [past] (C1) и-л-зы́разы-з / и-л-зы́разы-мыз, (C2) сы-з-зы́разы-з / сы-з-зы́разы-мыз.

а́иҕь-заа-ра 'to be better': Fin. [pres.] д-р-е́иҕь-уп / д-р-е́иҕьы-м, [past] д-р-е́иҕьы-н / д-р-е́иҕьы-мызт; Non-fin. [pres.] (C1) и-р-е́иҕь-у / и-р-е́иҕьы-м, (C2) д-з-е́иҕь-у / д-з-е́иҕьы-м, [past] (C1) и-р-е́иҕьы-з / и-р-е́иҕьы-мы-з, (C2) д-з-е́иҕьы-з / д-з-е́иҕьы-мыз (cf. а́иҕь 'better').

а-ха́ан-заа-ра 'to be a contemporary of': Fin. [pres.] с-а-ха́ан-уп, с-и-ха́ан-уп / с-а-ха́аны-м, [past] с-а-ха́аны-н / с-а-ха́аны-мызт; Non-fin. [pres.] (C1) и-а-ха́ан-у / и-а-ха́аны-м, (C2) сы-з-ха́ан-у / сы-з-ха́аны-м, [aor.] (C1) и-а-ха́аны-з / и-а-ха́аны-мыз, (C2) сы-з-ха́аны-з / сы-з-ха́аны-мыз (cf. а-ха́ан 'in the time of').

а-ха́ра-заа-ра 'to be guilty': Fin. [pres.] и-с-ха́ро-уп, и-л-ха́ро-уп / и-с-ха́ра-м, и-л-ха́ра-м, [past] и-л-ха́ра-н / и-л-ха́ра-мызт; Non-fin. [pres.] (C1) и-л-ха́ро-у / и-л-ха́ра-м, (C2) и-з-ха́ро-у / и-з-ха́ра-м (cf. а-ха́ра 'fault, guilt').

а-ҩы́за-ра 'to be like': Fin. [pres.] сы-л-ҩы́зо-уп / сы-л-ҩы́за-м, [past] сы-л-ҩы́за-н / сы-л-ҩы́за-мызт; Non-fin. [pres.] (C1) и-л-ҩы́зо-у / и-л-ҩы́за-м, (C2) сы-з-ҩы́зо-у / сы-з-ҩы́за-м, [past] (C1) и-л-ҩы́за-з / и-л-ҩы́за-мыз, (C2) сы-з-ҩы́за-з / сы-з-ҩы́за-мыз (cf. а-ҩы́за 'like').

3.2.4.2. Inflection of AP b

а́-мазаара /á-ma-zaa-ra/ 'to have'

Finite forms

	Affirmative	Negative
Present		
C1-C2		
Sg.1-2.F	с-бы́-мо-уп /s-bə́-ma-wp'/ I(C1)-you.F(C2)-have-Stat.Pres.Fin 'you-F have me'	с-бы́-ма-м /s-bə́-ma-m/
Sg.1-2.M	с-у́-мо-уп	с-у́-ма-м
Sg.1-3.Human.M	с-и́-мо-уп	с-и́-ма-м
Sg.1-3.F	с-лы́-мо-уп	с-лы́-ма-м
Sg.1-3.Non-Human	с-а́-мо-уп	с-а́-ма-м
Sg.1-Pl.2	с-шәы́-мо-уп	с-шәы́-ма-м
Sg.1-Pl.3	с-ры́-мо-уп	с-ры́-ма-м
Sg.2.M-1	у-сы́-мо-уп	у-сы́-ма-м
Sg.2.M-3.M	у-и́-мо-уп	у-и́-ма-м

Sg.2.M-3.F	у-лы́-мо-уп	у-лы́-ма-м
Sg.2.M-3.Non-Hum.	у-á-мо-уп	у-á-ма-м
Sg.2.M-Pl.1	у-ҳá-мо-уп	у-хá-ма-м
Sg.2.M-Pl.3	у-ры́-мо-уп	у-ры́-ма-м
Sg.2.F-1	б-сы́-мо-уп	б-сы́-ма-м
Sg.2.F-3.M	б-и́-мо-уп	б-и́-ма-м
Sg.2.F-3.F	б-лы́-мо-уп	б-лы́-ма-м
Sg.2.F-3.Non-Hum.	б-á-мо-уп	б-á-ма-м
Sg.2.F-Pl.1	б-ҳá-мо-уп	б-хá-ма-м
Sg.2.F-Pl.3	б-ры́-мо-уп	б-ры́-ма-м
Sg.3.Human-1	д-сы́-мо-уп	д-сы́-ма-м
Sg.3.Human-2.M	д-ý-мо-уп	д-ý-ма-м
Sg.3.Human-2.F	д-бы́-мо-уп	д-бы́-ма-м
Sg.3.Human-3.M	д-и́-мо-уп	д-и́-ма-м
Sg.3.Human-3.F	д-лы́-мо-уп	д-лы́-ма-м
Sg.3.Human-3.Non-Hum.	д-á-мо-уп	д-á-ма-м
Sg.3.Human-Pl.1	д-ҳá-мо-уп	д-ҳá-ма-м
Sg.3.Human-Pl.2	д-шəы́-мо-уп	д-шəы́-ма-м
Sg.3.Human-Pl.3	д-ры́-мо-уп	д-ры́-ма-м
Sg.3.Non.Human-1	и-сы́-мо-уп	и-сы́-ма-м
Sg.3.Non.Human-2.M	и-ý-мо-уп	и-ý-ма-м
Sg.3.Non.Human-2.F	и-бы́-мо-уп	и-бы́-ма-м
Sg.3.Non-Hum.-Sg.3.M	и́-мо-уп (< и-и́-мо-уп)	и́-ма-м
Pl.3-Sg.3.M	и́-мо-уп (< и-и́-мо-уп)	и́-ма-м
Sg.3.Non-Hum./Pl.3-Sg.3.Non-Hum.	и-á-мо-уп	и-á-ма-м
Sg.3.Non-Hum./Pl.3-Pl.1	и-ҳá-мо-уп	и-хá-ма-м
Sg.3.Non-Hum./Pl.3-Pl.2	и-шəы́-мо-уп	и-шəы́-ма-м
Sg.3.Non-Hum./Pl.3-Pl.3	и-ры́-мо-уп	и-ры́-ма-м
Pl.1-Sg.2.F	ҳ-бы́-мо-уп	х-бы́-ма-м
Pl.1-Sg.2.M	ҳ-ý-мо-уп	х-ý-ма-м
Pl.1-Sg.3.M	ҳ-и́-мо-уп	х-и́-ма-м
Pl.1-Sg.3.F	ҳ-лы́-мо-уп	х-лы́-ма-м
Pl.1-Sg.3.Non-Human	ҳ-á-мо-уп	х-á-ма-м
Pl.1-Pl.2	ҳ-шəы́-мо-уп	х-шəы́-ма-м
Pl.1-Pl.3	ҳ-ры́-мо-уп	х-ры́-ма-м
Pl.2-Sg.1	шə-сы́-мо-уп	шə-сы́-ма-м
Pl.2-Sg.3.M	шə-и́-мо-уп	шə-и́-ма-м
Pl.2-Sg.3.F	шə-лы́-мо-уп	шə-лы́-ма-м
Pl.2-Sg.3.Non-Human	шə-á-мо-уп	шə-á-ма-м
Pl.2-Pl.1	шə-ҳá-мо-уп	шə-ҳá-ма-м
Pl.2-Pl.3	шə-ры́-мо-уп	шə-ры́-ма-м

etc.

Past		
Sg.1-2.F	с-бы́-ма-н	с-бы́-ма-мы-зт
	/s-bə́-ma-n/	
	'you-F had me'	
Sg.1-3.Non-Human	с-á-ма-н	с-á-ма-мы-зт
etc.		

Non-Finite forms

	Affirmative	Negative
Present		
C1-C2		
Rel-Sg.1	и-сы́-мо-у	и-сы́-ма-м
	/jə-sə́-ma-w/	/jə-sə́-ma-m/
	Rel(C1)-me(C2)-have-Stat.Pres.NF	
	'which I have'	
Rel-Sg.2.F	и-бы́-мо-у	и-бы́-ма-м
Rel-Sg.2.M	и-у́-мо-у	и-у́-ма-м
Rel-Sg.3.F	и-лы́-мо-у	и-лы́-ма-м
Rel-Sg.3.M	и́-мо-у (< и-и́-мо-у)	и́-ма-м
Rel-Sg.3.Non-Human	и-á-мо-у	и-á-ма-м
Rel-Pl.1	и-хá-мо-у	и-хá-ма-м
Rel-Pl.2	и-шәы́-мо-у	и-шәы́-ма-м
Rel-Pl.3	и-ры́-мо-у	и-ры́-ма-м
Sg.1-Rel	сы-з-мо́-у	сы-з-мá-м
	/sə-z-má-w/	
	I(C1)-Rel(C2)-have-Stat.Pres.NF	
	'who has me'	
Sg.2.F-Rel	бы-з-мо́-у	бы-з-мá-м
Sg.2.M-Rel	у-з-мо́-у	у-з-мá-м
Sg.3.Human-Rel	ды-з-мо́-у	ды-з-мá-м
Sg.3.Non-Human/Pl.3-Rel	и-з-мо́-у	и-з-мá-м
Pl.1-Rel	ҳа-з-мо́-у	ҳа-з-мá-м
Pl.2.-Rel	шәы-з-мо́-у	шәы-з-мá-м
Past		
C1-C2		
Rel-Sg.1	и-лы́-ма-з	и-лы́-ма-мы-з
	/jə-lə́-ma-z/	
	'which she had'	
Sg.3.Human-Rel	ды-з-мá-з	ды-з-мá-мы-з
Sg.3.Non-Human/Pl.3-Rel	и-з-мá-з	и-з-мá-мы-з
etc.		

Notes:

1. а́-мазаара /á-ma-zaa-ra/ 'to have' is an 'inversive verb' (see §5.10). The verb root is an intransitive verb with a meaning close to the Russian *иметься* 'to be, to be present'. Accordingly, сбы́моуп /s-bə́-ma-wp'/ 'you have me' is close in meaning to the Russian 'у тебя есть я', lit. 'I am present at your place'. See also исы́гуп /jə-sə́-gə-wp'/ 'I lack it/them' discussed above.

2. The accent goes here when the Column II slot is filled by a pronominal prefix. The accent is placed on the root-final (stem-final) when the Column II slot is filled by a relative prefix.

3. When both Columns I and II have the pronominal prefix и- (or the relative prefix и- and the pronominal prefix и-) thus producing и́моуп /jə́-ma-wp'/, only one и- is written down and the result is pronounced [i:].

Other examples:

а́-г-заа-ра 'to be short of': Fin. [pres.] и-сы́-г-уп / и-сы́-гы-м, [past] и-сы́-гы-н / и-сы́-гы-мызт; Non-fin. [pres.] (C1) и-сы́-г-у / и-сы́-гы-м, (C2) и-зы́-г-у / и-зы́-гы-м, [past] (C1) и-сы́-гы-з / и-сы́-г-мыз, (C2) и-зы́-гы-з / и-зы́-г-мыз *or* и-з-гы́-мы-з (cf. а-г-ра́ 'shortage').

а́-д-заа-ра 'to lie near': Fin. [pres.] и-а́-д-уп, б-сы́-д-уп / и-а́-ды-м, б-сы́-ды-м, [past] и-а́-ды-н, б-сы́-ды-н / и-а́-д(ы)-мызт, б-сы́-д(ы)-мызт; Non-fin. [pres.] (C1) и-а́-д-у / и-а́-ды-м, (C2) и-з-д-у́ / и-з-ды́-м.

а́-қәиҭ-заа-ра 'to be entitled to': Fin. [pres.] д-а́-қәиҭ-уп / д-а́-қәиҭы-м (-қәиҭ-ӡа-м), [past] д-а́-қәиҭы-н / д-а́-қәиҭ-мызт.

а́-ла-заа-ра 'to be in': Fin. [pres.] и-а́-ло-уп *or* ы́-ло-уп / и-а́-ла-м, [past] и-а́-ла-н / и-а́-ла-мызт; Non-fin. [pres.] (C1) и-а́-ло-у / и-а́-ла-м, [past] и-а́-ла-з / и-а́-ла-мыз (cf. ла [peverb] 'in').

а́-лахәы-заа-ра 'to take part in': Fin. [pres.] д-а́-лахә-уп / д-а́-лахәы-м, [aor.] д-а́-лахәы-н / д-а́-лахәы-мызт; Non-fin. [pres.] (C1) и-ры́-лахә-у / и-ры́-лахәы-м, (C2) ды-з-лахә-у́ / ды-з-лахәы́-м, [past] (C1) и-ры́-лахәы-з / и-ры́-лахәы-мыз, (C2) ды-з-лахәы́-з / ды-з-лахәы́-мыз.

а́-мҕа-заа-ра 'to be girdled': Fin. [pres.] и-сы́-мҕо-уп / и-сы́-мҕа-м (-ӡа-м), [past] и-сы́-мҕа-н / и-сы́-мҕа-мызт; Non-fin. [pres.] (C1) и-сы́-мҕо-у / и-сы́-мҕа-м, (C2) и-зы-мҕо́-у / и-зы-мҕа́-м, [past] (C1) и-сы́-мҕа-з / и-сы́-мҕа-мыз, (C2) и-зы-мҕа́-з / и-зы-мҕа́-мыз (cf. -мҕа- [preverb]).

а́-мтца-заа-ра 'to be under': Fin. [pres.] и-а́-мтцо-уп, и-ры́-мтцо-уп, и́-мтцо-уп; Non-fin. [past] (C1) и-ры́-мтца-з (cf. -(а)мтца- [preverb] 'under').

а́-шьа-заа-ра 'to be shod in': Fin. [pres.] и-сы́-шьо-уп / и-сы́-шьа-м, [past] и-сы́-шьа-н / и-сы́-шьа-мызт; Non-fin. [pres.] (C1) и-сы́-шьо-у / и-сы́-шьа-м.

а́-шьҭа-заа-ра 'to be on the trail of': Fin. [pres.] и-а́-шьҭо-уп / и-а́-шьҭа-м, [past] и-а́-шьҭа-н; Non-fin. [pres.] (C1) и-сы́-шьҭо-у / и-сы́-шьҭа-м, (C2) д-зы-шьҭо́-у / д-зы-шьҭа́-м, [past] (C1) и-сы́-шьҭа-з / и-сы́-шьҭа-мыз, (C2) д-зы-шьҭа́-з / д-зы-шьҭа́-мыз (cf. а́-шьҭа 'trail').

а́-шьцыла-ра 'to be used to': Fin. [pres.] д-сы́-шьцыло-уп / д-сы́-шьцыла-м, [past] д-сы́-шьцыла-н / д-сы́-шьцыла-мызт; Non-fin. [pres.] (C1) и-лы́-шьцыло-у / и-лы́-шьцыла-м, (C2) д-зы-шьцы́ло-у / д-зы-шьцы́ла-м, [past] (C1) и-лы́-шьцыла-з / и-лы́-шьцыла-мыз, (C2) д-зы-шьцы́ла-з / д-зы-шьцы́ла-мыз.

Some of these verbs can also be considered Class F verbs. That is to say, we can think of -д-, -ла-,

-мҕа-, -мҵа-, and -шьа- as preverbs, with the resulting structure being 'Column I + Column II + preverb + zero-root'. See §3.2.9.4.3.

3.2.4.3. Inflection of AP c

а-кра́ /a-k'-rá/ 'to hold'

Finite forms

	Affirmative	Negative
Present		
C1-C2		
Sg.1-2.F	сы-б-к-у́п /sə-b-k'ə́-wp'/ 'you-F hold me'	сы-б-кы́-м /sə-b-k'ə́-m/
Sg.1-2.M	с-у-к-у́п	с-у-кы́-м
Sg.1-3.M	сы-и-к-у́п	сы-и-кы́-м
Sg.1-3.F	сы-л-к-у́п	сы-л-кы́-м
Sg.1-3.Non-Human	с-а-к-у́п	с-а-кы́-м
Sg.1-Pl.2	сы-шә-к-у́п	сы-шә-кы́-м
Sg.1-Pl.3	сы-р-к-у́п	сы-р-кы́-м
Sg.2.M-1	у-с-к-у́п	у-с-кы́-м
Sg.2.M-3.M	у-и-к-у́п	у-и-кы́-м
Sg.2.M-3.F	у-л-к-у́п	у-л-кы́-м
Sg.2.M-3.Non-Human	у-а-к-у́п	у-а-кы́-м
Sg.2.M-Pl.1	у-х-к-у́п	у-х-кы́-м
Sg.2.M-Pl.3	у-р-к-у́п	у-р-кы́-м
Sg.2.F-1	бы-с-к-у́п	бы-с-кы́-м
Sg.2.F-3.M	б-и-к-у́п	б-и-кы́-м
Sg.2.F-3.F	бы-л-к-у́п	бы-л-кы́-м
Sg.2.F-3.Non-Human	б-а-к-у́п	б-а-кы́-м
Sg.2.F-Pl.1	б-ах-к-у́п	б-ах-кы́-м
Sg.2.F-Pl.3	бы-р-к-у́п	бы-р-кы́-м
Sg.3.F-1	ды-с-к-у́п	ды-с-кы́-м
Sg.3-2.M	д-у-к-у́п	д-у-кы́-м
Sg.3-2.F	ды-б-к-у́п	ды-б-кы́-м
Sg.3-3.M	д-и-к-у́п	д-и-кы́-м
Sg.3-3.F	ды-л-к-у́п	ды-л-кы́-м
Sg.3-3.Non-Human	д-а-к-у́п	д-а-кы́-м
Sg.3-Pl.1	д-ах-к-у́п	д-ах-кы́-м
Sg.3-Pl.2	ды-шә-к-у́п	ды-шә-кы́-м
Sg.1-Pl.3	ды-р-к-у́п	ды-р-кы́-м
Sg.3.Non-Hum./Pl.3-1	и-с-к-у́п	и-с-кы́-м
Sg.3.Non-Hum./Pl.3-2.M	и-у-к-у́п	и-у-кы́-м
Sg.3.Non-Hum./Pl.3-2.F	и-б-к-у́п	и-б-кы́-м
Sg.3.Non-Hum./Pl.3-3.M	и-к-у́п (< и-и-к-у́п)	и-с-кы́-м

Sg.3.Non-Hum./Pl.3-3.F	и-л-к-у́п	и-л-кы́-м
Sg.3.Non-Hum./Pl.3-3.Non-Hum.	и-а-к-у́п	и-а-кы́-м
Sg.3.Non-Hum./Pl.3-Pl.1	и-аҳ-к-у́п	и-аҳ-кы́-м
Sg.3.Non-Hum./Pl.3-Pl.2	и-шә-к-у́п	и-шә-кы́-м
Sg.3.Non-Hum./Pl.3-Pl.3	и-р-к-у́п	и-р-кы́-м
Pl.1-Sg.2.M	ҳа-у-к-у́п	ҳа-у-кы́-м
Pl.1-Sg.2.F	ҳа-б-к-у́п	ҳа-б-кы́-м
Pl.1-Sg.3.M	ҳа-и-к-у́п	ҳа-и-кы́-м
Pl.1-Sg.3.F	ҳа-л-к-у́п	ҳа-л-кы́-м
Pl.1-Sg.3.Non-Hum.	ҳ-а-к-у́п	ҳ-а-кы́-м
Pl.1-Pl.2	ҳа-шә-к-у́п	ҳа-шә-кы́-м
Pl.1-Pl.3	ҳа-р-к-у́п	ҳа-р-кы́-м
Pl.2-Sg.1	шәы-с-к-у́п	шәы-с-кы́-м
Pl.2-Sg.3.M	шә-и-к-у́п	шә-и-кы́-м
Pl.2-Sg.3.F	шәы-л-к-у́п	шәы-л-кы́-м
Pl.2-Sg.3.Non-Hum.	шә-а-к-у́п	шә-а-кы́-м
Pl.2-Pl.1	шә-аҳ-к-у́п	шә-аҳ-кы́-м
Pl.2-Pl.3	шәы-р-к-у́п	шәы-р-кы́-м

Past

Sg.1-2.F	сы-б-кы́-н	сы-б-кы́-мы-зт
	/sə-b-k’ə́-n/	/sə-b-k’ə́-mə-zt’/
	‘you-F held me’	‘you-F did not hold me’
Sg.1-3.Non-Human	с-а-кы́-н	с-а-кы́-мы-зт
etc.		

Non-Finite forms

	Affirmative	Negative
Present		
C1-C2		
Rel-Sg.1	и́-с-к-у	и́-с-кы-м
	/jə́-s-k’ə-w/	/jə́-s-k’ə-m/
	‘which I hold’	‘which I do not hold’
Rel-Sg.3.F	и́-л-к-у	и́-л-кы-м
Rel-Sg.3.M	и́-к-у	и́-кы-м
Sg.3.Non-Hum./Pl.3-Rel	и-з-к-у́	и-з-кы́-м
	/jə-z-k’ə́-w/	/jə-z-k’ə́-m
	‘who holds it/them’	‘who does not hold it/them’
Past		
Rel-Sg.1	и́-с-кы-з ‘which I held’	и́-с-кы-мы-з
Rel-Sg.3.F	и́-л-кы-з	и́-л-кы-мы-з
Sg.3.Non-Hum./Pl.3-Rel	и-з-кы́-з ‘who held it/them’	и-з-кы́-мы-з

Notes:

1. а-кра́ /a-k'-rá/ 'to hold' is an inversive verb.

2. The 'и' in ику́п is pronounced as a short [i].

3. If there is an accent on the masdar, an accent is placed on the end of the root in finite forms. For non-finite forms, on the other hand, the tendency is to place an accent on the relative prefix when it is in Column I and in the root-final position when it is in Column II.

Other examples:

а-ҭахы́-заа-ра 'to want': Fin. [pres.] и-с-ҭахы́-уп *or* и-с-ҭах-у́п, и-ах-ҭахы́-уп, и-а-ҭахы́-уп / и-с-ҭахы́-м (-ҭах-ӡа́-м), ды-с-ҭахы́-м, [past] и-с-ҭахы́-н, д-л-ҭахы́-н / и-с-ҭахы́-мызт; Non-fin. [pres.] (C1) и́-л-ҭахы-у / и́-л-ҭахы-м, (C2) и-з-ҭахы́-у / и-з-ҭахы́-м, [past] (C1) и́-л-ҭахы-з / и́-л-ҭахы-мыз, (C2) и-з-ҭахы́-з / и-з-ҭахы́-мыз.

а-тәы́-заа-ра 'to belong to': Fin. [pres.] и-л-тә-у́п, сы-шә-тә-у́п (*I am yours-PL*), да-х-тә-у́п (*he/she belongs us*) / и-л-тәы́-м, [past] и-л-тәы́-н / и-л-тәы́-мызт; Non-fin. [pres.] (C1) и́-л-тә-у́ / и-л-тәы́-м, (C2) ды-з-тә-у́ / ды-з-тәы́-м. [past] (C1) и́-л-тәы́-з / и-л-тәы́-мыз, (C2) ды-з-тәы́-з / ды-з-тәы́-мыз (cf. а-тәы́ 'slave').

а-ԥса-ра́ 'to cost': Fin. [pres.] и-а-ԥсо́-уп / и-а-ԥса́-м, [past] и-а-ԥса́-н / и-а-ԥса́-мызт; Non-fin. [pres.] (C1) и-а-ԥсо́-у / и-а-ԥса́-м, (C2) и-з-ԥсо́-у / и-а-ԥса́-м, [past] (C1) и-а-ԥса́-з / и-а-ԥса́-мыз, (C2) и-з-ԥса́-з / и-а-ԥса́-мыз.

а-ҭа́-заа-ра 'to be a guest of': Fin. [pres.] ды-с-ҭо́-уп / ды-с-ҭа́-м, [past] ды-с-ҭа́-н / ды-с-ҭа́-мызт.

аитцбы́-заа-ра 'to be younger': Fin. [pres.] д-(с)-еитцб-у́п / д-(с)-еитцбы́-м (cf. аитцбы́ 'younger').

а-ны́-заа-ра 'to be on': Fin. [pres.] и-а-н-у́п / и-а-ны́-м (*or* и-а-н-ӡа́-м), [past] и-а-ны́-н / и-а-ны́-мызт; Non-fin. [pres.] (C1) и-а-н-у́ / и-а-ны́-м, (C2) ха-з-н(ы́)-у́ / ха-з-ны́-м, [past] (C1) и-а-ны́-з / и-а-ны́-мыз, (C2) ха-з-ны́-з / ха-з-ны́-мыз.

а-ха́-заа-ра 'to be in headgear': Fin. [pres.] и-с-хо́-уп / и-с-ха́-м, [past] и-с-ха́-н / и-с-ха́-мызт; Non-fin. [pres.] (C2) и-з-хо́-у / и-з-ха́-м, [past] и-з-ха́-з / и-з-ха́-мыз (cf. -ха- [preverb] 'above, on').

а-хәҭа-ра́ 'to need': Fin. [pres.] и-сы-хәҭо́-уп / и-сы-хәҭа́-м, [past] и-сы-хәҭа́-н / и-сы-хәҭа́-мызт; Non-fin. [pres.] (C1) и-сы-хәҭо́-у / и-сы-хәҭа́-м, (C2) и-зы-хәҭо́-у / и-зы-хәҭа́-м, [past] (C1) и-сы-хәҭа́-з / и-сы-хәҭа́-мыз, (C2) и-зы-хәҭа́-з / и-зы-хәҭа́-мыз. (cf. а-хәҭа́ 'part')

а-ҿы́-заа-ра 'to be engaged in': Fin. [pres.] д-а-ҿ-у́п *or* д-а-ҿы́-уп / д-а-ҿы́-м (-ҿ-ӡа́-м), [past] д-а-ҿы́-н / д-а-ҿы́-мызт (-ҿ-ӡа́-мызт); Non-fin. [pres.] (C1) и-а-ҿ-у́ / и-а-ҿы́-м, (C2) ды-з-ҿы́-у (ды-з-ҿ-у́) / ды-з-ҿы́-м; [past] (C1) и-а-ҿы́-з / и-а-ҿы́-мыз; (C2) ды-з-ҿы́-з / ды-з-ҿы́-мыз.

а-шәы́-заа-ра 'to be dressed': Fin. [pres.] и-с-шә-у́п / и-с-шәы́-м, [past] и-с-шәы́-н / и-с-шәы́-мызт, Non-fin. [pres.] (C1) и-с-шә-у́ / и-с-шәы́-м, (C2) и-з-шә-у́ / и-з-шәы́-м, [past] (C1) и-с-шәы́-з, (C2) и-з-шәы́-з (cf. а-шәы́ 'mourning').

3.2.4.4. Stative Verbs of the "д-сы́-сас-уп '(s)he is my guest'" Type

Verbal complexes in which 'possessive prefix + noun' has been made into a stative verb can also be included in Class B-1. For example, when the possessive prefix у- /wə/ 'your-M' is added to the noun áсас /á-sas/ 'guest' (see §2.2.2), the Column I pronominal prefix с- /s/ 'I' that will be the subject is added to that, and then the present tense stative suffix -уп is added as the suffix, the result is сýсасуп /s-wə́-sasə-wp'/ [I(C1)-your.M-guest-Stat.Pres.Fin] 'I am your guest'. This possessive pronoun has the same form as the Column II pronominal prefix of a verb (see §2.2.2 and §3.1.6). Accordingly, morphologically this structure is the same as that of Class B-1. For this reason, as noted in §3.2.4 there are researchers who say that the origin of Abkhaz stative verbs lies in this 'possessive prefix + noun' pattern. We will describe this structure by dividing it into groups AP a, AP b, and AP c based on accent type. These stative verb accent types all depend on noun accent types. If the noun has an accent fixed on the stem (fixed accent type), then the accent is also fixed on the stem for verbs that derive from it (AP a). If the noun has an accent on the article (moving accent type), the verbs derived from it will have an accent on the possessive prefix (AP b). If the noun has an accent on the word-ending position (final-position accent type), the verbs derived from it will have an accent in the root-final (stem-final) position (AP c).

3.2.4.4.1. Type суɷы́зоуп (AP a)

а-ɷы́за /a-jʷə́za/ 'friend'

Finite forms

	Affirmative	Negative
Present		
C1-Possessive		
Sg.1-2.M	с-у-ɷы́зо-уп /sə-w-jʷə́za-wp'/ 'I am your-M friend'	с-у-ɷы́за-м /sə-w-jʷə́za-m/
Sg.1-2.F	сы-б-ɷы́зо-уп	сы-б-ɷы́за-м
Sg.1-3.M	с-и-ɷы́зо-уп	с-и-ɷы́за-м
Sg.1-3.F	сы-л-ɷы́зо-уп	сы-л-ɷы́за-м
Sg.1-3.Non-Human	с-а-ɷы́зо-уп	с-а-ɷы́за-м
Sg.1-Pl.2	сы-шә-ɷы́зо-уп	сы-шә-ɷы́за-м
Sg.1-Pl.3	сы-р-ɷы́зо-уп	сы-р-ɷы́за-м
Sg.2.M-Sg.1	у-с-ɷы́зо-уп	у-с-ɷы́за-м
Sg.2.M-Pl.1	у-ах-ɷы́зо-уп	у-аҳ-ɷы́за-м
Sg.2.F-Sg.1	бы-с-ɷы́зо-уп	бы-с-ɷы́за-м
Sg.3.Human-Sg.1	ды-с-ɷы́зо-уп	ды-с-ɷы́за-м
Sg.3.Non-Human-Sg.1	и-с-ɷы́зо-уп	и-с-ɷы́за-м
Sg.3.N.Hum./Pl.3-Sg.3.M	и-ɷы́зо-уп (< и-и-ɷы́зо-уп)	и-ɷы́за-м
Pl.1.-Sg.2.F	ха-б-ɷы́зо-уп[111]	ҳа-б-ɷы́за-м
Pl.2.-Sg.1	шәы-с-ɷы́зо-уп	шәы-с-ɷы́за-м
Pl.3-Sg.1	и-с-ɷы́зо-уп	и-с-ɷы́за-м

111. The root does not absolutely need to take the plural form when the subject is plural.

Past		
Sg.1-2.M	с-у-ҩы́за-н	с-у-ҩы́за-мы-зт
	/sə-w-jʷə́za-n/	/sə-w-jʷə́za-mə-zt'/
	'I was your-M friend'	
Sg.1-2.F	сы-б-ҩы́за-н	сы-б-ҩы́за-мы-зт

3.2.4.4.2. Type с-у́-сас-уп (<u>AP b</u>)

á-сас /á-sas/ 'guest'

Finite forms

	<u>Affirmative</u>	<u>Negative</u>
Present		
C1-Possessive		
Sg.1-2.M	с-у́-сас-уп	с-у́-сасы-м
	/s-wə́-sasə-wp'/	/s-wə́-sasə-m/
	'I am your-M guest'	
Sg.1-2.F	с-бы́-сас-уп	с-бы́-сасы-м
Sg.1-3.M	с-и́-сас-уп	с-и́-сасы-м
Sg.1-3.F	с-лы́-сас-уп	с-лы́-сасы-м
Sg.1-3.Non-Human	с-á-сас-уп	с-á-сасы-м
Sg.1-Pl.2	с-шəы́-сас-уп	с-шəы́-сасы-м
Sg.1-Pl.3	с-ры́-сас-уп	с-ры́-сасы-м
Sg.2.M-Sg.1	у-сы́-сас-уп	у-сы́-сасы-м
Sg.2.F-Sg.1	б-сы́-сас-уп	б-сы́-сасы-м
Sg.3.Human-Sg.1	д-сы́-сас-уп	д-сы́-сасы-м
Sg.3.Non-Human-Sg.1	и-сы́-сас-уп	и-сы́-сасы-м
Sg.3.Non-Human-Sg.3.M	и́-сас-уп (< и-и́-сас-уп)	и́-сасы-м
Pl.1-Sg.2.F	х-бы́-сас-уп	х-бы́-сасы-м
Pl.2-Sg.1	шə-сы́-сас-уп	шə-сы́-сасы-м
Pl.3-Sg.1	и-сы́-сас-уп	и-сы́-сасы-м
Past		
Sg.1-2.M	с-у́-сасы-н	с-у́-сасы-мы-зт
	/s-wə́-sasə-n/	/s-wə́-sasə-mə-zt'/
	'I was your-M guest'	
Sg.1-2.F	с-бы́-сасы-н	с-бы́-сасы-мы-зт

3.2.4.4.3. Type с-у-ԥó-уп (<u>AP c</u>)

а-ԥá /a-pá/ 'son'

Finite forms

	<u>Affirmative</u>	<u>Negative</u>
Present		
C1-Possessive		

Sg.1-2.M	с-у-пҕó-уп /sə-w-pá-wp'/ 'I am your-M son'	с-у-пҕá-м /sə-w-pá-m/
Sg.1-2.F	сы-б-пҕó-уп	сы-б-пҕá-м
Sg.1-3.M	с-и-пҕó-уп	с-и-пҕá-м
Sg.1-3.F	сы-л-пҕó-уп	сы-л-пҕá-м
Sg.1-3.Non-Human	с-а-пҕó-уп	с-а-пҕá-м
Sg.1-Pl.2	сы-шә-пҕó-уп	сы-шә-пҕá-м
Sg.1-Pl.3	сы-р-пҕó-уп	сы-р-пҕá-м
Sg.2.M-1	у-с-пҕó-уп	у-с-пҕá-м
Sg.3.Human-1	ды-с-пҕó-уп	ды-с-пҕá-м
Sg.3.Non-Human-1	и-с-пҕó-уп	и-с-пҕá-м
Pl.1-Sg.2.M	ҳа-у-пҕó-уп[112]	ҳа-у-пҕá-м
Pl.2-Sg.1	шәы-с-пҕó-уп	шәы-с-пҕá-м
Pl.3-Sg.1	и-с-пҕó-уп	и-с-пҕá-м
Aorist		
Sg.1-2.M	с-у-пҕá-н /sə-w-pá-n/ 'I was your-M son'	с-у-пҕá-мы-зт /sə-w-pá-mə-zt'/
Sg.1-2.F	сы-б-пҕá-н	сы-б-пҕá-мы-зт

3.2.5. Class B-2

Class B-2 verbs are two-place intransitive dynamic verbs that have the subject (S) prefix in Column I and the indirect object (IO) prefix in Column II. Verbs in this class include for example ones like á-хәара /á-xʷa-ra/ 'to help' that would be intransitive (cf. the Russian *помогать* 'to help') or transitive (cf. the English 'help') even in accusative-type languages, but it also includes verbs like á-сра /á-s-ra/ 'to hit', á-пҕхьара /á-pxʲa-ra/ 'to read' that would be transitive in accusative-type languages. G.A. Klimov argues that the semantic feature of this series of verbs lies in the fact that they characteristically 'convey the fact that the effect the subject has on its object is superficial' in the verbal lexeme of ergative languages.[113] The following verbs belong to this class in Abkhaz: á-гәара /á-gʷa-ra/ 'to push', á-хара /á-xa-ra/ 'to pull, to smoke', á-хәара /á-xʷa-ra/ 'to help', á-ҳәара /á-ħʷa-ra/ 'to request', á-цхара /á-cħa-ra/ 'to bite, to sting', á-сра /á-s-ra/ 'to hit', á-пҕхьара /á-pxʲa-ra/ 'to read, to call', áбжьара /[á-]abžʲa-ra/ 'to advise', а-иáаира /a-jáaj-ra/ 'to defeat', á-ҭәҳәара /á-tʷħʷa-ra/ 'to blow at', а-фыԥрá /a-fəjʷ-rá/ 'to smell', á-хьра /á-xʲ-ra/ 'to happen to', áура /á-aw-ra/ 'to receive', etc.

112. Cf. хпҕацәóуп /ħ-pa-cʷá-wp'/ [we(C1)-son-Pl-Stat.Pres.Fin] 'we are sons', хпҕацәáн /ħ-pa-cʷá-n/'we were sons', шәпҕацәóуп /šʷ-pa-cʷá-wp'/ 'you-Pl were sons', ипҕацәóуп /jə-pa-cʷá-wp'/ 'they are sons'.

113. Климов Г.А. (1983) *Принципы контенсивной типологии.* Москва. с. 95–97.

3.2.5.1. Inflection of <u>AP a</u>

áура /á-aw-ra/ 'to receive; to obtain'

Finite forms

	Affirmative	Negative
Dynamic Group I		
Present		
C1-C2		
Sg.3.Non-Human/Pl.3-1	и-с-óу-е-ит /jə-s-áw-wa-jt'/ it/they(C1)-me(C2)-receive-Dyn-Fin 'I receive it/them'	и-с-óу-а-м /jə-s-áw-wa-m/
Sg.3.Non-Human/Pl.3-Sg.2.F	и-б-óу-е-ит	и-б-óу-а-м
Sg.3.Non-Human/Pl.3-Sg.2.M	и-у-óу-е-ит	и-у-óу-а-м
Sg.3.Non-Human/Pl.3-Sg.3.M	и-óу-е-ит (< /jə-j-áw-wa-jt'/)	и-óу-а-м
Sg.3.Non-Human/Pl.3-Sg.3.F	и-л-óу-е-ит	и-л-óу-а-м
Sg.3.Non-Hum./Pl.3-Sg.3.Non-Hum.	и-á-у-е-ит (< /j-a-áw-wa-jt'/)	и-á-у-а-м
Sg.3.Non-Human/Pl.3-Pl.1	и-ах-áу-е-ит /j-aħ-áw-wa-jt'/	и-ах-áу-а-м
Sg.3.Non-Human/Pl.3-Pl.2	и-шә-óу-е-ит	и-шә-óу-а-м
Sg.3.Non-Human/Pl.3-Pl.3	и-р-óу-е-ит	и-р-óу-а-м
Aorist		
C1-C2		
Sg.3.Non-Human/Pl.3-1	и-с-óу-ит /jə-s-áwə-jt'/	и-с-м-óу-ит
Sg.3.Non-Human/Pl.3-Sg.2.F	и-б-óу-ит	и-б-м-óу-ит
Sg.3.Non-Human/Pl.3-Sg.2.M	и-у-óу-ит	и-у-м-óу-ит
Sg.3.Non-Human/Pl.3-Sg.3.F	и-л-óу-ит	и-л-м-óу-ит
Sg.3.Non-Human/Pl.3-Sg.3.M	и-óу-ит (< и-и-óу-ит)	и-м-óу-ит
Sg.3.Non-Hum./Pl.3-Sg.3.Non-Hum.	и-á-у-ит (< /j-a-áwə-jt'/)	и-а-м-óу-ит
Sg.3.Non-Human/Pl.3-Pl.1	и-ах-áу-ит	и-ах-м-óу-ит
Sg.3.Non-Human/Pl.3-Pl.2	и-шә-óу-ит	и-шә-м-óу-ит
Sg.3.Non-Human/Pl.3-Pl.3	и-р-óу-ит	и-р-м-óу-ит
Sg.3.Non-Human/Pl.3-Sg.3.F		
Future I	и-л-óу-п	и-л-óу-ры-м
Future II	и-л-óу-шт	и-л-óу-ша-м
Perfect	и-л-óу-хье-ит	и-л-м-óу-цт
Dynamic Group II		
Imperfect	и-л-óу-а-н (< /jə-l-áw-wa-n/)	и-л-óу-а-мы-зт
Past Indefinite	и-л-óуы-н	и-л-м-óуы-зт
Conditional I	и-л-óу-ры-н	и-л-óу-ры-мы-зт
Conditional II	и-л-óу-ша-н	и-л-óу-ша-мы-зт
Pluperfect	и-л-óу-хьа-н	и-л-м-óу-цы-зт

Non-Finite forms
Dynamic Group I
Present
C1-C2

Rel-Sg.1	и-с-óу-а /jə-s-áw-wa/ 'which I receive'	и-с-м-óу-а
Rel-Sg.2.F	и-б-óу-а	и-б-м-óу-а
Rel-Sg.2.M	и-у-óу-а	и-у-м-óу-а
Rel-Sg.3.F	и-л-óу-а	и-л-м-óу-а
Rel-Sg.3.M	и-óу-а (< /jə-j-áw-wa/)	и-м-óу-а
Rel-Sg.3.Non-Human	и-áу-а (< /j-a-áw-wa/)	и-а-м-óу-а
Rel-Pl.1	и-х-áу-а	и-ах-м-óу-а
Rel-Pl.2	и-шә-óу-а	и-шә-м-óу-а
Rel-Pl.3	и-р-óу-а	и-р-м-óу-а
Sg.1-Rel	с-з-оу-á /s-z-aw-wá/ 'who receives me'	сы-з-м-оу-á
Sg.2.F-Rel	б-з-оу-á	бы-з-м-оу-á
Sg.2.M-Rel	у-з-оу-á	у-з-м-оу-á
Sg.3.Human-Rel	д-з-оу-á	ды-з-м-оу-á
Sg.3.Non-Human/3-Pl-Rel	и-з-оу-á	и-з-м-оу-á
Pl.1-Rel	х-з-оу-á	ха-з-м-оу-á
Pl.2-Rel	шә-з-оу-á	шәы-з-м-оу-á

Aorist

Rel-Sg.1	и-с-óу	и-с-м-óу

Dynamic Group II
Imperfect

Rel-Sg.1	и-с-óу-а-з	и-сы-м-óу-а-з

Past Indefinite

Rel-Sg.1	и-с-óу-з	и-сы-м-óу-з

Notes:

1. áура /[a-]aw-ra/ is an inversive verb (see §5.10). Example:
 ашәҟәы́ лóуит
 /a-šʷq'ʷə́   ø-l-áw-jt'/
 the-letter/book   it(C1)-]her(C2)-receive-(aor)-Fin
 'She received a letter/book.'

2. Note that <u>-ааук-</u> /-a-aw-/ becomes <u>-ау-</u>, and does not become <u>-оу-</u>.

3. The accent in finite forms is placed within the stem.

Other examples:

а́бжьа-ра 'to advise': Fin. [pres.] с-б-а́бжьо-ит, с-а́бжьо-ит (< с-а-а́бжьо-ит), д-х-а́бжьо-ит / с-б-а́бжьо-м, [aor.] с-б-а́бжье-ит / сы-б-м-а́бжье-ит, [fut.1] с-б-а́бжьа-п / с-б-а́бжьа-рым, [fut.2] с-б-а́бжьа-шт / с-б-а́бжьа-шам, [perf.] с-б-а́бжьа-хьеит / сы-б-м-а́бжьа-ц(т), [impf.] с-б-а́бжьо-н / с-б-а́бжьо-мызт, [past indef.] с-б-а́бжьа-н / сы-б-м-а́бжьа-зт, [cond.1] с-б-а́бжьа-рын / с-б-а́бжьа-рымызт, [cond.2] с-б-а́бжьа-шан / с-б-а́бжьа-шамызт, [plupf.] с-б-а́бжьа-хьан / сы-б-м-а́бжьа-цызт; Non-fin. [pres.] (C1) и-л-а́бжьо / и-л-м-а́бжьо, (C2) д-з-а́бжьо / ды-з-м-а́-бжьо, [aor.] (C1) и-л-а́бжьа / и-л-м-а́бжьа, (C2) д-з-а́бжьа / ды-з-м-а́бжьа, [fut.1] (C1) и-л-а́бжьа-ра / и-л-м-а́бжьа-ра, (C2) д-з-а́бжьа-ра / ды-з-м-а́бжьа-ра, [fut.2] (C1) и-л-а́бжьа-ша / и-л-м-а́бжьа-ша, (C2) д-з-а́бжьа-ша / ды-з-м-а́бжьа-ша, [perf.] (C1) и-л-а́бжьа-хьоу (-хьа(ц)) / и-л-м-а́бжьа-хьоу (-хьа(ц)), (C2) д-з-а́бжьа-хьоу (-хьа(ц)) / ды-з-м-а́бжьа-хьоу (-хьа(ц)), [impf.] (C1) и-л-а́бжьо-з / и-л-м-а́бжьо-з, (C2) д-з-а́бжьо-з / ды-з-м-а́бжьо-з, [past indef.] (C1) и-л-а́бжьа-з / и-л-м-а́бжьа-з, (C2) д-з-а́бжьа-з / ды-з-м-а́бжьа-з, [cond.1] (C1) и-л-а́бжьа-ры-з / и-л-м-а́бжьа-ры-з, (C2) д-з-а́бжьа-ры-з / ды-з-м-а́бжьа-ры-з, [cond.2] (C1) и-л-а́бжьа-ша-з / и-л-м-а́бжьа-ша-з, (C2) д-з-а́бжьа-ша-з / ды-з-м-а́бжьа-ша-з, [plupf.] (C1) и-л-а́бжьа-хьа-з / и-л-м-а́бжьаъхьа-з, (C2) д-з-а́бжьа-хьа-з / ды-з-м-а́бжьа-хьа-з.

а-иа́аи-ра 'to defeat': Fin. [pres.] ды-с-иа́аи-уе-ит, д-и-[и]а́аи-уе-ит / ды-с-иа́аи-уа-м, [aor.] ды-с-иа́а-ит / д-сы-м-иа́а-ит, д-иа́а-ит; Non-fin. [pres.] (C1) и-л-иа́аи-уа / и-лы-м-иа́аи-уа, (C2) ды-з-иа́аи-уа / д-зы-м-иа́аи-уа, [aor.] (C1) и-л-иа́аи / и-лы-м-иа́аи, (C2) ды-з-иа́аи / д-зы-м-иа́аи, [impf.] (C1) и-л-иа́аи-уа-з / и-лы-м-иа́аи-уа-з, (C2) ды-з-иа́аи-уа-з / д-зы-м-иа́аи-уа-з, [past indef.] (C1) и-л-иа́аи-з / и-лы-м-иа́аи-з, (C2) ды-з-иа́аи-з / д-зы-м-иа́аи-з.

а-ҭа́а-ра 'to stay with': Fin. [pres.] ды-л-ҭа́а-уе-ит, и-а-та́а-уе-ит / ды-л-ҭа́а-уа-м, [aor.] ды-л-ҭа́а-ит / д-лы-м-ҭа́а-ит; Non-fin. [pres.] (C1) и-л-ҭа́а-уа / и-лы-м-ҭа́а-уа, (C2) ды-з-ҭа́а-уа / д-зы-м-ҭа́а-уа.

а-ны́р-ра 'to influence': Fin. [pres.] и-с-ны́р-уе-ит / и-с-ны́р-уа-м, [aor.] и-с-ны́р-ит / и-сы-м-ны́р-ит; Non-fin. [pres.] (C1) и-с-ны́р-уа / и-сы-м-ны́р-уа, (C2) ды-з-ны́р-уа / д-зы-м-ны́р-уа.

3.2.5.2. Inflection of <u>AP b</u>

а́-сра /á-s-ra/ 'to hit'

Finite forms

	<u>Affirmative</u>	<u>Negative</u>
Dynamic Group I		
Present		
C1-C2		
Sg.1-2.F	с-бы́-с-уе-ит /s-bə́-s-wa-jt'/ 'I am hitting you-F'	с-бы́-с-уа-м /s-bə́-s-wa-m/
Sg.1-2.M	с-у́-с-уе-ит	с-у́-с-уа-м

Sg.1-3.M	с-и́-с-уе-ит	с-и́-с-уа-м
Sg.1-3.F	с-лы́-с-уе-ит	с-лы́-с-уа-м
Sg.1-3.Non-Human	с-а́-с-уе-ит	с-а́-с-уа-м
Sg.1-Pl.2	с-шәы́-с-уе-ит	с-шәы́-с-уа-м
Sg.1-Pl.3	с-ры́-с-уе-ит	с-ры́-с-уа-м
Sg.2.F-1	б-сы́-с-уе-ит	б-сы́-с-уа-м
Sg.3.Human-1	д-сы́-с-уе-ит	д-сы́-с-уа-м
Sg.3.Human-Pl.1	д-ҳа́-с-уе-ит	д-ҳа́-с-уа-м
Sg.3.Non-Human/Pl.3-Sg.1	и-сы́-с-уе-ит	и-сы́-с-уа-м
Sg.3.Non-Human/Pl.3-Sg.3.M	и́-с-уе-ит (< и-и́-с-уе-ит)	и́-с-уа-м
Pl.1-Sg.3.F	ҳ-лы́-с-уе-ит	ҳ-лы́-с-уа-м
Pl.1-Sg.3.Non-Human	ҳ-а́-с-уе-ит	ҳ-а́-с-уа-м
Pl.2-Sg.1	шә-сы́-с-уе-ит	шә-сы́-с-уа-м
Aorist		
C1-C2		
Sg.1-2.F	с-бы́-с-ит /s-bə́-sə-jt'/ 'I hit you-F'	сы-б-мы́-с-ит
Sg.2.F-Pl.1	б-ҳа́-с-ит	б-аҳ-мы́-с-ит
Sg.3.Human-3.Non-Human	д-а́-с-ит	д-а-мы́-с-ит
Pl.1-Sg.2.F	ҳ-бы́-с-ит	ҳа-б-мы́-с-ит
Sg.3.Non-Human/Pl.3-Sg.3.Non-Hum.	и-а́-с-ит	и-а-мы́-с-ит
Sg.1-2.F		
Future I	с-бы́-сы-п	с-бы́-с-ры-м
Future II	с-бы́-сы-ш-т	с-бы́-с-ша-м
Perfect	с-бы́-с-хье-ит	сы-б-мы́-сы-ц(т)
Dynamic Group II		
Imperfect	с-бы́-с-уа-н	с-бы́-с-уа-мы-зт
Past Indefinite	с-бы́-сы-н	сы-б-мы́-сы-зт
Conditional I	с-бы́-с-ры-н	с-бы́-с-ры-мы-зт
Conditional II	с-бы́-с-ша-н	с-бы́-с-ша-мы-зт
Pluperfect	с-бы́-с-хьа-н	сы-б-мы́-с-цы-зт
Non-Finite forms		
Dynamic Group I		
Present		
C1-C2		
Rel-Sg.1	и-сы́-с-уа /jə-sə́-s-wa/ 'who is hitting me'	и-с-мы́-с-уа
Rel-Sg.2.F	и-бы́-с-уа	и-б-мы́-с-уа

Rel-Sg.2.M	и-у́-с-уа	и-у-мы́-с-уа
Rel-Sg.3.F	и-лы́-с-уа	и-л-мы́-с-уа
Rel-Sg.3.M	и́-с-уа (< и-и́-с-уа)	и-мы́-с-уа
Rel-Sg.3.Non-Human	и-а́-с-уа	и-а-мы́-с-уа
Rel-Pl.1	и-ҳа́-с-уа	и-аҳ-мы́-с-уа
Rel-Pl.2	и-шәы́-с-уа	и-шә-мы́-с-уа
Rel-Pl.3	и-ры́-с-уа	и-р-мы́-с-уа
Sg.1-Rel	с-зы-с-уа́ /s-zə-s-wá/ 'whom/which I am hitting'	сы-з-мы́-с-уа
Sg.2.F	б-зы-с-уа́	бы-з-мы́-с-уа
Sg.2.M	у-зы-с-уа́	у-з-мы́-с-уа
Sg.3.Human-Rel	д-зы-с-уа́	ды-з-мы́-с-уа
Sg.3.Non-Human/Pl.3-Rel	и-зы-с-уа́	и-з-мы́-с-уа
Pl.1-Rel	х-зы-с-уа́	ҳа-з-мы́-с-уа
Pl.2-Rel	шә-зы-с-уа́	шәы-з-мы́-с-уа
Aorist		
Rel-Sg.3.F	и-лы́-с	и-л-мы́-с
Sg.3.Human-Rel	д-зы́-с	ды-з-мы́-с
Future I		
Rel-Sg.3.F	и-лы́-с-ра	и-л-мы́-с-ра
Sg.3.Human-Rel	д-зы-с-ра́	ды-з-мы́-с-ра
Future II		
Rel-Sg.3.F	и-лы́-с-ша	и-л-мы́-с-ша
Sg.3.Human-Rel	д-зы-с-ша́	ды-з-мы́-с-ша
Perfect		
Rel-Sg.3.F	и-лы́-с-хьо-у/хьа(ц)	и-л-мы́-с-хьо-у/хьа(ц)
Sg.3.Human-Rel у/хьа(ц)	д-зы-с-хьо́-у/хьа́(ц)	ды-з-мы́-с-хьо-
Dynamic Group II		
Imperfect		
Rel-Sg.3.F	и-лы́-с-уа-з	и-л-мы́-с-уа-з
Sg.3.Human-Rel	д-зы-с-уа́-з	ды-з-мы́-с-уа-з
Past Indefinite		
Rel-Sg.3.F	и-лы́-с-з	и-л-мы́-сы-з
Sg.3.Human-Rel	д-з-сы́-з	ды-з-мы́-сы-з
Conditional I		

Rel-Sg.3.F	и-лы́-с-ры-з	и-л-мы́-с-ры-з
Sg.3.Human-Rel	д-зы-с-ры́-з	ды-з-мы́-с-ры-з
Conditional II		
Rel-Sg.3.F	и-лы́-с-ша-з	и-л-мы́-сы-ша-з
Sg.3.Human-Rel	д-з-сы́-ша-з	ды-з-мы́-с-ша-з
Pluperfect		
Rel-Sg.3.F	и-лы́-с-хьа-з	и-л-мы́-с-хьа-з
Sg.3.Human-Rel	д-зы-с-хьа́-з	ды-з-мы́-с-хьа-з

Note: The accent in finite forms goes on the Column II pronominal prefix, or on the negative marker in forms like the aorist where the negative marker is before the root. As to non-finite affirmative forms, the accent goes on уа-(з), ра, ша, ры-з, хьа-(з) when the relative prefix -з is in Column II.

Other examples:

а́-гәара /á-g^{w}a-ra/ 'to push': Fin. [pres.] с-лы́-гәо-ит, с-а́-гәо-ит / с-лы́-гәо-м, [aor.] с-лы́-гәе-ит / сы-л-мы́-гәе-ит; Non-fin. [pres.] (C1) и-лы́-гәо, и-сы́-гәо, и-бы́-гәо, и-у́-гәо, и-а́-гәо, и́-гәо, и-ха́-гәо, и-шәы́-гәо, и-ры́-гәо / и-л-мы́-гәо, и-с-мы́-гәо, и-б-мы́-гәо, и-у-мы́-гәо, и-а-мы́-гәо, и-мы́-гәо, и-ах-мы́-гәо, и-шә-мы́-гәо, и-р-мы́-гәо, (C2) д-зы́-гәо *or* д-зы-гәо́, с-зы-гәо́, б-зы-гәо́, у-зы-гәо́, и-зы-гәо́, х-зы-гәо́, шә-зы-гәо́ / ды-з-мы́-гәо, сы-з-мы́-гәо, бы-з-мы́-гәо, у-з-мы́-гәо, и-з-мы́-гәо, ха-з-мы́-гәо, шәы-з-мы́-гәо, [aor.] (C1) и-лы́-гәа / и-л-мы́-гәа, (C2) д-зы́-гәа / ды-з-мы́-гәа, [fut.1] (C1) и-лы́-гәа-ра / и-л-мы́-гәа-ра, (C2) д-зы́-гәа-ра / ды-з-мы́-гәа-ра, [fut.2] (C1) и-лы́-гәа-ша / и-л-мы́-гәа-ша, (C2) д-зы́-гәа-ша / ды-з-мы́-гәа-ша, [perf.] (C1) и-лы́-гәа-хьоу (-хьа(ц)) / и-л-мы́-гәа-хьоу (-хьа(ц)), (C2) д-зы́-гәа-хьоу (-хьа(ц)) / ды-з-мы́-гәа-хьоу (-хьа(ц)), [impf.] (C1) и-лы́-гәо-з / и-л-мы́-гәо-з, (C2) д-зы́-гәо-з / ды-з-мы́-гәо-з, [past indef.] (C1) и-лы́-гәа-з / и-л-мы́-гәа-з, (C2) д-зы́-гәа-з / ды-з-мы́-гәа-з, [cond.1] (C1) и-лы́-гәа-ры-з / и-л-мы́-гәа-ры-з, (C2) д-зы́-гәа-ры-з / ды-з-мы́-гәа-ры-з, [cond.2] (C1) и-лы́-гәа-ша-з / и-л-мы́-гәа-ша-з, (C2) д-зы́-гәа-ша-з / ды-з-мы́-гәа-ша-з, [plupf.] (C1) и-лы́-гәа-хьа-з / и-л-мы́-гәа-хьа-з, (C2) д-зы́-гәа-хьа-з / ды-з-мы́-гәа-хьа-з.

а́-ҧхьара /á-px^{j}a-ra/ 'to read; to call': Fin. [pres.] с-а́-ҧхьо-ит, д-а́-ҧхьо-ит, д-ры́-ҧхьо-ит / с-а́-ҧхьо-м, [aor.] с-а́-ҧхье-ит / с-а-мы́-ҧхье-ит, [fut.1] с-а́-ҧхьа-п / с-а́-ҧхьа-рым, [fut.2] с-а́-ҧхьа-шт / с-а́-ҧхьа-шам, [perf.] с-а́-ҧхьа-хьеит / с-а-мы́-ҧхьа-ц(т), [impf.] с-а́-ҧхьо-н / с-а́-ҧхьо-мызт, [past indef.] с-а́-ҧхьа-н / с-а-мы́-ҧхьа-зт, [cond.1] с-а́-ҧхьа-рын / с-а́-ҧхьа-рымызт, [cond.2] с-а́-ҧхьа-шан / с-а́-ҧхьа-шамызт, [plupf.] с-а́-ҧхьа-хьан / с-а-мы́-ҧхьа-цызт; Non-fin. [pres.] (C1) и-а́-ҧхьо / и-а-мы́-ҧхьо, (C2) д-зы-ҧхьо́ / ды-з-мы́-ҧхьо, [aor.] (C1) и-а́-ҧхьа / и-а-мы́-ҧхьа, (C2) д-зы-ҧхьа́ / ды-з-мы́-ҧхьа, [fut.1] (C1) и-а́-ҧхьа-ра / и-а-мы́-ҧхьа-ра, (C2) д-зы-ҧхьа-ра́ / ды-з-мы́-ҧхьа-ра, [fut.2] (C1) и-а́-ҧхьа-ша / и-а-мы́-ҧхьа-ша, (C2) д-зы-ҧхьа́-ша / ды-з-мы́-ҧхьа-ша, [perf.] (C1) и-а́-ҧхьа-хьоу (-хьа(ц)) / и-а-мы́-ҧхьа-хьоу (-хьа(ц)), (C2) д-зы-ҧхьа-хьо́у (-хьа́(ц)) / ды-з-мы́-ҧхьа-хьоу (-хьа(ц)), [impf.] (C1) и-а́-ҧхьо-з / и-а-мы́-ҧхьо-з, (C2) д-зы-ҧхьо́-з / ды-з-мы́-ҧхьо-з, [past indef.] (C1) и-а́-ҧхьа-з / и-а-мы́-ҧхьа-з, (C2) д-зы-ҧхьа́-з / ды-з-мы́-ҧхьа-з, [cond.1] (C1) и-а́-ҧхьа-ры-з / и-а-мы́-ҧхьа-ры-з, (C2) д-зы-ҧхьа-ры́-з / ды-з-мы́-ҧхьа-ры-з, [cond.2] (C1) и-а́-ҧхьа-ша-з / и-а-мы́-ҧхьа-ша-з, (C2) д-зы-ҧхьа́-ша-з / ды-з-мы́-ҧхьа-ша-з, [plupf.] (C1) и-а́-ҧхьа-хьа-з / и-а-мы́-ҧхьа-хьа-з, (C2) д-зы-ҧхьа-хьа́-з / ды-з-мы́-ҧхьа-хьа-з.

а́-ҭәхәара /á-tʷħʷa-ra/ 'to blow at': Fin. [pres.] д-а́-ҭәхәо-ит / д-а́-ҭәхәо-м (-ҭәхәа-ӡо-м), [aor.] д-а́-ҭәхәе-ит / д-а-мы́-ҭәхәе-ит (-ҭәхәа-ӡе-ит); Non-fin. [pres.] (C1) и-а́-ҭәхәо / и-а-мы́-ҭәхәо, (C2) д-зы-ҭәхәо́ / ды-з-мы́-ҭәхәо, [aor.] (C1) и-а́-ҭәхәа / и-а-мы́-ҭәхәа, (C2) д-зы-ҭәхәа́ / ды-з-мы́-ҭәхәа, [impf.] (C1) и-а́-ҭәхәо-з / и-а-мы́-ҭәхәо-з, (C2) д-зы-ҭәхәо́-з / ды-з-мы́-ҭәхәо-з, [past indef.] (C1) и-а́-ҭәхәа-з / и-а-мы́-ҭәхәа-з, (C2) д-зы-ҭәхәа́-з / ды-з-мы́-ҭәхәа-з.

а́-хара /á-xa-ra/ 'to pull': Fin. [pres.] с-бы́-хо-ит, д-а́-хо-ит, д-ха́-хо-ит, х-лы́-хо-ит, и́-хо-ит / с-бы́-хо-м, [aor.] с-бы́-хе-ит / сы-б-мы́-хе-ит, с-а-мы́-хе-ит, д-ах-мы́-хе-ит, [fut.1] с-бы́-ха-п; [fut.2] с-бы́-ха-шт; [perf.] с-бы́-ха-хьеит; [impf.] с-бы́-хо-н / с-бы́-хо-мызт, [past indef.] с-бы́-ха-н / сы-б-мы́-ха-зт, [cond.1] с-бы́-ха-рын / с-у-ха-ры́мызт, [cond.2] с-у́-ха-шан / с-у-ха-ша́мызт, [plupf.] с-у́-ха-хьан / с-у-мы́-ха-цызт; Non-fin. [pres.] и-лы́-хо (*тот, который тянет ее*) / и-л-мы́-хо, (C2) д-зы́-хо́ (i.e. д-зы́-хо *or* д-зы-хо́) / ды-з-мы́-хо, [aor.] (C1) и-лы́-ха / и-л-мы́-ха, (C2) д-зы́-ха́ / ды-з-мы́-ха, [fut.1] (C1) и-лы́-ха-ра / и-л-мы́-ха-ра, (C2) д-зы́-ха-ра / ды-з-мы́-ха-ра, [fut.2] (C1) и-лы́-ха-ша / и-л-мы́-ха-ша, (C2) д-зы́-ха-ша / ды-з-мы́-ха-ша, [perf.] (C1) и-лы́-ха-хьоу (-хьа(п)) / и-л-мы́-ха-хьоу (-хьа(п)), (C2) д-зы́-ха-хьоу (-хьа(п)) / ды-з-мы́-ха-хьоу (-хьа(п)), [impf.] (C1) и-лы́-хо-з / и-л-мы́-хо-з, (C2) д-зы́-хо́-з / ды-з-мы́-хо-з, [past indef.] (C1) и-лы́-ха-з / и-л-мы́-ха-з, (C2) д-зы́-ха́-з / ды-з-мы́-ха-з, [cond.1] (C1) и-лы́-ха-ры-з / и-л-мы́-ха-ры-з, (C2) д-зы́-ха-ры-з / ды-з-мы́-ха-ры-з, [cond.2] (C1) и-лы́-ха-ша-з / и-л-мы́-ха-ша-з, (C2) д-зы́-ха-ша-з / ды-з-мы́-ха-ша-з, [plupf.] (C1) и-лы́-ха-хьа-з / и-л-мы́-ха-хьа-з, (C2) д-зы́-ха-хьа-з / ды-з-мы́-ха-хьа-з.

а́-хьра /á-xʲ-ra/ 'to ache, to hurt': Fin. [pres.] и-сы́-хь-уе-ит, и-а́-хь-уе-ит / и-сы́-хь-уа-м, [aor.] и-сы́-хь-ит / и-с-мы́-хь-ит; Non-fin. [pres.] (C1) и-лы́-хь-уа / и-л-мы́-хь-уа, (C2) и-зы́-хь-уа / и-з-мы́-хь-уа, [aor.] (C1) и-лы́-хь / и-л-мы́-хь, (C2) и-зы́-хь / и-з-мы́-хь, [impf.] (C1) и-лы́-хь-уа-з / и-л-мы́-хь-уа-з, (C2) и-зы́-хь-уа-з / и-з-мы́-хь-уа-з, [past indef.] (C1) и-лы́-хьы-з / и-л-мы́-хьы-з, (C2) и-зы́-хьы-з / и-з-мы́-хьы-з.

а́-хәара /á-xʷa-ra/ 'to help': Fin. [pres.] с-бы́-хәо-ит, с-а́-хәо-ит, б-ха́-хәо-ит / с-бы́-хәо-м, [aor.] с-бы́-хәе-ит / сы-б-мы́-хәе-ит, у-а-мы́-хәе-ит, ды-л-мы́-хәе-ит, [fut.1] с-бы́-хәа-п / с-бы́-хәа-рым, [fut.2] с-бы́-хәа-шт / с-бы́-хәа-шам, [perf.] с-бы́-хәа-хье́ит / сы-б-мы́-хәа-ц(т), [impf.] с-бы́-хәо-н / с-бы́-хәо-мызт, [past indef.] с-бы́-хәа-н / сы-б-мы́-хәа-зт, [cond.1] с-бы́-хәа-рын / с-бы́-хәа-рымызт, [cond.2] с-бы́-хәа-шан / с-бы́-хәа-ша́мызт, [plupf.] с-бы́-хәа-хьан / сы-б-мы́-хәа-цызт; Non-fin. [pres.] (C1) и-лы́-хәо / и-л-мы́-хәо, (C2) д-зы́-хәо / ды-з-мы́-хәо, [aor.] (C1) и-лы́-хәа / и-л-мы́-хәа, (C2) д-зы́-хәа / ды-з-мы́-хәа, [fut.1] (C1) и-лы́-хәа-ра / и-л-мы́-хәа-ра, (C2) д-зы́-хәа-ра / ды-з-мы́-хәа-ра, [fut.2] (C1) и-лы́-хәа-ша / и-л-мы́-хәа-ша, (C2) д-зы́-хәа-ша / ды-з-мы́-хәа-ша, [perf.] (C1) и-лы́-хәа-хьоу (-хьа(п)) / и-л-мы́-хәа-хьоу (-хьа(п)), (C2) д-зы́-хәа-хьоу (-хьа(п)) / ды-з-мы́-хәа-хьоу (-хьа(п)), [impf.] (C1) и-лы́-хәо-з / и-л-мы́-хәо-з, (C2) д-зы́-хәо-з / ды-з-мы́-хәо-з, [past indef.] (C1) и-лы́-хәа-з / и-л-мы́-хәа-з, (C2) д-зы́-хәа-з / ды-з-мы́-хәа-з, [cond.1] (C1) и-лы́-хәа-ры-з / и-л-мы́-хәа-ры-з, (C2) д-зы́-хәа-ры-з / ды-з-мы́-хәа-ры-з, [cond.2] (C1) и-лы́-хәа-ша-з / и-л-мы́-хәа-ша-з, (C2) д-зы́-хәа-ша-з / ды-з-мы́-хәа-ша-з, [plupf.] (C1) и-лы́-хәа-хьа-з / и-л-мы́-хәа-хьа-з, (C2) д-зы́-хәа-хьа-з / ды-з-мы́-хәа-хьа-з; с-бы́-хәа-ны / сы-б-мы́-хәа-кәа.

а́-ҳәара /á-ħʷa-ra/ 'to request; to beg, to ask': Fin. [pres.] с-лы́-ҳәо-ит / с-лы́-ҳәо-м (-ҳәа-ӡо-м), [aor.] с-лы́-ҳәе-ит / сы-л-мы́-ҳәе-ит; Non-fin. [pres.] (C1) и-лы́-ҳәо / и-л-мы́-ҳәо, (C2) д-зы́-ҳәо / ды-з-мы́-ҳәо, [aor.] (C1) и-лы́-ҳәа / и-л-мы́-ҳәа, (C2) д-зы́-ҳәа / ды-з-мы́-ҳәа, [impf.] (C1) и-лы́-ҳәо-з / и-л-мы́-ҳәо-з, (C2) д-зы́-ҳәо-з / ды-з-мы́-ҳәо-з, [past indef.] (C1) и-лы́-ҳәа-з / и-л-мы́-ҳәа-з, (C2) д-зы́-ҳәа-з / ды-з-мы́-ҳәа-з.

а-цхы́раара /a-cxə́raa-ra/ 'to help': Fin. [pres.] д-лы́-цхраа-уе-ит / д-лы́-цхраа-уа-м, [aor.] д-лы́-цхраа-ит / ды-л-мы́-цхраа-ит; Non-fin. [pres.] (C1) и-лы́-цхраа-уа / и-л-мы́-цхраа-уа, (C2) д-зы́-цхраа-уа / ды-з-мы́-цхраа-уа, [aor.] (C1) и-лы́-цхраа / и-л-мы́-цхраа, (C2) д-зы́-цхраа / ды-з-мы́-цхраа, [fut.1] (C1) и-лы́-цхраа-ра / и-л-мы́-цхраа-ра, (C2) д-зы-цхраа-ра́ / ды-з-мы́-цхраа-ра, [fut.2] (C1) и-лы́-цхраа-ша / и-л-мы́-цхраа-ша, (C2) д-зы-цхраа́-ша / ды-з-мы́-цхраа-ша, [perf.] (C1) и-лы́-цхраа-хьоу (-хьа(ц)) / и-л-мы́-цхраа-хьоу (-хьа(ц)), (C2) д-зы́-цхраа-хьоу (-хьа(ц)) / ды-з-мы́-цхраа-хьоу (-хьа(ц)), [impf.] (C1) и-лы́-цхраа-уа-з / и-л-мы́-цхраа-уа-з, (C2) д-зы́-цхраа-уа-з / ды-з-мы́-цхраа-уа-з, [past indef.] (C1) и-лы́-цхраа-з / и-л-мы́-цхраа-з, (C2) д-зы́-цхраа-з / ды-з-мы́-цхраа-з, [cond.1] (C1) и-лы́-цхраа-ры-з / и-л-мы́-цхраа-ры-з, (C2) д-зы́-цхраа-ры-з / ды-з-мы́-цхраа-ры-з, [cond.2] (C1) и-лы́-цхраа-ша-з / и-л-мы́-цхраа-ша-з, (C2) д-зы́-цхраа-ша-з / ды-з-мы́-цхраа-ша-з, [plupf.] (C1) и-лы́-цхраа-хьа-з / и-л-мы́-цхраа-хьа-з, (C2) д-зы́-цхраа-хьа-з / ды-з-мы́-цхраа-хьа-з.

а́-цхара /á-cħa-ra/ 'to bite': Fin. [pres.] с-бы́-цха-уе-ит, д-а́-цха-уе-ит, х-а́-цха-уе-ит / и-сы́-цха-уа-м (-цха-ӡо-м), [aor.] д-сы́-цха-ит, х-шәы́-цха-ит / ды-с-мы́-цха-ит, ха-шә-мы́-цха-ит, [fut.1] и-сы́-цха-п / и-сы́-цха-рым, [fut.2] и-сы́-цха-шт / и-сы́-цха-шам, [perf.] и-сы́-цха-хьеит / и-с-мы́-цха-ц(т), [impf.] и-сы́-цха-уа-н / и-сы́-цха-уа-мызт, [past indef.] и-сы́-цха-н / и-с-мы́-цха-зт, [cond.1] и-сы́-цха-рын / и-сы́-цха-рымызт, [cond.2] и-сы́-цха-шан / и-сы́-цха-ша́мызт, [plupf.] и-сы́-цха-хьан / и-с-мы́-цха-цызт; Non-fin. [pres.] (C1) и-лы́-цха-уа / и-л-мы́-цха-уа, (C2) д-зы-цха-уа́ / ды-з-мы-цха-уа́, [aor.] (C1) и-лы́-цха / и-л-мы́-цха, (C2) д-зы-цха́ / ды-з-мы-цха́, [impf.] (C1) и-лы́-цха-уа-з / и-л-мы́-цха-уа-з, (C2) д-зы-цха-уа́-з / ды-з-мы-цха-уа́-з, [past indef.] (C1) и-лы́-цха-з / и-л-мы́-цха-з, (C2) д-зы-цха́-з / ды-з-мы-цха́-з.

а́-шьцылара /á-šʲcəla-ra/ 'to get used to': Fin. [pres.] д-лы́-шьцыло-ит, и-а́-шьцыло-ит / д-лы́-шьцыло-м, [aor.] д-лы́-шьцыле-ит / ды-л-мы́-шьцыле-ит; Non-fin. [pres.] (C1) и-лы́-шьцыло / и-л-мы́-шьцыло, (C2) д-зы-шьцы́ло / ды-з-мы-шьцы́ло, [aor.] (C1) и-лы́-шьцыла / и-л-мы́-шьцыла, (C2) д-зы-шьцы́ла / ды-з-мы-шьцы́ла, [impf.] (C1) и-лы́-шьцыло-з / и-л-мы́-шьцыло-з, (C2) д-зы-шьцы́ло-з / ды-з-мы-шьцы́ло-з, [past indef.] (C1) и-лы́-шьцыла-з / и-л-мы́-шьцыла-з, (C2) д-зы-шьцы́ла-з / ды-з-мы-шьцы́ла-з.

3.2.5.3. Inflection of AP c

а-фыԥра́ /a-fəjʷ-rá/ 'to smell'

Finite forms

	Affirmative	Negative
Dynamic Group I		
Present		
C1-C2		
Sg.3.Human-1	ды-с-фыԥ-уе́-ит	ды-с-фыԥ-уа́-м

	/də-s-fəjʷ-wá-jt'/ '(s)he smells me'	
Sg.3.Human-3.Non-Hum.	д-а-фыҩ-уé-ит	д-а-фыҩ-уá-м
Sg.3.Human-Pl.1	д-ах-фыҩ-уé-ит	д-ах-фыҩ-уá-м
Aorist		
Sg.3.Human-1	ды-с-фыҩ-и́т	д-сы-м-фҩ-и́т
Sg.3.Human-3.Non-Hum.	д-а-фыҩ-и́т	д-а-м-фыҩ-и́т *or* д-м-а-фҩ-и́т

Notes:
1. Note the presence or absence of the schwa in the root in the aorist: -фыҩ- /fəjʷ/: -фҩ- /fjʷ/.
2. There are very few verbs for the AP c type.

Other examples:

а-крá /a-k'-rá/ 'to feel; to shut': Fin. [pres.] д-а-к-уé-ит / д-а-к-уá-м, [aor.] д-а-к-и́т / д-á-м-к-ит; Non-fin. [pres.] (C1) и-а-к-уá / и-á-м-к-уа, [aor.] (C1) и-а-кы́ / и-á-м-к.

а-хәарá /a-xʷa-rá/ 'to take a sip of': Fin. [pres.] д-а-хәо́-ит / д-а-хәо́-м (-хәа-ӡо́-м), [aor.] д-а-хәé-ит / д-а-мы́-хәе-ит (-хәа-ӡе-ит); Non-fin. [pres.] (C1) и-á-хәо / и-а-мы́-хәо, [aor.] (C1) и-á-хәа / и-а-мы́-хәа.

3.2.6. Class C

Two-place transitive verbs that take the direct object (DO) pronominal prefix in Column I and the pronominal prefix indicating A in Column III comprise this class. The voiced variant sg.1 з- /z/, pl.1 аа- /aa/, pl.2 жә- /žʷ/ of the Column III pronominal prefix appears when the initial consonant of the transitive verb root is voiced.[114] See, for example, the Column III pronominal prefix voiced variants of а-барá /a-ba-rá/ 'to see': дызбо́ит /də-z-ba-wá-jt'/ [him/her(C1)-I(C3)-see-Dyn-Fin] 'I see him/her', даабо́ит /d-aa-ba-wá-jt'/ [him/her(C1)-we(C3)-see-Dyn-Fin] 'we see him/her', дыжәбо́ит /də-žʷ-ba-wá-jt'/ [him/her(C1)-you.Pl(C3)-see-Dyn-Fin] 'you-Pl see him/her'. This voicing of the prefix does not take place for intransitive verbs. For example, сбáхауеит /s-báħa-wa-jt'/ [I(C1)-dig-Dyn-Fin] 'I am engaged in digging'. This contrast is most clearly apparent for labile verbs that can be conjugated as both transitive and intransitive verbs. Compare, for example, the transitive and intransitive forms of á-ӡахра /á-ʒax-ra/ 'sew': сӡахуéит /s-ʒax-wá-jt'/ [I(C1)-sew-Dyn-Fin] [intr.] 'I am sewing' vs. изӡахуéит /jə-z-ʒax-wá-jt'/ [it/them(C1)-I(C3)-sew-Dyn-Fin] [tr.] 'I am sewing it/them'.

The voicing of the pronominal prefix is the standard for concluding that it is to be counted as a Column III prefix (that is to say, that it is a pronominal prefix that indicates the agent of a transitive verb). In other words, it is a standard for determining the transitivity of a verb. However, this is not to say—as was also noted in §3.1.6, Note 5—this voicing phenomenon occurs strictly for all transitive verbs. The Column III pronominal prefix is not voiced for certain transitive verbs even if the initial consonant of the root is voiced. For example, а-ҕалáтра /a-ɣalát'-ra/ 'to betray': дысҕалáтуеит /də-s-ɣalát'-wa-jt'/ [him/her(C1)-I(C3)-betray-Dyn-Fin] 'I betray him/her' (*дызҕалáтуеит /*də-z-ɣalát'-

114. Pl.1 aa is the product of the voicing aa < *aʕ < aħ.

wa-jt'/ is ungrammatical, cf. imperative: дҕалáт! /d-ɣalát'/). Furthermore, there are also verbs like the following that are voiced or not voiced (or can either be voiced or unvoiced) even if they have the same root: а-гарá /a-ga-rá/ 'to take': бызгóит /bə-z-ga-wá-jt'/ [you.F(C1)-I(C3)-take-Dyn-Fin] 'I take you-F' vs. аагарá /aa-ga-rá/ 'to fetch': иааз/сгóит /j-aa-z/s-ga-wá-jt'/ [it/them(C1)-Prev-I(C3)-fetch-Dyn-Fin] 'I fetch it/them'. Voicing Column III pronominal prefixes based on voiced initial consonant at the root does not hold true for every transitive verb; however, we should note that this never occurs for all intransitive verbs under the same conditions.[115]

Class C verbs can be split up into the following two types according to accent type: AP a and AP c. There basically are none of the AP b type-verbs found in Classes A and B, that is to say, none in which the accent is placed on the pronominal prefix in the finite forms of present and aorist. However, as noted in §1.2.2.2, sometimes an accent is placed only on the Column III third-person singular, non-human prefix a-, depending on the type of verb. We treat that as a variant of AP c and use the following subordinate classifications:

(i) а-ба-рá 'to see' (or а-га-рá 'to take') type: The accent is placed on the prefix in this type only for those forms that have the third-person, non-human agent prefix a- in the aorist negative (as well as perfect, past indefinite, and pluperfect): дабéит /d-a-bá-jt'/ 'it saw him/her'; дáмбеит /d-á-m-ba-jt'/ 'it did not see him/her'.

(ii) á-фа-ра 'to eat' type: The accent for this type is placed on the prefix in all tenses: иáфоит /j-

115. We must also pay attention to the structure of the verbal root. When the transitive verb root has a CV(C) structure, the schwa does not appear on the Column III pronominal prefix. The prefix in general is easily voiced in such cases. For example, а-барá /a-ba-rá/ 'to see': бызбóит /bə-z-ba-wá-jt'/ 'I see you-F', а-былрá /a-bəl-rá/ 'to burn': избылуéит /jə-z-bəl-wá-jt'/ 'I burn it/them', а-гарá /a-ga-rá/ 'to take': бызгóит /bə-z-ga-wá-jt'/ 'I take you-F', а-ды́рра /a-dә́r-ra/ 'to know': бызды́руеит /bə-z-dә́r-wa-jt'/ 'I know you-F', а-ӡарá /a-ʒa-rá/ 'to steal': изӡóит /jə-z-ʒa-wá-jt'/ 'I steal it/them', (but иах/ааӡóм /j-aħ/aa-ʒa-wá-m/ 'we do not steal it/them'). The schwa is not generated on the Column III pronominal prefix and the prefix is easily voiced even when the root has a C structure: а-жрá /a-ž-rá/ 'to dig': изжуéит /jə-z-ž-wá-jt'/ 'I dig it/them', á-жәра /á-žʷ-ra/ 'to drink': изжәуéит /jə-z-žʷ-wá-jt'/ 'I drink it/them', а-жәрá /a-žʷ-rá/ 'to boil': изжәуéит /jə-z-žʷ-wá-jt'/ 'I boil it/them', а-ӡрá /a-ʒ-rá/ 'to roast': изӡуéит /jə-z-ʒ-wá-jt'/ 'I roast it/them', а-ҩрá /a-jʷ-rá/ 'to write': изҩуéит /jə-z-jʷ-wá-jt'/ 'I write it/them', (but иахҩи́т /j-aħ-jʷә́-jt'/ 'we wrote it/them', ишәҩи́т /jə-šʷ-jʷә́-jt'/ 'you-Pl wrote it/them'), а-џьрá /a-ǯʲ-rá/ 'to roast': изџьуéит /jə-z-ǯʲ-wá-jt'/ 'I roast it/them'. In contrast, the schwa is generated easily on the Column III pronominal prefix when the root has a CC(V) structure (for this see Rule III in §1.1.1.1). The prefix is difficult to voice in such cases. For example, á-бжьарá /á-bžʲa-rá/ 'to break in (*a horse*)': исыбжьéит /jə-sə-bžʲá-jt'/ 'I train it/them', á-жьжьара /á-žʲžʲa-ra/ 'to soothe': дсыжьжьéит /d-sə-žʲžʲá-jt'/ 'I soothed him/her', á-ӡбара /á-ʒba-ra/ 'to decide': исыӡбóит /jə-sə-ʒba-wá-jt'/ 'I decide it/them', á-ӡ(ы)бра /á-ʒ(ə)b-ra/ 'to decide/judge': исыӡбуéит /jə-sə-ʒb-wá-jt'/ 'I decide it/them', а-ӡры́жәра /a-ʒrә́žʷ-ra/ 'to temper': исӡры́жәуеит /jə-s-ʒrә́žʷ-wa-jt'/ 'I temper it/them', аӡҩарá /a-ʒjʷa-rá/ 'to dilute': исыӡҩóит /jə-sə-ʒjʷa-wá-jt'/ 'I dilute it/them', á-ӡәӡәара /á-ʒʷʒʷa-ra/ 'to wash': бсыӡәӡәóит /b-sə-ʒʷʒʷa-wá-jt'/ 'I wash you-F'. Also, the Column III pronominal prefix of roots that begin with ӡә- /ʒʷ/ tend to be difficult to voice: а-ӡәарá /a-ʒʷa-rá/ 'to vomit': исӡәóит /jə-s-ʒʷa-wá-jt'/ (*и-з-ӡәó-ит).

Furthermore, note also the differences between the affirmative and negative forms of verbs. According to our informant, despite the fact that the Column III pronominal prefix is voiced in ижәӡóит /jə-žʷ-ʒa-wá-jt'/ 'you-Pl steal it/them'—the present affirmative form of аӡарá /a-ʒa-rá/ 'to steal'—the two variants of ижәӡóм /jə-žʷ-ʒa-wá-m/ and ишәӡóм /jə-šʷ-ʒa-wá-m/ are both possibilities for the present negative form.

á-fa-wa-jt'/ 'it eats it/them'; иáфеит /j-á-fa-jt'/ 'it ate it/them'; иáмфеит /j-á-m-fa-jt'/ 'it did not eat it/them'.

(iii) а-ша-рá 'to divide' type: The accent for this type is placed in every stem-final position in the aorist form: иашéит /j-a-šá-jt'/ 'it divided it/them', иамшéит /j-a-m-šá-jt'/ 'it did not divide it/them'.

Below, based on this standard we describe each of the above variants as AP c-i, AP c-ii, and AP c-iii.

3.2.6.1. Inflection of AP a

а-ды́рра /a-dә́r-ra/ 'to know'

Finite forms

	Affirmative	Negative
Dynamic Group I		
Present		
	C1-C3	C1-C2-Pot
Sg.2.F-1	бы-з-ды́р-уе-ит /bә-z-dә́r-wa-jt'/ you.F(C1)-I(C3)-know-Dyn-Fin 'I know you-F'	б-сы-з-ды́р-уа-м[116] 'I do not know you-F'
Sg.2.M-1	у-з-ды́р-уе-ит	у-сы-з-ды́р-уа-м
Sg.3.Human-1	ды-з-ды́р-уе-ит	д-сы-з-ды́р-уа-м
Sg.3.Non-Human-1	и-з-ды́р-уе-ит	и-сы-з-ды́р-уа-м
Pl.2-Sg.1	шәы-з-ды́р-уе-ит	шә-сы-з-ды́р-уа-м
Sg.1-2.F	сы-б-ды́р-уе-ит	с-бы-з-ды́р-уа-м
Sg.1-3.M	с-и-ды́р-уе-ит	с-и-з-ды́р-уа-м
Sg.3.N.Hum./Pl.3-Sg.3.M	и-ды́р-уе-ит (< и-и-ды́р-уе-ит)	и-з-ды́р-уа-м
Sg.1-3.Non-Human	с-а-ды́р-уе-ит	с-а-з-ды́р-уа-м
Sg.2F-Pl.1	б-аа-ды́р-уе-ит	б-ха-з-ды́р-уа-м
Sg.1-Pl.2	сы-жә-ды́р-уе-ит	с-шәы-з-ды́р-уа-м
Sg.1-Pl.3	сы-р-ды́р-уе-ит	с-ры-з-ды́р-уа-м

Aorist		
C1-C2		
Sg.2.F-1	бы-з-ды́р-ит	бы-с-зы́-м-дыр-ит
Sg.2.M-1	у-з-ды́р-ит	у-с-зы́-м-дыр-ит
Sg.3.Non-Human/Pl.3-1	и-з-ды́р-ит	и-с-зы́-м-дыр-ит
Sg.2.F-3.Non-Human	б-а-ды́р-ит	бы-а-зы́-м-дыр-ит
Sg.2.M-1		

116. The potential form is used for the negative form of а-ды́рра /a-dә́r-ra/: бсызды́руам /b-sә-z-dә́r-wa-m/ [you.F(C1)-me(C2)-Pot-know-Dyn-Neg] 'I do not know you-F'. For the potential, see §4.2.4.

Future I	у-з-ды́р-п	у-сы-з-ды́р-ры-м
Future II	у-з-ды́р-шт	у-сы-з-ды́р-ша-м
Perfect	у-з-ды́р-хье-ит	у-с-зы́-м-дыр-т
Dynamic Group II		
Imperfect	у-з-ды́р-уа-н	у-сы-з-ды́р-уа-мы-зт
Past Indefinite	у-з-ды́ры-н	у-с-зы́-м-дыр-зт
Conditional I	у-з-ды́р-ры-н	у-сы-з-ды́р-ры-мы-зт
Conditional II	у-з-ды́р-ша-н	у-сы-з-ды́р-ша-мы-зт
Pluperfect	у-з-ды́р-хьа-н	у-с-зы́-м-дыр-цы-зт

Non-Finite forms

	Affirmative	Negative
Dynamic Group I		
Present		
	C1-C3	C1-C2-Pot
Rel-Sg.1	и́-з-дыр-уа /jə́-z-dər-wa/ Rel(C1)-I(C3)-know-Dyn.NF 'which/whom I know'	и-с-зы́-м-дыр-уа /jə-s-zə́-m-dər-wa/ Rel(C1)-me(C2)-Pot-Neg-know-Dyn.NF 'which/whom I do not know'
Rel-Sg.2.M	и́-у-дыр-уа	и-у-зы́-м-дыр-уа
Rel-Sg.2.F	и́-б-дыр-уа	и-б-зы́-м-дыр-уа
Rel-Sg.3.M	и́-и-дыр-уа[117]	и-зы́-м-дыр-уа
Rel-Sg.3.Non-Human	и-а-ды́р-уа	и-а-зы́-м-дыр-уа
Rel-Pl.1	и-а́а-дыр-уа	и-ах-зы́-м-дыр-уа
Rel-Pl.2	и́-жə-дыр-уа	и-шə-зы́-м-дыр-уа
Rel-Pl.3	и́-р-дыр-уа	и-р-зы́-м-дыр-уа
Sg.1-Rel	сы-з-ды́р-уа /sə-z-də́r-wa/ me(C1)-Rel(C3)-know-Dyn.NF 'who knows me'	сы-з-зы́-м-дыр-уа /sə-z-zə́-m-dər-wa/ I(C1)-Rel(C2)-Pot-Neg-know-Dyn.NF 'who does not know me'
Sg.2.F-Rel	бы-з-ды́р-уа	бы-з-зы́-м-дыр-уа
Sg.2.M-Rel	у-з-ды́р-уа	у-з-зы́-м-дыр-уа
Sg.3.Human-Rel	ды-з-ды́р-уа	ды-з-зы́-м-дыр-уа
Sg.3.Non-Human/Pl.3-Rel	и-з-ды́р-уа[118]	и-з-зы́-м-дыр-уа
Pl.1-Rel	ха-з-ды́р-уа	ха-з-зы́-м-дыр-уа
Pl.2-Rel	шəы-з-ды́р-уа	шəы-з-зы́-м-дыр-уа

117. Note that и́-и- is not contracted into a single 'и-'.

118. Distinguish between издыŕуа /jə-z-də́r-wa/ [it/them(C1)-Rel(C3)-know-Dyn.Non-Fin] '(the one) who knows it/them' and и́здыруа /jə́-z-dər-wa/ [Rel(C1)-I(C3)-know-Dyn.Non-Fin] '(the one) whom/which I know'.

Future I	C-C3	C1-C2
Rel-Sg.3.F	и́-л-дыр-ра	и-л-зы́-м-дыр-ра
Sg.3.Human-Rel	ды-з-ды́р-ра	ды-з-зы́-м-дыр-ра
Future II		
Rel-Sg.3.F	и́-л-дыр-ша	и-л-зы́-м-дыр-ша
Sg.3.Human-Rel	ды-з-ды́р-ша	ды-з-зы́-м-дыр-ша
Perfect		
Rel-Sg.3.F	и́-л-дыр-хьоу (-хьа(ц))	и-л-зы́-м-дыр-хьоу (-хьа(ц))
Sg.3.Human-Rel	ды-з-ды́р-хьоу (-хьа(ц))	ды-з-зы́-м-дыр-хьоу (-хьа(ц))
Dynamic Group II		
Imperfect		
Rel-Sg.3.F	и́-л-дыр-уа-з	и-л-зы́-м-дыр-уа-з
Sg.3.Human-Rel	ды-з-ды́р-уа-з	ды-з-зы́-м-дыр-уа-з
Past Indefinite		
Rel-Sg.3.F	и́-л-дыры-з	и-л-зы́-м-дыры-з
Sg.3.Human-Rel	ды-з-ды́ры-з	ды-з-зы́-м-дыры-з
Conditional I		
Rel-Sg.3.F	и́-л-дыр-ры-з	и-л-зы́-м-дыр-ры-з
Sg.3.Human-Rel	ды-з-ды́р-ры-з	ды-з-зы́-м-дыр-ры-з
Conditional II		
Rel-Sg.3.F	и́-л-дыр-ша-з	и-л-зы́-м-дыр-ша-з
Sg.3.Human-Rel	ды-з-ды́р-ша-з	ды-з-зы́-м-дыр-ша-з
Pluperfect		
Rel-Sg.3.F	и́-л-дыр-хьа-з	и-л-зы́-м-дыр-хьа-з
Sg.3.Human-Rel	ды-з-ды́р-хьа-з	ды-з-зы́-м-дыр-хьа-з

Note: Verbs of this type have stems made up of CVC, CVV, CCVC, and CVCV(C). The accent as a rule is placed on the stem for all finite forms (though the accent is placed on the potential marker for certain negative forms of one such example, ады́рра /a-də́r-ra/). The accent is placed on the relative prefix for non-finite forms when the relative prefix is in Column I. The accent tends to be placed on the stem when a relative prefix is in Column III.

Other examples:

а-ба́ха-ра 'to dig': Fin. [pres.] и-с-ба́ха-уе-ит (preferred) *or* и-з-ба́ха-уе-ит / и-с-ба́ха-уа-м, [aor.] и-с-ба́ха-ит / и-сы-м-ба́ха-ит; Non-fin. [pres.] (C1) и-с-ба́ха-уа / и-сы-м-ба́ха-уа, (C3) и-з-ба́ҳа-уа / и-зы-м-ба́ҳа-уа.

а-ҕала́т-ра 'to betray': Fin. [pres.] ды-с-ҕала́т-уе-ит (*ды-з-ҕала́т-уе-ит is unacceptable) / ды-с-ҕала́т-уа-м, [aor.] ды-с-ҕала́т-ит / д-сы-м-ҕала́т-ит; Non-fin. [pres.] (C1) и-с-ҕала́т-уа / и-сы-м-ҕала́т-уа, (C1) ды-з-ҕала́т-уа / д-зы-м-ҕала́т-уа.

а-ҕәы́х-ра 'to destroy': Fin. [pres.] ды-р-ҕәы́х-уе-ит / ды-р-ҕәы́х-уа-м, [aor.] ды-р-ҕәы́х-ит / д-ры-м-ҕәы́х-ит; Non-fin. [pres.] (C1) и-р-ҕәы́х-уа / и-ры-м-ҕәы́х-уа, (C1) ды-з-ҕәы́х-уа / д-зы-м-ҕәы́х-уа.

а-ӡры́жә-ра 'to temper': Fin. [pres.] и-с-ӡры́жә-уе-ит, и-аҳ-ӡры́жә-уе-ит / и-с-ӡры́жә-уа-м (-ӡры́жә-ӡо-м), [aor.] и-с-ӡры́жә-ит, и-аҳ-ӡры́жә-ит / и-сы-м-ӡры́жә-ит (-ӡры́жә-ӡе-ит), и-ҳа-м-ӡры́жә-ит; Non-fin. [pres.] (C1) и́-л-ӡрыжә-уа / и́-лы-м-ӡрыжә-уа, (C3) и-з-ӡры́жә-уа / и-зы-м-ӡры́жә-уа, [aor.] (C1) и́-л-ӡрыжә / и́-лы-м-ӡрыжә, (C3) и-з-ӡры́жә / и-зы-м-ӡры́жә, [impf.] (C1) и́-л-ӡрыжә-уа-з / и́-лы-м-ӡрыжә-уа-з, (C3) и-з-ӡры́жә-уа-з / и-зы-м-ӡры́жә-уа-з, [past indef.] (C1) и́-л-ӡрыжәы-з / и́-лы-м-ӡрыжәы-з, (C3) и-з-ӡры́жәы-з / и-зы-м-ӡры́жәы-з.

а́-ԥсах-ра 'to change'; а-ԥса́х-ра 'to borrow': Fin. [pres.] и-лы-ԥса́х-уе-ит, и-а́-ԥсах-уе-ит / и-лы-ԥса́х-уа-м, [aor.] и-лы-ԥса́х-ит / и-лы-м-ԥса́х-ит (-ԥса́х-ӡе-ит), [imper.] и-ԥса́х! / и-бы-м-ԥса́хы-н!, и-шәы-ԥса́х! / и-шәы-м-ԥса́хы-н!; Non-fin. [pres.] (C1) и́-лы-ԥсах-уа / и́-лы-м-ԥсах-уа, (C3) и-зы-ԥса́х-уа, д-зы-ԥса́х-уа / и-зы-м-ԥса́х-уа, д-зы-м-ԥса́х-уа, [aor.] (C1) и́-лы-ԥсах / и́-лы-м-ԥсах, (C3) и-зы-ԥса́х, д-зы-ԥса́х-уа / и-зы-м-ԥса́х, д-зы-м-ԥса́х, [impf.] (C1) и́-лы-ԥсах-уа-з / и́-лы-м-ԥсах-уа-з, (C3) и-зы-ԥса́х-уа-з, д-зы-ԥса́х-уа-з / и-зы-м-ԥса́х-уа-з, д-зы-м-ԥса́х-уа-з, [past indef.] (C1) и́-лы-ԥсахы-з / и́-лы-м-ԥсахы-з, (C3) и-зы-ԥса́хы-з, д-зы-ԥса́хы-з / и-зы-м-ԥса́хы-з, д-зы-м-ԥса́хы-з.

а-ра́а-ра 'to cut down': Fin. [pres.] и-с-ра́а-уе-ит / и-с-ра́а-уа-м, [aor.] и-с-ра́а-ит, и-а-ра́а-ит / и-сы-м-ра́а-ит, и-а-м-ра́а-ит; Non-fin. [pres.] (C1) и́-с-раа-уа / и́-сы-м-раа-уа, (C3) и́-з-раа-уа / и́-зы-м-раа-уа.

а-ха́ха-ра 'to spin': Fin. [pres.] и-л-ха́хо-ит / и-л-ха́хо-м (-ха́ха-ӡо-м), [aor.] и-л-ха́хе-ит / и-лы-м-ха́хе-ит; Non-fin. [pres.] (C1) и́-л-хахо / и́-лы-м-хахо, (C3) и-з-ха́хо / и-зы-м-ха́хо, [aor.] (C1) и́-л-хаха / и́-лы-м-хаха, (C3) и-з-ха́ха / и-зы-м-ха́ха, [impf.] (C1) и́-л-хахо-з / и́-лы-м-хахо-з, (C3) и-з-ха́хо-з / и-зы-м-ха́хо-з, [past indef.](C1) и́-л-хаха-з / и́-лы-м-хаха-з, (C3) и-з-ха́ха-з / и-зы-м-ха́ха-з.

а-хы́б-ра 'to cover a roof': Fin. [pres.] и-с-хы́б-уе-ит / и-с-хы́б-уа-м, [aor.] и-с-хы́б-ит / и-сы-м-хы́б-ит; Non-fin. [pres.] (C1) и-с-хы́б-уа / и-сы-м-хы́б-уа, (C3) и-з-хы́б-уа / и-зы-м-хы́б-уа, [aor.] (C1) и-с-хы́б / и-сы-м-хы́б, (C3) и-з-хы́б / и-зы-м-хы́б. (cf. а-хы́б 'roof')

а-хәы́ц-ра[1] 'to think of': Fin. [pres.] и-с-хәы́ц-уе-ит / и-с-хәы́ц-уа-м, [aor.] и-с-хәы́ц-ит / и-сы-м-хәы́ц-ит (-хәы́ц-ӡе-ит); Non-fin. [pres.] (C1) и́-с-хәыц-уа / и́-сы-м-хәыц-уа, (C3) и-з-хәы́ц-уа / и-зы-м-хәы́ц-уа.

а-хәы́ц-ра[2] 'to invent': Fin. [pres.] и-с-хәы́ц-уе-ит / и-с-хәы́ц-уа-м, [aor.] и-с-хәы́ц-ит / и-сы-м-хәы́ц-ит; Non-fin. [pres.] (C1) и-с-хәы́ц-уа / и-сы-м-хәы́ц-уа, (C3) и-з-хәы́ц-уа / и-зы-м-хәы́ц-уа.

а́-ҳасаб-ра 'to solve': Fin. [pres.] и-с-ҳаса́б-уе-ит, [aor.] и-с-ҳаса́б-ит / и-сы-м-ҳаса́б-ит; Non-fin. [pres.] (C1) и́-л-ҳасаб-уа / и́-лы-м-ҳасаб-уа, (C3) и-з-ҳаса́б-уа / и-зы́-м-ҳасаб-уа, [aor.]

(C1) и́-л-хасаб / и́-лы-м-хасаб, (C3) и-з-хаса́б / и-зы́-м-хасаб, [impf.] (C1) и́-л-хасаб-уа-з / и́-лы-м-хасаб-уа-з, (C3) и-з-хаса́б-уа-з / и-зы́-м-хасаб-уа-з, [past indef.] (C1) и́-л-хасабы-з / и́-лы-м-хасабы-з, (C3) и-з-хаса́бы-з / и-зы́-м-хасабы-з.

а-ча́лт-ра 'to harrow': Fin. [pres.] и-с-ча́лт-уе-ит / и-с-ча́лт-уа-м, [aor.] и-с-ча́лт-ит / и-сы-м-ча́лт-ит; Non-fin. [pres.] (C1) и-с-ча́лт-уа / и-сы-м-ча́лт-уа, (C3) и-з-ча́лт-уа / и-зы-м-ча́лт-уа.

а-ча́б-ра 'to stick': Fin. [pres.] и-л-ча́б-уе-ит / и-л-ча́б-уа-м, [aor.] и-л-ча́б-ит / и-лы-м-ча́б-ит; Non-fin. [pres.] (C1) и-л-ча́б-уа / и-лы-м-ча́б-уа *or* и́-лы-м-чаб-уа, (C3) и-з-ча́б-уа / и-зы-м-ча́б-уа. (cf. а-ча́б 'glue')

3.2.6.2. Inflection of AP c-i

For this type, the accent is placed on the element after the root in finite forms, though it is placed on the prefix when there is a Column III third person, non-human pronominal prefix а- in the negative forms of the aorist, perfect, past indefinite, and pluperfect.

а-бара́ /a-ba-rá/ 'to see'

Finite forms

	Affirmative	Negative
Dynamic Group I		
Present		
C1-C3		
Sg.2.F-1	бы-з-бо́-ит /bə-z-ba-wá-jt'/ you.F(C1)-I(C3)-see-Dyn-Fin 'I see you-F'[119]	бы-з-бо́-м /bə-z-ba-wá-m/
Sg.2.M-1	у-з-бо́-ит	у-з-бо́-м
Sg.3.Human-1	ды-з-бо́-ит	ды-з-бо́-м
Sg.3.Non-Human/Pl.3-1	и-з-бо́-ит	и-з-бо́-м
Pl.2-Sg.1	шәы-з-бо́-ит	шәы-з-бо́-м
Sg.1-2.F	сы-б-бо́-ит	сы-б-бо́-м
Pl.1-Sg.2.F	ха-б-бо́-ит	ха-б-бо́-м
Sg.1-Sg.3.M	с-и-бо́-ит	с-и-бо́-м
Sg.3.Non-Human/Pl.3-Sg.3.M	и-бо́-ит (< и-и-бо́-ит)	и-бо́-м
Sg.1-Sg.3.F	сы-л-бо́-ит	сы-л-бо́-м
Sg.3.Human-Sg.3.Non-Human	д-а-бо́-ит	д-а-бо́-м
Sg.3.Non-Hum./Pl.3-Sg.3.Non-Hum.	и-а-бо́-ит	и-а-бо́-м
Pl.1-Sg.3.Non-Human	х-а-бо́-ит	х-а-бо́-м
Sg.3.Human-Pl.1	д-аа-бо́-ит	д-аа-бо́-м
Sg.1-Pl.2	сы-жә-бо́-ит	сы-жә-бо́-м

119. The dynamic marker -уа /wa/ is contracted to become о because the root ends in the vowel а: /a + wa/ > [ɔ]. On this point, see §1.1.1.5. Compare with verbs that end in a consonant: дысшьуе́ит /də-s-ʃʲ-wá-jt'/ 'I'll kill him/her'.

Sg.3.Human-Pl.2	ды-жә-бó-ит	ды-жә-бó-м
Pl.1-Pl.2	ҳа-жә-бó-ит	ҳа-жә-бó-м
Sg.1-Pl.3	сы-р-бó-ит	сы-р-бó-м
Pl.1-Pl.3	ҳа-р-бó-ит	ҳа-р-бó-м
Aorist		
C1-C3		
Sg.2.F-1	бы-з-бé-ит /bə-z-bá-jt'/ 'I saw you-F'	б-сы-м-бé-ит /b-sə-m-bá-jt'/
Sg.2.M-1	у-з-бé-ит	у-сы-м-бé-ит
Sg.3.Human-1	ды-з-бé-ит	д-сы-м-бé-ит
Sg.3.Non-Human/Pl.3-1	и-з-бé-ит	и-сы-м-бé-ит
Pl.2-Sg.1	шәы-з-бé-ит	шә-сы-м-бé-ит
Sg.1-2.F	сы-б-бé-ит	с-бы-м-бé-ит
Pl.1-Sg.2.F	ҳа-б-бé-ит	ҳ-бы-м-бé-ит
Sg.1-Sg.3.M	с-и-бé-ит	с-и-м-бé-ит
Sg.3.Non-Human/Pl.3-Sg.3.M	и-бé-ит (< и-и-бé-ит)	и-м-бé-ит
Sg.1-Sg.3.F	сы-л-бé-ит	с-лы-м-бé-ит
Sg.1-Sg.3.Non-Human	с-а-бé-ит	с-á-м-бе-ит[120]
Sg.2.M-Sg.3.Non-Human	у-а-бé-ит	у-á-м-бе-ит
Sg.2.F-Sg.3.Non-Human	б-а-бé-ит	б-á-м-бе-ит
Sg.3.Human-Sg.3.Non-Human	д-а-бé-ит	д-á-м-бе-ит
Sg.3.Non-Hum./Pl.3-Sg.3.Non-Hum.	и-а-бé-ит	и-á-м-бе-ит
Pl.1-Sg.3.Non-Human	ҳ-а-бé-ит	ҳ-á-м-бе-ит
Pl.2-Sg.3.Non-Human	шә-а-бé-ит	шә-á-м-бе-ит
Sg.3.Human-Pl.1	д-аа-бé-ит	д-ҳа-м-бé-ит
Sg.3.Non-Hum./Pl.3-Pl.1	и-аа-бé-ит	и-ҳа-м-бé-ит
Pl.2-Pl.1	шә-аа-бé-ит	шә-ҳа-м-бé-ит
Sg.1-Pl.2	сы-жә-бé-ит	с-шәы-м-бé-ит
Pl.1-Pl.2	ҳа-жә-бé-ит	ҳ-шәы-м-бé-ит
Sg.1-Pl.3	сы-р-бé-ит	с-ры-м-бé-ит
Pl.1-Pl.3	ҳа-р-бé-ит	ҳ-ры-м-бé-ит
Future I		
Sg.2.F-Sg.1	бы-з-бá-п	бы-з-ба-ры́-м
Future II	бы-з-бá-шт	бы-з-бá-ша-м
Perfect		
Sg.2.F-Sg.1	бы-з-ба-хьé-ит	б-сы-м-бá-ц(т)
Sg.3.Non-Hum./Pl.3-Sg.3.Non-Hum.	и-а-ба-хьé-ит	и-á-м-ба-ц(т)

120. The forms where the accent is placed on the third-person singular, non-human prefix a- are underlined.

Sg.3.Non-Hum./Pl.3-Pl.1	и-аа-ба-хьé-ит	и-ха-м-бá-ц(т)
Sg.3.Non-Hum./Pl.3-Pl.2	и-жә-ба-хьé-ит	и-шәы-м-бá-ц(т)
Sg.3.Non-Hum./Pl.3-Pl.3	и-р-ба-хьé-ит	и-ры-м-бá-ц(т)
Dynamic Group II		
C1-C3		
Imperfect		
Sg.2.F-Sg.1	бы-з-бó-н	бы-з-бó-мы-зт
Past Indefinite		
Sg.2.F-Sg.1	бы-з-бá-н	б-сы-м-бá-зт
Sg.3.Non-Hum./Pl.3-Sg.3.Non-Hum.	и-а-бá-н	и-á-м-ба-зт
Sg.3.Non-Hum./Pl.3-Pl.1	и-аа-бá-н	и-ха-м-бá-зт
Conditional I		
Sg.2.F-Sg.1	бы-з-ба-ры́-н	бы-з-ба-ры́-мы-зт
Conditional II	бы-з-бá-ша-н	бы-з-бá-ша-мы-зт
Pluperfect		
Sg.2.F-Sg.1	бы-з-ба-хьá-н	б-сы-м-бá-цы-зт
Sg.3.Non-Hum./Pl.3-Sg.3.Non-Hum.	и-а-ба-хьá-н	и-á-м-ба-цы-зт
Sg.3.Non-Hum./Pl.3-Pl.1	и-аа-ба-хьá-н	и-ха-м-бá-цы-зт

Non-Finite forms

	<u>Affirmative</u>	<u>Negative</u>
Dynamic Group I		
Present		
C1-C3		
Rel-Sg.1	и́-з-бо /jə́-z-ba-wa/ Rel(C1)-I(C3)-see-Dyn.NF 'which/whom I see'	и́-зы-м-бо /jə́-zə-m-ba-wa/
Rel-Sg.2.F	и́-б-бо	и́-бы-м-бо
Rel-Sg.2.M	и́-у-бо	и́-у-м-бо
Rel-Sg.3.F	и́-л-бо	и́-лы-м-бо
Rel-Sg.3.M	и́-и-бо	и́-и-м-бо
Rel-Sg.3.Non-Human	и-а-бó	и-á-м-бо
Rel-Pl.1	и-áҳ-бо /já-ħ-ba-wa/	и-áҳа-м-бо /já-ħa-m-ba-wa/
Rel-Pl.2	и́-жә-бо	и́-жәы-м-бо
Rel-Pl.3	и́-р-бо	и́-ры-м-бо
Sg.1-Rel	сы-з-бó /sə-z-ba-wá/ me(C1)-Rel(C3)-see-Dyn.NF 'who sees me'	с-зы-м-бó /s-zə-m-ba-wá/
Sg.2.F-Rel	бы-з-бó	б-зы-м-бó

Sg.2.M-Rel	у-з-бо́	у-зы-м-бо́
Sg.3.Human-Rel	ды-з-бо́	д-зы-м-бо́
Sg.3.Non-Hum./Pl.3-Rel	и-з-бо́ /jə-z-ba-wá/ it/them(C1)-Rel(C3)-see-Dyn.NF '(the one) who sees it/them'	и-зы-м-бо́
Pl.1-Rel	ха-з-бо́	х-зы-м-бо́
Pl.2-Rel	шәы-з-бо́	шә-зы-м-бо́
Future I		
Rel-Sg.3.F	и́-л-ба-ра	и́-лы-м-ба-ра
Sg.3.Human-Rel	ды-з-ба-ра́	д-зы-м-ба-ра́
Future II		
Rel-Sg.3.F	и́-л-ба-ша	и́-лы-м-ба-ша
Sg.3.Human-Rel	ды-з-ба́-ша	д-зы-м-ба́-ша
Perfect		
Rel-Sg.3.F	и́-л-ба-хьоу/хьа(п)	и́-лы-м-ба-хьоу/хьа(п)
Sg.3.Human-Rel /хьа́(п)	ды-з-ба-хьо́у/хьа́(п)	д-зы-м-ба-хьо́у
Dynamic Group II		
C1-C3		
Imperfect		
Rel-Sg.3.F	и́-л-бо-з	и́-лы-м-бо-з
Sg.3.Human-Rel	ды-з-бо́-з	д-зы-м-бо́-з
Past Indefinite		
Rel-Sg.3.F	и́-л-ба-з	и́-лы-м-ба-з
Sg.3.Human-Rel	ды-з-ба́-з	д-зы-м-ба́-з
Conditional I		
Rel-Sg.3.F	и́-л-ба-ры-з	и́-лы-м-ба-ры-з
Sg.3.Human-Rel	ды-з-ба-ры́-з	д-зы-м-ба-ры́-з
Conditional II		
Rel-Sg.3.F	и́-л-ба-ша-з	и́-лы-м-ба-ша-з
Sg.3.Human-Rel	ды-з-ба-ша́-з	д-зы-м-ба́-ша-з
Pluperfect		
Rel-Sg.3.F	и́-л-ба-хьа-з	и́-лы-м-ба-хьа-з
Sg.3.Human-Rel	ды-з-ба-хьа́-з	д-зы-м-ба-хьа́-з

Notes:

1. For <u>AP c-i</u> the accent is placed on the Column III third-person singular, non-human prefix <u>a-</u> in the negative forms of finite forms aorist, perfect, past indefinite, and pluperfect. For non-finite forms, the accent is placed on the relative prefix in Column I when there is a relative prefix in that column, and on the root or the element after the root when there is a relative prefix in Column III.

However, accent moves to after the root when there is a relative prefix in Column I and the third-person singular, non-human prefix a- in Column III: иабо́ /j-a-ba-wá/ [Rel(C1)-it(C3)-see-Dyn.Non-Fin] 'which it is seeing'. The accent in a masdar is placed on the suffix.

2. The conjugation of the verb а-шьра́ /a-šʲ-rá/ 'to kill' whose root ends in a consonant is as follows:

Finite forms

Present

Affirmative: ды-с-шь-уе́-ит /də-s-šʲ-wá-jtʼ/ 'I'll kill him/her', у-с-шь-уе́-ит, бы-с-шь-уе́-ит, и-с-шь-уе́-ит, шәы-с-шь-уе́-ит, с-у-шь-уе́-ит, ды-б-шь-уе́-ит, ха-б-шь-уе́-ит, с-и-шь-уе́-ит, и-шь-уе́-ит (< и-и-шь-уе́-ит), ҳа-и-шь-уе́-ит, сы-л-шь-уе́-ит, ҳа-л-шь-уе́-ит, шәы-л-шь-уе́-ит, с-а-шь-уе́-ит, д-а-шь-уе́-ит, и-а-шь-уе́-ит, д-аҳ-шь-уе́-ит, сы-шә-шь-уе́-ит, сы-р-шь-уе́-ит, ха-р-шь-уе́-ит. Negative: ды-с-шь-уа́-м (ды-с-шь-ӡо́-м /də-s-šʲ-ʒa-wá-m/), у-с-шь-уа́-м, бы-с-шь-уа́-м, с-у-шь-уа́-м, сы-б-шь-уа́-м, с-и-шь-уа́-м, сы-л-шь-уа́-м, с-а-шь-уа́-м, и-а-шь-уа́-м, у-аҳ-шь-уа́-м, сы-шә-шь-уа́-м, сы-р-шь-уа́-м.

Aorist

Affirmative: ды-с-шь-и́т /də-s-šʲə́-jtʼ/ 'I killed him/her', у-с-шь-и́т, бы-с-шь-и́т, и-с-шь-и́т, шәы-с-шь-и́т, с-у-шь-и́т, и-у-шь-и́т, ха-у-шь-и́т, сы-б-шь-и́т, с-и-шь-и́т, д-и-шь-и́т, и-шь-и́т (< и-и-шь-и́т), ха-и-шь-и́т, шә-и-шь-и́т, сы-л-шь-и́т, с-а-шь-и́т, у-а-шь-и́т, д-а-шь-и́т, и-а-шь-и́т, х-а-шь-и́т, шә-а-шь-и́т, у-аҳ-шь-и́т, д-аҳ-шь-и́т, и-аҳ-шь-и́т, шә-аҳ-шь-и́т, сы-шә-шь-и́т, ха-шә-шь-и́т, сы-р-шь-и́т, ды-р-шь-и́т. Negative: д-сы-м-шь-и́т /d-sə-m-šʲə́-jtʼ/ 'I did not kill him/her', у-сы-м-шь-и́т, б-сы-м-шь-и́т, и-сы-м-шь-и́т, шә-сы-м-шь-и́т, с-у-м-шь-и́т, с-бы-м-шь-и́т, х-бы-м-шь-и́т, с-и-м-шь-и́т, и-м-шь-и́т (< и-и-м-шь-и́т), х-и-м-шь-и́т, с-лы-м-шь-и́т, с-а́-м-шь-ит, б-а́-м-шь-ит, д-а́-м-шь-ит, и-а́-м-шь-ит, х-а́-м-шь-ит, шә-а́-м-шь-ит, у-ха-м-шь-и́т, д-ха-м-шь-и́т, с-шәы-м-шь-и́т, с-ры-м-шь-и́т.

Future I

Affirmative: ды-с-шьы́-п, с-у-шьы́-п, сы-б-шьы́-п, с-и-шьы́-п, и-шьы́-п (< и-и-шьы́-п), сы-л-шьы́-п, с-а-шьы́-п, у-а-шьы́-п, д-а-шьы́-п, и-а-шьы́-п, х-а-шьы́-п, шә-а-шьы́-п, у-аҳ-шьы́-п, сы-шә-шьы́-п, сы-р-шьы́-п. Negative: у-с-шь-ры́-м, ды-с-шь-ры́-м, и-у-шь-ры́-м, сы-б-шь-ры́-м, с-и-шь-ры́-м, и-шь-ры́-м (< и-и-шь-ры́-м), сы-л-шь-ры́-м, с-а́-шь-ры-м, у-а́-шь-ры-м, б-а́-шь-ры-м, д-а́-шь-ры-м, и-а́-шь-ры-м, х-а́-шь-ры-м, шә-а́-шь-ры-м, у-аҳ-шь-ры́-м, сы-шә-шь-ры́-м, сы-р-шь-ры́-м.

Future II

Affirmative: ды-с-шьы́-шт, у-с-шьы́-шт, бы-с-шьы́-шт, и-с-шьы́-шт, шәы-с-шьы́-шт, с-у-шьы́-шт, ха-у-шьы́-шт, сы-б-шьы́-шт, и-б-шьы́-шт, и-шьы́-шт (< и-и-шьы́-шт), ха-и-шьы́-шт, сы-л-шьы́-шт, с-а-шьы́-шт, у-а-шьы́-шт, д-а-шьы́-шт, и-а-шьы́-шт, х-а-шьы́-шт, шә-а-шьы́-шт, у-аҳ-шьы́-шт, сы-шә-шьы́-шт, сы-р-шьы́-шт. Negative: ды-с-шьы́-ша-м, у-с-шьы́-ша-м, бы-с-шьы́-ша-м, с-у-шьы́-ша-м, ха-у-шьы́-ша-м, сы-б-шьы́-ша-м, с-и-шьы́-ша-м, и-шьы́-ша-м (< и-и-шьы́-ша-м), ҳа-и-шьы́-ша-м, сы-л-шьы́-ша-м, с-а-шьы́-ша-м, у-а-шьы́-ша-м, д-а-шьы́-ша-м, и-а-шьы́-ша-м, х-а-шьы́-ша-м, шә-а-шьы́-ша-м, у-аҳ-шьы́-ша-м, сы-шә-шьы́-ша-м, сы-р-шьы́-ша-м.

Perfect

Affirmative: ды-с-шь-хье́-ит, у-с-шь-хье́-ит, бы-с-шь-хье́-ит, и-с-шь-хье́-ит, шәы-с-шь-хье́-ит, с-у-шь-хьé-ит, сы-б-шь-хьé-ит, с-и-шь-хьé-ит, и-шь-хьé-ит (< и-и-шь-хьé-ит), ҳа-и-шь-хьé-ит, сы-л-шь-хьé-ит, с-á-шь-хье-ит, у-á-шь-хье-ит, б-á-шь-хье-ит, д-á-шь-хье-ит, и-á-шь-хье-ит, ҳ-á-шь-хье-ит, шә-á-шь-хье-ит, у-аҳ-шь-хьé-ит, сы-шә-шь-хьé-ит, сы-р-шь-хьé-ит. Negative: д-сы-м-шьы́-ц(т), у-сы-м-шьы́-ц(т), б-сы-м-шьы́-ц(т), и-сы-м-шьы́-ц(т), шә-сы-м-шьы́-ц(т), с-у-м-шьы́-ц(т), с-бы-м-шьы́-ц(т), с-и-м-шьы́-ц(т), и-м-шьы́-ц(т) (< и-и-м-шьы́-ц(т)), с-лы-м-шьы́-ц(т), с-á-м-шьы-ц(т), у-á-м-шьы-ц(т), б-á-м-шьы-ц(т), д-á-м-шьы-ц(т), и-á-м-шьы-ц(т), ҳ-á-м-шьы-ц(т), шә-á-м-шьы-ц(т), у-ҳа-м-шьы́-ц(т), б-ҳа-м-шьы́-ц(т), с-шәы-м-шьы́-ц(т), с-ры-м-шьы́-ц(т).

Imperfect

Affirmative: ды-с-шь-уá-н, у-с-шь-уá-н, бы-с-шь-уá-н, и-с-шь-уá-н, шәы-с-шь-уá-н, с-у-шь-уá-н, сы-б-шь-уá-н, с-и-шь-уá-н, и-шь-уá-н (< и-и-шь-уá-н), ҳа-и-шь-уá-н, сы-л-шь-уá-н, с-а-шь-уá-н, у-а-шь-уá-н, б-а-шь-уá-н, д-а-шь-уá-н, и-а-шь-уá-н, ҳ-а-шь-уá-н, шә-а-шь-уá-н, у-аҳ-шь-уá-н, сы-шә-шь-уá-н, сы-р-шь-уá-н. Negative: ды-с-шь-уá-мы-зт, у-с-шь-уá-мы-зт, бы-с-шь-уá-мы-зт, и-с-шь-уá-мы-зт, шәы-с-шь-уá-мы-зт, д-у-шь-уá-мы-зт, ҳа-у-шь-уá-мы-зт, сы-б-шь-уá-мы-зт, с-и-шь-уá-мы-зт, и-шь-уá-мы-зт (< и-и-шь-уá-мы-зт), ҳа-и-шь-уá-мы-зт, сы-л-шь-уá-мы-зт, с-а-шь-уá-мы-зт, у-а-шь-уá-мы-зт, б-а-шь-уá-мы-зт, д-а-шь-уá-мы-зт, и-а-шь-уá-мы-зт, ҳ-а-шь-уá-мы-зт, шә-а-шь-уá-мы-зт, б-аҳ-шь-уá-мы-зт, сы-шә-шь-уá-мы-зт, сы-р-шь-уá-мы-зт.

Past Indefinite

Affirmative: ды-с-шьы́-н, у-с-шьы́-н, бы-с-шьы́-н, и-с-шьы́-н, шәы-с-шьы́-н, с-у-шьы́-н, сы-б-шьы́-н, ҳа-б-шьы́-н, с-и-шьы́-н, и-шьы́-н (< и-и-шьы́-н), ҳа-и-шьы́-н, сы-л-шьы́-н, с-а-шьы́-н, у-а-шьы́-н, б-а-шьы́-н, д-а-шьы́-н, и-а-шьы́-н, ҳ-а-шьы́-н, шә-а-шьы́-н, у-аҳ-шьы́-н, сы-шә-шьы́-н, сы-р-шьы́-н. Negative: д-сы-м-шьы́-зт, у-сы-м-шьы́-зт, б-сы-м-шьы́-зт, и-сы-м-шьы́-зт, шә-сы-м-шьы́-зт, с-у-м-шьы́-зт, ҳ-у-м-шьы́-зт, с-бы-м-шьы́-зт, с-и-м-шьы́-зт, и-м-шьы́-зт (< и-и-м-шьы́-зт), ҳ-и-м-шьы́-зт, с-лы-м-шьы́-зт, с-á-м-шьы-зт, у-á-м-шьы-зт, б-á-м-шьы-зт, д-á-м-шьы-зт, и-á-м-шьы-зт, ҳ-á-м-шьы-зт, шә-á-м-шьы-зт, у-ҳа-м-шьы́-зт, б-ҳа-м-шьы́-зт, с-шәы-м-шьы́-зт, с-ры-м-шьы́-зт.

Conditional I

Affirmative: ды-с-шь-ры́-н, у-с-шь-ры́-н, бы-с-шь-ры́-н, и-с-шь-ры́-н, шәы-с-шь-ры́-н, с-у-шь-ры́-н, сы-б-шь-ры́-н, ҳа-б-шь-ры́-н, с-и-шь-ры́-н, и-шь-ры́-н (< и-и-шь-ры́-н), сы-л-шь-ры́-н, с-а-шь-ры́-н, у-а-шь-ры́-н, б-а-шь-ры́-н, д-а-шь-ры́-н, и-а-шь-ры́-н, ҳ-а-шь-ры́-н, шә-а-шь-ры́-н, у-аҳ-шь-ры́-н, сы-шә-шь-ры́-н, сы-р-шь-ры́-н. Negative: ды-с-шь-ры́-мы-зт, у-с-шь-ры́-мы-зт, бы-с-шь-ры́-мы-зт, и-с-шь-ры́-мы-зт, шәы-с-шь-ры́-мы-зт, с-у-шь-ры́-мы-зт, сы-б-шь-ры́-мы-зт, с-и-шь-ры́-мы-зт, и-шь-ры́-мы-зт (< и-и-шь-ры́-мы-зт), ҳа-и-шь-ры́-мы-зт, сы-л-шь-ры́-мы-зт, с-а-шь-ры́-мы-зт, у-а-шь-ры́-мы-зт, б-а-шь-ры́-мы-зт, д-а-шь-ры́-мы-зт, и-а-шь-ры́-мы-зт, ҳ-а-шь-ры́-мы-зт, шә-а-шь-ры́-мы-зт, у-аҳ-шь-ры́-мы-зт, сы-шә-шь-ры́-мы-зт, сы-р-шь-ры́-мы-зт.

Conditional II

Affirmative: ды-с-шьы́-ша-н, у-с-шьы́-ша-н, бы-с-шьы́-ша-н, и-с-шьы́-ша-н, шәы-с-шьы́-ша-н, с-у-шьы́-ша-н, ҳа-у-шьы́-ша-н, сы-б-шьы́-ша-н, с-и-шьы́-ша-н, и-шьы́-ша-н (< и-и-шьы́-ша-н), ҳа-и-шьы́-ша-н, сы-л-шьы́-ша-н, с-а-шьы́-ша-н, у-а-шьы́-ша-н, б-а-шьы́-ша-н, д-а-шьы́-ша-н, и-а-шьы́-ша-н, ҳ-а-шьы́-ша-н, шә-а-шьы́-ша-н, у-аҳ-шьы́-ша-н, сы-шә-шьы́-ша-н, сы-р-шьы́-ша-н. Negative: ды-с-шьы́-ша-мы-зт, у-с-шьы́-ша-мы-зт, бы-с-шьы́-ша-мы-зт, и-с-шьы́-ша-мы-зт, шәы-с-шьы́-ша-мы-зт, с-у-шьы́-ша-мы-зт, ха-у-шьы́-ша-мы-зт, сы-б-шьы́-ша-мы-зт, с-и-шьы́-ша-мы-зт, и-шьы́-ша-мы-зт (< и-и-шьы́-ша-мы-зт), сы-л-шьы́-ша-мы-зт, с-а-шьы́-ша-мы-зт, у-а-шьы́-ша-мы-зт, б-а-шьы́-ша-мы-зт, д-а-шьы́-ша-мы-зт, и-а-шьы́-ша-мы-зт, х-а-шьы́-ша-мы-зт, шә-а-шьы́-ша-мы-зт, у-ах-шьы́-ша-мы-зт, сы-шә-шьы́-ша-мы-зт, сы-р-шьы́-ша-мы-зт.

Pluperfect

Affirmative: ды-с-шь-хьа́-н, у-с-шь-хьа́-н, бы-с-шь-хьа́-н, и-с-шь-хьа́-н, шәы-с-шь-хьа́-н, с-у-шь-хьа́-н, сы-б-шь-хьа́-н, с-и-шь-хьа́-н, и-шь-хьа́-н (и-и-шь-хьа́-н), ха-б-шь-хьа́-н, с-и-шь-хьа́-н, сы-л-шь-хьа́-н, с-а-шь-хьа́-н, у-а-шь-хьа́-н, б-а-шь-хьа́-н, д-а-шь-хьа́-н, и-а-шь-хьа́-н, х-а-шь-хьа́-н, шә-а-шь-хьа́-н, у-ах-шь-хьа́-н, сы-шә-шь-хьа́-н, сы-р-шь-хьа́-н. Negative: д-сы-м-шьы́-цы-зт, у-сы-м-шьы́-цы-зт, б-сы-м-шьы́-цы-зт, и-сы-м-шьы́-цы-зт, шә-сы-м-шьы́-цы-зт, с-у-м-шьы́-цы-зт, с-бы-м-шьы́-цы-зт, с-и-м-шьы́-цы-зт, и-м-шьы́-цы-зт (< и-и-м-шьы́-цы-зт), с-лы-м-шьы́-цы-зт, с-а́-м-шьы-цы-зт, у-а́-м-шьы-цы-зт, б-а́-м-шьы-цы-зт, д-а́-м-шьы-цы-зт, и-а́-м-шьы-цы-зт, х-а́-м-шьы-цы-зт, шә-а́-м-шьы-цы-зт, у-ха-м-шьы́-цы-зт, с-шәы-м-шьы́-цы-зт, с-ры-м-шьы́-цы-зт.

Non-Finite forms

Dynamic Group I

Present

C1(Rel)-C3:

Affirmative: и́-л-шь-уа 'whom/which she kills', и́-с-шь-уа, и́-у-шь-уа, и́-б-шь-уа, и-а́-шь-уа, и́-и-шь-уа, и-а́х-шь-уа, и́-шә-шь-уа, и́-р-шь-уа. Negative: и́-лы-м-шь-уа, и́-сы-м-шь-уа, и́-у-м-шь-уа, и́-бы-м-шь-уа, и-а́-м-шь-уа, и́-и-м-шь-уа, и-а́ха-м-шь-уа, и́-шәы-м-шь-уа, и́-ры-м-шь-уа,

C1-C3(Rel):

Affirmative: ды-з-шь-уа́ 'who/which kills him/her', сы-з-шь-уа́, бы-з-шь-уа́, у-з-шь-уа́, и-з-шь-уа́, ха-з-шь-уа́, шәы-з-шь-уа́. Negative: д-зы-м-шь-уа́, с-зы-м-шь-уа́, б-зы-м-шь-уа́, у-зы-м-шь-уа́, и-зы-м-шь-уа́, х-зы-м-шь-уа́, шә-зы-м-шь-уа́.

Aorist

C1(Rel)-C3: Affirmative: и́-л-шь. Negative: и́-лы-м-шь

C1-C3(Rel): Affirmative: ды-з-шьы́. Negative: д-зы-м-шьы́

Future I

C1(Rel)-C3: Affirmative: и́-л-шь-ра. Negative: и́-лы-м-шь-ра

C1-C3(Rel): Affirmative: ды-з-шь-ра́. Negative: д-зы-м-шь-ра́

Future II

C1(Rel)-C3: Affirmative: и́-л-шь-ша. Negative: и́-лы-м-шь-ша

C1-C3(Rel): Affirmative: ды-з-шь-ша́. Negative: д-зы-м-шь-ша́

Perfect

C1(Rel)-C3: Affirmative: и́-л-шь-хьа(ц) (-хьо-у). Negative: и́-лы-м-шь-хьа(ц) (-хьоу)

C1-C3(Rel): Affirmative: ды-з-шь-хьа́(ц) (-хьо́-у). Negative: д-зы-м-шь-хьа́(ц) (-хьо́-у)

Dynamic Group II

Imperfect

C1(Rel)-C3: Affirmative: и́-л-шь-уа-з. Negative: и́-лы-м-шь-уа-з

C1-C3(Rel): Affirmative: ды-з-шь-уа́-з. Negative: д-зы-м-шь-уа́-з

Past Indefinite

C1(Rel)-C3: Affirmative: и́-л-шьы-з. Negative: и́-лы-м-шьы-з
C1-C3(Rel): Affirmative: ды-з-шьы́-з. Negative: д-зы-м-шьы́-з
Conditional I
C1(Rel)-C3: Affirmative: и́-л-шь-ры-з. Negative: и́-лы-м-шь-ры-з
C1-C3(Rel): Affirmative: ды-з-шь-ры́-з. Negative: д-зы-м-шь-ры́-з
Conditional II
C1(Rel)-C3: Affirmative: и́-л-шь-ша-з. Negative: и́-лы-м-шь-ша-з
C1-C3(Rel): Affirmative: ды-з-шьы́-ша-з. Negative: д-зы-м-шьы́-ша-з
Pluperfect
C1(Rel)-C3: Affirmative: и́-л-шь-хьа-з. Negative: и́-лы-м-шь-хьа-з
C1-C3(Rel): Affirmative: ды-з-шь-хьа́-з. Negative: д-зы-м-шь-хьа́-з

3. а-ура́ /a-w-rá/ 'to do; to make' is also the same type as AP c-i. The root and dynamic marker уа /wa/ are contracted because the root is у /w/:

Fin. [pres.] и-з/с-у-е́-ит (< /jə-z/s-w-wá-jt'/), и-б-у-е́-ит, и-у-у-е́-ит 'you-M do it/them', и-у-е́-ит, и-л-у-е́-ит, и-а-у-е́-ит, и-аа/ах-у-е́-ит, и-жә/шә-у-е́-ит, и-р-у-е́-ит / и-з-у-а́-м (*и-с-у-а́-м) *or* и-з-у-ʒо́-м, и-у-а́-м, и-а-у-а́-м, и-аа/ах-у-а́-м, и-жә/шә-у-а́-м, [aor.] и-з/с-у-и́т /jə-z/s-wə́-jt'/, и-у-у-и́т, и-б-у-и́т, и-л-у-и́т, и-у-и́т, и-а-у-и́т, и-аа-у-и́т, и-жә-у-и́т, и-р-у-и́т / и-сы/зы-м-у-и́т, и-у-м-у-и́т, и-бы-м-у-и́т, и-м-у-и́т, и-лы-м-у-и́т, и-а́-м-у-ит, и-ха/аа-м-у-и́т, и-шәы/жәы-м-у-и́т, и-ры-м-у-и́т, [fut.1] и-л-уы́-п / и-л-у-ры́-м, [fut.2] и-л-уы́-шт / и-л-уы́-ша-м, [perf.] и-л-у-хье́-ит / и-лы-м-уы́-цт, [impf.] и-л-у-а́-н (< jə-l-w-wá-n/) / и-л-у-а́-мы-зт (< jə-l-w-wá-mə-zt'/), [past indef.] и-л-уы́-н / и-лы-м-уы́-зт, [cond.1] и-л-у-ры́н / и-л-у-ры́мызт, [cond.2] и-л-уы́-ша-н / и-л-уы́-ша-мы-зт, [plupf.] и-л-у-хьа́-н / и-лы-м-уы́-цы-зт; Non-fin. [pres.] (C1) и́-л-у-а, и́-з/с-у-а, и́-б-у-а, и́-у-у-а, и́-и-у-а, и-а-у-а́, и-а́х-у-а, и́-жә/шә-у-а, и́-р-у-а / и́-лы-м-у-а, и́-сы/зы-м-у-а, и́-бы-м-у-а, и́-у-м-у-а, и́-и-м-у-а, и-а́-м-у-а, и-а́ха-м-у-а, и́-шәы/жәы-м-у-а, и́-ры-м-у-а, (C3) и-з-у-а́ / и-зы-м-у-а́, [aor.] (C1) и́-л-у / и́-лы-м-у, (C3) и-з-уы́ / и-зы-м-уы́, [impf.] (C1) и́-л-у-а-з / и́-лы-м-у-а-з, (C3) и-з-у-а́-з / и-зы-м-у-а́-з, [past indef.] (C1) и́-л-уы-з / и́-лы-м-уы-з, (C3) и-з-уы́-з / и-зы-м-уы́-з.

Other examples:

а-га-ра́ 'to take; to carry': Fin. [pres.] бы-з-го́-ит, и-го́-ит, б-а-го́-ит, д-аа-го́-ит, ды-жә-го́-ит, ха-л-го́-ит / бы-з-го́-м, бы-а-го́-м, [aor.] бы-з-ге́-ит, б-а-ге́-ит / б-сы-м-ге́-ит, б-а́-м-ге-ит, [fut.1] бы-з-га́-п, б-а-га́-п / бы-з-га-ры́-м, б-а-га-ры́-м, [fut.2] бы-з-га́-шт, б-а-га́-шт / бы-з-га́-ша-м, б-а-га́-ша-м, [perf.] бы-з-га-хье́-ит, б-а-га-хье́-ит / б-сы-м-га́-ц(т), б-а́-м-га-ц(т), [impf.] бы-з-го́-н, б-а-го́-н / бы-з-го́-мызт, б-а-го́-мызт, [past indef.] бы-з-га́-н, б-а-га́-н / б-сы-м-га́-зт, б-а́-м-га-ц(т), [cond.1] бы-з-га-ры́-н, б-а-га-ры́-н / бы-з-га-ры́-мы-зт, б-а-га-ры́-мы-зт, [cond.2] бы-з-га́-шан, б-а-га́-шан / бы-з-га́-ша-мы-зт, б-а-га́-ша-мы-зт, [plupf.] бы-з-га-хьа́-н, б-а-га-хьа́-н / б-сы-м-га́-цы-зт, б-а́-м-га-цы-зт; Non-fin. [pres.] (C1) и́-л-го / и́-лы-м-го, (C3) ды-з-го́ / д-зы-м-го́, [aor.] (C1) и́-л-га / и́-лы-м-га, (C3) ды-з-га́ / д-зы-м-га́, [fut.1] и́-л-га-ра / и́-лы-м-га-ра, (C3) ды-з-га-ра́ / д-зы-м-га-ра́, [fut.2] и́-л-га-ша / и́-лы-м-га-ша, (C3) ды-з-га́-ша / д-зы-м-га́-ша, [perf.] и́-л-га-хьа(ц) *or* и́-л-га-хьо-у / и́-лы-м-га-хьа(ц) *or* и́-лы-м-га-хьо-у, (C3) ды-з-га-хьа́(-ц) *or* ды-з-га-хьо́-у / д-зы-м-га-хьа́(-ц) *or* д-зы-м-га-хьо́-у, [impf.] (C1) и́-л-го-з / и́-лы-м-го-з, (C3) ды-з-го́-з / д-зы-м-го́-з, [past indef.] (C1) и́-л-га-з / и́-лы-м-га-з, (C3) ды-з-га́-з / д-зы-м-га́-з, [cond.1] (C1) и́-л-га-ры-з / и́-лы-м-га-ры-з, (C3) ды-з-га-ры́-з / д-зы-м-га-ры́-з, [cond.2] (C1) и́-л-га-ша-з / и́-лы-м-га-ша-з, (C3) ды-з-га́-ша-з / д-зы-м-га́-ша-з, [plupf.] и́-л-га-хьа-з / и́-лы-м-га-хьа-з, (C3) ды-з-га-хьа́-з / д-зы-м-га-хьа́-з.

а-ӡа-ра́ 'to hide': Fin. [pres.] и-с-ӡо́-ит, и-ах/аа-ӡо́-ит, и-шә/жә-ӡо́-ит, и-а-ӡо́-ит / и-с-ӡо́-м, [aor.] и-с-ӡе́-ит, и-а-ӡе́-ит / и-сы-м-ӡе́-ит, и-а́-м-ӡе-ит; Non-fin. [pres.] (C1) и́-л-ӡо / и́-лы-м-ӡо, (C3) и-з-ӡо́ / и-зы-м-ӡо́, [aor.] (C1) и́-л-ӡа / и́-лы-м-ӡа, (C3) и-з-ӡа́ / и-зы-м-ӡа́, [impf.] (C1) и́-л-ӡо-з / и́-лы-м-ӡо-з, (C3) и-з-ӡо́-з / и-зы-м-ӡо́-з, [past indef.] (C1) и́-л-ӡа-з / и́-лы-м-ӡа-з, (C3) и-з-ӡа́-з / и-зы-м-ӡа́-з.

а-к-ра́ 'to catch': Fin. [pres.] ды-с-к-уе́-ит (-к-ӡо-м), д-а-к-уе́-ит / ды-с-к-уа́-м, [aor.] ды-с-к-и́т, д-а-к-и́т / д-сы-м-к-и́т, д-а́-м-к-ит, [fut.1] ды-с-кы́-п / ды-с-к-ры́м, [fut.2] ды-с-кы́-шт / ды-с-кы́-ша-м, [perf.] ды-с-к-хье́-ит / д-сы-м-кы́-ц(т), д-а́-м-кы-ц(т), [impf.] ды-с-к-уа́-н / ды-с-к-уа́-мы-зт, [past indef.] ды-с-кы́-н / д-сы-м-кы́-зт, [cond.1] ды-с-к-ры́-н / ды-с-к-ры́-мы-зт, [cond.2] ды-с-кы́-ша-н / ды-с-кы́-ша-мы-зт, [plupf.] ды-с-к-хьа́-н / д-сы-м-кы́-цы-зт; Non-fin. [pres.] (C1) и́-л-к-уа / и́-лы-м-к-уа, (C3) и-з-к-уа́, ды-з-к-уа́ / и-зы-м-к-уа́, д-зы-м-к-уа́, [aor.] (C1) и́-л-к / и́-лы-м-к, (C3) ды-з-кы́ / д-зы-м-кы́, [fut.1] (C1) и́-л-к-ра / и́-лы-м-к-ра, (C3) ды-з-к-ра́ / д-зы-м-к-ра́, [fut.2] (C1) и́-л-к-ша / и́-лы-м-к-ша, (C3) ды-з-кы́-ша / д-зы-м-кы́-ша, [perf.] (C1) и́-л-к-хьо-у (-хьа(ц)) / и́-лы-м-к-хьо-у (-хьа(ц)), (C3) ды-з-хьо́-у (-хьа́(ц)) / д-зы-м-к-хьо́-у (-хьа́(ц)), [impf.] (C1) и́-л-к-уа-з / и́-лы-м-к-уа-з, (C3) ды-з-к-уа́-з / д-зы-м-к-уа́-з, [past indef.] (C1) и́-л-кы-з / и́-лы-м-кы-з, (C3) ды-з-кы́-з / д-зы-м-кы́-з, [cond.1] (C1) и́-л-к-ры-з / и́-лы-м-к-ры-з, (C3) ды-з-к-ры́-з / д-зы-м-к-ры́-з, [cond.2] (C1) и́-л-к-ша-з / и́-лы-м-к-ша-з, (C3) ды-з-кы́-ша-з / д-зы-м-кы́-ша-з, [plupf.] (C1) и́-л-к-хьа-з / и́-лы-м-к-хьа-з, (C3) ды-з-к-хьа́-з / д-зы-м-к-хьа́-з.

а-кәа-ра́ 'to shape stones (millstones)': Fin. [pres.] и-с-кәо́-ит, и-а-кәо́-ит / и-с-кәо́-м, и-а-кәо́-м, [aor.] и-с-кәе́-ит, и-а-кәе́-ит / и-сы-м-кәе́-ит, и-а́-м-кәе-ит; Non-fin. [pres.] (C1) и́-л-кәо / и́-лы-м-кәо, (C3) и-з-кәо́ / и-зы-м-кәо́, [aor.] (C1) и́-л-кәа / и́-лы-м-кәа, (C3) и-з-кәа́ / и-зы-м-кәа́, [impf.] (C1) и́-л-кәо-з / и́-лы-м-кәо-з, (C3) и-з-кәо́-з / и-зы-м-кәо́-з, [past indef.] (C1) и́-л-кәа-з / и́-лы-м-кәа-з, (C3) и-з-кәа́-з / и-зы-м-кәа́-з.

а-ҟьа-ра́ 'to wave, to flap': Fin. [pres.] и-с-ҟьо́-ит, и-а-ҟьо́-ит / и-с-ҟьо́-м, и-а-ҟьо́-м, [aor.] и-с-ҟье́-ит, и-а-ҟье́-ит / и-сы-м-ҟье́-ит, и-а́-м-ҟье-ит; Non-fin. [pres.] (C1) и́-л-ҟьо / и́-лы-м-ҟьо, (C3) и-з-ҟьо́ / и-зы-м-ҟьо́, [aor.] (C1) и́-л-ҟьа / и́-лы-м-ҟьа, (C3) и-з-ҟьа́ / и-зы-м-ҟьа́, [impf.] (C1) и́-л-ҟьо-з / и́-лы-м-ҟьо-з, (C3) и-з-ҟьо́-з / и-зы-м-ҟьо́-з, [past indef.] (C1) и́-л-ҟьа-з / и́-лы-м-ҟьа-з, (C3) и-з-ҟьа́-з / и-зы-м-ҟьа́-з.

а-ҧа-ра́ 'to knit': Fin. [pres.] и-л-ҧо́-ит, и-а-ҧо́-ит / и-л-ҧо́-м, и-а-ҧо́-м, [aor.] и-л-ҧе́-ит, и-а-ҧе́-ит / и-лы-м-ҧе́-ит, и-а́-м-ҧе-ит; Non-fin. [pres.] (C1) и́-л-ҧо / и́-лы-м-ҧо, (C3) и-з-ҧо́ / и-зы-м-ҧо́, [aor.] (C1) и́-л-ҧа / и́-лы-м-ҧа, (C3) и-з-ҧа́ / и-зы-м-ҧа́, [impf.] (C1) и́-л-ҧо-з / и́-лы-м-ҧо-з, (C3) и-з-ҧо́-з / и-зы-м-ҧо́-з, [past indef.] (C1) и́-л-ҧа-з / и́-лы-м-ҧа-з, (C3) и-з-ҧа́-з / и-зы-м-ҧа́-з.

а-са-ра́ 'to shave': Fin. [pres.] и-с-со́-ит, ды-с-со́-ит, и-а-со́-ит / ды-с-со́-м, и-а-со́-м, [aor.] ды-с-се́-ит, и-а-се́-ит / д-сы-м-се́-ит, и-а́-м-се-ит, [fut.1] ды-с-са́-п, и-а-са́-п / ды-с-са-ры́-м, и-а-са-ры́-м, [fut.2] ды-с-са́-шт, и-а-са́-шт / ды-с-са́-ша-м, и-а-са́-ша-м, [perf.] ды-с-са-хье́-ит, и-а-са-хье́-ит / д-сы-м-са́-ц(т), и-а́-м-са-ц(т), [impf.] ды-с-со́-н, и-а-со́-н / ды-с-со́-мы-зт, и-а-со́-мы-зт, [past indef.] ды-с-са́-н, и-а-са́-н / д-сы-м-са́-зт, и-а́-м-са-зт, [cond.1] ды-с-са-ры́-н, и-а-са-ры́-н / ды-с-са-ры́-мы-зт, и-а-са-ры́-мы-зт, [cond.2] ды-с-са́-ша-н, и-а-са́-ша-н / ды-с-са́-ша-мы-зт, и-а-са́-ша-мы-зт, [plupf.] ды-с-са-хьа́-н, и-а-са-хьа́-н / д-сы-м-са́-цы-зт, и-а́-м-са-цызт; Non-fin. [pres.] (C1) и́-л-со / и́-лы-м-со, (C3) и-з-со́, ды-з-со́ / и-зы-м-со́, д-зы-м-со́, [aor.] (C1) и́-л-са / и́-лы-м-са, (C3) и-з-са́, ды-з-са́ / и-зы-м-са́, д-зы-м-са́, [fut.1] (C1) и́-л-са-ра / и́-лы-м-са-ра, (C3) и-з-са-ра́, ды-з-са-ра́ / и-зы-м-са-ра́, д-зы-м-са-ра́, [fut.2] (C1) и́-л-са-ша / и́-лы-м-са-ша, (C3) ды-з-са́-ша / д-зы-м-са́-ша, [perf.] (C1) и́-л-са-хьоу (-хьа(п)) / и́-лы-м-са-хьоу (-хьа(п)), (C3) ды-з-са-хьо́у (-хьа́(п)) / д-зы-м-са-хьо́у (-хьа́(п)), [impf.] (C1) и́-л-со-з / и́-лы-м-со-з, (C3) ды-з-со́-з / д-зы-м-со́-з, [past indef.] (C1) и́-л-са-з / и́-лы-м-са-з, (C3) ды-з-са́-з / д-зы-м-са́-з, [cond.1] (C1) и́-л-са-ры-з / и́-лы-м-са-ры-з, (C3) ды-з-са-ры́-з / д-зы-м-са-ры́-з, [cond.2] (C1) и́-л-са-ша-з / и́-лы-м-са-ша-з, (C3) ды-з-са́-ша-з / д-зы-м-са́-ша-з, [plupf.] (C1) и́-л-са-хьа-з / и́-лы-м-са-хьа-з, (C3) ды-з-са-хьа́-з / д-зы-м-са-хьа́-з.

а-х-ра́ 'to sharpen': Fin. [pres.] и-с-х-уе́-ит, и-а-х-уе́-ит / и-с-х-уа́-м, и-а-х-уа́-м, [aor.] и-с-х-и́т, и-а-х-и́т / и-сы-м-х-и́т, и-а́-м-х-ит, [fut.1] и-с-хы́-п, и-а-хы́-п / и-с-х-ры́м, и-а-х-ры́м, [fut.2] и-с-хы́-шт, и-а-хы́-шт / и-с-хы́-шам, и-а-хы́-шам, [perf.] и-с-х-хье́-ит, и-а-х-хье́-ит / и-сы-м-хы́-ц(т), и-а́-м-хы-ц(т), [impf.] и-с-х-уа́-н, и-а-х-уа́-н / и-с-х-уа́-мы-зт, и-а-х-уа́-мы-зт, [past indef.] и-с-хы́-н, и-а-хы́-н / и-сы-м-хы́-зт, и-а́-м-хы-зт, [cond.1] и-с-х-ры́-н, и-а-х-ры́-н / и-с-х-ры́-мы-зт, и-а-х-ры́-мы-зт, [cond.2] и-с-хы́-ша-н, и-а-хы́-ша-н / и-с-хы́-ша-мы-зт, и-а-хы́-ша-мы-зт, [plupf.] и-с-х-хьа́-н, и-а-х-хьа́-н / и-сы-м-хы́-цы-зт, и-а-м-хы́-цызт; Non-fin. [pres.] (C1) и́-л-х-уа / и́-лы-м-х-уа, (C3) и-з-х-уа́ / и-зы-м-х-уа́, [aor.] (C1) и́-л-х / и́-лы-м-х, (C3) и-з-хы́ / и-зы-м-хы́, [fut.1] (C1) и́-л-х-ра / и́-лы-м-х-ра, (C3) и-з-х-ра́ / и-зы-м-х-ра́, [fut.2] (C1) и́-л-х-ша / и́-лы-м-х-ша, (C3) и-з-хы́-ша / и-зы-м-хы́-ша, [perf.] (C1) и́-л-х-хьоу (-хьа(ц)) / и́-лы-м-х-хьоу (-хьа(ц)), (C3) и-з-х-хьо́у (-хьа́(ц)) / и-зы-м-х-хьо́у (-хьа́(ц)), [impf.] (C1) и́-л-х-уа-з / и́-лы-м-х-уа-з, (C3) и-з-х-уа́-з / и-зы-м-х-уа́-з, [past indef.] (C1) и́-л-хы-з / и́-лы-м-хы-з, (C3) и-з-хы́-з / и-зы-м-хы́-з, [cond.1] (C1) и́-л-х-ры-з / и́-лы-м-х-ры-з, (C3) и-з-х-ры́-з / и-зы-м-х-ры́-з, [cond.2] (C1) и́-л-х-ша-з / и́-лы-м-х-ша-з, (C3) и-з-хы́-ша-з / и-зы-м-хы́-ша-з, [plupf.] (C1) и́-л-х-хьа-з / и́-лы-м-х-хьа-з, (C3) и-з-х-хьа́-з / и-зы-м-х-хьа́-з.

а-хәа-ра́ 'to mix/blend': Fin. [aor.] и-л-хәе́-ит / и-лы-м-хәе́-ит, и-а-хәе́-ит / и-а́-м-хәе-ит; Non-fin. [pres.] (C1) и́-л-хәо / и́-лы-м-хәо, (C3) и-з-хәо́ / и-зы-м-хәо́, [aor.] (C1) и́-л-хәа / и́-лы-м-хәа, (C3) и-з-хәа́ / и-зы-м-хәа́, [impf.] (C1) и́-л-хәо-з / и́-лы-м-хәо-з, (C3) и-з-хәо́-з / и-зы-м-хәо́-з, [past indef.] (C1) и́-л-хәа-з / и́-лы-м-хәа-з, (C3) и-з-хәа́-з / и-зы-м-хәа́-з.

а-хә-ра́ 'to hurt, to injure': Fin. [pres.] ды-с-хә-уе́-ит / ды-с-хә-уа́-м, [aor.] ды-с-хә-и́т, д-а-хә-и́т / д-сы-м-хә-и́т, д-а́-м-хә-ит; Non-fin. [pres.] (C1) и́-с-хә-уа / и́-сы-м-хә-уа, (C3) ды-з-хә-уа́ / д-зы-м-хә-уа́, [aor.] (C1) и-с-хәы́ / и-сы-м-хәы́, (C3) ды-з-хәы́ / д-зы-м-хәы́.

а-цәа-ра́ 'to suck': Fin. [pres.] и-с-цәо́-ит, и-а-цәо́-ит / и-с-цәо́-м, и-а-цәо́-м, [aor.] и-с-цәе́-ит, и-а-цәе́-ит / и-сы-м-цәе́-ит, и-а́-м-цәе-ит, [fut.1] и-с-цәа́-п / и-с-цәа-ры́-м, [fut.2] и-с-цәа́-шт / и-с-цәа́-ша-м, [perf.] и-с-цәа-хье́-ит, и-а-цәа-хье́-ит / и-сы-м-цәа́-ц(т), и-а́-м-цәа-ц(т), [impf.] и-с-цәо́-н / и-с-цәо́-мы-зт, [past indef.] и-с-цәа́-н, и-а-цәа́-н / и-сы-м-цәа́-зт, и-а́-м-цәа-зт, [cond.1] и-с-цәа-ры́-н / и-с-цәа-ры́-мы-зт, [cond.2] и-с-цәа́-ша-н / и-с-цәа́-ша-мы-зт, [plupf.] и-с-цәа-хьа́-н / и-сы-м-цәа́-цы-зт, и-а́-м-цәа-цы-зт; Non-fin. [pres.] (C1) и́-л-цәо / и́-лы-м-цәо, (C3) и-з-цәо́ / и-зы-м-цәо́, [aor.] (C1) и́-л-цәа / и́-лы-м-цәа, (C3) и-з-цәа́ / и-зы-м-цәа́, [impf.] (C1) и́-л-цәо-з / и́-лы-м-цәо-з, (C3) и-з-цәо́-з / и-зы-м-цәо́-з, [past indef.] (C1) и́-л-цәа-з / и́-лы-м-цәа-з, (C3) и-з-цəá-з / и-зы-м-цəá-з.

а-шəа-рá 'to pay': Fin. [pres.] и-с-шəó-ит / и-с-шəó-м, [aor.] и-с-шəé-ит, и-а-шəé-ит / и-сы-м-шəé-ит (-шəа-ӡé-ит), и-á-м-шəе-ит; Non-fin. [pres.] (C1) и́-л-шəо / и́-лы-м-шəо, (C3) и-з-шəó / и-зы-м-шəó, [aor.] (C1) и́-л-шəа / и́-лы-м-шəа, (C3) и-з-шəá / и-зы-м-шəá, [impf.] (C1) и́-л-шəо-з / и́-лы-м-шəо-з, (C3) и-з-шəó-з / и-зы-м-шəó-з, [past indef.] (C1) и́-л-шəа-з / и́-лы-м-шəа-з, (C3) и-з-шəá-з / и-зы-м-шəá-з.

3.2.6.3. Inflection of AP c-ii

This inflection type places the accent on the postradical element in finite forms, but through all tenses only the third-person singular non-human prefix a- in Column III places an accent on this prefix.

á-шьҭра /á-š^j^t-ra/ 'to send'

Finite forms

	Affirmative	Negative
Dynamic Group I		
Present		
C1-C3		
Sg.2.F-1	б-сы-шьҭ-уé-ит /b-sə-šʲt-wá-jt'/ you.F(C1)-I(C3)-send-Dyn-Fin 'I send you-F'	б-сы-шьҭ-уá-м /b-sə-šʲt-wá-m/
Sg.2.M-1	у-с(ы)-шьҭ-уé-ит	у-с(ы)-шьҭ-уá-м
Sg.3.Human-1	д-сы-шьҭ-уé-ит	д-сы-шьҭ-уá-м
Sg.3.Non-Human-1	и-сы-шьҭ-уé-ит	и-сы-шьҭ-уá-м
Pl.2-Sg.1	шə-сы-шьҭ-уé-ит	шə-сы-шьҭ-уá-м
Sg.1-2.M	с-у-шьҭ-уé-ит	с-у-шьҭ-уá-м
Sg.1-2.F	с-бы-шьҭ-уé-ит	с-бы-шьҭ-уá-м
Sg.1-3.M	с-и-шьҭ-уé-ит	с-и-шьҭ-уá-м
Sg.3.Non-Human/Pl.3-Sg.3.M	и-шьҭ-уé-ит (< и-и-шьҭ-уé-ит)	и-шьҭ-уá-м
Sg.1-3.F	с-лы-шьҭ-уé-ит	с-лы-шьҭ-уá-м
Pl.1-3.F	ҳ-лы-шьҭ-уé-ит	ҳ-лы-шьҭ-уá-м
Sg.1-3.Non-Human	с-á-шьҭ-уе-ит	с-á-шьҭ-уа-м
Sg.2.M-3.Non-Human	у-á-шьҭ-уе-ит	у-á-шьҭ-уа-м
Sg.2.F-3.Non-Human	б-á-шьҭ-уе-ит	б-á-шьҭ-уа-м
Sg.3.Human-3.Non-Human	д-á-шьҭ-уе-ит	д-á-шьҭ-уа-м
Sg.3.Non-Human-3.Non-Human	и-á-шьҭ-уе-ит	и-á-шьҭ-уа-м
Pl.1-3.Non-Human	ҳ-á-шьҭ-уе-ит	ҳ-á-шьҭ-уа-м
Pl.2-3.Non-Human	шə-á-шьҭ-уе-ит	шə-á-шьҭ-уа-м
Sg.2.M-Pl.1	у-ҳа-шьҭ-уé-ит	у-ҳа-шьҭ-уá-м
Sg.1-Pl.2	с-шəы-шьҭ-уé-ит	с-шəы-шьҭ-уá-м
Sg.1-Pl.3	с-ры-шьҭ-уé-ит	с-ры-шьҭ-уá-м

Aorist

Sg.2.F-1	б-сы-шьҭ-и́т /b-sə-šʲtə́-jt'/ 'I sent you-F'	бы-с-мы-шьҭ-и́т /bə-s-mə-šʲtə́-jt'/
Sg.2.M-1	у-сы-шьҭ-и́т	у-с-мы-шьҭ-и́т
Sg.3.Human-1	д-сы-шьҭ-и́т	ды-с-мы-шьҭ-и́т
Sg.3.Non-Human/Pl.3-1	и-сы-шьҭ-и́т	и-с-мы-шьҭ-и́т
Pl.2.M-Sg.1	шә-сы-шьҭ-и́т	шәы-с-мы-шьҭ-и́т
Sg.1-2.M	с-у-шьҭ-и́т	с-у-мы-шьҭ-и́т
Pl.1-2.M	ҳ-у-шьҭ-и́т	ҳа-у-мы-шьҭ-и́т
Sg.1-2.F	с-бы-шьҭ-и́т	сы-б-мы-шьҭ-и́т
Sg.1-3.M	с-и-шьҭ-и́т	с-и-мы-шьҭ-и́т
Sg.3.Non-Human/Pl.3-Sg.3.M	и-шьҭ-и́т (< и-и-шьҭ-и́т)	и-мы-шьҭ-и́т
Sg.1-3.F	с-лы-шьҭ-и́т	сы-л-мы-шьҭ-и́т
Sg.1-3.Non-Human	с-а́-шьҭ-ит	с-а́-мы-шьҭ-ит
Sg.2.M-3.Non-Human	у-а́-шьҭ-ит	у-а́-мы-шьҭ-ит
Sg.2.F-3.Non-Human	б-а́-шьҭ-ит	б-а́-мы-шьҭ-ит
Sg.3.Human-3.Non-Human	д-а́-шьҭ-ит	д-а́-мы-шьҭ-ит
Sg.3.Non-Human/Pl.3-3.Non-Human	и-а́-шьҭ-ит	и-а́-мы-шьҭ-ит
Pl.1-3.Non-Human	ҳ-а́-шьҭ-ит	ҳ-а́-мы-шьҭ-ит
Pl.2-3.Non-Human	шә-а́-шьҭ-ит	шә-а́-мы-шьҭ-ит
Sg.2.F-Pl.1	б-ҳа-шьҭ-и́т	б-аҳ-мы-шьҭ-и́т
Sg.1-Pl.2	с-шәы-шьҭ-и́т	сы-шә-мы-шьҭ-и́т
Sg.1-Pl.3	с-ры-шьҭ-и́т	сы-р-мы-шьҭ-и́т

Future I

Sg.2.F-1	б-сы-шьҭы́-п	б-сы-шьҭ-ры́-м
Sg.1-2.F	с-бы-шьҭы́-п	с-бы-шьҭ-ры́-м
Sg.1-3.M	с-и-шьҭы́-п	с-и-шьҭ-ры́-м
Sg.3.Non-Human/Pl.3-Sg.3.M	и-шьҭы́-п (< и-и-шьҭы́-п)	и-шьҭ-ры́-м
Sg.1-3.F	с-лы-шьҭы́-п	с-лы-шьҭ-ры́-м
Sg.1-3.Non-Human	с-а́-шьҭы-п	с-а́-шьҭ-ры-м
Sg.2.F-3.Non-Human	б-а́-шьҭы-п	б-а́-шьҭ-ры-м
Sg.3.Human-3.Non-Human	д-а́-шьҭы-п	д-а́-шьҭ-ры-м
Sg.3.Non-Human/Pl.3-3.Non-Human	и-а́-шьҭы-п	и-а́-шьҭ-ры-м
Pl.1-3.Non-Human	ҳ-а́-шьҭы-п	ҳ-а́-шьҭ-ры-м
Pl.2-3.Non-Human	шә-а́-шьҭы-п	шә-а́-шьҭ-ры-м
Sg.2.M-Pl.1	у-ҳа-шьҭы́-п	у-ҳа-шьҭ-ры́-м
Sg.1-Pl.2	с-шәы-шьҭы́-п	с-шәы-шьҭ-ры́-м
Sg.1-Pl.3	с-ры-шьҭы́-п	с-ры-шьҭ-ры́-м

Future II

Sg.2.F-1	б-сы-шьҭы́-шт	б-сы-шьҭы́-ша-м
Sg.1-3.F	с-лы-шьҭы́-шт	с-лы-шьҭы́-ша-м

Sg.1-3.Non-Human	с-а́-шьҭы-шт	с-а́-шьҭы-ша-м
Sg.2.M-3.Non-Human	у-а́-шьҭы-шт	у-а́-шьҭы-ша-м
Sg.3.Human-3.Non-Human	д-а́-шьҭы-шт	д-а́-шьҭы-ша-м
Pl.1-3.Non-Human	ҳ-а́-шьҭы-шт	ҳ-а́-шьҭы-ша-м
Pl.2-3.Non-Human	шә-а́-шьҭы-шт	шә-а́-шьҭы-ша-м
Sg.2.F-Pl.1	б-ҳа-шьҭы́-шт	б-ҳа-шьҭы́-ша-м
Sg.1-Pl.2	с-шәы-шьҭы́-шт	с-шәы-шьҭы́-ша-м
Sg.1-Pl.3	с-ры-шьҭы́-шт	с-ры-шьҭы́-ша-м

Perfect

Sg.2.F-1	б-сы-шьҭ-хьé-ит	бы-с-мы-шьҭы́-ц(т)
Sg.1-2.M	с-у-шьҭ-хьé-ит	с-у-мы-шьҭы́-ц(т)
Pl.1-2.F	ҳ-бы-шьҭ-хьé-ит	ҳа-б-мы-шьҭы́-ц(т)
Sg.3.Non-Human/Pl.3-Sg.3.M	и-шьҭ-хьé-ит (< и-и-шьҭ-хьé-ит)	и-мы-шьҭы́-ц(т)
Sg.1-3.F	с-лы-шьҭ-хьé-ит	сы-л-мы-шьҭы́-ц(т)
Sg.1-3.Non-Human	с-а́-шьҭ-хье-ит	с-а́-мы-шьҭы-ц(т)
Sg.2.M-3.Non-Human	у-а́-шьҭ-хье-ит	у-а́-мы-шьҭы-ц(т)
Sg.2.F-3.Non-Human	б-а́-шьҭ-хье-ит	б-а́-мы-шьҭы-ц(т)
Sg.3.Human-3.Non-Human	д-а́-шьҭ-хье-ит	д-а́-мы-шьҭы-ц(т)
Sg.3.Non-Hum./Pl.3-Sg.3.Non-Hum.	и-а́-шьҭ-хье-ит	и-а́-мы-шьҭы-ц(т)
Pl.1-Sg.3.Non-Human	ҳ-а́-шьҭ-хье-ит	ҳ-а́-мы-шьҭы-ц(т)
Pl.2-Sg.3.Non-Human	шә-а́-шьҭ-хье-ит	шә-а́-мы-шьҭы-ц(т)
Sg.2.F-Pl.1	б-ҳа-шьҭ-хьé-ит	б-аҳ-мы-шьҭы́-ц(т)
Sg.1-Pl.2	с-шәы-шьҭ-хьé-ит	сы-шә-мы-шьҭы́-ц(т)
Sg.1-Pl.3	с-ры-шьҭ-хьé-ит	сы-р-мы-шьҭы́-ц(т)

Dynamic Group II

Imperfect

Sg.2.F-1	б-сы-шьҭ-уа́-н	б-сы-шьҭ-уа́-мы-зт
Sg.3.Human-3.M	д-и-шьҭ-уа́-н	д-и-шьҭ-уа́-мы-зт
Sg.3.Non-Hum./Pl.3-Sg.3.M	и-шьҭ-уа́-н (< и-и-шьҭ-уа́-н)	и-шьҭ-уа́-мы-зт
Sg.1-3.Non-Human	с-а́-шьҭ-уа-н	с-а́-шьҭ-уа-мы-зт
Sg.2.M-3.Non-Human	у-а́-шьҭ-уа-н	у-а́-шьҭ-уа-мы-зт
Sg.2.F-3.Non-Human	б-а́-шьҭ-уа-н	б-а́-шьҭ-уа-мы-зт
Sg.3.Human-3.Non-Human	д-а́-шьҭ-уа-н	д-а́-шьҭ-уа-мы-зт
Sg.3.Non-Hum./Pl.3-3.Non-Hum.	и-а́-шьҭ-уа-н	и-а́-шьҭ-уа-мы-зт
Pl.1-3.Non-Human	ҳ-а́-шьҭ-уа-н	ҳ-а́-шьҭ-уа-мы-зт
Pl.2-3.Non-Human	шә-а́-шьҭ-уа-н	шә-а́-шьҭ-уа-мы-зт
Sg.2.M-Pl.1	у-ҳа-шьҭ-уа́-н	у-ҳа-шьҭ-уа́-мы-зт
Sg.1-Pl.2	с-шәы-шьҭ-уа́-н	с-шәы-шьҭ-уа́-мы-зт
Sg.1-Pl.3	с-ры-шьҭ-уа́-н	с-ры-шьҭ-уа́-мы-зт

Past Indefinite

Sg.2.F-1	б-сы-шьҭы́-н	бы-с-мы-шьҭы́-зт
Sg.3.Non-Hum./Pl.3-Sg.2.M	и-у-шьҭы́-н	и-у-мы-шьҭы́-зт
Sg.3.Human-2.F	д-бы-шьҭы́-н	ды-б-мы-шьҭы́-зт
Sg.3.Non-Hum./Pl.3-Sg.3.M	и-шьҭы́-н (< и-и-шьҭы́-н)	и-мы-шьҭы́-зт
Pl.1-Sg.3.M	ҳ-и-шьҭы́-н	ҳа-и-мы-шьҭы́-зт
Pl.1-Sg.3.F	ҳ-лы-шьҭы́-н	ҳа-л-мы-шьҭы́-зт
Sg.1-3.Non-Huma	с-á-шьҭы-н	с-á-мы-шьҭы-зт
Sg.2.M-3.Non-Huma	у-á-шьҭы-н	у-á-мы-шьҭы-зт
Sg.3.Human-3.Non-Huma	д-á-шьҭы-н	д-á-мы-шьҭы-зт
Sg.3.Non-Hum./Pl.3-3.Non-Hum.	и-á-шьҭы-н	и-á-мы-шьҭы-зт
Pl.1-3.Non-Human	ҳ-á-шьҭы-н	ҳ-á-мы-шьҭы-зт
Pl.2-3.Non-Human	шә-á-шьҭы-н	шә-á-мы-шьҭы-зт
Sg.2.M-Pl.1	у-ҳа-шьҭы́-н	у-аҳ-мы-шьҭы́-зт
Sg.1-Pl.2	с-шәы-шьҭы́-н	сы-шә-мы-шьҭы́-зт
Conditional I		
Sg.2.F-1	б-сы-шьҭ-ры́н	б-сы-шьҭ-ры́-мы-зт
Sg.1-2.M	с-у-шьҭ-ры́н	с-у-шьҭ-ры́-мы-зт
Sg.1-3.M	с-и-шьҭ-ры́н	с-и-шьҭ-ры́-мы-зт
Sg.3.Non-Hum./Pl.3-Sg.3.M	и-шьҭ-ры́н (< и-и-шьҭ-ры́н)	и-шьҭ-ры́-мы-зт
Sg.1-3.Non-Human	с-á-шьҭ-рын	с-á-шьҭ-ры-мызт
Sg.2.F-3.Non-Human	б-á-шьҭ-рын	б-á-шьҭ-ры-мызт
Sg.3.Human-3.Non-human	д-á-шьҭ-рын	д-á-шьҭ-ры-мызт
Sg.3.Non-Hum./Pl.3-3.Non-Hum.	и-á-шьҭ-рын	и-á-шьҭ-ры-мызт
Pl.1-Sg.3.Non-Human	ҳ-á-шьҭ-рын	ҳ-á-шьҭ-ры-мызт
Pl.2-Sg.3.Non-Human	шә-á-шьҭ-рын	шә-á-шьҭ-ры-мызт
Sg.2.M-Pl.1	у-ҳа-шьҭ-ры́н	у-ҳа-шьҭ-ры́-мы-зт
Sg.1-Pl.2	с-шәы-шьҭ-ры́н	с-шәы-шьҭ-ры́-мы-зт
Conditional II		
Sg.2.M-1	у-сы-шьҭы́-ша-н	у-сы-шьҭы́-ша-мы-зт
Sg.1-2.M	с-у-шьҭы́-ша-н	с-у-шьҭы́-ша-мы-зт
Sg.1-2.F	с-бы-шьҭы́-ша-н	с-бы-шьҭы́-ша-мы-зт
Sg.1-3.M	с-и-шьҭы́-ша-н	с-и-шьҭы́-ша-мы-зт
Sg.3.Non-Hum./Pl.3-Sg.3.M	и-шьҭы́-ша-н (< и-и-шьҭы́шан)	и-шьҭы́-ша-мы-зт
Sg.1-3.F	с-лы-шьҭы́-ша-н	с-лы-шьҭы́-ша-мы-зт
Sg.1-3.Non-Human	с-á-шьҭ(ы)-ша-н	с-á-шьҭ(ы)-ша-мы-зт
Sg.2.M-3.Non-Human	у-á-шьҭ(ы)-ша-н	у-á-шьҭ(ы)-ша-мы-зт
Sg.3.Human-3.Non-Human	д-á-шьҭ(ы)-ша-н	д-á-шьҭ(ы)-ша-мы-зт
Sg.3.Non-Hum./Pl.3-Sg.3.Non-Hum.	и-á-шьҭ(ы)-ша-н	и-á-шьҭ(ы)-ша-мы-зт
Pl.1-Sg.3.Non-Human	ҳ-á-шьҭ(ы)-ша-н	ҳ-á-шьҭ(ы)-ша-мы-зт
Pl.2-Sg.3.Non-Human	шә-á-шьҭ(ы)-ша-н	шә-á-шьҭ(ы)-ша-мы-зт

Sg.2.M-Pl.1	у-ха-шьҭы́-ша-н	у-ха-шьҭы́-ша-мы-зт
Sg.1-Pl.2	с-шәы-шьҭы́-ша-н	с-шәы-шьҭы́-ша-мы-зт
Pluperfect		
Sg.2.M-1	у-сы-шьҭ-хьа́-н	у-с-мы-шьҭы́-цы-зт
Pl.1-Sg.2.M	х-у-шьҭ-хьа́-н	ха-у-мы-шьҭы́-цы-зт
Sg.1-2.F	с-бы-шьҭ-хьа́-н	сы-б-мы-шьҭы́-цы-зт
Sg.2.M-1	у-сы-шьҭ-хьа́-н	у-с-мы-шьҭы́-цы-зт
Sg.3.Non-Hum./Pl.3-Sg.3.M	и-шьҭ-хьа́-н (и-и-шьҭ-хьа́-н)	и-мы-шьҭы́-цы-зт
Sg.3.Human-3.F	д-лы-шьҭ-хьа́-н	ды-л-мы-шьҭы́-цы-зт
Sg.1-3.Non-Human	с-а́-шьҭ-хьа-н	с-а́-мы-шьҭы-цы-зт
Sg.2.F-3.Non-Human	б-а́-шьҭ-хьа-н	б-а́-мы-шьҭы-цы-зт
Sg.3.Human-3.Non-Human	д-а́-шьҭ-хьа-н	д-а́-мы-шьҭы-цы-зт
Sg.3.Non-Hum./Pl.3-Sg.3.Non-Hum.	и-а́-шьҭ-хьа-н	и-а́-мы-шьҭы-цы-зт
Pl.1-3.Non-Human	ҳ-а́-шьҭ-хьа-н	ҳ-а́-мы-шьҭы-цы-зт
Pl.2-3.Non-Human	шә-а́-шьҭ-хьа-н	шә-а́-мы-шьҭы-цы-зт
Sg.2.M-Pl.1	у-ха-шьҭ-хьа́-н	у-аҳ-мы-шьҭы́-цы-зт
Pl.1-Pl.2	ҳ-шәы-шьҭ-хьа́-н	ҳа-шә-мы-шьҭы́-цы-зт
Sg.1-Pl.3	с-ры-шьҭ-хьа́-н	сы-р-мы-шьҭы́-цы-зт

Non-Finite forms

	Affirmative	Negative
Dynamic Group I		
C1-C3		
Present		
Rel-Sg.3.F	и́-л-шьҭ-уа /jə́-l-šʲt-wa/ Rel(C1)-she(C3)-send-Dyn.NF 'which/whom she sends'	и́-л-мы-шьҭ-уа
Sg.3.Human-Rel	ды-з-шьҭ-уа́ /də-z-šʲt-wá/ him/her(C1)-Rel(C3)-send-Dyn.NF 'who sends him/her'	ды-з-мы-шьҭ-уа́
Aorist		
Rel-Sg.3.F	и́-л-шьҭ	и́-л-мы-шьҭ
Sg.3.Human-Rel	ды-з-шьҭы́	ды-з-мы-шьҭы́
Future I		
Rel-Sg.3.F	и́-л-шьҭ-ра	и́-л-мы-шьҭ-ра
Sg.3.Human-Rel	ды-з-шьҭ-ра́	ды-з-мы-шьҭ-ра́
Future II		
Rel-Sg.3.F	и́-л-шьҭ-ша	и́-л-мы-шьҭ-ша
Sg.3.Human-Rel	ды-з-шьҭы́-ша	ды-з-мы-шьҭы́-ша

Perfect		
Rel-Sg.3.F	и́-л-шьҭ-хьа(ц)/-хьо-у	и́-л-мы-шьҭ-хьа(ц)/-хьо-у
Sg.3.Human-Rel	ды-з-шьҭ-хьа́(ц)/-хьо́-у	ды-з-мы-шьҭ-хьа́(ц)/-хьо́-у
Dynamic Group II		
C1-C3		
Imperfect		
Rel-Sg.3.F	и́-л-шьҭ-уа-з	и́-л-мы-шьҭ-уа-з
Sg.3.Human-Rel	ды-з-шьҭ-уа́-з	ды-з-мы-шьҭ-уа́-з
Past Indefinite		
Rel-Sg.3.F	и́-л-шьҭы-з	и́-л-мы-шьҭы-з
Sg.3.Human-Rel	ды-з-шьҭы́-з	ды-з-мы-шьҭы́-з
Conditional I		
Rel-Sg.3.F	и́-л-шьҭ-ры-з	и́-л-мы-шьҭ-ры-з
Sg.3.Human-Rel	ды-з-шьҭ-ры́-з	ды-з-мы-шьҭ-ры́-з
Conditional II		
Rel-Sg.3.F	и́-л-шьҭ-ша-з	и́-л-мы-шьҭ-ша-з
Sg.3.Human-Rel	ды-з-шьҭы́-ша-з	ды-з-мы-шьҭы́-ша-з
Pluperfect		
Rel-Sg.3.F	и́-л-шьҭ-хьа-з	и́-л-мы-шьҭ-хьа-з
Sg.3.Human-Rel	ды-з-шьҭ-хьа́-з	ды-з-мы-шьҭ-хьа́-з

Notes:

1. The masdar of the AP c-ii type places the accent on the article or the suffix -ра.

2. In а-былра́ /a-bəl-rá/ 'to burn', which belongs to the AP c-ii type, the schwa in the root of this word generally disappears when there is a schwa immediately after the root: -bəl-wa-, -bəl-rən, -bəl-xʲajt' vs. -blə-jt', -blə-p', -blə-št', -blə-šam, -blə-ct', -blə-cəzt'. In Abkhaz, the phenomenon of a presence or absence of a schwa in the root has already been seen in several examples. See the example in §3.2.3.3 á-ҧырра /á-pər-ra/ 'to fly': сҧыруе́ит /s-pər-wá-jt'/, сыҧры́п /sə-prə́-p'/, also see Note 1 in §3.2.5.3. However, likewise regardless if there is a schwa in the root, there are also verbs where the root is stable. For example, despite á-дыд-ра /á-dəd-ra/ 'to thunder' fulfilling the same conditions as those above, the loss of a schwa in the root cannot be seen at all: идыдуе́ит /jə-dəd-wá-jt'/ 'it thunders', идыди́т /jə-dədə́-jt'/ 'it thundered/, and the absence of a schwa absolutely cannot occur when the accent is on the schwa in the root: а-ды́рра /a-də́r-ra/ 'to know', а-гы́ла-ра /a-gə́la-ra/ 'to stand'.

The inflection of а-былра́ /a-bəl-rá/ 'to burn' is as follows:

Fin. [pres.] и-з-был-уе́-ит, и-á-был-уе-ит / и-з-был-уа́-м, и-á-был-уа-м, [aor.] и-з-бл-и́т, и-á-бл-ит / и-сы-м-бл-и́т, и-á-м-бл-ит, [fut.1] и-з-блы́-п, и-á-блы-п / и-з-был-ры́м, и-á-был-рым, [fut.2] и-з-блы́-шт, и-á-блы-шт / и-з-блы́-шам, и-á-блы-шам, [perf.] и-з-был-хье́ит, и-á-был-хьеит / и-сы-м-блы́-ц(т), и-á-м-блы-ц(т), [impf.] и-з-был-уа́н, и-á-был-уан / и-з-был-уа́мызт, и-á-был-уамызт, [past indef.] и-з-блы́-н, и-á-блы-н / и-сы-м-блы́-зт, и-á-м-блы-зт, [cond.1] и-з-был-ры́н, и-á-был-рын / и-з-был-ры́мызт, и-á-был-рымызт, [cond.2] и-з-блы́-шан, и-á-блы-шан / и-з-блы́-шамызт, и-á-блы-шамызт, [plupf.] и-з-был-хьа́н, и-á-был-хьан / и-с-м-блы́-

цызт, и-á-м-блы-цызт, Non-fin. [pres.] (C1) и́-л-б(ы)л-уа / и́-лы-м-бл-уа, (C3) и-з-бл-уа́ / и-зы-м-бл-уа́, [aor.] (C1) и́-л-бл / и́-лы-м-бл, (C3) и-з-блы́ / и-зы-м-блы́, [impf.] (C1) и́-л-бл-уа-з / и́-лы-м-бл-уа-з, (C3) и-з-бл-уа́-з / и-зы-м-бл-уа́-з, [past indef.] (C1) и́-л-блы-з / и́-лы-м-блы-з, (C3) и-з-блы́-з / и-зы-м-блы́-з.

3. áфара /á-fa-ra/ 'to eat' can be cited as an example of a root that ends with the vowel a. When the postradical element does not take an accent, the accent is placed on the vowel at the end of the root. Its inflection is as follows:

Finite forms

Dynamic Group I

Present

Affirmative: и-с-фó-ит /jə-s-fa-wá-jt'/ 'I eat it/them', у-с-фó-ит, бы-с-фó-ит, ды-с-фó-ит, шəы-с-фó-ит, с-у-фó-ит, с-бы-фó-ит, с-и-фó-ит, и-фó-ит (< и-и-фó-ит), ҳа-и-фó-ит, сы-л-фó-ит, с-á-фо-ит, у-á-фо-ит, б-á-фо-ит, д-á-фо-ит, и-á-фо-ит, х-á-фо-ит, шə-á-фо-ит, у-аҳ-фó-ит, и-ҳ-фó-ит, сы-шə-фó-ит, сы-р-фó-ит. Negative: и-с-фó-м /jə-s-fa-wá-m/ 'I do not eat it/them', (-фа-ӡó-м /-fa-ʒa-wá-m/), у-с-фó-м, бы-с-фó-м, и-á-фо-м, с-á-фо-м, у-аҳ-фó-м, сы-шə-фó-м, сы-р-фó-м.

Aorist

Affirmative: и-с-фé-ит /jə-s-fá-jt'/ 'I ate it/them', у-с-фé-ит, бы-с-фé-ит, ды-с-фé-ит, шəы-с-фé-ит, с-у-фé-ит, с-бы-фé-ит, с-и-фé-ит, и-фé-ит (< и-и-фé-ит), ҳа-и-фé-ит, сы-л-фé-ит, с-á-фе-ит, у-á-фе-ит, б-á-фе-ит, д-á-фе-ит, и-á-фе-ит, х-á-фе-ит, шə-á-фе-ит, у-аҳ-фé-ит, и-ҳ-фé-ит, сы-шə-фé-ит, сы-р-фé-ит. Negative: и-сы-м-фé-ит /jə-sə-m-fá-jt'/ 'I did not eat it/them', у-сы-м-фé-ит, б-сы-м-фé-ит, д-сы-м-фé-ит, шə-сы-м-фé-ит, д-бы-м-фé-ит, и-м-фé-ит (< и-и-м-фé-ит), х-лы-м-фé-ит, с-á-м-фе-ит, у-á-м-фе-ит, б-á-м-фе-ит, д-á-м-фе-ит, и-á-м-фе-ит, х-á-м-фе-ит, шə-á-м-фе-ит, у-ҳа-м-фé-ит, с-шəы-м-фé-ит, и-ры-м-фé-ит.

Future I

Affirmative: и-с-фá-п, у-с-фá-п, бы-с-фá-п, ды-с-фá-п, шəы-с-фá-п, с-у-фá-п, сы-б-фá-п, с-и-фá-п, и-фá-п (< и-и-фá-п), сы-л-фá-п, с-á-фа-п, у-á-фа-п, б-á-фа-п, д-á-фа-п, и-á-фа-п, х-á-фа-п, шə-á-фа-п, у-аҳ-фá-п, сы-шə-фá-п, сы-р-фá-п. Negative: и-с-фа-ры́-м, у-с-фа-ры́-м, бы-с-фа-ры́-м, ды-с-фа-ры́-м, и-с-фа-ры́-м, шəы-с-фа-ры́-м, с-у-фа-ры́-м, сы-б-фа-ры́-м, с-и-фа-ры́-м, и-фа-ры́-м (< и-и-фа-ры́-м), сы-л-фа-ры́-м, с-á-фа-рым, у-á-фа-рым, б-á-фа-рым, д-á-фа-рым, и-á-фа-рым, х-á-фа-рым, шə-á-фа-рым, у-аҳ-фа-ры́-м, сы-шə-фа-ры́-м, сы-р-фа-ры́-м.

Future II

Affirmative: и-с-фá-шт, бы-с-фá-шт, у-с-фá-шт, ды-с-фá-шт, шəы-с-фá-шт, ҳа-у-фá-шт, с-и-фá-шт, и-фá-шт (< и-и-фá-шт), сы-л-фá-шт, с-á-фа-шт, у-á-фа-шт, б-á-фа-шт, д-á-фа-шт, и-á-фа-шт, х-á-фа-шт, шə-á-фа-шт, у-аҳ-фá-шт, сы-шə-фá-шт, сы-р-фá-шт. Negative: бы-с-фá-ша-м, у-с-фá-ша-м, бы-с-фá-ша-м, и-с-фá-ша-м, шəы-с-фá-ша-м, с-у-фá-ша-м, сы-б-фá-ша-м, с-и-фá-ша-м, и-фá-ша-м (< и-и-фá-ша-м), сы-л-фá-ша-м, с-á-фа-ша-м, у-á-фа-ша-м, д-á-фа-ша-м, и-á-фа-ша-м, х-á-фа-ша-м, шə-á-фа-ша-м, у-аҳ-фá-ша-м, сы-шə-фá-ша-м, сы-р-фá-ша-м.

Perfect

Affirmative: и-с-фа-хьé-ит, бы-с-фа-хьé-ит, у-с-фа-хьé-ит, ды-с-фа-хьé-ит, шәы-с-фа-хьé-ит, с-у-фа-хьé-ит, сы-б-фа-хьé-ит, с-и-фа-хьé-ит, и-фа-хьé-ит (< и-и-фа-хьé-ит), сы-л-фа-хьé-ит, с-á-фа-хье-ит, у-á-фа-хье-ит, б-á-фа-хье-ит, д-á-фа-хье-ит, и-á-фа-хье-ит, х-á-фа-хье-ит, шә-á-фа-хье-ит, у-аҳ-фа-хьé-ит, сы-шә-фа-хьé-ит, сы-р-фа-хьé-ит. Negative: и-сы-м-фá-ц(т), у-сы-м-фá-ц(т), б-сы-м-фá-ц(т), д-сы-м-фá-ц(т), шә-сы-м-фá-ц(т), с-у-м-фá-ц(т), с-бы-м-фá-ц(т), с-и-м-фá-ц(т), и-м-фá-ц(т) (< и-и-м-фá-ц(т)), с-лы-м-фá-ц(т), с-á-м-фа-ц(т), у-á-м-фа-ц(т), б-á-м-фа-ц(т), и-á-м-фа-ц(т), х-á-м-фа-ц(т), шә-á-м-фа-ц(т), у-ҳа-м-фá-ц(т), с-шәы-м-фá-ц(т), с-ры-м-фá-ц(т).

Dynamic Group II

Imperfect

Affirmative: и-с-фó-н, бы-с-фó-н, у-с-фó-н, ды-с-фó-н, шәы-с-фó-н, с-у-фó-н, и-б-фó-н, с-и-фó-н, и-фó-н (< и-и-фó-н), сы-л-фó-н, с-á-фо-н, у-á-фо-н, б-á-фо-н, д-á-фо-н, и-á-фо-н, х-á-фо-н, шә-á-фо-н, и-аҳ-фó-н, и-шә-фó-н, и-р-фó-н. Negative: и-с-фó-мы-зт, у-с-фó-мы-зт, бы-с-фó-мы-зт, шәы-с-фó-мы-зт, с-у-фó-мы-зт, сы-б-фó-мы-зт, с-и-фó-мы-зт, и-фó-мы-зт (< и-и-фó-мы-зт), сы-л-фó-мы-зт, с-á-фо-мы-зт, у-á-фо-мы-зт, б-á-фо-мы-зт, д-á-фо-мы-зт, и-á-фо-мы-зт, х-á-фо-мы-зт, шә-á-фо-мы-зт, у-аҳ-фó-мы-зт, сы-шә-фó-мы-зт, сы-р-фó-мы-зт.

Past Indefinite

Affirmative: и-с-фá-н, бы-с-фá-н, у-с-фá-н, ды-с-фá-н, шәы-с-фá-н, с-у-фá-н, и-б-фá-н, с-и-фá-н, и-фá-н (< и-и-фá-н), сы-л-фá-н, с-á-фа-н, у-á-фа-н, б-á-фа-н, д-á-фа-н, и-á-фа-н, х-á-фа-н, шә-á-фа-н, и-аҳ-фá-н, и-шә-фá-н, и-р-фá-н. Negative: и-сы-м-фá-зт, у-сы-м-фá-зт, б-сы-м-фá-зт, д-сы-м-фá-зт, шә-сы-м-фá-зт, с-у-м-фá-зт, с-бы-м-фá-зт, с-и-м-фá-зт, и-м-фá-зт (< и-и-м-фá-зт), с-лы-м-фá-зт, с-á-м-фа-зт, у-á-м-фа-зт, б-á-м-фа-зт, и-á-м-фа-зт, х-á-м-фа-зт, шә-á-м-фа-зт, у-ҳа-м-фá-зт, с-шәы-м-фá-зт, с-ры-м-фá-зт.

Conditional I

Affirmative: и-с-фа-ры́н, бы-с-фа-ры́н, у-с-фа-ры́н, ды-с-фа-ры́н, шәы-с-фа-ры́н, с-у-фа-ры́н, сы-б-фа-ры́н, с-и-фа-ры́н, и-фа-ры́н (< и-и-фа-ры́н), сы-л-фа-ры́н, с-á-фа-рын, у-á-фа-рын, б-á-фа-рын, д-á-фа-рын, и-á-фа-рын, х-á-фа-рын, шә-á-фа-рын, у-аҳ-фа-ры́н, сы-шә-фа-ры́н, сы-р-фа-ры́н. Negative: и-с-фа-ры́-мы-зт, бы-с-фа-ры́-мы-зт, у-с-фа-ры́-мы-зт, ды-с-фа-ры́-мы-зт, шәы-с-фа-ры́-мы-зт, с-у-фа-ры́-мы-зт, сы-б-фа-ры́-мы-зт, с-и-фа-ры́-мы-зт, и-фа-ры́-мы-зт (< и-и-фа-ры́-мы-зт), сы-л-фа-ры́-мы-зт, с-á-фа-ры-мы-зт, у-á-фа-ры-мы-зт, б-á-фа-ры-мы-зт, д-á-фа-ры-мы-зт, и-á-фа-ры-мы-зт, х-á-фа-ры-мы-зт, шә-á-фа-ры-мы-зт, у-аҳ-фа-ры́-мы-зт, сы-шә-фа-ры́-мы-зт, сы-р-фа-ры́-мы-зт.

Conditional II

Affirmative: и-с-фá-ша-н, бы-с-фá-ша-н, у-с-фá-ша-н, ды-с-фá-ша-н, шәы-с-фá-ша-н, с-у-фá-ша-н, сы-б-фá-ша-н, с-и-фá-ша-н, и-фá-ша-н (< и-и-фá-ша-н), сы-л-фá-ша-н, с-á-фа-ша-н, у-á-фа-ша-н, б-á-фа-ша-н, д-á-фа-ша-н, и-á-фа-ша-н, х-á-фа-ша-н, шә-á-фа-ша-н, у-аҳ-фá-ша-н, сы-шә-фá-ша-н, сы-р-фá-ша-н. Negative: бы-с-фá-ша-мы-зт,

и-с-фá-ша-мы-зт, бы-с-фá-ша-мы-зт, у-с-фá-ша-мы-зт, ды-с-фá-ша-мы-зт, шәы-с-фá-ша-мы-зт, с-у-фá-ша-мы-зт, сы-б-фá-ша-мы-зт, с-и-фá-ша-мы-зт, и-фá-ша-мы-зт (< и-и-фá-ша-мы-зт), сы-л-фá-ша-мы-зт, с-á-фа-ша-мы-зт, у-á-фа-ша-мы-зт, б-á-фа-ша-мы-зт, д-á-фа-ша-мы-зт, и-á-фа-ша-мы-зт, х-á-фа-ша-мы-зт, шә-á-фа-ша-мы-зт, у-аҳ-фá-ша-мы-зт, сы-шә-фá-ша-мы-зт, сы-р-фá-ша-мы-зт.

Pluperfect
Affirmative: и-с-фа-хьá-н, бы-с-фа-хьá-н, у-с-фа-хьá-н, ды-с-фа-хьá-н, шəы-с-фа-хьá-н, с-у-фа-хьá-н, сы-б-фа-хьá-н, с-и-фа-хьá-н, и-фа-хьá-н (< и-и-фа-хьá-н), сы-л-фа-хьá-н, с-á-фа-хьа-н, у-á-фа-хьа-н, б-á-фа-хьа-н, д-á-фа-хьа-н, и-á-фа-хьа-н, х-á-фа-хьа-н, шə-á-фа-хьа-н, у-ах-фа-хьá-н, сы-шə-фа-хьá-н, сы-р-фа-хьá-н. Negative: и-сы-м-фá-цы-зт, у-сы-м-фá-цы-зт, б-сы-м-фá-цы-зт, д-сы-м-фá-цы-зт, шə-сы-м-фá-цы-зт, с-у-м-фá-цы-зт, с-бы-м-фá-цы-зт, с-и-м-фá-цы-зт, и-м-фá-цы-зт (< и-и-м-фá-цы-зт), с-лы-м-фá-цы-зт, с-á-м-фа-цы-зт, у-á-м-фа-цы-зт, б-á-м-фа-цы-зт, д-á-м-фа-цы-зт, и-á-м-фа-цы-зт, х-á-м-фа-цы-зт, шə-á-м-фа-цы-зт, у-ха-м-фá-цы-зт, с-шəы-м-фá-цы-зт, с-ры-м-фá-цы-зт.

Non-Finite forms
Dynamic Group I
Present
C1(Rel)-C3:
Affirmative: и́-с-фо /jə́-s-fa-wa/ 'which I eat', и́-б-фо, и́-у-фо, и-á-фо, и́-и-фо, и́-л-фо, и-áх-фо, и́-шə-фо, и́-р-фо. Negative: и́-сы-м-фо, и́-бы-м-фо, и́-у-м-фо, и-á-м-фо, и́-и-м-фо, и́-лы-м-фо, и-áха-м-фо, и́-шəы-м-фо, и́-ры-м-фо.
C1-C3(Rel):
Affirmative: и-з-фó /jə-z-fa-wá/ 'who eats it/them', сы-з-фó, бы-з-фó, у-з-фó, ды-з-фó, ха-з-фó, шы-з-фó. Negative: и-зы-м-фó, с-зы-м-фó, б-зы-м-фó, у-зы-м-фó, д-зы-м-фó, х-зы-м-фó, шə-зы-м-фó.
Aorist
C1(Rel)-C3: Affirmative: и́-с-фа. Negative: и́-сы-м-фа
C1-C3(Rel): Affirmative: и-з-фá. Negative: и-зы-м-фá
Future I
C1(Rel)-C3: Affirmative: и́-с-фа-ра. Negative: и́-сы-м-фа-ра
C1-C3(Rel): Affirmative: и-з-фа-рá. Negative: и-зы-м-фа-рá
Future II
C1(Rel)-C3: Affirmative: и́-с-фа-ша. Negative: и́-сы-м-фа-ша
C1-C3(Rel): Affirmative: и-з-фá-ша. Negative: и-зы-м-фá-ша
Perfect
C1(Rel)-C3: Affirmative: и́-с-фа-хьоу (-хьа(ц)). Negative: и́-сы-м-фа-хьоу (-хьа(ц))
C1-C3(Rel): Affirmative: и-з-фа-хьóу (-хьá(ц)). Negative: и-зы-м-фа-хьóу (-хьá(ц))

Dynamic Group II
Imperfect
C1(Rel)-C3: Affirmative: и́-с-фо-з. Negative: и́-сы-м-фо-з
C1-C3(Rel): Affirmative: и-з-фó-з. Negative: и-зы-м-фó-з
Past Indefinite
C1(Rel)-C3: Affirmative: и́-с-фа-з. Negative: и́-сы-м-фа-з
C1-C3(Rel): Affirmative: и-з-фá-з. Negative: и-зы-м-фá-з
Conditional I

C1(Rel)-C3: Affirmative: и́-с-фа-ры-з. Negative: и́-сы-м-фа-ры-з
C1-C3(Rel): Affirmative: и-з-фа-ры́-з. Negative: и-зы-м-фа-ры́-з
Conditional II
C1(Rel)-C3: Affirmative: и́-с-фа-ша-з. Negative: и́-сы-м-фа-ша-з
C1-C3(Rel): Affirmative: и-з-фа́-ша-з. Negative: и-зы-м-фа́-ша-з
Pluperfect
C1(Rel)-C3: Affirmative: и́-с-фа-хьа-з. Negative: и́-сы-м-фа-хьа-з
C1-C3(Rel): Affirmative: и-з-фа-хьа́-з. Negative: и-зы-м-фа-хьа́-з

Other examples:

а́-ҕьҕьа-ра 'to scrape': Fin. [pres.] и-лы-ҕьҕьо́-ит / и-лы-ҕьҕьо́-м (*or* и-лы-ҕьҕьа́-ӡо-м), [aor.] и-лы-ҕьҕье́-ит, и-а́-ҕьҕье-ит / и-л-мы-ҕьҕье́-ит, и-а́-мы-ҕьҕье-ит; Non-fin. [pres.] (C1) и́-лы-ҕьҕьо / и́-л-мы-ҕьҕьо, (C3) и-зы-ҕьҕьо́ / и-з-мы-ҕьҕьо́, [aor.] (C1) и́-лы-ҕьҕьа / и́-л-мы-ҕьҕьа, (C3) и-зы-ҕьҕьа́ / и-з-мы-ҕьҕьа́, [impf.] (C1) и́-лы-ҕьҕьо-з / и́-л-мы-ҕьҕьо-з, (C3) и-зы-ҕьҕьо́-з / и-з-мы-ҕьҕьо́-з, [past indef.] (C1) и́-лы-ҕьҕьа-з / и́-л-мы-ҕьҕьа-з, (C3) и-зы-ҕьҕьа́-з / и-з-мы-ҕьҕьа́-з.

а-ж-ра́ 'to dig': Fin. [pres.] и-з-ж-уе́-ит, и-ж-уе́-ит, и-а́-ж-уе-ит, и-аа-ж-уе́-ит (< и-аҳ-ж-уе́-ит), и-жә-ж-уе́-ит, сы-жә-ж-уе́-ит / и-з-ж-уа́-м, [aor.] и-з-ж-и́т, и-а́-ж-ит / и-сы-м-ж-и́т, и-а́-м-ж-ит, [fut.1] и-з-жы́-п, и-а́-жы-п / и-з-ж-ры́м, [fut.2] и-з-жы́-шт, и-а́-жы-шт / и-з-жы́-шам, [perf.] и-з-ж-хье́ит, и-а́-ж-хьеит / и-сы-м-жы́-ц(т), [impf.] и-з-ж-уа́-н / и-з-ж-уа́-мызт, [past indef.] и-з-жы́-н / и-сы-м-жы́-зт, [cond.1] и-з-ж-ры́н / и-з-ж-ры́мызт, [cond.2] и-з-жы́-шан / и-з-жы́-шамызт [plupf.] и-з-ж-хьа́н / и-сы-м-жы́-цызт; Non-fin. [pres.] (C1) и́-л-ж-уа / и́-лы-м-ж-уа, (C3) и-з-ж-уа́ / и-зы-м-ж-уа́, [aor.] (C1) и́-л-ж / и́-лы-м-ж, (C3) и-з-жы́ / и-зы-м-жы́, [fut.1] (C1) и́-л-ж-ра / и́-лы-м-ж-ра, (C3) и-з-ж-ра́ / и-зы-м-ж-ра́, [fut.2] (C1) и́-л-ж-ша / и́-лы-м-ж-ша, (C3) и-з-жы́-ша / и-зы-м-жы́-ша, [perf.] (C1) и́-л-ж-хьоу (-хьа(ц)) / и́-лы-м-ж-хьоу (-хьа(ц)), (C3) и-з-ж-хьо́у (-хьа́(ц)) / и-зы-м-ж-хьо́у (-хьа́(ц)), [impf.] (C1) и́-л-ж-уа-з / и́-лы-м-ж-уа-з, (C3) и-з-ж-уа́-з / и-зы-м-ж-уа́-з, [past indef.] (C1) и́-л-жы-з / и́-лы-м-жы-з, (C3) и-з-жы́-з / и-зы-м-жы́-з, [cond.1] (C1) и́-л-ж-ры-з / и́-лы-м-ж-ры-з, (C3) и-з-ж-ры́-з / и-зы-м-ж-ры́-з, [cond.2] (C1) и́-л-ж-ша-з / и́-лы-м-ж-ша-з, (C3) и-з-жы́-ша-з / и-зы-м-жы́-ша-з, [plupf.] (C1) и́-л-ж-хьа-з / и́-лы-м-ж-хьа-з, (C3) и-з-ж-хьа́-з / и-зы-м-ж-хьа́-з.

а́-жә-ра 'to drink': Fin. [pres.] и-з-жә-уе́-ит, и-а́-жә-уе-ит, и-аа-жә-уе́-ит, и-жә-жә-уе́-ит / и-з-жә-уа́-м (-жә-ӡо́-м), [aor.] и-з-жә-и́т, и-а́-жә-ит / и-сы-м-жә-и́т, и-а́-м-жә-ит, [fut.1] и-з-жәы́-п, и-а́-жәы-п / и-з-жә-ры́м, и-а́-жә-рым, [fut.2] и-з-жәы́-шт, и-а́-жәы-шт / и-з-жәы́-шам, и-а́-жә-шам, [perf.] и-з-жә-хье́.ит, и-а́-жә-хье-ит / и-сы-м-жәы́-ц(т), [impf.] и-з-жә-уа́-н / и-з-жә-уа́-мызт, [past indef.] и-з-жәы́-н, и-а́-жәы-н / и-сы-м-жәы́-зт, и-а́-м-жәы-зт, [cond.1] и-з-жә-ры́н, и-а́-жә-рын / и-з-жә-ры́мызт, и-а́-жә-рымызт, [cond.2] и-з-жәы́-шан / и-з-жәы́-шамызт, и-а́-жә-шамызт, [plupf.] и-з-жә-хьа́.н, и-а́-жә-хьа-н / и-сы-м-жәы́-цызт, и-а́-м-жәы-цызт; Non-fin. [pres.] (C1) и́-л-жә-уа, и́-з/с-жә-уа, и́-б-жә-уа, и́-и-жә-уа, и-а́-жә-уа, и-а́ҳ/а́а-жә-уа, и́-шә/жә-жә-уа, и́-р-жә-уа / и́-лы-м-жә-уа, и́-зы/сы-м-жә-уа, и-а́-м-жә-уа, и́-бы-м-жә-уа, и́-и-м-жә-уа, и-а́ҳа/а́а-м-жә-уа, и́-шәы/жәы-м-жә-уа, и́-р-м-жә-уа, (C3) и-з-жә-уа́ / и-зы-м-жә-уа́, [aor.] (C1) и́-л-жә, и-а́-жә, и́-з/с-жә, и́-и-жә, и-а́ҳ/а́а-жә, и́-шә/жә-жә, и́-р-жә / и́-лы-м-жә, и-а́-м-жә, и́-сы/зы-м-жә, и́-и-м-жә, и-а́ҳа/а́а-м-жә, и́-шәы/жәы-м-жә, и́-р-м-жә, (C3) и-з-жәы́ / и-зы-м-жәы́, [fut.1] (C1) и́-л-жә-ра / и́-лы-м-жә-ра, (C3) и-з-жә-ра́ / и-зы-м-жә-ра́, [fut.2] (C1) и́-л-жә-ша / и́-лы-м-жә-ша, (C3) и-з-жәы́-ша / и-зы-м-жәы́-ша, [perf.] (C1) и́-л-жә-хьоу (-хьа(п)) / и́-лы-м-жә-хьоу (-хьа(п)), (C3) и-з-жә-хьо́у (-хьа́(п)) / и-зы-м-жә-хьо́у (-хьа́(п)), [impf.] (C1) и́-л-жә-уа-з / и́-лы-м-жә-уа-з, (C3) и-з-жә-уа́-з / и-зы-м-жә-уа́-з, [past indef.] (C1) и́-л-жәы-з / и́-лы-м-жәы-з, (C3) и-з-жәы́-з / и-зы-м-жәы́-з, [cond.1] (C1) и́-л-жә-ры-з / и́-лы-м-жә-ры-з, (C3) и-з-жә-ры́-з / и-зы-м-жә-ры́-з, [cond.2] (C1) и́-л-жә-ша-з / и́-лы-м-жә-ша-з, (C3) и-з-жәы́-ша-з / и-зы-м-жәы́-ша-з, [plupf.] (C1) и́-л-жә-хьа-з / и́-лы-м-жә-хьа-з, (C3) и-з-жә-хьа́-з / и-зы-м-жә-хьа́-з.

а́-ӡ(ы)б-ра 'to decide; to judge': Fin. [pres.] и-сы-ӡб-уе́-ит, и-а́-ӡб-уе-ит / и-сы-ӡб-уа́-м, [aor.] и-сы-ӡб-и́т, и-а́-ӡб-ит / и-с-мы-ӡб-и́т, и-а́-мы-ӡб-ит; Non-fin. [pres.] (C1) и́-лы-ӡб-уа / и́-л-мы-ӡб-уа, (C3) и-зы-ӡб-уа́ / и-з-мы-ӡб-уа́, [aor.] и́-лы-ӡб / и́-л-мы-ӡб, (C3) и-зы-ӡбы́ / и-з-мы-ӡбы́, [impf.] (C1) и́-лы-ӡб-уа-з / и́-л-мы-ӡб-уа-з, (C3) и-зы-ӡб-уа́-з / и-з-мы-ӡб-уа́-з, [past indef.] и́-лы-ӡбы-з / и́-л-мы-ӡбы-з, (C3) и-зы-ӡбы́-з / и-з-мы-ӡбы́-з.

а-ӡ-ра́ 'to roast': Fin. [pres.] и-з-ӡ-уе́-ит, ды-з-ӡ-уе́-ит, и-а́-ӡ-уе-ит / и-з-ӡ-уа́-м, и-а́-ӡ-уа-м, [aor.] и-з-ӡ-и́т, ды-з-ӡ-и́т, и-а́-ӡ-ит / и-сы-м-ӡ-и́т, д-сы-м-ӡ-и́т, и-а́-м-ӡ-ит, [fut.1] и-з-ӡы́-п, ды-з-ӡы́-п, и-а́-ӡы-п / и-з-ӡ-ры́м, ды-з-ӡ-ры́м, и-а́-ӡ-рым, [perf.] и-з-ӡ-хье́-ит, ды-з-ӡ-хье́-ит, и-а́-ӡ-хье́-ит / и-сы-м-ӡы́-ц(т), д-сы-м-ӡы́-ц(т), и-а́-м-ӡы-ц(т), [impf.] и-з-ӡ-уа́-н, ды-з-ӡ-уа́-н, и-а́-ӡ-уа-н / и-з-ӡ-уа́-мызт, ды-з-ӡ-уа́-мызт, и-а́-ӡ-уа-мызт, [past indef.] и-з-ӡы́-н, ды-з-ӡы́-н, и-а́-ӡы-н / и-сы-м-ӡы́-зт, д-сы-м-ӡы́-зт, и-а́-м-ӡы-зт, [plupf.] и-з-ӡ-хьа́н, ды-з-ӡ-хьа́н, и-а́-ӡ-хьан / и-сы-м-ӡы́-цызт, д-сы-м-ӡы́-цызт, и-а́-м-ӡы-цызт; Non-fin. [pres.] (C1) и́-л-ӡ-уа / и́-лы-м-ӡ-уа, (C3) и-з-ӡ-уа́ / и-зы-м-ӡ-уа́, [aor.] (C1) и́-л-ӡ / и́-лы-м-ӡ, (C3) и-з-ӡы́ / и-зы-м-ӡы́, [fut.1] (C1) и́-л-ӡ-ра / и́-лы-м-ӡ-ра, (C3) и-з-ӡ-ра́ / и-зы-м-ӡ-ра́, [fut.2] (C1) и́-л-ӡ-ша / и́-лы-м-ӡ-ша, (C3) и-з-ӡы́-ша / и-зы-м-ӡы́-ша, [perf.] (C1) и́-л-ӡ-хьо-у (-хьа-(п)) / и́-лы-м-ӡ-хьо-у (-хьа-(п)), (C3) и-з-ӡ-хьо́-у (-хьа́-(п)) / и-зы-м-ӡ-хьо́-у (-хьа́-(п)), [impf.] (C1) и́-л-ӡ-уа-з / и́-лы-м-ӡ-уа-з, (C3) и-з-ӡ-уа́-з / и-зы-м-ӡ-уа́-з, [past indef.] (C1) и́-л-ӡы-з / и́-лы-м-ӡы-з, (C3) и-з-ӡы́-з / и-зы-м-ӡы́-з, [cond.1] (C1) и́-л-ӡ-ры-з / и́-лы-м-ӡ-ры-з, (C3) и-з-ӡ-ры́-з / и-зы-м-ӡ-ры́-з, [cond.2] (C1) и́-л-ӡ-ша-з / и́-лы-м-ӡ-ша-з, (C3) и-з-ӡы́-ша-з / и-зы-м-ӡы́-ша-з, [plupf.] (C1) и́-л-ӡ-хьа-з / и́-лы-м-ӡ-хьа-з, (C3) и-з-ӡ-хьа́-з / и-зы-м-ӡ-хьа́-з.

а-ӡҩа-ра́ 'to dilute': Fin. [pres.] и-сы-ӡҩо́-ит, и-а́-ӡҩо-ит / и-сы-ӡҩо́-м, [aor.] и-сы-ӡҩе́-ит, и-а́-ӡҩе-ит / и-с-мы-ӡҩе́-ит, и-а́-мы-ӡҩе-ит; Non-fin. [pres.] (C1) и́-лы-ӡҩо / и́-л-мы-ӡҩо, (C3) и-зы-ӡҩо́ / и-з-мы-ӡҩо́, [aor.](C1) и́-лы-ӡҩа / и́-л-мы-ӡҩа, (C3) и-зы-ӡҩа́ / и-з-мы-ӡҩа́, [impf.] (C1) и́-лы-ӡҩо-з / и́-л-мы-ӡҩо-з, (C3) и-зы-ӡҩо́-з / и-з-мы-ӡҩо́-з, [past indef.] (C1) и́-лы-ӡҩа-з / и́-л-мы-ӡҩа-з, (C3) и-зы-ӡҩа́-з / и-з-мы-ӡҩа́-з.

а́-ҟаҟа-ра 'to chew': Fin. [pres.] и-л-ҟаҟо́-ит, и-а́-ҟаҟо-ит / и-л-ҟаҟо́-м (-ҟаҟа-ӡо́-м), и-а́-ҟаҟо́-м, [aor.] и-л-ҟаҟе́-ит, и-а́-ҟаҟе-ит / и-лы-м-ҟаҟе́-ит (-ҟаҟа-ӡе́-ит), и-а́-м-ҟаҟе-ит; Non-fin. [pres.] (C1) и́-л-ҟаҟо / и́-лы-м-ҟаҟо, (C3) и-з-ҟаҟо́ / и-зы-м-ҟаҟо́, [aor.] (C1) и́-л-ҟаҟа / и́-лы-м-ҟаҟа, (C3) и-з-ҟаҟа́ / и-зы-м-ҟаҟа́, [impf.] (C1) и́-л-ҟаҟо-з / и́-лы-м-ҟаҟо-з, (C3) и-з-ҟаҟо́-з / и-зы-м-ҟаҟо́-з, [past indef.] (C1) и́-л-ҟаҟа-з / и́-лы-м-ҟаҟа-з, (C3) и-з-ҟаҟа́-з / и-зы-м-ҟаҟа́-з.

а́-ҟәшәа-ра 'to gather': Fin. [pres.] и-сы-ҟәшәо́-ит, и-а́-ҟәшәо-ит / и-сы-ҟәшәо́-м, [aor.] и-сы-ҟәшәе́-ит, и-а́-ҟәшәе-ит / и-с-мы-ҟәшәе́-ит, и-а́-мы-ҟәшәе-ит; Non-fin. [pres.] (C1) и́-лы-ҟәшәо / и́-л-мы-ҟәшәо, (C3) и-зы-ҟәшәо́ / и-з-мы-ҟәшәо́, [aor.] (C1) и́-лы-ҟәшәа / и́-л-мы-ҟәшәа, (C3) и-зы-ҟәшәа́ / и-з-мы-ҟәшәа́, [impf.] (C1) и́-лы-ҟәшәо-з / и́-л-мы-ҟәшәо-з, (C3) и-зы-ҟәшәо́-з / и-з-мы-ҟәшәо́-з, [past indef.] (C1) и́-лы-ҟәшәа-з / и́-л-мы-ҟәшәа-з, (C3) и-зы-ҟәшәа́-з / и-з-мы-ҟәшәа́-з.

а-ҧшьа-ра́ ‘to consecrate’: Fin. [pres.] и-сы-ҧшьо́-ит, и-а́-ҧшьо-ит / и-сы-ҧшьо́-м, [aor.] и-сы-ҧшье́-ит, и-а́-ҧшье-ит / и-сы-м-ҧшье́-ит, и-а́-м-ҧшье-ит; Non-fin. [pres.] (C1) и́-лы-ҧшьо / и́-лы-м-ҧшьо, (C3) и-зы-ҧшьо́ / и-зы-м-ҧшьо́, [aor.] (C1) и́-лы-ҧшьа / и́-лы-м-ҧшьа, (C3) и-зы-ҧшьа́ / и-зы-м-ҧшьа́, [impf.] (C1) и́-лы-ҧшьо-з / и́-лы-м-ҧшьо-з, (C3) и-зы-ҧшьо́-з / и-зы-м-ҧшьо́-з, [past indef.] (C1) и́-лы-ҧшьа-з / и́-лы-м-ҧшьа-з, (C3) и-зы-ҧшьа́-з / и-зы-м-ҧшьа́-з.

а́-ҭи-ра ‘to sell’: Fin. [pres.] и-л-ҭи-уе́-ит, и-а́-ҭи-уе-ит, и-ах-ҭи-уе́-ит / и-л-ҭи-уа́-м, и-а́-ҭи-уа-м, [aor.] и-л-ҭи́-ит, и-а́-ҭи-ит / и-лы-м-ҭи́-ит, и-а́-м-ҭи-ит, [fut.1] и-с-ҭи́-п, и-а́-ҭи-п / и-с-ҭи-ры́м, и-а́-ҭи-рым, [fut.2] и-с-ҭи́-шт, и-а́-ҭи-шт / и-с-ҭи́-шам, и-а́-ҭи-шам, [perf.] и-с-ҭи-хье́ит, и-а́-ҭи-хьеит / и-сы-м-ҭи́-ц(т), и-а́-м-ҭи́-ц(т), [impf.] и-с-ҭи-уа́-н, и-а́-ҭи-уа-н / и-с-ҭи-уа́-мызт, и-а́-ҭи-уа-мызт, [past indef.] и-с-ҭи́-н, и-а́-ҭи-н / и-сы-м-ҭи́-зт, и-а́-м-ҭи-зт, [cond.1] и-с-ҭи-ры́н, и-а́-ҭи-рын / и-с-ҭи-ры́мызт, и-а́-ҭи-рымызт, [cond.2] и-с-ҭи́-шан, и-а́-ҭи-шан / и-с-ҭи́-шамызт, и-а́-ҭи-шамызт, [plupf.] и-с-ҭи-хьа́н, и-а́-ҭи-хьан / и-сы-м-ҭи́-цызт, и-а́-м-ҭи-цызт; Non-fin. [pres.] (C1) и́-л-ҭи-уа / и́-лы-м-ҭи-уа, (C3) и-з-ҭи-уа́ / и-зы-м-ҭи-уа́, [aor.] (C1) и́-л-ҭи / и́-лы-м-ҭи, (C3) и-з-ҭи́ / и-зы-м-ҭи́, [fut.1] (C1) и́-л-ҭи-ра / и́-лы-м-ҭи-ра, (C3) и-з-ҭи-ра́ / и-зы-м-ҭи-ра́, [fut.2] (C1) и́-л-ҭи-ша / и́-лы-м-ҭи-ша, (C3) и-з-ҭи́-ша / и-зы-м-ҭи́-ша, [perf.] (C1) и́-л-ҭи-хьоу (-хьа(п)) / и́-лы-м-ҭи-хьоу (-хьа(п)), (C3) и-з-ҭи-хьо́у (-хьа́(п)) / и-зы-м-ҭи-хьо́у (-хьа́(п)), [impf.] (C1) и́-л-ҭи-уа-з / и́-лы-м-ҭи-уа-з, (C3) и-з-ҭи-уа́-з / и-зы-м-ҭи-уа́-з, [past indef.] (C1) и́-л-ҭи-з / и́-лы-м-ҭи-з, (C3) и-з-ҭи́-з / и-зы-м-ҭи́-з, [cond.1] (C1) и́-л-ҭи-ры-з / и́-лы-м-ҭи-ры-з, (C3) и-з-ҭи-ры́-з / и-зы-м-ҭи-ры́-з, [cond.2] (C1) и́-л-ҭи-ша-з / и́-лы-м-ҭи-ша-з, (C3) и-з-ҭи́-ша-з / и-зы-м-ҭи́-ша-з, [plupf.] (C1) и́-л-ҭи-хьа-з / и́-лы-м-ҭи-хьа-з, (C3) и-з-ҭи-хьа́-з / и-зы-м-ҭи-хьа́-з.

а-уанҭа-ра́ ‘to iron’: Fin. [pres.] и-с-уанҭо́-ит / и-с-уанҭо́-м, [aor.] и-с-уанҭе́-ит, и-а́-уанҭе-ит / и-сы-м-уанҭе́-ит, и-а́-м-уанҭе-ит; Non-fin. [pres.] (C1) и́-л-уанҭо / и́-лы-м-уанҭо, (C3) и-з-уанҭо́ / и-зы-м-уанҭо́, [aor.] (C1) и́-л-уанҭа / и́-лы-м-уанҭа, (C3) и-з-уанҭа́ / и-зы-м-уанҭа́, [impf.] (C1) и́-л-уанҭо-з / и́-лы-м-уанҭо-з, (C3) и-з-уанҭо́-з / и-зы-м-уанҭо́-з, [past indef.] (C1) и́-л-уанҭа-з / и́-лы-м-уанҭа-з, (C3) и-з-уанҭа́-з / и-зы-м-уанҭа́-з.

а́-фа-ра ‘to bite’: Fin. [pres.] с-а́-фо-ит, сы-б-фо́-ит / с-а́-фо-м (-фа-ӡо-м), сы-б-фо́-м, [aor.] с-а́-фе-ит, сы-б-фе́-ит / с-а́-м-фе-ит (-фа-ӡе-ит), с-бы-м-фе́-ит; Non-fin. [pres.] (C1) и-а́-фо, и́-с-фо / и-а́-м-фо, и́-сы-м-фо, (C3) сы-з-фо́ / с-зы-м-фо́, [aor.] (C1) и-а́-фа, и-с-фо́ / и-а́-м-фа, и-сы-м-фа́, (C3) сы-з-фа́ / с-зы-м-фа́.

а́-хьча-ра ‘to guard’: Fin. [pres.] с-лы-хьчо́-ит, с-а́-хьчо-ит / с-лы-хьчо́-м, [aor.] с-лы-хьче́-ит, с-а́-хьче-ит / сы-л-мы-хьче́-ит, с-а́-мы-хьче-ит; Non-fin. [pres.] (C1) и́-лы-хьчо / и́-л-мы-хьчо, (C3) д-зы-хьчо́, и-зы-хьчо́ / ды-з-мы-хьчо́, и-з-мы-хьчо́, [aor.] (C1) и́-лы-хьча / и́-л-мы-хьча, (C3) д-зы-хьча́ / ды-з-мы-хьча́, [impf.] (C1) и́-лы-хьчо-з / и́-л-мы-хьчо-з, (C3) д-зы-хьчо́-з / ды-з-мы-хьчо́-з, [past indef.] (C1) и́-лы-хьча-з / и́-л-мы-хьча-з, (C3) д-зы-хьча́-з / ды-з-мы-хьча́-з.

а́-ҵәах-ра ‘to hide’: Fin. [aor.] и-с-ҵәах-и́т, и-а́-ҵәах-ит / и-сы-м-ҵәах-и́т, и-а́-м-ҵәах-ит; Non-fin. [pres.] (C1) и́-л-ҵәах-уа / и́-лы-м-ҵәах-уа, (C3) и-з-ҵәах-уа́ / и-зы-м-ҵәах-уа́, [aor.] (C1) и́-л-ҵәах / и́-лы-м-ҵәах, (C3) и-з-ҵәахы́ / и-зы-м-ҵәахы́, [impf.] (C1) и́-л-ҵәах-уа-з / и́-лы-м-ҵәах-уа-з, (C3) и-з-ҵәах-уа́-з / и-зы-м-ҵәах-уа́-з, [past indef.] (C1) и́-л-ҵәахы-з / и́-лы-м-ҵәахы-з, (C3) и-з-ҵәахы́-з / и-зы-м-ҵәахы́-з.

а-шә-ра́ 'to dye': Fin. [pres.] и-с-шә-уе́-ит, и-а́-шә-уе-ит / и-с-шә-уа́-м, и-а́-шә-уа-м, [aor.] и-с-шә-и́т, и-а́-шә-ит / и-сы-м-шә-и́т, и-а́-м-шә-ит; Non-fin. [pres.] (C1) и́-л-шә-уа / и́-лы-м-шә-уа, (C3) и-з-шә-уа́ / и-зы-м-шә-уа́, [aor.] (C1) и́-л-шә / и́-лы-м-шә, (C3) и-з-шәы́ / и-зы-м-шәы́, [impf.] (C1) и́-л-шә-уа-з / и́-лы-м-шә-уа-з, (C3) и-з-шә-уа́-з / и-зы-м-шә-уа́-з, [past indef.] (C1) и́-л-шәы-з / и́-лы-м-шәы-з, (C3) и-з-шәы́-з / и-зы-м-шәы́-з.

а-ҩ-ра́ 'to write': Fin. [pres.] и-з-ҩ-уе́-ит, и-ҩ-уе́-ит, и-л-ҩ-уе́-ит, и-а́-ҩ-уе-ит, и-ҳа-ҩ-уе́-ит, и-шәы-ҩ-уе́-ит / и-з-ҩ-уа́-м; [aor.] и-з-ҩ-и́т, и-а́-ҩ-ит, и-аҳ-ҩ-и́т, и-шә-ҩ-и́т / и-сы-м-ҩ-и́т, [fut.1] и-з-ҩы́-п / и-з-ҩ-ры́м, [fut.2] и-з-ҩы́-шт / и-з-ҩы́-шам, [perf.] и-з-ҩ-хье́ит / и-сы-м-ҩы́-ц(т), [impf.] и-з-ҩ-уа́н / и-з-ҩ-уа́мызт, [past indef.] и-з-ҩы́-н / и-сы-м-ҩы́-зт, [cond.1] и-з-ҩы-ры́н / и-з-ҩ-ры́мызт, [cond.2] и-з-ҩы́-шан / и-з-ҩы́-шамызт, [plupf.] и-з-ҩ-хьа́н / и-сы-м-ҩы́-цызт; Non-fin. [pres.] (C1) и́-л-ҩ-уа, и́-с-ҩ-уа, и́-б-ҩ-уа, и́-у-ҩ-уа, и́-и-ҩ-уа, и-а́-ҩ-уа, и-а́ҳ-ҩ-уа, и́-шә-ҩ-уа, и́-р-ҩ-уа / и́-лы-м-ҩ-уа, и́-сы-м-ҩ-уа, и́-бы-м-ҩ-уа, и́-у-м-ҩ-уа, и́-и-м-ҩ-уа, и-а́-м-ҩ-уа, и-а́ҳа-м-ҩ-уа, и́-шәы-м-ҩ-уа, и́-ры-м-ҩ-уа, (C3) и-з-ҩ-уа́ / и-зы-м-ҩ-уа́, [aor.] (C1) и́-л-ҩы, и́-з/с-ҩы, и́-б-ҩы, и́-у-ҩы, и́-и-ҩы, и-а-ҩы́, и-а́ҳ-ҩы, и́-жә/шә-ҩы, и́-р-ҩы / и́-лы-м-ҩы, и́-зы /сы-м-ҩы, и́-бы-м-ҩы, и́-у-м-ҩы, и́-и-м-ҩы, и-а́-м-ҩы, и-а́ҳа-м-ҩы, и́-жәы/шәы-м-ҩы, и́-ры-м-ҩы, (C3) и-з-ҩы́ / и-зы-м-ҩы́, [fut.1] (C1) и́-лы-ҩ-ра, и́-зы/сы-ҩ-ра, и́-бы-ҩ-ра, и́-у-ҩ-ра, и-а-ҩ-ра́, и́-и-ҩ-ра, и-а́ҳа-ҩ-ра *or* и́-ҳа-ҩ-ра, и́-шәы-ҩ-ра, и́-ры-ҩ-ра / и́-л-м-ҩ-ра, и́-с/з-м-ҩ-ра, и́-б-м-ҩ-ра, и́-у-м-ҩ-ра, и-а́-м-ҩ-ра, и́-и-м-ҩ-ра, и́-(а)ҳ-м-ҩ-ра, и́-шә-м-ҩ-ра, и́-р-м-ҩ-ра, (C3) и-з-ҩ-ра́ / и-з-мы-ҩ-ра́, [fut.2] (C1) и́-л-ҩ-ша, и́-з/с-ҩ-ша, и́-б-ҩ-ша, и́-у-ҩ-ша, и́-и-ҩ-ша, и-а-ҩы́-ша, и-а́ҳ-ҩ-ша, и́-жә/шә-ҩ-ша, и́-р-ҩ-ша / и́-лы-м-ҩы-ша, и́-сы/зы-м-ҩы-ша, и́-бы-м-ҩы-ша, и́-у-м-ҩы-ша, и́-и-м-ҩы-ша, и-а́-м-ҩы-ша, и-а́ҳа-м-ҩы-ша, и́-шәы/жәы-м-ҩы-ша, и́-ры-м-ҩы-ша, (C3) и-з-ҩы́-ша / и-зы-м-ҩы́-ша, [perf.] (C1) и́-л-ҩ-хьоу (-хьа(ц)), и́-з/с-ҩ-хьоу (-хьа(ц)), и́-б-ҩ-хьоу (-хьа(ц)), и́-у-ҩ-хьоу (-хьа(ц)), и́-и-ҩ-хьоу (-хьа(ц)), и-а́-ҩ-хьоу (-хьа(ц)), и-а́ҳ-ҩ-хьоу (-хьа(ц)), и́-жә/шә-ҩ-хьоу (-хьа(ц)), и́-р-ҩ-хьоу (-хьа(ц)) / и́-лы-м-ҩ-хьоу (-хьа(ц)), и́-сы/зы-м-ҩ-хьоу (-хьа(ц)), и́-бы-м-ҩ-хьоу (-хьа(ц)), и́-у-м-ҩ-хьоу (-хьа(ц)), и́-и-м-ҩ-хьоу (-хьа(ц)), и-а́-м-ҩ-хьоу (-хьа(ц)), и-а́ҳа-м-ҩ-хьоу (-хьа(ц)), и́-шәы/жәы-м-ҩ-хьоу (-хьа(ц)), и́-ры-м-ҩ-хьоу (-хьа(ц)), (C3) и-з-ҩ-хьо́у (-хьа́(ц)) / и-зы-м-ҩ-хьо́у (-хьа́(ц)), [impf.] (C1) и́-л-ҩ-уа-з, и́-з/с-ҩ-уа-з, и́-б-ҩ-уа-з, и́-у-ҩ-уа-з, и́-и-ҩ-уа-з, и-а́-ҩ-уа-з, и-а́ҳ-ҩ-уа-з, и́-жә/шә-ҩ-уа-з, и́-р-ҩ-уа-з / и́-лы-м-ҩ-уа-з, и́-сы/зы-м-ҩ-уа-з, и́-бы-м-ҩ-уа-з, и́-у-м-ҩ-уа-з, и́-и-м-ҩ-уа-з, и-а́-м-ҩ-уа-з, и-а́ҳа-м-ҩ-уа-з, и́-шәы/жәы-м-ҩ-уа-з, и́-ры-м-ҩ-уа-з, (C3) и-з-ҩ-уа́-з / и-зы-м-ҩ-уа́-з, [past indef.] (C1) и́-л-ҩы-з, и́-з/с-ҩы-з, и́-б-ҩы-з, и́-у-ҩы-з, и́-и-ҩы-з, и-а́-ҩы-з, и-а́ҳ-ҩы-з, и́-жә/шә-ҩы-з, и́-р-ҩы-з / и́-лы-м-ҩы-з, и́-сы/зы-м-ҩы-з, и́-бы-м-ҩы-з, и́-у-м-ҩы-з, и́-и-м-ҩы-з, и-а́-м-ҩы-з, и-а́ҳа-м-ҩы-з, и́-шәы/жәы-м-ҩы-з, и́-ры-м-ҩы-з, (C3) и-з-ҩы́-з / и-зы-м-ҩы́-з, [cond.1] (C1) и́-л-ҩ-ры-з, и́-з/с-ҩ-ры-з, и́-б-ҩ-ры-з, и́-у-ҩ-ры-з, и-а́-ҩ-ры-з, и-а́-ҩ-ры-з, и-а́ҳ-ҩ-ры-з, и́-жә/шә-ҩ-ры-з, и́-р-ҩ-ры-з / и́-лы-м-ҩ-ры-з, и́-сы/зы-м-ҩ-ры-з, и́-бы-м-ҩ-ры-з, и́-у-м-ҩ-ры-з, и-а́-м-ҩ-ры-з, и-а́ҳа-м-ҩ-ры-з, и́-шәы/жәы-м-ҩ-ры-з, и́-ры-м-ҩ-ры-з, (C3) и-з-ҩ-ры́-з / и-з-мы-ҩ-ры́-з, [cond.2] (C1) и́-л-ҩ-ша-з, и́-з/с-ҩ-ша-з, и́-б-ҩ-ша-з, и́-у-ҩ-ша-з, и́-и-ҩ-ша-з, и-а́-ҩ-ша-з, и-а́ҳ-ҩ-ша-з, и́-жә/шә-ҩ-ша-з, и́-р-ҩ-ша-з / и́-лы-м-ҩ-ша-з, и́-сы/зы-м-ҩ-ша-з, и́-бы-м-ҩ-ша-з, и́-у-м-ҩ-ша-з, и́-и-м-ҩ-ша-з, и-а́-м-ҩ-ша-з, и-а́ҳа-м-ҩ-ша-з, и́-шәы/жәы-м-ҩ-ша-з, и́-ры-м-ҩ-ша-з, (C3) и-з-ҩы́-ша-з / и-з-мы-ҩы́-ша-з, [plupf.] (C1) и́-л-ҩ-хьа-з, и́-з/с-ҩ-хьа-з, и́-б-ҩ-хьа-з, и́-у-ҩ-хьа-з, и́-и-ҩ-хьа-з, и-а́-ҩ-хьа-з, и-а́ҳ-ҩ-хьа-з, и́-жә/шә-ҩ-хьа-з, и́-р-ҩ-хьа-з / и́-лы-м-ҩ-хьа-з, и́-сы/зы-м-ҩ-хьа-з, и́-бы-м-ҩ-хьа-з, и́-у-м-ҩ-хьа-з, и́-и-м-ҩ-хьа-з, и-а́-м-ҩ-хьа-з, и-а́ҳа-м-ҩ-хьа-з, и́-шәы/жәы-м-ҩ-хьа-з, и́-ры-м-ҩ-хьа-з, (C3) и-з-ҩ-хьа́-з / и-з-мы-ҩ-хьа́-з;

а-ц̦ь-ра́ ‘to to roast’: Fin. [pres.] и-з-ц̦ь-уе́-ит, и-аа-ц̦ь-уе́-ит, и-жә-ц̦ь-уе́-ит, и-а́-ц̦ь-уе-ит / и-з-ц̦ь-уа́-м, [aor.] и-з-ц̦ь-и́т, и-а́-ц̦ь-ит / и-сы-м-ц̦ь-и́т, и-а́-м-ц̦ь-ит; Non-fin. [pres.] (C1) и́-л-ц̦ь-уа / и́-лы-м-ц̦ь-уа, (C3) и-з-ц̦ь-уа́ / и-зы-м-ц̦ь-уа́, [aor.] (C1) и́-л-ц̦ь / и́-лы-м-ц̦ь, (C3) и-з-ц̦ьы́ / и-зы-м-ц̦ьы́, [impf.] (C1) и́-л-ц̦ь-уа-з / и́-лы-м-ц̦ь-уа-з, (C3) и-з-ц̦ь-уа́-з / и-зы-м-ц̦ь-уа́-з, [past indef.] (C1) и́-л-ц̦ьы-з / и́-лы-м-ц̦ьы-з, (C3) и-з-ц̦ьы́-з / и-зы-м-ц̦ьы́-з.

3.2.6.4. Inflection of AP c-iii

This type places an accent on postradical elements through all inflections in finite forms.

а-сара́ /a-sa-rá/ ‘to cut out’

Finite forms

	Affirmative	Negative
C1-C3		
Present		
Sg.3.Non-Human/Pl.3-Sg.1	и-с-со́-ит	и-с-со́-м
Sg.3.Non-Hum./Pl.3-Sg.3.Non-Hum.	и-а-со́-ит	и-а-со́-м
Aorist		
Sg.3.Non-Human/Pl.3-Sg.1	и-с-се́-ит	и-сы-м-се́-ит
Sg.3.Non-Hum./Pl.3-Sg.3.Non-Hum.	и-а-се́-ит	и-а-м-се́-ит

Finite forms

Present		
Rel-Sg.1	и́-л-со	и́-лы-м-со
Sg.3.Non-Human/Pl.3-Rel	и-з-со́	и-зы-м-со́
Aorist		
Rel-Sg.1	и́-л-са	и́-лы-м-са
Sg.3.Non-Human/Pl.3-Rel	и-з-са́	и-зы-м-са́
Imperfect		
Rel-Sg.1	и́-л-со-з	и́-лы-м-со-з
Sg.3.Non-Human/Pl.3-Rel	и-з-со́-з	и-зы-м-со́-з
Past Indefinite		
Rel-Sg.1	и́-л-са-з	и́-лы-м-са-з
Sg.3.Non-Human/Pl.3-Rel	и-з-са́-з	и-зы-м-са́-з

Other examples:

а-ша-ра́ ‘to divide’: Fin. [pres.] и-с-шо́-ит / и-с-шо́-м, [aor.] и-с-ше́-ит, и-а-ше́-ит / и-сы-м-ше́-ит, и-а-м-ше́-ит; Non-fin. [pres.] (C1) и́-с-шо / и́-сы-м-шо, (C3) и-з-шо́ / и-зы-м-шо́.

а-с-ра́ ‘to weave’: Fin. [pres.] и-с-с-уе́-ит, и-а-с-уе́-ит / и-с-с-уа́-м, [aor.] и-с-с-и́т, и-а-с-и́т / и-сы-м-с-и́т, и-а-м-с-и́т; Non-fin. [pres.] (C1) и́-л-с-уа / и́-лы-м-с-уа, (C3) и-з-с-уа́ / и-зы-м-с-уа́, [aor.] (C1) и́-л-с / и́-лы-м-с, (C3) и-з-сы́ / и-зы-м-сы́, [impf.] (C1) и́-л-с-уа-з / и́-лы-м-с-уа-з, (C3) и-з-с-уа́-з / и-зы-м-с-уа́-з, [past indef.] (C1) и́-л-сы-з / и́-лы-м-сы-з, (C3) и-з-сы́-з / и-зы-м-сы́-з.

а-та-ра́ 'to draw, to scoop': Fin. [pres.] и-л-то́-ит, и-а-то́-ит / и-л-то́-м (-та-ӡо́-м), и-а-то́-м, [aor.] и-л-те́-ит, и-а-те́-ит / и-лы-м-те́-ит, и-а-м-те́-ит; Non-fin. [pres.] (C1) и́-л-то / и́-лы-м-то, (C3) и-з-то́ / и-зы-м-то́, [aor.] (C1) и́-л-та / и́-лы-м-та, (C3) и-з-та́ / и-зы-м-та́, [impf.] (C1) и́-л-то-з / и́-лы-м-то-з, (C3) и-з-то́-з / и-зы-м-то́-з, [past indef.] (C1) и́-л-та-з / и́-лы-м-та-з, (C3) и-з-та́-з / и-зы-м-та́-з.

а-хәа-ра́ 'to press': Fin. [aor.] и-л-хәе́-ит / и-лы-м-хәе́-ит, и-а-хәе́-ит / и-а-м-хәе́-ит; Non-fin. [pres.] (C1) и́-л-с-хәо / и́-лы-м-хәо, (C3) и-з-хәо́ / и-зы-м-хәо́, [aor.] (C1) и́-л-с-хәа / и́-лы-м-хәа, (C3) и-з-хәа́ / и-зы-м-хәа́, [impf.] (C1) и́-л-с-хәо-з / и́-лы-м-хәо-з, (C3) и-з-хәо́-з / и-зы-м-хәо́-з, [past indef.] (C1) и́-л-с-хәа-з / и́-лы-м-хәа-з, (C3) и-з-хәа́-з / и-зы-м-хәа́-з.

а-хә-ра́ 'to sift': Fin. [pres.] и-с-хә-уе́-ит / и-с-хә-уа́-м, [aor.] и-с-хә-и́т, и-а-хә-и́т / и-сы-м-хә-и́т, и-а-м-хә-и́т; Non-fin. [pres.] (C1) и-с-хә-уа́ / и-сы-м-хә-уа́, (C3) и-з-хә-уа́ / и-зы-м-хә-уа́.

а-ҳа-ра́ 'to plait': Fin. [pres.] и-с-ҳа-уе́-ит, и-а-ҳа-уе́-ит / и-с-ҳа-уа́-м (-ҳа-ӡо́-м), [aor.] и-с-ҳа-и́т, и-а-ҳа-и́т / и-сы-м-ҳа-и́т (-ҳа-ӡе́-ит), и-а-м-ҳа-и́т; Non-fin. [pres.] (C1) и́-л-ҳа-уа / и́-лы-м-ҳа-уа, (C3) и-з-ҳа-уа́ / и-зы-м-ҳа-уа́, [aor.] (C1) и́-л-ҳа / и́-лы-м-ҳа, (C3) и-з-ҳа́ / и-зы-м-ҳа́, [impf.] (C1) и́-л-ҳа-уа-з / и́-лы-м-ҳа-уа-з, (C3) и-з-ҳа-уа́-з / и-зы-м-ҳа-уа́-з, [past indef.] (C1) и́-л-ҳа-з / и́-лы-м-ҳа-з, (C3) и-з-ҳа́-з / и-зы-м-ҳа́-з.

а-ҳәа-ра́ 'to comb': Fin. [pres.] и-с-ҳәо́-ит / и-с-ҳәо́-м, [aor.] и-с-ҳәе́-ит, и-а-ҳәе́-ит / и-сы-м-ҳәе́-ит, и-а-м-ҳәе́-ит; Non-fin. [pres.] (C1) и́-л-ҳәо / и́-лы-м-ҳәо, (C3) и-з-ҳәо́ / и-зы-м-ҳәо́, [aor.] (C1) и́-л-ҳәа / и́-лы-м-ҳәа, (C3) и-з-ҳәа́ / и-зы-м-ҳәа́, [impf.] (C1) и́-л-ҳәо-з / и́-лы-м-ҳәо-з, (C3) и-з-ҳәо́-з / и-зы-м-ҳәо́-з, [past indef.] (C1) и́-л-ҳәа-з / и́-лы-м-ҳәа-з, (C3) и-з-ҳәа́-з / и-зы-м-ҳәа́-з.

а-ҵаа-ра́ 'to salt': Fin. [aor.] и-с-ҵаа-и́т, и-а-ҵаа-и́т / и-сы-м-ҵаа-и́т, и-а-м-ҵаа-и́т; Non-fin. [pres.] (C1) и́-л-ҵаа-уа / и́-лы-м-ҵаа-уа, (C3) и-з-ҵаа-уа́ / и-зы-м-ҵаа-уа́, [aor.] (C1) и́-л-ҵаа / и́-лы-м-ҵаа, (C3) и-з-ҵаа́ / и-зы-м-ҵаа́, [impf.] (C1) и́-л-ҵаа-уа-з / и́-лы-м-ҵаа-уа-з, (C3) и-з-ҵаа-уа́-з / и-зы-м-ҵаа-уа́-з, [past indef.] (C1) и́-л-ҵаа-з / и́-лы-м-ҵаа-з, (C3) и-з-ҵаа́-з / и-зы-м-ҵаа́-з.

а-ҿа-ра́ 'to hoe': Fin. [pres.] и-с-ҿо́-ит / и-с-ҿо́-м, [aor.] и-с-ҿе́-ит, и-а-ҿе́-ит / и-сы-м-ҿе́-ит, и-а-м-ҿе́-ит; Non-fin. [pres.] (C1) и́-л-ҿо / и́-лы-м-ҿо, (C3) и-з-ҿо́ / и-зы-м-ҿо́, [aor.] (C1) и́-л-ҿа / и́-лы-м-ҿа, (C3) и-з-ҿа́ / и-зы-м-ҿа́, [impf.] (C1) и́-л-ҿо-з / и́-лы-м-ҿо-з, (C3) и-з-ҿо́-з / и-зы-м-ҿо́-з, [past indef.] (C1) и́-л-ҿа-з / и́-лы-м-ҿа-з, (C3) и-з-ҿа́-з / и-зы-м-ҿа́-з.

а-шәа-ра́ 'to measure': Fin. [pres.] и-с-шәо́-ит / и-с-шәо́-м, [aor.] и-с-шәе́-ит, и-а-шәе́-ит / и-сы-м-шәе́-ит, и-а-м-шәе́-ит; Non-fin. [pres.] (C1) и́-л-шәо / и́-лы-м-шәо, (C3) и-з-шәо́ / и-зы-м-шәо́, [aor.] (C1) и́-л-шәа / и́-лы-м-шәа, (C3) и-з-шәа́ / и-зы-м-шәа́, [impf.] (C1) и́-л-шәо-з / и́-лы-м-шәо-з, (C3) и-з-шәо́-з / и-зы-м-шәо́-з, [past indef.] (C1) и́-л-шәа-з / и́-лы-м-шәа-з, (C3) и-з-шәа́-з / и-зы-м-шәа́-з.

3.2.6.5. The Class C Type Verbs of Causative Derivative

In verbs that can take the same structure as the distribution of a pronominal prefix in a Class C verb, there are also causative derivation verbs from one-place intransitive verbs and adjectives. These verbs all have the causative marker р- /r/ attached to the head of the root. For example, а-ргы́лара /a-r-gə́la-ra/ 'to build' is a two-place transitive verb causatively derived from the one-place intransitive verb а-гы́лара /a-gə́la-ra/ 'to stand': исыргы́лоит /jə-sə-r-gə́la-wa-jt'/ [it/them(C1)-I(C3)-Caus-stand-Dyn-Fin] 'I am building it/them'. Here, the Column III pronominal prefix с(ы)- 'I', which is the agent, is placed before the causative marker, and the Column I pronominal prefix и- /jə/ 'it/them', which is the direct object, is placed at the beginning of the word. Therefore, this becomes a Class C type structure (C1+C3+Stem) where C1-C3 pronominal prefixes are placed before the stem ргыла /rgəla/ 'build'. Also, in the aorist negative form the negative marker м- /m/ is placed directly before the causative marker р- /r/: исмыргы́леит /jə-s-mə-r-gə́la-jt'/ [it/them(C1)-I(C3)-Neg-Caus-stand-Dyn-Fin] 'I did not build it/them'. The structure of this negative form is also the same as Class C type: C1+C3+Neg+Stem (for the causative see §4.1). No element can be inserted between this causative marker and the root. Therefore, in the text that follows we have opted not to insert the morpheme separator dash '-' between the causative marker and the root when transcribing 'causative + root'.

As previously mentioned in §3.1.6, Note 6, morphologically, something to take note of with Class C type causatives is that the third-person plural Column II and Column III pronominal prefixes р(ы)- /r(ə)/ alternates with д(ы)- /d(ə)/. Aside from that, they are basically not different from Class C type verbs. However, in regards to accent, there are three types of accent paradigms for causative derived verbs (cf. for non-causative type Class C verbs, there is only AP a and AP c). These three types are: AP a, which fixes its accent on the stem, and AP b, which places the accent on the pronominal prefix before the stem, and AP c, which places the accent on the postradical element. We will describe their respective inflections below.

3.2.6.5.1. Inflection of AP a

The accent paradigm of this verb is a type where the accent is fixed on the stem in all forms.

а-ргы́лара /a-rgə́la-ra/ 'to build' (cf. агы́лара /a-gə́la-ra/ 'to stand up')

Finite forms

	Affirmative	Negative
Dynamic Group I		
Present		
C1-C3		
Sg.3.Non-Human/Pl.3-Sg.1	и-сы-ргы́ло-ит /jə-sə-rgə́la-wa-jt'/ it/them(C1)-I(C3)-build-Dyn-Fin 'I build it/them'	и-сы-ргы́ло-м
Sg.3.Non-Human/Pl.3-Sg.2.M	и-у-ргы́ло-ит	и-у-ргы́ло-м
Sg.3.Non-Hum./Pl.3-Sg.3.M	и-ргы́ло-ит (< и-и-ргы́ло-ит)	и-ргы́ло-м
Sg.3.Non-Human/Pl.3-Sg.3.F	и-лы-ргы́ло-ит	и-лы-ргы́ло-м
Sg.3.Non-Hum./Pl.3-Sg.3.Non-Hum.	и-а-ргы́ло-ит	и-а-ргы́ло-м
Sg.3.Non-Human/Pl.3-Pl.1	и-ха-ргы́ло-ит	и-ха-ргы́ло-м
Sg.3.Non-Human/Pl.3-Pl.2	и-шәы-ргы́ло-ит	и-шәы-ргы́ло-м
Sg.3.Non-Human/Pl.3-Pl.3	и-ды-ргы́ло-ит /jə-də-rgə́la-wa-jt'/ it/them(C1)-they(C3)-build-Dyn-Fin	и-ды-ргы́ло-м /jə-də-rgə́la-wa-m/

	'They build it/them'	'They do not build it/them'
Aorist		
Sg.3.Non-Human/Pl.3-Sg.1	и-сы-ргы́ле-ит	и-с-мы-ргы́ле-ит
Sg.3.Non-Hum./Pl.3-Sg.3.Non-Hum.	и-а-ргы́ле-ит	и-а-мы-ргы́ле-ит
Sg.3.Non-Human/Pl.3-Pl.3	и-ды-ргы́ле-ит	и-д-мы-ргы́ле-ит
Future I		
Sg.3.Non-Human/Pl.3-Sg.1	и-сы-ргы́ла-п	и-сы-ргы́ла-ры-м
Future II		
Sg.3.Non-Human/Pl.3-Sg.1	и-сы-ргы́ла-шт	и-сы-ргы́ла-ша-м
Perfect		
Sg.3.Non-Human/Pl.3-Sg.1	и-сы-ргы́ла-хье-ит	и-с-мы-ргы́ла-ц(т)
Dynamic Group II		
Imperfect		
Sg.3.Non-Human/Pl.3-Sg.1	и-сы-ргы́ло-н	и-сы-ргы́ло-мы-зт
Past Indefinite		
Sg.3.Non-Human/Pl.3-Sg.1	и-сы-ргы́ла-н	и-сы-ргы́ла-зт
Conditional I		
Sg.3.Non-Human/Pl.3-Sg.1	и-сы-ргы́ла-ры-н	и-сы-ргы́ла-ры-мы-зт
Conditional II		
Sg.3.Non-Human/Pl.3-Sg.1	и-сы-ргы́ла-ша-н	и-сы-ргы́ла-ша-мы-зт
Pluperfect		
Sg.3.Non-Human/Pl.3-Sg.1	и-сы-ргы́ла-хьа-н	и-с-мы-ргы́ла-цы-зт

Non-Finite forms

	Affirmative	Negative
C1-C3		
Present		
Rel-Sg.3.F	и-лы-ргы́ло /jə-lə-rgə́la-wa/ Rel(C1)-she(C3)-build-Dyn.NF 'which she builds'	и-л-мы-ргы́ло /jə-l-mə-rgə́la-wa/ 'which she does not build'
Sg.3.Non-Human/Pl.3-Rel	и-зы-ргы́ло /jə-zə-rgə́la-wa/ it/them(C1)-Rel(C3)-build-Dyn.NF '(the one) who builds it/them'	и-з-мы-ргы́ло
Imperfect		
Rel-Sg.3.F	и-лы-ргы́ло-з	и-л-мы-ргы́ло-з
Sg.3.Non-Human/Pl.3-Rel	и-зы-ргы́ло-з	и-з-мы-ргы́ло-з
Past Indefinite		
Rel-Sg.3.F	и-лы-ргы́ла-з	и-л-мы-ргы́ла-з
Sg.3.Non-Human/Pl.3-Rel	и-зы-ргы́ла-з	и-з-мы-ргы́ла-з

Other examples:

а-рбе́иа-ра 'to enrich' (cf. а-бе́иа 'rich'): Fin. [aor.] и-ды-рбе́ие-ит / и-д-мы-рбе́ие-ит.

а-рбзи́а-ра 'to make good' (cf. а-бзи́а 'good'): Fin. [pres.] и-лы-рбзи́о-ит / и-лы-рбзи́о-м (-рбзи́а-ӡо-м), [aor.] и-лы-рбзи́е-ит / и-л-мы-рбзи́е-ит; Non-fin. [pres.] (C1) и-лы-рбзи́о / и-л-мы-рбзи́о, (C3) и-зы-рбзи́о / и-з-мы-рбзи́о, [aor.] (C1) и-лы-рбзи́а / и-л-мы-рбзи́а, (C3) и-зы-рбзи́а / и-з-мы-рбзи́а, [impf.] (C1) и-лы-рбзи́о-з / и-л-мы-рбзи́о-з, (C3) и-зы-рбзи́о-з / и-з-мы-рбзи́о-з, [past indef.] (C1) и-лы-рбзи́а-з / и-л-мы-рбзи́а-з, (C3) и-зы-рбзи́а-з / и-з-мы-рбзи́а-з.

а-ргəа́а-ра 'to make angry' (cf. а-гəа́а-ра 'to get angry'): Fin. [pres.] д-сы-ргəа́а-уе-ит (*я сержу его/ее*) / д-сы-ргəа́а-уа-м (-ӡо-м), [aor.] д-сы-ргəа́а-ит / ды-с-мы-ргəа́а-ит (-ӡе-ит); Non-fin. [pres.] (C1) и-лы-ргəа́а-уа / и-л-мы-ргəа́а-уа, (C3) д-зы-ргəа́а-уа / ды-з-мы-ргəа́а-уа, [aor.] (C1) и-лы-ргəа́а / и-л-мы-ргəа́а, (C3) д-зы-ргəа́а / ды-з-мы-ргəа́а, [impf.] (C1) и-лы-ргəа́а-уа-з / и-л-мы-ргəа́а-уа-з, (C3) д-зы-ргəа́а-уа-з / ды-з-мы-ргəа́а-уа-з, [past indef.] (C1) и-лы-ргəа́а-з / и-л-мы-ргəа́а-з, (C3) д-зы-ргəа́а-з / ды-з-мы-ргəа́а-з.

а-ргəа́ҟ-ра 'to torment' (cf. а-гəа́ҟ-ра 'to torment oneself, to suffer'): Fin. [pres.] д-сы-ргəа́ҟ-уе-ит (*я мучу его/ее*) / д-сы-ргəа́ҟ-уа-м, [aor.] д-сы-ргəа́ҟ-ит / ды-с-мы-ргəа́ҟ-ит (-ӡе-ит); Non-fin. [pres.] (C1) и-лы-ргəа́ҟуа / и-л-мы-ргəа́ҟуа, (C3) д-зы-ргəа́ҟуа / ды-з-мы-ргəа́ҟ-уа, [aor.] (C1) и-лы-ргəа́ҟ / и-л-мы-ргəа́ҟ, (C3) д-зы-ргəа́ҟ / ды-з-мы-ргəа́ҟ, [impf.] (C1) и-лы-ргəа́ҟ-уа-з / и-л-мы-ргəа́ҟ-уа-з, (C3) д-зы-ргəа́ҟ-уа-з / ды-з-мы-ргəа́ҟ-уа-з, [past indef.] (C1) и-лы-ргəа́ҟы-з / и-л-мы-ргəа́ҟы-з, (C3) д-зы-ргəа́ҟы-з / ды-з-мы-ргəа́ҟы-з.

а-ргəа́мц-ра 'to bother' (cf. а-гəа́мц-ра 'to suffer'): Fin. [pres.] д-сы-ргəа́мц-уе-ит / д-сы-ргəа́мц-уа-м, [aor.] д-сы-ргəа́мц-ит / ды-с-мы-ргəа́мц-ит; Non-fin. [pres.] (C1) и-сы-ргəа́мц-уа / и-с-мы-ргəа́мц-уа, (C3) д-зы-ргəа́мц-уа / ды-з-мы-ргəа́мц-уа.

а-ргəы́рӷьа-ра 'to make happy' (cf. а-гəы́рӷьа-ра 'to be glad, to be happy'): Fin. [pres.] д-сы-ргəы́рӷьо-ит (*я радую ее/его*) / д-сы-ргəы́рӷьо-м (-ргəы́рӷьа-ӡо-м), [aor.] д-сы-ргəы́рӷье-ит / ды-с-мы-ргəы́рӷье-ит (-ргəы́рӷьа-ӡе-ит); Non-fin. [pres.] (C1) и-лы-ргəы́рӷьо / и-л-мы-ргəы́рӷьо, (C3) д-зы-ргəы́рӷьо / ды-з-мы-ргəы́рӷьо, [aor.] (C1) и-лы-ргəы́рӷьа / и-л-мы-ргəы́рӷьа, (C3) д-зы-ргəы́рӷьа / ды-з-мы-ргəы́рӷьа, [impf.] (C1) и-лы-ргəы́рӷьо-з / и-л-мы-ргəы́рӷьо-з, (C3) д-зы-ргəы́рӷьо-з / ды-з-мы-ргəы́рӷьо-з, [past indef.] (C1) и-лы-ргəы́рӷьа-з / и-л-мы-ргəы́рӷьа-з, (C3) д-зы-ргəы́рӷьа-з / ды-з-мы-ргəы́рӷьа-з.

а-риа́ша-ра 'to correct; to set a watch' (cf. а-иа́ша 'right; straight; truth'): Fin. [pres.] и-сы-риа́шо-ит / и-сы-риа́шо-м, [aor.] и-сы-риа́ше-ит / и-с-мы-риа́ше-ит; Non-fin. [pres.] (C1) и-сы́-риа́шо / и-с-мы-риа́шо, (C3) и-зы́-риа́шо / и-з-мы-риа́шо.

а-ркьа́ҭа-ра 'to to put out, to extinguish' (cf. а-кьа́ҭа-ра 'to be extinguished'): Fin. [pres.] и-сы-ркьа́ҭо-ит / и-сы-ркьа́ҭо-м, [aor.] и-сы-ркьа́ҭе-ит / и-с-мы-ркьа́ҭе-ит; Non-fin. [pres.] (C1) и-сы-ркьа́ҭо / и-с-мы-ркьа́ҭо, (C3) и-зы-ркьа́ҭо / и-з-мы-ркьа́ҭо.

а-рма́ч-ра 'to lower, to reduce' (cf. а-ма́ч 'little, few'): Fin. [pres.] и-сы-рма́ч-уе-ит / и-сы-рма́ч-уа-м, [aor.] и-сы-рма́ч-ит / и-с-мы-рма́ч-ит; Non-fin. [pres.] (C1) и-сы-рма́ч-уа / и-с-мы-рма́ч-уа, (C3) и-зы-рма́ч-уа / и-з-мы-рма́ч-уа.

а-рӷа́гьа-ра 'to make *sb* haughty/proud' (cf. а-ӷа́гьа 'proud'): Fin. [aor.] ды-ды-рӷа́гье-ит / ды-д-мы-рӷа́гье-ит.

а-ртáта-ра ‘to soften’ (cf. а-тáта ‘soft’): Fin. [aor.] и-ртáте-ит / и-мы-ртáте-ит.

а-рҭы́нч-ра ‘to calm; to quiet’ (cf. а-ҭы́нч ‘calm, quiet’): Fin. [pres.] д-сы-рҭы́нч-уе-ит / д-сы-рҭы́нч-уа-м (-рҭы́нч-ӡо-м), [aor.] д-сы-рҭы́нч-ит / ды-с-мы-рҭы́нч-ит (-рҭы́нч-ӡе-ит); Non-fin. [pres.] (C1) и-лы-рҭы́нч-уа / и-л-мы-рҭы́нч-уа, (C3) д-зы-рҭы́нч-уа / ды-з-мы-рҭы́нч-уа, [aor.] (C1) и-лы-рҭы́нч / и-л-мы-рҭы́нч, (C3) д-зы-рҭы́нч / ды-з-мы-рҭы́нч, [impf.] (C1) и-лы-рҭы́нч-уа-з / и-л-мы-рҭы́нч-уа-з, (C3) д-зы-рҭы́нч-уа-з / ды-з-мы-рҭы́нч-уа-з, [past indef.] (C1) и-лы-рҭы́нчы-з / и-л-мы-рҭы́нчы-з, (C3) д-зы-рҭы́нчы-з / ды-з-мы-рҭы́нчы-з.

а-рхәмáр-ра ‘to make play’ (cf. á-хәмар-ра ‘to play’): Fin. [pres.] и-сы-рхәмáр-уе-ит / и-сы-рхәмáр-уа-м (-ӡо-м), [aor.] и-сы-рхәмáр-ит / и-с-мы-рхәмáр-ит (-рхәмáр-ӡе-ит); Non-fin. [pres.] (C1) и-сы́-рхәмар-уа / и-с-мы́-рхәмар-уа, (C3) и-зы́-рхәмар-уа / и-з-мы́-рхәмар-уа.

а-рцáа-ра ‘to freeze’ (cf. а-цáа-ра ‘to freeze’): Fin. [pres.] и-сы-рцáа-уе-ит / и-сы-рцáа-уа-м, [aor.] и-сы-рцáа-ит / и-с-мы-рцáа-ит; Non-fin. [pres.] (C1) и-сы-рцáа-уа / и-с-мы-рцáа-уа, (C3) и-зы-рцáа-уа / и-з-мы-рцáа-уа.

а-рцәы́уа-ра ‘to make cry’ (cf. а-цәы́уа-ра ‘to cry’): Fin. [pres.] д-сы-рцәы́уо-ит / д-сы-рцәы́уо-м, [aor.] д-сы-рцәы́уе-ит / ды-с-мы-рцәы́уе-ит; Non-fin. [pres.] (C1) и-сы-рцәы́уо / и-с-мы-рцәы́уо, (C3) д-зы-рцәы́уо / ды-з-мы-рцәы́уо, [aor.] (C1) и-сы-рцәы́уа / и-с-мы-рцәы́уа.

а-рҿы́ха-ра ‘to waken’ (cf. а-ҿы́-ха-ра ‘to wake up’): Fin. [pres.] д-ды-рҿы́хо-ит *they wake him/her* / ды-ды-рҿы́хо-м, [aor.] д-сы-рҿы́хе-ит / ды-с-мы-рҿы́хе-ит; Non-fin. [pres.] (C1) и-сы-рҿы́хо / и-с-мы-рҿы́хо, (C3) д-зы-рҿы́хо / ды-з-мы-рҿы́хо.

а-рҿы́ц-ра ‘to renew, to restore’ (cf. а-ҿы́ц ‘new’): Fin. [pres.] и-сы-рҿы́ц-уе-ит / и-сы-рҿы́ц-уа-м, [aor.] и-сы-рҿы́ц-ит / и-с-мы-рҿы́ц-ит; Non-fin. [pres.] (C1) и-сы-рҿы́ц-уа / и-с-мы-рҿы́ц-уа, (C3) и-зы-рҿы́ц-уа / и-з-мы-рҿы́ц-уа.

а-ры́цқьа-ра ‘to clean’ (cf. á-цқьа ‘clean’): Fin. [pres.] и-с-ры́цқьо-ит, и-д-ры́цқье-ит / и-с-ры́цқьо-м, [aor.] ды-с-ры́цқье-ит, и-с-ры́цқье-ит, и-а-ры́цқье-ит / и-сы-м-ры́цқье-ит, и-а-м-ры́цқье-ит; Non-fin. [pres.] (C1) и́-л-рыцқьо / и́-лы-м-рыцқьо, (C3) и-з-ры́цқьо / и-зы-м-ры́цқьо, [aor.] (C1) и́-л-рыцқьа / и́-лы-м-рыцқьа, (C3) и-з-ры́цқьа / и-зы-м-ры́цқьа, [impf.] (C1) и́-л-рыцқьо-з / и́-лы-м-рыцқьо-з, (C3) и-з-ры́цқьо-з / и-зы-м-ры́цқьо-з, [past indef.] (C1) и́-л-рыцқьа-з / и́-лы-м-рыцқьа-з, (C3) и-з-ры́цқьа-з / и-зы-м-ры́цқьа-з.

а-рҩáшьа-ра ‘to delude, to mislead; to mistake’ (cf. а-ҩáшьа-ра ‘to make a mistake’): Fin. [aor.] д-и-рҩáшье-ит / д-и-мы-рҩáшье-ит.

3.2.6.5.2. Inflection of AP b

The accent paradigm of this verb is a type where the accent is placed on the Column III pronominal prefix before the stem in all forms. The masdar accent is generally placed on the article.

á-рлаша-ра /á-rlaša-ra/ ‘to illuminate’ (cf. á-лаша-ра /á-laša-ra/ ‘to shine’)

Finite forms		
C1-C3	Affirmative	Negative
Present		
Sg.3.Non-Human/Pl.3-Sg.1	и-сы́-рлашо-ит	и-сы́-рлашо-м

	/jə-sə́-rlaša-wa-jt'/ 'I illuminate it/them'	
Sg.3.Non-Hum./Pl.3-Sg.3.Non-Hum.	и-а́-рлашо-ит	и-а́-рлашо-м
Aorist		
Sg.3.Non-Human/Pl.3-Sg.1	и-сы́-рлаше-ит	и-с-мы́-рлаше-ит
Non-Finite forms		
C1-C3		
Present		
Rel-Sg.3.F	и-лы́-рлашо	и-л-мы́-рлашо
Sg.3.Non-Human/Pl.3-Rel	и-зы́-рлашо	и-з-мы́-рлашо
Aorist		
Rel-Sg.3.F	и-лы́-рлаша	и-л-мы́-рлаша
Sg.3.Non-Human/Pl.3-Rel	и-зы́-рлаша	и-з-мы́-рлаша
Imperfect		
Rel-Sg.3.F	и-лы́-рлашо-з	и-л-мы́-рлашо-з
Sg.3.Non-Human/Pl.3-Rel	и-зы́-рлашо-з	и-з-мы́-рлашо-з
Past Indefinite		
Rel-Sg.3.F	и-лы́-рлаша-з	и-л-мы́-рлаша-з
Sg.3.Non-Human/Pl.3-Rel	и-зы́-рлаша-з	и-з-мы́-рлаша-з

Other examples:

а́-рааҧса-ра 'to tire' (cf. а́аҧса-ра 'to become tired'): Fin. [aor.] б-сы́-рааҧсе-ит / д-и-мы́-рааҧсе-ит.

а́-рбааӡа-ра 'to wet' (cf. а-бааӡа-ра́ 'to get soaked, to get drenched'): Fin. [pres.] и-сы́-рбааӡо-ит / и-сы́-рбааӡо-м (-рбааӡа-ӡо-м), [aor.] и-сы́-рбааӡе-ит / и-с-мы́-рбааӡе-ит; Non-fin. [pres.] (C1) и-сы́-рбааӡо / и-с-мы́-рбааӡо, (C3) и-зы́-рбааӡо / и-з-мы́-рбааӡо.

а́-ргьежь-ра 'to return' (cf. а́-гьежь-ра 'to go back'): Fin. [pres.] и-сы́-ргьежь-уе-ит / и-сы́-ргьежь-уа-м, [aor.] и-сы́-ргьежь-ит / и-с-мы́-ргьежь-ит; Non-fin. [pres.] (C1) и-сы́-ргьежь-уа / и-с-мы́-ргьежь-уа, (C3) и-зы́-ргьежь-уа / и-з-мы́-ргьежь-уа.

а́-рҕьаца-ра '(*of plants*) to promote the growth of' (cf. а́-ҕьаца-ра 'to grow'): Fin. [pres.] и-а́-рҕьацо-ит / и-а́-рҕьацо-м, [aor.] и-а́-рҕьаце-ит / и-а-мы́-рҕьаце-ит.

а́-рдыд-ра 'to make thunder' (cf. а́-дыд-ра 'to thunder'): Fin. [pres.] и-а́-рдыд-уе-ит, и-сы́-рдыд-уе-ит / и-а́-рдыд-уа-м, [aor.] и-а́-рдыд-ит / и-а-мы́-рдыд-ит; Non-fin. [pres.] (C3) и-зы́-рдыд-уа / и-з-мы́-рдыд-уа.

а́-рзаза-ра 'to rock, to sway' (cf. а-заза-ра́ 'to sway'): Fin. [pres.] и-сы́-рзазо-ит, и-а́-рзазо-ит / и-сы́-рзазо-м (-рзаза-ӡо-м), и-а́-рзазо-м (-рзаза-ӡо-м), [aor.] и-сы́-рзазе-ит / и-с-мы́-рзазе-ит (-рзаза-ӡе-ит); Non-fin. [pres.] (C1) и-лы́-рзазо / и-л-мы́-рзазо, (C3) и-зы́-рзазо / и-з-мы́-рзазо, [aor.] (C1) и-лы́-рзаза / и-л-мы́-рзаза, (C3) и-зы́-рзаза / и-з-мы́-рзаза, [impf.] (C1) и-лы́-рзазо-з / и-л-мы́-рзазо-з, (C3) и-зы́-рзазо-з / и-з-мы́-рзазо-з, [past indef.] (C1) и-лы́-рзаза-з / и-л-мы́-рзаза-з, (C3) и-зы́-рзаза-з / и-з-мы́-рзаза-з.

á-рӡ-ра 'to lose' (cf. á-ӡ-ра 'to disappear'): Fin. [pres.] и-сы́-рӡ-уе-ит, и-á-рӡ-уе-ит / и-сы́-рӡ-уа-м, [aor.] и-лы́-рӡ-ит / и-л-мы́-рӡ-ит; Non-fin. [pres.] (C1) и-лы́-рӡ-уа / и-л-мы́-рӡ-уа, (C3) и-зы́-рӡ-уа / и-з-мы́-рӡ-уа, [aor.] (C1) и-лы́-рӡ / и-л-мы́-рӡ, (C3) и-зы́-рӡ / и-з-мы́-рӡ, [impf.] (C1) и-лы́-рӡ-уа-з / и-л-мы́-рӡ-уа-з, (C3) и-зы́-рӡ-уа-з / и-з-мы́-рӡ-уа-з, [past indef.] (C1) и-лы́-рӡы-з / и-л-мы́-рӡы-з, (C3) и-зы́-рӡы-з / и-з-мы́-рӡы-з.

а-ркә-рá 'to make *sb* swear' (cf. а-кә-рá 'to swear'): Fin. [aor.] д-сы́-ркә-ит / д-с-мы́-ркә-ит; Non-fin. [past indef.] (C3) д-зы-ркәы́-з / ды-з-мы-ркәы́-з.

á-рлас-ра 'to lighten; to hurry' (cf. á-лас 'light; fast, quick'): Fin. [pres.] и-сы́-рлас-уе-ит / и-сы́-рлас-уа-м, [aor.] и-сы́-рлас-ит / и-с-мы́-рлас-ит; Non-fin. [pres.] (C1) и-сы́-рлас-уа / и-с-мы́-рлас-уа, (C3) и-зы́-рлас-уа / и-з-мы́-рлас-уа.

á-рлашьца-ра 'to darken' (cf. á-лашьца-ра 'to get dark'): Fin. [pres.] и-сы́-рлашьцо-ит / и-сы́-рлашьцо-м, [aor.] и-сы́-рлашьце-ит, и-á-рлашьце-ит / и-с-мы́-рлашьце-ит; Non-fin. [pres.] (C1) и-сы́-рлашьцо / и-с-мы́-рлашьцо, (C3) и-зы́-рлашьцо / и-з-мы́-рлашьцо.

á-рмазеи-ра 'to prepare': Fin. [pres.] и-сы́-рмазеи-уе-ит / и-сы́-рмазеи-уа-м, [aor.] и-сы́-рмазеи-т / и-с-мы́-рмазеи-т; Non-fin. [pres.] (C1) и-сы́-рмазеи-уа / и-с-мы́-рмазеи-уа, (C3) и-зы́-рмазеи-уа / и-з-мы́-рмазеи-уа.

á-рмацәыс-ра 'to make it lighten' (cf. á-мацәыс-ра 'to lighten'): Fin. [pres.] и-á-рмацәыс-уе-ит, и-сы́-рмацәыс-уе-ит / и-á-рмацәыс-уа-м, [aor.] и-á-рмацәыс-ит / и-а-мы́-рмацәыс-ит; Non-fin. [pres.] (C3) и-зы́-рмацәыс-уа / и-з-мы́-рмацәыс-уа.

á-рнаа-ра 'to bend (down)' (cf. á-наа 'crooked'): Fin. [pres.] и-сы́-рнаа-уе-ит / и-сы́-рнаа-уа-м (-рнаа-ӡо-м), [aor.] и-сы́-рнаа-ит / и-с-мы́-рнаа-ит (-рнаа-ӡе-ит); Non-fin. [pres.] (C1) и-лы́-рнаа-уа / и-л-мы́-рнаа-уа, (C3) и-зы́-рнаа-уа / и-з-мы́-рнаа-уа, [aor.] (C1) и-лы́-рнаа / и-л-мы́-рнаа, (C3) и-зы́-рнаа / и-з-мы́-рнаа, [impf.] (C1) и-лы́-рнаа-уа-з / и-л-мы́-рнаа-уа-з, (C3) и-зы́-рнаа-уа-з / и-з-мы́-рнаа-уа-з, [past indef.] (C1) и-лы́-рнаа-з / и-л-мы́-рнаа-з, (C3) и-зы́-рнаа-з / и-з-мы́-рнаа-з.

á-рҧа-ра 'to make jump' (cf. á-ҧа-ра 'to jump'): Fin. [aor.] и-лы́-рҧе-ит / и-л-мы́-рҧе-ит; Non-fin. [pres.] (C1) и́-рҧо / и-мы́-рҧо.

а-рҧсаа-рá 'to wet; to moisten' (cf. а-ҧсаа-рá 'to get wet'): Fin. [pres.] и-сы́-рҧсаа-уе-ит / и-сы́-рҧсаа-уа-м, [aor.] и-сы́-рҧсаа-ит / и-с-мы́-рҧсаа-ит; Non-fin. [pres.] (C1) и-сы́-рҧсаа-уа / и-с-мы́-рҧсаа-уа, (C3) и-зы́-рҧсаа-уа / и-з-мы́-рҧсаа-уа.

á-рҭбаа-ра 'to extend, to spread' (cf. á-ҭбаа 'wide'): Fin. [pres.] и-сы́-рҭбаа-уе-ит / и-сы́-рҭбаа-уа-м (-рҭбаа-ӡо-м), [aor.] и-сы́-рҭбаа-ит / и-с-мы́-рҭбаа-ит (-рҭбаа-ӡе-ит); Non-fin. [pres.] (C1) и-сы́-рҭбаа-уа / и-с-мы́-рҭбаа-уа, (C3) и-зы́-рҭбаа-уа / и-з-мы́-рҭбаа-уа.

á-рхәашь-ра 'to make muddy' (cf. á-хәашь 'muddy'): Fin. [pres.] и-сы́-рхәашь-уе-ит / и-сы́-рхәашь-уа-м, [aor.] и-сы́-рхәашь-ит / и-с-мы́-рхәашь-ит; Non-fin. [pres.] (C1) и-лы́-рхәашь-уа / и-л-мы́-рхәашь-уа, (C3) и-зы́-рхәашь-уа / и-з-мы́-рхәашь-уа, [aor.] (C1) и-лы́-рхәашь / и-л-мы́-рхәашь, (C3) и-зы́-рхәашь / и-з-мы́-рхәашь, [impf.] (C1) и-лы́-рхәашь-уа-з / и-л-мы́-рхәашь-уа-з, (C3) и-зы́-рхәашь-уа-з / и-з-мы́-рхәашь-уа-з, [past indef.] (C1) и-лы́-рхәашьы-з / и-л-мы́-рхәашьы-з, (C3) и-зы́-рхәашьы-з / и-з-мы́-рхәашьы-з.

á-рцәаак-ра 'to moisten' (cf. á-цәаак 'damp, humid'): Fin. [pres.] и-сы́-рцәаак-уе-ит / и-сы́-

рцәаак-уа-м, [aor.] и-сы́-рцәаак-ит / и-с-мы́-рцәаак-ит; Non-fin. [pres.] (C1) и-сы́-рцәаак-уа / и-с-мы́-рцәаак-уа, (C3) и-зы́-рцәаак-уа / и-з-мы́-рцәаак-уа, [aor.] (C1) и-сы́-рцәаак / и-с-мы́-рцәаак.

а́-рцәа-ра 'to put out': Fin. [pres.] и-сы́-рцәо-ит / и-сы́-рцәо-м, [aor.] и-сы́-рцәе-ит / и-с-мы́-рцәе-ит; Non-fin. [pres.] (C1) и-сы́-рцәо / и-с-мы́-рцәо, (C3) и-зы́-рцәо / и-з-мы́-рцәо. (cf. а́-цәа-ра 'to be extinguished')

а́-рцәа-ра 'to put to sleep': Fin. [pres.] с-лы́-рцәо-ит / с-лы́-рцәо-м, [aor.] с-лы́-рцәе-ит / сы-л-мы́-рцәе-ит; Non-fin. [pres.] (C1) и-лы́-рцәо / и-л-мы́-рцәо, (C3) д-зы́-рцәо / ды-з-мы́-рцәо, [aor.] (C1) и-лы́-рцәа / и-л-мы́-рцәа, (C3) д-зы́-рцәа / ды-з-мы́-рцәа. (cf. а́-цәа-ра 'to sleep')

а́-рчча-ра 'to make laugh': Fin. [pres.] д-сы́-рччо-ит / д-сы́-рччо-м, [aor.] д-сы́-рччe-ит / ды-с-мы́-рччe-ит, д-ды́-рччe-ит / ды-д-мы́-рччe-ит. (cf. а́-чча-ра 'to laugh')

а́-ршанха-ра 'to charm'(cf. а́-шанха-ра 'to be surprised'): Fin. [pres.] д-сы́-ршанхо-ит / д-сы́-ршанхо-м, [aor.] д-сы́-ршанхе-ит / ды-с-мы́-ршанхе-ит; Non-fin. [pres.] (C1) и-лы́-ршанхо / и-л-мы́-ршанхо, (C3) с-зы́-ршанхо / сы-з-мы́-ршанхо.

а́-ршкәакәа-ра 'to whiten' (cf. а́-шкәакәа 'white'): Fin. [pres.] и-сы́-ршкәакәо-ит / и-сы́-ршкәакәо-ит, [aor.] и-сы́-ршкәакәе-ит / и-с-мы́-ршкәакәе-ит; Non-fin. [pres.] (C1) и-сы́-ршкәакәо / и-с-мы́-ршкәакәо, (C3) и-зы́-ршкәакәо / и-з-мы́-ршкәакәо.

а́-ршә-ра 'to throw': Fin. [pres.] и-сы́-ршә-уе-ит / и-сы́-ршә-уа-м (-ӡо-м), [aor.] и-сы́-ршә-ит / и-с-мы́-ршә-ит (-ӡе-ит); Non-fin. [pres.] (C1) и-лы́-ршә-уа / и-л-мы́-ршә-уа, (C3) и-зы́-ршә-уа / и-з-мы́-ршә-уа, [aor.] (C1) и-лы́-ршә / и-л-мы́-ршә, (C3) и-зы́-ршә / и-з-мы́-ршә, [impf.] (C1) и-лы́-ршә-уа-з / и-л-мы́-ршә-уа-з, (C3) и-зы́-ршә-уа-з / и-з-мы́-ршә-уа-з, [past indef.] (C1) и-лы́-ршәы-з / и-л-мы́-ршәы-з, (C3) и-зы́-ршәы-з / и-з-мы́-ршәы-з.

а́-рҩ-ра 'to make run' (cf. а́-ҩ-ра 'to run'): Fin. [pres.] д-лы́-рҩ-уе-ит / д-лы́-рҩ-уа-м, [aor.] д-лы́-рҩ-ит / ды-л-мы́-рҩ-ит; Non-fin. [pres.] (C1) и-лы́-рҩ-уа / и-л-мы́-рҩ-уа, (C3) д-зы́-рҩ-уа / ды-з-мы́-рҩ-уа, [aor.] (C1) и-лы́-рҩ / и-л-мы́-рҩ.

3.2.6.5.3. Inflection of AP c

The accent paradigm for this verb is a type where the accent is placed on the element following the stem in all forms. The masdar accent is placed on the suffix -ра /ra/.

а-ртәара́ /a-rt'ʷa-rá/ 'to seat' (cf. атәара́ /a-t'ʷa-rá/ 'to sit down')

Finite forms
Dynamic Group I

C1-C3	Affirmative	Negative
Present		
Sg.3.Human-Sg.1	д-сы-ртәо́-ит /d-sə-rt'ʷa-wá-jt'/ him/her(C1)-I(C1)-seat-Dyn-Fin 'I seat him/her'	д-сы-ртәо́-м
Sg.1-Sg.3.F	с-лы-ртәо́-ит	с-лы-ртәо́-м
Pl.1-Pl.3	х-ды-ртәо́-ит	х-ды-ртәо́-м

Sg.2.F-Pl.1	б-ҳа-ртәӧ-ит	б-ҳа-ртәӧ-м
Aorist		
Sg.3.Human-Sg.1	д-сы-ртәé-ит	ды-с-мы-ртәé-ит
Sg.2.F-Pl.1	б-ҳа-ртәé-ит	б-аҳ-мы-ртәé-ит
Future I		
Sg.3.Human-Sg.1	д-сы-ртәá-п	д-сы-ртәа-ры́-м
Future II		
Sg.3.Human-Sg.1	д-сы-ртәá-шт	д-сы-ртәá-ша-м
Perfect		
Sg.3.Human-Sg.1	д-сы-ртәа-хьé-ит	ды-с-мы-ртәá-ц(т)
Dynamic Group II		
Imperfect		
Sg.3.Human-Sg.1	д-сы-ртәӧ-н	д-сы-ртәӧ-мы-зт
Past Indefinite		
Sg.3.Human-Sg.1	д-сы-ртәá-н	ды-с-мы-ртәá-зт
Conditional I		
Sg.3.Human-Sg.1	д-сы-ртәа-ры́-н	д-сы-ртәа-ры́-мы-зт
Conditional II		
Sg.3.Human-Sg.1	д-сы-ртәá-ша-н	д-сы-ртәá-ша-мы-зт
Pluperfect		
Sg.3.Human-Sg.1	д-сы-ртәа-хьá-н	ды-с-мы-ртәá-цы-зт

Non-Finite forms
Dynamic Group I

C1-C3	Affirmative	Negative
Present		
Rel-Sg.1	и-сы-ртәӧ /jə-sə-rt’ʷa-wá/ Rel(C1)-I(C3)-seat-Dyn.NF ‘whom I seat’	и-с-мы-ртәӧ
Rel-Sg.3.M	и-и-ртәӧ	и-и-мы-ртәӧ
Rel-Sg.3.Non-Human	и-а-ртәӧ	и-а-мы-ртәӧ
Rel-Pl.1	и-ҳа-ртәӧ	и-аҳ-мы-ртәӧ
Rel-Pl.2	и-шәы-ртәӧ	и-шә-мы-ртәӧ
Rel-Pl.3	и-ды-ртәӧ	и-д-мы-ртәӧ
Sg.3.Human-Rel	д-зы-ртәӧ /d-zə-rt’ʷa-wá/ him/her(C1)-Rel(C3)-seat-Dyn.NF ‘who seats him/her’	ды-з-мы-ртәӧ
Aorist		
Rel-Sg.3.F	и-лы-ртәá	и-л-мы-ртәá
Sg.3.Human-Rel	д-зы-ртәá	ды-з-мы-ртәá

Future I		
Rel-Sg.3.F	и-лы-ртәа-ра́	и-л-мы-ртәа-ра́
Sg.3.Human-Rel	д-зы-ртәа-ра́	ды-з-мы-ртәа-ра́
Future II		
Rel-Sg.3.F	и-лы-ртәа́-ша	и-л-мы-ртәа́-ша
Sg.3.Human-Rel	д-зы-ртәа́-ша	ды-з-мы-ртәа́-ша
Perfect		
Rel-Sg.3.F	и-лы-ртәа-хьо́у/-хьа́(ц)	и-л-мы-ртәа-хьо́у/-хьа́(ц)
Sg.3.Human-Rel	д-зы-ртәа-хьо́у/-хьа́(ц)	ды-з-мы-ртәа-хьо́у/-хьа́(ц)

Dynamic Group II		
Imperfect		
Rel-Sg.3.F	и-лы-ртәо́-з	и-л-мы-ртәо́-з
Sg.3.Human-Rel	д-зы-ртәо́-з	ды-з-мы-ртәо́-з
Past Indefinite		
Rel-Sg.3.F	и-лы-ртәа́-з	и-л-мы-ртәа́-з
Sg.3.Human-Rel	д-зы-ртәа́-з	ды-з-мы-ртәа́-з
Conditional I		
Rel-Sg.3.F	и-лы-ртәа-ры́-з	и-л-мы-ртәа-ры́-з
Sg.3.Human-Rel	д-зы-ртәа-ры́-з	ды-з-мы-ртәа-ры́-з
Conditional II		
Rel-Sg.3.F	и-лы-ртәа́-ша-з	и-л-мы-ртәа́-ша-з
Sg.3.Human-Rel	д-зы-ртәа́-ша-з	ды-з-мы-ртәа́-ша-з
Pluperfect		
Rel-Sg.3.F	и-лы-ртәа-хьа́-з	и-л-мы-ртәа-хьа́-з
Sg.3.Human-Rel	д-зы-ртәа-хьа́-з	ды-з-мы-ртәа-хьа́-з

Other examples:

а-рба-ра́ 'to dry; to wipe' (cf. а-ба-ра́ 'to dry (out)'): Fin. [pres.] и-сы-рбо́-ит, и-ды-рбо́-ит / и-сы-рбо́-м (-рба-ӡо́-м), и-ды-рбо́-м (-рба-ӡо́-м), [aor.] и-сы-рбе́-ит, и-ха-рбе́-ит / и-с-мы-рбе́-ит (-рба-ӡе́-ит), и-ах-мы-рбе́-ит (-рба-ӡе́-ит); Non-fin. [pres.] (C1) и-сы-рбо́ / и-с-мы-рбо́, (C3) и-зы-рбо́ / и-з-мы-рбо́.

а-рбга-ра́ 'to destroy' (cf. а-бга-ра́ 'to collapse'): Fin. [aor.] и-ды-рбге́-ит / и-д-мы-рбге́-ит.

а-р(ы)бза-ра́ 'to lick' (cf. а́-бз 'a tongue'): Fin. [pres.] д-сы-рбзо́-ит / д-сы-рбзо́-м (-рбза-ӡо́-м), [aor.] д-сы-рбзе́-ит / ды-с-мы-рбзе́-ит (-рбза-ӡе́-ит); Non-fin. [pres.] (C1) и-сы-рбзо́ / и-с-мы-рбзо́, (C3) д-зы-рбзо́ / ды-з-мы-рбзо́.

а-рбыц-ра́ 'to knead': Fin. [pres.] и-лы-рбыц-уе́-ит / и-лы-рбыц-уа́-м (-рбыц-ӡо́-м), [aor.] и-лы-рбыц-и́т, и-ҳа-рбыц-и́т / и-л-мы-рбыц-и́т (-рбыц-ӡе́-ит), и-аҳ-мы-рбыц-и́т (-рбыц-ӡе́-ит); Non-fin. [pres.] (C1) и-лы-рбыц-уа́ / и-л-мы-рбыц-уа́, (C3) и-зы-рбыц-уа́ / и-з-мы-рбыц-уа́, [aor.] (C1) и-лы-рбыцы́ / и-л-мы-рбыцы́, (C3) и-зы-рбыцы́ / и-з-мы-рбыцы́, [impf.] и-лы-рбыц-уа́-з / и-л-мы-рбыц-уа́-з, (C3) и-зы-рбыц-уа́-з / и-з-мы-рбыц-уа́-з, [past indef.] (C1) и-лы-рбыцы́-з / и-л-мы-рбыцы́-з, (C3) и-зы-рбыцы́-з / и-з-мы-рбыцы́-з.

а-рҕәҕәа-ра́ ‘to strengthen’ (cf. а́-ҕәҕәа ‘strong’): Fin. [pres.] и-сы-рҕәҕәо́-ит / и-сы-рҕәҕәо́-м, [aor.] и-сы-рҕәҕәе́-ит / и-с-мы-рҕәҕәе́-ит; Non-fin. [pres.] (C1) и-сы-рҕәҕәо́ / и-с-мы-рҕәҕәо́, (C3) и-зы-рҕәҕәо́ / и-з-мы-рҕәҕәо́.

а-риа-ра́ ‘to lay’ (cf. а-иа-ра́ ‘to lie’): Fin. [pres.] д-сы-рио́-ит / д-сы-рио́-м, [aor.] д-сы-рие́-ит / ды-с-мы-рие́-ит; Non-fin. [pres.] (C1) и-сы-рио́ / и-с-мы-рио́, (C3) д-зы-рио́ / ды-з-мы-рио́.

а-ркь-ра́ ‘to make sigh’ (а-кь-ра́ ‘to sigh’): Fin. [pres.] д-ды-р-кь-уе́-ит / д-ды-р-қь-уа́-м, [aor.] д-сы-рқь-и́т / ды-с-мы-ркь-и́т; Non-fin. [pres.] (C1) и-лы-ркь-уа́ / и-л-мы-рқь-уа́, (C3) д-зы-рқь-уа́ / ды-з-мы-рқь-уа́, [aor.] (C1) и-лы-рқьы́ / и-л-мы-рқьы́, (C3) д-зы-рқьы́ / ды-з-мы-рқьы́, [impf.] (C1) и-лы-ркь-уа́-з / и-л-мы-ркь-уа́-з, (C3) д-зы-ркь-уа́-з / ды-з-мы-ркь-уа́-з, [past indef.] (C1) и-лы-рқьы́-з / и-л-мы-рқьы́-з, (C3) д-зы-рқьы́-з / ды-з-мы-рқьы́-з.

а-рҟәыд-ра́ ‘to cut (the) hair’: Fin. [pres.] д-сы-рҟәыд-уе́-ит / д-сы-рҟәыд-уа́-м, [aor.] д-сы-рҟәыд-и́т / ды-с-мы-рҟәыд-и́т; Non-fin. [pres.] (C1) и-сы-рҟәыд-уа́ / и-с-мы-рҟәыд-уа́, (C3) д-зы-рҟәыд-уа́ / ды-з-мы-рҟәыд-уа́.

а-рҧс-ра́ ‘to put out, to extinguish’ (cf. а-ҧс-ра́ ‘to die; to go out’): Fin. [pres.] и-сы-рҧс-уе́-ит / и-сы-рҧс-уа́-м, [aor.] и-сы-рҧс-и́т / и-с-мы-рҧс-и́т; Non-fin. [pres.] (C1) и-сы-рҧс-уа́ / и-с-мы-рҧс-уа́, (C3) и-зы-рҧс-уа́ / и-з-мы-рҧс-уа́, [aor.] (C1) и-сы-рҧсы́ / и-с-мы-рҧсы́, (C3) и-зы-рҧсы́ / и-з-мы-рҧсы́.

а-рҧха-ра́ ‘to warm’ (cf. а-ҧха́ ‘warm’): Fin. [pres.] д-сы-рҧхо́-ит / д-сы-рҧхо́-м (-рҧха-ӡо́-м), [aor.] д-сы-рҧхе́-ит, д-ҳа-рҧхе́-ит / ды-с-мы-рҧхе́-ит (-рҧха-ӡе́-ит), д-аҳ-мы-рҧхе́-ит (-рҧха-ӡе́-ит); Non-fin. [pres.] (C1) и-лы-рҧхо́ / и-л-мы-рҧхо́, (C3) и-зы-рҧхо́ / и-з-мы-рҧхо́, [aor.] (C1) и-лы-рҧха́ / и-л-мы-рҧха́, (C3) и-зы-рҧха́ / и-з-мы-рҧха́, [impf.] (C1) и-лы-рҧхо́-з / и-л-мы-рҧхо́-з, (C3) и-зы-рҧхо́-з / и-з-мы-рҧхо́-з, [past indef.] (C1) и-лы-рҧха́-з / и-л-мы-рҧха́-з, (C3) и-зы-рҧха́-з / и-з-мы-рҧха́-з.

а-рҧш-ра́ ‘to make wait’ (cf. а-ҧш-ра́ ‘to wait’): Fin. [pres.] шә-ҳа-рҧш-уе́-ит / шә-ҳа-рҧш-уа́-м, [aor.] шә-ҳа-рҧш-и́т / шә-аҳ-мы-рҧш-и́т; Non-fin. [pres.] (C1) и-ҳа-рҧш-уа́ / и-аҳ-мы-рҧш-уа́, (C3) с-зы-рҧш-уа́ / сы-з-мы-рҧш-уа́, [aor.] (C1) и-ҳа-рҧшы́ / и-аҳ-мы-рҧшы́.

а-рҭәа-ра́ ‘to melt’ (cf. а-ҭәа-ра́ [intr.] ‘to melt’): Fin. [pres.] и-сы-рҭәо́-ит, и-ды-рҭәо́-ит / и-сы-рҭәо́-м, [aor.] и-сы-рҭәе́-ит / и-с-мы-рҭәе́-ит; Non-fin. [pres.] (C1) и-лы-рҭәо́ / и-л-мы-рҭәо́, (C3) и-зы-рҭәо́ / и-з-мы-рҭәо́, [aor.] (C1) и-лы-рҭәа́ / и-л-мы-рҭәа́, (C3) и-зы-рҭәа́ / и-з-мы-рҭәа́, [impf.] (C1) и-лы-рҭәо́-з / и-л-мы-рҭәо́-з, (C3) и-зы-рҭәо́-з / и-з-мы-рҭәо́-з, [past indef.] (C1) и-лы-рҭәа́-з / и-л-мы-рҭәа́-з, (C3) и-зы-рҭәа́-з / и-з-мы-рҭәа́-з.

а-рҭә-ра́ ‘to fill’ (cf. а-ҭә-ра́ ‘to fill’): Fin. [pres.] и-сы-рҭә-уе́-ит / и-сы-рҭә-уа́-м (-ӡо́-м), [aor.] и-сы-рҭә-и́т / и-с-мы-рҭә-и́т (-ӡе́-ит); Non-fin. [pres.] (C1) и-лы-рҭә-уа́ / и-л-мы-рҭә-уа́, (C3) и-зы-рҭә-уа́ / и-з-мы́-рҭә-уа́, [aor.] (C1) и-лы-рҭәы́ / и-л-мы-рҭәы́, (C3) и-зы-рҭәы́ / и-з-мы́-рҭәы́, [impf.] (C1) и-лы-рҭә-уа́-з / и-л-мы-рҭә-уа́-з, (C3) и-зы-рҭә-уа́-з / и-з-мы́-рҭә-уа́-з, [past indef.] (C1) и-лы-рҭәы́-з / и-л-мы-рҭәы́-з, (C3) и-зы-рҭәы́-з / и-з-мы́-рҭәы́-з.

а-рха-ра́ ‘to wear out’ (cf. а-ха-ра́ ‘(*of clothes*) to wear out’): Fin. [pres.] и-сы-рхо́-ит / и-сы-рхо́-м (-рха-ӡо́-м), [aor.] и-сы-рхе́-ит / и-с-мы-рхе́-ит (-рха-ӡе́-ит); Non-fin. [pres.] (C1) и-лы-рхо́ / и-л-мы-рхо́, (C3) и-зы-рхо́ / и-з-мы-рхо́, [aor.] (C1) и-лы-рха́ / и-л-мы-рха́, (C3) и-зы-рха́ / и-з-мы-рха́, [impf.] (C1) и-лы-рхо́-з / и-л-мы-рхо́-з, (C3) и-зы-рхо́-з / и-з-мы-рхо́-з, [past indef.] (C1) и-лы-рха́-з / и-л-мы-рха́-з, (C3) и-зы-рха́-з / и-з-мы-рха́-з.

а-рхиа-ра́ 'to prepare' (cf. а-хиа-ра́ 'to be ready'): Fin. [pres.] и-сы-рхио́-ит / и-сы-рхио́-м, [aor.] и-сы-рхие́-ит / и-с-мы-рхие́-ит; Non-fin. [pres.] (C1) и-лы-рхио́ / и-л-мы-рхио́, (C3) и-зы-рхио́ / и-з-мы-рхио́, [aor.] (C1) и-лы-рхиа́ / и-л-мы-рхиа́, (C3) и-зы-рхиа́ / и-з-мы-рхиа́, [impf.] (C1) и-лы-рхио́-з / и-л-мы-рхио́-з, (C3) и-зы-рхио́-з / и-з-мы-рхио́-з, [past indef.] (C1) и-лы-рхиа́-з / и-л-мы-рхиа́-з, (C3) и-зы-рхиа́-з / и-з-мы-рхиа́-з.

а-рх-ра́ 'to mow; to reap': Fin. [pres.] и-сы-рх-уе́-ит / и-сы-рх-уа́-м, [aor.] и-сы-рх-и́т / и-с-мы-рх-и́т; Non-fin. [pres.] (C1) и-сы-рх-уа́ / и-с-мы-рх-уа́, (C3) и-зы-рх-уа́ / и-з-мы-рх-уа́, [aor.] (C1) и-сы-рхы́ / и-с-мы-рхы́.

а-рхәыч-ра́ 'to reduce, to diminish' (cf. а-хәычы́ 'little'): Fin. [aor.] и-шәы-рхәыч-и́т / и-шә-мы-рхәыч-и́т.

а-рхә-ра́ 'to pasture' (cf. а-ҳә-ра́ 'to graze'): Fin. [pres.] и-сы-рхә-уе́-ит / и-сы-рхә-уа́-м (-ӡо́-м), [aor.] и-сы-рхә-и́т / и-с-мы-рхә-и́т (-ӡе́-ит); Non-fin. [pres.] (C1) и-сы-рхә-уа́ / и-с-мы-рхә-уа́, (C3) и-зы-рхә-уа́ / и-з-мы-рхә-уа́, [aor.] (C1) и-сы-рхәы́ / и-с-мы-рхәы́.

а-рца-ра́ 'to warm up' (cf. а-ца́ 'hot'): Fin. [pres.] и-сы-рцо́-ит / и-сы-рцо́-м, [aor.] и-сы-рце́-ит / и-с-мы-рце́-ит; Non-fin. [pres.] (C1) и-сы-рцо́ / и-с-мы-рцо́, (C3) и-зы-рцо́ / и-з-мы-рцо́, [aor.] (C1) и-сы-рца́ / и-с-мы-рца́.

а-ртцыс-ра́ 'to roll, to swing; to sway' (cf. а-тцыс-ра́ 'to swing'): Fin. [pres.] с-лы-ртцыс-уе́-ит / с-лы-ртцыс-уа́-м (-ӡо́-м), [aor.] с-лы-ртцыс-и́т / сы-л-мы-ртцыс-и́т (-ӡе́-ит); Non-fin. [pres.] (C1) и-лы-ртцыс-уа́ / и-л-мы-ртцыс-уа́, (C3) д-зы-ртцыс-уа́ / ды-з-мы-ртцыс-уа́, [aor.] (C1) и-лы-ртцысы́ / и-л-мы-ртцысы́, (C3) д-зы-ртцысы́ / ды-з-мы-ртцысы́, [impf.] (C1) и-лы-ртцыс-уа́-з / и-л-мы-ртцыс-уа́-з, (C3) д-зы-ртцыс-уа́-з / ды-з-мы-ртцыс-уа́-з, [past indef.] (C1) и-лы-ртцысы́-з / и-л-мы-ртцысы́-з, (C3) д-зы-ртцысы́-з / ды-з-мы-ртцысы́-з.

а-рч-ра́ 'to inflate' (cf. а-ч-ра́ 'to swell'): Fin. [pres.] и-сы-рч-уе́-ит / и-сы-рч-уа́-м, [aor.] и-сы-рч-и́т / и-с-мы-рч-и́т; Non-fin. [pres.] (C1) и-сы-рч-уа́ / и-с-мы-рч-уа́, (C3) и-зы-рч-уа́ / и-з-мы-рч-уа́, [aor.] (C1) и-сы-рчы́ / и-с-мы-рчы́, (C3) и-зы-рчы́ / и-з-мы-рчы́.

а-рᵒехәа-ра́ 'to praise' (cf. а́-ᵒехәа-ра 'to boast'): Fin. [pres.] с-лы-рᵒехәо́-ит / с-лы-рᵒехәо́-м, [aor.] с-лы-рᵒехәе́-ит / сы-л-мы-рᵒехәе́-ит; Non-fin. [pres.] (C1) и-лы-рᵒехәо́ / и-л-мы-рᵒехәо́, (C3) с-зы-рᵒехәо́ / сы-з-мы-рᵒехәо́.

а-рш-ра́ 'to boil' (cf. а-ш-ра́ 'to boil'): Fin. [pres.] и-сы-рш-уе́-ит / и-сы-рш-уа́-м (-рш-ӡо́-м), [aor.] и-сы-рш-и́т / и-с-мы-рш-и́т (-рш-ӡе́-ит); Non-fin. [pres.] (C1) и-лы-рш-уа́ / и-л-мы-рш-уа́, (C3) и-зы-рш-уа́ / и-з-мы-рш-уа́, [aor.] (C1) и-лы-ршы́ / и-л-мы-ршы́, (C3) и-зы-ршы́ / и-з-мы-ршы́, [impf.] (C1) и-лы-рш-уа́-з / и-л-мы-рш-уа́-з, (C3) и-зы-рш-уа́-з / и-з-мы-рш-уа́-з, [past indef.] (C1) и-лы-ршы́-з / и-л-мы-ршы́-з, (C3) и-зы-ршы́-з / и-з-мы-ршы́-з.

а-ршәа-ра́ 'to frighten' (cf. а-шәа-ра́ 'to be frightened'): Fin. [pres.] д-сы-ршәо́-ит / д-сы-ршәо́-м, [aor.] д-сы-ршәе́-ит / д-с-мы-ршәе́-ит; Non-fin. [pres.] (C1) и-сы-ршәо́ / и-с-мы-ршәо́, (C3) д-зы-ршәо́ / д-з-мы-ршәо́, [aor.] (C1) и-сы-ршәа́ / и-с-мы-ршәа́.

а-рҩа-ра́ 'to dry' (cf. а-ҩа-ра́ 'to wither'): Fin. [pres.] и-сы-рҩо́-ит / и-сы-рҩо́-м, [aor.] и-ды-рҩе́-ит / и-д-мы-рҩе́-ит; Non-fin. [pres.] (C1) и-лы-рҩо́ / и-л-мы-рҩо́, (C3) и-зы-рҩо́ / и-л-мы-рҩо́, [aor.] (C1) и-лы-рҩа́ / и-л-мы-рҩа́, (C3) и-зы-рҩа́ / и-л-мы-рҩа́, [impf.] (C1) и-лы-рҩо́-з / и-л-мы-рҩо́-з, (C3) и-зы-рҩо́-з / и-л-мы-рҩо́-з, [past indef.] (C1) и-лы-рҩа́-з / и-л-мы-рҩа́-з, (C3) и-зы-рҩа́-з / и-л-мы-рҩа́-з

3.2.7. Class D

This class takes the direct object pronominal prefix (DO) in Column I, the indirect object pronominal prefix (IO) in Column II, and the agent pronominal prefix (A) in Column III. The only Class D verb with a pure root in Abkhaz is а́-ҭара /á-ta-ra/ 'to give'.

For example:

(189) илы́сҭеит
/jə-lə́-s-ta-jt'/
it/them(C1)-her(C2)-I(C3)-give-(Aor)-Fin
'I gave it/them to her.'

Here, the Column II pronominal prefix л(ы)- /l(ə)/, which indicates the indirect object, is merely inserted between the pronominal prefixes in Columns I and III, and there is no marker present which indicates any grammatical relationship. When we express the English 'I carried it to her' in Abkhaz, we cannot use a verbal complex such as a Class D structure. In that case, the version marker з- /z/ must be inserted into the verb ана́гара /a-ná-ga-ra/ 'to take there' as follows:

(190) илызна́згеит
/jə-lə-z-ná-z-ga-jt'/
it/them (C1)-her(C2)-Version-Prev(there)-I(C3)-take-(Aor)-Fin

This version marker з- /z/ roughly corresponds to English 'for', and the literal meaning is close to 'I took it/them there for her'.[121] Also, when we express an English phrase like 'I said something to her' in Abkhaz, it must be:

(191) ила́схәеит
/jə-l-á-s-ħ^{w}a-jt'/
it/them(C1)-her(C2)-to-I(C3)-say-(Aor)-Fin

After the prefix л- /l/ 'her' there is a dative relation marker a here as well.

In this way, the verb а́ҭара /á-ta-ra/ 'to give', which can express a dative relation with just a Column II pronominal prefix, is an extremely peculiar verb in Abkhaz.

Three-place transitive verbs, verbs other than а́ҭара 'to give' above that are secondary derivatives produced by causative derivation from two-place transitive verbs, can have the same column distribution as Class D. For example, the causative form арбара́ /a-r-ba-rá/ 'to show' of абара́ /a-ba-rá/ 'to see' has a Class D structure:

(192) илсырбе́ит
/jə-l-sə-r-bá-jt'/
it/them(C1)-her(C2)-I(C3)-Caus-see-(Aor)-Fin
'I showed it/them to her.'

121. For the version, see §4.3.

Also, Class D three-place transitive verbs can be derived from some two-place intransitive verbs as well. For example, the intransitive verb аҳара́ /a-ħa-rá/ 'to hear' has the following causative form:[122]

(193) илсырҳауе́ит
/jə-l-sə-r-ħa-wá-jt'/
it/them(C1)-her(C2)-I(C3)-Caus-hear-Dyn-Fin
'I report it/them to her.' or 'I let her hear it/them.'

We shall first describe the verb а́ҭара /á-ta-ra/ in detail, and later describe the Class D verbs causatively derived.

3.2.7.1. The Class D verb: а́-ҭара 'to give'

3.2.7.1.1 We have already mentioned that when the agent of a three-place transitive verb is a third-person singular non-human, the Column III pronominal prefix is not а-, but becomes на- /na/ (see §3.1.6, Note 7). For example:

(194) бысна́ҭеит
/bə-s-ná-ta-jt'/
you.F(C1)-I(C2)-it(C3)-give-(Aor)-Fin
'It gave you-F to me.'

Also, if there is the third person plural pronominal prefix р- /r/ in Column II and there is the third person singular non-human pronominal prefix на- /na/ in Column III and if the accent is placed on a Column II pronominal prefix (variants where the accent is placed on a Column III pronominal prefix are also possible), after this р- /r/ an а-, not a schwa appears:

(195) ира́наҭоит
/jə-rá-na-ta-wa-jt'/
it/them(C1)-them(C2)-it(C3)-give-Dyn-Fin
'It gives it/them to them'

According to our informant, ирна́ҭоит /jə-r-ná-ta-wa-jt'/ is preferable to (195) above, but *иры́наҭоит /jə-rə́-na-ta-wa-jt'/ is unacceptable.

When the pronominal prefix in Column I and Column II is и-, only one и- is written:

(196) и́бҭеит /jə́-b-ta-jt'/ < ии́бҭеит /j-jə́-b-ta-jt'/ 'you-F gave it/them to him'

On the other hand, when the pronominal prefix in Column II and Column III is и-, и- is written twice:

(197) сии́ҭеит /s-jə́-j-ta-jt'/ 'he gave me to him'

When all of pronominal prefixes in Columns I, II and III are и-, и- is only written twice:

---

122. The conjugation of аҳара́ /a-ħa-rá/ 'to hear' is исаҳауе́ит /jə-s-a-ħa-wá-jt'/ [it/they(C1)-me(C2)-to-hear/be audible-Dyn-Fin] 'I hear it/them', lit. 'it/they is/are audible to me'. The fact that the root of this verb is ҳа /ħa/ is clear from the stem of the causative form above рҳа /r-ħa/. For the causative form of two-place intransitives, the causee is placed in Column I (e.g. дысбы́рсит /də-s-bə́-r-sə-jt'/ [him/her(C1)-me(C2)-you.F(C3)-Caus-hit-(Aor)-Fin] 'you made him/her hit me'), but in Example (193) above, the causee is placed in Column II. This is the same column placement as the causative form derived from two-place transitive verbs. Perhaps the reason is because аҳара́ /a-ħa-rá/ is *an inversive verb* (for inversive verbs, see §5.10).

(198) ии́т̦еит < иии́т̦еит /jə-jə́-j-ta-jt'/ 'he gave it/them to him'

3.2.7.1.2. Regarding the accent of finite forms in а́т̦ара /á-ta-ra/ 'to give', there is the following hierarchy of prefixes that determine the position of accents:

а /a/, ха /ħa/, ра /ra/ in Column II >

на /na/ in Column III >

Column II prefixes other than а, ха /ħa/, ра /ra/

This hierarchy indicates the following:

(1) First, when there are the pronominal prefixes а, ха, ра in Column II, the accent is placed on the Column II pronominal prefix regardless of the pronominal prefix in the other columns. However, when the Column II pronominal prefix is ха (also а?) and the Column III pronominal prefix is на, the accent can be placed on either column. Examples: иа́ст̦еит /j-á-s-ta-jt'/ 'I gave it/them to it', бх̦а́рт̦оит /b-ħá-r-ta-wa-jt'/ 'they give you-F to us', дх̦а́нат̦оит /d-ħá-na-ta-wa-jt'/ (*or* дх̦на́т̦оит /d-ħ-ná-ta-wa-jt'/) 'it gaves him/her to us', ира́нат̦оит /jə-rá-na-ta-wa-jt'/ 'it gaves it/them to them', да́нат̦оит /d-á-na-ta-wa-jt'/ 'it gives him/her to it' (cf. дана́т̦еит /d-a-ná-ta-jt'/ 'it gave him/her to it').

(2) Next, when the Column II pronominal prefix is a prefix other than а, ха, ра, and the Column III pronominal prefix is на, the accent is placed on the Column III pronominal prefix: бысна́т̦оит /bə-s-ná-ta-wa-jt'/ 'it gives you-F to me', иуна́т̦оит /jə-w-ná-ta-wa-jt'/ 'it gives it/them to you-M', ина́т̦оит /jə-ná-ta-wa-jt'/ (< иина́т̦оит) 'it gives it/them to him', х̦аина́т̦оит /ħa-j-ná-ta-wa-jt'/ 'it gives us to him', ишәна́т̦оит /jə-šʷ-ná-ta-wa-jt'/ 'it gives it/them to you-Pl', ирна́мт̦еит /jə-r-ná-m-ta-jt'/ 'it gave it/them to them', дыбна́мт̦еит /də-b-ná-m-ta-jt'/ 'it did not give him/her to you-F'.

(3) Finally, in cases other than those described above, the accent is placed on the Column II pronominal prefix: исы́лт̦оит /jə-sə́-l-ta-wa-jt'/ 'she gives it/them to me', сии́т̦оит /s-jə́-j-ta-wa-jt'/ 'he gives me to him', дба́х̦т̦оит < д-бы́-х̦-т̦о-ит /d-bə́-ħ-ta-wa-jt'/ 'we gives him/her to you-F', дуа́х̦т̦оит /d-wá-ħ-ta-wa-jt'/ 'we give him/her to you-M', х̦бы́рт̦оит /ħ-bə́-r-ta-wa-jt'/ 'they give us to you-F', иры́рт̦оит /jə-rə́-r-ta-wa-jt'/ 'they give it/them to them', дли́т̦ом /d-lə́-j-ta-wa-m/ 'he does not give him/her to her', дбы́сымт̦еит /d-bə́-sə-m-ta-jt'/ 'I did not give him/her to you-F'.

There are the following general rules regarding the accent on non-finite forms:

(1) When the relative prefix is in Column I, the accent follows the general rule for assigning accents to finite forms: илы́ст̦о /jə-lə́-s-ta-wa/ 'which I give to her', илна́т̦о /jə-l-ná-ta-wa/ 'which it gives to her', ила́х̦т̦о [i-lá-ħ-to:] /j-lə́-ħ-ta-wa/ 'which we give to her', и́ст̦о (< и-и́-с-т̦о /j-jə́-s-ta-wa/) 'which I give to him', иа́ст̦о /j-á-s-ta-wa/ 'which I give to it', их̦а́бт̦о [i-ħá-b-to:] < /j-ħə́-b-ta-wa/ 'which you-F give to us', илна́т̦о /jə-l-ná-ta-wa/ 'which it gives to her', иа́нат̦о /j-á-na-ta-wa/ 'which it gives to it', иах̦на́т̦о [ja-ħ-ná-to:] /jə-ħ-ná-ta-wa/ 'which it gives to us', илы́сымт̦о /jə-lə́-sə-m-ta-wa/ 'which I do not give to her', илна́мт̦о /jə-l-ná-m-ta-wa/ 'which it does not give to her'. Note: илах̦а́мт̦о [i-la-ħá-m-to:] < /j-lə-ħə́-m-ta-wa/ 'which we do not give to her'.

(2) When the relative prefix is in Column II, the accent is placed on the postradical element (when there is not one, it is placed at the end of the root). However, when there is на- /na/ in Column III, the accent is placed there: изылт̦о́ /jə-zə-l-ta-wá/ 'whom she gives it/them to', дзах̦т̦о́ [d-za-ħ-tó:] < /d-

zə-ħ-ta-wá/ ‘whom we give him/her’ to’, дзырҭо́ /d-zə-r-ta-wá/ ‘whom they give him/her to’, изна́ҭо /jə-z-ná-ta-wa/ ‘whom it gives it/them to’, сызлымҭо́ /sə-z-lə-m-ta-wá/ ‘whom she does not give me to’, дызна́мҭо /də-z-ná-m-ta-wa/ ‘whom it does not give him/her to’, дызҳамҭо́ /də-z-ħə-m-ta-wá/ ‘whom we do not give him/her to’, дызрымҭо́ /də-z-rə-m-ta-wá/ ‘whom they do not give him/her to’.

(3) When the relative prefix is in Column III, the accent is placed on the pronominal prefix in Column II: илы́зҭо /jə-lə́-z-ta-wa/ ‘(the one) who gives it/ them to her’, да́зҭо /d-á-z-ta-wa/ ‘(the one) who gives him/her to it’, дҳа́зҭо /d-ħə́-z-ta-wa/ ‘(the one) who gives him/her to us’, илы́зымҭо /jə-lə́-zə-m-ta-wa/ ‘(the one) who does not give it/them to her’.

3.2.7.1.3. Inflection of á-ҭара /á-ta-ra/ ‘to give’

Finite forms

Dynamic Group I

C1-C2-C3	<u>Affirmative</u>	<u>Negative</u>
Present		
Sg.3.Hum.-2.F-1	д-бы́-с-ҭо-ит /d-bə́-s-ta-wa-jt’/ him/her(C1)-you.F(C2)-I(C3)-give-Dyn-Fin ‘I give him/her to you-F’	д-бы́-с-ҭо-м /d-bə́-s-ta-wa-m/
Sg.3.Hum.-2.M-1	д-у́-с-ҭо-ит	д-у́-с-ҭо-м
Sg.3.N.-Hum./Pl.3-2.M-1	и-у́-с-ҭо-ит	и-у́-с-ҭо-м
Sg.2.M-3.M-1	у-и́-с-ҭо-ит	у-и́-с-ҭо-м
Sg.3.N.-Hum./Pl.3-3.M-1	и́-с-ҭо-ит (< и-и́-с-ҭо-ит)	и́-с-ҭо-м
Sg.2.F-3.Non-Hum.-1	б-а́-с-ҭо-ит	б-а́-с-ҭо-м
Sg.3.N.-Hum./Pl.3-Pl.2-1	и-шәы́-с-ҭо-ит	и-шәы́-с-ҭо-м
Sg.3.N.-Hum./Pl.3-Pl.3-1	и-ры́-с-ҭо-ит	и-ры́-с-ҭо-м
Sg.3.N.H/Pl.3-Sg.1-2.M	и-сы́-у-ҭо-ит	и-сы́-у-ҭо-м
Sg.3.N.H/Pl.3-Pl.1-Sg.2.F	и-ҳа́-б-ҭо-ит	и-ҳа́-б-ҭо-м
Sg.3.N.H/Pl.3-Pl.1-3.M	и-шә-и́-ҭо-ит /jə-šʷə́-j-ta-wa-jt’/	и-шә-и́-ҭо-м
Sg.1-3.M-3.M	с-и́-и-ҭо-ит	с-и́-и-ҭо-м
Sg.1-3.Non-Hum.-3.M	с-а́-и-ҭо-ит	с-а́-и-ҭо-м
Pl.1-3-Sg.3.M	ҳ-р-и́-ҭо-ит /ħ-rə́-j-ta-wa-jt’/	ҳ-р-и́-ҭо-м
Sg.2.F-1-3.F	б-сы́-л-ҭо-ит	б-сы́-л-ҭо-м
Sg.2.F-1-3.Non-Hum.	бы-с-на́-ҭо-ит	бы-с-на́-ҭо-м
Sg.3.N.H/Pl.3-2.M-3.N.H	и-у-на́-ҭо-ит	и-у-на́-ҭо-м
Sg.3.N.H/Pl.3-3.M-3.N.H	и-на́-ҭо-ит (< и-и-на́-ҭо-ит)	и-на́-ҭо-м
Sg.1-3.N.H.-3.N.H	с-а́-на-ҭо-ит	с-а́-на-ҭо-м
Sg.3.N.H/Pl.3-3.N.H.-N.H	и-а́-на-ҭо-ит	и-а́-на-ҭо-м
Sg.2.F-Pl.1-Sg.3.N.H	б-ҳа́-на-ҭо-ит	б-ҳа́-на-ҭо-м
Sg.1-Pl.2-Sg.3.N.H	сы-шә-на́-ҭо-ит	сы-шә-на́-ҭо-м
Pl.1-Pl.2-Sg.3.N.H	ҳа-шә-на́-ҭо-ит	ҳа-шә-на́-ҭо-м
Sg.1-Pl.3-Sg.3.N.H	с-ра́-на-ҭо-ит	с-ра́-на-ҭо-м
Sg.3.N.H/Pl.3-Pl.3-Sg.3.N.H	и-ра́-на-ҭо-ит	и-ра́-на-ҭо-м

Pl.1-Pl.3-Sg.3.N.H	ҳ-ра́-на-ҭо-ит	ҳ-ра́-на-ҭо-м
Sg.3.Hum-Sg.2.M-Pl.1	д-уа́-ҳ-ҭо-ит	д-уа́-ҳ-ҭо-м
Sg.3.N.H/Pl.3-Sg.3.M-Pl.1	иа́-ҳ-ҭо-ит (< и-иа́-ҳ-ҭо-ит)	иа́-ҳ-ҭо-м
Sg.3.Hum.-Sg.3.M-Pl.1	д-иа́-ҳ-ҭо-ит	д-иа́-ҳ-ҭо-м
Sg.3.Hum.-Sg.3.F-Pl.1	д-ла́-ҳ-ҭо-ит	д-ла́-ҳ-ҭо-м
Sg.3.Hum.-Sg.1-Pl.2	д-сы́-шә-ҭо-ит	д-сы́-шә-ҭо-м
Pl.1-Sg.3.M-Pl.2	ҳ-и́-шә-ҭо-ит	ҳ-и́-шә-ҭо-м
Sg.2.F-Sg.1-Pl.3	б-сы́-р-ҭо-ит	б-сы́-р-ҭо-м
Sg.1-Sg.3.N.H-Pl.3	с-а́-р-ҭо-ит	с-а́-р-ҭо-м
Sg.3.N.H/Pl.3-Pl.1-Pl.3	и-ҳа́-р-ҭо-ит	и-ҳа́-р-ҭо-м
Sg.3.N.H/Pl.3-Pl.3-Pl.3	и-ры́-р-ҭо-ит	и-ры́-р-ҭо-м
Aorist		
Sg.3.Hum-2.F-1	д-бы́-с-ҭе-ит	д-бы́-сы-м-ҭе-ит
	/d-bə́-s-ta-jt'/	/d-bə́-sə-m-ta-jt'/
	'I gave him/her to you-F'	
Sg.3.Hum.-2.M-1	д-у́-с-ҭе-ит	д-у́-сы-м-ҭе-ит
Sg.3.N.H/Pl.3-Sg.2.F-1	и-бы́-с-ҭе-ит	и-бы́-сы-м-ҭе-ит
Sg.3.N.H/Pl.3-Sg.3.F-1	и-лы́-с-ҭе-ит	и-лы́-сы-м-ҭе-ит
Sg.3.N.H/Pl.3-Sg.3.N.H-1	и-а́-с-ҭе-ит	и-а́-сы-м-ҭе-ит
Sg.3.Hum-2.F-3.N.H	ды-б-на́-ҭе-ит	ды-б-на́-м-ҭе-ит
Sg.3.Hum-3.N.H-3.N.H	д-а-на́-ҭе-ит	д-а-на́-м-ҭе-ит
Sg.3.N.H/Pl.3-Pl.3-Sg.3.N.H	и-р-на́-ҭе-ит	и-р-на́-м-ҭе-ит
	(*or* и-ра́-на-ҭе-ит)	(*or* и-ра́-на-м-ҭе-ит)
Future I		
Sg.3.N.H/Pl.3-Sg.2.F-1	и-бы́-с-ҭа-п	и-бы́-с-ҭа-ры-м
Future II		
Sg.3.N.H/Pl.3-Sg.2.F-1	и-бы́-с-ҭа-шт	и-бы́-с-ҭа-ша-м
Perfect		
Sg.3.N.H/Pl.3-Sg.2.F-1	и-бы́-с-ҭа-хье-ит	и-бы́-сы-м-ҭа-ц(т)
Sg.3.N.H/Pl.3-Sg.2.F-3.N.H	и-б-на́-ҭа-хье-ит	и-б-на́-м-ҭа-ц(т)
Dynamic Group II		
C1-C2-C3	<u>Affirmative</u>	<u>Negative</u>
Imperfect		
Sg.3.N.H/Pl.3-Sg.2.F-1	и-бы́-с-ҭо-н	и-бы́-с-ҭо-мы-зт
Past Indefinite		
Sg.3.N.H/Pl.3-Sg.2.F-1	и-бы́-с-ҭа-н	и-бы́-сы-м-ҭа-зт
Conditional I		
Sg.3.N.H/Pl.3-Sg.2.F-1	и-бы́-с-ҭа-ры-н	и-бы́-с-ҭа-ры-мы-зт
Conditional II		
Sg.3.N.H/Pl.3-Sg.2.F-1	и-бы́-с-ҭа-ша-н	и-бы́-с-ҭа-ша-мы-зт
Pluperfect		

Sg.3.N.H/Pl.3-Sg.2.F-1	и-бы́-с-т̣а-хьа-н	и-бы́-сы-м-т̣а-цы-зт
Sg.3.N.H/Pl.3-Sg.2.F-3.N.H	и-б-на́-т̣а-хьа-н	и-б-на́-м-т̣а-цы-зт

Non-Finite forms
Dynamic Group I

C1-C2-C3	Affirmative	Negative
Present		
Rel-Sg.3.F-1	и-лы́-с-т̣о /jə-lə́-s-ta-wa/ Rel(C1)-her(C2)-I(C3)-give-Dyn.NF 'which/whom I give to her'	и-лы́-сы-м-т̣о
Rel-Sg.3.F-2.F	и-лы́-б-т̣о	и-лы́-бы-м-т̣о
Rel-Sg.3.F-3.M	и-лы́-и-т̣о	и-лы́-и-м-т̣о
Rel-Sg.3.F-3.F	и-лы́-л-т̣о	и-лы́-лы-м-т̣о
Rel-Sg.3.F-3.Non-Hum.	и-л-на́-т̣о	и-л-на́-м-т̣о
Rel-Sg.3.F-Pl.1	и-л-а́х̣-т̣о (= и-ла́-х̣-т̣о)	и-л-ах̣а́-м-т̣о (= и-ла-х̣а́-м-т̣о)
Rel-Sg.2.F-1	и-бы́-с-т̣о	и-бы́-сы-м-т̣о
Rel-Sg.2.M-1	и-у́-с-т̣о	и-у́-сы-м-т̣о
Rel-Sg.3.M-1	и́-с-т̣о (< и-и́-с-т̣о)	и́-сы-м-т̣о
Rel-Sg.3.N.H-1	и-а́-с-т̣о	и-а́-сы-м-т̣о
Rel-Pl.1-Sg.2.F	и-х̣а́-б-т̣о	и-х̣а́-бы-м-т̣о
Rel-Pl.2-Sg.1	и-шәы́-с-т̣о	и-шәы́-сы-м-т̣о
Rel-Pl.3-Sg.1	и-ры́-с-т̣о	и-ры́-сы-м-т̣о
Rel-Sg.2.F-3.N.H	и-б-на́-т̣о	и-б-на́-м-т̣о
Rel-Sg.3.N.H-3.N.H	и-а́-на-т̣о	и-а́-на-м-т̣о
Rel-Sg.3.M-3.N.H	и-и-на́-т̣о	и-и-на́-м-т̣о
Rel-Pl.1-Sg.3.N.H	и-ах̣-на́-т̣о (= иа-х̣-на́-т̣о)	и-ах̣-на́-м-т̣о
Rel-Pl.2-Sg.3.N.H	и-шә-на́-т̣о	и-шә-на́-м-т̣о
Rel-Pl.3-Sg.3.N.H	и-р-на́-т̣о	и-р-на́-м-т̣о
Sg.3.Hum.-Rel-Sg.3.F	д-зы-л-т̣о́ /d-zə-l-ta-wá/ him/her(C1)-Rel(C2)-she(C3)-give-Dyn.NF 'whom she gives him/her to'	ды-з-лы-м-т̣о́
Sg.3.N.H/Pl.3-Rel-Sg.3.F	и-зы-л-т̣о́	и-з-лы-м-т̣о́
Sg.3.Hum.-Rel-Sg.1	д-зы-с-т̣о́	ды-з-сы-м-т̣о́
Sg.3.Hum.-Rel-Sg.2.F	д-зы-б-т̣о́	ды-з-бы-м-т̣о́
Sg.3.Hum.-Rel-Sg.3.M	д-з-и-т̣о́	ды-з-и-м-т̣о́
Sg.3.Hum.-Rel-Sg.3.N.H	ды-з-на́-т̣о	ды-з-на́-м-т̣о
Sg.3.Hum.-Rel-Pl.1	д-з-ах̣-т̣о́ (= д-за-х̣-т̣о́)	ды-з-х̣а-м-т̣о́
Sg.3.Hum.-Rel-Pl.2	д-зы-шә-т̣о́	ды-з-шәы-м-т̣о́
Sg.3.Hum.-Rel-Pl.3	д-зы-р-т̣о́	ды-з-ры-м-т̣о́
Sg.1-Rel-Sg.3.N.H	сы-з-на́-т̣о	сы-з-на́-м-т̣о

Sg.2.M-Rel-Sg.3.N.H	у-з-на́-т̣о	у-з-на́-м-т̣о
Pl.1-Rel-Sg.3.N.H	х̣а-з-на́-т̣о	х̣а-з-на́-м-т̣о
Sg.3.N.H/Pl.3-Rel-Sg.3.N.H	и-з-на́-т̣о	и-з-на́-м-т̣о
Sg.3.Hum-3.F-Rel	д-лы́-з-т̣о	д-лы́-зы-м-т̣о
	/d-lə́-z-ta-wa/	/d-lə́-zə-m-ta-wa/
	him/her(C1)-her(C2)-Rel(C3)-give-Dyn.NF	
	'(the one) who gives him/her to her'	
Sg.3.Hum-1-Rel	д-сы́-з-т̣о	д-сы́-зы-м-т̣о
Sg.3.Hum-2.F-Rel	д-бы́-з-т̣о	д-бы́-зы-м-т̣о
Sg.3.Hum-3.N.H-Rel	д-а́-з-т̣о	д-а́-зы-м-т̣о
Sg.3.Hum-3.M-Rel	д-и́-з-т̣о	д-и́-зы-м-т̣о
Sg.3.Hum-Pl.1-Rel	д-х̣а́-з-т̣о	д-х̣а́-зы-м-т̣
Sg.3.Hum-Pl.2-Rel	д-шәы́-з-т̣о	д-шәы́-зы-м-т̣о
Sg.3.Hum-Pl.3-Rel	д-ры́-з-т̣о	д-ры́-зы-м-т̣о
Sg.1-3.F-Rel	с-лы́-з-т̣о	с-лы́-зы-м-т̣о
Sg.2.F-3.F-Rel	б-лы́-з-т̣о	б-лы́-зы-м-т̣о
Sg.3.N.H/Pl.3-Sg.3.F-Rel	и-лы́-з-т̣о	и-лы́-зы-м-т̣о
Pl.1-Sg.3.F-Rel	х̣-лы́-з-т̣о	х̣-лы́-зы-м-т̣о
Pl.2-Sg.3.F-Rel	шә-лы́-з-т̣о	шә-лы́-зы-м-т̣о
Aorist		
Rel-Sg.3.F-1	и-лы́-с-т̣а	и-лы́-сы-м-т̣а
Sg.3.N.H/Pl.3-Rel-Sg.3.F	и-зы-л-т̣а́	и-з-лы-м-л-т̣а́
Sg.3.N.H/Pl.3-Sg.3.F-Rel	и-лы́-з-т̣а	и-лы́-зы-м-т̣а
Future I		
Rel-Sg.3.F-1	и-лы́-с-т̣а-ра	и-лы́-сы-м-т̣а-ра
Sg.3.N.H/Pl.3-Rel-Sg.3.F	и-зы-л-т̣а-ра́	и-з-лы-м-л-т̣а-ра́
Sg.3.N.H/Pl.3-Sg.3.F-Rel	и-лы́-з-т̣а-ра	и-лы́-зы-м-т̣а-ра
Future II		
Rel-Sg.3.F-1	и-лы́-с-т̣а-ша	и-лы́-сы-м-т̣а-ша
Sg.3.N.H/Pl.3-Rel-Sg.3.F	и-зы-л-т̣а́-ша	и-з-лы-м-л-т̣а́-ша
Sg.3.N.H/Pl.3-Sg.3.F-Rel	и-лы́-з-т̣а-ша	и-лы́-зы-м-т̣а-ша
Perfect		
Rel-Sg.3.F-1	и-лы́-с-т̣а-хьо-у/хьа(-ц)	и-лы́-сы-м-т̣а-хьо-у/хьа(-ц)
Sg.3.N.H/Pl.3-Rel-Sg.3.F	и-зы-л-т̣а-хьо́-у/хьа́(-ц)	и-з-лы-м-л-т̣а-хьо́-у/хьа́(-ц)
Sg.3.N.H/Pl.3-Sg.3.F-Rel	и-лы́-з-т̣а-хьо-у/хьа(-ц)	и-лы́-зы-м-т̣а-хьо-у/хьа(-ц)
Dynamic Group II		
C1-C2-C3	Affirmative	Negative
Imperfect		

Rel-Sg.3.F-1	и-лы́-с-ҭо-з	и-лы́-сы-м-ҭо-з
Sg.3.N.H/Pl.3-Rel-Sg.3.F	и-зы-л-ҭо́-з	и-з-лы-м-л-ҭо́-з
Sg.3.N.H/Pl.3-Sg.3.F-Rel	и-лы́-з-ҭо-з	и-лы́-зы-м-ҭо-з
Past Indefinite		
Rel-Sg.3.F-1	и-лы́-с-ҭа-з	и-лы́-сы-м-ҭа-з
Sg.3.N.H/Pl.3-Rel-Sg.3.F	и-зы-л-ҭа́-з	и-з-лы-м-л-ҭа́-з
Sg.3.N.H/Pl.3-Sg.3.F-Rel	и-лы́-з-ҭа-з	и-лы́-зы-м-ҭа-з
Conditional I		
Rel-Sg.3.F-1	и-лы́-с-ҭа-ры-з	и-лы́-сы-м-ҭа-ры-з
Sg.3.N.H/Pl.3-Rel-Sg.3.F	и-зы-л-ҭа-ры́-з	и-з-лы-м-ҭа-ры́-з
Sg.3.N.H/Pl.3-Sg.3.F-Rel	и-лы́-з-ҭа-ры-з	и-лы́-зы-м-ҭа-ры-з
Conditional II		
Rel-Sg.3.F-1	и-лы́-с-ҭа-ша-з	и-лы́-сы-м-ҭа-ша-з
Sg.3.N.H/Pl.3-Rel-Sg.3.F	и-зы-л-ҭа́-ша-з	и-з-лы-м-л-ҭа́-ша-з
Sg.3.N.H/Pl.3-Sg.3.F-Rel	и-лы́-з-ҭа-ша-з	и-лы́-зы-м-ҭа-ша-з
Pluperfect		
Rel-Sg.3.F-1	и-лы́-с-ҭа-хьа-з	и-лы́-сы-м-ҭа-хьа-з
Sg.3.N.H/Pl.3-Rel-Sg.3.F	и-зы-л-ҭа-хьа́-з	и-з-лы-м-л-ҭа-хьа́-з
Sg.3.N.H/Pl.3-Sg.3.F-Rel	и-лы́-з-ҭа-хьа-з	и-лы́-зы-м-ҭа-хьа-з

3.2.7.2. The Class D Verbs of Causative Derivation

Class D verbs can be also derived by causativizing two-place transitive verbs (or two-place intransitive verbs). They are no major differences with the verb а́ҭара /á-ta-ra/ 'to give' examined above, but that the pronominal prefix of third person plural in Column II and Column III is д(ы)- /d(ə)/ and their accentuation is different. As a general rule, the accent is based on the accentuation of the underlying two-place verbs. If the accent of the underlying form is fixed within the stem, the accent of the derived form is also fixed in the stem (AP a): илсырдырует /jə-l-sə-r-də́r-wa-jt'/ 'I inform her of it/them', cf. адырра /a-dér-ra/ 'to know'. Next, if the masdar accent of the underlying form is on the article, the accent of the derived form is placed on the element directly before the causative marker (AP b): илсы́ржәуеит /jə-l-sə́-r-žʷ-wa-jt'/ 'I give her something to drink', cf. а́жәра /á-žʷ-ra/ 'to drink'. Finally, if the accentuation of the underlying form is AP c, the derived form has the accent on the element after the stem: илсырбо́ит /jə-l-sə-r-ba-wá-jt'/ 'I show it/them to her', cf. абара́ /a-ba-rá/ 'to see (AP c)'.

3.2.7.2.1. AP a

а-рды́рра /a-rdér-ra/ 'to inform of, to introduce *sb* to *sb*' (cf. а-ды́рра /a-dér-ra/ 'to know')

Finite forms

C1-C2-C3	<u>Affirmative</u>	<u>Negative</u>
Present		
Sg.3.N.H/Pl.3-Sg.3.F-Sg.1	и-л-сы-рды́р-уе-ит	и-л-сы-рды́р-уа-м
	/jə-l-sə-rdə́r-wa-jt'/	/jə-l-sə-r-də́r-wa-m/
	it/them(C1)-her(C2)-I(C3)-Caus+know-Dyn-Fin	
	'I inform her of it/them'	
Sg.3.Hum.-Sg.2.F-Pl.3	ды-б-ды-рды́р-уе-ит	ды-б-ды-рды́р-уа-м
	/də-b-də-rdə́r-wa-jt'/	
	'they introduce him/her to you-F'	
Aorist		
Sg.3.N.H/Pl.3-Sg.3.F-Sg.1	и-л-сы-рды́р-ит	и-л(ы)-с-мы-рды́р-ит
Sg.3.Hum.-Sg.2.F-1	ды-б-сы-рды́р-ит	ды-б-с-мы-рды́р-ит
Sg.3.N.H/Pl.3-Pl.1-Pl.3	и-ах-ды-рды́р-ит	и-ха-д-мы-рды́р-ит

Non-Finite forms		
C1-C2-C3	<u>Affirmative</u>	<u>Negative</u>
Present		
Rel-Sg.3.F-Sg.1	и-л-сы-рды́р-уа	и-л(ы)-с-мы-рды́р-уа
	/jə-l-sə-rdə́r-wa/	
	'which I inform her of'	
Rel-Sg.2.F-1	и-б-сы-рды́р-уа	и-б-с-мы-рды́р-уа
	/jə-b-sə-rdə́r-wa/	
	'(the one) whom I introduce to you-F'	
Sg.3.N.H/Pl.3-Rel-Sg.1	и-з-сы-рды́р-уа	и-з(ы)-с-мы-рды́р-уа
	/jə-z-sə-rdə́r-wa/	
	'(the one) whom I inform of it/them'	
Sg.3.Hum.-Rel-Sg.1	ды-з-сы-рды́р-уа	ды-з-с-мы-рды́р-уа
	/də-z-sə-rdə́r-wa/	
	'(the one) whom I introduce him/her to'	
Sg.3.N.H/Pl.3-Sg.3.F-Rel	и-л-зы-рды́р-уа	и-л(ы)-з-мы-рды́р-уа
	/jə-l-zə-rdə́r-wa/	
	'(the one) who informs her of it/them'	
Sg.3.Hum.-Sg.2.F-Rel	ды-б-зы-рды́р-уа	ды-б-з-мы-рды́р-уа
	/də-b-zə-rdə́r-wa/	
	'(the one) who introduces him/her to you-F'	
Past Indefinite		
Rel-Sg.3.F-Sg.1	и-л-сы-рды́ры-з	и-л(ы)-с-мы-рды́ры-з
Rel-Sg.2.F-1	и-б-сы-рды́ры-з	и-б-с-мы-рды́ры-з
Sg.3.N.H/Pl.3-Rel-Sg.1	и-з-сы-рды́ры-з	и-з(ы)-с-мы-рды́ры-з
Sg.3.Hum.-Rel-Sg.1	ды-з-сы-рды́ры-з	ды-з-с-мы-рды́ры-з
Sg.3.N.H/Pl.3-Sg.3.F-Rel	и-л-зы-рды́ры-з	и-л(ы)-з-мы-рды́ры-з
Sg.3.Hum.-Sg.2.F-Rel	ды-б-зы-дры́ры-з	ды-б-з-мы-дры́ры-з

3.2.7.2.2. <u>AP b</u>

а́-ржəра /á-r-žʷ-ra/ ‘to give *sth* to drink’ (cf. а́-жəра /á-žʷ-ra/ ‘to drink’)

Finite forms

C1-C2-C3	<u>Affirmative</u>	<u>Negative</u>
Present		
Sg.3.N.H/Pl.3-Sg.3.F-Sg.1	и-л-сы́-ржə-уе-ит /jə-l-sə́-r-žʷ-wa-jtʼ/ ‘I give her somrthing to drink’	и-л-сы́-ржə-уа-м
Aorist		
Sg.3.N.H/Pl.3-Sg.3.F-Sg.1	и-л-сы́-ржə-ит	и-л(ы)-с-мы́-ржə-ит

Non-Finite forms

Present		
Rel-Sg.3.F-Sg.1	и-л-сы́-ржə-уа ‘which I give her to drink’ /jə-l-sə́-r-žʷ-wa/	и-л(ы)-с-мы́-ржə-уа
Sg.3.N.H/Pl.3-Rel-Sg.1	и-з-сы́-ржə-уа ‘(the one) whom I give something to drink’	и-з(ы)-с-мы́-ржə-уа
Sg.3.N.H/Pl.3-Sg.3.F-Rel	и-л-зы́-ржə-уа ‘(the one) who gives her something to drink’	и-л(ы)-з-мы́-ржə-уа

Other examples:

а́-рааӡа-ра ‘to make *sb* educate *sb*’ (cf. а́аӡа-ра ‘to bring up’): Fin. [aor.] д-и-ды́-рааӡе-ит / д-и-д-мы́-рааӡе-ит.

а́-рҧсах-ра ‘to lend’ (cf. а-ҧса́х-ра ‘to borrow’): Fin. [pres.] и-л-сы́-рҧсах-уе-ит, и-шə-сы́-рҧсах-уе-ит / и-л-сы́-рҧсах-уа-м (-ӡо-м), [aor.] и-л-сы́-рҧсах-ит / и-л(ы)-с-мы́-рҧсах-ит (-ӡе-ит); Non-fin. [pres.] (C1) и-л-сы́-рҧсах-уа / и-л(ы)-с-мы́-рҧсах-уа, (C2) и-з-сы́-рҧса́х-уа / и-з(ы)-с-мы́-рҧсах-уа, (C3) и-л-зы́-рҧсах-уа / и-л(ы)-з-мы́-рҧсах-уа, [aor.] (C1) и-л-сы́-рҧсах / и-л(ы)-с-мы́-рҧсах, (C2) и-з-сы́-рҧсах / и-з(ы)-с-мы́-рҧсах, (C3) и-л-зы́-рҧсах / и-л(ы)-з-мы́-рҧсах, [impf.] (C1) и-л-сы́-рҧсах-уа-з / и-л(ы)-с-мы́-рҧсах-уа-з, (C2) и-з-сы́-рҧсах-уа-з / и-з(ы)-с-мы́-рҧсах-уа-з, [past indef.] (C1) и-л-сы́-рҧсахы-з / и-л(ы)-с-мы́-рҧсахы-з, (C2) и-з-сы́-рҧсахы-з / и-з(ы)-с-мы́-рҧсахы-з, (C3) и-л-зы́-рҧсахы-з / и-л(ы)-з-мы́-рҧсахы-з.

а́-рҧхьа-ра ‘to make *sb* read *sth*; to teach’: Fin. [pres.] д-а-й-рҧхьо-ит / д-а-й-рҧхьо-м.

3.2.7.2.3. <u>AP c</u>

а-рбара́ /a-r-ba-rá/ ‘to show’ (cf. а-бара́ /a-ba-rá/ ‘to see’)

Finite forms

C1-C2-C3	<u>Affirmative</u>	<u>Negative</u>
Present		
Sg.3.N.H/Pl.3-Sg.3.F-Sg.1	и-л-сы-рбо́-ит	и-л-сы-рбо́-м (-рба-ӡо́-м)

	/jə-l-sə-r-ba-wá-jt'/	/jə-l-sə-r-ba-wá-m(-r-ba-ʒa-wá-m)/
	it/them(C1)-her(C2)-I(C3)-Caus+see-Dyn-Fin	
	'I show it/them to her'	'I do not show it/them to her'
Sg.3.N.H/Pl.3-Pl.1-Sg.3.F	и-аҳ-лы-рбó-ит	и-аҳ-лы-рбó-м (-рба-ӡó-м)
Sg.3.N.H/Pl.3-Sg.3.F-3.N.H	и-л-на-рбó-ит	и-л-на-рбó-м
Aorist		
Sg.3.N.H/Pl.3-Sg.3.F-Sg.1	и-л-сы-рбé-ит	и-л(ы)-с-мы-рбé-ит
Non-Finite forms		
Present		
Rel-Sg.3.F-Sg.1	и-л-сы-рбó	и-л-с-мы-рбó
	/jə-l-sə-rba-wá/	
	'which/whom I show to her'	
Sg.3.N.H/Pl.3-Rel-Sg.1	и-з-сы-рбó	и-з-с-мы-рбó
	/jə-z-sə-rba-wá/	
	'(the one) whom I show it/them to'	
Sg.3.N.H/Pl.3-Sg.3.F-Rel	и-л-зы-рбó	и-л-з-мы-рбó
	/jə-l-zə-rba-wá/	
	'(the one) who shows it/them to her'	
Past Indefinite		
Rel-Sg.3.F-Sg.1	и-л-сы-рбá-з	и-л-с-мы-рбá-з
Sg.3.N.H/Pl.3-Rel-Sg.1	и-з-сы-рбá-з	и-з-с-мы-рбá-з
Sg.3.N.H/Pl.3-Sg.3.F-Rel	и-л-зы-рбá-з	и-л-з-мы-рбá-з

Other examples:

а-рк-ра́ 'to hand' (cf. а-к-ра́ 'to catch'): Fin. [pres.] и-л-сы-рк-уé-ит / и-л-сы-рк-уá-м (-рк-ӡó-м), [aor.] и-л-сы-рк-и́т / и-л(ы)-с-мы-рк-и́т (-рк-ӡé-ит); Non-fin. [pres.] (C1) и-л-сы-рк-уа́ / и-л(ы)-с-мы-рк-уа́, (C2) и-з-сы-рк-уа́ / и-з(ы)-с-мы-рк-уа́, (C3) и-л-зы-рк-уа́ / и-л(ы)-з-мы-рк-уа́, [aor.] (C1) и-л-сы-ркы́ / и-л(ы)-с-мы-ркы́, (C2) и-з-сы-ркы́ / и-з(ы)-с-мы-ркы́, (C3) и-л-зы-ркы́ / и-л(ы)-з-мы-ркы́, [impf.] (C1) и-л-сы-рк-уá-з / и-л(ы)-с-мы-рк-уá-з, (C2) и-з-сы-рк-уá-з / и-з(ы)-с-мы-рк-уá-з, (C3) и-л-зы-рк-уá-з / и-л(ы)-з-мы-рк-уá-з, [past indef.] (C1) и-л-сы-ркы́-з / и-л(ы)-с-мы-ркы́-з, (C2) и-з-сы-ркы́-з / и-з(ы)-с-мы-ркы́-з, (C3) и-л-зы-ркы́-з / и-л(ы)-з-мы-ркы́-з; и-лы-рк-ны́ / и-л-мы-ркы́-кәа.

а-рҳа-ра́ 'to communicate; to make *sb* hear *sth*' (cf. а-ҳа-ра́ 'to hear'): Fin. [pres.] и-л-сы-рҳа-уé-ит / и-л-сы-рҳа-уá-м, [aor.] и-л-сы-рҳá-ит / и-л-с-мы-рҳá-ит; Non-fin. [pres.] (C1) и-л-сы-рҳа-уа́ / и-л-с-мы-рҳа-уа́, (C2) и-з-сы-рҳа-уа́ / и-з-с-мы-рҳа-уа́, (C3) и-л-зы-рҳа-уа́ / и-л-з-мы-рҳа-уа́.

а-рҵа-ра́ 'to teach' (cf. а-ҵа-ра́ 'to study, to learn'): Fin. [pres.] и-л-сы-рҵó-ит / и-л-сы-рҵó-м (-рҵа-ӡó-м), и-с-лы-рҵó-ит / и-с-лы-рҵó-м (-рҵа-ӡó-м), и-д-сы-рҵó-ит / и-д-сы-рҵó-м (-рҵа-ӡó-м), [aor.] д-лы-рҵé-ит *or* и-л-сы-рҵé-ит, и-а-сы-рҵé-ит, и-с-на-рҵé-ит / ды-л-мы-рҵé-ит *or* и-л-с-мы-рҵé-ит, и-а-с-мы-рҵé-ит, и-с-на-мы-рҵé-ит (-рҵа-ӡé-ит); Non-fin. [pres.] (C1) и-л-сы-рцó / и-л-с-мы-рцó, (C2) и-з-сы-рцó / и-з-с-мы-рцó, (C3) и-л-зы-рцó / и-л-з-мы-рцó, [aor.] (C1) и-л-сы-рцá / и-л-с-мы-рцá, (C2) и-з-сы-рцá / и-з-с-мы-рцá, (C3) и-л-зы-рцá / и-л-з-мы-рцá, [fut.1] (C1) и-л-сы-рца-рá / и-л-с-мы-рца-рá, (C2) и-з-сы-рца-рá / и-з-с-мы-рца-рá, (C3) и-л-зы-рца-рá / и-л-з-мы-рца-рá, [fut.2] (C1) и-л-сы-рцá-ша / и-л-с-мы-рцá-ша, (C2) и-з-сы-рцá-ша / и-з-с-мы-рцá-ша, (C3) и-л-зы-рцá-ша / и-л-з-мы-рцá-ша, [perf.] (C1) и-л-сы-рца-хьóу (-хьá(ц)) / и-л-с-мы-рца-хьóу (-хьá(ц)), (C2) и-з-сы-рца-хьóу (-хьá(ц)) / и-з-с-мы-рца-хьóу (-хьá(ц)), (C3) и-л-зы-рца-хьóу (-хьá(ц)) / и-л-з-мы-рца-хьóу (-хьá(ц)), [impf.] (C1) и-л-сы-рцó-з / и-л-с-мы-рцó-з, (C2) и-з-сы-рцó-з / и-з-с-мы-рцó-з, (C3) и-л-зы-рцó-з / и-л-з-мы-рцó-з, [past indef.] (C1) и-л-сы-рцá-з / и-л-с-мы-рцá-з, (C2) и-з-сы-рцá-з / и-з-с-мы-рцá-з, (C3) и-л-зы-рцá-з / и-л-з-мы-рцá-з, [cond.1] (C1) и-л-сы-рца-ры́-з / и-л-с-мы-рца-ры́-з, (C2) и-з-сы-рца-ры́-з / и-з-с-мы-рца-ры́-з, (C3) и-л-зы-рца-ры́-з / и-л-з-мы-рца-ры́-з, [cond.2] (C1) и-л-сы-рцá-ша-з / и-л-с-мы-рцá-ша-з, (C2) и-з-сы-рцá-ша-з / и-з-с-мы-рцá-ша-з, (C3) и-л-зы-рцá-ша-з / и-л-з-мы-рцá-ша-з, [plupf.] (C1) и-л-сы-рца-хьá-з / и-л-с-мы-рца-хьá-з, (C2) и-з-сы-рца-хьá-з / и-з-с-мы-рца-хьá-з, (C3) и-л-зы-рца-хьá-з / и-л-з-мы-рца-хьá-з.

а-ршəа-рá ‘to make pay (back)’ (cf. а-шəа-рá ‘to pay back’): Fin. [pres.] и-ах-ды-ршəó-ит / и-ах-ды-ршəó-м, [aor.] и-ах-ды-ршəé-ит / и-ха-д-мы-ршəé-ит; Non-fin. [pres.] (C1) и-л-сы-ршəó / и-л-с-мы-ршəó, (C2) и-з-сы-ршəó / и-з-с-мы-ршəó, и-л-зы-ршəó / и-л-з-мы-ршəó.

3.2.8. Class E

Class E verbs are those with a preverb before the verbal root and are intransitive verbs which place S in Column I. As previously discussed in the section on preverbs in §3.1.2.1, these Class E verbs are verbs that cannot insert any pronominal prefix before the preverb (in Spruit’s description, they are verbs that belong to Type C). Verbs that can insert a type of pronominal prefix before the preverb (verbs that belong to Type A and Type B in Spruit’s description) will be handled in the chapter on Class F verbs.

An example of a Class E verb is а-нхарá /a-n-xa-rá/ ‘to live’. This verb cannot take any pronominal prefix governed by the preverb н- /n/ ‘on’.[123]

(199) Уажəы́ сарá сынхóит Аҟəа.
/wažʷə́ sará sə-n-xa-wá-jt’ áq’ʷa/
now I I(C1)-Prev-live-Dyn-Fin Sukhum
‘I live in Sukhum now.’

(200) Тáмшьи Цыгъáрдеи инхóит. (*ирнхоит)
/támšʲə-j ǯʲgʲárda-j jə-n-xa-wá-jt’/ (*jə-r-n-xa-wa-jt’)
Tamsh-and Dzhgjarda-and they(C1)-Prev-live-Dyn-Fin (*they(C1)-them(C2)-Prev-live-Dyn-Fin)
‘They live in Tamsh and Dzhgjarda.’

In (199) and (200) above, pronominal prefixes agreeing with ‘Sukum’ and ‘Tamsh and Dzhgjarda’ cannot be inserted before the preverb (the absences of a third person plural prefix before a preverb in

123. However, there are also verbs which absolutely insert a Column II pronominal prefix before the preverb н- /n/. For example, а-нгы́лара /a-n-gə́la-ra/ ‘to stand on’: дангы́леит /d-a-n-gə́la-jt’/ ‘he/she stood on it’.

(200) shows that this verb is not Spruit's Type B verb). According to our informant, the form in (200), where a third-person plural marker р- /r/ is inserted, is ungrammatical. Also, the nouns in these sentences which indicate location also do not have postpositions indicating locatives. In Abkhaz, when nouns (here, place names) actively display locality, a locative postposition is not attached to the noun. This will be argued in detail in §5.6.3.

In describing Class E verbs (as well as Class F, G and H verbs), here we will not describe them with the accent paradigms used thus far. This is because verbs that have preverbs have derivative-form accents, and these accents must be examined independently.

3.2.8.1. Inflection of а-пхарá /a-n-xa-rá/ 'to live'

Finite forms

		Affirmative	Negative
Dynamic Group I			
Present			
Sg	1	сы-н-хó-ит /sə-n-xa-wá-jt'/ I(C1)-Prev-live-Dyn-Fin 'I live'	сы-н-хó-м /sə-n-xa-wá-m/
	2.M	у-н-хó-ит	у-н-хó-м
	2.F	бы-н-хó-ит	бы-н-хó-м
	3.Human	ды-н-хó-ит	ды-н-хó-м
	3.Non-Human	и-н-хó-ит	и-н-хó-м
Pl	1	ха-н-хó-ит	ха-н-хó-м
	2	шәы-н-хó-ит	шәы-н-хó-м
	3	и-н-хó-ит	и-н-хó-м
Aorist			
Sg	1	сы-н-хé-ит /sə-n-xá-jt'/	с-ны́-м-хе-ит /s-nə́-m-xa-jt'/
	2.M	у-н-хé-ит	у-ны́-м-хе-ит
	2.F	бы-н-хé-ит	б-ны́-м-хе-ит
	3.Human	ды-н-хé-ит	д-ны́-м-хе-ит
	3.Non-Human	и-н-хé-ит	и-ны́-м-хе-ит
Pl	1	ха-н-хé-ит	х-ны́-м-хе-ит
	2	шәы-н-хé-ит	шә-ны́-м-хе-ит
	3	и-н-хé-ит	и-ны́-м-хе-ит
Future I			
Sg	1	сы-н-хá-п	сы-н-ха-ры́-м
	2.M	у-н-хá-п	у-н-ха-ры́-м
	2.F	бы-н-хá-п	бы-н-ха-ры́-м
	3.Human	ды-н-хá-п	ды-н-ха-ры́-м
	3.Non-Human	и-н-хá-п	и-н-ха-ры́-м

Pl	1	ҳа-н-ха́-п	ҳа-н-ха-ры́-м
	2	шәы-н-ха́-п	шәы-н-ха-ры́-м
	3	и-н-ха́-п	и-н-ха-ры́-м

Future II

Sg	1	сы-н-ха́-шт	сы-н-ха́-ша-м
	2.M	у-н-ха́-шт	у-н-ха́-ша-м
	2.F	бы-н-ха́-шт	бы-н-ха́-ша-м
	3.Human	ды-н-ха́-шт	ды-н-ха́-ша-м
	3.Non-Human	и-н-ха́-шт	и-н-ха́-ша-м
Pl	1	ҳа-н-ха́-шт	ҳа-н-ха́-ша-м
	2	шәы-н-ха́-шт	шәы-н-ха́-ша-м
	3	и-н-ха́-шт	и-н-ха́-ша-м

Perfect

Sg	1	сы-н-ха-хьé-ит	с-ны́-м-ха-ц(т)
	2.M	у-н-ха-хьé-ит	у-ны́-м-ха-ц(т)
	2.F	бы-н-ха-хьé-ит	б-ны́-м-ха-ц(т)
	3.Human	ды-н-ха-хьé-ит	д-ны́-м-ха-ц(т)
	3.Non-Human	и-н-ха-хьé-ит	и-ны́-м-ха-ц(т)
Pl	1	ҳа-н-ха-хьé-ит	ҳ-ны́-м-ха-ц(т)
	2	шәы-н-ха-хьé-ит	шә-ны́-м-ха-ц(т)
	3	и-н-ха-хьé-ит	и-ны́-м-ха-ц(т)

Dynamic Group II
Imperfect

Sg	1	сы-н-хо́-н	сы-н-хо́-мы-зт
	2.M	у-н-хо́-н	у-н-хо́-мы-зт
	2.F	бы-н-хо́-н	бы-н-хо́-мы-зт
	3.Human	ды-н-хо́-н	ды-н-хо́-мы-зт
	3.Non-Human	и-н-хо́-н	и-н-хо́-мы-зт
Pl	1	ҳа-н-хо́-н	ҳа-н-хо́-мы-зт
	2	шәы-н-хо́-н	шәы-н-хо́-мы-зт
	3	и-н-хо́-н	и-н-хо́-мы-зт

Past Indefinite

Sg	1	сы-н-ха́-н	с-ны́-м-ха-зт
	2.M	у-н-ха́-н	у-ны́-м-ха-зт
	2.F	бы-н-ха́-н	б-ны́-м-ха-зт
	3.Human	ды-н-ха́-н	д-ны́-м-ха-зт
	3.Non-Human	и-н-ха́-н	и-ны́-м-ха-зт
Pl	1	ҳа-н-ха́-н	ҳ-ны́-м-ха-зт
	2	шәы-н-ха́-н	шә-ны́-м-ха-зт
	3	и-н-ха́-н	и-ны́-м-ха-зт

Conditional I

Sg	1	сы-н-ха-ры́-н	сы-н-ха-ры́-мы-зт
	2.M	у-н-ха-ры́-н	у-н-ха-ры́-мы-зт
	2.F	бы-н-ха-ры́-н	бы-н-ха-ры́-мы-зт
	3.Human	ды-н-ха-ры́-н	ды-н-ха-ры́-мы-зт
	3.Non-Human	и-н-ха-ры́-н	и-н-ха-ры́-мы-зт
Pl	1	ха-н-ха-ры́-н	ха-н-ха-ры́-мы-зт
	2	шәы-н-ха-ры́-н	шәы-н-ха-ры́-мы-зт
	3	и-н-ха-ры́-н	и-н-ха-ры́-мы-зт

Conditional II

Sg	1	сы-н-ха́-ша-н	сы-н-ха́-ша-мы-зт
	2.M	у-н-ха́-ша-н	у-н-ха́-ша-мы-зт
	2.F	бы-н-ха́-ша-н	бы-н-ха́-ша-мы-зт
	3.Human	ды-н-ха́-ша-н	ды-н-ха́-ша-мы-зт
	3.Non-Human	и-н-ха́-ша-н	и-н-ха́-ша-мы-зт
Pl	1	ха-н-ха́-ша-н	ха-н-ха́-ша-мы-зт
	2	шәы-н-ха́-ша-н	шәы-н-ха́-ша-мы-зт
	3	и-н-ха́-ша-н	и-н-ха́-ша-мы-зт

Pluperfect

Sg	1	сы-н-ха-хьа́-н	с-ны́-м-ха-цы-зт
	2.M	у-н-ха-хьа́-н	у-ны́-м-ха-цы-зт
	2.F	бы-н-ха-хьа́-н	б-ны́-м-ха-цы-зт
	3.Human	ды-н-ха-хьа́-н	д-ны́-м-ха-цы-зт
	3.Non-Human	и-н-ха-хьа́-н	и-ны́-м-ха-цы-зт
Pl	1	ха-н-ха-хьа́-н	ҳ-ны́-м-ха-цы-зт
	2	шәы-н-ха-хьа́-н	шә-ны́-м-ха-цы-зт
	3	и-н-ха-хьа́-н	и-ны́-м-ха-цы-зт

Non-Finite forms

	Affirmative	Negative
Dynamic Group I		
Present	и-н-хо́ /jə-n-xa-wá/ Rel(C1)-Prev-live-Dyn.NF '(the one) who lives'	и-ны́-м-хо
Aorist	и-н-ха́	и-ны́-м-ха
Future I	и-н-ха-ра́	и-ны́-м-ха-ра
Future II	и-н-ха́-ша	и-ны́-м-ха-ша
Perfect	и-н-ха-хьо́у (-хьа́(ц))	и-ны́-м-ха-хьоу (-хьа(ц))
Dynamic Group II		
Imperfect	и-н-хо́-з	и-ны́-м-хо-з

Past Indefinite	и-н-ха́-з	и-ны́-м-ха-з
Conditional I	и-н-ха-ры́-з	и-ны́-м-ха-ры-з
Conditional II	и-н-ха́-ша-з	и-ны́-м-ха-ша-з
Pluperfect	и-н-ха-хьа́-з	и-ны́-м-ха-хьа-з

Other examples:

Preverbs

-бна-:

а-бна́-ла-ра 'to hide (oneself)': Fin. [pres.] ды-бна́-ло-ит / ды-бна́-ло-м (-ла-ӡо-м), [aor.] ды-бна́-ле-ит / ды-бна́-м-ле-ит; Non-fin. [pres.] (C1) и-бна́-ло / и-бна́-м-ло, [aor.] (C1) и-бна́-ла / и-бна́-м-ла, [impf.] (C1) и-бна́-ло-з / и-бна́-м-ло-з, [past indef.] (C1) и-бна́-ла-з / и-бна́-м-ла-з.

аа-:

аа-гы́ла-ра 'to stop': Fin. [pres.] с-аа-гы́ло-ит / с-аа-гы́ло-м, [aor.] с-аа-гы́ле-ит / с-аа-м-гы́ле-ит; Non-fin. [pres.] (C1) и-аа-гы́ло / и-аа-м-гы́ло, [aor.] и-аа-гы́ла / и-аа-м-гы́ла, [impf.] и-аа-гы́ло-з / и-аа-м-гы́ло-з, [past indef.] и-аа-гы́ла-з / и-аа-м-гы́ла-з.

а́ан-гыла-ра (< а́а-н-гыла-ра Prev-Prev-R) 'to remain; to stop': Fin. [pres.] с-аан-гы́ло-ит / с-аан-гы́ло-м (-гы́ла-ӡо-м), [aor.] с-аан-гы́ле-ит / с-ааны́-м-гыле-ит (-гыла-ӡе-ит); Non-fin. [pres.] (C1) и-аа́н-гыло / и-ааны́-м-гыло, [aor.] и-аа́н-гыла / и-ааны́-м-гыла, [impf.] и-аа́н-гыло-з / и-ааны́-м-гыло-з, [past indef.] и-аа́н-гыла-з / и-ааны́-м-гыла-з.

бжьы-:

а-бжьы́-с-ра 'to go bad': Fin. [pres.] ды-бжьы́-с-уе-ит / ды-бжьы́-с-уа-м, и-бжьы́-с-уе-ит / и-бжьы́-с-уа-м, [aor.] ды-бжьы́-с-ит / ды-бжьы́-м-с-ит, [imper.] бы-бжьы́-с! / бы-бжьы́-м-сы-н!; Non-fin. [pres.] (C1) и-бжьы́-с-уа / и-бжьы́-м-с-уа, [aor.] (C1) и-бжьы́-с / и-бжьы́-м-с, [impf.] (C1) и-бжьы́-с-уа-з / и-бжьы́-м-с-уа-з, [past indef.] (C1) и-бжьы́-сы-з / и-бжьы́-м-сы-з. (cf. а-бжьы́-с-ра 'to go/pass between' (C1-C2-Prev-R): д-ры-бжьы́-с-уе-ит 'he is passing between them')

-гәар-:

а-гәа́р-ла-ра '(*of cattle*) to return home (from a pasture)': Fin. [pres.] и-гәа́р-ло-ит / и-гәа́р-ло-м, [aor.] и-гәа́р-ле-ит / и-гәа́ры-м-ле-ит; Non-fin. [pres.] (C1) и-гәа́р-ло / и-гәа́ры-м-ло.

а-гәа́р-ҵ-ра 'to go out to pasturage': Fin. [pres.] и-гәа́р-ҵ-уе-ит, х-гәа́р-ҵ-уе-ит / и-гәа́р-ҵ-уа-м (-ӡо-м), [aor.] и-гәа́р-ҵ-ит / и-гәа́ры-м-ҵ-ит (-ӡеит); Non-fin. [pres.] (C1) и-гәа́р-ҵ-уа / и-гәа́ры-м-ҵ-уа, [aor.] (C1) и-гәа́р-ҵ / и-гәа́ры-м-ҵ, [impf.] (C1) и-гәа́р-ҵ-уа-з / и-гәа́ры-м-ҵ-уа-з, [past indef.] (C1) и-гәа́р-ҵы-з / и-гәа́ры-м-ҵы-з.

-дәы́қә- (< дәы-қә- 'field-on'):

а-дәы́қә-ла-ра 'to set out, to depart': Fin. [pres.] д-дәы́қә-ло-ит / д-дәы́қә-ло-м, [aor.] д-дәы́қә-ле-ит / д-дәы́қә-м-ле-ит; Non-fin. (C1) [pres.] и-дәы́қә-ло / и-дәы́қә-м-ло, [aor.] и-дәы́қә-ла / и-дәы́қә-м-ла, [fut.1] и-дәы́қә-ла-ра / и-дәы́қә-м-ла-ра, [fut.2] и-дәы́қә-ла-ша / и-дәы́қә-м-ла-ша, [perf.] и-дәы́қә-ла-хьоу (-хьа(п)) / и-дәы́қә-м-ла-хьоу (-хьа(п)), [impf.] и-дәы́қә-ло-з / и-дәы́қә-м-ло-з, [past indef.] и-дәы́қә-ла-з / и-дәы́қә-м-ла-з, [cond.1] и-дәы́қә-ла-ры-з / и-дәы́қә-м-ла-ры-з, [cond.2] и-дәы́қә-ла-ша-з / и-дәы́қә-м-ла-ша-з, [plupf.] и-дәы́қә-ла-хьа-з / и-дәы́қә-м-ла-хьа-з.

-ка-:

а-ка-ҧса-ра́ 'to be scattered': Fin. [pres.] и-ка-ҧсо́-ит / и-ка-ҧсо́-м (*or* и-ка-ҧса-ӡо́-м), [aor.] и-ка-ҧсе́-ит / и-ка́-м-ҧсе-ит (и-ка́-м-ҧса-ӡе-ит); Non-fin. (C1) [pres.] и-ка-ҧсо́ / и-ка́-м-ҧсо, [aor.] и-ка-ҧса́ / и-ка́-м-ҧса, [impf.] и-ка-ҧсо́-з / и-ка́-м-ҧсо-з, [past indef.] и-ка-ҧса́-з / и-ка́-м-ҧса-з.

а-ка́-ҳа-ра 'to fall': Fin. [pres.] д-ка́-ҳа-уе-ит / д-ка́-ҳа-уа-м, [aor.] д-ка́-ҳа-ит / д-ка́-м-ҳа-ит *(preferred) or* ды-м-ка́-ҳа-ит, [fut.1] д-ка́-ҳа-п / д-ка́-ҳа-рым, [fut.2] д-ка́-ҳа-шт / д-ка́-ҳа-шам, [perf.] д-ка́-ҳа-хьеит / ды-м-ка́-ҳа-ц(т), [impf.] д-ка́-ҳа-уа-н / д-ка-ҳа-уа́-мызт, [past indef.] д-ка́-ҳа-н / --, [cond.1] д-ка́-ҳа-рын / д-ка-ҳа-ры́мызт, [cond.2] д-ка́-ҳа-шан / д-ка́-ҳа-шамызт, [plupf.] д-ка́-ҳа-хьан / ды-м-ка́-ҳа-цызт; Non-fin. (C1) [pres.] и-ка́-ҳа-уа / и-ка́-м-ҳа-уа *or* и-м-ка́-ҳа-уа, [aor.] и-ка́-ҳа / и-ка́-м-ҳа, [fut.1] и-ка́-ҳа-ра / и-ка́-м-ҳа-ра, [fut.2] и-ка́-ҳа-ша / и-ка́-м-ҳа-ша, [perf.] и-ка́-ҳа-хьоу (-хьа(ц)) / и-ка́-м-ҳа-хьоу (-хьа(ц)), [impf.] и-ка́-ҳа-уа-з / и-ка́-м-ҳа-уа-з, [past indef.] и-ка́-ҳа-з / и-ка́-м-ҳа-з, [cond.1] и-ка́-ҳа-ры-з / и-ка́-м-ҳа-ры-з, [cond.2] и-ка́-ҳа-ша-з / и-ка́-м-ҳа-ша-з, [plupf.] и-ка́-ҳа-хьа-з / и-ка́-м-ҳа-хьа-з.

а-ка-шәа-ра́ 'to fall': Fin. [pres.] и-ка-шәо́-ит / и-ка-шәо́-м, [aor.] и-ка-шәе́-ит / и-ка́-м-шәе-ит; Non-fin. (C1) [pres.] и-ка-шәо́ / и-ка́-м-шәо, [aor.] и-ка-шәа́ / и-ка́-м-шәа, [impf.] и-ка-шәо́-з / и-ка́-м-шәо-з, [past indef.] и-ка-шәа́-з / и-ка́-м-шәа-з.

-ҟа-:

а́-ҟа-ла-ра 'to become; to happen': Fin. [pres.] д-ҟа-ло́-ит / д-ҟа-ло́-м (-ла-ӡо́-м), [aor.] д-ҟа-ле́-ит / д-ҟа-м-ле́-ит (-ла-ӡе́-ит), [imper.] б-ҟа-ла́! / б-ҟа-м-ла́-н!, шә-ҟа-ла́! / шә-ҟа-м-ла́-н!, [vers.1] и-а-зы́-ҟа-ле-ит, [subj.] б-ҟа-ла́-аит; Non-fin. (C1) [pres.] и́-ҟа-ло / и́-ҟа-м-ло, [aor.] и́-ҟа-ла / и́-ҟа-м-ла, [impf.] и́-ҟа-ло-з / и́-ҟа-м-ло-з, [past indef.] и́-ҟа-ла-з / и́-ҟа-м-ла-з.

-лбаа-:

а́-лбаа-ҧа-ра 'to jump down': Fin. [pres.] ды-лбаа-ҧо-ит / ды-лба́а-ҧо-м, [aor.] ды-лба́а-ҧе-ит / ды-лба́а-м-ҧе-ит, [imper.] бы-лба́а-ҧа! / бы-лба́а-м-ҧа-н!; Non-fin. [pres.] (C1) и-лба́а-ҧо / и-лба́а-м-ҧо.

а́-лбаа-ҧш-ра 'to look down': Fin. [pres.] ды-лбаа-ҧш-уе́-ит / ды-лбаа-ҧш-уа́-м (-ҧш-ӡо́-м), [aor.] ды-лба́а-ҧш-и́т / ды-лба́а-м-ҧш-ит (-ҧш-ӡе-ит); Non-fin. (C1) [pres.] и́-лба́а-ҧш-уа / и́-лба́а-м-ҧш-уа, [aor.] и́-лба́а-ҧш / и́-лба́а-м-ҧш, [impf.] и́-лбаа-ҧш-уа-з / и́-лбаа-м-ҧш-уа-з, [past indef.] и́-лбаа-ҧшы-з / и́-лбаа-м-ҧшы-з.

-мҩа-:

а́-мҩа-с-ра 'to pass by, to go through': Fin. [pres.] ды-мҩа́-с-уе-ит / ды-мҩа́-с-уа-м, [aor.] ды-мҩа́-с-ит / ды-мҩа́-м-с-ит; Non-fin. [pres.] (C1) и-мҩа́-с-уа / и-мҩа́-м-с-уа, [aor.] (C1) и-мҩа́-с / и-мҩа́-м-с.

-на-:

а-на́-гәа-ра 'to push thither': Fin. [pres.] с-на́-гәо-ит / с-на́-гәо-м, [aor.] с-на́-гәе-ит / с-на́-м-гәе-ит; Non-fin. [pres.] (C1) и-на́-гәо / и-на́-м-гәо.

а́-на-ӡа-ра 'to arrive at': Fin. [pres.] д-на-ӡо́-ит / д-на-ӡо́-м, [aor.] д-на-ӡе́-ит / д-на-м-ӡе́-ит *or* д-м-на-ӡе́-ит; Non-fin. (C1) [pres.] и́-на-ӡо / и́-на-м-ӡо, [aor.] и́-на-ӡа (*or* и-на-ӡа́) / и́-на-м-ӡа, [impf.] и́-на-ӡо-з / и́-на-м-ӡо-з, [past indef.] и́-на-ӡа-з / и́-на-м-ӡа-з.

а́-на-ԥш-ра 'to look thither': Fin. [pres.] д-на-ԥш-уе́-ит / д-на-ԥш-уа́-м, [aor.] д-на-ԥш-и́т / д-на-м-ԥш-и́т *or* д-м-на-ԥш-и́т; Non-fin. (C1) [pres.] и́-на-ԥш-уа / и́-на-м-ԥш-уа *or* и́-м-на-ԥш-уа, [aor.] и́-на-ԥш / и́-на-м-ԥш, [impf.] и́-на-ԥш-уа-з / и́-на-м-ԥш-уа-з, [past indef.] и́-на-ԥшы-з / и́-на-м-ԥшы-з.

а́-на-ҳә-ра 'to turn thither': Fin. [aor.] д-на-ҳә-и́т / д-на-м-ҳә-и́т *or* д-м-на-ҳә-и́т; Non-fin. (C1) [pres.] и́-на-ҳә-уа / и́-на-м-ҳә-уа *or* и́-м-на-ҳә-уа, [aor.] и́-на-ҳә / и́-на-м-ҳә *or* и́-м-на-ҳә, [impf.] и́-на-ҳә-уа-з / и́-на-м-ҳә-уа-з *or* и́-м-на-ҳә-уа-з, [past indef.] и́-на-ҳәы-з / и́-на-м-ҳәы-з *or* и́-м-на-ҳәы-з.

а-на́-ҩ-ра 'to reach there': Fin. [pres.] и-на́-ҩ-уе-ит / и-на́-ҩ-уа-м, [aor.] и-на́-ҩ-ит / и-на́-м-ҩ-ит *or* и-м-на́-ҩ-ит; Non-fin. (C1) [pres.] и-на́-ҩ-уа / и-на́-м-ҩ-уа, [aor.] и-на́-ҩ / и-на́-м-ҩ, [impf.] и-на́-ҩ-уа-з / и-на́-м-ҩ-уа-з, [past indef.] и-на́-ҩы-з / и-на́-м-ҩы-з.

-х-:

а-х-т-ра́ 'to open': Fin. [pres.] и-х-т-уе́-ит / и-х-т-уа́-м, [aor.] и-х-т-и́т / и-хы́-м-т-ит; Non-fin. [pres.] (C1) и-х-т-уа́ / и-хы́-м-т-уа, [aor.] (C1) и-х-ты́ / и-хы́-м-т.

-шьҭа-:

а-шьҭа́-ла-ра 'to lie (down)': Fin. [aor.] сы-шьҭа́-ле-ит (-ла-ӡо-м) / сы-шьҭа́-л-т, ды-шьҭа́-ле-ит / д-шьҭа́-м-ле-ит *or* д-мы-шьҭа́-ле-ит, [perf.] ды-шьҭа́-ла-хье-ит; Non-fin. (C1) [pres.] и-шьҭа́-ло / и-шьҭа́-м-ло (*or* и-мы-шьҭа́-ло), [aor.] и-шьҭа́-ла / и-шьҭа́-м-ла, [impf.] и-шьҭа́-ло-з / и-шьҭа́-м-ло-з, [past indef.] и-шьҭа́-ла-з / и-шьҭа́-м-ла-з.

3.2.9. Class F

Class F verbs are two-place intransitive verbs that have preverbs. The distribution of the pronominal prefixes is in Column I for pronominal prefix which indicates S and in Column II for pronominal prefix which indicates IO. This preverb governs the Column II pronominal prefix. The normal morpheme arrangement order for this type of verb is 'S+IO+Prev+R'. For example: а́-хәаԥшра /á-x^{w}a-pš-ra/ 'to watch, to look at':

(201) Ателеви́зор ҳа́хәаԥшуеит.
/a-t'elevə́jzor ħ-á-x^{w}a-pš-wa-jt'/
the-television we(C1)-it(C2)-Prev-look-Dyn-Fin
'We are watching television.'

However, as an exception, there are some verbs that become 'S+Prev+IO+R'. For example, аа́ԥхьара /aá-px^{j}a-ra/ 'to summon':[124]

124. This verb becomes a transitive verb by changing its accent pattern: аа́ԥхьара /aá-px^{j}a-ra/'to invite':
Ҳара́ уаха́ аҩны́ҟа шәаа́ҳаԥхьоит. (IC)
/ħará waxá a-j^{w}nə́-q'a š^w-aá-ħa-px^{j}a-wa-jt'/

(202) Ачы́мазаҩ иа́хь аҳақьы́м саайҧхьеит.
/a-čʲə́mazajʷ j-axʲ a-ħakʲə́m s-aa-jə́-pxʲa-jt'/
the-sick person his-to the-doctor I(C1)-Prev-him(C2)-call-(Aor)-Fin
'I summoned the doctor to see the sick person.'

There are very few verbs which take this arrangement pattern, and here are examples: ана́хара /a-ná-xa-ra/ 'to move': сналы́хоит /s-na-lə́-xa-wa-jt'/ 'I will move her', ана́цхара /a-ná-cħa-ra/ 'to bite': сналы́цхауеит /s-na-lə́-cħa-wa-jt'/ 'I am biting her', аҩа́хара /a-jʷá-xa-ra/ 'to raise': сҩалы́хеит /s-jʷa-lə́-xa-jt'/ 'I raised her'.

As already discussed in §3.1.2.1, Spruit classifies preverbs as 1 the relational preverbs а- /a/, аи /aj/, хәа- /xʷa/, 2 the directional preverbs аа- /aa/ 'hither', на- /na/ 'thither', ла- /la/ 'downwards', ҩа- /jʷa/ 'upwards', and 3 the local preverbs. The preverbs related to Class F verbs that we are now looking at are the preverbs in 1 and 3.

3.2.9.1. In 1 above, the roots that attach to relational preverbs а-, аи-, хәа- are limited, and there are the following in Class F verbs. Examples display the aorist form:[125]

Preverb а-:

а́-бжьара /á-bžʲa-ra/ 'to advise': сба́бжьеит /s-b-á-bžʲa-jt'/ [I(C1)-you.F(C2)-Prev-advise-(Aor)-Fin] 'I advised you-F', а́-цлабра /á-clab-ra/ 'to to compete with': сба́цлабит /s-b-á-clabə-jt'/ 'I competed with you-F', а́-цәхара /á-cʷħa-ra/ 'to scold, to swear at': сба́цәхаит /s-b-á-cʷħa-jt'/ 'I scolded you-F', а́-цәажәара /á-cʷažʷa-ra/ 'to speak to, to talk with': сба́цәажәеит /s-b-á-cʷažʷa-jt'/ 'I spoke to you-F', а-хара́ /a-ħa-rá/ 'to hear, to be audible': исаха́ит /j-s-a-ħá-jt'/ 'I heard it/them', lit. 'it/they was/were audible to me', а-хәытхәы́тра /a-xʷətxʷə́t-ra/ 'to whisper to *sb*': сба́хәытхәытит /s-b-á-xʷətxʷətə-jt'/ 'I whispered to you-F', а́-лацәҟәысра /á-lacʷq'ʷəs-ra/ 'to wink at': сла́лацәҟәысит /s-l-á-lacʷq'ʷəsə-jt'/ 'I winked at her', а́-ҭәара /á-tʷa-ra/ 'to correspond': иса́ҭәоуп /jə-s-á-tʷa-wp'/ 'it suits me'.

Examples where there are two preverbs: а́-шьапкра /á-šʲa-p'k'-ra/ 'to pray to': сба́шьапкит /s-b-á-šʲa-p'k'ə-jt'/ [I(C1)-you-F(C2)-Prev-Prev-pray-(Aor)-Fin] 'I prayed to you-F', а́-қәҧара /á-kʷ-pa-ra/ 'to fight against': хиа́қәҧеит /ħ-j-á-kʷ-pa-jt'/ 'we fought against him', а́-макарра /á-ma-kar-ra/ 'to threaten': сба́макарит /s-b-á-ma-karə-jt'/ 'I threatened you-F', а-ҧы́зара /a-pə́-za-ra/ 'to lead': сбаҧы́зеит /s-b-a-pə́-za-jt'/ 'I led you-F', а́-ҩ(ы)сра /á-jʷ(ə)-s-ra/ 'to pass by': диа́ҩсит /d-j-á-jʷ-sə-jt'/ 'he/she passed by him'.

Preverb аи- /aj/:

we this evening the-house-to you.Pl(C1)-Prev-we(C3)-invite-Dyn-Fin
'We invite you-Pl to our house this evening'.
For detailed discussion see Hewitt (2008b: 78).

125. Take note of the fact that the distribution position of the negative marker м- in the aorist negative form differs from verbs which have the preverbs а-, аи- and verbs that have the preverb хәа-. In the former, the negative marker is placed directly before the preverb, while in the latter, it is placed directly after the preverb: сыбма́цәхаит /sə-b-m-á-cʷħa-jt'/ 'I did not scold you-F', исме́ишит /jə-s-m-áj-šə-jt'/ 'it/they did not bark at me' vs. сбы́хәамҧшит /s-bə́-xʷa-m-pšə-jt'/ 'I did not look at you-F'.

áишра /áj-š-ra/ 'to bark at': исéишит /jə-s-áj-šə-jt'/ 'it/they barked at me', áихсра /áj-xs-ra/ 'to shoot at': дсéихсит /d-s-áj-xsə-jt'/ 'he/she shot at me', áипҳхызра /áj-pxəʒ-ra/ 'to dream of': сбéипҳхызит /s-b-áj-pxəʒə-jt'/ 'I dreamed of you-F', áисра /áj-s-ra/ 'to quarrel with': сбéисит /s-b-áj-sə-jt'/ 'I quarreled with you-F', áиканра /áj-k'an-ra/ 'to compete with': сбéиканит /s-b-áj-k'anə-jt'/ 'I competed with you-F'.

Preverb хәа- /xʷa/:

á-хәапҳшра /á-xʷa-pš-ra/ 'to watch, to look at': сбы́хәапҳшит /s-bə́-xʷa-pšə-jt'/ 'I looked at you-F', á-хәаччара /á-xʷa-čʲčʲa-ra/ 'to smile at': сбы́хәаччеит /s-bə́-xʷa-čʲčʲa-jt'/ 'I smiled at you-F'.

These relational preverbs manifest all of the Column II pronominal prefixes they govern in the same way as the Type A local preverbs handled in §3.2.9.2. For example: á-хәа-пҳш-ра /á-xʷa-pš-ra/ 'to watch, to look at': сбы́хәапҳшуеит /s-bə́-xʷa-pš-wa-jt'/ [I(C1)-you.F(C2)-Prev-look-Dyn-Fin] 'I am looking at you-F'. сýхәапҳшуеит /s-wə́-xʷa-pš-wa-jt'/, с-и́-хәа-пҳш-уе-ит, с-лы́-хәа-пҳш-уе-ит, с-á-хәа-пҳш-уе-ит, с-шәы́-хәа-пҳш-уе-ит, с-ры́-хәа-пҳш-уе-ит, у-сы́-хәа-пҳш-уе-ит, у-хá-хәа-пҳш-уе-ит, ды-з-хәа-пҳш-уá [(s)he(C1)-Rel(C2)-Prev-look-Dyn.NF] 'which he/she is looking at'.

3.2.9.2. As already discussed in §3.1.2.1, according to Spruit (1983: 61) the type of Column II pronominal prefix governed by local preverbs appears to be as follows (the Type C among these has been described as Class E verbs (e.g. а-нхарá /a-n-xa-rá/ 'to live') in our classification):

	A	B	C
1 sg.	s-	-	-
3 sg. irr.[126]	a-	(ø-)	-
3 pl.	r-	(r-)	-
rel.	z-	(z-)	-

Type A indicates that every person and class prefix appears before a preverb. For example, in the verb á-ватәара /á-va-t'ʷa-ra/ 'to sit down next to', which has the preverb ва- /va/ 'next to' that is considered by Spruit to be Type A, all of the Column II prefixes appear as seen in the following (а- in 3 sg. non-human): дсы́ватәоит /d-sə́-va-t'ʷa-wa-jt'/ [he/she(C1)-me(C2)-Prev-sit-Dyn-Fin] 'he/she sits down next me', дбы́ватәоит /d-bə́-va-t'ʷa-wa-jt'/, длы́ватәоит /d-lə́-va-t'ʷa-wa-jt'/, дáватәоит /d-á-va-t'ʷa-wa-jt'/, дҳáватәоит /d-ħá-va-t'ʷa-wa-jt'/, дшәы́ватәоит /d-šʷə́-va-t'ʷa-wa-jt'/, дры́ватәоит /d-rə́-va-t'ʷa-wa-jt'/. In contrast to this, for Type B, the third-person singular non-human pronominal prefix а- does not appear. For example, in the verb а-кы́лсра /a-k'ə́l-s-ra/ 'to go through', which has the preverb кыл /k'əl/ 'through' that is considered by Spruit to be Type B, the third-person singular non-human pronominal prefix in Column II has a zero-prefix as seen in the following:

(203) Афлы́ка аӡы́ кы́лст.

a-flə́k'a a-ʒə́ ø-ø-k'ə́l-s[ə-j]t'

the-boat the-water [it(water,C1)-it(the boat, C2)-]Prev-go through-(Aor)-Fin

126. Take note that in this study we express Spruit' '3 sg. irr(ational)' as '3 sg. non-human'.

'Water seeped into the boat.'

Moreover, the same one preverb can take both Type A and Type B. Spruit (ibid.: 67) gives the preverb кә- /kʷ/ 'on' as an example. His example sentence is as follows:

(204) Type A: a-xə́za ø-sə́-kʷə-ø-w-p' 'the blanket is on me'[127]

a-xáħʷ ø-sə́-kʷ-ħa-jt' 'the stone fell on me'

(205) Type B: a-st'ól, s-gʷə́ j-øə́-kʷə-ø-w-p' 'it is on the table, my breast'

Spruit explains the difference between Type A and Type B for them in the following way:

> The difference between type A and type B of the P's (i.e. the local preverbs) kʷ- and c'(a)- may be described as 'effective local' vs. 'plain local', compare the following examples:
> a-wardə́n d-á-kʷə-ø-w-p' 'he is on the cart (and ready for transportation)'
> vs. á-mjʷa d-øə́-kʷə-ø-w-p' 'he is on the road'. (Spruit ibid.: 71)

This observation by Spruit is extremely thought-provoking. We will take a look at this from our own data. For example, Type A and Type B sentences with the verb á-кә-тәа-ра /á-kʷ-t'ʷa-ra/ 'to sit down on' are as follows:

Type A:

(206) Аҽы́ да́кәтәеит.
/a-čə́ d-á-kʷ-t'ʷa-jt'/ 'He/She mounted the horse.'

(207) Ауарды́н да́кәымтәаӡеит.
/a-wardə́n d-á-kʷə-m-t'ʷa-ʒa-jt'/ 'He/She did not get on the (ox-)cart.'

Type B:

(208) Аҟәа́рдә ды́кәтәеит.
/a-q'ʷárdʷ d-øə́-kʷ-t'ʷa-jt'/ 'He/She sat down on the chair.'

(209) Акды́ ды́кәтәеит.
/a-kdə́ d-øə́-kʷ-t'ʷa-jt'/ 'He/She sat down on the log.'

Between (206) above of Type A and (208) above of Type B, is it possible to observe a difference between the 'effective local' and the 'plain local'?[128] Also see examples (227)–(231) in §3.2.11.2.

Moreover, let us take up the verb á-кәхара /á-kʷ-ħa-ra/ 'to fall on', which displays a mixed form of

---

127. ø-sə́-kʷə-ø-w-p' ([it(the blanket, C1)]-me(C2)-Prev-be-Stat.-Fin). Spruit considers the stem кә(ы)- /kʷ(ə)/ of a stative verb like áкәзаара 'to exist on a surface' as 'preverb kʷə- + copula ø-'. This idea of his is insightful. If we follow this line of thought, stative verbs whose stem is formed from a noun or adjective, etc. such as сушы́зоуп 'I am your-M friend', which we have already examined, will have to be recognized as zero-copula: сушы́зоуп < sə-w-jʷə́za-ø-w-p' [I-your-friend-copula-Stat.Pres-Fin].

128. Regarding this, Hewitt (1979c: 210–211) also makes the following statement: 'The following pair of sentences where the use or non-use of this pronominal affix with one and the same preverb is apparently determined solely by the difference in the noun representing the direct object:

a-xaħʷ á-šaq'a jə́-kʷə-j-c'e-jt' 'He put the stone on the pillar.'

vs. a-xaħʷcʷ'áħʷ á-šaq'a j-á-kʷə-j-c'e-jt' 'He put the beam on the pillar.'

Type A and Type B:

(210) дсы́кәҳаит
/d-sə́-kʷ-ħa-jt'/
he/she-me-Prev(on)-fall-(Aor)-Fin
'He/She fell on me.'

(211) Ахәычы́ аҕәра́ ды́кәҳаит.
/a-xʷəč'ʲə́ a-ɣʷrá d-ǿə-kʷ-ħa-jt'/
the-child the-floor he(C1)-it(C2)-Prev-fall-(Aor)-Fin
'The child fell on the floor.'

(212) Акаранда́шькәа асто́лқәа ирықәҳаит.
/a-k'arandášʲ-kʷa a-st'ól-kʷa jə-rə́-kʷ-ħa-jt'/
the-pencil-Pl the-table-Pl they(= pencils, C1)-them(= tables, C2)-Prev-fall-(Aor)-Fin
'The pencils fell on the tables.'

In this way, the problem of the local preverbs and the pronominal prefixes they govern demonstrates a complex form. Below, when describing the inflection of intransitive verbs with local preverbs, our description will center on the Type A and Type B third person singular and plural.

3.2.9.3. Inflection with a relational preverb

3.2.9.3.1. á-хәаԥшра /á-xʷa-pš-ra/ 'to look at'

Finite forms

	Affirmative	Negative
Dynamic Group I		
C1-C2-		
Present		
1Sg.-2F.Sg	с-бы́-хәа-ԥш-уе-ит /s-bə́-xʷa-pš-wa-jt'/ I(C1)-you.F(C2)-Prev-look at-Dyn-Fin 'I am looking at you-F'	с-бы́-хәа-ԥш-уа-м
1Sg-2M.Sg	с-у́-хәа-ԥш-уе-ит	с-у́-хәа-ԥш-уа-м
1Sg-3M.Sg	с-и́-хәа-ԥш-уе-ит	с-и́-хәа-ԥш-уа-м
1Sg-3F.Sg	с-лы́-хәа-ԥш-уе-ит	с-лы́-хәа-ԥш-уа-м
1Sg-3Non-Hum.Sg	с-á-хәа-ԥш-уе-ит	с-á-хәа-ԥш-уа-м
1Sg-2Pl	с-шәы́-хәа-ԥш-уе-ит	с-шәы́-хәа-ԥш-уа-м
1Sg-3Pl	с-ры́-хәа-ԥш-уе-ит	с-ры́-хәа-ԥш-уа-м
2F.Sg-1Pl	б-ҳá-хәа-ԥш-уе-ит	б-ҳá-хәа-ԥш-уа-м
3Hum.Sg-1Sg	д-сы́-хәа-ԥш-уе-ит	д-сы́-хәа-ԥш-уа-м
3Non-Hum.Sg/3Pl-1Sg	и-сы́-хәа-ԥш-уе-ит	и-сы́-хәа-ԥш-уа-м
3N.H.Sg/3Pl-3N.H.Sg	и́-хәа-ԥш-уе-ит (< и-и́-хәа-ԥш-уе-ит)	и́-хәа-ԥш-уа-м
1Pl-3 Pl	ҳ-ры́-хәа-ԥш-уе-ит	ҳ-ры́-хәа-ԥш-уа-м
2Pl-1 Pl	шә-ҳá-хәа-ԥш-уе-ит	шә-ҳá-хәа-ԥш-уа-м

Aorist		
1Sg.-2F.Sg	с-бы́-хәа-ҧш-ит	с-бы́-хәа-м-ҧш-ит
1Sg.-2M.Sg	с-у́-хәа-ҧш-ит	с-у́-хәа-м-ҧш-ит
1Sg.-3M.Sg	с-и́-хәа-ҧш-ит	с-и́-хәа-м-ҧш-ит
1Sg.-3F.Sg	с-лы́-хәа-ҧш-ит	с-лы́-хәа-м-ҧш-ит
1Sg.-3Non-Hum.Sg	с-а́-хәа-ҧш-ит	с-а́-хәа-м-ҧш-ит
1Sg.-2Pl	с-шәы́-хәа-ҧш-ит	с-шәы́-хәа-м-ҧш-ит
1Sg.-3Pl	с-ры́-хәа-ҧш-ит	с-ры́-хәа-м-ҧш-ит
Future I		
1Sg.-2F.Sg	с-бы́-хәа-ҧшы-п	с-бы́-хәа-ҧш-ры-м
Future II		
1Sg.-2F.Sg	с-бы́-хәа-ҧшы-шт	с-бы́-хәа-ҧш-ша-м
Perfect		
1Sg.-2F.Sg	с-бы́-хәа-ҧш-хьеит	с-бы́-хәа-м-ҧшы-ц(т)
Dynamic Group II		
Imperfect		
1Sg.-2F.Sg	с-бы́-хәа-ҧш-уа-н	с-бы́-хәа-ҧш-уа-мы-зт
Past Indefinite		
1Sg.-2F.Sg	с-бы́-хәа-ҧшы-н	с-бы́-хәа-м-ҧшы-зт
Conditional I		
1Sg.-2F.Sg	с-бы́-хәа-ҧш-ры-н	с-бы́-хәа-ҧш-ры-мы-зт
Conditional II		
1Sg.-2F.Sg	с-бы́-хәа-ҧш-ша-н	с-бы́-хәа-ҧш-ша-мы-зт
Pluperfect		
1Sg.-2F.Sg	с-бы́-хәа-ҧш-хьа-н	с-бы́-хәа-м-ҧшы-цы-зт

Non-Finite forms

	Affirmative	Negative
Dynamic Group I		
C1-C2-		
Present		
Rel-1Sg	и-сы́-хәа-ҧш-уа /jə-sə́-xʷa-pš-wa/ Rel(C1)-me(C2)-Pev-look at-Dyn.NF '(the one) who is looking at me'	и-сы́-хәа-м-ҧш-уа
Rel-2F.Sg	и-бы́-хәа-ҧш-уа	и-бы́-хәа-м-ҧш-уа
Rel-2M.Sg	и-у́-хәа-ҧш-уа	и-у́-хәа-м-ҧш-уа
Rel-3M.Sg	и́-хәа-ҧш-уа (< и-и́-хәа-ҧш-уа)	и́-хәа-м-ҧш-уа
Rel-3F.Sg	и-лы́-хәа-ҧш-уа	и-лы́-хәа-м-ҧш-уа
Rel-3Non-Hum.Sg	и-а́-хәа-ҧш-уа	и-а́-хәа-м-ҧш-уа
Rel-1Pl	и-ха́-хәа-ҧш-уа	и-ха́-хәа-м-ҧш-уа
Rel-2Pl	и-шәы́-хәа-ҧш-уа	и-шәы́-хәа-м-ҧш-уа

Rel-3Pl	и-ры́-хәа-ҧш-уа	и-ры́-хәа-м-ҧш-уа
1Sg-Rel	сы-з-хәа-ҧш-уа́	сы-з-хәа́-м-ҧш-уа
	/sə-z-xʷa-pš-wá/	
	I(C1)-Rel(C2)-Prev-look at-Dyn.NF	
	'(the one) whom I am looking at'	
2F.Sg-Rel	бы-з-хәа-ҧш-уа́	бы-з-хәа́-м-ҧш-уа
2M.Sg-Rel	у-з-хәа-ҧш-уа́	у-з-хәа́-м-ҧш-уа
3Human.Sg-Rel	ды-з-хәа-ҧш-уа́	ды-з-хәа́-м-ҧш-уа
3N.H.Sg/3Pl-Rel	и-з-хәа-ҧш-уа́	и-з-хәа́-м-ҧш-уа
1Pl-Rel	ха-з-хәа-ҧш-уа́	ха-з-хәа́-м-ҧш-уа
2Pl-Rel	шәы-з-хәа-ҧш-уа́	шәы-з-хәа́-м-ҧш-уа
Aorist		
Rel-3F.Sg	и-лы́-хәа-ҧш	и-лы́-хәа-м-ҧш
3Human.Sg-Rel	ды-з-хәа-ҧшы́	ды-з-хәа́-м-ҧш
Future I		
Rel-3F.Sg	и-лы́-хәа-ҧш-ра	и-лы́-хәа-м-ҧш-ра
3Human.Sg-Rel	ды-з-хәа-ҧш-ра́	ды-з-хәа́-м-ҧш-ра
Future II		
Rel-3F.Sg	и-лы́-хәа-ҧш-ша	и-лы́-хәа-м-ҧш-ша
3Human.Sg-Rel	ды-з-хәа-ҧшы́-ша	ды-з-хәа́-м-ҧшы-ша
Perfect		
Rel-3F.Sg	и-лы́-хәа-ҧш-хьо-у (-хьа(-ц))	и-лы́-хәа-м-ҧш-хьо-у (-хьа(-ц))
3Human.Sg-Rel	ды-з-хәа-ҧш-хьо́-у (-хьа́(-ц))	ды-з-хәа́-м-ҧш-хьо-у (-хьа(-ц))
Dynamic Group II		
Imperfect		
Rel-3F.Sg	и-лы́-хәа-ҧш-уа-з	и-лы́-хәа-м-ҧш-уа-з
3Human.Sg-Rel	ды-з-хәа-ҧш-уа́-з	ды-з-хәа́-м-ҧш-уа-з
Past Indefinite		
Rel-3F.Sg	и-лы́-хәа-ҧшы-з	и-лы́-хәа-м-ҧшы-з
3Human.Sg-Rel	ды-з-хәа-ҧшы́-з	ды-з-хәа́-м-ҧшы-з
Conditional I		
Rel-3F.Sg	и-лы́-хәа-ҧш-ры-з	и-лы́-хәа-м-ҧш-ры-з
3Human.Sg-Rel	ды-з-хәа-ҧш-ры́-з	ды-з-хәа́-м-ҧш-ры-з
Conditional II		
Rel-3F.Sg	и-лы́-хәа-ҧшы-ша-з	и-лы́-хәа-м-ҧшы-ша-з
3Human.Sg-Rel	ды-з-хәа-ҧшы́-ша-з	ды-з-хәа́-м-ҧшы-ша-з

Pluperfect		
Rel-3F.Sg	и-лы́-хәа-ҧш-хьа-з	и-лы́-хәа-м-ҧш-хьа-з
3Human.Sg-Rel	ды-з-хәа-ҧш-хьа́-з	ды-з-хәа́-м-ҧш-хьа-з

3.2.9.3.2. а́-цәажәара /á-cʷažʷa-ra/ 'to speak to'

Finite forms		
	<u>Affirmative</u>	<u>Negative</u>
Dynamic Group I		
C1-C2-		
Present		
1Sg.-2F.Sg	с-б-а́-цәажәо-ит	с-б-а́-цәажәо-м
	/s-b-á-cʷažʷa-wa-jt'/	
	I(C1)-you.F(C2)-to-speak-Dyn-Fin	
	'I speak to you-F'	
Aorist		
1Sg.-2F.Sg	с-б-а́-цәажәе-ит	сы-б-м-а́-цәажәе-ит
Future I		
1Sg.-2F.Sg	с-б-а́-цәажәа-п	с-б-а́-цәажәа-ры-м
Future II		
1Sg.-2F.Sg	с-б-а́-цәажәа-шт	с-б-а́-цәажәа-ша-м
Perfect		
1Sg.-2F.Sg	с-б-а́-цәажәа-хье-ит	сы-б-м-а́-цәажәа-ц(т)
Dynamic Group II		
Imperfect		
1Sg.-2F.Sg	с-б-а́-цәажәо-н	с-б-а́-цәажәо-мы-зт
Past Indefinite		
1Sg.-2F.Sg	с-б-а́-цәажәа-н	сы-б-м-а́-цәажәа-зт
Conditional I		
1Sg.-2F.Sg	с-б-а́-цәажәа-ры-н	с-б-а́-цәажәа-ры-мы-зт
Conditional II		
1Sg.-2F.Sg	с-б-а́-цәажәа-ша-н	с-б-а́-цәажәа-ша-мы-зт
Pluperfect		
1Sg.-2F.Sg	с-б-а́-цәажәа-хьа-н	сы-б-м-а́-цәажәа-цы-зт

Non-Finite forms		
	<u>Affirmative</u>	<u>Negative</u>
Dynamic Group I		
C1-C2-		
Present		
Rel-3F.Sg	и-л-а́-цәажәо	и-л-м-а́-цәажәо
	/jə-l-á-cʷažʷa-wa/	

	Rel(C1)-her(C2)-to-speak-Dyn.NF '(the one) who speaks to her'	
3Human.Sg-Rel	д-з-á-цəажəо /d-z-á-cʷažʷa-wa/ he/she(C1)-Rel(C2)-to-speak-Dyn.NF '(the one) whom he/she speaks to'	ды-з-м-á-цəажəо
Aorist		
Rel-3F.Sg	и-л-á-цəажəа	и-л-м-á-цəажəа
3Human.Sg-Rel	д-з-á-цəажəа	ды-з-м-á-цəажəа
Future I		
Rel-3F.Sg	и-л-á-цəажəа-ра	и-л-м-á-цəажəа-ра
3Human.Sg-Rel	д-з-á-цəажəа-ра	ды-з-м-á-цəажəа-ра
Future II		
Rel-3F.Sg	и-л-á-цəажəа-ша	и-л-м-á-цəажəа-ша
3Human.Sg-Rel	д-з-á-цəажəа-ша	ды-з-м-á-цəажəа-ша
Perfect		
Rel-3F.Sg	и-л-á-цəажəа-хьо-у (-хьа(-п))	и-л-м-á-цəажəа-хьо-у (-хьа(-п))
3Human.Sg-Rel	д-з-á-цəажəа-хьо-у (-хьа(-п))	ды-з-м-á-цəажəа-хьо-у(-хьа(-п))
Dynamic Group II		
Imperfect		
Rel-3F.Sg	и-л-á-цəажəо-з	и-л-м-á-цəажəо-з
3Human.Sg-Rel	д-з-á-цəажəо-з	ды-з-м-á-цəажəо-з
Past Indefinite		
Rel-3F.Sg	и-л-á-цəажəа-з	и-л-м-á-цəажəа-з
3Human.Sg-Rel	д-з-á-цəажəа-з	ды-з-м-á-цəажəа-з
Conditional I		
Rel-3F.Sg	и-л-á-цəажəа-ры-з	и-л-м-á-цəажəа-ры-з
3Human.Sg-Rel	д-з-á-цəажəа-ры-з	ды-з-м-á-цəажəа-ры-з
Conditional II		
Rel-3F.Sg	и-л-á-цəажəа-ша-з	и-л-м-á-цəажəа-ша-з
3Human.Sg-Rel	д-з-á-цəажəа-ша-з	ды-з-м-á-цəажəа-ша-з
Pluperfect		
Rel-3F.Sg	и-л-á-цəажəа-хьа-з	и-л-м-á-цəажəа-хьа-з
3Human.Sg-Rel	д-з-á-цəажəа-хьа-з	ды-з-м-á-цəажəа-хьа-з

3.2.9.3.3. áишра /áj-š-ra/ 'to bark at'

Finite forms

	Affirmative	Negative
C1-C2-		
Present		
3Non-Hum.Sg/3Pl-1Sg	и-с-éи-ш-уе-ит /jə-s-áj-š-wa-jt'/	и-с-éи-ш-уа-м

	it/they(C1)-me(C2)-Prev-bark at-Dyn.Fin	
	‘it/they bark(s) at me’	
3Non-Hum.Sg/3Pl-2F.Sg	и-б-éи-ш-уе-ит	и-б-éи-ш-уа-м
3Non-Hum.Sg/3Pl-3M.Sg	(и-)éи-ш-уе-ит (< и-и-éи-ш-уе-ит)	(и-)éи-ш-уа-м
3Non-Hum.Sg/3Pl-3F.Sg	и-л-éи-ш-уе-ит	и-л-éи-ш-уа-м
3N.H.Sg/3Pl-3N.H.Sg	éи-ш-уе-ит (< и-а-éи-ш-уе-ит)	éи-ш-уа-м
3Non-Hum.Sg/3Pl-1Pl	и-х-áи-ш-уе-ит	и-х-áи-ш-уа-м
3Non-Hum.Sg/3Pl-2Pl	и-шә-éи-ш-уе-ит	и-шә-éи-ш-уа-м
3Non-Hum.Sg/3Pl-3Pl	и-р-éи-ш-уе-ит	и-р-éи-ш-уа-м

Aorist		
3Non-Hum.Sg/3Pl-1Sg	и-с-éи-ш-ит	и-с-м-éи-ш-ит
3N.H.Sg/3Pl-3N.H.Sg	éи-ш-ит (< и-а-éи-ш-ит)	и-а-м-éи-ш-ит

Non-Finite forms

	Affirmative	Negative
C1-C2-		
Present		
Rel-1Sg	и-л-éи-ш-уа	и-л-м-éи-ш-уа
3Non-Hum.Sg/3Pl-Rel	и-з-éи-ш-уа	и-з-м-éи-ш-уа
Imperfect		
Rel-1Sg	и-л-éи-ш-уа-з	и-л-м-éи-ш-уа-з
3Non-Hum.Sg/3Pl-Rel	и-з-éи-ш-уа-з	и-з-м-éи-ш-уа-з
Past Indefinite		
Rel-1Sg	и-л-éи-шы-з	и-л-м-éи-шы-з
3Non-Hum.Sg/3Pl-Rel	и-з-éи-шы-з	и-з-м-éи-шы-з

3.2.9.4. Inflection with a local preverb

3.2.9.4.1. á-ватәара /á-va-t’ʷa-ra/ ‘to sit down next to’

Finite forms

	Affirmative	Negative
C1-C2-		
Present		
3Hum.Sg-1Sg	д-сы́-ва-тәо-ит	д-сы́-ва-тәо-м
	/d-sə́-va-t’ʷa-wa-jt’/	
	he/she(C1)-me(C2)-Prev-sit-Dyn-Fin	
	‘he/she is sitting down next to me’	
3Hum.Sg-3F.Sg	д-лы́-ва-тәо-ит	д-лы́-ва-тәо-м
3Hum.Sg-3Non-Hum.Sg	д-á-ва-тәо-ит	д-á-ва-тәо-м
3Hum.Sg-1Pl	д-хá-ва-тәо-ит	д-хá-ва-тәо-м
3Hum.Sg-3Pl	д-ры́-ва-тәо-ит	д-ры́-ва-тәо-м
1Pl-3F.Sg	х-лы́-ва-тәо-ит	х-лы́-ва-тәо-м
3N.H.Sg/3Pl-3N.H.Sg	и-á-ва-тәо-ит	и-á-ва-тәо-м

Aorist		
3Hum.Sg-3F.Sg	д-лы́-ва-тәе-ит	д-лы́-ва-м-тәе-ит
3Hum.Sg-3Non-Hum.Sg	д-а́-ва-тәе-ит	д-а́-ва-м-тәе-ит
3N.H.Sg/3Pl-3N.H.Sg	и-а́-ва-тәе-ит	и-а́-ва-м-тәе-ит

Non-Finite forms

	<u>Affirmative</u>	<u>Negative</u>
C1-C2-		
Present		
Rel-3F.Sg	и-лы́-ва-тәо /jə-lə́-va-t'ʷa-wa/ Rel(C1)-her(C2)-Prev-sit-Dyn.NF '(the one) who is sitting down next to her'	и-лы́-ва-м-тәо
3Hum.Sg-Rel	д-зы́-ва-тәо /d-zə́-va-t'ʷa-wa/ he/she(C1)-Rel(C2)-Prev-sit-Dyn.NF '(the one) whom he/she is sitting down next to'	д-зы́-ва-м-тәо
Imperfect		
Rel-3F.Sg	и-лы́-ва-тәо-з	и-лы́-ва-м-тәо-з
3Hum.Sg-Rel	д-зы́-ва-тәо-з	д-зы́-ва-м-тәо-з
Past Indefinite		
Rel-3F.Sg	и-лы́-ва-тәа-з	и-лы́-ва-м-тәа-з
3Hum.Sg-Rel	д-зы́-ва-тәа-з	д-зы́-ва-м-тәа-з

3.2.9.4.2. а́-лагара /á-la-ga-ra/ 'to begin'

Finite forms

Dynamic Group I

	<u>Affirmative</u>	<u>Negative</u>
C1-C2-		
Present		
3Hum.Sg-3Non-Hum.Sg	д-а́-ла-го-ит /d-á-la-ga-wa-jt'/ he/she(C1)-it(C2)-Prev-begin-Dyn-Fin 'he/she begin it'	д-а́-ла-го-м
1Sg-3Non-Hum.Sg	с-а́-ла-го-ит	с-а́-ла-го-м
Aorist		
3Hum.Sg-3Non-Hum.Sg	д-а́-ла-ге-ит	д-а́-ла-м-ге-ит
Future I		
3Hum.Sg-3Non-Hum.Sg	д-а́-ла-га-п	д-а́-ла-га-ры-м
Future II		
3Hum.Sg-3Non-Hum.Sg	д-а́-ла-га-шт	д-а́-ла-га-ша-м
Perfect		

3Hum.Sg-3Non-Hum.Sg	д-á-ла-га-хье-ит	д-á-ла-м-га-ц(т)
Dynamic Group II		
Imperfect		
3Hum.Sg-3Non-Hum.Sg	д-á-ла-го-н	д-á-ла-го-мы-зт
Past Indefinite		
3Hum.Sg-3Non-Hum.Sg	д-á-ла-га-н	д-á-ла-м-га-зт
Conditional I		
3Hum.Sg-3Non-Hum.Sg	д-á-ла-га-ры-н	д-á-ла-га-ры-мы-зт
Conditional II		
3Hum.Sg-3Non-Hum.Sg	д-á-ла-га-ша-н	д-á-ла-га-ша-мы-зт
Pluperfect		
3Hum.Sg-3Non-Hum.Sg	д-á-ла-га-хьа-н	д-á-ла-м-га-цы-зт

Non-Finite forms

Dynamic Group I

	Affirmative	Negative
C1-C2-		
Present		
Rel-3Non-Hum.Sg	и-á-ла-го /j-á-la-ga-wa/ Rel(C1)-it(C2)-Prev-begin-Dyn.NF '(the one) who begins it'	и-á-ла-м-го
3Hum.Sg-Rel	ды-з-ла-гó /də-z-la-ga-wá/ he/she(C1)-Rel(C2)-Prev-begin-Dyn.NF 'which he/she begins'	ды-з-лá-м-го
Aorist		
Rel-3Non-Hum.Sg	и-á-ла-га	и-á-ла-м-га
3Hum.Sg-Rel	ды-з-ла-гá	ды-з-лá-м-га
Future I		
Rel-3Non-Hum.Sg	и-á-ла-га-ра	и-á-ла-м-га-ра
3Hum.Sg-Rel	ды-з-ла-га-рá	ды-з-лá-м-га-ра
Future II		
Rel-3Non-Hum.Sg	и-á-ла-га-ша	и-á-ла-м-га-ша
3Hum.Sg-Rel	ды-з-ла-гá-ша	ды-з-лá-м-га-ша
Perfect		
Rel-3Non-Hum.Sg	и-á-ла-га-хьоу (-хьа(ц))	и-á-ла-м-га-хьоу (-хьа(ц))
3Hum.Sg-Rel	ды-з-ла-га-хьóу (-хьá(ц))	ды-з-лá-м-га-хьоу (-хьа(ц))

Dynamic Group II

Imperfect		
Rel-3Non-Hum.Sg	и-á-ла-го-з	и-á-ла-м-го-з
3Hum.Sg-Rel	ды-з-ла-гó-з	ды-з-лá-м-го-з

Past Indefinite		
Rel-3Non-Hum.Sg	и-á-ла-га-з	и-á-ла-м-га-з
3Hum.Sg-Rel	ды-з-ла-гá-з	ды-з-лá-м-га-з
Conditional I		
Rel-3Non-Hum.Sg	и-á-ла-га-ры-з	и-á-ла-м-га-ры-з
3Hum.Sg-Rel	ды-з-ла-га-ры́-з	ды-з-лá-м-га-ры-з
Conditional II		
Rel-3Non-Hum.Sg	и-á-ла-га-ша-з	и-á-ла-м-га-ша-з
3Hum.Sg-Rel	ды-з-ла-гá-ша-з	ды-з-лá-м-га-ша-з
Pluperfect		
Rel-3Non-Hum.Sg	и-á-ла-га-хьа-з	и-á-ла-м-га-хьа-з
3Hum.Sg-Rel	ды-з-ла-га-хьá-з	ды-з-лá-м-га-хьаа-з

3.2.9.4.3. á-қәзаара /á-kʷ-zaa-ra/ 'to be on (a surface)'

Finite forms		
	<u>Affirmative</u>	<u>Negative</u>
C1-C2-		
Present		
3Hum.Sg-3Non-Hum.Sg	ды́-қә-уп /də́-kʷə-wp'/ < /d-øə́-kʷ-øə-wp'/ he/she(C1)-it(C2)-Prev(on)-be-Stat.Pres.Fin 'he/she is on it'	ды́-қә-м (ды́-қә-ӡа-м)
3N.H.Sg/3Pl-3N.H.Sg	и́-қә-уп /j-øə́-kʷə-ø-wp'/ 'it is/they are on it'	и́-қә-м
3Pl-3N.H.Sg	и-ры́-қә-уп /j-rə́-kʷə-ø-wp'/ 'they are on them'	и-ры́-қә-м
Past		
3Hum.Sg-3Non-Hum.Sg	ды́-қә-н	ды́-қә-мы-зт
3N.H.Sg/3Pl-3N.H.Sg	и́-қәы-н	и́-қә-мы-зт

Non-Finite forms		
Present		
Rel-3Non-Hum.Sg	и́-қә-у /j-øə́-kʷə-w/ 'which is on it'	и́-қәы-м
3N.H.Sg/3Pl-Rel	и-з-қә(ы́)-ý /jə-z-kʷə́-w/ 'which it is/they are on'	и-з-қәы́-м
Past		
Rel-3Non-Hum.Sg	и́-қәы-з	и́-қәы-мы-з
3N.H.Sg/3Pl-Rel	и-з-қәы́-з	и-з-қәы́-мы-з

Note: For this type of stative verb which indicates presence, -кә- /kʷ/ is not seen as a root, but as a preverb, and by regarding the root as ø-, it can achieve consistency with other verbs with the preverb -ҟә-. Compare the following verb а́ҟәгылазаара /á-kʷ-gəla-zaa-ra/ 'to stand on *sth*' which has the preverb -кә- 'on' and the root гыла /gəla/ 'stand'.

(213) Ашәҟәы́ астол и́кәуп.
/a-šʷq'ʷə́ a-st'ól j-øə́-kʷə-ø-wp'/
the-book the-table it(= the book, C1)-it(= the table, C2)-Prev(on)-be-Stat.Pres.Fin
'The book lies on the table.'

(214) Ашәҟәқәа́ астолқәа ирыкәуп.
/a-šʷq'ʷ-kʷá a-st'ól-kʷa j-rə́-kʷə-ø-wp'/
the-book-Pl the-table-Pl they(= the books, C1)-them(= the tables, C2)-Prev(on)-be-Stat.Pres.Fin
'The books lie on the tables.'

(215) Ахахә дыкәгылоуп. (ARD)
/a-xáħʷ d-øə́-kʷ-gəla-wp'/
the-stone he/she(C1)-it(C2)-Prev(on)-stand-Stat.Pres.Fin
'He/She is standing on the stone.'

(216) Ахахәкәа ирыкәгылоуп.
/a-xáħʷ-kʷa jə-rə́-kʷ-gəla-wp'/
the-stone-Pl they(C1)-them(C2)-Prev(on)-stand-Stat.Pres.Fin
'They are standing on the stones.'

Similar verbs are below:

а-гәы́ла-заа-ра 'to be inside': и-а-гәы́ло-уп 'it is/they are inside it', а-ҕра́-заа-ра 'to lie in': д-а-ҕро́-уп 'he/she lies in it', а́-д-заа-ра 'to lie/is near': и-а́-д-уп 'it is/they are is near it', а-кы́д-заа-ра 'to exist/be on a vertical, inclined plane, to hang on': и-ø-кы́д-уп 'it is/they are (in the sky/on the slope), it is hanging on it', а́-ла-заа-ра 'to be in (the field/forest): и-а́-ло-уп 'it is/they are in it', а́-мҕа-заа-ра 'to be wearing (a belt)': и-сы́-мҕо-уп 'I am wearing it', а́-мтца-заа-ра 'to be under': и-а́-мтцо-уп 'it is/they are under it', а-ны́-заа-ра 'to be on': и-а-н-у́п 'it is/they are on it', а-ҭа́-заа-ра 'to be in (the box, the pocket)': и-ø-ҭо́-уп 'it is/they are in it', а-ха́-заа-ра 'to be on': и-с-хо́-уп 'it is on me, I wear it', а́-ц-заа-ра 'to be together with': д-лы́-ц-уп 'he/she is together with her', а́-тца-заа-ра 'to be under': д-а́-тцо-уп 'he/she is under it', а-ҿы́-заа-ра 'to be engaged in': д-а-ҿ-у́п/д-а-ҿы́-уп 'he/she is engaged in it', а́-шьҭа-заа-ра 'to be on the trail of': д-а́-шьҭо-уп 'he/she is on the trail of it', а-ҩна́-заа-ра 'to be in premises': сы-ҩно́-уп 'I am in it'.

3.2.10. Class G

Class G verbs are two-place transitive verbs that have preverbs. The preverbs used in this class differ from preverbs used in Class F verbs and do not govern any Column II indirect objects. For example, they are the ones that indicate direction such as аа- /aa/ 'hither', на- /na/ 'thither', ла- /la/ 'downwards', ҩа- /jʷa/ 'upward', in addition to ҟа- /q'a/, бжьа- /bžʲa/, бжьы- /bžʲə/, гәа- /gʷa/, гәар-

/gʷar/, гән- /gʷn/, дәыкә- /dʷəkʷ/, гәын- /gʷən/, ӡаа- /ʒaa/, ка- /k'a/, лбаа- /lbaa/, мҩа- /mjʷa/, н(ы)- /n(ə)/, нықә(ы)- /nə́q'ʷ(ə)/, ԥ(ы)- /p(ə)/, т(ы)- /t(ə)/, ха- /xa/, х(ы)- /x(ə)/, ц(ы)- /c'(ə), ҿ(ы)- /č'(ə)/, шьҭа- /šʲta/, etc. These Class G verbs are derived from both intransitive and transitive verbs. For example, if the preverb на- 'thither' is attached to the intransitive ацара́ /a-ca-rá/ 'to go', а́нацара /á-na-ca-ra/ 'to drive thither' is derived. This is a two-place transitive verb which has only two arguments: A and DO. For example:

(217) Аԥшәма а́жәкәа ахка́арахь ине́ицеит.
/a-pšʷma á-žʷ-kʷa a-xk'áara-[a-a]xʲ jə-ná-j-ca-jt'/
the-owner the-cow-Pl the-pasture-to them(C1)-Prev(thither)-he(C3)-drive-(Aor)-Fin
'The owner drove the cows to the pasture.'

Also, when the same preverb is attached to the transitive агара́ /a-ga-rá/ 'to take, to carry', ана́гара /a-ná-ga-ra/ 'to take thither, to bring, to convey' is derived. This is also a two-place transitive verb that has only two arguments: A and DO. For example:

(218) Асалам шәҟәкәа́ аҩнкәа́ рахь ина́згоит.
/á-salam šʷq'ʷ-kʷá a-jʷn-kʷá r-axʲ jə-ná-z-ga-wa-jt'/
the-greeting letter-Pl the-house-Pl their-to them(C1)-Prev-I(C3)-bring-Dyn-Fin
'I am delivering the letters to the houses.'

The two и- /jə/ before the preverb in the verbal complexes in (217) and (218) above are not prefixes governed by the preverb на- /na/ (if they were governed, that would be expected to become a Column II pronominal prefix р- /r/), but a Column I pronominal prefix indicating the direct object. No pronominal prefixes attach themselves to the directional preverb на- /na/. Directional relations are indicated by the postposition -ахь /axʲ/ 'to' outside the verbal complex.

As previously discussed in §3.1.2.1, distinguishing a preverb and a root can be done by the method of inserting the negative marker -м- /m/ in the aorist negative form between the preverb and the root. Also, in transitive verbs, the pronominal prefix which indicates the Column III agent is inserted between the preverb and the root, and by splitting these two as well the preverb and root can be distinguished. Pronominal prefixes which indicate the Column III agent in this manner are always placed between a preverb and the root. This is something characteristic of only transitive verbs, and it is one of the criteria for judging transitivity (in contrast to this, the Class F intransitive verbs examined above have a distribution order of 'Column I + Column II + preverb + root', and the insertion of a Column II prefix between a preverb and root does not occur, aside from some exceptions.[129]) Furthermore, the causative marker р- /r/ is inserted between the preverb and the root (more precisely, between the Column III prefix and the root), and by doing that the preverb and the root can be split. For example:

(219) илна́смырцеит
/jə-l-ná-s-mə-r-ca-jt'/
it/them(C1)-her(C2)-Prev-I(C3)-Neg-Caus-go-(Aor)-Fin
'I did not make her convey it/them.'

129. The exception is аа́ԥхьара /aá-pxʲa-ra/ 'to summon', саары́ԥхьеит /s-aa-rə́-pxʲa-jt'/ [I(C1)-Prev-them(C2)-summon-(Aor)-Fin] 'I summoned them'. See §3.2.9.

Class G verbs have a causative marker inserted between the preverb and the root as in (219) above, but there are two examples of verbs that do not fit into this general principle. These verbs are á-ҟацара /á-q'a-c'a-ra/ 'to do, to make' and á-лацара /á-la-c'a-ra/ 'to sow' (see Spruit 1983: 74). See the following causative forms:

(220) ислы́рҟацеит
/jə-s-lə́-r-q'a-c'a-jt'/
it/them(C1)-me(C2)-she(C3)-Caus-Prev-do-(Aor)-Fin)
'She made me do it/them.'

Cf. иҟасымцéит
/jə-q'a-sə-m-c'á-jt'/
it/them(C1)-Prev-I(C3)-Neg-do-(Aor)-Fin
'I did not do it/them.'

(221) ислы́рлацеит
/jə-s-lə́-r-la-c'a-jt'/
it/them(C1)-me(C2)-she(C3)-Caus-Prev-sow-(Aor)-Fin
'She made me sow it/them.'

Cf. иласымцéит
/jə-la-sə-m-c'á-jt'/
it/them(C1)-Prev-I(C3)-Neg-sow-(Aor)-Fin
'I did not sow it/them.'

Also, the Column III third-person, singular, non-human prefix which indicates the agent in Class G verbs uses на- /na/:

(222) ина́нагеит
/j-ná-na-ga-jt'/
it/them(C1)-Prev-it(C3)-take-(Aor)-Fin
'It conveyed it/them.'

3.2.10.1. Inflection of á-ҟа-ца-ра 'to do, to make'

In finite forms, the accent is basically placed on the postradical element.

Finite forms

	Affirmative	Negative
Dynamic Group I		
C1-Prev-C3-		
Present		
3N.H.Sg/3Pl-1Sg	и-ҟа-с-цó-ит /jə-q'a-s-c'a-wá-jt'/ 'I am doing/making it/them'	и-ҟа-с-цó-м
3N.H.Sg/3Pl-2M.Sg	и-ҟа-у-цó-ит	и-ҟа-у-цó-м
3N.H.Sg/3Pl-2F.Sg	и-ҟа-б-цó-ит	и-ҟа-б-цó-м
3N.H.Sg/3Pl-3M.Sg	и-ҟа-и-цó-ит	и-ҟа-и-цó-м
3N.H.Sg/3Pl-3F.Sg	и-ҟа-л-цó-ит	и-ҟа-л-цó-м

3N.H.Sg/3Pl-3N.H.Sg	и-ҟа-на-ҵо́-ит	и-ҟа-на-ҵо́-м
3N.H.Sg/3Pl-1Pl	и-ҟа-ҳ-ҵо́-ит	и-ҟа-ҳ-ҵо́-м
3N.H.Sg/3Pl-2Pl	и-ҟа-шә-ҵо́-ит	и-ҟа-шә-ҵо́-м
3N.H.Sg/3Pl-3Pl	и-ҟа-р-ҵо́-ит	и-ҟа-р-ҵо́-м

Aorist

3N.H.Sg/3Pl-1Sg	и-ҟа-с-ҵе́-ит	и-ҟа-сы-м-ҵе́-ит (-ҵа-ӡе́-ит)
3N.H.Sg/3Pl-2M.Sg	и-ҟа-у-ҵе́-ит	и-ҟа-у-м-ҵе́-ит
3N.H.Sg/3Pl-2F.Sg	и-ҟа-б-ҵе́-ит	и-ҟа-бы-м-ҵе́-ит
3N.H.Sg/3Pl-3M.Sg	и-ҟа-и-ҵе́-ит	и-ҟа-и-м-ҵе́-ит
3N.H.Sg/3Pl-3F.Sg	и-ҟа-л-ҵе́-ит	и-ҟа-лы-м-ҵе́-ит
3N.H.Sg/3Pl-3N.H.Sg	и-ҟа-на-ҵе́-ит	и-ҟа-на́-м-ҵе-ит
3N.H.Sg/3Pl-1Pl	и-ҟа-ҳ-ҵе́-ит	и-ҟа-ҳа-м-ҵе́-ит
3N.H.Sg/3Pl-2Pl	и-ҟа-шә-ҵе́-ит	и-ҟа-шәы-м-ҵе́-ит
3N.H.Sg/3Pl-3Pl	и-ҟа-р-ҵе́-ит	и-ҟа-ры-м-ҵе́-ит

Future I

3N.H.Sg/3Pl-1Sg	и-ҟа-с-ҵа́-п	и-ҟа-с-ҵа-ры́-м
3N.H.Sg/3Pl-3N.H.Sg	и-ҟа-на-ҵа́-п	и-ҟа-на-ҵа-ры́-м

Future II

3N.H.Sg/3Pl-1Sg	и-ҟа-с-ҵа́-шт	и-ҟа-с-ҵа́-ша-м
3N.H.Sg/3Pl-3N.H.Sg	и-ҟа-на-ҵа́-шт	и-ҟа-на-ҵа́-ша-м

Perfect

3N.H.Sg/3Pl-1Sg	и-ҟа-с-ҵа-хье́-ит	и-ҟа-сы-м-ҵа́-ц(т)
3N.H.Sg/3Pl-3N.H.Sg	и-ҟа-на-ҵа-хье́-ит	и-ҟа-на́-м-ҵа-ц(т)

Dynamic Group II
Imperfect

3N.H.Sg/3Pl-1Sg	и-ҟа-с-ҵо́-н	и-ҟа-с-ҵо́-мы-зт
3N.H.Sg/3Pl-3N.H.Sg	и-ҟа-на-ҵо́-н	и-ҟа-на-ҵо́-мы-зт

Past Indefinite

3N.H.Sg/3Pl-1Sg	и-ҟа-с-ҵа́-н	и-ҟа-сы-м-ҵа́-зт
3N.H.Sg/3Pl-3N.H.Sg	и-ҟа-на-ҵа́-н	и-ҟа-на́-м-ҵа-зт

Conditional I

3N.H.Sg/3Pl-1Sg	и-ҟа-с-ҵа-ры́-н	и-ҟа-с-ҵа-ры́-мы-зт
3N.H.Sg/3Pl-3N.H.Sg	и-ҟа-на-ҵа-ры́-н	и-ҟа-на-ҵа-ры́-мы-зт

Conditional II

3N.H.Sg/3Pl-1Sg	и-ҟа-с-ҵа́-ша-н	и-ҟа-с-ҵа́-ша-мы-зт
3N.H.Sg/3Pl-3N.H.Sg	и-ҟа-на-ҵа́-ша-н	и-ҟа-на-ҵа́-ша-мы-зт

Pluperfect		
3N.H.Sg/3Pl-1Sg	и-ҟа-с-ҵа-хьа́-н	и-ҟа-сы-м-ҵа́-цы-зт
3N.H.Sg/3Pl-3N.H.Sg	и-ҟа-на-ҵа-хьа́-н	и-ҟа-на́-м-ҵа-цы-зт
Non-Finite forms		
	Affirmative	Negative
Dynamic Group I		
C1-Prev-C3-		
Present		
Rel-1Sg	и́-ҟа-с-ҵо	и́-ҟа-сы-м-ҵо
	/jə́-q'a-s-c'a-wa/	
	'which I am doing/making'	
Rel-2F.Sg	и́-ҟа-б-ҵо	и́-ҟа-бы-м-ҵо
Rel-2M.Sg	и́-ҟа-у-ҵо	и́-ҟа-у-м-ҵо
Rel-3F.Sg	и́-ҟа-л-ҵо	и́-ҟа-лы-м-ҵо
Rel-3M.Sg	и́-ҟа-и-ҵо	и́-ҟа-и-м-ҵо
Rel-3Non-Hum.Sg	и́-ҟа-на-ҵо	и́-ҟа-на-м-ҵо
Rel-1Pl	и́-ҟа-х-ҵо	и́-ҟа-ха-м-ҵо
Rel-2Pl	и́-ҟа-шә-ҵо	и́-ҟа-шәы-м-ҵо
Rel-3Pl	и́-ҟа-р-ҵо	и́-ҟа-ры-м-ҵо
3N.H.Sg/3Pl-Rel	и-ҟа-з-ҵо́	и-ҟа-зы-м-ҵо́
	/jə-q'a-z-c'a-wá/	
	'(the one) who is doing/making it/them'	
Aorist		
Rel-3F.Sg	и́-ҟа-л-ҵа	и́-ҟа-лы-м-ҵа
3N.H.Sg/3Pl-Rel	и-ҟа-з-ҵа́	и-ҟа-зы-м-ҵа́
Future I		
Rel-3F.Sg	и́-ҟа-л-ҵа-ра	и́-ҟа-лы-м-ҵа-ра
3N.H.Sg/3Pl-Rel	и-ҟа-з-ҵа-ра́	и-ҟа-зы-м-ҵа-ра́
Future II		
Rel-3F.Sg	и́-ҟа-л-ҵа-ша	и́-ҟа-лы-м-ҵа-ша
3N.H.Sg/3Pl-Rel	и-ҟа-з-ҵа́-ша	и-ҟа-зы-м-ҵа́-ша
Perfect		
Rel-3F.Sg	и́-ҟа-л-ҵа-хьо-у (-хьа(-ц))	и́-ҟа-лы-м-ҵа-хьо-у (-хьа(-ц))
3N.H.Sg/3Pl-Rel	и-ҟа-з-ҵа-хьо́-у (-хьа́(-ц))	и-ҟа-зы-м-ҵа-хьо́-у (-хьа́(-ц))
Dynamic Group II		
Imperfect		
Rel-3F.Sg	и́-ҟа-л-ҵо-з	и́-ҟа-лы-м-ҵо-з

3N.H.Sg/3Pl-Rel	и-ҟа-з-ҵó-з	и-ҟа-зы-м-ҵó-з
Past Indefinite		
Rel-3F.Sg	и́-ҟа-л-ҵа-з	и́-ҟа-лы-м-ҵа-з
3N.H.Sg/3Pl-Rel	и-ҟа-з-ҵá-з	и-ҟа-зы-м-ҵá-з
Conditional I		
Rel-3F.Sg	и́-ҟа-л-ҵа-ры-з	и́-ҟа-лы-м-ҵа-ры-з
3N.H.Sg/3Pl-Rel	и-ҟа-з-ҵа-ры́-з	и-ҟа-зы-м-ҵа-ры́-з
Conditional II		
Rel-3F.Sg	и́-ҟа-л-ҵа-ша-з	и́-ҟа-лы-м-ҵа-ша-з
3N.H.Sg/3Pl-Rel	и-ҟа-з-ҵá-ша-з	и-ҟа-зы-м-ҵá-ша-з
Pluperfect		
Rel-3F.Sg	и́-ҟа-л-ҵа-хьа-з	и́-ҟа-лы-м-ҵа-хьа-з
3N.H.Sg/3Pl-Rel	и-ҟа-з-ҵа-хьá-з	и-ҟа-зы-м-ҵа-хьá-з

Note: Take note of the underlined accents. The accent pattern in the perfect, past indefinite, and pluperfect follow the aorist accent pattern.
Other verbs with similar accent patterns:
аа-га-рá 'to fetch', áа-ҭи-ра 'to send', а-ка-ҿа-рá 'to cut off branches', á-ла-ҵа-ра 'to sow', á-на-гӡа-ра 'to complete', а-х-та-рá 'to scoop', а-х-ҽ-рá 'to weaken; to ease'.

3.2.10.2. Inflection of á-на-ца-ра 'to drive thither'

Accents in finite forms are placed on the preverb directly before the Column III pronominal prefix, but where there is no Column III pronominal prefix, the accent is placed on the element following the root (cf. Imperative: и-на-цá!, Absolutive: д-на-ца-ны́).

Finite forms

	Affirmative	Negative
Dynamic Group I		
C1-Prev-C3-		
Present		
3N.H.Sg/3Pl-1Sg	и-нá-с-цо-ит /jə-ná-s-ca-wa-jt'/ 'I am driving it/them thither'	и-нá-с-цо-м
3N.H.Sg/3Pl-2M.Sg	и-нá-у-цо-ит	и-нá-у-цо-м
3N.H.Sg/3Pl-2F.Sg	и-нá-б-цо-ит	и-нá-б-цо-м
3N.H.Sg/3Pl-3M.Sg	и-нé-и-цо-ит	и-нé-и-цо-м
3N.H.Sg/3Pl-3F.Sg	и-нá-л-цо-ит	и-нá-л-цо-м
3N.H.Sg/3Pl-3N.H.Sg	и-нá-на-цо-ит	и-нá-на-цо-м
3N.H.Sg/3Pl-1Pl	и-нá-х-цо-ит	и-нá-х-цо-м
3N.H.Sg/3Pl-2Pl	и-нá-шә-цо-ит	и-нá-шә-цо-м

3N.H.Sg/3Pl-3Pl	и-ná-р-цо-ит	и-ná-р-цо-м
3Hum.Sg-1.Sg	д-ná-с-цо-ит	д-ná-с-цо-м
2Pl-3Pl	х-ná-р-цо-ит	х-ná-р-цо-м
Aorist		
3N.H.Sg/3Pl-1Sg	и-ná-с-це-ит	и-ná-сы-м-це-ит
3N.H.Sg/3Pl-2M.Sg	и-ná-у-це-ит	и-ná-у-м-це-ит
3N.H.Sg/3Pl-2F.Sg	и-ná-б-це-ит	и-ná-бы-м-це-ит
3N.H.Sg/3Pl-3M.Sg	и-né-и-це-ит	и-né-и-м-це-ит
3N.H.Sg/3Pl-3F.Sg	и-ná-л-це-ит	и-ná-лы-м-це-ит
3N.H.Sg/3Pl-3N.H.Sg	и-ná-на-це-ит	и-ná-на-м-це-ит
3N.H.Sg/3Pl-1Pl	и-ná-х-це-ит	и-ná-ха-м-це-ит
3N.H.Sg/3Pl-2Pl	и-ná-шә-це-ит	и-ná-шәы-м-це-ит
3N.H.Sg/3Pl-3Pl	и-ná-р-це-ит	и-ná-ры-м-це-ит
3Hum.Sg-1.Sg	д-ná-с-це-ит	д-ná-сы-м-це-ит
2Pl-3Pl	х-ná-р-це-ит	х-ná-ры-м-це-ит
Future I		
3N.H.Sg/3Pl-3F.Sg	и-ná-л-ца-п	и-ná-л-ца-ры-м
Future II		
3N.H.Sg/3Pl-3F.Sg	и-ná-л-ца-шт	и-ná-л-ца-ша-м
Perfect		
3N.H.Sg/3Pl-3F.Sg	и-ná-л-ца-хьеит	и-ná-лы-м-ца-ц(т)
Dynamic Group II		
Imperfect		
3N.H.Sg/3Pl-3F.Sg	и-ná-л-цо-н	и-ná-л-цо-мы-зт
Past Indefinite		
3N.H.Sg/3Pl-3F.Sg	и-ná-л-ца-н	и-ná-лы-м-ца-зт
Conditional I		
3N.H.Sg/3Pl-3F.Sg	и-ná-л-ца-ры-н	и-ná-л-ца-ры-мы-зт
Conditional II		
3N.H.Sg/3Pl-3F.Sg	и-ná-л-ца-ша-н	и-ná-л-ца-ша-мы-зт
Pluperfect		
3N.H.Sg/3Pl-3F.Sg	и-ná-л-ца-хьа-н	и-ná-лы-м-ца-цы-зт

Non-Finite forms

	Affirmative	Negative
Dynamic Group I		
C1-Prev-C3-		
Present		

Rel-3F.Sg	й-на́-л-цо[130] /jə́-ná-l-ca-wa/ 'whom/which she is driving thither'	й-на́-лы-м-цо
3Hum.Sg-Rel	д-на́-з-цо /d-ná-z-ca-wa/ '(the one) who is driving her thither'	д-на́-зы-м-цо
Aorist		
Rel-3F.Sg	й-на́-л-ца	й-на́-лы-м-ца
3Hum.Sg-Rel	д-на́-з-ца	д-на́-зы-м-ца
Future I		
Rel-3F.Sg	й-на́-л-ца-ра	й-на́-лы-м-ца-ра
3Hum.Sg-Rel	д-на́-з-ца-ра	д-на́-зы-м-ца-ра
Future II		
Rel-3F.Sg	й-на́-л-ца-ша	й-на́-лы-м-ца-ша
3Hum.Sg-Rel	д-на́-з-ца-ша	д-на́-зы-м-ца-ша
Perfect		
Rel-3F.Sg	й-на́-л-ца-хьо-у (-хьа(-ц))	й-на́-лы-м-ца-хьо-у (-хьа(-ц))
3Hum.Sg-Rel	д-на́-з-ца-хьо-у (-хьа(-ц))	д-на́-зы-м-ца-хьо-у (-хьа(-ц))
Dynamic Group II		
Imperfect		
Rel-3F.Sg	и-на́-л-цо-з	и-на́-лы-м-цо-з
3Hum.Sg-Rel	д-на́-з-цо-з	д-на́-зы-м-цо-з
Past Indefinite		
Rel-3F.Sg	и-на́-л-ца-з	и-на́-лы-м-ца-з
3Hum.Sg-Rel	д-на́-з-ца-з	д-на́-зы-м-ца-з
Conditional I		
Rel-3F.Sg	и-на́-л-ца-ры-з	и-на́-лы-м-ца-ры-з
3Hum.Sg-Rel	д-на́-з-ца-ры-з	д-на́-зы-м-ца-ры-з
Conditional II		
Rel-3F.Sg	и-на́-л-ца-ша-з	и-на́-лы-м-ца-ша-з
3Hum.Sg-Rel	д-на́-з-ца-ша-з	д-на́-зы-м-ца-ша-з
Pluperfect		
Rel-3F.Sg	и-на́-л-ца-хьа-з	и-на́-лы-м-ца-хьа-з
3Hum.Sg-Rel	д-на́-з-ца-хьа-з	д-на́-зы-м-ца-хьа-з

Other verbs that have similar accent patterns:

а-бжьа-к-ра́ 'to hold *sth* between', а-гәцара-к-ра́ 'to take care of *sb*', а́ила-ҳәа-ра 'to dress', а́ила-ҵа-ра 'to mix, to blend', а́ил-ца-ра 'to separate', а́иҩ-ша-ра 'to split', а-ка-ҭәа-ра́ 'to pour out', а-ка-ца-ра́ 'to drive (*cattle*)', а́-мҩан-ҵа-ра 'to swing (*an arm*)', а-мҩах-га-ра́ 'to call in', а-ҧ-жәа-ра́ 'to tear, to break', а-ҧ-ҟа-ра́ 'to cut', а-ҧхаста-тә-ра́ 'to spoil', а-ҧха-ҵа-ра́ 'to drive

130. The accent can be placed on either the relative prefix or the preverb.

off', аҧ-ҵа-ра́ 'to create', а-ҧ-ҵәа-ра́ 'to break', а-ҧ-ҿ-ра́ 'to smash', а-ҭ-га-ра́ '(*of a voice*) to raise', а-ҭ-ҵаа-ра́ 'to study', а-ха-ҵа-ра́ 'to believe', а-х-жәа-ра́ 'to break', а-х-каа-ра́ 'to fence in', а-х-са-ра́ 'to cut down', а-х-т-ра́ 'to open', а-хҭа-к-ра́ 'to pester', а-х-шәа-ра́ 'to take off', а-х-ҩа-ра́ 'to cover from above', а-ҵәы-ҧсса-ра́ 'to peel', а-ҵәын-ҵа-ра́ 'to ferment', á-шьҭа-ҵа-ра 'to put *sth* down *on* the ground/floor', а-ҩна-к-ра́ 'to lock in', а-ҵь-шьа-ра́ 'to thank'.

3.2.10.3. Inflection of á-на-шьҭ-ра 'to send thither, to admit, to let go'

In finite forms, the accent is placed on the Column III prefix.

Finite forms

	Affirmative	Negative
Dynamic Group I		
C1-Prev-C3-		
Present		
3Hum.Sg-3F.Sg	д-на-лы́-шьҭ-уе-ит /d-na-lə́-šʲt-wa-jt'/ him/her(C1)-Prev-she(C3)-send-Dyn-Fin 'She is sending him/her thither'	д-на-лы́-шьҭ-уа-м
3Hum.Sg-3N.H.Sg	д-на-на́-шьҭ-уе-ит	д-на-на́-шьҭ-уа-м
3Hum.Sg-1Pl	д-на-ха́-шьҭ-уе-ит	д-на-ха́-шьҭ-уа-м
3Hum.Sg-3Pl	д-на-ры́-шьҭ-уе-ит	д-на-ры́-шьҭ-уа-м
Aorist		
3Hum.Sg-3F.Sg	д-на-лы́-шьҭ-ит	д-на-л-мы́-шьҭ-ит
3Hum.Sg-3N.H.Sg	д-на-на́-шьҭ-ит	д-на-на́-мы-шьҭ-ит
3Hum.Sg-1Pl	д-на-ҳа́-шьҭ-ит	д-на-ҳ-мы́-шьҭ-ит
3Hum.Sg-3Pl	д-на-ры́-шьҭ-ит	д-на-р-мы́-шьҭ-ит
Future I		
3Hum.Sg-3F.Sg	д-на-лы́-шьҭы-п	д-на-лы́-шьҭ-ры-м
Future II		
3Hum.Sg-3F.Sg	д-на-лы́-шьҭы-шт	д-на-лы́-шьҭ-ша-м
Perfect		
3Hum.Sg-3F.Sg	д-на-лы́-шьҭ-хьеит	д-на-л-мы́-шьҭ-ц(т)
Dynamic Group II		
Imperfect		
3Hum.Sg-3F.Sg	д-на-лы́-шьҭ-уа-н	д-на-лы́-шьҭ-уа-мы-зт
Past Indefinite		
3Hum.Sg-3F.Sg	д-на-лы́-шьҭы-н	д-на-л-мы́-шьҭы-зт
Conditional I		
3Hum.Sg-3F.Sg	д-на-лы́-шьҭ-ры-н	д-на-лы́-шьҭ-ры-мы-зт
Conditional II		
3Hum.Sg-3F.Sg	д-на-лы́-шьҭ-ша-н	д-на-лы́-шьҭ-ша-мы-зт
Pluperfect		
3Hum.Sg-3F.Sg	д-на-лы́-шьҭ-хьа-н	д-на-л-мы́-шьҭ-цы-зт

Non-Finite forms

	Affirmative	Negative
Dynamic Group I		
C1-Prev-C3-		
Present		
Rel-1Sg	и́-на-сы-шьҭ-уа /jə́-na-sə-šʲt-wa/ Rel(C1)-Prev-I(C3)-send-Dyn.NF 'whom/which I am sending thither'	и́-на-с-мы-шьҭ-уа
Rel-2F.Sg	и́-на-бы-шьҭ-уа	и́-на-б-мы-шьҭ-уа
Rel-2M.Sg	и́-на-у-шьҭ-уа	и́-на-у-мы-шьҭ-уа
Rel-3F.Sg	и́-на-лы-шьҭ-уа	и́-на-л-мы-шьҭ-уа
Rel-3M.Sg	и́-на-и-шьҭ-уа	и́-на-и-мы-шьҭ-уа
Rel-1Pl	и́-на-ҳа-шьҭ-уа	и́-на-ҳ-мы-шьҭ-уа
Rel-2Pl	и́-на-шәы-шьҭ-уа	и́-на-шә-мы-шьҭ-уа
Rel-3Pl	и́-на-ры-шьҭ-уа	и́-на-р-мы-шьҭ-уа
1Sg-Rel	с-на-зы́-шьҭ-уа /s-na-zə́-šʲt-wa/ me(C1)-Prev-Rel(C3)-send-Dyn.NF '(the one) who is sending me thither'	с-на-з-мы́-шьҭ-уа
2F.Sg-Rel	б-на-зы́-шьҭ-уа	б-на-з-мы́-шьҭ-уа
2M.Sg-Rel	у-на-зы́-шьҭ-уа	у-на-з-мы́-шьҭ-уа
3N.H.Sg/3Pl-Rel	и-на-зы́-шьҭ-уа	и-на-з-мы́-шьҭ-уа
1Pl-Rel	ҳ-на-зы́-шьҭ-уа	ҳ-на-з-мы́-шьҭ-уа
2Pl-Rel	шә-на-зы́-шьҭ-уа	шә-на-з-мы́-шьҭ-уа
Aorist		
Rel-3F.Sg	и́-на-лы́-шьҭ	и́-на-л-мы́-шьҭ
3N.H.Sg/3Pl-Rel	и-на-зы́-шьҭ	и-на-з-мы́-шьҭ
Future I		
Rel-3F.Sg	и́-на-лы́-шьҭ-ра	и́-на-л-мы́-шьҭ-ра
3N.H.Sg/3Pl-Rel	и-на-зы́-шьҭ-ра	и-на-з-мы́-шьҭ-ра
Future II		
Rel-3F.Sg	и́-на-лы́-шьҭ-ша	и́-на-л-мы́-шьҭ-ша
3N.H.Sg/3Pl-Rel	и-на-зы́-шьҭ-ша	и-на-з-мы́-шьҭ-ша
Perfect		
Rel-3F.Sg	и́-на-лы́-шьҭ-хьо-у (-хьа(-ц))	и́-на-л-мы́-шьҭ-хьо-у (-хьа(-ц))
3N.H.Sg/3Pl-Rel	и-на-зы́-шьҭ-хьо-у (-хьа(-ц))	и-на-з-мы́-шьҭ-хьо-у (-хьа(-ц))

Dynamic Group II

Imperfect		
Rel-3F.Sg	и́-на-лы́-шьҭ-уа-з	и́-на-л-мы́-шьҭ-уа-з
3N.H.Sg/3Pl-Rel	и-на-зы́-шьҭ-уа-з	и-на-з-мы́-шьҭ-уа-з
Past Indefinite		
Rel-3F.Sg	и́-на-лы́-шьҭы-з	и́-на-л-мы́-шьҭы-з
3N.H.Sg/3Pl-Rel	и-на-зы́-шьҭы-з	и-на-з-мы́-шьҭы-з
Conditional I		
Rel-3F.Sg	и́-на-лы́-шьҭ-ры-з	и́-на-л-мы́-шьҭ-ры-з
3N.H.Sg/3Pl-Rel	и-на-зы́-шьҭ-ры-з	и-на-з-мы́-шьҭ-ры-з
Conditional II		
Rel-3F.Sg	и́-на-лы́-шьҭ-ша-з	и́-на-л-мы́-шьҭ-ша-з
3N.H.Sg/3Pl-Rel	и-на-зы́-шьҭ-ша-з	и-на-з-мы́-шьҭ-ша-з
Pluperfect		
Rel-3F.Sg	и́-на-лы́-шьҭ-хьа-з	и́-на-л-мы́-шьҭ-хьа-з
3N.H.Sg/3Pl-Rel	и-на-зы́-шьҭ-хьа-з	и-на-з-мы́-шьҭ-хьа-з

3.2.11. Class H

Class H verbs are three-place transitive verbs that have preverbs. The arrangement order of the morphemes within the verb 'C1+C2+Prev+C3+R' is strictly followed. Here, (i) relational preverbs and (ii) local preverbs in Types A and B (or D) are used as preverbs, and they govern the pronominal prefixes in Column II directly before it.

(i) For an example which uses relational preverb -а- 'to', see the example of а-ҳәарá /a-ħʷa-rá/ 'to say' that uses three arguments:[131]

(223) исáлҳәеит
/jə-s-á-l-ħʷa-jt'/
it/them(C1)-me(C2)-Prev(to)-she(C3)-say-(Aor)-Fin
'She said it/them to me.'

Also, as an example which uses (ii) local preverb -ҟә- /kʷ/ 'on', see the example of á-ҟәҵара /á-kʷ-c'a-ra/ 'to put *sth* on':

(224) исы́ҟәылҵеит
/jə-sə́-kʷə-l-c'a-jt'/
it/them(C1)-me(C2)-Prev(on)-she(C3)-put-(Aor)-Fin
'She put it/them on me.'

In (223), the preverb а- /a/ governs the Column II pronominal prefix с- /s/ 'me' directly before it and

131. а-ҳәарá 'to say' can also be used as a two-place transitive verb: исҳәéит /jə-s-ħʷá-jt'/ [it/them(C1)-I(C3)-say-(Aor)-Fin] 'I said it/them'.

indicates a dative relation. Aslo, in (224) the preverb кә(ы)- /kʷ(ə)/ governs the Column II pronominal prefix с(ы)- /s(ə)/ 'me' directly before it and indicates the location of the action expressed by the verb. The preverbs used in Class H verbs are practically the same as the preverbs used in Class F verbs.

(i) Relational preverb: -а- /a/ 'to', -аи- /aj/ 'to', -з- /z/ 'for, about', -цә(ы)- /cʷ(ə)/ 'from.

(ii) Local preverb:

Type A: -ва-, -в-, -вҵа-, -гәы́д-, -гәы́ла-, -гәы́л-, -ҕра-, -ҕр(ы)-, -д-, -жә-,-кә-, -ҟә(ы)-, -ла-, -л-, ма-, -м-, -мҕа-, -мҕы-, -мпы́ҵ-, -мҵа-, -мҵ-, -н(ы)-, -ҧ-, -ҧы́р-, -ха-, -х(ы)-, -хьӡ-, хәла-, -ц-, -цыр-, -ҵа-, -ҵ-, -ҿа-, -шьҭа-, -шь-, -шә-, -ҵьа-.

Type B: -дәы́л-, -кна-, -кы́д-, -кы́ла-, -кы́л-, -қә-, -ла-, -л-, -ҭа-, -ҭ(ы)-, -ҵ-, -ҩна-.

Regarding preverbs with the vocalic alteration -а : -ø (example: -ва- /va/: -в- /v/, etc.), see §3.1.2.4.

When describing the verbal inflections below, the Column II third-person singular non-human (3 sg. N.H) prefixes in verbs with Type B local preverbs will be transcribed as -ø-. For example, the Column II prefix in аҭаҧсара́ /a-ta-psa-rá/ 'to to pour into' is transcribed as follows:

(225) Ашы́ла ааҵәа́ иøҭа́сҧсеит.
/a-šə́la [a-]aac'ʷá jə-ø-ta-s-psá-jt'/
the-flour the-sack it(= flour, C1)-it(= the sack, C2)-Prev(into)-I(C3)-pour-(Aor)-Fin
'I poured flour into the sack'.

(226) Ашы́ла ааҵәақәа́ ирҭа́сҧсеит.
/a-šə́la [a-]aac'ʷa-kʷá jə-r-tá-s-psá-jt'/
the-flour the-sack-Pl it(= flour, C1)-them(the sacks, C2)-Prev(into)-I(C3)-pour-(Aor)-Fin
'I poured flour into the sacks.'

3.2.11.1. Inflection of а-ҳәа-ра́ 'to say *sth* to *sb*'

Finite forms

	Affirmative	Negative
Dynamic Group I		
C1-C2-Prev-C3- Present		
3N.H.Sg/3Pl-2F.Sg-1Sg	и-б-а́-с-ҳәо-ит /jə-b-á-s-ħʷa-wa-jt'/ it/them(C1)-you.F(C2)-to-I(C3)-say-Dyn-Fin 'I am saying it/them to you-F'	и-б-а́-с-ҳәо-м
3N.H.Sg/3Pl-2M.Sg-1Sg	и-у-а́-с-ҳәо-ит	и-у-а́-с-ҳәо-м
3N.H.Sg/3Pl-3F.Sg-1Sg	и-л-а́-с-ҳәо-ит	и-л-а́-с-ҳәо-м
3N.H.Sg/3Pl-3M.Sg-1Sg	и-а́-с-ҳәо-ит (< и-и-а́-с-ҳәо-ит)	и-а́-с-ҳәо-м
3N.H.Sg/3Pl-3N.H.Sg-1Sg	и-а́-с-ҳәо-ит (< и-а-а́-с-ҳәо-ит)	и-а́-с-ҳәо-м
3N.H.Sg/3Pl-2Pl-1Sg	и-шә-а́-с-ҳәо-ит	и-шә-а́-с-ҳәо-м
3N.H.Sg/3Pl-3Pl-1Sg	и-р-а́-с-ҳәо-ит	и-р-а́-с-ҳәо-м
3N.H.Sg/3Pl-1Sg-2F.Sg	и-с-а́-б-ҳәо-ит	и-с-а́-б-ҳәо-м
3N.H.Sg/3Pl-1Sg-2M.Sg	и-с-о́-у-ҳәо-ит	и-с-а́-у-ҳәо-м

3N.H.Sg/3Pl-1Sg-3F.Sg	и-с-á-л-ҳәо-ит	и-с-á-л-ҳәо-м
3N.H.Sg/3Pl-1Pl-3M.Sg	и-ҳ-á-и-ҳәо-ит	и-х-á-и-ҳәо-м
3N.H.Sg/3Pl-1Sg-3M.Sg	и-с-é-и-ҳәо-ит	и-с-á-и-ҳәо-м
3N.H.Sg/3Pl-3M.Sg-3M.Sg	é-и-ҳәо-ит (< и-и-á-и-хәо-ит)	é-и-ҳәо-м
3N.H.Sg/3Pl-3N.H.Sg-3M.Sg	и-á-и-ҳәо-ит (< и-а-á-и-ҳәо-ит)	и-á-и-ҳәо-м
3N.H.Sg/3Pl-1Sg-3N.H.Sg	и-с-á-на-ҳәо-ит	и-с-á-на-ҳәо-м
3N.H.Sg/3Pl-3M.Sg-3N.H.Sg	и-á-на-хәо-ит (< и-и-á-на-хәо-ит)	и-á-на-ҳәо-м
3N.H.Sg/3Pl-3N.H.Sg-3N.H.Sg	и-á-на-хәо-ит (< и-а-á-на-ҳәо-ит)	и-á-на-хәо-м
3N.H.Sg/3Pl-2.M.Sg-1Pl	и-у-á-ҳ-ҳәо-ит	и-у-á-ҳ-ҳәо-м
3N.H.Sg/3Pl-1Sg-2Pl	и-с-á-шә-ҳәо-ит	и-с-á-шә-ҳәо-м
3N.H.Sg/3Pl-1Sg-3Pl	и-с-á-р-ҳәо-ит	и-с-á-р-ҳәо-м
Aorist		
3N.H.Sg/3Pl-1Sg-3F.Sg	и-с-á-л-ҳәе-ит	и-с-á-лы-м-ҳәе-ит
3N.H.Sg/3Pl-1Sg-2M.Sg	и-с-ó-у-ҳәе-ит	и-с-ó-у-м-ҳәе-ит
3N.H.Sg/3Pl-1Sg-3M.Sg	и-с-é-и-ҳәе-ит	и-с-é-и-м-ҳәе-ит
3N.H.Sg/3Pl-3M.Sg-3M.Sg	é-и-ҳәе-ит (< и-и-á-и-хәе-ит)	é-и-м-ҳәе-ит
3N.H.Sg/3Pl-2F.Sg-1Pl	и-б-á-ҳ-ҳәе-ит	и-б-á-ҳа-м-ҳәе-ит
Future I		
3N.H.Sg/3Pl-1Sg-3F.Sg	и-с-á-л-ҳәа-п	и-с-á-л-ҳәа-ры-м
Future II		
3N.H.Sg/3Pl-1Sg-3F.Sg	и-с-á-л-ҳәа-шт	и-с-á-л-ҳәа-ша-м
Perfect		
3N.H.Sg/3Pl-1Sg-3F.Sg	и-с-á-л-ҳәа-хьe-ит	и-с-á-лы-м-ҳәа-ц(т)
Dynamic Group II		
C1-C2-Prev-C3-		
Imperfect		
3N.H.Sg/3Pl-1Sg-3F.Sg	и-с-á-л-ҳәо-н	и-с-á-л-ҳәо-мы-зт
Past Indefinite		
3N.H.Sg/3Pl-1Sg-3F.Sg	и-с-á-л-ҳәа-н	и-с-á-лы-м-ҳәа-зт
Conditional I		
3N.H.Sg/3Pl-1Sg-3F.Sg	и-с-á-л-ҳәа-ры-н	и-с-á-л-ҳәа-ры-мы-зт
Conditional II		
3N.H.Sg/3Pl-1Sg-3F.Sg	и-с-á-л-ҳәа-ша-н	и-с-á-л-ҳәа-ша-мы-зт
Pluperfect		
3N.H.Sg/3Pl-1Sg-3F.Sg	и-с-á-л-ҳәа-хьа-н	и-с-á-лы-м-ҳәа-цы-зт

Non-Finite forms

	<u>Affirmative</u>	<u>Negative</u>
Dynamic Group I		
C1-C2-Prev-C3-		

Present		
Rel-1Sg-3F.Sg	и-с-á-л-ҳәо	и-с-á-лы-м-ҳәо
	/jə-s-á-l-ħʷa-wa/	
	Rel(C1)-me(C2)-to-she(C3)-say-Dyn.NF	
	‘which she is saying to me’	
Rel-1Sg-3Non-Hum.Sg	и-с-á-на-ҳәо	и-с-á-на-м-ҳәо
Rel-3M.Sg-3F.Sg	и-á-л-ҳәо (< и-и-á-л-ҳәо)	и-á-лы-м-ҳәо
Rel-1Pl-3F.Sg	и-ҳ-á-л-ҳәо	и-ҳ-á-лы-м-ҳәо
3N.H.Sg/3Pl-Rel-3F.Sg	и-з-а-л-ҳәó	и-з-á-лы-м-ҳәо
	/jə-z-a-l-ħʷa-wá/	
	it/them(C1)-Rel(C2)-to-she(C3)-say-Dyn.NF	
	‘(the one) whom she is saying it/them to’	
3N.H.Sg/3Pl-Rel-1Sg	и-з-а-с-ҳәó	и-з-á-сы-м-ҳәо
3N.H.Sg/3Pl-Rel-3M.Sg	и-з-а-и-ҳәó	и-з-á-и-м-ҳәо
3N.H.Sg/3Pl-Rel-3Non-Hum.Sg	и-з-á-на-ҳәо	и-з-á-на-м-ҳәо
3N.H.Sg/3Pl-Rel-1Pl	и-з-а-ҳ-ҳәó	и-з-á-ҳа-м-ҳәо
3N.H.Sg/3Pl-Rel-3Pl	и-з-а-р-ҳәó	и-з-á-ры-м-ҳәо
3N.H.Sg/3Pl-1Sg-Rel	и-с-á-з-ҳәо	и-с-á-зы-м-ҳәо
	/jə-s-á-z-ħʷa-wa/	
	it/them(C1)-me(C2)-to-Rel(C3)-say-Dyn.NF	
	‘(the one) who is saying it/them to me’	
3N.H.Sg/3Pl-2F.Sg-Rel	и-б-á-з-ҳәо	и-б-á-зы-м-ҳәо
3N.H.Sg/3Pl-3F.Sg-Rel	и-л-á-з-ҳәо	и-л-á-зы-м-ҳәо
3N.H.Sg/3Pl-3M.Sg-Rel	и-á-з-ҳәо (< и-и-á-з-ҳәо)	и-á-зы-м-ҳәо
3N.H.Sg/3Pl-1Pl-Rel	и-ҳ-á-з-ҳәо	и-ҳ-á-зы-м-ҳәо
3N.H.Sg/3Pl-3Pl-Rel	и-р-á-з-ҳәо	и-р-á-зы-м-ҳәо
Aorist		
Rel-1Sg-3F.Sg	и-с-á-л-ҳәа	и-с-á-лы-м-ҳәа
3N.H.Sg/3Pl-Rel-3F.Sg	и-з-á-л-ҳәа	и-з-á-лы-м-ҳәа
3N.H.Sg/3Pl-1Sg-Rel	и-с-á-з-ҳәа	и-с-á-зы-м-ҳәа
Future I		
Rel-1Sg-3F.Sg	и-с-á-л-ҳәа-ра	и-с-á-лы-м-ҳәа-ра
3N.H.Sg/3Pl-Rel-3F.Sg	и-з-á-л-ҳәа-ра	и-з-á-лы-м-ҳәа-ра
3N.H.Sg/3Pl-1Sg-Rel	и-с-á-з-ҳәа-ра	и-с-á-зы-м-ҳәа-ра
Future II		
Rel-1Sg-3F.Sg	и-с-á-л-ҳәа-ша	и-с-á-лы-м-ҳәа-ша
3N.H.Sg/3Pl-Rel-3F.Sg	и-з-á-л-ҳәа-ша	и-з-á-лы-м-ҳәа-ша
3N.H.Sg/3Pl-1Sg-Rel	и-с-á-з-ҳәа-ша	и-с-á-зы-м-ҳәа-ша
Perfect		
Rel-1Sg-3F.Sg	и-с-á-л-ҳәа-хьо-у (-хьа(-ц))	и-с-á-лы-м-ҳәа-хьо-у (-хьа(-ц))

3N.H.Sg/3Pl-Rel-3F.Sg	и-з-á-л-ҳәа-хьо-у (-хьа(-ц))	и-з-á-лы-м-ҳәа-хьо-у (-хьа(-ц))
3N.H.Sg/3Pl-1Sg-Rel	и-с-á-з-ҳәа-хьо-у (-хьа(-ц))	и-с-á-зы-м-ҳәа-хьо-у (-хьа(-ц))
Dynamic Group II		
Imperfect		
Rel-1Sg-3F.Sg	и-с-á-л-ҳәо-з	и-с-á-лы-м-ҳәо-з
3N.H.Sg/3Pl-Rel-3F.Sg	и-з-á-л-ҳәо-з	и-з-á-лы-м-ҳәо-з
3N.H.Sg/3Pl-1Sg-Rel	и-с-á-з-ҳәо-з	и-с-á-зы-м-ҳәо-з
Past Indefinite		
Rel-1Sg-3F.Sg	и-с-á-л-ҳәа-з	и-с-á-лы-м-ҳәа-з
3N.H.Sg/3Pl-Rel-3F.Sg	и-з-á-л-ҳәа-з	и-з-á-лы-м-ҳәа-з
3N.H.Sg/3Pl-1Sg-Rel	и-с-á-з-ҳәа-з	и-с-á-зы-м-ҳәа-з
Conditional I		
Rel-1Sg-3F.Sg	и-с-á-л-ҳәа-ры-з	и-с-á-лы-м-ҳәа-ры-з
3N.H.Sg/3Pl-Rel-3F.Sg	и-з-á-л-ҳәа-ры-з	и-з-á-лы-м-ҳәа-ры-з
3N.H.Sg/3Pl-1Sg-Rel	и-с-á-з-ҳәа-ры-з	и-с-á-зы-м-ҳәа-ры-з
Conditional II		
Rel-1Sg-3F.Sg	и-с-á-л-ҳәа-ша-з	и-с-á-лы-м-ҳәа-ша-з
3N.H.Sg/3Pl-Rel-3F.Sg	и-з-á-л-ҳәа-ша-з	и-з-á-лы-м-ҳәа-ша-з
3N.H.Sg/3Pl-1Sg-Rel	и-с-á-з-ҳәа-ша-з	и-с-á-зы-м-ҳәа-ша-з
Pluperfect		
Rel-1Sg-3F.Sg	и-с-á-л-ҳәа-хьа-з	и-с-á-лы-м-ҳәа-хьа-з
3N.H.Sg/3Pl-Rel-3F.Sg	и-з-á-л-ҳәа-хьа-з	и-з-á-лы-м-ҳәа-хьа-з
3N.H.Sg/3Pl-1Sg-Rel	и-с-á-з-ҳәа-хьа-з	и-с-á-зы-м-ҳәа-хьа-з

3.2.11.2. Inflection of á-қә-тҵа-ра 'to put *sth* on, to load *sth* into'

Finite forms

	Affirmative	Negative
Dynamic Group I		
C1-C2-Prev-C3-		
Present		
3N.H.Sg/3Pl-1Sg-3F.Sg	и-сы́-қәы-л-тҵо-ит /jə-sə́-kʷə-l-c'a-wa-jt'/ it/them(C1)-me(C2)-Prev(on)-she(C3)-put-Dyn-Fin 'she is putting it/them on me'	и-сы́-қәы-л-тҵо-м
3N.H.Sg/3Pl-2F.Sg-3F.Sg	и-бы́-қәы-л-тҵо-ит	и-бы́-қәы-л-тҵо-м
3N.H.Sg/3Pl-2M.Sg-3F.Sg	и-ý-қәы-л-тҵо-ит	и-ý-қәы-л-тҵо-м
3N.H.Sg/3Pl-3F.Sg-3F.Sg	и-лы́-қәы-л-тҵо-ит	и-лы́-қә-л-тҵо-м
3N.H.Sg/3Pl-3M.Sg-3F.Sg	и́-қәы-л-тҵо-ит (< и-и́-қәы-л-)	и́-қәы-л-тҵо-м

3N.H.Sg/3Pl-3N.H.Sg-3M.Sg	и-а́-кə-и-тцо-ит	и-а́-кə-и-тцо-м
3N.H.Sg/3Pl-3N.H.Sg-3M.Sg	и́-ø-кə-и-тцо-ит	и́-ø-кə-и-тцо-м
3N.H.Sg/3Pl-1Pl-3F.Sg	и-ха́-кəы-л-тцо-ит	и-ха́-кəы-л-тцо-м
3N.H.Sg/3Pl-2Pl-3F.Sg	и-шəы́-кəы-л-тцо-ит	и-шəы́-кəы-л-тцо-м
3N.H.Sg/3Pl-3Pl-3F.Sg	и-ры́-кəы-л-тцо-ит	и-ры́-кəы-л-тцо-м
3N.H.Sg/3Pl-1Sg-3Non-Hum.Sg	и-сы́-кə-на-тцо-ит	и-сы́-кə-на-тцо-м
3N.H.Sg/3Pl-3Pl-3Pl	и-ры́-кə-р-тцо-ит	и-ры́-кə-р-тцо-м

Aorist

3N.H.Sg/3Pl-1Sg-3F.Sg	и-сы́-кəы-л-тце-ит	и-сы́-кə-лы-м-тце-ит
3N.H.Sg/3Pl-3N.H.Sg-1Sg	и-а́-кəы-с-тце-ит	и-а́-кə-сы-м-тце-ит
3N.H.Sg/3Pl-3N.H.Sg-3M.Sg	и-а́-кə-и-тце-ит	и-а́-кə-и-м-тце-ит

Non-Finite forms

	Affirmative	Negative
Dynamic Group I		
C1-C2-Prev-C3-		
Present		
Rel-1Sg-3F.Sg	и-сы́-кəы-л-тцо /jə-sə́-kʷə-l-c'a-wa/ Rel(C1)-me(C2)-Prev(on)-she(C3)-put-Dyn.NF 'which she is putting on me'	и-сы́-кə-лы-м-тцо
3N.H.Sg/3Pl-Rel-3F.Sg	и-з-кəы́-л-тцо /jə-z-kʷə́-l-c'a-wa/ it/them(C1)-Rel(C2)-Prev(on)-she(C3)-put-Dyn.NF 'which/whom she is putting it/them on'	и-з-кəы́-лы-м-тцо
3N.H.Sg/3Pl-1Sg-Rel	и-сы́-кəы-з-тцо /jə-sə́-kʷə-z-c'a-wa/ it/them(C1)-me(C2)-Prev(on)-Rel(C3)-put-Dyn.NF '(the one) who is putting it/them on me'	и-сы́-кə-зы-м-тцо

Aorist

Rel-1Sg-3F.Sg	и-сы́-кəы-л-тца	и-сы́-кə-лы-м-тца
3N.H.Sg/3Pl-Rel-3F.Sg	и-з-кəы́-л-тца	и-зы́-кə-лы-м-тца *or* и-з-кəы́-лы-м-тца
3N.H.Sg/3Pl-1Sg-Rel	и-сы́-кəы-з-тца	и-сы́-кə-зы-м-тца

Imperfect

Rel-1Sg-3F.Sg	и-сы́-кəы-л-тцо-з	и-сы́-кə-лы-м-тцо-з
3N.H.Sg/3Pl-Rel-3F.Sg	и-з-кəы́-л-тцо-з	и-зы́-кə-лы-м-тцо-з *or* и-з-кəы́-лы-м-тцо-з
3N.H.Sg/3Pl-1Sg-Rel	и-сы́-кəы-з-тцо-з	и-сы́-кə-зы-м-тцо-з

Past Indefinite		
Rel-1Sg-3F.Sg	и-сы́-кәы-л-тца-з	и-сы́-кә-лы-м-тца-з
3N.H.Sg/3Pl-Rel-3F.Sg	и-з-кәы́-л-тца-з	и-зы́-кә-лы-м-тца-з *or* и-з-кәы́-лы-м-тца-з
3N.H.Sg/3Pl-1Sg-Rel	и-сы́-кәы-з-тца-з	и-сы́-кә-зы-м-тца-з

Examples:

(227) Амра ла́н илы́кәылтцеит ахы́за.
/ámra l-án jə-lə́-kʷə-l-c'a-jt' a-xə́za/
name her-mother it(C1)-her(C2)-Prev-she(C3)-put-(Aor)-Fin the-blanket
'Amra put a blanket on her mother.'

(228) Ахра ала́ ахы́за а́кәитцеит.
/áxra a-lá a-xə́za ø-á-kʷə-j-c'a-jt'/
name the-dog the-blanket [it(= the blanket, C1)-]it(= the dog, C2)-Prev-he(C3)-(Aor)-Fin
'Akhra put the blanket on the dog.'

(229) Ау́суцәа авагóн акартóш а́кәыртцоит.
/a-wə́swə-cʷa a-vagón a-k'art'óš ø-á-kʷə-r-c'a-wa-jt'/
the-worker-Pl the-car the-potato(es) [it (C1)-]it(= the car, C2)-Prev-they(C3)-put-Dyn-Fin
'The workers are loading the (railroad) car with potatoes.'

(230) Ау́суцәа ахабырза́кь амашьы́накәа иры́кәртцоит.
/a-wə́swə-cʷa a-ħabərzák'ʲ a-mašʲə́na-kʷa jə-rə́-kʷ-r-c'a-wa-jt'/
the-worker-Pl the-watermelon the-car-Pl it(C1)-them(C2)-Prev-they(C3)-put-Dyn-Fin
'The workers are loading watermelons into the cars.'

(231) Ашәҟәы́ астóл и́кәтца!
/a-šʷq'ʷə́ a-st'ól jə́-ø-kʷ-c'a/
the-book the-table it(= the book, C1)-it(= the table, C2)-Prev(on)-put.Imp
'Put the book on the table!'

Note: For the difference between the Column II third person singular, non-human prefix -a- in Examples (228) and (229) above and the zero-prefix -ø- in Example (231), see §3.2.9.2.

3.2.11.3. Inflection of а-ты́-х-ра 'to take *sth* out of, to drag/pull out'

Finite forms

	Affirmative	Negative
Dynamic Group I		
C1-C2-Prev-C3-		
Present		
3N.H.Sg/3Pl-3N.H.Sg-1Sg	и-ø-ты́-с-х-уе-ит /jə-ø-tə́-s-x-wa-jt'/ it/them(C1)-[it(C2)-]Prev-I(C3)-take out of-Dyn-Fin 'I am taking it/them out of it'	и-ø-ты́-с-х-уа-м
3N.H.Sg/3Pl-3Pl-1Sg	и-р-ты́-с-х-уе-ит	и-р-ты́-с-х-уа-м

	/jə-r-tə́-s-x-wa-jt'/	
	'I am taking it/them out of them'	
Aorist		
3N.H.Sg/3Pl-3N.H.Sg-1Sg	и-ø-ҭы́-с-х-ит	и-ø-ҭы́-сы-м-х-ит
Future I		
3N.H.Sg/3Pl-3N.H.Sg-1Sg	и-ø-ҭы́-с-хы-п	и-ø-ҭы́-с-х-ры-м
Future II		
3N.H.Sg/3Pl-3N.H.Sg-1Sg	и-ø-ҭы́-с-хы-шт	и-ø-ҭы́-с-хы-ша-м
Perfect		
3N.H.Sg/3Pl-3N.H.Sg-1Sg	и-ø-ҭы́-с-х-хье-ит	и-ø-ҭы́-сы-м-хы-ц(т)

Dynamic Group II

C1-C2-Prev-C3-

Imperfect		
3N.H.Sg/3Pl-3N.H.Sg-1Sg	и-ø-ҭы́-с-х-уа-н	и-ø-ҭы́-с-х-уа-мы-зт
Past Indefinite		
3N.H.Sg/3Pl-3N.H.Sg-1Sg	и-ø-ҭы́-с-хы-н	и-ø-ҭы́-сы-м-хы-зт
Conditional I		
3N.H.Sg/3Pl-3N.H.Sg-1Sg	и-ø-ҭы́-с-х-ры-н	и-ø-ҭы́-с-х-ры-мы-зт
Conditional II		
3N.H.Sg/3Pl-3N.H.Sg-1Sg	и-ø-ҭы́-с-хы-ша-н	и-ø-ҭы́-с-хы-ша-мы-зт
Pluperfect		
3N.H.Sg/3Pl-3N.H.Sg-1Sg	и-ø-ҭы́-с-х-хьа-н	и-ø-ҭы́-сы-м-хы-цы-зт

Non-Finite forms

	Affirmative	Negative
Dynamic Group I		
C1-C2-Prev-C3-		
Present		
Rel-3N.H.Sg-3F.Sg	и-ø-ҭы́-л-х-уа	и-ø-ҭы́-лы-м-х-уа
	/jə-ø-tə́-l-x-wa/	
	Rel(C1)-[it(C2)-]Prev-she(C3)-take out of-Dyn.NF	
	'which she is taking out of it'	
3N.H.Sg/3Pl-3N.H.Sg-Rel	и-ø-ҭы́-з-х-уа	и-ø-ҭы́-зы-м-х-уа
	/jə-ø-tə́-z-x-wa/	
	it/them(C1)-[it(C2)-]Prev-Rel(C3)-take out of-Dyn.NF	
	'(the one) who is taking it/them out of it'	
Aorist		
Rel-3N.H.Sg-3F.Sg	и-ø-ҭы́-л-х	и-ø-ҭы́-лы-м-х
3N.H.Sg/3Pl-3N.H.Sg-Rel	и-ø-ҭы́-з-х	и-ø-ҭы́-зы-м-х
Future I		
Rel-3N.H.Sg-3F.Sg	и-ø-ҭы́-л-х-ра	и-ø-ҭы́-лы-м-х-ра

3N.H.Sg/3Pl-3N.H.Sg-Rel	и-ø-ҭы́-з-х-ра	и-ø-ҭы́-зы-м-х-ра
Future II		
Rel-3N.H.Sg-3F.Sg	и-ø-ҭы́-л-х-ша	и-ø-ҭы́-лы-м-х-ша
3N.H.Sg/3Pl-3N.H.Sg-Rel	и-ø-ҭы́-з-х-ша	и-ø-ҭы́-зы-м-х-ша
Perfect		
Rel-3N.H.Sg-3F.Sg	и-ø-ҭы́-л-х-хьо-у (-хьа(-ц))	и-ø-ҭы́-лы-м-х-хьо-у(-хьа(-ц))
3N.H.Sg/3Pl-3N.H.Sg-Rel	и-ø-ҭы́-з-х-хьо-у (-хьа(-ц))	и-ø-ҭы́-зы-м-х-хьо-у (-хьа(-ц))

Dynamic Group II

Imperfect		
Rel-3N.H.Sg-3F.Sg	и-ø-ҭы́-л-х-уа-з	и-ø-ҭы́-лы-м-х-уа-з
3N.H.Sg/3Pl-3N.H.Sg-Rel	и-ø-ҭы́-з-х-уа-з	и-ø-ҭы́-зы-м-х-уа-з
Past Indefinite		
Rel-3N.H.Sg-3F.Sg	и-ø-ҭы́-л-хы-з	и-ø-ҭы́-лы-м-хы-з
3N.H.Sg/3Pl-3N.H.Sg-Rel	и-ø-ҭы́-з-хы-з	и-ø-ҭы́-зы-м-хы-з
Conditional I		
Rel-3N.H.Sg-3F.Sg	и-ø-ҭы́-л-х-ры-з	и-ø-ҭы́-лы-м-х-ры-з
3N.H.Sg/3Pl-3N.H.Sg-Rel	и-ø-ҭы́-з-х-ры-з	и-ø-ҭы́-зы-м-х-ры-з
Conditional II		
Rel-3N.H.Sg-3F.Sg	и-ø-ҭы́-л-х-ша-з	и-ø-ҭы́-лы-м-х-ша-з
3N.H.Sg/3Pl-3N.H.Sg-Rel	и-ø-ҭы́-з-х-ша-з	и-ø-ҭы́-зы-м-х-ша-з
Pluperfect		
Rel-3N.H.Sg-3F.Sg	и-ø-ҭы́-л-х-хьа-з	и-ø-ҭы́-лы-м-х-хьа-з
3N.H.Sg/3Pl-3N.H.Sg-Rel	и-ø-ҭы́-з-х-хьа-з	и-ø-ҭы́-зы-м-х-хьа-з

Examples:

(232) Лџьы́ба иҭы́лхит аҧа́ра.

/l-ǯʲə́ba jə-ø-tə́-l-xə-jt’ a-pára/
her-pocket it(= money, C1)-[it(= her pocket, C2)-]Prev-she(C3)-take out-(Aor)-Fin the-money
‘She took some money out of her pocket.’

(233) Лџьы́бақәа ирҭы́лхит аҧа́рақәа.

/l-ǯʲə́ba-kʷa jə-r-tə́-l-xə-jt’ a-pára-kʷa/
her-pocket-Pl them(C1)-them(C2)-Prev-she(C3)-take out-(Aor)-Fin the-money-Pl
‘She took some money out of her pockets.’

3.2.11.4. Verbal Complexes That Form Structures Similar to Class H

Verbal complexes with the objective version (abbreviated hereafter as ‘OV’, for the objective version see §§4.3.2–4.3.5) markers -з(ы)- /z(ə)/, -цә(ы)- /cʷ(ə)/ or the subjective version (abbreviated hereafter as ‘SV’, for the subjective version see §§4.3.6–4.3.8) markers -х(ы)- /x(ə)/, -гәа́ла- /gʷála/, -бжьа- /bžʲa/, -д- /d/, -ха- /xa/, -ҿы /č’ə/, -шә(ы)- /šʷ(ə)/ also have a structure similar to Class H: ‘DO+IO+OV+A+R’ and ‘DO+Poss+SV+A+R’, respectively. In the objective version vrebal complexes, different pronominal prefixes must be used for A and IO. For example, an example sentence which uses а-цәгара́ /a-cʷ-ga-rá/ 'to take away from' (cf. агара́ /a-ga-rá/ 'to take') has different pronominal prefixes for A and IO:

(234) Уи сара́ аҧа́ра сцәйгеит.
/wəj sará a-pára ϕ-s-cʷə́-j-ga-jt'/
he I the-money [it(C1)-]me(C2)-OV(against one's will)-he(C3)-take-(Aor)-Fin
'He took the money away from me.' (lit. 'He took the money against my will')

Also, in the verb азура́ /a-zə-w-rá/ 'to do *sth* for *sb*', which uses the the objective version marker з- /z/ in the two-place transitive verb аура́ /a-w-rá/ 'to do', the pronominal prefixes for A and IO are different:

(235) Ау́с ду́ хзйуит.
/a-wə́s dəw ϕ-ħ-zə́-j-wə-jt'/
the-job big [it(C1)-]us(C2)-OV(for)-he(C3)-do-(Aor)-Fin
'He did a big job for us.'

These objective version markers -цә- /cʷ/, -з- /z/ work in the same way as a preverb, so there is also a view that does not recognize them as the objective version but considers them as preverbs. However, we follow the traditional view and regard the objective version as a grammatical category (see §4.3 for details). The two-place transitive verb а-ура́ /a-w-rá/ 'to do' seen above does not have preverbs, but the objective version markers can also attach to two-place transitive verbs with prevebs as well. For example, а-зы́ӄатцара /a-zə́-q'a-c'a-ra/ 'to do *sth* for *sb*', the form of а́-ӄатцара /á-q'a-c'a-ra/ 'to do' with the objective version marker -з- attached, is inflected as follows:

(236) илзы́ӄастцоит
/jə-l-zə́-q'a-s-c'a-wa-jt'/
it/them(C1)-her(C2)-OV(for)-Prev-I(C3)-Dyn-Fin
'I am doing it/them for her.'

The objective version maker -з- /z/ and the pronominal prefix it governs are placed after the Column I pronominal prefix. The structure of this verbal complex is different from Class H verbs, but if the OV and preverb are viewed as a compound preverb (cf. -гәыд- < -гәы + д-), this can be probably be considered Class H as well.

The subjective version is different from the objective version and A and IO must be the same person. For example, in the following sentence the fact that the person in A and IO in the verb а-хгара́ /a-x-ga-rá/ 'to spend', which has the subjective version marker -х(ы)- /x(ə)/ (cf. а-гара́ /a-ga-rá/ 'to take'), is the same is clear:

(237) Сара́ а́ҧхынра акы́тан исхы́згеит.
/sará á-pxənra a-kə́ta-n jə-s-xə́-z-ga-jt'/
I the-summer the-village-in it(C1)-my(Poss)-SV-I(C3)-spend-(Aor)-Fin
'I spent the summer in the village.'

Here, taking the the с- /s/ directly before the subjective version marker х(ы)- /x(ə)/ as a possessive (abbreviated hereafter as 'Poss') prefix is due to the reason why this marker has its origins in (а-)хы́ /(a-)xə́/ '(the/a-)head': in other words, схы /s-xə/ 'my head'. The details of the subjective version will be examined in §4.3.6.

3.2.11.4.1. Inflection of Class H Verbs with Objective Version Markers

3.2.11.4.1.1. Inflection of а-зы́-ҟа-ҵа-ра ‘to do *sth* for *sb*’

Finite forms

	Affirmative	Negative
Dynamic Group I		
C1-C2-OV-Prev-C3-		
Present		
3N.HSg/3Pl-2F.Sg-1Sg	и-б-зы́-ҟа-с-ҵо-ит	и-б-зы́-ҟа-с-ҵо-м
	/jə-b-zə́-q’a-s-c’a-wa-jt’/	
	it/them(C1)-you.F(C2)-OV-Prev-I(C3)-do/make-Dyn-Fin	
	‘I am doing/making it/them for you-F’	
3N.H.Sg/3Pl-2M.Sg-1Sg	и-у-зы́-ҟа-с-ҵо-ит	и-у-зы́-ҟа-с-ҵо-м
3N.H.Sg/3Pl-3M.Sg-1Sg	и-зы́-ҟа-с-ҵо-ит (< и-и-зы́-)	и-зы́-ҟа-с-ҵо-м
3N.H.Sg/3Pl-3F.Sg-1Sg	и-л-зы́-ҟа-с-ҵо-ит	и-л-зы́-ҟа-с-ҵо-м
3N.H.Sg/3Pl-3N.H.Sg-1Sg	и-а-зы́-ҟа-с-ҵо-ит	и-а-зы́-ҟа-с-ҵо-м
3N.H.Sg/3Pl-1Pl-2F.Sg	и-ах-зы́-ҟа-б-ҵо-ит	и-ах-зы́-ҟа-б-ҵо-м
3N.H.Sg/3Pl-2Pl-1Sg	и-шә-зы́-ҟа-с-ҵо-ит	и-шә-зы́-ҟа-с-ҵо-м
3N.H.Sg/3Pl-3Pl-1Sg	и-р-зы́-ҟа-с-ҵо-ит	и-р-зы́-ҟа-с-ҵо-м
3N.HSg/3Pl-2F.Sg-3N.H.Sg	и-б-зы́-ҟа-на-ҵо-ит	и-б-зы́-ҟа-на-ҵо-м
Aorist		
3N.HSg/3Pl-2F.Sg-1Sg	и-б-зы́-ҟа-с-ҵе-ит	и-б-зы́-ҟа-сы-м-ҵе-ит
3N.H.Sg/3Pl-1Pl-3F.Sg	и-ах-зы́-ҟа-л-ҵе-ит	и-ах-зы́-ҟа-лы-м-ҵе-ит
3N.H.Sg/3Pl-3F.Sg-1Pl	и-л-зы́-ҟа-х-ҵе-ит	и-л-зы́-ҟа-ха-м-ҵе-ит
3N.HSg/3Pl-1Sg-3N.H.Sg	и-с-зы́-ҟа-на-ҵе-ит	и-с-зы́-ҟа-на-м-ҵе-ит
3N.H.Sg/3Pl-3N.H.Sg-1Sg	и-а-зы́-ҟа-с-ҵе-ит	и-а-зы́-ҟа-сы-м-ҵе-ит

Non-Finite forms

	Affirmative	Negative
Dynamic Group I		
C1-C2-OV-Prev-C3-		
Present		
Rel-3F.Sg-1Sg	и-л-зы́-ҟа-с-ҵо	и-л-зы́-ҟа-сы-м-ҵо
	/jə-l-zə́-q’a-s-c’a-wa/	
	Rel(C1)-her(C2)-OV-Prev-I(C3)-do/make-Dyn.NF	
	‘which I am doing/making for her’	
3N.H.Sg/3Pl-Rel-1Sg	и-з-зы́-ҟа-с-ҵо	и-з-зы́-ҟа-сы-м-ҵо
	/jə-z-zə́-q’a-s-c’a-wa/	
	it/them(C1)-Rel(C2)-OV-Prev-I(C3)-do/make-Dyn.NF	
	‘(the one) whom I am doing/making it/them for’	
3N.H.Sg/3Pl-3F.Sg-Rel	и-л-зы́-ҟа-з-ҵо	и-л-зы́-ҟа-зы-м-ҵо
	/jə-l-zə́-q’a-z-c’a-wa/	
	it/them(C1)-her(C2)-OV-Prev-Rel(C3)-do/make-Dyn.NF	

'(the one) who is doing/making it/them for her'

3.2.11.4.1.2. Inflection of а-цә-га-ра́ 'to take away from'

Finite forms

	Affirmative	Negative
Dynamic Group I		
C1-C2-OV-C3-		
Present		
3N.HSg/3Pl-2F.Sg-1Sg	и-б-цәы́-з-го-ит /jə-b-cʷə́-z-ga-wa-jt'/ it/them(C1)-you.F(C2)-OV-I(C3)-taka away-Dyn-Fin 'I am taking it/them away from you-F'	и-б-цәы́-з-го-м
3N.HSg/3Pl-2M.Sg-1Sg	и-у-цәы́-з-го-ит	и-у-цәы́-з-го-м
3N.HSg/3Pl-3M.Sg-1Sg	и-цәы́-з-го-ит (< и-и-цәы́-)	и-цәы́-з-го-м
3N.HSg/3Pl-3F.Sg-1Sg	и-л-цәы́-з-го-ит	и-л-цәы́-з-го-м
3N.HSg/3Pl-3N.H..Sg-1Sg	и-а-цәы́-з-го-ит	и-а-цәы́-з-го-м
3N.HSg/3Pl-1Pl-2F.Sg	и-аҳ-цәы́-б-го-ит	и-аҳ-цәы́-б-го-м
3N.HSg/3Pl-2Pl-1Sg	и-шә-цәы́-з-го-ит	и-шә-цәы́-з-го-м
3N.HSg/3Pl-3Pl-1Sg	и-р-цәы́-з-го-ит	и-р-цәы́-з-го-м
3N.HSg/3Pl-2F.Sg-1Pl	и-б-цә-а́а-го-ит	и-б-цә-а́а-го-м
3N.HSg/3Pl-1Sg-3N.H.Sg	и-с-цә-а́-го-ит	и-с-цә-а́-го-м
3N.HSg/3Pl-3N.H.Sg-3N.H.Sg	и-а-цә-на́-го-ит	и-а-цә-на́-го-м
3N.HSg/3Pl-2Pl-3Pl	и-аҳ-цәы́-р-го-ит	и-аҳ-цәы́-р-го-м
Aorist		
3N.HSg/3Pl-2F.Sg-1Sg	и-б-цәы́-з-ге-ит	и-б-цәы́-зы-м-ге-ит
3N.HSg/3Pl-3M.Sg-3F.Sg	и-цәы́-л-ге-ит (< и-и-цәы́-)	и-цәы́-лы-м-ге-ит
3N.HSg/3Pl-1Pl-2F.Sg	и-аҳ-цәы́-б-ге-ит	и-аҳ-цәы́-бы-м-ге-ит
3N.HSg/3Pl-3F.Sg-1Pl	и-л-цә-а́а-ге-ит	и-л-цә-а́ҳа-м-ге-ит
3N.HSg/3Pl-1Sg-3N.H.Sg	и-с-цә-а-ге́-ит	и-с-цә-а́-м-ге-ит
3N.HSg/3Pl-3N.H.Sg-3N.H.Sg	и-а-цә-на-ге́-ит	и-а-цә-на́-м-ге-ит
3N.HSg/3Pl-2Pl-3Pl	и-ах-цәы́-р-ге-ит	и-ах-цәы́-ры-м-ге-ит

Non-Finite forms

	Affirmative	Negative
Dynamic Group I		
C1-C2-OV-Prev-C3-		
Present		
Rel-2F.Sg-3F.Sg	и-б-цәы́-л-го /jə-b-cʷə́-l-ga-wa/ Rel(C1)-you.F(C2)-OV-she(C3)-take away-Dyn.NF 'which she is taking away from you-F'	и-б-цәы́-лы-м-го
3N.HSg/3Pl-Rel-3F.Sg	и-з-цәы́-л-го	и-з-цәы́-лы-м-го

	/jə-z-cʷә́-l-ga-wa/	
	it/them(C1)-Rel(C2)-OV-she(C3)-take away-Dyn.NF	
	'(the one) whom she is taking it/them away from'	
3N.HSg/3Pl-2F.Sg-Rel	и-б-цәы́-з-го	и-б-цәы́-зы-м-го
	/jə-b-cʷә́-z-ga-wa/	
	it/them(C1)-you.F(C2)-OV-Rel(C3)-take away-Dyn.NF	
	'(the one) who is taking it/them away from you-F'	

3.2.11.4.2. Inflection of Class H Verbs with Subjective Version Markers

3.2.11.4.2.1. Inflection of а-ха-тца-рá 'to put on (headgear)'

Finite forms

	Affirmative	Negative
Dynamic Group I		
C1-Poss-SV-Prev-C3-Present		
3N.HSg/3Pl-1Sg-1Sg	и-с-хá-с-тцо-ит	и-с-хá-с-тцо-м
	/jə-s-xá-s-c'a-wa-jt'/	
	it/them(C1)-my(Poss)-SV-I(C3)-put on-Dyn-Fin	
	'I am putting on it/them'	
3N.HSg/3Pl-2F.Sg-2F.Sg	и-б-хá-б-тцо-ит	и-б-хá-б-тцо-м
3N.HSg/3Pl-2M.Sg-2M.Sg	и-у-хá-у-тцо-ит	и-у-хá-у-тцо-м
3N.HSg/3Pl-3M.Sg-3M.Sg	и-хé-и-тцо-ит (< и-и-хé-)	и-хé-и-тцо-м
3N.HSg/3Pl-3M.Sg-3M.Sg	и-л-хá-л-тцо-ит	и-л-хá-л-тцо-м
3N.HSg/3Pl-3N.H.Sg-3N.H.Sg	и-а-ха-на-тцó-ит	и-а-ха-на-тцó-м
3N.HSg/3Pl-1Pl-1Pl	и-ах-хá-х-тцо-ит	и-ах-хá-х-тцо-м
3N.HSg/3Pl-2Pl-2Pl	и-шә-хá-шә-тцо-ит	и-шә-хá-шә-тцо-м
3N.HSg/3Pl-3Pl-3Pl	и-р-хá-р-тцо-ит	и-р-хá-р-тцо-м
Aorist		
3N.HSg/3Pl-1Sg-1Sg	и-с-хá-с-тце-ит	и-с-хá-сы-м-тце-ит
3N.HSg/3Pl-3N.H.Sg-3N.H.Sg	и-а-ха-на-тцé-ит	и-а-ха-нá-м-тце-ит
3N.HSg/3Pl-1Pl-1Pl	и-ах-хá-х-тце-ит	и-ах-хá-ха-м-тце-ит

Non-Finite forms

	Affirmative	Negative
Dynamic Group I		
C1-C2-OV-Prev-C3-Present		
Rel-3F.Sg-3F.Sg	и-л-хá-л-тцо	и-л-хá-лы-м-тцо
	/jə-l-xá-l-c'a-wa/	
	Rel(C1)-her(Poss)-SV-she(C3)-put on-Dyn.NF	
	'which she is putting on'	

3N.HSg/3Pl-Rel-Rel	и-з-хá-з-тцо	и-з-хá-зы-м-тцо
	/jə-z-xá-z-c’a-wa/	
	it/them(C1)-Rel(Poss)-SV-Rel(C3)-put on-Dyn.NF	
	‘(the one) who is putting on it/them’	
Aorist		
Rel-3F.Sg-3F.Sg	и-л-хá-л-тца	и-л-хá-лы-м-тца
3N.HSg/3Pl-Rel-Rel	и-з-хá-з-тца	и-з-хá-зы-м-тца
Future I		
Rel-3F.Sg-3F.Sg	и-л-хá-л-тца-ра	и-л-хá-лы-м-тца-ра
3N.HSg/3Pl-Rel-Rel	и-з-хá-з-тца-ра	и-з-хá-зы-м-тца-ра
Future II		
Rel-3F.Sg-3F.Sg	и-л-хá-л-тца-ша	и-л-хá-лы-м-тца-ша
3N.HSg/3Pl-Rel-Rel	и-з-хá-з-тца-ша	и-з-хá-зы-м-тца-ша
Perfect		
Rel-3F.Sg-3F.Sg	и-л-хá-л-тца-хьо-у (-хьа(-ц))	и-л-хá-лы-м-тца-хьо-у (-хьа(-ц))
3N.HSg/3Pl-Rel-Rel	и-з-хá-з-тца-хьо-у (-хьа(-ц))	и-з-хá-зы-м-тца-хьо-у (-хьа(-ц))

Dynamic Group II		
C1-C2-OV-Prev-C3-		
Imperfect		
Rel-3F.Sg-3F.Sg	и-л-хá-л-тцо-з	и-л-хá-лы-м-тцо-з
3N.HSg/3Pl-Rel-Rel	и-з-хá-з-тцо-з	и-з-хá-зы-м-тцо-з
Past Indefinite		
Rel-3F.Sg-3F.Sg	и-л-хá-л-тца-з	и-л-хá-лы-м-тца-з
3N.HSg/3Pl-Rel-Rel	и-з-хá-з-тца-з	и-з-хá-зы-м-тца-з
Conditional I		
Rel-3F.Sg-3F.Sg	и-л-хá-л-тца-ры-з	и-л-хá-лы-м-тца-ры-з
3N.HSg/3Pl-Rel-Rel	и-з-хá-з-тца-ры-з	и-з-хá-зы-м-тца-ры-з
Conditional II		
Rel-3F.Sg-3F.Sg	и-л-хá-л-тца-ша-з	и-л-хá-лы-м-тца-ша-з
3N.HSg/3Pl-Rel-Rel	и-з-хá-з-тца-ша-з	и-з-хá-зы-м-тца-ша-з
Pluperfect		
Rel-3F.Sg-3F.Sg	и-л-хá-л-тца-хьа-з	и-л-хá-лы-м-тца-хьа-з
3N.HSg/3Pl-Rel-Rel	и-з-хá-з-тца-хьа-з	и-з-хá-зы-м-тца-хьа-з

3.3. Reduplicative Verbs

In Abkhaz, there are verbs that have roots that are reduplicated. These reduplicative verbs can be divided into the following types based on their meaning.

(i) They are used in onomatopoeia. For example:

á-чырчырра /á-č’ʲərč’ʲər-ra/ ‘to chirp, to twitter’ (cf. а-чырчы́р /a-č’ʲərč’ʲə́r/ ‘a twitter/chirping of birds’):

Ацáракәа чырчы́руа áшәа рхәóит.
/a-c'ára-kʷa č'ʲərč'ʲə́r-wa [a-]ášʷa ∅-r-ħʷa-wá-jt'/
the-bird-Pl chirp-Abs the-song [it(C1)-]they(C3)-say-Dyn-Fin
'Chirping, the birds are singing.'

áкашәкашәара /á-kašʷkašʷa-ra/ '(of young grass) to rustle, to sway':

С-чáи хазы́на кашәкашәó, мшы́нцас ицәкәрҧóит. (AFL)
/s-čʲáj xazə́na ∅-kašʷ-kašʷa-wá mšə́n-c'as jə-cʷkʷrpa-wá-jt'/
my-tea fine it-sway-Abs sea-like it-billow-Dyn-Fin
'My beautiful tea leaves, swaying like the sea, makes waves.'

á-ччаччара /á-čʲčʲačʲčʲa-ra/ 'to chuckle' (cf. á-чча-ра /á-čʲčʲa-ra/ 'to laugh', áчча /á-čʲčʲa/ 'laugh')

á-цыҕәцыҕә-ра /á-č'ʲəɣʷč'ʲəɣʷ-ra/ 'to yap' (cf. áцыҕәцыҕәхәа /á-č'ʲəɣʷč'ʲəɣʷħʷa/ 'with yaps')

а-чча-рá /a-č'ʲč'ʲa-rá/ 'to crack' (cf. а-ччáхәа /a-č'ʲč'ʲáħʷa/ 'chirpingly', аччá /a-č'ʲč'ʲá/ 'crunching sound')

а-хәытхәы́т-ра /a-xʷətxʷə́t-ra/ 'to whisper'

а-заза-рá /a-zaza-rá/ 'to sway'

(ii) They indicate a repeated action or a continuous action. For example:

а-хáхара /a-xáxa-ra/ 'to spin' (cf. á-хара /á-xa-ra/ 'to pull'):

Анду́ áласа лхáхоит.
/[a-]andə́w á-lasa ∅-l-xáxa-wa-jt'/
the-grandmother the-wool [it(C1)-]she(C3)-spin-Dyn-Fin
'The grandmother is spinning wool.'

á-ҧырҧырра /á-pərpər-ra/ 'to flutter, to flap wings' (cf. á-ҧырра /á-pər-ra/ 'to fly'):

Аҧырҧалы́кькәа ҧырҧыруá алә́ы ины́кәло-ит. (AFL)
/a-pərpalə́kʲ-kʷa ∅-pərpər-wá a-dʷə́ jə-nə́kʷ-la-wa-jt'/
the-butterfly-Pl [they(C1)-]flutter-Abs the-field they(C1)-Prev-set off-Dyn-Fin
'The butterflies, fluttering, are setting off for the field.'

а-цысцысрá /a-c'əsc'əs-rá/ 'to swing, to shake' (cf. а-цысрá /a-c'əs-rá/ 'to move, to shake'):

Аҧшá ахьáсуаз áцлакәа ры́махәкәа цысцысуáн.
/a-pšá ∅-axʲ-á-s-wa-z á-c'la-kʷa rə́-maxʷ-kʷa ∅-c'əsc'əs-wa-n
the-wind [it(C1)-]where-Dummy-blow-Impf.NF the-tree-Pl their-branch-Pl [they(C1)-]shake-Impf-Fin
'The branches of the trees were shaking from the wind.'

а-шәыршәыррá /a-šʷəršʷər-rá/ 'to flap, to rustle':

Абирáҟкәа аҧшá иáршәыршәыруеит.
/a-bəjráq'-kʷa a-pšá j-á-r-šʷəršʷər-wa-jt'/
the-flag-Pl the-wind them(C1)-it(C3)-Caus-flap-Dyn-Fin
'The wind is fluttering the flags.'

а-кәáкәара /a-k'ʷák'ʷa-ra/ 'to loosen the ground, to crumble':

Аýтракәа рҿóит, иркәакәóит. (AFL)

/a-wə́tra-kʷa ø-r-ča-wá-jt' jə-r-kʷakʷa-wá-jt'/
the-market garden-Pl [them(C1)-]they(C3)-hew-Dyn-Fin them(C1)-they(C3)-crumble-Dyn-Fin
'They are cultivating a market garden, and they are loosening the soil.'

á-ҟаҟара /á-q'aq'a-ra/ 'to chew', 'to gnaw':

Алá áбаҩ áҟаҟоит.
/a-lá á-bajʷ ø-á-q'aq'a-wa-jt'/
the-dog the-bone [it(C1)-]it(C3)-gnaw-Dyn-Fin
'The dog is gnawing a bone.'

A meaning of repetition or emphasis can be expressed by reduplicating part of the verb root. Here is an example where a part of the root in the verb а-ҧҵəарá /a-p-c'ʷa-rá/ 'to break' is reduplicated:

Абна бзи́а избó, атҵлакəá ҧи́ҵəҵəом. (AFL)
/a-bna bzə́ja jə-z-ba-wá a-c'la-kʷá ø-pə́-j-c'ʷ-c'ʷa-wa-m/
the-forest well it(C1)-Rel(C3)-see-Dyn.NF the-tree-Pl [them(C1)-]Prev-he(C3)-break-Dyn-Neg
'The person who loves the forest usually does not break the trees.'

(iii) They emphasize the meaning, or indicate a specialized meaning. For example:

á-цырцырра /á-cərcər-ra/ 'to glitter':

Аӡáӡа áмраҟны ицырцы́руеит.
/a-ʒáʒa á-mra-q'nə jə-cər-cə́r-wa-jt'/
the-dew the-sun-in it(C1)-glitter-Dyn-Fin
'The dew is glittering in the sun.'

á-хəхəара /á-ħʷħʷa-ra/ 'to shout, to scream' (cf. а-хəарá /a-ħʷa-rá/ 'to say')

а-ҧхеиҧхéира /a-pxajpxáj-ra/ 'to be iridescent' (cf. а-ҧхеиҧхéи /a-pxajpxáj/ 'transparent, clear', а-ҧхарá /a-pxa-rá/ 'to shine')

á-хыҭхыҭра /á-xətxət-ra/ 'to worry, to be excited'

(iv) A few verbs change their preverb and reduplicate the root. For example:

á-нахаáахара /á-na-xa-áa-xa-ra/ 'to move to different sides/places' (cf. а-нá-ха-ра /a-ná-xa-ra/ 'to move there', аá-ха-ра /aá-xa-ra/ 'to move here')

а-наҧшаáҧшра /a-na-pš-aá-pš-ra/ 'to look here and there' (cf. á-на-ҧш-ра /á-na-pš-ra/ 'to look there', áа-ҧш-ра /áa-pš-ra/ 'to look here')

4. Morphosyntax

4.1. Causativity

In Abkhaz, the causative is produced by inserting the causative marker р- /r/ into the verbal complex. This causative marker is always placed immediately before the verbal root.[132] The distribution order of the morphemes within the general slots is as follows:

DO(C1)-{IO(C2)-OV}-{IO(C2)-Instr}-IO(C2)-Prev-A(C3)-Neg-Caus-R-Tense/Aspect-Fin

Below, we shall demonstrate the method in which the causative form is derived from each class of underlying verbs.

4.1.1. Causative Forms Produced from One-Place Intransitive Verbs

When a new subject of a transitive verb (A) is inserted in an underlying one-place verb (S+R) and a causative form is produced, the subject of the underlying intransitive verb (S) is transformed into a direct object (DO) by the causative form and becomes a two-place transitive verb:

[underlying]	S(C1) + R
	(S → DO)
[causative]	DO(C1) + A(C3) + Caus + R

For example:

(238) ды́ҩуеит [underlying]
/də́-jʷ-wa-jt'/
he/she(C1)-run-Dyn-Fin
'He/She is running.'

(239) дсы́рыҩуеит [causative]
/d-sə́-rə-jʷ-wa-jt'/
him/her(C1)-I(C3)-Caus-run-Dyn-Fin
'I am making him/her run.'

In the aorist negative form, the negative marker is placed before the causative marker:

(240) дысмы́рҩит [causative-aorist-negative]

132. Exceptions are the two verbs with preverbs: а́-лацара /á-la-c'a-ra/ 'to sow' and а́-кацара /á-q'a-c'a-ra/ 'to do, to make'. For these verbs, the causative marker is placed before the preverb. See fn. 134.

/də-s-mə́-r-jʷə-jt'/
him/her(C1)-I(C3)-Neg-Caus-run-(Aor)-Fin
'I did not make him/her run.'

In the causative form, when the pronominal prefix for A is in the third person plural (also when the pronominal prefix for the indirect object IO is in the third person plural), the original prefix р- /r/ is replaced by д- /d/ (see §3.1.6 Note 6):

(241) ддырыҩуеит [causative]
/d-dé-rə-jʷ-wa-jt'/ (< */d-ré-rə-jʷ-wa-jt'/)
him/her(C1)-they(C3)-Caus-run-Dyn-Fin
'They are making him/her run.'

This replacement is not a phonetically occurring dissimilative phenomenon but a morphophonological one, and is seen only in the causative form.[133] In verbal complexes that are not causative forms, even if there are two consonants р- р- /r- r-/, this type of consonant replacement does not occur. Look at the following example where third-person plural pronominal prefixes appear in Column II and Column III:

(242) ирыртеит
/jə-rə́-r-ta-jt'/
it/them(C1)-them(C2)-they(C3)-give-(Aor)-Fin
'They gave it/them to them.'

Except for the replacement of the third-person plural pronominal prefix, the function of the causative form pronominal prefixes derived from the one-place intransitive verbs examined above are not different from that of Class C verbs. Consequently, this causative derivation has the function of transitivizing intransitive verbs. This was already discussed in §3.2.6.5. For example, а-ргы́лара /a-rgə́la-ra/ 'to build' is derived from а-гы́лара /a-gə́la-ra/ 'to stand (up)'. In Abkhaz, there are a great many transitive verbs that are produced by this kind of causative derivation (Regarding this, see §§3.2.6.5.1–3.2.6.5.3, §§3.2.7.2.1–3.2.7.2.3).

4.1.2. Causative Forms Produced From One-Place Intransitive Verbs with Preverbs (Class E)

Among one-place intransitive verbs there are Class E verbs (S+Prev+R) that have a preverb. When a causative form is produced by inserting A into an underlying form, it takes on the structure of 'DO+Prev+A+Caus+R'. For example, the underlying form (243) of а́-наҧшра /á-na-pš-ra/ 'to look thither' and its causative form (244) are as follows:

(243) днаҧшуе́ит [underlying]
/d-na-pš-wá-jt'/
he/she(C1)-Prev(thither)-look-Dyn-Fin
'He/she is looking thither.'

133. The personal pronoun дара́ /dará/ 'they' is probably originally the same consonant replacement. For this, see §2.2.1.1, fn. 77.

(244) днасырпҽшуе́ит [causative]
/d-na-sə-r-pš-wá-jt'/
him/her(C1)-Prev-I(C3)-Caus-look-Dyn-Fin
'I am making him/her look thither.'

In (244) above, the agent prefix сы- /sə/ is inserted between the preverb and the causative marker. If the causative marker and root are regarded as a single stem, it will have prefix distribution structure similar to the Class G verbs (DO+Prev+A+R) already discussed above. As already discussed, when a transitive verb has a preverb, the agent must come in between the preverb and the root (or the causative marker). This is one of the criteria for determining transitivity (for transitivity see §5.9).

4.1.3. Causative Forms Produced from Two-Place Intransitive Verbs (Class B)

When the causative form is produced by inserting A in an underlying two-place intransitive verb (S+IO+R), the subject S of the two-place intransitive verb is transformed into direct object DO (C1) and takes the structure 'DO+IO+A+Caus+R'.

[underlying]	S + IO + R
	(S → DO, IO = IO)
[causative]	DO + IO + A + Caus + R

For example, the underlying form (245) of á-хара /á-xa-ra/ 'to pull' and its causative form (246) are as follows:

(245) са́хоит [underlying]
/s-á-xa-wa-jt'/
I(C1)-it(C2)-pull-Dyn-Fin
'I am pulling it.'

(246) салы́рхоит [causative]
/s-a-lə́-r-xa-wa-jt'/
I(C1)-it(C2)-she(C3)-Caus-pull-Dyn-Fin
'She is making me pull it.'

As discussed above, in the causative form when the Column II and Column III pronominal prefixes are in the third person plural, р /r/ is replaced by д /d/ for these pronominal prefixes:

(247) сыдды́рхоит [causative]
/sə-d-də́-r-xa-wa-jt'/ (< */sə-r-rə́-r-xa-wa-jt'/)
I(C1)-them(C2)-they(C3)-Caus-pull-Dyn-Fin
'They are making me pull them.'

The negative marker м(ы) /m(ə)/ in the aorist is placed immediately before the causative marker:

(248) сдыдмы́рхеит [causative]
/s-də-d-mə́-r-xa-jt'/
I(C1)-them(C2)-they(C3)-Neg-Caus-pull-(Aor)-Fin

'They did not make me pull them.'

Furthermore, when the objective version (OV) is included in the causative form, the 'pronominal prefix governed by the objective version + objective version marker' is placed immediately after the pronominal prefix in Column I (for the objective version, see §4.3.2):

(249) дышәзасы́рсит [causative]
/də-š^{w}-z-a-sə́-r-sə-jt'/
him/her(C1)-{you.Pl-OV(for)}-it(C2)-I(C3)-Caus-hit-(Aor)-Fin
'I made him/her hit it for you-Pl.'

4.1.4. Causative Forms Produced From Two-Place Intransitive Verbs with a Preverb

When causative forms are produced by inserting A into a Class F verb (S+IO+Prev+R), the introduced A goes between the preverb and root, and the subject S of the underlying form is transformed into a direct object DO (C1):

[underlying]	S + IO + Prev + R
	(S → DO, IO = IO)
[causative]	DO + IO + Prev + A + Caus + R

For example, the underlying form (250) of а́-хәаҧшра /á-x^{w}a-pš-ra/ 'to look at' and its causative form (251) are as follows:

(250) сбы́хәаҧшит [underlying]
/s-bə́-x^{w}a-pšə-jt'/
I(C1)-you.F(C2)-Prev-look-(Aor)-Fin
'I looked at you-F.'

(251) сбы́хәалырҧшит [causative]
/s-bə́-x^{w}a-lə-r-pšə-jt'/
me(C1)-you.F(C2)-Prev-she(C3)-Caus-look-(Aor)-Fin
'She made me look at you-F.'

4.1.5. Causative Forms Produced from Two-Place Transitive Verbs (Class C)

When a new A is inserted in a two-place transitive Class C verb and made into a causative form, the A of the underlying form is transformed into an indirect object (IO), and the direct object (DO) of the underlying form remains as a direct object (DO).

[underlying]	DO + A + R
	(DO = DO, A → IO)
[causative]	DO + IO + A + Caus + R

For example, the underlying form (252) of а-ҩра́ /a-j^{w}-rá/ 'to write' and its causative form (253) are as follows:

(252) изҩит [underlying]
/jə-z-jʷə́-jt'/
it/them(C1)-I(C3)-write-(Aor)-Fin
'I wrote it/them.'

(253) ислы́рҩит [causative]
/jə-s-lə́-r-jʷə-jt'/
it/them(C1)-me(C2)-she(C3)-Caus-write-(Aor)-Fin
'She made me write it/them.'

(253) above is a three-place transitive verb and this has the same argument distribution as Class D. Also, the negative marker in the aorist form is placed between the Column III pronominal prefix and the causative marker, and the Columns II and III third-person plural prefixes in the causative form are replaced by д- /d/:

(254) иддмы́рҩит [causative]
/jə-d-d-mə́-r-jʷə-jt'/ (< *jə-r-r-mə́-r-jʷə-jt')
it/them(C1)-them(C2)-they(C3)-Neg-Caus-write-(Aor)-Fin
'They did not make them write it/them.'

Furthermore, when the objective version is used in the causative form, the third-person plural pronominal prefix, which is governed by this objective version marker, is not replaced with д /d/:

(255) ирзылсы́рҩит [causative]
/jə-r-zə-l-sə́-r-jʷə-jt'/
it/them(C1)-{them(C2)-OV(for)}-her(C2)-I(C3)-Caus-write-(Aor)-Fin
'I made her write it/them for them.'

It is also possible to insert the instrumental affix -ла- /la/, which indicates means or method, into the causative form:

(256) (сара́) ркьырмы́т амашьы́на иа́ладсыргеит
/(sará) r-kʲərmə́t' a-mašʲə́na j-á-la-d-sə-r-ga-jt'/
I their-brick the-car it(C1)-{it(C2)-with}-them(C2)-I(C3)-Caus-take-(Aor)-Fin
'I made them take their brick(s) in a car.'

4.1.6. Causative Form Produced From Two-Place Transitive Verbs with a Preverb (Class G)

In the causative form produced from two-place transitive verbs (Class G) with a preverb, the pronominal prefix for the newly introduced A is inserted between the preverb and causative marker:[134]

[underlying] DO(C1) + Prev + A(C3) + R

134. When producing a causative form from a Class G verb, there are two verbs where the preverb and root are not split by the causative marker: а́-ҟацара /á-q'a-c'a-ra/ 'to do; to make' and а́-ла-ца-ра /á-la-c'a-ra/ 'to sow'. In their causative forms, they are: ислы́рҟатцеит /jə-s-lə́-r-q'a-c'a-jt'/ [it/them(C1)-me(C2)-she(C3)-Caus-Prev-do/make-(Aor)-Fin] 'she made me do/make it/them'; ислы́рлатцеит /jə-s-lə́-r-la-c'a-jt'/ [it/them(C1)-me(C2)-she(C3]-Caus-Prev-sow-(Aor)-Fin) 'she made me sow it/them'.

(DO = DO, A → IO)

[causative] DO(C1) + IO(C2) + Prev + A(C3) + Caus + R

For example, the underlying form (257) of а-пҟара́ /a-p-q'a-rá/ 'to cut' and its causative form (258) are as follows:

(257) ипҕы́сҟеит [underlying]
/jə-pə́-s-q'a-jt'/
it/them(C1)-Prev-I(C3)-cut-(Aor)-Fin
'I cut it/them.'

(258) испҕлырҟе́ит [causative]
/jə-s-p-lə-r-q'á-jt'/
it/them(C1)-me(C2)-Prev-she(C3)-Caus-cut-(Aor)-Fin
'She made me cut it/them.'

(258) above resembles the causative form (251) сбы́хәалырпҕшит /s-bə́-xʷa-lə-r-pšə-jt'/ 'she made me look at you' formed from the intransitive verb discussed in §4.1.4, but take note of the fact that the function of the pronominal prefixes in Columns I and II are different.

4.1.7. Causative Forms Produced from Three-Place Transitive Verbs (Class D)

The only pure three-place transitive verb is а́-ҭара /á-ta-ra/ 'to give'. When A is added to this underlying form and a causative form is produced, it takes on the following schema:

[underlying] DO(C1) + IO(C2) + A(C3) + R

(DO = DO, IO → IO', A → IO")

[causative] DO(C1) + IO'(C2) + IO"(C2) + A(C3) + Caus + R

As an example of this, the underlying form (259) and its causative form (260) are as follows:

(259) илы́бҭеит [underlying]
/jə-lə́-b-ta-jt'/
it/them(C1)-her(C2)-you.F(C3)-give-(Aor)-Fin
'You-F gave it/them to her.'

(260) илы́бдырҭеит [causative]
/jə-lə́-b-də-r-ta-jt'/ (< /jə-lə́-b-rə-r-ta-jt'/)
it/them(C1)-her(C2)-you.F(C2)-they(C3)-Caus-give-(Aor)-Fin
'They made you-F give it/them to her.'

Abkhaz does not tolerate four-place causative forms, and in that case periphrastic expressions using the resultative form and the verb а́-ҟаҵара /á-q'a-c'a-ra/ 'do' are normally used.[135] However, in

135. Cf. the example of a periphrastic causative construction: Аҵаҩы́ ла́ни ла́би лыртҵаҩы́ аҵәа́ и́лҭартә ҟарҵе́ит (/лды́рҟаҵеит). (ACST) 'The pupil's parents got her to give an apple to her teacher'.

Abkhaz folklore texts four-place causative forms like (260) above are used:

(261) аны́шә да́дхарҭом
/a-nə́ŝʷ d-á-d-ħa-r-ta-wa-m/
the-earth him/her(C1)-it(= the earth,C2)-them(C2)-we(C3)-Caus-give-Dyn-Neg
lit. 'We do not make them give him/her to it (= the earth)', i.e. 'We do not make them bury him/her.'

4.1.8. Causative Forms Produced from Three-Place Transitive Verbs with a Preverb (Class H)

The causative derivation produced by introducing a new A into a Class H verb takes on the following schema:

[underlying] DO(C1) + IO(C2) + prev + A(C3) + R
(DO = DO, IO → IO', A → IO")
[causative] DO(C1) + IO'(C2) + Prev + IO"(C2) + A(C3) + Caus + R

For example, the underlying form (262) of а-хәара́ /a-ħʷa-ra/ 'to say' and its causative form (263) are as follows:

(262) иса́лхәеит [underlying]
/jə-s-á-l-ħʷa-jt'/
it/them(C1)-me(C2)-Prev-she(C3)-say-(Aor)-Fin
'She said it/them to me.'

(263) иса́лдырхәеит [causative]
/jə-s-á-l-də-r-ħʷa-jt'/
it/them(C1)-me(C2)-Prev-her(C2)-they(C3)-Caus-say-(Aor)-Fin
'They made her say it/them to me.'

4.1.9. Other Causative Forms

The causative form of verbs with the subjective version have the same structure as the causative form of the Class H verbs previously discussed, the A of the underlying form becomes an indirect object IO in the causative form, and the possessive prefix and the objective version marker join together and are placed after the Column I pronominal prefix. Moreover, in the causative form the third-person plural possessive prefix р- /r/ is not replaced by д- /d/. The causative derivations take on the following schema:

[underlying] DO(C1) + Poss + SV + A(C3) + R
(DO = DO, A → IO)
[causative] DO(C1) + Poss + SV + IO(C2) + A(C3) + Caus + R

The possessive prefix (Poss) and the referent of indirect object (IO) above must be the same. For example, the underlying form (264) of а́-дкылара /á-d-k'əla-ra/ 'to take (medicine)' and its causative form (265) are as follows:

(264) áхəшəқəа ры́дыркылеит [underlying]
/á-xʷʂ̌ʷ-kʷa ϕ-rə́-də-r-k'ə-la-jt'/
the-medicine-Pl [it/them(C1)-]their(Poss)-SV-they(C3)-hold-Introvert-(Aor)-Fin
'They took the medicine.'

(265) áхəшəқəа ры́ддсыркылеит [causative]
/á-xʷʂ̌ʷ-kʷa ϕ-rə́-d-d-sə-r-k'ə-la-jt'/
the-medicine-Pl [it/them(C1)-]their(Poss)-SV-them(C2)-I(C3)-Caus-hold-Introvert-(Aor)-Fin
'I made them take the medicine.'

4.1.10. Causative Forms

а-гы́лара /a-gə́la-ra/ 'to stand':

Finite forms

Present

C1-C3-Caus-R-	Affirmative	Negative
3Sg.Human-1Sg	д-сы-р-гы́ло-ит /d-sə-r-gə́la-wa-jt'/ him/her(C1)-I(C3)-Caus-stand-Dyn-Fin 'I am making him/her stand.'	д-сы-р-гы́ло-м
3Sg.Human-2Sg.F	д-бы-р-гы́ло-ит	д-бы-р-гы́ло-м
3Sg.Human-3Sg.M	д-и-р-гы́ло-ит	д-и-р-гы́ло-м
3Sg.Human-3Sg.F	д-лы-р-гы́ло-ит	д-лы-р-гы́ло-м
3Sg.Human-3Pl	д-ды-р-гы́ло-ит	д-ды-р-гы́ло-м

Aorist

C1-C3-Caus-R-	Affirmative	Negative
3Sg.Human-1Sg	д-сы-р-гы́ле-ит	ды-с-мы-р-гы́ле-ит
3Sg.Human-2Sg.F	д-бы-р-гы́ле-ит	ды-б-мы-р-гы́ле-ит
3Sg.Human-3Sg.M	д-и-р-гы́ле-ит	д-и-мы-р-гы́ле-ит
3Sg.Human-3Sg.F	д-лы-р-гы́ле-ит	ды-л-мы-р-гы́ле-ит
3Sg.Human-3Pl	д-ды-р-гы́ле-ит	ды-д-мы-р-гы́ле-ит

á-хара /á-xa-ra/ 'to pull':

Finite forms

Present

C1-C2-C3-Caus-R-	Affirmative	Negative
3Sg.H-3Sg.N.H-1Sg	д-а-сы́-р-хо-ит /d-a-sə́-r-xa-wa-jt'/ him/her(C1)-it(C2)-I(C3)-Caus-pull-Dyn-Fin 'I am making him/her pull it.'	д-а-сы́-р-хо-м
3Sg.H-3Sg.N.H-2Sg.F	д-а-бы́-р-хо-ит	д-а-бы́-р-хо-м
3Sg.H-3Sg.N.H-3Sg.F	д-а-лы́-р-хо-ит	д-а-бы́-р-хо-м
3Sg.H-3Sg.N.H-3Sg.M	д-а-й-р-хо-ит	д-а-й-р-хо-м
3Sg.H-3Sg.N.H-1Pl	д-а-ха́-р-хо-ит	д-а-ха́-р-хо-м

3Sg.H-3Sg.N.H-2Pl	д-а-шәы́-р-хо-ит	д-а-шәы́-р-хо-м
3Sg.H-3Sg.N.H-3Pl	д-а-ды́-р-хо-ит	д-а-ды́-р-хо-м
1Sg-2Sg.F-3Sg.F	сы-б-лы́-р-хо-ит	сы-б-лы́-р-хо-м
1Sg-3Pl-2Sg.F	сы-д-бы́-р-хо-ит	сы-д-бы́-р-хо-м

Aorist

C1-C2-C3-Caus-R-	<u>Affirmative</u>	<u>Negative</u>
3Sg.H-3Sg.N.H-1Sg	д-а-сы́-р-хе-ит	д-а-с-мы́-р-хе-ит
3Sg.H-3Sg.N.H-3Sg.M	д-а-й-р-хе-ит	д-а-и-мы́-р-хе-ит
1Sg-2Sg.F-3Sg.F	сы-б-лы́-р-хе-ит	с-бы-л-мы́-р-хе-ит
1Sg-3Pl-2Sg.F	сы-д-бы́-р-хе-ит	с-ды-б-мы́-р-хе-ит

а-ҩрá /a-j^{w}-rá/ 'to write':

Finite forms

Aorist

C1-C2-C3-Caus-R-	<u>Affirmative</u>	<u>Negative</u>
3Sg.N.H/3Pl-3Sg.F-1Sg	и-л-сы́-р-ҩ-ит /jə-l-sə́-r-j^{w}ə-jr'/ it/them(C1)-her(C2)-I(C3)-write-(Aor)-Fin 'I made her write it/them.'	и-л-с-мы́-р-ҩ-ит
3Sg.N.H/3Pl-1Sg-3Pl	и-с-ды́-р-ҩ-ит	и-с-д-мы́-р-ҩ-ит
3Sg.N.H/3Pl-1Pl-3Sg.F	и-аҳ-лы́-р-ҩ-ит	и-ҳа-л-мы́-р-ҩ-ит

á-ҟаҵара /á-q'a-c'a-ra/ 'to do; to make':

Finite forms

Aorist

C1-C2-C3-Caus-Prev-R-	<u>Affirmative</u>	<u>Negative</u>
3Sg.N.H/3Pl-2Sg.F-1Sg	и-б-сы́-р-ҟа-ҵе-ит /jə-b-sə́-r-q'a-c'a-jt'/ it/them(C1)-you.F(C2)-I(C3)-Caus-Prev-do/make-(Aor)-Fin 'I made you-F do/make it/them.'	и-бы-с-мы́-р-ҟа-ҵе-ит
3Sg.N.H/3Pl-3Pl-1Sg	и-д-сы́-р-ҟа-ҵе-ит	и-ды-с-мы́-р-ҟа-ҵе-ит
3Sg.N.H/3Pl-3Pl-3Pl	и-д-ды́-р-ҟа-ҵе-ит	и-ды-д-мы́-р-ҟа-ҵе-ит

а-ҧҟарá /a-p-q'a-rá/ 'to cut':

Finite forms

Aorist

C1-C2-Prev-C3-Caus-R-	<u>Affirmative</u>	<u>Negative</u>
3Sg.N.H/3Pl-1Sg-3Sg.F	и-л-ҧ-сы-р-ҟé-ит /jə-l-p-sə-r-q'á-jt'/ it/them(C1)-her(C2)-Prev-I(C3)-Caus-cut-(Aor)-Fin 'I made her cut it/them.'	и-л-ҧы-с-мы-р-ҟé-ит
3Sg.N.H/3Pl-3Pl-3Sg.F	и-д-ҧ-сы-р-ҟé-ит	и-д-ҧы-с-мы-р-ҟé-ит

3Sg.N.H/3Pl-1Sg-3Sg.F	и-с-ҧ-лы-р-ќé-ит	и-с-ҧы-л-мы-р-ќé-ит
3Sg.N.H/3Pl-2Sg.F-3Pl	и-б-ҧ-ды-р-ќé-ит	и-б-ҧы-д-мы-р-ќé-ит

4.2. Moods

There are seven moods in Abkhaz: (i) indicative, (ii) imperative, (iii) subjunctive, (iv) optative, (v) potential, (vi) non-volitional, (vii) evidential. The verb form described thus far is (i) indicative. The indicative mood is the one that represents real events that have occurred/are occurring/will likely occur in the past, present or foreseeable future. Also, this is used to make general factual statements. We will discuss the forms from (ii) to (vii).

4.2.1. Imperative

4.2.1.1. The Second-Person Imperative

The second-person imperative in Abkhaz is formed in an extremely regular way. The formation of the imperative form differs according to differences in the type of verb, its transitivity, whether the verb is affirmative or negative, and whether the person is singular or plural. The distribution of the imperative mood's pronominal prefixes and suffixes are as follows:

1. Stative Verbs:
    - affirmative: S[C1] + (IO[C2] + Prev) + R+ -z
    - negative: S[C1] + (IO[C2] + Prev) + R+ -mə-z
2. Dynamic Verbs:
    - a) Intransitive Verbs
        - affirmative: S[C1] + (IO[C2] + Prev) + R + ø
        - negative: S[C1] + (IO[C2] + Prev) + Neg + R + -n
    - b) Transitive Verbs
        - affirmative (sg.): DO[C1] + (IO[C2] + Prev) + R + ø
        - affirmative (pl.): DO[C1] + (IO[C2] + Prev) + A[C3] + R + ø
        - negative: DO[C1] + (IO[C2] + Prev) + A[C3] +Neg + R + -n

Below, we will describe the imperative mood in this order.

4.2.1.1.1. Imperative Mood of Stative Verbs

The affirmative imperative form of stative verbs takes the same pronominal prefixes as the indicative form, and is formed by attaching <u>-з-</u> /z/ to the root. The negative form takes the same pronominal prefix as the affirmative form and <u>-мы-з</u> /mə-z/ is added to the root. In short, it is 'Column I + (Column II) + root + -з/-мы-з'. The accent is placed in the same place as the indicative finite form of Class A-1 and Class B-1 described above.

<u>The imperative form of Class A-1 verbs</u>:

AP a: а-гы́лазаара /a-gə́la-zaa-ra/ 'to stand, to be standing': Aff. 2F.Sg. бгы́лаз! /b-gə́la-z/ [you.F(C1)-stand-Stat.Imp] 'stand!, be standing! (to a woman)', Aff. 2M.Sg. угы́лаз! /wə-gə́la-z/ [you.M(C1)-stand-Stat.Imp] 'stand!, be standing! (to a man)', Aff. 2Pl. шәгы́лаз! /šʷ-gə́la-z/ [you.Pl(C1)-stand-Stat.Imp] 'stand!, be standing! (to multiple people)', Neg.2F.Sg. бгы́ламыз! /b-gə́la-mə-z/ [you.F(C1)-stand-Neg-Stat.Imp] 'don't stand!, don't be standing! (to a woman)', Neg.2M.Sg. угы́ламыз! /wə-gə́la-mə-z/ [you.M(C1)-stand-Neg-Stat.Imp], Neg.2Pl. шәгы́ламыз! /šʷ-gə́la-mə-z/ [you.Pl(C1)-stand-Neg-Stat.Imp]

AP b: а́-цәара /á-cʷa-ra/ 'to sleep, to be sleeping': Aff. 2F.Sg. бы́цәаз! /bə́-cʷa-z/ [you.F(C1)-sleep-Stat.Imp] 'sleep!, be sleeping! (to a woman)', Aff. 2M.Sg. у́цәаз!, Aff. 2Pl. шәы́цәаз!, Neg.2F.Sg. бы́цәамыз! /bə́-cʷa-mə-z/ [you.F(C1)-sleep-Neg-Stat.Imp] 'don't sleep!, don't be sleeping!', Neg.2M.Sg. у́цәамыз!, Neg.2Pl. шәы́-цәа-мы-з!

AP c: а-тәара́ /a-t'ʷa-rá/ 'to be sitting': Aff. 2F.Sg. бтәа́з! /b-t'ʷá-z/ 'sit!, be sitting! (to a woman)', Aff. 2M.Sg. утәа́з!, Aff. 2Pl. шәтәа́з!, Neg.2F.Sg. бтәа́мыз! /b-t'ʷá-mə-z/ 'don't sit!, don't be sitting!', Neg.2M.Sg. утәа́мыз!, Neg.2Pl. шә-тәа́-мы-з!

The imperative form of Class B-1 verbs:

AP b: а́-мазаара /á-ma-zaa-ra/ [inverse] 'to have': Aff. 2F.Sg. ибы́маз! /jə-bə́-ma-z/ [it/they(C1)-you.F(C2)-have-Stat.Imp] 'have it/them! (to a woman)', Aff. 2M.Sg. иу́маз! /jə-wə́-ma-z/ [it/they(C1)-you.M(C2)-have-Stat.Imp], Aff. 2Pl. ишәы́маз! /jə-šʷə́-ma-z/ [it/they(C1)-you.Pl(C2)-have-Stat.Imp], Neg.2F.Sg. ибы́мамыз! /jə-bə́-ma-mə-z/ [it/they(C1)-you.F(C2)-have-Neg-Stat.Imp] 'don't have it/them!', Neg.2M.Sg. иу́мамыз! /jə-wə́-ma-mə-z/ [it/they(C1)-you.M(C2)-have-Neg-Stat.Imp], Neg.2Pl. ишәы́мамыз! /jə-šʷə́-ma-mə-z/ [it/they(C1)-you-Pl (C2)-have-Neg-Stat.Imp]

AP c: а-ҭахы́заара /a-taxə́-zaa-ra/ [inverse] 'to want': Aff. 2F.Sg. ибҭахы́з! /jə-b-taxə́-z/ [it/they(C1)-you.F(C2)-want-Stat.Imp] 'want it/them! (to a woman)', Aff. 2M.Sg. иуҭахы́з!, Aff. 2Pl. ишәҭахы́з!, Neg.2F.Sg. ибҭахы́мыз! /jə-b-taxə́-mə-z/ [it/they(C1)-you.F(C2)-want-Neg-Stat.Imp], Neg.2M.Sg. иуҭахы́мыз!, Neg.2Pl. и-шә-ҭахы́-мы-з!

Also, stative verbs which can be included in Class F verbs:

а-ҿы́заара /a-č'ə́-zaa-ra/ 'to be engaged in': Aff. 2F.Sg. баҿы́з! /b-a-čʲə́-z/ [you.F(C1)-it(C2)-do-Stat.Imp] 'be doing it! (to a woman)', Aff. 2M.Sg. уаҿы́з!, Aff. 2Pl. шәаҿы́з!, Neg.2F.Sg. баҿы́мыз! /b-a-č'ə́-mə-z/ [you.F(C1)-it(C2)-do-Neg-Stat.Imp], Neg.2M.Sg. уаҿы́мыз!, Neg.2Pl. шәаҿы́мыз!

4.2.1.1.2. Imperative Mood of Dynamic Verbs

The formation of the imperative mood of dynamic verbs differs in transitive and intransitive verbs. The difference is that in the singular, affirmative imperative form of transitive verbs the Column III pronominal prefix indicating A can be absent. This is one of the criteria for classifying verbs into transitive and intransitive.

4.2.1.1.2.1. Imperative Mood of Dynamic Intransitive Verbs

The affirmative imperative mood takes the same pronominal prefixes as the indicative finite form and the root remains as it is, without having any suffix elements attached to it. When the root ends in a vowel a, in many cases the final vowel will disappear if it has no accent: e.g. бгы́л! /b-gə́l/ 'stand up!'

(cf. а-гы́лара /a-gə́la-ra/ 'to stand up'). On the other hand, the negative imperative mood takes the same pronominal prefix as the affirmative imperative mood, the negative marker -м- /m/ is inserted before the root, and the prohibition (abbreviated as 'Proh') suffix -н /n/ is attached to the root. The position of the accent is the same as that of the indicative finite form.

The imperative form of Class A-2 verbs

AP a: а-гы́лара /a-gə́la-ra/ 'to stand up': Aff. 2F.Sg. бгы́л! /b-gə́l/ [you.F(C1)-stand.Imp] 'stand up! (to a woman)', Aff. 2M.Sg. угы́л! /wə-gə́l/ [you.M(C1)-stand.Imp] 'stand up! (to a man)', Aff. 2Pl. шәгы́л! /ŝʷ-gə́l/ [you.Pl(C1)-stand.Imp] 'stand up! (to multiple people)', Neg.2F.Sg. бымгы́лан! /bə-m-gə́la-n/ [you.F(C1)-Neg-stand-Proh] 'don't stand up! (to a woman)', Neg.2M.Sg. умгы́лан!, Neg.2Pl. шәымгы́лан!

AP b: á-ҧара /á-pa-ra/ 'to jump': Aff. 2F.Sg. бы́ҧ! /bə́-p/ [you.F(C1)-jump.Imp] 'jump! (to a woman)', Aff. 2M.Sg. ýҧ! /wə́-p/ [you.M(C1)-jump.Imp] 'jump! (to a man)', Aff. 2Pl. шәы́ҧ! /sʷə́-p/ [you.Pl(C1)-jump.Imp] 'jump! (to multiple people)', Neg.2F.Sg. бмы́ҧан! /b-mə́-pa-n/ [you.F(C1)-Neg-jump-Proh] 'don't jump!' (to a woman), Neg.2M.Sg. умы́ҧан!, Neg.2Pl. шәмы́ҧан!

AP c: а-кьрá /a-kʲ-rá/ 'to sigh': Aff. 2F.Sg. бкьы́! /b-kʲə́/ [you.F(C1)-sigh.Imp] 'sigh! (to a woman)', Aff. 2M.Sg. укьы́!, Aff. 2Pl. шәкьы́!, Neg.2F.Sg. бымкьы́н! /bə-m-kʲə́-n/ [you.F(C1)-Neg-sigh-Proh] 'don't sigh!', Neg.2M.Sg. умкьы́н! /wə-m-kʲə́-n/ [you.M-Neg-sigh-Proh], Neg.2Pl. шәымкьы́н! /ŝʷə-m-kʲə́-n/ [you.Pl-Neg-sigh-Proh]

When the root of the AP c word has a CVC structure (C = any consonant, V = schwa), since the accent is placed on the end of the root, a schwa develops here. Due to this, the schwa in the root disappears, and the root becomes CC (see §3.2.6.3, Note 2). For example:

á-ҧырра /á-pər-ra/ 'to fly': Aff. 2F.Sg. бырҧы́! /bə-prə́/ [you.F-fly.Imp] 'fly! (to a woman)', Aff. 2Pl. шәыҧры́! /ŝʷə-prə́/ [you.Pl(C1)-fly.Imp], Neg.2F.Sg. бымҧыры́н! /bə-m-pərə́-n/ [you.F(C1)-Neg-fly-Proh] 'don't fly!' (to a woman, Neg.2M.Sg. умҧыры́н! /wə-m-pərə́-n/ [you.M(C1)-Neg-fly-Proh], Neg.2Pl. шәымҧыры́н! /ŝʷə-m-pərə́-n/ [you.Pl(C1)-Neg-fly-Proh] 'don't fly! (to multiple people)'.[136]

Imperative form of Class B-2 verbs

AP a: áура /[a-]aw-ra/ [inverse] 'to to receive; to obtain': Aff. 2F.Sg. ибóу! /jə-b-áw/ [it/they(C1)-you.F(C2)-receive.Imp] 'receive it/them! (to a woman)', Aff. 2M.Sg. иуóу!, Aff. 2Pl. ишәóу!, Neg.2F.Sg. ибмóун! /jə-b-m-áw-n/ [it/they(C1)-you.F(C2)-Neg-receive-Proh] 'don't receive it/them! (to a woman)', Neg.2M.Sg. и-у-м-óу-н!, Neg.2Pl. и-шә-мó-у-н!

AP b: á-сра /á-s-ra/ 'to hit': Aff. 2F.Sg. бсы́с! /b-sə́-s/ [you.F(C1)-me(C2)-hit.Imp] 'hit me! (to a woman)', Aff. 2M.Sg. усы́с!, Aff. 2Pl. шәсы́с!, Neg.2F.Sg. бысмы́сын! /bə-s-mə́-sə-n/ [you.F(C1)-me(C2)-Neg-hit-Proh] 'don't hit me!' (to a woman), Neg.2M.Sg. усмы́сын!, Neg.2Pl. шәы-с-мы́-сы-н!

AP c: а-фыҩрá /a-fəjʷ-rá/ 'to smell': Aff. 2F.Sg. бсыфҩы́! /b-sə-fjʷə́/ [you.F(C1)-me(C2)-smell.Imp]

136. The schwa in the root disappears even in the negative form in the imperative mood of the Class C verb а-былрá /a-bəl-rá/ 'to burn' (AP c): Aff. 2F.Sg. иблы́! /jə-blə́/ [it/them(C1)-burn.Imp] 'burn it/them!', Neg.2F.Sg. ибымблы́н! /jə-bə-m-blə́-n/ [it/them(C1)-you.F(C3)-Neg-burn-Proh] 'don't burn it/them!'

'smell me! (to a woman)', Aff. 2M.Sg. усыфԜы́!, Aff. 2Pl. шә-сы-фԜы́!, Neg.2F.Sg. бсымфԜы́н! /b-sə-m-fjʷə́-n/ [you.F(C1)-me(C2)-Neg-smell-Proh] 'don't smell me! (to a woman)', Neg.2M.Sg. усымфԜы́н!, Neg.2Pl. шә-сы-м-фԜы́-н!

Imperative form of Class E verbs

а-нхара́ /a-n-xa-rá/ 'to live': Aff. 2F.Sg. бынха́! [you.F(C1)-Prev-live.Imp] /bə-n-xá/ 'live! (to a woman)', Aff. 2M.Sg. унха́!, Aff. 2Pl. шәынха́!, Neg.2F.Sg. бнымха́н! /b-nə-m-xá-n/ [you.F(C1)-Prev-Neg-live-Proh] 'don't live!' (to a woman), Neg.2M.Sg. унымха́н!, Neg.2Pl. шә-ны-м-ха́-н!

Imperative form of Class F verbs

а́-хәаҧшра /á-xʷa-pš-ra/ 'to look at': Aff. 2F.Sg. ба́хәаҧш! /b-á-xʷa-pš/ [you.F(C1)-it(C2)-Prev-look at.Imp] 'look at it! (to a woman)', Aff. 2M.Sg. уа́хәаҧш! /w-á-xʷa-pš/ 'look at it! (to a man)', Aff. 2Pl. шәа́хәаҧш!, Neg.2F.Sg. ба́хәамҧшын! /b-á-xʷa-m-pšə-n/ [you.F(C1)-it(C2)-Prev-Neg-look at-Proh] 'don't look at it! (to a woman)', Neg.2M.Sg. уа́хәамҧшын!, Neg.2Pl. шәа́хәамҧшын!

а́ишра /áj-š-ra/ 'to bark at': Aff. 2M.Sg. уле́иш! /wə-l-áj-š/ [you.M(C1)-her(C2)-Prev-bark.Imp] 'bark at her!', Neg.2M.Sg. улме́ишын! /wə-l-m-áj-šə-n/ [you.M(C1)-her(C2)-Prev-bark-Proh] 'don't bark at her!'[137]

а́-лагара /á-la-ga-ra/ 'to begin': Aff. 2F.Sg. ба́лага! /b-á-la-ga/ [you.F(C1)-it(C2)-Prev-begin.Imp] 'begin it! (to a woman)', Aff. 2M.Sg. уа́лага!, Aff. 2Pl. шәа́лага!, Neg.2F.Sg. ба́ламган! /b-á-la-m-ga-n/ [you.F(C1)-it(C2)-Prev-Neg-begin-Proh] 'don't begin it! (to a woman)', Neg.2M.Sg. уа́ламган!, Neg.2Pl. шәа́ламган!

4.2.1.1.3. Imperative Mood of Transitive Verbs

In the imperative form of transitive verbs, agent (i.e. the Column III) pronominal prefixes are absent in the singular affirmative form. The ending of the imperative form is the same as the dynamic and intransitive verbs seen above. Therefore, its morphosyntactic structure in the most basic Class C verbs is 'DO + R'. In contrast, in the affirmative, plural imperative form, the agent pronominal prefix appears. Therefore, its morphosyntactic structure in the most basic Class C verbs is 'DO + A + R'. In the negative imperative form, the agent pronominal prefix appears in all persons. The negative marker -м- /m/ is placed before the root, and the prohibition suffix -н- /n/ is attached to the root. Also, when the consonant at the head of the root is voiced, the Column III pronominal prefix шә- /šʷ/ changes into its voiced variant жә- /žʷ/, but this is not something that necessarily occurs in all cases (see §3.2.6). Generally, when the head consonant in the root is ӡ /ʒ/, ж /ž/, жә /žʷ/, it appears that the Column III pronominal prefix шә /šʷ/ is always voiced.

Regarding accent, the following are worthy of note. Class C verbs do not take accent type AP b (see §3.2.6), but in the imperative mood an accent is placed on the pronominal prefix in the singular affirmative form. Also, the unaccented -a at the end of the root disappears easily.

137. Person for addressing an animal and a thing (for example, thunder, wind, etc) uses the second-person masculine singular. Therefore, the Column I pronominal prefix is у- /wə/.

Imperative form of Class C verbs

AP a: а-дырра /a-dә́r-ra/ 'to know':

Aff. 2F.Sg. идыр! /jә-dә́r/ [it/them(C1)-know.Imp] 'know it/them! (to a man/woman)'

Aff. 2M.Sg. идыр!

Aff. 2Pl. ишәдыр! /jә-šʷ-dә́r/ [it/them(C1)-you.Pl(C3)-know.Imp] 'know it/them! (to multiple people)'

Neg.2F.Sg. ибымдырын! /jә-bә-m-dә́rә-n/ [it/them(C1)-you.F(C3)-Neg-know-Proh] 'don't know it/them! (to a woman)'[138]

Neg.2M.Sg. иумдырын! /jә-wә-m-dә́rә-n/ [it/them(C1)-you.M(C3)-Neg-know-Proh] 'don't know it/them! (to a man)'

Neg.2Pl. ишәымдырын! /jә-šʷә-m-dә́rә-n/ [it/them(C1)-you.PL(C3)-Neg-know-Proh] 'don't know it/them! (to multiple people)'

AP b: а́-фара /á-fa-ra/ 'to eat': Aff. 2F.Sg. и́фа! *or* и́ф! /jә́-f(a)/ [it/them(C1)-eat.Imp] 'eat it/them!', Aff. 2M.Sg. и́фа! *or* и́ф!, Aff. 2Pl. ишәфа́! /jә-šʷ-fá/ [it/them(C1)-you.Pl(C3)-eat.Imp], Neg.2F.Sg. ибымфа́н! /jә-bә-m-fá-n/ [it/them(C1)-you.F(C3)-Neg-eat-Proh] 'don't eat it/them! (to a woman)', Neg.2M.Sg. иумфа́н!, Neg.2Pl. ишәымфа́н!

а́-жәра /á-zʷ-ra/ 'drink': Aff. 2F.Sg. и́жә! /jә́-žʷ/ [it/them(C1)-drink.Imp] 'drink it/them!', Aff. 2M.Sg. и́жә!, Aff. 2Pl. ижәжәы́! /jә-žʷ-zʷә́/ [it/them(C1)-you.Pl(C3)-drink.Imp] 'drink it/them!' (to multiple people), Neg.2F.Sg. ибымжәы́н! /jә-bә-m-žʷә́-n/ [it/them(C1)-you.F(C3)-Neg-drink-Proh] 'don't drink it/them! (to a woman)', Neg.2M.Sg. иумжәы́н! /jә-wә-m-žʷә́-n/, Neg.2Pl. ишәымжәы́н! /jә-šʷә-m-žʷә́-n/ [it/them(C1)-you.Pl(C3)-Neg-drink-Proh] 'don't drink it/them! (to multiple people)'.

AP c-i: а-бара́ /a-ba-rá/ 'to see': Aff. 2F.Sg. дба́! /d-bá/ 'see him/her!', Aff. 2M.Sg. дба́!, Aff. 2Pl. дыжәба́! /dә-žʷ-bá/ [him/her(C1)-you.Pl(C3)-see.Imp] 'see him/her!' *or* дышәба́! /dә-sʷ-bá/, Neg.2F.Sg. дбымба́н! /d-bә-m-bá-n/ [him/her(C1)-you.F(C3)-Neg-see-Proh] 'don't see him/her! (to a woman)', Neg.2M.Sg. думба́н! /d-wә-m-bá-n/ [him/her(C1)-you.M(C3)-Neg-see-Proh] 'don't see him/her! (to a man)', Neg.2Pl. дшәымба́н! /d-šʷә-m-bá-n/ [him/her(C1)-you.Pl(C3)-Neg-see-Proh] 'don't see him/her! (to multiple people)'.

AP c-ii: а́-шьтра /á-šʲt-ra/ 'to send': Aff. 2F.Sg. ишьты́! /jә-šʲtә́/ [it/them(C1)-send.Imp] 'send it/them!', Aff. 2M.Sg. ишьты́!, Aff. 2Pl. ишәышьты́! /jә-šʷә-šʲtә́/ [it/them(C1)-you.Pl(C3)-send.Imp], Neg.2F.Sg. ибмышьты́н! /jә-b-mә-šʲtә́-n/ [it/them(C1)-you.F(C3)-Neg-send-Proh] 'don't send it/them! (to a woman)', Neg.2M.Sg. иумышьты́н! /jә-w-mә-šʲtә́-n/ [it/them(C1)-you.M(C3)-Neg-send-Proh], Neg.2Pl. ишәмышьты́н! /jә-šʷ-mә-šʲtә́-n/ [it/them(C1)-you.Pl(C3)-Neg-send-Proh].

а-ӡра́ /a-ʒ-rá/ 'to roast': Aff. 2F.Sg. иӡы́! /jә-ʒә́/ [it/them(C1)-roast.Imp] 'roast it/them!', Aff. 2M.Sg. иӡы́!, Aff. 2Pl. ижәӡы́! /jә-žʷ-ʒә́/ [it/them(C1)-you.Pl(C3)-roast.Imp], Neg.2F.Sg. ибымӡы́н! /jә-bә-m-ʒә́-n/ [it/them(C1)-you.F(C3)-Neg-roast-Proh] 'don't roast it/them! (to a woman)', Neg.2M.Sg. иумӡы́н!, Neg.2Pl. ишәымӡы́н! /jә-šʷә-m-ʒә́-n/ [it/them(C1)-you.Pl(C3)-Neg-roast-Proh].

138. Take note of the fact that the negative and imperative forms of а-дырра /a-dә́r-ra/ do not become a potential form (cf. §3.2.6.1. Fn. 116).

а-жрá /a-ž-rá/ 'to dig': Aff. 2F.Sg. ижы́! /jə-žə́/ [it/them(C1)-dig.Imp] 'dig it/them!', Aff. 2M.Sg. ижы́!, Aff. 2Pl. ижəжы́! /jə-žʷ-žə́/ [it/them(C1)-you.Pl(C3)-dig.Imp], Neg.2F.Sg. ибымжы́н! /jə-bə-m-žə́-n/ [it/them(C1)-you.F(C3)-Neg-dig-Proh] 'don't dig it/them! (to a woman)', Neg.2M.Sg. иумжы́н!, Neg.2Pl. ишəымжы́н! /jə-šʷə-m-žə́-n/ [it/them(C1)-you.Pl(C3)-Neg-dig-Proh].

Imperative form of Class C type verbs causatively derived

AP a: а-ргы́лара /a-rgə́la-ra/ 'to build': Aff. 2F.Sg. иргы́л(а)! /jə-rgə́l(a)/ [it/them(C1)-build.Imp] 'build it/them!', Aff. 2M.Sg. иргы́л(а)!, Aff. 2Pl. ишəыргы́ла! /jə-šʷə-rgə́la/ [it/them(C1)-you.Pl(C3)-buid.Imp], Neg.2F.Sg. ибмыргы́лан! /jə-b-mə-rgə́la-n/ [it/them(C1)-you.F(C3)-Neg-build-Proh] 'don't build it/them! (to a woman)', Neg.2M.Sg. иумыргы́лан! /jə-w-mə-rgə́la-n/ [it/them(C1)-you.M(C3)-Neg-build-Proh], Neg.2Pl. ишəмыргы́лан! /jə-šʷ-mə-rgə́la-n/ [it/them(C1)-you.Pl(C3)-Neg-build-Proh].

AP b: á-рлашара /á-rlaša-ra/ 'to light up, to illuminate': Aff. 2F.Sg. и́рлаша! /jə́-rlaša/ [it/them(C1)-light up.Imp] 'light it/them up!', Aff. 2M.Sg. и́рлаша!, Aff. 2Pl. ишəы́рлаша! /jə-šʷə́-rlaša/ [it/them(C1)-you.Pl(C3)-light up.Imp], Neg.2F.Sg. ибмы́рлашан! /jə-b-mə́-rlaša-n/ [it/them(C1)-you.F(C3)-Neg-light up-Proh] 'don't light it/them up! (to a woman)', Neg.2M.Sg. иумы́рлашан! /jə-wə-mə́-rlaša-n/ [it/them(C1)-you.M(C3)-Neg-light up-Proh], Neg.2Pl. ишəмы́рлашан! /jə-šʷ-mə́-rlaša-n/ [it/them(C1)-you.Pl(C3)-Neg-light up-Proh]

AP c: а-ртəарá /a-rt'ʷa-rá/ 'to seat': Aff. 2F.Sg. дыртəá! /də-rt'ʷá/ [him/her(C1)-seat.Imp] 'seat him/her!', Aff. 2M.Sg. дыртəá!, Aff. 2Pl. дшəыртəá! /d-šʷə-rt'ʷá/ [him/her(C1)-you.Pl(C3)-seat.Imp], Neg.2F.Sg. дыбмыртəáн! /də-b-mə-rt'ʷá-n/ [him/her(C1)-you.F(C3)-Neg-seat-Proh] 'don't seat him/her! (to a woman)', Neg.2M.Sg. думыртəáн! /də-w-mə-rt'ʷá-n/ [him/her(C1)-you.M(C3)-Neg-seat-Proh], Neg.2Pl. дышəмыртəáн! /də-šʷ-mə-rt'ʷá-n/ [him/her(C1)-you.Pl(C3)-Neg-seat-Proh]

Imperative form of Class D verbs

á-ҭара /á-ta-ra/ 'to give':

Aff. 2F/M.Sg. и́ҭ! /jə́-t/ (< /j-jə́-t/ [it/tehm(C1)-him(C2)-give.Imp]) 'give it/them (to him)!', исы́ҭ! /jə-sə́-t/ [it/them(C1)-me(C2)-give.Imp] 'give it/them to me!', дсы́ҭ! /d-sə́-t/ [him/her(C1)-me(C2)-give.Imp] 'give him/her to me!' (to a man/woman)

Aff. 2Pl. и́шəҭ! /jə́-šʷ-t/ (< /j-jə́-šʷ-t/ [it/them(C1)-him(C2)-you.Pl(C3)-give.Imp]) 'give it/them to him!', исы́шəҭ! /jə-sə́-šʷ-t/ [it/them(C1)-me(C2)-you.Pl(C3)-give.Imp] 'give it/them to me!'

Neg.2F.Sg. исы́бымҭан! /jə-sə́-bə-m-ta-n/ [it/them(C1)-me(C2)-you.F(C3)-Neg-give-Proh] 'don't give it/them to me! (to a woman)'

Neg.2M.Sg. исы́умҭан! /jə-sə́-wə-m-ta-n/ [it/them(C1)-me(C2)-you.M(C3)-Neg-give-Proh] 'don't give it/them to me! (to a man)'

Neg.2Pl. ииры́шəымҭан! /jə-rə́-šʷə-m-ta-n/ [it/them(C1)-them(C2)-you.Pl(C3)-Neg-give-Proh] 'don't give it/them to them! (to multiple people)'

Imperative form of Class D type verbs that are causatively derived

AP a: а-рды́рра /a-r-də́r-ra/ 'to inform, to introduce': Aff. 2F.Sg. исырды́р! /jə-sə-rdə́r/ [it/them(C1)-

me(C2)-inform.Imp] 'inform me of it/them!', Aff. 2M.Sg. исырдыр́!, Aff. 2Pl. исшәырдыр́! /jə-s-šʷə-rdə́r/ [it/them(C1)-me(C2)-you.Pl(C3)-inform.Imp], Neg.2F.Sg. ис(ы)бмырдыр́ын! /jə-s(ə)-b-mə-rdə́rə-n/ [it/them(C1)-me(C2)-you.F(C3)-Neg-inform-Proh] 'don't inform me of it/them! (to a woman)', Neg.2M.Sg. исумырдыр́ын! /jə-sə-w-mə-rdə́rə-n/ [it/them(C1)-me(C2)-you.M(C3)-Neg-inform-Proh], Neg.2Pl. ис(ы)шәмырдыр́ын! /jə-s(ə)-šʷ-mə-rdə́rə-n/ [it/them(C1)-me(C2)-you.Pl(C3)-Neg-inform-Proh]

<u>AP b</u>: а́-ржәра /á-r-žʷ-ra/ 'to give *sth* to drink': Aff. 2F.Sg. исыр́жә! /jə-sə́-ržʷ/ [it/them(C1)-me(C2)-give (*sth*) to drink.Imp] 'give me it/them to drink!', Aff. 2M.Sg. исыр́жә!, Aff. 2Pl. исшәыр́жә! /jə-s-šʷə́-ržʷ/ [it/them(C1)-me(C2)-you.Pl(C3)-give (*sth*) to drink.Imp], Neg.2F.Sg. исбмыр́жәын! /jə-s-b-mə́-ržʷə-n/ [it/them(C1)-me(C2)-you.F(C3)-Neg-give (*sth*) to drink-Proh] 'don't give me it/them to drink! (to a woman)', Neg.2M.Sg. исумыр́жәын!, Neg.2Pl. и-с-шә-мы́-ржәы-н!

<u>AP c</u>: а-рбара́ /a-r-ba-rá/ 'to show': Aff. 2F.Sg. илырба́! /jə-lə-rbá/ [it/them(C1)-her(C2)-show.Imp] 'show it/them to her!', Aff. 2M.Sg. илырба́!, Aff. 2Pl. илшәырба́! /jə-l-šʷə-rbá/ [it/them(C1)-her(C2)-you.Pl(C3)-show.Imp], Neg.2F.Sg. илбмырба́н! /jə-l-b-mə-rbá-n/ [it/them(C1)-her(C2)-you.F(C3)-Neg-show-Proh] 'don't show it/them to her! (to a woman)', Neg.2M.Sg. илумырба́н!, Neg.2Pl. ил(ы)шәмырба́н!

<u>Imperative form of Class G verbs</u>

а́-ҟацара /á-q'a-c'a-ra/ 'to do, to make': Aff. 2F.Sg. иҟаца́! /jə-q'a-c'á/ [it/them(C1)-Prev-do/make.Imp] 'do/make it/them!', Aff. 2M.Sg. иҟаца́!, Aff. 2Pl. иҟашәца́! /jə-q'a-šʷ-c'á/ [it/them(C1)-Prev-you.Pl(C3)-do/make.Imp], Neg.2F.Sg. иҟабымца́н! /jə-q'a-bə-m-c'á-n/ [it/them(C1)-Prev-you.F(C3)-Neg-do/make-Proh] 'don't do/make it/them! (to a woman)', Neg.2M.Sg. иҟаумца́н!, Neg.2Pl. иҟашәымца́н!

а́-нацара /á-na-ca-ra/ 'to drive thither': Aff. 2F.Sg. инаца́! /jə-na-cá/ [it/them(C1)-Prev(thither)-drive.Imp] 'drive it/them thither!', Aff. 2M.Sg. инаца́!, Aff. 2Pl. ина́шәца! /jə-ná-šʷ-ca/ [it/them(C1)-Prev(thither)-you.Pl-drive.Imp], Neg.2F.Sg. ина́бымца́н! /jə-ná-bə-m-cá-n/ [it/them(C1)-Prev(thither)-you.F(C3)-Neg-drive-Proh] 'don't drive it/them thither! (to a woman)', Neg.2M.Sg. ина́умца́н!, Neg.2Pl. ина́шәымца́н!

а́-нашьҭра /á-na-šʲt-ra/ 'to send thither': Aff. 2F.Sg. инашьҭы́! /jə-na-šʲtə́/ [it/them(C1)-Prev-send.Imp] 'send it/them thither!', Aff. 2M.Sg. инашьҭы́!, Aff. 2Pl. инашәышьҭы́! /jə-na-šʷə-šʲtə́/ [it/them(C1)-Prev-you.Pl(C3)-send.Imp], Neg.2F.Sg. инабмы́шьҭын! /jə-na-b-mə́-šʲtə-n/ [it/them(C1)-Prev-you.F(C3)-Neg-send-Proh] 'don't send it/them thither! (to a woman)', Neg.2M.Sg. инаумы́шьҭын!, Neg.2Pl. инашәмы́шьҭын!

<u>Imperative form of Class H verbs</u>

а-хәара́ /a-ħʷa-rá/ 'to say': Aff. 2F.Sg. иса́хәа! /jə-s-á-ħʷa/ [it/them(C1)-me(C2)-Prev-say.Imp] 'say it/them to me!', Aff. 2M.Sg. иса́хәа!, Aff. 2Pl. иса́шәхәа! /jə-s-á-šʷ-ħʷa/ [it/them(C1)-me(C2)-to-you.Pl(C3)-say.Imp], Neg.2F.Sg. иса́бымхәан! /jə-s-á-bə-m-ħʷa-n/ [it/them(C1)-me(C2)-to-you.F(C3)-Neg-say-Proh] 'don't say it/them to me! (to a woman)', Neg.2M.Sg. иса́умхәан!, Neg.2Pl. иса́шәымхәан!

á-кәтцара /á-kʷ-c'a-ra/ 'to put *sth* on': Aff. 2F.Sg. исы́кәтца! /jə-sə́-kʷ-c'a/ [it/them(C1)-me(C2)-Prev-put.Imp] 'put it/them on me!' (to a man/woman), Aff. 2M.Sg. исы́кәтца!, Aff. 2Pl. исы́кәышәтца! /jə-sə́-kʷə-šʷ-c'a/ [it/them(C1)-me(C2)-Prev-you.Pl(C3)-put.Imp], Neg.2F.Sg. исы́кәбымтцан! /jə-sə́-kʷ-bə-m-c'a-n/ [it/them(C1)-me(C2)-Prev-you.F(C3)-Neg-put-Proh] 'don't put it/them on me! (to a woman)', Neg.2M.Sg. исы́кәумтцан!, Neg.2Pl. исы́кәшәымтцан!

а-ҭы́хра /a-tə́-x-ra/ 'to take out *sth* from': Aff. 2F.Sg. иҭы́х! /jə-ø-tə́-x/ [it/them(C1)-[it(C2)-]Prev-take out.Imp] 'take out it/them from it!', Aff. 2M.Sg. иҭы́х!, Aff. 2Pl. и-ø-ҭы́-шә-х! /jə-ø-tə́-šʷ-x/ [it/them(C1)-[it(C2)-]Prev-you.Pl(C3)-take out.Imp], Neg.2F.Sg. иҭыбымхы́н! /jə-ø-tə-bə-m-xə́-n/ [it/them(C1)-[it(C2)-]you.F(C3)-take out-Proh] 'don't take out it/them from it! (to a woman)', Neg.2M.Sg. иҭыумхы́н!, Neg.2Pl. иҭышәымхы́н!

Imperative form of verb complexes that form structures similar to Class H

а-зы́ҟатцара /a-zə́-q'a-c'a-ra/ 'to do/make *sth* for *sb*': Aff. 2F.Sg. илзы́ҟатца! /jə-l-zə́-q'a-c'a/ [it/them(C1)-her(C2)-OV(for)-Prev-do/make.Imp] 'do/make it/them for her!', Aff. 2M.Sg. илзы́ҟатца!, Aff. 2Pl. илзы́ҟашәтца! /jə-l-zə́-q'a-šʷ-c'a/ [it/them(C1)-her(C2)-for-Prev-you,Pl(C3)-do.Imp], Neg.2F.Sg. илзы́ҟабымтцан! /jə-l-zə́-q'a-bə-m-c'a-n/ [it/them(C1)-her(C2)-for-Prev-you.F(C3)-Neg-do-Proh] 'don't do/make it/them for her! (to a woman)', Neg.2M.Sg. илзы́ҟаумтцан!, Neg.2Pl. илзы́ҟашәымтцан!

а-цәгара́ /a-cʷ-ga-rá/ 'to take away from': Aff. 2F.Sg. ицәга́! (< /j-jə-cʷ-gá/) [it/them(C1)-him(C2)-Prev-take (away from).Imp] 'take it/them away from him!', Aff. 2M.Sg. ицәга́!, Aff. 2Pl. ицәыжәга́! /jə-cʷə-žʷ-gá/ [it/them(C1)-[him(C2)-]Prev-you.Pl(C3)-take (away from).Imp], Neg.2F.Sg. ицәы́бымган! /jə-cʷə́-bə-m-ga-n/ [it/them(C1)-[him(C2)-]Prev-you.F(C3)-Neg-take (away from)-Proh] 'don't take it/them away from him! (to a woman)', Neg.2M.Sg. ицәы́умган!, Neg.2Pl. ицәы́шәымган!

а-хатцара́ /a-xa-c'a-rá/ 'to put on (headgear)': Aff. 2F.Sg. ибхатца́! /jə-b-xa-c'á/ [it/them(C1)-your.F(Poss)-SV-put (on).Imp] 'put on it/them!' (to a woman), Aff. 2M.Sg. иухатца́! /jə-w-xa-c'á/ [it/them(C1)-your.M(Poss)-SV-put (on).Imp] 'put on it/them! (to a man)', Aff. 2Pl. ишәха́шәтц! /jə-šʷ-xá-šʷ-c'/ [it/them(C1)-your.Pl(Poss)-SV-you.Pl(C3)-put (on).Imp] 'put on it/them! (to multiple people)', Neg.2F.Sg. ибха́бымтцан! /jə-b-xá-bə-m-c'a-n/ [it/them(C1)-you.F(Poss)-SV-you.F(C3)-Neg-put (on)-Proh] 'don't put on it/them! (to a woman)', Neg.2M.Sg. иуха́умтцан!, Neg.2Pl. ишәха́шәымтцан!

4.2.1.2. The First-Person Plural Imperative

The first-person plural imperative is expressed by the Future I Indicative, which has the first-person plural pronominal prefix х- /ħ/ for the subject or agent. This imperative form expresses an invitation or suggestion by the speaker to the addressee to perform an action. In other words, it can be translated as 'let us DO!' in English.

(266) Ҳцап!
/ħ-ca-p'/
we(C1)-go-Fut I.Fin
'Let's go!'

(267) Ҳаибады́рып!
/ħ-ajba-dә́rә-p'/
we(C1)-each other-know-Fut I.Fin 'Let's get acquainted with each other!'

(268) Акаҳуа́ еицәа́ажәып! (GAL)
/a-k'aħwá ø-ajc-áa-žʷә-p'/
the-coffee [it(C1)-]together-we(C3)-drink-Fut I.Fin
'Let's drink coffee together!'

(269) Уара́ абри́ ахуҷы́ дахшьы́п! (Abkhaz text)
/wará abrә́j a-xʷәč'ʲә́ d-aħ-šʲә́-p'/
you.M this the-child him(C1)-we(C3)-kill-Fut.I.Fin
'You, let's kill this child!'

4.2.1.3. For the third-person imperative, see §4.2.2.

4.2.2. Subjunctive

The subjunctive (abbreviated as 'Subj') in Abkhaz is produced by attaching the suffix -ааит /aajt'/ to the stems of dynamic verbs (normally, an aorist stem) (suffix -зааит /zaajt'/ to the stems of stative verbs). The following meanings are expressed by the subjunctive:

(i) Third person imperative: the subjunctive expresses (to the addressee) the speaker's desire for a human in the third person (he/her) to perform an action. In English, it can be translated as 'let him/her DO!'

(270) дца́аит (< д-ца-ааит)
/d-c[a-]áajt'/ (he/she(C1)-go-Subj)
'Let him/her go!'

(271) Лара́ аӡы́ аалга́аит.
/lará a-ʒә́ ø-aa-l-gá-aajt'/
she the-water [it(C1)-]Prev(here)-she(C3)-take-Subj
'Let her bring some water.'

(272) Уи уа́ дгы́лазаит.
/wәj wa d-gә́la-zaajt'/
he/she there he/she(C1)-stand-Subj
'Let him/her stand there.'

(ii) The subjunctive expresses to the addressee the speaker's desire for a second- or third-person (or thing) to accomplish an action (or a certain state). The subject (or agent) of the subjunctive is 'a person who will accomplish a certain action', or the 'subject of the state':

(273) Акәра ду́кәа шәы́шәцааит! (GAL)
/á-kʷra dә́w-kʷa ø-nә́-šʷ-c'-aajt'
the-age big-Pl [it(C1)-]Prev-you.Pl(C3)-live to-Subj
'May you-Pl live long!'

(274) Нагӡара́ а́қәзаит атәы́нчра адунеи зе́гь аҟны́!

/nagʒará ∅-á-kʷ-∅-zaajt' a-tə́nčʲra a-də́wnaj zagʲ a-q'nə́
fulfillment [it-]it(C2)-on-be-Subj the-peace the-world all its-in
'Long live peace throughout the whole world!'

(iii) The subjunctive of the negative form is used together with a speech particle (SP) хәа /ħʷa/ and expresses the object clause of the verb а-шәара́ /a-šʷa-rá/ 'to fear'.

(275) Дка́мхааит хәа сшәоит. (ACST)
/d-k'á-m-ħa-[a]ajt' ħʷa s-šʷa-wá-jt'
he/she-Prev-Neg-fall-Subj SP I-feel fear-Dyn-Fin
'I am afraid that he/she will fall.'

4.2.3. Optative

The optative (abbreviated as 'Opt') in Abkhaz is produced by attaching the suffix -нда(з) /nda(z)/ to the stems of dynamic verbs in the aorist, present and perfect of the non-finite form (in the perfect form, the ending -у of the non-finite form is removed and the suffix -нда(з) is added). In the present form of stative verbs, the ending -у of the non-finite form is removed and the suffix -нда(з) is added. Optatives indicate 'a wish'.

(276) Акәа́ аýндаз!
/a-kʷá ∅-a-wə́-ndaz
the-rain [it-]Dummy-fall.Aor.NF-Opt
'If only it would rain!'

(277) Ҭа́ца бзы́иак дбы́манда(з)!
/táca bzə́ja-k' d-bə́-ma-nda(z)/
daughter-in-law good-one her(C1)-you.F(C2)-have.Pres.NF-Opt
'Would that you had a good daughter-in-law!'

(278) Исшәырбо́ндаз, иааигәаны́ са́хәаԥшыр стахыу́п! (AFL)
/jə-s-šʷə-r-ba-wá-ndaz j-aajgʷanə́ s-á-xʷa-pšə-r
it(C1)-me(C2)-you.Pl(C3)-Caus-see-Dyn-Opt it-closely I(C1)-it(C2)-Prev-look at-if
∅-s-taxə́-wp'/
[it(C1)-]I(C2)-want-Stat.Pres.Fin
'If only you had showed it to me, I want to see it closely!'

4.2.4. Potential

The potential mood (abbreviated as 'Pot') is generally used with the negative marker, and indicates the impossibility of performing a certain action.[139] In other words, it means 'cannot DO'. The

---

139. The potential mood is generally used with negative forms, but there are also cases where it is not necessarily accompanied by a negative marker. The following is an example from the text of a folk tale. (1) below is used in the affirmative form, (2) below is used in a question, and they express probability.

(1) Ус ра́хәаны, а́чкунцәа изны́ҟуаз ла́ԥхьа иларгы́ланы, ... (Abkhaz text)
Wəs ∅-r-á-ħʷa-nə, á-č'ʲk'ʷən-cʷa jə-z-nə́q'ʷ-wa-z
so [it-]them-to-say-Past.Abs the-boy/son-Pl Rel-Pot-walk-Dyn+Impf.NF

potential mood is produced by inserting the potential marker -з(ы)- /z(ə)/ into a verbal complex. The potential mood does not change the distribution order of the pronominal prefixes in intransitive verbs, but does change it in transitive verbs. First, we shall take a look at the potential mood derived from intransitive verbs.

4.2.4.1. Method of Deriving the Potential from Intransitive Verbs

The potential mood of intransitive verbs is produced by just inserting the potential marker -з(ы)- /z(ə)/ immediately after the Column I pronominal prefix of the underlying form, and there is no change to the distribution order of the other pronominal prefixes.

The potential mood of the one-place intransitive verb á-ҩра /á-jʷ-ra/ 'to run' is as follows:

(279) дзы́ҩуам [potential]
/d-zə́-jʷ-wa-m/
he/she(C1)-Pot-run-Dyn-Neg
'He/She cannot run.'

Cf. ды́ҩуеит [underlying]
/də́-jʷ-wa-jt'/
'He/She is running.'

(280) дызмы́ҩит [potential]
/də-z-mə́-jʷə-jt'/
he/she-Pot-Neg-run-(Aor)-Fin
'He/She could not run.'

Cf. дмы́ҩит [underlying]
/d-mə́-jʷə-jt'/
he/she(C1)-Neg-run-(Aor)-Fin
'He/She did not run.'

Verbs that have preverbs, such as Class E verbs, also have the potential marker -з(ы)- /z(ə)/ placed after the Column I prefix and before the preverb:

(281) сзынхо́м [potential]
/s-zə-n-xa-wá-m/

---

l-ápxʲa j-la-r-gə́la-nə, ...
she-ahead of them-Par-Caus-stand-Abs
'After having said so to them, she made the sons who were able to be on their feet walk ahead of her, ...'

(2) Да́ара а́мла сакны́ сы́ҟоуп, изӡа́ргьы иаҧса́м, хучы́к бзысҿатцару́шь? — ихәи́т. (Abkhaz text)
Dáara á-mla s-a-k'-nə́ sə́-q'a-wp', jə-z-ʒá-r-gʲə
very the-hunger I-it-feel-Past.Abs I-be-Stat.Pres.Fin it-I-hide-Masd-even
j-a-psá-m, xʷəč'ʲə́-k' ø-b-zə-s-c̓a-c̓a-rə́.wšʲ?
it-it-be worth-Neg.Stat.Pres.Fin a.little [it-]you.F-Pot-me-Prev-feed-even if
— ø-jə-ħʷə́-jt'.
[it-]he-say-(Aor)-Fin
'I'm very hungry. I cannot hide my suffering from hunger [lit. It is not worth while hiding it]. Cannot you feed me a little food?', he said.

I(C1)-Pot-Prev-live-Dyn-Neg
'I cannot live.'

Cf. сынхóм [underlying]
/sə-n-xa-wá-m/
I(C1)-Prev-live-Dyn-Neg
'I live.'

Verbs with Column II pronominal prefixes, such as Class B-2 and Class F verbs, also have the potential marker -з(ы)- /z(ə)/ placed immediately after the Column I prefix:

(282) сызбы́суам [potential]
/sə-z-bə́-s-wa-m/
I(C1)-Pot-you.F(C2)-hit-Dyn-Neg
'I cannot hit you-F.'

Cf. áсра /á-s-ra/ 'to hit' [Class B-2] [underlying]
сбы́суеит
/s-bə́-s-wa-jt'/
I(C1)-you.F(C2)-hit-Dyn-Fin
'I am hitting you-F.'

(283) сызбы́хәаҧшуам [potential]
/sə-z-bə́-xʷa-pš-wa-m/
I(C1)-Pot-you.F(C2)-Prev-look at-Dyn-Neg
'I cannot look at you-F.'

Cf. áхәаҧшра /á-xʷa-pš-ra/ 'to look at' [Class F] [underlying]
сбы́хәаҧшуеит
/s-bə́-xʷa-pš-wa-jt'/
I(C1)-you.F(C2)-Prev-look at-Dyn-Fin
'I am looking at you-F.'

(284) изахьы́мӡеит (Abkhaz text) [potential]
/jə-z-a-xʲə́-m-ʒa-jt'/
they(C1)-Pot-it(C2)-Prev-Neg-catch up with-(Aor)-Fin
'They could not follow it (= the horse).'

Cf. ахьӡара́ /a-xʲ-ʒa-rá/ 'to catch up with' [Class F] [underlying]
сыбхьы́мӡеит
/sə-b-xʲə́-m-ʒa-jt'/
I(C1)-you.F(C2)-Prev-Neg-catch up with-(Aor)-Fin
'I did not catch up with you.'

4.2.4.1.1. Potential Forms of Intransitive Verbs

а-цара́ /a-ca-rá/ 'to go':
Finite forms
C1-Pot-R- Present Aorist

1Sg	сы-з-цó-м	с-зы́-м-це-ит
	/sə-z-ca-wá-m/	/s-zə́-m-ca-jt'/
	I(C1)-Pot-go-Dyn-Neg	
	'I cannot go'	'I could not go'
2Sg.M	у-з-цó-м	у-зы́-м-це-ит
2Sg.F	бы-з-цó-м	б-зы́-м-це-ит
3Sg.Human	ды-з-цó-м	д-зы́-м-це-ит
3Sg.N.H/3Pl	и-з-цó-м	и-зы́-м-це-ит
1Pl	ҳа-з-цó-м	ҳ-зы́-м-це-ит
2Pl	шәы-з-цó-м	шә-зы́-м-це-ит

а-ҩра́ /a-j^{w}-rá/ 'to write' [intr.]

Finite forms

C1-Pot-R-	Present	Aorist
1Sg	с-зы-ҩ-уа́-м	с-зы́-м-ҩ-ит
	/s-zə-j^{w}-wá-m/	/s-zə́-m-j^{w}ə-jt'/
	I(C1)-Pot-write-Dyn-Neg	
	'I cannot write'	
	Future I	Future II
	с-зы-ҩ-ры́-м	сы-з-ҩы́-ша-м
	Perfect	Imperfect
	с-зы́-м-ҩы-ц(т)	с-зы-ҩ-уа́-мы-зт
	Past Indefinite	Conditional I
	с-зы́-м-ҩы-зт	с-зы-ҩ-ры́-мы-зт
	Conditional II	Pluperfect
	сы-з-ҩы́-ша-мы-зт	с-зы́-м-ҩы-цы-зт

4.2.4.2. Method of Deriving the Potential from Transitive Verbs

The potential mood of transitive verbs can basically be produced in the following way. The Column pronominal prefix indicating A of the underlying form is placed immediately before the potential marker and is changed into a Column II pronominal prefix. Then, this 'Column II pronominal prefix + potential marker' is placed immediately after the Column I pronominal prefix. Since the Column III pronominal prefix, which indicates the agent, changed into a pronominal prefix indicating a Column II indirect object (IO), the form of the potential mood becomes an intransitive verb form, and the previous Column I direct object (DO) changes into the subject (S) of the intransitive verb.

4.2.4.2.1. The schematization of the derivation of the potential mood in Class C verbs, which are the most basic of transitive verbs, appears in the following way:

[underlying] DO(C1) + A(C3) + R
(DO → S, A → IO)
[potential] S(C1) + IO(C2) + Pot + R

For example, а-дырра /a-dər-ra/ 'to know':

(285) издыруеит [underlying]
/jə-z-dər-wa-jt'/
it/them(C1)-I(C3)-know-Dyn-Fin
'I know it/them.'

(286) исыздыруам [potential]
/jə-sə-z-dər-wa-m/
it/they(C1)-{me(C2)-Pot}-know-Dyn-Neg
'I do not know it/them.'[140]

Similarly, the potential aorist form of the verb а-шьра́ /a-š^j-rá/ 'to kill', an AP c-i Class C verb, is as follows:

(287) дсымшьи́т [underlying]
/d-sə-m-š^jə́-jt'/
him/her(C1)-I(C3)-Neg-kill-(Aor)-Fin
'I did not kill him/her.'

(288) дысзы́мшьит [potential]
/də-s-zə́-m-š^jə-jt'/
he/she(C1)-{me(C2)-Pot}-Neg-kill-(Aor)-Fin
'I could not kill him/her.'

4.2.4.2.2. The derivation of the potential mood in Class D verbs can be schematized as follows:

[underlying]	DO(C1) +IO(C2) + A(C3) + R
	(DO → S, A → IO', IO = IO)
[potential]	S(C1) + {IO'(C2) + Pot} + IO(C2) + R

For example, а́-тара /á-ta-ra/ 'to give':

(289) дбы́сымҭеит [underlying]
/d-bə́-sə-m-ta-jt'/
him/her(C1)-you.F(C2)-I(C3)-Neg-give-(Aor)-Fin
'I did not give him/her to you-F.'

(290) дсызбы́мҭеит [potential]
/d-sə-z-bə́-m-ta-jt'/
he/she(C1)-{me(C2)-Pot}-you.F(C2)-Neg-give-(Aor)-Fin
'I could not give him/her to you-F.'

4.2.4.2.3. The derivation of the potential mood in Class G verbs can be schematized as follows:

140. The negative form of а-дырра /a-dər-ra/ must use the potential form. This is probably because one cannot consciously produce 'not knowing'.

[underlying] DO(C1) + Prev + A(C3) + R
(DO → S, A → IO)
[potential] S(C1) + {IO(C2) + Pot} + Prev + R

For example,
á-ҟатцара /á-q'a-c'a-ra/ 'to do, to make':

(291) иҟасымтцéит [underlying]
/jə-q'a-sə-m-c'á-jt'/
it/them(C1)-Prev-I(C3)-Neg-do/make-(Aor)-Fin
'I did not do/make it/them.'

(292) исзы́ҟамтцеит [potential]
/jə-s-zə́-q'a-m-c'a-jt'/
it/they(C1)-{me(C2)-Pot}-Prev-Neg-do/make-(Aor)-Fin
'I could not do/make it/them.'

á-нашьҭра /á-na-šʲt-ra/ 'to send thither':

(293) днасмы́шьҭит [underlying]
/d-na-s-mə́-šʲtə-jt'/
him/her(C1)-Prev-I(C3)-Neg-send-(Aor)-Fin
'I did not send him/her thither.'

(294) дысзы́намышьҭит [potential]
/də-s-zə́-na-mə-šʲtə-jt'/
he/she(C1)-{I(C2)-Pot}-Prev-Neg-send-(Aor)-Fin
'I could not send him/her thither.'

4.2.4.2.4. The derivation of the potential mood in Class H verbs can be schematized as follows:

[underlying] DO(C1) + IO(C2) + Prev + A(C3) + R
(DO → S, A → IO', IO = IO)
[potential] S(C1) + {IO'(C2) + Pot} + IO(C2) + Prev + R

For example, а-хәарá /a-ħʷa-rá/ 'to say':

(295) исáлымхәеит [underlying]
/jə-s-á-lə-m-ħʷa-jt'/
it/them(C1)-me(C2)-Prev-she(C3)-Neg-say-(Aor)-Fin
'She did not say it/them to me.'

(296) илызсáмхәеит [potential]
/jə-lə-z-s-á-m-ħʷa-jt'/
it/they(C1)-{her(C2)-Pot}-me(C2)-Prev-Neg-say-(Aor)-Fin
'She could not say it/them to me.'

á-кәтцара /á-kʷ-c'a-ra/ 'to put *sth* on *sth*':

(297) исы́ҟәлымтцеит [underlying]
/jə-sə́-kʷ-lə-m-c'a-jt'/
it/them(C1)-me(C2)-Prev(on)-she(C3)-Neg-put-(Aor)-Fin
'she did not put it/them on me'

(298) илызсы́ҟәмтцеит [potential]
/jə-lə-z-sə́-kʷ-m-c'a-jt'/
it/them(C1)-{her(C2)-Pot}-me(C2)-Prev(on)-Neg-put-(Aor)-Fin
'She could not put it/them on me.'

4.2.4.2.5. The derivation of the potential mood of the causative form can be schematized as follows:

[underlying]	DO(C1) + A(C3) + R
	(DO = DO, A → IO)
[causative]	DO(C1) + IO(C2) + A(C3) + Caus + R
	(DO → S, A → IO', IO = IO)
[potential]	S(C1) + {IO'(C2) + Pot} + IO(C2) + Caus + R

For example,

а-ҩрá /a-jʷ-rá/ 'to write' (Class C):

(299) илымҩи́т [underlying]
/jə-lə-m-jʷə́-jt'/
it/them(C1)-she(C3)-Neg-write-(Aor)-Fin
'She did not write it/them.'

(300) илсмы́рҩит [causative]
/jə-l-s-mə́-r-jʷə-jt'/
it/them(C1)-her(C2)-I(C3)-Neg-Caus-write-(Aor)-Fin
'I did not make her write it/them.'

(301) исзылмы́рҩит [causative-potential]
/jə-s-zə-l-mə́-r-jʷə-jt'/
it/they(C1)-{me(C2)-Pot}-her(C2)-Neg-Caus-write-(Aor)-Fin
'I could not make her write it/them.'

á-ҟатцара /á-q'a-c'a-ra/ 'to do, to make':

(302) иҟартцóит [underlying]
/jə-q'a-r-c'a-wá-jt'/
it/them(C1)-Prev-they(C3)-do/make-Dyn-Fin
'I am doing/making it/them.'

(303) идсы́рҟатцоит [causative]
/jə-d-sə́-r-q'a-c'a-wa-jt'/
it/them(C1)-them(C2)-I(C3)-Caus-Prev-do/make-Dyn-Fin

'I am making them do it/them.'

(304) исыздыр́ҟацом [causative-potential]
/jə-sə-z-də́-r-q'a-c'a-wa-m/
it/they(C1)-{me(C2)-Pot}-them(C2)-Caus-Prev-do/make-Dyn-Neg
'I cannot make them do it/them.'

The verb á-ҟацара /á-q'a-c'a-ra/ used above is a special verb in which a causative marker does not come between the preverb and the root in the causative form (see (303) above. For this, see fn. 134). In contrast, in the causative form of verbs with regular preverbs the causative marker splits the preverb and the root. For example, the causative form of а-ҧҟара́ /a-p-q'a-rá/ 'to cut' as well as its potential form is as follows:

(305) иҧи́ҟом [underlying]
/jə-pə́-j-q'a-wa-m/
it/them(C1)-Prev-he(C3)-cut-Dyn-Neg
'He does not cut it/them.'

(306) иҧсырҟо́м [causative]
/jə-j-p-sə-r-q'a-wá-m/
it/them(C1)-him(C2)-Prev-I(C3)-Caus-cut-Dyn-Neg
'I do not make him cut it/them.'

(307) исызирҧҟо́м [causative-potential]
/jə-sə-zə-j-r-p-q'a-wá-m/
it/they(C1)-{me(C2)-Pot}-him(C2)-Caus-Prev-cut-Dyn-Neg
'I cannot make him cut it/them.'

As can be seen in (304) and (307) above, both causative potential forms assume the same structure. This means that a formation rule for the causative form must be added to the potential formation rules discussed in §4.2.4.2: when potentializing the causative form of verbs with preverbs, the causative marker does not split the preverb and root.

4.2.4.2.6. Potential Forms of Transitive Verbs

á-фара /á-fa-ra/ 'to eat':

Finite forms

C1-C2-Pot-R-	Present	Aorist
3Sg.N.H/3Pl-1Sg	и-с-зы́-фо-м /jə-s-zə́-fa-wa-m/ it/they(C1)-me(C2)-Pot-eat-Dyn-Neg 'I cannot eat it/them'	и-с-зы́-м-фе-ит
3Sg.N.H/3Pl-2Sg.F	и-б-зы́-фо-м	и-б-зы́-м-фе-ит
3Sg.N.H/3Pl-2Sg.M	и-у-зы́-фо-м	и-у-зы́-м-фе-ит
3Sg.N.H/3Pl-3Sg.F	и-л-зы́-фо-м	и-л-зы́-м-фе-ит
3Sg.N.H/3Pl-3Sg.M	и-зы́-фо-м (< и-и-зы́-фо-м)	и-зы́-м-фе-ит
3Sg.N.H/3Pl-3Sg.N.H	и-а-зы́-фо-м	и-а-зы́-м-фе-ит
3Sg.N.H/3Pl-1Pl	и-аҳ-зы́-фо-м	и-аҳ-зы́-м-фе-ит

3Sg.N.H/3Pl-2Pl	и-шә-зы́-фо-м	и-шә-зы́-м-фе-ит
3Sg.N.H/3Pl-3Pl	и-р-зы́-фо-м	и-р-зы́-м-фе-ит

а-бара́ ‘to see’:

Finite forms

C1-C2-Pot-R-	Present	Aorist
2Sg.F-1Sg	б-сы-з-бо́-м ‘I cannot see you’	бы-с-зы́-м-бе-ит
3Sg.Hum.-1Sg	д-сы-з-бо́-м	ды-с-зы́-м-бе-ит
1Sg-3Sg.F	с-лы-з-бо́-м	сы-л-зы́-м-бе-ит
1Pl-3Sg.Non-Hum	ҳ-а-з-бо́-м	ҳ-а-зы́-м-бе-ит

а́-ҭара ‘to give’:

Finite forms

C1-C2-Pot-C2-R-	Present	Aorist
3Sg.N.H/3Pl-1Sg-2Sg.F	и-сы-з-бы́-ҭо-м /jə-sə-z-bə́-ta-wa-m/ it/they(C1)-me(C2)-Pot-you.F(C2)-give-Dyn-Neg ‘I cannot give it/them to you-F’	и-сы-з-бы́-м-ҭе-ит
3Sg.N.H/3Pl-3Sg.M-1Sg	и-з-сы́-ҭо-м (< и-и-з-сы́-ҭо-м)	и-з-сы́-м-ҭе-ит
3Sg.N.H/3Pl-3Sg.F-1Sg	и-лы-з-сы́-ҭо-м	и-лы-з-сы́-м-ҭе-ит
3Sg.N.H/3Pl-1Pl-2Sg.F	и-ҳа-з-бы́-ҭо-м	и-ҳа-з-бы́-м-ҭе-ит
3Sg.N.H/3Pl-2Pl-3Pl	и-шәы-з-ры́-ҭо-м	и-шәы-з-ры́-м-ҭе-ит
3Sg.Hum-1Sg-2Sg.F	д-сы-з-бы́-ҭо-м	д-сы-з-бы́-м-ҭе-ит

а́-ҟаҵара ‘to do, to make’:

Finite forms

C1-C2-Pot-Prev-R-	Present	Aorist
3Sg.N.H/3Pl-1Sg	и-с-зы́-ҟа-ҵо-м jə-s-zə́-q’a-c’a-wa-m it/they(C1)-me(C2)-Pot-Prev-do/make-Dyn-Neg ‘I cannot do/make it/them’	и-с-зы́-ҟа-м-ҵе-ит
3Sg.N.H/3Pl-2Sg.F	и-б-зы́-ҟа-ҵо-м	и-б-зы́-ҟа-м-ҵе-ит
3Sg.N.H/3Pl-3Sg.F	и-л-зы́-ҟа-ҵо-м	и-л-зы́-ҟа-м-ҵе-ит
3Sg.N.H/3Pl-3Sg.N.H	и-а-зы́-ҟа-ҵо-м	и-а-зы́-ҟа-м-ҵе-ит
3Sg.N.H/3Pl-1Pl	и-аҳ-зы́-ҟа-ҵо-м	и-аҳ-зы́-ҟа-м-ҵе-ит
3Sg.N.H/3Pl-3Pl	и-р-зы́-ҟа-ҵо-м	и-р-зы́-ҟа-м-ҵе-ит

4.2.4.2.7. Periphrastic Expression of ‘Cannot’

The expression of ‘cannot do X’ can be expressed by not only the potential mood but by a periphrastic expression as well. Namely, it is expressed by ‘masdar + а́-лшара /á-l-ša-ra/ ‘to be able’’. For example, a periphrastic expression with а́-ҟаҵара /á-q’a-c’a-ra/ ‘to do/make’ is as follows:

(308) а́ҟаҵара сы́лшом

/á-q’a-c’a-ra ø-sə́-l-ša-wa-m/

its-Prev-do-Masd [it(C1)-]me(C2)-Prev-be able-Dyn-Fin
'I cannot do it'

Cf. (309) исызы́қатцом [potential]
/jə-sə-zə́-q'a-c'a-wa-m/
it(C1)-me(C2)-Pot-Prev-do-Dyn-Neg
'I cannot do it'

According to our informant, periphrastic expression (308) above implies 'I am unable to do it because the surrounding conditions do not permit it, for example, I am very busy, or I am physically unable to do, or unable to do it because I caught a cold today', etc. In contrast, potential mood expression (309) above is used in circumstances that are uncontrollable by the person in question: 'I do not want to, so I cannot do it'.

4.2.5. Non-Volitional Mood

Abkhaz has a non-volitional mood, which expresses 'the coincidental performance of an action regardless of the subject's intent'. This non-volitional mood is produced by inserting the non-volitional (abbreviated here as 'Nonvol') marker -амха- /amxa/ in the verbal complex. The method in which the non-volitional mood is derived from the underlying form is the same as that of the potential mood examined above. This non-volitional mood is usually used in the affirmative form.

4.2.5.1. Method of Deriving the Non-Volitional Mood from Intransitive Verbs

The non-volitional marker -амха- /amxa/ is inserted immediately after subject S. For example, а-цара́ /a-ca-rá/ 'to go':

(310) са́мхацеит
/s-ámxa-ca-jt'/
I(C1)-Nonvol-go-(Aor)-Fin
'I went against my own volition.'

4.2.5.2. Method of Deriving the Non-Volitional Mood from Transitive Verbs

The schematization of the derivation of the non-volitional mood of Class C verbs, which are the most basic of transitive verbs, appears in the following way:

[underlying]	DO(C1) + A(C3) + R
	(DO → S, A → IO)
[non-volitional]	S(C1) + {IO(C2) + Nonvol} + R

For example,
Class C verb а́-фара /á-fa-ra/ 'to eat':

(311) исфе́ит [underlying]
/jə-s-fá-jt'/
it/them(C1)-I(C3)-eat-(Aor)-Fin

'I ate it/them.'

(312) иса́мхафеит [non-volitional]
/jə-s-ámxa-fa-jt'/
it/they(C1)-{me(C2)-Nonvol}-eat-(Aor)-Fin
'I involuntarily ate it/them.'

Class G verb а-ԥҟара́ /a-p-q'a-rá/ 'to cut':

(313) иԥы́сҟеит [underlying]
/jə-pə́-s-q'a-jt'/
it/them(C1)-Prev-I(C3)-cut-(Aor)-Fin
'I cut it/them.'

(314) иса́мхаԥҟеит [non-volitional]
/jə-s-ámxa-p-q'a-jt'/
it/they(C1)-{me(C2)-Nonvol}-Prev-cut-(Aor)-Fin
'I involuntarily cut it/them.'

Class D verb а́-ҭара /á-ta-ra/ 'to give':

(315) илы́сҭеит [underlying]
/jə-lə́-s-ta-jt'/
hit/them(C1)-her(C2)-I(C3)-give-(Aor)-Fin
'I gave it/them to her.'

(316) исамхалы́ҭеит [non-volitional]
/jə-s-amxa-lə́-ta-jt'/
it/they(C1)-{me(C2)-Nonvol}-her(C2)-give-(Aor)-Fin
'I involuntarily gave it/them to her.'

Class H verb а-хәара́ /a-ħʷa-rá/ 'to say':

(317) иба́схәеит [underlying]
/jə-b-á-s-ħʷa-jt'/
it/them(C1)-you.F(C2)-Prev-I(C3)-say-(Aor)-Fin
'I said it/them to you-F.'

(318) иса́мхабахәеит [non-volitional]
/jə-s-ámxa-b-a-ħʷa-jt'/
it/they(C1)-{me(C2)-Nonvol}-you.F(C2)-Prev-say-(Aor)-Fin
'I involuntarily said it/them to you-F.'

The derivation of the non-volitional mood from the causative form has the same structure as the potential mood.

(319) ислы́рҟацеит [causative]
/jə-s-lə́-r-q'a-c'a-jt'/
it/them(C1)-me(C2)-she(C3)-Caus-Prev-do/make-(Aor)-Fin
'She made me do/make it/them.'

(320) иламхасы́рҟацеит [causative-non-volitional]
/jə-l-amxa-sə́-r-q'a-c'a-jt'/

it/they(C1)-{her(C2)-Nonvol}-me(C2)-Caus-Prev-do/make-(Aor)-Fin
'She involuntarily made me do/make it/them.'

4.2.5.3. Non-volitional Forms

а-гы́лара /a-gə́la-ra/ 'to stand':

Finite forms

C1-C2-Nonvol-R-	Aorist
1Sg	с-амха-гы́ле-ит
2Sg.F	б-амха-гы́ле-ит
2Sg.M	у-амха-гы́ле-ит
3Sg.Human	д-амха-гы́ле-ит
3Sg.Non-Human/3Pl	и-амха-гы́ле-ит
1Pl	х-амха-гы́ле-ит
2Pl	шә-амха-гы́ле-ит

а́-фара /á-fa-ra/ 'to eat':

Finite forms

C1-C2-Nonvol-R-	Aorist
3Sg.N.H/3Pl-1Sg1	и-с-а́мха-фе-ит
3Sg.N.H/3Pl-2Sg.F	и-б-а́мха-фе-ит
3Sg.N.H/3Pl-2Sg.M	и-у-а́мха-фе-ит
3Sg.N.H/3Pl-3Sg.F	и-л-а́мха-фе-ит
3Sg.N.H/3Pl-3Sg.M	и-а́мха-фе-ит (< и-и-а́мха-фе-ит)
3Sg.N.H/3Pl-3Sg.Non-Hum	и-а́мха-фе-ит (< и-а-а́мха-фе-ит)
3Sg.N.H/3Pl-1Pl	и-х-а́мха-фе-ит
3Sg.N.H/3Pl-2Pl	и-шә-а́мха-фе-ит
3Sg.N.H/3Pl-3Pl	и-р-а́мха-фе-ит

а-пҟара́ /a-p-q'a-rá/ 'to cut':

Finite forms

C1-C2-Nonvol-R-	Aorist
3Sg.N.H/3Pl-1Sg1	и-с-а́мха-пҟе-ит
Non-Finite forms	Past Indefinite
Rel-1Sg1	и-с-а́мха-пҟа-з
3Sg.N.H/3Pl-Rel	и-з-а́мха-пҟа-з

Examples:

(321) сара́ снапы́ са́мхапҟеит
/sará s-nap'ə́ ø-s-ámxa-p-q'a-jt'/
I my-hand [it(C1)-]me(C2)-Nonvol-Prev-cut-(Aor)-Fin
'I accidentally cut my hand.'

(322) сара́ иса́мхапҟаз с-напы́
/sará jə-s-ámxa-p-q'a-z s-nap'ə́/

I Rel(C1)-me(C2)-Nonvol-Prev-cut-Past Ind.NF my-hand
'my hand which I accidentally cut'

(323) знапы́ за́мхаҧҟаз атцаҩы́
/z-nap'ə́ ϕ-z-ámxa-p-q'a-z a-c'ajʷə́/
Rel(Poss)-hand [it(C1)-]Rel(C2)-Nonvol-Prev-cut-Past Ind.NF the-pupil
'the pupil who accidentally cut his own hand'

4.2.6. Evidential Mood

The evidential mood is used in order to express conjecture or speculation. To produce this, the evidential suffix -заап /zaap'/ (abbreviated as 'Evid') is added to the non-finite stem of the aorist, perfect and present. For example:

(324) Сара́ атцәы́ць сы́маҙамзаап.
/sará a-c'ʷə́ʒʲ ϕ-sə́-ma-ʒa-m-zaap'/
I the-match [it(C1)-]I(C2)-have-Emph-Neg-Evid
'Apparently I don't have matches.'

(325) Ахәычы́ илба́заап ари́.
/a-xʷəčʲ'ə́ jə-l-bá-zaap' arə́j/
the-child it(C1)-she(C)-see.Aor.NF-Evid this
'The child apparently saw this.'

(326) Дачеазны́к ди́сыр, алау́ иҧсы́ ҭа́лозаап. (Abkhaz text)
/dača-znə́k' d-jə́-sə-r a-dawə́ jə-psə́ ϕ-ϕ-tá-la-wa-zaap'/
once more he(C1)-him(C2)-hit-if the-ogre his-soul [it(C1)-it(C2)-]Prev-go into-Dyn-Evid
'If he hits him once more, the ogre will apparently come back to life.'

Furthermore, it is also possible to produce the evidential mood by means of the suffix -заарын /zaarən/.[141] This suffix is attached to the non-finite stem. If -з /z/ from Dynamic Group II is at the end of this non-finite stem, it disappears before the suffix -заарын. For example:

(327) Ҳәынҭка́рк ды́ҟан, жәаҩы́к а́ҧхацәа и́мазаарын. (Abkhaz text)
/ħʷəntkár-k' də́-q'a-n žʷa-jʷə́-k' á-pħa-cʷa ϕ-jə́-ma-zaarən/
king-one he(C1)-be-Stat.Past 10-Hum-NS the-daughter-Pl [them(C1)-]he(C2)-have-Evid
'There was a King. They say that he had ten daughters.'

(328) Усҟан а́шьха асы́, ақуа́, акы́рцх а́муазаарын. (Abkhaz text)
/wəsq'an á-šʲxa a-sə́ a-kʷá a-k'ə́rcx ϕ-á-m-w-[w]a-[z-]zaarən/
at that time the-mountain the-snow the-rain the-hail [they(C1)-]Dummy-Neg-fall-Dyn+Impf.NF-Evid
'In those days, they say that there was neither snow, nor rain nor hail in the mountains.'

(329) Дара́ иа́рбанзаалакгьы акы́ у́сс иры́мамкуа, акы́ иацәы́мшәо и́ҟазаарын. (Abkhaz text)
/dará járbanzaalák'-gʲə ak'ə́ wə́s-s jə-rə́-ma-m-k'ʷa ak'ə
they anything-also something work-as it(C1)-they(C2)-have-Neg-Abs something
j-a-cʷə́-m-šʷa-wa jə́-q'a-[z]-zaarən/
they(C1)-it(C2)-Prev-Neg-fear-Abs they(C1)-be-Stat.Past.NF-Evid

141. For -заарын, see Chirikba (2003a: 47).

'Apparently, they didn't have any work and yet they feared nothing.'

4.3. Version

4.3.1. Categories of Version

Version ('версия' in Russian) is a unique grammatical category seen in Caucasian languages. The term version ('kceba' in Georgian) was introduced into Georgian grammar by Shanidze in 1930.[142] We have observed this category in Abkhaz as well, and they are the objective version (abbreviated as 'OV') and the subjective version (abbreviated as 'SV'). These two versions have markers which express their specialized versions in the verbal complex. We shall discuss their forms and functions below.

4.3.2. Definition of the Objective Version

Scholars have defined the objective version in Abkhaz in the following way. For example, according to Aristava, et al, it is considered 'a grammatical category that expresses a mutual relationship between subject and object, or a mutual relationship between objects'.[143] Also, according to Lomtatidze, 'the objective version refers to actions or states of verbs that are joined to indirect objects, then, as a matter of course, the person of the indirect object is indicated in the verb form'.[144]

In the present volume, we define the objective version in Abkhaz as a grammatical category which has the following characteristics:

(i) The objective version forms can be produced from both intransitive and transitive verbs.

(ii) In the objective version, the person governed by the objective version marker and the person of the subject must be different.

(iii) The objective version must be expressed in the verbal complex. Even if the same meaning is expressed outside the verbal complex, it is not called the objective version.

(iv) When producing the objective version, a Column II pronominal prefix governed by the objective version marker is placed before the objective version marker. This 'Column II Prefix + Objective Version Marker' (in the present section, a union is expressed with { }) is placed immediately after the Column I prefix.

(v) There are two objective version markers: з(ы)- /z(ə)/ and цә(ы)- /c^w(ə)/. The former expresses 'for' or a dative meaning along with the indirect object. The latter indicates contradiction to the indirect object's volition or an action separated from the indirect object. These can be translated as 'against one's will' and 'from'.

(vi) The objective version marker з(ы)- /z(ə)/ used in transitive verbs can express a possessive relationship between the direct and indirect objects.

---

142. Hewitt, B.G. 1996. *Georgian: A Structural Reference Grammar.* Amsterdam/Philadelphia: John Benjamins. p. 170.

143. Аристава Ш.К. и др. 1968. *Грамматика абхазского языка: фонетика и морфология.* Сухуми. с. 138.

144. Ломтатидзе К.В. 1976. Категория версии в картвельских и абхазско-адыгских языках. *Ежегодник иберийско-кавказского языкознания.* III. с. 99.

4.3.3. Forms of the Objective Version

Examples of the objective version derived from intransitive verbs:

(330) слызцо́ит [objective version]
/s-lə-z-ca-wá-jt'/
I(C1)-{her(C2)-OV}-go-Dyn-Fin 'I am going for her'

Cf. сцо́ит /s-ca-wá-jt'/ 'I am going.' [underlying]

(331) сылзы́мцеит [objective version]
/sə-l-zə́-m-ca-jt'/
I(C1)-{her(C2)-OV}-Neg-go-(Aor)-Fin 'I did not go for her.'

(332) сбыцәцо́ит [objective version]
/s-bə-cʷ-ca-wá-jt'/
I(C1)-{you.F(C2)-OV}-go-Dyn-Fin 'I am going against your-F will.'

(333) сбызлы́суеит [objective version]
/s-bə-z-lə́-s-wa-jt'/
I(C1)-{you.F(C2)-OV}-her(C2)-hit-Dyn-Fin 'I am hitting her for you-F'

Cf. слы́суеит /s-lə́-s-wa-jt'/ 'I am hitting her.' [underlying]

(334) сылцәамы́сит [objective version]
/sə-l-cʷ-a-mə́-sə-jt'/
I(C1)-{her(C2)-OV}-it(C2)-Neg-hit-(Aor)-Fin 'I did not hit it against her will.'

Examples of the objective version derived from transitive verbs:

(335) илзы́ӄастцоит [objective version]
/jə-l-zə́-q'a-s-c'a-wa-jt'/
it/them(C1)-{her(C2)-OV}-Prev-I(C3)-do/make-Dyn-Fin
'I am doing/making it/them for her.'

Cf. иӄастцо́ит /jə-q'a-s-c'a-wá-jt'/ 'I am doing/making it/them' [underlying]

(336) иахцәы́ӄалымтцеит [objective version]
/j-aħ-cʷə́-q'a-lə-m-c'a-jt'/
it/them(C1)-{us(C2)-OV}-Prev-she(C3)-Neg-do/make-(Aor)-Fin
'She did not do/make it/them against our will.'

(337) ибызлы́сымтеит [objective version]
/jə-bə-z-lə́-sə-m-ta-jt'/
it/them(C1)-{you.F(C2)-OV}-her(C2)-I(C3)-Neg-give-(Aor)-Fin
'I did not give it/them to her for you-F.'

Cf. илы́сымтеит /jə-lə́-sə-m-ta-jt'/ 'I did not give it/them to her.' [underlying]

(338) Уи сара́ аҧа́ра сцәы́игеит.
/wəj sará a-pára [ø-]s-cʷə́-j-ga-jt'/
he I the-money [it(C1)]-{me(C2)-OV}-he(C3)-take-(Aor)-Fin
'He took the money away from me.'

As the examples above make clear, the transitivity does not change in derivations by the objective version. In other words, the form of objective version derived from intransitive verbs is an intransitive verb, and the form of the objective version derived from transitive verbs is a transitive verb. Here, we shall investigate the transitivity of the verb а-цәы́ӡра /a-cʷə́-ʒ-ra/ 'to lose', which has the objective version marker цә(ы)- /cʷ(ə)/. This is clearly a derivation by the objective version from а́-ӡра /á-ʒ-ra/ 'to disappear' (Class A-2). This а-цәы́ӡра /a-cʷə́-ʒ-ra/ can take two pronominal prefixes:

(339) Сара́ аҧа́ра сцәы́ӡит.
/sará a-pára ø-s-cʷə́-ʒə-jt'/
I the-money [it-]-I/me-OV-lose/disappear-(Aor)-Fin
'I lost money.'

In the English translation of (339) above, the verb is translated as though it is transitive, but is this verb really transitive? In the objective version (338) derived from the transitive verb above, the Column III pronominal prefix is between the objective version marker (OV) and the root. In contrast, in (339) the subject 'I' in the English translation is before the objective version marker. Therefore, this 'I' is not the agent of the verb; it must be regarded as a pronominal prefix governed by the objective version marker. Here, no agent exists. Also, the imperative mood of this verb is as follows:

(340) ибцәы́ӡ!
/jə-b-cʷə́-ʒ/
it-you.F-OV-lost/disappear.Imp
'Lose it/them!'

In the imperative mood of the singular, affirmative form of transitive verbs, since the agent does not appear, this verb is intransitive from the standpoint of the imperative mood. As in the examples above, from the position of these pronominal prefixes and the form of the imperative mood, (339) can be considered intransitive, so 'the money disappeared against my will' can be seen as its original meaning. However, according to the academic version of the *Dictionary of the Abkhaz Language*,[145] this verb is listed as 'transitive'. According to their interpretation, the transitivity of this verb was not determined from its morphological features, but semantically as in its English translation (in their Russian translation, it is *терять* 'to lose'). Verbs such as these are called inversive verbs (see §5.10).

4.3.4. Usage of the Objective Version

In the objective version discussed above, the person of the subject (or agent) and the indirect object governed by the objective version marker must be different:

(341) Сара́ сҩы́за а́фатә лзы́ҟастцоит.
/sará s-jʷə́za á-fat'ʷ ø-l-zə́-q'a-s-c'a-wa-jt'/
I my-friend the-meal [it(C1)-]{her(C2)-OV}-Prev-I(C3)-make-Dyn-Fin
'I am preparing a meal for my friend.'

In (341) above, the agent с- /s/ 'I' and the person л- /l/ 'her' governed by the objective version marker

145. Шакрыл К.С., Конджария В.Х. Чкадуа Л.П. (ed.) 1987. *Словарь абхазского языка. (Аҧсуа бызшәа ажәа).* т. 2. Сухуми: Алашара. However, according to the most recently published Касландзия В.А. (ед.) 2005. *Абхазско-русский словарь.* т. I, т. II. Сухум: ОЛМА-ПРЕСС, it is listed as an 'intransitive verb'.

are different. It is possible for the sentence using this objective version to change into the following sentence (342) which does not use the objective form. In that case, the objective version marker з(ы)- in the verbal complex in (341) above is placed outside the verbal complex, and a possessive prefix meaning 'her' is added to it:

(342) Сара́ сҩы́за лзы а́фатә ҟастцо́ит.
/sará s-jʷə́za l-zə á-fat'ʷ ø-q'a-s-c'a-wá-jt'/
I my-friend her-for the-meal [it(C1)-]Prev-I(C3)-make-Dyn-Fin
'I am preparing a meal for my friend.'

In the verbal complex in (342) above, there is no marker indicating any version. This type of verb form that does not have any version marker has no restriction in which the agent person and the person governed by the objective version marker must be different as in (341). Therefore, in (343) below these can be the same person:

(343) Сара́ сзы а́фатә ҟастцо́ит.
/sará s-zə á-fat'ʷ ø-q'a-s-c'a-wá-jt'/
I my-for the-meal [it(C1)-]Prev-I(C3)-make-Dyn-Fin
'I am preparing a meal for myself.'

The sentence in (343) above cannot be expressed by the objective version.

In the case of the third person, if the subject (or agent) person and the person governed by the objective version marker are different, sentences below using the objective version are possible. For example:

(344) Дара́ ирзы́ҟартцеит.
/dará jə-r-zə́-q'a-r-c'a-jt'/
they it/them(C1)-{them$_j$ (C2)-OV}-Prev-they$_i$ (C3)-do/make(Aor)-Fin
'They$_i$ did/made it/them for them$_j$.'

4.3.5. Other Usage of the Objective Version

As seen above, the objective version marker з(ы)- /z(ə)/ actively indicates that the action is not limited to the inside of the subject (or agent), but the action is directed outside the subject (or agent) as if to say 'the subject (or agent) is performing an action for someone'. For this reason, the objective version also indicates an action heading in someone's direction, in other words, a dative expression. For example, since а-гара́ /a-ga-rá/ 'to take, to carry' is a Class C verb, it can only take two arguments, A and DO: изго́ит /jə-z-ga-wá-jt'/ [it/them (C1)-I(C3)-take/carry-Dyn-Fin] 'I am taking/carrying it/them'. Therefore, as in а́-тара /á-ta-ra/ 'to give' (Class D) which can take three arguments, inserting one more argument into изго́ит /jə-z-ga-wá-jt'/ and making it a three-actant structure C1-C2-C3-R is not tolerated in Abkhaz. If one wanted to add a dative argument and express the meaning of 'I am taking it to her', as seen in the following example, the preverb на- /na/ 'thither' has to be added to this verb, and in addition, the objective version has to be used:

(345) илызна́згоит
/jə-lə-z-ná-z-ga-wa-jt'/
it/them(C1)-{her(C2)-OV}-Prev-I(C3)-take-Dyn-Fin

In this way, by using the preverb meaning 'thither' which indicates direction and the objective version in the underlying verb, it is possible to add the dative argument. Similarly, the objective version can be used and the dative argument can be added to the verb аа́хәара /aá-xʷa-ra/ 'to buy' which has the preverb <u>аа-</u> /aa/ 'hither':

(346) Сара́ лара́ а́хәшәкәа лзаа́схәеит.
 /sará lará á-xəšʷ-kʷa ø-l-z-aá-s-xʷa-jt'/
 I she the-medicine-Pl [them(C1)]-{her(C2)-OV}-Prev-I(C3)-buy-(Aor)-Fin
 'I bought the medicine for her.'

Also, the verb а́-шьтра /á-šʲt-ra/ 'to send', which does not take a preverb, can also have a dative argument by using the objective version.

(347) Сара́ сан дыбзы́сышьҭит.
 /sará s-an də-b-zə́-sə-šʲtə-jt'/
 I my-mother her(C1)-{you.F(C2)-OV}-I(C3)-send-(Aor)-Fin
 'I sent my mother to you-F.'

In contrast, there are verbs in which the objective version cannot indicate a dative meaning and can only express the meaning of 'for X'. For example, а-дәы́кәҵара /a-dʷə́kʷ-c'a-ra/ 'to send':

(348) илызлдәы́кә(ы)сҵеит
 /jə-lə-z-dʷə́kʷ(ə)-s-c'a-jt'/
 it/them(C1)-{her(C2)-OV}-Prev-I(C3)-send-(Aor)-Fin
 'I send it/them for her.', *'I send it to her.'

In order to express the dative meaning using this verb, the postposition <u>-ахь</u> /axʲ/ 'toward' indicating the direction of motion is placed with an affix agreeing with the indirect object outside the verb:

(349) Сара́ сҩы́за иахь ателеграмма дәы́кәсҵеит.
 /sará s-jʷə́za j-axʲ a-t'elegramma ø-dʷə́kʷ-s-c'a-jt'/
 I my-friend his-toward the-telegram [it(C1)-]Prev-I(C3)-(Aor)-Fin
 'I sent my friend a telegram.'

Furthermore, according to our informant, even if the objective version is placed in the verbal complex, or if the postposition <u>-ахь</u> is used as in (349) above, there is a verb which cannot express a dative meaning. This is the verb а́-ҭира /á-təj-ra/ 'to sell', and it is not possible to express 'X sells *sth* to Y' or 'X sells *sth* for Y' using this verb. If the objective version is used with this verb, it takes on the separate meaning of 'X sells Y's *sth*' or 'X sends *sth* to Y'. For example:

(350) Сара́ лара́ а́хәшәкәа лзы́сҭиуеит.
 /sará lará á-xʷšʷ-kʷa ø-l-zə́-s-təj-wa-jt'/
 I she the-medicine-Pl [them(C1)-]{her(C2)-OV}-I(C3)-sell-Dyn-Fin
 'I am selling her medicine' (Я продаю ее лекарства) or 'I am sending the medicine to her.'

In Abkhaz, if it is assumed that the phrase 'X sells *sth* to Y' cannot be expressed with this verb, the problem of how to express this arises. According to our informant, this phrase is expressed by using the causative form of the verb аа́хәара /aá-xʷa-ra/, which means 'buy'. For example, 'I sold the book to my friend' would be expressed in Abkhaz in the following manner:

(351) Сара́ сҩы́за ашәҟәы́ иаа́сырхәеит.
 /sará s-jʷə́za a-šʷq'ʷə́ ø-j-aá-sə-r-xʷa-jt'/

I　my-friend　the-book　[it(C1)-]him(C2)-Prev-I(C3)-Caus-buy-(Aor)-Fin
'I made my friend buy the book.'

4.3.6. Definition and Usage of the Subjective Version (SV)

According to Lomtatidze, the subjective version in Kartvelian languages indicates the following two relationships between the subject and direct object:[146]

(i) That the 'closest object' belongs to the subject.

(ii) The subject extends an action for oneself to the 'closest object'.

Compare examples (352) with (353) from Georgian:

(352) i-ban-s　is　xel-s.
SV-wash-3Sg　he　hand-Dat
'He is washing his (own) hand.' (Он моет себе руку, Он моет свою руку.)

(353) i-šen-eb-s　is　saxl-s.
SV-build-TS-3Sg　he　house-Dat　(TS = thematic suffix)
'He is buiding his house', 'He is building a house for himself.' (Он строит себе (для себе) дом.)

The subjective version marker *i* in (352) above joins together the subject and its bodily part, and indicates that 'hand', which is the 'closest object', belongs to the subject. In (353) as well not only is the affiliation relationship indicated by the subjective version, as in (352), it also indicates that an action is performed 'for one's own benefit'. Abkhaz also has a subjective version function like (i). In Georgian, this subjective version marker *i* is a marker which has only an abstracted grammatical function, but in Abkhaz this marker indicating the subjective version has not yet been completely abstracted. Abkhaz frequently uses a radical element which indicates a bodily part as this marker. For example, the subjective version maker xa- in а-хатцара́ /a-xa-c'a-rá/ 'to put headgear on *sb*' is related to ахы́ /a-xə́/ 'head' (cf. Bzyp dialect, а-х̌ы́ < а-х̌а 'head'). The subjective version marker шьа- /šʲa/ in а́-шьатцара /á-šʲa-c'a-ra/ 'to put footwear on *sb*' is related to а-шьапы́ /a-šʲap'ə́/ 'foot'. In Abkhaz personal possessive prefixes same as the subject (or agent) are attached to this marker, and the possessive prefix and subjective version marker are placed after the Column I pronominal prefix. For example, the sentence 'I put on my hat' is expressed in the following way:

(354) Ахы́лпҕа схáстцеит.
/a-xə́lpa　ø-s-xá-s-c'a-jt'/
the-hat　[it(C1)-]{my(Poss)-SV}-I(C3)-put-(Aor)-Fin

In (354) above the 'head', which is 'the closest object' is incorporated in the verbal complex. A 'distant object' is placed outside the verb and the pronominal prefix cross-referenced by this is placed in the Column I position in the verb.[147] Look at the example that uses а́-шьатцара 'to put footwear on

146. Ломтатидзе К.В. 1976. Категория версии в картвельских и абхазско-адыгских языках. *Ежегодник иберийско-кавказского языкознания*. III. с. 91.

147. The structure of this subjective version in Abkhaz is similar to the middle voice in Indo-European languages: cf. Gr. *περιτίθεται στέφανον* 'he puts on a crown'. Furthermore, cf. the opinion of T.V. Gamkrelidze and Vjach.V. Ivanov, who hypothesize on the centripetal marker *o-* in Indo-European.

sb' in a similar way:

(355) Убáрт áимаакәа бы́шьатца!
/wəbárt ájmaa-kʷa ø-bə́-šʲa-c'a/
those shoe-Pl [them(C1)-]your.F(Poss)-SV-put.Imp
'Put on those shoes!'

The two verbs above are examples in which the subjective version markers for 'head' and 'foot' appear rather clearly, but in а-хгарá /a-x-ga-rá/ 'to spend (time)', which uses the same subjective version marker -х-, in this marker -х- the meaning of 'head(?)' practically vanishes and only has the meaning of a grammaticalized subjective version marker. The subjective version marker here indicates that 'the subject is in a process, and is itself influenced by it and does something' (Benveniste, É. 1966. *Problemes de Linguistique Générale*, 1. Gallimard. p. 173) like the 'middle voice' in Indo-European languages. For example:

(356) Сарá áԥхынра акы́тан исхы́згеит.
/sará á-pxənra a-kə́ta-n jə-s-xə́-z-ga-jt'/
I the-summer the-village-in it(C1)-my(Poss)-SV-I(C3)-spend-(Aor)-Fin
'I spent the summer in the village.'

Next, let us examine Lomtatidze's definition (ii) of the subjective version in Georgian, "the subject extends an action to the 'closest object' for one's own benefit". According to our informant, in Abkhaz, generally statements such as 'he is building a house for himself' cannot be expressed using the subjective version (cf. the example of the Georgian subjective version (353) above). Namely, in Abkhaz, a method of generally expressing 'a subject (or agent) performing something for himself' cannot be expressed in the verbal complex. Also, as already discussed in the section on the objective version, in Abkhaz the objective version marker -з- /z/ cannot be used to express 'subject (or agent) performs something for himself':

(357) *Сарá áфатә сзыҟастцóит. [ungrammatical]
/sará á-fat'ʷ ø-s-zə-q'a-s-c'a-wá-jt'/
I the-meal [it(C1)-]me-OV-Prev-I(C3)-do-Dyn-Fin
'I am preparing a meal for myself.'

In order to express this, there is no other option other than to place the postposition -з(ы) /z(ə)/ outside the verbal complex as in example (343) in §4.3.4 above:

(358) Сарá сзы áфатә ҟастцóит.
/sará s-zə á-fat'ʷ ø-q'a-s-c'a-wá-jt'/
I my-for the-meal [it(C1)-]Prev-I(C3)-make-Dyn-Fin
'I am preparing a meal for myself.'

In order to further clarify that the agent performs an action for himself, the form with -ха- /xa/ before the postposition -з(ы) is used:

(359) Сарá схазы́ áфатә ҟастцóит.
/sará s-xa-zə́ á-fat'ʷ ø-q'a-s-c'a-wá-jt'/

[Гамкрелидзе, Т.В., Иванов Вяч. Вс. 1984. *Индоевропейский язык и индоевропейцы*. Тбилиси: издательство тбилисского университета. с. 333–336.]

I my-head-for the-meal [it(C1)-]Prev-I(C3)-make-Dyn-Fin

Above, we explained that a general method of expressing 'a subject (or an agent) performs something for himself' like in Georgian does not exist in Abkhaz, but this type of expression is possible in some verbs. For example, the verb á-дкылара /á-d-k'əla-ra/ 'to take (medicine)', has the verbal root -к- /k'/ 'hold' and the introvertive suffix -ла- /la/ added to the original preverb -д- /d/ 'next to'. It means 'the agent takes (medicine) for oneself', and its inflection is as follows:

(360) еснáгь áхәшә сы́дыскылоит
/asnágʲ á-xʷšʷ ø-sә́-dә-s-k'ә-la-wa-jt'/
always the-medicine [it(C1)]-me(C2)-Prev-I(C3)-hold-Introvert-Dyn-Fin
'I always take the medicine.'

The Column II prefix before the preverb -д- /d/ here must be the same person as the Column III pronominal prefix. Since the Column II prefix and the possessive prefix have the same form, this verb form can be regarded as that of the subjective version. In other words, the preverb -д- is regarded as the subjective version marker, and it is possible to interpret it in the following way:

(361) сы́дыскылоит
/ø-sә́-dә-s-k'ә-la-wa-jt'/
[it(C1)]-my(Poss)-SV-I(C3)-hold-Introvert-Dyn-Fin

From what was seen above, we define the 'subjective version' in Abkhaz as follows:

(i) There is a subjective version marker in the verbal complex, and the person for the possessive prefix attached to it must be the same person as the agent.

(ii) The agent is in the process, and performs an action himself while receiving its influence. Also, the agent extends the action to the object for his own benefit.

4.3.7. Other Verbs that Take the Form of the Subjective Version

The following are verbs in the subjective form besides the ones described above:

а-бжьацарá /a-bžʲa-c'a-rá/ 'to conclude (a treaty)':

(362) Ҳарá áиқәшаҳатра ҳабжьáҳцеит. (GAL)
/ħará [a-]ajkʷšaħatra ø-ħa-bžʲá-ħ-c'a-jt'/
we [the-]treaty [it(C1)-]our(Poss)-SV-we(C3)-conclude-(Aor)-Fin
'We concluded the treaty.'

а-гәáларшәара /a-gʷála-ršʷa-ra/ 'to remember':

(363) исгәáласыршәеит
/jә-s-gʷála-sә-ršʷa-jt'/
it/them(C1)-my(Poss)-Prev-I(C3)-remember-(Aor)-Fin
'I remembered it/them.'

á-дгалара /á-d-gala-ra/ 'to prepare for':

(364) Амҿы́ ры́дыргалоит.
/a-mč'ә́ ø-rә́-dә-r-gala-wa-jt'/
the- firewood [it(C1)-]their(Poss)-SV-they(C3)-prepare for-Dyn-Fin

'They are stockpiling the firewood.'

а-ҿы́нахара /a-č'ə́-na-xa-ra/ 'to set out':

(365) лҿы́налхоит
/l-č'ə́-na-l-xa-wa-jt'/
her(Poss)-SV-Prev-she(C3)-set out-Dyn-Fin
'She sets out there.' (cf. а-ҿы́ /a-č'ə/ 'mouth')

а-ҿы́ҩахара /a-č'ə́-jʷa-xa-ra/ 'to set out':

(366) Иҿы́ҩаханы дце́ит. (ARD)

/jə-č'ə́-jʷa-xa-nə	d-cá-jt'/
his(Poss)-SV-Prev-set out-Abs	he(C1)-go-(Aor)-Fin/

'He set out suddenly.'

а-шәҵара́ /a-šʷ-c'a-rá/ 'to put on (clothes)':

(367) Сы́маҭәақәа сшәысҵо́ит. (AFL)

/sé-matʷa-kʷa	ø-s-šʷə-s-c'a-wá-jt'/
my-clothes-Pl	[them(C1)-]my(Poss)-SV-I(C3)-put on-Dyn-Fin

'I am putting on some clothes.'

а-шәы́хра /a-sʷə́-x-ra/ 'to to take off (clothes):

(368) Наа́ла лыҵкы́ ҟа́ԥшь лшәы́лхит.

/naála	lə-c'k'ə́	q'ápšʲ	ø-l-šʷə́-l-xə-jt'/
name(F)	her-dress	red	[it(C1)-]her(Poss)-SV-she(C3)-take off-(Aor)-Fin

'Naala took off her red dress.'

4.3.8. Morphology of the Subjective Version

а-хаҵара́ /a-xa-c'a-rá/ 'to put on (headgear)':

Finite forms

C1-Poss-SV-C3-R-	Affirmative	Negative
Present		
3Sg.N.H/3Pl-1Sg-1Sg	и-с-ха́-с-ҵо-ит /jə-s-xá-s-c'a-wa-jt'/ it/them(C1)-my(Poss)-SV-I(C3)-put on-Dyn-Fin 'I am putting on it/them.'	и-с-ха́-с-ҵо-м
3Sg.N.H/3Pl-3Sg.M-3Sg.M	и-хе́-и-ҵо-ит (< и-и-хе́-и-ҵо-ит)	и-хе́-и-ҵо-м
3Sg.N.H/3Pl-3Sg.N.H-3Sg.N.H	и-а-ха-на-ҵо́-ит	и-а-ха-на-ҵо́-м
3Sg.N.H/3Pl-1Pl-1Pl	и-ах-ха́-х-ҵо-ит	и-ах-ха́-х-ҵо-м
Aorist		
3Sg.N.H/3Pl-1Sg-1Sg	и-с-ха́-с-ҵе-ит	и-с-ха́-сы-м-ҵе-ит
3Sg.N.H/3Pl-3Sg.N.H-3Sg.N.H	и-а-ха-на-ҵе́-ит	и-а-ха-на́-м-ҵе-ит
3Sg.N.H/3Pl-1Pl-1Pl	и-ах-ха́-х-ҵе-ит	и-ах-ха́-ха-м-ҵе-ит

Non-Finite forms

C1-Poss-SV-C3-R- Present	Affirmative	Negative
Rel-3Sg.F-3Sg.F	и-л-ха́-л-тцо /jə-l-xá-l-c'a-wa/ Rel(C1)-her(Poss)-SV-she(C3)-put on-Dyn.NF 'which she is putting on'	и-л-ха́-лы-м-тцо
3Sg.N.H/3Pl-Rel-Rel	и-з-ха́-з-тцо /jə-z-xá-z-c'a-wa/ it/them(C1)-Rel(Poss)-SV-Rel(C3)-put on-Dyn.NF '(the one) who is putting on it/them'	и-з-ха́-зы-м-тцо

Imperative		
C1-Poss-SV-C3-R-	Affirmative	Negative
3Sg.N.H/3Pl-2Sg.F-[2Sg.F]	и-б-ха-тца́! /jə-b-xa-c'á/ it/them(C1)-you.F(Poss)-put on.Imp 'Put on it/them!'	и-б-ха́-бы-м-тца-н! /jə-b-xá-bə-m-c'a-n/
3Sg.N.H/3Pl-2Pl-2Pl	и-шә-ха́-шә-тц!	и-шә-ха́-шәы-м-тца-н!

Potential		
C1-C2-Pot-Poss-SV-(Neg)-R	Present	Aorist
3Sg.N.H/3Pl-1Sg-1Sg	и-сы-з-с-ха-тцо́-м /jə-sə-z-s-xa-c'a-wá-m/ it/them(C1)-me(C2)-Pot-my(Poss)-SV-put on-Dyn-Neg 'I cannot put on it/them.'	и-сы-з-с-ха́-м-тце-ит /jə-sə-z-s-xá-m-c'a-jt'/

4.4. Reflexive

4.4.1. The reflexive in Abkhaz is produced by attaching a possessive prefix of the same person as the agent to the reflexive marker -ҽ(ы)- /č(ə)/ (abbreviated as 'Self') and placing them at the head of the word. For example, from the form (369) of а́-кәабара /á-k'ʷaba-ra/ 'to wash' (Class C) the reflexive form (370) can be derived in the following way:

(369) дылкәабо́ит
/də-l-k'ʷaba-wá-jt'/
him/her(C1)-she(C3)-wash-Dyn-Fin
'She is washing him/her.'

(370) лҽы́лкәабоит
/l-čə́-l-k'ʷaba-wa-jt'/
her(Poss)-Self-she(C3)-wash-Dyn-Fin
'She is washing herself.'

The reflexive form of verbs with preverbs is also produced in a similar manner by attaching a possessive prefix of the same person as the agent to the reflexive marker and placing them at the head of the verb. For example, from the form (371) of áилахәара /ájla-ħʷa-ra/ 'to dress' the the reflexive form (372) can be derived in the following way:

(371) деилáсхәеит
/d-ajlá-s-ħʷa-jt'/
him/her(C1)-Prev-I(C3)-dress-(Aor)-Fin
'I dressed him/her.'

(372) сҿеéиласхәеит
/s-č-ájla-s-ħʷa-jt'/
my(Poss)-Self-Prev-I(C3)-dress-(Aor)-Fin
'I dressed myself.'

The reflexive form of verbs with the objective version is produced in a similar manner by attaching a possessive prefix of the same person as the agent to the reflexive maker and placing them at the head of the word. For example, the following is the reflexive form (373) of а-зы́қатцара /a-zə́-q'a-c'a-ra/ 'to do/make *sth* for'.

(373) сҿа/рзы́қастцоит
/s-č-a/r-zə́-q'a-s-c'a-wa-jt'/
my(Poss)-Self-it/them(C2)-OV-Prev-I(C3)-do/make-Dyn-Fin
'I am preparing myself for it/them.'

Cf. илзы́қастцоит
/jə-l-zə́-q'a-s-c'a-wa-jt'/
it/them(C1)-her(C2)-OV-Prev-I(C3)-do/make-Dyn-Fin
'I am doing/making it/them for her.'

As can be seen from examples (369)–(373) above, in order to derive the reflexive form the Column I pronominal prefix of the underlying forms should be replaced by the 'possessive prefix + reflexive marker'. When the agent of the reflexive form is in the third-person singular/non-human, a is used as the agent pronominal prefix.

(374) аҿáкәабоит
/a-č-á-k'ʷaba-wa-jt'/
its(Poss)-Self-it(C3)-wash-Dyn-Fin
'It is washing itself.'

From this, it is clear that the function of the reflexive marker differs from a preverb (in two-place transitive verbs with preverbs, the agent indicated by the third-person singular/non-human is на- /na/). Furthermore, observe the following forms that causatively derive the reflexive form:

(375) рҿыдлы́ркәабеит
/r-čə-d-lə́-r-k'ʷaba-jt'/
their(Poss)-Self-them(C2)-she(C3)-Caus-wash-(Aor)-Fin
'She made them wash themselves.'

In example (375) above, the third-person plural prefix р- /r/ changes to д- /d/ in Column II, but the р- /r/ at the head of the word does not change. Here, there is reason to regard the prefix attached to the reflexive marker as a possessive prefix and not a pronominal prefix.[148]

4.4.2. Paradigm of the Reflexive Form

а-ҽешьра́ /a-č-šʲ-rá/ 'to kill oneself':

Finite forms

Poss-Self-C3-R-	Affirmative	Negative
Present		
3Sg.F	л-ҽы́-л-шь-уе-ит /l-čə́-l-šʲ-wa-jt'/ 'She is killing herself.'	л-ҽы́-л-шь-уа-м
Aorist		
3Sg.F	л-ҽы́-л-шь-ит	л-ҽы́-лы-м-шь-ит
3Sg.M	и-ҽ-и́-шь-ит	и-ҽ-и́-м-шь-ит
1Pl	х-ҽа́-х-шь-ит	х-ҽа́(*or* -ҽы́)-ха-м-шь-ит
3Pl	р-ҽы́-р-шь-ит	р-ҽы́-ры-м-шь-ит

Non-Finite forms

Rel(Poss)-Self-Rel(C3)-R-	Affirmative	Negative
Present	з-ҽы́-з-шь-уа /z-čə́-z-šʲ-wa/ Rel(Poss)-Self-Rel(C3)-kill-Dyn.NF '(the one) who is killing oneself'	з-ҽы́-зы-м-шь-уа /z-čə́-zə-m-šʲ-wa/
Past Indefinite	з-ҽы́-з-шьы-з	з-ҽы́-зы-м-шьы-з

Imperative

Poss-Self-[C3]-R-	Affirmative	Negative
2Sg.F	бы-ҽ-шьы́! /bə-č-šʲə́/ you.F(Poss)-Self-kill.Imp 'kill yourself-F!'	б-ҽы́-бы-м-шьы-н! /b-čə́-bə-m-šʲə-n/ you.F(Poss)-Self-you.F(C3)-Neg-kill-Proh 'don't kill yourself-F!'
2Pl	шә-ҽы́-шә-шь! /šʷ-čə́-šʷ-šʲ/ you.Pl(Poss)-Self-you.Pl(C3)-kill.Imp 'kill yourselves!'	шә-ҽы́-шәы-м-шьы-н! /šʷ-čə́-šʷə-m-šʲə-n/

Potential

Poss-Self-C2-Pot-(Neg)-R-	Present	Aorist
3Sg.F	л-ҽы-л-зы́-шь-уа-м	л-ҽы-л-зы́-м-шь-ит

148. Cf. идҧлырҟе́ит /jə-d-p-lə-r-q'á-jt'/ (it/them(C1)-them(C2)-Prev-she(C3)-Caus-cut-(Aor)-Fin) 'she made them cut it/them'. Here, the third-person plural prefix in Column II directly before the preverb changes to д-/d/.

/l-čə-l-zə́-šʲ-wa-m/	/l-čə-l-zə́-m-šʲə-jt'/
her(Poss)-Self-her(C2)-Pot-kill-Dyn-Neg	her(Poss)-Self-her(C2)-Pot-Neg-kill-(Aor)-Fin
'She cannot kill herself.'	'She could not kill herself.'

4.5. Labile Verbs

In Abkhaz, there is a class of verbs called 'labile verbs' (or 'diffuse verbs'). These verbs can become both transitive and intransitive in the same lexeme. In many Caucasian languages, these verbs are those that express basic production activity.[149] In Abkhaz as well this verbal class is also those that indicate traditional agricultural labor, household production labor and various human activities, but other than these, verbs that indicate changes in phenomenon are also included. In describing labile verbs in Abkhaz, we shall divide our description on these verbs into (i) verbs that indicate productive labor and various human activities, and (ii) verbs that indicate change in phenomenon.

4.5.1. Labile Verbs which Indicate Productive Labor and Human Activities

The first group of labile verbs, those which indicate traditional agricultural labor or household production labor, as well as various human activities are as follows:

а-ба́ҳара /a-báħa-ra/ [intr.] 'to dig' [tr.] 'to dig up'

а́-ӡахра /á-ʒax-ra/ [intr.] 'to sew, to be engaged in sewing' [tr.] 'to sew'

а́-ӡәӡәара /á-ʒʷʒʷa-ra/ [intr.] 'to wash, to do the washing' [tr.] 'to wash'

а́-кәӡахра /á-kʷ-ʒax-ra/ [intr.] 'to be engaged in sewing, to sew' [tr.] 'to sew on'

а-кәҵара́ /a-kʷc'a-rá/ [intr.] 'to embroider' [tr.] 'to embroider'

а́-лагара /á-laga-ra/ [intr.] 'to grind', [tr.] to mill, to grind'

а-ҧара́ /a-pa-rá/ [intr.] 'to knit, to be busy with knitting' [tr.] 'to knit'

а́-рашәара /á-rašʷa-ra/ [intr.] 'to weed' [tr.] 'to weed'

а-сара́ /a-sa-rá/ [intr.] 'to be engaged in cutting' [tr.] 'to cut out'

а-сра́ /a-s-rá/ [intr.] 'to weave' [tr.] 'to weave'

а-уанҭара́ /a-wanta-rá/ [intr.] 'to iron' [tr.] 'to iron'

а-ха́хара /a-xáxa-ra/ [intr.] 'to be engaged in spinning' [tr.] 'to spin'

а-хәа́рхьра /a-xʷárxʲ-ra/ [intr.] 'to saw' [tr.] 'to saw'

а́-цәаҕәара /á-cʷaɣʷa-ra/ [intr.] 'to be engaged in ploughing' [tr.] 'to plough'

---

149. Cf. the following statement by G.A. Klimov: "The majority of (labile) verbs are those that express activities socially important to people: 'sow', 'plough', 'graze', 'braid', 'weave', 'spin', 'cut out', 'sew', 'tie', 'pound', 'weed', 'mow', etc. Therefore, to a certain degree, we can agree with Yakovlev and Ashkhamaf's view [Яковлев Н.Ф., Ашхамаф Д.А. 1941. *Грамматика адыгейского литературного языка.* М.-Л., с.216] that 'based on their actual content, this verbal class are largely the names of the oldest agricultural production and household production activities, namely those related to cultivating land, animal husbandry, and the processing of food, wool, and trees, etc.' (Климов Г.А. 1973. *Очерк общей теории эргативности.* Москва. стр. 122)

а-ча́лтра /a-čʲált'-ra/ [intr.] 'to be engaged in harrowing' [tr.] 'to harrow'
а-ча́чра /a-č'ʲáč'ʲ-ra/ [intr.] 'to do needlework' [tr.] 'to string, to thread'
а-ҽара́ /a-ča-rá/ [intr.] 'to hoe' [tr.] 'to hoe'
а-ҿырпра́ /a-č'ə-rp'-rá/ [intr.] 'to be engaged in husking' [tr.] 'to husk'
а-ҕьы́чра /a-ɣʲə́čʲ-ra/ [intr.] 'to steal, to be engage in stealing/theft' [tr.] 'to steal'
а-ӡәара́ /a-ʒʷa-rá/ [intr.] 'to vomit' [tr.] 'to vomit, to throw up'
а-ны́хәара /a-nə́ħʷa-ra/ [intr.] 'to pray' [tr.] 'to bless'
а-рҟәыдра́ /a-rq'ʷəd-rá/ [intr.] 'to have a haircut' [tr.] 'to cut (the) hair'
а-хәы́цра /a-xʷə́c-ra/ [intr.] 'think' [tr.] 'to think up, to devise, to plan, to intend, to think of'
а́-хасабра /á-ħasab-ra/ [intr.] 'to solve' [tr.] 'to solve'
а́-чапшьара /á-č'ʲapšʲa-ra/ [intr.] 'to (keep) watch, to guard' [tr.] 'to watch, to guard'
а́-шәира /á-šʷəj-ra/ [intr.] 'to curse' [tr.] 'to curse'
а-ҩра́ /a-jʷ-rá/ [intr.] 'to write' [tr.] 'to write'
а́-џьабара /á-ǯʲaba-ra/ [intr.] 'to mourn' [tr.] 'to mourn over'

For example, the intransitive (376) and transitive (377) inflections of а́-ӡахра /á-ʒax-ra/ are as follows:

(376) сӡахуе́ит
/s-ʒax-wá-jt'/
I(C1)-sew-Dyn-Fin
'I am sewing.'

(377) изӡахуе́ит
/jə-z-ʒax-wá-jt'/
it/them(C1)-I(C3)-sew-Dyn-Fin
'I am sewing it/them.'

Here, in example (377) take note of the voicing of the first-person prefix in Column III: this voicing indicates that this verb is transitive.

As seen in (376) and (377) above, this type of labile verb expresses the meaning of 'a person does X' in intransitive verbs, and expressing the meaning of 'a person does X to something' in transitive verbs. Therefore, in intransitive verbs of this type, the subject (S) is the person who performs the action of that verb, and is the same person (or thing capable of performing that action) as A. If S is regarded as an active subject, it can then be called 'S-active'. This type of labile verb can be schematized in the following way:

[intr.]	<u>S-active</u> + R
[tr.]	O + <u>A</u> + R

Since S-active and A are treated in the same way, this type of verb can be regarded as what Dixon calls 'S=A ambitransitives'.[150]

---

150. Dixon, R.M.W. and Aikhenvald, Alexandra Y. 2000. *Changing valency: case studies in transitivity.*

4.5.2. Labile Verbs Indicating Phenomenon Change

The following are verbs in the second group which express changes in phenomenon:

а-былра́ /a-bəl-rá/ [intr.] 'to burn' [tr.] 'to burn'

а-жәра́ /a-žʷ-rá/ [intr.] 'to be boiled, to cook' [tr.] 'to boil, to cook'

а-ӡра́ /a-ʒ-rá/ [intr.] 'to fry, to roast' [tr,] 'to roast; to fry'

а́илаҧсара /ájla-psa-ra/ [intr.] 'to be mixed' [tr.] 'to mix'

а́илахәара /ájla-xʷa-ra/ [intr.] '(*of thread*) to be twisted' [tr.] 'to tangle'

а-каҧсара́ /a-k'a-psa-rá/ [intr.] 'to be scattered' [tr.] 'to scatter'

а-каҭәара́ /a-k'a-tʷa-rá/ [intr.] 'to flow, to run' [tr.] 'to pour out'

а-кы́лцәара /a-k'ə́l-c'ʷa-ra/ [intr.] 'to wear through, to get a hole' [tr.] 'to make a hole in'

а́-кәблаара /á-kʷ-blaa-ra/ [intr.] 'to be burnt down completely' [tr.] 'to burn the surface of *sth*'

а́-кәҧсара /á-kʷ-psa-ra/ [intr.] 'to fall on' [tr.] 'to sprinkle from above'

а-нҟьара́ /a-n-q'ʲa-rá/ [intr.] 'to hit/strike against' [tr.] 'to hit, to strike'

а-ҧжәара́ /a-p-žʷa-rá/ [intr.] 'to tear, to break, to explode' [tr.] 'to tear, to break'

а-ҧцәара́ /a-p-c'ʷa-rá/ [intr.] 'to be broken' [tr.] 'to break'

а-ҧҽра́ /a-p-č-rá/ [intr.] 'to be broken' [tr.] 'to smash, to break'

а-ҧыҽҽра́ /a-pə-čč-rá/ [intr.] 'to get broken into pieces' [tr.] 'to break into pieces'

а-ҭаҭәара́ /a-ta-tʷa-rá/ [intr.] 'to pour in, to run in' [tr.] 'to pour into'

а-хблаара́ /a-x-blaa-rá/ [intr.] 'to be burnt/scorched' [tr.] 'to wither, to dry up'

а-хжәара́ /a-x-žʷa-rá/ [intr.] 'to be broken' [tr.] 'to break'

а-хҟьара́ /a-x-q'ʲa-rá/ [intr.] 'to be covered' [tr.] 'to cover'

а-хҩара́ /a-x-jʷa-rá/ [intr.] 'to be covered' [tr.] 'to cover'

а-ча́бра /a-č'ʲáb-ra/ [intr.] 'to become sticky' [tr.] 'to stick, to seal'

а-шара́ /a-ša-rá/ [intr.] 'to be divided' [tr.] 'to divide'

For example, compare the intransitive verb sentence (378) with the transitive verb sentence (379) for а-былра́ /a-bəl-rá/ 'to burn':

(378) Амҿы́ бзи́аны ибылуе́ит. (RAD)
/a-mč'ə́ bzə́janə jə-bəl-wá-jt'/
the-firewood well it(C1)-burn-Dyn-Fin
'The firewood burns well.'

(379) Амра сы́бӷа а́былуеит. (RAD)
/á-mra sə́-bɣa ø-á-bəl-wa-jt'/
the-sun my-back [it(C1)-]it(C3)-burn-Dyn-Fin
'The sun is burning my back.'

Cambridge, UK: Cambridge University Press. p. 5.

As seen in example (378) above, in the second type of libile verbs the subject S of the intransitive verb is not the person performing the action, it is the target. If this is taken to be an inactive subject (S-inactive), this type of labile verb can be schematized as follows:

[intr.] S-inactive + R

[tr.] O + A + R

Since S-inactive and O are treated in the same way, the second type of libile verbs can be regarded as what Dixon calls 'S=O ambitransitives'.

Intransitive verbs in this second type of verbs indicates natural phenomenon — actions taken by the subject itself, which is a thing, or states. For example, observe the following intransitive sentences with а-каҧсара́ /a-k'a-psa-rá/ 'to scatter, to be scattered' (380) and а-ӡра́ /a-ʒ-rá/ 'to fry' (381).

(380) Абыҕьқәа́ каҧсе́ит.
/a-bəɣʲ-kʷá ϕ-k'a-psá-jt'/
the-leaf-Pl [they(C1)-]Pev-fall-(Aor)-Fin
'The leaves fell down.'

Cf. Сара́ абыҕьқәа́ ка́сыҧсоит.
/sará a-bəɣʲ-kʷá ϕ-k'á-sə-psa-wa-jt'/
I the-leaf-Pl [them(C1)-]Prev-I(C3)-scatter-Dyn-Fin
'I am scattering the leaves.'

(381) Акәа́ц ӡуа́н.
/a-k'ʷác ϕ-ʒ-wá-n/
the-meat [it(C1)-]fry-Dyn-Impf
'The meat was frying.'

Cf. Акәа́ц лӡит.
/a-k'ʷác ϕ-l-ʒə-jt'/
the-meat [it(C1)-]I(C3)-fry-(Aor)-Fin
'She fried the meat.'

Also, intransitive verbs can express a passive meaning:[151]

(382) Алаба́ ҧҵәе́ит. [intr.]

151. Take note that the Abkhaz verbal system lacks a passive voice. However, a passive meaning can be expressed by means of (i) the intransitive form of a libile verb discussed above, (ii) the stative form derived from a transitive verb (e.g. а-кна́ҳара /a-k'ná-ħa-ra/ 'to hang': Аса́ркьа абна́ икна́ҳауп. (IC) /a-sárk'ʲa abná jə-k'ná-ħa-wp'/ the-mirror there it(C1)-Prev-hang-Stat.Pres.Fin 'The mirror is suspended there'. Cf. Аҭӡа́мцқәа рҿы́ аса́хьақәа кна́сҳаит. /a-tʒámc-kʷa r-č'ə́ a-sáxʲa-kʷa ϕ-k'ná-s-ħa-jt'/the-wall-Pl their-on the-picture-Pl [it(C1)-]Prev-I(C3)-hang-(Aor)-Fin 'I hung the pictures on the walls'. Also see Text (3), Note (1)), and (iii) the active form which uses the non-specific third-person plural subject of a transitive verb (see §3.1.6, Note 10. Cf. in Russan: *этого писателя любят* 'this writer is loved'). Also the suffix -xa-, which is used to derive a dynamic intransitive form from a transitive/intransitve verb, provides a pseudo-passive meaning for the intransitive form: e.g. иҟалцахо́ит /jə-q'a-c'a-xa-wá-jt'/ 'it/they will be done', lit. 'то сделанным становится/станет'. For this suffix, see Hewitt (2010: 128).

/a-labá ø-p-c'ʷá-jt'/
the-stick [it(C1)-]Prev-be broken-(Aor)-Fin
'The stick was broken.'

Cf. Ацә ашá ҧнатцәéит. [tr.]
/a-cʷ a-šá ø-p-na-c'ʷá-jt'/
the-bull the-rope [it(C1)-]Prev-it(C3)-break-(Aor)-Fin
'The bull broke the rope.'

(383) Иҧҿéит асáан. [intr.]
/jə-p-čə́-jt' a-sáan
it(C1)-Prev-be broken-(Aor)-Fin the-plate
'A plate was broken.'

Cf. Иҧы́сҿеит асáан. [tr.]
/jə-pə́-s-čə-jt' a-sáan/
it(C1)-Prev-I(C3)-break-(Aor)-Fin the-plate
'I smashed the plate.'

(384) Жәабá ҩбá ры́ла, хәбá ры́ла, жәабá ры́ла ишóит. [intr.]
/žʷabá jʷba rə́-la xʷba rə́-la žʷabá rə́-la jə-ša-wá-jt'/
10 2 their-by 5 their-by 10 their-by it(C1)-be divided-Dyn-Fin
'10 is divisible by 2, 5 and 10.'

Cf. Урт рмáл ршéит. [tr.]
/wərt r-mal ø-r-šá-jt'/
they their-property [it(C1)-]they(C3)-divide-(Aor)-Fin
'They divided their property.'

4.6. Incorporation

As already discussed in §3.2.2, in Abkhaz the addition of pronominal prefixes to nouns and adjectives, etc and turning them into stative verbs is often seen: сҧы́уп /s-pá-wp'/ 'I am a son' (cf. аҧá /a-pá/ 'son'), дҕáруп /d-ɣárə-wp'/ 'he/she is poor' (cf. аҕáр /a-ɣár/ 'poor'), сýсасуп /s-wə́-sasə-wp'/ 'I am your guest' (ýсас /wə́-sas/ 'your guest'). Also, there are examples where the subjective version marker indicating a bodily part is incorporated into verbs (see §§4.3.6–4.3.7). Other than these, although it is not very productive, nouns can be incorporated into verbs. For example, а-хы́сра /a-xə́-s-ra/ 'to shoot' comes from а-хы́ /a-xə́/ 'bullet' and á-сра /á-s-ra/ 'to hit' and is inflected in the following manner:

(385) ухы́сит
/wə-xə́-sə-jt'/
you.M-bullet-hit-(Aor)-Fin
'She shot.'

Similarly, а-ҧсы́ӡкра /a-psə́ʒ-k'-ra/ 'to fish; to catch a fish' (cf. а-ҧсы́ӡ /a-psə́ʒ/ 'fish', акрá /a-k'-rá/ 'to catch') has a noun incorporated into it, and is inflected as both an intransitive verb (386) and a transitive verb (387):

(386) дыԥсы́ӡкуеит
/də-psə́ʒ-k'-wa-jt'/
he/she(C1)-fish-catch-Dyn-Fin
'He/She is fishing.'

(387) аԥсыӡлкит
/a-psəʒ-l-k'ə́-jt'/
the-fish-she(C3)-catch-(Aor)-Fin
'She caught a fish.'[152]

Cf. аԥсы́ӡкы!
/a-psə́ʒ-k'ə/
the-fish-catch.Imp
'Catch a fish!'

Examples of other nouns incorporated into verbs are а́шәахәара /áš^wa-ħ^wa-ra/ 'to sing a song' (cf. а́шәа /áš^wa/ 'a song', а-хәара́ /a-ħ^wa-rá/ 'to say'), а́-мцхәара /á-mc-ħ^wa-ra/ 'to tell a lie' (cf. а́мц /á-mc/ 'a lie'). According to our informant, these two verbs are inflected with a noun incorporated into it in the following way respectively:

(388) а́шәалхәоит
/[á-]aš^wa-l-ħ^wa-wá-jt'/
[the-]song-she(C3)-say-Dyn-Fin
'she is singing a song'

(389) а́мцсхәоит
/á-mc-s-ħ^wa-wá-jt'/
the-lie-I(C3)-say-Dyn-Fin
'I am telling a lie.'

However, these verbs are normally inflected in the following way without incorporating a noun:

(390) а́шәа лхәоит
/[á-]aš^wa ø-l-ħ^wa-wá-jt'
the-song [it(C1)-]she(C3)-say-Dyn-Fin
'She is singing a song.'

(391) а-мц схәоит
/a-mc ø-s-ħ^wa-wá-jt'/
the-lie [it(C1)-]I(C3)-say-Dyn-Fin
'I am telling a lie.'

One more type of incorporation in Abkhaz is found when -ла- /la/ 'with' is incorporated into the verb:

(392) Ажә а́хәызба иа́ласшьит.
/a-ž^w á-ħ^wəzba j-á-la-s-š^jə-jt'/
the-cow the-knife it(= the cow, C1)-it(= the knife, C2)-with-I(C3)-kill-(Aor)-Fin

152. This verb is usually written separately without incorporation: аԥсыӡ лкит.

'I killed the cow with a/the knife.'

The a- in front of -ла- /la/ in (392) above is a pronomonal prefix which agrees with 'knife', and is used with -ла- to indicate an instrumental meaning 'with it'. In Abkhaz this -ла- can also be placed outside the verbal complex as a postposition of a noun. According to our informant, rather than incorporating -ла-, placing it outside the verbal complex is preferable. An example of this is (393) below:

(393) Ажә ҳәы́збала исшьи́т.
/a-žʷ ħʷə́zba-la jə-s-šʲə́-jt'/
the-cow knife-with it(C1)-I(C3)-kill-(Aor)-Fin
'I killed the cow with a knife.'

4.7. Interrogatives

Interrogatives in Abkhaz will be described in the following order:

(i) 'Who?' Questions: §4.7.1

(ii) 'Whose?' Questions: §4.7.2

(iii) 'What?' Questions: §4.7.3

(iv) 'Where?' Questions: §4.7.4.1

(v) 'When?' Questions: §4.7.4.2

(vi) 'Why?' Questions: §4.7.4.3

(vii) 'How?' Question: §4.7.4.4

(viii) 'Whence?' Questions: §4.7.4.5

(ix) 'Yes-No' Questions: §4.7.5

4.7.1. 'Who?' Questions

4.7.1.1. The form of interrogatives expressing 'who' and 'whom' is produced by adding the interrogative suffix (abbreviated hereafter as 'Qu') -да /da/ to the non-finite stem of the verb. When adding this suffix, the -у /wə/ at the end of the stem of the present tense of stative verbs and the perfect tense of dynamic verbs is omitted. Also in the past tense of stative verbs and Group II dynamic verbs, the interrogative suffix -да /da/ is placed before the suffix -з /z/. On the other hand, pronominal prefixes are indicated in the following way: for example, when asking questions about subject of an intransitive verb, or the direct object of a transitive verb, the relative prefix и- /jə/ is placed in Column I. When asking questions about the subject of a transitive verb, or the indirect object, the relative prefix -з- /z/ is placed in Columns III and II respectively.

(a) Examples where the relative prefix и- /jə/ is placed in Column I:

Subject of an Intransitive Verb

Stative verb а-гы́лара /a-gə́la-ra/ 'to stand'

Affirmative Negative

Present		
Rel-R-Qu	и-гы́ла-да?	и-гы́ла-м-да?
	/jə-gə́la-da/	/jə-gə́la-m-da/
	Rel(C1)-stand.NF-Qu	
	'Who is standing?'	
Past	и-гы́ла-да-з?	и-м-гы́ла-да-з?
	/jə-gə́la-da-z/	
	'Who was standing?'	

Dynamic verb а́-пҕхьара /á-pxja-ra/ 'to read'

	Affirmative	Negative
Dynamic Group I		
Present		
Rel-3Sg.N.H-R-Qu	и-а́-пҕхьо-да?	и-а-мы́-пҕхьо-да?
	/j-á-px^{j}a-wa-da/	/j-a-mə́-px^{j}a-wa-da/
	Rel(C1)-it(C2)-read-Dyn.NF-Qu	
	'Who is reading it?'	
Aorist	и-а́-пҕхьа-да?	и-а-мы́-пҕхьа-да?
Future I	и-а-пҕхьа-ры́-да?	и-а-мы́-пҕхьа-ры-да?
Perfect	и-а́-пҕхьа-хьа-да?	и-а-мы́-пҕхьа-хьа-да?
Dynamic Group II		
Imperfect	и-а́-пҕхьо-да-з?	и-а-мы́-пҕхьо-да-з?
Conditional I	и-а-пҕхьа-ры́-да-з?	и-а-мы́-пҕхьа-ры-да-з?
Pluperfect	и-а́-пҕхьа-хьа-да-з?	и-а-мы́-пҕхьа-хьа-да-з?

<u>Object of a transitive verb</u>

а-ды́рра /a-də́r-ra/ 'to know'

	Affirmative	Negative
Dynamic Group I		
Present		
Rel-3Sg.F-R-Dyn-Qu	и́-л-дыр-уа-да?	и-л-зы́-м-дыр-уа-да?[153]
	/jə́-l-dər-wa-da/	
	Rel(C1)-she(C3)-know-Dyn.NF-Qu	
	'Whom does she know?'	
Aorist	и́-л-дыр-да?	и-л-зы́-м-дыр-да?
Dynamic Group II		
Imperfect	и́-л-дыр-уа-да-з?	и-л-зы́-м-дыр-уа-да-з?

а-шьра́ /a-š^j-rá/ 'to kill'

153. илзы́мдыруада? /jə-l-zə́-m-dər-wa-da/ [Rel(C1)-her(C2)-Pot-Neg-know-Dyn-Qu] 'whom doesn't she know?'

Present	и́-л-шь-уа-да? /jə́-l-š^j-wa-da/ Rel(C1)-she(C3)-kill-Dyn.NF-Qu 'Whom is she killing?'	и́-лы-м-шь-уа-да? /jə́-lə-m-š^j-wa-da/ Rel(C1)-she(C3)-Neg-kill-Dyn.NF-Qu 'Whom is she not killing?'
Aorist	и́-л-шьы-да? /jə́-l-š^{j}ə-da/ 'Whom did she kill?'	и́-лы-м-шьы-да? /jə́-lə-m-š^{j}ə-da/ 'Whom didn't she kill?'

(b) Examples where the relative prefix <u>-з(ы)-</u> /z(ə)/ is placed in Column II:

<u>Indirect object of a stative verb</u>

Stative verb а́-мазаара /á-ma-zaa-ra/ 'to have'

	Affirmative	Negative
Present		
3Sg.N.H/3Pl-Rel-R-Qu	и-з-ма́-да? /jə-z-má-da/ it/them(C1)-Rel(C2)-have.NF-Qu 'Who has it/them?'	и-з-ма́-м-да? /jə-z-má-m-da/
Past	и-з-ма́-да-з?	и-з-ма́-м-да-з?

<u>Indirect object of a dynamic verb</u>

а-цхы́раара /a-cxə́raa-ra/ 'to help'

	Affirmative	Negative
Present		
2Sg.F-Rel-R-Qu	б-зы́-цхраа-уа-да? /b-zə́-cxraa-wa-da/ you.F(C1)-Rel(C2)-help-Dyn.NF-Qu 'Whom are you-F helping?'	
Aorist	б-зы́-цхраа-да?	

Dynamic/transitive verb а́-ҭара /á-ta-ra/ 'to give'

	Affirmative	Negative
Present		
3Sg.N.H/3Pl-Rel-2Sg.F-R-Qu	и-зы-б-ҭо́-да? /jə-zə-b-ta-wá-da/ it/them(C1)-Rel(C2)-you.F-give-Dyn.NF-Qu 'Whom do you-F give it/them to?'	и-з-бы-м-ҭо́-да?
Aorist	и-зы-б-ҭа́-да?	и-з-бы-м-ҭа́-да?

<u>Indirect object of the objective version</u>

а-ҩра́ /a-j^w-rá/ 'to write':

	Affirmative	Negative

Aorist
3Sg.N.H/3Pl-Rel-OV-2Sg.F-R-Qu   и-з-зы́-б-ҩы-да?   и-з-зы́-бы-м-ҩы-да?
/jə-z-zə́-b-jʷə-da/
it/them(C1)-Rel(C2)-OV-you.F(C3)-write.Aor.NF-Qu
'Whom did you-F write it/them to?'

Indirect object of the comitative prefix -ц(ы)- 'with'

а́-ҭира /á-təj-ra/ 'to sell':

Affirmative

Present
3Sg.N.H/3Pl-Rel-Com-2Sg.F-R-Qu   и-з-цы́-б-ҭи-уа-да?
/jə-z-cə́-b-təj-wa-da/
it/them(C1)-Rel(C2)-with-you.F(C3)-sell-Dyn.NF-Qu
'Whom are you-F selling it/them with?'

(c) Examples where the relative prefix -з(ы)- /z(ə)/ is placed in Column III:

Subject of a transitive verb

а́-ҟаҵара /á-q'a-c'a-ra/ 'to do/make':

	Affirmative	Negative
Dynamic Group I		
Present		
3Sg.N.H/3Pl-Prev-Rel-R-Qu	и-ҟа-з-ҵо́-да?	и-ҟа-зы-м-ҵо́-да?
	/jə-q'a-z-c'a-wá-da/	/jə-q'a-zə-m-c'a-wá-da/
	it/them(C1)-Prev-Rel(C3)-do/make-Dyn.NF-Qu	
	'Who is doing/making it/them?'	
Aorist	и-ҟа-з-ҵа́-да?	и-ҟа-зы-м-ҵа́-да?
Dynamic Group II		
Imperfect	и-ҟа-з-ҵо́-да-з?	и-ҟа-зы-м-ҵо́-да-з?
Pluperfect	и-ҟа-з-ҵа-хьа́-да-з?	и-ҟа-зы-м-ҵа-хьа́-да-з?

а-шьра́ /a-šʲ-rá/ 'to kill'

Present	ды-з-шь-уа́-да?	д-зы-м-шь-уа́-да?
	/də-z-šʲ-wá-da/	/d-zə-m-šʲ-wá-da/
	him/her(C1)-Rel(C3)-kill-Dyn.NF-Qu	
	'Who is killing him/her?'	'Who is not killing him/her?'
Aorist	ды-з-шьы́-да?	д-зы-м-шьы́-да?
	/də-z-šʲə́-da/	/d-zə-m-šʲə́-da/
	him/her(C1)-Rel(C3)-kill.Aor.NF-Qu	
	'Who killed him/her?'	'Who didn't kill him/her?'

For example:

(394) Изды́зкылада а́хәшәқәа?
/jə-z-də́-z-k'ə-la-da   á-xʷšʷ-kʷa/

them(C1)-Rel(Poss)-SV-Rel(C3)-hold-Introvert.Aor.NF-Qu the-medicine-Pl
'Who took the medicine?'

Agent of a causative form

(395) исзы́рҭида?
/jə-s-zə́-r-təj-da/
it/them(C1)-me(C2)-Rel(C3)-Caus-sell-(Aor)-Qu
'Who made me sell it/them?'

4.7.1.2. Interrogative Sentences with Interrogative Pronouns

Other than the interrogative forms which include the interrogative suffixes discussed above in the verbal complex, in Abkhaz interrogative sentences using the interrogative pronoun да́рбан /dárban/ 'who', which indicates a human category, are also possible (this was already touched upon in §2.2.5.1). In this case, the verb form uses non-infinite forms and the pronominal prefix uses a relative prefix, which corresponds to да́рбан 'who/whom'. For example:

Examples using the stative verb а-тәара́ /a-t'ʷa-rá/ 'to sit':

Present

(396) да́рбан ара́ҟа итәо́у?
/dárban aráq'a jə-t'ʷá-w/
who here Rel(C1)-sit-Stat.Pres.NF
'Who is sitting here?'

Past

(397) да́рбан ара́ҟа итәа́з?
/dárban aráq'a jə-t'ʷá-z/
who here Rel(C1)-sit-Stat.Past.NF
'Who was sitting here?'

Examples using the transitive verb а-пҟара́ /a-p-q'a-rá/ 'to cut; to fell' and а-ҿы́заара /a-č'ə́-zaa-rá/ 'to have in mind':

Aorist

(398) да́рбан ари́ а́ҵла пы́зҟа?
/dárban arə́j á-c'la ∅-pə́-z-q'a/
who this the-tree [it(C1)-]Prev-Rel(C3)-fell.(Aor.Non-Fin)
'Who felled this tree?'

(399) Шәызҿу́ да́рбан?
/šʷə-z-č'ə́-w dárban/
you.Pl(C1)-Rel(C2)-have in mind-Stat.Pres.NF who
'Whom do you have in mind?'

4.7.1.3. Expressions with 'who am I', 'who are you', etc.

сара́ сы-зу́сҭо-у? / сы-зу́сҭа-да? 'Who am I?'
уара́ у-зу́сҭо-у? / у-зу́сҭа-да? 'Who are you-M?'

бара́ бы-зу́стo-у? / бы-зу́ста-да? 'Who are you-F?'
иара́ ды-зу́стo-у? / ды-зу́ста-да? 'Who is he?'
лара́ ды-зу́стo-у? / ды-зу́ста-да? 'Who is she?'
хара́ ха-зу́стo-у? / ха-зу́ста-да? 'Who are we?'
шәара́ шәы-зу́стo-у? / шәы-зу́ста-да? 'Who are you-Pl?'
дара́ зу́стo-у? / зу́ста-да? 'Who are they?'
сзакәи́? /s-z-ak'ʷə́-j/ 'Who am I?'

4.7.2. 'Whose?' Questions

The form of the interrogative 'whose' can be produced by the non-infinite form of the stative verb атәы́заара /a-t'ʷə́-zaa-ra/ 'to belong to' and the interrogative suffix -да /da/ (take note that in the present tense the end of the stem of the non-infinite form lacks -у). Since this verb is an intransitive verb that takes the subject pronominal prefix in Column I and the indirect object in Column II, in an interrogative sentence the relative prefix -з(ы)- /z(ə)/ is placed in Column II. For example:

(400) Ари́ ашәҟәы́ зтәы́да?
/arə́j a-šʷq'ʷə́ ø-z-t'ʷə́-da/
this the-book [it(C1)-]Rel(C2)-belong to-Qu
'Whose book is this?' (lit. 'Whom does this book belong to?')

Cf. Ари́ ашәҟәы́ сара́ истәу́п.
/arə́j a-šʷq'ʷə́ sará jə-s-t'ʷə́-wp'/
this the-book I it(C1)-me(C2)-belong to-Stat.Pres.Fin
'This book is mine.'

(401) Бзыԥхьо́ ашәҟәы́ зтәы́да?
/b-zə-pxʲa-wá a-šʷq'ʷə́ ø-z-t'ʷə́-da/
you.F(C1)-Rel(C2)-read-Dyn.NF the-book [it(C1)-]Rel(C2)-belong to-Qu
'Whose book are you-F reading?' (lit. 'Whom does the book you-F are reading belong to?')

4.7.3. 'What?' Questions

4.7.3.1. The form of the interrogative expressing 'what' is produced by means of non-infinite form of the verb. Its formation can be divided into the following two categories:

(i) In the forms of Dynamic Group I verbs and the present tense of stative verbs, it is produced by adding the interrogative suffix -и or -зеи to the non-infinite form. According to our informant, in this case the final -у in the perfect tense and the present tense of stative verbs is sometimes lost, but in this event the vowel a directly before it turns into an o.

(ii) In the forms of Dynamic Group II verbs and the past tense of stative verbs, it is formed with just the non-infinite form without adding the interrogative suffix.[154]

Regarding pronominal prefixes, similar to the 'who?' question presented above, in the column

154. However, in the past tense the suffix -зы- /zə/ can also be inserted. E.g. ицо́зыз? /jə-ca-wá-zə-z/ (Rel(C1)-go-Dyn-Qu-Impf.NF) 'what was going?'.

corresponding to 'what' the corresponding relative prefixes -и- (C1) or -з(ы)- (C2, C3) are inserted.

(a) Examples with the relative prefix и- /jə/ in Column I

Subject of a one-place intransitive verb

Stative verb а-гы́лара /a-gə́la-ra/ 'to stand'

	Affirmative	Negative
Present		
Rel-R-Qu	и-гы́ло-и? /jə-gə́la-[wə-]j/ Rel(C1)-stand-Pres.NF-Qu 'What is standing?'	и-гы́ла-м-и? /jə-gə́la-mə-j/
Past	и-гы́ла-з? /jə-gə́la-z/ Rel(C1)-stand-Past.NF 'What was standing?'	и-гы́ла-мы-з?

For example:

(402) и́-ҟо-у-зей ара́?
/jə́-q'a-w-zaj ará/
Rel(C1)-be-Stat.Pres.NF-Qu here
'What is happening here?'

Subject of a two-place intransitive verb

Stative verb а́-мазаара 'to have'

	Affirmative	Negative
Present		
Rel-2Sg.F-R-Qu	и-бы́-мо-(у)-зеи/-и? /jə-bə́-ma-w-zaj/əj Rel(C1)-you.F(C2)-have-Pres.NF-Qu 'What do you-F have?'	и-бы́-ма-м-и?
Past	и-бы́-ма-(зы)-з?	и-бы́-ма-м-зы-з?

(403) Уара́ уԥхәы́с илы́хьӡузеи?
/wará wə-phʷə́s jə-lə́-xʲʒə-w-zaj/
you.M your-wife Rel(C1)-her(C2)-be called-Stat.NF-Qu
'What is your wife's name?'

(404) Агәи́л ԥштәы́с иа́моузеи? (AFL)
/a-gʷjə́l pšt'ʷə́-s j-á-ma-w-zaj/
the-rose color-as Rel(C1)-it(C2)-have-Stat.NF-Qu
'What color is the rose?'

Direct object of a transitive verb

á-ҟаҵара /á-q'a-c'a-ra/ 'to do/make'

	Affirmative	Negative
Dynamic Group I		
Present		
Rel-Prev-3Sg.F-R-Qu	и́-ҟа-л-ҵо-и/зеи?	и́-ҟа-лы-м-ҵо-и?
	/jə́-q'a-l-c'a-wa-j/zaj	
	Rel(C1)-Prev-she(C3)-do/make-Dyn.NF-Qu	
	'What is she doing/making?'	
Aorist	и́-ҟа-л-ҵе-и?	и́-ҟа-лы-м-ҵе-и?
	и́-ҟа-л-ҵа-зеи?	и́-ҟа-лы-м-ҵа-зеи?
Dynamic Group II		
Imperfect	и́-ҟа-л-ҵо-з?	и́-ҟа-лы-м-ҵо-з?
	/jə́-q'a-l-c'a-wa-z/	
	'What was she doing/making?'	

а-шьра́ 'to kill'		
Present	и́-л-шь-уе-и?	и́-лы-м-шь-уе-и?
	/jə́-l-šʲ-wa-j/	/jə́-lə-m-šʲ-wa-j/
	Rel(C1)-she(C3)-kill-Dyn.NF-Qu	
	'What is she killing?'	'What isn't she killing?'

Examples:

(405) Шәангы́ло áшьҭахь и́ҟашәҵозеи? (AFL)
/šʷ-an-gə́la-wa á-šʲtaxʲ jə́-q'a-šʷ-c'a-wa-zaj/
you.Pl(C1)-when-get up-Dyn.NF its-after Rel(C1)-Prev-you.Pl(C3)-do-Dyn.NF-Qu
'After you get up, what do you do?'

(406) Аҵла ҧшӡакәа́с шәара́ и́жәдыруазеи? (AFL)
/á-c'la pšʒa-kʷá-s šʷará jə́-žʷ-dər-wa-zaj/
the-tree beautiful-Pl-as you.Pl Rel(C1)-you.Pl(C3)-know-Dyn.NF-Qu
'What beautiful trees do you know?' (lit. As beautiful trees, what do you know?')

(407) Ари́ ашәҟәы́ ацынхәра́с ису́ҭои?
/arə́j a-šʷq'ʷə́ a-cənxʷrás jə-sə́-w-ta-wa-j/
thei the-book its-instead of Rel(C1)-me(C2)-you.M(C3)-give-Dyn.NF-Qu
'What do you give me in exchange for this book?'

(b) Examples with the relative prefix <u>-з(ы)-</u> in Column II

<u>Indirect object of an intransitive verb</u>

á-ҧхьара /á-pxʲa-ra/ 'to read'

	Affirmative	Negative
Dynamic Group I		
Present		
3Sg.Human-Rel-R-Qu	д-зы-ҧхьó-и/зеи?	ды-з-мы́-ҧхьо-и/-зеи?

	/d-zə-pxʲa-wá-j/zaj/	
	(s)he(C1)-Rel(C2)-read-Dyn.NF-Qu	
	'What is he/she reading?'	
Aorist	д-зы-пҕхьé-и?	ды-з-мы́-пҕхье-и?
	д-зы-пҕхьá-зеи?	ды-з-мы́-пҕхьа-зеи?
Future II	д-зы-пҕхьá-ше-и?	ды-з-мы́-пҕхьа-ше-и?
	д-зы-пҕхьá-ша-зеи?	ды-з-мы́-пҕхьа-ша-зеи?
Perfect	д-зы-пҕхьа-хьó-и?	ды-з-мы́-пҕхьа-хьо-и?
	д-зы-пҕхьа-хьó-зеи?	
Dynamic Group II		
Imperfect	д-зы-пҕхьó-з?	ды-з-мы́-пҕхьо-з?
	/d-zə-pxʲa-wá-z/	
	'What was he/she reading?'	

Examples:

(408) Излáҟаутцеи?
/jə-z-lá-q'a-w-c'a-j/
it/them(C1)-Rel(C2)-with-Prev-you.M(C3)-do.Aor-NF-Qu
'What did you-M do it/them with?'

(409) Шәызлацәáжәоз шәарá?
/šʷə-z-la-cʷážʷa-wa-z šʷará/
you.Pl(C1)-Rel(C2)-Prev-talk about-Dyn-Impf.NF you.Pl
'What were you talking about?'

(c) Examples with the relative prefix <u>-з(ы)-</u> in Column III

<u>Subjects of two-place transitive verbs</u>

а-шьрá /a-šʲ-rá/ 'to kill'

	Affirmative	Negative
Dynamic Group I		
Present		
3Sg.Human-Rel-R-Qu	ды-з-шь-уé-и?	д-зы-м-шь-уé-и?
	/də-z-šʲ-wá-j	/d-zə-m-šʲ-wá-j/
	him/her(C1)-Rel(C3)-kill-Dyn.NF-Qu	
	'What is killing him/her?'	'What is not killing him/her?'
Aorist	ды-з-шь-и́? *or* ды-з-шьы́-зеи?	д-зы-м-шьы́-зеи?
	/də-z-šʲə́-j/zaj	/d-zə-m-šʲə́-zaj/
	him/her(C1)-Rel(C3)-kill.Aor.NF-Qu	
	'What killed him/her?'	'What didn't kill him/her?'

Examples:

(410) Бзы́раапҕсеи уиáҟара?
/b-zə́-raapsa-j wəjáq'ara/
you.F(C1)-Rel(C3)-tire.Aor-NF-Qu so much
'Why did you get so tired?' (lit. 'What tired you so much?')

(411) Ари́ ахәычы́ дзыртцәы́уозеи?
/arә́j a-xʷәč'ʲә́ d-zә-r-c'ʷә́wa-wa-zaj/
this the-child him/her(C1)-Rel(C3)-Caus-cry-Dyn.NF-Qu
'What is making this child cry?'

(412) Аýс узыруа́зеи?
/a-wә́s ø-wә-zә-r-w-wá-zaj/
the-work [it(C1)-]you(C2)-Rel(C3)-Caus-do-Dyn.NF-Qu
'What is making you work?'

4.7.3.2. Interrogative Sentences with Interrogative Pronouns

Other than the method of adding interrogative suffixes to the verbal complex discussed above, interrogative sentences can be made using the interrogative pronoun иа́рбан /járban/ 'what'. Similar to the formation of interrogative sentences with да́рбан /dárban/ 'who' discussed in §4.7.1.2, the verb uses the non-infinite form. Here are some examples that use the stative verb а-гы́лара /á-gә́la-ra/ 'to stand' and the dynamic verb а́-ҟатцара /á-q'a-c'a-ra/ 'to do, to make':

(413) иа́рбан игы́лоу?
/járban jә-gә́la-w/
what Rel(C1)-stand-Stat.Pres.NF
'What is standing?'

(414) иа́рбан игы́лаз?
/járban jә-gә́la-z/
what Rel(C1)-stand-Stat.Past.NF
'What was standing?'

(415) иа́рбан и́ҟалтца?
/járban jә́-q'a-l-c'a/
what Rel(C1)-Prev-she(C3)-do/make.Aor.NF
'What did she do/make?'

Also, the phrase 'what is this?' can be expressed using закәи́ /zak'ʷә́j/ or закәы́зеи /zak'ʷә́zaj/ as in the following:

(416) ари́ закәи́? / закәы́з(е)и?
/arә́j z-ak'ʷә́-j / z-ak'ʷә́-z(a)j/
this Rel(C2)-be-Qu (cf. а́кәзаара 'to be')

(417) Бызлацәа́жәо закәи́?
/bә-z-la-cʷážʷa-wa z-ak'ʷә́-j/
you.F(C1)-Rel(C2)-Prev-talk about-Dyn.NF Rel(C2)-be-Qu
'What are you-F talking about?'
(= Бызлацәа́жәозеи?)

(418) иутахы́у закәы́зеи?
/jә-w-taxә́-w z-ak'ʷә́-z(a)j/
Rel(C1)-you.M(C2)-want-Stat.Pres.NF Rel(C2)-be-Qu

'What do you-M want?'

4.7.4. 'Where?', 'When?', 'Why?', 'How?', 'Whence?' Questions

In order to express sentences using interrogative adverbs such as 'where?', 'when?', 'why?', 'how?', and 'whence?' in Abkhaz, an interrogative marker indicating the meaning of the respective interrogative adverb must be inserted in the verbal complex. In this case, these interrogative markers are inserted immediately after the pronominal prefixes in Column I. The verb form takes the non-infinitive form, but there are also cases where the suffix -и is added. Generally, it appears that in the aorist and future forms the addition of the suffix -и is preferred.

4.7.4.1. 'Where?' Questions

The interrogative marker for 'where' is -аба- /aba/. The formation of the verbal stem is as follows: (i) in Dynamic Group I, it is also possible to add the suffix -и /j/ except in the perfect tense. (ii) In Dynamic Group II, a variant where the -зы- /zə/ is inserted before the non-infinitive suffix -з /z/ is also possible. The verbal stem remains in the non-infinitive form in stative verbs.

Stative verb а-гы́лара /a-gə́la-ra/ 'to stand':

	Affirmative	Negative
3Sg.Hum.-where-R-		
Present	д-аба́-гылоу? /d-abá-gəla-w/ he/she(C1)-where-stand-Stat.Pres.NF 'Where is he/she standing?'	д-аба́-гыла-м?
Past	д-аба́-гыла-з?	д-аба́-гыла-мы-з?

The placement of the interrogative marker -аба- between the Column I and II pronominal prefixes is clear in the following example:

(419) иаба́бымаз ашәҟәы́?
/j-abá-bə-ma-z a-šʷq'ʷə́/
it(C1)-where-you.F(C2)-have-Past.NF the-book
'Where did you-F have the book?'

Dynamic/intransitive verb а-цара́ /a-ca-rá/ 'to go'

	Affirmative	Negative
2Sg.F-where-R-		
Present	б-аба́-цо-(и)? /b-abá-ca-wa-(j)/ you.F(C1)-where-go-Dyn.NF-Qu 'Where are you-F going?'	б-аба́-м-цо-(и)?
Aorist	б-аба́-це-и? / б-аба́-ца?	б-аба́-м-ца?
Perfect	б-аба́-ца-хьоу?	

Dynamic/transitive verb а-шьра́ /a-šʲ-rá/ 'to kill'; а́-ҭира /á-təj-ra/ 'to sell':

	Affirmative	Negative
Dynamic Group I		
3Sg.N.H/3Pl-where-3Sg.F-R-		
Present	д-аба́-л-шь-уе-и?	д-аба́-лы-м-шь-уе-и?
	/d-abá-l-šʲ-wa-j/	/d-abá-lə-m-šʲ-wa-j/
	him/her(C1)-where-she(C3)-kill-Dyn.NF-Qu	
	'Where is she killing him/her?'	
	и-аба́-л-ҭи-уе-и?	
	/j-abá-l-təj-wa-j/	
	'Where is she sell it/them?'	
Aorist	д-аба́-л-шь?	д-аба́-лы-м-шь?
	/d-abá-l-šʲ/	/d-abá-lə-m-šʲ/
	'Where did she kill him/her?'	
	и-аба́-л-ҭи?	
Dynamic Group II		
Imperfect	и-аба́-л-ҭи-уа-з?	

Examples:

(420) Уан ау́с аба́луеи?

/w-an a-wə́s ø-abá-l-w-wa-j/

your.M-mother the-work [it(C1)-]where-she(C3)-do-Dyn-Qu

'Where is your-M mother working?'

(421) аҵа́ракәа а́шәа аба́рҳәо?

/a-c'ára-kʷa á-šʷa ø-abá-r-ħʷa-wa/

the-bird-Pl the-song [it(C1)-]where-they(C3)-say-Dyn.NF

'Where are the birds singing a song?'

4.7.4.2. 'When?' Question

The interrogative marker for 'when' is <u>-анба-</u> /anba/. The formation of the verbal stem is as follows: (i) In Dynamic Group I it is the non-infinitive form or 'non-infinitive form + -и' (in the aorist and future the latter is preferable). (ii) In Dynamic Group II and stative verbs, the verbal stem is the same as in the 'where' questions.

<u>Stative verb</u> а́-ҟазаара /á-q'a-zaa-ra/ 'to be; to exist'

Present	и-анба́-ҟо-у?
	/j-anbá-q'a-w/
	it/they(C1)-when-be-Stat.Pres.NF
	'When is it?/When are they?'
Past	и-анба́-ҟа-з?
	/j-anbá-q'a-z/

For example:

(422) Ры́хә анба́цәгьоу ауҭраҭы́хкәа? (AFL)

/rə́-xʷ	ø-anbá-cʷgʲa-w	a-wtratə́x-kʷa/
their-cost	[it(C1)-]when-be expensive-Stat.Pres.NF	the-vegetable-Pl

'When is the cost of vegetables expensive?'

Dynamic verb а-шьрá /a-šʲ-ra/ 'to kill'; а-царá /a-ca-rá/ 'to go'

	Affirmative	Negative
Dynamic Group I		
Present	д-анбá-л-шь-уе-и? /d-anbá-l-šʲ-wa-j/ him/her(C1)-when-she(C3)-kill-Dyn.NF-Qu 'When does she kill him/her?'	д-анбá-лы-м-шь-уе-и? /d-anbá-lə-m-šʲ-wa-j/
	б-анбá-цо-(и)? /b-anbá-ca-wa-(j)/ 'Where are you-F going?'	
Aorist	д-анбá-л-шь-и? /d-anbá-l-šʲə-j/ 'When did she kill him/her?'	д-анбá-лы-м-шь-и? /d-anbá-lə́-m-šʲə-j/
	б-анбá-ца? / б-анбá-це-и?	
Perfect	б-анбá-ца-хьо-у? / б-анбá-ца-хье-и?	
Dynamic Group II		
Imperfect	б-анбá-цо-з? / б-анбá-цо-зы-з?	

The placement of the interrogative marker -анба- /anba/ between the Column I and II pronominal prefixes is clear in the following examples:

(423) Ианбáбымаз ашәk̄əы́?

/j-anbá-bə-ma-z	a-šʷq'ʷə́/
it(C1)-when-you.F(C2)-have-Stat.Past.NF	the-book

'When did you-F have the book?'

4.7.4.3. 'Why?' Questions

The interrogative marker for 'why' is -з(ы)-. Verbs with this interrogative marker are produced in the following way: (i) in forms in Dynamic Group I and the present tense of stative verbs, the suffix -и or -зеи is attached to the non-finitive form. According to our informant, when the suffix -и is added to the non-finitive form, the -у /w/ at the end of the perfect and present tense of the stative verbs disappears, but the vowel a immediately before it changes to an o (in the perfect tense there is only the variant with the suffix -и). (ii) In forms in Dynamic Group II and the past tense of stative verbs a suffix is not attached to the non-infinitive form.

Stative verb а-гы́лара /a-gə́la-ra/ 'to stand'; á-мазаара /á-ma-zaa-ra/ 'to have'

	Affirmative	Negative
2Sg.F-why-R-Qu		
Present	бы-з-гы́ло-и? /bə-z-gə́la-[w-]j/	бы-з-гы́ла-м-и?

'why are you-F standing?'

и-з-бы́-мо-и / и-з-бы́-мо-у-зеи?
/jə-z-bə́-ma-(w)-j / jə-z-bə́-ma-w-zaj
it/them(C1)-why-you.F(C2)-have-Stat.Pres.NF-Qu
'Why do you-F have it/them?'

Past бы-з-гы́ла-з? бы-з-гы́ла-мы-з?

Dynamic/intransitive verb á-пҕхьара /á-pxʲa-ra/ 'to read':

	Affirmative	Negative
3Sg.H-why-3Sg.N.H-R-Qu		
Present	д-з-á-пҕхьо-и? /d-z-á-pxʲa-wa-j/ he/she(C1)-why-it(C2)-read-Dyn-Qu 'Why is he/she reading it?'	д-з-а-мы́-пҕхьо-и?
Aorist	д-з-á-пҕхье-и?	д-з-а-мы́-пҕхье-и?

Dynamic/transitive verb á-ҟатцара /á-q'a-c'a-ra/ 'to do/make'; á-ҭара /á-ta-ra/ 'to give':

	Affirmative	Negative
3Sg.N.H/3Pl-why-Prev-3Sg.F-R-		
Present	и-зы́-ҟа-л-тцо-и? /jə-zə́-q'a-l-c'a-wa-j/ 'Why is she doing/making it/them?'	и-зы́-ҟа-лы-м-тцо-и?
Aorist	и-зы́-ҟа-л-тце-и? и-з-сы́-л-ҭе-и? /jə-z-sə́-l-ta-j/ it/them(C1)-why-me(C2)-she(C3)-give.Aor.NF.-Qu 'Why did she give the book to me?'	и-зы́-ҟа-лы-м-тце-и? и-з-сы́-лы-м-ҭе-и? /jə-z-sə́-lə-m-ta-j/

The suffixes -и and -зеи can be alternated. Look at the following examples which use the stative verb áмазаара /á-ma-zaa-ra/ 'to have' and the dynamic verb аáира /aá-j-ra/ 'to come':

(424) Избы́мои / Избы́моузеи ашәҟәы́?
/jə-z-bə́-ma-[w-]j / jə-z-bə́-ma-w-zaj a-šʷq'ʷə́/
it(C1)-why-you.F(C2)-have-Non-Fin-Qu the-book
'Why do you have the book?'

(425) Мура́т иахьа́ дзы́мааи? / дзы́мааизеи?
/məwrát jaxʲá d-zə́-m-aa-jə-j / d-zə́-m-aa-j-zaj/
name today he-why-Neg-Prev-come.Aor.NF-Qu
'Why didn't Murat come here today?'

4.7.4.4. 'How?' Questions

The interrogative marker for 'how' is -шԥа- /špa/.[155] The interrogative form is produced by placing the interrogative marker after the Column I prefix, and its stem and suffix are formed in the following manner: (i) in Dynamic Group I of dynamic verbs, it is 'non-finite form + -и' and (ii) in Dynamic Group II of dynamic verbs and in stative verbs, it is just the non-finite form.

Stative verb а-гы́лара /a-gə́la-ra/ 'to stand':

	Affirmative	Negative
3Sg.Hum-how-R-		
Present	ды-шԥá-гыло-у? /də-špá-gəla-w/ (s)he(C1)-how-stand-Pres-.Stat.NF 'How is he/she standing?'	ды-шԥá-гыла-м?
Past	ды-шԥá-гыла-з?	ды-шԥá-гыла-мы-з?

Two-place dynamic verb á-ҭира /á-təj-ra/ 'to sell':

	Affirmative	Negative
3Sg.N.H/3Pl-how-3Sg.F-R-		
Dynamic Group I		
present	и-шԥá-л-ҭи-уе-и? /jə-špá-l-təj-wa-j/ it/them(C1)-how-she(C3)-sell-Dyn.NF-Qu 'How is she selling it/them?'	и-шԥá-лы-м-ҭи-уе-и?
Aorist	и-шԥá-л-ҭи? (< и-шԥá-л-ҭи-и?)	и-шԥá-лы-м-ҭи?
Dynamic Group II		
Imperfect	и-шԥá-л-ҭи-уа-з?	и-шԥá-лы-м-ҭи-уа-з?

Three-place dynamic verb á-ҭара /á-ta-ra/ 'to give':

3Sg.N.H/3Pl-how-3Sg.F-1Sg-R-	
Dynamic Group I	
Present	и-шԥá-лы-с-ҭо-и? /jə-špá-lə-s-ta-wa-j/ it/them(C1)-how-her(C2)-I(C3)-give-Dyn.NF-Qu 'How am I giving it/them to her?'
Aorist	и-шԥá-лы-с-ҭе-и?
Dynamic Group II	

155. The interrogative marker -шԥа- /špa/ is also used when producing exclamatory forms:
Ишԥáԥшӡоу асасаáирҭа ахы́бра!
/jə-špá-pšʒa-w a-sasaájərta a-xə́bra
it-how-beauty-Stat.NF the-hotel its-building
'How beautiful the building of the hotel is!'

Imperfect и-шҧá-лы-с-ҭо-з?
Pluperfect и-шҧá-лы-с-ҭа-хьа-з?

Also, in verbs with the subjective version the interrogative marker -шҧа- /špa/ is inserted in between the Column I prefix and the possessive prefix. For example, look at an example sentence using the verb а-хгарá /a-x-ga-rá/ 'to spend':

(426) Амш шҧоухýгеи?
/a-mš ø-špa-w-xə́-w-ga-j/
the-day [it(C1)-]how-your.M(Poss)-SV-you.M(C3)-take.Aor.NF-Qu
'How did you-M spend the day?'

Also, in verbs with preverbs the interrogative marker -шҧа- is inserted between the Column I prefix and the preverb. Look at an example sentence using á-ҟаҵара /á-q'a-c'a-ra/ 'to do/make':

(427) Ишҧáҟабҵеи ари́?
/jə-špá-q'a-b-c'a-j arə́j/
it(C1)-how-Prev-you.F-do/make-(Aor)-Qu this
'How did you-F do/make this?'

4.7.4.5. 'Whence?' Questions

The interrogative marker for 'whence' is -абáнтәи- /abánt'ʷəj/ (cf. -аба- 'where', -нтә 'from'). The suffix -и is attached to the stems of Dynamic Group I. Example sentences using аарá /aa-rá/ 'to come' and а-ды́рра /a-də́r-ra/ 'to know' are given in (428) and (429):

(428) дабáнтәáауеи?
/d-abánt'ʷ-áa-wa-j/
he/she(C1)-whence-come-Dyn-Qu
'Where is he/she coming from?'

Cf. бабáнтәи áаи? 'where did you-F come from?'

(429) сабáнтәилды́ри?
/s-abánt'ʷəj-l-də́rə-j/
me(C1)-whence-she(C3)-know-(Aor)-Qu
'Where did she know me from?'

4.7.5. 'Yes-No' Questions

Different suffixes are used in the formation of the affirmative and negative forms of 'yes-no' questions in Abkhaz. Affirmative interrogative sentences are produced by adding the interrogative suffix -ма /ma/ (rarely -у /w/) to the non-finite form. The suffix -ма is added after -з at the end of the non-finite form in Dynamic Group II as well. In contrast to this, negative interrogative sentences are produced by adding -(ӡа)-и to the non-finitive form, but in the past tense of stative verbs, the present tense of dynamic verbs and Dynamic Group II forms it is possible to omit the -и.

Stative Verbs á-мазаара /á-ma-zaa-ra/ 'to have':

	Affirmative	Negative
3Sg.N.H/3Pl-2Sg.F-R-		

Present и-бы́-мо-у-ма? и-бы́-ма-ʒа-м-и?[156]
/jə-bə́-ma-w-ma/
it/them(C1)-you.F(C2)-have-Pres.Stat.NF-Qu
'Do you-F have it/them?'
Past и-бы́-ма-з-ма? и-бы́-ма-ʒа-м-з?

Dynamic Verbs а-ды́рра /a-də́r-ra/ 'to know':

	Affirmative	Negative
3Sg.N.H/3Pl-3Sg.F-R-Dynamic Group I		
Present	сы-л-ды́р-уа-ма?	сы-л-зы́-м-дыр-ʒо?
	/sə-l-də́r-wa-ma/	/sə-l-zə́-m-dər-ʒa-wa/
	me(C1)-she(C3)-know-Dyn.NF-Qu	I(C1)-her(C2)-Pot-Neg-know-Emph-Dyn.NF
	'Does she know me?'	'Doesn't she know me?'
Aorist	сы-л-ды́р-ма?	сы-л-зы́-м-дыр-ʒе-и?
		/sə-l-zə́-m-dər-ʒa-j/
Dynamic Group II		
Imperfect	сы-л-ды́р-уа-з-ма?	сы-л-зы́-м-дыр-ʒо-з?
		/sə-l-zə́-m-dər-ʒa-wa-z/

Examples:

(430) Исы́лтама / Исы́лымтаʒеи ашәҟәы́?
/jə-sə́-l-ta-ma / jə-sə́-lə-m-ta-ʒa-j a-šʷq'ʷə́/
it(C1)-me(C2)-she(C3)-give-(Aor)-Qu / it(C1)-me(C2)-she(C3)-Neg-give-(Aor)-Emph-Qu the-book
'Did/Didn't she give a/the book to me?'

(431) Исзы́бҩыма / Исзы́бмыҩʒеи ашәҟәы́?
/jə-s-zə́-b-jʷə-ma / jə-s-zə́-b-mə-jʷ-ʒa-j a-šʷq'ʷə́/
it(C1)-me(C2)-OV-you.F(C3)-write-(Aor)-Qu / -Neg-write-(Aor)-Qu the-letter
'Did/Didn't you-F write a letter to me?'

(432) Уара́ иахьа́ а́калакь ахь уцо́у? (Яковлев 2006: 10)
/wará jaxʲá á-kalakʲ [a-]axʲ wə-ca-wá-w/
you.M today the-city its-to you.M(C1)-go-Dyn-Qu
'Will you-M go to the city today?'

(433) Уара́ иахьа́ а́калакь ахь умцо́и? (ibid. 10)
/wará jaxʲá á-kalakʲ [a-]axʲ wə-m-ca-wá-j/
you.M today the-city its-to you.M(C1)-Neg-go-Dyn-Qu
'Will you-M not go to the city today?'

The intonation of yes-no questions falls when there is a verb at the end of the sentence. For example:

(434) Ашәҟәы́ бы́моума? ↘ /ašʷq'ʷə́ bə́mawma?/ 'Do you have the book?'

---

156. -ʒа- is an 'Emph(asis)' marker.

The intonation of negative interrogative sentences does not display as sudden a fall in intonation as in affirmative interrogative sentences. For example:

(435) Ашәҟәы́ бы́мазами? ↘ /ašʷq'ʷə́ bə́mazaməj?/ 'Don't you have the book?'

4.7.6. Other Interrogative Sentences

To produce interrogative sentences indicating 'how many', the interrogative шаҟа /šaq'a/ (or заҟа /zaq'a/) is used. For the number of the noun modified by the interrogative, there is a tendency for the plural form to be used in the word order of 'noun + шаҟа' and for the singular form (without an article) to be used in the word order of 'шаҟа + noun'. Also, when this interrogative шаҟа modifies a noun of a human class, the suffix -ҩ /jʷ/, which indicates the human class, is attached to this interrogative. For the verb form in this interrogative sentence, when the noun modified by the interrogative is of a human class, it takes the same form as a 'who' question (in other words, attaching the suffix -да /da/ to the non-finite form) and on the other hand, when the noun is of a class other than human, it is the same form as a 'what' question (in other words, the suffix -и/-зеи is attached to the non-finite form). Look at the examples using the verb а́-мазаара /á-ma-zaa-ra/ 'to have':

(436) Шаҟа́ тцәа у́мои?
/šaq'á c'ʷa ø-wə́-ma-w-j/
how many apple [it/they(C1)-]you.M(C2)-have-Stat.Pres.NF-Qu
'How many apples do you-M have?'

Cf. Атцәакәа́ шаҟа́ у́мои?
/a-c'ʷa-kʷá šaq'a ø-wə́-ma-w-j/
the-apple-Pl how many [they(C1)-]you.M(C2)-have-Stat.NF-Qu
'How many apples do you-M have?'

(437) Уа́рма шьапы́ шаҟа́ шьацәкьы́с амо́узеи?
/w-árma šʲap'ə́ šaq'á šʲacʷk'ʲə́s ø-a-má-w-zaj/
your.M-left foot how many toe [they(C1)-it(C2)-have-Stat.Pres.NF-Qu
'How many toes does your-M left foot have?'

(438) Ахәычкәа́ шаҟа́ҩ у́мада?
/a-xʷəč'-kʷá šaq'á-jʷ ø-wə́-ma-da/
the-child-Pl how many-Human [they(C1)-]you.M(C2)-have-Qu
'How many children do you-M have?'

(439) Уара́ а́шьыжь асаа́т шаҟа́ рзы́ угы́лои?
/wará ášʲəžʲ a-saát šaq'á r-zə w-gə́la-w-j/
you.M morning the-o'clock how many their-at you.M(C1)-get up-Stat.Pres.NF-Qu
'What time do you-M get up?'

In order to produce interrogative sentences indicating 'how much', the interrogative шаҟа /šaq'a/ (or заҟа́ /zaq'á/) is used alone. The verb form is the same as that of a 'what' question (in other words, the suffix -и/-зеи is attached to the non-finite form). Look at an example using the stative verb а-ԥсара́ /a-psa-rá/ 'to cost':

(440) Шаҟа́ иаԥсо́и ашәҟәы́?

/šaq'á j-a-psá-w-j a-šʷq'ʷə́/
how much it(C1)-it(C2)-cost-Stat.Pres.NF-Qu the-book
'How much does this book cost?'

(441) Шаҟа́ иаԥсо́узеи абри́ атцкы́ ҩе́ижь? (AFL)
/šaq'á j-a-psá-w-zaj abrə́j a-c'k'ə́ jʷájžʲ
how much it(C1)-it(C2)-cost-Stat.Pres.NF-Qu this the-dress yellow
'How much does this yellow dress cost?'

4.7.7. Indirect Interrogative Sentences

When the direct interrogative sentences shown above are used as a subordinate clause in indirect interrogative sentences, the verb form of the direct interrogative sentence must be changed in the following way. Regarding (i) interrogative sentences with 'what', 'who' and 'whose', the interrogative suffixes (-и/-зеи /jə/zaj/, -да /da/) used in direct interrogative sentences are not used and the interrogative sentences change into relative clauses. (ii) The interrogative markers used in direct interrogative sentences -аба- /aba/ 'where', -анба- /anba/ 'when', -шԥа- /špa/ 'how', -аба́нтәи /abánt'ʷəj/ 'whence' are changed into -ахь- /axʲ/, -ан- /an/, -ш(ы)- /š(ə)/, -ахьынтәи- /axʲənt'ʷəj/ respectively.[157] The verb form is a non-finite form that does not have an interrogative suffix attached to it. Below, we will describe indirect interrogatives using the verb а-ды́рра 'to know' in the main clause. In Abkhaz, there is no 'sequence of tenses' phenomenon like that in English.

4.7.7.1. 'I know what ...'

A direct interrogative sentence (442) using а́-ҟатцара /á-q'a-c'a-ra/ 'to do/make' and its indirect interrogative sentence (443) are as follows:

(442) и́ҟабтцеи?
/jə́-q'a-b-c'a-j/
Rel(C1)-Prev-you.F(C3)-do/make-(Aor)-Qu
'What did you-F do/make?'

(443) Иацы́ бара́ и́ҟабтцаз здырусит.
/jacə́ bará jə́-q'a-b-c'a-z ø-z-də́r-wa-jt'/
yesterday you.F Rel(C1)-Prev-you.F(C3)-do/make-Past.Ind.NF [it(C1)-]I(C3)-know-Dyn-Fin
'I know what you did yesterday.'

The subordinate clause и́ҟабтцаз /jə́-q'a-b-c'a-z/ of sentence (443) above is in the past indefinite non-finite form, and here verb forms with the suffix -и, like that in (442), cannot be used.

When the tense of a direct interrogative sentence belongs to Dynamic Group II, as there is no suffix -и in the verb, the verb form of the subordinate clause of the indirect interrogative sentence is the same as the verb form of the direct interrogative sentence. In the following examples, direct interrogative sentence (444) is imperfect, and the verb form of the subordinate clause in indirect interrogative sentence (445) is also imperfect:

157. Taking into accouunt the compounded marker an-ba, we can consider špa to come from š-ba, aba to come from axʲ-ba.

(444) и́ҟабцоз?
/jə́-q'a-b-c'a-wa-z/
Rel(C1)-Prev-you.F(C3)-do/make-Dyn-Impf.NF
'What were you-F doing/making?'

(445) Иацы́ бара́ и́ҟабцоз сыздры́руам.
/jacə́ bará jə́-q'a-b-c'a-wa-z ø-sə-z-də́r-wa-m/
yesterday you.F Rel(C1)-Prev-you.F(C3)-do-Dyn-Impf.NF [it(C1)-]me(C2)-Pot-know-Dyn-Neg
'I do not know what you were doing yesterday.'

4.7.7.2. 'I know who ...'

A direct interrogative sentence (446) using а́-тара /á-ta-ra/ 'to give' and its indirect interrogative sentence (447) are as follows:

(446) Ашәҟәы́ зылта́ла?
/a-š^wq'^wə́ ø-zə-l-tá-da/
the-book [it(C1)-]Rel(C2)-she(C3)-give.Aor.NF-Qu
'Whom did she give the book to?'

(447) Ашәҟәы́ зылта́з сыздры́руам.
/a-š^wq'^wə ø-zə-l-tá-z ø-sə-z-də́r-wa-m/
the-book [it(C1)-Rel(C2)-she(C3)-give-Past.Ind.NF [it(C1)-]me(C2)-Pot-know-Dyn-Neg
'I do not know whom she gave the book to.'

The subordinate clause зылта́з /zə-l-tá-z/ in sentence (447) above is in the past indefinite non-finite form, and here a verb form with the suffix -да, like that in (446), cannot be used.

For interrogative sentences using the independent interrogative да́рбан /dárban/ 'who', the interrogative remains as is even when it is made into an indirect interrogative sentence. Look at the following example:

(448) Бара́ бҩы́за да́рбан сыздры́руам.
/bará b-j^wə́za dárban ø-sə-z-də́r-wa-m/
you.F your-friend who [it(C1)-]me(C2)-Pot-know-Dyn-Neg
'I do not know who your friend is.'

4.7.7.3. 'I know whose ...'

Interrogative sentences with 'whose' are also produced in the same way as the indirect interrogative sentences shown above. Look at the following direct interrogative sentence (449) and its indirect interrogative sentence (450):

(449) Ари́ ашәҟәы́ зтәы́да?
/arə́j a-š^wq'^wə́ ø-z-t'^wə́-da/
this the-book [it(C1)-]Rel(C2)-belong to-Qu
'Whose book is this?'

(450) Ари́ ашәҟәы́ зтәу́ сыздры́руам.
/arə́j a-š^wq'^wə́ ø-z-t'^wə́-w ø-sə-z-də́r-wa-m/

this the-book [it(C1)-]Rel(C2)-belong to-Stat.Pres.NF [it(C1)-]me(C2)Pot-know-Dyn-Neg
'I do not know whose book this is.'

4.7.7.4. 'I know where ...'

The interrogative marker <u>-аба-</u> /aba/ turns into the relative adverb marker <u>-ахь-</u> /ax^{j}/, and the verb form of the subordinate clause changes into a non-finite form without interrogative suffixes. (451) and (453) are direct interrogative sentences, and their respective indirect interrogative sentences are (452) and (454):

(451) дабáҵеи?
/d-abá-ca-j/
he/she(C1)-where-go-(Aor)-Qu
'Where did he/she go?'

(452) Дахьҵáз сызды́руам.
/d-ax^{j}-cá-z ϕ-sə-z-də́r-wa-m/
he/she(C1)-where-go-Past.Ind.NF [it(C1)-]me(C2)Pot-know-Dyn-Neg
'I do not know where he/she went.'

(453) Иацы́ дабáҟаз?
/jacə́ d-abá-q'a-z/
yesterday he/she(C1)-where-be-Stat.Past.NF.Qu
'Where was he/she yesterday?'

(454) Иацы́ дахьы́ҟаз сызды́руам.
/jacə́ d-ax^{j}ə́-q'a-z ϕ-sə-z-də́r-wa-m/
yesterday he/she(C1)-where-be-Stat.Past.NF [it(C1)-]me(C2)Pot-know-Dyn-Neg
'I do not know where he/she was yesterday.'

The <u>-ахь(ы)-</u> /ax^{j}(ə)/ in the verbal complex in (452) and (454) above can be seen as expressing 'the place in/to which' (cf. in English: *this is <u>where</u> I used to live*). This can be confirmed by the following sentence, whose subordinate clause is not an indirect interrogative sentence but has <u>-ахь(ы)-</u> /ax^{j}(ə)/ in its verbal complex:

(455) Нас сáни сарéи áфатә ахьы́рҭиуаз ҳнеит.
/nas s-ánə-j sará-j á-fat'^{w} ϕ-ax^{j}ə́-r-təj-wa-z
then my-mother-and I-and the-food [it(C1)-]where-they(C3)-sell-Dyn-Impf.NF
ħ-na-jə-jt'/
we(C1)-Prev(thither)-go-(Aor)-Fin
'Then my mother and I went to where they were selling food.'

4.7.7.5. 'I know whence ...'

The interrogative marker <u>-абáнтәи-</u> /abánt'^{w}əj/ changes into <u>-ахьынтәи-</u> /ax^{j}ənt'^{w}əj/, and the verb form of the subordinate clause is changed into a non-finite form without an interrogative suffix:

(456) бабáнтәи áаи?
/b-abá-nt'^{w}əj áa-j/

you.F-where-from come-(Aor)-Qu
'Where did you-F come from?'

(457) Бахьы́нтәи а́аз сыздды́руам.
/b-axʲə́-nt'ʷəj áa-z ø-sə-z-də́r-wa-m/
you.F-where-from come-Past Ind.NF [it(C1)-]me(C2)-Pot-know-Dyn-Fin
'I do not know where you-F came from.'

4.7.7.6. 'I know when ...'

The interrogative marker -анба- /anba/ changes into the relative adverb marker -ан- /an/, and the verb form of the subordinate clause changes into an non-finite form without interrogative suffixes:[158]

(458) банба́гыло(и)?
/b-anbá-gə́la-wa-j/
you.F-when-get up-Dyn.NF-Qu
'When do you-F wake up?'

(459) Бара́ шьыжьла́ бангы́ло здь́ірырц стаху́п.
/bará šʲəžʲlá b-an-gə́la-wa ø-z-də́rə-rc
you.F in the morning you.F(C1)-when-get up-Dyn.NF [it(C1)-]I(C3)-know-in order to
ø-s-taxə́-wp'/
[it(C1)-]I(C2)-want-Stat.Pres.Fin
'I want to know when you-F wake up in the morning.'

4.7.7.7. 'I know how ...'

The interrogative marker -шҧа- /špa/ changes into the relative adverb marker -ш(ы)- /š(ə)/, and the verb form of the subordinate clause changes into a non-finite form without interrogative suffixes:

(460) ишҧа́ҟабтцеи
/jə-špá-q'a-b-c'a-j/
it/them(C1)-how-Prev-you.F-do/make-(Aor)-Qu
'How did you-F do/make it/them?'

(461) Ишы́ҟабтцаз сыздды́руам.
/jə-šə́-q'a-b-c'a-z ø-sə-z-də́r-wa-m/
it/them(C1)-how-Prev-you.F(C3)-do/make-Past.Ind.NF [it(C1)-]me(C2)-Pot-know-Dyn-Fin
'I do not know how you-F did it/them.'

The position of ш(ы)- /š(ə)/ in (461) above is inserted immediately after the Column I prefix (before the Column II prefix), similar to direct interrogative sentence. For example, this is clear by the form of the subordinate clause in the following intransitive verb а́-ҧхьара /á-pxʲa-ra/ 'to read':

158. The marker -ан- /an/ 'when' is also used as a time conjunction: Сара́ ашәҟәы́ сана́ҧхьо дысгәа́лашәоит. /sará a-šʷq'ʷə́ s-an-á-pxʲa-wa də-s-gʷálašʷa-wa-jt'/ [I the-book I(C1)-when-it(C2)-read-Dyn.NF him/her(C1)-me(C2)-remember-Dyn-Fin] 'When I read the book, I remember him/her'.

(462) Сара́ ашәҟәы́ сшáпҕхьоз сáлацәажәоит.
/sará a-šʷq'ʷə́ s-š-á-pxʲa-wa-z s-á-la-cʷažʷa-wa-jt'/
I the-book I(C1)-how-it(C2)-read-Dyn-Impf.NF I(C1)-it(C2)-Prev-talk about-Dyn-Fin
'I am talking about how I was reading the book.'

4.7.7.8. 'I know whether ...'

When inserting a 'yes-no' question into a subordinate clause, the direct interrogative suffix -ма /ma/ is removed and the verb form is made into the non-finite form. The direct interrogative sentence and its indirect interrogative sentence are given in (463) and (464) respectively:

(463) Аса́бшаҽены быҧсы́ бшьóма?
/asábša-čnə bə-psə́ ø-b-šʲa-wá-ma/
Sunday-on your.F(Poss)-soul [it(C1)-]you.F(C3)-rest-Dyn-Qu
'Do you-F take a rest on Sunday?'

(464) Аса́бшаҽены быҧсы́ бшьóибымшьó сыздырүам.
/asábša-čnə bə-psə́ ø-b-šʲa-wá-j-bə-m-šʲa-wá
Sunday-on your.F(Poss)-soul [it(C1)-]you.F(C3)-rest-Dyn-it(C1)-you.F(C3)-Neg-rest-Dyn.NF
ø-sə-z-də́r-wa-m/
[it(C1)-]me(C2)-Pot-know-Dyn-Fin
'I do not know whether or not you-F take a rest on Sunday.'

However, according to our informant, in aorist indirect interrogative sentences, -у, which can be considered an interrogative suffix, is added to the stem of the non-infinitive form:

(465) Ашәҟәы́ лҩы́ма?
/a-šʷq'ʷə́ ø-l-jʷə́-ma/
the-letter [it(C1)-]she(C3)-write-(Aor)-Qu
'Did she write a/the letter?'

(466) Ашәҟәы́ лҩуилымҩу́ сыздырүам.
/a-šʷq'ʷə́ ø-l-jʷə-w-jə-lə-m-jʷə́-w ø-sə-z-də́r-wa-m/
the-letter [it(C1)-]she(C3)-write-Qu-it(C1)-she(C3)-Neg-write-Qu [it(C1)-]me(C2)-Pot-know-Dyn-Fin
'I do not know whether or not she wrote a/the letter.'

5. Syntax

5.1. Noun Phrases

5.1.1. Possession

Possessive constructions in Abkhaz follow a head-marking pattern. As already described in §2.2.2, possessive constructions are expressed by adding a possessive prefix indicating the possessor to the possessed noun:

(467) (сара́) сҩы́за
/(sará) s-jʷə́za/
I my-friend
'my friend'

(The personal pronoun сара́ /sará/ 'I' does not appear except when emphasizing this pronoun.)

(468) иҩы́зцәа
/jə-jʷə́z-cʷa/
his-friend-Pl
'his friends'

Also, 'Shwarax's friends' is expressed as 'Shwarax his-friends,' with the addition of the possessive prefix и- /jə/ 'his' which relates to Shwarax:

(469) Шәара́х иҩы́зцәа
/šʷaráx jə-jʷə́z-cʷa/
Shwarax his-friend-Pl

Here is an even more complex example:

(470) Сара́ а́гызмалкәа рхәынҭка́р иҧа́ со́уп. (Abkhaz text)
/sará á-gəzmal-kʷa r-ħʷəntkár jə-pá s-á-wp'/
I the-demon-Pl their-king his-son I(C2)-be-Pres.Stat.Fin
'I am a son of the king of the demons.'

When demonstrative adjectives modify the possessive expressions above, the pronouns are placed before its possessive syntagm (for demonstrative adjectives, see §2.3.2). For example:

(471) у́рҭ са́н лышәҟәкәа́
/wə́rt s-án lə-šʷq'ʷ-kʷá
those my-mother her-book-Pl
'those books of my mother's'

When additional numerals are attached to the phrases above, the numerals are separated and placed after the head noun, or directly join to the front of the noun (for the placement of numerals and nouns, see §2.6.1.2):

(472) у́рҭ са́н лышәҟәкәа́ хәба́ *or* урт сан лыхушәҟу(-к)

/wért s-án lə-šʷq'ʷ-kʷá xʷ-bá *or* wért s-án lə-xʷ-šʷq'ʷə-(k')/
those my-mother her-book-Pl five-Non.Hum those my-mother her-5-book-(NS)
'those five books of my mother's'

When an adjective modifies a possessive syntagm, possessive prefixes are not added to the adjective (for the word order of adjectives modifying nouns, see §§2.4.2.2, 2.4.2.3, 2.4.3):

(473) сҩы́за бзи́а
/s-jʷə́za bzə́ja/
my-friend good
'my good friend'

5.1.2. Adjective Phrases

The relationship between nouns and adjectives is as follows:

<u>(i)</u> Many non-derived adjectives are placed after the noun which they modify:

(474) а́шьха ԥшӡаҟəа́
/á-šʲxa pšʒa-kʷá/
the-mountain beautiful-Pl
'the beautiful mountains'

In this case, articles and possessive prefixes are added to nouns, and plural markers are added to adjectives (or adjectives and nouns) (for details, see §2.4.2.3). Also, the indefinite marker, postpositions, and conjunctive affixes are added to adjectives. For example:

(475) шəҟəы́ ҿы́ц с
/šʷq'ʷə́ č'ə́c-s
book new-as
'as a new book'

(476) ха́цəа ӷəӷəаҟəа́ки иаре́и
/xá-cʷa ɣʷɣʷa-kʷá-k'ə-j jará-j/
man-Pl strong-Pl-one-and he-and
'some strong men and he'

When the 'noun-adjective' syntagm is modified by да́ара /dáara/ 'very', да́ара is placed before this syntagm:

(477) да́ара анхара́ бзи́а
/dáara a-nxará bzə́ja/
very the-living good
'a very good life'

<u>(ii)</u> Adjectives formed by means of the suffixes <u>-тə</u> and <u>-тəи</u> are placed before the nouns they modify. (For details, see §§2.4.3.2, 2.4.3.3):

(478) абна́тə ԥстəҟəа́
/a-bnát'ʷ pst'ʷ-kʷá
the-wild animal-Pl
'wild animals'

(479) ажəы́тə сҩы́за
/a-žʷə́t'ʷ s-jʷə́za/
the-old my-friend
'my old friends'

(480) кавка́зтəи абызшəакəа́
/k'avk'ázt'ʷəj a-bəzšʷa-kʷá/
Caucasian the-language-Pl
'the Caucasian languages'

(iii) Relativized adjectives are placed in front of the nouns they modify (see §2.4.2.4):

(481) иаҭахкəо́у ашəҟəкəа́
/j-a-tax-kʷá-w a-šʷq'ʷ-kʷá/
Rel-it-want-Pl-Stat.Pres.NF the-book-Pl
'the necessary books'

Relative clauses modifying nouns are placed before nouns in many cases similar to (iii) above (for relative clauses, see §§5.4.5.1, 5.4.5.2):

(482) уи́ аҧҳəы́с и́лдыруа арҵаҩы́
/wə́j a-pħʷə́s jə́-l-dər-wa a-rc'ajʷə́/
that the-woman Rel(C1)-she(C3)-know-Dyn.NF the-teacher
'the teacher whom that woman knows'

(483) Да́ара анхара́ бзи́а ры́ман уа инх'уа́з зегьы́, ҧҳəы́сеибак лы́да. (Abkhaz text)
/Dáara a-nxará bzə́ja ø-rə́-ma-n wa jə-n-x-wá-z
very the-living good [it-]they-have-Stat.Past.Fin there Rel(C1)-Prev-live-Dyn+Impf.NF
zagʲə́, pħʷə́sajba-k' lə́-da/
all widow-one her-except
'All the people who lived there lived a good life except for one widow.'

5.2. Copula Construction and Nominal Sentence

5.2.1. Copula Construction

The Abkhaz copula construction is expressed by the verb а́-ҟазаара /á-q'a-zaa-ra/ 'to be'. Spruit (1983: 60) regards this verb as consisting of the preverb ҟа- /q'a/, which indicates existence, and the zero-root (cf. а́-ҟаҵара /á-q'a-c'a-ra/ 'to do', lit. 'to move X into existence'). In Abkhaz, when constructing the sentence 'Y is Z' using this verb, the postposition -с /s/ 'as' must be added to the noun corresponding to 'Z'. Also, this noun does not have the article а-. For example:

(484) Уи́ рҵаҩы́с ды́ҟоуп.
/wəj rc'ajʷə́-s də́-q'a-wp' (< dé-q'a-øə-wp')/
he/she teacher-as he/she(C1)-be-Stat.Pres.Fin (< he/she-Prev-be-Stat.Pres.Fin)
'He/She is a teacher.'

The original meaning of the sentence above is 'he/she exists as a teacher', and the root -ҟа- /q'a/ in this verbal complex cannot be regarded as a pure copula. Following Spruit, what expresses the copula should be regarded as a zero-root. If we postulate that the copula is a zero-root, structures which have a pronominal prefix and stative predicate suffixes attached to the noun (а-)поéт /(a-)p'oét'/ 'poet', as in example (485) below, can be understood as a structure including a zero-root copula, and structural coherence can be given to Abkhaz verb structure.

(485) Пушкин дпоéтуп.
/p'ušk'in d-p'oét'ə-wp' (< d-p'oét'-øə-wp')/
Pushkin he(C1)-poet-Stat.Pres.Fin (< he-poet-be-Stat.Pres.Fin)
'Pushkin is a poet.'

Other than these, -а- /a/ and -акә(ы)- /ak'ʷ(ə)/ are also roots, which express the copula in Abkhaz. These two roots are in complementary distribution, with -а- used for present, affirmative sentences, and -акә(ы)- used for present, negative sentences, past sentences and interrogative sentences. When constructing the sentence 'Y is Z', only a Column II pronominal prefix which cross-references Z is added to the verbal root, and a pronominal prefix which cross-references Y does not appear at all in the verbal complex. In the following examples, (486) and (487) are present, affirmative sentences, (488) is a past sentence and (489) is a present, negative sentence:

(486) Арй Кáма лóуп.
/arə́j k'áma l-á-wp'/
this name.F her(C2)-be-Stat.Pres.Fin
'This is Kama.'

(487) Аҧсны́ сарá сыҧсáдгьыл áуп.
/apsnə́ sará sə-psádgʲəl [a-]a-wp'/
Abkhazia I my-homeland [it(C2)-]be-Stat.Pres.Fin
'Abkhazia is my homeland.'

(488) Уи саб иáкәын.
/wəj s-ab j-ák'ʷə-n/
that my-father him(C2)-be-Stat.Past.Fin
'That was my father.'

(489) Уи саб иáкәым.
/wəj s-ab j-ák'ʷə-m/
that my-father him(C2)-be-Neg(.Pres.Fin)
'That is not my father.'

5.2.2. Nominal Sentence

As seen above, when saying 'Pushkin is a poet', Abkhaz attaches pronominal prefixes which cross-reference the subject and stative verbal suffixes to all common nouns. Furthermore, in the sentence 'This pupil is good', which uses an adjective as the predicate, pronominal prefixes which cross-reference the subject and stative verbal suffixes are attached to the adjective 'good', and the adjective is made into a stative verb:

(490) Абри́ атцаҩы́ дыбзи́оуп.
/abrə́j a-c'ajʷə́ də-bzə́ja-wp'/
this the-pupil he(C1)-good-Stat.Pres.Fin
'This pupil is good.'

The plural form in (490) above is as follows:

(491) Абри́ атцаоцəá бзи́акəоуп.
/abrə́j a-c'ajʷ-cʷá ∅-bzə́ja-kʷa-wp'/
this the-pupil-Pl [they(C1)-]good-Pl-Stat.Pres.Fin
'These pupils are good.'

Other examples:

(492) Исхьа́ амш бзи́ан.
/jəsxʲá a-mš ∅-bzə́ja-n/
today the-weather [it(C1)-]good-Stat.Past.Fin
'Today the weather was good.'

(493) Аҧсны́ аҧсаба́ра да́ара иҧшӡо́уп.
/apsnə́ a-psabára dáara jə-pšʒá-wp'/
Abkhazia its-nature very it(C1)-beautiful-Stat.Pres.Fin
'The nature of Abkhazia is very beautiful.'

Example (493) above demonstrates the fact that the pronominal prefix и- /jə/ 'it/they' originally exists before the adjective бзи́а /bzəja/ in (491) and (492) above (this prefix и- /jə/ does not appear as the noun which cross-references и- /jə/ is immediately before it).

Also, when the nominal phrase (а-)ртцаҩ бзи́а /(a-)rc'ajʷ bzə́ja/ 'a good teacher' is made into the predicate, a pronominal prefix which cross-references the subject is attached to the beginning of the nominal phrase, and a stative verbal suffix is attached to the adjective portion:

(494) Сара́ сыртцаҩ бзи́оуп.
/sará sə-rc'ajʷ bzə́ja-wp'/
I I(C1)-teacher good-Stat.Pres.Fin
'I am a good teacher.'

In addition, the plural form of (494) above is as follows:

(495) Ҳара́ хартцаҩцəа́ бзи́акəоуп.
/ħará ħa-rc'ajʷ-cʷá bzə́ja-kʷa-wp'/
we we(C1)-teacher-Pl good-Pl-Stat.Pres.Fin
'We are good teachers.'

Other examples:

(496) Абри́ да́ҧсуа ха́тцоуп. (cf. а́ҧсуа ха́тца 'an Abkhazian man')
/abrə́j d-ápswa xác'a-wp'/
this he(C1)-Abkhazian man-Stat.Pres.Fin
'This is an Abkhazian man.'

(497) Абри́ са́хəалоуп дшы́сшьыз. (Abkhaz text)
/abrə́j ∅-s-áħʷa-la-wp' d-šə́-s-šʲə-z/
this [it(C1)-]my-sword-with-Stat.Pres.Fin him(C1)-how/that-I(C3)-kill-Past.Ind.NF
'It is this, my sword with which I killed him.'

(497) above has 'with my sword' as the predicate.

5.3. Simple Sentences

As described in §3.1.4, simple declarative sentences end with the finite form of the verb. Arguments expressing the subject and object of the verb are cross-referenced with their constituents (pronouns and nominal phrases) outside the verb in person, number, gender, and class.

5.3.1. When there is one constituent which agrees with the pronominal prefix, it is a subject:

(498) Ҳәынтҟарк дыҟан. (Abkhaz text)
/ħʷəntkár-k' dǝ́-q'a-n/
king-one he(C1)-be-Stat.Past.Fin
'There was a King.' lit. 'One king was.'

The subject in (498) above хәынтҟарк /ħʷəntkár-k'/ 'one king' cross-references the pronominal prefix inside the verb ды- /də-/ in the person (third person), number (singular) and the class (human). The word order of the subject (S)[159] and verb (V) is normally SV, but VS is also possible:

(499) Дыҟан нхаҩык. (Abkhaz text)
/dǝ́-q'a-n nxajʷǝ́-k'/
he-be-Stat.Past peasant-one
'There was once a peasant.'

Pronouns that are subjects normally do not appear other than when they are emphatic:

(500) Асаáт фба рзы́ аҩны́ҟа сцóит.
/asaát fba r-zǝ́ a-jʷnǝ́-q'a s-ca-wá-jt'/
o'clock 6 their-at the-home-to I-go-Dyn-Fin
'I return home at 6 o'clock.'

5.3.2. When pronominal prefixes in the verbal complex cross-reference two constituents, the following sentences can be conceived:

(i) (a) Intransitive verbal sentences with a subject and an indirect object,
(b) Intransitive verbal sentences with a subject and a circumstantial word.
(ii) Transitive verbal sentences with a subject and a direct object.

Below, let us examine these sentences based on this sequence.

5.3.2.1. Examples of (i)–(a). These are intransitive sentences:

(501) Какáшьа Ҭарáшь дúҧхьеит.
/K'ak'áš^ja Taráš^j d-jǝ́-px^ja-jt'/
Kakasha(F) Tarash(M) she(C1)-him(C2)-call-(Aor)-Fin
'Kakasha called Tarash.'

In the examples above, Какáшьа /K'ak'áš^ja/ 'Kakasha' cross-references д- /d/ 'she', the pronominal prefix in the verbal complex, and Ҭарáшь /Taráš^j/ 'Tarash' cross-references -и- /jə/ 'him'. In this case, the nominal phrase and the pronominal prefix in the verbal complex have a one-to-one correspondence. In Abkhaz, when these types of correspondence relationships are clear, the word

159. 'Subject (S)' here is a universal grouping of A and S in Dixon's terminology.

order is rather free. The following is an example of a word order our informant found acceptable:

(502) Ҭара́шь Кака́шьа ди́ҧхьеит.
/Tarášʲ K’ak’ášʲa d-jə́-pxʲa-jt’/

(503) Ҭара́шь ди́ҧхьеит Кака́шьа.
/Tarášʲ d-jə́-pxʲa-jt’ K’ak’ášʲa/

(504) Кака́шьа ди́ҧхьеит Ҭара́шь.
/K’ak’ášʲa d-jə́-pxʲa-jt’ Tarášʲ/

In contrast, example (505) below shows that both nouns, ‘Pakhwala’ and ‘Tarash’, belong to the same third-person, singular, masculine class:

(505) Пахуа́ла Ҭара́шь ди́суеит.
/P’axwála Tarášʲ d-jə́-s-wa-jt’/
Paxwala(M) Tarash(M) he(C1)-him(C2)-hit-Dyn-Fin
‘Pakhwala is hitting Tarash’

In this case, the nouns cross-referencing д- /d/ ‘he’ in Column I of the verbal complex and the и- /jə/ ‘him’ in Column II are *Pakhwala* and *Tarash*, respectively. According to our informant, (505) cannot be interpreted as ‘Tarash is hitting Pakhwala’. From this, we can see that in cases where either of the nominal phrases can be cross-referenced by a pronominal prefix, the position order of the nominal phrases (in other words, the word order) determines the meaning of the sentence.

5.3.2.2. Examples of (i)–(b):

(506) Атцәцакәа ашә(ы)ҟәкәа́ ирыі́кәгылоуп.
/á-c’ʷca-kʷa a-šʷəq’ʷ-kʷá jə-rə́-kʷ-gəla-wp’/
the-glass-Pl the-book-Pl they(C1)-them(C2)-Prev(on)-stand-Stat.Pres.Fin
‘The glasses are standing on the books.’

In the example above, it is clear that а-тцәцакәа /á-c’ʷca-kʷa/ ‘the glasses’ cross-references the pronominal prefix и- /jə/ in the verbal complex, and that а-шә(ы)ҟәкәа /a-šʷəq’ʷ-kʷa/ ‘the books’ cross-references ры- /rə/. The reason is that the presence of verb-initial prefix и- /jə/ indicates that it does not cross-reference the word immediately preceding it (see §3.1.1). Also, when the circumstantial word is singular and the Column II pronominal prefix in the verbal complex is zero, the relationship between the subject and the circumstantial word is clear.[160] In the example below, similar

160. Even if a circumstantial word does not cross-reference a prefix in the verbal complex, the relationship between the subject and the circumstantial word is clear. Cf. the following examples with a postposition after the circumstantial word (1) and without a postposition after it (2):

(1) Ашәҟәы́ асто́л аҿы́ и́ҟоуп.
/a-šʷq’ʷə́ a-st’ól a-č’ə́ jə́-q’a-wp’/
the-book the-desk its-in it(C1)-be-Stat.Pres.Fin
‘The book is in the desk’.

(2) Аҧсуаа Аҧсны́ инхо́ит.
/ápswaa apsnə́ jə-n-xa-wá-jt’/
Abkhazians Abkhazia they(C1)-Prev-live-Dyn-Fin
‘Abkhazians live in Abkhazia’.

to (506) above, the presence of the Column I pronominal prefix и- /jə/ in the verbal complex shows that the word immediately preceding it does not cross-reference this prefix:

(507) Атцəца ашə(ы)ҟəы́ и́кəгылоуп.
/á-c'ʷca a-šʷəq'ʷə́ jə́-ø-kʷ-gəla-wp'/
the-glass the-book it(C1)-[it(C2)-]Prev(on)-stand-Stat.Pres.Fin
'The glass is standing on the book.'

5.3.2.3. Examples of (ii).

(508) Кака́шьа Ҭара́шь дылшьи́т. (SOV) (For 'S' see fn. 159)
/K'ak'áʃʲa Taráʃʲ də-l-ʃʲə́-jt'/
Kakasha(F) Tarash(M) him(C1)-she(C3)-kill-(Aor)-Fin
Kakasha killed Tarash.'

In the example above, the nominal phrase and the pronominal prefix in the verbal complex cross-reference each other in a one-to-one relationship, and their relationship is clear. In cases like this, the word order is rather free, and according to our informant, the word order below is possible:

(509) Ҭара́шь Кака́шьа дылшьи́т. (OSV)
/Taráʃʲ K'ak'áʃʲa də-l-ʃʲə́-jt'/

(510) Кака́шьа дылшьи́т Ҭара́шь. (SVO)
/K'ak'áʃʲa də-l-ʃʲə́-jt' Taráʃʲ/

(511) Ҭара́шь дылшьи́т Кака́шьа. (OVS)
/Taráʃʲ də-l-ʃʲə́-jt' K'ak'áʃʲa/

In contrast, when the subject and direct object belong to the third-person, singular, masculine class, the freedom of the word order above is restricted. According to our informant, the word order in (512) below only means 'Pakhwala killed Tarash.'

(512) Пахуа́ла Ҭара́шь дишьи́т.
/P'axwála Taráʃʲ də-j-ʃʲə́-jt'/
Pakhwala(M) Tarash(M) him(C1)-he(C3)-kill-(Aor)-Fin
'Pakhwala killed Tarash.'

Here, if the word order between Пахуа́ла /P'axwála/ and Ҭара́шь /Taráʃʲ/ is reversed, it means 'Tarash killed Pakhwala':

(513) Ҭара́шь Пахуа́ла дишьи́т.
/Taráʃʲ P'axwála də-j-ʃʲə́-jt'/

Furthermore, according to our informant, if the word order is arranged like (514) below, its meaning becomes ambiguous:

(514) Пахуа́ла дишьи́т Ҭара́шь.
/P'axwála də-j-ʃʲə́-jt' Taráʃʲ/
'Pakhwala killed Tarash.' *or* 'Tarash killed Pakhwala.'

On the other hand, when the subject and object are nominal phrases belonging to the third-person non-human class, there is no ambiguity if the nominal phrase is placed directly before the Column I pronominal prefix in the verbal complex. For example, the following four examples mean 'the wolves ate his pigs', but none of these sentences have an ambiguous cross-reference relationship between the nominal phrase and the verbal pronominal prefix:

(515) Абгақәа иҳәақәа́ рфе́ит.
/á-bga-kʷa jə-ħʷa-kʷá ϕ-r-fá-jt' (< jə-r-fá-jt')/
the wolf-Pl his-pig-Pl them(= his pigs, C1)-they(= the wolf, C3)-eat-(Aor)-Fin

(516) Иҳәақәа́ рфе́ит а́бгақәа.
/jə-ħʷa-kʷá ϕ-r-fá-jt' á-bga-kʷa/
his-pig-Pl them(= his pigs, C1)-they(= the wolf, C3)-eat-(Aor)-Fin the wolf-Pl

(517) Иҳәақәа́ а́бгақәа ирфе́ит.
/jə-ħʷa-kʷá á-bga-kʷa jə-r-fá-jt'/
his-pig-Pl the wolf-Pl them(= his pigs, C1)-they(= the wolf, C3)-eat-(Aor)-Fin

(518) Абгақәа ирфе́ит иҳәақәа́.
/á-bga-kʷa jə-r-fá-jt' jə-ħʷa-kʷá/
the wolf-Pl them(= his pigs, C1)-they(= the wolf, C3)-eat-(Aor)-Fin his-pig-Pl

What determines the subject and object relationship in the four sentences above is the presence or absence of the Column I pronominal prefix и- /jə/ in the verbal complex: in other words, when the и- /jə/ is absent, the immediately preceding nominal phrase is the object, and when the и- /jə/ is present, the nominal phrase immediately preceding it is not the object.[161]

5.3.3. When the pronominal prefixes in the verbal complex cross-reference three constituents, the following sentences can be conceived:

(iii) Sentences with a subject, indirect object and direct object.

(iv) Sentences with a subject, direct object and circumstantial word.

We shall examine these cases.

5.3.3.1. Examples of (iii):

(519) Кака́шьа Ҭара́шь аҵәа́ и́лҭеит.
/K'ak'ášʲa Tarášʲ a-c'ʷá ϕ-jə́-l-ta-jt'/
Kakasha(F) Tarash(M) the-apple it(C1)-him(C2)-she(C3)-give-(Aor)-Fin
'Kakasha gave the/an apple to Tarash.'

In the examples above, Кака́шьа /K'ak'ášʲa/ 'Kakasha' cross-references the Column III pronominal prefix л- /l/, Ҭара́шь /Tarášʲ/ 'Tarash' cross-references the Column II pronominal prefix и- /jə/, and аҵәа /a-c'ʷá/ 'the apple' cross-references the Column I zero prefix. In this way, when there is a one-to-

161. In the case of an intransitive verb, the opposite occurs. Namely, when the Column I pronominal prefix и- /jə/ is present, the nominal phrase immediately preceding it is the indirect object, and when the и- /jə/ is absent, the immediately preceding nominal phrase is the subject. For example:
(аҳәажә) ацә иахьӡо иалагеит. (Abkhaz text)
/(a-ħʷá-žʷ) á-cʷ j-a-xʲ-ʒa-wá j-á-la-ga-jt'/
the-pig-bad the-bull it(bad pig, C1)-it(bull, C2)-Prev-catch up with-Abs it-it-Prev-begin-(Aor)-Fin
'The bad pig started to catch up with the bull'.

one cross-reference relationship between the noun phrases and the pronominal prefixes in the verbal complex, the word order is permitted a certain degree of freedom. The following is an example accepted by our informant:

(520) Ҭара́шь атцәа́ и́лҭеит Кака́шьа.
/Tarášʲ a-c'ʷá ø-jə́-l-ta-jt' K'ak'ášʲa/
Tarash(M) the-apple [it(C1)-]hem(C2)-she(C3)-give-(Aor)-Fin Kakasha(F)
'Kakasha gave the/an apple to Tarash.'

However, when the subject and indirect object belong to the same third-person, a certain degree of ambiguity arises due to the word order. (521) below follows the S-IO-DO-V word order, and in this case, there is no ambiguity in the meaning of the sentence:

(521) Пахуа́ла Ҭара́шь атцәа́ и́иҭеит.
/P'axwála Tarášʲ a-c'ʷá ø-jə́-j-ta-jt'/
Pakhwala(M) Tarash(M) the-apple [it(C1)-]him(C2)-he(C3)-give-(Aor)-Fin
'Pakhwala gave the/an apple to Tarash.'
*'Tarash gave the/an apple to Pakhwala.'

However, our informant says that there is ambiguity in the meaning of the sentence with the following word order:

(522) Пахуа́ла атцәа́ и́иҭеит Ҭара́шь.
/P'axwála a-c'ʷá ø-jə́-j-ta-jt' Tarášʲ/
Pakhwala(M) the-apple [it(C1)-]him(C2)-he(C3)-give-(aor)-Fin Tarash(M)
'Pakhwala gave the/an apple to Tarash.' *or* 'Tarash gave the/an apple to Pakhwala.'

(523) Атцәа́ и́иҭеит Пахуа́ла Ҭара́шь.
/a-c'ʷá ø-jə́-j-ta-jt' P'axwála Tarášʲ /
the-apple [it(C1)-]him(C2)-he(C3)-give-(aor)-Fin Pakhwala(M) Tarash(M)
'Pakhwala gave the/an apple to Tarash.' *or* 'Tarash gave the/an apple to Pakhwala.'

Examples of the causative form taking the same structure as (iii):

(524) Сара́ атцаҩцәа́ а́ҧсуа бызшәа́ дсырҵо́ит.
/sará a-c'ajʷə-cʷá ápswa bəzšʷá ø-d-sə-r-c'a-wá-jt'/
I the-pupil-Pl Abkhaz language [it(C1)-]them(C2)-I(C3)-Caus-study-Dyn-Fin
'I am teaching the pupils the Abkhaz language.'

(525) Са́н [акы́ҭа шко́л аҿы́ аўс луе́ит,] а́ҧсуа абызшәе́и алитерату́реи атцаҩцәа́ идлырҵо́ит. (AFL)
/s-án [a-kə́ta šk'ól a-č'ə́ a-wə́s ø-l-w-wá-jt'] ápswa a-bəzšʷá-j
my-mother the-village school its-in the-work [it(C1)-]she(C3)-do-Dyn-Fin Abkhaz the-language-and
a-ləjt'erat'ə́wra-j a-c'ajʷ-cʷá jə-d-lə-r-c'a-wá-jt'/
the-literature-and the-pupil-Pl them(C1)-them(C2)-she(C3)-Caus-study-Dyn-Fin
'My mother [works at the village school, and she] teaches the pupils the Abkhaz language and literature.'

The Column I prefix in verb in the sentences above cross-reference а́ҧсуа бызшәа́ /ápswa bəzšʷá/ 'the Abkhaz language' immediately preceding the prefix in (524) and a nominal phrase not immediately preceeding it, а́ҧсуа абызшәе́и алитерату́реи /ápswa a-bəzšʷá-j a-lit'erat'úra-j/ 'the

Abkhaz language and literature' in (525). The word orders are S-IO-DO-V and S-DO-IO-V respectively.

5.3.3.2. Examples of (iv):

(526) Алак̧ə́а а́ашьарак̧əа аҭы́ҩрак̧əа ирҭа́рцалеит.

/a-la-kʷá [á-]aašʲara-kʷa a-tə́jʷra-kʷa jə-r-tá-r-ca-la-jt'/

the-dog-Pl the-badger-Pl the-nest-Pl them(C1)-them(C2)-Prev-they(C3)-drive-Introvert-(Aor)-Fin

'The dogs drove the badgers into the holes.'

The pronominal prefixes in the verbal complex in the sentence above are all in the third-person plural. The Column I pronominal prefix in this verbal complex, и- /jə/, cross-references а́ашьарак̧əа /[á-]aašʲarakʷa/ 'the badgers', the Column II pronominal prefix р- /r/ cross-references аҭы́ҩрак̧əа /atə́jʷrakʷa/ 'the nests', and the Column III pronominal prefix р- /r/ cross-references а-лак̧əа /alakʷá/ 'the dogs'. The presence of the pronominal prefix и- /jə/ makes it evident that the Column I pronominal prefix does not cross-reference аҭы́ҩрак̧əа /atə́jʷrakʷa/ 'the nests' immediately preceding it, but here it is the word order which determines which nominal phrases the Column III and Column I pronominal prefixes cross-reference. Namely, it is the constituent which appears at the beginning of the three nominal phrases which cross-references the Column III pronominal prefix which expresses the subject of the transitive verb (more precisely, it is positioned first in the nominal phrase which can become an agent). Consequently, here, а-лак̧ə́а /alakʷá/ 'the dogs' becomes the subject. As we can see in example (521) above, the change in the word order for а-лак̧ə́а /alakʷá/ 'the dogs'and а́ашьарак̧əа /[á-]aašʲarakʷa/ 'the badgers' makes it mean 'The badgers drove the dogs into the holes'.

In summary, the basic word order in Abkhaz can be regarded in the following way:

a) S-IO-V in intransitive sentences

b) S-DO-V in transitive sentences.

c) S-IO-DO-V / S-DO-ID-V in transitive sentences.

(For 'S' see fn. 159.)

5.4. Complex Sentences: Clauses

Complex sentences consist of main clauses and subordinate clauses. In Indo-European languages, the main clause and subordinate clause are joined by conjugations and relatives, but these do not exist in Abkhaz. In Abkhaz, affixes in the verbal complex fulfill these functions. For example, for temporal subordinate clauses affixes meaning 'when', 'while', 'as soon as', 'until', 'since', etc. are inserted into the verbal complex. Similarly, for subordinate clauses expressing 'condition', 'reason', 'relatives', and 'indirect statement' the corresponding prefixes are inserted into the verbal complex. The formation of subordinate clauses by incorporating conjunctive affixes or relative affixes into this type of verbal complex was already discussed in §4.7.7.

Generally, subordinate clauses precede main clauses. This is related to the basic constituent order in Abkhaz being subject-object-verb (SOV). Also, relative clauses normally precede the word it modifies, but in Abkhaz texts this also is not necessarily the case: it is not unusual for the word it modifies to be placed before the relative clause.

In this chapter, we will describe the following subordinate clauses:

i. Temporal Clauses: §5.4.1.
ii. Conditional Clauses: §5.4.2.
iii. Causal Clauses: §5.4.3.
iv. Concessive Clauses: §5.4.4.
v. Relative Clauses: §5.4.5.
vi. Indirect Statements: §5.4.6.
vii. Purposive Clauses: §5.4.7.

5.4.1. Temporal Clauses

The following are conjunctive affixes which indicate time: -ан- 'when', -ахьы́нӡа- 'while', -натцы 'while, as long as', -ш(ы)—цәҟьа 'as soon as', -ан—цәҟьа 'as soon as', -аанӡа 'before, until', -ижьтеи 'since; after', -иште 'since', -ц(ы)ҧхьаӡа 'as soon as ... (always); every time', -зар аахы́с 'since', -ма 'as soon as', -зар нахы́с 'since', -зар инаркны́ 'since'.

5.4.1.1. Prefix -ан- 'when'

This affix is placed immediately after the Column I pronominal prefix of the non-finite verbal form in the subordinate clause. The simultaneity or succession of the actions in the main clause and subordinate clause is indicated by the relationship of the tense in the main clause and the tense in the subordinate clause. When the main clause and subordinate clause are in the imperfective aspect (i.e. present and imperfect, see §3.1.7), it indicates the simultaneity of the action (examples are given in (527), (528), (529) and (530)). On the other hand, when the subordinate clause and main clause are aorist, it indicates that the action occurs in succession (examples are given in (531), (532) and (533a)):

(527) Ашәҟәы́ аны́сыҩуа сан дуанҭо́ит.
/a-šʷq'ʷə́ ϕ-anə́-sə-jʷ-wa s-an d-wanta-wá-jt'/
the-letter [it(C1)-]when-I-write-Dyn.NF my-mother she(C1)-iron-Dyn-Pres.Fin
'When I am writing a letter, my mother is ironing.'

(528) Сара́ сҽыаны́скәабо сан дуанҭо́ит.
/sará s-čə-anə́-s-k'ʷaba-wa s-an d-wanta-wá-jt'/
I my(Poss)-Self-when-I(C3)-bethe-Dyn.NF my-mother she(C1)-iron-Dyn-Pres.Fin
'When I am bathing, my mother is ironing.'
(Note that the prefix аны- /anə/ is placed after the reflexive marker.)

(529) Ашәҟәы́ сана́ҧхьоз сан дуанҭо́н.
/a-šʷq'ʷə́ s-an-á-pxʲa-wa-z s-an d-wanta-wá-n/
the-book I(C1)-when-it(C2)-read-Dyn-Impf.NF my-mother she(C1)-iron-Dyn-Impf.Fin
'When I was reading a book, my mother was ironing.'

(530) Ка́ма аҩны́ даны́ҟаз лан а́фатәқәа лҭиуа́н аҵьырмы́кь аҿы́.
/k'ama a-jʷnə́ d-anə́-q'a-z l-an á-fat'ʷ-kʷa
name (F) the-home she(C1)-when-be-Stat.Past.NF her-mother the-food-Pl
ϕ-l-təj-wá-n a-ǯʲərmə́k'ʲ a-č'ə́/
[them(C1)-]she(C3)-sell-Dyn-Impf.Fin the-market its-at

'When Kama was at home, her mother was selling food at the market.'

(531) Мурáҭ данчмазаҩхá ахаҟьы́м даáит.
/məwrát d-an-čʲmazajʷ-xá a-ħakʲə́m d-aá-jt'/
name (M) he-when-ill-become.(Aor.NF) the-doctor he(C1)-come-(Aor)-Fin
'When Murat fell ill, a doctor came.'

(532) Аҩны́ӄа санхынҳәы́ аҟәоурá иáлагеит.
/ajʷnə́q'a s-an-xən-ħʷə́ a-kʷawrá j-á-la-ga-jt'/
home I(C1)-when-Prev-return.(Aor.NF) the-rain it(C1)-it(C2)-Prev-begin-(Aor)-Fin
'When I had returned home, it began to rain.'

(533a) Аҩны́ӄа санхынҳәы́ сҩы́за дысԥы́леит.
/ajʷnə́q'a s-an-xən-ħʷə́ s-jʷə́za də-s-pə́-la-jt'/
home I(C1)-when-Prev-return.(Aor.NF) my-friend he(C1)-me(C2)-Prev-meet-(Aor)-Fin
'When I had returned home, I met my friend.'

When the subordinate clause is imperfect, and the main clause is aorist, it differs from (533a) above and means 'On my way home I met him':

(533b) Аҩны́ӄа санхынҳәуáз сҩы́за сы́ӄәшәеит.
/ajʷnə́q'a s-an-xən-ħʷ-wá-z s-jʷə́za s-jə́-kʷ-šʷa-jt'/
home I-when-Prev-return-Dyn-Impf.NF my-friend I(C1)-him(C2)-Prev-meet-(Aor)-Fin
'When I was returning home, I met my friend.'

In cases where the subordinate clause is aorist and the main clause is pluperfect, when the action in the subordinate clause occured, the action in the main clause had already been completed:

(534) Сарá аҩны́ӄа санхынҳәы́ сабду́ дыԥсхьáн.
/sará ajʷnə́q'a s-an-xən-ħʷə́ s-abnə́w də-ps-xʲá-n/
I home I(C1)-when-Prev-return.(Aor.NF) my-grandfather he(C1)-die-Plupf-Fin
'When I returned home, my grandfather had already died.'

5.4.1.2. In order to express 'after', the postposition á-шьҭахь /á-šʲtaxʲ/ is frequently placed after the subordinate clause using the prefix -ан- /an/ 'when'. (535) below is an example with a postposition attached to the aorist form, and (536) is an example with a postposition attached to the present form:

(535) Даны́иба áшьҭахь дыцéит.
/d-anə́-j-ba á-šʲtaxʲ də-cá-jt'/
him/her(C1)-when-he(C3)-see.(Aor.NF) its-after he(C1)-go-(Aor)-Fin
'After he saw him/her, he left.'

(536) Шәангы́ло áшьҭахь и́ӄашәҵозеи? (AFL)
/šʷ-an-gə́la-wa á-šʲtaxʲ jə́-q'a-šʷ-c'a-wa-zaj/
you.Pl(C1)-when-stand-Dyn.NF its-after Rel(C1)-Prev-you.Pl(C3)-do-Dyn-Qu
'After you get up, what do you do?'

5.4.1.3. Prefix -ахьы́нӡа- 'while'

This prefix is placed immediately after the pronominal prefix in Column I of the non-finite form, and is used in stative verbs and dynamic verbs of non-motion. For example:

(537) Аҩны́ сахьы́нӡаҟо́у (/сы́ҟанатцы) ашәҟәы́ са́ԥхьоит.
/a-jʷnə́ s-axʲə́nʒa-q'á-w (/sə́-q'a-nac'ə) a-šʷq'ʷə́ s-á-pxʲa-wa-jt'/
the-house I(C1)-while-be-Stat.Pres.NF the-book I(C1)-it(C2)-read-Dyn-Fin
'While I am at home, I read.'

(538) Лара́ дахьы́нӡацәаз (/ды́цәанатцы) ажурна́л са́ԥхьон.
/lará d-axʲə́nʒa-cʷa-z (/də́-cʷa-nac'ə) a-žəwrnál s-á-pxʲa-wa-n/
she she(C1)-while-sleep-Stat.Past.N.F the-magazine I(C1)-it(C2)-read-Dyn-Impf.Fin
'While she was sleeping, I was reading a magazine.'

All of the examples above can be expressed by the suffix -натцы /nac'ə/.

5.4.1.4. Suffix -натцы 'while'

This suffix is attached to the present stem of dynamic verbs in the non-finite form or the root of stative verbs regardless of the tense of the main clause. (537) and (538) in §5.4.1.3 above, and (539) below are examples with this suffix attached to stative verbs. Examples of this suffix attached to dynamic verbs are given in (540) and (541):

(539) Адуне́и ы́ҟанатц шәы́ҟазааит!
/a-dəwnáj ə́-q'a-nac' šʷə́-q'a-zaajt'/
the-world [it(C1)-]be-as long as you.Pl-be-Subj
'Let it be that you all exist as long as the world exists!'

(540) Акрысфонатцы лара́ ашәҟәы́ да́ԥхьон.
/ak'rə-s-fa-wa-nac'ə́ lará a-šʷq'ʷə́ d-á-pxʲa-wa-n/
Dummy-I(C3)-eat-Dyn-while she the-book sh(C1)-it(C2)-read-Dyn-Impf
'While I was eating, she was reading a book.'

(541) Ашәҟәы́ зыҩуанатцы́ лара́ ажурна́л да́ԥхьон.
/a-šʷq'ʷə́ ø-zə-jʷ-wa-nac'ə́ lará a-žəwrnál d-á-pxʲa-wa-n/
the-letter [it(C1)-]I(C3)-write-Dyn-while she the-magazine she(C1)-it(C2)-read-Dyn-Impf
'While I was writing the letter, she was reading a magazine.'

5.4.1.5. Affix -ш(ы)—тцәҟьа, -ан(ы)—тцәҟьа 'as soon as'

Prefix -ш(ы)-/-ан(ы)- /š(ə)/an(ə)/ is placed immediately after the Column I pronominal prefix, and the intensifying suffix -тцәҟьа- /c'ʷq'ʲa/ 'just' is placed after the root or at the end of the word. If the sentence indicates a past event, the stem of the subordinate clause with the prefix -ш(ы)- uses the past indefinite stem, and the stem of the subordinate clause with the prefix -ан- uses the aorist stem. If the sentence indicates a future event, the stem of the subordinate clause uses the aorist stem, and the future suffix -лакь /lak'ʲ/ is attached after it (-лакь is possible immediately after the verb stem or after 'the verb stem + -тцәҟьа-'). For example:

(542) Сшы́лбазтцәҟьа дце́ит.
/s-šə́-l-ba-z-c'ʷq'ʲa d-cá-jt'/
me(C1)-how-she(C3)-see-Past Ind.NF-just she(C1)-go-(Aor)-Fin
'As soon as she saw me, she went.'

(543) Бара́ акы́ҭа ахь бышне́илакьцәḱьа, ашәḱәы́ сызҩы́.
/bará a-kə́ta [a-]axʲ bə-š-n-áj-lak'ʲ-c'ʷq'ʲa
you.F the-village its-to you.F(C1)-how-Prev-go there.(Aor.NF)-LA-just
a-šʷq'ʷə́ ø-sə́-z-jʷə́/
the-letter [it(C1)-]me(C2)-OV(for)-write.Imp
'As soon as you arrive at the village, write a letter to me!'

(544) Ашҭа данааҭа́лацәкьа дызды́рит. (ARD)
/a-šta d-an-aa-tá-la-c'ʷq'ʲa də-z-də́rə-jt'/
the-yard he/she(C1)-when-Par-Prev-go into(Aor.NF)-just him/her(C1)-I(C3)-know-(Aor)-Fin
'As soon as he/she came into the yard, I recognized him/her.'

5.4.1.6. Suffix -аанӡа 'until'

This suffix is attached to the aorist stem of dynamic verbs. The sentence tense is determined by the tense of the main clause. Examples:

(545) Сара́ сиа́анӡа сабду́ дыпсхьа́н.
/sará s-j-áanʒa s-abdə́w də-ps-xʲá-n/
I I(C1)-be born(Aor.NF)-until my-grandfather he(C1)-die-Plupf-Fin
'My grandfather had already died before I was born.'

(546) Ааԥын ааиа́анӡа сара́ акы́ҭаҿы саанхо́ит.
/áapən ø-áa-j-áanʒa sará a-kə́ta-č'ə s-aa-n-xa-wá-jt'/
spring [it(C1)-]Prev-come(Aor.NF)-until I the-village-in I(C1)-Par-Prev-live-Dyn-Fin
'I will stay in the village until spring comes.'

(547) Аибашьра ḱала́анӡа, Та́мшь да́араӡа ауа́а рацәаҩны́ инхо́н. (AFL)
/[á-]ajbašʲra ø-q'a-lá-[a]anʒa támšʲ dáaraʒa awáa racʷajʷnə́ jə-n-xa-wá-n/
the-war [it(C1)-]Prev-begin-until place-name very people many they(C1)-Prev-live-Dyn-Impf.Fin
'Very many people lived in Tamsh until the war began.'

(548) Ари́ а́хәшә ужәа́анӡа еилу́рхроуп.
/arə́j á-xʷšʷ ø-wə-žʷ-áanʒa j-ajl-wé-rx-r-a-wp'/
this the-medicine [it(C1)-]you(C3)-drink(Aor.NF)-until it(C1)-Prev-you(C3)-shake-must-be-Stat.Pres.Fin
'Before using this medicine, it is necessary to shake it.'

5.4.1.7. Suffix -ижьҭеи 'since'

This suffix is attached to the non-finite stem. (549), (550) and (551) below are examples of this suffix attached to the aorist stem, and (552) is an example of it attached to the present non-finite stem of the stative verb:

(549) Ка́ма ашко́л да́лгеижьҭеи кы́р аацуе́ит.
/k'áma a-šk'ól d-á-l-ga-jəžʲtaj k'ə́r ø-aa-c'-wá-jt'/
name.F the-school she(C1)-it(C2)-Prev-finish.(Aor.NF)-since a lot [it(C1)-]Prev-pass-Dyn-Pres.Fin
'A lot of time has passed since Kama finished school.'

(550) Иара́ да́аиижьҭеи дсымба́шт. (RAD)
/jará d-áa-j-jəžʲtaj d-sə-m-bá-ct'/

he he(C1)-Prev-come.(Aor.NF)-since him(C1)-I(C3)-Neg-see-Perf.Fin
'I have not seen him since returning.'

(551) Жәáмш ҵи́т дцéижьҭеи.
/žʷá-mš ø-c'ə́-jt' d-cá-jəžʲtaj/
10-day [they-]pass-(Aor)-Fin he/she-go(Aor.NF)-since
'Ten days have passed since he/she left.'

(552) Арá ды́ҟоижьҭеи áԥхьара даҿы́уп. (ACST)
/ará də́-q'a-w-jəžʲtaj á-pxʲara d-a-č'ə́-wp'/
here he/she(C1)-be(Pres.NF)-since the-reading he/she(C1)-it(C2)-be engaged in-Stat.Pres.Fin
'Since he/she has been here, he/she has been busy reading.'

5.4.1.8. Suffixes -ишҭе, -зар аахы́с, нахы́с 'since'

The suffix -ишҭе attaches to the non-finite stem. An example of this suffix attached to the present stem is given in (553):

(553) Кáма Џьгьáрда дынхóишҭе ҩы́шықәса ҵуéит.
/k'áma ǯʲgʲársa də-n-xa-wá-jəšte jʷə́-šəkʷsa ø-c'-wá-jt'/
name.F place-name she(C1)-Prev-live-Dyn(Pres.NF)-since two-year [it(C1)]-pass-Dyn-Pres.Fin
'Kama has been living in Dzhgjarda for two years.'

The suffixes -зар аахы́с, нахы́с and -инаркны 'since' also attach to the non-finite stem in the appropriate tense in the same way as the example above:

(554) Кáма Џьгьáрда дынхóзар аахы́с ҩы́шықәса ҵуéит.
/k'áma ǯʲgʲársa də-n-xa-wá-zar aaxə́s jʷə́-šəkʷsa ø-c'-wá-jt'/
name.F place-name she-Prev-live-Dyn-that clause since two-year [it(C1)]-pass-Dyn-Pres.Fin
'Kama has been living in Dzhgjarda for two years.'

(555) Дхәычҷы́з нахы́с дыхьчáн. (ACST)
/d-xʷəč'ʲə́-z naxə́s də-xʲčʲá-n/
he/she(C1)-child-Stat.Past.NF since he/she(C1)-shepherd/shepherdess-Stat.Past.Fin
'From childhood he/she was a shepherd/shepherdess.'

5.4.1.9. Suffix -ц(ы)ԥхьаӡа 'as soon as ... (always), every time'

This suffix attaches to the verb root. The tense of the sentence depends on the tense of the main clause. In the following examples, (556) is in the present tense, and (557) is in the imperfect tense:

(556) Аҩны́ҟа схынҳәы́цԥхьаӡа, еснáгь áхәшә сы́дыскылоит.
/ajʷnə́q'a s-xən-ħʷə́-cpxʲaʒa esnágʲ á-xʷšʷ ø-sə́-də-s-k'əla-wa-jt'/
home I(C1)-Prev-return-as soon as always the-medicine [it(C1)-]my(Poss)-SV-I(C3)-take-Dyn-Pres.Fin
'As soon as I return home, I always take medicine.'

(557) Ашкóлынтә аҩны́ҟа сцáцыԥхьаӡа áмпыл сáсуан /сáслон.
/a-šk'ólə-nt'ʷ ajʷnə́q'a s-cá-cəpxʲaʒa á-mp'əl
the-school-from home I(C1)-go.Aor.NF-every time the-ball
s-á-s-(la-)wa-n/
I(C1)-it(C2)-hit-(Iterative-)Dyn-Impf.Fin

'Whenever I got home from school, I used to play ball.'

5.4.2. Conditional Clauses

Conditional clauses are produced by adding the suffixes -р /r/, -зар /zar/, -ӡҭгьы /ztgʲə/ to the protasis verb stem. -р is added to the non-finite aorist stem, whereas -зар and -ӡҭгьы are added to the non-finite present stem of dynamic verbs or the root of stative verbs. In our description below, they will be divided into sentences indicating simple conditional clauses and sentences indicating contrary-to-fact conditional clauses.

5.4.2.1. Simple Conditions

In order to express simple future conditional sentences, the suffixes -р /r/ and -зар /zar/ are used for the protasis. The tense of the apodosis is either the present tense or the Future I tense (for the future meaning of the present tense, see §3.1.7.2.3):

(558) Ауаҩы́ ари́ ашәҟәы́ да́пҳьар, акы́р еилы́икаауеит.
/a-wajʷə́ arə́j a-šʷq'ʷə́ d-á-pxʲa-r a-k'ə́r ϕ-ajlə́-j-k'aa-wa-jt'/
the-person this the-book he(C1)-it(C2)-read(Aor.NF)-if something [it(C1)-]Prev-he(C3)-learn-Dyn-Fin
'If a person reads this book, he will learn something.'

(559) Ақалақь ахь дыца́р, а́имаақәа а́аихәап.
/á-kalakʲ [a-]axʲ də-cá-r [a-]ájmaa-kʷa ϕ-áa-j-xʷa-p'/
the-town [its-]to he(C1)-go.(Aor.NF)-if the-shoe-Pl [it(C1-]Prev-he(C3)-buy-Fut.I
'If he goes to town, he will buy some shoes.'

(560) Иҟало́зар исы́шәҭ ашәҟәы́!
/jə-q'a-la-wá-zar jə-sə́-šʷ-t a-šʷq'ʷə́/
it(C1)-Prev-be possible-Dyn.NF-if it(C1)-me(C2)-you.Pl(C3)-give.Imp the-book
'If it is possible, please give me the book!'

(561) Аҽы́ урхәма́руазар, ирхәма́р. (Abkhaz text)
/a-čə́ ϕ-wə-r-xʷmár-wa-zar jə-r-xʷmár/
the-horse [it(C1)-]you.M(C3)-Caus-play-Dyn.NF-if it(C1)-Caus-play.Imp
'If you-M want to ride a horse, please do so.'

Sentences using -ӡҭгьы /ztgʲə/ indicate past conditionals:

(562) Аматәақәа лыӡәӡәоӡҭгьы, хы́мҧада шәахьа́н. (ACST)
/á-matʷa-kʷa ϕ-lə-ʒʷʒʷ-wa-ztgʲə xə́mpada šʷaxʲá-n/
the-cloth-Pl [them(C1)-]she(C3)-wash-Dyn.NF-if surely Monday-Stat.Past.Fin
'If she was washing clothes, it was surely Monday.'

5.4.2.2. Contrary-to-Fact Conditions

In order to express contrary-to-fact conditional clauses, the protasis uses the suffix -р /r/, and for the apodosis, the imperfect or Conditional I tense is used:

(563) Уатцәы́ акәа́ а́мур, хаанеиҩе́ирын.
/wac'ʷə́ a-kʷá ϕ-á-m-wə-r ħ-aa-naj-jʷáj-rən/
tomorrow the-rain [it(C1-]Dummy-Neg-fall(Aor.NF)-if we(C1)-Par-Prev-take a walk-Cond.I.Fin

'If it were not to rain tomorrow, we could take a walk.'

(564) Уаха́ бца́р, уаҵәы́ Аҟәа бҟало́н.
/waxá b-ca-r wac'ʷə́ aq'ʷa b-q'a-la-wá-n/
this evening you.F(C1)-go(Aor.NF)-if tomorrow Sukhum you.F(C1)-Prev-be-Dyn-Impf.Fin
'If you-F went this evening, you-F would be at Sukhum tomorrow.'

(565) Уаҵәы́ амш бзи́ахар, а́қалақь а́хь сцары́н.
/wac'ʷə́ á-mš ø-bzə́ja-xa-r á-kalakʲ [a-]axʲ s-ca-rə́n/
tomorrow the-weather [it(C1)-]fine-become(Aor.NF)-if the-town [its-]to I(C1)-go-Cond.I.Fin
'If the weather cleared up tomorrow, I would go to the town.'

Sentences using -зҭгьы /ztgʲə/ (or -зар /zar/) express past contrary-to-fact conditional clauses (this corresponds to the past subjunctive in English). For the apodosis, the imperfect or Conditional I tense is used. Examples of these suffixes attached to a stative verb and dynamic verbs are given in (566) and (567)–(568) respectively:

(566) Иаҵы́ а́мш бзи́азҭгьы (*or* бзи́азар), а́қалақь а́хь сцо́н.
/jacə́ á-mš ø-bzə́ja-ztgʲə (*or* ø-bzə́ja-zar) á-kalakʲ [a-]axʲ s-ca-wá-n/
yesterday the-weather [it(C1)-]fine-if the-town [its-]to I(C1)-go-Dyn-Impf.Fin
'If the weather had been fine yesterday, I would have gone to town.'

(567) Ари́ сзымдыруазҭгьы (*or* сзымдыруазар), иаҵы́ ақы́ҭа ахь сцары́н.
/arə́j ø-s-zə-m-dər-wa-ztgʲə (*or* -zar) jacə́ a-kə́ta [a-]axʲ s-ca-rə́n/
this [it(C1)-]me(C2)-Pot-Neg-know-Dyn.NF-if yesterday the-village [its-]to I(C1)-go-Cond.I.Fin
'If I had not known this, I would have gone to the village yesterday.'

(568) Ари́ здыры́уазар, саауа́мызт. (RAD)
/arə́j ø-z-də́r-wa-zar s-aa-wá-mə-zt'/
this [it(C1)-]I(C3)-know-Dyn.NF-if I(C1)-come-Dyn-Neg-Impf.Fin
'If I had known this, I would not have come.'

5.4.3. Causal Clauses

Causal clauses are produced by inserting the conjunctional prefix -ахь- /axʲ/ into the non-finite form and placing the postposition а-ҟны́тә/а-ҟы́нтә /a-q'nə́t'ʷ/a-q'ə́nt'ʷ/ 'its-from' or а-зы́ /a-zə́/ 'its-for' after it:

(569) Акәа́ ахьауа́з аҟны́тә аҩны́ҟа ҳзы́мцеит.
/a-kʷá ø-axʲ-a-w-wá-z a-q'nə́t'ʷ ajʷnə́q'a ħ-zə́-m-ca-jt'/
the-rain [it(C1)-]that-Dummy-fall-Dyn-Impf.NF its-from home we(C1)-Pot-Neg-go-(Aor)-Fin
'We could not come home due to the rain.' (Lit. 'From that it was raining, we could not come here')

(570) Бара́ бахьца́з азы́ /аҟы́нтә сара́ ара́ саанхе́ит.
/bará b-axʲ-cá-z a-zə́/a-q'ə́nt'ʷ sará ará s-aan-xá-jt'/
you.F you.F(C1)-that-go-Past.Ind.NF its-for/its-from I here I(C1)-Prev-stay here-(Aor)-Fin
'Because you-F went, I stayed here.'

The meaning of sentence (570) above can also be expressed by the subordinate clause with 'finite form+ а-зы́/а-ҟны́тә':

(571) Бара́ бце́ит азы́ /аҟынтә сара́ ара́ саанхе́ит.

/bará b-cá-jt' a-zə́/a-q'ə́nt'ʷ sará ará s-aan-xá-jt'/
you.F you.F(C1)-go-(Aor)-Fin its-for/its-from I here I(C1)-Prev-stay here-(Aor)-Fin

5.4.4. Concessive Clauses

Concessive clauses can be produced by the following methods:

(i) By adding the manner-indicating prefix -ш(ы)- /š(ə)/ 'how' and the suffix -гьы /gʲə/ 'even' to the verbal non-finite form:

(572) Амра шыҧхогьы́ ихьҭо́уп. (ACST)
/á-mra ø-šə-pxa-wa-gʲə́ jə-xʲtá-wp'/
the-sun [it(C1)-]how-shine-Dyn.NF-even it(Dummy)-cold-Stat.Pres.Fin
'Although the sun is shining, it is cold.'

(ii) By using the subjunctive suffix -заит /zaajt'/:

(573) Аҳасабтә цәгьа́зааит, ахá сарá исҳаса́буеит.
/á-ħasabt'ʷ ø-cʷgʲá-zaajt' axá sará jə-s-ħasáb-wa-jt'/
the-problem [it(C1)-]difficult-even if but I it(C1)-I(C3)-solve-Dyn-Fin
'Even if the problem is difficult, I will solve it.'

(iii) With the aorist finite form + хәа /ħʷa/:[162]

(574) Зны́к иа́аурхеит хәа иарá иара́знак дыҧсзо́м. (Abkhaz text)
/znə́k' j-áa-wə-rxa-jt' ħʷa jará jaráznak' də-ps-ʒa-wá-m/
once it(C1)-Prev-you.M(C3)-whip-(Aor)-Fin SP it/he instantly he-die-Emph-Dyn-Neg
'Even if you-M hit it once, it/he won't die right away.'

(iv) With the compound suffix -зар-гьы /zar-gʲə/ (lit. 'if-even'):

(575) Уа́гхазаргьы уаа́ит.
/w-á-g-xa-zargʲə w-aá-jt'/
you.M(C1)-it(C2)-Prev-be late-even if you.M(C1)-come-(Aor)-Fin
'Although you-M were late, you-M came.'

(576) Амра ҧхо́заргьы хьҭо́уп.
/á-mra ø-pxa-wá-zargʲə xʲtá-wp'/[163]
the-sun [it(C1)-]shine-Dyn.NF-even if cold-Stat.Pres.Fin
'Although the sun is shining, it's cold.'

(v) With the compound suffix -ргьы /r-gʲə/ (lit. 'if-even'):

(577) Амра ҧха́ргьы хьҭахо́ит.
/á-mra ø-pxá-rgʲə xʲta-xa-wá-jt'/
the-sun [it(C1)-]shine.(Aor.NF)-even if cold-become-Dyn-Fin
'Although (even if) the sun shines, it will become cold.'

(578) Аҧха́ дба́ургьы ҧсыхәа́к бза́ауп. (Abkhaz text)

162. For Speech-Particle (SP) хәа, see §5.5.

163. Note that in xʲtá-wp' 'it is cold' there is no dummy prefix и- /jə/. Cf. fn. 106.

/a-pħá d-b-áw-rg^{j}ə psəx^{w}á-k’ ø-b-z-áa-wə-p’/
the-daughter her(C1)-you(C2)-receive.Aor.NF-even if aid-one [it(C1)-]you(C2)-for-we(C3)-do-Fut.I.Fin
‘Even if you-F have a girl, we shall help you-F.’

The compound suffix -(за)ргьы /(za)rg^{j}ə/ is used with the adverbs егьа́ /ag^{j}á/, иага́ /jagá/, иагьа́ /jag^{j}á/ and expresses concession:

(579) Аха́ иагьа́ ирдыды́ргьы, иагьа́ ирмацәы́сыргьы, уара́ аҳаҳа́и акы́ уацәы́мшәан. (Abkhaz text)
/axá jag^{j}á jə-rdədə́-rg^{j}ə jag^{j}á jə-rmac^{w}ə́sə-rg^{j}ə
but even it-he-make thunder-even if even it-he-make lightning-even if
wará aħaħáj ak’ə́ w-a-c^{w}ə́-m-š^{w}a-n/
you.M hey something you.M(C1)-it(C2)-Prev-Neg-fear-Proh
‘But, even if he (i.e. the ogre) makes thunder, and even if he makes lightning, you-M have nothing to fear.’

5.4.5. Relative Clauses

5.4.5.1. Relative-Adjective Clauses

In Abkhaz, prefixes inserted in the verbal complex perform the function of relatives, and these shall be called relative (abbreviated as ‘Rel’ below) prefixes. There are two types of relative prefixes: и- /jə/ and з(ы)- /z(ə)/. The prefix и- is placed in the position of the Column I pronominal prefix, and performs the relative functions of the subject of an intransitive verb and the direct object of a transitive verb. On the other hand, the prefix з(ы)- is placed in the position of the pronominal prefixes in Columns II and III, and it performs the relative functions of the indirect object of both intransitive and transitive verbs, and the subject of a transitive verb, respectively. This can be schematized in the following way:

Intransitive:	C1-(C2)-R	C1-C2-R	
	и-(C2)-R	C1-з(ы)-R	
Transitive:	C1-(C2)-C3-R	C1-C2-C3-R	C1-(C2)-C3-R
	и-(C2)-C3-R	C1-з(ы)-C3-R	C1-(C2)-з(ы)-R

5.4.5.2. (580) below is an example of и- /jə/ used as the subject of an intransitive verb. Also, (581) below is an example of и- used as the direct object of a transitive verb:

(580) Ашко́лахь ицо́ а́чкәын дыздыруеит.
/a-šk’ól-[a-]ax^{j} jə-ca-wá á-č’^{j}k’^{w}ən də-z-də́r-wa-jt’/
the-school-[its-]to Rel(C1)-go-Dyn.NF the-boy him(C1)-I(C3)-know-Dyn-Fin
‘I know the/a boy who is going to school.’

(581) Уи́ аԥхәы́с и́лҩыз ашәҟәы́ сы́ртеит.
/wəj a-pħ^{w}ə́s jə́-l-j^{w}ə-z a-š^{w}q’^{w}ə́ ø-sə́-r-ta-jt’/
that the-woman Rel(C1)-she(C3)-write-Past.Ind.NF the-letter [it(C1)-]me(C2)-they(C3)-give-(Aor)-Fin
‘They gave me the letter which that woman wrote.’

The relative clause in (580) above modifies the following а́-чкәын /á-č’^{j}k’^{w}ən/ ‘the boy’. The relative clause in (581) modifies the following ашәҟәы́ /a-šʷq'ʷə́/ 'the letter'.

The examples (582) and (583) below show з(ы)- /z(ə)/ used as the indirect object of a transitive verb and з(ы)- used as the subject of an transitive verb, respectively:

(582) Ашәҟәы́ зытәа́з а́чкәын да́пҳьоит.
/a-šʷq'ʷə́ ø-zə-l-tá-z á-č'ʲk'ʷən d-á-pxʲa-wa-jt'/
the-book [it(C1)-]Rel(C2)-she(C3)-give-Past.Ind.NF the-boy he(C1)-it(C2)-read-Dyn-Fin
'The boy to whom she gave the book is reading it.'

(583) Ашәҟәы́ сы́зтаз а́чкәын дыздыруеит.
/a-šʷq'ʷə́ ø-sə́-z-ta-z á-č'ʲk'ʷən də-z-də́r-wa-jt'/
the-book [it(C1)-]me(C2)-Rel(C3)-give-Past.Ind.NF the-boy him(C1)-I(C3)-know-Dyn-Fin
'I know the boy who gave me the book.'

The relative clauses in (582) and (583) above modify the following á-чкәын /á-č'ʲk'ʷən/ 'the boy'.

The relative prefix з(ы)- is also used when it is joined to the preverb or version marker; this is because the pronominal prefix joined to the preverb or version marker takes the Column II pronominal prefix. Example (584) below is an example of a relative prefix which becomes an indirect object before the preverb, and example (585) is an example of a relative prefix which is used in the subjective version:

(584) Уара́ узлацәа́жәо сара́ исха́штхьеит. (AAD)
/wará wə-z-la-cʷážʷa-wa sará jə-s-xá-št-xʲa-jt'/
you.M you.M(C1)-Rel(C2)-Prev-talk about-Dyn.NF I it(C1)-I(C2)-Prev-forget-Perf-Fin
'I have already forgotten what you-M are talking about.'

(585) Ахәшә зыды́зкыло а́чкәын дыздыруеит.
/á-xʷšʷ ø-zə-də́-z-k'əla-wa á-č'ʲk'ʷən də-z-də́r-wa-jt'/
the-medicine [it(C1)-]Rel(Poss)-SV-Rel(C3)-take-Dyn.NF the-boy him(C1)-I(C3)-know-Dyn-Fin
'I know the boy who is taking medicine.'

In example (584) above, no word modified by the relative clause appears. In Abkhaz, it is possible to express the meaning of the modified word with the relative prefix itself. This corresponds to the 'what' in the compound relative pronoun in the English translation 'what are you talking about?'. In example (585) above, the two relative prefixes з(ы)- are inserted in the position of the possessive prefix before the subjective version marker and in the position of Column III, which indicates the agent.

As already discussed in §3.2.9.2, in verbs with Type B local preverbs, з(ы)- /z(ə)/ is used as the relative prefix joined to the preverb. Example (586) below is an example of this:

(586) а́матәа зты́лгаз ачамада́н
/á-matʷa ø-z-tə́-l-ga-z a-čʲamadán/
the-cloth(es) [it(C1)-]Rel(C2)-Prev-she(C3)-take out of-Past.Ind.NF the-suitcase
'the suitcase from which she took out the clothes'

Cf. Лара́ лы́матәакәа ачамада́н иты́лгеит.
/lará lə́-matʷa-kʷa a-čʲamadán jə-ø-tə́-l-ga-jt'/
she her-cloth(es)-Pl the-suitcase them(C1)-[it(C2)-]Prev-she(C3)-take out of-(Aor)-Fin
'She took her clothes out of the suitcase.'

In order to express relative clauses of possession, the relative prefix з(ы)- /z(ə)/ is attached to the noun that is possessed, and the subordinate clause (including this word) is put into the non-finite form:

(587) зегьы́ зы́хьз рды́руа афырха́тца
/zagʲə́ zə́-xʲʒ ø-r-də́r-wa a-fərxác'a/
all Rel(Poss)-name [it(C1)-]they(C3)-know-Dyn.NF the-hero
'the hero whose name is well known to all'

(588) Зыгура́ лго́з а́ҳәса бы́ргцәа (Abkhaz text)
/zə-gʷrá ø-l-ga-wá-z á-ħʷsa bə́rg-cʷa/
Rel(Poss)-heart [it-]she-take-Dyn-Impf.NF the-women elderly-Pl
'some wise old women that she trusted'
(Cf. а-гәрагара́ /a-gʷra-ga-rá/ 'to believe', быгәра́ лге́ит /bə-gʷrá ø-l-gá-jt'/ 'she believed you'.)

5.4.5.3. Relative-Adverbial Clauses

In order to form relative-adverbial subordinate clauses, the verbal prefix -ахь- /axʲ/ 'where' is used. Examples are given in (589) and (590) below:

(589) Сара́ издьі́руеит Амра дахьынхо́ аҩны́.
/sará jə-z-də́r-wa-jt' ámra d-axʲə-n-xa-wá a-jʷnə́/
I it(C1)-I(C3)-know-Dyn-Fin name(F) she(C1)-where-Prev-live-Dyn.NF the-house
'I know the house where Amra lives.'

(590) Сара́ атцара́ ахьы́стцоз ашко́л, акы́ҭа агәҭаны́ игы́лоуп. (AFL)
/sará a-c'ará ø-axʲə́-s-c'a-wa-z a-šk'ól a-kə́ta a-gʷtanə́
I the-study [it(C1-]where-I(C3)-study-Dyn-Impf.NF the-school its-village its-in the center
jə-gə́la-wp'/
it(C1)-stand-Stat.Pres.Fin
'The school where I studied stands in the center of the village.'

We already saw the prefix -ахь- used in indirect interrogative sentences in §4.7.7.4. For example:

(591) Иацы́ дахьы́ҟаз сыздьі́руам.
/jacə́ d-axʲə́-q'a-z ø-sə-z-də́r-wa-m/
yesterday he/she(C1)-where-be-Stat.Past.NF [it(C1)-]me(C2)-Pot-know-Dyn-Neg
'I don't know where he/she was yesterday.'

We regarded иацы́ дахьы́ҟаз /jacə́ d-axʲə́-q'a-z/ in (591) above as a transformation from the direct interrogative sentence иацы́ дабá́ҟаз? /jacə́ d-abá-q'a-z/ 'Where was he/she yesterday?' (see examples (453) and (454) in §4.7.7.4). However, strictly speaking, example (591) above can be considered as a relative-adverbial subordinate clause similar to (589) and (590) above. However, in (591) the word modified by the subordinate clause can be considered omitted or not appearing on the surface. An example that demonstrates this more clearly is (592) below, which is taken from Hewitt (1998a):

(592) Аази́з а́мпыл иахьа́суаз ибе́ит. (ANR)
/aazə́jz á-mp'əl j-axʲ-á-s-wa-z ø-jə-bá-jt'/
name(M) the-ball he(C1)-where-it(C2)-play-Dyn-Impf it(C1)-he(C3)-see-(Aor)-Fin
'Aaziz saw where they were playing football.'

(592) above is not an indirect interrogative sentence. Here, the word modified by the subordinate clause does not appear on the surface, but is included in the prefix -ахь- /ax^{j}/. (Cf. English: This is *where* I used to live.)

5.4.6. Indirect Statements

5.4.6.1. Indirect statements are expressed by inserting the verbal prefix -ахь- /ax^{j}/ 'that' as a complementizer for subordinate clauses. Subordinate clauses including this prefix can come before or after the main clause. Examples are given in (593), (594) and (595):

(593) Бахьаа́з бзи́оуп.
/b-ax^{j}-aá-z   ϕ-bzə́ja-wp'/
you.F(C1)-that-come-Past.Ind.NF   [it(C1)-]good-Stat.Pres.Fin
'It is good that you-F came.'

(594) Се́игәырӷьоит иахьугәаԥха́з.
/s-áj-g^{w}ərɣ^{j}a-wa-jt'   j-ax^{j}ə-w-g^{w}a-pxá-z/
I(C1)-Prev-rejoice-Dyn-Fin   it/they(C1)-that-you.M(C2)-Prev-like-Past.Ind.NF
'I am glad that you-M liked it/them.'

(595) Уи́ ауниверсите́т дахьҭашәа́з игәы́ иахәаны́ ды́ҟоуп.
/wə́j   a-wənəjversəjt'ét'   d-ax^{j}-ϕ-ta-š^{w}á-z
he   the-university   he(C1)-that-[it(C2)-]Prev-enter-Past.Ind.NF
jə-g^{w}ə́   j-a-x^{w}a-nə́   də́-q'a-wp'/
his-heart   it(C1)-it(C2)-help-Abs   he(C1)-be-Stat.Pres.Fin
'He is pleased that he got into the university.'

5.4.6.2. When verbs of perception such as 'seeing, knowing, etc.' are used in the main clause, the prefix -ш(ы)- /š(ə)/ 'that/how' is used as a complementizer in the subordinate clause:

(596) Ааԥсара шыбны́ԥшуа збо́ит.
/áapsara   ϕ-šə-b-nə́-pš-wa   ϕ-z-ba-wá-jt'/
fatigue   [it(C1)-]that-you.F(C2)-Prev-be reflected in-Dyn.NF   [it(C1)-]I(C3)-see-Dyn-Fin
'It seems that you-F are tired.' (lit. 'I see that you are tired.')

(597) Сшычҟәы́нам ааилы́каар, са́нгьы саргьы́ хаишьуе́ит са́б (...). (Abkhaz text)
/s-šə-č'^{j}k'^{w}ə́na-m   ϕ-a[a-]ajlə́-j-k'aa-r   s-án-g^{j}ə
I(C1)-that-boy-Neg.(NF)   [it(C1)-]Par-Prev-he(C3)-understand-if   my-mother-and
sar-g^{j}ə́   ħa-j-š^{j}-wá-jt'   s-áb/
I-and   us(C1)-he(C3)-kill-Dyn-Fin   my-father
'If my father know that I am not a boy, he will kill my mother and me (...).'

(598) Сара́ сы́шьҭахьҟа санхьа́ԥш, ха́цак дсы́шьҭаланы дшаауа́з збеит. (IC)
/sará   sə́-š^{j}tax^{j}q'a   s-an-x^{j}á-pš   xác'a-k'
I   my-back   I(C1)-when-Prev-look back(Aor.NF)   man-one
/d-sə́-š^{j}ta-la-nə   d-š-aa-wá-z   ϕ-z-ba-jt'/
he(C1)-me(C2)-Prev-trail after-Abs   he(C1)-that-come-Dyn-Impf.NF   [it(C1)-]I(C3)-see-(Aor)-Fin
'When I looked back, I saw that a man was coming along trailing after me.'

The prefix -ш(ы)- /š(ə)/ 'that/how' is also used in subordinate clauses in reported speech constructions:

(599) Аҧсуаа реихабы́ е́ихәеит Анцәа́ дышии́ҧхьаз. (AF)
/ápswaa r-ajħabə́ j-j-á-j-ħʷa-jt' a-ncʷá
the Abkhazians their-leader it(C1)-hem(C2)-to-he(C3)-say-(Aor)-Fin the-God
də-ş-jə́-pxʲa-z/
he(C1)-that-him(C2)-invite-Past.Ind.NF
'He told the leader of the Abkhazians that God had invited him.'

5.4.6.3. When the subordinate clause indicates possibility, the suffix -зар /zar/ is attached to the subordinate clause and is followed by the speech particle хәа /ħʷa/:

(600) Дычмазаҩха́зар хәа гәыҩа́рас исы́моуп.
/də-čʲmazajʷ-xá-zar ħʷa gʷajʷára-s jə-sə́-ma-wp'/
he/she(C1)-ill-become(Aor.NF)-if SP suspicion-as it(C1)-I(C2)-have-Stat.Pres.Fin
'I suspect that he/she fell ill.'

(601) Лара́ дца́зар хәа сы́ҟоуп.
/lará d-cá-zar ħʷa sə́-q'a-wp'/
she she(C1)-go(Aor.NF)-that SP I(C1)-be-Stat.Pres.Fin
'It seems to me that she left.'

The subordinate clause that becomes a complement for the verb а-шәара́ /a-šʷa-rá/ 'to fear' is produced by the suffix -р /r/ and the speech particle хәа:[164]

(602) Адәы́ҕба са́гхар хәа сшәо́ит. (AAD)
/a-dʷə́ɣba s-á-g-xa-r ħʷa s-šʷa-wá-jt'/
the-train I(C1)-it(C2)-Prev-be late-if SP I(C1)-fear-Dyn-Fin
'I am afraid to be late for the train.'

5.4.7. Purposive Clauses

In order to form purposive clauses, suffixes expressing purpose -рц /rc/, -разы /ra-zə/ (or -зарц /za-rc/) (< -ра 'non-finite Future I suffix' + -зы 'for') are attached to the aorist stem of dynamic verbs regardless of the tense of the main clause. Examples:

(i) -рц /rc/:

(603) Сҩы́за дыртцаҩны́ дҟала́рц [/дҟалаеразы́] дта́леит аинститу́т.
/s-jʷə́za də-rc'ajʷ-nə́ d-q'alá-rc [/ d-q'ala-razə́]
my-friend he(C1)-teacher-as he(C1)-become-in order to [/ he(C1)-become-in order to]
d-ø-tá-la-jt' a-jənst'əjt'əwt'/

164. 'Finite form + хәа' can also become a complement for а-шәара́ /a-šʷa-rá/ 'to fear'.
Бка́хауеит хәа сшәоит.
/b-k'áħa-wa-jt' ħʷa s-šʷa-wá-jt'/
you.F(C1)-Prev-fall-Dyn-Fin SP I(C1)-fear-Dyn-Fin
'I am afraid that you-F will fall'.

he(C1)-[it(C2)-]Prev-enter-(Aor)-Fin the-college
'My friend entered college in order to become a teacher.'

(604) Афатә аáсхәарц абазáрахь сцóит.
/a-fat'ʷ ø-aá-s-xʷa-rc a-bazár-[a-]axʲ s-ca-wá-jt'/
the-food [it(C1)-]Prev-I(C3)-buy-in order to the-bazaar-[its-]to I(C1)-go-Dyn-Fin
'I am going to the bazaar in order to buy food.'

азы́ 'it-for' can be added after the suffix -рц:

(605) Сҩы́за дсымбáрц азы́ аҩны́ сы́ҟоуп.
/s-jʷə́za d-sə-m-bá-rc a-zə́ a-jʷnə́ sə́-q'a-wp'/
my-friend him(C1)-I(C3)-Neg-see-in order to it-for the-house I(C1)-be-Stat.Pres.Fin
'I am at home in order that I may not see my friend.'

(ii) -разы /ra-zə/:

(606) Амца éиқәылаpазы сáҭәхәеит.
/á-mca ø-ájkʷə-la-razə s-á-tʷħʷa-jt'/
the-fire [it(C1)-]Prev-be kindled-in order to I(C1)-it(C2)-blow at-(Aor)-Fin
'I blew on the fire so that it flared up.'

When the main clause is a verb of motion, forms without -зы can also be used:

(607) Аҩны́ аргы́лара[/аргы́лазы] хáаит.
/a-jʷnə́ a-rgə́la-ra[/a-rgə́la-zə] ħ-áa-jt'/
the-house its-build-Masd[-for] we(C1)-come-(Aor)-Fin
'We came to build a house.'

Also, according to Chirikba (Chirikba 2003a: 65), purposive clauses can also be produced by 'masdar + хәа':

(608) рбарá хәа
/r-ba-rá ħʷa/
them-see-Masd SP
'in order to see them'

5.5. Speech-Particle (SP) хәа

5.5.1. Abkhaz has the particle хәа /ħʷa/ for quoting the content of thought or speech.[165] Hewitt calls it a 'speech-particle', and Chrikba calls it a 'quotative particle'. Here, we will follow Hewitt and call it a 'speech-particle' (abbreviated as 'SP'). This particle хәа is placed immediately after the quoted sentence. The quoted sentence is an independent, complete sentence (a sentence that ends in a finite form, an interrogative sentence, or an imperative sentence). In the examples of quoted sentences below, (609) and (610) are affirmative sentences, (611) is an interrogative sentence, and (612) is an imperative sentence:

165. According to Hewitt (AF 237) 'the speech-particle is a fossilized form of the Past Absolutive' of а-хәарá /a-ħʷa-rá/ 'to say'.

(609) Сара́ уи́ и́рласны дааує́ит хәа́ сахáит.
/sará wəj jə́rlasnə d-aa-wá-jt' ħʷa ø-s-a-ħá-jt'/
I he soon he-come-Dyn-Fin SP [it(C1)-]me(C2)-to-hear-(Aor)-Fin
'I heard that he would come soon.'

(610) Дырми́т Гәли́а ишәҟәы́ сҭаху́п ҳәа се́иҳәеит.
/dərmə́jt' gʷlə́ja jə-šʷq'ʷə́ ø-s-taxə́-wp' ħʷa
name(M) his-book [it(C1)-]I(C2)-want-Stat.Pres.Fin SP
ø-s-á-j-ħʷa-jt'/
[it(C1)-]me(C2)-to-he(C3)-say-(Aor)-Fin
"I need Dmitry Gulia's book,' he said to me.'

(611) Бара́ баба́нхои?, хәа сара́ дсызҵаа́ит Амра.
/bará d-abá-n-xa-wa-j ħʷa sará d-sə-z-c'aá-jt' ámra/
you.F you.F-where-Prev-live-Dyn-Qu SP I she(C1)-me(C2)-Prev-ask-(Aor)-Fin name(F)
"Where do you-F live?' Amra asked me.'

(612) Абри́ а́чкун би́шца хәа анла́сҳәа, уаха́к ахы́цха сы́шәҭ, а́шьжьымҭан аҭа́к шәы́сҭоит хәа са́лҳәеит. (Abkhaz text)
/abrə́j á-č'ʲk'ʷən b-jə́-c-ca ħʷa ø-an-l-á-s-ħʷa
this the-boy you.F(C1)-him(C2)-with-go.Imp SP [it(C1)-]when-her(C2)-to-I(C3)-say.Aor.NF
waxá-k' a-xʷə́cxa ø-sə́-šʷ-t áš'ʲž'ʲəmtan a-ták'
tonight-one the-meditation [it(C1)-]me(C2)-you.Pl(C3)-give.Imp in the morning the-answer
ø-šʷə́-s-ta-wa-jt' ħʷa ø-s-á-l-ħʷa-jt'/
[it(C1)-]you.Pl(C2)-I(C3)-give-Dyn-Fin SP [it(C1)-]me(C2)-to-she(C3)-say-(Aor)-Fin
"When I told her 'Go away as a bride to this boy', she said to me 'Let me consider it for one night tonight. I will give you-Pl my answer in the morning."

In sentence (610) above, since the Column I pronominal prefix at the head of an introductory verb such as '(she) said' does not appear, we know that the portion up to 'dərmə́jt' gʷlə́ja jə-šʷq'ʷə́ ø-s-taxə́-wp' ħʷa' is the direct object of the introductory verb. Also, the sentence quoted in example (611) above is a direct interrogative sentence (for the equivalent indirect interrogative sentence, see §4.7.7.4). As can be seen from this, this speech particle is not used when direct speech is converted into indirect speech.

The position of the speech particle ҳәа is placed immediately after the quoted sentence as seen above. Introductory verbs, such as '(she) said' or '(Arma) asked (me)' do not necessarily need to be placed after the speech particle. Look at the following example:

(613) Ана́ҩс ирҭы́нчны ҿа́алҭуеит: «Исзы́лашәҳәа, аҵкы́ сара́ изго́ит!», ҳәа́. (AFL)
/anájʷs jərtə́nčʲnə č'áa-l-t-wa-jt'
and then quietly mouth-Prev-she(C3)-speak-Dyn-Fin
jə-s-zə́-la-šʷ-ħʷa a-c'k'ə́ sará jə-z-ga-wá-jt' ħʷa
it(C1)-me(C2)-for-Prev-you.Pl(C3)-wrap up.Imp the-dress I it(C1)-I(C3)-take-Dyn-Fin SP
'And then she quietly said: "Wrap it for me, I am getting the dress."'

In addition to sentences, the speech particle ҳәа can also quote noun phrases. In the sentences below, the speech particles quote 'Indian summer' in (614), 'Kama' in (615), and 'Ts'an' in (616):

(614) Ҭага́лантәи а́мш бзи́а "ҕхы́нчкән" ҳәа́ иа́шьтоуп. (AFL)

/tagálant'ʷəj á-mš bzə́ja pxə́nč'ʲk'ʷn ħʷa j-á-šʲta-wp'/
autumnal the-day good Indian summer SP it(C1)-it(C2)-be called-Stat.Pres.Fin
'Good autumn days are called an "Indian summer."'

(615) Ка́ма (хəа́) са́шəхəалар ҟало́ит. (AFL)
/k'áma ħʷa ø-s-á-šʷ-ħʷa-la-r
name(F) SP [it(C1)-]me(C2)-to-you.Pl(C3)-say-Iterative-if/that
ø-q'a-la-wá-jt'/
[it(C1)-]Prev-be possible-Dyn-Fin
'You can call me Kama.'

(616) Ажəы́тə атца́н хəа цьоукы́ ы́ҟан. (Abkhaz text)
/ažʷə́t'ʷ a-c'án ħʷa ǯʲawk'ə́ ə́-q'a-n/
in olden times the-Ts'an SP people [they(C1)-]be-Stat.Past.Fin
'In the olden times, there lived a people called the Ts'an.'

According to our informant, the хəа in (615) above can be omitted.

5.5.2. Regarding using the speech particle хəа for the subordinate clause indicating possibility, see §5.4.6.3.

5.5.3. Regarding using the speech particle хəа for concessive clauses, see §5.4.4.

5.5.4. The speech particle хəа is also used as a component of onomatopoetic words and adverbs. For details of the adverbs produced by means of the speech particle, see 2.5.2.1.

5.6. Verbal Prefixes Expressing the Location of an Action

As already mentioned in §3.1.2.1, in Abkhaz local preverbs (Spruit 1983: 55) can be divided into three types: Type A, Type B, and Type C. Following these three types, prefixes which indicate the location where the action is performed or its direction appear in the verbal complex. The following is an illustration of these types (ibid.: 61):

	A	B	C
1 sg.	s-	-	-
3 sg. irr.[166]	a-	(ø-)	-
3 pl.	r-	(r-)	-
rel.	z-	(z-)	-

We have already discussed this pattern in §3.2.9.2. To reiterate, Type A indicates the pattern in which every pronominal prefix appears before a preverb: for example, the preverb ва- /va/ 'next to'. In Type B ø- instead of the pronominal prefix a- appears in the case of 3 sg. non-human, while the pronominal

166. Spruit's 3sg. irr(ational) is listed as '3 sg. non-human' in the present work.

prefix р- /r/ appears in the case of 3 pl.: for example, the preverb кыл- /k'əl/ 'through'. In Type C, no pronominal prefix appears before the preverb. Below, we will examine locational expressions for verbs with Type A, B and C preverbs.

5.6.1. Locational Expressions for Verbs with Type A Preverbs

In verbs with this type of preverb, all pronominal prefixes appear before the preverb. Examples of verbs with the preverb ва- /va/ 'next to' are given in (617), (618) and (619):

(617) Дсы́вагылоуп.
/d-sə́-va-gəla-wp'/
he/she(C1)-me(C2)-Prev(next to)-stand-Stat.Pres.Fin
'He/She is standing next to me.'

(618) Абóра давагы́ланы акьажы́ҳәа атцәы́уара да́лагеит. (Abkhaz text)
/a-bóra d-a-va-gə́la-nə ak'ʲažə́-ħʷa a-c'ʷə́wa-ra d-á-la-ga-jt'/
the-stable she(C1)-it(C2)-Prev-stand-Abs cry on and on-Masd she-it-Prev-start-(Aor)-Fin
'She, having stood by the stable, started to sob out loud.'

(619) Сара́ ахәчы́ иа́н длы́васыртәеит.
/sará a-xʷč'ʲə́ j-án d-lə́-va-sə-r-t'ʷa-jt'/
I the-child his-mother him(C1)-her(C2)-Prev-I(C3)-Caus-sit down-(Aor)-Fin
'I made the child sit down next to his mother.'

As discussed in §3.2.9.2, there are cases where the same preverb can take Type A and Type B. Using the preverb -кә- /kʷ/ 'on' as an example, Spruit (1983: 67) regards the difference between Type A and Type B as that of an 'effective local' versus a 'plain local'. However, can a difference between an 'effective local' versus a 'plain local' be observed between Types A and B? (Furthermore, cf. examples (206) and (208) in §3.2.9.2.) Here, we will cite data obtained from our informant on verb а́кәҧҿра /á-kʷ-č-ra/ 'to break/smash *sth* on', which has the preverb -кә- /kʷ/ (verbs with an asterisk in the parenthesis are forms that our informant deemed inappropriate).

Type A

(620) Атцәа ихы́ иа́кәпҧырҿеит. (*и́кәпҧырҿеит)
/á-c'ʷca jə-xə́ j-á-kʷ-pə-r-čə-jt' (*jə́-ø-kʷ-pə-r-čə-jt')/
the-glass his-head it(the glass, C1)-it(his head, C2)-Prev(on)-Prev-they(C3)-break-(Aor)-Fin
'They broke the glass on his head.'

Type B

(621) Акака́н адашьма́ и́кәпҧиҿеит. (*иа́кәпҧиҿеит) (ARD)
/a-k'ak'án a-dašʲmá jə́-ø-kʷ-pə-j-čə-jt' (*j-á-kʷ-pə-j-čə-jt')/
the-nut the-floor it(the nut, C1)-[it(the floor, C2)-]Prev(on)-Prev-he(C3)-break-(Aor)-Fin
'He smashed the walnut on the floor.'

5.6.2. Locational Expressions for Verbs with Type B Preverbs

In verbs with this type of preverb, the third-person singular/non-human pronominal prefix which cross-references the noun indicating the location does not appear (or has a zero prefix), whereas the third-person plural pronominal prefix р- /r/, which cross-references the noun indicating the locations, appears. For example, compare the nouns indicating the location of the intransitive verb а-ҭатәара́ /a-ta-t’ʷa-rá/ ‘to sit inside’, which has the preverb ҭа- /ta/ ‘in, into’, when they are singular (622) and plural (623):

(622) Ачкәын амашьы́на дҭатәе́ит.
/á-č’ʲk’ʷən a-mašʲə́na d-ø-ta-t’ʷá-jt’/
the-boy the-car he(C1)-[it(= the car, C2)-]Prev(in)-sit-(Aor)-Fin
‘The boy sat in the car.’

(623) Ачкәынцәа амашьы́накәа ирҭатәе́ит.
/á-č’ʲk’ʷən-cʷa a-mašʲə́na-kʷa jə-r-ta-t’ʷá-jt’/
the-boy-Pl the-car-Pl they(C1)-them(= the cars, C2)-Prev(in)-sit-(Aor)-Fin
‘The boys sat in the cars.’

In sentence (622) above, амашьы́на /a-mašʲə́na/ ‘the car’ and the Column II pronominal prefix ø- cross-reference each other, and in (623), the plural form амашьы́накәа /a-mašʲə́na-kʷa/ ‘the cars’ and the Column II pronominal prefix р- /r/ ‘them’ cross-reference each other. Also, compare the nouns indicating the location of the transitive verb а-ҭацара́ /a-ta-c’a-rá/ ‘to put in’, which has the same preverb ҭа- /ta/, when they are singular (624) and plural (625):

(624) Сара́ снапы́ сџьы́ба итáсцеит.
/sará s-nap’ə́ s-ǯʲə́ba jə-ø-tá-s-c’a-jt’/
I my-hand my-pocket it(=my hand, C1)-[it(= my pocket, C2)-]Prev(in)-I(C3)-put-(Aor)-Fin
‘I put my hand into my pocket.’

(625) Сара́ снапкәа́ сџьы́бакәа ирҭáсцеит.
/sará s-nap’-kʷá s-ǯʲə́ba-kʷa jə-r-tá-s-c’a-jt’/
I my-hand-Pl my-pocket-Pl them(my hands, C1)-them(= my pockets, C2)-Prev-I(C3)-put-(Aor)-Fin
‘I put my hands into my pockets.’

In sentence (624) above, the Column II pronominal prefix ø- is cross-referenced with the singular сџьы́ба /s-ǯʲə́ba/ ‘my pocket’. On the other hand, the Column II pronominal prefix р- /r/ in (625) is cross-referenced with the plural сџьы́бакәа /s-ǯʲə́ba-kʷa/ ‘my pockets’. In addition, the following sentence (626) is an example with the relative prefix з- /z/ in the Column II slot:

(626) снапы́ зҭáсцаз аџьы́ба
/s-nap’ə́ ø-z-tá-s-c’a-z a-ǯʲə́ba/
my-hand [it(= my hand, C1)-]Rel(C2)-Prev(in)-I(C3)-put-Past.Ind.NF the-pocket
‘the pocket into which I put my hand’

Furthermore, in Abkhaz there is a stative verb а-ҭáзаара /a-tá-zaa-ra/ ‘to be in an enclosed space’ which is formed solely from the preverb ҭа- /ta/ ‘in’. Stative verbs with this type of preverb as its root can be analyzed as ‘preverb ҭа- + copula ø-’, as previously discussed in §3.2.9.2, fn.127 and §5.2.1. Examples:

(627) Ацаҧхá аџьы́ба иҭóуп.
/a-capxá a-ǯʲə́ba jə-ø-tá-øə-wp’/
the-key the-pocket it(= the key, C1)-[it(= the pocket, C2)-]Prev(in)-be-Stat.Pres.Fin
‘The key is in the pocket.’

(628) Ацаҧхакәá аџьы́бакәа ирҭóуп.

/a-capxa-kʷá a-ǯʲә́ba-kʷa jә-r̠-tá-øә-wp'/
the-key-Pl the-pocket-Pl they(= the keys, C1)-[them(= the pockets, C2)-]Prev(in)-be-Stat.Pres.Fin
'The keys are in the pockets.'

In sentence (627) above, the Column II pronominal prefix ø- is cross-referenced with the singular a-цьы́ба /a-ǯʲә́ba/ 'the pocket'. On the other hand, in sentence (628) the Column II pronominal prefix р- /r/ is cross-referenced with the plural ацьы́бақәа /a-ǯʲә́ba-kʷa/ 'the pockets'. Sentence (627) above can also be expressed with a structure using the root -ҟа- /q'a/ 'to be'. In this case, a postposition indicating a locative meaning is attached to the noun 'pocket':

(629) Ацаҧха́ ацьы́баҿы и́ҟоуп.
/a-capxá a-ǯʲә́ba-č'ә jә́-q'a-wp'/
the-key the-pocket-in it(= the key, C1)-be-Stat.Pres.Fin
'The key is in the pocket.'

Other verbs with the preverb ҭа- /ta/ also indicate the same function as we discussed above. For example, а-ҭаҧсра́ /a-ta-ps-rá/ 'to die inside':

(630) Ажра иҭаҧси́т.
/á-žra jә-ø̠-ta-psә́-jt'/
the-hole it/they(C1)-[it(= the hole, C2)-]Prev(in)-die-(Aor)-Fin
'It/They died in the hole.'

(631) Ажрақәа ирҭаҧси́т.
/á-žra-kʷa jә-r̠-ta-psә́-jt'/
the-hole-Pl they(C1)-them(= the holes, C2)-Prev(in)-die-(Aor)-Fin
'They died in the holes.'

The following are verbs with the preverb ҭа- /ta/, which has a similar structure:

а-ҭагы́лара /a-ta-gә́la-ra/ 'to stand in', а-ҭа́жьра /a-tá-žʲ-ra/ 'to throw *sb/sth* heavy into', а-ҭаӡара́ /a-ta-ʒa-rá/ 'to fit into', а-ҭаиара́ /a-ta-ja-rá/ 'to lie (down) in', а-ҭа́лара /a-tá-la-ra/ 'to go into (an enclosed area)', а-ҭа́ҧалара /a-tá-pala-ra/ 'to jump into', а-ҭаҧсара́ /a-ta-psa-rá/ 'to pour in', а-ҭаҧшра́ /a-ta-pš-rá/ 'to look into', а-ҭаргы́лара /a-ta-rgә́la-ra/ 'to cause to stand in', а-ҭаҭәара́ /a-ta-tʷa-rá/ 'to pour into', а-ҭахара́ /a-ta-xa-rá/ 'to remain in', а-ҭа́хара /a-tá-ħa-ra/ 'to fall in', а-ҭаца́лара /a-ta-cála-ra/ 'to drive into', а-ҭашьра́ /a-ta-šʲ-rá/ 'to kill in', а-ҭашәара́ /a-ta-šʷa-rá/ 'to enter', etc.

Also, the following are Type B preverbs:

ҭ(ы)- /t(ә)/ 'out of': а-ҭгара́ /a-t-ga-rá/ 'to take out of'

(632) Сцьы́ба аҧа́ра ҭы́згеит.
/s-ǯʲә́ba a-pára ø-ø̠-tә́-z-ga-jt'/
my-pocket the-money [it(= money, C1)-it(= my pocket, C2)-]Prev-I(C3)-take-(Aor)-Fin
'I took money out of my pocket.'

(633) Сцьы́бақәа аҧа́ракәа рҭы́згеит.
/s-ǯʲә́ba-kʷa a-pára-kʷa ø-r̠-tә́-z-ga-jt'/
my-pocket-Pl the-money-Pl [them(C1)-]them(my pockets, C2)-Prev-I(C3)-take-(Aor)-Fin
'I took money out of my pockets.'

дәы́л- /dʷə́l/ 'outside a building' (Spruit 1983): а-дәы́лҟьара /a-dʷə́l-q'ʲa-ra/ 'to rush out from (the premises)'

(634) Алá ауаҭáх идәы́лҟьеит. (RAD)
/a-lá a-watáx jə-ø-dʷə́l-q'ʲa-jt'/
the-dog the-room it(= the dog, C1)-[it(= the room, C2)-]Prev-run out from-(Aor)-Fin
'The dog ran out from the room.'

(635) Алакәá ауаҭáхкәа ирдәы́лҟьеит.
/a-la-kʷá a-watáx-kʷa jə-r-dʷə́l-q'ʲa-jt'/
the-dog-Pl the-room-Pl they(= the dogs, C1)-[them(= rooms, C2)-]Prev-run out from-(Aor)-Fin
'The dogs ran out from the rooms.'

кы́д- /k'ə́d/ 'on a slope/incline': акы́дбгара /a-k'ə́d-bga-ra/ 'to fall off'

(636) Аҭӡы́ ашьы́х кы́дбгеит. (ARD)
/a-tʒə́ a-šʲə́x ø-ø-k'ə́d-bga-jt'/
the-wall the-plaster [it(= the plaster, C1)-it(= the wall, C2)-]Prev-fall off-(Aor)-Fin
'The plaster fell off (of) the wall.'

(637) Аҭӡкәá ашьы́х ркы́дбгеит.
/a-tʒ-kʷá a-šʲə́x ø-r-k'ə́d-bga-jt'/
the-wall-Pl the-plaster [it(= the plaster, C1)-]them(= the walls, C2)-Prev-fall off-(Aor)-Fin
'The plaster fell off (of) the walls.'

кы́л- /k'əl/ 'through, out from': акы́лҟьара /a-k'ə́l-q'ʲa-ra/ 'to go through'

(638) Ахы́ аӷәы́ икы́лҟье-ит (/ иáлҟьеит). (ARD)
/a-xə́ a-ɣʷə́ jə-ø-k'ə́l-q'ʲa-jt' (/ j-á-k'əl-q'ʲa-jt')/
the-bullet the-board it(= the bullet, C1)-[it(= the board, C2)-]Prev-go through-(Aor)-Fin
'The bullet went through the board.'

(639) Ахкәá аӷәкәá иркы́лҟьеит.
/a-x-kʷá a-ɣʷ-kʷá jə-r-k'ə́l-q'ʲa-jt'/
the-bullet-Pl the-board-Pl they(= the bullets, C1)-them(= the boards, C2)-Prev-go through-(Aor)-Fin
'The bullets went through the boards.'

кә- /kʷ/ 'on': á-кәгылазаара /á-kʷ-gəla-zaa-ra/ 'to stand on'[167]

(640) Ахáхә ды́кәгылоуп. (ARD)
/a-xáħʷ də́-ø-kʷ-gəla-wp'/
the-stone he/she(C1)-[it(= the stone, C2)-]Prev(on)-stand-Stat.Pres.Fin
'He/She is standing on the stone.'

(641) Ахáхәкәа ирыкәгылоуп.
/a-xáħʷ-kʷa jə-rə́-kʷ-gəla-wp'/
the-stone-Pl they(C1)-them(= the stones, C2)-Prev(on)-stand-Stat.Pres.Fin
'They are standing on the stones.'

167. кә- is also used as Type A. See §3.2.9.2 for the difference between Type A and Type B.

ла- /la/ 'in': а́-лаҳәара /á-la-ħʷa-ra/ 'to wrap *sth* (up) in'

(642) Ашәҟәы́ акьаа́д и́ласхәеит.
/a-šʷq'ʷə́ a-kʲaád jə́-ø-la-s-ħʷa-jt'/
the-book the-paper it(= the book, C1)-[it(= the paper, C2)-]Prev(in)-I(C3)-wrap-(Aor)-Fin
'I wrapped the book in the paper.'

(643) Ашәҟәқәа́ акьаа́дкәа иры́ласхәеит.
/a-šʷq'ʷ-kʷá a-kʲaád-kʷa jə-rə́-la-s-ħʷa-jt'/
the-book-Pl the-paper-Pl them(= the books, C1)-them(= the papers, C2)-Prev(in)-I(C3)-wrap-(Aor)-Fin
'I wrapped the books up in (some pieces of) paper.'

тц(ы)- /c'(ə)/ 'from under': а́-тц(ы)тцра /á-c'(ə)-c'-ra/ 'to go/come out from under'

(644) Ацгәы́ астол и́тцытцит.
/a-cgʷə́ a-st'ól jə́-ø-c'ə-c'ə-jt'/
the-cat the-table it(= the cat, C1)-[it(= the table, C2)-]Prev(from under)-go out-(Aor)-Fin
'The cat came out from under the table.'

(645) Ацгәқәа́ асто́лкәа ирытцытцит.
/a-cgʷ-kʷá a-st'ól-kʷa jə-rə́-c'ə-c'ə-jt'/
the-cat-Pl the-table-Pl they(= the cats, C1)-them(= the tables, C2)-Prev(from under)-go out-(Aor)-Fin
'The cats came out from under the tables.'

ҩна- /jʷna/ 'inside (a house)': а-ҩнаххра́ /a-jʷna-xx-rá/ 'to run off to'

(646) Ауаҭа́х дыҩнаххи́т.
/a-watáx də-ø-jʷna-xxə́-jt'/
the-room he/she(C1)-[it(= the room, C2)-]run off-(Aor)-Fin
'He/She ran off to the room.'

(647) Ауаҭа́хқәа хрыҩнаххи́т.
/a-watáx-kʷa ħ-rə-jʷna-xxə́-jt'/
the-room-Pl we(C1)-them(= the rooms, C2)-run off-(Aor)-Fin
'We ran off to the rooms.'

5.6.3. Locational Expressions for Verbs with Type C Preverbs

In the verbs of this type a pronominal prefix expressing location or direction does not appear before the preverb. The preverb -н- /n/ in анхара́ /a-n-xa-rá/ 'to live' is typical of the type C preverbs:

(648) Аԥсуаа Аԥсны́ инхо́ит.
/ápswaa apsnə́ jə-n-xa-wá-jt'/
Abkhazians Abkhazia they(C1)-Prev-live-Dyn-Fin
'Abkhazians live in Abkhazia.'

(649) Уажәы́ сара́ сынхо́ит Аҟәа.
/wažʷə́ sará sə-n-xa-wá-jt' áq'ʷa/
now I I(C1)-Prev-live-Dyn-Fin Sukhum
'I live in Sukhum now.'

(650) Та́мшьи Цыгъа́рдеи инхо́ит. (*ирнхоит)

/t'ámšʲə-j ǯʲgʲárda-j jə-n-xa-wá-jt'/ (*jə-r-n-xa-wa-jt')
Tamsh-and Dzhgjarda-and(village name) they(C1)-Prev-live-Dyn-Fin
'They live in Tamsh and Dzhgjarda.'

In (648), (649) and (650) above, in all cases pronominal prefixes a- /a/ 'it' or р- /r/ 'them' cross-referenced to Аԥсны́ /apsnə́/ 'Abkhazia', Аҟәа /áq'ʷa/ 'Sukhum', Та́мшьи Џьгьа́рдеи /t'ámšʲə-j ǯʲgʲárda-j/ 'Tamsh and Dzhgjarda' do not appear in the verbal complexes. Also, there are no postpositions indicating a locative meaning attached to the nouns. However, in the following examples using the same verb postpositions indicating a locative meaning appear:

(651) Сара́ сынхо́ит Аҟәа а́калакь аҟны́.
/sará sə-n-xa-wá-jt' áq'ʷa á-kalakʲ a-q'nə́/
I I(C1)-Prev-live-Dyn-Fin Sukhum its-city its-in
'I live in the city of Sukhum.'

(652) Ҳара́ аԥсшьа́рта ҩнаҿы́ ханхо́н. (AFL)
/ħará a-psšʲárta jʷn-a-č'ə́ ħa-n-xa-wá-n/
we the-place for a rest house-its-in we(C1)-Prev-live-Dyn-Impf
'We lived in a vacation home.'

It seems that the difference between (648–650) and (651–652) above is that in the former, nouns with a locative meaning are the proper names of places, and in the latter, they are common nouns. It is a general tendency of language to require explicit marking for common nouns.[168] In contrast, proper nouns easily express locative meaning without explicit marking. This can also be seen in the following sentences using the stative verb á-ҟазаара /á-q'a-zaa-ra/ 'to be, to exist':

(653) Ҭемы́р Москва́ ды́ҟан. (GAL)
/temə́r mosk'vá də́-q'a-n/
name(M) Moscow he(C1)-be-Stat.Past.Fin
'Temyr was in Moscow.'

(654) Аб аҩны́ ды́ҟоуп.
/[a-]ab a-jʷnə́ də́-q'a-wp'/
the-father the-home he(C1)-be-Stat.Pres.Fin
'The father is at home.'

In (653) above, no postposition indicating a locative meaning is attached to the proper noun Москва́ 'Moscow' (cf. (629)). Also, in (654), no postposition indicating a locative meaning is attached to a-ҩны́ /a-jʷnə́/ 'home'. This word, like the English 'home', is a special noun with a locative meaning.[169]

---

168. For the discussion of the marking of peripheral arguments see Dixon (2010: 127). [Dixon, R.M.W. 2010, *Basic Linguistic Theory*. Volume 1 Methodology. Oxford University Press.]

169. Cf. Dixon (ibid. 127): 'As mentioned under (a), absolutive or nominative (or, rarely, accusative) may receive zero marking. In contrast, peripheral NPs with a common noun as head generally require some explicit marking. However, there may be an exception in the case of proper names of places; these nouns may be used alone with either a locative or allative meaning, depending on the nature of the accompanying verb (for example, 'stay [at] Split Rock' or 'go [to] Split Rock'). In English there is just one noun, *home*, which can be used alone with allative or locative sense; for example. *She's going home* (rather than **She's going to home*) and—just in some dialects—*He's staying home* (*He's staying at home* is an alternative).'

In contrast, in common nouns a postposition indicating a locative meaning is necessary. In the following example, the postpostion а-ҿы́ /a-č'ə/ 'its-in' is attached after араио́н /a-rajón/ 'region':

(655) Уи́ Очамчы́ра араио́н аҿы́ и́ҟоуп. (AFL)
/wəj očʲamčʲə́ra a-rajón a-č'ə́ jə́-q'a-wp'/
this city-name the-region its-in it(C1)-be-Stat.Pres.Fin
'This is in the Ochamchira region.'

This tendency for a locative marking to occur in common nouns and to be absent in proper nouns appears obvious, but there are also exceptions. As the following examples demonstrate, when a noun with locative meaning is a country name other than Abkhazia, a postposition indicating a locative meaning is attached to it:

(656) Сара́ Ҟырҭтәы́лан / Урыстәы́лан / Ҭырқәтәы́лан сынхо́ит.
/sará kərtt'ʷə́la-n /wərəst'ʷə́la-n /tərkʷt'ʷə́la-n sə-n-xa-wá-jt'/
I Georgia-in /Russia-in /Turkey-in I(C1)-Prev-live-Dyn-Fin
'I live in Georgia/Russia/Turkey.'

5.7. Reciprocal Construction

We use reciprocal constructions in order to express structures such as 'Tom hit Mary and Mary hit Tom', in other words, 'Tom and Mary hit each other'. In Abkhaz, this construction can be expressed by inserting two reciprocal (abbreviated as 'Rec') markers аи- /aj/ and аиба- /ajba/ in the verbal complex. These reciprocal markers are normally inserted into the slot after the Column I pronominal prefix in the verbal complex. The reciprocal marker аи- is inserted into intransitive verbs, and the reciprocal marker аиба- is inserted into transitive verbs. Below, we will describe the derivational processes and usage of reciprocal constructions.

5.7.1. Reciprocal Construction with -аи-

In order to make a two-place intransitive verb a reciprocal construction, the Column II pronominal prefix expressing the indirect object of the two-place intransitive verb must be changed by the reciprocal marker -аи-. Compare the aorist form (657) of the two-place intransitive verb а́-қәшәара /á-kʷ-šʷa-ra/ 'to meet' with the form (658) produced by means of the reciprocal marker -аи-:

(657) слы́қәшәеит
/s-lə́-kʷ-šʷa-jt'/
I(C1)-her(C2)-Prev-meet-(Aor)-Fin
'I met her.'

(658) хаиқәшәе́ит
/ħ-aj-kʷ-šʷá-jt'/
we(C1)-Rec-Prev-meet-(Aor)-Fin
'We met each other.'

The Column II pronominal prefix -лы- /lə/ in (657) is changed to -аи- /aj/ and the subject is made plural. The verb forming this reciprocal construction, а́иқәшәара /áj-kʷ-šʷa-ra/ 'to meet each other', is conjugated in the following manner:

	Affirmative	Negative
Finite forms		
Present		
1Pl-Rec-Prev-R-	ҳ-аи-қә-шәб-ит	ҳ-аи-қә-шәб-м
2Pl-	шә-еи-қә-шәб-ит	шә-еи-қә-шәб-м
3Pl-	(и)еи-қә-шәб-ит	(и)еи-қә-шәб-м
Aorist		
1Pl-	ҳ-аи-қә-шәé-ит	ҳ-аи-қә-м-шәé-ит
Non-Finite forms		
Present		
Rel-Rec-Prev-R-	и-éи-қә-шәо	и-éи-қә-м-шәо
Imperative	шә-еи-қә-шәá!	шә-еи-қә-м-шәá-н!

When there is an interrogative prefix, the reciprocal prefix <u>-аи-</u> is placed after it:

(659) Шәанбéиқәшәо?
/šʷ-anbá-[a]j-kʷ-šʷa-wa/
you.Pl(C1)-when-Rec-Prev-meet-Dyn.NF(Qu)
'When will you-Pl meet each other?'

Examples of other verbs using the reciprocal marker <u>-аи-</u>:

áицхыраара /áj-c-xəraa-ra/ 'to help/aid each other' (cf. ацхы́раара /a-cxə́raa-ra/ [intr.] 'to help'):

(660) Уарéи сарéи ҳаицхы́раауеит.
/wará-j sará-j ħ-aj-c-xə́raa-wa-jt'/
you.M-and I-and we(C1)-Rec-Prev-help-Dyn-Fin
'You-M and I help each other.'

áицлабра /áj-clab-ra/ 'to compete with each other' (cf. áцлабра /á-clab-ra/ [intr.] 'to compete with'):

(661) Ҳаицлáбуеит.
/ħ-aj-cláb-wa-jt'/
we(C1)-Rec-compete-Dyn-Fin
'We are competing with each other.'

Cf. сбáцлабуеит
/s-b-á-clab-wa-jt'/
I(C1)-you.F(C2)-with-compete-Dyn-Fin
'I am competing with you-F' (Note that in (5) above there is no preverb <u>a</u> after the reciprocal marker.)

áизыԥшра /áj-zə-pš-ra/ 'to wait for each other' (cf. азыԥшрá /a-zə-pš-rá/ [intr.] 'to wait for'):

(662) Ҳаизыԥши́т.
/ħ-aj-zə-pšə́-jt'/
we(C1)-Rec-Prev-wait-(Aor)-Fin
'We waited for each other.'

Cf. сыбзыԥшуéит

/sə-b-zə-pš-wá-jt'/
I(C1)-you.F(C2)-Prev-wait-Dyn-Fin
'I am waiting for you-F.'

áихәаԥшра /áj-xʷa-pš-ra/ 'to look at each other' (cf. áхәаԥшра /á-xʷa-pš-ra/ [intr.] 'to look at'):

(663) Ҳаихәаԥшуе́ит.
/ħ-aj-xʷa-pš-wá-jt'/
we(C1)-Rec-Prev-watch-Dyn-Fin
'We are looking at each other.'

Cf. сбы́хәаԥшуеит
/s-bə́-xʷa-pš-wa-jt'/
I(C1)-you.F(C2)-Prev-look at-Dyn-Fin
'I am looking at you-F.'

áицәажәара /áj-cʷažʷa-ra/ 'to talk with each other' (cf. ацәа́жәара /a-cʷážʷa-ra/ 'to speak to'):

(664) Урҭ еицәа́жәоит.
/wərt ø-aj-cʷážʷa-wa-jt'/
they [they(C1)-]Rec-talk-Dyn-Fin
'They are talking with each other.'

Cf. сба́цәажәоит
/s-b-á-cʷažʷa-wa-jt'/
I(C1)-you.F(C2)-to-talk-Dyn-Fin
'I am speaking to you.' (Note that in (8) above there is no preverb a after the reciprocal marker.)

5.7.2. Reciprocal Construction with -аиба-

5.7.2.1. In order to transform a two-place transitive verb into a reciprocal construction, the Column III pronominal prefix of the two-place transitive verb is changed by the reciprocal maker -аиба- /ajba/ and placed after Column I. For example, compare the underlying form (665) of the two-place transitive verb а-шьра́ /a-šʲ-rá/ 'to kill' with the reciprocal form (666) derived by means of -аиба-:

(665) дахшьуе́ит
/d-aħ-šʲ-wá-jt'/
him/her(C1)-we(C3)-kill-Dyn-Fin
'We are killing him/her.'

(666) хаибашьуе́ит
/ħ-ajba-šʲ-wá-jt'/
we(C1)-Rec-kill-Dyn-Fin
'We are killing each other.'

Examples of other verbs using the reciprocal marker -аиба-:

а́ибадырра /ájba-dər-ra/ 'to get acquainted with each other'(cf. а-ды́рра /a-dər-ra/ [tr.] 'to know'):

(667) Ҳара́ ҳаибады́руеит.
/ħará ħ-ajba-dər-wa-jt'/
we we(C1)-Rec-know-Dyn-Fin

'We are acquainted with each other.'

(668) Шәеибадыр́!
/š^{w}-ajba-dә́r/
you.Pl(C1)-Rec-know.Imp
'Get acquainted with each other!'

Cf. бызды́руеит
/bә-z-dә́r-wa-jt'/
you.F(C1)-I(C3)-know-Dyn-Fin
'I know you-F.'

а́ибабара /ájba-ba-ra/ 'to see each other' (cf. а-бара́ /a-ba-rá/ [tr.] 'to see'):

(669) Бзи́а хаибабо́ит.
/bzә́ja ħ-ajba-ba-wá-jt'/
well we(C1)-Rec-see-Dyn-Fin
'We love each other.'

а́ибаӡәӡәара /ájba-ʒ^{w}ʒ^{w}a-ra/ 'to wash each other' (cf. а́-ӡәӡәара /á-ʒ^{w}ʒ^{w}a-ra/ 'to wash'):

(670) Напи́ напи́ еиба́ӡәӡәоит.
/nap'ә́-j nap'ә́-j ø-ajbá-ʒ^{w}ʒ^{w}a-wa-jt'/
hand-and hand-and [they(C1)-]Rec-wash-Dyn-Fin
'A hand washes a hand.'

5.7.2.2. In order to transform a three-place transitive verb into a reciprocal construction, the Column II pronominal prefix expressing the indirect object of the three-place transitive verb is changed by the reciprocal marker -аиба- /ajba/.[170] Compare the present tense form (671) of the three-place transitive verb арбара́ /a-rba-rá/ 'to show' with the reciprocal form (672) produced by means of -аиба-:

(671) ислырбо́ит
/jә-s-lә-r-ba-wá-jt'/
it/them(C1)-me(C2)-she(C3)-Caus-see-Dyn-Fin
'She is showing it/them to me.'

(672) хаибалырбо́ит
/ħ-ajba-lә-r-ba-wá-jt'/
us(C1)-Rec-she(C3)-Caus-see-Dyn-Fin
'She is showing us to each other.'

Other example:

170. Also, it is possible that the Column III pronominal prefix expressing the subject of the three-place transitive verb is changed by the reciprocal marker -аиба- /ajba/. See the examples below, which are taken from Hewitt (1979c: 86): a-j^{w}ә́ ø-ħ-ájba-te-jt' (the-wine it-to us(C2)-each other-give-Fin) 'We gave the wine to each other'. Cf. a-j^{w}ә́ ø-ejbá-ħ-te-jt' (the-wine it-to each other-we(C3)-give-Fin) 'We gave the wine to each other'.

а́ибыхəара /ájbə-ħʷa-ra/[171] 'to tell *sth* to each other' (cf. а-хəара́ /a-ħʷa-rá/ [tr.] 'say'):

(673) (И)еиба́ххəоит.
/j-ajb[a-]áħ-ħʷa-wa-jt'/
it/them(C1)-Rec-we(C3)-say-Dyn-Fin
'We are telling it/them to each other.'

Cf. иса́лхəоит
/jə-s-á-l-ħʷa-wa-jt'/
it/them(C1)-me(C2)-to-she(C3)-say-Dyn-Fin
'She say it/them to me.'

5.7.2.3. а́ибашьра /ájba-šʲ-ra/ 'to kill each other' is conjugated in the following way:

	Affirmative	Negative
Finite Forms		
Present		
1Pl-Rec-R-	ҳ-аиба-шь-уе́-ит	ҳ-аиба-шь-уа́-м
2Pl-	шə-еиба-шь-уе́-ит	шə-еиба-шь-уа́-м
3Pl-	(и)еиба-шь-уе́-ит	(и)еиба-шь-уа́-м
Aorist		
1Pl-	ҳ-аиба́-шь-ит	ҳ-аиба́-м-шь-ит[172]
2Pl-	шə-еиба-шь-и́т	шə-еиба́-м-шь-ит[173]
3Pl-	(и)еиба-шь-и́т	(и)еиба́-м-шь-ит[174]
Causative	ҳ-аиба-ды-р-шь-и́т /ħ-ajba-də-r-šʲə́-jt'/ we(C1)-Rec-they(C3)-Caus-kill-(Aor)-FIn 'They made us kill each other.'	ҳ-аиба-д-мы-р-шь-и́т
Non-Finite Forms		
Present		
Rel-Rec-R-	и-е́иба-шь-уа	и-е́иба-м-шь-уа
Past Indefinite	и-е́иба-шьы-з	и-е́иба-м-шьы-з

а́ибарбара /ájba-rba-ra/ 'to show *sb*/*sth* to each other' is conjugated in the following manner:

	Affirmative	Negative
Finite Forms		
Present		
1Pl-Rec-3Sg.F-Caus-R-	ҳ-аиба-лы-рбо́-ит	ҳ-аиба-лы-рбо́-м
3Pl-Rec-1Pl-Caus-R-	еиба-ҳа-рбо́-ит	еиба-ҳа-рбо́-м

---

171. Here, -аиба- /ajba/ causes the weakening of a vowel.
172. Cf. ҳ-м-еиба-шь-и́т 'we did not make war'.
173. Cf. шə-м-еиба-шь-ит 'you did not make war'.
174. Cf. и-м-еиба-шь-ит 'they did not make war'.

Aorist		
1Pl-Rec-3Sg.F-Caus-R-	ҳ-аиба-лы-рбé-ит	ҳ-аиба-л-мы-рбé-ит
Non-Finite Forms		
Present		
Rel-Rec-3Sg.F-Caus-R-	и-éиба-лы-рбо	и-éиба-л-мы-рбо
	/j-ájba-lə-rba-wa/ '(the one) whom she is showing to each other'	
1Pl-Rec-Rel-Caus-R-	ҳ-аиба-зы-рбó	ҳ-аиба-з-мы-рбó
	/ħ-ajba-zə-rba-wa/ '(the one) who is showing us to each other'	
Past Indefinite		
Rel-Rec-3Sg.F-Caus-R-	и-éиба-лы-рба-з	и-éиба-л-мы-рба-з
1Pl-Rec-Rel-Caus-R-	ҳ-аиба-зы-рбá-з	ҳ-аиба-з-мы-рбá-з
Imperative	(и)еиба-шәы-рбá!	(и)еиба-шә-мы-рбá-н!

5.8. Absolutive Construction

5.8.1. Absolutive (abbreviated as 'Abs') is a form which works in the same way as the Russian *деепричастие* 'gerund' in that it functions as a verb and adverb combined. As the function of the absolutive construction is to join two sentences into one, there must be a sentence in the finite form. Now, if two sentences named S_1 and S_2 have a logical relation, and if S_1 is changed into the absolutive and S_2 is made the main sentence (in the finite form), the following temporal relationships between S_1 and S_2 are conceivable:

(i) After performing the action in S_1 the action in S_2 is/will be/was performed.

(ii) The actions in S_1 and S_2 is/will be/were performed at the same time.

5.8.2. Past Absolutive

The past absolutive (abbreviated as 'Past Abs') expresses the temporal relationship in (i) above.[175] This absolutive is produced by attaching the absolutive marker -ны /-nə/ (affirmative), -кәа(н) /-k'ʷa(n)/ (negative) to the aorist stem of dynamic verbs (i.e. the form with -ит removed from the aorist finite form). In this case, when the verb is a transitive verb, in the affirmative form the Column III pronominal prefix expressing an agent disappears.[176] On the other hand, when the verb is a transitive verb in the negative form, the appearance of this Column III pronominal prefix is optional (in the examples below, the Column III pronominal prefix is not displayed). Examples:

175. The temporal relationship between S_1 and S_2 can also be expressed by the past indefinite: Сарá сашьá ашәҟәы́ изы́зҩын апóчҭахь сцéит. /sará s-ašʲá a-šʷq'ʷə́ jə-zə́-z-jʷə-n a-p'óčʲta-[a-]xʲ s-ca-wá-jt'/ 'I wrote a letter to my brother and went to the post office' (see §3.1.7.5). However, regarding this usage, in Abkhaz texts the past absolutive appears with greater frequency than the past indefinite.

176. On rare occasions, the absolutive marker -ны /nə/ weakens and becomes -н /n/. For this reason, the end of the past absolutive and the end of the past indefinite have the same form. However, the two forms are distinguised by whether there is a pronominal prefix for the agent or not.

	Affirmative	Negative
Intransitive verbs		
а-ца-ра́ 'to go'	д-ца-ны́ /d-ca-nə́/ (s)he(C1)-go-Past Abs 'he/she, having gone' Cf. Aorist Finite: д-цé-ит /d-cá-jt'/ 'he/she went' ды-м-цé-ит /də-m-cá-jt'/ 'he/she did not go'	ды-м-ца́-кәа /də-m-cá-k'ʷa/
а-гы́ла-ра 'to stand'	д-гы́ла-ны /d-gə́la-nə/ 'he/she having stood up'	ды-м-гы́ла-кәа
а́-с-ра 'to hit'	с-бы́-с-ны /s-bə́-s-nə/ 'I having hit you-F' Cf. Aorist Finite: с-бы́-с-ит (C1-C2-R-Fin) 'I hit you-F'	сы-б-мы́-с-кәа
а́-г-ха-ра 'to be late'	д-а́-г-ха-ны /d-á-g-xa-nə/ 'he/she having been late for it' Cf. Aorist Finite: д-а́-г-хе-ит 'he/she was late for it'	д-а́-гы-м-ха-кәа
а́-хәа-ҧш-ра 'to look at'	с-бы́-хәа-ҧш-ны /s-bə́-xʷa-pš-nə/ 'I having looked at you-F' Cf. Aorist Finite: с-бы́-хәа-ҧш-ит 'I looked at you-F'	с-бы́-хәа-м-ҧш-кәа
Transitive verbs		
а-ба-ра́ 'to see'	д-ба-ны́ /d-ba-nə́/ him/her(C1)-ø-see-Past Abs 'having seen him/her' Cf. Aorist Finite: ды-з-бé-ит (C1-C3-R-Fin) 'I saw him/her' д-сы-м-бé-ит 'I did not see him/her'	ды-м-ба́-кәа /də-m-bá-k'ʷa/
а́-жә-ра 'to drink'	и́-жә-ны /jə́-žʷ-nə/ 'having drunk it/them' Cf. Aorist Finite: и-з-жә-и́т 'I drank it/them'	и-мы́-жә-кәа *or* и́-жәы-м-кәа
а-ргы́ла-ра 'to build'	и-ргы́ла-ны /jə-rgə́la-nə/ 'having built it/them' Cf. Aorist Finite: и-сы-ргы́ле-ит 'I built it/them'	и-мы-ргы́ла-кәа
а́-ҟа-ҵа-ра 'to do/make'	и-ҟа-ҵа-ны́ /jə-q'a-c'a-nə́/ 'having done/made it/them' Cf. Aorist Finite: и-ҟа-с-ҵé-ит 'I did/made it/them'	и-ҟа-м-ҵа́-кәа

á-ҭа-ра ‘to give’	и-ры́-ҭа-ны /jə-rə́-ta-nə/ ‘having given it/them to them’ Cf. Aorist Finite: и-ры́-с-ҭе-ит ‘I gave it/them to them’	и-ры́-м-ҭа-кәа
а-хәа-рá ‘to say’	и-хәа-ны́ /jə-ħʷa-nə́/ ‘having said it/them’ Cf. Aorist Finite: и-с-хәé-ит ‘I said it/them’	и-м-хәá-кәа / и-с-á-м-хәа-кәа
Labile verbs		
á-ӡах-ра ‘to sew’	л-ӡах-ны́ /d-ӡах-nə́/ ‘he/she having sewn’	ды-м-ӡахы́-кәа
	и-ӡах-ны́ /jə-ӡах-nə́/ ‘having sewn it/them’	и-м-ӡахы́-кәа
а-был-рá ‘to burn’	и-был-ны́ /jə-bəl-nə́/ ‘it having burned’ or ‘having burned it/them’	и-м-б(ы)лы́-кәа

The examples below use the past absolutive with the intransitive verb (674) and the transitive verb (675):

(674) Ашәҟәы́ лáҧхьаны сарá сахь лаáит.
/a-šʷq’ʷə́ d-á-pxʲa-nə sará s-axʲ d-aá-jt’/
the-book he/she(C1)-it(C2)-read-Abs I me-to he/she-come-(Aor)-Fin
‘Having read the book, he/she came to me.’

(675) Ашәҟәы́ ɸны́ апóчҭахь дцéит.
/a-šʷq’ʷə́ ϕ-jʷ-nə́ a-p’óčʲta-[a]xʲ d-cá-jt’/
the-letter [it(C1)-]write-Abs the-post office-to he/she-go-(Aor)-Fin
‘Having written a letter, he/she went to the post office.’

In the sentences above, since it is possible for the main clause to be in any tense, so for example, main clause S_2 in (674) above can be put into the present tense as shown in (676) below:

(676) Ашәҟәы́ лáҧхьаны сарá сахь лаауéит.
/a-šʷq’ʷə́ d-á-pxʲa-nə sará s-axʲ d-aa-wá-jt’/
the-book he/she(C1)-it(C2)-read-Abs I me-to he/she-come-Dyn-Fin
‘Having read the book, he/she will come to me.’

As can be seen in these examples, the tense of the sentence is dependant on main clause S_2 and the past absolutive indicates only a temporal successional relationship (namely, that the action in main clause S_2 occurs after the action in subordinate clause S_1).

The tense of main clause S_2 in both (674) and (675) above is aorist. In this way, when main clause S_2 is aorist, the tense of subordinate clause S_1 can also be in the past indefinite tense without using the absolutive. For example, if (675) is put in the past indefinite tense, it becomes (677) below. In that case, take note of the appearance of the III pronominal prefix indicating an agent in the verbal complex of clause S_1:

(677) Ашәƙәы́ лҩы́н апо́чтахь дце́ит.
/a-šʷq'ʷə́ ø-l̲-jʷə́-n a-p'óčʲta-[a]xʲ d-cá-jt'/
the-letter [it(C1)-]she(C3)-write-Past.Ind.Fin the-post office-to she-go-(Aor)-Fin
'She wrote a letter and went to the post office.'

In the absolutive constructions in (674–676) above, the agent (subject) of the subordinate clause and the subject of the main sentence are the same. While examining more complex sentences (678–680), we shall investigate whether the agent (subject) of the subordinate clause and the subject of the main clause are the same. Sentence (678) below is a form with the two-place transitive verb абара́ /a-ba-rá/ 'to see' in the subordinate clause:

(678) Али Мура́т дбаны́ дце́ит.
/áləj məwrát d-ø-ba-nə́ d-cá-jt'/
name(M) name(M) him(C1)-ø(C3)-see-Abs he(C1)-go-(Aor)-Fin
'Having seen Murat, Ali went.'

According to our informant, the agent of the subordinate clause in (678) above is *Ali*, not *Murat*. Also, the subject of the main clause is *Ali*. Therefore, since A and S are treated as the same here, its syntactic pivot is an S/A pivot[177]. Now, let us look at the same thing in the absolutive negative. Since the appearance of an agent in the absolutive negative form is optional, the agent of the subordinate clause is even more evident. Sentence (679) below presents a form where the agent appears in the absolutive:

(679) Амра Мура́т длымба́кәан[178] дце́ит.
/ámra məwrát d-lə-m-bá-k'ʷan d-cá-jt'/
name(F) name(M) him(C1)-she(C3)-Neg-see-Abs she(C1)-go-(Aor)-Fin
'Amra, not having seen Murat, went.'

The agent of the subordinate clause in (679) above is *Arma*, and the subject of the main sentence is also *Arma*, so it is an S/A pivot. Next, let us examine the relationship between subject of the subordinate clause and the main clause examined above using the two-place intransitive verb á-пҳара /á-cħa-ra/ 'to bite' in the subordinate clause:

(680) Сла а́мшә иа́мцҳакәан ице́ит.
/s-la á-mšʷ j-á-m-cħa-k'ʷan jə-cá-jt'/
my-dog the-bear it(dog,C1)-it(bear, C2)-Neg-bite-Abs it(C1)-go-(Aor)-Fin
'My dog, not having bitten the bear, went.'

In (680) above, as already mentioned in §3.1.6, Note 3, the referent which cross-references the subject и- /jə/ of the subordinate clause is сла /s-la/ 'my dog', not а́мшә /á-mšʷ/ 'the bear'. Furthermore, according to our informant, the subject of the main clause is сла /s-la/ 'my dog'. The subject of the subordinate clause and the subject of the main clause are the same here as well.[179]

177. For syntactic pivots see Dixon (1994: §6.2).

178. The form дымба́кәан /də-m-bá-k'ʷan/, where an agent does not appear, is also possible.

179. The relationship between the subject of the subordinate clause (or the agent) and the subject of the main clause can be an S/A pivot in sentences using the past indefinite tense as well. Compare the sentence (680)

5.8.3. Absolutive of Stative Verbs

The absolutive, which attaches -ны /nə/ to the affirmative form and -кәа(н) /k'ʷa(n)/ to the negative form of the root of stative verbs, expresses the temporal relationship in (ii) above (a relationship where the action in the main clause and the subordinate clause are performed at the same time). Absolutives formed from stative verbs normally do not omit the pronominal prefix which appears there. Example:

	Affirmative	Negative
а́-ма-заа-ра 'to have'	и-сы́-ма-ны[180] /jə-sə́-ma-nə/ it/them(C1)-I(C2)-have-Abs 'I, having it/them'	и-сы́-ма-м-кәа /jə-sə́-ma-m-k'ʷa/
а-тәа-ра́ 'to sit'	д-тәа-ны́ /d-t'ʷa-nə́/ 'he/she, sitting'	ды-м-тәа́-кәа *or* д-тәа́-м-кәа
а-гы́ла-заа-ра 'to stand'	и-гы́ла-ны /jə-gə́la-nə/ 'it/they, standing'	и-гы́ла-м-кәа
а́-ла-заа-ра 'to be in'	и-а́-ла-ны /j-á-la-nə/ 'it/they, being in it'	и-а́-ла-м-кәа
а-ҿы́-заа-ра 'to be engaged in'	д-а-ҿ-ны́ /d-a-č'-nə́/ 'he/she, being engaged in it'	д-а-ҿы́-м-кәа
а-шьҭа́-заа-ра 'to lie'	ды-шьҭа-ны́ /də-šʲta-nə́/ 'he/she, lying'	ды-шьҭа́-м-кәа
а-шәы́-заа-ра 'to be wearing'	и-с-шәы-ны́ /jə-s-šʷə-nə́/ 'I, being wearing'	и-с-шәы́-м-кәа

Example sentences with the absolutive of stative verbs:

---

with the following sentence:

Сла а́мшә аба́н ицéит.

/s-la	á-mšʷ	ø-a-bá-n	jə-cé-jt'/
my-dog	the-bear	[it(= bear, C1)-]it(= dog, C3)-see-Past.Ind.Fin	it(= dog, C1)-go-(Aor)-Fin

'My dog saw the bear and (my dog) went'.

180. In this verb, there are also the variants ма /ma/, маны́ /ma-nə́/ where the pronominal prefix does not appear.

(681) Сҩы́за дтәаны́, ашәҟәы́ да́пҳхьоит.[181]
/s-jʷə́za d-t'ʷa-nə́ a-šʷq'ʷə́ d-á-pxʲa-wa-jt'/
my-friend he/she(C1)-sit-Abs the-book he/she(C1)-it(C2)-read-Dyn-Fin
'My friend is reading a book, sitting.'

(682) Сҩы́за дтәаны́, ашәҟәы́ да́пҳхьон.
/s-jʷə́za d-t'ʷa-nə́ a-šʷq'ʷə́ d-á-pxʲa-wa-n/
my-friend he/she(C1)-sit-Abs the-book he/she(C1)-it(C2)-read-Dyn-Impf
'My friend was reading a book, sitting.'

(683) Сҩы́зцәа сы́ма(ны) саа́ит.
/s-jʷə́z-cʷa ø-sə́-ma(-nə) s-aá-jt'/
my-friend-Pl [them(C1)-]I(C2)-have-Abs I(C1)-come-(Aor)-Fin
'I came with my friends.'

In examples (681) and (682) above, both indicate that the state in subordinate clause S_1 and the action in main clause S_2 are being performed simultaneously. The literal meaning of (683) is 'I, having my friends, came', and the action in the main clause is supplemented by the situation expressed by the absolutive.

5.8.4. Present Absolutive

The temporal relationship in (ii) above can also be expressed by the present stem of dynamic verbs (namely, forms ending in -уа /wa/). We shall call this form the 'present absolutive' (abbreviated as 'Pres.Abs'). In this case, the appearance or absence of the Column III pronominal prefix indicating the agent of a transitive verb is optional. For example:

Intransitive Verb: а-ца-ра́ 'to go': дцо́ /d-ca-wá/ 'he/she, going', а́-пҳхьа-ра 'to read': са́пҳхьо /s-á-pxʲa-wa/ 'I, reading it', а-тҵәы́уа-ра 'to cry': дтҵәы́уо /d-c'ʷə́wa-wa/ 'he/she, crying', а́-ҩ-ра 'to run': сы́ҩуа /sə́-jʷ-wa/ 'I, running'.

Transitive Verb: а-ҩ-ра́ 'to write': изҩуа́ /jə-z-jʷ-wá/ 'I, writing it/them', а́-фа-ра 'to eat': исфо́ /jə-s-fa-wá/ 'I, eating it/them', а-ба-ра́ 'to see': илбо́ /jə-l-ba-wá/ 'she, seeing it/them', а́-жә-ра 'to drink': изжәуа́ /jə-z-žʷ-wá/ 'I, drinking it/them', а-х-ра́ 'to sharpen': исхуа́ /jə-s-x-wá/ 'I, sharpening'; а-пҳ-ҟа-ра́ 'to cut': ипҳҟо́ /jə-p-q'a-wá/ 'cutting it/them', а-пҳ-тҵәа-ра́ 'to break': ипҳтҵәо́ /jə-p-c'ʷa-wá/ 'breaking it/them', а-ргы́ла-ра 'to build': иргы́ло /jə-rgə́la-wa/ 'building it/them'.
The following are examples of the present absolusive of dynamic verbs:

(684) Атҵа́ракәа чырчы́руа а́шәа рҳәо́ит.
/a-c'ára-kʷa ø-č'ʲərč'ʲə́r-wa á-šʷa ø-r-ħʷa-wá-jt'/
the-bird-Pl [they(C1)-]chirp-Pres.Abs the-song [it(C1)-]they(C3)-say-Dyn-Fin
'Chirping, the birds are singing.'

181. Take note of the difference with the dynamic verb а-тәара́ /a-t'ʷa-rá/ 'to sit down':
Сҩы́за дтәан, ашәҟәы́ да́пҳхьеит.
/s-jʷə́za d-t'ʷa-n a-šʷq'ʷə́ d-á-pxʲa-jt'/
my-friend he/she(C1)-sit-Past Ind the-book he/she(C1)-it(C2)-read-(Aor)-Fin
'My friend sat down and read a/the book'.

(685) Сыҧҳәы́с дуанҭо́, а́шәа лҳәо́н.
/sə-pħ^{w}ə́s d-wanta-wá á-š^{w}a ø-l-ħ^{w}a-wá-n/
my-wife she-iron-Pres.Abs the-song [it(C1)-]she(C3)-say-Dyn-Impf.Fin
'My wife, ironing, was singing a song.'

(686) Ашәҟәы́ (л)ҩуа́, аму́зыка дазы́ӡырҩуан.
/a-š^{w}q'^{w}ə́ ø-(l)-j^{w}-wá a-mə́wzək'a d-a-zə́-ʒərj^{w}-wa-n/
the-letter [it(C1)-](she(C3))-write-Pres.Abs the-music she(C1)-it(C2)-Prev-listen-Dyn-Impf.Fin
'Writing a letter, she was listening to music.'

(687) Аҽы́ а́ӡҕаб хәычы́ да́маны ицо́, ицо́ акы́р хара́ ице́ит. (Abkhaz text)
/a-čə́ á-ʒɣab x^{w}əč'^{j}ə́ d-á-ma-nə jə-ca-wá, jə-ca-wá
the-horse the-girl little her(C1)-it(C2)-have-Abs it(C1)-go-Pres.Abs it(C1)-go-Pres.Abs
ak'ə́r xará jə-cá-jt'/
very far it(C1)-go-(Aor)-Fin
'The horse, running and running, ran far, far away, taking the little girl with him.'

(688) Аҧе́нџьыр а́шә аалырты́н, ҳәы́ҳәк ҧырҧыруа́ иааҩнашы́лт. (Abkhaz text)
/a-pénǯ^{j}ər a-š^{w} ø-aa-[a-]lə-rt'ə́-n ħ^{w}ə́ħ^{w}-k'
the-window its-door [it(C1)-Par-?-she(C3)-open-Past.Ind.Fin dove-one
ø-pərpər-wá j-aaj^{w}na-šə́l[a-j]t'/
[it(C1)-]flap-Pres.Abs it(C1)-Prev-go inside-(Aor)-Fin
'When she opened the door window, a dove flew in flapping its wings.'

Examples (684–686) above indicate that the action in the subordinate clause and the action in the main clause co-occur since the main clause is in the present or imperfect (i.e. in the imperfective aspect). On the other hand, in examples (687) and (688) where the main clause is aorist, the present absolutive depicts the circumstances and indicates a collateral condition on the main clause. Other than these sentences using the present absolutive, the co-occurrence of the actions in the subordinate and main clauses can be expressed in Abkhaz even when the temporal conjunctional prefix -ан- /an/ 'when' is used. Compare (685) above with (689) below:

(689) Сыҧҳәы́с даныуанҭо́з, а́шәа лҳәо́н.
/sə-pħ^{w}ə́s d-anə-wanta-wá-z á-š^{w}a ø-l-ħ^{w}a-wá-n/
my-wife she-when-iron-Dyn-Impf.NF the-song [it(C1)-]she(C3)-say-Dyn-Impf.Fin
'When my wife was ironing, she would usually sing a song.'

According to our informant, (685) expresses a one-time action, and (689) indicates a repeated action.

5.8.5. The absolusive can be used as a complement to verbs such as а́-лгара /á-l-ga-ra/ 'to finish', а́-лагара /á-la-ga-ra/ 'to begin'. The former takes the past absolutive that has -ны /nə/, and the latter takes the present absolutive that has -уа /wa/, as a complement. The masdar can also work as a complement of these verbs. Examples (the masdar forms are in parenthesis) are given in (690–693):

(690) Сара́ ашәҟәы́ ҩны (*or* аҩра́) са́лгеит.
/sará a-š^{w}q'^{w}ə́ ø-j^{w}-nə́ (*or* a-j^{w}-rá) s-á-l-ga-jt'/
I the-letter [it(C1)-]write-Past Abs (*or* its-write-Masd) I(C1)-it(C2)-Prev-finish-(Aor)-Fin

'I finished writing the letter.'

(691) Сара́ са́жәахә кы́ԥхьны са́лгеит.
/sará s-áž^w^ax^w^ ø-k'^j^ə́px^j^-nə s-á-l-ga-jt'/
I my-report [it(C1)-]print-Past Abs I(C1)-it(C2)-Prev-finish-(Aor)-Fin
'I finished printing my report.'

(692) Ашәҟәы́ лҩуа́ да́лагеит.
/a-š^w^q'^w^ə́ ø-l-j^w^-wá d-á-la-ga-jt'/
the-letter [it(C1)-]she(C3)-write-Pres.Abs she(C1)-it(C2)-Prev-begin-(Aor)-Fin
'She started writing the/a letter.'

(693) А-жьа́ шьҭа́ ишкәакәахо (*or* а́шкәакәахара) иа́лагоит.
/a-ž^j^á š^j^tá jə-šk'^w^ak'^w^a-xa-wa (*or* á-šk'^w^ak'^w^a-xa-ra)
the-hare already it(C1)-white-become-Pres.Abs (*or* its-white-become-Masd)
j-á-la-ga-wa-jt'/
it(C1)-it(C2)-Prev-begin-Dyn-Pres.Fin
'The hare is already beginning to turn white.'

According to our informant, while the masdar complement states simple facts, the nuance of 'must do…' and 'it is difficult to do…' is implied when the absolusive is the complement. However, this nuance cannot be confirmed in Abkhaz texts. It appears to be used with virtually the same meaning. Look at the following examples taken from Abkhaz texts:

(694) Аҵәы́ргакәҵа баны́ сана́лга а́шьҭахь, сара́ сце́ит Аԥсуа ҳәынҭқа́рратә музе́и а́хь.
/a-c^w^ə́rgak^w^c'a ø-ba-nə́ s-an-á-l-ga á-š^j^tax^j^ sará
the-exhibition [it(C1)-]see-Past Abs I(C1)-when-it(C2)-Prev-finish-(Aor.NF) its-after I
s-cá-jt' ápswa ħ^w^əntkárrat'^w^ məwzéj [a-]ax^j^
I(C1)-go-(Aor)-Fin Abkhazian state museum [its-]to
'After I had finished seeing the exhibition, I went to the Abkhazian State Museum.'

In addition, the absolutive is used with the verb а́-ҟазаара /á-q'a-zaa-ra/ 'to be' and indicates a state:

(695) Уи́ дзакә́тәу ды́рны ҳа́ҟоуп.
/wəj d-zak'^w^t'^w^ə-w ø-də́r-nə ħá-q'a-wp'/
he he-what sort of-Stat.NF [it(C1)-]know-Abs we(C1)-be-Stat.Pres.Fin
'We know who he is.'

(696) Ҩажәа́ шыкәса́ хша́ра димаӡа́мкәа(н) (еиԥш) ды́ҟан.
/j^w^až^w^á šək^w^sá xšára də-j-ma-ʒá-m-k'^w^a(n) (ajpš) də́-q'a-n/
20 year child him/her(C1)-he(C2)-have-Emph-Neg-Abs (like) he(C1)-be-Stat.Past.Fin
'For 20 years he was without offspring.'

5.9. Transitivity of Verbs

5.9.1. The transitivity of Abkhaz verbs can be determined by the following criteria:

(i) With the Imperative Form

Since the Column III pronominal prefix indicating an agent is absent in the singular affirmative imperative form of transitive verbs (see §4.2.1.1.3), the transitivity of verbs can be determined by forming a singular, affirmative imperative. For example, the singular affirmative imperative form of á-фара /á-fa-ra/ 'to eat' is и́ф(а) /jə́-f(a)/ [it/them(C1)-eat.Imp] 'eat it/them!', and this verb is transitive from the fact that the Column III pronominal prefix б-/у- /b-/wə/ indicating an agent is absent (cf. ибфе́ит /jə-b-fá-jt'/ [it/them(C1)-you.F(C3)-eat-(Aor)-Fin] 'you-F ate it/them'). On the other hand, the singular affirmative imperative form of а-хшара́ /a-x-ša-rá/ 'to give birth to' is дбыхша́ /d-bə-x-šá/ [him/her-you.F-Prev-give birth to.Imp] 'give birth to him/her!', and due to the appearance of the prefix бы- /bə/ this verb is intransitive (for this verb see §5.10). And the singular affirmative imperative form of á-сра /á-s-ra/ 'to hit' is бсы́с /b-sə́-s/ [you.F(C1)-me(C2)-hit.Imp] 'hit me! (to a woman)', усы́с /wə-sə́-s/ [you.M(C1)-me(C2)-hit.Imp] 'hit me! (to a man)', and due to the appearance of the Column I pronominal prefix б-/у- /b-/wə/ indicating a subject this verb is also intransitive (cf. бсы́сит /b-sə́-sə-jt'/ [you.F(C1)-me(C2)-hit-(Aor)-Fin] 'you hit me').

(ii) With the Past Absolutive

In the affirmative form of the past absolutive of transitive verbs, the transitivity of the verb can be determined from the fact that the Column III pronominal prefix indicating an agent does not appear (see §5.8.2). For example, the affirmative past Absolutive of á-фара /á-fa-ra/ 'to eat' is и́фаны /jə́-fa-nə/ [it/them(C1)-eat-Abs] 'having eaten it/them', and this verb is transitive because the Column III pronominal prefix indicating an agent does not appear. On the other hand, the past absolutive form of а-хшара́ /a-x-ša-rá/ 'to give birth to' is дсыхшаны́ /d-sə-x-ša-nə́/ [him/her-I-Prev-give birth to-Past Abs] 'I, having given birth to him/her', and this verb is intransitive because the prefix сы- /sə/ 'I' appears. And the past absolutive form of á-сра /á-s-ra/ 'to hit' in an affirmative form is усы́сны /wə-sə́-s-nə/ [you.M(C1)-me(C2)-hit-Abs] 'you-M, having hit me', and this verb is intransitive from the fact that the Column I pronominal prefix у- /wə/ indicating a subject appears.

(iii) By the insertion position of the pronominal prefix of verbs with preverbs

In transitive verbs with preverbs, the pronominal prefix of the agent is inserted in between the preverb and the root (cf. Class G verbs in §3.2.1 and §3.2.10 as well as Class H verbs in §3.2.11). For example, the aorist form of á-ҟацара /á-q'a-c'a-ra/ 'to do' is иҟасце́ит /jə-q'a-s-c'á-jt'/ [it/them(C1)-Prev-I(C3)-do-(Aor)-Fin] 'I did it/them'. On the other hand, in intransitive verbs with preverbs, the pronominal prefix does not split the preverb and root. For example, the aorist form of á-хәаԥшра /á-xʷa-pš-ra/ 'to watch; to look at' (Class F) is сбы́хәаԥшит /s-bə́-xʷa-pšə-jt'/ [I(C1)-you.F(C2)-Prev-look at-(Aor)-Fin] 'I looked at you-F'.[182]

(iv) By voicing the pronominal prefix immediately before an initial-voiced consonant in the root

When the initial consonant in the root of a transitive verb is voiced, the pronominal prefix of the unvoiced consonant immediately before it (namely, the first-person singular prefix с- /s/, the first person plural prefix х- /ħ/, and the second-person plural prefix шә- /šʷ/) would be voiced. For the first-

182. We know that хәа- is a preverb on the basis of the division of the preverb and root by the negative marker м-: сбы́хәамԥшит /s-bə́-xʷa-m-pšə-jt'/.

person plural, it further changes into aa (see §3.2.6). For example, the aorist forms of а-бара́ /a-ba-rá/ 'to see': дызбе́ит /də-z-bá-jt'/ 'I saw him/her', даабе́ит /d-aa-bá-jt'/ 'we saw him/her', дыжәбе́ит /də-žʷ-bá-jt'/ 'you-Pl saw him/her'. However, even under the same conditions, there are cases where the pronominal prefixes mentioned above will not be voiced (for this, see §3.2.6, fn. 115). On the other hand, even if the initial consonant in the root of an intransitive verb is voiced, the pronominal prefix immediately before it will never be voiced. For example, сӡахуе́ит /s-ʒax-wá-jt'/ 'I am sewing'.

(v) By the differences in the position of the potential marker

In the potential derivation, there are the following differences in the position of the potential marker in transitive and intransitive verbs (see §4.2.4):

Two-Place Intransitive: C1-C2-R- → C1-Pot-C2-R-:

сбы́суеит /s-bə́-s-wa-jt'/ 'I am hitting you'

→ сызбы́суам /sə-z-bə́-s-wa-m/ 'I cannot hit you' [potential]

Two-Place Transitive: C1-C3-R- → C1-C2-Pot-R-:

издьы́руеит /jə-z-də́r-wa-jt'/ 'I know it/them'

→ исыздьы́руам /jə-sə-z-də́r-wa-m/ 'I do not know it/them' [potential]

We shall examine whether the criteria for (i) through (v) above applies to intransitive and transitive verbs ('--' indicates that form does not exist, or is unclear, or its criterion is not applicable).

Intransitive verbs

а-нхара́ 'live' (i) бынха́! (ii) дынханы́ (iii) -- (iv) -- (v) --

а́-сра 'hit' (i) бсы́с! 1(ii) сбы́сны (iii) -- (iv) -- (v) сызбы́суам

а́-цхара 'bite' (i) блы́цха! (ii) сбы́цханы (iii) -- (iv) -- (v) ?

а́-хәара 'help' (i) бсы́хәа! (ii) сбы́хәаны (iii) -- (iv) -- (v) дызлы́хәом

а́-хәаҧшра 'look at' (i) ба́хәаҧш! (ii) сбы́хәаҧшны (iii) сбы́хәаҧшит (iv) --
(v) сызбы́хәаҧшуам

а-зы́ӡырҩра 'listen to' (i) бысзы́ӡырҩ! (ii) сыбзы́ӡырҩны (iii) сыбзы́мӡырҩит (iv) --
(v) сызбзы́ӡырҩуам

а́-ҧхьара 'read' (i) ба́ҧхь(а)! (ii) да́ҧхьаны (iii) -- (iv) -- (v) сза́ҧхьом

Inversive verbs

а-хара́ 'hear' (i) ибаха́! (ii) сбаханы́ (iii) сбахауе́ит (iv) -- (v) ?

а-гәаҧхара́ 'like' (i) сыбгәаҧха́з! (ii) илгәаҧханы́ (iii) сыбгәа́мҧхеит
(iv) cf. дысгәаҧхо́ит (v) сызбгәаҧхо́м

а́ура 'receive' (i) ибо́у! (ii) исо́уны (iii) -- (iv) -- (v) изсоуам (?)

а-хшара́ 'give birth to' (i) дбыхша! (ii) дсыхшаны́ (iii) дылхы́мшеит (iv) -- (v)?

Transitive verbs

а-гарá 'take' (i) игá! (cf. ибымгáн!) (ii) дганы́ (iii) -- (iv) бызгóит (v) бысзы́гом

а-ды́рра 'know' (i) иды́р! (cf. ибымды́рын!) (ii) дды́рны (iii) -- (iv) бызды́руеит
(v) исызды́руам

á-жәра 'drink' (i) и́жә! (cf. ибымжәы́н!) (ii) и́жәны (iii) -- (iv) изжәуéит
(v) исызы́жәуам

á-ӡбара 'decide' (i) иӡбá! (cf. ибмыӡбáн!) (ii) иӡбаны́ (iii) -- (iv) исыӡбóит (v) ?

á-ҟаҵара 'do/make' (i) иҟаҵá! (cf. иҟабымҵáн!) (ii) иҟаҵаны́ (iii) иҟасымҵéит
(iv) -- (v) исзы́ҟаҵом

а-ҧжәарá 'tear' (i) иҧжәá! (cf. иҧы́бымжәан!) (ii) иҧжәаны́
(iii) иҧы́зы/сымжәеит (iv) иҧы́з/сжәоит (v) ?

á-ҭира 'sell' (i) иҭиӣ! (cf. ибымҭиӣн!) (ii) иҭины́ (iii) -- (iv) -- (v) исзы́мҭи(ӡе)ит

á-фара 'eat' (i) и́ф(а)! (cf. ибымфáн!) (ii) и́фаны (iii) -- (iv) -- (v) исзы́фом

а-шьрá 'kill' (i) ишьы́! (cf. ибмшьы́н!) (ii) д(ы)шьны́ (iii) -- (iv) -- (v) дысзы́шьуам

а-ҩрá 'write' (i) иҩы́! (cf. ибымҩы́н!) (ii) иҩны́ (iii) -- (iv) изҩуéит (v) иаҳзыҩуáм

а-ҧҟарá 'cut' (i) иҧҟá! (cf. иҧы́бымҟан!) (ii) иҧҟаны́ (iii) иҧы́сымҟеит (iv) --
(v) исызҧҟóм

In the examples of intransitive and transitive verbs above, there is no inconsistency between the transitivity criteria from (i) through (v) and the examples. In the imperative form of inversive verbs, the pronominal prefix expressing the subject appears in the position after the Column I pronominal prefix, unlike cases in intransitive verbs. In the second-person, singular, affirmative and imperative forms in transitive verbs, the pronominal prefix which expresses the Column III agent does not appear, so the second-person pronominal prefix which appears in the imperative form of an inversive verb cannot be regarded as the agent of a transitive verb. Inversive verbs should be regarded as anomalous intransitive verbs.

5.9.2. The transitivity of Abkhaz verbs can be determined based on the criteria in (i) through (v) above. According to these criteria, verbs in Abkhaz have a slightly different shape from the Indo-European languages we are familiar with. First, some of the transitive verbs in Indo-European languages are intransitive verbs in Abkhaz (see §3.2.5). For example, á-сра /á-s-ra/ 'to hit', áгәара /á-gʷa-ra/ 'to push', á-цхара /á-čha-ra/ 'to bite, to sting', á-хара /á-xa-ra/ 'to pull; to smoke', á-ҧхьара /á-pxʲa-ra/ 'to read; to call', á-хәара /á-xʷa-ra/ 'to help', áура /[a-]aw-ra/ 'to receive', etc. In addition inversive verbs such as *verba sentiendi, verba affectuum, verba habendi* are also intransitive verbs (see §5.10 for this), where in some Indo-European languages (such as English) they are transitive; in other Indo-European languages (such as Russian), some of them are intransitive verbs. Also, in Abkhaz, verbs whose stem begins with р- /r/ are virtually all causative forms, and this derivation process is fairly productive. For example, as in а-рӡрá /a-r-ʒ-rá/ 'to lose' (cf. á-ӡра /á-ʒ-ra/ 'to disappear'), а-ргы́лара /a-r-gə́la-ra/ 'to build' (cf. а-гы́лара /a-gə́la-ra/ 'to stand'), а-ртрá /a-r-t'-rá/ [tr.] 'to open' (cf. а-трá /a-t'-ra/ [intr.] 'to open'), a derivation from intransitive to transitive verb and derivations which increase the valency from a transitive verb, such as а-рбарá /a-r-ba-rá/ 'to show' (cf. а-бара́ /a-ba-rá/ 'to see'), а-рды́рра /a-r-də́r-ra/ 'to inform' (cf. а-ды́рра /a-də́r-ra/ 'to know') are fairly productive as well.

5.10. Inversive Construction

5.10.1. Similar to other Caucasian languages,[183] Abkhaz also has 'inversive verbs' which occupy a neutral position between intransitive and transitive verbs. These inversive verbs form an inversive construction. Verbs well-known as inversive verbs in Abkhaz are *verba affectuum*, *verba sentienda*, and *verba habendi*.[184] For example, а-гəаҧхара́ /a-g^{w}a-pxa-rá/ 'to like', а-ҭахха-ра́ /a-tax-xa-rá/ 'to want', а-хара́ /a-ħa-rá/ 'to hear', а-гəа́лашəара /a-g^{w}ála-š^{w}a-ra/ 'to remember', а-ха́шҭра /a-xá-št-ra/ 'to forget', а́-мазаара /á-ma-zaa-ra/ 'to have'. In addition, there are the following verbs: а́ура /[a-]aw-ra/ 'to receive', а-хша-ра́ /a-x-ša-rá/ 'to bear, to give birth to', а-хы́лҵра /a-xə́l-c'-ra/ 'to give birth to', а-ҧхара́ /a-p-xa-rá/ 'to lose, to be deprived of', etc. Let us look at how these verb groups are different from other verbs.

For example, the aorist negative form of а-гəаҧхара́ /a-g^{w}a-pxa-rá/ 'to like' becomes сыбгəа́мҧхеит /sə-b-g^{w}á-m-pxa-jt' / 'you-F did not like me', and since the negative marker -м- /m/ splits гəа /g^{w}a/ and ҧха /pxa/, гəа /g^{w}a/ can be regarded as a preverb and ҧха /pxa/ as the root. In addition, since there is no pronominal prefix inserted between the preverb and root, the б- /b/ here is not the Column III pronominal prefix indicating an agent, but can be regarded as the Column II pronominal prefix indicating an indirect object (see transitivity criteria (iii) in §5.9.1). Examples using

183. Inversive constructions are observed throughout the Caucasian languages. In almost all of the Caucasian languages which have declension structures, this construction appears as a sentence indicating its logical subject with the dative. 'In Georgian, there is a whole group of verbs that have an inversive construction in all their conjugated forms. These are called *affective stative verbs* and tend to express emotions and perceptions typically experienced only by human beings. e.g.

me (DAT) is (NOM) m-i-q'var-s 'I love Y',

me (DAT) is (NOM) m-a-kv-s 'I have Y',

me (DAT) is (NOM) m-c'-am-s 'I trust Y',

me (DAT) is (NOM) m-jul-s 'I hate Y',

me (DAT) is (NOM) mo=m-c'on-s 'I like Y',

me (DAT) is (NOM) m-i-č'ir-s 'I find Y difficult'.

kal-s (DAT) švil-i (NOM) u-q'var-s 'the woman (DAT) loves (her) child (NOM).'

(Melikishvili, D., Humphries, D., Kupunia, M. 2008. *The Georgian Verb: A Morphosyntactic Analysis*. Dunwoody. pp. 123–127).

Furthermore, in the Avar language as well logical subjects appear as datives. For example: инсуе жиндирго лъимер б-окьула (insu-e (DAT) žindirgo l'imer b-okula) 'the father (DAT) loves his child', инсуе жиндирго вас в-окьула 'the father loves his son', эбелалъе жиндирго вас в-окьула 'the mother loves her son', лъималазе жодорго эбел й-окьула 'the children love their mother' (Бокарев, А.А. 1949. *Синтаксис аварского языка*. Москва-Ленинград. с. 34).

184. Inversive constructions produced by this inversive verb are also known as 'affective constructions' or 'dative constructions' in other Caucasian languages. From a semantic viewpoint, inversive constructions in Abkhaz are constructions which express an involuntary action or a state which occurs in the subject regardless of the subject's wishes.

this verb are as follows:

(697) Ари́ арти́ст и́хәмаршьа сгәаԥхе́ит. (RAD)
/arə́j [a-]art'ə́jst' jə́-xʷmaršʲa ø-s-gʷa-pxá-jt'/
this the-artist his-performance [it(C1)-]me(C2)-Prev-like-(Aor)-Fin
'I liked this artist's performance.' 'Мне понравилась игра этого артиста.'

In English, the subject is translated as 'I' and the object as 'this artist's performance', but in Abkhaz this sentence must be interpreted as 'it' (= this artist's performance) as the subject, and 'me' as the indirect object (the Russian translation above has many points in common with Abkhaz: *мне* dat. sg. 'to me', *игра* nom. sg. 'performance'). In addition, the past absolutive and potential forms of this verb are as follows:

(698) илгәаԥханы́
/jə-l-gʷa-pxa-nə́/
it/they(C1)-her(C2)-Prev-like-Past Abs
'she, having liked it/them'

(699) сызбгәаԥхо́м
/sə-z-b-gʷa-pxa-wá-m/
I(C1)-Pot-you.F(C2)-Prev-like-Dyn-Neg
'you-F cannot like me'

As л- /l/ 'her' in (698) above does not disappear here, this cannot be regarded as a pronominal prefix indicating the agent (see transitivity criterion (ii) in §5.9.1). Also, the distribution position of the potential marker in (699) indicates that its form is derived from an intransitive verb due to transitivity criterion (v) in §5.9.1. Therefore, the criteria we determined for transitivity in §5.9.1 indicate that this verb а-гәаԥхара́ /a-gʷa-pxa-rá/ is intransitive.[185] What happens to the imperative form for criterion (i) in §5.9.1? According to our informant, the imperative form is as follows:

(700) сыбгәаԥха́з!
/sə-b-gʷa-pxá-z/
I(C1)-you.F(C2)-Prev-like-Stat.Imp

185. P.K. Uslar (1887 [2002]: 55–56) regards this verb а-гәаԥхара́ /a-gʷa-pxa-rá/ 'to like' as a transitive verb on the basis of the regularity of the person/class prefixes, the independent personal pronouns placed before the verb, and the word order of the nouns. The reason Uslar interprets it as a transitive verb is as follows: the mirror-image distribution of the relationship between the sentence's word order and the distribution order of the pronominal prefixes in the verbal complex is the reason that this sentence can be regarded as a transitive verb sentence. See the examples used by Uslar:

Сара уара усгуаԥхуеjт.
/sara wara wə-s-gʷapx-wa-jt'/
I you.M you.M-I-like-Dyn-Fin 'I like you-M'

The sentence above has the same mirror-image relationship to the sentence below which uses the transitive verb а-бара́ /a-ba-rá/ 'to see'

Сара уара узбо́ит.
/sara wara wə-z-ba-wá-jt'/
I you.M you.M-I-see-Dyn-Fin 'I am seeing you-M'.

'пусть я тебе нравлюсь!'

In (700) above, б- /b/ 'you-F' appears, but it appears in Column II, not Column I, where the subject of intransitive verbs normally appears (cf. бсы́с! /b-sə́-s/ [you.F(C1)-me(C2)-hit.Imp] 'hit me! (to a woman)'). Furthermore, the ending of the imperative form is -з /z/, as in the ending of the imperative form of stative verbs. We can see a similar shape in а-гәа́лашәара /a-gʷála-šʷa-ra/ 'to remember' as well:

(701) Сара́ шәа́к сгәа́лашәеит.
/sará šʷa-k' ø-s-gʷála-šʷa-jt'/
I song-one [it(C1)-]me(C2)-Prev-remember-(Aor)-Fin
'I remembered one song.' 'Мне вспомнилась одна песня.'
(Cf. the negative form исгәа́ламшәеит /jə-s-gʷála-m-šʷa-jt'/ 'I did not remember it/them')

(702) ибгәа́лашәа!
/jə-b-gʷála-šʷa/
it/they(C1)-you.F(C2)-Prev-remember.Imp
'remember it/them (to a women)!', 'вспомни!'

According to our informant, the negative imperative form in (702) above is said in the following way using the causative form:

(703) ибгәа́лабмыршәан!
/jə-b-gʷála-b-mə-r-šʷa-n/
it/them(C1)-you.F(C2/Poss)-Prev/SV-you.F(C3)-Neg-Caus-remember-Proh
'don't remember it/them!', 'не вспоминай!' lit. 'don't make you-F remember it/them!'

Here as well the formation of the imperative form differs from other verbs. In addition, let us examine example (704) below, which uses а-хы́лцра /a-xə́l-c'-ra/ 'to give birth to':

(704) Хәҩы́к а́чкәынцәа лхы́лцит.
/xʷ-jʷə́k' á-č'ʲk'ʷən-cʷa ø-l-xə́l-c'ə-jt'/
5-Hum the-boy-Pl [they(C1)-]her(C2)-Prev-give birth to-(Aor)-Fin
'She gave birth to five boys.'
(Cf. дылхы́лмцит /də-l-xə́l-m-c'ə-jt'/ 'she did not give birth to him/her')

According to our informant, the imperative form of this verb cannot be produced. This is because the action in the verb can be considered to express unintentionality, so (704) above should be literally interpreted as 'Пять мальчиков родилось у нее', lit. 'Five boys were born at her place'.

Finally, we shall examine the possessive verb а́мазаара /á-ma-zaa-ra/ 'to have':

(705) Сара́ дсы́моуп ҩы́за бзи́ак. (AFL)
/sará d-sə́-ma-wp' jʷə́za bzə́ja-k'/
I he/she(C1)-me(C2)-have-Stat.Pres.Fin friend good-one
'I have one good friend.' 'У меня есть один хороший друг/одна хорошая подруга.'

(706) ибы́маз!
/jə-bə́-ma-z/
it/they(C1)-you.F(C2)-have-Stat.Imp
'have it/them! (to a woman)'

(707) исы́маны
/jə-sə́-ma-nə/
it/they(C1)-me(C2)-have-Abs
'I, having had it/them'

We know that this verb is intransitive from the presence of бы- /bə/ in the imperative form in (706) above and сы- /sə/ in the past absolutive form in (707). Therefore, the verb in (705) should be interpreted as an intransitive verb as in the Russian translation 'у меня есть один хороший друг/одна хорошая подруга', not as a transitive verb which uses the verb 'have' in English. From a morphological point of view, inversive verbs can be regarded as intransitive verbs as above.

The word order of an inversive construction is S-IO-V (S-V-IO is also possible) as described by Uslar (see fn. 185 above) (also see examples (701) and (705) above). The following examples demonstrate that the basic word order in an inversive construction is S-IO-V:

(708) Амра Серҧи́ль дылгэаҧхо́ит.
/Amra Serpə́jlʲ də-l-gʷa-pxa-wá-jt'/
name(F) name(F) she(C1)-her(C2)-Prev-like-Dyn-Fin
'Amra likes Serpil.' (*'Serpil likes Amra.')

(709) Амра дылгэаҧхо́ит Серҧи́ль.
/Amra də-l-gʷa-pxa-wá-jt' Serpə́jlʲ/
name(F) she(C1)-her(C2)-Prev-like-Dyn-Fin name(F)
'Amra likes Serpil.'

(710) Амра Мура́ҭ дылгэаҧхо́ит.
/Amra Məwrát də-l-gʷa-pxa-wá-jt'/
name(F) name(M) he(C1)-her(C2)-Prev-like-Dyn-Fin
'Amra likes Murat'

(711) *Мура́ҭ Амра дылгэаҧхо́ит.
/*Məwrát Amra də-l-gʷa-pxa-wá-jt'/

The Column I pronominal prefix д(ы)- /d(ə)/ in the verbal complex in (708) above is cross-referenced with Серҧи́ль /Serpə́jlʲ/ 'Serpil', and the Column II pronominal prefix л- /l/ is cross-referenced with Амра /Amra/ 'Amra'. As described by Ulsar, the word order of the nouns here and the distribution order of the pronominal prefixes in the verbal complex they cross-reference is in a reflection in the mirror relationship. The word order in (709) is also possible. In (710), there is no dispute as to which pronominal prefix 'Amra' and 'Murat' cross-reference. Nonetheless, our informant regards (711) as an ungrammatical sentence. The similarity of this situation to transitive constructions becomes obvious when the following transitive construction (712) and intransitive construction (713) are compared to (710) above:

(712) Амра Мура́ҭ дылшьи́т.
/ámra məwrát də-l-šʲə́-ø-jt'/
name(F) name(M) him(C1)-she(C3)-kill-Aor-Fin
'Amra killed Murat'

(713) Амра Мура́ҭ ди́сит.
/ámra məwrát d-jə́-sə-ø-jt'/

name(F) name(M) she(C1)-him(C2)-hit-Aor-Fin
'Amra hit Murat'

These syntactical and semantic circumstances demonstrate that inversive constructions in Abkhaz are drawing closer to transitive verbs.

5.11. Prefixal Particles

5.11.1. Abkhaz has several prefixal particles (abbreviated as 'Par') which express various nuances of an action or a mood. The prefixal particles used in Abkhaz folktale texts are as follows: <u>n(a)</u> /n(a)/, <u>л(a)</u> /l(a)/, <u>aa</u> /aa/, 'quickly', <u>ҩ(a)</u> /jʷ(a)/.[186] Though in standard literary Abkhaz they are rare, they are often found in folktale texts. Grammatically, these particles are not necessary for building verbal complexes. Since they are placed before the verbal root and resemble the preverbs which specify the direction or location of a verbal action, some investigators regard the particles as the preverbs.[187] However, the latter cannot be dropped. In this regard there is a distinct difference between the particle and the preverb. These particles have seldom been referred to in detail in the Abkhaz grammars and dictionaries. This may be because it is difficult to describe their subtle meanings and most of them are found in the colloquial speech of the folktale texts. However, in order to understand a language deeper, we should know how a grammatical category such as a particle is used in the sentences, and what nuances it gives to the sentences.

5.11.2. The Position of Particles in the Verbal Complex

If a verbal complex has the prefixal particle in question, it is inserted after Column I pronominal prefix. Compare the example of a one-place intransitive (714) and the example of a three-place transitive which contains Column I, Column II and Column III pronominal prefixes (715):

(714) Адәкьа́н дындәы́лтцуеит аҧхәы́зба. (Abkhaz text)[188]
/a-dʷkʲán də-<u>n</u>-ø-dʷə́l-c'-wa-jt' a-pħʷə́zba/

---

186. According to Hewitt (2005a), the open vowel in the modal preverb [= the prefixal particle] is dropped before 'a non-human 3rd person singular affix that is governed by the locational preverb': e.g. wə.ɥ.ø.ta.¹ja.j(.)ʃ 'you(-Masc).Prev.it-in-lie.Hort' (ibid. 153). It is likely that this means that the open vowel in a modal preverb is dropped before the zero-affix of Column II that is governed by the locational preverb. See also jə.n.ø.¹ta.sə.ø.n 'it.Prev.it.in.hit.Past.Fin(-P/I)' (ibid. 101), d.¹lə.ø.kʷ.pʂə.ø.n 'he.down.it.on.look. Past.Fin(-P/I)' (ibid. 161). Again the open vowel in the modal preverb is lost 'in front of an incorporated nominal root, itself dependent upon the locational preverb that follows it': də.n.¹χə.kʷ.gəla.ø.r 'he.Prev.head.on.stand.Past(-N/F-Aor).if' (ibid. 185).

187. According to Chirikba (2003a: 43), preverbs which do not make up a part of the verbal stem can be called 'free preverbs', cf. d-aa-x°ə́cə-ø-jt' '(s)he thought a bit' vs. d-x°ə́cə-ø-jt' '(s)he thought' (stem x°ə́c*(ə)* 'to think'). On the other hand, the preverbs which are a part of the stem (a-p+q'a-rá 'to cut', the stem p+q'a) can be called 'stem (or bound) preverbs'. We do not use the term 'free preverbs' for the prefixal elements which do not make up a part of the verbal stem. This is because, though preverbs and prefixal particles have a same origin, they are not functionally equivalent.

188. The examples of sentences cited below are from the texts 'Сергеи Зыхуба (ed.) *Аҧсуа лакуқуа*. Аҟуа: Алашара. 1997'.

the-store he/she(C1)-Par-[it(C2)-]Prev(outside)-go-Dyn-Fin the-girl
'The girl is going out of the shop at once/gladly.'

(715) шәызҕаб даасшәмырбар, ... (Abkhaz text)
/š^wә́-ʒɣab d-aa-s-š^w-mә-r-bá-r/
your-daughter her(C1)-Par-me(C2)-you(C3)-Caus-see-if
'if you show me your daughter, ...'

Furthermore, if there is both a prefixal particle and a relative adverbial prefix in a verbal complex, the particle is placed after the relative adverbial prefix, e.g.,

(716) Аҩны́ лахьы́ныҩналаз ауаа́ рацәаҩны́ исикушаны́ иштәа́з ибе́ит. (Abkhaz text)
/a-j^wnә́ d-ax^jә́-nә-ø-j^wna-la-z awáa rac^wa-j^wnә́ j-ajk'^wša-nә́
the-house he-where-Par-[it(C2)-]Prev(into)-enter-Past.Ind.Fin people many-Hum they-surround-Abs
jә-š-t'^wá-z ø-jә-bá-ø-jt'/
they(C1)-how-sit-Stat.Past.NF [it(C1)-]he(C3)-see-(Aor)-Fin
'He saw that in the house where he entered rapidly many people were sitting around.'

If a verbal complex has both the reflexive prefix and the particle, the latter is placed after the former, e.g.,

(717) аӡы́ аҽы́нтнашьын (Abkhaz text)
/a-ʒә́ a-čә́-n-ø-t-na-s^jә-n/
the water its(Poss)-Self-Par-[it(C2)-]Prev-it(C3)-dip-Past.Ind.Fin
'it dipped itself into the water and ...'

If the prefixal particle is used in a relative adjective clause, it is placed after the relative adjective marker which functions as Column I pronominal prefix, e.g.,

(718) иа́ахауа (Abkhaz text)
/j-áa-ħ-aw-[w]a/
Rel(C1)-Par-we-receive-Dyn.NF
'all that we receive'

Compare the example above (718) and the following example (719) with the relative adjective marker which functions as C2:

(719) дынзахҭо́, уаха́ дыпсуе́ит (Abkhaz text)
/dә-n-z-aħ-ta-wá, waxá dә-ps-wá-jt'/
her(C1)-Par-Rel(C2)-we-give-Dyn.NF tonight he(C1)-die-Dyn-Fin
'the person to whom we will give her (in marriage) will die tonight'

5.11.3. The Usages and Meanings of Prefixal Particles in Abkhaz Folktale Texts

As mentioned above, these particles are not always grammatically necessary to build a sentence. Therefore, though it is difficult to describe their meaning, the primary use, perhaps, is to intensify an action. Furthermore, they indicate that an action has started quickly or has been rapidly completed. When the particles in question are used in the folktale texts, the forms of the verbal complex involving them usually have Absolutive which are marked by -ны /nә/, Past Indefinite in -н /n/, and a finite form of Aorist in -ит /-ø-jt'/ or non-finite form of Aorist in -ø. These particles are remarkably similar in meaning, and they are often interchangeable, e.g. d-lә́-j^wna-la-jt' or d-nә́-j^wna-la-jt' (he/she-

Par-Prev-enter-Fin) 'he/she entered at once'. The following are examples:

(720) Ашарҧаз ачы́мазаҩ дынҭа́ҳаны ды́цәеит. (AAD)
/a-šarpaz a-čə́mazajʷ də-n-ø-tá-ħa-nə də́-cʷa-ø-jt'/
early morning the-sick person he/she-Par-[it(C2)-]Prev(in)-fall-Abs he/she(C1)-sleep-(Aor)-Fin
'The sick person slept soundly early in the morning.'

(721) Ахәчы́ а́мба днакьы́сын, шьҭахьҟа́ ды́ҩит.
/a-xʷč'ʲə́ á-mba d-na-[a]-k'ʲə́-sə-n šʲtaxʲq'á də́-jʷə-ø-jt'/
the-boy the-goal he-Par-it-Prev-touch-Past.Ind.Fin back he(C1)-run-(Aor)-Fin
'As soon as the child touched the target, he ran back.'

(722) Нас а́фырхәа иҿы́неихан, ани́ изыдгы́лаз аҩн ду длы́ҩналеит. (Abkhaz text)
/nas áfərhʷa jə-č'ə́-na-j-xa-n, anə́j jə-zə-d-gə́la-z
then quickly his-SV-Prev-he-start-Past.Ind.Fin that they-Rel-Prev(by)-stand-Stat.Past.NF
a-jʷn dəw d-lə́-jʷna-la-ø-jt'/
the-house big he-Par-Prev-enter-(Aor)-Fin
'Then he quickly set out and (at once) entered that big house by which they stood.'

(723) Ибзи́оуп, са́б, и́ухәаз саҳа́ит,—ихәа́н, дыҩҽы́жәлан иҽы́ да́сны дце́ит.
/jə-bzə́ja-wp', s-áb, jə́-w-ħʷa-z ø-s-a-ħá-ø-jt', j-ħʷá-n,
it-good-Stat.Pres.Fin my-father Rel-you-say-Past.Ind.NF [it]-me-to-hear-(Aor)-Fin he-say-Past.Ind.Fin
də-jʷ-čə́-žʷ-la-n jə-čə́ d-á-s-nə d-cá-ø-jt'/
he-Par-Prev-mount a horse-Past.Ind.Fin his-horse he-it-hit-Abs he-go-(Aor)-Fin
'It is good, my father, I see what you said, — said he, and he (quickly) mounted his horse, and having struck it (with the whip), he went away.'

(724) Ибзи́оуп, са́б, и́ухәаз саҳа́ит, — ихәе́ит у́игьы, иҽы́ да́асны дце́ит.
/jə-bzə́ja-wp', s-áb, jə́-w-ħʷa-z ø-s-a-ħá-jt', — j-ħʷá-jt'
wə́j-gʲə, jə-čə́ d-áa-[a]-s-nə d-cá-ø-jt'/
this-also his-horse he(C1)-Par-it(C2)-hit-Abs he(C1)-go-(Aor)-Fin
'It is good, my father, I see what you said, — said he and having struck it (quickly) (with the whip), he went away.'

From the examples given above (see also the examples below) it will be seen that in many cases these particles are used in the forms of the Past Indefinite and Absolutive. Since Abkhaz lacks a coordinate conjunction, the Past Indefinite and Absolutive play the role of clause linkage. For this reason, in order to express various nuances of an action in clause-chaining the particles are mainly used in the Past Indefinite and Absolutive.

We find that two different particles are used in one sentence, e.g.,

(725) Ибзи́оуп, — ихәа́н, а́хәа а́ашьҭихын «а́чкун» ахәынҭқа́р иҩны́ дныҩна́лт.
/jə-bzjə́a-wp' j-ħʷá-n, [a-]áħʷa ø-áa-šʲtə-j-xə-n
it-good-Stat.Pres.Fin he-say-Past.Ind.Fin [the]-sword [it]-Par-Prev-he-pick up-Past.Ind.Fin
á-č'k'ʷən a-ħʷəntkár jə-jʷnə́ d-nə-ø-jʷná-l-t' (< d-nə-jʷná-la-ø-jt')/
the-boy the-king his-house he(C1)-Par-[it(C2)-]Prev-enter-(Aor)-Fin
'It is good, — the «boy» said, and he picked up the sword at once and quickly entered the king's house.'

(726) Нас ари́ «а́чкун» иџьы́ба иааҭи́хын адау́ илы́мха нагаы́ ра́ђхьа иныќуитцеит.

/nas arə́j á-č'k'ʷən jə-ʒʲə́ba j-aa-tə́-j-xə-n a-dawə́ jə-lə́mħa
then this the-boy his-pocket it(C1)-Par-Prev-he(C3)-take out-Past.Ind.Fin the-ogre his-ear
ϕ-na-ga-nə́ r-ápxʲa jə-nə́-kʷə-j-c'a-ϕ-jt'/
[it(C1)]-Prev(thither)-take-Abs their-in front of it(C1)-Par-Prev(on)-he(C3)-put-(Aor)-Fin

'Then as soon as this «boy» removed an ear of the ogre from his pocket, he took it thither and put it in front of them.'

(727) Аҳәы́ҳә иа́аиз алаха́нка ианы́з аʒы́ аҿы́нҭнашьын амҵәы́жәҩакуа ан-**а́а**-рышәшәа а́-рђызба ђшʒа́-к, а́-рђызба зама́на-к д-аа-ҭы́-ҵт.

/a-ħʷə́ħʷ j-aa-j-z a-laxánk'a j-a-nə́-z a-ʒə́
the-pigeon Rel-Prev-come-Past.Ind.NF the-washtub Rel(C1)-it(C2)-be on-Stat.Past.NF the-water
a-čə́-n-ϕ-t-na-šʲə-n a-mc'ʷə́žʷjʷa-kʷa ϕ-an-á[a]-a-rəšʷšʷa,
its-Self-Par-[it-]Prev-it-dip-Past.Ind.Fin the-wing-Pl [them]-when-Par-it-wave.Aor.NF
á-rpəzba pšʒá-k', á-rpəzba zamána-k' d-aa-tə́c'-t'/
a-young man beautiful-one a-young.man fine-one he-Prev-go out-(Aor)-Fin

'The pigeon which had come here dipped itself into the water on the washtub, and as soon as it waved its wings, it turned into a beautiful and fine young man.'

(728) Адау́ уа иђсы́ ааихы́тцын, а́гуарахәа дылка́хаит.

/a-dawə́ wa jə-psə́ ϕ-aa-j-xə́c'ə-n,
the-ogre there his-soul [it]-Par-him-cross-Past.Ind.Fin (= he breathed his last)
ágʷaraħʷa də-l-ϕ-k'á-ħa-jt'/
in a heap he-Par-[it-]Prev-fall-(Aor)-Fin

'The moment the ogre breathed his last there, he fell in a heap.'

(729) Ари́ адау́ дызшьы́тцәҟьаз «а́чкун» дылдәы́лтцын иҽы́ ахӯцкуа аайди́кшалан ...

/arə́j a-dawə́ də-z-šʲə́-c'ʷq'ʲa-z á-č'k'ʷən də-l-ϕ-dʷə́l-c'ə-n
this the-ogre him-Rel(C3)-kill-indeed-Past.Ind.NF the-boy he-Par-[it-]Prev-go out-Past.Ind.Fin
jə-čə́ a-xʷə́c-kʷa ϕ-a[a]-aj-də́-jə-k'šala-n/
his-horse its-hair-Pl [them]-Par-one onother-Prev-he-bump-Past.Ind.Fin

'As soon as the «boy» who had indeed killed this ogre went out, he rubbed his horse's hair, ...'

(730) «Ачкун» дылҽы́жәђан адаукуа́ харантәы́ данрыхуа́ђш, ры́лакуа хтны́ ибан, д**лы́**шьҭасын аха́ҳә мтца́рсны ды́ҩт.

/a-č'k'ʷən də-l-ϕ-čə́žʷ-pa-n a-daw-kʷá xara-nt'ʷə́
the-boy he-Par-[it-]Prev(out of horse)-jump-Past.Ind.Fin the-ogre-Pl far-from
d-an-rə-xʷá-pš, rə́-la-kʷa ϕ-x-t'-nə́ [jə-]j-bá-n,
he-when-them-Prev-look at.Aor.NF their-eye-Pl [they]-Prev-open-Abs [it]-he-see-Past.Ind.Fin
d-lə́-šʲta-sə-n a-xáħʷ ϕ-mc'á-rs-nə də́-jʷ-t'/
he-Par-Prev-touch the ground-Past.Ind.Fin the-stone [it]-Prev-snatch-Abs he-run-(Aor)-Fin

'When the «boy» quickly jumped down off the horse and looked at the ogres from afar, he saw that their eyes were open. And at once he lay down on the ground, snatched the stone and started to run.'

Here is an example where two verbs with a similar meaning have different particles:

(731) Анцәа́ иаҳђы́хьаиршәаз, куты́к ҳа́ургьы, иеиҟараны́ илеиҩаҳшоит, капе́к ҳа́ургьы еиҟараны́ иааиҟуҳарчча́роуп.

/a-ncʷá j-ah-pə́xʲa-jə-r-šʷa-z, k'ʷt'ə́-k' ø-ħ-áw-r-gʲə,
the-God Rel-us-Prev-he-Caus-come into-Past.Ind.NF hen-one [it]-we-receive-if-even
j-ajq'ara-nə́ jə-l-ajjʷ-áħ-ša-wa-jt', k'ap'ék' ø-ħ-áw-r-gʲə
it-equally-adv it-Par-Prev-we-divide-Dyn-Fin kopeck [it]-we-receive-if-even
ajq'ara-nə́ j-a[a]-ajq'ʷ-ħa-rč'č'á-r-a-wp'/
equally-Adv it-Par-Prev-we-divide-must-be-Stat.Pres.Fin
'Whatever God gave us — even if we receive one hen —, we shall divide it equally, even if we receive a kopeck, we must divide it equally.'

We can also provide an example of different particles in the same roots:

(732) anáxʲ-aráxʲ d-aa-nə́q'ʷa-n, d-lə́-kʷpš-jʷə́-kʷpšə-n,
thither-hither he-Par-walk-Past.Ind.Fin he-Par-watch-Par-watch-Past.Ind.Fin
awáa-gʲ ø-j-bá-ø-jt'
people-also [them]-he-see-(Aor)-Fin
'he walked thither and hither, looked around, and he also saw people ...'

5.11.4. Conclusion

The prefixal particles н(а) /n(a)/, л(а) /l(a)/, аа /aa/, ҩ(а) /jʷ(a)/, which are often found particularly in the Abkhaz folktale texts, are not preverbs but a peculiar grammatical category. Grammatically, Abkhaz can do without these particles to build a sentence. In standard literary Abkhaz they are rarely found. They are inserted after the Column I pronominal prefix or the relative adverbial prefix in the verbal complex, and they are mainly used in the forms of Past Indefinite and Absolutive. The basic meaning of the particles used in these forms is to connect more than two clauses closely by intensifying an action. From this basic meaning come several individual meanings, e.g., quickness of an action, rapid completion of an action, the mood of contentment as a result of an action, etc. However, most of the examples in the folktale texts indicate that an action has been done quickly.

5.12. Other Affixes in the Verbal Complex

In addition to the prefix discussed in §5.11, the following affixes appear in verbal complexes:

5.12.1. Prefixes

1. -ц- /c/ 'together with'

'The Column II pronominal prefix + ц' is inserted after the Column I pronominal prefix. For example:

(733) Сара́ Ка́ма акы́ҭа а́хь слы́ццеит.
/sará k'áma a-kə́ta [a-]áxʲ s-lə́-c-ca-jt'/
I Kama the-village [its-]to I(C1)-her(C2)-with-go-(Aor)-Fin
'I went to the village with Kama.'

(734) илы́ц(ы)сфоит
/jə-lə́-c(ə)-s-fa-wa-jt'/
it/them(C1)-her(C2)-with-I(C3)-eat-Dyn-Fin
'I am eating it/them with her'

When there is a potential marker, 'the Column II pronominal prefix + ц' is inserted after it:

(735) исызу́цгом
/jə-sə-z-wə́-c-ga-wa-m/
it/them(C1)-me(C2)-Pot-you.M(C2)-with-carry-Dyn-Neg
'I cannot carry it/them with you-M.'

2. -аиц-/-еиц- /ajc/ (Rec-together with) 'together'

This prefix is placed after the Column I pronominal prefix:

(736) иеиццо́ит
/j-ajc-ca-wá-jt'/
they(C1)-together-go-Dyn-Fin
'they will go together'

(737) Ашәҟәы́ ҳаица́ԥхьоит.
/a-šʷq'ʷə́ ħ-ajc-á-pxʲa-wa-jt'/
the-book we(C1)-together-it(C2)-read-Dyn-Fin
'We are reading the book together.'

(738) иеица́ҳфоит
/j-ajc-áħ-fa-wa-jt'/
it/them(C1)-together-we(C3)-eat-Dyn-Fin
'we are eating it/them together'

3. а́иҭа- /ájta/

This prefix expresses the repetition of an action and is intensified by the suffix -х-. The prefix is placed after the Column I pronominal prefix:

(739) Арахи, аӡахәе́и еиҭа́ҿиахма?
/a-raxə-j a-ʒaxʷá-j ø-ajtá-č'ja-x-ma/
the-reed-and the-vine-and [they-]again-grow up-(Aor)-Emph-Qu
'Have the reeds and vines grown up again?'

4. -ау- /aw/

This prefix expresses a rhetorical question and is intensified by the suffix -х-. The prefix is placed after the Column I pronominal prefix:

(740) Аҿены́ шьыжьымҭа́н ша́анӡа даумгы́лахʻуаз (Abkhaz text)
/ačnə́ šʲəžʲəmtán šáanʒa d-awə-m-gə́la-x-wa-z/
on that day in the morning very early in the morning she-Rhetorical.Qu-Neg-get up-Emph-Dyn-Impf.NF
'Didn't she get up early in the morning of the following day?' (Of course she got up very early in the morning of the following day.)

(741) Убри́ а́ҟара има́ҷын лкьы́ра, ахá акры́ ау́лхәахуаз, илхәа́ргьы илóуамызт лџьы́руан. (Abkhaz text)
/wəbrə́j áq'ara jə-máč'ʲə-n l-kʲə́ra, axá ak'rə́
so much it-little-Stat.Past.Fin her-wage but anything
ø-awə́-l-ħʷa-x-wa-z, jə-l-ħʷá-rgʲə
[it-]Rhetorical Qu-she-say-Emph-Dyn-Impf.NF it-she-say-even if

j-l-áw-[w]a-mə-zt' ø-l-də́r-wa-n/
them-she-obtain-Dyn-Neg-Impf.Fin [it-]she-know-Dyn-Impf.Fin
'Her wages were so very small, but how could she say anything? She knew that even if she said anything, she could obtain nothing more.'

5.12.2. Suffixes

1. -aa /aa/

This suffix expresses 'extrovert' (Spruit 1983) or 'the meaning of a complete action' (Chirikba): и́-кə-з-бл-аа-ит /jə́-kʷ-z-bl-aa-jt'/ (it/them(C1)-Prev-I(C3)-(Aor)-completely-Fin) 'I burnt it completely on the surface'.

2. -гəы́шьа- /gʷə́šʲa/

This suffix is placed after the verb stem, and expresses the meaning of 'misfortune, regret, pity, wretchedness':

(742) Аԥшəма дыќагəышьам.
/á-pšʷma də́-q'a-gʷəšʲa-m/
the-host he(C1)-be-unfortunately-Neg
'Sadly the host is not here.'

(743) Ааи, ҳҳəынтқáр ры́цха, адаý дифагəы́шьеит. (Abkhaz text)
/aaj ħ-ħʷəntkár rə́cħa a-dawə́ də-j-fa-gʷə́šʲa-jt'/
oh our-king wretched the-ogre him(C1)-he(C3)-eat-(Aor)-unfortunately-Fin
'Oh no. The ogre has eaten our poor King.'

3. -жь- /žʲ/

This suffix is attached to the verb root -ма- /ma/ 'have', it expresses the meaning of 'many/much':

(744) Амáл ры́мажьуп. (ACST)
a-mál ø-ré-ma-žʲə-wp'/
the-wealth [it-]they-have-many-Stat.Pres.Fin
'They have wealth in abundance.'

4. -зар /zar/

With a copula -а- or -акə(ы)-, this suffix forms a 'deontic construction' (Chirikba 2003a: 53). In this structure, an agent does not appear (cf. -р 'must'). For example:

(745) Аҩы́за дҩы́зазароуп áцəгьараҿгьы, абзи́араҿгьы. (AFL)
/a-jʷə́za d-jʷə́za-zar-a-wp' á-cʷgʲara-č'-gʲə a-bzə́jara-č'-gʲə/
the-friend he-friend-must-be-Stat.Pres.Fin the-misfortune-in-and the-joy-in-and
'A friend must be a friend both in misfortune and in joy.'

(746) Аҩны́ дыќазарóуп.
/a-jʷnə́ də-q'a-zar-á-wp'/
the-house he/she(C1)-be-must-be-Stat.Pres.Fin
'He/She must be at home.'

(747) с-гы́лазар áкəын

/s-gə́la-zar ák'ʷə-n/
I(C1)-stand-must be-Stat.Past.Fin
'I had to stand'

(748) сгы́ламзар áкәын
/s-gə́la-m-zar ák'ʷə-n/
I(C1)-stand-Neg-must be-Stat.Past.Fin
'I didn't have to stand'

5. -зтгы /ztgʲə/

This suffix is added to the non-finite stem and expresses the nuance of 'maybe' or 'perhaps' (cf. §5.4.2.2):

(749) Акы́ уаҿы́зтгы?
/ak'ə́ w-a-č'ə́-ztgʲə/
something you.M(C1)-it(C2)-be engaged in-maybe
'Maybe, were you-M busy with something?'

6. -ӡа- /ʒa/

This suffix is used to emphasize a negative meaning. However, in the present Abkhaz language this suffix does not always emphasize the negative; it is used as a variant of the simple negative form. This suffix is placed immediately after the verbal root:

(750) дсыздырӡомызт
/d-sə-z-də́r-ʒa-wa-mə-zt'/
he/she(C1)-me(C2)-Pot-know-Emph-Dyn-Neg-Impf
'I did not know him/her at all.'

Also, on rare occasions this suffix is used to express emphasis in the affirmative form as well. For example:

(751) Иарá и́пҳацәа ри́тар áкәымзи, ахá иарá аӡәы́ лáкәӡан и́маз.
/jará jə́-pħa-cʷa ∅-rə́-j-ta-r ák'ʷə-m-zəj
he his-daughter-Pl [them(C1)-]them(C2)-he(C3)-give-must be-Neg-Qu
axá jará aʒʷə́ l-ák'ʷ-ʒa-n j-jə́-ma-z/
but he one her(C2)-be-Emph-Stat.Past.Fin Rel(C1)-he(C2)-have-Stat.Past.NF
'He had to give his daughters to them, but he had only one daughter.'

(752) Аҽы анлырхумар, егьи апҟаоҳәа иоҭҟьан, даманы, еес, илтакукуа ипеит, ипаӡеит. (Abkhaz text)
/a-čə́ ∅-an-lə́-rxʷmar, agʲə́j ap'q'ájʷħʷa
the-horse [it]-when-she-gallop-(Aor.NF) that instantly
jə-jʷ-t-q'ʲá-n, d-á-ma-nə, ées, jəltak'ʷk'ʷwá
it-Par-Prev-jump out-Past.Ind.Fin she-it-have-Abs Interjection without trace
jə-cá-jt', jə-ca-ʒá-jt'./
it-go-(Aor)-Fin it-go-Emph-(Aor)-Fin.
'When she made the horse gallop, it suddenly flew up into the air, and taking her along, disappeared into the blue, running away into nothing, leaving no trace.'

7. -ишь(т) /jš^{j}(t’)/

This suffix is attached to the imperative form, and works to modify the force of an imperative:

(753) Исырбе́ишь!
/jə-sə-r-bá-jš^{j}/
it/them(C1)-me(C2)-Caus-see.Imp-just
‘Just let me see!’, ‘Дай-ка мне посмотреть!’

Also, it indicates an unwilling action when attached to the Future I finite form.

8. -кь /k’^{j}/

This suffix expresses the meaning of ‘all that’:

(754) Иуҿашәáкь зегьы́ умҳәáроуп.
/jə-w-č’a-š^{w}á-k’^{j} zag^{j}ə́ ø-wə-m-ħ^{w}á-r-a-wp’/
Rel(C1)-you(C2)-Prev(to mouth)-get into-all that all [it(C1)-]you.M(C3)-Neg-say-must-be-Stat.Pres.Fin
‘You-M must not say everything that comes to the tongue.’

9. -кәа- /k^{w}a/

(a) Generally this suffix is used in the aorist, and indicates the plurality of an action. This suffix is placed immediately after the verb root:

(755) Ицакәе́ит.
/jə-ca-k^{w}á-jt’/
they(C1)-go.Aor-Pl-Fin
‘They gradually left.’

(b) It is also used to express the plurality of the arguments within a verb. This is an archaic expression. The plurality of the subject (756) below, the indirect object (757–758), and of the direct object (759) is expressed in these examples:

(756) Ачкәынцәа áмпыл áсра ицакәе́ит.
/a-č’^{j}k’^{w}ən-c^{w}a á-mp’əl á-s-ra jə-ca-k^{w}á-jt’/
the-boy-Pl the-ball its-hit-Masd they(C1)-go.Aor-Pl-Fin
‘The boys went to play football.’

(757) Уи́ ахáцәа áхәша ры́итакәеит.
/wə́j a-xác^{w}a á-x^{w}ša ø-rə́-j-ta-k^{w}a-jt’/
he the-men the-butter [it(C1)-]them(C2)-he(C3)-give.(Aor)-Pl-Fin
‘He gave butter to the men.’

(758) сры́ццакәеит
/s-rə́-c-ca-k^{w}a-jt’/
I(C1)-them(C2)-with-go.Aor-Pl-Fin
‘I went with them’

(759) Сарá ахáтца ашәҟәкәá и́стакәеит.
/sará a-xác’a a-š^{w}q’^{w}-k^{w}á ø-jə́-s-ta-k^{w}a-jt’/
I the-man the-book-Pl [them(C1)-]him(C2)-I(C3)-give.(Aor)-Pl-Fin
‘I gave the books to the man.’

In addition, this suffix is also used to express the plurality of a relativized argument. (28) below is an example of a Column III relative prefix expressing a plural:

(760) Зы́злан дызккәахьбугьы ы́ҟан. (AF)
/ʒə́zlan də-z-k'-kʷa-xʲá-w-gʲə ə́-q'a-n/
name(F) her(C1)-Rel(C3)-catch-Pl-Perf-NF-even [they(C1)-]be-Stat.Past.Fin
'And there have been those who have even captured Dzyzlan.'

10. -ла-[1] /la/

This suffix is added immediately after the verb root or after -кәа /kʷa/, which indicates the plurality of an action, and indicates that an action occurs regularly (also known as the 'iterative'). This suffix is used with verb forms in the imperfective aspect (i.e. imperfect and present) (see §3.1.7). The differences in aspect between verb forms with this suffix attached and those without it attached are readily visible in the differences between the following Russian translations ((761) is imperfective and (762) is perfective):

(761) иҟашәцала́!
/jə-q'a-šʷ-c'a-lá/
it/them(C1)-Prev-you.Pl-do.Imp-Iterative
'do it/them (always)!', 'его(нрз.)/их делайте (всегда)!'

(762) иҟашәцá!
/jə-q'a-šʷ-c'á/
it/them(C1)-Prev-you.Pl-do.Imp
'do it/them!', 'его(нрз.)/их сделайте!'

Other examples:

(763) Аҧхын амшы́н ахь сцало́ит.
/á-pxən a-mšə́n [a-]axʲ s-ca-la-wá-jt'/
the-summer the-sea [its-]to I(C1)-go-Iterative-Dyn-Fin
'I (usually) go to the sea in the summer.' 'Летом я езжу на море.'

(764) Ашко́лынтә аҩны́ҟа сца́цыҧхьаӡа а́мпыр са́слон.
/a-šk'ólə-nt'ʷ a-jʷnə́-q'a s-cá-cəpxʲaʒa á-mp'ər s-á-s-la-wa-n/
the-school-from the-house-to I(C1)-go-every time the-ball I(C1)-it(C2)-hit-Iterative-Dyn-Impf
'Every time I got home from school, I used to play ball.'

(765) Ишәыхьчала́ а́бна! (AFL)
/jə-šʷə-xʲčʲa-lá á-bna/
it(C1)-you.Pl(C3)-guard.Imp-Iterative the-forest
'Take care of the forest!'

11. -ла-[2] /la/

(a) This suffix is used in certain verbs and constructs a hortative sentence:

(766) уаала́ (M)
/w-aa-lá/
you.M(C1)-come.Imp-let's
'let's go!'

(b) It is used to emphasize imperative forms:

(767) Аа, амц схәа́зар, уҧшла́! (AF)
/aa a-mc ø-s-ħʷa-wá-zar wə-pš-lá/
ah the-lie [it(C1)-]I(C3)-say-Dyn-if you.M(C1)-look.Imp-Emph
'Ah, just watch if I'm telling lies!'

12. -ла-[3] /la/

This suffix is used with the present stem and expresses the progressive aspect (Hewitt 1979c: 181–182):

(768) дыхәма́рлоит
/də-xʷmár-la-wa-jt'/
he/she(C1)-play-Progress-Dyn-Fin
'he will be playing'

13. -ла-[4] /la/

This suffix xpresses the meaning of introvert (cf. (360) in §4.3.6):

(769) Сара́ а́хәшәкәа сы́дыскылоит.
/sará á-xʷšʷ-kʷa ø-sə́-də-s-k'ə-la-wa-jt'/
I the-medicine-Pl [them(C1)-]Poss-SV-I(C3)-hold-Introvert-Dyn-Fin
'I take the medicine.'

14. -лак /lak'/

(a) This suffix is attached to the aorist stem of dynamic verbs in temporal clauses and expresses the meaning of 'when..., always'. For example:

(770) Ашьыжь уангы́лалак и́ҟаутцои?[189]
/ašʲəžʲ w-an-gə́la-lak' jə́-q'a-w-c'a-wa-j/
morning you.M-when-stand.Aor-always Rel(C1)-Prev-you.M(C3)-do-Dyn-Qu
'What do you-M always do when you-M get up in the morning?'

(771) Шәанызбзи́ахалак, аҭаҭы́н шәа́халап, ары́жәтә жәжәла́п. (IC)
/šʷ-anə-bzə́ja-xa-lak' a-tatə́n šʷ-á-xa-la-p'
you.Pl-when-good-become-always the-tobacco you.Pl(C1)-it(C2)-smoke-Iterative-Fut.I
a-rə́žʷt'ʷ ø-žʷ-žʷ-lá-p'/
the-drink [it(C1)-]you.Pl(C3)-drink-Iterative-Fut.I
'When you recover, you will always smoke and drink (spirits).'

(b) It expresses the simple future:

(772) Бара́ ауниверсите́т бана́лгалак бзакәхо́и?
/bará a-wənəjversəjt'ét' b-an-á-l-ga-lak' b-z-ak'ʷ-xa-wá-j/

---

189. Cf. Ашьыжь уангы́ло и́ҟаутцои?
/ašʲəžʲ w-an-gə́la-wa jə́-q'a-w-c'a-wa-j/
morning you.M(C1)-when-stand-Dyn.NF Rel(C1)-Prev-you.M(C3)-do-Dyn-Qu
'What do you-M do when you-M get up in the morning?'

you the-university you(C1)-when-it(C2)-Prev-finish.Aor-future you(C1)-Rel(C2)-be-become-Dyn-Qu
'What will you-F become after finishing unversity?'

15. -лакь /lak'ʲ/

This suffix -лакь (abbreviated as 'LA') is attached to the aorist stem of dynamic verbs in temporal clauses and expresses (i) the future (cf. Hewitt 1979c: 39–40) or (ii) the indefinite future:

(773) Адаў данáаилакь, áҳәа рыххá ихы́ уáс. (Abkhaz text)
/a-dawə́ d-an-áaj-lak'ʲ [a-]áħʷa ø-rəxxá jə-xə́ w-á-s/
the-ogre he(C1)-when-come-LA [the-]sword [it(C1)-]stretch.Imp his-head you.M(C1)-it(C2)-hit.Imp
'When the ogre comes, take out your sword and strike it on the head.'

(774) Барá ақы́та ахь бышнéилакьцәҟьа, ашәҟәы́ сызҩы́.
/bará a-kə́ta [a-]axʲ bə-š-n-áj-lak'ʲ-c'ʷq'ʲa a-šʷq'ʷə́ ø-sə-z-jʷə́/
you.F the-village [its-]to you.F(C1)-how-Prev-go there-LA-just the-letter [it(C1)-]me(C2)-for-write.Imp
'As soon as you-F arrive in the village, write a letter to me.'
(For ш-...-цәҟьа 'as soon as' see §5.4.1.5).

(775) дахьубалакь (Bgažba (1964))
/d-axʲ-w-ba-lak'ʲ/
him/her(C1)-where-you.M(C3)-see-LA
'wherever you-M see him/her'

16. -лац /lac/

This suffix is attached to the verb root and expresses the past iterative:

(776) Аўха ани́ иаáилац аҳәы́ҳә аáин, иáрҧызбаны ишы́ҟалац иáаҟалан иарéи ларéи еицәáжәеит. (Abkhaz text)
/awə́xa anə́j j-aá-j-lac a-ħʷə́ħʷ ø-aá-jə-n
that night that it-Prev-come-always the-dove [it-]Prev-come-Past.Ind.Fin
j-á-rpəzba-nə jə-šə́-q'a-lac j-áa-q'a-la-n jará-j lará-j
it-its-young man-Abs it-how-be-always it-Par-Prev-become-Past.Ind.Fin he-and she-and
j-aj-cʷážʷa-jt'/
they-each other-talk with-(Aor)-Fin
'That night, the dove came as usual and, as usual, turned into a young man. And then he talked with her.'

17. -ма /ma/

This suffix expresses the meaning of 'as soon as' (see ACST: 194): Урт цáма, аҽцәá áшҭа иааҭáлеит. (ACST) 'As soon as they went, lo! the horsemen came into the yard!'

18. -р /r/

Along with the copular radical -а- /a/, -акәы- /ak'ʷə/, this suffix expresses the meaning of 'must' or 'should'. This suffix is placed after the verb root. Unlike the suffix -зар /zar/ mentioned above, it is possible for an agent to appear in verbs with this suffix. For example:

(777) Ашәҟәы́ зҩы́роуп.
/a-šʷq'ʷə́ ø-z-jʷə́-r-a-wp'/
the-letter [it(C1)-]I(C3)-write-must-be-Stat.Pres.Fin

'I must write a letter.'

(778) Астатиа́ зҩы́р а́кәын асаа́ҭ хҧа рҟы́нӡа.
/a-st'at'əjá ø-z-jʷə́-r ák'ʷə-n a-saát xpa r-q'ə́nʒa/
the-article [it(C1)-]I(C3)-write-must be-Stat.Past the-o'clock three their-by
'I had to write the article by three o'clock.'

19. -ртә /rt'ʷ/

This suffix is attached to the non-finite aorist stem and is used to express the resultative. еиҧш /ajpš/ 'like it' often comes after verbs with this suffix. For example:

(779) Иара́знак ды́цәартә еиҧш дааҧсаны́ ды́ҟан.
/jaráznak' də́-cʷa-rt'ʷ ajpš d-aapsa-nə́ də́-q'a-n/
suddenly he/she-sleep-Resultative it-like he/she-become tired-Abs he/she-be-Stat.Past.Fin
'He was so tired that he suddenly fell asleep.'

For periphrastic causative expressions using this suffix, see §4.1.7.

20. -ст /st'/ [dialect]

This suffix is added to the imperative form and it modifies the force of an imperative:

(780) ихәаст!
/jə-ħʷa-st'/
it/them-say.Imp-just
'Just say it/them!', 'скажи-ка его(нрз.)/их!' (= и-хәе́-ишь!)

21. -тәы- /t'ʷə/

The combination of this suffix and the suffix of a stative verb expresses the meaning 'be to be DONE':

(781) Ари́ ҟацатәу́п.[190]
/arə́j ø-q'a-c'a-t'ʷə́-wp'/

---

190. In examples (781) and (782) above, the verb's Column I pronominal prefix does not appear because there is a referent which cross-references it immediately before it. However, although the following example meets the same condition above, a Column I pronominal prefix does appear:

Ажәлар рма́л ихьчатәу́п.
/a-žʷlar r-mal jə-xʲčʲa-t'ʷə́-wp'/
the-people their-property it(C1)-protect-to be done-Stat.Pres.Fin
'The people's property is to be protected'.

In Abkhaz, examples which deviate from the general principle in this manner occur on rare occasions. Look at the following example:

Рыҩны́ а́ҧхьа азы́ ииасуеит.
/rə-jʷnə́ [a-]ápxʲa a-ʒə́ jə́-ja-s-wa-jt'/
their-house [its-]before the-river it(C1)-Prev-flow-Dyn-Fin
'The river flows in front of their house'.

Regarding the example above, according to Hewitt and Z. Khiba (personal communication), 'и- is better, but schwa is possible'.

this [it(C1)-]Prev-do-to be done-Stat.Pres.Fin
'This is to be done.'

(782) Хынҩажәи хәба мааҭ шәатәуп.
/xənjʷažʷəj xʷba maát ϕ-šʷa-t'ʷə́-wp'/
60-and 5 rouble [it(C1)-]pay-to be done-Stat.Pres.Fin
'It is necessary to pay 65 roubles.'

22. -тәыс /t'ʷəs/

This suffix is a compound suffix formed by joining two suffixes, -тәы 'be to be DONE' and с- 'as'.

(783) Ҟаҵатәыс ибоуеит.
/q'a-c'a-t'ʷə́s jə-b-áw-wa-jt'/
Prev-do-to be done-as it(C1)-you.F(C2)-receive-Dyn-Fin
'You-F have to do it/them.' lit. 'You-F receive it/them as something to be done.'

23. -х- /x/

(a) This suffix is added to the verb root, it expresses 'emphasis' or 'surprise':

(784) Аҳәынҭкар иԥҳа ас аныҳәа, иҟаиҵахуаз. (Abkhaz text)
/a-ħʷəntkár jə-pħá as ϕ-anə́-l-ħʷa
the-king his-daughter so [it(C1)-]when-she(C3)-say.Aor.NF
jə́-q'a-j-c'a-x-wa-z/
Rel(C1)-Prev-he(C3)-do-Emph-Dyn-Impf.NF(Qu)
'What on earth could the King have done, when his daughter told him this?'

(b) This suffix is added to the verb root, and indicates 'a repetitive action' (Chirikba: 5):

(785) Зегьы еиҭагылахит. (ACST)
/zagʲə́ j-ajtá-gə́la-xə-jt'/
all they-again-stand-(Aor)-Repetitive-Fin
'Ecverybody stood up again.'

24. -ха- /xa/

(a) This suffix is used to derive dynamic intransitive verbs from nouns and adjectives, and expresses the meaning of 'become':

(786) Баҭал итахыуп дфизикхарц. (AFL)
/batál [j-]jə-taxə́-wp' d-fə́jzəjk'-xa-rc/
name(M) it(C1)-he(C2)-want-Stat.Pres.Fin he(C1)-physicist-become-in order to
'Batal wants to become a physicist.' (cf. афизик 'a physicist')

(787) Ачкәын дыӷәӷәахеит.
/a-č'ʲk'ʷən də-ɣʷɣʷa-xá-jt'/
the-boy he-strong-become-(Aor)-Fin
'The boy became stronger.' (cf. аӷәӷәа /á-ɣʷɣʷa/ 'strong')

(b) This suffix derives intransitive verbs from transitive or intransitive verbs (cf. fn. 151):

(788) иҟаҵахоит
/jə-q'a-c'a-xa-wá-jt'/

it/they(C1)-Prev-do-become-Dyn-Fin
'it is/they are happening', lit. 'то сделанным становится/станет'

25. -ахa /aћa/

This suffix is attached to the subjunctive suffixes -р/-зар /r/zar/, and expresses the meaning of 'far from' or 'let alone' (Hewitt 1979c: 233):

(789) Акәáц ифáраха, акгьы́ дáламкьысит. (ACST)
/a-k'ʷác ϕ-jə-fá-r-aћa ak'gʲə́ d-á-la-m-k'ʲəsə-jt'/
the-meat [it-]he(C3)-eat-Sub-far from nothing he(C1)-it(C2)-Prev-Neg-touch-(Aor)-Fin
'Far from eating the meat, he did not even touch anything.'

26. -цы /cə/

Masdar plus -цы /cə/ indicates purpose:

(790) Уи́ сиҿáмхарацы, сарá даҿá мҩáкала сцéит. (RAD)
/wə́j sə-j-č'á-m-ћa-ra-cə sará dačá mjʷá-k'-a-la s-cá-jt'/
he I(C1)-him(C2)-Prev-Neg-meet-Masd-in order to I another way-one-its-by I-go-(Aor)-Fin
'In order to avoid an encounter with him, I went along a different road.'

27. -цәа- /cʷa/

(a) This suffix is attached immediately after the verb root and expresses the excessive performance of an action:

(791) акрысфцәéит
/ak'rə-s-f-cʷá-jt'/
Dummy-I(C3)-eat-too much-(Aor)-Fin
'I ate too much'

(b) This suffix is attached immediately after the verb root and indicates that a state is excessive:

(792) Ишбурацәоуп иахьá.
jə-šáwra-cʷa-wp' jaxʲá/
it-hot-extremely-Stat.Pres.Fin today
'It is extremely hot today.'

28. -шь /šʲ/

This suffix is attached to the interrogative form and works to intensify the interrogative meaning:

(793) сифацәҟьары́машь?! (ACST)
/sə-j-fa-c'ʷq'ʲa-rə́-ma-šʲ/
me(C1)-he(C3)-eat-indeed-Fut.I-Qu-really
'Will he really indeed eat me?!'

29. -шьа-[1] /šʲa/

This suffix serves to derive transitive verbs:

(794) дры́цхалшьеит
/d-rə́cћa-l-šʲa-jt'/
him/her(C1)-Prev-she(C3)-pity-(Aor)-Fin

'she felt sorry for him/her.' (cf. а-ры́цха 'pitiful')

30. -шьа-[2] /šʲa/

This suffix is attached to the verbal root, and derives a noun which means 'the manner of doing':

(795) Уара́ а́ӡсашьа уды́руама? (AFL) (cf. а́ӡсара /á-ʒsa-ra/ 'to swim')
/wará á-ʒsa-šʲa ɸ-wə-dә́r-wa-ma/
you.M the-swim-manner [it(C1)-]you.M(C3)-know-Dyn-Qu
'Do you-M know how to swim?'

31. -шәа /šʷa/

This suffix is attached to the non-finite stem and expresses the meaning of 'as if':

(796) Ихаҭа́ иба́зшәа иҳәбит. (RAD)
/jə-xatá ɸ-jə-bá-z-šʷa ɸ-jə-ħʷa-wá-jtʼ/
his-oneself it/them(C1)-he(C3)-see-Past.Ind.NF-as if [it(C1)-]he(C3)-say-Dyn-Fin
'He speaks as if he saw it/them himself.' 'Он говорит, будто сам видел.'

6. Features of the Bzyp Dialect

6.1. The Bzyp Dialect and its Subdialects

Thus far, we have described standard Abkhaz (abbreviated as 'SA'). Standard Abkhaz was created based on the Abzhywa dialect, and this dialect spreads to the south from the capital of Sukhum. In contrast, the dialect which spreads out to the north is the Bzyp dialect, and according to materials from 1959, there are approximately 30,000 speakers, and the central city in this region is Гудаута (G°dauta). In this chapter, we will present an outline of this dialect primarily using Bgazhba's 1964 materials.[191]

It is possible to further divide the Bzyp dialect into two subdialects based on its phonetic features: i.e. the Kaldakhvara subdialect (Калдахварский говор) and the Aatsi(n) subdialect (Аацинский говор) (Bgazhba, ibid. 22). The Kaldakhvara subdialect takes its name from a village along the right bank of the Bzyb' (Бзыбь) River, and it retains somewhat older linguistic features. On the other hand, the Aatsi(n) subdialect is spoken in an area closer to Sukhum than the Kaldakhvara subdialect, and is the dialect spoken in the villages between the Aapsta and Anukhava rivers, as well as the villages in the Aapsta River valley.

The Kaldkhvara subdialect retains all seven sounds particular to the Bzyb dialect: the chuintante/plato-alveolan and the sifflante/sibilant fricatives and affricates: ć, ӡ́, ц́, ҙ́, тц́, с°, з° /ś, ź, ć, ҙ́, ć', ś°, ź°/, and the velar-pharyngeal fricatives: х̫, х̫°. On the other hand, among the aforementioned chuintante/plato-avelolan and sifflantes/sibilants, the Aatsi(n) subdialect lacks ć, ӡ́, ц́, ҙ́, тц́ /ś, ź, ć, ҙ́, ć'/.

6.2. Phonological System

6.2.1. Vowels

This dialect has the same two vowels as standard Abkhaz: а /a/ and ы /ə/. These vowels produce the following sounds when they come into contact with the semiconsonants й /j/ and ў /w/.

(1) а becomes е when it is next to й, and а becomes о when it is next to ў. For example:

Аҧćыҙ ҳа-к-ўе-йт (< ҳа-к-ўа-йт) каҭ-ла. (мы ловим рыбу неводом, 156),

Cf. а-ҧćыҙк-ц°а а-ҧćыҙ ры-к-ўа-йт. (рыбаки ловят рыбу, 166).

а-доў 'big' < а-да́ў,

и-сы-ӡ́-дыр-о-м 'I do not know it/them' < и-сы-ӡ́-дыр-ўо-м (я не знаю. 105) < и-сы-ӡ́-дыр-ўа-м.

оҩы < а-ўаҩы́ 'man, person'.

(2) и [i] is produced due to the merger of ы [ə] and й [j], and у [u] is produced due to the merger of ы [ə] and ў [w]. For example:

191. Бгажба Х.С. *Бзыбский диалект абхазского языка: исследование и тексты*. Тбилиси. 1964] (The numbers below indicate the page in Bgazhba's work).

ды-ц°-ит (< ды-ц°ы-йт < ды-ц°а-йт) (он заснул, 163),
Cf. и-ć-ак°ы́-м и-ќалы-йт (< и-ќала-йт) (вышло не так (как должно быть), 182).
Саргьы с-ўаꙩ-уп (< с-ўаꙩы-ўп) х̣а с-х̮ы сы-ђхьаӡ́-ўейт. (и я считаю себя человеком, 156),
Cf. й-ах̣ракы-ўп (< их̣аракы-ўп) ‘высоко’.

6.2.2. Consonants

The system of consonant phonemes is as follows (ibid. 93):

	Stops	Affricates	Fricatives	Resonants	Semivowels
Labials:					
bilabial	b p p’			m	w
dentolabial			v f 【f’】		
Dentals					
simple	d t t’	ʒ c c’	z s	n r	
labialized	d° t° t’°	ʒ° c° c’°			
Alveolars					
simple [retroflex]		ǯ č č’	ž š		
labialized			ž° š°		
palatalized [palato-alveolar]		ǯʲ čʲ č’ʲ	žʲ šʲ		
Palato-alveolars		ʒ́ (ӡ́) ć (џ́) ć’(т́џ)	ź (ʒ́) ś (ć)		
labialized			ź° (ʒ°) ś° (c°)		
Palatals					
simple					j (й)
labialized					j° (ꙩ)
Laterals					
simple				l	
Velars					
simple	g k k’				
labialized	g° k° k’°				
palatalized	gʲ kʲ k’ʲ				
Uvulars					
simple	q’		ɣ x		
labialized	q’°		ɣ° x°		
palatalized	q’ʲ		ɣʲ xʲ		
Velar-pharyngeals			x̮ (х̮)		
labialized			x̮° (х̮°)		
Pharyngals	ʔ (ъ)				
simple			ħ		
labialized			ħ°		

Notes:

1. Here, labialized consonants use the symbol °.
2. The characters in the parenthesis are Abkhaz characters particular to the Bzyp dialect.
3. There are scholars who regard the phonetic features of x̬ and x̬° as pharyngealised uvulars. For more on this, cf. Chirikba (1996: 17).
4. ʔ can be seen in аъ 'where', which is used as a verbal prefix: с-аъ-т°ó-ў 'where I am sitting', (там, где я сижу, 180). с-аъ-цо 'where I am going', (куда я иду, 180). с-аъы́-ъо-ў 'where I am' (где я нахожусь, 180). The origins of ʔ can be found in ҟ (cf. Abaza. ъа < аъ < аҟ (180)).

6.3. Phonetic Process

6.3.1. Assimilation

6.3.1.1. Vowel Assimilation

(1) a becomes e when it is adjacent to й:
йахьа /jaxʲa/ 'today' → йехьа [jexʲa] → ехьá [exʲá] (95),
дцаўайт /dćawajt'/ 'he/she is going' → дцўайт [dćwajt'] → дцўейт [dćwejt'] (95).

(2) a becomes o when it is adjacent to ў :
ўах̬а /wax̬a/ 'this night' → ўох̬á [wox̬á],
амардўан /amardwan/ 'ladder' → амардўон [amardwon] → амардóн [amardón],
ашáўра /ašáwra/ 'heat' → ашоўра [ašowra] → ашора [ašora].

6.3.1.2. Consonant Assimilation

6.3.1.2.1. Regressive Assimilation

The following types of regressive assimilation occur:

(1) Voiced Consonant + Unvoiced Consonant → Unvoiced Consonant + Unvoiced Consonant:
абх°а [abħ°a] → аҧх°á [apħ°á] 'plum'

(2) Unvoiced Consonant + Voiced Consonant → Voiced Consonant + Voiced Consonant:
арҧыс́ба [arpəśba] → áрҧыз́ба [árpəźba] 'youth'
аҧх°ыс́ба [apħ°əćба] → аҧх°ыз́ба [apħ°əźба] 'girl' (cf. аҧх°ыс́ 'woman')

(3) Ejective + Non-ejective → Non-ejective + Non-ejective:
аҵ°ц́а [ac'°ća] → áц°ц́а [ác°ća] 'a glass' (cf. SA áҵәца)

(4) Non-ejective + Ejective → Ejective + Ejective:
абты [abt'ə] → апты [ap't'ə] 'wood bug'

(5) Others:
бн → мн : абнахь [abnaxʲ] → амнáхь [amnáxʲ] 'there'
сшь → шьшь : аҧсшьара [apsšʲara] → аҧшьшьáра [apšʲšʲára] 'to be resting', etc.

6.3.1.2.2. Progressive Assimilation

абас́ҟак [abaśq'ak'] → абас́ҟаҟ [abaśq'aq'] 'so much'

аҵ́кьыć [aćʼkʼʲəś] → аҵ́ҵыć [aćʼćʼəś] ‘than’
аҧьжьымҭан [ašʲžʲəmtan] → áшьшьымҭан [ášʲšʲəmtan] ‘in the morning’

6.3.2. Consonant Dissimilation

(1) ejective + ejective → non-ejective + ejective:
ачк°ын [ačʼkʼ°ən] → ачк°ын [ačkʼ°эн] ‘boy’,
аҵкы [acʼkʼə] → ацкы [ackʼə] ‘dress’.

6.3.3. Metathesis

(1) Metathesis occurring between resonants, or between resonants and other sounds:
аҟ°арыл [aqʼ°arəl] → аҟ°алы́р [aqʼ°alə́r] ‘capon’, cf. SA аҟәрыл,
аўалыр [awalər] → аўлыр [awlər] → аўры́л [awrə́l] ‘barrel’,
адырҩагь [adərj°agʲ] → адыҩра́гь [adəj°rágʲ] ‘again’,
аказарма [akʼazarma] → акарза́ма [akʼarzáma] ‘barrack’, etc.

(2) Metathesis occurring between consonants other than resonants:
аш°ашьыр [aš°ašʲər] → ашьаш°ы́р [ašʲaš°ə́r] ‘shade’, cf. SA ашәшьыра,
есышык°са [esəšək°sa] → ешысы́к°са [ešəsə́k°sa] ‘evry year’, cf. SA есы́шықәса.

6.3.4. Sound Alternation

(1) Alternation of н and м:
аҟамчы → аҟанчы́ ‘lash’, cf. SA а-ҟамчы́,
аг°амҵ́ра → аг°а́нҵ́ра ‘suffering’,
амӡанра → а́нӡанра ‘wonderful’, cf. SA амӡанра,
шаҟант°ы → шаҟамт°ы́ ‘how many’,
ачамг°ы́р / ачанг°ыр ‘chonguri [a Georgian stringed instrument]’, cf. SA ачамгәы́р.

(2) Other alternations:
м → б : абага́на ‘sickle’, cf. SA амага́на, Megr. magána.
б → м : аҟамла́ ‘young animals’, cf. SA а́ҟабла, Megr. kabla.
ҧ → м : акьа́мш, cf. акьаҧш ‘slanting’.
н / л : а́нҧхыҧрак / алҧхыҧрак ‘all summer long’.
кь / к : аҵ́кьы́ć ‘much than’, cf. SA аҵкыс.
Cf. -ц°ҟа ‘just, indeed’, SA -ҵәҟьа-.
т / ҭ : аша́тара, cf. SA ашаҭара ‘to spare’.
б → ҧ → п : аҳабыш → аҳаҧыш → аҳапы́ш ‘tooth’, cf. SA ахаҧы́ц.
ҟ → а : д-аба-ҟа-ў → д-аба́-а-ў ‘where is she?’.
ҳ → а : акы́лҳара → акылаара ‘aperture’,
Cf. Bzyp. аҭахц°а́ ‘family’, SA аҭаацәа́.

Other consonant alternations: к°/ҟ°, ц/ҿ, п°/ц°, ч/ц°, ц/ҵ, ӡь/жь, с/шь, ш/с, х°/ҩ, х/х°, х/хь.

(3) Delabialization

ɷ [j°] → й [j] : аз°ɷан → áз°йан 'sky', cf. SA áжəɷан; ат°ыɷа → ат°ы́йа, cf. SA а-тəы́ɷа 'horn'.
йаж°а '20', cf. SA ɷажəá.

х° [ħ°] → ҳ [ħ] : х°а → ха 'speech-particle', cf. SA ҳəа,

т° [t'°] → т [t'] : у-т°а → у-тá 'sit down!', cf. SA у-тəá; áж°ы́т 'in olden times', cf. SA ажəы́тə.

ц° [c'°] → ц [c'] : амц°ыз°йа → амцы́з°йа 'wing',

ҟ° [q'°] → ҟ [q'] : ашºҟ°ы / ашºҟы 'book', cf. SA ашəҟəы́,

у-л-ҟá-ц (< у-л-ҟ°а-ц) 'Lose touch with her!', cf. SA у-л-ҟəá-ц,

к° [k'°] → к [k'] : -м-к°а → -м-ка 'marker of Negative Absolutive',

cf. к° [k'°] → к° [k°] : с°ы-м-с°á-к°а → с°ы-м-с°á-қ°а 'You not feeling fear', SA шəы-м-шəá-кəа.

6.3.5. Epenthesis

Primarily, the resonants л, н, м, р are inserted:

л : а-ҳшлы́баɷ, cf. SA а-хшыбаɷ 'skull',

н : ашпаҕьы́нч, cf. SA ашпаҕьыч 'titmouse',

м : амшьандáл, cf. SA ашьандал 'candlestick',

р : асáржан, cf. Russ. сажень 'sazhen', SA асацьáн.

6.3.6. Sound Dropping and Weakening

Compared to the standard language, sound dropping is frequently seen in the Bzyp dialect. Resonant dropping is frequently seen in cases where consonants drop. In vowels, a phenomenon is seen where the word-final а is weakened and becomes ы.

6.3.6.1. Consonant Dropping

The following resonant dropping is seen in Abkhaz:

р : афáхь < афархь 'brushwood',

н : асарáць, SA асарáнц 'honeycomb',

л : ды-баа-йт < д-лыбаа-йт 'He/She descended', cf. SA ды-лбаá-ит, etc.

In addition, dropping of the й /j/ in verbal aorist suffix -йт is often seen:

д-и-м-бы-т 'He did not see him/her', cf. SA д-и-м-бé-ит,

д-гыл-т 'He/She stood up', cf. SA д-гы́ле-ит,

и-л-дыр-т (166) 'She knew it/them', cf. SA и-л-ды́р-ит,

д-а-ла-г-т (157) 'He/She began it', cf. SA д-á-ла-ге-ит,

ды-чмазаɷхы-т (165) 'He/She fell ill', cf. SA ды-чмазаɷхé-ит,

йеж°йж°аба маат с-и-ты-т (113) 'He gave me 300 rubles', cf. SA и-с-и́-те-ит,

У-йаша-м ха й-а-л-х°ы-т (165) 'She said to him, "you are not right"'; cf. SA и-á-л-ҳəе-ит,

айдра шьты-л-х-т 'She lifted the burden up', cf, SA и-шьты́-л-х-ит,

ды-ɷ-т 'he/she ran', cf. SA ды́-ɷ-ит, etc.

6.3.6.2. Weakening and Dropping of Vowels

(1) Weakening of an unaccented a to ы:

ақаҕц°а → ақáҕц°ы 'chin',

занцлы → зынцьы́ 'once, recently',

абаҩ → áбыҩ 'bone', cf. SA áбаҩ,

асалдат → асылдáҭ 'soldier', cf. Russ. солдат,

ацаҕха → ацыҕхá 'key', cf. SA ацаҕхá, etc.

(2) Dropping of an unaccented word-final a:

аҩаша → аҩáш 'Tuesday', cf. SA аҩáша,

ачаҕьа → ачы́ҕь 'food, provisions', cf. SA ачáҕьа,

аҳ°аша → аҳ°áш 'Friday', cf. SA áхәаша,

аамҭа → áамҭ 'time', cf. SA áамҭа, etc.

NB: Due to the dropping of word-final a in the Bzyp dialect, there are cases where ы is inserted word-medial:

áбыл, cf. SA áбла 'eye', áмыр, cf. SA áмра 'sun', áшьҭыр, cf. SA áшьҭра 'relatives', etc.

(3) Dropping of unaccented non word-final a:

аҕатца → аҕтцы́ 'beard', cf. SA а-ҕатцá,

ақ°араан → ақ°рáан 'crow',

аҳарак → áҳрак 'high', cf. SA á-харак(ы),

атцақа → áтцқа 'under', cf. SA á-тцақа,

алада → áлда 'down', cf. SA áлада, etc.

(4) Dropping of unaccented a in a verbal form:

In verbal forms other than the masdar, dropping of a is a phenomenon frequently seen in the Bzyp dialect. What is seen the most is the dropping of the unaccented a at the end of a verbal root before the dynamic suffix ў̈а:

и-л-ба-ў̈éйт → и-л-б-ў̈éйт 'She is seeing it/them', cf. SA и-л-бó-ит /jə-l-ba-wá-jt'/,

д-ńа-ў̈ейт → д-ń-ў̈éйт 'He/She is going', cf. у-ńа (197) 'go! (to a man)', SA д-цó-ит /d-ca-wá-jt'/

ды-ʒ́-ńа-ў̈а-м → ды-ʒ́-ń-ў̈а-м (175) 'He/She cannot go', cf. SA сы-з-цó-ма?/sə-z-ca-wá-ma/ 'Can I go?',

ды-нха-ў̈а-н → ды-нх-ў̈а-н (153) 'He/She was living', cf. SA ды-нхó-н /də-n-xa-wá-n/,

и-қа-л-тца-ў̈ейт → и-қа-л-тц-ў̈éйт 'She is doing it/them', cf. и-қа-тца (186) 'Do it/them!', SA и-қа-л-тцó-ит /jə-q'a-l-c'a-wá-jt'/,

ды-с-ф-ў̈áт (157) 'I'll eat him/her', cf. SA ды-с-фó-ит /də-s-fa-wá-jt'/,

й-аҳ-фа-ў̈а → й-аҳ-ф-ў̈а 'the one which we are eating', cf. SA и-áҳ-фо /j-áħ-fa-wa/,

бзиа ейба-ба-ў̈ан → бзиа ейба-б-ў̈ан 'They loved each other', cf. айбабара 'to see each other', SA х-аиба-бó-н /ħ-ajba-ba-wá-n/, etc.

Also, dropping of the unaccented a at the end of a verbal root is seen in the aorist form:

й-аа-й-х°-т (179) 'He bought it', cf. SA и-аа́-и-хәе-ит /j-aá-j-xʷa-jt'/,

ха й-е-й-х°а-ит → ха й-е-й-х°-т (114) 'He said to him, '...', cf. SA и-с-е́-и-ҳәе-ит /jə-s-á-j-ħʷa-jt'/,

д-гы́ла-йт → д-гыл-т (166) 'He/She stood up', cf. SA д-гы́ле-ит /d-gə́la-jt'/,

и-на́-л-ге-йт → и-на-л-г-т (166) 'She brought it/them', cf. SA и-на́-л-ге-ит /jə-ná-l-ga-jt'/,

д-а-ла-га-ит → д-а-ла-г-т (157) 'He/She began it', cf. д-а́-ла-ге-ит /d-á-la-ga-jt'/, etc.

(5) Weakening of accented <u>a</u> to <u>ы</u>:

(i) Weakening of word-final <u>a</u> to <u>ы</u>:

аҕша → аҕшы́ 'wind', cf. SA аҕша́,

аꚏеада → аꚏеады́ 'donkey', cf. SA аꚏеада́,

сах°шьа → сах°шьы́ 'my sister', cf. SA с-аҳәшьа́.

NB: there are also examples where <u>a</u> is preserved in the Bzyp dialect, and in standard Abkhaz it becomes <u>ы</u>: Bzyp айхаба́, cf. SA аиҳабы́ 'elder', Bzyp айтҵба́, cf. айтҵбы́ 'younger', etc.

(ii) Weakening of non word-final <u>a</u> to <u>ы</u>:

ахак → ахы́к 'one prince', cf. SA ахы́к/аха́к

мач → мыч 'little', cf. SA а-ма́ч,

д-ҭа-м-ла-ӡы́-к°а (< д-ҭа-м-ла-ӡа-к°а) 'He, not going into', etc.

NB: there are also examples where <u>a</u> is preserved in the Bzyp dialect, and in the standard language it becomes <u>ы</u>: Bzyp аҵа́ба, cf. SA аҵьы́ба 'pocket', Bzyp аҕа́хьа, cf. аҕы́хьа 'before', etc.

(iii) Change from <u>a</u> to <u>ы</u> in the verbal root:

д-аанхы-йт (153) 'He stayed', cf. SA д-аан-хе́-ит /d-aan-xá-jt'/,

ды-з°-ба → ды-з°-бы́ 'You-Pl see him/her!', cf. SA ды-жә-ба́,

д-ба → д-бы 'see him/her!', cf. SA д-ба́,

д-и-м-бы-т (159) 'He did not see him/her', cf. SA д-и-м-бе́-ит,

и-м-бы-йт (164) 'He did not see it/them', cf. SA и-м-бе́-ит,

и-га → и-гы́ 'Take it/them!', cf. SA и-га́ /jə-gá/,

ды-р-гы-йт (164) 'They took him/her', cf. SA ды-р-ге́-ит /də-r-gá-jt'/,

и-ҟалы-йт (182) 'It/They happened', cf. SA и-ҟале́-ит /jə-q'alá-jt'/,

и-х°ы 'Say it/them!', cf. SA и-ҳәа́ /jə-ħʷá/, etc.

6.4. Sound Correspondences Between the Bzyp Dialect and Standard Abkhaz

Sounds correspond in the following ways in the Bzyp dialect and standard Abkhaz:

Bzyp dial.:	SA	Examples:
с /s/ :	с /s/,	сара : сара́ 'I', с : с 'the 1st sg. pronominal prefix', а-сыс : а-сы́с 'lamb'.
ć /ś/ :	ш /š/,	д-ć-ú-ў а : д-ш-цо 'how he/she is going', ćейбак°ы : шеибакәы́ 'all'.
ć /ś/ :	с /s/,	а-ćы́ : а-сы́ 'snow', ćымт°а́ : сынтәа́ 'in this year', а-ć-ра : а́-с-ра 'to hit'.
с° /ś°/ :	шә /š°/,	с°ара : шәара́ 'you-Pl', а́с°а : а́шәа 'song'.

As can be seen from the examples above, с /s/ and ć /ś/ in the Bzyp dialect correspond to с /s/ in standard Abkhaz. According to Nikolayev and Starostin (1994), as Proto-Northwest-Caucasian sounds, the sounds from the Bzyp dialect are considered to be older when reconstructed: W.-Cauc. *sA 'I' (ibid. 1084), *śə 'snow' (ibid. 675).

з /z/ :	з /z/,	з-ны : з-ны 'once', зегь(ы́)/загь(ы) : зегь(ы́) 'all', зкьы : зкьы́ 'thousand'.
(з /z/ :	ӡ /ʒ/,	азы : аӡы́ 'river').
з́ /ź/ :	з /z/,	и-сы-з́-дыр-ў̆о-м : и-сы-з-ды́р-уа-м 'I do not know', з́ы : зы 'for'.
(з́ /ź/ :	ш /š/,	з́ейбак° : шеибакы́ 'all').
з° /ẑ°/ :	жә /ž°/,	áз° : áжә 'cow', áз°а : áжәа 'word', аз°ра : áжәра 'to drink'.

z /z/ and з́ /ź/ in the Bzyp dialect correspond to з /z/ in standard Abkhaz. The sounds in Proto-Northwest-Caucasian are reconstructed as follows: W.-Cauc. *zV 'one', Abkh. z-nə, (Nikolayev and Starostin: 324), W.-Cauc. *z^{w}A 'to drink' (ibid. 263).

ӡ /ʒ/ :	ӡ /ʒ/,	а-ӡы́ : а-ӡы́ 'water; river', аӡбах̬° : áӡбахә 'news'.
ӡ́ /ʒ́/ :	ӡ /ʒ/,	á-ӡ́ы́н : á-ӡын 'winter', аӡ́ахра : áӡахра 'to sew'.
ӡ° /ʒ°/ :	ӡә /ʒ°/,	аӡ° : аӡәы́ 'someone'.

ӡ /ʒ/ and ӡ́ /ʒ́/ in the Bzyp dialect correspond to ӡ /ʒ/ in standard Abkhaz. The sounds in Proto-Northwest-Caucasian are reconstructed as follows: PAT (Proto-Abkhaz-Tapant) *ʒə 'water' (ibid. 872); PAT *ʒ́ə-nə 'winter' (ibid. 327).

ц /c/ :	ц /c/,	ацха : áцха 'bridge', ацламх°ы́ : а-цламхәá 'chin'.
(ц /c/ :	с /s/,	и-ц-хы́ччейт : и-с-хыччейт 'they mocked me').
(ц /c/ :	ҵ /c'/,	ацкы : аҵкы́ 'dress').
ц́ /ć/ :	ц /c/,	ац́ара : ацарá 'to go', ац́г°ы : ацгәы́ 'cat'.
ц° /c°/ :	цә /c°/,	áц° : áцә 'bull', ац°ҟьа : ацәҟьá 'trap'.

ц /c/ and ц́ /ć/ in the Bzyp dialect correspond to ц /c/ in standard Abkhaz. The sounds in Proto-Northwest-Caucasian are reconstructed as follows: W.-Cauc. *ća 'to go' (Nikolayev and Starostin: 253), W.-Cauc. *cA 'hot', SA a-cá, Bzyb. a-cá (ibid. 416).

ҵ /c'/ :	ҵ /c'/,	а-ҵы́х̬° : а-ҵы́хәа 'tail', áҵла : áҵла 'tree'.
ҵ́ /ć'/ :	ҵ /c'/,	аҵ́ыć : аҵы́с 'bird', аҵ́ра : аҵрá 'to pass'.
ҵ° /c'°/ :	ҵ /c'°/,	аҵ°á : аҵәá 'apple', аҵ°ы : аҵәы́ 'skewer'.

ҵ /c'/ and ҵ́ /ć'/ in the Bzyp dialect correspond to ҵ /c'/ in standard Abkhaz. The sounds in Proto-Northwest-Caucasian are reconstructed as follows: PAT *c'əq^{w}a < W.-Cauc. *c'əq:^{w}a 'tail' (ibid. 934); PAT *ć'ə-śə < W-Cauc. *ć'ə 'small bird' (ibid. 525).

х /x/ :	х /x/,	хы-мш 'three days' : х-ҧа 'three', а-хан : а-хáн 'palace', áхаш : á-хаша

		'Wednesday'.
хь /xʲ/ :	хь /xʲ/,	ахьамта : áхьанҭа 'heavy', ахьча : áхьча 'shepherd'.
х° /x°/ :	хә /x°/,	х°-ба : хә-бá 'five', ах°ачы́ : ахәычы́ 'child; little'.
х̬ /χ/ :	х /x/,	á-х̬а-ра : á-ха-ра 'to pull', ах̬áҭа : ахáҵа 'man', а-х̬ах° : а-хáхә 'stone', ах̬ы́ : ахы́ 'head'.
х̬° /χ°/ :	хә /x°/,	а-х̬°ы-ц : а-хәы́-ц 'hair', ах̬°ара : áхәара 'to help', а-х̬°áш : á-хәаша 'Friday'.

х /x/ and х̬ /χ/ in the Bzyp dialect correspond to х /x/ in standard Abkhaz. Also, х° /x°/ and х̬° /χ°/ in the Bzyp dialect correspond to х° /x°/ in standard Abkhaz. The sounds in Proto-Northwest-Caucasian are reconstructed as follows: PAT *хә 'three' (ibid. 768); PAT *qV 'to pull, drag' (ibid. 576); PAT *xʷә- < W.-Cauc. *s-xʷә 'five' (ibid. 426); PAT *qʷә < W.-Cauc. *qIʷә 'hair' (ibid. 931).

ъ /ʕ/ :	хь /xʲ/,	с-аъ-цо : с-ахь-цо 'where I am going'.
ъ /ʕ/ :	ҟ /q'/,	с-аъы́-ъо-ӱ : с-ахьы́-ҟо-у 'where I am'.

For all other consonants, there is a one-to-one correspondence between the Bzyp dialect and standard Abkhaz. For example:

Bzyp dial.	SA	Bzyp dial.	SA
ш /š/	ш /š/	ашх̬°а	á-шхәа 'canoe'
шь /šʲ/	шь /šʲ/	ашьра	ашьрá 'to kill'.
ш° /š°/	шә /š°/	аш°ҟ°ы́	ашәҟәы́ 'book', аш° : áшә 'door'
к /k'/	к /k'/	акы	акы́ 'one'
кь /k'ʲ/	кь /k'ʲ/	акьы́сра	акьы́сра 'to touch'
к° /k'°/	кә /k'°/	ак°ац	акәáц 'meat'
қ /k/	қ /k/	ақыҭа	ақы́ҭа 'village'
қь /kʲ/	қь /kʲ/	ақьр	ақьрá 'to sigh'
қ° /k°/	қә /k°/	ақ°лара	áқәлара 'to set off'
ҟ /q'/	ҟ /q'/	аҟáма	аҟáма 'dagger'
ҟ° /q'°/	ҟә /q'°/	аҟ°áҟ°	аҟәáҟәа 'back'
т /t'/	т /t'/	аты́ш(а)	аты́ша 'deep hole'
т° /t'°/	тә /t'°/	ат°ы́йа	атәы́ҩа 'horn'
ҭ /t/	ҭ /t/	аҭаац°а	аҭаацәá 'family'
ҭ° /t°/	ҭә /t°/	аҭ°а	аҭәá 'hay'
ҽ /č/	ҽ /č/	аҽы́	аҽы́ 'horse'
ҿ /č'/	ҿ /č'/	аҿырпáн	аҿырпы́н/аҿарпы́н 'reed-pipe; flute'
ҩ /j°/	ҩ /j°/	ҩ-ба	ҩ-бá 'two'
ць /ʒ̆ʲ/	ць /ʒ̆ʲ/	аџьáба	аџьы́ба 'pocket'
б /b/	б /b/	аб	áб 'father'
в /v/	в /v/	авҟ°ыла	áваҟәыла 'companion-in-arms'

г /g/	г /g/	ага́р	ага́ра ‘cradle’
гь /gʲ/	гь /gʲ/	-гьы	-гьы ‘also’
г° /g°/	гә /g°/	аг°а́	агәа́ра ‘ fence; hedge’
ҕ /ɣ/	ҕ /ɣ/	аҕа	аҕа́ ‘enemy’
ҕь /ɣʲ/	ҕь /ɣʲ/	а-ҕьыч	а-ҕьы́ч ‘thief’
(ҕ° /ɣ°/	ҕ /ɣ/	аҕ°а	аҕа́ ‘enemy’)
д /d/	д /d/	ада́ў	аду́ ‘big’
д° /d°/	дә /d°/	ад°ы́	адәы́ ‘field’
ж /ž/	ж /ž/	ажы́га	ажы́га ‘shovel; spade’
жь /žʲ/	жь /žʲ/	ажьа́	ажьа́ ‘hare, rabbit’
ж° /ž°/	жә /ž°/	аж°ла	а́жәла ‘seed’; аж° : ажә ‘old’
й /j/	и /j/	а-йаша	аиа́ша ‘straight; just; right’
л /l/	л /l/	ала́	ала́ ‘dog’
м /m/	м /m/	амш	а́мш ‘day’
н /n/	н /n/	а́н	а́н ‘mother’
п /p’/	п /p’/	-п	-п ‘suffix of Future I’
(п /p’/	б /b/	апжы	абжы́ ‘beetle’)
ҧ /p/	ҧ /p/	аҧа	аҧа́ ‘son’; аҧс́ра : аҧсра́ ‘to die’
р /r/	р /r/	арах°	а́рахә ‘cattle’
ў /w/	у /w/	аўаса	ауаса́ ‘sheep’
ф /f/	ф /f/	афат°	а́фатә ‘food’
х /ħ/	х /ħ/	аха́	аха́ ‘pear’
х° /ħ°/	хә /ħ°/	ах°ынаҧ	ахәы́наҧ ‘mouse’
ч /čʲ/	ч /čʲ/	а-чара	а-ча́ра ‘wedding’
ч /čʲ’/	ч /čʲ’/	а́-чк°ын	а́-чкәын ‘boy

6.5. The Morphological Features of the Bzyp Dialect

6.5.1. Nouns

For nouns, there are virtually no differences seen in the Bzyp dialect and standard Abkhaz.

6.5.1.1. Plural Forms

The plural marker for the non-human class is -к°а, and the human class is -ц°а:

а-ўаса-к°а́ ‘sheep’, cf. SA а-уаса-кәа́.
а-чк°ын-ц°а ‘boys’, cf. SA а́-чкәын-цәа.
NB: The non-human class marker -к°а is used for some groups of people:
а-кы́рт-к°а ‘Georgians’, cf. SA а-кы́рт-цәа/-кәа, sg. а́-кырту.

Plural forms with these markers joined together can also be seen:

чк°ы́н-ц°а-к°а-к (144) (boy-Pl-Pl-one) ‘some boys’, cf. SA ӡӷа́б-цәа-кәа-к ‘some girls’.

There is also a suffix -ар which expresses collective nouns:

а-ҵ́ар ‘a flock of birds’ (sg. а-ҵ́ыс́ ‘bird’), cf. SA а-ҵа́р (sg. а-ҵы́с).

6.5.1.2. Noun Accent

Accentuation in the Bzyp dialect and standard Abkhaz is basically the same. For example, compare the following examples:

Bzyp dialect:	а-ла́ ‘dog’, а-ла-к̦°а́ ‘dogs’, ла́-к ‘one dog’, ла-к̦°а́-к ‘some dogs’,
SA:	а-ла́ ‘dog’, а-ла-кәа́, ла́-к, ла-кәа́-к.
Bzyp dialect:	а́-бла ‘eye’, бла́-к/бла-кы́ ‘one eye’, ры́-бла-к°а ‘their eyes’,
SA:	а́-бла ‘eye’, бла́-к/бла-кы́, а́-бла-кәа, сы́-бла-кәа.

6.5.2. Pronouns

6.5.2.1. Personal Pronouns

If the sound changes in personal pronouns in the Bzyp dialect are not taken into consideration, there is no difference with the ones in standard Abkhaz.

	Sg.	Pl.
1st person	сара / са	хара / ха
2nd person (male)	ўара / ўа	с°ар (с°арҭ) / с°а
2nd person (female)	бара	с°ар (с°арҭ) / с°а
3rd person (human male)	йара (йера)	дара
3rd person (human female)	лара	дара
3rd person (non-human)	йара	дара

6.5.2.2. Possessive Prefixes

The possessive prefixes in the Bzyp dialect are no different from the ones in standard Abkhaz:

	Sg.	Pl.
1st person	с-	х-
2nd person (male)	ў-	с°-
2nd person (female)	б-	с°-
3rd person (human male)	и-	р(ы)-
3rd person (human female)	л-	р(ы)-
3rd person (non-human)	а-	р(ы)-

6.5.2.3. Demonstrative Pronouns

	Sg.		Pl.
(α)	аб(р)и́	'this'	аба́(р)ҭ 'these'
(β)	амни́	'that' (cf. SA абни́)	
(γ)	уи/убри́	'that'	урҭ/ў̆ҭ 'those'

6.5.2.4. Other Pronouns

акгы 'nothing',
ры́ззагь 'all',
ры́ўаӡ° 'one of them', cf. SA руа́ӡəы́ 'one of them',
ры́ўак 'one of them', cf. SA руа́к (руакы́) 'one (*thing*) of them',
а-х̯аҭа́ 'oneself', cf. хаҭа́ 'oneself',
шьоўкы́ [pron] (= цьоўкы́) некоторые,
цьукы [pron] какие.

6.5.3. Verbs

6.5.3.1. Pronomional Prefixes in Verbs

If sound changers are not considered, the pronominal prefixes in the Bzyp dialect are no different from the ones in standard Abkhaz:

Column I

Person	Sg.	Pl.
1	с-	х-
2 (M)	ў-	с°-
2 (F)	б-	с°-
3 (Human)	д-	и-
3 (Non-Human)	и-/ø-	и-/ø-

Column II

Person	Sg.	Pl.
1	с(ы)-	х-
2 (M)	ў-	с°-
2 (F)	б-	с°-
3 (Human, M)	й-	р-
3 (Human, F)	л(ы)-	р-
3 (Non-Human)	а-	р-

Column III

Person	Sg.	Pl.

1	с-/з-	х̮-/аа-
2 (M)	ў-	с°-/з°-
2 (F)	б-	с°-/з°-
3 (Human, M)	й-	р-/д-
3 (Human, F)	л-	р-/д-
3 (Non-Human)	а-	р-/д-

6.5.3.2. Verbal Paradigms

No differences can be seen between the Bzyp dialect and standard Abkhaz in verbal paradigms as well if the sound changes (dropping of the root-final sound, etc.) between the two dialects are excluded. No changes can be seen in the placement order of the pronominal prefixes between the two dialects either. The following represents an incomplete paradigm as the examples were taken from texts:

6.5.3.2.1. Class A-1/B-1 (intransitive/stative verbs)

Finite
Present
д-ўы-мо-ўп (182) 'You-M have him/her.' (cf. а-ма-(заа)-ра 'to have')
и-х̮ы д-а-к̦°и́т̦-уп 'He is free.' (cf. а-к°ит̦-(заа)-ра 'to be free')
ейтц°а кыд-уп аз°йан (151–2) 'There are stars on the sky.' (cf. а-кыд-(заа)-ра 'to be on')
Past
д-гыла-н 'He/She was standing.' (cf. а-гыла-(заа)-ра 'to stand')
рах° ха-ма-ӡы-мызт (192) 'We did not have cattle.'

Non-Finite
Present
и-ć-ак°ы́-м (182) 'How it is not/they are not'
Past
ды-ш-гы́ла-з 'How he/she was standing'
д-ах(ы́)-шьт̦а-з (178) 'Where he/she was lying'

Absolutive
ры-мыйныф ры-ма-ны 'They, having their travelling food'

6.5.3.2.2. Class A-2 (intransitive/dynamic verbs)

а-ц́а-ра 'to go':
Finite
Present
с-ц́-ўо-йт (192) 'I am going.' ды-ӡ́-ц́-ўа-м (175) 'He/She cannot go.'
д-ц́-ўе́йт (< д-ц́а-ўе́йт) (124) 'He/She is going.'
Aorist
д-ц́е-йт (153)
Future I
х̮-ай-ц́-ц́а-п (175) 'Let's go together!'

Pluperfect
сы-м-п́а́-п́ы-зт

Non-Finite
Present
и-п́-ўа́ (< и-п́а-ўа) ‘the one who is going’
Imperfect
х-аќ-п́-ўа́-з (180) ‘where we were going’

Imperative
у-п́а (197) ‘you-Sg.M go!’
у-лы́-п́-п́а (175) ‘you-Sg.M go with her!’

6.5.3.2.3. Class C (transitive/dynamic verbs)

а-ба-ра ‘to see’:
Finite
Present
и-л-б-ўе́-йт ‘She is seeing it/them.’
Aorist
д-и-б-ит ‘He saw him/her.’ д-и-м-бы-т (159) ‘He did not see him/her.’
и-с-б-ит (168) ‘I saw it/them’ д-лы-м-б-ит (162) ‘She did not see him/her.’
и-з-бы-т (178) ‘I saw it/them’
и-бы-йт (182) ‘He saw it/them.’ д-ры-м-б-ит (179) ‘They did not see him/her.’
Future I
ø-аа-ба-п (185) ‘We shall see [it/them].’
Perfect
и-з-ба-хьа-т (165) ‘I have seen it/them.’ д-сы-м-ба-ӡа́-п́-т (175) ‘I have not seen him/her.’

Non-Finite
Present
и́-р-б-ўа ‘which they are seeing’
д-аба́-з-б-ўа? (192) ‘where shall I see him/her?’
Aorist
д-ан-ах-ба (168) ‘when we saw him/her’
Pluperfect
И-й-ба-п́ы-з (cf. SA и-й-ба-хьа-з) (167) ‘the one who he had seen’
Imperative
д-бы (< д-ба) ‘You-Sg see him/her!’
ды-з°-бы́ (< ды-з°-ба) ‘You-Pl see him/her!’
Absolutive
бзиа и-б-ны́ (< и-ба-ны) ‘having fallen in love with them’

6.5.3.2.4. Class D (transitive verbs)

а-ҭа-ра ‘to give’
Finite

Present
зегь й-аҳ-ҭ-ўойт (158) 'We shall give all to him.'
Aorist
йеж°йж°аба мааҭ с-и-ҭы-т (113) 'He gave me 13 rubles.'
и-на-лы-й-ҭы-т (100) 'He gave it to her.'
Imperfect
аҭ°а ры-р-ҭ-ўан (146) 'They were giving hay to them.'

Non-Finite
Present
с-аҳ°шьа ды-з́ба-ры́-с-ҭ-ўа (196) 'how I shall give my sister to them'
Aorist
зкьы манаҭ у-с-ҭе-йшьҭей 'since I gave 1000 rubles to you'

Imperative
и-сы-ҭ (149) 'Give it/them to me!'
д-ҳа-ҭ (153) 'Give him/her to us!'
ат°ан сы-с°-ҭ (114) 'You-Pl give me broth!'

6.5.3.2.5. Class F (intransitive/dynamic verbs)

а-ҳа-ра 'to hear':
Finite
Present
и-с-а-ҳ-ўе́йт (< и-с-а-ҳа-ўе́йт) 'I hear it.'
и-ў-а-ҳ-ўа-йт 'You hear it.'
Aorist
й-а-ҳа-йт (113) 'He heard it.'
и-с-а-ҳа-т (165) 'I heard it.'
Imperfect
и-с-а-ҳ-он 'I was hearing it.'
и-л-а-ҳ-ўо-н 'She was hearing it.'

Non-Finite
Present
и-б-а-ҳ-ўа-зи? (190) 'what are you heraing?'
Aorist
и-ан-й-а-ҳа (184) 'when she heard it'
Imperfect
й-а-ҳ-ўа-з 'which he was hearing'
Past Indefinite
и-с-с-а-ҳа́-з 'how I heard it'

6.5.3.2.6. Class G (transitive verbs)

а-к̆а-ҵа-ра 'to do':
Finite

Present
и-ƙа-л-тц-ўéйт 'She is doing it/them.'
Aorist
и-ƙа-р-тц-ит 'They did it/them.'
Imperfect
и-ƙа-р-тц-ўа-н 'They were doing it/them.'

Non-Finite
Present
и́-ƙа-л-тц-ўа '(that) which she is doing'
и-ƙа-з-тц-уá '(one) who is doing it/them'

Imperative
и-ƙа-тцы́ / и-ƙа-тца (186) 'you-Sg do it/them!'

6.5.3.2.7. Class H/C (transitive verbs)

а-х°а-рá 'to say':
Finite
Future I
и-б-а-с-х°а-п (186) 'I shall say it/them to you-F.'
и-ў-а-с-х°а-п (186) 'I shall say it/them to you-M.'
Aorist
и-л-а-р-х°-т (185) 'They said it/them to her.'
й-а-л-х°ы-т (187) 'She said it/them to him.'
и-р-е-й-х°ы-йт / и-р-е-й-х°ы-т / и-р-е-й-х°-т (< и-р-é-й-х°е-йт) (166) 'He said it/them to them.'
и-л-е-й-м-х°а-ӡ-ит (184) 'He did not say it/them to her.'
и-сы-з́-й-а-м-х°-т (175) 'I could not say it/them to him.'

Non-Finite
Present
и-р-х°-ўа (166) '(that) which they say'
Imperfect
и-ахы́нӡа-л-х°-ўа-з (189) 'while she was saying it/them'
Past Indefinite
и-л-а-х̧-х°а-з (193) '(that) which we said to her'
и-з́-р-é-й-х°а-з (185) 'how he said it/them to them'

Imperative
и-х°а / и-х°ы 'Say!'
и-л-а-х° 'Say it/them to her!'

6.5.3.3. Derived Forms

6.5.3.3.1. Imperative

The imperative form in the Bzyb dialect is produced in the same way as in the standard language. In the imperative form of intransitive verbs the subject also appears in cases where it is in the singular, but in the imperative form of transitive verbs the singular agent does not appear in the affirmative

form.
у-ц́а (197) 'Go!' (to a man)
д-бы (< д-ба) 'See him/her!' (to a man/woman)
ды-з°-бы́ < ды-з°-ба 'See him/her!' (to multiple people)

6.5.3.3.2. Subjunctive

The subjunctive is produced by adding the suffix -аайт to the aorist stem. Examples:

(797) а-дуней ў-аќы́-нӡа-к° чмазара у-мы-хь-аайт (180)
the-world you-where-until-Abs illness [it-]you-not-hurt-Sub
'May you not become ill as long as you live in this world!'

6.5.3.3.3. Potential

The potential marker uses ӡ́- (cf. SA з-). The potential form is produced in the same method as in the standard language. In intransitive verbs, ӡ́- is inserted after the pronominal prefix which expresses the subject of the intransitive verb. In transitive verbs, ӡ́- is inserted after the pronominal prefix which expresses the agent.
Examples in Intransitive Verbs:

(798) сара ўахь сы-ӡ́-ц́-ўа-м (162)
I there I-Pot-go-Dyn-Neg
'I cannot go there.'

Examples in Transitive Verbs:

(799) и-сы-ӡ́-дыр-ўо-м (105)
it/they-I-Pot-know-Dyn-Neg
'I do not know it/them.'

(800) и-ӡ́-и-ӡ́ы-м-дыр-о-зи (191)
it-why-he-Pot-Neg-know-Dyn-Qu
'Why don't he know it?'

(801) уи аӡ́бах̯° и-сы-ӡ́-й-а-м-х°-т (175)
this news it-I-Pot-hem-to-Neg-say-(Aor)-Fin
'I could not tell him this news.'

6.5.3.3.4. Causativity

The causative marker uses р. The causative form in the Bzyp dialect is produced in the same method as in the standard language. Examples:

(802) и-с-ўы-р-ў-[ў]а-ма? (196)
it-me-you-Caus-do-Dyn-Qu
'Do you make me do it?'

(803) а-мла с-а-ў-мы-р-га-ра-ц́ы с-у-х°-ўа-йт (169)
hunger me-it-you-Neg-Caus-take-Masd-in order to I-you-ask-Dyn-Fin
'I ask you not to starve me.'

6.5.4. Syntax

6.5.4.1. Simple Sentences

Similar to the standard language, the Byzp dialect has finite and non-finite forms. Simple sentences always have predicates in the finite form:

(804) А-ҧш°ма д-гаӡ́-уп, егь и-ӡ́-дыр-ў̈о-м. (162)
the-master he-stupid-Pres.Stat.Fin nothing [ø-]he-Pot-know-Dyn-Neg
'The master is stupid; he knows nothing.'

Since the negative form of the present form ends the sentences with the negative marker м-, it is probably possible to view this marker as expressing both the negative and finite forms. In the Bzyp dialect as well, it is possible to express the finite form with the following tenses, just as in the standard language:

Stative verbs	Affirmative	Negative
Present	-уп	-м
Past	-н	-мызт

Dynamic verbs	Affirmative	Negative
Present	-(ў̈а)-йт	-(ў̈а)-м
Aorist	-(й)т	-м--(й)т

However, it is possible to produce interrogative sentences with just the non-finite form:

(805) Уҫ́ шбо́-ў̈-ҳ°-ў̈а (< и-ш-ба-ў̈-ҳ°-ў̈а)? (193)
so [ø-]how-you.M-say-Dyn.Non-Fin
'How do you say so?'

6.5.4.2. Complex Sentences

In complex sentences, the verb in the subordinate clause uses the non-finite form, and the verb in the main clause uses the finite form:

(806) А-йаша ззегь ϕ-аны-й-дыр д-г°аа-йт. (176)
the-truth all [it-]when-he-know.Aor.NF he-become angry-(Aor)-Fin
'When he knew the whole truth, he became angry.'

The conjunctional verbal prefix ан(ы)- 'when' used in (3) above often becomes н- (< ын(ы) < ен) in the Bzyp dialect :

(807) Убри аз°а ϕ-н-и́-ҳ°а [< й-ан-и-ҳ°а], загь р-г°ы й-а-х̬°-т. (177)
that word [it-]when-he-say.Aor.NF all their-heart it-it-help-(Aor)-Fin
'When he said that word, all of them liked it.'

The conjunctional verbal prefix expressed by ш- 'how/that' in the standard language is expressed by ӡ́ (or ҫ́) in the Bzyb dialect:

(808) Й-аб д-ӡ́-а́айы-з ϕ-ан-й-а-ҳа д-г°ы(р)ҕь-ит. (184)
his-father he-how/that-come-Past.Ind.NF [it-]when-him-to-hear.Aor.NF he-rejoice-(Aor)-Fin

'When he heard that his father returned, he rejoiced.'

(809) Аҩны д-ах-ней-з   и-пҳ°ыс́   и-л-е-й-м-х°а-ӡ-ит   а-пҳара-к°а
home   he-where-come-Past.Ind.NF   his-wife   it-her-to-he-Neg-say-Emph-(Aor)-Fin   the-money-Pl
ϕ-ӡ́-й-а́ӯ-з. (184)
[them-]how/that-he-receive-Past.Ind.NF
'When he came home, he did not tell his wife that he had received the money.'

Moreover, cases can be seen using ш- in the Bzyp dialect as well:

(810) Анҭица   а-сас   д-ш-аа́-з   л-аб   й-а-л-х°ы-т. (187)
Antitsa   the-guest   he-how/that-come-Past.Ind.Non-Fin   her-father   [it-]him-to-she-say-(Aor)-Fin
'Antitsa told her father that the guest came.'

However, in the Bzyp dialect, cases can be seen where the subordinate clause is put into the finite form without using the conjunctional verbal prefix ӡ́- seen above:

(811) У-аба́-ц́-ӯа   ϕ-аны-л-х°а,   Аҟ°а-нӡа   с-ц́-ӯо-йт   и-ҳ°ы-йт. (192)
you-where-go-Dyn.NF   [it-]when-she-say.Aor.N.F   Sukhum-to   I-go-Dyn-Fin   he-say-(Aor)-Fin
'When she said, "where will you go?", he said, "I will go to Sukhum."'

In sentence structures using relative prefixes, the verbal form of the subordinate clause uses the non-finite form:

(812) Уара   сы-з-ӡ́ы́-ӯ-шьҭы-з   д-аа-з-г-ӯо-йт. (188)
you   me-Rel-for-you-send-Past.Ind.Non-Fin   him-Prev-I-take-Dyn-Fin
'I will bring the one whom you had sent me to.'

In sentence structures using relative adverbial prefixes as well, the verbal form of the subordinate clause uses the non-finite form:

(813) А-пҳ°ызба   д-ахь-гы́ла-з   а-шҟа   ды-пҳш-он. (179)
the-girl   she-where-stand-Stat.Past.Non-Fin   it-towards   he-look-Impf.Fin
'He was looking at the side where the girl was standing.'

Part II : Abkhaz Texts

1. Ts'an

Text

(1) Ажәытә атцан хәа ҵьоукы ыҟан.

(2) Урҭ ашьха инхон, уаа ссан, аҭырас иқуланы икарҿон.

(3) Усҟан ашьха асы, ақуа, акырцх амуазаарын.

(4) Аҧшацәгьа асуамызт.

(5) Дара иарбанзаалакгьы акы усс ирымамкуа, акы иацәымшәо иҟазаарын.

(6) Анцәагьы дрымамызт, «ҳара ҳада уаха ҧсызхоу дарбану?!» ҳәа акун ишыҟаз.

(7) Ус ишыҟаз зны атцан-гуара иахьҭатәаз аҽнышьыбжьон ахьтәы куаса ахьтәы гара анырглыланы, аҧшқа даниаланы, хыхьтәи акы дылбаанашьҭит, дылбаазышьҭыз закуу уаҩы изымдыруа.

(8) Атцан ари ахуҷы данырба игурҕьатцәа иҟалеит.

(9) Даашьҭырхын драаӡеит.

(10) Ахуҷы мшызҳа изҳауа, даара иҵьоушьаратәы лассы изҳаит.

(11) Дандуха зны ус дрызтцааит дзааӡаз:

(12) —Абри шәара акы шәацәымшәо шәыҟоуп, абри шәара ишәиааира мчыс иҟоузеи? — ҳәа дрызтцааит.

(13) Атцан рабду, хышә шықуса зхытцуаз, ус ихәеит:

(14) —Ҳара хатцкьыс ииааиуаны иҟоу уи ауп: абамба-сы ауны, амца ацрашәар ҳаблыр ҟалап, уаҳа ҳара хатцкьыс иаиааиуа акы адунеи аҿы изыҟаларым, — ихәеит.

(15) Ус иштәаз, ахуҷы дахьца-дахьаа рымбаӡакуа, дныцашәкуа дцеит.

(16) Дабацеи ҳхуҷы, анахь-арахь рхәеит, аха уатцәы дубар дааху — дрымбеит.

(17) Ишыҧшуаз, ҧыҭрак ашьҭахь, атцан реиҳабы данынаҧш, аҵьмақуа атцангуара иахьҭатәаз, баҕьык аҧатцақуа лахьхьынӡа илаӡо иштцысуаз ибеит.

(18) —Ҳаи, шәанацьалбеит! Ҳақутцра аазаап, ҳара ахуҧха дҳааӡама, ҳақузхышаз дҳааӡеит, ҳақуихит шәымбои! — ихәан, атцан нарҧшны идирбеит абаҕь аҧатца шытцысуаз.

(19) —Ари закузеи? — рхәан ианизтцаа, ус реихәеит:

(20) —Ҳара хҟны иахьа уажәраанӡа, ишыжәдыруа еиҧш, аҧша амысцызт, уажәы ари абаҕь аҧатца зыртцысуа аҧшоуп.

(21) Ҳақутцрац хаҟазаап, шьҭа ҳара иҟаҳтцо егьыҟам, — ихәеит.

(22) Аҧша иаҳа-иаҳа аҽарҕуҕуон.

(23) Абамба-сы аура иалагеит.

(24) Асы ауа, асы ауа, ҩбаҟа сацьан рҟынӡа абамба-сы ауит.

(25) Нас амца лацрашәан зегьы иаразнак илықублаа иагеит.

(26) Абасала, иқутцит атцан.

(27) Уажәгьы ашьха иҟоуп ҩадарак, Аҽагылара ҳәа иахьашьҭоу.

(28) Ас захьӡу уи ауп: аҵан дашьҭалазаап шьамхыла иск‘уеит хәа абнҿа.

(29) Иҕхаҵаны иманы дышнеиуаз, абри Аҿагылара хәа иахьашьҭоу ианҩеи, убра длаҵрасны, аҵыхуа кны иааникылеит.

(30) Аҵан-уаа абас шьамхылагьы иҕуҕуан, акы иацәшәомызт, дара ириааиуаз хәа акгьы ыҟамызт.

Transcription

(1) ažʷə́t’ʷ a-c’án ħʷa ʒ̆ʲawk’ə́ ə́-q’a-n.
in olden times the-Ts’an SP some people they-be-Stat.Past.Fin
In the olden times, there lived a people called the Ts’an (mythological aboriginal inhabitants of Abkhazia).

(2) wərt á-šʲxa jə-n-xa-wá-n waá ssá-n a-tə́ras
they the-mountain they-Prev-dwell-Dyn-Impf people small-Stat.Past.Fin the-fern
jə́-kʷ-la-nə j-k’á-r-č’a-wa-n.
they-Prev-climb-Abs it-Prev-they-cut off (a branch of)-Dyn-Impf
They were a tiny people who lived in the mountains. They clambered up ferns and cut off the fronds.

(3) wə́sq’an á-šʲxa a-sə́ a-kʷá a-k’ə́rcx ∅-á-m-w-[w]a-[z]-zaarən.
at that time the-mountain the-snow the-rain the-hail [they]-Dummy-Neg-fall-Dyn-Impf.NF-Evid
In those days, they say that there was neither snow, nor rain nor hail in the mountains.

(4) a-pšá-cʷgʲa ∅-á-s-wa-mə-zt’.
the-wind-bad/strong [it]-Dummy-blow-Dyn-Neg-Impf.Fin
Nor was there was any strong wind.

(5) dará járbanzaalák’-gʲə ak’ə́ wə́s-s j-rə́-ma-m-k’ʷa
they anything-also something work-as it-they-have-Neg-Abs
ak’ə j-a-cʷə́-m-šʷa-wa jə́-q’a-[z]-zaarən.
something they-it-Prev-Neg-fear-Abs they-be-Stat.Past.NF-Evid
They had no need to work, nor had they anything to fear.

(6) a-ncʷa-gʲə́ d-rə́-ma-mə-zt ‘ħará ħá-da wáħa psəzxáw
the-God-even him-they-have-Neg-Stat.Past.Fin we us-without more creature
dárbanə-w’ ħʷa [a]-ak’ʷə́-n j-šə́-q’a-z.
who-Stat.NF.Pres SP [it]-be-Stat.Past.Fin they-how-be-Stat.Past.NF
They did not even have a God. ‘What is alive apart from us?!’ they said, and so they passed their days.

(7) wəs j-šə́-q’a-z znə́ á-c’an-gʷára
so they-how-be-Stat.Past.NF one day the-Ts’an-courtyard
j-axʲ-ta-t’ʷá-z a-čnə́-šʲəbžʲon a-xʲt’ʷə́ k’ʷasá a-xʲt’ʷə́
they-where-Prev-sit inside-Stat.Past.NF on that day-at noon the-golden basket the-golden
gára ∅-a-nə-rgə́la-nə á-pška d-a-n-jála-nə xəxʲt’ʷə́j ak’ə́

cradle [it]-it-Prev-stand onto-Abs the-baby he-it-Prev-lie on-Abs upper something
də-lbáa-na-šʲtə-jt' də-lbáa-zə-šʲtə-z
him-Prev-it-bring down-(Aor)-Fin him-Prev-Rel-bring down-Past.Ind.NF
z-ak'ʷə́-w wajʷə́ jə-j-zə́-m-dər-wa.
Rel-be-Stat.Pres.NF person it-him-Pot-Neg-know-Abs

While they were living in this way, one day at noon, as they were sitting in the Ts'an courtyard, [they noticed that] there was a golden cradle with a baby asleep in it, placed on a golden basket. Someone had placed the child there from out of the heavens. No one knew who had placed the baby there.

(8) a-c'án arə́j a-xʷəč'ʲə́ d-anə́-r-ba j-gʷə́ɣʲa-c'ʷa
the-Ts'an this the-baby him-when-they-see.(Aor).NF they-merrily-very
j-q'a-lá-jt'.
they-Prev-become-(Aor)-Fin

The Ts'an became very happy when they saw the baby there.

(9) d-aa-šʲtə-r-xə-n d-r-aaʒá-jt'.
him-Par-Prev-they-take up-Past.Ind.Fin him-they-bring up-(Aor)-Fin

They picked him up, and brought him up.

(10) a-xʷəč'ʲə́ mšə-zħá j-jə-z-ħa-wá dáara
the-baby day-growing Dummy-him-Prev-grow-Abs very
j-ǯʲá-w-šʲa-ra-t'ʷə lassə́ j-jə-z-ħá-jt'.
it/him-Prev-you-feel suprised-Resultative rapidly Dummy-him-Prev-grow-(Aor)-Fin

The baby grew day by day, and grew so quickly that you would be very surprised.

(11) d-an-də́w-xa znə wəs d-rə-z-c'aá-jt'
he-when-big-become-(Aor.NF) one day as follows he-them-Prev-ask-(Aor)-Fin
d-z-aaʒá-z.
him-Rel-bring up-Past.Ind.NF

One day, when the baby had grown up, he questioned the people who had brought him up:

(12) — abrə́j šʷará ak'ə́ šʷ-a-cʷə́-m-šʷa-wa šʷə́-q'a-wp' abrə́j
this you.Pl something you.Pl-it-Prev-Neg-fear-Abs you.Pl-be-Stat.Pres this
šʷará jə-šʷ-jaáj-ra mčʲə́-s jə́-q'a-w-zaj
you.Pl Rel-you.Pl-overcome-Fut.I.NF power-as what-be-Stat.NF-Qu
— ħʷa d-rə-z-c'aá-jt'.
SP he-them-Prev-ask-(Aor)-Fin

'You people don't seem to be afraid of anything. Is there nothing that can defeat you?' he asked them.

(13) a-c'án r-abdə́w xə́šʷ šəkʷsá ø-z-xə́-c'-wa-z
the-Ts'an their-grandfather 300 year [they]-Rel-Prev-be X-years-Dyn-Impf.NF
wəs ø-j-ħʷá-jt':
as follows [it]-he-say-(Aor)-Fin

The oldest man among them, who was 300 years old, said:

(14) — ħará ħ-ác'k'ʲəs j-jaáj-wa-nə jə́-q'a-w wəj

we us-than it-overcom-Dyn-Abs Rel-be-Stat.Pres.NF as follows
[a]-á-wp': a-banba-sə́ ø-a-w-nə́ á-mca
[it]-be-Stat.Pres.Fin the-cotton-snow [it-]Dummy-fall-Abs the-fire
ø-a-cra-šʷá-r ħa-blə́-r ø-q'á-la-p'
[it]-it-Prev-start to burn.(Aor.NF)-if we-burn.(Aor.NF)-Conditonal [it-]Prev-become-Fut.I.Fin
wáħa ħará ħ-ac'k'ʲə́s j-a-jaáj-wa ak'ə́ a-də́wnáj a-č'ə́
more we us-than Rel-it-overcome-Dyn.(Pres.NF) something the-world its-in
j-zə́-q'-la-rə-m — ø-j-ħʷá-jt'.
it-Pot-Prev-happen-Fut.I-Neg.Fin [it-]he-say-(Aor)-Fin

'There is this one thing that is stronger than us: when *cotton snow* falls, if it catches fire, we will be burnt up. I think that there is nothing stronger than that for us in the entire world,' he said.

(15) wəs jə-š-t'ʷá-z a-xʷəč'ʲə́ d-axʲ-cá=d-axʲ-aá
thus they-as-sit-Stat.Past.NF the-child he-where-go=he-where-come.(Aor.NF)
ø-rə-m-ba-ʒá-k'ʷa d-nə́-c'a-šʷk'ʷa d-cá-jt'.
[it]-they-Neg-see-Emph-Abs he-Par-Prev-disappear.(Abs?) he-go-(Aor)-Fin

As they were sitting together in this manner, they realized that they did not know where the child had gone, he had disappeared.

(16) d-abá-ca-j ħ-xʷəč'ʲə́, anáxʲ-aráxʲ r-ħʷá-jt',
he-where to-go-(Aor)-Qu our-child thither-hither they-say-(Aor)-Fin
(= they went this way and that)
axá wac'ʷə́ də-w-bá-r d-aá-xʷ — d-rə-m-bá-jt'.
but tomorrow him-you-see-if him-Prev-buy.Imp him-they-Neg-see-(Aor)-Fin

'Where has our child gone?' they cried. They searched high and low for him, but they could not find him.

(17) j-šə-pš-wá-z pə́trak' á-šʲtaxʲ a-c'án r-ajħabə́
they-how-wait-Dyn-Impf.NF a little while it-after the-Ts'an their-leader/elder
d-anə́-na-pš á-ǯʲma-kʷa á-c'an-gʷára
he-when-Prev-look thither-(Aor.NF) the-goat-Pl the-Ts'an-courtyard
j-axʲ-ta-t'ʷá-z baɣʲə́-k' a-pac'a-kʷá laxʲxʲə́nʒa
they-where-Prev-sit inside-Stat.Past.NF billy goat-one its-beard-Pl far
j-la-ʒa-wá jə-š-c'əs-wá-z ø-j-bá-jt'.
they-Prev-reach-Abs they-how/that-swing-Dyn-Impf.NF [it-]he-see-(Aor)-Fin

After they been waiting for a little while, the Ts'an chief looked at the billy goats in the middle of the Ts'an courtyard, and noticed that the beard of one of the goats was almost touching the ground, and that it was swaying in the wind.

(18) — ħaj šʷ-an-aǯʲá-l-ba-jt' ħá-kʷ-c'-ra
oh! your.Pl-mother-labor-she-see-(Aor)-Fin we-Prev-abandan one's countryside-Masd
ø-aá-zaap', ħará á-xʷpħa d-ħ-aaʒá-ma
[it]-come-(Aor)-Evid we the-adopted.child him-we-bring up-Qu
ħa-kʷə-z-xə́-šaz d-ħ-aaʒá-jt', ħá-kʷə-j-xə-jt'
us-Prev-Rel-exterminate-Cond.II.NF him-we-bring up-(Aor)-Fin us-Prev-he-exterminate-(Aor)-Fin
ø-šʷə-m-ba-wá-j — ø-j-ħʷá-n, a-c'án ø-na-r-pš-nə́
[it]-you.Pl-Neg-see-Dyn-Qu [it-]he-say-Past.Ind.Fin the-Ts'an [them-]Prev-Caus-look thither

jə-d-jə-r-bá-jt' á-baɣʲ a-pac'á ∅-šə́-c'əs-wa-z.
it-them-he-Caus-see(= show)-(Aor)-Fin the-billy goat its-beard [it-]how/that-sway-Dyn-Impf.NF

'Oh no! What's this? The time for us to abandon our land has come. We raised our adopted child, didn't we? We have brought up the one being who will destroy us. He will drive us out. Can't you see?!' he said, pointing to the spot on the ground where the goat's beard was swaying.

(19) — arə́j ∅-z-ak'ʷə́-zaj? — ∅-r-ħʷá-n j-an-jə-z-c'aá,
this [it-]Rel-be-what [it-]they-say-Past.Ind.Fin they-when-him-Prev-ask.Aor.NF
wəs ∅-r-á-j-ħʷa-jt':
as.follows [it]-them-to-he-say-(Aor)-Fin

'What on earth does this mean?' they asked him, their chief, and he replied:

(20) — ħará ħ-q'nə́ jaxʲá wažʷráanʒa, j-šə́-žʷ-dər-wa ájpš,
we us-at today till now it-how-you.Pl-know-Dyn.NF [it]-like
[a]-a-pšá ∅-a-mə́-s-cəzt', wažʷə́ arə́j á-baɣʲ a-pac'á
the-wind [it-]?-Neg-blow-Plupf.Fin now this the-billy goat its-beard
∅-zə-r-c'əs-wá ∅-a-pšá-wp'.
[it]-Rel-Caus-swing-Dyn.NF [it]-the-wind-Stat.Pres.Fin

'As you all know, in our place, until today, the wind has never blown. Now, that wind is moving the billy goat's beard.'

(21) ħá-kʷ-c'-rac ħá-q'a-zaap', šʲtá ħará
we-Prev-abandan one's countryside-Purp we-be-Evid now we
jə́-q'a-ħ-c'a-wa agʲə́-q'a-m — ∅-j-ħʷá-jt'.
Rel-Prev-we-do-Dyn.NF nothing-be-Neg [it-]he-say-(Aor)-Fin

'We will have to abandon our land. Now there is nothing that we can do,' he said.

(22) a-pšá jaħá-jaħá a-č-a-r-ɣʷɣʷa-wá-n.
the-wind more and more its-Self-it-Caus-strengthen-Dyn-Impf
The wind was growing stronger and stronger.

(23) a-bamba-sə́ a-w-rá j-á-la-ga-jt'.
the-cotton-snow the-fall-Masd it/they-it-Prev-begin-(Aor)-Fin
Then the cotton snow started to fall.

(24) a-sə́ ∅-a-w-[w]á a-sə́ ∅-a-w-[w]a, jʷba-q'a
the-snow [it]-Dummy-fall-Abs the-snow [it]-Dummy-fall-Abs 2-about
saǯʲán r-q'ə́nʒa a-bamba-sə́ ∅-a-wə́-jt'.
sazhen (2.13m.) them-up to the-cotton-snow [it]-Dummy-fall-(Aor)-Fin
The snow, the cotton snow, fell and fell to a depth of about two *sazhen* (4.26 metres).

(25) nas á-mca ∅-l-a-cra-šʷá-n zagʲə́ jaráznak'
then the-fire [it-]Par-it-Prev-start to burn-Past.Ind.Fin all suddenly
j-lə́-kʷ-blaa j-a-gá-jt'.
they-Par-Prev-be burned completely them-it-take-(Aor)-Fin

Then it caught fire, and soon everything around it burnt up.

(26) abásala jə́-kʷ-c'ə-jt' a-c'án.
in.this.way they-Prev-abandan one's homeland-(Aor)-Fin the-Ts'an
This is how the Ts'an people abandoned their homeland.

(27) wáž̌ʷ-gʲə á-šʲxa jə́-q'a-wp' jʷadára-k' Ačagə́lara
now-also the-mountain it-be-Stat.Pres.Fin hill-one Achagylara (*lit.* the-horse-standing)
ħʷa j-axʲ-á-šʲta-w.
SP they-where-it-call-Stat.Pres.NF
Even today, in the middle of the mountains, there is a place called *Achagylara, The Place Where The Horse Stands*.

(28) as ø-z-á-xʲʒə-w wəj [a]-a-wp': a-c'án
so [it-]why-it-be called-Stat.Pres.NF that it-be-Stat.Pres.Fin the-Ts'an
d-a-šʲta-la-záap' šʲamxə́-la jə-s-k'-wá-jt' ħʷa a-bnča.
he-it-Prev-track-(Aor)-Evid knee-Instr it-I-catch-Dyn-Fin SP the-deer
The reason why it is so called is as follows: Apparently a Ts'an once chased a deer saying, 'I'll catch you because I can outrun you'.

(29) jə-pxa-c'a-nə j-jə́-ma-nə də-š-ná-j-wa-z, abrə́j
it-Prev-follow-Abs it-he-have-Abs he-how-Prev-go thither-Dyn-Impf.NF this
ačagə́lara ħʷa j-axʲ-á-šʲta-w j-an-jʷá-j,
Achagylara SP they-where-it-call-Stat.Pres.NF they-when-Prev-go up.(Aor.NF)
wəbrá d-l-a-crá-s-nə, a-c'ə́xʷa ø-k'-nə́ j-aa-n-jə́-k'əla-jt'.
there he-Par-it-Prev-touch-Abs the-tail [it-]catch-Abs it-Prev-Prev-he-hold down-(Aor)-Fin
He chased the deer very fast, until he reached and climbed up to the place that is called *Achagylara, The Place Where The Horse Stands*, touching the deer there, and grabbing hold of it by its tail.

(30) a-c'án-waa abás šʲamxə́-la-gʲə jə-ɣʷɣʷá-n,
the-Ts'an-people in this way knee-Instr-also they-strong-Stat.Past.Fin
ak'ə́ j-a-cʷ-šʷa-wá-mə-zt', dará jə-r-jáaj-wa-z
something they-it-Prev-fear-Dyn-Neg-Impf.Fin they Rel-them-overcome-Dyn-Impf.NF
ħʷa ak'-gʲə́ ə́-q'a-məzt'.
SP something-also it-be-Neg.Stat.Past.Fin (= it did not seem that)
The Ts'an people were indefatigable walkers in this way. It seems too that they never feared anything, and that there was nothing that could defeat them either.

Notes

* The text is taken from «Ш. Хь. Салаҟаиа. Аҧсуа жәлар рҿаҧыщтә рҿиамҭа, Ахрестоматиа. Аҟиа: Алашара», 1975. pp. 121–123.

(1) **1.** ac'án = 'низкорослые мифические жители Абхазии' (Kaslandzia 2005). **2.** ə́-q'a-n: masd. á-q'a-zaa-ra [intr.] 'to be, to exist'.

(2) **1.** á-šʲxa jə-n-xa-wá-n 'they lived in the mountain': masd. a-n-xa-rá [intr.] 'to dwell'. Cf. Apswa kə́tak' a-č'ə́ jə-n-xa-wá-n 'they lived in an Abkhazian village'. Also see Hewitt (2005a: 20). **2.** ssá-n:

á-ssa 'small'. **3**. jə́-kʷ-la-nə: masd. á-kʷ-la-ra [intr.]. **4**. j-k'á-r-č'a-wa-n: masd. a-k'a-č'a-rá [tr.] 'to cut off branches of'.

(3) **1**. Here á-šʲxa 'the-mountain' expresses a locative meaning, i.e. 'in the mountain(s)'. **2**. ø-á-m-w-[w]a-[z]-zaarən: masd. a-w-rá [intr.] 'to fall', cf. a-sə́ ø-a-w-wá-jt' or j-a-w-wá-jt' a-sə́ 'it snows': (C1(snow)-C2(Dummy)-fall-Dyn-Fin). **3**. For -zaarən, see Chirikba (2003a: 47).

(4) ø-á-s-wa-mə-zt': masd. á-s-ra [intr.] 'to blow'; cf. a-pšá ø-á-s-wa-jt' (C1(wind)-C2(Dummy)-blow-Dyn-Fin) 'the wind blows'. The verb á-s-ra meaning 'to blow' is cognate with the intransitive verb á-s-ra meaning 'to hit'. Therefore, a-pšá ø-á-s-wa-jt' is interpretable as 'the wind is hitting it' (C1(wind)-C2(it)-hit-Dyn-Fin). As regards the meaning of Column II here, Hewitt (2005a: 117, fn. 2) states that the (indirect) object will originally have been 'the earth'.

(5) **1**. j-rə́-ma-m-k'ʷa: masd. á-ma-zaa-ra [intr. inverse] 'to have'. **2**. j-a-cʷə́-m-šʷa-wa: masd. a-cʷ-šʷa-rá [intr.] 'to be afraid of'.

(6) **1**. d-rə́-ma-məzt: (he(C1)-them(C2)-be-Neg.Past.Fin), lit. 'he(God) was not by them', i.e. 'they did not have a God'. **2**. dárbanəw (= dárban) is a colloquial expression (Kaslandzia 2005). **3**. ħʷa: *SP* (Speech-Particle) 'saying, having said; that ...', cf. masd. a-ħʷa-rá 'to say'. *SP* is an archaic form of the Past Absolute (Hewitt 2005a: 47). **4**. [a]-ak'ʷə́-n: (it(C2)-be-Stat.Past) 'X was it'. **5**. [a]-ak'ʷə́-n j-šə́-q'a-z: 'вот так они жили'.

(7) **1**. á-c'an-gʷára 'the-Ts'an-courtyard'. According to our informant, however, the meaning for this word is 'a fence of stones build by the Ts'an'; cf. a-gʷára 'the fence', 'the courtyard [bzyp dialect]'. **2**. j-axʲ-ta-t'ʷá-z: masd. a-ta-t'ʷá-zaa-ra [intr.] 'to sit inside'. **3**. ø-a-nə-rgə́la-nə < [j]-a-nə-ø-r-gə́la-nə ([it (cradle, C1)-]it(basket, C2)-Prev(onto)-[C3]-Caus-stand-Abs): masd. a-nə-rgə́la-ra [tr.] 'to stand *sth* onto'. **4**. d-a-n-jála-nə: masd. a-n-jála-ra [intr.] 'to lie on'. **5**. də-lbáa-na-šʲtə-jt' (him(C1)-Prev-it(something, (C3))-let down-(Aor)-Fin): masd. á-lbaa-šʲt-ra [tr.]. **6**. də-lbáa-zə-šʲtə-z (him(C1)-Prev-Rel(C3)-let down-Past.Ind.NF). **7**. z-ak'ʷə́-w (Rel(C2)-be-Stat.Pres.NF), cf. (6)-4. **8**. jə-j-zə́-m-dər-wa (it(C1)-him(C2)-Pot-Neg-know-Abs): masd. a-də́r-ra [tr.] 'to know'.

(8) **1**. Here the form a-c'án is plural. Note that this noun has the same form for both the singular and the plural. **2**. d-anə́-r-ba (him(C1)-when-they(C3)-see.Aor.NF): masd. a-ba-rá [tr.] 'to see'. **3**. j-q'a-lá-jt': masd. á-q'a-la-ra [intr.] 'to become'.

(9) **1**. d-aa-šʲtə-r-xə-n (him(C1)-Par-Prev-they(C3)-take up-Past.Ind.Fin): masd. á-šʲtə-x-ra [tr.] 'to pick up'. Also for Particle *-aa-* see §5.11. **2**. d-r-aaʒá-jt' (him(C1)-they(C3)-bring up-(Aor)-Fin): masd. áaʒa-ra [tr.] 'to bring up'.

(10) **1**. j-jə-z-ħa-wa (Dummy(C1)-him(C2)-Prev-grow-Abs) lit. 'he growing': masd. a-z-ħa-rá [intr.] 'to grow', cf. a-xʷəč̣ʲ-kʷá ø-rə-z-ħa-wá-jt' 'the children are growing'. **2**. mšə-zħá j-jə-z-ħa-wa 'he growing day by day'. **3**. j-ǯʲá-w-šʲa-ra-t'ʷə 'на удивление': masd. a-ǯʲa-šʲa-rá [tr.] 'to feel surprised'.

(11) **1**. d-an-də́w-xa: masd. a-də́w-xa-ra [intr.] 'to become big', cf. a-də́w 'big'. **2**. d-rə-z-c'aá-jt' (he(C1)-them(C2)-Prev-ask-(Aor)-Fin): masd. a-z-c'aa-rá [intr.] 'to ask'. **3**. d-z-aaʒá-z (him(C1)-Rel(C3)-bring up-Past.Ind.NF) 'the one who brought him up', cf. 9-2.

(12) **1**. jə-šʷ-jaáj-ra: masd. a-jaáj-ra [intr.] 'to overcome'.

(13) **1**. ø-z-xə́-c'-wa-z < [jə]-z-xə́-c'-wa-z (they(300 years, (C1))-Rel(C2)-Prev-be X-years-Dyn-Impf.NF) 'the one who was 300 years old': masd. a-xə́-c'-ra [intr.] 'to be X years old'. **2**. ø-j-ħʷá-jt' ([it(C1)]-he(C3)-say-(Aor)-Fin): masd. a-ħʷa-rá [tr.] 'to say'.

(14) **1**. [a]-a-wp' ([it(C2)-]copula-Stat.Pres.Fin) 'X is it'. **2**. ø-a-w-nə́: masd. a-w-rá, cf. (3)-2. **3**. ø-a-cra-šʷá-r < j-a-cra-šʷá-r (it(fire, C1)-it(cotton-snow, C2)-Prev-burn-if) 'if feathery snowflakes catch fire':

masd. a-cra-šʷa-rá [intr.] 'to catch fire'. **4.** ħa-blə́-r: masd. a-bəl-rá [intr.] 'to burn'. 5. ħa-blə́-r ø-q'á-la-p' 'we will probably burn'.

(15) **1.** jə-š-t'ʷá-z: masd. a-t'ʷa-rá [intr.] 'to sit'. **2.** d-nə́-c'a-šʷk'ʷa: masd. á-c'a-šʷk'ʷa-ra [intr.] 'to disappear'. **3.** d-cá-jt': masd. a-ca-rá [intr.] 'to go'.

(16) **1.** d-aá-xʷ (him(C1)-Prev-buy.Imp): masd. aá-xʷa-ra [tr.] 'to buy'. **2.** wac'ʷə́ də-w-bá-r d-aá-xʷ lit. 'if you see him tomorrow, buy him!', i.e. 'searched for him, but in vain'.

(17) **1.** j-šə-pš-wá-z: masd. a-pš-rá [intr.] 'to wait; to look'. **2.** d-anə́-na-ps: masd. á-na-pš-ra [intr.] 'to look thither'. **3.** j-la-ʒa-wá: masd. á-la-ʒa-ra [intr.] 'to reach'. **4.** jə-š-c'əs-wá-z: masd. a-c'əs-rá [intr.] 'to swing'.

(18) **1.** šʷ-an-aǯʲá-l-ba-jt' 'my God, боже мой!'. **2.** ħá-kʷc'-ra: masd. á-kʷc'-ra [intr.] 'to move; to abandan one's countryside'. **3.** ø-aá-zaap': masd. aa-rá [intr.] 'to come'. **4.** ħá-kʷə-j-xə-jt: masd. á-kʷ-x-ra [tr.] 'to exterminate'. **5.** ø-na-r-pš-nə́: masd. á-na-r-pš-ra [tr.] 'to make look thither'. **6.** jə-d-jə-rbá-jt': masd. a-rba-rá [tr.] 'to show' < a-r-ba-rá 'to make see'.

(19) **1.** ø-r-á-j-ħʷa-jt' ([it(C1)-]them(C2)-to-he(C3)-say-(Aor)-Fin) 'he said it to them': masd. a-ħʷa-rá [tr.] 'to say'.

(20) **1.** ø-zə-r-c'əs-wá: masd. a-rc'əs-rá [tr.] 'to swing; to sway', cf. (17)-4 above. a-c'əs-rá [intr.] 'to swing'. **2.** ø-a-pšá-wp' ([it(C1)-]the-wind-Stat.Pres.Fin) 'it is the wind': cf. a-pšá 'the-wind'.

(21) **1.** ħá-kʷ-c'-rac ħá-q'a-zaap' 'мы должны исчезнуть'. The suffix *-rac* is the Bzyp variant of *-rc* expressing Purpose. Cf. -рацы 'чтобы'. See Bgazhba (1964: 189). **2.** jə́-q'a-ħ-c'a-wa (Rel(C1)-Prev-we(C3)-do-Dyn.NF) 'that which we will do': masd. á-q'a-c'a-ra [tr.] 'to do'.

(22) a-č-a-r-ɣʷɣʷa-wá-n (its(Poss)-Self-it(C3)-Caus-strong-Dyn-Impf) 'it was strengthening'; cf. a-r-ɣʷɣʷa-rá [tr.] 'to strengthen'.

(23) **1.** j-á-la-ga-jt' (it/they(C1)-it(fall of cotton-snow, C2)-Prev-begin-(Aor)-Fin) 'cotton-snow (=feathery snowflakes) began to fall': masd. á-la-ga-ra [intr.] 'to begin'.

(24) **1.** ø-a-w-[w]á ([it(=snow, C1-]Dummy(C2)-fall-Abs) 'it falling': masd. a-w-rá [intr.] 'to fall'.

(25) **1.** j-lə́-kʷ-blaa: masd. á-kʷ-bl-aa-ra [intr.] 'to be burned completely'. For Particle -lə- see §5.11. **2.** j-a-gá-jt': masd. a-ga-rá [tr.] 'to take'.

(27) **1.** Here á-šʲxa denotes the locative meaning 'in the mountain(s)'. **2.** Ačagə́lara < A-č-agə́lara (lit. 'the-horse-standing'). **3.** j-axʲ-á-šʲta-w : masd. á-šʲta-zaa-ra 'to be called; cf. *Górk'əj jə́-wlica ħʷa j-á-šʲta-wp'*. 'It is called the Gorky Street'.

(28) **1.** ø-z-á-xʲʒə-w ([it(C1)-why-it(C2)-be called-Stat.Pres.NF], lit. (it(C1)-why-its(Poss)-name-be.NF) 'the reason why it is called so': masd. á-xʲʒ-zaa-ra [intr.] 'to be called'. **2.** wəj [a]-a-wp' 'is as follows'. **3.** d-a-šʲta-la-záap': masd. á-šʲta-la-ra [intr.] 'to track'. **4.** jə-s-k'-wá-jt': masd. a-k'-rá [tr.] 'to catch'.

(29) **1.** jə-pxa-c'a-nə́ (it(C1)-Prev-[ø(C3)-]follow-Abs) 'following it': a-pxa-c'a-rá [tr.] 'to follow'. **2.** j-jə́-ma-nə (it(C1)-he(C2)-have-Abs), lit. (it(C1)-him-be by-Abs) 'he having it': masd. á-ma-zaa-ra [intr.] 'to have', cf. (6)-1. **3.** də-š-ná-j-wa-z: masd. a-ná-j-ra [intr.] 'go thither'. **4.** j-an-jʷá-j : masd. a-jʷá-j-ra [intr.] 'to go up'. **5.** d-l-a-crá-s-nə (he(C1)-Par-it(C2)-Prev-touch-Abs) 'he quickly having touched it': masd. a-crá-s-ra [intr.] 'to touch'. **6.** ø-k'-nə́ < ø-ø-k'-nə́ ([it(tail, C1)-he(C3)-]catch-Abs) 'having caught [it]': masd. a-k'-rá [tr.] 'to catch'. **7.** j-aan-jə́-k'əla-jt': masd. aa-n-kə́la-ra [tr.] 'to hold down'.

(30) **1.** a-c'án-waa: cf. a-waá pl. 'people', sg. a-wajʷə́ 'man, person'. **2.** jə-ɣʷɣʷá-n: cf. á-ɣʷɣʷa 'strong', cf. 22. **3.** ħʷa á-q'a-zaa-ra 'to seem'.

2. Lake Rits'a

Text

(1) Рица аӡыгьажь уажәы иахыҟоу анкьа адәы ҧшӡараны, ауаа ықунх'уа иҟан хәа рҳәоит.

(2) Абни аҟара адә-ду иҟаз иӡытҟуаны изыҟала ҳәа ирҳәуа абас ауп.

(3) Ана аҧаса ианҧсуа дгьылыз инх'уаз Ҧшысаа ракун.

(4) Даара анхара бзиа рыман уа инх'уаз зегьы, ҧхәысеибак лыда.

(5) Аҧхәысеиба аҷкунцәа рацәаны илыман, аха зегьы хуҷкуан, «иааг» ада, уаха ак рыздыруамызт.

(6) Аҧҳәысеба есымша аашаргьы лхы ныцахуа акрылуан лгулацәа рҟны.

(7) Илуазгьы уи акун: ашы, абысҭа, ача, лара лыда, егьырҭ зегьы ирацәаны ироуан, алаҳәара аныршаанхалагь, ани ргула ҧҳәыс аҟьыра азы илырҭуан, аха аҟьыра маҷӡан:

(8) Убри аҟара имаҷын лҟьыра, аха акры аулҳәах'уаз, илхәаргьы илоуамызт лдыруан.

(9) Убас рыщхарыла иааизылг'уа ала акун лыҷкунцәа зланыҟулг'уаз.

(10) Зны, еизылгаз анынтцәа, лыҷкунцәа «амла, амла» ҳәа дыркит.

(11) Ҩ-цьара хы-цьара, исоуп ахылгуахуаз днеин ча хуҷык хәа, аха аӡәгьы даахәны длыху-амҧшит.

(12) Агьирахь уиазгьы исылмоуаз лдыруан.

(13) Иҟалтцах'уази, даагьажьит.

(14) Дааин, авырҳәа ачуан ахаҳә лҭаҧсаны иҩкналҳан, амца аҟуҟуаҳәа иҩатцалтцт.

(15) Ааиха лымҭакуа, аҷкунцәа «амла, амла» ҳәа илыкушаны игылт.

(16) — Ааи, нан дшәыкухшоуп, ожәытцәҟьа акырзымои, — лҳәан, рыхҟуа аалшьшьит.

(17) Анҭ ачуан анырба, иакушаны илатәеит, ожәы-ошьҭан абысҭа аабарушь ҳәа, аха акры аур-бах'уа.

(18) Ахуларагь уи акун.

(19) Аҷкунцәа ҵьоукгьы ицәт, ҵьоукгьы ацәа иаарымнахаанӡа, итцәуан, ран: «Ожәытцәҟьа, нан ожәытцәҟьа шәымтцәыуан», — лҳәуан.

(20) Лыҷкунцәа рҽынкаҧса-ҩкаҧсаны, икарауараха ицәт, ларгьы дхуцуа, лчуан мтцәахы ҧшаа ҳәа дызҭаҧшуаз, «аҧшәма!» ҳәа аӡәы ибжьы геит адәахьы.

(21) — Ау! — лҳәан, дыҩдәылтцын.

(22) — Бзиала уаабеит! — лҳәан аҩныҟа длалгит.

(23) Дсылатәаз аиҧш ус иҳәит:

(24) — Даара амла сакны сыҟоуп, изӡаргьы иаҧсам, хуҷык бзысҿатцарушь? — иҳәит.

(25) — Унан, уажәытцәҟьа, — лҳәит, аха дахҧшуа ани аҟуаб ахаҳә зҭоу ашҟа ауп:

(26) Ани адҩрагь ус иҳәит:

(27) — Ҵьоушьҭ, ари иҭоугь хаҳәушәа збуот, анахь цьара тцәахык бымамзар, уаха исҿабтцуази? — иҳәит.

(28) — Уахгьы тцәахыс исымоу егьыҟам, аха анцәа исиҭалагь збап, уаамццакын, сукухшоуп, — лҳәыхт адрҩагь.

(29) Ус-ус сылҳәауаз, лхаҳә ишылаханы иҟьат-ҟьатуа иалагеит.

(30) Амҳаԥ атцылшьын абысҭа луит.

(31) Иаакнылхын, лысас хуҷык иҿалтцан дышьҭалтцит.

(32) Ашьҭахь лыҷкунцәа аалырԥшын хучык рҿалтцан ишьҭалтцит.

(33) Аҽны шьыжьымҭан шаанӡа даумгылахʻуаз, данаарԥш, лысас длымбит, аҩнгьы аӡы ааҩнажжуа иҟан.

(34) «Иҟалазеи?!» хәа даныҩгыла, лылаԥш ахынӡанаӡауаз зегьы иӡытҟуаны, игазуа иҭажьын, аҩны иамариашаны мҩахуасҭа хучык ган акумзар.

(35) Авырҳәа даагьажьын, лыҷкунцәа аалырԥшын, идлырбит.

(36) — Ари амҩахуасҭа алганы изыҟоу — шәара шәамгар анцәа иҭахыуп, — лҳәит.

(37) Ус раҳәаны, аҷкунцәа изныҟууаз лаԥхьа иларгыланы, ахуҷкуа лара иаашьҭыхны, амҩахуасҭа хуҷы иалгаз дыкуланы дләыкулт.

(38) Есааира наҟ дцацыԥхьаӡа, лышьҭахьҟа еимаҳуан.

(39) Аԥхәыс еибагь дысҭаҳцәаз дналтцит, аӡгьы иааилаҩеиласын, игазгʻуа илҭатәеит.

(40) Убри анахыс Рица ӡыжь цәгьаны, итцыданы иааҟалт.

(41) Абни аԥхәысеиба лыҷкунцәа иаархылтцыз роуп ожә Ԥшысаа ирыжәланы иҟоу.

(42) Ииашаны, Ԥшысбаны иҟоу Рица ибар, думкыр схы асҭуеит хәа далагоит рҳәоит.

Transcription

(1) Rə́jc'a a-ʒə́g^{j}až^{j} waž^{w}ə́ j-axə́-q'a-w ánk'^{j}a a-d^{w}ə́ pšʒá-ranə
Rits'a the-lake now it-where-be-Pres.NF before the-field beautiful-around
awáa ə́-ϕ-k^{w}ə-n-x-wa jə́-q'a-n ħ^{w}a ϕ-r-ħ^{w}a-wá-jt'.
people they-[it-]Prev-Prev-live on-Dyn.Abs it-be-Stat.Past.Fin SP [it-]they-say-Dyn-Fin
It is said that the area where Lake Rits'a now lies was once beautiful populated farmland.

(2) Abnə́j áq'ara a-d^{w}-də́w jə́-q'a-z jə-ʒət'q'^{w}a-nə́
that so the-field-big Rel-be-Stat.Past.NF it-place of water-as
jə-zə́-q'a-la ħ^{w}a jə́-r-ħ^{w}-wa abás [a-]-á-wp'.
it-why-Prev-become.Aor.NF SP Rel-they-say-Dyn.Pres.NF like this it-be-Pres.Stat
What they say about the reason why that wide farmland became a lake is as follows.

(3) Aná apása j-an-pswá dg^{j}ə́lə-z jə-n-x-wá-z
there early it-when-Abkhazian earth-Stat.Past.NF Rel-Prev-live-Dyn-Impf.NF
Pšə́s-aa r-ák'^{w}ə-n.
Pshys-Pl them-be-Stat.Past.Fin
When long ago the area was Abkhazian land, the people who lived there were the tribe called Psysaa [note: 'Psysaa' is the plural form of 'Psysba'.].

(4) Dáara a-nxará bzə́ja ∅-rə́-ma-n wa jə-n-x-wá-z
very the-living good [it-]they-have-Stat.Past.Fin there Rel-Prev-live-Dyn-Impf.NF
zagʲə́, pħʷə́sajba-k' lə́-da.
all widow-one her-except
All the people who lived there lived a good life except for one widow.

(5) A-pħʷə́sajba á-č'ʲk'ʷən-cʷa racʷanə́ jə-lə́-ma-n, axá zagʲə́
the-widow the-boy/son-Pl many them-she-have-Stat.Past.Fin but all
∅-xʷəč'ʲ-kʷá-n, «j-aá-g» á-da, wáħa ak'
[they-]little-Pl-Stat.Past.Fin it/them-Prev-give.Imp it-except more something
∅-rə-z-də́r-wa-mə-zt'.
[it-]them-Pot-know-Dyn-Neg-Impf.Fin
This widow had many sons, but all the sons were still small. They knew nothing except one word, 'give!'

(6) A-pħʷə́sajba esəmšá ∅-aa-šá-rgʲə l-xə ∅-nə́-c'ax-wa
the-widow every day [it-]Par-dawn-even if her-head [it-]Par-hang-Dyn.Abs
ak'rə-l-w-[w]á-n l-gʷə́la-cʷa r-q'nə.
Dummy-she-work-Dyn-Impf.Fin her-neighbor-Pl their-at
Every day, as soon as dawn broke, the widow, hanging her head, went to work at her neighbors' houses.

(7) Jə́-l-w-[w]a-z-gʲə wəj [a-]ák'ʷə-n: a-šə́, a-bə́sta,
Rel-she-do-Dyn-Impf.NF-even that it-be-Stat.Past.Fin the-millet the-polenta
a-čá, lará lə́-da, agʲə́rt zagʲə́ j-racʷanə́ jə-r-áw-[w]a-n,
the-bread she her-except other everything they-many them-they-obtain-Dyn-Impf.Fin
á-laħʷara ∅-anə-r-záa-n-xa-lagʲ, anə́j r-gʷə́la pħʷəs
the-remains [it-]when-them-Prev-Prev-remain-(Aor)-LA that their-neighbor woman
a-kʲə́ra a-zə́ j-lə́-r-t-wa-n, axá a-kʲə́ra ∅-máč'ʲ-ʒa-n.
the-wage it-for it-her-they-give-Dyn-Impf.Fin but the-wage [it-]little-Emph-Stat.Past.Fin
What she was doing was this. All the neighbors except her used to obtain millet, polenta, bread, and many other things. When they had leftover food, they used to give it to the widow woman as wages.

(8) <u>Wəbrə́j áq'ara</u> jə-máč'ʲə-n l-kʲə́ra, axá ak'rə́
so much it-little-Stat.Past.Fin her-wage but anything
∅-<u>awə́</u>-l-ħʷa-<u>x</u>-wa-z, jə-l-ħʷá-rgʲə
[it-]Rhetorical.Qu-she-say-Emph-Dyn-Impf.NF it-she-say-even if
j-l-áw-[w]a-mə-zt' ∅-l-də́r-wa-n.
them-she-obtain-Dyn-Neg-Impf.Fin [it-]she-know-Dyn-Impf.Fin
Her wages were so very small, but how could she say anything? She knew that even if she said anything, she could obtain nothing more.

(9) Wbás rə́cħarəla j-a[a]-ajzə-l-g-wa á-la [a-]-ak'ʷə́-n

in this way with difficulty Rel-Par-Prev-she-gather-Dyn.NF it-with it-be-Stat.Past.Fin
lə́-č'ʲk'ʷən-cʷa ϕ-zla-nə́q'ʷə-l-g-wa-z.
her-boy/son-pl [them-]how-Prev-she-feed-Dyn-Impf.NF
In this way, she used to feed her sons what she was gathering with difficulty.

(10) Znə, j-ájzə-l-ga-z ϕ-anə-n-c'ʷá, lə́-č'ʲk'ʷən-cʷa
one.day Rel-Prev-she-gather-Past.Ind.NF [it-]when-Prev-run out.Aor.NF her-son-Pl
«á-mla, á-mla» ħʷa də-r-k'ə́-jt'.
the-hunger the-hunger SP her-they-bother-(Aor)-Fin
One day, when what she had gathered ran out, her sons bothered her saying, 'I'm hungry, I'm hungry!'

(11) Jʷ-ʒ̆ʲará xə́-ʒ̆ʲara, j-s-áw-p' ϕ-axə-l-gʷá-xʷ-wa-z
2-somewhere 3-somewhere it-I-receive-Fut.I [it-]where-she-Prev-think-Dyn-Impf.NF
d-ná-j-n čʲa xʷəč'ʲə-k' ħʷa, axá aʒʷgʲə́
she-Prev-go thither-Past.Ind.Fin bread a little-one SP but nobody
d-áa-ħʷ-nə d-lə-xʷa-m-pšə-jt'.
he-Prev-turn this way-Past.Abs he-her-Prev-Neg-look at-(Aor)-Fin
She thought that she would be able to obtain some food at two or three places, and went there. Though she asked them to give her a little bread, nobody turned to her, nor paid her any attention.

(12) Agʲə́jraxʲ wjazgʲə́ jə-sə-l-m-áw-[w]a-z
on the other side all the same it-how-she-Neg-obtain-Dyn-Impf.NF
ϕ-l-də́r-wa-n.
[it-]she-know-Dyn+Impf.Fin
She knew that even though she went to the other places, she would still not be able to obtain food in either case.

(13) Jə-q'a-l-c'á-x-wa-zəj, d-aa-gʲažʲə́-jt'.
Rel-Prev-she-do-Emph-Dyn-what she-Par-return-(Aor)-Fin
Whatever should she have done? She returned home fruitlessly.

(14) D-aá-jə-n, avə́rħʷa a-čʲwán a-xáħʷ
she-Prev-come-Past.Ind.Fin quickly the-caldron the-stone
ϕ-l-ϕ-ta-psa-nə́ jə-jʷ-k'na-l-ħá-n, á-mca
[it-]Par-it-Prev-pour into-Past.Abs it-Par-Prev-she-hang on-Past.Ind.Fin the-fire
aq'ʷq'ʷáħʷa jə-jʷ-á-c'a-l-c'-t'.
plop-plop it-Par-it-Prev(under)-she-put-(Aor)-Fin
She came home and quickly poured stones into a caldron. Then she hung it up and lit the fire under it.

(15) <u>Aáj-xa ϕ-lə́-m-ta-k'ʷa,</u> á-č'ʲk'ʷən-cʷa «á-mla, á-mla» ħʷa
come-Masd [it-]her-Neg-give-Past.Abs the-boy/son-Pl the-hunger the-hunger SP
jə-lə́-k'ʷ-ša-nə jə-gə́l-t'.

they-her-Prev-surround-Past.Abs they-stand up-(Aor)-Fin
No sooner had she come back home than her sons followed her about saying, 'I'm hungry, I'm hungry!'

(16) — Aaj, nan d-šʷə́-k'ʷxša-wp', ožʷə́c'ʷq'ʲa
Oh young man he-yourPl-to alleviate pain-Pres.Stat.Fin at once
ak'ər-zə-m-w-wá-j, — ø-l-ħʷá-n, rə́-x-kʷa
Dummy-I-Neg-prepare-Dyn-Qu [it-]she-say-Past.Ind.Fin their-head-Pl
ø-aa-l-šʲšʲə́-jt'.
[them-]Par-she-stroke-(Aor)-Fin
'Oh, poor children! I'll prepare a meal at once!' she said, and stroked their heads.

(17) Ant a-čʲwán ø-anə́-r-ba, j-á-k'ʷ-ša-nə
those the-caldron [it-]when-they-see.Aor.NF they-it-Prev-surround-Past.Abs
j-la-t'ʷá-jt', ožʷə́-ošʲtán a-bə́sta [a-]áa-ba-rə.wšʲ ħʷa,
they-Prev-sit down-(Aor)-Fin now-then (= at once) the-polenta it-Par-see-even if SP
axá ak'rə́ ø-awə́-r-ba-x-wa.
but something [it-]Rhetorical Qu-they-see-Emph-Dyn.NF
When they saw the caldron, at once they surrounded it and sat down there hoping to see the polenta. But of course they could see nothing.

(18) A-xʷla-ra-gʲ wəj [a-]ák'ʷə-n.
the-become evening-Masd-also that it-be-Stat.Past.Fin
It became dark.

(19) A-č'ʲk'ʷən-cʷa ǯʲawk'-gʲə́ jə́-cʷ-t', ǯʲawk'-gʲə́
the-boy/son-Pl some people-also they-fall asleep-(Aor)-Fin some people-also
á-cʷa j-aa-rə-m-na-x-aanʒa, jə-c'ʷə́wa-n, r-an:
the-sleep it-Par-them-Prev(from)-it-take-(Aor)-until they-cry-Past.Ind.Fin their-mother
«ožʷə́c'ʷq'ʲa, nan ožʷə́c'ʷq'ʲa šʷə-m-c'ʷə́wa-n», — ø-l-ħʷ-wá-n.
at once young man at once you.Pl-Neg-cry-Proh [it-]she-say-Dyn-Impf.Fin
Some of the boys fell asleep, others were crying until they too fell asleep. Their mother said, 'Boys, now, stop crying at once!'

(20) Lə́-č'ʲk'ʷən-cʷa r-čə́-n-k'apsa=jʷ-k'apsa-nə́,
her-boy/son-Pl their-Self-Par-scatter=Par-scatter-Past.Abs
jə-k'arawára-xa jə́-cʷ-t', lar-gʲə́ d-xʷə́c-wa,
Rel-exhausted-become.Abs they-fall asleep-(Aor)-Fin she-also she-think-Dyn.Abs
l-čʲwán m-c'ʷaxə́ pšáa ħʷa də-z-ø-ta-pš-wá-z,
her-caldron Neg-hide find SP she-how-[it-]Prev(into)-look-Dyn-Impf.NF
«á-pšʷma!» ħʷa aʒʷə́ jə-bžʲə́ ø-gá-jt' adʷaxʲə́.
the-master SP someone his-voice [it-]be heard-(Aor)-Fin outdoors
The boys who had become very tired, having lain down just anywhere, fell asleep. She, thinking about

the future, said, 'I hid nothing, I am looking for something', and looked into the caldron. Just then she heard someone's voice outside saying 'Master!'

(21) — Aw! — ∅-l-ħʷa-n, dǝ-jʷ-dʷǝ́l-c'ǝ-n.
yes [it-]she-say-Past.Ind.Fin she-Par-Prev-go out-Past.Ind.Fin
'Yes', she said and went out.

(22) — Bzǝ́ja-la w-aa-bá-jt'! — ∅-l-ħʷá-n a-jʷnǝ-q'a
good-by you.M-we-see-(Aor)-Fin [it-]she-say-Past.Ind.Fin the-home-to
d-lá-l-gǝ-jt'.
him-Prev-she-take thither-(Aor)-Fin
'Welcome!' she said to the man who stood there, and took him back inside.

(23) D-sǝ́-la-t'ʷa-z ájpš wǝs ∅-jǝ-ħʷǝ́-jt':
he-how-Par-sit down-Past.Ind.NF as soon as as follows [it-]he-say-(Aor)-Fin
As soon as he had sat down, he said as follows:

(24) — Dáara á-mla s-a-k'-nǝ́ sǝ́-q'a-wp', jǝ-z-ʒá-r-gʲǝ
very the-hunger I-it-feel-Past.Abs I-be-Stat.Pres.Fin it-I-hide-Masd-even
j-a-psá-m, xʷǝč'ʲǝ́-k' ∅-b-zǝ-s-č'a-c'a-rǝ́.wšʲ?
it-it-be worth-Neg.Stat.Pres.Fin a little [it-]you.F-Pot-me-Prev-feed-even.if
— ∅-jǝ-ħʷǝ́-jt'.
[it-]he-say-(Aor)-Fin
'I am very hungry. I cannot hide how I am suffering from hunger [lit. It is not worth while hiding it]. Cannot you give me a little food?' he asked.

(25) — Wǝ́nan, wažʷǝ́c'ʷq'ʲa, — ∅-l-ħʷǝ́-jt', axá d-ax-pš-wá
of course at once/now [it-]she-say-(Aor)-Fin but she-where-look-Dyn.NF
anǝ́j a-kʷáb a-xáħʷ ∅-z-tá-w á-šq'a [a-]á-wp':
that the-caldron the-stone [it-]Rel-be in-Pres.Stat.NF it-toward it-be-Pres.Stat.Fin
'Of course, at once', she said. But she did nothing but look toward the caldron in which were the stones.

(26) Anǝ́j adjʷrágʲ wǝs ∅-jǝ-ħʷǝ́-jt':
that once more as follows [it-]he-say-(Aor)-Fin
The guest spoke again as follows:

(27) — ǯʲáwšʲt, arǝ́j jǝ-∅-tá-w-gʲ ∅-xaħʷǝ́-w-šʷa
well this Rel-[it-]be in-Pres.Stat.NF -even [it-]stone-Stat.Pres.NF-just like
∅-z-bwa-wá-t', anáxʲ ǯʲará c'ʷaxǝ́-k' ∅-bǝ́-ma-m-zar, waxá
[it-]I-see-Dyn-Pres.Fin there somewhere stock-one [it-]you.F-have-Neg-if this evening
jǝ-s-č'á-b-c'-wa-zǝj? — ∅-jǝ-ħʷǝ́-jt'.
Rel-me-Prev-you.F-feed-Dyn-Qu [it-]he-say-(Aor)-Fin

'Well, whatever is in that looks like stones to me. If you do not have a stock of food somewhere, what will you feed me with this evening?' he said.

(28) — Wáxʲ-gʲə c'ʷaxə́-s jə-sə́-ma-w agʲə́-q'a-m, axá
there-also stock-as Rel-I-have-Pres.Stat.NF nothing-be-Neg.Pres.Fin but
a-ncʷá jə-sə́-j-ta-lagʲ ø-z-bá-p', w-aa-m-ccak'ə́-n,
the god Rel-me-he-give-LA [it-]I-see-Fut.I.Fin you.M-Par-Neg-hurry-Proh
s-wə́-k'ʷxša-wp', — ø-l-ħʷə́-x-t' adrjʷágʲ.
I-your.M-to alleviate pain-Pres.Stat.Fin [it-]she-say-Emph-(Aor)-Fin once more
'I have no stock of food, but I'll see what God will give me. Do not hurry, my friend', she said once more.

(29) Wəs=wəs ø-sə́-l-ħʷ-wa-z, l-xaħʷ jə-šə́la-xa-nə
so [it-]how-she-say-Dyn-Impf.NF her-stone it-cornmeal-become-Past.Abs
jə-q'ʲat'=q'ʲát'-wa j-á-la-ga-jt'.
it-mush/kasha-Dyn.Abs it-it-Prev-begin-(Aor)-Fin
As she was saying so, the stones became cornmeal, and it began to turn into mush.

(30) A-mħáp ø-á-c'ə-l-šʲə-n a-bə́sta ø-l-wə́-jt'.
the-spoon for mush [it-]it-Prev-she-mix-Past.Ind.Fin the-polenta [it-]she-make-(Aor)-Fin
She mixed the mush with a spoon and made polenta.

(31) J-aa-k'nə́-l-xə-n, lə-sas xʷəč'ʲə́-k'
it-Par-Prev-she-put away-Past.Ind.Fin her-guest little-one
ø-jə-č'á-l-c'a-n də-šʲtá-l-c'ə-jt'.
[it-]him-Prev-she-feed-Past.Ind.Fin him-Prev-she-put down-(Aor)-Fin
She took out the polenta and gave her guest a little, and then she gave him a place on the floor to sleep.

(32) A-šʲtaxʲ lə́-č'ʲk'ʷən-cʷa ø-aa-lə-r-pšə́-n xʷəč'ʲə́-k'
it-after her-boy/son-Pl [them-]Prev-she-Caus-wake-Past.Ind.Fin little-one
ø-r-č'á-l-c'a-n jə-šʲtá-l-c'ə-jt'.
[it-]them-Prev-she-feed-Past.Ind.Fin them-Prev-she-put down-(Aor)-Fin
Then she woke up her sons and fed them a little polenta, and gave each of them in turn a place on the floor.

(33) Ačnə́ šʲəžʲəmtán šáanʒa
on that day in the morning very early in the morning
d-awə-m-gə́la-x-wa-z, d-an-áa-pš,
she-Rhetorical Qu-Neg-get up-Emph-Dyn-Impf.NF she-when-Prev-awake.Aor.NF
lə́-sas d-lə-m-bə́-jt', a-jʷn-gʲə́ a-ʒə́
her-guest him-she-Neg-see-(Aor)-Fin the-house-also the-water
ø-aa-jʷna-žž-wá jə́-q'a-n.

[it-]Prev-Prev-percolate-Dyn.Abs it-be-Stat.Past.Fin
Did she get up early in the morning of the following day? (Of course she got up very early in the morning of the following day.) When she awoke, she found that her guest was gone, and that water was seeping into the house.

(34) «Jә́-q'a-la-zaj?!» ħʷa d-anә́-jʷ-gәla, lә́-lapš
Rel-Prev-happen-(Aor)-what SP she-when-Par-stand up.Aor.NF her-gaze
ø-axә-nʒa-na-ʒá-wa-z zagʲә́ jә-ʒәt'q'wa-nә́
[it-]where-as far as-Prev-reach thither-Dyn-Impf.NF all it-place of water-as
j-gaz-wá jә-ø-tá-žʲә-n, a-jʷnә́ j-a-ma-rjaša-nә
it-be ruffled-Dyn.Abs it-[it-]Prev-lie in-Stat.Past.Fin the-house it-it-Prev-direct to-Past.Abs
mjʷaxʷásta xʷәč'ʲә́-k' ø-ga-n ák'ʷәmzar.
path little-one [it-]lead-Stat.Past.Fin only
'What has happened?!' she cried. When she stood up, she found that as far as the eye could see, everything was rippling water and that only one narrow path led to her house.

(35) Avәrħʷa d-aa-gʲažʲә́-n, lә́-č'ʲk'ʷәn-cʷa
quickly she-Par-return-Past.Ind.Fin her-boy/son-Pl
ø-aa-lә-r-pšә́-n jә-d-lә-rbә́-jt'.
[them-]Prev-she-Caus-wake-Past.Ind.Fin it-them-she-show-(Aor)-Fin
She hurried back, woke her sons and showed them the little path.

(36) Arә́j a-mjʷaxʷásta ø-á-l-ga-nә jә-zә́-q'a-w
this the-path [it-]it-Prev-lead from-Past.Abs it-why-be-Pres.Stat.NF
— šʷará šʷ-á-m-ga-r a-ncʷá jә-[j-]taxә́-wp', — ø-l-ħʷә́-jt'.
you.Pl you.Pl-it-Neg-kill-if the-god it-he-want-Pres.Stat.Fin [it-]she-say-(Aor)-Fin
'The reason why this path was laid down is because God does not want you to die', she said.

(37) Wәs ø-r-á-ħʷa-nә, á-č'ʲk'ʷәn-cʷa jә-z-nә́q'ʷ-wa-z
so [it-]them-to-say-Past.Abs the-boy/son-Pl Rel-Pot-walk-Dyn-Impf.NF
l-ápxʲa j-la-r-gә́la-nә, a-xʷәč'ʲ-kʷá lará
her-ahead of them-Par-Caus-stand-Past.Abs the-baby-Pl she
j-áa-šʲtә-x-nә, a-mjʷaxʷásta xʷәč'ʲә́ j-á-l-ga-z
them-Par-Prev-pick up-Past.Abs the-path little Rel-it-Prev-lead-Stat.Past.NF
dә́-kʷ-la-nә d-dʷә́kʷ-l-t'.
she-Prev-set off-Past.Abs she-Prev-depart-(Aor)-Fin
Having said so, she made the sons who were old enough to go on their own feet walk ahead of her, and carried her babies. Then she made her way along the little path.

(38) Esaájra naq' d-cá-cәpxʲaʒa, lә́-šʲtaxʲq'a j-ajmáħ-wa-n.
gradually there she-go-every time her-behind it-collapse-Dyn-Impf.Fin
As she was progressing along it, the little path was gradually collapsing behind her.

(39) A-pħʷə́s ajbá-gʲ d-ná-l-c'ə-jt', a-ʒ-gʲə́
the-widow-also she-Prev-Prev-go out-(Aor)-Fin the-water-also
j-a[a-]ajlajʷajlá-sə-n, jə-gazg-wá
Dummy-Par-Prev-seethe-Past.Ind.Fin it-be ruffled-Dyn.Abs
jə-l-ø-ta-tʷá-jt'.
it-Par-[it-]Prev-pour into-(Aor)-Fin
As soon as the widow had finished crossing over the path, the water, being churned up, poured over it.

(40) Wəbrə́j á-naxəs Rə́jc'a ʒə́žʲ ø-cʷgʲa-nə́, jə-c'ə́da-nə
that its-after Rits'a backwater [it-]awfully deep-Abs it-bottomless-Abs
j-áa-q'a-l-t'.
it-Par-Prev-become-(Aor)-Fin
After that Rits'a's backwater became an unfathomably deep, bottomless lake.

(41) Abnə́j a-pħʷə́sajba lə́-č'ʲk'ʷən-cʷa j-aa-r-xə́l-c'ə-z
that the-widow her-boy/son-Pl Rel-Par-they-Prev-give birth to-Past.Ind.NF
r-á-wp' ožʷ Pšə́saa jə-rə́-žʷla-nə jə́-q'a-w.
them-be-Pres.Stat.Fin now Pshys-Pl it-their-surname-as Rel-be-Pres.Stat.NF
The people to whom the widow's sons gave birth now go by the surname of Psysaa.

(42) Jəjášanə, Pšə́sba-nə jə́-q'a-w Rə́jc'a ø-jə-bá-r, d-wə-m-k'ə́-r
in fact Pshysba-as Rel-be-Pres.Stat.NF Rits'a [it-]he-see-if him-you-Neg-hold-if
s-xə ø-á-s-t-wa-jt' ħʷa d-á-la-ga-wa-jt' ø-r-ħʷa-wá-jt'.
my-head [it-]it-I-give-Dyn-Fin SP he-it-Prev-begin-Dyn-Fin [it-]they-say-Dyn-Fin
In fact, they say that if a person named Psysba sees Lake Rits'a, he will begin to say 'If you don't hold me back, I'll plunge into it.'

Notes

* The text is taken from «Ш. Хь. Салаҟаиа. Аҧсуа жәлар рҿаҧыцтә рҿиамҭа, Ахрестоматиа. Аҟиа: Алашара», 1975. pp. 125–126.

** This text is written in the Bzyp (Gudauta) dialect. For this dialect can be characterized as the weakening of the open vowel in the final position of the verbal root (see §6.3.6).

(1) ə́-kʷə-n-x-wa (dial.) = ə́-kʷə-n-xa-wa: masd. á-kʷə-n-xa-ra 'to live on'.

(2) **1.** jə-zə́-q'a-la: masd. á-q'a-la-ra [intr.] 'to become'. **2.** jə́-r-ħʷ-wa (dial.) = jə́-r-ħʷa-wa: masd. a-ħʷa-ra [tr.] 'to say'. For the dropping of the radical vowel, see §6.3.6.2.

(3) **1.** j-an-pswá = j-an-psə́wa. j-an-pswá dgʲə́lə-z, cf. ápswa matʷá 'Abkhazian clothes'. **2.** Pšə́s-aa: Pšə́s-ba [sg.] (surname). **3.** r-ák'ʷə-n (them(C2)-be-Stat.Past.Fin) '[people who lived there] were the tribe called Pshysbas': masd. ák'ʷ-zaa-ra 'to be'.

(4) **1.** a-nxa-rá or a-nxá-ra.

(5) **1.** j-aá-g (it/them(C1)-Prev-give.Imp) 'give it/them!': masd. aá-ga-ra [tr.] 'to give'. **2.** ø-rə-z-də́r-wa-mə-zt' (it(C1)-them(C2)-Pot-know-Dyn-Neg-Impf.Fin) 'they did not know it': masd. a-də́r-ra [tr.] 'to know'.

(6) **1.** aa-šá-rg^{j}ə: masd. a-ša-rá [intr.] 'to dawn', cf. jə-ša-wá-jt' (Dummy(C1)-dawn-Dyn-Fin) 'it dawns'. **2.** ak'rə-l-w-[w]á-n (Dummy-she(C3)-work-Dyn-Impf.Fin) 'she was working': masd. ak'rə-w-rá [tr.] 'to work'.

(7) **1.** jə́-l-w-[w]a-z-g^{j}ə (Rel(C1)-she(C3)-do-Dyn-Impf.NF-even) 'one which she was doing': masd. a-w-rá [tr.] 'to do'. **2.** jə-r-áw-[w]a-n (them(C1)-they(C2)-obtain-Dyn-Impf.Fin) 'they used to obtain them': masd. á-aw-ra [intr.] 'to receive, obtain'. **3.** ø-anə-r-záa-n-xa-lag^{j} = ø-anə-r-záa-n-xa-lak'^{j} (it(C1)-when-them(C2)-Prev-Prev-remain-(Aor)-LA) 'when they had remains': masd. a-záan-xa-ra [intr.] 'to remain'. **4.** j-lə́-r-t-wa-n (dial.) = j-lə́-r-ta-wa-n (it(C1)-her(C2)-they(C3)-give-Dyn-Impf.Fin) 'they used to give it to her': masd. á-ta-ra [tr.] 'to give'.

(8) **1.** ø-awə́-l-ħ^{w}a-x-wa-z (it(anything)-Rhetorical.Qu-she-say-Emph-Dyn-Impf.NF) 'Could she say anything?' = 'Of course she could not say anything'.: masd. a-ħ^{w}a-rá [tr.] 'to say'. Of the affix of the rhetorical question see Hewitt (2010: 271).

(9) **1.** j-a[a]-ajzə-l-g-wa = j-a[a]-ajzə-l-ga-wa (Rel(C1)-Par-Prev-she(C3)-gather-Dyn.NF) 'what she is gathering': masd. ájz-ga-ra [tr.] 'to gether'. **2.** ø-zla-nə́q'^{w}ə-l-g-wa-z = ø-zla-nə́q'^{w}ə-l-ga-wa-z (them(C1)-how-Prev-she(C3)-feed-Dyn-Impf.NF) 'how she was feeding them': masd. a-nə́q'^{w}-fa-ra [tr.] 'to feed'.

(10) **1.** ø-anə-n-c'^{w}a (it-when-Prev-run out.Aor.NF) 'when it ran out': masd. a-n-c'^{w}a-rá [intr.] 'to finish, to run out'. **2.** á-mla = á-mla sak'wájt' 'I'm hungry'. **3.** də-r-k'ə́-jt' (her(C1)-they(C3)-pester-(Aor)-Fin) 'they bothered her': masd. a-k'-rá [tr.] 'to bother'.

(11) **1.** ø-axə-l-g^{w}á-x^{w}-wa-z (it(C1)-where-she(C2)-Prev-think-Dyn-Impf.NF) 'to the place where she thought that (she would receive the food)': masd. a-g^{w}á-x^{w}-ra [intr.] 'to think'. **2.** d-áa-ħ^{w}-nə (he-Prev-turn this way-Past.Abs) 'he, having turned this way': masd. áa-ħ^{w}-ra [intr.] 'to turn this way'. **3.** d-lə-x^{w}a-m-pšə-jt' (he(C1)-her(C2)-Prev-Neg-look at-(Aor)-Fin) 'he did not look at her': masd. á-x^{w}a-pš-ra [intr.] 'to look at'.

(12) **1.** wjazg^{j}ə́ (dial.) = wajzg^{j}ə́ 'all the same'. **2.** jə-sə-l-m-áw-[w]a-z (dial.) = jə-šə-l-m-áw-[w]a-z (it-how-she-Neg-obtain-Dyn-Impf.NF) '(she knew) that she could not obtain it': masd. á-aw-ra [intr.] 'to receive, obtain'.

(13) **1.** d-aa-g^{j}až^{j}ə́-jt' (she-Par-return-(Aor)-Fin) 'she returned': masd. á-g^{j}až^{j}-ra/á-g^{j}ež^{j}-ra [intr.] 'to return'.

(14) **1.** D-aá-jə-n (she-Prev-come-Past.Ind.Fin) 'she came and': masd. aá-j-ra [intr.] 'to come, to arrive'. **2.** ø-l-ø-ta-psa-nə́ (it(the stone, C1)-Par-it(the caldron, C2)-Prev(into)-pour-Abs) lit. 'having poured stones into a caldron': masd. a-ta-psa-rá [tr.] 'to pour into'. **3.** jə-j^{w}-k'na-l-ħá-n (it(the caldron, C1)-Par-Prev-she(C3)-hang.on-Past.Ind.Fin) 'she hung the caldron': masd. a-k'ná-ħa-ra [tr.] 'to hang on'. **4.** jə-j^{w}-á-c'a-l-c'-t' = jə-j^{w}-á-c'a-l-c'a-jt' (it(the fire, C1)-Par-it(the caldron, C2)-Prev(under)-she(C3)-put-(Aor)-Fin) 'she put the fire under the caldron': masd. á-c'a-c'a-ra [tr.] 'to put under'.

(15) **1.** aáj-xa = aáj-ra 'coming'. **2.** Aáj-xa ø-lə́-m-ta-k'^{w}a 'no sooner had she come back'. **3.** jə-lə́-k'^{w}-ša-nə (they(C1)-her(C2)-Prev-surround-Abs) 'they surrounded her': masd. á-lə́-k'^{w}-ša-ra [intr.] 'to surround'. **4.** jə-gə́l-t' = jə-gə́la-jt' (they(C1)-stand up-(Aor)-Fin) 'they stood up': masd. a-gə́la-ra [intr.] 'to stand up'.

(16) **1.** d-š^{w}ə́-k'^{w}xša-wp': á-кәхшазаара 'ласковое обращение: «чтобы твои болезни перешли на меня»' (AAD). **2.** ož^{w}ə́c'^{w}q'^{j}a = waž^{w}ə́c'^{w}q'^{j}a; cf. 25. **3.** ak'ər-zə-m-w-wá-j (Dummy-I-Neg-prepare-Dyn-Qu)

‘don’t I prepare a meal?’: masd. a-k’rə-w-ra [tr.] ‘to prepare; to work’. **4.** ø-aa-l-š^{j}š^{j}ə́-jt’ (them(their heads, C1)-Par-she(C3)-stroke-(Aor)-Fin) ‘she stroked them’: masd. a-š^{j}š^{j}-ra [tr.] ‘to stoke’.

(17) **1.** j-la-t’^{w}á-jt’ (they-Prev-sit down-(Aor)-Fin) ‘they sat down’: masd. á-la-t’^{w}a-ra [intr.] ‘to sit down’. **2.** [a-]áa-ba-rə-wš^{j} ħ^{w}a ‘only to see it’. **3.** ø-awə́-r-ba-x-wa (it(something, C1)-Rhetorical.Qu-they(C3)-see-Emph-Dyn.NF) ‘Can they see anything?’, ‘Of course they can see nothing’: masd. a-ba-rá [tr.] ‘to see’.

(19) **1.** jə́-c^{w}-t’ = jə́-c^{w}a-jt’ (they(C1)-fall asleep-(Aor)-Fit) ‘they fell aspleep’: masd. á-c^{w}a-ra [intr.] ‘to sleep’. **2.** j-aa-rə-m-na-x-aanʒa (it(C1)-Par-them(C2)-Prev(from)-it(sleep, C3)-take-(Aor)-until) lit. ‘until a sleep took it from them’, i.e. ‘until they grew sleepy’: masd. á-m-x-ra [tr.] ‘to take from’. **3.** jə-c’^{w}ə́wa-n (they(C1)-cry-Past.Ind.Fin): a-c’^{w}ə́wa-ra [intr.] ‘to cry’.

(20) **1.** r-čə́-n-k’apsa=j^{w}-k’apsa-nə́ ‘they, having lain down everywhere’: masd. a-k’a-psa-rá [labile] ‘to scatter’. **2.** jə-k’arawára-xa: masd. a-k’arawára-xa-ra [intr.] ‘to become exhausted’. **3.** d-x^{w}ə́c-wa (she-think-Dyn.Abs) ‘she, thinking’: masd. a-x^{w}ə́c-ra [intr.] ‘to think’. **4.** m-c’^{w}axə́ pšáa is not analysable. According to our informant, its phrase was translated as ‘ничего не спрятала, а ищет’. Cf. the masdars á-c’^{w}ax-ra [tr.] ‘to hide’, á-pšaa-ra [tr.] ‘to find’. **5.** də-z-ø-ta-pš-wá-z = də-š-ø-ta-pš-wá-z (she(C1)-how-it(C2)-Prev(into)-look-Dyn-Impf.NF) lit. ‘how she was looking into it’: masd. a-ta-pš-rá [intr.] ‘to look into’. **6.** ø-gá-jt’ (it(C1)-be heard-(Aor)-Fin) ‘it was heard’: masd. a-ga-rá [intr.] ‘to be audible’.

(21) **1.** də-j^{w}-d^{w}ə́l-c’ə-n: masd. a-d^{w}ə́l-c’-ra [intr.] ‘to go out’.

(22) **1.** bzə́ja-la w-aa-bá-jt’! ‘(addressed to a male person) welcome!’: masd. a-ba-rá [tr.] ‘to see’. **2.** d-lá-l-gə-jt’ = d-ná-l-ga-jt’ (him-Prev-she-take thither-(Aor)-Fin) ‘she took him there’: masd. a-ná-ga-ra [tr.] ‘to take thither’.

(23) **1.** d-sə́-la-t’^{w}a-z = d-šə́-la-t’^{w}a-z: masd. á-t’^{w}a-ra [intr.] ‘to sit down’. **2.** ø-jə-ħ^{w}ə́-jt’ = ø-jə-ħ^{w}á-jt’.

(24) **1.** s-a-k’-nə́ (I(C1)-it(C2)-feel-Abs): masd. a-k’-rá [intr.] ‘to feel’. Cf. 10-2. **2.** j-a-psá-m (it(C1)-it(hiding, C2)-be worth-Neg.Stat.Pres.Fin) ‘it is not worth hiding’: masd. a-psa-rá [intr.] ‘to be worth’. **3.** ø-b-zə-s-č^{j}a-c’a-rə́.wš^{j} (it(C1)-you.F(C2)-Pot-me(C2)-Prev-feed-even if) ‘Cannot you feed me some food?’: masd. a-č^{j}a-c’a-rá [tr.] ‘to feed’.

(25) **1.** d-ax-pš-wá = d-ax^{j}-pš-wá (she-where-look-Dyn.NF) ‘where she is looking’: masd. a-pš-rá [intr.] ‘to look’. **2.** ø-z-tá-w (it(the stone, C1)-Rel(C2)-be in-Pres.Stat.NF) ‘which the stone is in’: masd. a-tá-zaa-ra [intr.] ‘to be in’.

(27) **1.** jə-ø-tá-w-g^{j} (Rel(C1)-it(this, C2)-be in-Pres.Stat.NF-even) ‘what is in it’: masd. a-tá-zaa-ra [intr.] ‘to be in’. **2.** ø-z-bwa-wá-t’ = ø-z-ba-wá-jt’: masd. a-ba-rá [tr.] ‘to see’. **3.** jə-s-č’á-b-c’-wa-zəj? = jə-s-č’á-b-c’a-wa-zaj? (Rel(C1)-me(C2)-Prev-you.F(C3)-feed-Dyn-Qu) ‘What will you feed me with?’: masd. a-č^{j}a-c’a-rá [tr.] ‘to feed’. Cf. 25-2.

(28) **1.** jə-sə́-j-ta-lag^{j} (Rel(C1)-me(C2)-he(C3)-give-LA) (= Abzh. dialect: jə-sə́-j-ta-lak’^{j}) ‘what he will give me’. For the future suffix lag^{j} in the Bzyb dialect, see Bgazhba (1964a: 198-199, 177). **2.** w-aa-m-ccak’ə́-n (you.M-Par-Neg-hurry-Proh) ‘don’t hurry up!’: masd. á-ccak’-ra [intr.] ‘to hurry’. **3.** s-wə́-k’^{w}xša-wp’ ‘my dear!’: masd. á-кəхшазаара ‘ласковое обращение’; cf. 16-1 above. **4.** adrj^{w}ág^{j} = ad-j^{w}rág^{j}, see (26).

(29) **1.** ø-sə́-l-ħ^{w}-wa-z = ø-šə́-l-ħ^{w}a-wa-z (it(C1)-how-she(C3)-say-Dyn-Impf.NF) lit. ‘how she was saying so’. **2.** q’^{j}at’=q’^{j}át’ ‘каша из кукурузной крупы’.

(30) **1.** ø-á-c’ə-l-š^{j}ə-n: masd. á-c’-š^{j}-ra [tr.] ‘to mix’. **2.** ø-l-wə́-jt’: masd. a-w-rá [tr.] ‘to make; to do’.

(31) **1.** j-aa-k’nə́-l-xə-n: masd. a-k’nə́-x-ra [tr.] ‘to take down; to put away (the polenta)’. **2.** də-š^{j}tá-l-c’ə-jt’ = də-š^{j}tá-l-c’a-jt’ (him(C1)-Prev-she(C3)-put down-(Aor)-Fin): masd. á-š^{j}ta-c’a-ra [tr.] ‘to put down’.

(32) **1.** ϕ-aa-lə-r-pšə́-n (them-Prev-she-Caus-wake-Past.Ind.Fin) 'she woke them up and': masd. áa-rpš-ra [tr.] 'to wake up'; cf. 33-2.

(33) **1.** d-awə-m-gə́la-x-wa-z (she(C1)-Rhetorical.Qu-Neg-get up-Emph-Dyn-Impf.NF) 'didn't she get up': masd. a-gə́la-ra [intr.] 'to get up'. **2.** d-an-áa-pš (she(C1)-when-Prev-awake.Aor.NF) 'when she awoke': masd. áa-pš-ra [intr.] 'to awake'. **3.** d-lə-m-bə́-jt' = d-lə-m-bá-jt' (him(C1)-she(C3)-Neg-see-(Aor)-Fin) 'she did not see him'. **4.** ϕ-aa-jʷna-žž-wa: masd. aa-jʷna-žž-rá [intr.] 'to percolate'.

(34) **1.** jə́-q'a-la-zaj (Rel-Prev-happen-(Aor)-what) 'what happened?': masd. á-q'a-la-ra [intr.] 'to happen'. **2.** ϕ-axə-nʒa-na-ʒá-wa-z = ϕ-axʲə-nʒa-na-ʒá-wa-z (it(her gaze, C1)-where-as.far.as-Prev-reach.thither-Dyn-Impf.NF) 'as far as her eye could see': masd. á-na-ʒa-ra [intr.] 'to reach thither'. **3.** j-gaz-wá = j-gazga-wá: masd. a-gazga-rá [intr.] 'to be ruffled'. For this form see j-gazga-wá in 39. **4.** jə-ϕ-tá-žʲə-n (it(C1)-it(C2)-Prev(in)-lie-Stat.Past.Fin) 'it lay in it': masd. a-tá-žʲ-zaa-ra [intr.] 'to lie in'. **5.** j-a-ma-rjaša-nə (it(C1)-it(the house, C2)-Prev-direct to-Abs) lit. 'having directed it to the house': masd. á-ma-rjaša-ra [tr.] 'to direct to'. **6.** ϕ-ga-n: masd. a-gá-zaa-ra [intr.] 'to lead'.

(35) **1.** jə-d-lə-rbə́-jt' = jə-d-lə-rbá-jt' < jə-r-lə-r-bá-jt' (it(the path, C1)-them(C2)-she(C3)-Caus-see-(Aor)-Fin) 'she showed it to them': masd. a-r-ba-rá [tr.] ' to show'.

(36) **1.** ϕ-á-l-ga-nə (it(the path, C1)-it(C2)-Prev-lead from-Past.Abs) 'having led the path from it': masd. á-la-ga-ra [tr.] 'to lead from'. **2.** šʷ-á-m-ga-r (you.Pl(C1)-it(C3)-Neg-kill-if) jə-[j-]taxə́-wp' '[God] does not want it to kill you': masd. a-ga-rá [tr.] 'to kill, убить'.

(37) **1.** wəs ϕ-r-á-ħʷa-nə (it(C1)-them(C2)-to-say-Abs) 'having said so to them': masd. a-ħʷa-rá [tr.] 'to say'. **2.** jə-z-nəq'ʷ-wa-z = jə-z-nəq'ʷa-wa-z (Rel-Pot-walk-Dyn-Impf.NF) '[the boys] who could walk': masd. a-nə́q'ʷa-ra [intr.] 'to walk, go (on foot)'. **3.** j-la-r-gə́la-nə (them(C1)-Par-Caus-stand up-Abs) 'having made them stand': masd. a-rgə́la-ra [tr.] 'make *sb* stand'. **4.** j-áa-šʲtə-x-nə (them-Par-Prev-pick up-Past.Abs) 'having picked them up': masd. á-šʲtə-x-ra [tr.] 'to pick up'. **5.** j-á-l-ga-z '[the little path] which was laid down'. **6.** də́-kʷ-la-nə: masd. á-kʷ-la-ra [intr.] 'to set off'. **7.** d-dʷə́kʷ-l-t' = d-dʷə́kʷ-la-jt': masd. a-dʷə́kʷ-ra [intr.] 'to depart'.

(38) **1.** j-ajmáħ-wa-n = j-ajmáħa-wa-n (it(C1)-collapse-Dyn-Impf.Fin) 'it was collapsing': masd. ájmaħa-ra [intr.] 'to collapse, to cave in'.

(39) **1.** A-pħʷə́s ajbá-gʲ: cf. (5) a-pħʷə́sajba 'the widow'. **2.** d-ná-l-c'ə-jt': masd. a-ná-l-c'-ra [intr.] 'to go out'. **3.** j-a[a-]ajlajʷajlá-sə-n: masd. ájlajʷajka-s-ra [intr.] 'to seethe; to crowd'. **4.** jə-l-ϕ-ta-tʷá-jt' (it(the water, C1)-Par-it(the path, C2)-Prev-pour into-(Aor)-Fin) 'the water poured into the path': masd. a-ta-tʷa-rá [labile] 'to pour into'.

(40) **1.** jə-c'ə́da-nə < jə-c'ə́-da-nə 'it-bottom-without-Abs', cf. á-c'a 'bottom'. **2.** j-áa-q'a-l-t' = j-áa-q'a-la-jt' (it-Par-Prev-become-(Aor)-Fin) 'it became': masd. á-q'a-la-ra [intr.] 'to become'.

(41) **1.** j-aa-r-xə́l-c'ə-z (Rel(C1)-Par-they(C2)-Prev-give birth to-Past.Ind.NF) 'one who they gave birth to': masd. a-xə́l-c'-ra [intr.] 'to give birth to'.

(42) **1.** d-wə-m-k'ə́-r (him(C1)-you(C2)-Neg-hold-if) 'if you do not hold him': masd. a-k'-rá [intr. inverse] 'to hold'. **2.** ϕ-á-s-t-wa-jt' = ϕ-á-s-ta-wa-jt' (it(my head, C1)-it(Lake, C2)-I(C3)-give-Dyn-Fin) 'I'll give my head to Lake Rits'a', i.e. 'I'll plunge into Lake Rits'a': masd. á-ta-ra [tr.] 'to give'.

3. The Boy Brought up by a Bull

Text

(1) Ацә иааӡаз аҷкун

(2) Дыҟан нхаҩык.

(3) Абри анхаҩы аҧх̣әыс диман, иҷкун дыҟан.

(4) Ишыҟаз акумкуа, абри анхаҩы иҧх̣әыс дыҧсит.

(5) Иҧх̣әыс даныҧсы ашьт̣ахь акыр аамт̣а дц̣ьабеит, дгурҩеит егьит, аха ат̣цыхутәан аӡә дааимгар ҟамлазт, даҽа ҧх̣әыск дааигеит.

(6) Иааигаз аҧх̣әыс ани иҷкун даалбар ҟамлаӡеит.

(7) — Уара абри ахуҷы дах̣шьып, иоух̣әои, ц̣ьара х̣ант̣ытцны х̣цозаргьы, уск аауазаргьы иара дах̣ҧырхагоуп, — х̣әа лхатца иалх̣әо далагеит лассы-лассы.

(8) Ари зны илх̣әеит, ҩынтә илх̣әеит, хынтә илх̣әеит, аха анхаҩы рыцха иҷкун дызыгуаҕьуам, иҟаитцари, димгуаҕьыргьы иҧх̣әыс дитцытцны дцар х̣әа дшәоит.

(9) Ашьт̣ахь игу анҧылтцәаӡа, «сыҷкун затцәы исымоу дабаст̣ахыу, дысшьып, сыҧх̣әыс сыматц луеит» их̣әан, ари анхаҩы рыцх̣а иҷкун дызлаишьышаз ах̣әызба ахра далагеит.

(10) Ах̣әызба ахра даҿуп уажәы ашьашәыраҿы дтәаны.

(11) Амак̣ьа ик̣ушьуа иах̣әызба ахра даҿуп.

(12) Ари цәкы иман, ахуҷы игуарихлон, игуараитцалон, акраҿеитцон, акраиржәуан.

(13) Ари аҽены ахуҷы ацә акраҿатцаны, иманы ашьашәыраҿы данааи, «саб, ари ах̣әызба иух‘уа иалаухи, изут̣ахи?» х̣әа иаб дизтцааит.

(14) — Х̣ацә х̣шьып, акуац х̣фап, убри азоуп сах̣әызба зысх‘уа, — их̣әеит аб, ахуҷы дижьарц ауп изих̣әо уажәы.

(15) Аб ацә х̣шьуеит аних̣әа, ахуҷы акьажых̣әа атцәуара далагеит.

(16) — Закуузеи, уара узыртцәуо, атцәуара уаҟутцны, уцаны аӡартцәи аага, — их̣әеит аб.

(17) Иаб даникуцәҟьа, аӡартцәи аазгоит х̣әа ахуҷы дтцәуо дышнеиуаз ацә дабеит.

(18) — Узыртцәуозеи, иухьзеи? — ах̣әан ацә иазтцааит.

(19) — Сабамтцәуо, саб иах̣әызба амак̣ьа ик̣утцаны ахра даҿуп, аӡартцәи аага, ацә х̣шьып х̣әа сеих̣әеит, — их̣әеит ахуҷы.

(20) — Сара сакуӡам иршьуа, уижьеит акумзар, иишьырц иит̣ахыу уара уоуп, уаныҧса т̣аха илымт̣еит, уара иухырҟьаны ианагь ат̣ыӡшәа рылибах‘уеит, ухуҷы дшьы х̣әа иалх̣әоижьт̣еи акыр аатцуеит.

(21) «Дабах̣т̣ахыу, дах̣шьып, нас х̣ара ишах̣т̣ахыу хаҟалап» х̣әа дааҟумтцӡакуа уаб даныхт̣алкӡа, иаргьы игу аныҧтцәаӡа, дак̣ушах̣ат̣хеит, уишьырц иак̣уикит, — ах̣әеит ацә.

(22) — Нас ишҧасыҧсыхуоу, ишҧаҟастцари? — их̣әан, инеимат̣әаны иеих̣агьы атцәуара далагеит ахуҷы.

(23) — Иҟаутцара уи ауп, сахҿаухәо, убра хах̣әык шьт̣оуп, хх̣әакгьы убра икаршәуп, ҧат̣лыкакгьы, аҿарпынгьы убра иҟоуп, убарт̣ аашьт̣ыхны, иуманы уаа, нас уаби уаныҧсеи

уршьаанӡа са урцәызгоит, умшәан, — ахәеит аҵә.

(24) Аҵә днаҧызан, има иҿынеихан, дынкылсын, аҵә ахьҿеихәалоз атыҧ аҿы аҿарпынгьы, ахахәгьы, аххәагьы, аҧатлыкагьы аашьҭихын, дыҩны даакылсын, даннадгыла, «уҧаны усыкутәа!» ахәан, аҵә абҕа дҩакутәеит.

(25) Ахучы данҩакутәа, аҵә ҩатҟьан иҩт.

(26) Аҵә ҩатҟьан иҩны иандәыкула, ари ачкун ианыҧса иахуҭамыз ахьылхәахьаз азы дхәахеит, иаб ахәа дакутәаны ддәыкулеит.

(27) Ачкун иаб ахәа дакутәаны аҵә дашьҭалан дахьӡо далагеит.

(28) — Ҳаи, уаныҧса ажәрацәгьа дхәахан, ахәа уаб дакутәаны дхашьҭаланы даауеит, абар, абар уажәышьҭа дхахьӡоит.

(29) Уҧатлыка иҭоу аӡы катәа ҳашьҭахьҟа, — ахәеит аҵә.

(30) Аҵә ас анахәа, иҧатлыка иҭаз аӡы ишьҭахьҟа икеиҭәеит ачкун.

(31) Рышьҭахьҟа мшынхеит иҧатлыка иҭазаӡы анкеиҭәа.

(32) Имшынхеит, аха изхуарҭоузеи, ахәажә амшын аҿы иаангыло иҟоума, аҽҭанажьын иӡсаны идәыкулеит.

(33) Амшын ааимгухәаны ирын, аҵә иахьӡо иалагеит.

(34) — Ари ахәажә хахьӡоит умбо, уххәа каршә ушьҭахьҟа! — ахәеит аҵә.

(35) Аҵә ас анахәа, ачкун иххәа ишьҭахьҟа икаиршәит, иххәа анкаиршә, ишьҭахьҟа иахабалакь бнарахеит, аха ахәажә абнаҿ иаангыло, абна иннакыло иҟазма, абнара иласын, наҟ иҩылсын, аҵә иахьӡо иалагеит.

(36) — Уаныҧса ахәажәи уаби хахьӡоит еиҭах умбо, ушьҭахьҟа ухьаханы ухахә кажь! — хәа аҵә ахучы ус ианахәеит.

(37) Аҵә ас анахәа, ачкун хучы ихахә ишьҭахьҟа икаижьт.

(38) Ишьҭахьҟа ахахә анкаижь, ахахәгуара дукуа ҟалеит.

(39) Ахәа еихеит, еихеит, аха ахахәгуаракуа изырхымтцит.

(40) Уа инхеит, ахуч иабгьы нас дабаушьтуаз, уа даанхеит.

(41) Ачкун хучы аҵә даманы ицо, ицо, ицо, иахьынӡалшоз ицеит.

(42) Ианааҧса, ҧсҭа гуаҩак аҿы иаангылт.

(43) — Ахых, уажәышьҭа абра улбаа, саргьы абра акрысфап, уара абра утәа, иагьаҵьара сцаргьы, ара саауеит, усшьуам, амла уасырк'уам, ахахаи акы уаҵәымшәан, — хәа аҵә ачкун ус ианахәеит.

(44) — Ара стәар, гыгшәыгк ааир самфои, — ихәеит ачкун.

(45) Абра атцлаҿы ухунаны укутәа, амла уанаклакь, аҿарпын иумоу архәара уалага, аҿарпын архәара уаналагалакь, сахыҟазаалакгьы уара уҿарпын абжьы са исахауеит.

(46) Нас афатә са иузаазгоит.

(47) Амала, иуасхәо убри ауп, са саанӡа, са сыҟамкуа атцла улымбаан, — ахәеит аҵә.

(48) Аҵә аҿынанахан хәра ицеит.

(49) Ачкун амла данаклакь, аҿарпын архәара далагон, аҿарпын абжьы аҵә ахыҟазаалакь иахауан, амла дшакыз уи ала иадыруан, афатә ааганы иҿанатцон.

(50) Абас ишыҟаз акумкуа мызкы, ҩымз тцит.

(51) Ари ачкун аҿарпын аирхәо даналагалакь, аӆстa атцаракуа, ашәарах аҿарпын абжьы змахацыз рацәамзи, зегьы еизон.

(52) Аҿарпын абжьы хааӡа изахауаз иеизаны ачкун дзыкутәаз атцла ааигуа-сигуа иавагьыжьуа, иавагьыжьуа аумашәа ибаны, иргуаӆханы иазыӡырҩуан.

(53) Абри атыӆ ааигуара ахак дынхозаарын.

(54) Ани ах иќнытә аӡәы дшәарыцо аӆстa гуаҩа дталаны дышлеиуаз акумкуан, ани ачкун хучы иҿарпын абжьы иахаит.

(55) Ашәарыцаҩ аҿарпын абжьы аниаха, «абри иахсахауа снеип, изакуу еилыскаап» ихәан, ддәыкулан уа дазааигуахеит.

(56) Уа ааигуа длеит, аха ачкун дахьыќатцәќьаз дзымнеит, ари дзакуз изеилымкааит, агыгшәыг бааӆсны иќан, ашәарыцаҩ уахь днармышьтит.

(57) Ашәарыцаҩ ари зыбжьы гоз анизеилымкаа, ишьтахьќа дгьажьны дцеит.

(58) Дахьнеиз, «абас, абас ауп избаз, ассир збеит, сара акыр сныќуахьеит, аха ас еиӆш сымбацызт, абна агутаҿы аҿарпын абжьы сахаит, изакуу збап хәа сҿынасхан, аха абжьы исахауаз иахьсахауаз саназааигуаха, агыгшәыг акушаны иќан, снармышьтит.

(59) Снаӆшны еиргь хәа избон, цәкы неин зегьы ӆханатцеит, харантәи сахьыӆшуаз дуаҩӆсуп ухәартә чкуна тцәрышкуак атцла длалбаан, ацә акриҿанатцеит хәа сыќоуп, усшәа избеит.

(60) Аха избаз, исахаз цкьа иеилыскаартә ааигуа сзымнеит» — хәа реихәеит.

(61) — Нас ари иеилкаашьас иамоузеи? — хәа ауаа алацәажәеит.

(62) Аха еилкаашьас иамоу абри ауп хәа аӡәгьы акагьы изымхәеит.

(63) Убра ааигуа такуажәык, хуартлаӆьк дыќазаарын, «абас, абас ауп исбаз, исахаз, аха изакуу нагӡаны исзеилымкааит, абнараҿы иќоу еилкаашьас иамоу хәа акрыбдыруазар?» хәа ари ашәарыцаҩ днеин ахуартлаӆь длазтцааит.

(64) — Уи мариоуп, зызбаху ухәо дуаҩӆсызар ќалап, дуаҩӆсызаргьы, дуаҩӆсымкуа даҩыстаазаргьы дыкны ара дузаасгоит акыр сутозар, — лхәеит атакуажә.

(65) — Аа, банацьалбеит, ус еиӆш былшозар, акыр бызымтода, ибтахыу быстоит, — ихәеит ашәарыцаҩ.

(66) — Уасак ашаха нахатцаны исыт, хәызбак сыт уажәазы, уи абнараҿы иубаз иаагара споит, — лхәеит.

(67) Ашәарыцаҩ хәызбак имоуа дыќазма, ауасагьы ашаха нахатцаны илитеит, ахәызбагьы литеит.

(68) Ахуртлаӆь афырхәа ауасагьы лыманы, ахәызбагьы лыманы ани абнаҿы атцла икутәаны аҿарпын азырхәоз иҿы днеит.

(69) Иара дзыкутәаз атцла амтцан даннеи, ауаса лкалыжьын, ахәызбажә ала исшьуеит хәа далагеит.

(70) Аха ауаса зшьуа ахы ауп ихитцәо, ари атакуажә ашьапала илшьуа далагеит, ашьапкуа акакала ихытцәтцәаны исшьуеит хәа даҿуп.

(71) Ачкун атцла дахьыкутәаз ари иќалтцоз длаӆшны ибон.

(72) — Ди, иќабтцо закуузеи, ас аӡәыр иќаитцома, ауаса аныршьуа ахы ауп ихыртцәо, ашьапы хыртцәо цьаракар иббахьоума, ирыщхауп, иагьтцасым, ашьапы хыбымтцәан, ибшьуазар, ахы хтцәа, — ихәеит. (Ачкун атцла дахьыкуу ани атакуажә дзыхунаӡом, умбо!)

(73) — Ааи, нанхеит, ауаса ашьышьа здыруеит, аха сымч акухом уи аҟаракуа удыруазар, улбааны усыцхраарауазеи! — лҳәеит лыгҽрыҵхатәны.

(74) Аҭакуажә лыгуҭакы аҷкун иалидыраауеиз, ашырҳәа атҵла длалбаан, ауаса шьны илиҭеит.

(75) Уаткоума, спиртума, анцәа идырп, рыжәтәык лыман, «нан абри ыжә, абри ахьсзушьыз аҟнытә, аӡбагьы уамк‘уеи» ҳәа иалҳәан, арыжәтә дҩахан ижәит.

(76) Арыжәтә анижә ашьҭахь, ани асаби рыцҳа, иичҳауази, аминуҭк дашьит, дхылга-ӡылго дааҟалеит.

(77) Лара дааимтцасын, даанылкылан (арыжәтә данашьы имч мачымхеи, рыцҳа!), ауаса зланалгаз ашахала дԥахны дааҿалхәан, даашьҭылхын, аҳ иҿы дылгеит.

(78) Аҳ иҿы дахьналгаз быжь-уадак рышә аартны наҟ днаигуаны дыҩнеикит.

(79) Уажә уа дыҩнахеит аҷкун, иҟаитцои?

(80) Ицә нахьхьи аԥсара итцахеит, дызлацаз, дахьцаз, дызгаз ҳәа акагьы издырӡом.

(81) Алада аҳәеит, аҩада аҳәеит, анахь аҳәеит, арахь аҳәеит, атәыла ацәа ахнахит, аха ацә аҷкун дахьцаз абом, ишьҭа абом, дахага аллаҳ идырп.

(82) Ари аҷкун абжь-уадак дахьыҩнаркыз акриҿартцон, амла дадырк‘уамызт, аха изхуарҭоузеи, ицә хьаас икит, ицә адырра аиҭар иҭаххеит, аха излеиҭои?

(83) Дхыркуакуо ус дыштәаз акумкуа ҟураанк ԥырны иааин аԥенцьыр аҿы иаакутәеит.

(84) Аҟураан аԥенцьыр ианаакутәа, аҷкун дхыркуакуо, дтцәыуо, дыштәаз анаба, «иухьзеи уара, узыртцәуои?» ҳәа иазтцааит.

(85) — Сызыртцәуо убри ауп, абригь, абригь аԥсҭа гуаҩаҿы хьа тцла дук сыкутәан, сҿырпын убра ахьа тцла икухеит, исымазар сҭахын, сгу аласырҿыԥьуамызт.

(86) Арахь сахьынаԥшуа адәахьы ауаа збоит, аха ауааи сареи ҳаицәажәар ҟалом, аҳ сауишьҭуам, абас сгуаҟ‘уа абра сыҩнахеит, — иҳәеит.

(87) — Ус акузар, уҿырпын са иузаазгоит, — аҳәан, аҿынанахан ицан ахаԥыц ибжьакны иаманы иааит.

(88) Иаман иааин, аԥенцьыр икылыршәны аҷкун дахьыҩнакыз инаҭеит.

(89) Аҷкун знык иҿырпын анимԥыхьашәагушьа, аԥенцьыр дкылатәаны архәара далагеит.

(90) Уажә ицә аагароуп дзыргуаҟ‘уа, умбо!

(91) Аҿырпын абжьы анраҳа, ани аԥсараҿы ишеизоз еиԥш, гыгшәыгс, ԥсаатәыс иҟаз зегьы еизеит, ари аҳ игуара ҭәит.

(92) Аҿарпын абжьы ацәгьы иаҳаит.

(93) Аҿарпын абжьы ацә ианаҳа, аҟуакҳәа илаҭрысны иҩны икукуаӡа аҿаанахеит.

(94) Ишааиуаз ашәкуа иларысын, ԥышьба знык ала иԥнаҽит, даҽа хԥа нхеит, ацә азтәыҩак хжәеит.

(95) Аха иаанымҽаскуа иаанхаз ашәкуагьы иахо, иагуо иԥнаҽын, иныҩнашылан, аҷкун аҟуаҟу дҩыкутәан, иҩдәылԥан ицеит.

(96) Аха иалаухи, ацә ахы ахькыднаҟьаз егьиз ахбылҩышы тцысит.

(97) Аҷкун дама аԥсҭаҿы иахьнеиз, адырҩагь атцла дыкунатцеит.

(98) — Улымбаан ҳәа уасымҳәази, узылбаази?

(99) Ухунаны уҭыԥ аҿы укутәа, са смаакуа улымбаан, — ҳәа ус ианаҳәеит.

(100) Знык, ҩынтә ицеит, ачкун иху аанагеит, аха ахы бжьымсхьази, ҽенак иахьыҩҭытцыз, ацә ҭахеит, куарак аҿы ишнеиуаз аблахатц гьажьын, абни акуара иҭахан, уаха изҭымтцӡеит, уа иҭахеит.

(101) Ачкун атцла дахьыкутәаз амла дакит, дыҧшит, дыҧшит, аха ицә ибом, арахь егьааиуам, ахы ахьархаз издырӡом.

(102) Аҿарпын аирхәо далагеит, аха иабаќоу, ицә ыќаӡам.

(103) Алахәа ахьыкутәаз ус ахәеит: — Уара, уара узааӡаз уцә акуара иҭахан иҧсит.

(104) Иахьыҧсызгьы абригь, абригь аҭыҧ аҿоуп.

(105) Ачкун иќаитцагушьоиз, ҭынхас имаз ицә акун, уаха, хыхь ажәҩан, тцаќа адгьыл, дзыкугуҕʻуа хәа акагьы имаӡамызт.

(106) Ицә иҭахаз, иахьҭахаз алахәа ианианахәа, атцла дзыкутәаз длалбаан, иҿынеихан, ицә ахьҭахаз иҧшааит.

(107) Уаха ихы ахьигоз анимоу, ацә амгуацәа ааирќьан, хыла ацә амгуацәа дылҭалан, иаргьы уа ацә амгуацәа дылҭаҧсы дцеит.

(108) Анҧса «бзиа» лҧаҧса «дшылааӡаз» абас ауп.

Transcription

(1) A-cʷ j-áaʒa-z á-č’ʲk’ʷən
the-bull Rel-bring up-Stat.Past .NF the-boy
The Boy Brought up by a Bull

(2) Də́-q’a-n nxajʷə́-k’.
he-be-Stat.Past peasant-one
There was once a peasant.

(3) Abrə́j a-nxajʷə́ a-phʷə́s d-jə́-ma-n, jə́-č’ʲk’ʷən
this the-peasant the-wife her-he-have-Stat.Past.Fin his-boy
də́-q’a-n.
he-be-Stat.Past.Fin
This peasant had a wife and (he also had) a son.

(4) J-šə́-q’a-z [a-]ák’ʷə-m-k’ʷa, abrə́j a-nxajʷə́ jə-phʷə́s
they-how-be-Stat.Past.NF [it-]be-not-Abs this the-peasant his-wife
də-psə́-jt’.
she-die-(Aor)-Fin
One day, the man’s wife died. (*As they were living their life,* the man’s wife died).

(5) Jə-pħʷə́s d-anə-psə́ á-šʲtaxʲ ak’ə́r áamta d-ǯʲabá-jt’,
his-wife she-when-die-(Aor.NF) it-after a long time he-mourn-(Aor)-Fin
d-gʷərjʷá-jt’ agʲə́jt’, axá ac’əxʷt’ʷán áʒʷ
he-grieve-(Aor)-Fin and so on but after all someone
d-aa-jə-m-gá-r ϕ-q’a-m-lá-zt’,

her-Prev-he-Neg-bring-Cond. [it-]Prev-Neg-be possible-Past.Ind.Fin
dačá phʷə́s-k' d-aa-j-gá-jt'.
other wife-one her-Prev-he-bring-(Aor)-Fin

After his wife's death, for a long time the man mourned her and grieved for her, but finally he had to bring along another wife, so he brought along another wife.

(6) J-aa-j-gá-z a-pħʷə́s anə́j jə́-č'ʲk'ʷən
Rel-Prev-he-bring-Past.Ind.NF the-wife that his-boy
d-aa-l-bá-r ø-q'a-m-la-ʒá-jt'.
him-Par-she-care for-Cond [it-]Prev-Neg-become-Emph-(Aor)-Fin

The wife that he had brought along did not look after his son.

(7) — Wará abrə́j a-xʷəč'ʲə́ d-aħ-šʲə́-p', j-á-w-hʷa-wa-j,
you.M this the-child him-we-kill-Fut.1 what-[him?]-to-you-say-Dyn-Qu
ǯʲará ħa-n-tə́-c'-nə ħ-ca-wá-zargʲə, wə́s-k'
somewhere we-Par-Prev-go out-Abs we-go-Dyn-even if work-one
ø-aa-w-[w]á-zargʲə jará d-aħ-pərxága-wp', — ħʷa l-xác'a
[it]-we-do-Dyn-even if he he-us-disturb-Stat.Pres.Fin SP her-husband
j-a-l-ħʷa-wá d-á-la-ga-jt' lassə́-lassə́.
[it]-him-to-she-say-Abs she-it-Prev-begin-(Aor)-Fin often

'Hey! Let's kill this boy! What do you say to that? You see, wherever we go, whatever we do, he will only be a problem for us,' she started to ask her husband repeatedly.

(8) Arə́j znə́ jə-l-ħʷá-jt', jʷə́-nt'ʷ jə-l-ħʷá-jt', xə́-nt'ʷ
she once it-she-say-(Aor)-Fin two-times it-she-say-(Aor)-Fin three-times
jə-l-ħʷá-jt', axá a-nxajʷə́ rə́cħa jə́-č'ʲk'ʷən
it-she-say-(Aor)-Fin but the-peasant poor his-boy
də-j-zə́-gʷaɣʲ-wa-m, jə́-q'a-j-c'a-rə-j, d-jə-m-gʷaɣʲə́-rgʲə
he-him-Pot-dare-Dyn-Neg what-Prev-he-do-Fut.I-Qu him-he-Neg-dare-even if
jə-pħʷə́s d-jə́-c'ə-c'-nə d-cá-r ħʷa d-šʷa-wá-jt'.
his-wife she-him-Prev-go out from-Abs she-go-Cond SP he-worry-Dyn-Fin

She said it once. She said it twice, she said it three times. But the poor peasant couldn't kill his son. What could he do? If he didn't do it, he was afraid that his wife would leave him.

(9) Ašʲtaxʲ j-gʷə́ ø-an-pə́-l-c'ʷa-ʒa, «sə́-č'ʲk'ʷən zac'ʷə́
After that his-heart [it-]when-Prev-she-break-Emph-(Aor.NF) my-boy single
j-sə́-ma-w d-abá-s-taxə-w, də-s-šʲə́-p', sə-pħʷə́s
Rel-I-have-Stat.Pres.NF him-where-I-want-Stat.Pres.NF him-I-kill-Fut.I.Fin my-wife
sə́-mac' ø-l-w-[w]á-jt'» ø-j-ħʷá-n, arə́j a-nxajʷə́ rə́cħa
my-care [it-]she-do-Dyn-Fin [it-]he-say-(Aor)-Past.Ind.Fin this the-peasant poor
jə́-č'ʲk'ʷən də-z-lá-j-šʲə-šaz á-ħʷəzba a-x-rá
his-boy him-Rel-with-he-kill-Cond.2.NF the-knife the-sharpen- Masd
d-á-la-ga-jt'.

he-it-Prev-begin-(Aor)-Fin

Afterwards, he got really fed up with her, and said to her, 'I have only one son, why do I need him? I shall kill him. My wife will look after me'. Then the poor peasant started sharpening the knife that he was going to use to kill his son.

(10) A-ħʷəzba a-x-rá d-a-č'ə́-wp' wažʷə́
the-knife the-sharpen- Masd he-it-be engaged in-Stat.Pres now
a-šʲašʷə́r-a-č'ə d-t'ʷa-nə́.
the-shade-it-in he-sit-Abs

Now, he was sitting in the shade, sharpening the knife.

(11) A-mákʲa jə́-kʷ-šʲ-wa j-áħʷəzba a-x-rá
the-whetstone it-Prev-rub-Abs his-knife the-sharpen-Masd
d-a-č'ə́-wp'.
he-it-be engaged in-Stat.Pres.Fin

He sharpened the knife, rubbing it against a whetstone.

(12) Arə́j cʷ-k'ə́ jə́-ma-n, a-xʷəč'ʲə́ j-gʷárə-j-x-la-wa-n,
he bull-one [it]-he-have-Stat.Past the-child it-Prev-he-pasture-iterative-Dyn-Impf
j-gʷára-j-c'a-la-wa-n, ak'r-a-č'á-j-c'a-wa-n
it-Prev-he-drive into the farmyard-iterative-Dyn-Impf.Fin something-it-Prev-he-feed-Dyn-Impf.Fin
ak'r-a-jə́-r-žʷ-wa-n.
something-it-he-Caus-drink-Dyn-Impf.Fin

He had a bull. His child would often take the bull grazing, driving it into the farm, feeding it and giving it water to drink.

(13) Arə́j ačnə́ a-xʷəč'ʲə́ á-cʷ ak'r-a-č'a-c'a-nə́, jə́-ma-nə
this on that day the-child the-bull something-it-Prev-feed-Abs [it]-he-have-Abs
a-šʲašʷə́r-a-č'ə d-an-aá-j, «s-áb, arə́j á-ħʷəzba
the-shade-its-in he-when-Prev-come hither.Aor.NF my-father this the-knife
jə́-w-x-wa j-á-lə-w-xə-j, j-zə́-w-taxə-j?»
Rel-you-sharpen-Pres.NF what-it-Prev-you.M-choose-Qu it-why-you-want-Qu
ħʷa j-áb d-jə-z-c'aá-jt'.
SP his-father he-him-Prev-ask-(Aor)-Fin

One day, the boy fed the bull and when he lead it into the shade, the boy saw his father sharpening the knife and asked his father, 'Father, why are you sharpening the knife like that? What are you going to use it for?'

(14) — ħá-cʷ ∅-ħ-šʲə́-p', a-k'ʷác ∅-ħ-fá-p', wəbrə́j a-z-á-wp'
our-bull [it-]we-kill-Fut.I.Fin the-meat [it-]we-eat-Fut.I it it-for-be-Stat.Pres
s-áħʷəzba ∅-zə́-s-x-wa, — ∅-j-ħʷá-jt' [a-]áb, a-xʷəč'ʲə́
my-knife [it-]why-I-sharpen-Pres.NF [it-]he-say-(Aor)-Fin the-father the-child
də-j-žʲá-rc ∅-á-wp' j-zə́-j-hʷa-wa wažʷə́.

him-he-deceive-in order to [it-]be-Stat.Pres it-why-he-say-Dyn.NF now

'We are going to kill the bull and eat the meat. That's why I'm sharpening the knife'. He said it to fool the boy.

(15) Ab á-cʷ ø-ħ-šʲ-wá-jt' ø-anə́-j-ħʷa, a-xʷəčʼʲə́ akʼʲažə́hʷa
father the-bull [it-]we-kill-Dyn-Fin [it-]when-he-say.Aor.NF the-child bitter tears
a-cʼʷə́wa-ra d-á-la-ga-jt'.
the-cry-Masd he-it-Prev-begin-(Aor)-Fin

When the father said, 'We are going to kill the bull,' the boy burst out crying uncontrollably.

(16) — Z-akʼʷə́-w-zaj, wará w-zə-r-cʼʷə́wa-wa, a-cʼʷə́wa-ra
what-be-Stat.Pres.NF-Qu you.M you.M-Rel-Caus-cry-Pres.NF the-cry-Masd
w-a-qʼʷə́-cʼ-nə, w-ca-nə́ a-ʒarcʼʷə́j ø-aa-gá,
you-it-Prev-stop-Abs you.M-go-Abs the-bent twig [it-]Prev-bring.Imp
— ø-j-ħʷá-jt' [a-]áb.
[it-]he-say-(Aor)-Fin the-father

'What's wrong? Why are you crying? Stop crying. Come over here, bring me that bent twig,' his father said.

(17) J-áb d-an-jə́-kʷ-cʷqʼʲa, a-ʒárcʼʷə́j
his-father he-when-him-Prev-shout at.Aor.NF the-bent twig
[ø]-aa-z-ga-wá-jt' ħʷa a-xʷəčʼʲə́ d-cʼʷə́wa-wa
[it]-Prev-I-bring-Dyn-Fin SP the-child he-cry-Abs
də-š-ná-j-wa-z á-cʷ d-a-bá-jt'.
he-how-Prev-go thither-Impf.NF the-bull him-it-see-(Aor)-Fin

Because his father shouted at him, the boy said, 'I will bring the bent twig with me,' and he walked over with the twig, crying. The bull saw him going there.

(18) — W-zə-r-cʼʷə́wa-wa-zaj, j-wə́-xʲ-zaj? — ø-a-ħʷá-n
you.M-what-Caus-cry-Dyn-Qu what-you.M-happen to-(Aor)-Qu [it-]it-say-Past.Ind.Fin
á-cʷ ø-j-a-z-cʼáa-jt'.
the-bull [it-]him-to-Prev-ask-(Aor)-Fin

'Why are you crying? What has happened?' the bull said, asking him.

(19) — S-abá-m-cʼʷwa-wa, s-áb j-áħʷəzba a-mákʲa
I-how-Neg-cry-Dyn.NF my-father his-knife the-whetstone
jə́-kʷ-cʼa-nə a-x-rá d-a-čʼə́-wp',
[it]-him-Prev-put on-Abs the-sharpen-Masd he-it-be engaged in-Stat.Pres
a-ʒarcʼʷə́j ø-aa-gá, á-cʷ ø-ħ-šʲə́-p' ħʷa
the-bent twig [it]-Prev-bring.Imp the-bull [it-]we-kill-Fut.I SP
ø-s-á-j-ħʷa-jt', — ø-j-ħʷá-jt' á-xʷəčʼʲə.
[it-]me-to-he-say-(Aor)-Fin [it-]he-say-(Aor)-Fin the-child

The boy said to the bull, 'Why can't I stop crying? My father is sharpening his knife on the whetstone.

He said to me, 'Bring me that bent twig. Let's kill the bull."

(20) — Sará s-ák'ʷ-ʒa-m jǝ́-r-šʲ-wa, wǝ-j-žʲá-jt'
I me-be-Emph-Neg Rel-they-kill-Pres.NF you.M-he-deceive-(Aor)-Fin
ák'ʷǝmzar jǝ́-j-šʲǝ-rc jǝ́-j-taxǝ-w wará w-á-wp',
simply Rel-he-kill-in order to Rel-he-want-Stat.Pres.NF you.M you.M-be-Stat.Pres
w-ánǝpsa táxa jǝ́-lǝ-m-ta-jt', wará jǝ-w-xǝ-rq'ʲa-nǝ́
your.M-stepmother rest [it]-him-she-Neg-give-(Aor)-Fin you.M him-you.M-Prev-accuse-Abs
janágʲ a-tǝʒšʷá ø-rǝ́-lǝjbax-wa-jt', w-xʷǝč'ʲǝ́ d-šʲǝ́
always the-quarrel [it-]they-quarrel with each other-Dyn-Fin your.M-child him-kill.Imp
ħʷa j-á-l-ħʷa-wa-jžʲtaj a-k'ǝ́r ø-aa-c'-wá-jt'.
SP [it]-him-to-she-say-Dyn-since a long time [it-]Prev-pass-Dyn-Fin
'They aren't going to kill me. They have fooled you. You are the one that they want to kill. Your stepmother has been hounding him a lot. She has been complaining about you to him, and they have been arguing a lot with each other. It has been a long time since she said to him: 'Kill your child'.

(21) «D-abá-ħ-taxǝ-w, d-aħ-šʲǝ́-p', nas ħará
him-where-we-need-Stat.Pres.NF him-we-kill-Fut.1 then we
j-š-áħ-taxǝ-w ħ-q'a-lá-p'» ħʷa
it-how-we-want-Stat.Pres.NF we-Prev-become-Fut.I SP
d-a[a]-a-q'ʷǝ́-m-c'-ʒa-k'ʷa w-áb
he-Par-it-Prev-Neg-stop-Emph-Abs your.M-father
d-anǝ-xtá-l-k'-ʒa, jar-gʲǝ́ j-gʷǝ́
him-when-Prev-she-insist-Emph.Aor.NF he-also his-heart
anǝ-p-c'ʷa-ʒá, d-á-kʷ-šaħat-xa-jt',
[it]-when-Prev-be broken-Emph.Aor.NF he-it-Prev-agree-become-(Aor)-Fin
wǝ-j-šʲǝ́-rc j-á-kʷǝ-j-k'ǝ-jt', — ø-a-ħʷá-jt' á-cʷ.
you-he-kill-Purp it-it-Prev-he-decide-(Aor)-Fin [it-]it-say-(Aor)-Fin the-bull
The bull told him, 'She said, 'Why do we need that child? Let's kill him. If we do so, we'll be able to do whatever we like'. Your father couldn't stop her. She demanded it of your father, it broke his heart, and finally he agreed to it. He decided to kill you'.

(22) — Nas jǝ-špá-sǝ-psǝ́xʷa-w, jǝ-špá-q'a-s-c'a-rǝ-j?
then it-how-my-possibility-Stat.Pres.NF it-how-Prev-I-do-Fut.I.NF -Qu
— j-hʷá-n, jnajmatʷanǝ́ jejhágʲǝ a-c'ʷǝ́wa-ra
[it-]he-say-Past.Ind.Fin with tears of grief even more the-cry-Masd
d-á-la-ga-jt' a-xʷǝč'ʲǝ́.
he-it-Prev-begin-(Aor)-Fin the-child
'What can I do? What should I do?' the boy cried out aloud in tears of agony, crying even more.

(23) — Jǝ́-q'a-w-c'a-ra wǝj ø-á-wp', s-ax-č'á-w-ħʷa-wa,
Rel-Prev-you-do-should that [it-]be-Stat.Pres me-where-Prev-you.M-tie-Pres.NF
wbrá xaħʷǝ́-k' [ø]-šʲtá-wp', xħʷá-k'-gʲǝ wbrá j-k'á-ršʷǝ-wp',

there stone-one [it]-be lying-Stat.Pres.Fin comb-one-also there it-Prev-be thrown-Stat.Pres.Fin
patlə́k'a-k'-gʲə, a-č'arp'ə́n-gʲə wbrá jə́-q'a-wp', wbart
bottle-one-also the-flute-also there they-exist-Stat.Pres those
áa-šʲtə-x-nə, j-wə́-ma-nə w-aá, nas
[them]-Par-Prev-take up-Abs them-you.M-have-Abs you.M-come hither.Imp then
w-ábə-j w-ánpsa-j wə-r-šʲ-áanʒa sa
your.M-father-and your.M-stepmother-and you.M-they-kill-before I
wə-r-cʷə́-z-ga-wa-jt', wə-m-šʷá-n, — ø-a-ħʷá-jt'
you.M-them-Prev-I-take away from-Dyn-Fin you.M-Neg-fear-Proh [it-]it-say-(Aor)-Fin
á-cʷ.
the-bull

The bull told him, 'This is what you must do. See the stone over there that you tied me to? There is a comb over there. There are also a bottle and a flute over there. Pick them up and bring them over here! And before your father and stepmother kill you, I will lift you up from them. Don't fear!

(24) A-cʷ d-n-[a]-a-pə́-za-n, jə́-ma
the-bull he-Par-[it]-Prev-lead-Past.Ind.Fin it-have.Abs
j-č'ə́-na-j-xa-n, də-n-k'ə́l-sə-n, á-cʷ
his-SV-Prev-he-set out-Past.Ind.Fin he-Par-Prev-go out-Past.Ind.Fin the-bull
axʲ-čʲá-j-ħʷa-la-wa-z a-tə́p á-č'ə a-č'arp'ə́n-gʲə, a-xáħʷ-gʲə
[it]-where-Prev-he-tie-Iterative-Impf.NF the-place it-in the-flute-also the-stone-also
a-xhʷa-gʲə́, a-patlə́k'a-gʲə ø-áa-šʲtə-j-xə-n, də́-jʷ-nə
the-comb-also the-bottle-also [them-]Par-Prev-he-take up-Past.Ind he-run-Abs
d-aa-k'ə́l-sə-n, d-an-n-á-d-gəla,
he-Par-Prev-go through-Past.Ind he-when-Par-it-Prev-stand.by-(Aor.NF)
«wə́-pa-nə w-sə́-kʷ-t'ʷa!» ø-a-ħʷá-n, a-cʷ á-bɣa
you.M-jump-Abs you.M-me-Prev(on)-sit down.Imp [it-]it-say-Past.Ind.Fin the-bull the-back
d-jʷ-á-kʷ-t'ʷa-jt'.
he-Par-it-Prev(on)-sit down-(Aor)-Fin

He led the bull and left, going outside. And then at the place where he used to tie the bull up, he picked up the stone and the flute and comb and bottle, ran outside, and when he stood beside the bull, the bull said , 'Jump up on to my back!' and he got up onto the bull's back.

(25) A-xʷəč'ʲə́ d-an-jʷ-á-kʷ-t'ʷa, á-cʷ
the-child he-when-Par-it-Prev(on)-sit down-(Aor.NF) the-bull
ø-jʷá-c'q'ʲa-n jə́-jʷ-t'.
[it-]Prev-leap-Past.Ind.Fin it-run-(Aor)-Fin

When the boy sat down there, the bull rose up and flew away.

(26) A-cʷ ø-jʷá-c'q'ʲa-n jə́-jʷ-nə j-an-dʷə́kʷ-la,
the-bull [it-]Prev-leap-Past.Ind it-run-Abs it-when-Prev-set out-(Aor.NF)
arə́j á-č'ʲk'ʷən j-ánəpsa j-a-xʷtá-mə-z
this the-boy his-stepmother Rel-it-be necessary-Neg-Stat.Past.NF
ø-axʲə́-l-ħʷa-xʲa-z a-zə́ d-ħʷa-xá-jt', j-áb a-ħʷá

[it]-that-she-say-Plupf-NF it-for she-pig-become-(Aor)-Fin his-father the-pig
d-á-kʷ-t'ʷa-nə d-dʷə́kʷ-la-jt'.
he-it-Prev(on)-sit down-Abs he-Prev-set out-(Aor)-Fin
The bull rose up and flew away. The boys' stepmother turned into a pig because she had some something that she shouldn't have said. The boy's father sat down on the pig's back and set out.

(27) A-č'ʲk'ʷən j-áb a-ħʷá d-á-kʷ-t'ʷa-nə á-cʷ
the-boy his-father the-pig he-it-Prev(on)-sit down-Abs the-bull
d-á-šʲta-la-n d-a-xʲ-ʒa-wá d-á-la-ga-jt'.
he-it-Prev-track-Past.Ind.Fin he-it-Prev-catch up with-Abs he-it-Prev-begin-(Aor)-Fin
The boy's father sat down on the pig's back and chased after the bull, and started to catch up with the bull.

(28) — ħáj, w-ánəpsa á-[a]žʷra-cʷgʲa d-ħʷa-xá-n, a-ħʷá
oh your.M-stepmother the-old age-bad she-pig-become-Past.Ind.Fin the-pig
w-áb d-á-kʷ-t'ʷa-nə d-ħá-šʲta-la-nə
your.M-father he-it-Prev(on)-sit down-Abs he-us-Prev-track-Abs
d-aa-wá-jt', abár, abár wažʷəšʲtá d-ħa-xʲ-ʒa-wá-jt'.
he-come hither-Dyn-Fin look look now he-us-Prev-catch up with-Dyn-Fin
The bull said, 'Yes. Your old stepmother has turned into a pig. And your father has sat down on the back of that pig and has come looking for us. Look! Look! He is just about to catch up with us'.

(29) W-patlə́k'a j-ø-tá-w a-ʒə́ ø-k'a-tʷá
your.M-bottle Rel-[it-]be in-Stat.Pres.NF the-water [it-]Prev-sprinkle.Imp
há-šʲtaxʲq'a, — ø-a-hʷá-jt' á-cʷ.
us-behind [it-]it-say-(Aor)-Fin the-bull
'Sprinkle the water in your bottle behind us,' said the bull.

(30) A-cʷ as ø-an-a-ħʷá, j-patlə́k'a j-ø-tá-z
the-bull thus [it-]when-it-say-(Aor.NF) his-bottle Rel-[it-]be in-Stat.Past.NF
a-ʒə́ jə́-šʲtaxʲq'a j-k'á-j-tʷa-jt' á-č'ʲk'ʷən.
the-water him-behind it-Prev-he-sprinkle-(Aor)-Fin the-boy
And just as the bull was saying this, the boy sprinkled the water that was in the bottle behind him.

(31) Rə́-šʲtaxʲq'a ø-mšə́n-xa-jt' j-patlə́k'a j-ø-tá-z
them-behind [it-]sea-become-(Aor)-Fin his-bottle Rel-[it-]be in-Stat.Past.NF
a-ʒə́ ø-an-k'á-j-tʷa.
the-water [it-]when-Prev-he-sprinkle.Aor.NF
As he sprinkled the water that was in the bottle, it turned into a sea.

(32) Jə-mšə́n-xa-jt' axá jə-z-xʷartá-w-zaj, a-ħʷá-žʷ a-mšə́n
it-sea-become-(Aor)-Fin but it-what-aid-Stat.Pres.NF-Qu the-pig-bad the-sea
a-č'ə́ j-aan-gə́la-wa jə́-q'a-w-ma, a-č-ta-ná-žʲə-n

it-in it-Prev-stop-Abs it-be-Stat.Pres.NF-Qu its-self-Prev-it-throw-Past.Ind.Fin
jə-ʒsa-nə́ j-dʷə́kʷ-la-jt'.
it-swim-Abs it-Prev-set out-(Aor)-Fin
It turned into a sea. But what help would that be to them? Would the evil pig be stopped at the sea? The pig flung itself into the sea and started to swim.

(33) A-mšə́n ø-a[a]-ajmgʷ-ħʷa-nə́ jə́-rə-n, á-cʷ
the-sea [it-]Par-Prev-go through-Abs it-[it]-cross-Past.Ind.Fin the-bull
j-a-xʲ-ʒa-wá j-á-la-ga-jt'.
it-it-Prev-catch up with-Abs it-it-Prev-begin-(Aor)-Fin
The pig crossed the sea and started to catch up with the bull.

(34) — Arə́j a-ħʷá-žʷ ø-ħa-xʲ-ʒa-wá-jt' wəmbawá,
this the-pig-bad [it-]us-Prev-catch up with-Dyn-Fin look
wə-xħʷá ø-k'á-ršʷ wə́-šʲtaxʲq'a! — ø-a-ħʷá-jt' á-cʷ.
your.M-comb [it-]Prev-throw.Imp you.M-behind [it-]it-say-(Aor)-Fin the-bull
'Will this evil pig really be able to catch up with us? Throw your comb down behind you!' the bull said.

(35) A-cʷ as ø-an-a-ħʷá, a-č'ʲk'ʷən jə-xħʷá jə́-šʲtaxʲq'a
the-bull thus [it-]when-it-say.Aor.NF the-boy his-comb him-behind
j-k'a-jə́-ršʷə-jt', jə-xħʷá ø-an-k'a-jə́-ršʷ, jə́-šʲtaxʲq'a
it-Prev-he-throw-(Aor)-Fin his-comb [it-]when-Prev-he-throw-(Aor.NF) him-behind
jaxabalák'ʲ ø-bnara-xá-jt', axá a-ħʷá-žʷ á-bna-č'
everywhere [it-]luxuriant forest-become-(Aor)-Fin but the-pig-bad the-forest-in
j-aan-gə́la-wa, á-bna jə-n-na-k'ə́la-wa jə́-q'a-z-ma,
it-Prev-stop-Abs the-forest it-Prev-it-detain-Abs it-be-Stat.Past.NF-Qu
á-bnara j-l-á-sə-n, naq'
the-luxuriant forest it-Par-it-rush into-Past.Ind.Fin there
j-jʷə́-l-sə-n, á-cʷ j-a-xʲ-ʒa-wá
it-Par-Prev-pass through-Past.Ind.Fin the-bull it-it-Prev-catch up with-Abs
j-á-la-ga-jt'.
it-it-Prev-begin-(Aor)-Fin
Just as the bull was saying that, the boy threw the comb behind him. When he tossed his comb away behind him, the whole area behind turned into a luxuriant forest. Do you think the forest was able to stop the evil pig? The pig dashed into the forest and passed through it, and started to catch up with the bull.

(36) — W-ánəpsa a-ħʷá-žʷə-j w-ábə-j
your.M-stepmother the-pig-bad-and your.M-father-and
ø-ħa-xʲ-ʒa-wá-jt' ajtáx wəmbawá, wə́-šʲtaxʲq'a
[they-]us-Prev-catch up with-Dyn-Fin again look you.M-behind
w-xʲá-hʷ-nə w-xáhʷ ø-k'á-žʲ! — hʷa á-cʷ

you.M-Prev(back)-turn-Abs your.M-stone [it-]Prev(on surface)-throw.Imp SP the-bull
a-xʷəč'ʲə́ wəs ø-j-á-na-ħʷa-jt'.
the-child thus [it]-him-to-it-say-(Aor)-Fin
'Look. Your stepmother, the evil pig and your father are catching up with us again. Turn around and throw the stone out!' the bull said to the boy.

(37) A-cʷ as ø-an-a-ħʷá, á-č'ʲk'ʷən xʷəč'ʲə́ j-xáħʷ jə-šʲtaxʲq'a
the-bull thus [it-]when-it-say.Aor.NF the-boy little his-stone him-behind
j-k'a-jə́-žʲ-t'.
it-Prev-he-throw down-(Aor)-Fin
And just as the bull was speaking, the little boy threw the stone away down behind him.

(38) Jə́-šʲtaxʲq'a a-xaħʷ ø-an-k'a-jə́-žʲ, a-xaħʷ-gʷára
him-behind the-stone [it-]when-Prev-he-throw down.Aor.NF the-stone-fence
də́w-kʷa ø-q'a-lá-jt'.
big-Pl [they-]Prev-become-(Aor)-Fin
When he threw the stone down behind him, it turned into many big stone walls.

(39) A-ħʷá ø-ajxá-jt', ø-ajxá-jt', axá
the-pig [it-]be dying to go-(Aor)-Fin [it-]be dying to go-(Aor)-Fin but
a-xahʷ-gʷára-kʷa j-zə-r-xə́-m-c'ə-jt'.
the-stone-fence-Pl it-Pot-them-Prev-Neg-cross-(Aor)-Fin
The pig tried desperately to catch up with them, but it couldn't cross over the large stone walls.

(40) Wa jə-n-xá-jt', a-xʷə́č'ʲ j-áb-gʲə nas
there it-Prev-remain-(Aor)-Fin the-child his-father-also then
d-abá-wə-šʲt-wa-z, wa d-aan-xá-jt'.
him-where-Prev-let go-Dyn-Impf.NF there he-Prev-remain-(Aor)-Fin
The pig stopped there. Where do you think the boy's father could have gone at that time? He remained there as well.

(41) A-č'ʲk'ʷən xʷəč'ʲə́ á-cʷ d-á-ma-nə j-ca-wá, j-ca-wá, j-ca-wá,
the-boy little the-bull him-it-have-Abs it-go-Abs it-go-Abs it-go-Abs
j-axʲə́nʒa-[a]-l-ša-wa-z j-cá-jt'.
it-until-it-Prev-be able to-Impf.NF it-go-(Aor)-Fin
The bull led the boy, walking as far as it was able to.

(42) J-an-áapsa, pstá gʷájʷa-k' a-č'ə́ j-aan-gə́l-t'.
it-when-get tired-(Aor.NF) valley deep-one it-in it-Prev-stop-(Aor)-Fin
When the bull got tired, it stopped in a deep valley.

(43) — Aħə́h, wažʷəšʲtá abrá wə-l-baá, sar-gʲə́ abrá
now.then! now here you.M-Prev-get down.Imp I-also here

a-k'rə-s-fá-p, warā abrá w-t'ʷá, jagʲáǯʲara s-cá-r-gʲə,
the-Dummy-I-eat-Fut.I you.M here you.M-sit.Imp wherever I-go-if-even
ará s-aa-wá-jt', wə-s-šʲ-wá-m, á-mla w-a-sə-r-k'-wá-m,
here I-come-Dyn-Fin you.M-I-kill-Dyn-Neg the-hunger you.M-it-I-Caus-catch-Dyn-Neg
aħaħáj ak'ə́ w-a-cʷə́-m-šʷa-n, — ħʷa á-cʷ
Cheer up! something you.M-it-Prev-Neg-be afraid-Proh SP the-bull
á-č'ʲk'ʷən wəs ø-j-á-na-ħʷa-jt'.
the-boy so [it-]him-to-it-say-(Aor)-Fin

'Hey you! Please get off your horse here. I will have a meal here as well. Please sit here. Wherever I may go, I will return. I won't kill you. I won't starve you. Cheer up! You have nothing to fear,' the bull said to the boy.

(44) — Ará s-t'ʷa-r, gəgšʷə́g-k' aá-j-r s-a-m-fa-wá-j,
here I-sit-if wild animal-one Prev-come-if me-it-Neg-eat-Dyn-Qu
— ø-jə-ħʷá-jt' á-č'ʲk'ʷən.
[it-]he-say-(Aor)-Fin the-boy

'If I sit down here and a wild animal comes along, won't it eat me?' the boy asked.

(45) Abrá á-c'la-č'ə wə-xʷna-nə́ wə́-kʷ-t'ʷa, á-mla
here the-tree-at you-climb-Abs you-Prev (on)-sit.Imp the-hunger
w-an-a-k'-lák'ʲ, a-č'arp'ə́n j-wə́-ma-w a-rħʷa-rá
you-when-it-catch-LA the-flute Rel-you-have-NF the-to play-masd
w-á-la-ga, a-č'arp'ə́n a-rħʷa-rá w-an-á-la-ga-lak'ʲ,
you-it-Prev-begin.Imp the-flute to play-masd you-when-it-Prev-begin-Lak
s-axʲə́-q'azaa-lák'-gʲə warā w-č'arpə́n a-bžʲə́ sa
I-where-be-whenever-even you your-flute its-voice I
j-s-a-ħa-wá-jt'.
it-me-to-be audible-Dyn-Fin

'Climb this tree and sit in it. If you are hungry, begin to play the flute you have! When you start to play the flute, no matter where I am, I will hear it.

(46) Nas á-fat'ʷ sa jə-w-z-aa-z-ga-wá-jt'.
then the-food I it-you.M-for-Prev-I-bring-Dyn-Fin

Then I will bring you food.

(47) Amala, j-w-á-s-ħʷa-wa wəbrə́j [a-]á-wp', sa s-aá-nʒa, sa
only Rel-you.M-to-I-say-Dyn.NF it it-be-Stat.Fin I I-come-until I
sə́-q'a-m-k'ʷa á-c'la w-lə-m-baá-n, — ø-a-ħʷá-jt' á-cʷ.
I-be-Neg-Abs the-tree you.M-Prev-Neg-get down-Proh [it-]it-say-(Aor)-Fin the-bull

But I want to say this to you: Until I come back, don't come down from the tree!' the bull said.

(48) A-cʷ a-č'ə́-na-na-xa-n ħʷ-rá j-cá-jt'.
the-bull its-SV-Prev-it-depart-Past.Ind.Fin to feed-Masd it-go-(Aor)-Fin

The bull then went away to eat.

(49) A-č'ʲk'ʷən á-mla d-an-a-k'-lák'ʲ, a-č'arp'ə́n a-rħʷa-rá
the-boy the-hunger him-when-it-catch-LA the-flute the-play-Masd
d-á-la-ga-wa-n, a-č'arp'ə́n a-bžʲə́ á-cʷ ø-axʲə́-q'azaa-lak'ʲ
he-it-Prev-begin-Dyn-Impf the-flute its-voice the-bull [it-]where-be-Lak
j-a-ħa-wá-n, á-mla d-š-a-k'ə́-z wəj á-la
it-[it]-to-hear-Dyn-Impf.Fin the-hunger him-how-it-catch-Past.Ind.NF that it-by
j-a-də́r-wa-n, á-fat'ʷ ø-aa-ga-nə́ j-č'a-na-c'a-wá-n.
it-it-know-Dyn-Impf.Fin the-food [it-]Prev-bring-Abs it-[to him]-Prev-it-feed-Dyn-Impf.Fin
When the boy became hungry, he would start to play the flute. Wherever the bull was, when he heard the flute, from the sound of the flute, he would know how hungry the boy was. The bull would bring him food and give it to him.

(50) Abás jə-šə́-q'a-z [a-]ák'ʷə-m-k'ʷa məz-k'ə́,
thus they-how-be-Stat.Past.NF [it-]copula-Neg-Abs month-one
jʷə-mz ø-c'ə́-jt'.
two-months [they-]pass-(Aor)-Fin
In this way they lived for one month, then two.

(51) Arə́j á-č'ʲk'ʷən a-č'arp'ə́n ø-a-j-rħʷa-wá d-an-á-la-ga-lak'ʲ,
this the-boy the-flute [it-]it-he-play-Abs.Pres he-when-it-Prev-begin-Lak
a-pstá a-c'ára-kʷa, á-šʷarax a-č'arp'ə́n a-bžʲə́
the-valley its-bird-Pl its-wild animal the-flute its-voice
ø-z-m-a-ħá-cəz racʷá-m-zəj, zagʲə́ ø-ajza-wá-n.
[it]-Rel-Neg-to-hear-Plupf.NF many-Neg-Qu all [they]-gather-Dyn-Impf.Fin
When the boy started to play the flute, all the birds and animals in the valley, having never heard the sound of a flute, gathered together.

(52) A-č'arp'ə́n a-bžʲə́ xaaʒá jə-z-a-ħa-wá-z j-ájza-nə
the-flute its-voice pleasantly it-Rel-to-hear-Dyn-Impf.NF they-gather-Abs
á-č'ʲk'ʷən d-zə-kʷ-t'ʷá-z á-c'la aajgʷá-səjgʷa
the-boy he-Rel-Prev-sit-Stat.Past.NF the-tree around
j-á-va-gʲəžʲ-wa, j-á-va-gʲəžʲ-wa áwma-šʷa
they-it-Prev-go around-Abs.Pres they-it-Prev-go around-Abs.Pres many-how
j-bá-nə, jə-r-gʷa-pxa-nə́ j-a-zə́-ʒərjʷ-wa-n.
it-see-Abs (with surprise) it-they-Prev-like-Abs (joyfully) they-it-Prev-listen to-Dyn-Impf.Fin
Enjoying the sound of the flute, they gathered together and marched round and round the tree in which the boy was sitting, listening happily to it.

(53) Abrə́j a-tə́p [a-]aajgʷára aħá-k' də-n-xa-wá-zaarən.
this the-place [it-]near king-one he-Prev-live-Dyn-[Impf.NF]-Evidential
A king lived nearby.

(54) Anə́j [a-]aħ jə-q'nə́t'ʷ aʒʷə́ d-šʷarə́ca-wa á-psta gʷájʷa
that the-king him-from someone he-hunt-Abs.Pres the valley deep
d-ø-tá-la-nə də-š-lá-j-wa-z [a-]ák'ʷə-m-k'ʷan,
he-[it-]Prev-go into-Abs he-how-Prev-go down-Dyn-Impf.NF [it-]copula-Neg-Abs
anə́j á-č'ʲk'ʷən xʷəč'ʲə́ j-č'arp'ə́n a-bžʲə́ ø-j-a-ħá-jt'.
that the-boy little his-flute its-voice [it-]him-to-hear-(Aor)-Fin
One of the king's servants went hunting, and entered the deep valley, and when he descended into it, he heard the sound of the little boy's flute.

(55) A-šʷarəcajʷ a-č'arp'ə́n a-bžʲə́ ø-an-j-a-ħá, «abrə́j
the-hunter the-flute its-voice [it-]when-him-to-hear.Aor.NF this
j-ax-s-a-ħa-wá s-ná-j-p', j-zak'ʷə́w
it-where-me-to-hear-Dyn.NF I-Prev-go thither-Fut. I what is it?
ø-ajlə́-s-k'aa-p'» ø-j-ħʷá-n, d-dʷə́kʷ-la-n
[it]-Prev-I-understand-Fut.I [it-]he-say-(Aor)-Past.Ind.Fin he-Prev-depart-Past.Ind.Fin
wa d-a-záajgʷaxa-jt'.
there he-it-approach-(Aor)-Fin
When the hunter heard the sound of the flute, he said 'I must go there and find out what it is' and set out for it. And he got closer and closer to it.

(56) Wa áajgʷa d-lá-j-t', axá á-č'ʲk'ʷən
there near he-Prev-go down-(Aor)-Fin but the-boy
d-axʲə́-q'a-c'ʷq'ʲa-z d-zə́-m-na-j-t', arə́j
he-where-be-really-Stat.Past.NF he-Pot-Neg-Prev-go thither-(Aor)-Fin this
d-zak'ʷə́z ø-j-z-ájlə-m-k'aa-jt, a-gəgšʷə́g baapsnə́
who was he? [it-]him-Pot-Prev-Neg-know-(Aor)-Fin the-beast too many
jə́-q'a-n, á-šʷarəcajʷ waxʲ d-na-r-mə́-šʲtə-jt'.
they-be-Past.Fin the-hunter there him-Prev-they-Neg-let go-(Aor)-Fin
He went down near there, but couldn't reach the actual place where the boy was. The hunter didn't know who it was. There were too many animals and they would not let him go there.

(57) A-šʷarəcajʷ arə́j zə-bžʲə́ ø-ga-wá-z
the-hunter this whose-voice [it-]be heard-Dyn-Impf.NF
ø-anə-j-z-ájlə-m-k'aa, jə́-šʲtaxʲq'a d-gʲažʲ-nə́
[it]-when-him-Pot-Prev-Neg-know.(Aor.NF) he-back he-return-Abs
d-cá-jt'.
he-go-(Aor)-Fin
The hunter returned home without knowing whose voice he had heard.

(58) D-axʲ-ná-j-z, «abás, abás [a-]á-wp' jə́-z-ba-z,
he-where-Prev-go thither-Past.Ind.NF thus thus it-be-Stat.Pres Rel-I-see-Past.Ind.NF
á-ssəjr ø-z-bá-jt', sará ak'ə́r s-nə́q'ʷa-xʲa-jt', axá as

the-wonder [it-]I-see-(Aor)-Fin I extensively I-travel-Perf-Fin but such
éjpš ø-sə-m-bá-cəzt', á-bna a-gʷta-č'ə́ a-č'arp'ə́n a-bžʲə́
similar [it-]I-Neg-see-Plupf the-forest its-middle-in the-flute its-voice
ø-s-a-ħá-jt', j-zak'ʷə́w ø-z-bá-p' ħʷa
[it]-me-to-hear-(Aor)-Fin what is it? [it-]I-see-Fut.I SP
s-č'ə́-na-s-xa-n, axá a-bžʲə́ j-s-a-ħa-wá-z
my-SV-Prev-I-start-Past.Ind.Fin but the-voice Rel-me-to-hear-Dyn-Impf.NF
j-axʲ-s-a-ħa-wá-z s-an-a-záajgʷaxa, a-gəgšʷə́g
it-where-me-to-hear-Dyn-Impf.NF I-when-it-approach.Aor.NF the-beast
ø-á-k'ʷ-ša-nə jə́-q'a-n, s-na-r-mə́-šʲtə-jt'.
[they-]it-Prev-surround-Abs they-be-Past me-Prev-they-Neg-let go-(Aor)-Fin
When he arrived, he told everyone. 'This is what I saw. I saw something very unusual. I have traveled widely but I've never seen anything like this before. In the middle of a forest I heard the sound of a flute. I started toward it to see what it was, but when I approached the place where it was, I found wild animals surrounding it and they wouldn't let me go there.

(59) S-na-pš-nə́ éjrgʲ ħʷa jə-z-ba-wá-n, cʷ-k'ə
I-Prev-look thither-Abs barely it-I-see-Dyn-Impf.Fin bull-one
ø-ná-j-n zagʲə́ ø-pxa-na-c'á-jt', xaránt'ʷ
[it-]Prev-go thither-Past.Ind.Fin all [them-]Prev-it-drive off-(Aor)-Fin from a distance
s-axʲə-pš-wá-z d-wajʷpsə́-wp' w-ħʷá-rt'ʷ č'ʲk'əná c'ʷrə́šk'ʷa-k'
I-where-look-Dyn-Impf.NF he-person-Stat.Pres.Fin so to speak young very young-one
á-c'la d-lá-l-baa-n, á-cʷ ak'rə-j-č'a-na-c'á-jt'
the-tree he-Par-Prev-get down-Past.Ind.Fin the-bull something-him-Prev-it-feed-(Aor)-Fin
ħʷa sə́-q'a-wp', wə́šʷa jə-z-bá-jt'.
SP I-be-Stat.Pres.Fin (it seems to me) so it-I-see-(Aor)-Fin (I think so)
When I looked there, I was barely able to see. A bull walked in and drove out all the animals. I saw this from a distance, but it was a boy. Somehow, when a very young person climbed down from the tree, I thought that the bull seemed to give him some food to eat. That is what I saw'.

(60) Axá jə́-z-ba-z, jə-s-a-ħá-z ckʲa
but Rel-I-see-Past.Ind.NF Rel-me-to-hear-Past.Ind.NF well
j-ajlə́-s-k'aa-rt'ʷ áajgʷa s-zə́-m-na-j-t'» — ħʷa
them-Prev-I-know-in order to near I-Pot-Neg-Prev-go thither-(Aor)-Fin SP
ø-r-a-j-ħʷá-jt'.
[it-]them-to-he-say-(Aor)-Fin
But I couldn't get close enough to confirm what I had seen and heard,' he told them.

(61) — Nas arə́j j-ajl-k'áa-šʲa-s j-á-ma-w-zej? — ħʷa a-waá
then this it-Prev-know-way-as what-it-have-Pres.NF-Qu SP the-people
ø-á-la-cʷažʷa-jt'.
[they-]it-Prev-talk about-(Aor)-Fin
If that's the case, how do you know?' the people asked him.

(62) Axá ajl-k'áa-šʲa-s j-á-ma-w abrə́j [a-]a-wp' ħʷa
but Prev-know-way-as Rel-it-have-Pres.NF this it-be-Stat.Pres SP
aʒʷgʲə́ ak'agʲə́ ø-jə-zə́-m-ħʷa-jt'.
nobody nothing [it-]him-Pot-Neg-say-(Aor)-Fin
Nonetheless, there was no one who could say 'This is how we can find out about this'.

(63) Wəbrá áajgʷa tak'ʷažʷə́-k', xʷartláɣʲ-k' də́-q'a-zaarən,
there near old woman-one witch-one she-be-Evidential
«abás, abás [a-]a-wp' jə́-s-ba-z, jə-s-a-ħá-z,
thus thus it-be-Stat.Pres.Fin Rel-I-see-Past.Ind.NF Rel-me-to-hear-Past.Ind.NF
axá j-zak'ʷə́w nagʒanə́ jə-s-z-ájlə-m-k'aa-jt', á-bnara-č'ə
but what is it? completely it-me-Pot-Prev-Neg-know-(Aor)-Fin the-forest-in
jə́-q'a-w ø-ajl-k'áa-šʲa-s j-á-ma-w ħʷa
Rel-be-Pres.NF [it-]Prev-know-way-as Rel-it-have-Pres.NF SP
ak'rə-b-də́r-wa-zar?» ħʷa arə́j á-šʷarəcajʷ
something-you.F-know-Dyn-Subordinate.Suffix SP this the-hunter
d-ná-j-n a-xʷartláɣʲ d-l-á-z-c'aa-jt'.
he-Prev-go thither-Past.Ind.Fin the-witch he-her-it-Prev-ask-(Aor)-Fin
Apparently an old woman, a witch, lived nearby. 'This is what I saw. This is what I heard. But I have no idea what it was. Is there any way to find out who is in the middle of the forest? Do you know of a way?' The hunter went to the witch and asked her these things.

(64) — Wəj ø-marjá-wp', zə́-ʒbaxʷ ø-wə-ħʷa-wá
that [it-]easy-Stat.Pres Rel(Poss)-news [it-]you-say-Dyn.NF
d-wajʷpsə́-zar ø-q'a-lá-p',
he-person-Subordinate.Suffix [it-]Prev-be possible-Fut.I (it is likely that ...)
d-wajʷpsə́-zargʲə, d-wajʷpsə́-m-k'ʷa d-ajʷə́staa-zargʲə də-k'-nə́ ará
he-person-whether he-person-Neg-Abs he-devil-whether him-catch-Abs here
də-w-z-aa-s-ga-wá-jt' ak'ə́r ø-sə́-w-ta-wa-zar,
him-you-for-Prev-I-bring-Dyn-Fin something [it-]me-you-give-Dyn-if
— ø-l-ħʷa-jt' a-ták'ʷažʷ.
[it-]she-say-(Aor)-Fin the-old woman
'That's easy. Judging by what you say, he's probably a human. Whether he's human or a devil, if you bring me something, I could catch him and bring him back here to you,' said the old woman.

(65) — Aa, b-anaǯʲálbajt', wəs ájpš ø-bə́-l-ša-wa-zar, ak'ə́r
oh you.F-really thus like [it-]you-Prev-be possible-Dyn-if something
ø-bə́-zə-m-ta-wa-da, jə́-b-taxə-w ø-bə́-s-ta-wa-jt'
[it-]you-Rel-Neg-give-Dyn-Qu(who) Rel-you-want-Stat.NF [it-]you-I-give-Dyn-Fin
— ø-j-ħʷá-jt' á-šʷarəcajʷ.
[it-]he-say-(Aor)-Fin the-hunter
'Oh really? If you could do that, who wouldn't give you something? I'll give you what you want,'

said the hunter.

(66) — Wasá-k' a-šáxa ø-na-[a]-xa-c'a-nə́ j-sə́-t,
sheep-one the-rope [it-]Par-[its]-Poss-put on-Abs it-me-give.Imp
ħʷəzbá-k' ø-sə́-t wažʷazə́, wəj á-bnara-č'ə jə́-w-ba-z
knife-one [it-]me-give.Imp now that the-forest-in Rel-you-see-Past.Ind.NF
j-áa-ga-ra s-ca-wá-jt', — ø-l-ħʷá-jt'.
it-Prev-bring-in order to I-go-Dyn-Fin [it-]she-say(Aor)-Fin

'Tie up a sheep with a rope around its neck, and bring it to me! And bring me a knife! Then I will go and bring you back what you saw in the middle of the forest,' she said.

(67) A-šʷarəcajʷ ħʷəzbá-k' ø-j-m-áw-[w]a də́-q'a-z-ma,
the-hunter knife-one [it-]him-Neg-receive-Abs he-be-Past.NF-Qu
a-wasa-gʲə́ a-šáxa ø-na-[a-]xa-c'a-nə́ j-lə́-j-ta-jt',
the-sheep-also the-rope [it-]Par-[its-]Poss-put on-Abs it-her-he-give-(Aor)-Fin
á-ħʷəzba-gʲə ø-lə́-j-ta-jt'.
the-knife-also [it-]her-he-give-(Aor)-Fin

Is there a hunter who couldn't find a knife! He put a rope around the sheep's neck and gave it to her. And he also gave her a knife.

(68) A-xʷartláɣʲ áfərħʷa a-wasa-gʲə́ ø-lə-ma-nə́, á-ħʷəzba-gʲə
the-witch quickly the-sheep-and [it-]she-have-Abs the-knife-and
ø-lə-ma-nə́ anə́j á-bna-č'ə á-c'la jə́-ø-kʷ-t'ʷa-nə a-č'arp'ə́n
[it]-she-have-Abs that the-forest-in the-tree he-[it-]Prev-sit on-Abs the-flute
ø-a-zə-rħʷa-wá-z j-č'ə́ d-ná-j-t'.
[it-]it?-Rel-play-Dyn-Impf.NF him-to she-Prev-go thither-(Aor)-Fin

The witch quickly grabbed the sheep and the knife and set out for the place where the boy was sitting atop the tree, playing his flute.

(69) Jará d-zə-kʷ-t'ʷá-z á-c'la á-mc'an
he he-Rel-Prev-sit on-Past.NF the-tree it-under
d-an-ná-j, a-wasá ø-l-k'a-lə-žʲə́-n,
she-when-Prev-go thither.(Aor.NF) the-sheep [it-]Par-Prev-she-knock down-Past.Ind.Fin
á-ħʷəzba-žʷ á-la jə-s-šʲ-wá-jt' ħʷa d-á-la-ga-jt'.
the-knife-old it-with it-I-kill-Dyn-Fin SP she-it-Prev-begin-(Aor)-Fin

The witch went under the tree where the boy was sitting. Knocking down the sheep she said 'I'm going to kill the sheep with this old knife' and she began to kill it.

(70) Axá a-wasá ø-z-šʲ-wá a-xə́ [a]-á-wp'
but the-sheep [it-]Rel-kill-Dyn.NF the-head it-be-Stat.Pres
jə-xə́-j-c'ʷa-wa, arə́j a-ták'ʷažʷ a-šʲap'-á-la jə-l-šʲ-wá
Rel-Prev-he-cut-Dyn.NF this the-old woman the-leg-it-with it-she-kill-Abs.Pres
d-á-la-ga-jt', a-šʲap'-kʷá ak'ák'a-la jə-xə́-c'ʷc'ʷa-nə

she-it-Prev-begin-(Aor)-Fin the-leg-Pl one by one-with them-Prev-cut into sections-Abs
jə-s-šʲ-wá-jt' ħʷa d-a-č'ə́-wp'.
it-I-kill-Dyn-Fin SP she-it-be engaged in-Stat.Pres
Although people who kill sheep start with the neck, the old woman started to kill the sheep by cutting its legs. 'I'm going to kill this sheep by cutting the legs one by one,' she said and started to do so.

(71) A-č'ʲk'ʷən á-c'la d-axʲə́-kʷ-t'ʷa-z arə́j jə́-q'a-l-c'a-wa-z
the-boy the-tree he-where-Prev-sit on-Stat.Past.NF this Rel-Prev-she-do-Dyn-Impf
d-la-pš-nə́ ø-j-ba-wá-n.
he-Prev-look below-Abs [it-]he-see-Dyn-Impf
The boy watched what she was doing from where he was sitting atop the tree.

(72) Dəj, jə́-q'a-b-c'a-wa zak'ʷə́wzej, as aʒʷə́r
Grandmother! Rel-Prev-you-do-Dyn.NF what so anyone
jə-q'a-j-c'a-wá-ma, a-wasá ø-anə́-r-šʲ-wa a-xə́ [a]-á-wp'
it-Prev-he-do-Dyn-Qu the-sheep [it-]when-they-kill-Dyn.NF the-head it-be-Stat.Pres.Fin
jə-xə́-r-c'ʷa-wa, a-šʲap'ə́ ø-xə́-r-c'ʷa-wa ǯʲarák'ar
Rel-Prev-they-cut-Dyn.NF the-leg [it-]Prev-they-cut-Abs.Pres anywhere
jə-b-ba-xʲá-w-ma, j-rə́cħa-wp', j-agʲ-c'ásə-m, a-šʲap'ə́
it-you-see-Perf-NF-Qu it-pitiful-Stat.Pres it-even-custom-Stat.Neg the-leg
ø-xə́-bə-m-c'ʷa-n, jə-b-šʲ-wá-zar, a-xə́ ø-x-c'ʷá,
[it-]Prev-you-Neg-cut-Proh it-you-kill-Dyn.NF-if the-head [it-]Prev-cut.Imp
— ø-j-ħʷá-jt'. (a-č'ʲk'ʷən á-c'la d-axʲə́-kʷə-w anə́j
[it-]he-say-(Aor)-Fin the-boy the-tree he-where-be on-Stat.NF that
a-ták'ʷažʷ d-zə-xʷna-ʒa-wá-m, wəmbawá!)
the-old woman she-Pot-climb-Emph-Dyn-Neg really
'Grandmother! What are you doing? Who on earth would do such a thing? When people kill sheep, they first cut the neck. Where have you ever seen them cut the legs? I feel sorry for the sheep. That's not what we do. If you're going to kill a sheep, don't cut its legs. Cut the neck,' the boy said. (It was true that the old woman couldn't climb up the tree to where the boy was sitting.)

(73) — Aaj, nán-xajt', a-wasá a-šʲə́-šʲa ø-z-də́r-wa-jt', axá
yes, young man! the-sheep it-kill-way [it-]I-know-Dyn-Fin but
sə́-mčʲ ø-á-kʷ-xa-wa-m, wəj áq'ara-kʷa ø-w-də́r-wa-zar,
my-strength [it-]it-Prev-overpower-Dyn-Neg that so much-Pl [it-]you-know-Dyn-if
wə-l-baá-nə w-sə́-cxraa-rawázej! — ø-l-ħʷá-jt'
you-Prev-get down-Abs you.M-me-help.Imp-then [it-]she-say-(Aor)-Fin
lə-č-rə́cħa-t'ʷ-nə.
her-Self-Prev-pretend to be pitiful-Abs
'That's right, young man! I know how to kill a sheep. But I don't have the strength to do it. If you know so much about it, come down from the tree and help me!' the woman said, making herself sound pitiful.

(74) A-tákʼʷažʷ lə-gʷtakʼə́ á-čʼʲkʼʷən
the-old woman her-aim the-boy
j-alə-j-də́r-aa-wa-jz, ášərħʷa á-cʼla
it-where from (?)-he-know-completely-Dyn-Impf.NF quickly the-tree
d-lá-l-baa-n, a-wasá ø-šʲ-nə́ jə-lə́-j-ta-jtʼ.
he-Par-Prev-get down-Past.Ind.Fin the-sheep [it-]kill-Abs it-her-he-give-(Aor)-Fin

How was the boy to know the old woman's plans? He came down from the tree quickly, killed the sheep and gave it to the old woman.

(75) Wátʼkʼa-w-ma, spʼə́jrtʼ-w-ma, a-ncʷá jə-də́r-pʼ, rə́žʷtʼʷə-kʼ
vodka-Stat.NF-Qu spirits-Stat.NF -Qu the-god it-he-know-Fut.I.Fin drink-one
ø-lə́-ma-n, «nan, abrə́j ə́-žʷ, abrə́j
[it-]her-have-Stat.Past.Fin young man! this it-drink.Imp this
ø-axʲ-s-zə́-w-šʲə-z a-qʼnə́tʼʷ, a-ʒba-gʲə́
[it]-where-me-for-you-kill-Past.Ind.NF it-because the-thirst-also
w-á-m-kʼ-wa-j ħʷa ø-j-á-l-ħʷa-n, a-rə́žʷtʼʷ
you-it-Neg-catch-Dyn-Qu SP [it-]him-to-she-say-Past.Ind.Fin the-drink
d-jʷá-xa-n jə-žʷə́-jtʼ.
he-Prev-[it]-raise-Past.Ind.Fin it-he-drink-(Aor)-Fin (= he drank it up)

The old woman had a drink with her, but God only knows if it was vodka or spirits. 'Young man! Drink this! You helped me kill the sheep, so you must be thirsty, aren't you?' she said. And the boy drank it up.

(76) A-rə́žʷtʼʷ ø-ané-j-žʷ á-šʲtaxʲ anə́j á-sabəj rə́cħa,
the-drink [it-]when-he-drink.Aor.NF it-after that the-baby pitiful
jə́-jə-čʲħa-wa-zəj, a-məjnə́wt-kʼ d-a-šʲə́-jtʼ,
what-he-endure-Dyn-Qu in a minute him-it-kill-(Air)-Fin
d-xəlga-ʒə́lga-wa d-áa-qʼa-la-jtʼ.
he-staggering he-Par-Prev-begin-(Aor)-Fin

After he drank it, the poor child couldn't control himself and got drunk and started staggering about.

(77) Lará d-aa-jə́-mcʼa-sə-n, d-aa-nə́-l-kʼəla-n
she she-Par-him-Prev-seize-Past.Ind.Fin him-Par-Prev-she-hold-Past.Ind.Fin
(a-rə́žʷtʼʷ d-an-a-šʲə́ jə́-mčʲ ø-mačʼʲə-m-xá-j,
the-drink him-when-it-kill.Aor.NF his-strength [it-]weak-Neg-become-Qu
rə́cħa!) a-wasá ø-z-la-ná-l-ga-z a-šáxa-la
poor fellow! the-sheep [it-]Rel-with-Prev-she-take-Past.Ind.NF the-rope-with
d-páxnə d-aa-čʼá-l-ħʷa-n, d-áa-šʲtə-l-xə-n,
him-fast/strong him-Par-Prev-she-bind-Past.Ind.Fin him-Par-Prev-she-take.up-Past.Ind.Fin
[a]-áħ j-čʼə́ də-l-gá-jtʼ.
the-king him-to him-she-take-(Aor)-Fin

The old woman grabbed him and held him down. (The drink had made him weak, the poor thing!). Then she bound him up tightly with the rope that she had led the sheep with, and lifted him up and carried him off to the king.

(78) [A]-aħ j-č'ə́ d-axʲ-ná-l-ga-z bəžʲ-wáda-k'
the-king him-to him-where-Prev(there)-she-take-Past.Ind.NF 7-room-NS
rə́-šʷ ø-aa-rt'-nə́ naq' d-na-j-gʷa-nə́
their-door [it-]Prev-open-Abs there he-Prev(there)-him-push-Abs
də-jʷná-j-k'ə-jt'.
him-Prev-he-lock in-(Aor)-Fin
When she (the old woman) took him (the boy) to where the king was, the king opened the doors of seven rooms, and pushed him in there and locked him in.

(79) Wážʷ wa də-jʷna-xá-jt' á-č'ʲk'ʷən,
now there he-Prev-fall into-(Aor)-Fin the-boy
jə́-q'a-j-c'a-wa-j?
Rel-Prev-he-do-Dyn-Qu(what)
Now that the boy was down there, what on earth could he do?

(80) Jə́-cʷ naxʲxʲə́j á-psara
his-bull in the distance over there the-fir grove
jə́-c'a-xa-jt', də-z-la-cá-z,
it-Prev(under)-find oneself-(Aor)-Fin he-Rel-with-go-Past.Ind.NF
d-axʲ-cá-z, də-z-gá-z ħʷa ak'agʲə́
he-where-go-Past.Ind.NF him-Rel-take-Past.Ind.NF SP nothing
jə-z-də́r-ʒa-wa-m.
he-Pot-know-Emph-Dyn-Neg
His bull was far away in a distant fir grove. The bull knew nothing about how the boy had gone, where he had gone, or who had taken him away.

(81) A-lada a-ħʷá-jt', á-jʷada a-ħʷá-jt',
down it-say-(Aor)-Fin upward it-say-(Aor)-Fin
anáxʲ a-ħʷá-jt', aráxʲ a-ħʷá-jt',
there it-say-(Aor)-Fin here it-say-(Aor)-Fin
a-t'ʷə́la a-cʷá ø-a-x-ná-xə-jt',
the-world the-skin [it-]it-Prev-it-take off-(Aor)-Fin
axá á-cʷ á-č'ʲk'ʷən d-axʲ-cá-z ø-a-ba-wá-m, jə́-šʲta
but the-bull the-boy he-where-go-Past.Ind.NF [it-]it-see-Dyn-Neg his-footprint
ø-a-ba-wá-m, d-ax-a-gá alláħ ø-jə-də́r-p'.
[it]-it-see-Dyn-Neg him-where-it-take.Aor.NF Allah [it-]he-know-Fut.I.Fin
The bull looked around everywhere, here and there, high and low. He looked all over the world. But the bull didn't know where the boy had gone. He couldn't find any of the boy's footprints. Only Allah knew where the boy had been taken.

(82) Aréj á-č'ʲk'ʷən á-bžʲ-wáda-k' d-axʲə-jʷná-r-k'ə-z

this the-boy the-7-room-NS him-where-Prev-they-lock in-Past.Ind.NF
ak'rə-j-č'á-r-c'a-wa-n, á-mla
something-him-Prev-they-feed-Dyn-Impf the-hunger
d-a-də-r-k'-wá-mə-zt', axá jə-z-xʷárta-w-zaj,
him-it-they-Caus-catch-Dyn-Neg-Impf.Fin but it-Rel-help-Stat.NF -Qu(what)
jə́-cʷ xʲaá-s ø-j-k'ə́-jt', jə́-cʷ a-də́rra
his-bull pain-as [it-]he-catch-(Aor)-Fin (= he worried) his-bull the-knowledge
ø-á-j-ta-r ø-j-tax-xá-jt', axá jə-zlá-j-ta-wa-j?
[it-]to it-he-give-Subjunctive [it-]he-wish to-(Aor)-Fin but it-how-he-give-Dyn-Qu

They locked the boy up in the seven rooms, they gave him food, they were careful not to let him die of hunger. But what was the use of that? The boy was worried about the bull. He wanted to tell the bull about himself, but how could he tell him?

(83) D-xə́rkʷakʷa-wa wəs də-š-t'ʷá-z ak'ʷə-m-k'ʷá
he-grieve-Abs thus he-how-be sitting-Stat.Past.NF be-Neg-Abs
q'ʷráan-k' ø-pər-nə́ j-aá-j-n a-pénǯʲər a-č'ə́
crow-one [it-]fly-Abs it-Prev-come here-Past.Ind.Fin the-window it-at
j-áa-kʷ-t'ʷa-jt'.
it-Par-Prev(on)-sit down-(Aor)-Fin

He was feeling very sad and when he sat down, just at that moment a crow flew in and sat down on the windowsill.

(84) A-q'ʷráan a-pénǯʲər j-an-áa-[a]-kʷ-t'ʷa, á-č'ʲk'ʷən
the-crow the-window it-when-Par-[it]-Prev(on)-sit down.Aor.NF the-boy
d-xə́rkʷakʷa-wa, d-c'ʷə́wa-wa, də-š-t'ʷá-z
he-grieve-Abs he-cry-Abs he-how-be sitting-Stat.Past.NF
ø-an-a-bá, "j-wə́-xʲ-zaj wará,
[it-]when-it-see.(Aor.NF) Rel-you-happen-(Aor)-what you.M
w-zə-r-c'ʷə́wa-wa-j?" ħʷa ø-j-á-z-c'aa-jt'.
you.M-Rel-Caus-cry-Dyn-what SP [it-]him-it-Prev-ask-(Aor)-Fin

When the crow stopped on the windowsill, it saw the boy feeling very sad and sitting there crying, and asked him, 'What is the matter with you? What causes you to cry?'

(85) — Sə-zə-r-c'ʷə́wa-wa wəbrə́j [a]-á-wp', abrə́jgʲ, abrə́jgʲ
me-Rel-Caus-cry-Dyn.NF that it-be-Stat.Pres.Fin such and such
á-psta gʷájʷa-č'ə xʲa c'la də́w-k' sə́-kʷ-t'ʷa-n,
the-valley deep-in chestnut tree big-one I-Prev(on)-sit-Stat.Past.Fin
s-č'ərp'ə́n wəbrá á-xʲa c'la jə́-kʷ-xa-jt',
my-flute there the-chestnut tree it-Prev(on)-remain alone-(Aor)-Fin
j-sə́-ma-zar ø-s-taxə́-n, s-gʷə
it-I-have-Subjunctive [it-]I-want-Stat.Past.Fin my-heart
ø-a-la-sə-r-č'ə́ɣʲ-wa-mə-zt'.
[it-]it-with-I-Caus-be bored-Dyn-Neg-Impf.Fin

'This is why I'm crying. Deep in a valley somewhere, I was sitting on the top of a big chestnut tree. I left my flute at the top of that chestnut tree. If I had the flute, I wouldn't feel bored here.'

(86) Aráxʲ s-axʲə́-na-pš-wa adʷaxʲə́ awaá ø-z-ba-wá-jt',
here I-where-Prev(there)-look-Dyn.NF outside people [them-]I-see-Dyn-Fin
axá awaá-j sará-j ħ-aj-cʷážʷa-r ø-q'a-la-wá-m,
but people-and I-and we-each other-talk with-if [it]-Prev-be possible-Dyn-Neg
[á]-aħ s-á-w-jə-šʲt-wa-m, abás s-gʷáq'-wa abrá
the-king me-Dummy-Prev-he-release-Dyn-Neg so I-suffer-Abs here
sə-jʷna-xa-jt', — ø-j-ħʷá-jt'.
I-Prev-fall into-(Aor)-Fin [it-]he-say-(Aor)-Fin
'When I looked over there, I saw people, but we couldn't talk with each other. The king would not let me go. And I felt sad, and ended up in here', he said.

(87) — Wəs ák'ʷ-zar, wə-č'ərp'ə́n sa jə-w-z-aa-z-ga-wá-jt',
if so your.M-flute I it-you-for-Prev-I-bring-Dyn-Fin
— ø-a-ħʷá-n, a-č'ə́-na-na-xa-n j-cá-n a-xapə́c
[it-]it-say-Past.Ind.Fin its-SV-Prev-it-set out-Past.Ind.Fin it-go-Past.Ind.Fin the-tooth
jə-bžʲa-k'-nə́ j-á-ma-nə j-aá-j-t'.
it-Prev(between)-hold-Abs it-it-have-Abs it-Prev(here)-come-(Aor)-Fin
'If that is the case, I will bring your flute to you here', said the crow, and flew away. And then the crow brought the flute back, holding it in its beak.

(88) J-á-ma-n j-aá-j-n, a-pénǯʲər
it-it-have-Past.Fin it-Prev-come-Past.Ind.Fin the-window
j-ø-k'ə́lə-ršʷ-nə á-č'ʲk'ʷən d-axʲə-jʷna-k'ə́-z
it-[it-]Prev(through)-throw-Abs the-boy he-where-Prev-be locked in-Stat.Past.NF
ø-j-ná-ta-jt'.
[it-]him-it-give-(Aor)-Fin
The crow carried the flute and, throwing it into the place where the boy was locked up, he gave it to him.

(89) A-č'ʲk'ʷən znək' jə-č'ərp'ə́n ø-an-jə-mpə́xʲa-šʷa-gʷə́šʲa,
the-boy as soon as his-flute [it-]when-he-Prev-find-(Aor.NF)-at last
a-pénǯʲər d-k'ə́la-t'ʷa-nə a-rħʷa-rá d-á-la-ga-jt'.
the-window he-Prev-sit-Abs the-play-masd he-it-Prev-begin-(Aor)-Fin
The boy found his flute and, sitting on the windowsill, started to play it.

(90) Wažʷ jə́-cʷ ø-aa-ga-r-á-wp'
now his-bull [it-]Prev-bring-must-be-Stat.Pres.Fin
d-zə-rgʷáq'-wa, wəmbawá!
him-Rel-worry-Dyn.NF indeed
The bull that indeed must have been worrying about him would surely be brought here now.

(91) A-č'ərp'ə́n a-bžʲə́ ø-an-r-a-ħá, anə́j á-psara-č'ə
the-flute its-voice [it-]when-them-to-hear.Aor.NF that the-fir grove-at
j-š-ájza-wa-z ajpš, gəgšʷə́g-s, psaát'ʷə-s jə́-q'a-z
they-how-gather-Dyn-Impf.NF like wild animal-as bird-as Rel-be-Stat.Past.NF
zagʲə́ ø-ajzá-jt', arə́j [á]-aħ j-gʷára ø-tʷə́-jt'.
all [they]-gather-(Aor)-Fin this the-king his-residence [it-]be filled-(Aor)-Fin

When they heard the sound of the flute, all of the animals and birds that had come together in the fir grove gathered together and assembled at the king's residence.

(92) A-č'arp'ə́n a-bžʲə́ á-cʷ-gʲə j-[a]-a-ħá-jt'.
the-flute its-voice the-bull-also it-it-to-hear-(Aor)-Fin

The bull also heard the sound of the flute.

(93) A-č'arp'ə́n a-bžʲə́ á-cʷ j-an-[a]-a-ħá,
the-flute its-voice the-bull it-when-[it]-to-hear.Aor.NF
aq'ʷákħʷa j-la-trə́-s-nə jə́-jʷ-nə jə-k'ʷk'ʷaʒá
with a bump it-Par-Prev-break away-Abs it-run-Abs it-full tilt
a-č'-áa-na-xa-jt'.
its-SV-Par-it-set out-(Aor)-Fin

When the bull heard the sound of the flute, he made a loud bumping noise, stood up quickly, and ran off at a full tilt.

(94) J-š-aá-j-wa-z á-šʷ-kʷa j-la-rə́-sə-n,
it-how-Prev(here)-come-Dyn-Impf.NF the-door-Pl it-Par-them-hit-Past.Ind.Fin
pšʲ-ba <u>zn</u><u>ək' á-la</u> jə-p-na-čə́-jt', dačá
4-Non.Hum one time it-with them-Prev-it-break-(Aor)-Fin still.more
x-pa ø-n-xá-jt', a-cʷ á-z-t'ʷəjʷa-k'
3-Non.Hum [they-]Prev-remain-(Aor)-Fin the-bull its-one part of a pair-horn-one
ø-x-žʷá-jt'.
[it-]Prev-be broken-(Aor)-Fin

The bull arrived, opened the door, and broke down each of the four doors one by one. Three of the doors still remained. One of the bull's horns was broken.

(95) Axá j-aanə́-m-č'as-k'ʷa j-áan-xa-z á-šʷ-kʷa-gʲə
but it-Prev-Neg-stop-Abs Rel-Prev-remain-Past.Ind.NF the-door-Pl-also
j-á-xa-wa, j-á-gʷa-wa, jə-p-na-čə́-n,
it-it-pull-Abs it-it-push-Abs them-Prev-it-break-Past.Ind.Fin
j-nə-jʷna-šə́la-n, a-č'ʲk'ʷən a-q'ʷáq'ʷa d-jʷə́-kʷ-t'ʷa-n,
it-Par-Prev-go into-Past.Ind.Fin the-boy the-back he-Par-Prev(on)-sit-Past.Ind.Fin
jə-jʷ-dʷə́l-pa-n j-cá-jt'.
it-Par-Prev(out)-rush-Past.Ind.Fin it-go-(Aor)-Fin

But the bull did not give up. He broke down the remaining doors, pushed through them and ripped them up. And when he got through, he put the boy up on his back and rushed from there.

(96) Axá jálawxəj, a-cʷ a-xə́ ∅-axʲ-k'ə́d-na-q'ʲa-z
but what of it? the-bull the-head [it-]where-Prev-it-strike-Past.Ind.NF
agʲə́jz a-xbəljʷəšə́ ∅-c'əsə́-jt'.
and so on its-brain [it-]swing-(Aor)-Fin
But, somehow the bull had struck his head and his brain was badly damaged.

(97) A-č'ʲk'ʷən d-á-ma á-psta-č'ə j-axʲ-ná-j-z,
the-boy him-it-have.Abs the-valley-in it-where-Prev(there)-go-Past.Ind.NF
adərjʷágʲ á-c'la də́-kʷ-na-c'a-jt'.
again the-tree him-Prev(on)-it-put-(Aor)-Fin
The bull took the boy along with him and when they entered the valley, the bull put him up on top of the tree.

(98) — W-lə́-m-baa-n ħʷa ∅-w-a-sə-m-ħʷá-zə-j,
you.M-Prev-Neg-descend-Proh SP [it-]you.M-to-I-Neg-say-Past.Ind.NF-Qu
w-zə́-l-baa-zə-j?
you-why-Prev-descend-Past.Ind.NF-Qu
'Don't fall down from the tree! Didn't I tell you that? Why did you climb down?

(99) wə-xʷna-nə́ w-təp a-č'ə́
you-climb-Abs your.M-place it-at
wə́-kʷ-t'ʷa, sa s-m-aá-k'ʷa w-lə́-m-baa-n,
you.M-Prev(on)-sit down.Imp I I-Neg-come here-Abs you.M-Prev-Neg-descend-Proh
— ħʷa wəs ∅-j-á-na-ħʷa-jt'.
SP thus [it-]him-to-it-say-(Aor)-Fin
Climb the tree and sit in your spot. Don't climb down from the tree until I come back!' the bull said to him.

(100) *Znək'*, jʷə́nt'ʷ j-cá-jt', á-č'ʲk'ʷən j-xʷə́ ∅-aa-na-gá-jt',
once twice it-go-(Aor)-Fin the-boy his-food [it-]Prev-it-bring-(Aor)-Fin
axá a-xə́ ∅-bžʲə́-m-s-xʲa-zə-j, čnak'
but the-head [it-]Prev-Neg-be broken-Plupf-NF-Qu one day
j-axʲə́-jʷ-tə-c'ə-z, a-cʷ ∅-ta-xá-jt', k'ʷára-k'
it-where-Par-Prev-go out-Past.Ind.NF the-bull [it-]Prev-die-(Aor)-Fin stream-one
a-č'ə́ jə-š-ná-j-wa-z a-blaxác' gʲažʲə́-n, abnə́j
it-at it-how-Prev-come-Dyn-Impf.NF its-feel dizzy-Past.Ind.Fin that
a-k'ʷára j-∅-tá-ħa-n, wáħa
the-stream it-[it-]Prev(in)-fall-Past.Ind.Fin more
jə-z-tə́-m-c'-ʒa-jt', wa j-ta-xá-jt'.
it-Pot-Prev(out of)-Neg-go-Emph-(Aor)-Fin there it-Prev-die-(Aor)-Fin
The bull went away once, then twice, and brought some food back to the boy. But, the bull's head was

broken, wasn't it? Then once, when the bull went out, it ended up dying. The bull had come to a small stream and, feeling dizzy, he fell into the stream and was unable to climb out. He ended up dying there.

(101) A-č'ʲk'ʷən á-c'la d-axʲə́-ø-kʷ-t'ʷa-z á-mla
the-boy the-tree he-where-[it-]Prev(on)-sit-Stat.Past.NF the-hunger
d-a-k'ə́-jt', də-pšə́-jt', də-pšə́-jt',
him-it-catch-(Aor)-Fin (= he became hungry) he-wait-(Aor)-Fin he-wait-(Aor)-Fin
axá jə-cʷ ø-j-ba-wá-m, aráxʲ agʲ-aá-j-wa-m,
but his-bull [it-]he-see-Dyn-Neg here anything-Prev(here)-come-Dyn-Neg
a-xə́ ø-axʲ-a-rxá-z ø-jə-z-də́r-ʒa-wa-m.
the-head [it-]where-it-turn-Past.Ind.NF [it-]him-Pot-know-Emph-Dyn-Neg

When the boy sat up on the top of tree, he felt hungry. He waited and waited. However, he couldn't see his bull, and no one else would come, would they? The boy didn't know where the bull had gone off to.

(102) A-č'arp'ə́n ø-a-jə-rħʷa-wá d-á-la-ga-jt', axá
the-flute [it-]Dummy-he-play-Abs he-it-Prev-begin-(Aor)-Fin but
j-abá-q'a-w, jə-cʷ ə́-q'a-ʒa-m.
it-where-be-Stat.Pres.NF his-bull it-be-Emph-Neg

He started to play his flute. But where was his bull? His bull was nowhere to be found.

(103) A-laħʷa ø-axʲə́-kʷ-t'ʷa-z wəs ø-a-ħʷá-jt':
the-raven [it-]where-Prev(on)-sit down-Past.Ind.NF thus [it-]it-say-(Aor)-Fin
— Wará, wará wə-z-aaʒá-z wə́-cʷ a-k'ʷára
you.M you.M you.M-Rel-bring up-Past.Ind.NF your.M-bull the-stream
j-ø-]á-ħa-n jə-psə́-jt'.
it-[it-]Prev(in)-fall-Past.Ind.Fin it-die-(Aor)-Fin

A raven stopped on the tree and said, 'The bull that brought you up, your bull, has fallen into a stream and died.

(104) J-axʲə-psə́-z-gʲə abrə́jgʲ, abrə́jgʲ a-tə́p a-č'-a-wp'.
it-where-die-Past.Ind.NF-also such and such the-place it-in/at-be-Stat.Pres.Fin

The place where it died is over there in such and such a place.'

(105) A-č'ʲk'ʷən j-q'á-j-c'a-gʷə́šʲa-wa-jəz, tənxá-s
the-boy Rel-Prev-he-do-Suffix-Dyn-Qu(what) close relative-as
jə́-ma-z jə́-cʷ [a]-ák'ʷə-n, wáħa, xəxʲ á-žʷjʷan,
Rel-[he]-have-Stat.Past.NF his-bull it-be-Stat.Past.Fin more above the-sky
c'áq'a á-dgʲəl, d-zə-kʷ-gʷə́ɣ-wa ħʷa ak'agʲə́
under the-ground he-Rel-Prev-rely on-Dyn.NF SP nothing
ø-jə́-ma-ʒa-mə-zt'.
[it-]he-have-Emph-Neg-Stat.Past.Fin

What on earth could the poor boy do? The bull was his only close relative. There was no one he could rely on in Heaven or on Earth.

(106) Jə́-cʷ j-ta-ħá-z, j-axʲ-ta-xá-z
his-bull Rel-Prev(in)-fall-Past.Ind.NF it-where/that-Prev-die-Past.Ind.NF
á-laħʷa j-an-j-á-na-ħʷa, á-c'la d-zə-kʷ-t'ʷá-z
the-raven it-when-him-to-it-say.Aor.NF the-tree he-Rel-Prev(on)-sit-Stat.Past.NF
d-lá-l-baa-n, j-č'ə́-na-j-xa-n, jə́-cʷ
he-Par-Prev-descend-Past.Ind.Fin his-SV-Prev-he-set out-Past.Ind his-bull
ø-axʲ-ta-xá-z [j]-jə-pšaá-jt'.
[it]-where-Prev-die-Past.Ind.NF it-he-find-(Aor)-Fin

When the raven told him that the bull had fallen into the stream and died, the boy rushed down from the tree and ran off. He found the place where the bull had died.

(107) Wáħa j-xə́ ø-axʲə́-j-ga-wa-z ø-anə-j-má-w,
more his-head [it-]where-he-take-Dyn-Impf.NF [it-]when-he-have-Stat.Pres.NF
a-cʷ a-mgʷacʷá ø-aa-jə-rq'ʲá-n, xə́-la a-cʷ a-mgʷacʷá
the-bull its-belly [it-]Par-he-cut-Past.Ind.Fin head-with the-bull its-belly
də-l-ø-tá-la-n, jar-gʲə́ wa a-cʷ a-mgʷacʷa
he-Par-[it-]Prev(into)-go-Past.Ind.Fin he-also there the-bull its-belly
də-l-ø-ta-psə́ d-cá-jt'.
he-Par-[it-]Prev(inside)-die.(Abs.Past) he-go-(Aor)-Fin

As he didn't know any longer what to do with himself, he cut the bull's belly and climbed into the bull's belly headfirst, and he ended up dying there as well, inside the bull's belly.

(108) [A]-anpsa "bzə́ja" l-papsá "d-šə́-l-aaʒa-z"
the-stepmother good her-stepson him-how-she-bring up-Past.Ind.NF
abás [a]-á-wp'.
in.this.way it-be-Stat.Pres.Fin

This is the way that a 'good' stepmother 'raised' her stepson.

Notes

* The text is taken from «Сергеи Зыхуба (ed.), Аҧсуа лакукуа, Аҟуа, Алашара», 1997. pp. 383-388.

(1) **1.** j-áaʒa-z (Rel(C1)-bring up-Stat.Past.NF) 'the one who was brought up (by a bull)': masd. áaʒa-ra [tr.] 'to bring up', cf. d-s-aaʒa-wá-jt' (him/her(C1)-I(C3)-bring up-Dyn-Fin) 'I bring him/her up'. Because there is no passive voice in Abkhaz, the alternative constructions are used, that is, if the notional passive represents a state of affairs, the intransitive stative form derived from the relevant transitive is used.

(2) **1.** də́-q'a-n (he(C1)-be-Stat.Past): masd. á-q'a-zaa-ra [intr.] 'to exist, to be'.

(3) **1.** d-jə́-ma-n (she(C1)-him(C2)-have/be-Stat.Past.Fin) lit. 'she was by him', i.e. 'he had her'. masd. á-ma-zaa-ra [intr. inverse] 'to have'. For the inversive verbs see §5.10.

(4) **1**. j-šә́-q'a-z ák'ʷә-m-k'ʷa 'they were living like this': masd. ák'ʷ-zaa-ra 'to be'. For the copular root ák'ʷ see §5.2.1. **2**. dә-psә́-jt' < dә-psә́-ϕ-jt' (she(C1)-die-Aor-Fin) 'she died': masd. a-ps-rá [intr.] 'to die'.

(5) **1**. d-anә-psә́ < d-anә-psә́-ϕ (she(C1)-when-die-Aor.NF) 'when she died, ... ', for the masd. see (4)-2. **2**. d-ǯʲabá-jt': masd. á-ǯʲaba-ra [intr.] 'to mourn'. **3**. d-gʷәrjʷá-jt': masd. a-gʷәrjʷa-rá [intr.] 'to grieve'. **4**. d-aa-jә-m-gá-r (her(C1)-Prev(hither)-he(C3)-Neg-take (i.e. bring)-Cond.) 'he could not bring her': masd. aaga-rá [tr.] 'to bring'. **5**. ϕ-q'a-m-lá-zt' ([it(C1)-]Prev-Neg-be possible-Past.Ind.Fin) 'it was impossible that ... and': masd. á-q'ala-ra [intr.] 'to be possible'. **6**. d-aa-j-gá-jt' < d-aa-j-gá-ϕ-jt' (her(C1)-Prev-he(C3)-bring-Aor-Fin) 'he brought her'. For the masdar see **4** above.

(6) **1**. j-aa-j-gá-z (Rel(C1)-Prev-he(C3)-bring-Past.Ind.NF) 'the one whom he brought'. **2**. d-aa-l-bá-r (him(C1)-Par-she(C3)-care for-Cond.): masd. a-ba-rá [tr.] 'to care for; to see'. For the element *-aa-* see §5.11. **3**. ϕ-q'a-m-la-ʒá-jt' < [j]-q'a-m-la-ʒá-ϕ-jt' ([it(C1)-]Prev-Neg-become-Emph-Aor-Fin) 'it did not become', i.e. '*she* stopped *caring for him*': masd. á-q'ala-ra [intr.] 'to become; to begin'.

(7) **1**. d-ah-šʲә́-p' (him(C1)-we(C3)-kill-Fut.1) 'let's kill him': masd. a-šʲ-rá [tr.] 'to kill'. **2**. j-á-w-hʷa-wa-j < j-[j]-á-w-hʷa-wa-j (what-[him(C2)?-]to-you(C3)-say-Dyn-Qu) lit. 'what do you say to him?': masd. a-hʷa-rá [tr.] 'to say'. **3**. ha-n-tә́-c'-nә'we having gone out': masd. a-tә́c'-ra [intr.] 'to go out'. **4**. h-ca-wá-zargʲә: masd. a-ca-rá [intr.] 'to go'. **5**. ϕ-aa-w-[w]á-zargʲә < j-aa-w-wá-zargʲә ([it(C1)-]we(C3)-do-Dyn-even if) 'even if we do it': masd. a-w-rá [tr.] 'to do'. **6**. d-ah-pәrxága-wp' (he-us-disturb-Stat.Pres) 'he disturbs us': masd. a-pәrxága-ra [intr.] 'to disturb'. **7**. j-a-l-hʷa-wá < j-j-a-l-hʷa-wá (it(C1)-him(C2)-to-she(C3)-say-Pres.Abs) lit. 'she saying it to him': masd. a-hʷa-rá [tr.] 'to say'. **8**. For the ħʷa see §5.5. **9**. d-á-la-ga-jt' < d-á-la-ga-ϕ-jt' (she(C1)-it(C2)-Prev-begin-Aor-Fin) 'she began it': masd. á-laga-ra [intr.] 'to begin'.

(8) **1**. jә-l-hʷá-jt' < jә-l-hʷá-ϕ-jt' (it(C1)-she(C3)-say-Aor-Fin) 'she said it': masd. a-hʷa-rá [tr.] 'to say'. **2**. dә-j-zә́-gʷaɣʲ-wa-m (he(the peasant, C1)-him(his boy, C2)-Pot-dare-Dyn-Neg) 'he can not dare [to kill him]': masd. á-gʷaɣʲ-ra [tr.] 'to venture'. **3**. jә́-q'a-j-c'a-rә-j (what-Prev-he(C3)-do-Fut.I-Qu) 'what should he do?': masd. á-q'ac'a-ra [tr.] 'to do'. **4**. d-jә-m-gʷaɣʲә́-rgʲә (him(C1)-he(C3)-Neg-dare-even if) 'if he does not dare [to kill him]': á-gʷaɣʲ-ra [tr.] 'to venture'. **5**. d-jә́-c'ә-c'-nә (she(C1)-him(C2)-Prev-go.out-Past.Abs) 'she having left him': á-c'*(ә)*c'-ra [intr.] 'to go out from under'. **6**. d-cá-r : masd. a-ca-rá [intr.] 'to go'. **7**. d-šʷa-wá-jt' (he(C1)-worry-Dyn-Fin) 'he worries': masd. a-šʷa-rá [intr.] 'to worry'. d-cá-r hʷa d-šʷa-wá-jt' 'he worries that she might leave'.

(9) **1**. ϕ-an-pә́-l-c'ʷa-ʒa < [j]-an-pә́-l-c'ʷa-ʒa-ϕ ([it(C1)-]when-Prev-she(C3)-break-Emph-Aor.NF) 'when she broke it': masd. a-pc'ʷa-rá [tr.] 'to break'. j-gʷә́ (his-heart) ϕ-an-pә́-l-c'ʷa-ʒa: lit. 'when she broke his heart', i.e. 'when he got fed up with her' (= она очень надоела ему). **2**. j-sә́-ma-w (Rel(C1)-I(C2)-have-Stat.Pres.NF) lit. 'the one whom I have': masd. á-ma-zaa-ra [intr. inverse] 'to have'. **3**. d-abá-s-taxә-w (him(C1)-where-I(C2)-want-Stat.Pres.NF) lit. 'where do I want him?', i.e. 'why do I need him?': masd. a-taxә́-zaa-ra [intr. inverse] 'to want'. **4**. dә-s-šʲә́-p' (him(C1)-I(C3)-kill-Fut.1) 'I'll kill him', cf. (7)-1. **5**. sә́-mac' ϕ-l-w-[w]á-jt' ([it (C1)-]she(C3)-do-Dyn-Fin) lit. 'she will do my care', i.e. 'she will care for me': masd. a-w-rá [tr.] 'to do'. **6**. dә-z-lá-j-šʲә-šaz (him(C1)-Rel(C2)-Instr.-he(C3)-kill-Cond.2.NF) 'the one which he might kill him with': masd. a-šʲ-rá [tr.] 'to kill'. **7**. á-[a]ħʷәzba a-x-rá d-á-la-ga-jt' (he(C1)-it(C2)-Prev-begin-(Aor)-Fin) 'he started sharpening the knife': masd. á-laga-ra [intr.] 'to begin'.

(10) **1**. d-a-č'ә́-wp' (he(C1)-it(C2)-be engaged in-Stat.Pres) 'he is engaged in it (= sharpening the knife)': masd. a-č'ә́-zaa-ra [intr.] 'to devote oneself to'. **2**. d-t'ʷa-nә (he-sit-Abs) 'he, having sat down': masd. a-t'ʷa-rá [intr.] 'to sit down'.

(11) **1.** a-mákʲa jə́-kʷ-šʲ-wa (it(C1)-Prev-rub-Abs) ‘rubbing it with a whetstone’: masd. á-kʷ-šʲ-ra [tr.] ‘to rub’. Cf. и-аҳәызба а-макьа и-кә-и-шь-ит ‘он провел свой нож по точильному камню’ (ARD).

(12) **1.** j-gʷárə-j-x-la-wa-n (it(C1)-Prev-he(C3)-pasture-iterative-Dyn+Impf.Fin) ‘he used to pasture it’: masd. a-gʷár-x-ra [tr.] ‘to pasture’. **2.** j-gʷára-j-c’a-la-wa-n (it(C1)-Prev-he(C3)-drive into the farmyard-iterative-Dyn+Impf.Fin) ‘he used to drive it into the farmyard’: masd. a-gʷára-c’a-ra [tr.] ‘to drive into the farmyard’. **3.** ak’r-a-č’á-j-c’a-wa-n (something-it(the bull, C2)-Prev-he(C3)-feed-Dyn+Impf.Fin) ‘he used to feed it’: masd. a-č’ac’a-rá [tr.] ‘to feed’. **4.** ak’r-a-jə́-r-žʷ-wa-n (something-it(C2)-he(C3)-Caus-drink-Dyn+Impf.Fin) lit. ‘he used to make it drink something’, i.e. ‘he used to water it’: masd. á-ržʷ-ra [tr.] ‘to make *sb* drink’. Cf. á-žʷ-ra [tr.] ‘to drink’.

(13) **1.** ak’r-a-č’a-c’a-nə́ (something-it(C1)-Prev-feed-Past.Abs) ‘having fed it’: masd. a-k’rač’ac’a-rá [tr.] ‘to feed’. **2.** jə́-ma-nə < [j]-jə́-ma-nə ([it(C1)-]he(C2)-have-Abs) lit. ‘he having had it’, i.e. ‘he ... with it’. **3.** d-an-aá-j < d-an-aá-j-ø (he(C1)-when-Prev-come hither-Aor.NF) ‘when he came hither’: masd. aá-j-ra [intr.] ‘to come hither’. **4.** jə́-w-x-wa (Rel(C1)-you.M(C3)-sharpen-Pres.NF) ‘the one which you are sharpening’: masd. a-x-rá [tr.] ‘to sharpen’. **5.** j-á-lə-w-xə-j (it-it(C2)-Prev-you.M(C3)-choose-Qu) ‘what do you need it for?’: masd. á-l-x-ra [tr.] ‘to choose’. **6.** j-zə́-w-taxə-j (it(C1)-why-you.M(C2)-want-Qu) ‘why do you want it?’: masd. a-taxə́-zaa-ra [intr. inverse] ‘to want’. **7.** d-jə-z-c’aá-jt’ < d-jə-ø-z-c’aá-ø-jt’ (he(C1)-him(C2)-[it-]Prev (about)-ask-Aor-Fin) ‘he asked him (about it) ’: masd. a-z-c’aa-rá [intr.] ‘to ask’.

(14) **1.** h-fá-p’ < [ja]-h-fá-p’ < *[jə]-h-fá-p’ ([it(C1)-]we(C3)-eat-Fut.1) ‘let’s eat it’: masd. á-fa-ra [tr.] ‘to eat’. **2.** wəbrə́j a-z-á-wp’... < a-z-a-á-wp’ (it-for-it(C2)-copula-Stat.Pres.Fin) ‘that is the reason *why* ...’, cf. wəbrə́j a-zə́ ‘therefore’. For the copular root *-a-* see §5.2.1. **3.** zə́-s-x-wa < [j]-zə́-s-x-wa ([it(C1)]-why-I(C3)-sharpen-Pres.NF) ‘why I sharpen it’: masd. a-x-rá [tr.] ‘to sharpen’. **4.** də-j-žʲá-rc (him(C1)-he(C3)-deceive-in order to) ‘in order that he deceives him’: masd. a-žʲa-rá [tr.] ‘to deceive’. **5.** á-wp’ < a-á-wp’ (it(C2)-copula-Stat.Pres.Fin) ‘it is’. **6.** j-zə́-j-hʷa-wa (it(C1)-why-he(C3)-say-Dyn.NF) ‘(the reason) why he says it’: masd. a-hʷa-rá [tr.] ‘to say’.

(15) **1.** h-šʲ-wá-jt’ < [ja]-h-šʲ-wá-jt’ ([it(C1)-]we(C3)-kill-Dyn-Fin) ‘we'll kill it’: masd. a-šʲ-rá [tr.] ‘to kill’. **2.** anə́-j-hʷa < [j]-anə́-j-hʷa-ø ([it(that we’ll kill it, C1)-]when-he(C3)-say-Aor.NF) ‘when he said that ...’.

(16) **1.** z-ak’ʷə́-w-zaj (what(C2)-be-Stat.Pres.NF-Qu) ‘what happened?’: masd. ák’ʷ-zaa-ra [intr.] ‘to be’. **2.** w-zə-r-c’ʷə́wa-wa (you(C1)-Rel(C3)-Caus-cry-Pres.NF) lit. ‘the one who makes you cry’. Such an interrogative pronoun as dárban ‘who’ may be omitted here. If so, this means ‘who makes you cry?’: masd. a-r-c’ʷə́wa-ra [tr.] ‘to make *sb* cry’. **3.** w-a-q’ʷə́-c’-nə (you.M(C1)-it (C2)-Prev-stop-Abs) ‘you having stopped it’: masd. a-q’ʷə́-c’-ra [intr.] ‘to stop; to leave alone’. **4.** aa-gá < [j]-aa-gá ([it(C1)-]Prev-bring.Imp) ‘bring it!’: masd. aaga-rá [tr.] ‘bring’.

(17) **1.** d-an-jə́-kʷ-cʷq’ʲa < d-an-jə́-kʷ-cʷq’ʲa-ø (he(his father, C1)-when-him(the child, C2)-Prev-shout.at-Aor.NF) ‘when he (his father) shouted at him’: masd. á-kʷ-cʷq’ʲa-ra [intr.] ‘to shout at’. **2.** aa-z-ga-wá-jt’ < [j-]aa-z-ga-wá-jt’ ([it-]Prev-I-bring-Dyn-Fin) ‘I’ll bring it’. **3.** d-c’ʷə́wa-wa (he(C1)-cry-Abs) ‘he crying’: masd. a-c’ʷə́wa-ra [intr.] ‘to cry’. **4.** də-š-ná-j-wa-z (he-how-Prev-go.thither-Impf.NF) lit. ‘(it saw) how (that) he was going thither’, i.e. ‘it saw him going there’: masd. a-náj-ra [intr.] ‘to go thither’. **5.** d-a-bá-jt’ < d-a-bá-ø-jt’ (him(C1)-it(C3)-see-Aor-Fin) ‘it saw him’: a-ba-rá [tr.] ‘to see’.

(18) **1.** w-zə-r-c’ʷə́wa-wa-zaj (you(C1)-what(C3)-Caus-cry-Dyn-Qu) lit. ‘what makes you cry?’: For the masdar see (16)-2. **2.** j-wə́-xʲ-zaj < j-wə́-xʲ-ø-zaj (what(C1)-you(C2)-happen to-Aor-Qu) ‘what happened to you?’: masd. á-xʲ-ra [intr.] ‘to happen to’. **3.** j-a-z-c’áa-jt’ < [j]-j-a-z-c’áa-jt’ ([it (the bull, C1)-]him(C2)-to-Prev-ask-(Aor)-Fin) ‘it (the bull) asked him (about it)’: masd. a-z-c’aa-rá [intr.] ‘to

ask'.

(19) **1.** s-abá-m-c'ʷwa-wa (I(C1)-where/how-Neg-cry-Dyn.NF) 'how can't I cry?'. **2.** jə́-kʷ-c'a-n ə < [j]-jə́-kʷ-c'a-n ə ([it(C1)-]him(C2)-Prev-put on-Abs) lit. 'having put it on him': masd. á-kʷc'a-ra [tr.] 'to put on'. **3.** s-á-j-hʷa-jt' < [j]-s-á-j-hʷa-ø-jt' ([it-]me-to-he-say-Aor-Fin) 'he said it to me': masd. a-hʷa-rá [tr.] 'to say'. **4.** j-hʷá-jt' < [jə-]j-hʷá-ø-jt' ([it-]he-say-Aor-Fin) 'he said it'.

(20) **1.** s-ák'ʷ-ʒa-m (me(C2)-be-Emph-Neg): masd. ák'ʷ-zaa-ra [intr.] 'to be (copula)'. *S*ará s-ák'ʷ-ʒa-m jə́-r-šʲ-wa 'It is not me that they will kill'. **2.** wə-j-žʲá-jt' < wə-j-žʲá-ø-jt' (you(C1)-he(C3)-deceive-Aor-Fin) 'he deceived you': masd. a-žʲa-rá [tr.] 'to deceive'. **3.** jə́-j-taxə-w (Rel(C1)-he(C2)-want-Stat.Pres.NF) 'the one that he wants': masd. a-taxə́-zaa-ra [intr.] 'to want'. **4.** w-á-wp' (you(C2)-be-Stat.Pres). jə́-j-šʲə-rc jə́-j-taxə-w wará w-á-wp' 'it is you that he wants to kill'. **5.** táxa jə́-lə-m-ta-jt' < táxa [j-]jə́-lə-m-ta-ø-jt' ([it(C1)-]him (C2)-she(C3)-Neg-give-Aor-Fin) 'she followed him round': masd. á-ta-ra [tr.] 'to give'. **6.** jə-w-xə-rq'ʲa-nə (him (C1)-you(C2)-Prev-accuse-Abs) 'having accused him of your behavior': masd. a-xərq'ʲa-rá [tr.] 'to accuse'. **7.** rə́-ləjbax-wa-jt' < j-rə́-ləjbax-wa-jt' ([it(C1)-]they (C3)-quarrel with each other-Dyn-Fin) 'they quarrel with each other': masd. á-ləjbax-ra. **8.** d-šʲə́ (him(C1)-kill.Imp) 'kill him!': masd. a-šʲ-rá [tr.] 'to kill'. **9.** j-á-l-hʷa-wa-jžʲtaj < [j-]j-á-l-hʷa-wa-jžʲtaj ([it(C1)-]him(C2)-to-she(C3)-say-Dyn-since) 'since she has been saying it': masd. a-hʷa-rá [tr.] 'to say'. **10.** aa-c'-wá-jt' < [j-]aa-c'-wá-jt' ([it-]Prev-pass-Dyn-Fin) 'it has passed': masd. áac'-ra [intr.] 'to pass'.

(21) **1.** d-abá-h-taxə-w (him(C1)-where-we(C2)-need-Stat.Pres.NF) 'why do we need him?': masd. a-taxə́-zaa-ra [intr. inverse] 'to want'. **2.** h-q'a-lá-p' (we(C1)-Prev-become-Fut.1): masd. á-q'ala-ra [intr.] 'to become; to be possible'. **3.** d-a[a]-a-q'ʷə́-m-c'-ʒa-k'ʷa (he(C1)-Par-it(C2)-Prev-Neg-stop-Emph-Abs) lit. 'he not having stopped it': masd. a-q'ʷə́c'-ra [intr.] 'to stop'. **4.** d-anə-xtá-l-k'-ʒa < d-anə-xtá-l-k'-ʒa-ø (him(C1)-when-Prev-she(C3)-insist-Emph-Aor.NF) 'when she insisted *on it* to him': masd. a-xtak'-rá [tr.] 'to insist'. **5.** anə-p-c'ʷa-ʒá < [j]-anə-p-c'ʷa-ʒá-ø ([it(C1)-]when-Prev-be broken-Emph-Aor.NF) lit. 'when it (his heart) was broken', i.e. 'when he was disgusted': masd. a-pc'ʷa-rá [labile] 'to be broken; to break'. **6.** d-á-kʷšahat-xa-jt' < d-á-kʷšahat-xa-ø-jt' (he(C1)-it(C2)-consent to-become-Aor-Fin) 'he agreed to it': masd. á-kʷšahatxa-ra [intr.] 'to agree to'. 7. wə-j-šʲə́-rc (you(C1)-he(C3)-kill-Purp) j-á-kʷə-j-k'ə-jt' (it(C1)-it?(C2)-Prev-he(C3)-decide-(Aor)-Fin) 'he decided to kill you': masd. á-kʷ(ə)k'-ra [tr.] 'to decide'.

(22) **1.** jə-špá-sə-psə́xʷa-w (it(C1)-how-my-possibility-Stat.Pres.NF) 'how should I do it?'. **2.** jə-špá-q'a-s-c'a-rə-j (it(C1)-how-Prev-I(C3)-do-Fut.1.NF-Qu) lit. 'how shall I do it?', i.e. 'what am I to do?': masd. á-q'ac'a-ra [tr.] 'to do'.

(23) **1.** j-q'á-w-c'a-ra (Rel(C1)-Prev-you.M(C3)-do-should) 'what you should do': masd. á-q'ac'a-ra [tr.] 'to do'. **2.** wəj á-wp' < wəj a-á-wp' ([it(C2)-]copula-Stat.Pres.Fin) '(what you should do) is that'. Cf. wəj K'áma l-á-wp' (her(C2)-copula-Stat.Pres.Fin) 'that is Kama'. **3.** s-ax-č'á-w-hʷa-wa (me-where-Prev-you.M-tie-Pres.NF) '(the place) where you tie me': masd. a-č'ahʷa-rá [tr.] 'to tie'. The prefix *-ax-* 'where' is the Bzyp dialect form (by Dr. Chirikba's instruction). [Also see Bgazhba (1964a: 178).] Also for the Abzhwa dialect form -axʲ-, cf. (24)-5. **4.** šʲtá-wp' < [jə-]šʲtá-wp' ([it(C1)-]be ly ing-Stat.Pres.Fin) 'it is lying': masd. á-šʲta-zaa-ra [intr.] 'to lie'. **5.** j-k'á-ršʷə-wp' (it(C1)-Prev-be thrown+Stat.Pres.Fin) 'it is thrown': masd. a-k'áršʷ-ra [tr.] 'to throw'. **6.** jə́-q'a-wp' (they-exist-Stat.Pres.Fin) 'they are': masd. á-q'a-zaa-ra [intr.] 'to exist, to be'. 7. áa-šʲtə-x-nə ([them(C1)-]Par-Prev-take up-Abs) 'having taken them up': masd. á-šʲtəx-ra [tr.] 'to take up'. For Par[ticle] see (6)-2. **8.** j-wə́-ma-nə (them-you-have-Abs) lit. 'you having had them', i.e. 'with them': masd. á-ma-zaa-ra [intr. inverse] 'to have'. **9.** w-aá (you(C1)-come hither.Imp) 'come hither!': masd. aa-rá [intr.] 'to come hither'. **10.** wə-r-šʲ-áanʒa

< wə-r-šʲ-ø-áanʒa (you(C1)-they(C3)-kill-Aor.NF-before) 'before they kill you': masd. a-šʲ-rá [tr.] 'to kill'. **11**. wə-r-cʷə́-z-ga-wa-jt' (you(C1)-them(C2)-Prev-I(C3)-take away from-Dyn-Fin) 'I'll take you away from them': masd. a-cʷga-rá [tr.] 'to take away from'. **12**. wə-m-šʷá-n (you.M(C1)-Neg-worry-Proh) 'don't worry!': a-šʷa-rá [intr.] 'to worry'.

(24) **1**. d-n-[a]-a-pə́-za-n (he(C1)-Par-it (the bull, C2)-Prev-lead-Past.Ind.Fin) 'he led it and ...': masd. a-pə́za-ra [intr.] 'to lead'. **2**. jə́-ma (it(C1)-have.Abs) lit. 'having it', i.e. 'with it': masd. á-ma-zaa-ra [intr. inverse] 'to have'. **3**. j-č'ə́-na-j-xa-n (his(Poss)-SV-Prev-he(C3)-set out-Past.Ind.Fin) 'he set out and ... ': masd. a-č'ə́naxa-ra [tr.] 'to set out thither'. **4**. də-n-k'ə́l-sə-n (he-Par-Prev-go out-Past.Ind.Fin) 'he went out and ...': masd. a-k'ə́ls-ra [intr.] 'to go out; to go through'. **5**. ø-axʲ-čʲá-j-hʷa-la-wa-z < [j-]axʲ-čʲá-j-hʷa-la-wa-z ([it(C1)-]where-Prev-he (C3)-tie-Iterative-Impf.NF) '(the place) where he used to tie it': masd. a-č'ahʷa-rá [tr.] 'to tie'. **6**. ø-áa-šʲtə-j-xə-n < [j-]áa-šʲtə-j-xə-n ([them(C1)-]Par-Prev-he(C3)-take up-Past.Ind.Fin) 'he took them up and ...': masd. á-šʲtəx-ra [tr.] 'to take up'. **7**. də́-jʷ-nə (he(C1)-run-Abs) 'he having run': masd. á-jʷ-ra [intr.] 'to run'. **8**. d-aa-k'ə́l-sə-n (he-Par-Prev-go out-Past.Ind.Fin) 'he went out and ... ': masd. a-k'ə́ls-ra [intr.] 'to go out; to go through'. Cf. (24)-4. **9**. d-an-n-á-d-gəla < d-an-n-á-d-gəla-ø (he(C1)-when-Par-it(C2)-Prev-stand by-Aor.NF) 'when he stood by it': masd. á-dgəla-ra [intr.] 'to stand by'. **10**. wə́-pa-nə (you(C1)-jump-Abs) 'you having jumped': masd. á-pa-ra [intr.] 'to jump'. **11**. w-sə́-kʷ-t'ʷa (you(C1)-me(C2)-Prev(on)-sit down.Imp) 'sit down on me!': masd. á-kʷt'ʷa-ra [intr.] 'to sit down on'. **12**. d-jʷ-á-kʷ-t'ʷa-jt' < d-jʷ-á-kʷ-t'ʷa-ø-jt' (he(C1)-Par-it(C2)-Prev(on)-sit down-Aor-Fin) 'he sat down on it'. For Par[ticle] -jʷ- see §5.11.

(25) **1**. d-an-jʷ-á-kʷ-t'ʷa < d-an-jʷ-á-kʷ-t'ʷa-ø (he(C1)-when-Par-it(C2)-Prev(on)-sit down-Aor.NF) 'when he sat down on it'. **2**. ø-jʷá-c'q'ʲa-n < [j-]jʷá-c'q'ʲa-n ([it]-Prev-leap-Past.Ind.Fin) 'it leaped and ... ': masd. a-jʷác'q'ʲa-ra [intr.] 'to leap'. **3**. jə́-jʷ-t' = jə́-jʷə-jt' < jə́-jʷə-ø-jt' (it(C1)-run-Aor-Fin) 'it ran'.

(26) **1**. jə́-jʷ-nə j-an-dʷə́kʷ-la < jə́-jʷ-nə j-an-dʷə́kʷ-la-ø (it(C1)-when-Prev-set out-(Aor.NF) 'when it started running': masd. a-dʷə́kʷla-ra [intr.] 'to set out'. **2**. j-a-xʷtá-mə-z (Rel(C1)-it(C2)-be necessary-Neg-Stat.Past.NF) 'the one which was not necessary for it': masd. a-xʷta-rá [intr.] 'to be necessary'. **3**. axʲə́-l-hʷa-xʲa-z < [j]-axʲə́-l-hʷa-xʲa-z ([it(C1)-]-that-she(C3)-say-Plupf-NF) '(for the reason) that she had said it'. **4**. d-hʷa-xá-jt' < d-hʷa-xá-ø-jt' (she(C1)-pig-become-Aor-Fin) 'she turned into a pig'; see a-hʷá 'a pig'. **5**. d-á-kʷ-t'ʷa-nə (he(C1)-it(the pig, C2)-Prev(on)-sit down-Abs) 'he having sat down on it': masd. á-kʷt'ʷa-ra [intr.] 'to sit down on'. **6**. d-dʷə́kʷ-la-jt' < d-dʷə́kʷ-la-ø-jt' (he(C1)-Prev-set out-(Aor)-Fin) 'he set out'.

(27) **1**. d-á-šʲta-la-n (he(his father, C1)-it(the bull, C2)-Prev-track-Past.Ind.Fin) 'he tracked it and ...': masd. á-šʲtala-ra [intr.] 'to track'. **2**. d-a-xʲ-ʒa-wá (he(his father, C1)-it(the bull, C2)-Prev-catch up with-Abs) lit. 'he catching up with it': masd. a-xʲʒa-rá [intr.] 'to catch up with'. **3**. d-á-la-ga-jt' (he-it-Prev-begin-(Aor)-Fin) lit. 'he began it', i.e. 'he began to (catch up with it)': masd. á-laga-ra [intr.] 'to begin'.

(28) **1**. d-hʷa-xá-n (she(C1)-pig-become-Past.Ind.Fin) 'she turned into a pig and ...'. **2**. d-há-šʲta-la-nə (he(C1)-us(C2)-Prev-track-Abs) 'he having tracked us'. **3**. d-aa-wá-jt' (he(C1)-come hither-Dyn-Fin) 'he'll come hither': masd. aa-rá [intr.] 'to come hither'. **4**. d-ha-xʲ-ʒa-wá-jt' (he(C1)-us(C2)-Prev-catch up with-Dyn-Fin) 'he'll catch up with us'.

(29) **1**. j-tá-w < j-ø-tá-w (Rel(C1)-[it(your bottle, C2)-]be in[/Prev(in)-be(ø)]-Stat.Pres.NF) 'the one which is in it': masd. a-tá-zaa-ra/a-ta-rá [intr.] 'to be in'. w-patlə́k'a j-ø-tá-w a-ʒə́ 'the water which is in your bottle'. **2**. k'a-tʷá < [j-]k'a-tʷá ([it-]Prev-sprinkle.Imp) 'sprinkle it!': masd. a-k'atʷa-rá [tr.] 'to sprinkle'. **3**. a-hʷá-jt' < [j-]a-hʷá-ø-jt' ([it(C1)-]it (the bull, C3)-say-Aor-Fin) 'it said it'.

(30) **1.** ø-an-a-hʷa < [j-]an-a-hʷa-ø ([it(the bull, C1)-]when-it(C3)-say-Aor.NF) 'when it (the bull) said that'. **2.** j-tá-z < j-ø-tá-z (Rel(C1)-[it (your bottle, C2)-]be in-Stat.Past.NF) 'the one which was in it'. **3.** j-k'á-j-tʷa-jt' (it(C1)-Prev-he(C3)-sprinkle-(Aor)-Fin) 'he sprinkled it': masd. a-k'atʷa-rá [tr.] 'to sprinkle'.

(31) **1.** ø-mšə́n-xa-jt' < [jə-]mšə́n-xa-ø-jt' ([it(everything behind them, C1)-]sea-become-(Aor)-Fin) 'it turned into a sea'; cf. a-mšə́n 'the sea'. **2.** ø-an-k'á-j-tʷa < [j-]an-k'á-j-tʷa-ø ([it (water, C1)-]when-Prev-he (C3)-sprinkle-Aor.NF) 'when he sprinkled it'.

(32) **1.** jə-z-xʷartá-w-zaj (it(the sea, C1)-what-aid-Stat.Pres.NF-Qu) lit. 'what help is it? ', i.e. 'it will not be of any help'. **2.** j-aan-gə́la-wa (it(the pig, C1)-Prev-stop-Abs) lit. 'it stopping': masd. áangəla-ra [intr.] 'to stop'. **3.** jə́-q'a-w-ma (it(C1)-be-Stat.Pres.NF-Qu) lit. 'is it?': masd. á-q'a-zaa-ra [intr.] 'to be'. j-aan-gə́la-wa jə́-q'a-w-ma 'can it stop?'. **4.** a-č-ta-ná-žʲə-n (its(pig's, Poss)-Self-Prev-it(the pig, C3)-throw-Past.Ind.Fin) lit. 'it (the pig) threw itself and ...', i.e. 'it plunged into (the sea) and ...': masd. a-čtážʲ-ra [tr.] 'to throw oneself into'. **5.** jə-ʒsa-nə́ (it(the pig, C1)-swim-Abs) lit. 'it having swum': masd. á-ʒsa-ra [intr.] 'to swim'. jə-ʒsa-nə́ j-dʷə́kʷ-la-jt' 'it started to swim'.

(33) **1.** a[a]-ajmgʷ-hʷa-nə́ < [j]-a[a]-ajmgʷ-hʷa-nə́ ([it(the sea, C1)-]Par-Prev-go through-Abs) 'having gone through': masd. ájmgʷhʷa-ra [tr.] 'to go through'. **2.** jə́-rə-n < j-[ø]ə́-rə-n (it(the pig, C1)-[it(the sea, C2)-]cross-Past.Ind.Fin) 'it (the pig) crossed it (the sea) and ...': masd. á-r-ra [intr.] 'to cross'. **3.** j-a-xʲ-ʒa-wá (it(the pig, C1)-it(the bull, C2)-Prev-catch up with-Abs) 'it (the pig) catching up with it (the bull)'. j-a-xʲ-ʒa-wá j-á-la-ga-jt' 'it (the pig) started to catch up with it (the bull)'.

(34) **1.** ha-xʲ-ʒa-wá-jt' < [j-]ha-xʲ-ʒa-wá-jt' ([it(the bad pig, C1)-]us(C2)-Prev-catch.up.with-Dyn-Fin) 'it will catch up with us'. **2.** k'á-ršʷ < [j-]k'á-ršʷ ([it (your comb, C1)-]Prev-throw.Imp) 'throw it!': masd. a-k'áršʷ-ra [tr.] 'to throw *something light*'.

(35) **1.** j-k'a-jə́-ršʷə-jt' < j-k'a-jə́-ršʷə-ø-jt' (it(his comb, C1)-Prev-he(C3)-throw-Aor-Fin) 'he threw it'. **2.** ø-an-k'a-jə́-ršʷ < [j-]an-k'a-jə́-ršʷ-ø ([it (his comb, C1)-]when-Prev-he (C3)-throw-Aor.NF) 'when he threw it'. **3.** ø-bnara-xá-jt' < [jə-]bnara-xá-ø-jt' ([it-]luxuriant forest-become-Aor-Fin) 'it turned into a luxuriant forest'. **4.** jə-n-na-k'ə́la-wa (it(the pig, C1)-Prev-it(the forest, C3)-detain-Abs) lit. 'it (the forest) keeping it (the pig)': masd. a-nk'ə́la-ra [tr.] 'to detain'. jə-n-na-k'ə́la-wa jə́-q'a-z-ma lit. 'could it (the forest) keep it (the pig)?'. **5.** j-l-á-sə-n (it(the pig, C1)-Par-it(the forest, C2)-rush into-Past.Ind.Fin) 'it (the pig) rushed into it and ...': masd. á-s-ra [intr.] 'to rush'. For Par[ticle] *l* see §5.11. **6.** j-jʷə́-l-sə-n (it(the pig, C1)-Par-Prev-pass through-Past.Ind.Fin) 'it (the pig) passed through *it*': masd. á-ls-ra [intr.] 'to pass through'. **7.** j-a-xʲ-ʒa-wá (it(the pig, C1)-it(the bull, C2)-Prev-catch up with-Abs) lit. 'it (the pig) catching it (the bull)'. á-cʷ j-a-xʲ-ʒa-wá j-á-la-ga-jt' 'it began to catch up with the bull'.

(36) **1.** ø-ha-xʲ-ʒa-wá-jt' < [j-]ha-xʲ-ʒa-wá-jt' ([they(C1)-]us(C2)-Prev-catch up with-Dyn-Fin) 'they will catch up with us'. **2.** w-xʲá-hʷ-nə (you.M(C1)-Prev(back)-turn-Abs) 'you having turned back': masd. a-xʲáħʷ-ra [intr.] 'to turn back'. **3.** ø-k'á-žʲ < [j-]k'á-žʲ ([it (your stone, C1)-]Prev(on surface)-throw.Imp) 'throw it down!': masd. a-k'ážʲ-ra [tr.] 'to throw on'. **4.** j-á-na-hʷa-jt' < [j-]j-á-na-hʷa-ø-jt' ([it(C1)-]him(C2)-to-it (the bull, C3)-say-Aor-Fin) 'it (the bull) said to him that ...'.

(37) **1.** j-k'a-jə́-žʲ-t' = j-k'a-jə́-žʲə-jt' < j-k'a-jə́-žʲə-ø-jt' (it(C1)-Prev-he(C3)-throw down-Aor-Fin) 'he threw it down'.

(38) **1.** ø-an-k'a-jə́-žʲ < [j]-an-k'a-jə́-žʲ-ø ([it(your stone, C1)-]when-Prev-he(C3)-throw down-Aor.NF) 'when he threw it down'. **2.** ø-q'a-lá-jt' < [j]-q'a-lá-ø-jt' ([they(the big stone fences, C1)-]Prev-become-Aor-Fin) 'they was formed': masd. á-q'ala-ra [intr.] 'to become, to happen'.

(39) **1.** ajxá-jt' < [j-]ajxá-ø-jt' ([it(the pig, C1)-]be dying to.go-Aor-Fin) 'it was dying to go': masd. ájxa-ra [intr.] 'to be dying to go'. **2.** j-zə-r-xə́-m-c'ə-jt' (it(the pig, C1)-Pot-them(the stone fences, C2)-Prev-

Neg-cross-(Aor)-Fin) ‘it (the pig) could not cross them’: masd. a-xə́c’-ra [intr.] ‘to cross’. For the Pot[entail] see §4.2.4.

(40) **1**. jə-n-xá-jt’ (it(the pig, C1)-Prev-remain-Aor-Fin) ‘it remained’: masd. a-nxa-rá [intr.] ‘to remain, to stay’. **2**. d-abá-wə-šʲt-wa-z < d-abá-w-[w?]ə-šʲt-wa-z (him-where-Prev-[you?-]let.go-Impf.NF) ‘where did you let him go?’: masd. á-wəšʲt-ra [tr.] ‘to let *sb* go’. **3**. d-aan-xá-jt’ < d-aan-xá-ø-jt’ (he(C1)-Prev-remain-Aor-Fin) ‘he remained’: masd. áanxa-ra [intr.] ‘to stay here’.

(41) **1**. d-á-ma-nə (him(C1)-it(the bull, C2)-have-Abs) lit. ‘it having had him’, i.e. ‘with him’: masd. á-ma-zaa-ra [intr. inverse] ‘to have’. **2**. j-ca-wá (it(the bull, C1)-go-Abs) ‘it going’: masd. a-ca-rá [intr.] ‘to go’. **3**. j-axʲə́nʒa-[a]-l-ša-wa-z (it(going, C1)-until-it(the bull, C2)-Prev-be able to-Impf-NF) ‘as far as it could go’: masd. á-lša-ra [intr. inverse] ‘to be able to’. **4**. j-cá-jt’ (it(the bull, C1)-go-(Aor)-Fin) ‘it went’.

(42) **1**. j-an-áapsa < j-an-áapsa-ø (it(the bull, C1)-when-get tired-Aor.NF) ‘when it got tired’: masd. áapsa-ra [intr.] ‘to get tired’. **2**. j-aan-gə́l-t’ = j-aan-gə́la-jt’ < j-aan-gə́la-ø-jt’ (it(the bull, C1)-Prev-stop-(Aor)-Fin) ‘it stopped’: masd. áangəla-ra [intr.] ‘to stop’.

(43) **1**. aħə́ħ = aħə́ interjection, ‘now, now then’. **2**. wə-l-baá (you.M(C1)-Prev-get down.Imp) ‘get down!’. **3**. a-k’rə-s-fá-p (the-Dummy-prefix(C1)-I(C3)-eat-Fut.I) ‘I’ll have a meal’: masd. a-k’rə́-fa-ra [tr.] ‘to have a meal’. Cf. á-fa-ra [tr.] ‘to eat’. For the Dummy-prefix -k’rə- see Hewitt (1979c: 220-221). **4**. w-t’ʷá (you.M(C1)-sit.Imp) ‘sit!’: masd. a-t’ʷa-rá [tr.] ‘to sit’. **5**. jagʲáǯʲara = egʲáǯʲara. **6**. s-cá-r-gʲə (I(C1)-go-if-even): masd. a-ca-rá ‘to go’. jagʲáǯʲara s-cá-r-gʲə ‘wherever I may go’. **7**. s-aa-wá-jt’ (I(C1)-come.hither-Dyn-Fin) ‘I come, I’ll come’: masd. aa-rá [intr.] ‘to come’. **8**. wə-s-šʲ-wá-m (you.M(C1)-I(C3)-kill-Dyn-Neg) ‘I won’t kill you’: masd. a-šʲ-rá [tr.] ‘to kill’. **9**. w-a-sə-r-k’-wá-m (you.M(C1)-it(hunger, C2)-I(C3)-Caus-catch-Dyn-Neg) ‘I won’t let you go hungry’: masd. a-k’-rá [tr.] ‘to catch’. Cf. á-mla s-a-k’-wá-jt’ ‘I am hungry’. **10**. w-a-cʷə́-m-šʷa-n (you.M(C1)-it(C2)-Prev-Neg-be afraid of-Proh) ‘don’t be afraid of it!’: masd. a-cʷ-šʷa-rá [intr.] ‘to be afraid of’. **11**. ø-j-á-na-ħʷa-jt’ (it(C1)-him(C2)-to-it(the bull, C3)-say-(Aor)-Fin ‘the bull said it to him’: masd. a-ħʷa-rá [tr.] ‘to say’.

(44) **1**. aá-j-r < [j-]aá-j-r (it(C1)-Prev-come-if) ‘if it comes’: masd. aá-j-ra [intr.] ‘to come’. **2**. s-a-m-fa-wá-j (me(C1)-it(C3)-Neg-eat-Dyn-Qu) ‘won’t it eat me?’: masd. á-fa-ra [tr.] ‘to eat’. **3**. ø-jə-ħʷá-jt’ < jə-j-hʷa-ø-jt’ (it(C1)-he(C3)-say-(Aor)-Fin) ‘he said it’.

(45) **1**. wə-xʷna-nə́ (you.M(C1)-climb-Abs) ‘you, climbing’: masd. a-xʷna-rá ‘to climb’. **2**. wə́-kʷ-t’ʷa < wə́-ø-kʷ-t’ʷa (you.M(C1)-it(C2)-Prev-sit on.Imp) ‘sit down on it!’: masd. á-kʷ-t’ʷa-ra [intr.] ‘to sit down on’. **3**. w-an-a-k’-lák’ʲ (you.M(C1)-when-it(C3)-catch-LA) ‘when it catches you’. á-mla w-an-a-k’-lák’ʲ ‘when you are hungry’. The suffix lák’ʲ is used when the tense of the subordinate is the future tense. For the suffix, see §5.12.2. **4**. j-wə́-ma-w (Rel(C1)-you.M(C2)-have-Pres.NF) ‘(a flute) which you have’: masd. á-ma-zaa-ra [intr.] ‘to have’. **5**. w-á-la-ga (you.M(C1)-it(C2)-Prev-begin.Imp) ‘begin it!’, i.e. ‘start to play the flute!’: masd. á-la-ga-ra [intr.] ‘to begin’. **6**. w-an-á-la-ga-lak’ʲ (you.M(C1)-when-it(C2)-Prev-begin-LA) ‘when you start to play it’. **7**. s-axʲə́-q’azaa-lák’-gʲə (I(C1)-where-be-whenever-even) ‘wherever I may be’: masd. á-q’a-zaa-ra [intr.] ‘to be, to exist’. **8**. j-s-a-ħa-wá-jt’ (it(C1)-me(C2)-to-be audible to-Dyn-Fin) lit. ‘it will be audible to me’, ‘I’ll hear it’: masd. a-ħa-rá [intr.] ‘to hear’.

(46) **1**. jə-w-z-aa-z-ga-wá-jt’ (it(C1)-you.M(C2)-for-Prev-I(C3)-bring-Dyn-Fin) ‘I’ll bring it to you’: masd. aa-ga-rá [tr.] ‘to bring’.

(47) **1**. j-w-á-s-ħʷa-wa (Rel(C1)-you.M(C2)-to-I(C3)-say-Dyn.NF) ‘which I say to you’: masd. a-ħʷa-rá [tr.] ‘to say’. **2**. á-wp’ < a-á-wp’ (it(C2)-copula-Stat.Pres.Fin) ‘X (= j-w-á-s-ħʷa-wa) is it’. **3**. s-aá-nʒa

(I(C1)-come-until) 'until I come back': masd. aá-ra [int.] 'to come'. **4**. sə́-q'a-m-k'ʷa (I(C1)-be-Neg-Abs) 'I not being': masd. á-q'a-zaa-ra [intr.] 'to be, to exist'. **5**. w-lə-m-baá-n (you.M(C1)-Prev-Neg-get down-Proh) 'don't get down!': masd. á-l-baa-ra [intr.] 'to get down, to descend'. á-c'la w-lə-m-baá-n 'don't get down from the tree!'. Cf. á-raxʷ á-šʲxa-nt'ʷ jə-l-baa-wá-jt' (the-cattle the-mountain-from they(C1)-Prev-descend-Dyn-Fin) 'The cattle descend the mountain'.

(48) **1**. a-č'ə́-na-na-xa-n (its(Poss)-SV-Prev-it(C3)-depart-Past.Ind.Fin) 'it left and ...': masd. a-č'ə́-na-xa-ra [tr.] 'to depart'. **2**. ħʷ-rá j-cá-ø-jt' (it(C1)-go-(Aor)-Fin) 'it went to feed'.

(49) **1**. d-an-a-k'-lák'ʲ (him(C1)-when-it(hunger, C3)-catch-LA) lit. 'when hunger caught him', i.e. 'when he became hungry'. **2**. d-á-la-ga-wa-n (he(C1)-it(C2)-Prev-begin-Dyn-Impf) 'he was (always) beginning it'. **3**. ø-axʲə́-q'azaa-lak'ʲ < j-axʲə́-q'azaa-lak'ʲ (it(C1)-where-be-LA) 'wherever it may be'; cf. (45)-7. **4**. j-a-ħa-wá-n < j-a-a-ħa-wá-n (it(its voice, C1)-it(the bull, C2)-to-hear-Dyn-Impf.Fin) 'the bull heard the voice': masd. a-ħa-rá [intr.] 'to hear'. **5**. á-mla d-š-a-k'ə́-z (him(C1)-how-it(C3)-catch-Past.Ind.NF) 'how hungry he was'. **6**. j-a-də́r-wa-n (it(C1)-it(the bull, C3)-know-Dyn-Impf.Fin) 'the bull knew it': masd. a-də́r-ra [tr.] 'to know'. á-mla d-š-a-k'ə́-z wəj á-la j-a-də́r-wa-n. lit. 'The bull knew how hungry the boy was by that [from the sound of the flute]'. **7**. ø-aa-ga-nə́ < j-aa-ga-nə́ (it(C1)-Prev-bring-Abs) 'having brought it': masd. aa-ga-rá [tr.] 'to bring'. **8**. j-č'a-na-c'a-wá-n < jə-j-č'a-na-c'a-wá-n (it(food, C1)-him(C2)-Prev-it(the bull, C3)-feed-Dyn-Impf.Fin) 'The bull always gave him food'.: masd. a-č'a-c'a-rá [tr.] 'to feed'.

(50) **1**. abás jə-šə́-q'a-z ák'ʷə-m-k'ʷa 'they were living like this' **2**. c'ə́-jt' < j-c'ə́-ø-jt' (they(C1)-pass-(Aor)-Fin) 'they passed': masd. a-c'-rá [intr.] 'to pass'.

(51) **1**. ø-a-j-rħʷa-wá < j-a-j-rħʷa-wá (it(the flute, C1)-it?-he(C3)-play-Abs.Pres) 'he, playing the flute': masd. a-rħʷa-rá [tr.] 'to play'. a-č'arp'ə́n a-j-rħʷa-wá d-an-á-la-ga-lak'ʲ 'when he began to play the flute'. **2**. ø-z-m-a-ħá-cəz < j-z-m-a-ħá-cəz (it(C1)-Rel(C2)-Neg-to-hear-Plupf.NF) 'that had not heard it': masd. a-ħa-rá [intr.] 'to hear'. **3**. racʷá-m-zəj 'many'. **4**. ø-ajza-wá-n < j-ajza-wá-n (they(C1)-gather-Dyn-Impf.Fin) 'they were gathering': masd. ájza-ra [intr.] 'to gather'.

(52) **1**. jə-z-a-ħa-wá-z (it(C1)-Rel(C2)-to-hear-Dyn-Impf.NF) 'that was hearing it': masd. a-ħa-rá [intr.] 'to hear'. **2**. j-a!jza-n′ (they(C1)-gather-Abs) 'they, having gathered'. **3**. d-zə-kʷ-t'ʷá-z (he(C1)-Rel(C2)-Prev(on)-sit-Stat.Past.NF) 'which he was sitting on': masd. á-kʷ-t'ʷa-ra [intr.] 'to sit on'. **4**. j-á-va-gʲəžʲ-wa (they(C1)-it(the tree, C2)-Prev-go around-Abs.Pres) 'they, going around it': masd. á-va-gʲəžʲ-ra [intr.] 'to go around'. **5**. jə-r-gʷa-pxa-nə́ (it(C1)-they(C2)-Prev-like-Abs) lit. 'they, having liked it', i.e. 'joyfully': masd. a-gʷa-pxa-rá [intr.] 'to like'. **6**. j-a-zə́-ʒərjʷ-wa-n (they(C1)-it(C2)-Prev-listen to-Dyn-Impf.Fin) 'they were listening to it': masd. a-zə́-ʒərjʷ-ra [intr.] 'to listen to'.

(53) **1**. abrə́j a-tə́p aajgʷára (< a-aajgʷára) 'near this place'. **2**. də-n-xa-wá-zaarən < də-n-xa-wá-z-zaarən (he(C1)-Prev-live-Dyn-Impf.NF-Evidential) 'it is said that he was living': masd. a-n-xa-rá [intr.] 'to live'.

(54) **1**. aħ jə-q'nə́t'ʷ aʒʷə́ lit. 'someone from the king', i.e. 'a retainer of the king's'. **2**. d-šʷarə́ca-wa (he(C1)-hunt-Abs.Pres) 'he, hunting', i.e. 'while he was hunting': masd. a-šʷarə́ca-ra [intr.] 'to hunt'. **3**. d-ø-tá-la-nə (he(C1)-it(the deep valley, C2)-Prev-go into-Abs) lit. 'he, having gone into the deep valley': masd. a-tá-la-ra [intr.] 'to go into'. **4**. də-š-lá-j-wa-z (he(C1)-how-Prev-go down-Dyn-Impf.NF): masd. a-lá-j-ra [intr.] 'to go down'. də-š-lá-j-wa-z ák'ʷə-m-k'ʷan 'at that time when he was going down'. **5**. ø-j-a-ħá-jt' < j-j-a-ħá-ø-jt' (it(C1)-him(C2)-to-hear-(Aor)-Fin) 'he heard it'.

(55) **1**. ø-an-j-a-ħá < j-an-j-a-ħá (it(C1)-when-him(C2)-to-hear.Aor.NF) 'when he heard it'. **2**. j-ax-s-a-ħa-wá (= j-axʲ-s-a-ħa-wa!) (it(C1)-where-me(C2)-to-be audible to-Dyn.NF) lit. 'where it is audible to

me', i.e. 'whence it is audible to me'. The prefix *-ax-* is the Bzyp dialect form. See Note (23)-3 above. **3.** s-ná-j-p' (I(C1)-Prev-go thither-Fut.I.Fin) 'I'll go there': masd. a-ná-j-ra [intr.] 'to go thither'. **4.** ø-ajlə́-s-k'aa-p' < j-ajlə́-s-k'aa-p' (it(C1)-Prev-I(C3)-understand-Fut.I.Fin) 'I'll understand it': masd. ájl-k'aa-ra [tr.] 'to understand'. **5.** ø-j-ħʷá-n < jə-j-ħʷá-n (it(C1)-he(C3)-say-Past.Ind.Fin) 'he said it and ...': masd. a-ħʷa-rá [tr.] 'to say'. **6.** d-dʷə́kʷ-la-n (he(C1)-Prev-depart-Past.Ind.Fin) 'he departed and ...': masd. a-dʷə́kʷ-la-ra [intr.] 'to depart'. **7.** d-a-záajgʷaxa-jt' < d-a-záajgʷa-xa-ø-jt' (he(C1)-it(C2)-near-become [i.e. approach]-Aor-Fin) 'he approached it': masd. a-záajgʷa-xa-ra [intr.] 'to approach'.

(56) **1.** d-lá-j-t' < d-lá-jə-ø-jt' (he(C1)-Prev-go down-(Aor)-Fin) 'he went down': masd. a-lá-j-ra [intr.] 'to go down'. **2.** d-axʲə́-q'a-c'ʷq'ʲa-z (he(C1)-where-be-really-Past.NF) 'where he really was'. **3.** d-zə́-m-na-j-t' < d-zə́-m-na-jə-ø-jt' (he(C1)-Pot-Neg-Prev-go thither-(Aor)-Fin) 'he could not go thither'. **4.** ø-j-z-ájlə-m-k'aa-jt < jə-j-z-ájlə-m-k'aa-ø-jt (it(C1)-him(C2)-Pot-Prev-Neg-know-(Aor)-Fin) 'he could not know it': masd. ájl-k'aa-ra [tr.] 'to understand'. **5.** d-na-r-mə́-šʲtə-ø-jt' (him(C1)-Prev(thither)-they(C3)-Neg-let go-(Aor)-Fin) 'they didn't let him go there': á-na-šʲt-ra [tr.] 'to let go'.

(57) **1.** ø-ga-wá-z < j-ga-wá-z (it(C1)-be heard-Dyn-Impf.NF): masd. a-ga-rá [intr.] 'to be heard'. zə-bžʲə́ ø-ga-wá-z 'whose voice was heard'. **2.** ø-anə-j-z-ájlə-m-k'aa < j-anə-j-z-ájlə-m-k'aa-ø (it(C1)-when-him(C2)-Pot-Prev-Neg-know-Aor.NF) 'when he could not know it'. **3.** d-gʲažʲ-nə (he(C1)-return-Abs) 'he, having returned': masd. á-gʲažʲ-ra [intr.] 'to return'. **4.** d-cá-jt' (he(C1)-go-(Aor)-Fin) 'he went': masd. a-ca-rá [intr.] 'to go'.

(58) **1.** á-wp' < a-á-wp' (it(C2)-copula-Stat.Pres.Fin) 'X is it'. **2.** jə́-z-ba-z (Rel(C1)-I(C3)-see-Past.Ind.NF) 'that I saw': masd. a-бa-pá [tr.] 'to see'. abás á-wp' jə́-z-ba-z 'what I saw is the following'. **3.** s-nə́q'ʷa-xʲa-jt' (I(C1)-travel-Perf-Fin) 'I have traveled': masd. a-nə́q'ʷa-ra [intr.] 'to walk; to travel'. **4.** ø-sə-m-bá-cəzt' < j-sə-m-bá-cəzt' (it(C1)-I(C3)-Neg-see-Plupf) 'I had not seen it'. **5.** s-č'ə́-na-s-xa-n (my(Poss)-SV-Prev-I(C3)-start-Past.Ind.Fin) 'I started and ...': masd. a-č'ə́-na-xa-ra [tr.] 'to start'. **6.** j-s-a-ħa-wá-z (Rel(C1)-me(C2)-to-hear-Dyn-Impf.NF) 'that I was hearing'. **7.** j-axʲ-s-a-ħa-wá-z (it(C1)-where-me(C2)-to-hear-Dyn-Impf.NF); cf. Note (55)-1 above. **8.** s-an-a-záajgʷa-xa (I(C1)-when-it(C2)-near-become [i.e. approach].Aor.NF) 'when I approached it'. **9.** ø-á-k'ʷ-ša-nə < j-á-k'ʷ-ša-nə (they(C1)-it(C2)-Prev-surround-Abs) 'they, having surrounding it': masd. á-k'ʷ-ša-ra [intr.] 'to surround'. **10.** s-na-r-mə́-šʲtə-ø-jt' (me(C1)-Prev-they(C3)-Neg-let.go-(Aor)-Fin) 'they didn't let me go'.

(59) **1.** s-na-pš-nə́ (I(C1)-Prev-look thither-Abs) 'I, having looked thither': masd. á-na-pš-ra [intr.] 'to look thither, to observe'. **2.** ø-pxa-na-c'á-jt' < jə-pxa-na-c'á-ø-jt' (them(C1)-Prev-it(C3)-drive off-(Aor)-Fin) 'it drove them off': masd. a-pxa-c'a-rá [tr.] 'to drive off'. **3.** s-axʲə-pš-wá-z (I-where-look-Dyn-Impf.NF) 'where I was looking': masd. a-pš-rá [intr.] 'to look'. **4.** d-wajʷpsə́-wp' lit. 'he is a person': a-wajʷpsə́ = a-wajʷə́ 'a person'. **5.** d-lá-l-baa-n (he(C1)-Par-Prev-get down-Past.Ind.Fin) (= d-ná-l-baa-n) 'he got down': masd. á-l-baa-ra [intr.] 'to get down'. **6.** ak'rə-j-č'a-na-c'á-ø-jt' (something-him(C2)-Prev-it(C3)-feed-(Aor)-Fin) 'it fed something to him': masd. a-č'a-c'a-rá [tr.] 'to feed'.

(60) **1.** jə́-z-ba-z (Rel(C1)-I(C3)-see-Past.Ind.NF) 'what I saw'. **2.** jə-s-a-ħá-z (Rel(C1)-me(C2)-to-hear-Past.Ind.NF) 'what I heard'. **3.** j-ajlə́-s-k'aa-rt'ʷ (them(C1)-Prev-I(C3)-know-in order to) 'in order to know them'. **4.** s-zə́-m-na-j-t' < s-zə́-m-na-jə-ø-jt' (I(C1)-Pot-Neg-Prev-go thither-(Aor)-Fin) 'I could not go thither'. **5.** ø-r-a-j-ħʷá-jt' < j-r-a-j-ħʷá-ø-jt' (it(C1)-them(C2)-to-he(C3)-say-(Aor)-Fin) 'he said it to them'.

(61) **1.** j-ajl-k'áa-šʲa-s j-á-ma-w-zej? lit. 'what does it have as a way of knowing it?', i.e. 'is there any way

to find it out?'. **2.** ø-á-la-cʷažʷa-jt' < j-á-la-cʷažʷa-ø-jt' (they(C1)-it(C2)-Prev-talk about-(Aor)-Fin) 'they talked about it': masd. á-la-cʷažʷa-ra [intr.] 'to talk about'.

(62) **1.** ajl-k'áa-šʲa-s j-á-ma-w abrə́j a-wp' lit. 'this is what it has as the way of thinking', i.e. 'this is the way to find out about it'. **2.** ø-jə-zə́-m-ħʷa-jt' < jə-j-zə́-m-ħʷa-ø-jt' (it (nothing, C1)-him(nobody, C2)-Pot-Neg-say-(Aor)-Fin) 'he could not say it', i.e. 'nobody could say anything'.

(63) **1.** də́-q'a-zaarən < də́-q'a-z-zaarən (she(C1)-be-Past.NF-Evidential) 'it is said that she lived'. **2.** jə-s-z-ájlə-m-k'aa-ø-jt' (it(C1)-me(C2)-Pot-Prev-Neg-know-(Aor)-Fin) 'I could not know it'. **3.** ... ħʷa ak'rə-b-də́r-wa-zar (something-you.F-know-Dyn-Subordinate.Suffix) '[he asked her] whether you knew something about ...': masd. a-də́r-ra [tr.] 'to know'. **4.** d-l-á-z-c'aa-ø-jt' (he(C1)-her(C2)-it(C2)-Prev(about)-ask-(Aor)-Fin) 'he asked her about it': masd. a-z-c'aa-rá [intr.] 'to ask'.

(64) **1.** ø-marjá-wp' < j-marjá-wp' (it(C1)-easy-Stat.Pres.Fin) 'it is easy'; á-marja 'easy'. **2.** zə́-ʒbaxʷ ø-wə-ħʷa-wá lit. 'whose name you say'. **3.** d-wajʷpsə́-zar q'a-lá-p' 'it is likely that it is a person': masd. á-q'a-la-ra [intr.] 'to be possible'. **4.** də-k'-nə́ (him(C1)-catch-Abs) 'having caught him': masd. a-k'-rá [tr.] 'to catch'. **5.** də-w-z-aa-s-ga-wá-jt' (him(C1)-you.M(C2)-for-Prev-I(C3)-bring-Dyn-Fin) 'I'll bring him to you': masd. aa-ga-rá [tr.] 'to bring'. **6.** ø-sə́-w-ta-wa-zar < j-sə́-w-ta-wa-zar (it(C1)-me(C2)-you.M(C3)-give-Dyn-if) 'if you give it to me': á-ta-ra [tr.] 'to give'.

(65) **1.** ø-bə́-l-ša-wa-zar < j-bə́-l-ša-wa-zar (it(C1)-you.F(C2)-Prev-be possible-Dyn-if) 'if you could do so': masd. á-l-ša-ra [intr.] 'to be able to do'. **2.** ø-bə́-zə-m-ta-wa-da < j-bə́-zə-m-ta-wa-da (it(C1)-you.F(C2)-Rel(C3)-Neg-give-Dyn-Qu(who)) 'who on earth wouldn't give it to you?'. **3.** jə́-b-taxə-w (Rel(C1)-you.F(C2)-want-Stat.NF) 'what you want': masd. a-taxə́-zaa-ra [intr.] 'to want'. **4.** ø-bə́-s-ta-wa-jt' < j-bə́-s-ta-wa-jt' (it(C1)-you.F(C2)-I(C3)-give-Dyn-Fin) 'I'll give it to you'.

(66) **1.** ø-na-xa-c'a-nə́ < j-na-a-xa-c'a-nə́ (it(the rope, C1)-Par-its(sheep's, Poss)-Prev(head)-put-Abs) 'having put the rope on the sheep's head': masd. a-xa-c'a-rá [tr.] 'to put on'. **2.** j-sə́-t (it(C1)-me(C2)-give.Imp) 'give it to me!': masd. á-ta-ra [tr.] 'to give'. **3.** ø-sə́-t < j-sə́-t. **4.** jə́-w-ba-z (Rel(C1)-you.M(C3)-see-Ind.NF) j-áa-ga-ra (it(C1)-Prev-bring-in order to) 'in order to bring what you saw'. **5.** s-ca-wá-jt' (I(C1)-go-Dyn-Fin) 'I'll go'.

(67) **1.** ø-j-m-áw-[w]a < jə-j-m-áw-wa (it(C1)-him(C2)-Neg-receive-Abs) lit. 'he, not receiving it': masd. á-w-ra [intr.] 'to receive'. **2.** də́-q'a-z-ma (he(C1)-be-Past.NF-Qu(yes-no)), lit. 'didn't he exist?', i.e. 'where on earth was a hunter [who could not find a knife]?' **3.** j-lə́-j-ta-ø-jt' (it(C1)-her(C2)-he(C3)-give-(Aor)-Fin) 'he gave it to her'.

(68) **1.** ø-lə-ma-nə́ < j-lə-ma-nə́ (it(C1)-she(C2)-have-Abs) lit. 'she, having had it': masd. á-ma-zaa-ra [intr.] 'to have'. **2.** jə́-ø-kʷ-t'ʷa-nə < j-øə́-kʷ-t'ʷa-nə (he(C1)-it(C2)-Prev(on)-sit-Abs) 'he, having sat on it': masd. á-kʷ-t'ʷa-ra 'to sit on'. **3.** ø-a-zə-rħʷa-wa-z < j-a-zə-rħʷa-wa-z (it(the flute, C1)-it?-Rel(C3)-play-Dyn-Impf.NF) 'one who was playing the flute' : masd. a-rħʷa-rá [tr.] 'to play'.

(69) **1.** d-zə-kʷ-t'ʷá-z (he(C1)-Rel(C2)-Prev(on)-sit-Past.NF) '(the tree) which he sat on'. **2.** ø-l-k'a-lə-žʲə́-n < jə -l-k'a-lə-žʲə́-n (it(C1)-Par-Prev-she(C3)-knock down-Past.Ind.Fin) 'she knocked it down and ...': masd. a-k'á-žʲ-ra [tr.] 'to overthrow'. **3.** jə-s-šʲ-wá-jt' (it(C1)-I(C3)-kill-Dyn-Fin) 'I'll kill it' : masd. a-šʲ-rá [tr.] 'to kill'. jə-s-šʲ-wá-jt' ħʷa d-á-la-ga-jt' lit. 'having said, 'I'll kill it (with an old knife)', she began to do it'. **4.** d-á-la-ga-ø-jt' (she(C1)-it(C2)-Prev-begin-(Aor)-Fin) 'she began it': masd. á-la-ga-ra [intr.] 'to begin'.

(70) **1.** ø-z-šʲ-wá < jə-z-šʲ-wá (it(C1)-Rel(C3)-kill-Dyn.NF) 'one who kills it'. **2.** jə-xə́-j-c'ʷa-wa (Rel(C1)-Prev-he(C3)-cut-Dyn.NF) '(the part) which he (i.e. one who kills a sheep) cuts': masd. a-x-c'ʷa-rá [tr.] 'to cut'. a-xə́ [a]-á-wp' jə-xə́-j-c'ʷa-wa 'it is the head that he must cut first of all'. **3.** jə-xə́-

c'ʷc'ʷa-nə (them(C1)-Prev-cut into sections-Abs) 'having cut them into sections': masd. a-xə́-c'ʷc'ʷa-rá [tr.] 'cut into sections'. **4**. d-a-č'ə́-wp' (she(C1)-it(C2)-be engaged in-Stat.Pres.Fin) 'she is engaged in it': masd. a-č'ə́-zaa-ra [intr.] 'to be engaged in'.

(71) **1**. jə́-q'a-l-c'a-wa-z (Rel(C1)-Prev-she(C3)-do-Dyn-Impf.NF) 'what she was doing': masd. á-q'a-c'a-ra [tr.] 'to do'. **2**. d-la-pš-nə́ (he(C1)-Prev-look below-Abs) 'he, having looked below'. Cf. á-la-pš-ra [intr.] 'to peer at', d-á-la-pš-wa-jt' 'he/she peers at it'. **3**. j-ba-wá-n < jə-j-ba-wá-n (it(C1)-he(C3)-see-Dyn-Impf.Fin) 'he was seeing it'.

(72) **1**. jə́-q'a-b-c'a-wa (Rel(C1)-Prev-you.F(C3)-do-Dyn.NF) zak'ʷə́wzej 'what are you doing?'. **2**. as aʒʷə́r jə-q'a-j-c'a-wá-ma lit. 'does anyone do such a thing?', i.e. 'who would do such a thing?' **3**. ϕ-anə́-r-šʲ-wa < j-anə́-r-šʲ-wa (it(C1)-when-they(C3)-kill-Dyn.NF) 'when they kill it'. **4**. jə-b-ba-xʲá-w-ma (it(C1)-you.F(C3)-see-Perf-NF-Qu) 'have you seen it?'. **5**. j-agʲ-c'ásə-m (it(C1)-even-custom-Stat.Neg): lit. 'it is not even a custom', i.e. 'you are not supposed to do it'. **6**. ϕ-xə́-bə-m-c'ʷa-n < j-xə́-bə-m-c'ʷa-n (it(C1)-Prev-you.F(C3)-Neg-cut-Proh) 'don't cut it!'. **7**. ϕ-x-c'ʷá < jə-x-c'ʷá (it(C1)-Prev-cut.Imp) 'cut it!'. **8**. d-axʲə́-kʷə-w < d-axʲə́-kʷ-ϕə-w (he(C1)-where-Prev(on)-be-Stat.NF) '(the tree) which he is on': masd. á-kʷ-zaa-ra [intr.] 'to be on'. **9**. d-zə-xʷna-ʒa-wá-m (she(C1)-Pot-climb-Emph-Dyn-Neg) 'she cannot climb at all': masd. a-xʷna-rá [intr.] 'to climb'.

(73) **1**. nán-xajt' = nan. **2**. a-šʲə́-šʲa ϕ-z-də́r-wa-jt' (< jə-z-də́r-wa-jt') (it(C1)-I(C3)-know-Dyn-Fin) 'I know how to kill it'. **3**. sə́-mčʲ ϕ-á-kʷ-xa-wa-m ([it(C1)-]it(C2)-Prev-overpower-Dyn-Neg) 'I have no strength to do it': masd. á-kʷ-xa-ra [intr.] 'to overpower'. **4**. w-sə́-cxraa-rawázej = w-sə́-cxraa (you.M(C1)-me(C2)-help.Imp) 'then, help me!': masd. a-cxə́raa-ra [intr.] 'to help'. **5**. lə-č-rə́cħa-t'ʷ-nə (her(Poss)-Self-Prev-pretend to be pitiful-Abs) lit. '[she said] pretending to be pitiful': masd. a-č-rə́cħa-t'ʷ-ra [tr.] 'to pretend to be poor'.

(74) **1**. j-alə́-j-də́r-aa-wa-jz = j-alə́-j-də́r-aa-wa-z, lit. 'where did he know it from?': masd. a-də́r-ra [tr.] 'to know'. **2**. ϕ-šʲ-nə́ < jə -šʲ-nə́ (it(C1)-kill-Abs) 'having killed it'. **3**. jə-lə́-j-ta-ϕ-jt' (it(C1)-her(C2)-he(C3)-give-(Aor)-Fin) 'he gave it to her'.

(75) **1**. a-ncʷá jə-də́r-p' 'God knows it', 'nobody knows it'. Wát'k'a-w-ma, sp'ə́jrt'-w-ma, a-ncʷá jə-də́r-p' 'Nobody knows whether it's vodka or whether it's spirits'. **2**. ϕ-lə́-ma-n <jə-lə́-ma-n (it(C1)-her(C2)-have-Stat.Past.Fin) 'she had it'. **3**. ə́-žʷ < jə́-žʷ (it(C1)-drink.Imp) 'drink it!': masd. á-žʷ-ra [tr.] 'to drink'. **4**. ϕ-axʲ-s-zə́-w-šʲə-z < [j-]axʲ-s-zə́-w-šʲə-z ([it(C1)-]where-me(C2)-for-you.M(C3)-kill-Past.Ind.NF) a-q'nə́t'ʷ 'because you killed it for me'. **5**. a-ʒba-gʲə́ w-á-m-k'-wa-j (you.M(C1)-it(C3)-Neg-catch-Dyn-Qu), lit. 'doesn't the thirst catch you, too?', i.e. 'aren't you thirsty?'. **6**. d-jʷá-xa-n < d-jʷa-á-xa-n (he(C1)-Prev-it(C2)-raise-Past.Ind.Fin) 'he raised it and ...': masd. a-jʷá-xa-ra [intr.] 'to raise'. **7**. jə-žʷə́-jt' < jə-j-žʷə́-ϕ-jt' (it(C1)-he(C3)-drink-(Aor)-Fin) 'he drank it'. d-jʷá-xa-n jə-žʷə́-jt' 'he drank it up'.

(76) **1**. ϕ-ané-j-žʷ < j-ané-j-žʷ-ϕ (it(C1)-when-he(C3)-drink-Aor.NF) 'when he drank'. j-ané-j-žʷ á-šʲtaxʲ 'after he drank it'. **2**. jə́-jə-čʲħa-wa-zəj (what(C1)-he(C3)-endure-Dyn-Qu) lit. 'what does he endure?', i.e. 'he can no longer endure it': masd. á-čʲħa-ra [tr.] 'to endure'. **3**. a-məjnə́wt-k' d-a-šʲə́-jt' (him(C1)-it(the drink, C3)-kill-(Aor)-Fin), lit. 'it killed him in a minute', i.e. 'he got drunk in a minute'. **4**. d-xəlga-ʒə́lga-wa d-áa-q'a-la-jt' 'he began to stagger about': masd. á-q'a-la-ra [intr.] 'to begin'.

(77) **1**. d-aa-jə́-mc'a-sə-n (she(C1)-Par-him(C2)-Prev-seize-Past.Ind.Fin) 'she seized him quickly and ...': masd. á-mc'a-s-ra [intr.] 'to seize'. **2**. d-aa-nə́-l-k'əla-n (him(C1)-Par-Prev-she(C3)-hold-Past.Ind.Fin) 'she held him down and ...': masd. a-n-k'ə́la-ra [tr.] 'to hold'. **3**. jə́-mčʲ ϕ-mač'ʲə-m-xá-ϕ-j ([it(C1)]-weak-Neg-become-Aor.NF-Qu) 'he lost his strength': masd. a-máč'ʲ-xa-ra [intr.] 'to become weaker'.

4. ø-z-la-ná-l-ga-z < jə-z-la-ná-l-ga-z (it(the sheep, C1)-Rel(C2)-with-Prev-she(C3)-take-Past.Ind.NF) '[the rope] that she took the sheep with': masd. a-ná-ga-ra [tr.] 'to take thither'. **5.** d-aa-č'á-l-ħʷa-n (him(C1)-Par-Prev-she(C3)-bind-Past.Ind.Fin) 'she bound him up and ...': masd. a-č'a-ħʷa-rá [tr.] 'to bind'. **6.** d-áa-šʲtə-l-xə-n (him(C1)-Par-Prev-she(C3)-take up-Past.Ind.Fin) 'she took him up and ...': masd. á-šʲtə-x-ra [tr.] 'to take up'. **7.** də-l-gá-ø-jt' (him(C1)-she(C3)-take-(Aor)-Fin) 'she took him': masd. a-ga-rá [tr.] 'to take'. Cf. Note (57)-1.

(78) **1.** d-axʲ-ná-l-ga-z (him(C1)-where(there)-Prev-she(C3)-take-Past.Ind.NF): masd. a-ná-ga-ra [tr.] 'to take s.o. there'. **2.** ø-aa-rt'-nə (it(C1)-Prev-open-Abs): masd. áa-rt'-ra [tr.] 'to open'. **3.** d-na-j-gʷa-nə́ (he(the king, C1)-Prev-him(C2)-push-Abs): masd. a-ná-gʷa-ra [intr.] 'to push *someone in there*'. **4.** də-jʷná-j-k'ə-ø-jt' (him(C1)-Prev-he(the king, C3)-lock in-(Aor)-Fin): masd. a-jʷna-k'-rá [tr.] 'to lock *someone* in'.

(79) **1.** də-jʷna-xá-ø-jt' (he(C1)-Prev-fall into-(Aor)-Fin): masd. a-jʷna-xa-rá [intr.] 'to fall into'. **2.** jə́-q'a-j-c'a-wa-j (Rel(C1)-Prev-he(C3)-do-Dyn-what): masd. á-q'a-c'a-ra [tr.] 'to do'.

(80) **1.** jə́-c'a-xa-jt' (it(the bull, C1)-Prev(under)-find oneself-(Aor)-Fin): masd. á-c'a-xa-ra [intr.] 'to find oneself under'. **2.** də-z-la-cá-z (he(C1)-Rel(C2)-with-go-Past.Ind.NF) 'how he went': masd. a-ca-rá [intr.] 'to go'. **3.** d-axʲ-cá-z (he(C1)-where-go-Past.Ind.NF) 'where he went/had gone'. **4.** də-z-gá-z (him(C1)-Rel(C3)-take-Past.Ind.NF) 'who took him': masd. a-ga-rá [tr.] 'to take, carry'. **5.** jə-z-də́r-ʒa-wa-m < ø-jə-z-də́r-ʒa-wa-m (it(nothing, C1)-he(C2)-Pot-know-Emph-Dyn-Neg) 'he knows nothing': masd. a-də́r-ra [tr.] 'to know'.

(81) **1.** á-lada a-ħʷá-jt', á-jʷada a-ħʷá-jt' 'it (the bull) searched up and down (for the boy)'. anáxʲ a-ħʷá-jt', aráxʲ a-ħʷá-jt' 'it searched here, there, and everywhere'. **2.** a-t'ʷə́la a-cʷá ø-a-x-ná-xə-jt' lit. 'it (the bull) removed the skin from the world', i.e. 'the bull searched all over the world (for the boy)'. ø-a-x-ná-xə-jt' (it(the skin, C1)-it(the world, C2)-Prev-it(the bull, C3)-remove-(Aor)-Fin): masd. a-xə́-x-ra [tr.] 'to remove'. **3.** d-axʲ-cá-z ø-a-ba-wá-m (it(C1)-it(the bull, C3)-see-Dyn-Neg) lit. 'it (the bull) doesn't see it (= where the boy went)', i.e. 'the bull doesn't know where the boy went'. masd. a-ba-rá [tr.] 'to see'. **4.** d-ax-a-gá = d-axʲ-a-gá (him(C1)-where-it(C3)-take.Aor.NF). For the prefix *-ax-*, see Note (23-3). **5.** jə-də́r-p' < jə-j-də́r-p' (it(C1)-he(Allah, C3)-know-Fut.I.Fin) 'Allah will know it'.

(82) **1.** d-axʲə-jʷná-r-k'ə-z (him(C1)-where-Prev-they(C3)-lock.in-Past.Ind.NF), see Note (78-4) above. **2.** ak'rə-j-č'á-r-c'a-wa-n (something-him(C2)-Prev-they(C3)-feed-Dyn-Impf) 'they gave him some food to eat'. masd. a-k'ra-č'a-c'a-rá [tr.] 'to feed'. **3.** d-a-də-r-k'-wá-mə-zt' (him(C1)-it(hunger, C2)-they(C3)-Caus-catch-Dyn-Neg-Impf.Fin) lit. 'they didn't use to make hunger catch him', i.e. 'they didn't cause him to die of hunger'. masd. a-k'-rá [tr.] 'to catch'. Cf. á-mla s-a-k'-wá-jt' 'I am hungry'. **4.** jə-z-xʷárta-w-zaj 'it is good for nothing', cf. a-xʷárta 'help', 'useful'. **5.** xʲaá-s j-k'ə́-jt' < jə-j-k'ə́-ø-jt' (it(the bull, C1)-he(C3)-catch-(Aor)-Fin) 'he worried about the bull'. Cf. xʲaá-s jə-s-k'ə́-wp' 'I am anxious about it'. **6.** á-j-ta-r < [j]-á-j-ta-r ([it(the knowledge, C1)-]to it(the bull, C2)-he(C3)-give-Subjunctive): masd. á-ta-ra [tr.] 'to give'. **7.** j-tax-xá-jt' < [jə-]j-tax-xá-ø-jt' ([it(C1)]-he(C2)-wish to-(Aor)-Fin): masd. a-tax-xa-rá [inverse, intr.] 'to wish for'. **8.** jə-zlá-j-ta-wa-j (it(C1)-how-he(C3)-give-Dyn-Qu) 'How will he give it?'

(83) **1.** d-xə́rkʷakʷa-wa (he(C1)-grieve-Abs): masd. a-xə́rkʷakʷa [intr.] 'to grieve'. **2.** də-š-t'ʷá-z (he(C1)-how-be sitting-Stat.Past.NF) 'when he was sitting': masd. a-t'ʷa-rá [intr.] 'to be sitting'. **3.** wəs ak'ʷə-m-k'ʷa 'at the time'. **4.** ø-pər-nə́ < [j-]pər-nə́ ([it(C1)-]fly-Abs) 'having flown': masd. á-pər-ra [intr.] 'to fly'. **5.** j-aá-j-n (it(C1)-Prev-come here-Past.Ind.Fin): masd. aá-j-ra [intr.] 'to come here'. **6.** j-áa-kʷ-t'ʷa-jt' (it(a crow, C1)-Par-Prev(on)-sit down-(Aor)-Fin): masd. á-kʷ-t'ʷa-ra [intr.] 'to sit down on'.

(84) **1.** j-an-áa-[a]-kʷ-t'ʷa (it(the crow, C1)-when-Par-it(the window, C2)-Prev(on)-sit down.Aor.NF) lit.

'when the crow sat down on the window'. **2.** d-c'ʷə́wa-wa, 'he, crying': masd. a-c'ʷə́wa-ra [intr.] 'to cry'. **3.** də-š-t'ʷá-z (he-how-be sitting-Stat.Past.NF) 'how he was sitting': masd. a-t'ʷa-rá [intr.] 'to be sitting'. **4.** ø-an-a-bá < [j]-an-a-bá ([it(C1)-]when-it(the crow, C3)-see.Aor.NF): masd. a-ba-rá [tr.] 'to see'. **5.** j-wə́-xʲ-zaj (Rel(C1)-you.M(C2)-happen-(Aor)-what) 'What happened to you?': masd. á-xʲ-ra [intr.] 'to happen to'. **6.** w-zə-r-c'ʷə́wa-wa-j (you.M(C1)-Rel(C3)-Caus-cry-Dyn-what) 'What is making you cry?' **7.** j-á-z-c'aa-jt' < [j]-j-á-z-c'aa-jt' ([it(the crow, C1)-]him(C2)-it-Prev-ask-(Aor)-Fin) 'the crow asked him about it': masd. a-z-c'aa-rá [intr.] 'to ask'.

(85) **1.** *s*ə-zə-r-c'ʷə́wa-wa (me(C1)-Rel(C3)-Caus-cry-Dyn.NF) 'the one who makes me cry': masd. a-r-c'ʷə́wa-ra [tr.] 'to make s.o. cry'. **2.** [a]-a-wp' ([it(C2)-]copula-Stat.Pres.Fin) 'X is it'. See Notes (4)-1, (14)-5 and (23)-2. **3.** sə́-kʷ-t'ʷa-n < sə́-ø-kʷ-t'ʷa-n (I(C1)-it(a chestnut tree, C2)-Prev(on)-sit-Stat.Past.Fin) 'I was sitting on the top of a chestnut tree'.: masd. á-kʷ-t'ʷa-zaa-ra [intr.] 'to sit on'. **4.** jə́-kʷ-xa-jt' < jə́-ø-kʷ-xa-jt' (it(my flute, C1)-it(the chestnut tree, C2)-Prev(on)-remain alone-(Aor)-Fin) 'my flute has remained on the chestnut tree'.: masd. á-kʷ-xa-ra [intr.] 'to remain alone'. **5.** j-sə́-ma-zar (it(C1)-I(C2)-have-Subjunctive) 'if I had had it': masd. á-ma-zaa-ra [intr.] 'to have'. **6.** s-taxə́-n < jə-s-taxə́-n (it(C1)-I(C2)-want-Stat.Past.Fin) 'I wanted it': masd. a-taxə́-zaa-ra [intr.] 'to want'. **7.** a-la-sə-r-č'ə́ɣʲ-wa-mə-zt' < j-a-la-sə-r-č'ə́ɣʲ-wa-mə-zt' (it(my heart, C1)-it(my flute, C2)-with-I(C3)-Caus-be bored-Dyn-Neg-Impf.Fin) lit. 'I would not have bored my heart with my flute', i.e. 'my flute would not have bored me': masd. a-rč'ə́ɣʲ-ra [tr.] 'to bore'. Cf. s-gʷə č'ə́ɣʲ-wa-jt' 'I am bored'. The imperfect tense expresses the past subjunctive in an apodosis.

(86) **1.** s-axʲə́-na-pš-wa: masd. á-na-pš-ra [intr.] 'to look there'. **2.** ħ-aj-cʷážʷa-r: masd. áj-cʷažʷa-ra [intr.] 'to talk with each other'. **3.** q'a-la-wá-m: masd. á-q'a-la-ra [intr.] 'to be possible'. Cf. b-cá-r q'a-lo-wá-m 'it is impossible for you to go'. **4.** s-á-w-jə-šʲt-wa-m (me(C1)-Dummy-Prev-he(C3)-release-Dyn-Neg) 'he will not release me': masd. á-wə-šʲt-ra [tr.] 'to release'. **5.** s-gʷáq'-wa: masd. a-gʷáq'-ra [intr.] 'to suffer'. **6.** sə-jʷna-xa-jt', see Note (79-1) above.

(87) **1.** jə-w-z-aa-z-ga-wá-jt' (it(C1)-you(C2)-for-Prev-I(C3)-bring-Dyn-Fin) 'I'll bring it to you': masd. aa-ga-rá [tr.] 'to bring'. **2.** a-č'ə́-na-na-xa-n (its(Poss)-SV-Prev-it(C3)-set out-Past.Ind.Fin) 'it set out and': masd. a-č'ə́-na-xa-ra [tr.] 'to set out'. **3.** jə-bžʲa-k'-nə́ (it(the flute, C1)-Prev(between)-hold-Abs) 'having held it between [the beaks]': masd. a-bžʲa-k'-rá [tr.] 'to hold *sth* between'. **4.** j-á-ma-nə (it(the flute)-it(the crow, C2)-have-Abs) 'it (the crow), having had it (the flute)'. **5.** j-aá-j-t' (it(C1)-Prev(here)-come-(Aor)-Fin) 'it came here': masd. aá-j-ra [intr.] 'come here'.

(88) **1.** j-ø-kə́lə-ršʷ-nə (it(the flute, C1)-[it(the window, C2)]-Prev(through)-throw-Abs) 'having thrown the flute into the window', cf. á-ršʷ-ra [tr.] 'to throw'. **2.** d-axʲə-jʷna-k'ə́-z 'where he was locked in'. For masdar see Note (78-4). **3.** j-ná-ta-jt' < jə-j-ná-ta-jt' (it(the flute, C1)-him(C2)-it(the crow, C3)-give-(Aor)-Fin) 'the crow gave it to him': masd. á-ta-ra [tr.] 'to give'.

(89) **1.** [j]-an-jə-mpə́xʲa-šʷa-gʷə́šʲa (it(C1)-when-he(C2)-Prev-find-(Aor.NF)-at last) 'when he found it at last': masd. a-mpə́xʲa-šʷa-ra [intr. inverse] 'to find'. **2.** d-k'ə́la-t'ʷa-nə 'he, having sat on the windowsill': masd. a-k'ə́la-t'ʷa-ra [intr.] 'to sit in an aperture'. **3.** d-á-la-ga-jt' (he(C1)-it(to play, C2)-Prev-begin-(Aor)-Fin) 'he began to play the flute': masd. á-la-ga-ra [intr.] 'to begin'.

(90) **1.** aa-ga-r-á-wp' < j-aa-ga-r-á-wp' (it(C1)-Prev-bring-must-be-Stat.Pres.Fin) 'the bull must be brought': masd. aa-ga-rá [tr.] 'to bring'. **2.** d-zə-rgʷáq'-wa (him(C1)-Rel(C3)-worry-Dyn.NF) 'the one who worries him': masd. a-rgʷáq'-ra [tr.] 'to worry'. Cf. a-gʷáq'-ra [intr.] 'to suffer'.

(91) **1.** an-r-a-ħá < j-an-r-a-ħá (it(C1)-when-them(C2)-to-hear.Aor.NF) 'when they heard it': masd. a-ħa-rá [intr. inverse] 'to hear'. **2.** j-š-ájza-wa-z (they(C1)-how-gather-Dyn-Impf) ajpš 'as they used to gather (at that fir grove)': masd. ájza-ra [intr.] 'to gather'. **3.** jə́-q'a-z : masd. á-q'a-zaa-ra [intr.] 'to be'.

gəgšʷə́g-s, psaátʼʷə-s jə́-qʼa-z zagʲə́ ajzá-jtʼ 'all that were wild animals and birds gathered'. **4.** tʷə́-jtʼ < j-tʷə́-jtʼ 'it was filled': masd. a-tʷ-rá [intr.] 'to fill'.

(92) **1.** j-[a]-a-ħá-jtʼ (it(its voice, C1)-it(the bull, C2)-to-hear-(Aor)-Fin) 'the bull also heard the sound of the flute'.

(93) **1.** j-an-[a]-a-ħá (it(its voice, C1)-when-it(the bull, C2)-to-hear.Aor.NF) 'when the bull heard the sound of the flute'. **2.** j-la-trə́-s-nə (it(C1)-Par-Prev-break away-Abs): masd. a-trə́-s-ra [intr.] 'to break away'. **3.** jə́-jʷ-nə (it(C1)-run-Abs): masd. á-jʷ-ra [intr.] 'to run'. **4.** a-čʼ-áa-na-xa-jtʼ (its(Poss)-SV-Par-it(C3)-set out-(Aor)-Fin) 'it set out': masd. a-čʼə́-na-xa-ra [tr.] 'to set out'.

(94) **1.** j-š-aá-j-wa-z (it(C1)-how-Prev(here)-come-Dyn-Impf.NF) lit. 'how it was coming here'. **2.** j-la-rə́-sə-n (it(the bull, C1)-Par-them(the doors, C2)-hit-Past.Ind.Fin) 'it hit them': masd. á-s-ra [intr.] 'to hit'. **3.** znəkʼ á-la 'each time'. **4.** jə-p-na-čə́-jtʼ (them(C1)-Prev-it(the bull, C3)-break-(Aor)-Fin) 'it broke them': masd. a-p-č-rá [tr.] 'to break'. **5.** n-xá-jtʼ < jə-n-xá-jtʼ (they(C1)-Prev-remain-(Aor)-Fin) 'three doors remained': masd. a-n-xa-rá [intr.] 'to remain'. **6.** á-z-tʼʷəjʷa-kʼ 'one of its horns'. The affix *-z-* with the suffix *-kʼ-* is used to mark one part of a (body) pair; e.g., lə́-z-la-kʼ 'one of her eyes'. **7.** x-žʷá-jtʼ < jə-x-žʷá-jtʼ (it(C1)-Prev-be broken-(Aor)-Fin) 'it was broken': masd. a-x-žʷa-rá [labile] 'to break; to be broken'.

(95) **1.** j-aanə́-m-čʼas-kʼʷa (it(the bull, C1)-Prev-Neg-stop-Abs) 'it didn't stop': masd. áan-čʼas-ra [intr.] 'to stop; to remain'. **2.** j-áan-xa-z (Rel(C1)-Prev-remain-Past.Ind.NF) '(the doors) which remained': masd. áan-xa-ra [intr.] 'to remain'. **3.** j-á-xa-wa (it(the bull, C1)-it(the door, C2)-pull-Abs) 'the bull, pulling the door': masd. á-xa-ra [intr.] 'to pull'. **4.** j-á-gʷa-wa (it(the bull, C1)-it(the door, C2)-push-Abs) 'the bull, pushing the door': masd. á-gʷa-ra [intr.] 'to push'. **5.** jə-p-na-čə́-n (them(the doors, C1)-Prev-it(the bull, C3)-break-Past.Ind.Fin) 'it broke them and'. **6.** j-nə-jʷna-šə́la-n (it(C1)-Par-Prev-go into-Past.Ind.Fin) 'it went into and': masd. a-jʷna-šə́la-ra [intr.] 'to go into'. **7.** d-jʷə́-kʷ-tʼʷa-n (he(C1)-Par-Prev(on)-sit-Past.Ind.Fin) 'he got on (the bull's back)': masd. á-kʷ-tʼʷa-ra [intr.] 'to sit down on'. **8.** jə-jʷ-dʷə́l-pa-n (it(C1)-Par-Prev(out)-rush-Past.Ind.Fin) 'it rushed out': masd. a-dʷə́l-pa-ra [intr.] 'to rush out'.

(96) **1.** [j]-axʲ-kʼə́d-na-qʼʲa-z ([it(the head, C1)]-where-Prev-it(the bull, C3)-strike-Past.Ind.NF) 'the bull struck its head': masd. a-kʼə́d-qʼʲa-ra [tr.] 'to strike'. **2.** [j]-cʼəsə́-jtʼ ([it(its brain, C1)]-swing-(Aor)-Fin) 'it swung': masd. a-cʼəs-rá [intr.] 'to swing; to move'.

(97) **1.** d-á-ma (him(C1)-it(the bull, C2)-have.Abs) 'the bull, taking him': masd. á-ma-zaa-ra [intr.] 'to have'. **2.** j-axʲ-ná-j-z (it(C1)-where-Prev(there)-go-Past.Ind.NF) '(the valley) that it reached': masd. a-ná-j-ra [intr.] 'to go there'. **3.** də́-kʷ-na-cʼa-jtʼ < də́-ø-kʷ-na-cʼa-jtʼ (him(C1)-[it(the tree, C2)]-Prev(on)-it(the bull, C3)-put-(Aor)-Fin) 'the bull put him on the tree': masd. á-kʷ-cʼa-ra [tr.] 'to put on'.

(98) **1.** w-lə́-m-baa-n (you.M(C1)-Prev-Neg-descend-Proh) 'Don't climb down!': masd. á-l-baa-ra [intr.] 'to descend, to climb down'. **2.** [jə]-w-a-sə-m-ħʷá-zə-j ([it(C1)-]you.M(C2)-to-I(C3)-Neg-say-Past.Ind.NF-Qu) 'didn't I say it to you?': masd. a-ħʷa-rá [tr.] 'to say'. **3.** w-zə́-l-baa-zə-j (you(C1)-why-Prev-descend-Past.Ind.NF-Qu) 'Why did you climb down?'.

(99) **1.** wə-xʷna-nə́ (you.M(C1)-climb-Abs): masd. a-xʷna-rá [intr.] 'to climb down'. **2.** wə́-kʷ-tʼʷa (you.M-Prev(on)-sit down.Imp) 'sit down!': masd. á-kʷ-tʼʷa-ra [intr.] 'to sit down on'. **3.** s-m-aá-kʼʷa (I(C1)-Neg-come here-Abs) 'until I come back': masd. aa-rá [intr.] 'to come here'. **4.** [j]-j-á-na-ħʷa-jtʼ ([it(C1)]-him(C2)-to-it(the bull, C3)-say-(Aor)-Fin) 'the bull said it to him'.

(100) **1.** [jə]-bžʲə́-m-s-xʲa-zə-j ([it(C1)]-Prev-Neg-be.broken-Plupf-NF-Qu) 'Hadn't it been broken?': masd. a-bžʲə́-s-ra [intr.] 'to be broken; to go bad'. **2.** j-axʲə́-jʷ-tə-cʼə-z (it(the bull, C1)-where-Par-Prev-go.out-Past.Ind.NF) 'where the bull went out': masd. a-tə́-cʼ-ra [intr.] 'to go out'. **3.** [j]-ta-xá-jtʼ

([it(C1)]-Prev-die-(Aor)-Fin) 'it died': masd. a-ta-xa-rá [intr.] 'to perish'. **4**. jə-š-ná-j-wa-z (it(C2)-how-Prev(here)-come-Dyn-Impf.NF) lit. 'how it was coming here', i.e. 'when the bull was coming to (a stream)'. **5**. a-blaxác' gʲažʲə́-n 'it felt dizzy and': masd. a-blaxác'-gʲežʲ-ra [intr.] 'to feel dizzy', cf. sə-blaxác' gʲežʲ-wá-jt' 'I feel dizzy'. **6**. j-ø-tá-ħa-n (it(the bull, C1)-[it(the stream, C2)-]Prev(in)-fall-Past.Ind.Fin) 'the bull fell into the stream': á-ta-ħa-ra [intr.] 'to fall in'. **7**. jə-z-tə́-m-c'-ʒa-jt' (it(C1)-Pot-Prev(out of)-Neg-go-Emph-(Aor)-Fin) 'it was unable to go out (of the stream)': masd. a-tə́-c'-ra [intr.] 'to go out'.

(101) **1**. d-axʲə́-ø-kʷ-t'ʷa-z (he(C1)-where-[it (the tree, C2)]-Prev(on)-sit-Stat.Past.NF) 'when he was sitting on the tree': masd. á-kʷ-t'ʷa-zaa-ra [intr.] 'to sit on'. **2**. d-a-k'ə́-jt' (him(C1)-it(hunger, C3)-catch-(Aor)-Fin) lit. 'it caught him': masd. a-k'-rá [tr.] 'to catch'. **3**. də-pšə́-jt' (he(C1)-wait-(Aor)-Fin) 'he waited': masd. a-pš-rá [intr.] 'to wait'. **4**. j-ba-wá-m < [jə]-j-ba-wá-m ([it(C1)-]he(C3)-see-Dyn-Neg) 'he won't see it'. **5**. agʲ-aá-j-wa-m 'nothing will come here'. **6**. [j]-axʲ-a-rxá-z ([it(the head, C1)-]where-it(the bull, C3)-turn-Past.Ind.NF) lit. 'where the bull turned its head', i.e. '(he does not know) where the bull went away to': masd. a-rxa-rá [tr.] 'to turn, to aim'. **7**. ø-jə-z-də́r-ʒa-wa-m < [j-]jə-z-də́r-ʒa-wa-m ([it(C1)-]him(C2)-Pot-know-Emph-Dyn-Neg) 'he doesn't know it': masd. a-də́r-ra [tr.] 'to know'.

(102) **1**. a-jə-rħʷa-wa < [j-]a-jə-rħʷa-wa ([it(the flute, C1)-]Dummy-he(C3)-play-Abs) 'he (began to) play the flute': masd. a-rħʷa-rá [tr.] 'to play'. **2**. j-abá-q'a-w (it(C1)-where-be-Stat.Pres.NF) 'where is it?': masd. á-q'a-zaa-ra [intr.] 'to be'.

(103) **1**. wə-z-aaʒá-z (you.M(C1)-Rel(C3)-bring up-Past.Ind.NF) 'the one who brought you up': masd. áaʒa-ra [tr.] 'to bring up'. **2**. jə-psə́-jt' (it(C1)-die-(Aor)-Fin) 'it died': masd. a-ps-rá [intr.] 'to die'.

(104) **1**. a-č'-a-wp' 'X is at a certain place', cf. á-kalakʲ a-č'ə́ 'in the town'.

(105) **1**. j-q'á-j-c'a-gʷə́šʲa-wa-jəz (Rel(C1)-Prev-he(C3)-do-Suffix-Dyn-What) 'What could the poor boy do?': masd. á-q'a-č'a-ra [tr.] 'to do'. -gʷə́šʲa is used to express nuances of misfortune, regret, etc. **2**. jə́-ma-z < j-jə́-ma-z (Rel(C1)-he(C2)-have-Stat.Past.NF) '(the one) which he had'. **3**. [a-]ák'ʷə-n ([it(his bull, C2)-]be-Stat.Past.Fin) 'X was only a bull'. **4**. d-zə-kʷ-gʷə́ɣ-wa (he(C1)-Rel(C2)-Prev-rely on-Dyn.NF) 'the one upon which he relies': masd. a-kʷ-gʷə́ɣ-ra [intr.] 'to rely upon'. **5**. ħʷa ak'agʲə́ jə́-ma-ʒa-mə-zt' 'he had nothing to (rely upon)'.

(106) **1**. j-an-j-á-na-ħʷa (it(C1)-when-him(C2)-to-it(the raven, C3)-say.Aor.NF) 'when the raven told him that ...'. **2**. d-lá-l-baa-n (he(C1)-Par-Prev-descend-Past.Ind.Fin) 'he climbed down (from the tree) quickly': masd. á-l-baa-ra [intr.] 'to descend'. **3**. j-č'ə́-na-j-xa-n (his(Poss)-SV-Prev-he(C3)-set out-Past.Ind.Fin) 'he set out': masd. a-č'ə́-na-xa-ra [intr.] 'to set out'. **4**. [j-]jə-pšaá-jt' ([it(the place where his bull died, C1)-]he(C3)-find-(Aor)-Fin) 'he found it': masd. á-pšaa-ra [tr.] 'to find'.

(107) **1**. j-xə́ axʲə́-j-ga-wa-z anə-j-má-w 'when he does not know where to put himself'. **2**. [j-]aa-jə-rq'ʲá-n ([it(the belly, C1)-]Par-he(C3)-cut-Past.Ind.Fin) 'he cut it and ...': masd. a-rq'ʲa-ra [tr.] 'to cut'. **3**. də-l-ø-tá-la-n (he(C1)-Par-[it(the belly, C2)-]Prev(into)-go-Past.Ind.Fin) 'he went into the bull's belly': masd. a-tá-la-ra [intr.] 'to go into'. **4**. də-l-[ø-]ta-psə́ (he(C1)-Par-[it(the belly, C2)-]Prev(in)-die.Abs.Past) 'he died in the bull's belly': masd. a-ta-ps-rá [intr.] 'to die inside'.

(108) **1**. d-šə́-l-aaʒa-z (him(C1)-how-she(C3)-bring up-Past.Ind.NF) 'how she brought him up'.

4. How the king's daughter turned into a boy

Text

(1) Ахәынҭқар иӡха дшычкунхаз

(2) Ҳәынҭқарк дыҟан, жәаҩык аӡхацәа имазаарын, аӡа димаӡамызт.

(3) Иӡхәыс лцәа лтәымкуа дҟалеит.

(4) —Иагарааны исхәахьазаргьы иагараан исычҳахьазаргьы абаржәы аӡа даныбмоу, ибоуа аӡҳагьы баргьы шәысшьуеит, — ҳәа леиҳәеит аҳәынҭқар иӡхәыс.

(5) Аӡхәыс рыцҳа лара илҭахымкуа дыҟазма аӡа длоур, аха анцәа длиҭом, шәымбо!

(6) Ари лхатца ас аниҳәа, акьыжыҳәа инеимаҭәаны атцә(ы́)уара далагеит.

(7) Зыгура лгоз аҳәса быргцәа аалган драцәажәеит, «ӡсыхуа сышәҭ, схатца сишьуеит исыӡсыхуоузеи?» лхәеит.

(8) Ари анҭ аҳәсакуа анс анралҳәа, «бымшәан, банацьалбеит, макьана анцәа иҳәаны аӡа дбауазаргьы быздыруам, ус акумкуа, аӡха дбаургьы ӡсыхуак бзаауп» ҳәа ларҳәеит.

(9) Ус ишыҟаз акумкуан, ах иӡхәыс лаамҭа анааи, ахшара длоут, аха ажәеизаҩык илаузгьы дыӡҳахеит.

(10) Ари уажәгьы аӡха длоут, аха ауаа азыҟатцаны илымамзи, «ииз дычқуноуп» рҳәан аҳәынҭқар дыржьан, ларгьы деикухеит.

(11) Ари аӡӡаб ииз драаӡеит, абар уажә шьҭа жәаҩа шықуса лхытцуеит, ачкун маҭәа лшәуп.

(12) —Ари уажәшьҭа дхыжәӡа дыҟоуп, асунеҭ изызуеит, — иҳәеит аб (аҳәынҭқар, дычқуноу цьимшьои!)

(13) Ари аӡӡаб хучы лаб ас аниҳәа, лара дшәан, днеин, абора давагыланы акьажыҳәа атцәуара далагеит.

(14) Або́ра аҩну́тцҟа аҿы́ ҭакы́н.

(15) Уи иҭакы́з аҿы́ ахучы́ дкьы́зкьы́зуа лтцәы́уабжьы анаҳа́, ус аҳәе́ит:

(16) —О, уара́, уа иавагы́лоу ахучы́, узыртцәыуозеи?

(17) —Сызыртцәыуозеи ҳәа аҟоума, сабамтцәуо, саб сара сычқуноу цьишьоит, асунеҭ узызуеит ҳәа сеиҳәеит, сара сызӡабуп, сшычкунам аайликаар, сангьы саргьы ҳаишьуеит саб, — лҳәеит.

(18) —Аҳаҳаи акы уацәымшәан, уаб асунеҭ анузиуша аламҭала хучык аҿы сырхумарыр сҭахыуп ҳәа иаҳәа, нас аҿырхумарра азин шӡауимҭари.

(19) Аҿырхумарра азин ануиҭалакь, уааины сара усықутәа, сара усырхумарып.

(20) Знык уааuны сара усықутәар, нас сара́ уе́иқурхашьа зды́руеит, — аҳәеит аҿы.

(21) Ари́ а́ӡӡаб хучы́ аҿы́ иаҳәа́з аагәны́лкыкан, дгурӡьан ды́ҩны ла́н лҿы́ дне́ин илалҳәеит абас, абас аҿы исабжьанагаз, исанаҳәаз абри ауп ҳәа.

(22) Ла́нгьы дгәы́рӡьатцәа дҟале́ит.

(23) Аҳәынҭқар ачара ажәра, иуит.

(24) —Ба́ба, уара́, уажәшьҭа́ ушьҭа́стцоит, — иҳәеит, — уажәшьҭа иазхоит, — иҳәеит. (Ари уажәы ахучы лоуп изеиҳәо).

(25) —Саб, ибзиоуп, иухәо сакушахатәуп, аха аказы сухеар атахын, азин сыт, иќалозар аҿы сырхумарыр стахыуп, — ихәеит «ачкун». (Ачкун ххәоит уажәшьта, ачкун дабаќоу, дызҕабуп, аха дшызҕабу лаб издырӡом ауп.)

(26) —Ибзиоуп, аҿы урхумаруазар, ирхумар, — ихәеит ахәынтқар.

(27) Нас аҿырхумарра азин анлоу, чкýна матәала деилахәан уеизгьы, днеин аҿы дѳакутәан, алала илырѳит, аѳада илырѳит, аҿы лырхумарт, аха жәлары ицьаршьо илырхумарит.

(28) Аҿы анлырхумар, егьи апќаѳхәа иѳтқьан, даманы, еес, илтакукуа ипеит, ипаӡеит.

(29) Ахәынтқар ицәымыҕхан ауаа ашьтеитцеит аҿы, аха иабахьӡоз, изахьымӡеит.

(30) Аҿы азҕаб хучы даманы ицо, ицо акыр хара ипеит, ишнеиуаз даҿа калакьк аҿы даманы инеит.

(31) Дахьнанагаз акалакь аҿы ѳн дук абан, аѳн ду ааигуара инеит.

(32) —Улбаа шьта абра, абра аѳн ду аќны умеи схупкуа ѳба аасылхны ига, санутаххо схупкуа ѳба ааихьушьыр, уара уҿы сааиуеит, — ахәеит аҿы.

(33) «Ачкун» хучы дааҿыжәтцын, аҿы ахупкуа ѳба аалихын ицьыба интеитцеит.

(34) Нас афырхәа иҿынеихан, ани изыдгылаз аѳн ду длыѳналеит.

(35) Аѳны дахьныѳналаз ауаа рапәаѳны иеикушаны иштәаз ибеит.

(36) —Иќоузеи ара, арсќаѳык ауаа, шәеизаны шәызтәоузеи? — ихәан, дразтцааит.

(37) —Иќоу уи ауп, ажәлар еизаны итәоуп, рхәынткар адау дааины дифараны дыќоуп, иќахтцара, ҧсыхуас иахтара хаздырам, — рхәеит дзызтцаакуаз.

(38) Ари «ачкун» ас аниаха, дѳагыжьын, аѳны даалдәылтцын, ахупкуа аайниќьан, иҿы ааины иаҧхьа иаагылт.

(39) —Уахьнеиз иубазеи, иеилукаазеи? — ахәан аҿы иазтцааит.

(40) —Иќоу уи ауп, ажәлар еизаны итәоуп, рхәынткар адау даaины дифараны дыќоуп, иќартцара, рыздырам, игужәáжәо еилатәоуп, — ихәеит.

(41) —Ус акузар, иќаутцаша уи ауп, аа, уст ахәа, абри ахәа кны, ашьшьы́хәа уне́ины ахәынтқар дахьыќоу иуалаҿы уштал, уеӡаны цьара куакьк аҿы ухәытцатәа.

(42) Адау данаaиуа, ирдылуа ирмацәысуа даауеит, аха иагьа ирдылыргьы, иагьа ирмацәы́сыргьы, уара ахахаи акы уацәымшәан, уҿырҕуҕуа, акагьы ухьуам.

(43) Адау данаaилакь, ахәа рыхха ихы уас.

(44) Знык иааурхеит хәа иара иаразнак дыҧсӡом.

(45) «Уара уи аќара ухатца ҕуҕуазар, даҿа знык гьы усыс» хәа уеихәоит адау, аха уара «иауази, иараби сызусуа?» хәа иумун, знык ала уимысын (даҿа-знык дисыр, адау иҧсы талозаап) — ахәеит аҿы.

(46) —Ибзиоуп, — ихәан, ахәа аашьтихын «ачкун» ахәынтқар иѳны дныѳналт.

(47) Ахәынтқар дзыѳназ ауалаҿы днеиаанӡа ауалакуа днарыѳныс-ааѳнысуа иеимидан, хуалак ибеит, уалапыҧхьаӡа аӡәаӡәа ахәынтқар иҧхапәа ѳнатәан.

(48) Абант ахәынткар иҧхапәа иибаз рахьтә ѳыцьа ашәы рыпәны руалакуа ирыѳнатәан, илаҕырӡышаха, ахҧатәи ашәы лышәӡáмызт, шкуакуа матәала деилахәан, дгу́рҕьатцәа луáда дыѳнатәáн.

(49) Арт ас ибеит ари, аха изакузаалакь акагьы рхымхәааӡакуа, ашьшьыхәа днеин ахәынтқар

иуада иҧшаан, иҽӡаны џьара даатәеит.

(50) Ана ани аҟара ауаа еилаҟь иахьтәаз ари лымкаала дгуазҭодаз?

(51) Ус уа дыштәаз акумкуа, аҵхыбжьон агур-гурҳәа абжьы бааҧс го, идыдуа имацәысуа, атәыла бго иа́лагеит.

(52) Ари «аҷкун» идырт — адау даауеит уажәы.

(53) Аха иҽырҕуҕуаны игу мышьҭыкуа дтәбуп.

(54) Аҕьеҩхәа ашә аарты адау данааҩнала, ари «аҷкун» ишилшоз иаҳәа рыхха аҟуакҳәа дист.

(55) Абри згуаҕьыз уара уҳаҵаҵәҟьоуп дҽеа знык укшозар! — иҳәеит адау, аха ари «аҷкун» ҿимҭӡеит, уаҳагьы адау сисуеит хәангьы даламгеит.

(56) А-дау уа иҧсы ааихыҵын, агуараҳәа дылкаҳаит.

(57) «Аҷкун» днеин днеихаххын, адау илымҳа аахиҵәан иџьыба илҭаҵаны и́ма дцеит.

(58) —Ааи, ҳҳәынҭкар рыцҳа, адау дифагушьеит, уажәшьҭа ишҧаҳаҧсыхуоу, — рҳәеит ажәлар.

(59) Аҳәынҭкар данааҧш, адау дышьны, иаҧхьа дышкажьыз дибеит.

(60) Аа, абаакуа, сыҧсы еиқузырхада, ари сара сызшьраны иҟаз саҕа ихы хызҵәада? — иҳәан, аҳәынҭкар ажәлар дразҵааит.

(61) Абзиара аагоит ҳәа «сара иҟасҵеит» ҳәа ауаа аӡәымкуа ҩыџьамкуа ицәыртқуеит, аха иҟазҵаҵәҟьаз дләылҵны дцахьан.

(62) А-дау дызшьыҵәҟьаз аиаша рзеилымкааит.

(63) Ари адау дызшьыҵәҟьаз «аҷкун» дылдәылҵын иҽы ахуцқуа ааидикшалан, иҽы анааи, дазҵааит «уажә шьҭа ишҧаҟасҵари?» ҳәа.

(64) Иҟаиҵашаз ианаҳәеит.

(65) Нас иара ажәлар еизаны адау иахьихагылаз зегьы рҵыхутәаны даацәырҵит.

(66) Ашьшьыҳәа днеин днарыдгылан, «ари дызшьыз дазусҭзаалакгьы адау илымҳақуа руак иџьыба иҭоуп» иҳәеит. (Ари иахьихуаҧшуа дыҷкуноу џьыршьоит).

(67) Адау дышьны дахькажьыз цҟьа ианылаихуаҧш, ҵабыргынгьы илымҳақуа акы шамамыз рбеит.

(68) «Ари дызшьыз са соуп» зҳәаз рахьтә аӡәгьы алымҳа изцәырымгеит.

(69) Нас ари «аҷкун» иџьыба иааҭихын адау илымҳа наганы раҧхьа иныҟуиҵеит.

(70) «Абри сахәалоуп дшысшьыз» иҳәа́н, иаҳәа аҭра иааҭыхны ашьаршәы аҿатата идирбеит.

(71) —Аа, уанаџьалбеит, уара сыҧсы еиқуурхеит, сыҧсаанӡа уара узы сыҟоуп, амал иуҭазыу, заҟа уҭахыу усҭоит, — иҳәеит аҳәынҭкар.

(72) Моумоу, сара амал егьи ҳәа акагьы сҭахӡам, уакушаҳаҭзар, абри ашкуакуа маҭәа зышәҵаны ауада иҩнатәоу уҧха дсыҭ, — иҳәеит «акун».

(73) —Уа, уара, уанаџьалбеит, уи сара слеигӡом, аха лара дхуарҭам, уи илеиҕьу аҧҳацәа бзиакуа сымоуп, урыларҧшны иреиҕьу дусҭап, уи илзууазеи ? — иҳәеит аҳәынҭка́р.

(74) —Моумоу, уи лоуп исҭахыу, даҽаӡә дысҭахым, дсуҭозар, лара дсыҭ егьырҭ аӡәгьы дысҭахым, — иҳәеит «аҷкун».

(75) «Аҷкун» ианимуӡа, аҳәынҭкар ашкуакуа маҭәа зшәыз иҧха лҿы днеин леиҳәеит:

(76) —Ҳаи, дад, абааҧсы, сара сыҧсы еиқузырхаз абри аҷкун иоуп, иуҭахыу амал усҭап ҳәа

иасҳәан, акагьы стахым хәа сеиҳәеит, бара биҭаххеит, сбыхәоит мап иҵәымкыкуа бишьарц.

(77) —Ибзиоуп, саб, уара изухәо сиҵоит, аха иќалозар, уаха затцәык исажәараӡа уаха ахупха сышәт, — лҳәеит ларá.

(78) —Абри абас дыќоуп, дмараҳәуеит, убри́ азбуп дхуáрҭам ҳәа зуáсҳәаз.

(79) Абри акун бишьа хәа анласҳәа, уахак ахупха сышәт, ашьжьымтан атак шәыстоит хәа салҳәеит, — иҳәеит аҳәынҭкáр «ачкун» иҿы днеин.

(80) —Иаҧырхагам, урткуа сара еихагьы бзиа избоит, — иҳәеит «ачкун».

(81) Ауха ари «ачкун» дмыцәаӡакуа маӡала ани аӡҕаб иќалтцо збоит хәа луадаҿы аҵаҧха акылтцәараҿы дкылҧшуа далагеит.

(82) Ари ара дкылҧшуа дыштәаз акумкуа атцх акыр инеигуахьан еиҧшаан, ахьтәы лаханка ауала агута илалыргылт, алаханка аӡы нанылтәалт.

(83) Аҧенцьыр апә аалыртын, хәыҳәк ҧырҧыруа иаафнашылт.

(84) Аҳәыҳә иааиз алаханка ианыз аӡы аҿынҭнашьын амтцәыжәфакуа анаарышәшәа арҧызба ҧшӡак, арҧызба заманак даатытц.

(85) Ари арҧызба данаатытц, ари аӡҕаб инеиматәаны атцәуара далагеит.

(86) —Ибыхьзеи, бызтцәыуозеи? — иҳәáн, ани аҳәыҳә иалтцыз арҧызба длазтцааит.

(87) — Абра чкуна хучык дааин саб дызфарц иќаз адау дишьит.

(88) Ачкун са ситаххаит, уажәшьта ишҧазури? — лҳәеит.

(89) —Ќох! — иҳәеит ани аҳәыҳә иалтцыз ачкун.

(90) —Сара агызмалкуа рҳәынҭкар иҧа соуп.

(91) Ани ахучы бара бышҧасцәиго, дысшьыроуп, дышҧасзымшьуеи! — иҳәеит.

(92) —Нас ишҧазури, уатцәы аашар атак расҳәароуп? — лҳәеит.

(93) —Уатцәы баб убас иаҳәа (худук ахьӡ иҳәеит).

(94) Абригь, абригь атыҧ аҿы аху ду икууп ахахә ду.

(95) Убри аху икуу ахахә сзааигааит, нас сиҵоит уи ачкун ҳәа иаҳәа, — иҳәеит.

(96) Арт иеибырхәакуаз ари иаҳаит, нас ани аҳәыҳә иалтцыз ситах дҳәыҳәхан аҧенцьыр дыкылҧраан дцеит.

(97) Ашьыжь ианааша, ари аӡҕаб лаб иҿы днеит.

(98) — Саб, иаха иуҳәаз сазхупын сакушахатуп, аха аачкун сызутараны иќоу абригь, абригь аху ду аҿы дцаны, убра ишьтоу ахахә ҧшӡа сзааигааит, нас сиҵоит, мамзар сызиҵом, — лҳәеит.

(99) Аҳәынҭкар иҧха ас анылҳәа, иќаитцахуаз, ани адау дызшьыз «ачкун» диҧхьан даагеит.

(100) —Ҳаи, далхеит, ари дхуарҭам, улыхуом улќуатц ҳәа зуасҳәаз абри акуп.

(101) Уажә илҳәаз убри ауп, уара лушьар мап лымкит, аха абригь абригь аху ду аҿы дьшаны убра икуу ахахә ҧшӡа сзааигаанӡа сиҵом, — лҳәеит.

(102) —Аҳәынҭкар, уара азин сутозар, уи иззылҳәаз ахахә са иаазгоит, иҳәеит «ачкун».

(103) —Азин зусымтозеи, аха уи аагара уадафуп, — иҳәет аҳәынҭкар.

(104) «Ачкун» даадәылтцын, иҿы даҧхьан аҳәынҭкар иҿы дахьыќаз иаҳаз ажәабжь аиҳәеит.

(105) —Уи ахахә аагара иуадафу усуп, адаукуа ахылаҧшуеит.

(106) Аха, уаала, ҳалагап, иаҳзаагозар аабап.

(107) Амала, уа хахьнеиша ҳаннеилакь, адаукуа рылакуа хтызар, ицәоуп ауп иаанаго, уара иаразнак ахаҳә аашьтӷьааны иуманы удәыкула.

(108) Адаукуа угуартар, иҟаапт иҳәҳәапт, аха иагьа иҳәҳәаргьы, иагьа иҟааргьы, ушьҭаахьҟа ухьамӷьшын.

(109) Адаукуа рылакуа хԥазар, ицәаӡам, иааӷьшуп ауп иаанаго, урбоит иаразнак, рааигуара узнеиӡом, снеиуеит ҳәагьы уаламган, — аҳәеит аҽы.

(110) Ари «ачкун» иҽы даманы ани аҳәынҭкар иззиҳәаз ахаҳә ӷьпза ахьыҟаз аху ду аҽы адаукуа рааигуара инеит.

(111) «Ачкун» дыҭҽыжәҵан адаукуа харантәы данрыхуаӷьш, рылакуа хтны ибан, дльшьҭасын ахаҳә мтцарсны дыԥт.

(112) Ари даныԥ, адаукуа дгуарҭан иҳәҳәеит, иҟааит, аха ари иҽы даашьҭнаӷьаан даманы илҭакукуа ицеит.

(113) Ахаҳә иманы даакылсын, дԥахунан, инаганы аҳәынҭкар ииҭеит.

(114) —Абар уажәшьҭа уԥха илҳәаз насыгӡеит, дызгоит, — иҳәеит.

(115) Ари «ачкун» иааигаз ахаҳә наганы аҳәынҭкар иӷьха иналиҭан, «уашьҭа бишьа, дад!» ҳәа леиҳәеит.

(116) —Ибзиоуп, сищоит, уашьҭа уаха акагьы сҳәом, аха уаха затцәык аӡара сышәҭ, — лҳәеит лара худахтцәа еиҭах.

(117) —Ибзиагушьоуп, — иҳәеит лабгьы.

(118) Аҽны ианыхула, ари дызгараны иҟаз «ачкун» еиҭах аӷьхьан еиӷьш дкылыӷьшны ла дызҽыз ибеит.

(119) Аӷьхьан еиӷьш уи аухагьы, атцх неигуон еиӷьш, ани лыхьтәы лаханка аацәырылгеит, ауада агуҭаны инаганы иналыргылт, аӡы наныҭәалеит.

(120) Аӷьенцьыр аалыртын, аҳәыхә ӷьырӷьыруа иааԥналт.

(121) Инеины ани алаханка ианыз аӡы аҽыԥҭнашьын, дарӷьыс бзиаха даакугылы.

(122) Аҳәынҭкар иӷьха дтәаны акьажыхәа атцәуара даҽыуп.

(123) —Ибыхьзеи, бзыртцәыуозеи? — иҳәан, ани аҳәыхә иалтцыз ачкун длазтцааит.

(124) —Саб сызиҭо ачкун адтца исҭаз наигӡеит адаукуа рхаҳә ааигеит, — лҳәеит.

(125) —Абригь, абригь адгьыл аҽы даукуак ыҟоуп, убарҭ адаукуа саркьак рымоуп, убри асаркьа ааигааит.

(126) убри асаркьа аазгаз акагьы иҳуом, хуарҭаӷьшь имам, — иҳәеит ани аҳәыхә иалтцыз ачкун.

(127) Нас иара дҳәыхәхан днықуӷьраан дцеит.

(128) Арҭ иеибырҳәакуоз ани адау дызшьхьаз ачкун дахьызыртцуаз зегь иаҳаит.

(129) Алырԥаҽны ианаапа, ари аӡӷьаб лаб иҟны днеит.

(130) —Абригь, абригь адгьыл аҽы адаукуа нхоит, убарҭ адаукуа саркьак рымоуп, убарҭ рсаркьа рымхны иааигар, нас сищоит сызуҭарц иуҭахыу ачкун, — ҳәа иалҳәеит лаб.

(131) Ари лаб (аҳәынҭкар) иҟаитцахʻуаз, ани «ачкун» дааиӷьхьан, «абас абас, ари ахудахтцәа, абригь, абригь адгьыл аҽы инхо адауцәа асаркьа рымоуп, убри асаркьа рымхны иааигар сищоит, мамзар сищом» ҳәа лҳәеит иҳәеит.

(132) —Ибзиоуп, — иҳәеит ари «ачкун».

(133) Ари «аҷкун» даадәылтцын, ажәабжь ҿыш иаҳаз иҽы иаихәеит.

(134) —Ҳаи, аллаҳ, ахаҳә змаҳхыз адаукуагьы ҕуҕуан, аха уажәы ари асаркьа змоу рлеишәа бааҧсӡоуп, егьырҭ иреиҧшым, хахьнеира ҳаннеилакь, егьырҭ ишырзууз еиҧш, рылакуа тхны иубозар, асаркьа аарымтцҧааны, иаразнак усиханы уҩ.

(135) Адаукуа угуарҭашт, иҳәҳәашт, иҟаашт, ашәиҧшьира иалагашт, аха иагьа рҳәаргьы ичҳаны, изакузаалакь ухьаҧшны урыхуамҧшын, ажәакгьы расҳәоит ҳәа уаламган.

(136) Амала, уӡырҩла, иухаумырштын, ашәира ианалагалакь, ирхәо гуынкыла, — аҳәеит аҽы.

(137) Аҽы ас анаҳәа, апҟаҩҳәа дыҩҽыжәлан, асаркьа змаз адаукуа рҿы днеит.

(138) Дыҩҽыжәтцын нахьхьи ахахә змихыз адаукуа рҿы ишыҟаитцаз еиҧш, адаукуа рыла хтызшәа аниба, днеин асаркьа аарымтциҧаан дыҩт.

(139) Даныҩ дара шгуарҭан иҳәҳәеит, иҟааит, ашәира иалагеит.

(140) —Еҳ абра иааины ҳара ҳсаркьа згаз дхатцазар, дыҧхәысхааит, дыҧхәысзар, дхатцахааит, — рҳәан, дыршәиит. (Азаманала дыршәиит, умбо!)

(141) Ари асаркьа иманы иҽы аҟны данааи «иуарҳәазеи, ушҧаршәиит?» ҳәа иҽы иазтцааит.

(142) —Абра иааины ҳара ҳсаркьа згаз дхатцазар, дыҧхәысхааит, дыҧхәысзар, дхатцахааит ҳәа сыршәиит, — иҳәеит. (Ари иара ахатца маҭәа ишәын, аха дызҕабымзи, дхатцазар иҭахымзи, заманала дыршәиит урҭ адаукуа!)

(143) Ари уажәшьҭа дхатцахеит, адаукуа ирҳәаз наӡеит.

(144) Асаркьа ирцәигаз има иҿылеихан аҳәынтҟар инаган иитеит.

(145) Ахеынтҟар еиҭах иҵха длыҧхьан дааиган, «аа, дад, асаркьа ҳәа бызҿызгьы ааигеит, уашьта бицӡозар, бицша!» иҳәеит.

(146) —Иҟалозар, уахакгьы аӡара сышәҭ, — лҳәеит.

(147) —Ибзиоуп, ибаҳҭап аӡара, — иҳәеит лабгьы.

(148) Ауха ани иааилац аҳәыҳә ааин, иарҧызбаны ишыҟалап иааҟалан иареи лареи еиҧәажәеит.

(149) —Саб сызиҭарц иҭахыу аҷкун уара иззуҳәаз адауцәа рсаркьа ааигеит, — лҳәеит.

(150) —Ҟох, уа ицаз аӡәгьы сибгала дмааӡацызт, уи иара излаилшазеи, деибганы дызлаазеи? — иҳәеит ани аҳәыҳә иалтцыз арҧызба.

(151) —Излаилшаз сыздырам, аха илшеит, — лҳәеит.

(152) —Ус акузар, уатцәы бахьнеиуа убас иаҳәа баб.

(153) Аҳәынтҟар ибаҳчаҿы абиа шьаҭак ыҟоуп, атцытцмыць шьаҭакгьы ыҟоуп.

(154) Абиа унакьысыр, иччоит, атцытцмыць унакьысыр, итцәуоит.

(155) Убарҭ абиеи атцытцмыцьи ытцхны иааигаait, — иҳәеит.

(156) Адырҩаҽны ианааша ари аӡҕаб днеин лаб иалхәеит «абас, абас, абригь, абригь аҭыҧ аҿы иҟоу абиеи атцытцмыцьи ааигаait, нас уара сызуҭо аҷкун ситәуп» ҳәа.

(157) Ари аҷкун (анҭ асаркьа змихыз адауцәа даныршәиз аахыс усгьы дыҷкунахахьан) дыҩдәылтцын ажәабжь ҿыц иаҳаз иҽы иаиҳәеит.

(158) —Уаа, уи даара иуалаҩӡоуп, абиеи атцытцмыцьи ҳәа зызбаху уарҳәаз агьзмалкуа рбаҳчаҿоуп иахьыҟоу, аха ҳдәыкулап, иаҳзаагозар аабап, ҳҽазаҳшәап, — аҳәеит аҽы.

(159) Иҽы дҩакутәан дышнеиуаз акумкуа, хҩык аишьцәа раб иҭынхаз ҟамаки хыլҧарчыки, уапаки еимакны рылакуа штибах'уаз днарыдгылт.

(160) —Иҟашәҵо закуузеи, уара? — иҳәан, дразҵааит.

(161) —Абарҭ еимаҳк‘уеит, — рҳәан аҟамчи, ахылԥарчи, аупеи идырбеит.

(162) —Шәысзыӡырҩы, баша шәылакуа ҭибаҳ‘уеит.

(163) Уи аҵкысгьы сара ишшәасҳәо шәныҟуар, имариаӡаны ишәзысшоит, — иҳәеит аҷкун.

(164) —Ишԥаҳзушои?

(165) —Ишышәзысшо уи ауп, ахыц дәыкусҵоит, аԥхьа убри ахыц аазго итәуп аҟамчи, ахылԥарчи, аупеи, — иҳәеит.

(166) —Ибзиоуп, уара ишуҳәаз иҟаҳҵоит, — рҳәеит.

(167) Ари ахыц дәыкуиҵан, иааҳгоит ҳәа аишьцәа еибарҩны ианца, иааргаанӡа, ани иара уа дыԥшызма, аҟамчи, ахылҵарчи, аупеи аашьҭихын, иман дцеит.

(168) —Аупа ааиҵыхны унылатәаны ҟамчыла уанаслакь, иаҳьаауҭахыу уагоит, ахылԥарч наухауҵар, аӡәгьы уибаӡом, — аҳәеит ари аҷкун иҽы.

(169) Дыпнеиуаз ани абиеи аҵыҵмыҵьи ахьгылаз аҩсҭаацәа рбаҳча дазааигуахеит.

(170) Дыԥшын, ани иара иигараны иҟаз аҳәынҭкар иԥҳагьы уа дыҟоуп, аҩсҭаацәа реиҳабы иԥагьы уа дыҟоуп, абиеи аҵыҵмыҵьи ршьапкуа ар рыкуршаны, иҭаххааны иҟаҵоуп.

(171) Ари аҷкун ихылԥарч ҩеихеиҵан, ашышьыхәа днеин (ахылԥарч анихеиҵа, нас дызбодаз?!) иччоз абиеи иҵәуоз аҵыҵмыҵьи ааҭихын, акы ччо, акы ҵәуо има ддәыкулеит, иҽегьы иаргьы аупа аиҵихын иҩангылан, аупа аҟамчы аныҩахиҟьа, ари зыԥха дигаран иҟаз аҳәынҭкар иҿы иааит.

(172) —Аҳәынҭкар, иуҳәаз зегьы насыгӡеит, иччо абиеи иҵәуо аҵыҵмыҵьи аазгеит, — иҳәеит.

(173) —Аҳәынҭкар иԥха длыԥхьан днеиган «аа, баба, иззыбҳәаз аҵлакуа ааигеит ари аҷкун» иҳәан ус леиҳәеит.

(174) —Ааҟ, уажәшьҭа, уаҳа акагьы сызхәом, сицщауеит, — лҳәеит ларгьы.

(175) Ачара рун, ажәра рун ари аҷкун аҳәынҭкар иԥха дирҭеит.

(176) Ачараҿы дҩагылан абри аҷкун иааихигаз зегьы акакала ажәлар иезаны итәаз иреиҳәеит.

(177) Абхуа аҷкун иаб иахь ашәҟу дәыкуиҵеит «уԥа аԥҳәыс диманы хьыӡлаԥшала дузнеиуеит» ҳәа.

(178) Аҷкун иԥҳәыс диманы иаб иҿы иахьааизгьы чарала иԥылеит.

(179) Зашәа шәаргьы убас абзиаракуа шәзыҟалаша.

Transcription

(1) a-ħʷəntkár jə-pħá d-šə-č’ʲk’ʷə́n-xa-z
the-king his-daughter she-how-boy-become-Past.Ind.NF

How the King’s daughter turned into a boy

(2) ħʷəntkár-k’ də́-q’a-n, žʷa-jʷə́-k’ á-pħa-cʷa ∅-jə́-ma-zaarən,
king-one he-be-Stat.Past.Fin 10-person-NS the-daughter-Pl [they-]him-have-Evidentiality
a-pá d-jə́-ma-ʒa-mə-zt’.
the-son he-him-have-Emph-Neg-Stat.Past.Fin

There was a King. They say that he had ten daughters. But he didn’t even have one son.

(3) jə-pħʷə́s l-cʷá ∅-l-t'ʷə́-m-k'ʷa d-q'á-la-jt'.
his-wife her-skin [it-]her-belong to-Neg-Abs she-Prev-became-Fin
His wife became pregnant.

(4) — jagáraanə jə-s-ħʷa-xʲá-zargʲə jagáraan j-sə-čʲħa-xʲá-zargʲə abəržʷə́
very often it-I-say-Perf-even if very often it-I-endure-Perf-even if now
a-pá d-anə-b-má-w, j-b-áw-[w]a a-pħa-gʲə́ bar-gʲə́
the-son he-when-you.F-have-Stat.NF Rel-you.F-receive-Dyn the-daughter-and you.F-and
šʷə-s-šʲ-wá-jt', — ħʷa ∅-l-a-j-ħʷá-jt' a-ħʷəntkár jə-pħʷə́s.
you.Pl-I-kill-Dyn-Fin SP [it-]her-to-he-say-(Aor)-Fin the-king his-wife.
'I've told you many times and I've have been patient many times, but this time when you give birth to a daughter, [Note: This speaker probably mistakes a-pħa 'a daughter' for a-pá 'a son'.] I will kill you and the daughter you have given birth to,' the King told his wife.

(5) a-pħʷə́s rə́cħa lará jə-l-taxə́-m-k'ʷa də́-q'a-z-ma a-pá
the-wife poor she it-her-want-Neg-Abs she-be-Stat.Past.NF-Qu the-son
d-l-áwə-r, axá a-ncʷá d-lə́-j-ta-wa-m, šʷə-m-ba-wa!
he-her-receive-Conditional but the-God him-to her-he-give-Dyn-Neg you.Pl-Neg-see-Dyn
The poor wife surely wished to give birth to a son. But God did not give her a son, as we can see below.

(6) arə́j l-xác'a as ∅-anə́-j-ħʷa, ak'ʲəžə́-ħʷa
this her-husband so [it-]when-he-say-(Aor.NF) boohoo
j-n-ajma-tʷa-nə́ a-c'ʷə́wa-ra d-á-la-ga-jt'.
?-Par-Prev-(tears) well up-Abs/Adv the-cry-Masd she-it-Prev-begin-(Aor)-Fin
When her husband told her this, she burst into tears crying out loud.

(7) zə-gʷrá ∅-l-ga-wá-z á-ħʷsa bə́rg-cʷa
Rel(Poss)-heart [it-]she-take-Dyn-Impf.NF the-women elderly-Pl
∅-aa-l-gá-n d-r-á-cʷažʷa-jt', «psə́xʷa
[them]-Prev-she-bring-Past.Ind.Fin she-them-to-speak-(Aor)-Fin help/aid
∅-sə́-šʷ-t, s-xác'a sə-j-šʲ-wá-jt'
[it]-to me-you.Pl-give.Imp my-husband me-he-kill-Dyn-Fin
j-sə-psə́xʷa-w-zaj?» ∅-l-ħʷá-jt'.
what-my-help-Stat.Pres.NF-Qu [it-]she-say-(Aor)-Fin
She had some wise old women that she trusted brought to her, and she told them, 'Please help me. My husband is going to kill me. Can anything be done to help me?'

(8) Arə́j ant á-ħʷsa-kʷa ans ∅-an-r-á-l-ħʷa,
she those the-woman-Pl so [it-]when-them-to-she-say.Aor.NF
«bə-m-šʷá-n, b-anaǯʲálbajt', mak'ʲána a-ncʷá j-∅-ħʷa-nə́
you.F-Neg-fear-Proh you.F-dear still the-god it-[he-]say-Abs
a-pá d-b-áw-[w]a-zargʲə ∅-bə-z-də́r-wa-m, wəs

the-son he-you.F-receive-Dyn-whether [it-]you.F-Pot-know-Dyn-Neg so
[a-]ák'ʷə-m-k'ʷa, a-pħá d-b-áw-r-gʲə psəxʷá-k'
it-be-Neg-Abs(= if not) the-daughter she-you.F-receive-if-also help-one
ø-b-z-áa-w-p'» ħʷa ø-l-á-r-ħʷa-jt'.
[it-]you.F-for-we-do-Fut.I.Fin SP [it-]her-to-they-say-(Aor)-Fin

When she told the women her story, they said, 'There's nothing to worry about. In keeping with God's will, you don't know now whether you will have a boy or a girl. If it's not a boy, and if you have a girl, we can help you'.

(9) wəs j-šə́-q'a-z [a-]ák'ʷ-m-k'ʷan, [á]-aħ jə-pħʷə́s
thus it-how-be-Stat.Past.NF it-be-Neg-Abs (= the time passed) the-king his-wife
l-áamta ø-an-aá-j, a-xšára d-l-aw-t', axá
her-time [it-]when-Prev-come.Aor.NF the-baby she-her-receive-(Aor)-Fin but
a-žʷájza-jʷə-k' j-l-áw-z-gʲə də-pħa-xá-jt'.
the-11-person-NS Rel-her-receive-Past.Ind.NF-also she-daughter-become-(Aor)-Fin

And so time passed. The time came for the King's wife to give birth. She gave birth to a child but it was another girl, her eleventh daughter.

(10) arə́j wažʷ-gʲə́ a-pħá d-l-áw-t', axá a-waá
this now-also the-daughter she-her-receive-(Aor)-Fin but the-people
ø-a-zə́-q'a-c'a-nə j-lə́-ma-m-zəj,
[them-]it-OV(for)-Prev-prepare/train-Abs what-she-have-Neg-Qu
«j-jə́-z də-č'ʲk'ʷə́na-wp'» ø-r-ħʷá-n a-ħʷəntkár
Rel-be born-Past.Ind.NF he-boy-Stat.Pres.Fin [it-]they-say-Past.Ind.Fin the-king
də-r-žʲá-n, lar-gʲə́ d-ajkʷxá-jt'.
him-they-deceive-Past.Ind.Fin she-also she-be saved-(Aor)-Fin

She had given birth to yet another girl. However, she made the people around her believe that she had given birth to a boy. The people said, 'The child born is a boy,' and deceived the King. And so she was able to save her own life as well.

(11) arə́j á-ʒɣab j-jə́-z d-r-aaʒá-jt', abár
this the-girl Rel-be born-Past.Ind.NF her-they-bring up-(Aor)-Fin look.here
wažʷšʲtá žʷá-jʷa šəkʷsá ø-l-xə́-c'-wa-jt', á-č'k'ʷən
now 12-Non.Hum year [it/they-]her-Prev-be years old-Dyn-Fin the-boy
matʷá ø-l-šʷə́-wp'.
clothes [it-]her-be on-Stat.Pres.Fin

They raised the girl that she had given birth to. Look, now, she is twelve years old and is wearing boys' clothes.

(12) — arə́j wažʷšʲtá d-xə́žʷʒa də́-q'a-wp', a-sunét
he now he-big he-be-Stat.Pres.Fin the-circumcision
ø-j-zə́-z-w-[w]a-jt', — ø-j-ħʷá-jt' á-[a]b.
[it-]him-for-I-do-Dyn-Fin [it-]he-say-(Aor)-Fin the-father
(a-ħʷəntkár, də-č'ʲk'ʷə́na-w ø-ǯʲə́-jə-m-šʲa-wa-j!)

the-king, he/she-boy-Stat.Pres.NF [it-]Prev-he-Neg/Emph-think-Dyn-just!
'Now you have grown up. I will perform the circumcision ceremony on you,' his father said. (The King thought that the child was a boy, you see).

(13) arə́j á-ʒɣab xʷč'ʲə́ l-ab as ø-anə́-j-ħʷa, lará
this the-girl little her-father so [it-]when-he-say.Aor.NF she
d-šʷá-n, d-ná-j-n, a-bóra
she-be frightened-Past.Ind.Fin she-Prev(thither)-go-Past.Ind.Fin the-stable
d-a-va-gə́la-nə ak'ʲažə́-ħʷa a-c'ʷə́wa-ra d-á-la-ga-jt'.
she-it-Prev(beside)-stand-Abs boohoo the-cry-Masd she-it-PREV-begin-(Aor)-Fin
When she heard the King say this, the little girl was surprised and ran away and stood in the corner of the stable and started to sob out loud.

(14) a-bóra a-jʷnwə́c'q'a a-čə́ ø-ø-ta-k'ə́-n.
the-stable it-inside the-horse [it-it-]Prev-be shut in-Stat.Past.Fin
There was a horse in the stable.

(15) wə́j j-ø-ta-k'ə́-z a-čə́ a-xʷəč'ʲə́
that Rel-[it-]Prev-be shut in-Stat.Past.NF the-horse the-child
d-kʲə́z-kʲə́z-wa l-c'ʷə́wabžʲə ø-an-a-[a]-ħá, wəs
she-sob-Abs her-tearful voice [it-]when-it-to-be audible-(Aor.NF) thus
ø-a-ħʷá-jt':
[it-]it-say-(Aor)-Fin
The horse that was in the stable heard the little girl crying and said to her.

(16) — o, wará, wa j-a-va-gə́la-w a-xʷč'ʲə́,
oh! you.M there Rel-it-Prev(beside)-stand-Stat.Pres.NF the-child
wə-zə-r-c'ʷə́wa-wa-zaj?
you.M-who-Caus-cry-Dyn-Qu?
'Hey, you, little girl standing over there. What is making you cry like this?'

(17) — sə-zə-r-c'ʷə́wa-wa-zaj ħʷa á-q'a-w-ma, s-abá-m-c'ʷəwa-wa,
I-who-Caus-cry-Dyn-Qu SP it-be-Stat.NF-Qu I-where-Neg-cry-Pres.NF
s-ab sará sə-č'ʲk'ʷə́na-w ø-ǯʲə́-j-šʲa-wa-jt', a-sunét
my-father I I-boy-Pres.NF [it-]Prev-he-think-Dyn-Fin the-circumcision
ø-w-zə́-z-w-[w]a-jt' ħʷa ø-s-á-j-ħʷa-jt', sará sə-ʒɣábə-wp',
[it-]you.M-for-I-do-Dyn-Fin SP [it-]me-to-he-say-(Aor)-Fin I I-girl-Stat.Pres.Fin
s-šə-č'ʲk'ʷə́na-m ø-a[a]-ajlə́-j-k'aa-r, s-án-gʲə sar-gʲə́
I-how-boy-Neg.NF [it-]Par-Prev-he-learn/know-if my-mother-and I-and
ħa-j-šʲ-wá-jt' s-ab, — ø-l-ħʷá-jt'.
us-he-kill-Dyn-Fin my-father, — [it-]she-say-(Aor)-Fin
'You ask me what is making me cry like this? Why can't I stop crying? My father thinks that I am a boy and told me, 'I will perform the rites of circumcision on you'. I am a girl. If my father finds out

that I am not a boy, he will kill me and my mother,' she said.

(18) — aħaħáj ak'ə́ w-a-cʷə́-m-šʷa-n, w-ab
encouraging.word something you.M-it-Prev-Neg-be afraid of-Proh your.M-father
a-sunét ø-anə-w-zə́-jə-w-ša á-lamtala xʷəč'ʲə́k' a-čə́
the-circumcision [it-]when-you.M-for-he-do-Fut.II.NF it-just before a little the-horse
ø-sə́-rxʷmarə-r ø-s-taxə́-wp' ħʷa ø-j-á-ħʷa, nas
[it-]I-gallop-Conditional [it-]I-want-Stat.Pres.Fin SP [it-]him-to-say.Imp then
a-čə-rxʷmár-ra a-zə́jn ø-špá-w-jə-m-ta-rə-j.
the-horse-gallop-Masd the-permission [it-]how-you.M-he-Neg-give-Fut.I.NF-Qu
'Cheer up. There's nothing to be afraid of. Before your father circumcises you, say to him 'I want to ride a horse for a while'. He won't be able to deny you permission to get up on a horse and gallop, will he?

(19) a-čə-rxʷmár-ra a-zə́jn ø-an-wə́-j-ta-lak'ʲ,
the-horse-gallop-Masd the-permission [it-]when-to you.M-he-give-Lak,
w-aá-j-nə sará w-sə́-kʷ-t'ʷa, sará
you.M-Prev-come hither.Imp I you.M-me-Prev(onto)-ride.Imp I
w-sə́-rxʷmarə-p'.
you.M-I-make *sb* play-Fut.I.Fin
When your father gives you permission to ride a horse, come here, and get on my back. I will fly away with you'.

(20) znək' w-aá-j-nə sará w-sə́-kʷ-t'ʷa-r, nas sará
as.soon.as you.M-Prev-come.hither-Abs I you.M-me-Prev-ride-if, then I
w-ájkʷə-rxa-šʲa ø-z-də́r-wa-jt', — ø-a-ħʷá-jt' a-čə́.
your.M-Prev-saving-manner [it-]I-know-Dyn-Fin, — [it-]it-say-(Aor)-Fin the-horse.
The horse said, 'As soon as you come here and mount me, I will tell you how I will save you'.

(21) arə́j á-ʒɣab xʷč'ʲə́ a-čə́ j-a-ħʷá-z
this the-girl little the-horse Rel-it-say-Past.Ind.NF
ø-aa-gʷnə́-l-k'əla-n, d-gʷə́rɣʲa-n də́-jʷ-nə l-án
[it-]Par-Prev-she-perceive-Past.Ind.Fin she-rejoice-Past.Ind.Fin she-run-Abs her-mother
l-č'ə́ d-ná-j-n j-l-á-l-ħʷa-jt' abás, abás a-čə́
her-to she-Prev-go thither-Past.Ind.Fin it-her-to-she-say-(Aor)-Fin in this way the-horse
j-s-á-bžʲa-na-ga-z, j-s-á-na-ħʷa-z
Rel-me-to-Prev-it-advise-Past.Ind.NF Rel-me-to-it-say-(Aor)-Past.Ind.NF
abrə́j á-[a]-wp' ħʷa.
this it-copula-Stat.Pres.Fin SP.
The girl listened to what the horse said and was happy and rushed off to where her mother was and told her, 'This is how the horse advised me and what the horse told me to do'.

(22) l-án-gʲə d-gʷə́rɣʲa-c'ʷa d-q'a-lá-jt'.

her-mother-also she-rejoice-Emph she-Prev-become-(Aor)-Fin

Her mother also rejoiced from the bottom of her heart.

(23) a-ħʷəntkár a-čʲára á-žʷra, ɸ-j-wə́-jt'.
the-king the-feast the-drinking [it-]he-do-(Aor)-Fin

The King held a feast.

(24) — bába, wará, wažʷšʲtá wə-šʲtá-s-c'a-wa-jt', — ɸ-j-ħʷá-jt',
sonny! you.M now you.M-Prev-I-put down-Dyn-Fin [it-]he-say-(Aor)-Fin
— wažʷšʲtá j-a-z-xa-wá-jt', — ɸ-j-ħʷá-jt'.
now it-it-for-enough-Dyn-Fin [it-]he-say-(Aor)-Fin
(arə́j wažʷə́ a-xʷəč'ʲə́ l-á-wp' j-z-a-j-ħʷa-wa.)
this now the-child her-copula-Stat.Pres.Fin it-Rel-to-he-say-Dyn.NF

He said, 'Son, please lie down now [so that I can perform the circumcision on you]'. 'Now it is time for the ceremony,' he said. (The King was speaking to the girl).

(25) — s-ab, jə-bzə́ja-wp', jə́-w-ħʷa-wa s-á-kʷšaħatə-wp',
my-father it-good-Stat.Pres.Fin Rel-you.M-say-Dyn.NF I-it-consent to-Stat.Pres
axá ak'azə́ s-wə́-ħʷa-r ɸ-s-taxə́-n, a-zə́jn ɸ-sə-t,
but one I-you.M-ask-if [it-]I-want-Stat.Past the-permission [it-]to me-give.Imp
j-q'ala-wá-zar a-čə́ ɸ-sə́-rxʷmarə-r ɸ-s-taxə́-wp',
it-be possible-Dyn-if the-horse [it-]I-gallop-if [it-]I-want-Stat.Pres.Fin
— ɸ-jə-ħʷá-jt' á-č'ʲk'ʷən. (a-č'ʲk'ʷən ɸ-ħ-ħʷa-wá-jt' wažʷšʲtá, á-č'ʲk'ʷən
[it-]he-say-(Aor)-Fin 'the-boy' the-boy [it-]we-say-Dyn-Fin now the-boy
d-abá-q'a-w, də́-ʒɣábə-wp', axá d-šə-ʒɣábə-w
he-where-be-Stat.Pres.NF he/she-girl-Stat.Pres.Fin but he/she-that-girl-Stat.Pres.NF
l-ab [j-]jə-z-də́r-ʒa-wa-m [a-]á-wp'.)
her-father [it-]him-Pot-know-Emph-Dyn-Neg it-copula-Stat.Pres.Fin

'Father, it's all right. I agree with what you say. But I have one thing to ask of you. Please forgive me. If I may, I would like to ride a horse around,' the 'boy' said. (We use the word 'boy' now. 'Where is the boy?' You might ask. This child is a girl but, however, in reality the father of the boy doesn't know that the child is a girl).

(26) — jə-bzə́ja-wp', a-čə́ ɸ-wə-rxʷmár-wa-zar, jə-rxʷmár,
it-good-Stat.Pres.Fin the-horse [it-]you.M-gallop-Dyn-if it-gallop.Imp
— ɸ-jə-ħʷá-jt' a-ħʷəntkár.
[it-]he-say-(Aor)-Fin the-king

'Fine. If you want to ride a horse, please do so,' the King said.

(27) nas a-čə-rxʷmár-ra a-zə́jn ɸ-an-l-áw,
then the-horse-gallop-Masd the-permission [it-]when-her-receive.Aor.NF
č'ʲk'ʷə́na matʷá-la d-ajla-ħʷá-n wajzgʲə́,
boy clothes-with she-Prev-be dressed in-Stat.Past.Fin all the same
d-ná-j-n a-čə́ d-jʷ-á-kʷ-t'ʷa-n, á-lada

she-Prev-go thither-Past.Ind.Fin the-horse she-Par-it-Prev(on)-ride-Past.Ind.Fin down
j-lə́-r-jʷə-jt', á-jʷada j-lə́-r-jʷə-jt', a-čə́
it-she-Caus-run-(Aor)-Fin upward it-she-Caus-run-(Aor)-Fin the-horse
ø-lə́-rxʷmar-t', axá žʷlarə́ j-ǯʲá-r-šʲa-wa
[it-]she-gallop-(Aor)-Fin (so...) that people it-Prev-they-be surprised-Abs
j-lə́-rxʷmarə-jt'.
it-she-gallop-(Aor)-Fin

When the girl was given permission to ride the horse, she was wearing boy's clothes and went to the place where the horse was, got up on the horse's back and rode the horse up and down. Everyone was surprised that she was able to ride the horse so skillfully.

(28) a-čə́ ø-an-lə́-rxʷmar, agʲə́j ap'q'ájʷħʷa
the-horse [it-]when-she-gallop-(Aor.NF) that instantly
jə-jʷ-t-q'ʲá-n, d-á-ma-nə, ées, jəltak'ʷk'ʷwá
it-Par-Prev-jump out-Past.Ind.Fin she-it-have-Abs Interjection without trace
j-cá-jt', j-ca-ʒá-jt'.
it-go-(Aor)-Fin it-go-Emph-(Aor)-Fin

When she made the horse gallop, it suddenly flew up into the air, and taking her along, disappeared into the blue, running away into nothing, leaving no trace.

(29) a-ħʷəntkár [jə]-j-cʷə́məɣ-xa-n a-waá
the-king [it-]him-become unpleasant-Past.Ind.Fin people
ø-á-šʲta-j-c'a-jt' a-čə́, axá
[them-]it-Prev-he-make pursue-(Aor)-Fin the-horse but
j-abá-[a]-xʲ-ʒa-wa-z, j-z-a-xʲə́-m-ʒa-jt'.
they-where-[it]-Prev-catch up with-Dyn-Impf.NF they-Pot-it-Prev-Neg-catch up with-(Aor)-Fin

The King was upset by this and made people chase after the horse. But where could they have chased the horse to? They could not follow the horse.

(30) a-čə́ á-ʒɣab xʷəč'ʲə́ d-á-ma-nə j-ca-wá, j-ca-wá ak'ə́r
the-horse the-girl little she-it-have-Abs it-go-Abs it-go-Abs considerably
xará j-cá-jt', jə-š-ná-j-wa-z dačá kalákʲ-k'
far they-go-(Aor)-Fin they-how-Prev-go thither-Dyn-Impf.NF other town-one
a-č'ə́ d-á-ma-nə j-ná-j-t'.
it-to she-it-have-Abs they-Prev-go thither-(Aor)-Fin

The horse ran far, far away, taking the girl with him. He took her far away to another village.

(31) d-axʲ-ná-na-ga-z á-kalakʲ a-č'ə́ jʷn də́w-k'
her-where-Prev-it-take thither-Past.Ind.NF the-town it-in house big-one
ø-a-bá-n, a-jʷn dəw [a]-áajgʷara j-ná-j-t'.
[it-]it-see-Past.Ind.Fin the-house big it-near to they-Prev-go thither-(Aor)-Fin

The horse took her to a village, and they saw a large house, and they went up to it.

(32) — wə-l-báa šʲtá abrá, abrá a-jʷn dəw a-q'nə́

you.M-Prev-descend.Imp now here here the-house big it-to
w-ná-j s-x^wə́c-k^wa j^w-ba ø-aa-sə́-l-x-nə
you.M-Prev-go thither.Imp my-hair-Pl 2-non.Hum [them-]Par-me-Prev-pull from-Abs
j-gá, s-anə́-w-tax-xa-wa s-x^wə́c-k^wa j^w-ba
them-take.Imp I-when-you.M-want-become-Dyn.NF my-hair-Pl 2-non.Hum
ø-aa-[a]j-x^jə́-w-š^jə-r, wará w-č'ə s-áa-j-wa-jt',
[them-]Par-Reciprocal-Prev-you.M-rub-if you.M you.M-at I-Prev-come hither-Dyn-Fin
— ø-a-ħ^wá-jt' a-čə́.
[it-]it-say-(Aor)-Fin the-horse
'Please get off here. Go into the big house. Pluck out two hairs from me and take them with you. When you need me, if you rub these two hairs together, I will come to your side,' the horse said.

(33) «á-č'^jk'^wən» x^wəč'^jə́ d-aa-čə́ž^w-c'ə-n, a-čə́
'the-boy' little he-Par-Prev-dismount from a horse-Past.Ind.Fin the-horse
a-x^wə́c-k^wa j^w-ba ø-áa-[a]-lə-j-xə-n j-ǯ^jə́ba
its-hair-Pl 2-Non.Hum [them]-Par-[it]-Prev-he-pull from-Past.Ind.Fin his-pocket
jə-n-ø-tá-j-c'a-jt'.
them-Par-[it(= his pocket)-]Prev-he-put into-(Aor)-Fin
The little 'boy' got down off the horse, and plucked out two strands of hair and put them in his pocket.

(34) nas áfə́r-ħ^wa j-č'ə́-na-j-xa-n, anə́j
then quickly his-SV-Prev(thither)-he-set out-Past.Ind.Fin that
j-zə-d-gə́la-z a-j^wn dəw d-lə́-ø-j^wna-la-jt'.
they-Rel-Prev(by)-stand-Stat.Past.NF the-house big he-Par-[it-]Prev-enter-(Aor)-Fin
After that, he left very quickly and went into the house that stood close to where they had been standing.

(35) a-j^wnə́ d-ax^jə́-nə-j^wna-la-z a-waá rac^wa-j^w-nə́
the-house he-where-Par-Prev-enter-Past.Ind.NF people many-people-adv
j-ajk'^wša-nə́ jə-š-t'^wá-z ø-j-bá-jt'.
they-surround-Abs they-how/that-be sitting-Stat.Past.NF [it-]he-see-(Aor)-Fin
He saw a large number of people inside the house, sitting in a circle.

(36) — jə́-q'a-w-zaj ará, arsq'aj^wə́k' a-waá, š^w-ajza-nə́
what-be-Stat.Pres.NF-Qu here so many people you.Pl-gather-Abs
š^wə-z-t'^wá-w-zaj? — ø-j-ħ^wá-n,
you.Pl-why-be sitting-Stat.Pres.NF-Qu? — [it-]he-say-(Aor)-Past.Ind.Fin
d-r-á-z-c'aa-jt'.
he-them-it-Prev-ask-(Aor)-Fin
'What's going on here? Such a lot of people. Why are you all sitting here together?' he asked them.

(37) — jə́-q'a-w wəj [a-]á-wp', á-ž^wlar ø-ajza-nə́
Rel-be-Stat.Pres.NF that it-be-Stat.Pres.Fin the-people [they-]gather-Abs
j-t'^wá-wp', r-ħ^wəntkár a-dawə́ d-aá-j-nə

they-be sitting-Stat.Pres.Fin their-king the-ogre he-Prev-come hither-Abs
də-j-fa-ranə́ də́-q'a-wp', jə́-q'a-ħ-c'a-ra, psə́xʷa-s
him-he-eat-must he-be-Stat.Pres.Fin Rel/what-Prev-we-do-Fut.I.NF possibility-as
j-á-ħ-ta-ra ø-ħa-z-də́r-[w]a-m, — ø-r-ħʷá-jt'
what/Rel-it-we-give-Fut.I.NF [it-]us-Pot-know-Dyn-Neg [it-]they-say-(Aor)-Fin
d-zə-z-c'aa-kʷá-z.
he-Rel-Prev-ask-Pl-Past.Ind.NF

'This is what is happening. People have come together and are sitting down. We are sure that an ogre is going to come and eat our King. [Note: This King was not the 'boy's' father. Rather, he was another King, from another Kingdom.] We don't know what we should do or what we can do,' they told the boy who had asked them.

(38) árəj «á-č'ʲk'ʷən» as ø-an-j-a-ħá, d-jʷa-gʲəžʲə́-n,
this 'the-boy' so [it-]when-him-to-be audible.(Aor.NF) he-Par-turn-Past.Ind.Fin
a-jʷnə́ d-aa-dʷə́l-c'ə-n a-xʷə́c-kʷa
the-house he-Par-Prev-go out of-Past.Ind.Fin the-hair-Pl
ø-aa-[a]j-nə́-j-q'ʲa-n, j-čə́ ø-aá-j-nə
[them-]Par-each other-Prev-he-hit against-Past.Ind.Fin his-horse [it-]Prev-come hither-Abs
j-ápxʲa j-aa-gə́l-t'.
him-in front of it-Par-stand-(Aor)-Fin

When the 'boy' heard this, he turned around and left the house, and rubbed the hairs together. And then the horse came and was standing in front of him.

(39) — w-axʲ-ná-j-z jə́-w-ba-zaj,
you.M-where-Prev-go thither-Past.Ind.NF what-you.M-see-(Aor)-Qu
j-ájlə-w-k'aa-zaj? — ø-a-ħʷá-n a-čə́
what-Prev-you.M-learn-(Aor)-Qu [it-]it-say-Past.Ind.Fin the-horse
ø-j-á-z-c'aa-jt'.
[it-]him-it-Prev-ask-(Aor)-Fin

'Where did you go? What did you see? What did you find out?' the horse asked the boy.

(40) — jə́-q'a-w wəj á-[a]-wp', á-žʷlar ø-ajza-nə́
Rel-be-Stat.Pres.NF that it-copula-Stat.Pres.Fin the-people [they-]gather-Abs
j-t'ʷá-wp', r-ħʷəntkár a-dawə́ d-áa-j-nə
they-be sitting-Stat.Pres.Fin their-king the-ogre he-Prev-come hither-Abs
də-j-fa-ranə́ də́-q'a-wp', jə́-q'a-r-c'a-ra,
him-he-eat-must he-be-Stat.Pres.Fin Rel/what-Prev-they-do-Fut.I.NF
ø-rə-z-də́r-[w]a-m, jə-gʷžʷážʷa-wa j-ajla-t'ʷá-wp',
[it-]them-Pot-know-Dyn-Neg they-grieve-Abs they-Prev-sit together-Stat.Pres.Fin
— ø-j-ħʷá-jt'.
[it-]he-say-(Aor)-Fin

'This is what's happening. The people have come together and are sitting down. They are sure that an ogre is going to come and eat their King. They don't know what they should do. They are all sitting down together, feeling sad,' he said.

(41) — wəs ák'ʷzar, jə́-q'a-w-c'a-ša wəj [a-]á-wp',
if so Rel-Prev-you.M-do-Fut.II.NF that it-copula-Stat.Pres.Fin
áa, wə-s-t á-[a]ħʷa, abrə́j á-[a]ħʷa ɸ-k'-nə́, ašʲšʲə́-ħʷa
oh here/take! the-sword this the-sword [it]-hold-Abs quietly
w-ná-j-nə a-ħʷəntkár d-axʲə́-q'a-w j-wáda-[a-]č'ə
you.M-Prev-go thither-Abs the-king he-where-be-Stat.Pres.NF his-room-its-in
wə-šʲtá-l, wə-č-ʒa-nə́ ǯʲará k'ʷák'ʲ-k'
you.M-Prev-lie down.Imp you.M-Self-conceal-Abs somewhere corner-one
a-č'ə́ w-xʷə́c'a-t'ʷa.
it-in you.M-Prev-sit down.Imp

'If this is so, this is what you must do. Look, pick up that sword. Take the sword and go quietly to the room where the King is, and lie down and hide yourself somewhere in a corner.

(42) a-dawə́ d-an-aá-j-wa, jə-r-dəd-wá jə́-r-macʷəs-wa
the-ogre he-when-Prev-come hither-Abs it-Caus-thunder-Abs it-Caus-lighten-Abs
d-aa-wá-jt', axá jagʲá jə-r-dədə́-rgʲə, jagʲá
he-come hither-Dyn-Fin, but however it-Caus-thunder-even if however
jə-r-macʷə́sə-rgʲə, wará aħaħáj ak'ə́
it-Caus-lighten-even if you.M encouraging word something
w-a-cʷə́-m-šʷa-n, w-čə-rɣʷɣʷá, ak'agʲə́
you.M-it-Prev-Neg-be afarid-Proh your.M-Self-hold out.Imp nothing
ɸ-wə́-xʲ-wa-m.
[it-]you.M-happen to-Dyn-Neg

When the ogre appears, he will come with bolts of thunder and lightning. But, even if the ogre makes thunder, and even if he makes lightning, you have nothing to fear. Be brave, nothing will happen to you.

(43) a-dawə́ d-an-aá-j-lak'ʲ, á-[a]ħʷa ɸ-rəxxá
the-ogre he-when-Prev-come hither-LA the-sword [it-]stretch.Imp
j-xə́ w-a-s.
his-head you.M-it-hit.Imp

When the ogre comes, take out your sword and strike it on the head.

(44) znək' [jə-]j-áa-wə-rxa-jt' ħʷa jará jaráznak'
one time [?-]it-Prev-you.M-hit-(Aor)-Fin SP(= although) he instantly
də-ps-ʒa-wá-m.
he-die-Emph-Dyn-Neg

Even if you hit it once, it won't die right away.

(45) «wará wəj áq'ara w-xác'a ɣʷɣʷá-zar, dačá znə́k'-gʲə
you.M this so much you.M-man strong-if again one time-also
w-sə-s» ħʷa ɸ-w-á-j-ħʷa-wa-jt' a-dawə́, axá wará
you.M-me-hit.Imp SP [it-]you.M-to-he-say-Dyn-Fin the-ogre but you.M

«jawázəj, járabəj sə-z-wə́-s-wa?» ħʷa j-wə-m-wə́-n,
why ever Interjection I-why-you.M-hit-Dyn.NF SP it-you.M-Neg-do-Proh
znək' á-da wə-j-mə́-sə-n (dača=znə́k' d-jə́-sə-r, a-dawə́
one.time it-except you.M-him-Neg-hit-Proh another-once he-him-hit-if the-ogre
jə-psə́ ø-tá-la-wa-zaap') — ø-a-ħʷá-jt' a-čə́.
his-soul [it-]Prev-go into (revive)-Dyn.NF-apparently [it-]it-say-(Aor)-Fin the-horse
'If you are such a strong man, hit me once more,' the ogre will say to you, but you should reply, 'Why on earth should I strike you?' Say this, and don't do it. Don't hit the ogre more than one time. If you hit it more than once, the ogre will come back to life,' the horse said.

(46) — jə-bzə́ja-wp', — j-ħʷá-n, á-[a]ħʷa
it-good-Stat.Pres.Fin he-say-Past.Ind.Fin the-sword
ø-áa-šʲtə-j-xə-n «á-č'ʲk'ʷən» a-ħʷəntkár jə-jʷnə́
[it-]Par-Prev-he-pick up-Past.Ind.Fin 'the-boy' the-king his-house
d-nə-ø-jʷná-l[a-j]t'.
he-Par-[it-]Prev-enter-(Aor)-Fin
'All right,' the 'boy' said and picked up the sword and went into the King's room.

(47) a-ħʷəntkár d-zə-jʷná-z a-wáda-[a-]č'ə d-ná-j-aanʒa
the-king he-Rel-live-Stat.Past.NF the-room-its-in he-Prev-go thither-(Aor)-before
a-wáda-kʷa d-na-rə-jʷnə́-s=aa-jʷnə́-s-wa
the-room-Pl he-Prev(thither)-them-Prev-pass the inside=Prev(hither)-Prev-pass the inside-Abs
j-ajmə́-j-da-n, x-wáda-k' ø-j-bá-jt', wáda-cəpxʲaʒá
them-Prev-he-walk all over-Past.Ind.Fin 3-room-NS [it-]he-see-(Aor)-Fin room-every
aʒʷáʒʷa a-ħʷəntkár jə́-pħa-cʷa ø-ø-jʷna-t'ʷá-n.
one by one the-king his-daughter-Pl [they-it-]Prev-sit inside-Stat.Past.Fin
While he was walking toward the room where the King was, he walked through many rooms and looked around. He saw three rooms. In each room one of the King's daughters was sitting.

(48) abánt a-ħʷəntkár jə́-pħa-cʷa jə́-j-ba-z r-áxʲt'ʷ jʷə́-ǯʲa
those the-king his-daughter-Pl Rel-he-see-Past.Ind.NF them-among 2-women
a-šʷə́ ø-rə-šʷ-nə́ r-wáda-kʷa
the-mourning [it-]them-be on/wear-Abs their-room-Pl
j-rə-jʷna-t'ʷá-n, j-laɣərʒə́-šaxa, á-xpat'ʷəj a-šʷə́
they-them-Prev-sit inside-Stat.Past.Fin they-tear-much the-third the-mourning
ø-lə-šʷ-ʒá-mə-zt', šk'ʷák'ʷa matʷá-la
[it-]her-be on/wear-Emph-Neg-Stat.Past.Fin white clothes-with
d-ajla-ħʷá-n, d-gʷə́rɣʲa-c'ʷa l-wáda
she-Prev-be dressed-Stat.Past.Fin she-joyfully-very her-room
də-ø-jʷna-t'ʷá-n.
she-[it-]Prev-sit inside-Stat.Past.Fin
Two of the King's daughters were in mourning dress, crying out loud, and sitting in the middle of their rooms. The third daughter wasn't wearing any mourning costume. She was wearing a white

dress. She was very happy and was sitting in the middle of her own room.

(49) art as ø-j-bá-jt' arə́j, axá j-zak'ʷə́zaalak'ʲ
these (people) thus [them/it-]he-see-(Aor)-Fin he but his-completely
ak'agʲə́ ø-r-xə-m-ħʷaa-ʒá-k'ʷa, ašʲšʲə́-ħʷa d-ná-j-n
nothing [it-]them-Prev(about)-Neg-say-Emph-Abs quietly he-Prev-go thither-Past.Ind.Fin
a-ħʷəntkár j-wáda ø-jə-pšáa-n, jə-č-ʒa-nə́ ǯʲará
the-king his-room [it-]he-find-Past.Ind.Fin his-Self-conceal-Abs somewhere
d-aa-t'ʷá-jt'.
he-Par-sit down-(Aor)-Fin
In this way, he saw them but he didn't say anything to them at all, and passed through (their rooms) quietly, and found the King's room and hid himself, sitting down somewhere.

(50) aná anə́j áq'ara a-waá ajlákʲ j-axʲ-t'ʷá-z arə́j
there that so many people many they-where-be sitting-Stat.Past.NF he
ləmk'áala d-gʷá-z-ta-wa-da-z?
particularly him-Prev-who-notice-Dyn-Qu-Impf.NF
There were so many people in the room that no one took particular notice of him.

(51) wəs wa də-š-t'ʷá-z [a-]ák'ʷ-m-k'ʷa, ac'xəbžʲón
thus there he-how-sit-Stat.Past.NF it-be-Neg-Abs in the middle of the night
agʷr=gʷə́r-ħʷa a-bžʲə́ báaps ø-ga-wá, j-dəd-wá, j-macʷə́s-wa,
din-din-SP the-voice terrible [it-]be heard-Abs it-thunder-Abs it-lighten-Abs
a-t'ʷə́la ø-bga-wá j-á-la-ga-jt'.
the-world [it-]collapse-Abs it-it-Prev-begin-(Aor)-Fin
He sat there and in the middle of the night there was a terrible noise like the end of the world, with bolts of thunder and lightning.

(52) arə́j «á-č'ʲk'ʷən» [jə]-j-də́r[ə-j]t' — a-dawə́ d-aa-wá-jt' wažʷə́.
this 'the-boy' it-he-know-(Aor)-Fin the-ogre he-come here-Dyn-Fin now
The 'boy' realized that the ogre was coming.

(53) axá j-čə-rɣʷɣʷa-nə́ j-gʷə́ mə-šʲtə́-k'ʷa d-t'ʷá-wp'.
but his-Self-endure-Abs his-heart Neg-be frightened-Abs he-sit-Stat.Pres.Fin
But he was patient and remained seated quietly.

(54) aɣʲájʷ-ħʷa a-šʷ ø-aa-r-t'ə́ a-dawə́
violently the-door [it-]Prev-Caus-open-(Abs) the-ogre
d-an-áa-jʷna-la, arə́j «á-č'ʲk'ʷən»
he-when-Prev-Prev-enter.Aor.NF this the-boy
jə-š-jə́-l-ša-wa-z j-áħʷa ø-rəxxá
Rel-how-he-Prev-be able to-Dyn-Impf.NF his-sword [it-]stretch.Abs
a-q'ʷák-ħʷa d-jə́-s-t'.

the-bang-SP he-him-hit-(Aor)-Fin
The door was flung open violently and when the ogre came into the room, the 'boy' picked up the sword with all his strength and hit the ogre making a loud banging noise.

(55) — abrə́j ø-z-gʷaɣʲə́-z warа́ w-xа́c'a-c'ʷq'ʲa-wp' dačа́
this [it-]Rel-dare-Past.Ind.NF you.M you.M-man-real-Stat.Pres.Fin again
znək' wə-k'ša-wа́-zar! — ø-j-ħʷа́-jt' a-dawə́, axа́ arə́j «а́-č'ʲk'ʷən»
once you.M-hit-Dyn-if [it-]he-say-(Aor)-Fin the-ogre but this the-boy
č'ə́-jə-m-t-ʒa-jt', wа́ħa-gʲə a-dawə́
Prev-he-Neg+call(= keep silence)-Emph-(Aor)-Fin some more-also the-ogre
s-jə́-s-wa-jt' ø-ħʷа́-n-gʲə d-а́-la-m-ga-jt'.
I-him-hit-Dyn-Fin [it-]say-Abs-also he-it-Prev-Neg-begin-(Aor)-Fin.
'If you hit me once again, you, who do so bravely, must be a real man,' the ogre said. But the 'boy' remained silent. After this, he didn't even start to say, 'I will hit the ogre'.

(56) a-dawə́ wa jə-psə́ ø-aa-j-xə́-c'ə-n,
the-ogre there his-spirit [it-]Par-him-Prev-hatch-Past.Ind.Fin (= he breathed his last)
a-gʷarа́-ħʷa də-l-k'а́-ħa-jt'.
the-plump-SP he-Par-Prev-fall down-(Aor)-Fin
At that, the ogre drew his last breath and collapsed.

(57) «а́-č'ʲk'ʷən» d-nа́-j-n d-na-j-xa-xxə́-n,
'the-boy' he-Prev-go.thither-Past.Ind.Fin he-Par-him-Prev-run up to-Past.Ind.Fin
a-dawə́ j-lə́mħa ø-а́a-xə-j-c'ʷa-n j-ǯʲə́ba
the-ogre his-ear [it-]Par-Prev-he-cut-Past.Ind.Fin his-pocket
jə-l-ø-ta-c'a-nə́ jə-jə́-ma d-cа́-jt'.
it-Pat-[it-]Prev-put into-Abs it-he-have.Abs he-go-(Aor)-Fin
The 'boy' rushed over to where the ogre was and cut off the ogre's ear and put it in his pocket and took it with him.

(58) — а́aj, ħ-ħʷəntkа́r rə́cħa, a-dawə́ də-j-fa-gʷə́šʲa-jt', wažʷšʲtа́
ah our-king pitiful the-ogre him-he-eat-unfortunately-(Aor)-Fin now
jə-špa-ħa-psə́xʷa-w, — ø-r-ħʷа́-jt' а́-žʷlar.
it(?)-how-us/our-possibility-Stat.Pres.NF [it-]they-say-(Aor)-Fin the-people
The people said, 'Oh no. The ogre has eaten our poor King. What should we do now?'

(59) a-ħʷəntkа́r d-an-а́a-pš, a-dawə́ də-šʲ-nə́
the-king he-when-Prev-wake up-(Aor.NF) the-ogre he-be killed-Abs
j-а́pxʲa də-š-k'а́-žʲə-z də-j-bа́-jt'.
him-in front of he-how-Prev-be thrown down-Stat.Past.NF him-he-see-(Aor)-Fin
When the King awoke, he saw that the ogre had been killed and tossed down before him.

(60) — а́a, abaakʷа́, sə-psə́ ø-ajkʷ-zə-rxа́-da, arə́j sarа́

oh everybody! my-soul [it-]PREV-who-save-(Aor)-Qu this I
sə-z-š^j-ranə́ jə́-q'a-z s-aɣá j-xə́ ɸ-xə́-z-c'^wa-da?
me-Rel-kill-must Rel-be-Stat.Past.NF my-enemy his-head [it-]Prev-who-cut-(Aor)-Qu
— ɸ-j-ħ^wá-n, a-ħ^wəntkár á-ž^wlar d-r-á-z-c'aa-jt'.
[it-]he-say-Past.Ind.Fin the-king people he-them-it-Prev-ask-(Aor)-Fin

The King spoke, asking the people, 'Oh. People! Who saved my life? Who cut off the head of this ogre, my enemy, who should have killed me?'

(61) a-bzə́jara ɸ-aa-ga-wá-jt' ħ^wa «sará j-q'a-s-c'á-jt'» ħ^wa
the-good deed [it-]Prev-bring-Dyn-Fin SP I it-Prev-I-do-(Aor)-Fin SP
a-waá aʒ^wə́-m-k'^wa j^wə́ʒ^ja-m-k'^wa j-c^wə́r-c'-k^wa-jt', axá
people one person-Neg-Adv two persons-Neg-Adv they-Prev-appear-Pl-(Aor)-Fin but
j-q'a-z-c'á-c'^wq'^ja-z d-d^wə́l-c'-nə d-ca-x^já-n.
it-Prev-Rel-do-really-Past.Ind.NF he-Prev-go out-Abs he-go-Plupf-Fin

Many people appeared, saying, 'I did it,' hoping to be recognized for this good deed, but 'the boy' who had in truth done it was outside.

(62) a-dawə́ də-z-š^jə́-c'^wq'^ja-z a-jáša
the-ogre him-Rel-kill-really-Past.Ind.NF the-truth
ɸ-r-z-ájlə-m-k'aa-jt'.
[it-]them-Pot-Prev-Neg-understand-(Aor)-Fin

No one knew who had really killed the ogre.

(63) arə́j a-dawə́ də-z-š^jə́-c'^wq'^ja-z «á-č'^jk'^wən»
this the-ogre him-Rel-kill-really-Past.Ind.NF the-boy
də-l-d^wə́l-c'ə-n j-čə́ a-x^wə́c-k^wa
he-Par-Prev-go out-Past.Ind.Fin his-horse the-hair-Pl
ɸ-a[a]-aj-d-jə́-k'šala-n, j-čə́ ɸ-an-aá-j,
[them-]Par-Reciprocal-Prev-he-rub-Past.Ind.Fin his-horse [it-]when-come hither.Aor.NF
d-a-z-c'áa-jt' «waž^wš^jtá jə-špá-q'a-s-c'a-rə-j?» ħ^wa.
he-it-Prev-ask-(Aor)-Fin now it-how-Prev-I-do-Fut.I.NF-Qu SP

The 'boy' who had in truth killed the ogre, went outside, and rubbed the hairs together. When his horse appeared, he asked the horse, 'What should I do now?'

(64) jə́-q'a-j-c'a-šaz ɸ-j-á-na-ħ^wa-jt'.
Rel-Prev-he-do-Conditional II.NF [it-]him-to-it-say-(Aor)-Fin

The horse told him what he should do next.

(65) nas jará á-ž^wlar ɸ-ajza-nə́ a-dawə́
then he the-people [they-]gather-Abs the-ogre
j-ax^j-j-xa-gə́la-z zag^jə́ r-c'ə́x^wt'^waná
they-where-him-Prev-stand near-Past.Ind.NF all them-last
d-aa-c^wə́r-c'ə-jt'.

he-Par-Prev-appear-(Aor)-Fin
After that he was the last to go to the place near the ogre where many people had gathered.

(66) ašʲšʲə́-ħʷa d-ná-j-n d-na-rə́-d-gəla-n,
quietly he-Prev-go thither-Past.Ind.Fin he-Par-them-Prev-stand by-Past.Ind.Fin
«arə́j də-z-šʲə́-z d-a-zwə́st-zaalák'-gʲə a-dawə́ j-lə́mħa-kʷa
this/he him-Rel-kill-Past.Ind.NF whoever he may be the-ogre his-ear-Pl
r-wa-k' j-ǯʲə́ba j-ø-tá-wp'» ø-j-ħʷá-jt'.
one.of.them his-pocket it-[it]-be in-Stat.Pres.Fin [it-]he-say-(Aor)-Fin
(arə́j j-axʲ-jə́-xʷa-pš-wa də-č'ʲk'ʷəná-w
he they-where-him-Prev-look at-Pres.NF he-boy-Stat.Pres.NF
ø-ǯʲə́-r-šʲa-wa-jt'.)
[it-]Prev-they-think-Dyn-Fin
He went up quietly and stood beside them and said, 'Whoever it is who killed the ogre will have one of the ogre's ears in his pocket'. (Judging from appearances, they thought that this was the boy.)

(67) a-dawə́ də-šʲ-nə́ d-axʲ-k'á-žʲə-z ckʲa
the-ogre he-be killed-Abs he-where-Prev-be thrown down-Stat.Past.NF well
j-anə́-la-j-xʷa-pš, c'abərgə́ngʲə j-lə́mħa-kʷa ak'ə́
they-when-Par-him-Prev-look.at.Aor.NF in fact his-ear-Pl one
ø-š-á-ma-mə-z ø-r-bá-jt'.
[it-]how/that-it-have-Neg-Stat.Past.NF [it-]they-saw-(Aor)-Fin
When they looked at the ogre that had been killed, lying there, they realized that, indeed, one of his ears was missing.

(68) «arə́j də-z-šʲə́-z sa s-á-wp'» ø-z-ħʷá-z
this/he him-Rel-kill-Past.Ind.NF I I-copula-Stat.Pres.Fin [it-]Rel-say-Past.Ind.NF
r-áxʲt'ʷ aʒʷgʲə́ a-lə́mħa ø-jə-z-cʷə́rə-m-ga-jt'.
them-among nobody the-ear [it-]them-Pot-Prev-Neg-show-(Aor)-Fin
Not one of the people who had said, 'I am the one who killed him' could produce the ear.

(69) nas arə́j «á-č'ʲk'ʷən» j-ǯʲə́ba j-aa-tə́-j-xə-n a-dawə́ j-lə́mħa
then this the-boy his-pocket it-Par-Prev-he-take out-Past.Ind.Fin the-ogre his-ear
ø-na-ga-nə́ r-ápxʲa j-nə́-kʷ-j-c'a-jt'.
[it-]Prev-take thither-Abs them-in front of it-Par-Prev-he-put on-(Aor)-Fin
Then, the 'boy' took the ogre's ear out of his pocket and placed it in front of them.

(70) «abrə́j s-áħʷa-la-[a]-wp' d-šə́-s-šʲə-z»
this my-sword-with-copula-Stat.Pres.Fin him-how-I-kill-Past.Ind.NF
ø-j-ħʷá-n, j-áħʷa a-trá j-aa-tə́-x-nə
[it-]he-say-Past.Ind.Fin his-sword the-sheath it-Par-Prev-take out-Abs
a-šʲaršʷə́ a-č'at'át'a jə-d-jə-rbá-jt'.
the-clotted blood the-dirty it-them-he-show-(Aor)-Fin

'I killed the ogre with this, my sword,' he said, and took his sword from its sheath and showed everyone the dirty, clotted blood on it.

(71) — áa, w-anaӡ̌ʲálbajt', wará sə-psə́ ø-ajkʷ-wə-rxá-jt',
oh you.M-dear you.M my-soul [it-]Prev-you.M-save-(Aor)-Fin,
sə-ps-áanӡa wará w-zə́ sə́-q'a-wp', a-mál
I-die-(Aor.NF)-until you.M you.M-for I-be-Stat.Pres.Fin the-wealth
jə́-w-taxə-w, zaq'á w-taxə́-w
Rel-you.M-want-Stat.Pres.NF as much as you.M-want-Stat.Pres.NF
ø-wə́-s-ta-wa-jt', — ø-j-ħʷá-jt' a-ħʷəntkár.
[it-]to you.M-I-give-Dyn-Fin [it-]he-say-(Aor)-Fin the-king.

The King said, 'So you saved my life. I will be here for you until I die. I will give you all the wealth that you want'.

(72) — mawmáw, sará a-mál agʲə́j ħʷa ak'agʲə́ ø-s-tax-ӡá-m,
no I the-wealth other SP nothing [it-]me-want-Emph-Neg
w-á-kʷšaħat-zar, abrə́j á-šk'ʷak'ʷa matʷá ø-zə-šʷ-c'a-nə́ a-wáda
you.M-it-concent to-if this the-white clothes [it-]Rel-SV-put on-Abs the-room
jə-ø-jʷna-t'ʷá-w wə-pħá d-sə́-t,
Rel-[it-]Prev-sit inside-Stat.Pres.NF your.M-daughter her-to me-give.Imp
— ø-j-ħʷá-jt' «á-č'ʲk'ʷən».
[it-]he-say-(Aor)-Fin 'the-boy'.

'No. I do not want your wealth. If you agree, I would like your daughter, in the middle of the room, who is wearing white clothes,' the 'boy' said.

(73) — wa, wará, w-anaӡ̌ʲálbajt', wəj sará s-l-ájg-ӡa-wa-m, axá lará
oh you.M you.M-dear she I I-her-Prev-grudge-Dyn-Neg but she
d-xʷárta-m, wəj j-l-ájɣʲə-w á-pħa-cʷa
she-useful-Neg she Rel-her-better than-Stat.Pres.NF the-daughter-Pl.Hum
bzə́ja-kʷa ø-sə́-ma-wp', w-rə́-la-r-pš-nə
good-Pl.Non.Hum [they-]me-have-Stat.Pres.Fin you.M-them-Prev-Caus-choose-Abs
j-r-ájɣʲə-w d-wə́-s-ta-p', wəj
Rel-them-better than-Stat.Pres.NF her-you.M-I-give-Fut.I.Fin she
jə-l-zə́-w-w-[w]a-zaj? — ø-j-ħʷá-jt' a-ħʷəntkár.
what-her-for-you.M-do-Dyn-Qu [it-]he-say-(Aor)-Fin the-king

'Oh my dear friend. I do not begrudge my daughter, but she is useless. I have daughters who are much better than her. If you choose them, I will give you the best from among them. Why do you need her?' the King asked.

(74) — mawmáw, wəj l-á-wp' jə́-s-taxə-w, dačáӡʷ
no she her-copula-Stat.Pres.Fin Rel-me-want-Stat.Pres.NF another
də-s-taxə́-m, d-sə́-w-ta-wa-zar, lará d-sə́-t agʲə́rt aӡʷgʲə́
she-me-want-Neg her-me-you.M-give-Dyn-if she her-me-give.Imp other nobody
də-s-taxə́-m, — ø-j-ħʷá-jt' «á-č'ʲk'ʷən».

she-me-want-Neg [it-]he-say-(Aor)-Fin 'the-boy'.

'No. What I want is that daughter. I do not want the other daughters. If you will give me any of your other daughters, please give me that one. I do not want the others,' the 'boy' said.

(75) «á-č'ʲk'ʷən» j-anə́-jə-m-w-ʒa, a-ħʷəntkár á-šk'ʷak'ʷa matʷá
'the-boy' it-when-he-Neg-do-Emph.Aor.NF the-king the-white clothes
ø-z-šʷə́-z jə-pħá l-č'ə́ d-ná-j-n
[it-]Rel-be on/wear-Stat.Past.NF his-daughter her-to he-Prev-go thither-Past.Ind.Fin
wəs l-á-j-ħʷa-jt':
so her-to-he-say-(Aor)-Fin

As the 'boy' didn't choose any of the other daughters (he was persistent), the King went to the place where the daughter wearing the white clothes was, and said to her:

(76) — ħaj, dad, abaapsə́, sará sə-psə́ ø-ajkʷ-zə-rxá-z abrə́j
hi dear please I my-soul [it-]Prev-Rel-save-Past.Ind.NF this
á-č'ʲk'ʷən j-á-wp', jə-w-taxə́-w a-mál
the-boy him-copula-Stat.Pres.Fin Rel-you.M-want-Stat.Pres.NF the-wealth
ø-wə́-s-ta-p' ħʷa ø-j-á-s-ħʷa-n, ak'agʲə́
[it-]to you.M-I-give-Fut.I.Fin SP [it-]him-to-I-say-Past.Ind.Fin nothing
ø-s-taxə́-m ħʷa ø-s-á-j-ħʷa-jt', bará
[it]-me-want-Neg SP [it-]me-to-he-say-(Aor)-Fin you.F
bə-j-tax-xá-jt', s-bə́-ħʷa-wa-jt' map'
you.F-him-want-become-(Aor)-Fin I-you.F-ask-Dyn-Fin no
ø-j-cʷə́-m-k'ə-k'ʷa b-jə́-c-ca-rc.
[it-]him-Prev-Neg-refuse-Abs you.F-him-with-go (= get married to)-Purposive

'Hello, my dear. This boy here is the one who saved my life. Even though I told him, 'I will give you all the wealth that you want,' he said, 'I don't want it'. He wants you. I ask this of you. Please don't refuse to go with him as his bride'.

(77) — jə-bzə́ja-wp', s-ab, wará j-zə-w-ħʷa-wá
it-good-Stat.Pres.Fin my-father you.M Rel-about-you.M-say-Pres.NF
s-jə́-c-ca-wa-jt', axá j-q'a-la-wá-zar, waxá zac'ʷə́k'
I-him-with-go-Dyn-Fin but it-Prev-be possible-Dyn-if tonight only
j-s-á-žʷ-raʒa, waxá a-xʷə́cxa
it-me-to-grant a postponement.Imp tonight the-meditation
ø-sə́-šʷ-t, — ø-l-ħʷá-jt' lará.
[it-]me-you.(formal/polite)Pl-give.Imp [it-]she-say-(Aor)-Fin she

She said, 'Father, I understand. I will go away as the bride of this person you have told me about. If it is possible, allow me one night's grace. Please let me consider it tonight'.

(78) — abrə́j abás də́-q'a-wp', d-maraħʷ-wa-jt', wəbrə́j
this in this way she-be-Stat.Pres.Fin she-be obstinate-Dyn-Fin it
a-z-á-wp' d-xʷárta-m ħʷa ø-z-w-á-s-ħʷa-z.
it-for-copula-Stat.Pres.Fin she-useful-Neg SP [it-]why-you.M-to-I-say-Past.Ind.NF

'See. This is how my daughter is. She is obstinate. That's why I told you 'She is useless.''

(79) abrə́j á-č'ʲk'ʷən b-jə́-c-ca ħʷa ø-an-l-á-s-ħʷa,
this the-boy you.F-him-with-go.Imp SP [it-]when-her-to-I-say.Aor.NF
waxá-k' a-xʷə́cxa ø-sə́-šʷ-t, á-šʲžʲəmtan
tonight-one the-meditation [it-]me-you.(formal/polite)Pl-give.Imp in the morning
[a-]aták' ø-šʷə́-s-ta-wa-jt' ħʷa ø-s-á-l-ħʷa-jt',
the-answer [it-]to.you.(formal/polite)Pl-I-give-Dyn-Fin SP [it-]me-to-she-say-(Aor)-Fin
— ø-j-ħʷá-jt' a-ħʷəntkár «á-č'ʲk'ʷən» j-č'ə́ d-ná-j-n.
[it-]he-say-(Aor)-Fin the-king the-boy him-to he-Prev-go thither-Past.Ind.Fin
The King went to where the boy was and said, 'When I told her 'Go away as this boy's bride,' she said to me, 'Let me consider it for one night tonight. I will give you my answer in the morning.''

(80) — j-a-pərxága-m, wə́rt-kʷa sará ajħagʲə́ bzə́ja jə-z-ba-wá-jt',
it-it disturb-Neg everything I even more well it-I-see-Dyn-Fin
— ø-j-ħʷá-jt' «á-č'ʲk'ʷən».
[it-]he-say-(Aor)-Fin the-boy
'That is all right. I like her even more,' the 'boy' said.

(81) awə́xa arə́j «á-č'ʲk'ʷən» d-mə́-cʷa-ʒá-k'ʷa maʒalá anə́j á-ʒɣab
that night this the-boy he-Neg-sleep-Emph-Abs secretly that the-girl
jə́-q'a-l-c'a-wa ø-z-ba-wá-jt' ħʷa l-wáda-[a-]č'ə a-capxá
Rel-Prev-she-do-Pres.NF [it-]I-see-Dyn-Fin SP her-room-its-in the-key
a-kə́lc'ʷara-[a-]č'ə d-k'ə́l-pš-wa d-á-la-ga-jt'.
its-hole-its-to he-Prev-peep-Abs he-it-Prev-begin-(Aor)-Fin
That night, the 'boy' was unable to sleep and crept up to the girl's room secretly and peeked through the keyhole to see what she was doing.

(82) arə́j ará d-k'ə́l-pš-wa də-š-t'ʷá-z [a-]ák'ʷə-m-k'ʷa
he here he-Prev-peep-Abs he-how-be sitting-Stat.Past.NF it-be-Neg-Abs
á-c'x ak'ə́r j-n-ajgʷa-xʲá.n ájpšaan, a-xʲt'ʷə́ laxánk'a
the-night considerably it-Par-pass-Plupf.Fin at the time the-gold(en) washtub
a-wáda a-gʷtá j-la-lə-rgə́l[a-j]t', a-laxánk'a a-ʒə́
the-room the-middle it-Par-she-place-(Aor)-Fin the-washtub the-water
ø-n-a-nə́-l-tʷal[a-j]t'.
[it-]Par-it-Prev-she-pour into-(Aor)-Fin
As he was sitting there peeping at her, the night got later and later. Then, she placed a golden washtub in the middle of her room and poured some water into it.

(83) a-pénǯʲər á-šʷ ø-aa-lə-r-t'ə́-n, ħʷəħʷ-k'
the-window the-door [it-]Prev-she-Caus-open-Past.Ind.Fin dove-one
ø-pər-pər-wá j-aa-jʷna-šə́l[a-j]t'.
[it-]flap one's wings-Abs it-Prev-Prev-go inside-(Aor)-Fin
When she opened the window in her room, a dove flew in flapping its wings.

(84) a-ħʷə́ħʷ j-aá-j-z a-laxánk'a j-a-nə́-z
the-dove Rel-Prev-come-Past.Ind.NF the-washtub Rel-it-be on-Stat.Past.NF
a-ʒə́ a-čə́-n-t-na-šʲə-n a-mc'ʷə́žʷjʷa-kʷa
the-water it-Self-Par-Prev-it-dip-Past.Ind.Fin the-wing-Pl
ø-an-á[a]-a-rəšʷšʷa, á-rpəzba pšʒa-k', á-rpəzba
[them-]when-Par-it-wave.Aor.NF the-young man beautiful-one the-young man
zamána-k' d-aa-tə́-c'[ə-j]t'.
fine-one he-Prev-Prev-go out-(Aor.)-Fin
The dove that had come dipped itself in the water in the washtub and when it flapped its wings, it turned into a fine, handsome young man.

(85) arə́j á-rpəzba d-an-áa-tə-c', arə́j á-ʒɣab
this the-young man he-when-Prev-Prev-go out.Aor.NF this the-girl
jnajmatʷanə́ a-c'ʷə́wa-ra d-á-la-ga-jt'.
violently the-cry-Masd he-it-Prev-begin-(Aor)-Fin
When the young man appeared, the girl started to cry.

(86) — j-bə́-xʲ-zaj, bə-z-c'ʷə́wa-wa-zaj?
what-you.F-happen to-(Aor)-Qu you.F-why-cry-Dyn-Qu
— ø-j-ħʷá-n, anə́j a-ħʷə́ħʷ j-á-l-c'ə-z
[it-]he-say-Past.Ind.Fin that the-dove Rel-it-Prev-go out of-Past.Ind.NF
á-rpəzba d-l-á-z-c'aa-jt'.
the-young man he-her-it-Prev-ask-(Aor)-Fin
'What's the matter? Why are you crying?' the young man who had come out of the dove asked.

(87) — abrá č'ʲk'ʷə́na xʷə́č'ʲə-k' d-áa-j-n s-ab
here boy little-one he-Prev-come hither-Past.Ind.Fin my-father
də-z-fá-rc jə́-q'a-z a-dawə́ də-j-šʲə́-jt'.
him-Rel-eat-must Rel-be-Stat.Past.NF the-ogre him-he-kill-(Aor)-Fin
'A little boy came here and killed the ogre that should have eaten my father.

(88) a-č'ʲk'ʷən sa sə-j-tax-xá-jt', wažʷšʲtá
the-boy I I-him-want-become-(Aor)-Fin (= he wanted me) now
jə-špá-zə-w-rə-j? — ø-l-ħʷá-jt'.
it-how-I-do-Fut.I.NF-Qu [it-]she-say-(Aor)-Fin
That boy wants me. What should I do now?' she said.

(89) — ʔoħ! — ø-j-ħʷá-jt' anə́j a-ħʷə́ħʷ j-á-l-c'ə-z
oh! [it-]he-say-(Aor)-Fin that the-dove Rel-it-Prev-go out of-Past.Ind.NF
á-č'ʲk'ʷən.
the-boy
'Oh no,' said the young man who had come out of the dove.

(90) — sará á-gəzmal-kʷa r-ħʷəntkár j-pá s-a-wp'.
I the-demon-Pl their-king his-son I-copula-Stat.Pres Fin
'I am the son of the King of the demons.

(91) anə́j a-xʷəč'ʲə́ bará bə-špa-s-cʷə́-j-ga-wa,
that the-child you.F you.F-how-me-Prev-he-take away from-Pres.NF
də-s-šʲə́-r-a-wp', də-špa-s-zə́-m-šʲ-wa-j!
him-I-kill-must-copula-Stat.Pres.Fin he-how-me-Pot-Neg-kill-Pres.NF-Qu
— ø-j-ħʷá-jt'.
[it-]he-say-(Aor)-Fin
Does that boy think he is going to take you away from me? I have to kill him. How can I not kill him?' he said.

(92) — nas jə-špá-zə-w-rə-j, wac'ʷə́ ø-aa-šá-r [a-]aták'
then it-how-I-do-Fut.I.NF-Qu tomorrow [it-]Prev(here)-dawn-if the-answer
ø-r-á-s-ħʷa-r-a-wp'? — ø-l-ħʷá-jt'.
[it]-them-to-I-say-must-copula-Stat.Pres.Fin [it-]she-say-(Aor)-Fin
She asked him, 'So what should I do? I have to give my answer tomorrow, in the morning'.

(93) — wac'ʷə́ b-ab wbas ø-j-á-ħʷa
tomorrow your.F-father thus [it-]him-to-say.Imp
(xʷə=də́w-k' a-xʲʒ ø-j-ħʷá-jt').
hill-big-one its-name [it-]he-say-(Aor)-Fin)
'Say this to your father tomorrow. (He told her the name of a large hill).

(94) abrə́jgʲ, abrə́jgʲ a-tə́p a-č'ə́ a-xʷə́ dəw jə́-ø-kʷə-wp' a-xáħʷ dəw.
<u>such and such</u> the-place it-at the-hill big it-[it-]on-Stat.Pres.Fin the-stone big
'On the top of the big hill at a certain place there is a big stone.

(95) wəbrə́j a-xʷə́ jə́-ø-kʷə-w a-xáħʷ
it the-hill Rel-[it-]be on-Stat.Pres.NF the-stone
ø-s-z-aa-j-gá-[a]ajt', nas
[it-]me-OV(for)-Prev-he-bring-Subjunctive then
s-jə́-c-ca-wa-jt' wə́j á-č'ʲk'ʷən ħʷa ø-j-á-ħʷa,
I-him-<u>with-go</u>(= get married to)-Dyn-Fin that the-boy SP [it-]him-to-say.Imp
— ø-j-ħʷá-jt'.
[it-]he-say-(Aor)-Fin
Have him [the 'boy'] bring the stone on the top of the hill here to me'. And tell your father, 'Then I will go as his bride," he [the demon King's son] said.

(96) art j-ajbə́-r-ħʷa-kʷa-z arə́j
these people Rel-Rec(each other)-they-talk with-Pl-Past.Ind.NF this
ø-j-a-ħá-jt', nas anə́j a-ħʷə́ħʷ j-á-l-c'ə-z
[it-]him-to-be audible-(Aor)-Fin then that the-dove Rel-it-Prev-go out of-Past.Ind.NF

ajtáx d-ħʷəħʷ-xá-n a-pénǯʲər də-n-k'ə́l-praa-n
once.more he-dove-become-Past.Ind.Fin the-window he-Par-Prev-fly out-Past.Ind.Fin
d-cá-jt'.
he-go-(Aor)-Fin
He [the 'boy'] listened to what they said to each other. Then the young man who had come out of the dove turned into a dove again and flew out the window.

(97) ášʲəžʲ j-an-áa-ša, arə́j á-ʒɣab l-ab j-č'ə
in the morning it-when-Par-dawn.Aor.NF this the-girl her-father him-to
d-ná-j-t'.
she-Prev-go thither-(Aor)-Fin
In the morning, as the dawn was breaking, the girl went to her father's room.

(98) — s-ab, jaxá j-wə́-ħʷa-z s-a-z-xʷə́cə-n
my-father last night Rel-you.M-say-Past.Ind.NF I-it-Prev(about)-think-Past.Ind.Fin
s-á-kʷšaħatə-wp', axá á-č'ʲk'ʷən sə-z-w-ta-ranə́ jə́-q'a-w
I-it-consent to-Stat.Pres.Fin but the-boy me-Rel-you.M-give-must Rel-be-Stat.Pres.NF
abrə́jgʲ, abrə́jgʲ a-xʷə́ dəw a-č'ə́ d-ca-nə́, wəbrá jə-šʲtá-w
such and such the-hill big it-to he-go-Abs there Rel-be situated-Stat.Pres.NF
a-xáħʷ pšʒa ø-s-z-aa-j-gá-[a]ajt', nas
the-stone beautiful [it-]me-OV(for)-Prev-he-bring-Subjunctive then
s-jə́-c-ca-wa-jt', mámzar
I-him-with-go(= get married to)-Dyn-Fin otherwise
sə-z-jə́-c-ca-wa-m, — ø-l-ħʷá-jt'.
I-Pot-him-with-go(= get married to)-Dyn-Neg [it-]she-say-(Aor)-Fin
'Father, I have thought about what you said to me last night. And I agree to it. But I ask you to have the person you are certainly going to give me away to as a bride go to a big hill and bring me back a certain beautiful stone from there. Then I will marry him. If not, I cannot marry him,' she said.

(99) a-ħʷəntkár jə-pħá as ø-anə́-l-ħʷa,
the-king his-daughter so [it-]when-she-say.Aor.NF
jə́-q'a-j-c'a-x-wa-z, anə́j a-dawə́ də-z-šʲə́-z
what-Prev-he-do-Par-Dyn-Impf.NF that the-ogre him-Rel-kill-Past.Ind.NF
«á-č'ʲk'ʷən» d-jə́-pxʲa-n d-aa-j-gá-jt'.
'the-boy' he-him-call-Past.Ind.Fin him-Prev-he-bring-(Aor)-Fin
What could the King do, when his daughter told him this? He called out, and had the 'boy' who killed the ogre brought to him.

(100) — ħaj, dádxajt', arə́j d-xʷárta-m, w-lə́-xʷa-wa-m,
unfortunately my dear she she-useful-Neg you.M-her-manage-Dyn-Neg,
wə-l-q'ʷá-c' ħʷa ø-zə-w-á-s-ħʷa-z abrə́j
you.M-her-leave alone.Imp SP [it-]why-you.M-to-I-say-Past.Ind.NF this
á-[a]k'ʷə-n.
it-copula-Stat.Past.Fin

'My dear friend, unfortunately, this girl is useless. You won't be able to manage her. That is why I told you 'Please leave her as she is'.

(101) wažʷ jə́-l-ħʷa-z wəbrə́j [a-]á-wp', wará
now Rel-she-say-Past.Ind.NF it it-copula-Stat.Pres.Fin you.M
d-wə́-c-ca-r map' ø-lə-m-k'ə́-jt', axá abrə́jgʲ abrə́jgʲ a-xʷə́
she-you.M-with-go-if no [it-]she-Neg-refuse-(Aor)-Fin but such and such the-hill
dəw a-č'ə́ d-ca-nə́ wəbrá jə́-kʷə-w a-xáħʷ pšʒa
big it-to he-go-Abs there Rel-be-Stat.Pres.NF the-stone beautiful
ø-s-z-aa-j-gá-[a]anʒa s-jə́-c-ca-wa-m,
[it-]me-OV(for)-Prev-he-bring.(Aor.NF)-until I-him-with-go(= get married to)-Dyn-Neg
— ø-l-ħʷá-jt'.
[it-]she-say-(Aor)-Fin
Now, what she has said is this. She hasn't refused to be your wife. But she said she will not consent to marry you until you go to some big hill and bring her back a beautiful stone'.

(102) — a-ħʷəntkár, wará a-zə́jn ø-sə́-w-ta-wa-zar, wəj
the-king you.M the-permission [it-]me-you.M-give-Dyn-if she
jə-z-zə́-l-ħʷa-z a-xáħʷ sa j-aa-z-ga-wá-jt',
it-Rel-about-she-say-Past.Ind.NF the-stone I it-Prev-I-bring-Dyn-Fin
— ø-j-ħʷá-jt' «á-č'ʲk'ʷən».
[it-]he-say-(Aor)-Fin the-boy
'Your Majesty, if you will give me permission, I will bring back the stone that she mentioned,' the 'boy' said.

(103) — a-zə́jn ø-z-wə́-sə-m-ta-wa-zaj, axá wəj
the-permission [it-]why-you.M-I-Neg-give-Dyn-Qu but that
ø-aa-ga-rá ø-wadájʷə-wp', — ø-j-ħʷá-jt' a-ħʷəntkár.
[it-]Prev-bring-Masd [it-]difficult-Stat.Pres.Fin [it-]he-say-(Aor)-Fin the-king
'How could I possibly refuse you? But it will be difficult,' the King responded.

(104) «á-č'ʲk'ʷən» d-aa-dʷə́l-c'ə-n, j-čə
the-boy he-Par-Prev-go out-Past.Ind.Fin his-horse
d-á-pxʲa-n a-ħʷəntkár j-č'ə d-axʲə́-q'a-z
he-it-call-Past.Ind.Fin the-king him-at he-where-be-Stat.Past.NF
j-[j-]a-ħá-z á-žʷabžʲ ø-[a-]á-j-ħʷa-jt'.
Rel-[him-]to-be audible-Past.Ind.NF the-story [it-]it-to-he-say-(Aor)-Fin
The 'boy' left right away, called his horse, and told the horse what he had been told when he was at the King's place.

(105) — wəj a-xáħʷ ø-aa-ga-rá j-wadájʷə-w
that the-stone [it-]Prev-bring-Masd Rel-difficult-Stat.Pres.NF
wə́sə-wp', a-daw-kʷá ø-a-xə́la-pš-wa-jt'.
work-Stat.Pres.Fin the-ogre-Pl [they-]it-Prev-watch-Dyn-Fin

'It will be difficult to bring back the stone. Ogres are guarding it.

(106) axá, w-aa-lá, ħ-á-la-ga-p',
but you.M-go-let's we-it-Prev-begin-Fut.I.Fin (= let's begin it!)
j-aħ-z-aa-ga-wá-zar ø-aa-bá-p'.
it-us-Pot-Prev-bring-Dyn-if [it]-we-see-Fut.I.Fin
But let's go. Let's set out. We'll probably be able to bring it back.

(107) ámala, wa ħ-axʲ-ná-j-ša ħ-an-ná-j-lak'ʲ,
but there we-where-Prev-go thither-Fut.II.NF we-when-Prev-go thither-Lak
a-daw-kʷá rə́-la-kʷa ø-x-t'ə́-zar, jə́-cʷa-wp'
the-ogre-Pl their-eye-Pl [they-]Prev-open-if, they-sleep-Stat.Pres.Fin
[a-]á-wp' j-aá-na-ga-wa, wará jaráznak'
it-copula-Stat.Pres.Fin Rel-Prev-mean-Pres.NF (= that is), you.M immediately
a-xáħʷ ø-áašʲt-paa-nə j-wə́-ma-nə w-dʷə́kʷ-la.
the-stone [it-]Prev-take up-Abs it-you.M-have-Abs you.M-Prev-set out.Imp
When we arrive at the place that we have to go to, even if the ogres have their eyes open, they will be sleeping. Please lift up the stone that is there and run away with it immediately.

(108) a-daw-kʷá w-gʷá-r-ta-r, j-q'áa-št',
the-ogre-Pl you.M-Prev-they-notice-if they-cry out-Fut.II.Fin,
jə-ħʷħʷá-št', axá jagʲá jə-ħʷħʷá-rgʲə, jagʲá j-q'áa-rgʲə,
they-bawl-Fut.II.Fin but however they-bawl-even if however they-cry out-even if
wə́-šʲtaxʲq'a w-xʲá-m-pšə-n.
you.M-back you.M-Prev-Neg-look back-Proh
If the ogres notice you, they will probably scream and wail. But even if they scream, even if they wail out loud, you must not look back behind you.

(109) a-daw-kʷá rə́-la-kʷa ø-x-jʷá-zar, jə́-cʷa-ʒa-m,
the-ogre-Pl their-eye-Pl [they-]Prev-be closed-if they-sleep-Emph-Neg
j-áa-pšə-wp' <u>[a-]á-wp' j-áana-ga-wa</u>, wə-r-ba-wá-jt'
they-Prev-be awake-Stat.Pres.Fin <u>that is</u> you.M-they-see-Dyn-Fin
jaráznak', r-áajgʷara wə-z-ná-j-ʒa-wa-m, s-ná-j-wa-jt'
immediately them-near you.M-Pot-Prev-reach-Emph-Dyn-Neg I-Prev-reach-Dyn-Fin
ħʷá-gʲə w-á-la-m-ga-n, — ø-a-ħʷá-jt' a-čə́.
SP-also you.M-it-Prev-Neg-begin-Proh [it-]it-say-(Aor)-Fin the-horse
If the ogres close their eyes, that means they're not asleep, they're awake. They will notice you in no time, so you won't be able to get near them. Even if I try to get close to them, you must not try to approach them,' the horse said.

(110) arə́j «á-č'ʲk'ʷən» j-čə d-á-ma-nə anə́j a-ħʷəntkár
this the-boy his-horse him-it-have-Abs that the-king
jə-z-zə́-j-ħʷa-z a-xáħʷ pšʒa ø-axʲə́-q'a-z
it-Rel-about-he-say-Past.Ind.NF the-stone beautiful [it-]where-be-Stat.Past.NF

a-xʷə́ dəw a-č'ə́ a-daw-kʷá r-áajgʷara j-ná-j[ə-j]t'.
the-hill big it-to the-ogre-Pl them-near they-Prev-go thither-(Aor)-Fin
The horse had the 'boy' get on his back and then they set off for the big hill where the King had told them that the beautiful stone would be, near the ogres.

(111) «á-č'ʲk'ʷən» də-l-čə́žʷ-pa-n a-daw-kʷá
the-boy he-Par-Prev-leap down from a horse-Past.Ind.Fin the-ogre-Pl
xara-nt'ʷə́ d-an-rə́-xʷa-pš, rə́-la-kʷa
far-from (= from afar) he-when-them-Prev-look at.Aor.NF their-eye-Pl
ø-x-t'-nə́ jə-j-bá-n, d-lə́-šʲta-sə-n a-xáħʷ
[they-]Prev-open-Abs it-he-see-Past.Ind.Fin he-Par-touch the ground-Past.Ind.Fin the-stone
ø-mc'á-rs-nə də́-jʷ[ə-j]t'.
[it-]Prev-snatch-Abs he-run-(Aor)-Fin
The 'boy' got down from the horse, and looking at the ogres from afar, saw that they had their eyes open, so he crawled along the ground and took the stone and ran off.

(112) arə́j d-anə́-jʷ, a-daw-kʷá d-gʷá-r-ta-n
he he-when-run.Aor.NF the-ogre-Pl him-Prev-they-notice-Past.Ind.Fin
jə-ħʷħʷá-jt', j-q'áa-jt', axá arə́j j-čə
they-bawl-(Aor)-Fin they-cry out-(Aor)-Fin but he his-horse
d-áašʲt-na-paa-n d-á-ma-nə jə-l-tak'ʷk'ʷá j-cá-jt'.
him-Prev-it-pick up-Past.Ind.Fin him-it-have-Abs they-Par-run down they-go-(Aor)-Fin
As he ran off, the ogres noticed him, and screamed and wailed. But his horse had him get on his back and they sped off with the stone.

(113) a-xáħʷ ø-jə́-ma-nə d-aa-k'ə́l-sə-n,
the-stone [it-]he-have-Abs he-Par-Prev-go through-Past.Ind.Fin
d-jʷa-xʷná-n, j-ná-ga-nə a-ħʷəntkár [j-]jə́-j-ta-jt'.
he-Par-go up-Past.Ind.Fin it-Prev-take thither-Abs the-king it-him-he-give-(Aor)-Fin
He took the stone over fields and across mountains. He took it to where the King was, and presented it to the King.

(114) — abár wažʷšʲtá wə-pħá jə́-l-ħʷa-z
look here now your.M-daughter Rel-she-say-Past.Ind.NF
ø-na-sə-gʒá-jt', də-z-ga-wá-jt', — ø-j-ħʷá-jt'.
[it-]Prev-I-carry out-(Aor)-Fin her-I-take-Dyn-Fin [it-]he-say-(Aor)-Fin
'Look here. Now I have accomplished what your daughter asked of me. I will take her away,' he said.

(115) arə́j «á-č'ʲk'ʷən» j-aa-j-gá-z a-xáħʷ
this 'the-boy' Rel-Prev-he-bring-Past.Ind.NF the-stone
ø-ná-ga-nə a-ħʷəntkár jə-pħá j-na-lə́-j-ta-n,
[it-]Prev-take thither-Abs the-king his-daughter it-Par-her-he-give-Past.Ind.Fin
«wašʲtá b-jə́-c-ca, dad!» ħʷa ø-l-á-j-ħʷa-jt'.
now you.F-him-<u>with-go</u>(= get married to).Imp dear SP [it-]her-to-he-say-(Aor)-Fin

The King took the stone that the 'boy' had brought him to his daughter's room, and gave it to his daughter, saying, 'My dear daughter, go and marry him'.

(116) — jə-bzə́ja-wp', s-jə́-c-ca-wa-jt', wašʲtá wáħa
it-good-Stat.Pres.Fin I-him-with-go(= get married to)-Dyn-Fin now more
ak'agʲə́ ϕ-s-ħʷa-wá-m, axá waxá zac'ʷə́k' á-ʒara
nothing [it-]I-say-Dyn-Neg but tonight one and only the-time
ϕ-sə́-šʷ-t, — ϕ-l-ħʷá-jt' lará xʷdaxc'ʷá ajtáx.
[it-]me-you.Polite-give.Imp [it]-she-say-(Aor)-Fin she obstinate once.more

'That is fine. I will marry him. I will not say anything more. But tonight, just once, please give me some time,' the obstinate daughter asked her father again.

(117) — jə-bzə́ja-gʷə́šʲa-wp', — ϕ-j-ħʷá-jt' l-áb-gʲə.
it-good-discontentedly-Stat.Pres.Fin [it-]he-say-(Aor)-Fin her-father-also

'Oh well, all right,' her father said.

(118) a-čnə́ j-anə́-xʷla, arə́j də-z-ga-ranə́ jə́-q'a-z
on that day it-when-get dark-(Aor.NF) this her-Rel-take-must Rel-be-Stat.Past.NF
«á-č'ʲk'ʷən» ajtáx apxʲán ajpš d-k'ə́lə-pš-nə la
the-boy once.more before like (= as before) he-Prev-peep-Abs she
də-z-č'ə́-z ϕ-j-bá-jt'.
she-Rel-be engaged in-Stat.Past.NF [it-]he-see-(Aor)-Fin

That night, when it got dark, the 'boy' who was supposed to take the daughter away, crept up as he had done before and spied on her.

(119) apxʲán ajpš wəj awə́xa-gʲə, a-c'x ϕ-n-ajgʷa-wá-n ajpš,
as before that that night-also the-night [it-]Par-pass-Dyn-Impf.Fin like as
anə́j lə-xʲt'ʷə́ laxánk'a ϕ-aa-cʷə́rə-l-ga-jt', a-wáda a-gʷtanə́
that her-gold(en) washtub [it-]Par-Prev-she-bring.out-(Aor)-Fin the-room the-middle
j-ná-ga-nə j-na-lə-rgə́l[a-j]t', a-ʒə́
it-Prev-take thither-Abs it-Par-she-place-(Aor)-Fin the-water
ϕ-n-a-nə́-l-tʷála-jt'.
[it-]Par-it-Prev-she-pour into-(Aor)-Fin

The night passed in the same manner as it had previously. She brought out the golden washtub, placed it in the middle of her room and then poured water into it.

(120) a-pénǯʲər ϕ-aa-lə-rt'ə́-n, a-ħʷə́ħʷ ϕ-pər-pər-wá
the-window [it-]Prev-she-open-Past.Ind.Fin the-dove [it-]flap one's wings-Abs
j-aa-jʷná-l[a-j]t'.
it-Prev-Prev-enter-(Aor)-Fin

When she opened the window, a dove came flapping in.

(121) j-ná-j-nə anə́j a-laxánk'a j-a-nə́-z a-ʒə́
it-Prev-go thither-Abs that the-washtub Rel-it-be on-Stat.Past.NF the-water

a-čə-jʷ-t-ná-šʲə-n, d-arpə́s bzə́ja-xa
it-Self-Par-Prev-it-dip-Past.Ind.Fin he-young man good-Adv
d-áa-kʷ-gəl[a-j]t'.
he-Par-Prev-appear-(Aor)-Fin
When the dove went there, diving into the water in the golden washtub, it turned into a fine young man.

(122) a-ħʷəntkár jə-pħá d-t'ʷa-nə́ a-k'ʲažə́-ħʷa a-c'ʷə́wa-ra
the-king his-daughter she-sit-Abs the-bitterly-Adv the-cry-Masd
d-a-č'ə́-wp'.
she-it-be engaged in-Stat.Pres.Fin
The King's daughter sat there and cried bitterly.

(123) — j-bə́-xʲ-zaj, b-zə-r-c'ʷə́wa-wa-zaj?
what-you.F-happen to-(Aor)-Qu you.F-Rel-Caus-cry-Dyn-Qu
— ø-j-ħʷá-n, anə́j a-ħʷə́ħʷ j-á-l-c'ə-z á-č'ʲk'ʷən
[it-]he-say-(Aor)-Fin that the-dove Rel-it-Prev-go out of-Past.Ind.NF the-boy
d-l-á-z-c'aa-jt'.
he-her-it-Prev-ask-(Aor)-Fin
'What happened? Who has made you cry like this?' the young man who had been the dove asked her.

(124) — s-ab sə-z-j-ta-wá á-č'ʲk'ʷən a-dc'á
my-father me-Rel-he-give-Pres.NF the-boy the-order
[j-]jə́-s-ta-z ø-na-jə-gʒá-jt' a-daw-kʷá
Rel-him-I-give-Past.Ind.NF [it-]Prev-he-carry out-(Aor)-Fin the-ogre-Pl
r-xaħʷ ø-aa-j-gá-jt', — ø-l-ħʷá-jt'.
their-stone [it-]Prev-he-bring-(Aor)-Fin [it-]she-say-(Aor)-Fin
'The boy who my father has asked me to marry has carried out the task that I set him and brought the stone back from the ogres,' she told him.

(125) — abrə́jgʲ, abrə́jgʲ á-dgʲəl a-č'ə́ daw-kʷá-k' ə́-q'a-wp',
such and such the-land it-at ogre-Pl-one they-be-Stat.Pres.Fin
wbárt a-daw-kʷá sárk'ʲa-k' ø-rə́-ma-wp', wəbrə́j a-sárk'ʲa
those the-ogre-Pl mirror-one [it]-they-have-Stat.Pres.Fin it the-mirror
ø-aa-j-gá-[a]ajt'.
[it-]Prev-he-bring-Subj
'In a certain place there are some ogres. At that place there is a mirror. Have him bring back that mirror.

(126) wəbrə́j a-sárk'ʲa ø-aa-z-gá-z ak'agʲə́ ø-jə́-xʷa-wa-m,
it the-mirror [it-]Prev-Rel-bring-Past.Ind.NF nothing [it-]him-help-Dyn-Neg
xʷartá-pšʲ ø-jə́-ma-m, — ø-j-ħʷá-jt' anə́j a-ħʷə́ħʷ
help-? [it-]he-have-Neg [it-]he-say-(Aor)-Fin that the-dove
j-á-l-c'ə-z á-č'ʲk'ʷən.

Rel-it-Prev-go out of-Past.Ind.NF the-boy
Nobody will be able to help the person who brings back that mirror. Nobody will be able to help him,' said the young man who had come out of the dove.

(127) nas jará d-ħʷə́ħʷ-xa-n d-nə́-kʷ-praa-n
then he he-dove-become-Past.Ind.Fin he-Par-Prev-fly away-Past.Ind.Fin
d-cá-jt'.
he-go-(Aor)-Fin
Then he turned back into a dove and flew away.

(128) art j-ájbə-r-ħʷa-kʷa-wa-z anə́j
these people Rel-Rec(each other)-they-talk with-Pl-Dyn-Impf.NF that
a-dawə́ də-z-šʲ-xʲá.z á-č'ʲk'ʷən d-axʲə́-ʒərjʷ-wa-z
the-ogre him-Rel-kill-Plupf.NF the-boy he-where-listen-Dyn-Impf.NF
zagʲ ø-j-a-ħá-jt'.
all [it-]him-to-be audible-(Aor)-Fin
When they were talking with each other, the 'boy' who had killed the ogre was listening to all that they said.

(129) ádərjʷačnə j-an-áa-ša, arə́j á-ʒɣab l-áb
the.next.day it-when-Par-dawn.Aor.NF this the-girl her-father
jə-q'nə́ d-ná-j-t'.
him-to he-Prev-go thither-(Aor)-Fin
At dawn the next day, the daughter went to her father's room.

(130) — abrə́jgʲ, abrə́jgʲ á-dgʲəl a-č'ə́ a-daw-kʷá ø-n-xa-wá-jt',
such and such the-land it-at the-ogre-Pl [they-]Prev-live-Dyn-Fin
wbárt a-daw-kʷá sárk'ʲa-k' ø-rə́-ma-wp', wbart r-sárk'ʲa
those the-ogre-Pl mirror-one [it-]they-have-Stat.Pres.Fin they their-mirror
ø-rə́-m-x-nə j-aa-j-gá-r, nas
[it-]them-Prev(from)-take-Abs it-Prev-he-bring-if then
s-jə́-c-ca-wa-jt' sə-z-w-tá-rc
I-him-with-go (= get married to)-Dyn-Fin me-Rel-you.M-give-Purposive
jə́-w-taxə-w á-č'ʲk'ʷən, — ħʷa ø-j-á-l-ħʷa-jt' l-ab.
Rel-you.M-want-Stat.Pres.NF the-boy SP [it-]him-to-she-say-(Aor)-Fin her-father
'In a certain place there are some ogres and they have a mirror. If he can take the mirror from them, then I will marry the boy you want me to marry,' the daughter said to her father.

(131) arə́j l-ab (a-ħʷəntkár) jə́-q'a-j-c'a-x-wa-z, anə́j «á-č'ʲk'ʷən»
this her-father (the-king) what-Prev-he-do-Par-Dyn-Impf.NF that the-boy
d-aa-jə́-pxʲa-n, «abás abás, arə́j a-xʷdaxc'ʷá, abrə́jgʲ, abrə́jgʲ
him-Prev-he-invite-Past.Ind.Fin in this way this the-bitch such and such
á-dgʲəl a-č'ə́ jə-n-xa-wá a-daw-cʷá a-sárk'ʲa ø-rə́-ma-wp',
the-land it-at Rel-Prev-live-Pres.NF the-ogre-Pl the-mirror [it-]they-have-Stat.Pres.Fin

wəbrə́j a-sárk'ʲa ø-rə́-m-x-nə j-aa-j-gá-r
it the-mirror [it-]them-Prev(from)-take-Abs it-Prev-he-bring-if
s-jə́-c-ca-wa-jt', mamzár s-jə́-c-ca-wa-m» ħʷa
I-him-with-go(= get married to)-Dyn-Fin otherwise I-him-with-go-Dyn-Neg SP
ø-l-ħʷá-jt' ø-j-ħʷá-jt'.
[it-]she-say-(Aor)-Fin [it-]he-say-(Aor)-Fin

There was nothing that the father (the King) could do. The King called the 'boy' and told him what his daughter had said. 'This is the way it is. This is a bitch. My daughter tells me 'There are ogres who live in a certain place who have a mirror. If the boy can steal the mirror from them and bring it back, I will marry him. If he cannot, I will not marry him."

(132) — jə-bzə́ja-wp', — ø-j-ħʷá-jt' arə́j «á-č'ʲk'ʷən».
it-good-Stat.Pres.Fin [it-]he-say-(Aor)-Fin this the-boy
'That is all right,' said the boy.

(133) arə́j «á-č'ʲk'ʷən» d-aa-dʷə́l-c'ə-n, á-žʷabžʲ č'əc
this the-boy he-Par-Prev-go out-Past.Ind.Fin the-story again
[j-]j-a-ħá-z j-čə́ j-[a-]á-j-ħʷa-jt'.
Rel-him-to-hear-Past.Ind.NF his-horse it-it-to-he-say-(Aor)-Fin
When the 'boy' went away, he repeated what he had heard to his horse.

(134) — ħaj, alláħ, a-xáħʷ ø-z-m-áħ-xə-z
unfortunately Allah the-stone [it-]Rel-Prev(from)-we-take-Past.Ind.NF
a-daw-kʷa-gʲə́ ø-ɣʷɣʷá-n, axá wažʷə́ arə́j a-sárk'ʲa
the-ogre-Pl-also [they-]strong-Stat.Past.Fin but now this the-mirror
ø-z-má-w r-lájsʷa ø-baaps-ʒá-wp', agʲə́rt
[it-]Rel-have-Stat.Pres.NF their-behavior [it-]bad-Emph-Stat.Pres.Fin other
j-r-ájpšə-m, ħ-axʲ-ná-j-ra ħ-an-ná-j-lak'ʲ,
they-them-resemble-Neg we-where-Prev-go thither-must we-when-Prev-go thither-Lak
agʲə́rt j-šə-r-zə́-w-wə-z ájpš, rə́-la-kʷa ø-x-t'-nə́
other it-how-them-for-you.M-do-Past.Ind.NF like their-eye-Pl [they/them-]Prev-open-Abs
jə-w-ba-wá-zar, a-sárk'ʲa ø-aa-rə́-m-c'-paa-nə,
them-you.M-see-Dyn-if the-mirror [it-]Par-them-Prev(from)-Prev-take-Abs
jaráznak' w-ajxa-nə́ wə́-jʷ.
instantly you.M-be dying to go-Abs (= at full speed) you.M-run.Imp

'Oh no! Allah. The ogres we stole the stone from were strong. But now, the ogres with the mirror have a character even worse and are not like any other ogres. When we reach the place we must go to, as you did before, if the ogres' eyes are open (if their eyes aren't shut), take the mirror away from them quickly and run away with all your might.

(135) a-daw-kʷá w-gʷá-r-ta-št', jə-ħʷħʷá-št',
the-ogre-Pl you.M-Prev-they-notice-Fut.II.Fin they-bawl-Fut.II.Fin
j-q'áa-št', a-šʷjə-pšʲjə́-ra j-á-la-ga-št', axá jagʲá
they-cry out-Fut.II.Fin the-curse-Masd they-it-Prev-begin-Fut.II.Fin but however

r-ħʷá-rgʲə   jə-čʲħa-nə́,   j-zák'ʷzaa-lak'ʲ   w-xʲá-pš-nə
they-say-even if   it-endure-Abs   whatever may happen   you.M-Prev-look back-Abs
w-rə́-xʷa-m-pšə-n,   a-žʷá-k'-gʲə   ϕ-r-á-s-ħʷa-wa-jt'   ħʷa
you.M-them-Prev-Neg-look at-Proh   the-word-one-even   [it-]them-to-I-say-Dyn-Fin   SP
w-á-la-m-ga-n.
you.M-it-Prev-Neg-begin-Proh

The ogres may notice you and cry out and wail. They might start to curse you. But you must be patient and put up with whatever they say. Whatever happens, you must not turn around and look at them. You must not say even one word to them.

(136) ámala,   w-ʒərjʷ-lá,   jə-w-xá-w-mə-r-štə-n,
only   you.M-listen-Iterative   it-you.M-Prev-you.M-Neg-Caus-forget-Proh
á-šʷj-ra   j-an-á-la-ga-lak'ʲ,   jə́-r-ħʷa-wa
the-curse-Masd   they-when-it-Prev-begin-LA   Rel-they-say-Pres.NF
ϕ-gʷən-k'ə́la,   —   ϕ-a-ħʷá-jt'   a-čə́.
[it-]Prev-remember.Imp   [it-]it-say-(Aor)-Fin   the-horse

And listen. Please remember this. When the ogres start to curse you, please remember what they say,' said the horse.

(137) a-čə́   as   ϕ-an-a-ħʷá,   ap'q'ájʷ-ħʷa
the-horse   thus   [it-]when-it-say-(Aor.NF)   instantly
də-jʷ-čə́žʷ-la-n,   a-sárk'ʲa   ϕ-z-má-z   a-daw-kʷá
he-Par-Prev-mount a horse-Past.Ind.Fin   the-mirror   [it-]Rel-have-Stat.Past.NF   the-ogre-Pl
r-č'ə   d-ná-j[ə-j]t'.
them-to   he-Prev-go thither-(Aor)-Fin

When the horse said this, the boy mounted the horse immediately and they left for the place where the ogres kept the mirror.

(138) də-jʷ-čə́žʷ-c'ə-n   naxʲxʲə́j   a-xáħʷ
he-Par-Prev-get down from a horse-Past.Ind.Fin   in the distance over there   the-stone
ϕ-z-mə́-j-xə-z   a-daw-kʷá   r-č'ə
[it-]Rel-Prev-he-take from-Past.Ind.NF   the-ogre-Pl   them-to
j-šə́-q'a-j-c'a-z   ájpš,   a-daw-kʷá   rə́-la   ϕ-x-t'ə́-z-šʷa
it-how-Prev-he-do-Past.Ind.NF   like   the-ogre-Pl   their-eye   [it-]Prev-open-Past.Ind.NF-as if
ϕ-anə́-j-ba,   d-ná-j-n   a-sárk'ʲa
[it-]when-he-see-(Aor.NF)   he-Prev-go thither-Past.Ind.Fin   the-mirror
ϕ-aa-rə́-m-c'ə-j-paa-n   də́-jʷ-t'.
[it-]Par-them-Prev(from)-Prev-he-take-Past.Ind.Fin   he-run-(Aor)-Fin

He got down from the horse at a distance from them and again he did what he had done to the ogres that he had stolen the stone from before. The ogres' eyes seemed to be open, and he went there and stole the mirror and rushed off with it.

(139) d-anə́-jʷ,   dará   d-gʷá-r-ta-n   jə-ħʷħʷá-jt',
he-when-run.Aor.NF   they   him-Prev-they-notice-Past.Ind.Fin   they-bawl-(Aor)-Fin

j-q'áa-jt', á-šʷəj-ra j-á-la-ga-jt'.
they-cry out-(Aor)-Fin the-curse-Masd they-it-Prev-begin-(Aor)-Fin
When he ran away, the ogres noticed and wailed, crying out aloud. They started to put a curse on him.

(140) — eħ, abrá j-aá-j-nə ħará ħ-sárk'ʲa
eh! hither they-Prev-come hither-Abs we our-mirror
ϕ-z-gá-z d-xác'a-zar, də-pħʷə́s-xa-[a]ajt', də-pħʷə́s-zar,
[it-]Rel-take-Past.Ind.NF he-man-if he-woman-become-Subj she-woman-if
d-xác'a-xa-[a]ajt', — ϕ-r-ħʷá-n, də-r-šʷəjə́-jt'.
she-man-become-Subj [it-]they-say-Past.Ind.Fin him-they-curse-(Aor)-Fin
(á-zamanala də-r-šʷəjə́-jt', wə-m-ba-wá!).
perfectly well him-they-curse-(Aor)-Fin you.M-Neg-see-Dyn (= indeed!)
'Hey! If the one who has come here and has our mirror is a man, he will be turned into a woman. If it's a woman, she will be turned into a man,' the ogres said, putting a curse on him. (And in fact, they actually did put a real curse on him).

(141) arə́j a-sárk'ʲa ϕ-jə́-ma-nə j-čə́ a-q'nə́
this the-mirror [it-]he-have-Abs his-horse it-to
d-an-áa-j, «j-w-á-r-ħʷa-zaj,
he-when-Prev-come hither.Aor.NF what-you.M-to-they-say-(Aor)-Qu
wə-špá-r-šʷəjə-j?» ħʷa j-čə ϕ-j-á-z-c'aa-jt'.
you.M-how-they-curse-(Aor)-Qu SP his-horse [it-]him-it-Prev-ask-(Aor)-Fin
When he took the mirror back to where the horse was, his horse asked him, 'What did they say to you? How did they curse you?'

(142) — abrá j-aá-j-nə ħará ħ-sárk'ʲa ϕ-z-gá-z
here they-Prev-come hither-Abs we our-mirror [it-]Rel-take-Past.Ind.NF
d-xác'a-zar, də-pħʷə́s-xa-[a]ajt', də-pħʷə́s-zar, d-xác'a-xa-[a]ajt'
he-man-if he-woman-become-Subjunctive she-woman-if she-man-become-Subjunctive
ħʷa sə-r-šʷəjə́-jt', — ϕ-j-ħʷá-jt'.
SP me-they-curse-(Aor)-Fin [it-]he-say-(Aor)-Fin
(arə́j jará a-xác'a matʷá ϕ-j-šʷə́-n, axá
this he the-man clothes [they-]him-be on (i.e. he wears them)-Stat.Past.Fin but
də-ʒɣábə-m-zəj, d-xác'a-zar ϕ-j-taxə́-m-zəj, zamánala
he-girl-Neg-Qu he-man-if [it-]him-want-Neg-Qu perfectly well
də-r-šʷəjə́-jt' wərt a-daw-kʷá!).
him-they-curse-(Aor)-Fin they the-ogre-Pl
He said, 'They cursed me saying 'If the one who has come here and has our mirror is a man, then he will turn into a woman, and if she is a woman, she will turn into a man.'' (This boy wore men's clothes, but wasn't he a girl? He didn't want to turn into a man, did he? The ogres had indeed put a clever curse on him).

(143) arə́j wažʷšʲtá d-xác'a-xa-jt', a-daw-kʷá
he now he-man-become-(Aor)-Fin the-ogre-Pl

jə-r-ħʷá-z ø-na-ʒá-jt'.
Rel-they-say-Past.Ind.NF [it-]Prev-reach-(Aor)-Fin
Now he was a man. The ogres' curse had come true.

(144) a-sárk'ʲa jə-r-cʷə́-j-ga-z ø-jə́-ma
the-mirror Rel-them-Prev-he-take away from-Past.Ind.NF [it-]he-have.Abs
j-č'ə́-la-j-xa-n a-ħʷəntkár j-na-ga-n
his-SV-Prev-he-set out thither-Past.Ind.Fin the-king it-Prev-take thither-Abs
[j-]jə́-j-ta-jt'.
it-to.him-he-give-(Aor)-Fin
He set out for the King's place with the mirror he had stolen from the ogres, and presented it to the King.

(145) a-ħʷəntkár ajtáx jə-pħá d-lə́-pxʲa-n
the-king once again his-daughter he-her-call-Past.Ind.Fin
d-aa-j-gá-n, «áa, dad, a-sárk'ʲa ħʷa
her-Prev-he-bring-Past.Ind.Fin oh dear the-mirror SP
bə-z-č'ə́-z-gʲə ø-aa-j-gá-jt', wašʲtá
you.F-Rel-be engaged in-Stat.Past.NF-even [it-]Prev-he-bring-(Aor)-Fin now
b-jə́-c-ca-wa-zar, b-jə́-c-ca!» ø-j-ħʷá-jt'.
you.F-him-with-go(= get married to)-Dyn-if you.F-him-with-go.Imp [it-]he-say-(Aor)-Fin
The King called for his daughter once more and had her come to him. 'Well, my daughter. He has brought you the mirror that you asked for. Well, if you are going to marry him, please marry him,' he said.

(146) — j-q'a-la-wá-zar, waxá-k'-gʲə á-ʒara
it-Prev-become-Dyn-if (= if possible) tonight-one-also the-time
ø-sə́-šʷ-t, — ø-l-ħʷá-jt'.
[it-]me-you.Polite-give.Imp [it-]she-say-(Aor)-Fin
'If it is possible, please give me some time tonight as well,' she said.

(147) — jə-bzə́ja-wp', j-b-áħ-ta-p' á-ʒara,
it-good-Stat.Pres.Fin it-to you.F-we-give-Fut.I.Fin the-time
— ø-j-ħʷá-jt' l-áb-gʲə.
[it-]he-say-(Aor)-Fin her-father-also
'All right. I will give you time,' her father said.

(148) awə́xa anə́j j-aá-j-lac a-ħʷə́ħʷ
that night that Rel-Prev-come hither-always the-dove
ø-aá-j-n, j-árpəzba-nə j-šə́-q'a-lac
[it-]Prev-come hither-Past.Ind.Fin it-the young man-as it-how-be-always
j-áa-q'a-la-n jará-j lará-j ø-aj-cʷážʷa-jt'.
it-Par-Prev-become-Past.Ind.Fin he-and she-and [they-]Reciprocal-talk together-(Aor)-Fin
That night, the dove came as usual and, as usual, turned into a young man. And then he talked with

the girl.

(149) — s-ab sə-z-j-tá-rc jə́-j-taxə-w á-č'ʲk'ʷən
my-father me-Rel-he-give-in order to Rel-him-want-Stat.Pres.NF the-boy
wará jə-z-zə́-w-ħʷa-z a-daw-cʷá r-sárk'ʲa
you.M it-Rel-about-you.M-say-Past.Ind.NF the-ogre-Pl their-mirror
ø-aa-j-gá-jt', — ø-l-ħʷá-jt'.
[it-]Prev-he-bring-(Aor)-Fin [it-]she-say-(Aor)-Fin
'The man that my father wants me to marry has brought me back the mirror from the ogres that you asked for,' she said.

(150) — ʔoħ, wa j-cá-z aʒʷgʲə́ ajbgá-la
oh there Rel-go-Past.Ind.NF nobody safe-with
d-m-aa-ʒá-cəzt', wəj jará jə-zla-jə́-l-ša-zaj,
he-Neg-come back-Emph-Plupf.Fin that he it-how-him-Prev-be possible-(Aor)-Qu
d-ajbga-nə́ də-zlá-[a]a-zaj? — ø-j-ħʷá-jt' anə́j a-ħʷə́ħʷ
he-safe-Adv he-how-come back-(Aor)-Qu [it-]he-say-(Aor)-Fin that the-dove
j-á-l-c'ə-z [a]-árpəzba.
Rel-it-Prev-go out of-Past.Ind.NF the-young man
'Oh no. No one has ever succeeded in coming back from there alive. How on earth did this man manage to do it? How on earth did he get back?' asked the young man who had come out of the dove.

(151) — jə-zla-jə́-l-ša-z ø-sə-z-də́r-[w]a-m, axá
it-how-him-Prev-be possible-Past.Ind.NF [it-]me-Pot-know-Dyn-Neg but
[j-]jə́-l-ša-jt', — ø-l-ħʷá-jt'.
it-him-Prev-be possible-(Aor)-Fin [it-]she-say-(Aor)-Fin
'I do not know how he managed to do it. But he has,' she said.

(152) — wəs ák'ʷzar, wac'ʷə́ b-axʲ-ná-j-wa wbas
if so tomorrow you.F-where-Prev-go thither-Pres.NF thus
ø-j-á-ħʷa b-ab.
[it-]him-to-say.Imp your-father
'If it is so, then you must go to your father's place tomorrow and tell him this.

(153) a-ħʷəntkár j-báħčʲa-[a-]č'ə a-bə́ja šʲatá-k' ə́-q'a-wp',
the-king his-garden-its-in the-quince root-one it-be-Stat.Pres.Fin
a-c'əc'mə́ǯʲ šʲatá-k'-gʲə ə́-q'a-wp'.
the-pomegranate root-one-also [it]-be-Stat.Pres.Fin
In the King's garden there are roots of the quince tree, and also roots of the pomegranate tree.

(154) a-bə́ja w-n-a-k'ʲə́-sə-r, jə-čʲčʲa-wá-jt', a-c'əc'mə́ǯʲ
the-quince you.M-Par-it-Prev-touch-if it-laugh-Dyn-Fin the-pomegranate
w-n-a-k'ʲə́-sə-r, j-c'ʷə́wa-wa-jt'.

you.M-Par-it-Prev-touch-if it-cry-Dyn-Fin
If a person touches the quince tree, it will laugh. If they touch the pomegranate, it will cry.

(155) wbart a-bə́ja-j a-c'əc'mə́ǯʲə-j ə́-c'-x-nə
those the-quince-and the-pomegranate-and [them-]Prev-pull out-Abs
j-aa-j-gá-[a]ajt', — ø-j-ħʷá-jt'.
them-Prev-he-bring-Subj [it-]he-say-(Aor)-Fin
Have him pull out these quinces and pomegranates and bring them to you,' he said.

(156) ádərjʷačnə j-an-áa-ša, arə́j á-ʒɣab
the.next.day it-when-Par-dawn.Aor.NF this the-girl
d-ná-j-n l-áb j-j-á-l-ħʷa-jt'
she-Prev-go thither-Past.Ind.Fin her-father it-him-to-she-say-(Aor)-Fin
«abás, abás, abrə́jgʲ, abrə́jgʲ a-tə́p a-č'ə́ jə́-q'a-w a-bə́ja-j
in this way and that such and such the-place it-in Rel-be-Stat.Pres.NF the-quince-and
a-c'əc'mə́ǯʲə-j ø-aa-j-gá-[a]ajt', nas wará
the-pomegranate-and [them-]Prev-he-bring-Subjunctive then you.M
sə-z-w-ta-wá á-č'ʲk'ʷən sə-j-t'ʷə́-wp'» ħʷa.
me-Rel-you.M-give-Pres.NF the-boy I-him-belong to-Stat.Pres.Fin SP
The next day at dawn, the girl went to her father and told him, 'Have him bring me quince and pomegranate trees from a certain area in a certain place. If he can do this, then I will marry the boy that you want me to marry'.

(157) arə́j á-č'ʲk'ʷən (ant a-sárk'ʲa ø-z-mə́-j-xə-z
this the-boy those the-mirror [it-]Rel-Prev(from)-he-take-Past.Ind.NF
a-daw-cʷá d-anə́-r-šʷəjə-z áaxəs wə́sgʲə də-č'ʲk'ʷə́na-xa-xʲa.n)
the-ogre-Pl him-when-they-curse-Past.Ind.NF since after all he-boy-become-Plupf.Fin
də-jʷ-dʷə́l-c'ə-n á-žʷabžʲ č'əc [j-]j-a-ħá-z
he-Par-Prev-go out-Past.Ind.Fin the-story again Rel-him-to-be audible-Past.Ind.NF
j-čə j-[a]-á-j-ħʷa-jt'.
his-horse it-it-to-he-say-(Aor)-Fin
The boy (and he was in fact a boy, having been turned into one after he had stolen the mirror from, and been cursed by, the ogres) went outside and repeated what he had heard to his horse.

(158) — wáa, wəj dáara j-wadájʷ-ʒa-wp', a-bə́ja-j
oh that very it-difficult-Emph-Stat.Pres.Fin the-quince-and
a-c'əc'mə́ǯʲə-j ħʷa zə́-ʒbaxʷ ø-w-á-r-ħʷa-z
the-pomegranate-and SP Rel.Poss-information [it-]you.M-to-they-say-Past.Ind.NF
á-gəzmal-kʷa r-báħčʲa-č'-a-wp' j-axʲə́-q'a-w, axá
the-demon-Pl their-garden-in-copula-Stat.Pres.Fin they-where-be-Stat.Pres.NF but
ħ-dʷə́kʷ-la-p', j-aħ-z-aa-ga-wá-zar aa-bá-p',
we-Prev-set out-Fut.I.Fin it-us-Pot-Prev-bring-Dyn-if Par-see-Fut.I.Fin
ħ-č-a-z-áħ-šʷa-p', — ø-a-ħʷá-jt' a-čə́.
our-Self-it-for-we-do one's best-Fut.I.Fin [it-]it-say-(Aor)-Fin the-horse

'Oh no. This is really difficult. The quinces and pomegranates they are talking about are in the ogres' garden. But let's set off, shall we. Let's see if we can bring them back. Let's do our best,' said the horse.

(159) j-čә d-jʷ-á-kʷ-t'ʷa-n dә-š-ná-j-wa-z
his-horse he-Par-it-Prev(on)-ride-Past.Ind.Fin he-how-Prev-go thither-Dyn-Impf,
[a-]ák'ʷә-m-k'ʷa, x-jʷә-k' ájšʲ-cʷa r-ab [jә-]j-tә-nxá-z
it-be-Neg-Abs 3-Hum-NS brother-Pl their-father Rel-him-Prev-remain after-Past.Ind.NF
q'áma-k'ә-j xәlparčʲә́-k'ә-j, wap'á-k'ә-j ø-ájma-k'-nә
dagger-one-and hat-one-and felt cloak-one-and [them-]Prev-argue-Abs
rә́-la-kʷa ø-š-tә́jbax-wa-z
their-eye-Pl [they-]how-they quarrel-Dyn-Impf (= how they were quarreling)
d-na-rә́-d-gәl[a-j]t'.
he-Par-them-Prev(by)-stand-(Aor)-Fin
He mounted the horse right away and rushed off there. At that time three brothers were arguing about a dagger [Note: This speaker probably mistakes a-q'áma 'a dagger' for a-q'amčʲә 'a whip'. Cf. (161), (165), etc.], a fur hat and felt cloak their father had bequeathed them, and the boy arrived at the place where they were arguing.

(160) — jә́-q'a-šʷ-c'a-wa zak'ʷә́wzaj, wará?
Rel-Prev-you.Pl-do-Dyn.NF what you.M
— ø-j-ħʷá-n, d-r-á-z-c'aa-jt'.
[it-]he-say-(Aor)-Past.Ind.Fin he-them-it-Prev(about)-ask-(Aor)-Fin
'What are you people doing?' he asked them.

(161) — abárt ø-ajmá-h-k'-wa-jt', — ø-r-ħʷá-n a-q'amčʲә́-j,
these [them-]Prev-we-argue-Dyn-Fin [it-]they-say-Past.Ind.Fin the-whip-and
a-xә́lparčʲә-j, a-wp'á-j ø-j-dә-rbá-jt'.
the-fur hat-and the-felt cloak-and [them-]him-they-show-(Aor)-Fin
'This is what we are arguing about,' they said, showing him the whip, the fur hat and the felt cloak.

(162) — šʷә-s-zә́-ʒәrjʷә, báša šʷә́-la-kʷa ø-tә́jbax-wa-jt'.
you.Pl-me-Prev-listen to.Imp in vain your.Pl-eye-Pl [they-]quarrel-Dyn-Fin (= you are quarreling)
'You people, please listen to what I have to say. Isn't it in vain to argue?

(163) wәj ác'k'әs-gʲә sará jә-š-šʷ-á-s-ħʷa-wa
that better than-also I it-how-you.Pl-to-I-say-Pres.NF
šʷ-nә́q'ʷa-r, jmarja-ʒa-nә́ jә-šʷ-zә́-s-ša-wa-jt',
you.Pl-act-if easy-Emph-Adv them-you.Pl-for-I-divide-Dyn-Fin
— ø-j-ħʷá-jt' á-č'ʲk'ʷәn.
[it-]he-say-(Aor)-Fin the-boy
Better than that, if you do as I say, I will divide these up for you very easily,' the boy said.

(164) — jə-špá-ħ-zə́-w-ša-wa-j?
them-how-us-for-you.M-divide-Dyn-Qu
'How will you divide these up for us?'

(165) — j-šə-šʷ-zə́-s-ša-wa wəj [a-]á-wp',
them-how-you.Pl-for-I-divide-Pres.NF that it-copula-Stat.Pres.Fin
a-xə́c ø-dʷə́kʷə-s-c'a-wa-jt', ápxʲa wəbrə́j a-xə́c ø-aa-z-ga-wá
the-bow [it-]Prev-I-draw-Dyn-Fin first it the-arrow [it-]Prev-Rel-bring-Pres.NF
[jə-]j-t'ʷə́-wp' a-q'amčʲə́-j, a-xə́lparčʲə-j, a-wp'á-j,
they-him-belong to-Stat.Pres.Fin the-whip-and the-fur hat-and the-felt cloak-and
— ø-j-ħʷá-jt'.
[it-]he-say-(Aor)-Fin
'This is how I will divide them up for you. I will shoot an arrow. Whoever brings me back the arrow first can have the whip, the fur hat and the felt cloak,' he said.

(166) — jə-bzə́ja-wp', wará j-šə́-w-ħʷa-z
it-good-Stat.Pres.Fin you.M it-how-you.M-say-Past.Ind.NF
j-q'a-ħ-c'a-wá-jt', — ø-r-ħʷá-jt'.
it-Prev-we-do-Dyn-Fin [it-]they-say-(Aor)-Fin
'That is good. Let's do as you have said,' they responded.

(167) arə́j a-xə́c ø-dʷə́+k'ʷə-j-c'a-n, j-aa-ħ-ga-wá-jt' ħʷa
this the-bow [it-]Prev-he-draw-Past.Ind.Fin it-Prev-we-bring-Dyn-Fin SP
ájšʲ-cʷa ø-ajbár-jʷ-nə j-an-cá,
brother-Pl [they-]Prev-race with one another-Abs they-when-go.Aor.NF
j-aa-r-gá-[a]anʒa, anə́j jará wa də-pšə́-z-ma,
them-Prev-they-bring-(Aor.NF)-before that he there he-wait-Stat.Past.NF-Qu
a-q'amčʲə́-j, a-xə́lparčʲə-j, a-wp'á-j ø-áa-šʲtə-j-xə-n,
the-whip-and the-fur hat-and the-felt cloak-and [them-]Par-Prev-he-pick up-Past.Ind.Fin
[j-]jə́-ma-n d-cá-jt'.
them-he-have-Past.Ind.Fin he-go-(Aor)-Fin
They said, 'When he shoots the arrow, we will bring it back to him' and ran off towards where the arrow had been shot. The boy didn't wait there until they brought the arrow back, but picked up the whip, fur hat and felt cloak and took them away.

(168) — a-wp'á ø-a[a]-ajc'ə́-x-nə w-nə́-la-t'ʷa-nə
the-felt cloak [it-]Par-Prev-stretch-Abs you.M-Par-Prev-sit down in-Abs
q'amčʲə́-la w-an-á-s-lak'ʲ, j-axʲ-áa-w-taxə-w
whip-Instr you.M-when-it-hit-LA it-where-Par-you.M-want-Stat.Pres.NF
w-a-ga-wá-jt', a-xə́lparčʲ ø-na-w-xá-w-c'a-r, aʒʷgʲə́
you.M-it-take-Dyn-Fin the-fur hat [it-]Par-your.M-SV-you.M-put on-if nobody
wə-j-ba-ʒa-wá-m, — ø-a-ħʷá-jt' arə́j á-č'ʲk'ʷən j-čə.
you.M-he-see-Emph-Dyn-Neg [it-]it-say-(Aor)-Fin this the-boy his-horse
'Spread out the cloak, and get on it, hit it with the whip and it will take you to the place where you

wish to go to. If you put on the fur hat, nobody will be able to see you,' the boy's horse said.

(169) də-š-ná-j-wa-z anə́j a-bə́ja-j a-c'əc'mə́ʒʲə-j
he-how-Prev-go thither-Dyn-Impf.NF that the-quince-and the-pomegranate-and
ϕ-axʲ-gə́la-z [á-]ajʷstaa-cʷa r-báħčʲa
[they-]where-stand-Stat.Past.NF the-devil-Pl their-garden
d-a-z-áa-[a]jgʷa-xa-jt'.
he-it-Prev-Prev-approach-(Aor)-Fin
The boy went to the place and approached the ogres' garden with the quince and pomegranate trees.

(170) də-pšə́-n, anə́j jará jə-j-ga-ranə́ jə́-q'a-z a-ħʷəntkár
he-look-Past.Ind.Fin that he Rel-he-take-must Rel-be-Stat.Past.NF the-king
jə-pħa-gʲə́ wa də́-q'a-wp', [á-]ajʷstaa-cʷa r-ajħabə́ j-pa-gʲə́
his-daughter-also there she-be-Stat.Pres.Fin the-devil-Pl their-leader his-son-also
wa də́-q'a-wp', a-bə́ja-j a-c'əc'mə́ʒʲə-j r-šʲap'-kʷá a-r
there he-be-Stat.Pres.Fin the-quince-and the-pomegranate-and their-root-Pl the-army
rə́-k'ʷ-rša-nə, j-táxk'aa-nə j-q'a-c'á-wp'.
them-Prev-fence-Abs them-encircle-Abs they-Prev-be done-Stat.Pres.Fin
When he saw it, the King's daughter that he was to take away with him was also there and the ogre chief's son was there as well. The roots of the quince and pomegranate trees were encircled by a fence and were surrounded by soldiers.

(171) arə́j á-č'ʲk'ʷən j-xə́lparčʲ ϕ-jʷa-j-xá-j-c'a-n, ašʲšʲə́-ħʷa
this the-boy his-fur hat [it-]Par-his-SV-he-put on-Past.Ind.Fin quietly
d-ná-j-n (a-xə́lparčʲ ϕ-an-j-xá-j-č'a, nas
he-Prev-go thither-Past.Ind.Fin the-fur hat [it-]when-his-SV-he-put on.Aor.NF then
də-z-ba-wá-da-z?!) jə́-čʲčʲa-wa-z a-bə́ja-j
him-who-see-Dyn-Qu-Impf.NF Rel-laugh-Dyn-Impf.NF the-quince-and
j-c'ʷə́wa-wa-z a-c'əc'mə́ʒʲə-j ϕ-áa-c'ə-j-xə-n,
Rel-cry-Dyn-Impf.NF the-pomegranate-and [them-]Par-Prev-he-pull out-Past.Ind.Fin
ak'ə́ ϕ-čʲčʲa-wá, ak'ə́ ϕ-c'ʷə́w[a]-wa [j-]jə́-ma
something [it-]laugh-Abs something [it-]cry-Abs them-he-have.Abs
d-dʷə́kʷ-la-jt', jə-č-gʲə́ jar-gʲə́ a-wp'á
he-Prev-set out-(Aor)-Fin his-horse-and he-and the-the-felt cloak
ϕ-a[a]-ajc'ə́-j-xə-n j-jʷa-[a]n-gə́la-n, a-wp'á
[it-]Par-Prev-he-stretch-Past.Ind.Fin they-Prev-when-stand up-Past.Ind.Fin the-felt cloak
a-q'amčʲə́ ϕ-anə́-jʷa-[a]-xə-j-q'ʲa, arə́j zə-pħá də-j-ga-rán
the-whip [it-]when-Par-it-Prev-he-lash.Aor.NF this Rel-daughter her-he-take-must
jə́-q'a-z a-ħʷəntkár j-č'ə j-aá-jt'.
Rel-be-Stat.Past.NF the-king him-to they-come-(Aor)-Fin
The boy put on the fur hat and went there quietly. (When he was wearing the fur hat, no one could see him). And so he pulled out the laughing quince and the crying pomegranate, and there was laughter and crying but he took them away with him. He and his horse spread open the felt cloak and got on it, and then hit it with the whip. And so he went back to the King's place, to where the daughter he was

to take away was.

(172) — a-ħʷəntkár, jə́-w-ħʷa-z zagʲə́ ɸ-na-sə-gʒá-jt',
the-king Rel-you.M-say-Past.Ind.NF all [it-]Prev-I-carry out-(Aor)-Fin
jə́-čʲčʲa-wa a-bə́ja-j j-c'ʷə́wa-wa a-c'əc'mə́ǯʲə-j
Rel-laugh-Pres.NF the-quince-and Rel-cry-Pres.NF the-pomegranate-and
ɸ-aa-z-gá-jt', — ɸ-j-ħʷá-jt'.
[them-]Prev-I-bring-(Aor)-Fin [it-]he-say-(Aor)-Fin
'Your Majesty, I have carried out all the things you said. I have brought you the laughing quince and the crying pomegranate,' he said.

(173) a-ħʷəntkár jə-pħá d-lə́-pxʲa-n d-ná-j-ga-n
the-king his-daughter he-her-call-Past.Ind.Fin her-Prev-he-take thither-Past.Ind.Fin
«áa, bába, jə-z-zə́-b-ħʷa-z á-c'la-kʷa ɸ-aa-j-gá-jt'
oh hi it-Rel-about-you.F-say-Past.Ind.Fin the-tree-Pl [them-]Prev-he-bring-(Aor)-Fin
arə́j «á-č'ʲk'ʷən» ɸ-j-ħʷá-n wəs ɸ-l-á-j-ħʷa-jt'.
this the-boy [it-]he-say-Past.Ind.Fin so [it-]her-to-he-say-(Aor)-Fin
The King called his daughter and took her there and said to her, 'Oh daughter. The boy has brought back the trees you talked about'.

(174) — áaq', wažʷšʲtá wáħa ak'agʲə́ ɸ-sə-z-ħʷa-wá-m,
Oh dear now some more nothing [it-]me-Pot-say-Dyn-Neg
s-jə́-c-ca-wa-jt', — ɸ-l-ħʷá-jt' lar-gʲə́.
I-him-with-go(= get married to)-Dyn-Fin [it-]she-say-(Aor)-Fin she-also
'Oh dear. Now, I have nothing to say. I will marry him,' she said.

(175) a-čʲára ɸ-r-wə́-n, á-žʷra ɸ-r-wə́-n arə́j
the-wedding [it-]they-do-Past.Ind.Fin the-drinking [it-]they-do-Past.Ind.Fin this
á-č'ʲk'ʷən a-ħʷə́ntkár jə-pħá d-jə́-r-ta-jt'.
the-boy the-king his-daughter her-him-they-give-(Aor)-Fin
They had a wedding ceremony, feasting and drinking, and the King gave his daughter to the boy.

(176) a-čʲára-[a-]č'ə d-jʷa-gə́la-n abrə́j á-č'ʲk'ʷən
the-wedding-it-at he-Prev-stand up-Past.Ind.Fin this the-boy
j-aa-j-xə́-j-ga-z zagʲə́ ak'ák'ala á-žʷlar
Rel-Par-his-SV-he-experience-Past.Ind.NF all one by one the-people
j-ajza-nə́ j-t'ʷá-z j-r-á-j-ħʷa-jt'.
they-gather-Abs Rel-be sitting-Stat.Past.NF it-them-to-he-say-(Aor)-Fin
At the wedding, the boy stood up and told the people who had come together and were seated there all the things he had experienced one by one.

(177) [á-]abxʷa á-č'ʲk'ʷən j-ab j-axʲ a-šʷq'ʷə́
the-father-in-law the-boy his-father him-to the-letter
ɸ-dʷə́kʷə-j-c'a-jt' «w-pa a-pħʷə́s d-jə́-ma-nə

[it-]Prev-he-send-(Aor)-Fin   your.M-son   the-wife   her-he-have-Abs
xʲə́ʒ-la=pšá-la   d-wə-z-ná-j-wa-jt'»   ħʷa.
name-with-wind-with (= with a great reputation)   he-you.M-for-Prev-go thither-Dyn-Fin   SP
His father-in-law sent the boy's father a letter. It said: 'Your son will come back to you, bringing a wife with him, and having made a great name for himself'.

(178) á-č'ʲk'ʷən   jə-pħʷə́s   d-jə́-ma-nə   j-ab   j-č'ə
the-boy   his-wife   her-he-have-Abs   his-father   him-to
j-axʲ-aá-j-z-gʲə   čʲára-la   j-pə́-la-jt'.
they-where-Prev-come hither-Past.Ind.NF -also   wedding-with   they-Prev-meet-(Aor)-Fin
The boy took his wife and went back to his father's place. And they had a wedding ceremony there as well.

(179) zašʷá   šʷar-gʲə́   wbas   a-bzjára-kʷa   ϕ-šʷ-zə́-q'a-la-ša.
may... you.Pl-also   like this   the-good-Pl   [they-]you.Pl-for-Prev-happen-Fut.II.NF
May you all also have good luck like this!

Notes

* The text was taken from «Сергеи Зыхуба (ed.), Аҧысуа лакукуа, Аҟуа, Алашара», 1997. pp. 302–311.

(1) **1**. d-šə-č'ʲk'ʷə́n-xa-z : cf. á-č'ʲk'ʷən 'a boy'.

(2) **1**. də́-q'a-n 'he was': masd. á-q'a-zaa-ra [intr.] 'to be, to exist'. **2**. á-pħa-cʷa ϕ-jə́-ma-zaarən < á-pħa-cʷa [j-]jə́-ma-zaarən ([they(C1)-]him(C2)-have-Evidential) 'he (C2) reportedly had (ten) daughters (C1)'. masd. á-ma-zaa-ra [intr. inverse] 'to have'. **3**. d-jə́-ma-ʒa-mə.zt' (he (C1)-him(C2)-have-Emph-Neg.Past.Fin) 'he(C2) never had him(the son, C1)'.

(3) **1**. jə-pħʷə́s l-cʷá l-t'ʷə́-m-k'ʷa d-q'á-la-jt' 'his wife became pregnant': ϕ-l-t'ʷə́-m-k'ʷa < [jə-]l-t'ʷə́-m-k'ʷa ([it (her skin, C1)-]her (C2)-belong to-Neg-Abs), masd. a-t'ʷə́-zaa-ra [intr. stative] 'to belong to'. **2**. d-q'á-la-jt' : masd. á-q'a-la-ra [intr.] 'to become, to happen'.

(4) **1**. jə-s-ħʷa-xʲá-zargʲə : masd. a-ħʷa-rá [tr.] 'to say'. **2**. j-sə-čʲħa-xʲá-zargʲə : masd. a-čʲħa-ra [tr.] 'to endure'. **3**. d-anə-b-má-w (him(C1)-when-you.F (C2)-have-Stat.NF) 'when you have him'. **4**. j-b-áw-wa (Rel(C1)-you.F(C2)-receive-Dyn) 'the one whom you receive': masd. á-[a]w-ra [intr. inverse] 'to receive'. **5**. šʷə-s-šʲ-wá-jt' (you.Pl(C1)-I(C3)-kill-Dyn-Fin) 'I will kill you': masd. a-šʲ-rá [tr.] 'to kill'. **6**. ϕ-l-a-j-ħʷá-jt' < [j-]l-a-j-ħʷá-ϕ-jt' ([it(C1)-]her (C2)-to-he (C3)-say-Aor-Fin) 'he said it to her, ' 'he told her': masd. a-ħʷa-rá [tr.] 'to say'.

(5) **1**. jə-l-taxə́-m-k'ʷa (it(C1)-her(C2)-want-Neg-Abs) də́-q'a-z-ma (she(C1)-be-Past.NF-Qu) 'didn't she want it?': masd. a-taxə́-zaa-ra [intr. inverse] 'to want'. **2**. d-l-áwə-r (he(the son, C1)-her(C2)-receive-Cond.) lit. 'if she receive him'. jə-l-taxə́-m-k'ʷa də́-q'a-z-ma a-pá d-l-áwə-r 'didn't she want to be blessed with a son?' **3**. d-lə́-j-ta-wa-m (him(the son, C1)-to her(C2)-he(God, C3)-give-Dyn-Neg) 'he(God) does not give him to her': masd. á-ta-ra [tr.] 'to give'. **4**. šʷə-m-ba-wá 'you see, видите': masd. [tr.] a-ba-rá 'to see'.

(6) **1**. ϕ-anə́-j-ħʷa < [j]-anə́-j-ħʷa-ϕ ([it(C1)-]when-he(C3)-say-Aor.NF) 'when he said so': masd. a-ħʷa-rá

[tr.] 'to say'. **2.** ak'ʲəžə́-ħʷa [onomatopoeia] 'boohoo'; cf. at'áx-ħʷa 'быстро', át'əq'-ħʷa 'быстро', agʷákʲ-ħʷa 'сразу'. For -ħʷa see §2.5.2.1. ak'ʲəžə́-ħʷa a-c'ʷə́wa-ra 'to cry bitterly'. **3.** j-n-ajma-tʷa-nə́ 'как без остановки что-то льется', i.e. '(плакать) горькими слезами'. **4.** d-á-la-ga-jt' (she(C1)-it(crying, C2)-Prev-begin-(Aor)-Fin) 'she began to cry': masd. á-laga-ra [intr.] 'to begin'.

(7) **1.** zə-gʷrá l-ga-wá-z 'the one whom she believed': masd. a-gʷra-ga-rá [tr.] 'to believe'. **2.** ø-aa-l-gá-n : masd. aa-ga-rá [tr.] 'to bring'. **3.** d-r-á-cʷažʷa-jt' (she(C1)-them(C2)-to-speak-(Aor)-Fin) 'she spoke to them': masd. a-čʷážʷa-ra [intr.] 'to speak to'. **4.** ø-sə́-šʷ-t ([it(C1)-]me(C2)-you.Pl(C3)-give.Imp) 'give it to me!': masd. á-ta-ra [tr.] 'to give'. psə́xʷa sə́-šʷ-t 'help me!, give aid to me!' **5.** sə-j-šʲ-wá-jt' (me(C1)-he(C3)-kill-Dyn-Fin) 'he will kill me': masd. a-šʲ-rá [tr.] 'to kill'. **6.** j-sə-psə́xʷa-w-zaj 'what helps me?', cf. Note (7)-4.

(8) **1.** á-ħʷsa-kʷa (the-women-Pl) 'the women,' cf. á-ħʷsa [pl.] 'women', a-pħʷə́s [sg.] 'woman'. **2.** bə-m-šʷá-n 'do not worry!': masd. a-šʷa-rá [intr.] 'to fear'. **3.** b-anaǯʲálbajt' 'дорогая, dear,' cf. w-anaǯʲálbajt' 'дорогой!' **4.** a-ncʷá j-ħʷa-nə́ : lit. 'God having said it', i.e. 'by God's will'. **5.** d-b-áw-[w]a-zargʲə (he(the son, C1)-you.F(C2)-receive-Dyn-whether) lit. 'whether you will receive him or not'. **6.** ø-bə-z-də́r-wa-m ([it(C1)]-you.F(C2)-Pot-know-Dyn-Neg) 'you cannot know it': masd. a-də́r-ra [tr.] 'to know'. **7.** wə́s ák'ʷə-m-k'ʷa 'если не так'. **8.** ø-b-z-áa-w-p' < ø-b-z-áħ-w-p' ([it(C1)-]you.F(C2)-for-we(C3)-do-Fut.I.Fin) 'we will do it for you': masd. a-zə-w-rá [tr.] 'to do for'. **9.** ħʷa 'SP = Speech-Particle'. **10.** ø-l-á-r-ħʷa-jt' ([it(C1)-]her(C2)-to-they(C3)-say-(Aor)-Fin) 'they said it to her': masd. a-ħʷa-rá [tr.] 'to say'.

(9) **1.** j-šə́-q'a-z (it-how-be-Stat.Past.NF) ák'ʷmk'ʷan 'the time passed'. **2.** ø-an-aa-j < [j]-an-aa-j-ø ([it (C1)-]when-Prev-come-Aor.NF) 'when it came': masd. aá-j-ra [intr.] 'to come'. **3.** a-xšára = a-xšáara 'a baby'. **4.** d-l-aw[ə-j]t' (she/he(C1)-her(C2)-receive-(Aor)-Fin) 'she(C2) received her/him (a baby, C1),' cf. (4)-4. **5.** a-žʷájza-jʷə-k' 'the eleventh'. **6.** j-l-áw-z-gʲə 'the one whom she also received'. **7.** də-pħa-xá-jt' (she(C1)-daughter-become-(Aor)-Fin): lit. 'she (whom she received) also became a daughter,' i.e. 'the child (that she gave birth to) was a daughter,' cf. a-pħá [n.] 'the daughter'.

(10) **1.** a-waá a-zə́-q'a-c'a-nə j-lə́-ma-m-zəj 'она же подготовила людей': masd. a-zə́-q'a-c'a-ra [tr.] 'to prepare/train'; masd. á-ma-zaa-ra [intr. inverse] 'to have'. **2.** j-jə́-z 'the one who was born': masd. a-jə-rá [intr.] 'to be born'. **3.** də-č'ʲk'ʷə́na-wp': cf. č'ʲk'ʷə́na [n.] 'a (little) boy'. **4.** də-r-žʲá-n (him(C1)-they(C3)-deceive-Past.Ind.Fin): masd. a-žʲa-rá [tr.] 'to deceive'. **5.** lar-gʲə́, cf. lará 'she'. **6.** d-ajkʷxá-jt' : masd. ájkʷxa-ra [intr.] 'to remain intact, to be saved'.

(11) **1.** d-r-aaʒá-jt': masd. áaʒa-ra [tr.] 'to bring up'. **2.** ø-l-xə́-c'-wa-jt' ([it/they(12 years, C1)]-her(C2)-Prev-be years old-Dyn-Fin) 'she is 21 years old': masd. a-xə́-c'-ra [intr.] 'исполниться'. **3.** á-č'k'ʷən matʷá 'boys' clothes'. **4.** ø-l-šʷə́-wp' ([it(C1)-]her(C2)-be on-Stat.Pres.Fin) lit. 'it is on her,' i.e. 'she wears it': masd. a-šʷə́-zaa-ra [intr.] 'to wear'.

(12)**1.** ø-j-zə́-z-w-[w]a-jt' ([it(C1)-]him(C2)-for-I(C3)-do-Dyn-Fin) lit. 'I will do it (= a circumcision) for him': masd. a-zə-w-rá [tr.] 'to do for *sb*'. **2.** ø-ǯʲə́-jə-m-šʲa-wa-j: masd. a-ǯʲ-šʲa-rá [tr.] 'to think'. də-č'ʲk'ʷə́na-w ø-ǯʲə́-jə-m-šʲa-wa-j*!* 'он ведь думает, что это мальчик'.

(13) **1.** d-šʷá-n : masd. a-šʷa-rá [intr.] 'to be frightened; to fear,' cf. Note (8)-2. **2.** d-ná-j-n : masd. a-ná-j-ra [intr.] 'to go thither'. **3.** d-a-va-gə́la-nə (she(C1)-it(the stable, C2)-Prev(beside)-stand-Abs) 'she having stood next to it': masd. á-va-gəla-ra [intr.] 'to stand next to'. **4.** d-á-la-ga-jt' (she(C1)-it(to cry, C2)-Prev-begin-(Aor)-Fin) 'she began it': masd. á-la-ga-ra [intr.] 'to begin'.

(14) **1.** ø-ø-ta-k'ə́-n < [j]-[ø]-ta-k'ə́-n ([it(a horse, C1)-it(the stable, C2)]-Prev-be shut-Stat.Past.Fin) 'it was shut in it': masd. a-ta-k'-rá [tr.] 'to shut *sb*. in'.

(15) **1.** d-kʲə́z-kʲə́z-wa, lit. 'she, sobbing': masd. á-kʲəz-kʲəz-ra [intr.] 'to sob'. **2.** ø-an-a-[a]-ħá < [j]-an-a-

a-ħá ([it(her tearful voice, C1)-]when-it(the horse, C2)-to-be audible.Aor.NF) lit. 'it (= her tearful voice) was audible to it (= the horse),' i.e. 'when the horse heard her sobbing': masd. a-ħa-rá [intr.] 'to be audible to, to hear'. **3.** ø-a-ħʷá-jt' : masd. a-ħʷa-rá [tr.] 'to say'.

(16) **1.** w-zə-r-c'ʷə́wa-wa-zaj (you.F(C1)-who/Rel(C3)-Caus-cry-Dyn-Qu) 'who/what makes you cry?': masd. a-r-c'ʷə́wa-ra [tr.] 'to make *sb* cry,' cf. a-c'ʷə́wa-ra [intr.] 'to cry'.

(17) **1.** á-q'a-w-ma : masd. á-q'a-zaa-ra [intr.] 'to be, to exist'. **2.** s-abá-m-c'ʷəwa-wa : lit. 'where don't I cry?', i.e., 'why can't I stop crying?' **3.** ø-ǯʲə́-j-šʲa-wa-jt' ([it(C1)-]Prev-he(C3)-think-Dyn-Fin) 'he thinks it': masd. a-ǯʲ-šʲa-rá [tr.] 'to think'. **4.** ø-w-zə́-z-w-[w]a-jt' ([it(the circumcision, C1)-]you.M(C2)-for-I(C3)-do-Dyn-Fin) 'I'll do it for you': masd. a-zə-w-rá [tr.] 'to do *sth* for *sb*'. **5.** ø-s-á-j-ħʷa-jt' ([it(C1)-]me(C2)-to-he(C3)-say-(Aor)-Fin) 'he said it to me': masd. a-ħʷa-rá [tr.] 'to say'. **6.** sə-ʒɣábə-wp' 'I am a girl'; cf. á-ʒɣab 'a girl'. **7.** ø-a[a]-ajlə́-j-k'aa-r 'if he knows that ...': masd. ájl-k'aa-ra [tr.] 'to learn, to know'. **8.** ħa-j-šʲ-wá-jt' (us(C1)-he(C3)-kill-Dyn-Fin) 'he will kill us': masd. a-šʲ-rá [tr.] 'to kill'.

(18) **1.** ak'ə́ w-a-cʷə́-m-šʷa-n 'there's nothing to be afraid of': masd. a-cʷ-šʷa-rá [intr.] 'to fear'. **2.** ø-sə́-rxʷmarə-r : masd. a-rxʷmár-ra [tr.] 'to make play; to gallop'. **3.** ø-s-taxə́-wp' ([it(C1)]-I(C2)-want-Stat.Pres.Fin) 'I want it': masd. a-taxə́-zaa-ra [intr. inverse] 'to want'. ø-sə́-rxʷmarə-r ø-s-taxə́-wp' 'I want to gallop (a horse)'. **4.** ø-j-a-ħʷa ([it(C1)-]him(C2)-to-say.Imp) 'say it to him!' **5.** ø-špá-w-jə-m-ta-rə-j ([it(C1)-]how-you.M(C2)-he(C3)-Neg-give-Fut.I.NF-Qu) lit. 'how won't he give it to you?': masd. á-ta-ra [tr.] 'to give'.

(19) **1.** ø-an-wə́-j-ta-lak'ʲ ([it(C1)-]when-you.M(C2)-he(C3)-give-LA) 'when he gives it to you, ... '. For -lak'ʲ see Hewitt (1979c: 39): 'if the tense of the subordinate clause is future, the non-finite form must end in -lak'ʲ'. **2.** w-sə́-kʷ-t'ʷa : masd. á-kʷ-t'ʷa-ra [intr.] 'to ride on, to mount'.

(20) **1.** w-ájkʷə-rxa-šʲa : masd. ájkʷə-rxa-ra [tr.] 'to save'.

(21) **1.** ø-aa-gʷnə́-l-k'əla-n ([it(C1)-]Par-Prev-she(C3)-perceive-Past.Ind.Fin) 'she perceived it and ...': masd. a-gʷən-k'ə́la-ra [tr.] 'to perceive'. **2.** d-gʷə́rɣʲa-n : masd. a-gʷə́rɣʲa-ra [intr.] 'to rejoice'. **3.** də́-jʷ-nə 'running, бегом': masd. á-jʷ-ra [intr.] 'to run'. **4.** abás, abás 'так и так'. **5.** j-s-á-bžʲa-na-ga-z (Rel(C1)-me(C2)-to-Prev-it(the horse, C3)-advise-Past.Ind.NF) 'that which it (= the horse) advised me on': masd. á-bžʲa-ga-ra [tr.] 'to advise'.

(22) **1.** á-[a]-wp' (it(C2)-copula-Stat.Pres.Fin). **2.** d-q'a-lá-jt': masd. á-q'a-la-ra [intr.] 'to become'.

(23) **1.** ø-j-wə́-jt': masd. a-w-rá [tr.] 'to do'.

(24) **1.** bába 'сынок!'. **2.** wə-šʲtá-s-c'a-wa-jt' (you.M(C1)-Prev-I(C3)-put down-Dyn-Fin) 'I'll have you lie down': masd. á-šʲta-c'a-ra [tr.] 'to put down'. **3.** j-a-z-xa-wá-jt' 'it is enough for it': masd. a-z-xa-rá [intr.] 'to be enough for'.

(25) **1.** jə-bzə́ja-wp' 'it is good'; cf. a-bzə́ja [adj.] 'good'. **2.** s-á-kʷšaħatə-wp' (I(C1)-it(C2)-consent to-Stat.Pres) 'I consent to it': masd. á-kʷšaħat-zaa-ra [intr.]. **3.** s-wə́-ħʷa-r (I(C1)-you.M(C2)-ask-if): masd. á-ħʷa-ra [intr.] 'to ask'; s-wə́-ħʷa-r ø-s-taxə́-n 'I wanted to ask you'. **4.** ø-sə́-t ([it(C1)]-to me(C2)-give.Imp) 'give it to me!': masd. á-ta-ra [tr.] 'to give'. **5.** j-q'ala-wá-zar 'if possible': masd. á-q'ala-ra [intr.] 'to be possible'. **6.** d-abá-q'a-w 'where is he?' **7.** [j]-jə-z-də́r-ʒa-wa-m ([it(C1)-]him(C2)-Pot-know-Emph-Dyn-Neg) 'he does not know it': masd. a-də́r-ra [tr.] 'to know'. **8.** á-[a]-wp' 'in actual fact'.

(27) **1.** ø-an-l-áw ([it(C1)-]when-her(C2)-receive.Aor.NF) 'when she received it': masd. á-[a]w-ra [intr. inverse]. **2.** d-ajla-ħʷá-n 'she was dressed in': masd. ájla-ħʷa-ra [tr.] 'to dress'. **3.** j-lə́-r-jʷə-jt' (it(C1)-she(C3)-Caus-run-(Aor)-Fin) 'she made it run': masd. á-r-jʷ-ra [tr.] 'to make *sb* run'. **4.** ø-lə́-rxʷmar-t'

= ϕ-lə́-rxʷmarə-jt'. **5.** j-ǯʲá-r-šʲa-wa : masd. a-ǯʲa-šʲa-rá [tr.] 'to feel surprised'.

(28) **1.** jə-jʷ-t-q'ʲá-n : masd. a-t-q'ʲa-rá [intr.] 'to jump out'. **2.** d-á-ma-nə (she(C1)-it(C2)-have-Abs) lit. 'it having her': masd. á-ma-zaa-ra [intr. inverse] 'to have'. **3.** ées [interjection]. **4.** j-cá-jt': masd. a-ca-rá [intr.] 'to go'.

(29) **1.** [jə]-j-cʷə́məɣ-xa-n ([it(C1)-]him(C2)-become unpleasant-Past.Ind.Fin) 'ему то не понравилось,' 'he became displeased by this': masd. a-cʷə́mɣ-xa-ra [intr.]. **2.** ϕ-á-šʲta-j-c'a-jt' ([them(C1)-]it(C2)-Prev-he(C3)-make pursue-(Aor)-Fin) 'he made them pursue it': masd. a-šʲta-c'a-ra [tr.] 'to make *sb* pursue'. **3.** j-abá-[a]-xʲ-ʒa-wa-z (they(C1)-where-it(C2)-Prev-catch up with-Dyn-Impf.NF) lit. 'where would they catch up with it?', 'how could they catch up with it?': masd. a-xʲ-ʒa-rá [intr.] 'to catch up with'. **4.** j-z-a-xʲə́-m-ʒa-jt' (they(C1)-Pot-it(C2)-Prev-Neg-catch up with-(Aor)-Fin) 'they could not catch up with it'.

(30) **1.** j-ná-j-t' < j-ná-jə-jt' : masd. a-ná-j-ra [intr.] 'to go thither'.

(31) **1.** d-axʲ-ná-na-ga-z : masd. a-ná-ga-ra [tr.] 'to take thither'. **2.** ϕ-a-bá-n ([it(a big house, C1)-]it(the horse, C3)-see-Past.Ind.Fin) 'it saw it': masd. a-ba-rá [tr.] 'to see'.

(32) **1.** wə-l-báa : masd. á-l-baa-ra [intr.] 'to descend'. **2.** ϕ-aa-sə́-l-x-nə ([them(C1)-]Par-me(C2)-Prev-pluck from-Abs) 'having plucked them out of me': masd. á-l-x-ra [tr.] 'to pluck *sth* out of'. **3.** j-gá ([them(C3)]-take.Imp) 'take them!': masd. a-ga-rá [tr.] 'to take'. **4.** s-anə́-w-tax-xa-wa (I(C1)-when-you.M(C2)-want-become-Dyn.NF) 'when you want me': masd. a-tax-xa-rá [intr. inverse] 'to want, захотеть '. **5.** ϕ-aa-j-xʲə́-w-šʲə-r : masd. a-xʲ-šʲ-rá [tr.] 'to rub'. **6.** s-aá-j-wa-jt' : masd. aá-j-ra [intr.] 'to come hither'.

(33) **1.** d-aa-čə́žʷ-c'ə-n : masd. a-čəžʷ-c'-rá [intr.] 'to dismount from a horse'. **2.** ϕ-áa-[a]-lə-j-xə-n ([them(C1)-]Par-it(C2)-Prev-he(C3)-pull from-Past.Ind.Fin) 'he plucked them out from it ...': cf. Note (32)-2. **3.** jə-n-ϕ-tá-j-c'a-jt' ([them(C1)]-Par-[it(his pocket, C2)]-Prev-he(C3)-put into-(Aor)-Fin) 'he put them into it': masd. a-ta-c'a-rá [tr.] 'to put *sth* into'.

(34) **1.** áfə́r-ħʷa [onomatopoeia] 'quickly'. **2.** j-č'ə́-na-j-xa-n (his(Poss)-SV-Prev(thither)-he(C3)-set out-Past.Ind.Fin) 'he set out thither ...': masd. a-č'ə́-na-xa-ra [tr.] 'to set out thither'. **3.** j-zə-d-gə́la-z (they(C1)-Rel(C2)-Prev(by)-stand-Stat.Past.NF) 'that which they stood by': masd. á-d-gəla-ra [intr.] 'to stand by'. **4.** d-lə-jʷná-la-jt' = d-nə-jʷná-la-jt' : masd. a-jʷná-la-ra [intr.] 'to come into'.

(35) **1.** j-ajk'ʷša-nə : masd. ájk'ʷša-ra [tr.] 'to surround'. **2.** jə-š-t'ʷá-z : masd. a-t'ʷa-rá [intr. stative] 'to be sitting'.

(36) **1.** jə́-q'a-w-zaj 'what happens?': masd. á-q'a-zaa-ra [intr.] 'to be'. **2.** šʷ-ajza-nə́ : masd. ájza-ra [intr.] 'to gather'. **3.** d-r-á-z-c'aa-jt' (he(C1)-them(C2)-it(C2)-Prev-ask-(Aor)-Fin) 'he asked them about it': masd. a-z-c'aa-rá [intr.] 'to ask'.

(37) **1.** jə́-q'a-w wəj á-[a]-wp' 'вот что происходит'. **2.** də-j-fa-ranə́ də́-q'a-wp' 'he(the ogre) must eat him(the king)': masd. á-fa-ra [tr.] 'to eat'. **3.** jə́-q'a-ħ-c'a-ra 'what should we do?': masd. á-q'a-c'a-ra [tr.] 'to do'. **4.** psə́xʷa-s j-á-ħ-ta-ra 'what can we do?' **5.** ϕ-ħa-z-də́r-[w]a-m 'we do not know that ...': masd. a-də́r-ra [tr.] 'to know'. **6.** d-zə-z-c'aa-kʷá-z (he(C1)-Rel(C2)-Prev-ask-Pl-Past.Ind.NF) 'those who he asked': masd. a-z-c'aa-rá [intr.] 'to ask'.

(38) **1.** ϕ-an-j-a-ħa ([it(C1)-]when-him(C2)-to-be audible.Aor.NF) 'when he heard it': masd. a-ħa-rá [intr. inverse] 'to be audible to, to hear'. **2.** d-jʷa-gʲəžʲə́-n : masd. á-gʲəžʲ-ra [intr.] 'to turn'. **3.** d-aa-dʷəl-c'ə́-n : masd. a-dʷə́l-c'-ra [intr.] 'to go out'. **4.** ϕ-aa-[a]j-nə́-j-q'ʲa-n : masd. áj-n-q'ʲa-ra [tr.] 'to hit *sth* against each other'. **5.** j-aa-gə́l-t' = j-aa-gə́la-jt'.

(39) **1.** j-ájlə-w-k'aa-zaj (what(C1)-Prev-you(C3)-learn-(Aor)-Qu) 'what did you learn?': masd. ájl-k'aa-ra [tr.] 'to learn'. **2.** ϕ-j-á-z-c'aa-jt' ([it(the horse, C1)-]him(the boy, C2)-it-Prev-ask-(Aor)-Fin) 'it asked

him'.

(40) **1**. jə-gʷžʷážʷa-wa : masd. a-gʷžʷážʷa-ra [intr.] 'to grieve; to mutte'.

(41) **1**. wəs ák'ʷzar 'if so'. **2**. jə́-q'a-w-c'a-ša wəj á-[a]-wp' 'вот что ты должен сделать'. **3**. wəst 'возьми!'. **4**. ϕ-k'-nə́ : masd. a-k'-rá [intr. inverse] 'to hold'. abrə́j á-[a]ħʷa ϕ-k'-nə́ 'с этой саблей'. **5**. wə-šʲtá-l : masd. a-šʲtá-la-ra [intr.] 'to lie down'. **6**. wə-č-ʒa-nə́ (you.M(Poss)-Self-conceal-Abs): masd. a-č-ʒa-rá [tr.] 'to conceal oneself'. **7**. w-xʷə́c'a-t'ʷa : masd. a-xʷə́c'a-t'ʷa-ra [intr.] 'сидеть под чем-н'.

(42) **1**. jə-r-dəd-wá ([it(C1)-]Caus-thunder-Abs) 'making thunder': masd. á-r-dəd-ra [tr.] 'to make thunder'. **2**. jə́-r-macʷəs-wa (it(C1)-Caus-lighten-Abs) 'making lighten': masd. á-r-macʷəs-ra [tr.] 'to make lighten'. **3**. d-aa-wá-jt' : masd. aa-rá [intr.] 'to come hither' (= aá-j-ra). **4**. jagʲá ...-rgʲə 'even if'. **5**. aħaħáj, cf. (18). **6**. w-a-cʷə́-m-šʷa-n (you.M(C1)-it(C2)-Prev-Neg-be afraid of-Proh) 'don't be afraid of it!': masd. a-cʷ-šʷa-rá [intr.]. **7**. w-čə-rɣʷɣʷá : masd. a-čə-rɣʷɣʷa-rá [tr.] 'to hold out; to endure'. **8**. ϕ-wə́-xʲ-wa-m ([it(nothing, C1)-]you.M(C2)-happen to-Dyn-Neg) 'nothing will happen to you': masd. á-xʲ-ra [intr.] 'to happen to'.

(43) **1**. d-an-aá-j-lak'ʲ: for -lak'ʲ, see §5.12.2. **2**. ϕ-rəxxá : masd. a-rxxa-rá [tr.] 'to stretch, to draw tight'. **3**. w-á-s (you.M(C1)-it(C2)-hit.Imp): masd. á-s-ra [intr.] 'to hit'.

(44) **1**. [jə]-j-áa-wə-rxa-jt' ħʷa 'even though you hit it'; see Hewitt (1979c: 174): 'Accompanied by the particle indicating a direct quote, <u>ħʷa</u>, an Aorist has concessive force'. Masd. áa-rxa-ra [tr.] 'to hit, to whip'. **2**. də-ps-ʒa-wá-m 'he will never die': masd. a-ps-rá [intr.] 'to die'.

(45) **1**. w-xác'a ɣʷɣʷá-zar 'if you are a strong man,' cf. á-ɣʷɣʷa [adj.] 'strong'. **2**. járabəj [intrerj.] (< Turkish < Arabic [according to Chirikba]). **3**. sə-z-wə́-s-wa (I(C1)-why-you.M(C2)-hit-Dyn.NF) 'why do I hit you?' **4**. j-wə-m-wə́-n (it(C1)-you.M(C3)-Neg-do-Proh) 'don't do it! (to a man)': masd. a-w-rá [tr.] 'to do'. **5**. 'znə́k' á-da' forms an accentual unity. **6**. jə-psə́ ϕ-tá-la-wa-zaap' 'he will apparently revive': masd. a-tá-la-ra [intr.] 'to go into'.

(46) **1**. ϕ-áa-šʲtə-j-xə-n ([it(C1)-]Par-Prev-he(C3)-take up-Past.Ind.Fin) 'he picked it up and ...': masd. á-šʲtə-x-ra [tr.] 'to pick up'. **2**. d-nə-jʷná-l[a-j]t' : masd. a-jʷná-la-ra [intr.] 'to enter, to come into'.

(47) **1**. d-zə-jʷná-z (he(C1)-Rel(C2)-live-Stat.Past.NF) '(the room) where he lived': masd. a-jʷná-zaa-ra [intr.] 'to stay, to live'. **2**. d-na-rə-jʷnə́-s=aa-jʷnə́-s-wa : masd. a-jʷnə́-s-ra [intr.] 'to pass the inside/room'. **3**. j-ajmə́-j-da-n (them(C1)-Prev-he(C3)-walk all over-Past.Ind.Fin) 'he walked all through them': masd. ájm-da-ra [tr.] 'to walk all over'. **4**. ϕ-ϕ-jʷna-t'ʷá-n ([they(C1)-it(the room, C2)-]Prev-sit inside-Stat.Past.Fin) 'they were sitting inside it': masd. a-jʷna-t'ʷa-rá [intr. stative] 'to sit inside'; cf. Note (48)-2.

(48) **1**. ϕ-rə-šʷ-nə́ ([it(C1)]-them(C2)-be on/wear-Abs) 'they wear it': masd. a-šʷə́-zaa-ra [intr.] 'to wear'. a-šʷə́ ϕ-rə-šʷ-nə 'in mourning'. **2**. j-rə-jʷna-t'ʷá-n (they(C1)-them(the rooms, C2)-Prev-sit inside-Stat.Past.Fin) 'they were sitting in them'. **3**. d-ajla-ħʷá-n (she(C1)-Prev-be dressed-Stat.Past.Fin) 'she was dressed (in white clothes)': masd. ájla-ħʷa-ra [tr.] 'to dress'.

(49) **1**. ϕ-r-xə-m-ħʷaa-ʒá-k'ʷa ([it(C1)-]them(C2)-Prev(about)-Neg-say-Emph-Abs) 'saying nothing about them': masd. a-x-ħʷaa-rá [tr.] 'to say *sth* about'. **2**. ϕ-jə-pšáa-n ([it(C1)-]he(C3)-find-Past.Ind.Fin) 'he found it ...': masd. á-pšaa-ra [tr.] 'to find'. **3**. jə-č-ʒa-nə́ : maasd. a-č-ʒa-rá [tr.] 'to conceal oneself'. **4**. d-aa-t'ʷá-jt' : masd. a-t'ʷa-rá [intr. dynamic] 'to sit down'.

(50) **1**. j-axʲ-t'ʷá-z : masd. a-t'ʷa-rá [intr. stative] 'to sit'. **2**. d-gʷá-z-ta-wa-da-z (him(C1)-Prev-who(C3)-notice-Dyn-Qu-Impf.NF) 'who noticed him?': masd. a-gʷá-ta-ra [tr.] 'to notice'.

(51) **1**. wəs wa də-š-t'ʷá-z ák'ʷmk'ʷa 'when he was sitting there'. **2**. agʷr=gʷə́r-ħʷa [onomatopoeia] 'с грохотом,' cf Note (6)–2. **3**. ϕ-ga-wá ([it(C1)-]be heard-Abs): masd. a-ga-rá [intr.] 'to be heard'. **4**. j-

dəd-wá : masd. á-dəd-ra [intr.] ‘to thunder’. **5.** j-macʷə́s-wa : masd. á-macʷəs-ra [intr.] ‘to lighten’. **6.** ø-bga-wá : masd. a-bga-rá [intr.] ‘to collapse’. **7.** j-á-la-ga-jt’ : masd. á-la-ga-ra [intr.] ‘to begin’.

(53) **1.** j-čə-rɣʷɣʷa-nə́ : masd. a-čə-rɣʷɣʷa-rá [tr.] ‘to endure’. **2.** j-gʷə́ mə-šʲtə́-k’ʷa ‘не пугаясь’: masd. a-gʷə́ á-šʲt-ra ‘to be frightened’.

(54) **1.** ø-áa-r-t’ə < ø-áa-ø-r-t’ə ([it(C1)-]Prev-[he(C3)]-Caus-open-(Abs)) ‘(he), having opened it’: masd. áa-r-t’-ra [tr.] ‘to open’. **2.** d-an-áa-jʷna-la : masd. aa-jʷná-la-ra [intr.] ‘to go inside, to enter’. **3.** jə-š-jə́-l-ša-wa-z ‘with all his strength’: masd. á-l-ša-ra [intr. inverse] ‘to be able to’. **4.** a-q’ʷák-ħʷa [onomatopoeia] ‘banging, bumping’. **5.** d-jə́-s-t’ = d-jə́-sə-jt’.

(55) **1.** ø-z-gʷaɣʲə́-z : masd. á-gʷaɣʲ-ra [tr.] ‘to dare to *do*’. **2.** wə-k’ša-wá-zar : masd. á-k’ša-ra [intr.] ‘to hit’. **3.** č’ə́-jə-m-t-ʒa-jt’ : masd. č’ə́-m-t-ra [tr.] ‘to keep silence’. **4.** ø-ħʷá-n-gʲə < ø-ħʷá-nə-gʲə.

(56) **1.** jə-psə́ ø-aa-j-xə́c’ə-n : masd. a-psə́ a-xə́-c’-ra [intr.] ‘to breathe one’s last’. **2.** á-gʷara-ħʷa [onomatopoeia] ‘plump’. For the onomatopoetic suffix ħʷa, see §2.5.2.1. **3.** də-l-k’á-ħa-jt’: masd. a-k’á-ħa-ra [intr.] ‘to fall down’.

(57) **1.** d-na-j-xa-xxə́-n : masd. a-xa-xx-rá [intr.] ‘to run up to’. **2.** ø-áa-xə-j-c’ʷa-n : masd. a-x-c’ʷa-rá [tr.] ‘to cut’. **3.** jə-l-ø-ta-c’a-nə́ (it(his ear, C1)-Pat-[it(his pocket, C2)-]Prev(into)-put-Abs) ‘having put it into it’: masd. a-ta-c’a-rá [tr.] ‘to put *sth* into’. **4.** jə́-ma ‘with it’: masd. á-ma-zaa-ra [intr.] ‘to have’.

(58) **1.** də-j-fa-gʷə́šʲa-jt’ : masd. á-fa-ra [tr.] ‘to eat’. **2.** jə-špa-ħa-psə́xʷa-w lit. ‘how should we do?’, i.e. ‘what should we do?’ For -psə́xʷa see Note (37)-4.

(59) **1.** d-an-áa-pš: masd. áa-pš-ra [intr.] ‘to wake up’. **2.** də-šʲ-nə́ : masd. a-šʲ-rá [tr.] ‘to kill’. **3.** də-š-k’á-žʲə-z : masd. a-k’á-žʲ-ra [tr.] ‘to throw down’.

(60) **1.** sə-psə́ ø-ajkʷ-zə-rxá-da ([it(my soul, C1)-]Prev-who(C3)-save-(Aor)-Qu) ‘who saved my life?’: masd. ájkʷ-rxa-ra [tr.] ‘to save’. **2.** sə-z-šʲ-ranə́ jə́-q’a-z ‘the one who would have killed me’.

(61) **1.** a-bzə́jara ø-aa-ga-wá-jt’ ħʷa ‘чтобы показаться хорошим’. **2.** aʒʷə́-m-k’ʷa jʷə́ǯʲa-m-k’ʷa lit. ‘ни один и ни два,’ i.e. ‘несколько человек, several people’. **3.** j-cʷə́r-c’-kʷa-jt’: masd. a-cʷə́r-c’-ra [intr.] ‘to appear’. **4.** j-q’a-z-c’á-c’ʷq’ʲa-z (it(C1)-Prev-Rel(C3)-do-really-Past.Ind.NF) ‘the one who really did it’. **5.** d-dʷə́l-c’-nə : masd. a-dʷə́l-c’-ra [intr.] ‘to go out’.

(62) **1.** də-z-šʲə́-c’ʷq’ʲa-z ‘the one who really killed him’: masd. a-šʲ-rá [tr.] ‘to kill’. **2.** ø-r-z-ájlə-m-k’aa-jt’ : masd. ájl-k’aa-ra [tr.] ‘to understand’.

(63) **1.** ø-a[a]-aj-d-jə́-k’šala-n : masd. aj-d-k’šála-ra [tr.] ‘to rub’.

(64) **1.** jə́-q’a-j-c’a-šaz ‘that which he must do’.

(65) **1.** j-axʲ-j-xa-gə́la-z (they(C1)-where-him(the ogre, C2)-Prev-stand over-Past.Ind.NF) ‘(*in the place*) where they stood near him’: masd. a-xa-gə́la-ra [intr.] ‘to stand near’. **2.** zagʲə́ r-c’ə́xʷt’ʷanə́ ‘last of all’.

(66) **1.** d-na-rə́-d-gəla-n (he(C1)-Par-them(C2)-Prev-stand by-Past.Ind.Fin) ‘he stood by them ...’: masd. á-d-gəla-ra [intr.] ‘to stand by’. **2.** d-a-zə́wst-zaalák’gʲə ‘кто бы он ни был’; for -zaalák’gʲə see Hewitt (1979c:40). **3.** j-ø-tá-wp’ (it(his ear, C1)-[it(his pocket, C2)-]be in-Stat.Pres.Fin) ‘his ear is in his pocket’: masd. a-tá-zaa-ra [intr.] ‘to be in’. **4.** j-axʲ-jə́-xʷa-pš-wa (they(C1)-where-him(C2)-Prev-look at-Pres.NF) lit. ‘where they looked at him,’ i.e. ‘judging by his appearance’: masd. á-xʷa-pš-ra [intr.] ‘to look at’. **5.** ø-ǯʲə́-r-šʲa-wa-jt’ ([it(C1)-]Prev-they(C3)-think-Dyn-Fin) ‘they think that ...’: masd. a-ǯʲ-šʲa-rá [tr.] ‘to think’.

(67) **1.** d-axʲ-k’a-žʲə́-z: masd. a-k’á-žʲ-ra [tr.] ‘to throw down’. **2.** ø-š-á-ma-mə-z ([it(an ear, C1)-]how/that-it(the ogre, C2)-have-Neg-Stat.Past.NF) ‘... that the ogre did not have an ear’: masd. á-ma-zaa-ra [intr. inverse] ‘to have’.

(68) **1.** arə́j də-z-šʲə́-z sá s-á-wp’ ‘it is I who killed him’. **2.** ø-jə-z-cʷə́rə-m-ga-jt’ ([it(the ear, C1)]-

them(C2)-Pot-Prev-Neg-show-(Aor)-Fin) 'they could not show it': masd. a-cʷə́r-ga-ra [tr.] 'to show, to bring out'.

(69) **1**. j-aa-tə́-j-xə-n: masd. a-tə́-x-ra [tr.] 'to take out'. **2**. j-nə́-kʷ-j-c'a-jt' (it(the ear, C1)-Par-Prev-he(C3)-put on-(Aor)-Fin) 'he put it (in front of them)': masd. á-kʷ-c'a-ra [tr.] 'to put *sth* on'.

(70) **1**. j-aa-tə́-x-nə, cf. Note (69)-1 above. **2**. a-č'at'át'a, cf. a-č'at'át'a-ra [tr.] 'to dirty'. **3**. jə-d-jə-rbá-jt' (it(C1)-them(C2)-he(C3)-show-(Aor)-Fin) < jə-r-jə-r-bá-jt' (it(C1)-them(C2)-he(C3)-Caus-see-(Aor)-Fin) 'he showed it to them': masd. a-rba-rá [tr.] 'to show'.

(71) **1**. sə-psə́ ø-ajkʷ-wə-rxá-jt'; cf. Note (60)-1. **2**. sə-ps-áanʒa : masd. a-ps-rá [intr.] 'to die'. **3**. jə́-w-taxə-w : masd. a-taxə́-zaa-ra [intr.] 'to want'. **4**. zaq'á w-taxə́-w 'as much as you want'.

(72) **1**. mawmáw = mamáw, maw. **2**. agʲáj ħʷa ak'agʲə́ 'nothing else'. **3**. w-á-kʷšahat-zar: masd. á-kʷšahat-zaa-ra [intr.] 'to concent to'. **4**. ø-zə-šʷ-c'a-nə́ ([it(C1)-]Rel(Poss)-SV-put on-Abs) 'having worn it': masd. a-šʷ-c'a-rá [tr.] 'to put on'. **5**. jə-ø-jʷna-t'ʷá-w : masd. a-jʷna-t'ʷa-rá [intr.] 'to sit inside'. **6**. d-sə́-t (her(C1)-me(C2)-give.Imp) 'give her to me!': masd. á-ta-ra [tr.] 'to give'.

(73) **1**. s-l-ájg-ʒa-wa-m (I(C1)-her(C2)-Prev-grudge-Dyn-Neg) 'I do not grudge her': masd. ájg-ʒa-ra [intr.] 'to spare, to grudge'. **2**. d-xʷárta-m, cf. a-xʷárta [adj.] 'useful'. **3**. j-l-ájɣʲə-w (Rel(C1)-her(C2)-better than-Stat.Pres.NF) 'the one who is better than her'; cf. ájɣʲə-wp' 'to be better'. **4**. ø-sə́-ma-wp' 'I have them'. **5**. w-rə́-la-r-pš-nə (you.M(C1)-them(C2)-Prev-Caus-choose-Abs) 'making you choose them': masd. á-la-r-pš-ra [tr.] 'to make choose'. **6**. j-r-ájɣʲə-w 'the one who is better than them', i.e. 'the one who is best'. **7**. jə-l-zə́-w-w-[w]a-zaj (what(C1)-her(C2)-for-you.M(C3)-do-Dyn-Qu) lit. 'what do you do for her?', i.e. 'why do you want her?': masd. a-zə-w-rá [tr.] 'to do for *sb*'.

(74) **1**. wəj l-á-wp' jə́-s-taxə-w 'it is her that I want'. **2**. də-s-taxə́-m (she(C1)-me(C2)-want-Neg) 'I do not want her': masd. á-ma-zaa-ra [intr. inverse] 'to have'.

(75) **1**. j-anə́-jə-m-w-ʒa: masd. a-w-rá [tr.] 'to do'. **2**. ø-z-šʷə́-z ([it(C1)-]Rel(C2)-be on/wear-Stat.Past.NF) lit. 'the one who was on it(= the white clothes),' i.e. 'the one who wore it': masd. a-šʷə́-zaa-ra [intr.] 'to wear'.

(76) **1**. j-á-wp' (him(C2)-copula-Stat.Pres.Fin): ø-ajkʷ-zə-rxá-z abrə́j á-č'ʲk'ʷən j-á-wp' 'it is this boy who saved my life'. **2**. bə-j-tax-xá-jt' (you.F(C1)-him(C2)-want-become-(Aor)-Fin) 'he wanted you': masd. a-tax-xa-rá [intr. inverse] 'to want, захотеть'. **3**. s-bə́-ħʷa-wa-jt' (I(C1)-you(C2)-ask-Dyn-Fin) 'I ask you': masd. á-ħʷa-ra [intr.] 'to ask'. **4**. map' ø-j-cʷə́-m-k'ə-k'ʷa 'not refusing him': masd. map' a-cʷ-k'-rá [tr.] 'to refuse'. **5**. b-jə́-c-ca-rc 'in order that you may get married to him': masd. á-c-ca-ra [intr.] 'to go with; to get married to'.

(77) **1**. j-zə́-w-ħʷa-wa 'the one who you are talking about': masd. a-z-ħʷa-rá [tr.] 'to say about'. **2**. j-q'a-la-wá-zar 'if possible'. **3**. j-s-á-žʷ-raʒa (it(C1)-me(C2)-to-[ø-agent]-grant a postponement.Imp) 'grant me a postponement!': masd. a-ráʒa-ra [tr.] 'to grant a postponement'. **4**. ø-sə́-šʷ-t ([it(C1)-]me(C2)-you.[formal/polite Pl](C3)-give.Imp) 'give it to me!': masd. á-ta-ra [tr.] 'to give'.

(78) **1**. d-maraħʷ-wa-jt': masd. á-maraħʷ-ra [intr.] 'to be restive'. **2**. wəbrə́j a-z-á-wp' ... ø-z-w-á-s-ħʷa-z 'that is why I told you that ... '.

(80) **1**. j-a-pərxága-m 'that is all right': masd. a-pərxága-ra [intr.] 'to disturb; to be injurious'. **2**. bzə́ja jə-z-ba-wá-jt' (it(C1)-I(C3)-see-Dyn-Fin) 'I like it': masd. a-ba-rá [tr.] 'to see'.

(81) **1**. d-mə́-cʷa-ʒá-k'ʷa: masd. á-cʷa-ra [intr.] 'to sleep, to fall asleep'. **2**. maʒa-lá: cf. á-maʒa [n.] 'secret'. **3**. d-k'ə́l-pš-wa: masd. a-k'ə́l-pš-ra [intr.] 'to peep'.

(82) **1**. d-k'ə́l-pš-wa də-š-t'ʷá-z ák'ʷəmkʷa 'at the time that he was sitting and was looking'. **2**. j-n-ajgʷa-xʲán : masd. ajgʷa-ra [intr.] '(*of time*) to pass'. **3**. j-la-lə-rgə́l[a-j]t' < j-la-lə-r-gə́l[a-j]t' (it-Par-she-Caus-

stand-(Aor)-Fin) 'she placed it': masd. a-rgə́la-ra [tr.] 'to place, to put'. **4.** ø-n-a-nə́-l-tʷal[a-j]t' ([it(the water, C1)-]Par-it(the washtub, C2)-Prev-she(C3)-pour into-(Aor)-Fin) 'she poured it into it': masd. a-n-tʷála-ra [tr.] 'to pour into'.

(83) **1.** ø-aa-lə-r-t'ə́-n : masd. áa-r-t'-ra [tr.] 'to open'; cf. áa-t'-ra [intr.] 'to open'. **2.** ø-pər-pər-wá : masd. á-pər-pər-ra [intr.] 'to fly; to flap one's wings'. **3.** j-aa-jʷna-šəl[a-j]t' : masd. áa-jʷna-šəla-ra [intr.] 'to go inside'.

(84) **1.** j-a-nə́-z (Rel(C1)-it(the washtub, C2)-be on-Stat.Past.NF) 'that which was on it': masd. a-nə́-zaa-ra [intr.] 'to be on'. **2.** a-čə́-n-t-na-šʲə-n 'it(the dove) dipped itself into it': masd. a-č-t-šʲ-rá [tr.] 'to dip oneself'. **3.** ø-an-á[a]-a-rəšʷšʷa: masd. a-ršʷšʷa-rá [tr.] 'to wave'. **4.** d-aa-tə́-c'[ə-j]t': masd. aa-tə́-c'-ra [intr.] 'to go out hither'.

(86) **1.** j-bə́-xʲ-zaj 'what happened to you?': masd. á-xʲ-ra [intr.] 'to happen to'. **2.** bə-z-c'ʷə́wa-wa-zaj 'why are you crying?': masd. a-c'ʷə́wa-ra [intr.] 'to cry'. **3.** j-á-l-c'ə-z (Rel(C1)-it(the dove, C2)-Prev-go out of-Past.Ind.NF) 'the one who came out of it': masd. á-l-c'-ra [intr.] 'to go out of'.

(87) **1.** According to V. A. Chirikba (personal communication), č'ʲk'ʷə́na 'boy' is etymologically derived from *č'ʲk'ʷə́-na with a diminutive suffix *-na*. See also Note 157-1. **2.** də-z-fá-rc jə́-q'a-z 'the one who must have eaten him'.

(88) **1.** sə-j-tax-xa-jt' : masd. a-tax-xa-rá [intr. inverse] 'to want'. **2.** jə-špá-zə-w-rə-j 'how will I do it?', i.e. 'what should I do?': masd. a-w-rá [tr.] 'to do'.

(89) ʔoħ 'oh' is written as q'oħ in the original text. See fn. 58.

(91) **1.** bə-špa-s-cʷə́-j-ga-wa (you.F(C1)-how-me(C2)-Prev-he(C3)-take away from-Pres.NF) 'how can he take you away from me?': masd. a-cʷ-ga-rá [tr.] 'to take away from'. **2.** də-s-šʲə́-r-a-wp' : masd. a-šʲ-rá [tr.] 'to kill'. **3.** də-špa-s-zə́-m-šʲ-wa-j (he(C1)-how-me(C2)-Pot-Neg-kill-Pres.NF-Qu) lit. 'how can't I kill him?'

(92) **1.** ø-aa-šá-r : masd. a-ša-rá [intr.] 'to dawn,' cf. j-ša-wá-jt' 'the morning dawns'. **2.** [a-]aták' ø-r-á-s-ħʷa-r-a-wp' 'I must answer them': masd. a-ħʷa-rá [tr.] 'to say'.

(94) **1.** abrə́jgʲ, abrə́jgʲ a-tə́p a-č'ə́ 'на таком-то месте'. **2.** jə́-ø-kʷə-wp' (it(a big stone, C1)-[it(a big hill, C2)-]on-Stat.Pres.Fin) 'there is a big stone on a big hill': masd. á-kʷ-zaa-ra [intr.] 'to exist on'.

(95) **1.** ø-s-z-aa-j-gá-[a]ajt' ([it(C1)-]me(C2)-OV(for)-Prev-he(C3)-bring-Subjunctive) 'let him bring it to me!': masd. aa-ga-rá [tr.] 'to bring'. **2.** ø-j-á-ħʷa 'say it to him!'

(96) **1.** j-ajbə́-r-ħʷa-kʷa-z: masd. ájbə-ħʷa-ra [tr.] 'to talk with each other'. **2.** ø-j-a-ħá-jt' ([it(C1)-]him(C2)-to-be audible-(Aor)-Fin) 'he heard it': masd. a-ħa-rá [intr. inverse] 'to hear'. **3.** də-k'ə́l-praa-n : masd. a-k'ə́l-praa-ra [intr.] 'to fly out'.

(97) **1.** j-an-áa-ša, cf. (92)-1. **2.** d-ná-j-t' < d-ná-j-jt'.

(98) **1.** s-a-z-xʷə́cə-n (I(C1)-it(C2)-Prev(about)-think-Past.Ind.Fin) 'I thought about it ...': masd. a-z-xʷə́c-ra [intr.] 'to think about'. **2.** s-á-kʷšaħatə-wp': masd. á-kʷšaħat-zaa-ra [intr.] 'to consent to'. **3.** sə-z-w-ta-ranə́ (me(C1)-Rel(C2)-you.M(C3)-give-must) jə́-q'a-w (Rel(C1)-be-Stat.Pres.NF) 'the one to whom you must give me'. **4.** jə́-šʲta-w: masd. á-šʲta-zaa-ra [intr.] 'to lie; to be situated'. **5.** sə-z-jə́-c-ca-wa-m (I(C1)-Pot-him(C2)-with-go-Dyn-Fin) 'I cannot marry him'.

(99) **1.** jə́-q'a-j-c'a-x-wa-z 'what should he have done?': masd. á-q'a-c'a-ra [tr.] 'to do'. The suffix/particle *-x* is added to a verbal root and expresses 'emphasis', 'surprise'. **2.** d-jə́-pxʲa-n (he(C1)-him(C2)-call-Past.Ind.Fin) 'he called him and ...': masd. á-pxʲa-ra [intr.] 'to call'.

(100) **1.** dádxajt' [interj.] 'обращение, выражающее недовольство, порицание' (Kaslandzia:2005). **2.** w-lə́-xʷa-wa-m (you(C1)-her(C2)-manage-Dyn-Neg) 'you cannot manage her': masd. á-xʷa-ra [intr.] 'to

manage'. **3.** wə-l-q'^{w}á-c' (you(C1)-her(C2)-leave alone.Imp) 'leave her alone!': masd. a-q'^{w}ə́-c'-ra [intr.] 'to leave alone'. **4.** ø-zə-w-á-s-ħ^{w}a-zabrə́j á-[a]k'^{w}ə-n 'this is why I told you that ... '.

(101) **1.** map' lə-m-k'ə́-jt' 'she did not refuse': masd. máp'-k'-ra [tr.] 'to refuse'.

(102) **1.** jə-z-zə́-l-ħ^{w}a-z '(the stone) that she speak of': masd. a-z-ħ^{w}a-rá [tr.] 'to speak of'; cf. Note (77)-1.

(103) **1.** ø-z-wə́-sə-m-ta-wa-zaj 'why don't I give it to you?'. **2.** ø-wadáj^{w}ə-wp', cf. á-wadaj^{w} [adj.] 'difficult'.

(104) **1.** j-[j]-a-ħá-z (Rel(C1)-[him(C2)-]to-be audible to-Past.Ind.NF) 'that which he heard'. **2.** ø-[a]-á-j-ħ^{w}a-jt' ([it(= the story, C1)]-[it(the horse, C2)]-to-he(C3)-say-(Aor)-Fin) 'he told the horse the story'.

(105) **1.** j-wadáj^{w}ə -w 'difficult'. **2.** wə́sə-wp' : cf. a-wə́s [n.] 'work'. **3.** ø-a-xə́la-pš-wa-jt' ([they(C1)-] it(C2)-Prev-watch-Dyn-Fin) 'they watch it': masd. a-xə́la-pš-ra [intr.] 'to watch'.

(106) **1.** w-aa-lá 'let's go'. The suffix *-la* indicates the hortative marker. See also Chirikba (2003a: 54). **2.** ħ-á-la-ga-p' (we(C1)-it(C2)-Prev-begin-Fut.I.Fin) 'let's begin it!' **3.** j-aħ-z-aa-ga-wá-zar (it(C1)-us(C2)-Pot-Prev-bring-Dyn-if) 'if we can bring it'; for -z- see Hewitt (1979c: 195).

(107) **1.** ø-x-t'ə́-zar ([they(C1)-]Prev-open-if) 'if they(their eyes) are open': masd. a-x-t'-rá [intr.] 'to open'. **2.** jə́-c^{w}a-wp' 'they are sleeping': masd. á-c^{w}a-ra [intr.] 'to sleep'. **3.** j-aá-na-ga-wa : masd. aá-na-ga-ra [intr.] 'to mean'. **4.** ø-áaš^{j}t-paa-nə : masd. aaš^{j}t-paa-ra [tr.] 'to take up'. **5.** w-d^{w}ə́k^{w}-la : masd. a-d^{w}ə́k^{w}-la-ra [intr.] 'to set out'.

(108) **1.** w-g^{w}á-r-ta-r (you.M(C1)-Prev-they(C3)-notice-if) 'if they notice you': masd. a-g^{w}á-ta-ra [tr.] 'to notice'. **2.** j-q'áa-št' 'they may cry out': masd. á-q'aa-ra [intr.] 'to cry out'. **3.** jə-ħ^{w}ħ^{w}á-št' 'they may bawl': masd. á-ħ^{w}ħ^{w}a-ra [intr.] 'to bawl; to shout'. **4.** jag^{j}á jə-ħ^{w}ħ^{w}á-rg^{j}ə jag^{j}á j-q'áa-rg^{j}ə 'even if they cry out, even if they bawl'. **5.** w-x^{j}á-m-pšə-n 'don't look back!': masd. a-x^{j}á-pš-ra [intr.] 'to look back'.

(109) **1.** ø-x-j^{w}á-zar ([they(C1)-]Prev-be closed-if) 'if they are closed': masd. a-x-j^{w}a-rá [intr.] 'to be closed'. **2.** j-áa-pšə-wp' 'they are awake': masd. áa-pš-ra [intr.] 'to wake up'. **3.** wə-z-ná-j-ʒa-wa-m 'you cannot reach': masd. a-ná-j-ra [intr.] 'to reach; to go thither'.

(111) **1.** də-l-čə́ž^{w}-pa-n: masd. a-čə́ž^{w}-pa-ra [intr.] 'to leap down from a horse'. **2.** d-an-rə-x^{w}á-pš (he(C1)-when-them(C2)-Prev-look at-(Aor.NF)) 'when he looked at them': masd. á-x^{w}a-pš-ra [intr.] 'to look at'. **3.** d-lə́-š^{j}ta-sə-n: masd. a-š^{j}tá-s-ra [intr.] 'to touch the ground'. **4.** ø-mc'á-rs-nə ([it(C1)]-Prev-snatch-Abs) 'having snatched it': masd. á-mc'a-rs-ra [tr.] 'to snatch'. **5.** də́-j^{w}[ə-j]t': masd. á-j^{w}-ra [intr.] 'to run'.

(112) **1.** d-áaš^{j}t-na-paa-n (him(C1)-Prev-it(C3)-pick up-Past.Ind.Fin) 'it picked him up': masd. aaš^{j}t-paa-ra [tr.] 'to pick up'. **2.** jə-l-tak'^{w}k'^{w}á j-cá-jt' 'they ran down'; cf. a-la-k^{w}á tak'^{w}k'^{w}á j-cá-jt' 'собаки быстро побежали вниз' (Kaslandzia 2005).

(113) **1.** d-aa-k'ə́l-sə-n: masd. a-k'ə́l-s-ra [intr.] 'to go through; to go out'. **2.** d-j^{w}a-x^{w}ná-n: masd. a-x^{w}na-rá [intr.] 'to climb'. **3.** jə́-j-ta-jt' < j-jə́-j-ta-jt' (it(C1)-him(C2)-he(C3)-give-(Aor)-Fin) 'he gave it to him'.

(114) **1.** ø-na-sə-gʒá-jt': masd. á-na-gʒa-ra [tr.] 'to carry out'.

(115) **1.** j-na-lə́-j-ta-n: masd. á-ta-ra [tr.] 'to give'.

(116) **1.** ø-sə́-š^{w}-t ([it(time, C1)-]me(C2)-you.formal/polite Pl(C3)-give.Imp) 'give it to me!': masd. á-ta-ra [tr.] 'to give'.

(118) **1.** j-anə́-x^{w}la : masd. á-x^{w}la-ra [intr.] 'to get dark'. **2.** də-z-ga-ranə́ jə́-q'a-z 'the one who must have taken her'. **3.** d-k'ə́lə-pš-nə: masd. a-k'ə́l-pš-ra [intr.] 'to peep'. **4.** də-z-č'ə́-z (she(C1)-Rel(C2)-be engaged in-Stat.Past.NF) 'that which she was engaged in': masd. a-č'ə́-zaa-ra [intr.] 'to be engaged in'.

(119) **1.** ø-n-ajg^{w}a-wá-n: cf. (82-2). **2.** ø-aa-c^{w}ə́rə-l-ga-jt': masd. a-c^{w}ə́r-ga-ra [tr.] 'to bring out'. **3.** ø-n-a-

nə́-l-tʷála-jt’: cf. (82-4).

(120) **1.** j-aa-jʷná-l[a-j]t’: masd. aa-jʷná-la-ra [intr.] ‘to go inside’. **2.** bzə́ja-xa: the suffix -xa is used to derive adverbs.

(121) **1.** a-čə-jʷ-t-ná-šʲə-n: cf. (84-2). **2.** d-áa-kʷ-gəl[a-j]t’: masd. á-kʷ-gəla-ra [intr.] ‘to stand; to make a speech’.

(122) **1.** a-k’ʲažə́-ħʷa = a-k’ʲəžə́-ħʷa.

(123) **1.** j-bə́-xʲ-zaj: masd. á-xʲ-ra [intr.] ‘to happen to’. **2.** b-zə-r-c’ʷə́wa-wa-zaj (you.F(C1)-Rel(C3)-Caus-cry-Dyn-Qu), lit. ‘what makes you cry?’, i.e. ‘who makes you cry?’: masd. a-rc’ʷə́wa-ra [tr.] ‘to make *sb* cry’.

(125) **1.** ø-rə́-ma-wp’ ([it]-them-have-Stat.Pres.Fin) ‘they have it’: masd. á-ma-zaa-ra [intr.] ‘to have’.

(126) **1.** ø-jə́-xʷa-wa-m ([it(C1)-]him(C2)-help-Dyn-Neg) ‘it does not help him’: masd. á-xʷa-ra [intr.] ‘to help’.

(127) **1.** d-nə́-kʷ-praa-n: masd. á-kʷ-praa-ra [intr.] ‘to fly away’.

(128) **1.** d-axʲə́-ʒərjʷ-wa-z: masd. a-ʒə́rjʷ-ra [intr.] ‘to listen’. **2.** ø-j-a-ħá-jt’ ([it(C1)-]him(C2)-to-be audible-(Aor)-Fin) ‘he heard it’: masd. a-ħa-rá [intr. inverse] ‘to hear’.

(129) **1.** j-an-áa-ša: masd. a-ša-rá [intr.] ‘to dawn’.

(130) **1.** ø-n-xa-wá-jt’ ([they-]Prev-live-Dyn-Fin) ‘they live’: masd. a-n-xa-rá [inrt.] ‘to live’. **2.** ø-rə́-m-x-nə ([it-]them-Prev(from)-take-Abs) ‘taking it from them’: masd. á-m-x-ra [tr.] ‘to take from’. **3.** sə-z-w-tá-rc jə́-w-taxə-w ‘the one whom you want to give me to’.

(131) **1.** d-aa-jə́-pxʲa-n (him(C1)-Prev-he(C3)-invite-Past.Ind.Fin) ‘he invited him’: masd. aá-pxʲa-ra [tr.] ‘to invite’. **2.** a-daw-cʷá: cf. a-daw-kʷá (130).

(133) **1.** j-[a]-á-j-ħʷa-jt’ (it(the story, C1)-[it(his horse, C2)-]to-he(C3)-say-(Aor)-Fin) ‘he said it to his horse’.

(134) **1.** ø-z-m-aħ-xə-z ([it-]Rel-Prev(from)-we-take-Past.Ind.NF) ‘the one whom we took it from’: masd. á-m-x-ra [tr.] ‘to take *sth* from’. **2.** ø-ɣʷɣʷá-n : cf. á-ɣʷɣʷa [adj.] ‘strong’. **3.** ħ-axʲ-ná-j-ra ‘куда мы должны прийти’. **4.** j-šə-r-zə́-w-wə-z (it(C1)-how-them(C2)-for-you(C3)-do-Past.Ind.NF) ‘how you did it for them’: masd. a-zə-w-rá [tr.] ‘to do for’. **5.** ø-x-t’-nə́ ([they/them]-Prev-open-Abs) ‘they opening/ opening them’: masd. a-x-t’-ra [tr./intr.] ‘to open’. **6.** ø-aa-rə́-m-c’-paa-nə ([it(C1)]-Par-them(C2)-Prev(from)-Prev-take-Abs) ‘taking it from them’: masd. á-m-c’-paa-ra [tr.] ‘to take’. **7.** w-ajxa-nə́: masd. ájxa-ra [intr.] ‘to be dying to go’. **8.** wə́-jʷ: masd. á-jʷ-ra [intr.] ‘to run’.

(135) **1.** a-šʷjə-pšʲjə́-ra: masd. á-šʷjə-pšʲj-ra [intr.] ‘to curse’. **2.** jə-čʲħa-nə́: masd. á-čʲħa-ra [tr.] ‘to endure’. **3.** j-zák’ʷzaa-lak’ʲ (= j-zak’ʷə́zaa-lak’ʲ) ‘ни за что’. **4.** w-xʲá-pš-nə: masd. a-xʲá-pš-ra [intr.] ‘to look back’. **5.** w-rə́-xʷa-m-pšə-n: masd. á-xʷa-pš-ra [intr.] ‘to look at’.

(136) **1.** w-ʒərjʷ-lá: masd. á-ʒərjʷ-ra [intr.] ‘to listen’. **2.** jə-w-xá-w-mə-r-štə-n (it(C1)-you(C2)-Prev-you.M(C3)-Neg-Caus-forget-Proh) lit. ‘don’t make you forget it,’ i.e. ‘don’t forget it!’: masd. a-xá-r-št-ra [tr.], cf. a-xá-št-ra [intr. inverse] ‘to forget’. **3.** ø-gʷən-k’ə́la: masd. a-gʷən-k’ə́la-ra [tr.] ‘to remember, to memorize’.

(137) **1.** də-jʷ-čə́žʷ-la-n: masd. a-čə́žʷ-la-ra [intr.] ‘to mount a horse’.

(138) **1.** də-jʷ-čə́žʷ-c’ə-n: masd. a-čəžʷ-c’-rá [intr.] ‘to get down from a horse’.

(139) **1.** á-šʷəj-ra [tr.] ‘to curse’.

(140) **1.** d-xác’a-zar ‘if he is a man,’ cf. a-xác’a [n.] ‘a man’. **2.** də-pħʷə́s-xa-[a]ajt’ ‘let him become a woman!,’ ‘make him a woman,’ cf. a-pħʷə́s [n.] ‘a woman’.

(141) **1.** j-w-á-r-ħʷa-zaj (what(C1)-you.M(C2)-to-they(C3)-say-(Aor)-Qu) ‘what did they say to you?’ **2.**

wə-špá-r-šʷəjə-j (you.M(C1)-how-they(C3)-curse-(Aor)-Qu) 'how did they curse you?'

(143) **1.** ϕ-na-ʒá-jt': masd. á-na-ʒa-ra [intr.] 'to reach'.

(144) **1.** jə-r-cʷə́-j-ga-z (Rel(C1)-them(C2)-Prev-he(C3)-take away from-Past.Ind.NF) 'that which he took away from them': masd. a-cʷ-ga-rá [tr.] 'to take away from'. **2.** j-č'ə́-la-j-xa-n (his(Poss)-SV-Prev-he(C3)-set out thither-Past.Ind.Fin) 'he set out thither': masd. a-č'ə́-na-xa-ra [tr.] 'to set out thither'.

(145) **1.** d-lə́-pxʲa-n (he(C1)-her(C2)-call-Past.Ind.Fin) 'he called her': masd. á-pxʲa-ra [intr.] 'to call'. **2.** bə-z-č'ə́-z-gʲə lit. 'that which you were engaged in', i.e. 'that which you spoke about': masd. a-č'ə́-zaa-ra [intr.] 'to be engaged in'.

(148) **1.** ϕ-aj-cʷážʷa-jt': masd. áj-cʷažʷa-ra [intr.] 'to talk together'.

(150) **1.** ajbgá-la 'in safety'. **2.** d-m-aa-ʒá-cəzt': masd. aa-rá [intr.] 'to come hither'. **3.** jə-zla-jə́-l-ša-zaj (it(C1)-how-him(C2)-Prev-be possible-Qu) 'how he could do it?': masd. á-l-ša-ra [intr. inverse] 'to be able to'. **4.** d-ajbga-nə́ 'in safety'.

(151) **1.** ϕ-sə-z-də́r-[w]a-m: masd. a-də́r-ra [tr.] 'to know'.

(152) **1.** wəs ák'ʷzar 'if so'.

(154) **1.** w-n-a-k'ʲə́-sə-r (you.M(C1)-Par-it(C2)-Prev-touch-if) 'if you touch it': masd. a-k'ʲə́-s-ra [intr.] 'to touch'. **2.** jə-čʲčʲa-wá-jt': masd. á-čʲčʲa-ra [intr.] 'to laugh'. **3.** j-c'ʷə́wa-wa-jt': masd. a-c'ʷə́wa-ra [intr.] 'to cry'.

(155) **1.** ə́-c'-x-nə (them(C1)-Prev-pull out-Abs) 'having pulled them out': masd. á-c'-x-ra [tr.] 'to pull out'.

(156) **1.** sə-j-t'ʷə́-wp' (I(C1)-him(C2)-belong to-Stat.Pres.Fin) 'I belong to him': masd. a-t'ʷə́-zaa-ra [intr.] 'to belong to'.

(157) **1.** də-č'ʲk'ʷə́na-xa-xʲan = də-č'ʲk'ʷə́n-xa-xʲan. **2.** j-[a]-á-j-ħʷa-jt' (it(C1)-it(the horse, C2)-to-he(C3)-say-(Aor)-Fin) 'he said it to his horse'.

(158) **1.** ħ-č-a-z-áħ-šʷa-p' (our(Poss)-Self-it(C2)-for-we(C3)-do one's best-Fut.I.Fin) lit. 'we shall attempt it,' i.e. 'let's try!': masd. a-č-a-zə́-šʷa-ra [tr.] 'to do one's best'.

(159) **1.** də-š-ná-j-wa-z ák'ʷəmk'ʷa 'вот он шел и в это время'. **2.** ájšʲ-cʷa: cf. ájašʲa [sg.] 'brother'. **3.** jə-j-tə-nxá-z (Rel(C1)-him(C2)-Prev-remain after-Past.Ind.NF) 'that which remained after him': masd. a-tə-nxa-rá [intr.] 'to remain after'. **4.** ϕ-ájma-k'-nə: masd. ájma-k'-ra [tr.] 'to argue'. **5.** rə́-la-kʷa ϕ-š-tə́jbax-wa-z 'how they quarreled': masd. a-tə́jbax-ra 'to quarrel'.

(160) **1.** jə́-q'a-šʷ-c'a-wa zak'ʷə́wzaj 'what are you (pl.) doing?'

(161) **1.** a-q'amčʲə-j: cf. (159) q'áma-k'ə-j. **2.** ϕ-j-də-rbá-jt' < ϕ-j-rə-r-bá-jt' ([them(C1)-]to him(C2)-they(C3)-Caus-see-(Aor)-Fin) 'they showed them to him': masd. a-r-ba-rá [tr.] 'to show'.

(162) **1.** šʷə-s-zə́-ʒərjʷə (you.Pl(C1)-me(C2)-Prev-listen to.Imp) 'listen to me!': masd. a-zə́-ʒərjʷ-ra [intr.] 'to listen to'. **2.** šʷə́-la-kʷa ϕ-tə́jbax-wa-jt' 'you are quarreling'. **3.** šʷ-nə́q'ʷa-r (you.Pl(C1)-act-if) 'if you act': masd. a-nə́q'ʷa-ra [intr.] 'to act'.

(163) **1.** šʷ-nə́q'ʷa-r: masd. a-nə́q'ʷa-ra [intr.] 'to act'. **2.** jə-šʷ-zə́-s-ša-wa-jt' (them(C1)-you.Pl(C2)-for-I(C3)-divide-Dyn-Fin) 'I will divide them for you': masd. a-ša-rá [tr.] 'to divide'.

(165) **1.** ϕ-dʷə́kʷə-s-c'a-wa-jt': masd. a-dʷə́kʷ-c'a-ra [tr.] 'to draw; to stretch'. **2.** jə-j-t'ʷə́-wp' (they(the whip, the hat and the felt cloak, C1)-him(C2)-belong to-Stat.Pres.Fin) 'they belong to him': masd. a-t'ʷə́-zaa-ra [intr.] 'to belong to'.

(167) **1.** ϕ-ajbár-jʷ-nə: masd. ájbar-jʷ-ra [intr.] 'to race with one another'. **2.** də-pšə́-z-ma, lit. 'was he waiting?,' i.e. 'he was not waiting there': masd. a-pš-rá [intr.] 'to wait'. **3.** jə-j-má-n (they(C1)-him(C2)-

have-Past.Ind.Fin) 'he had them ... '. **4.** ø-aa-šʲtə-j-xə́-n: masd. á-šʲtə-x-ra [tr.] 'to pick up'.

(168) **1.** ø-a[a]-ajc'ə́-x-nə: masd. ájc'ə́-x-ra [tr.] 'to stretch'. **2.** w-nə́-la-t'ʷa-nə: masd. á-la-t'ʷa-ra [intr.] 'to sit down in'. **3.** w-an-á-s-lak'ʲ (you.M(C1)-when-it(the felt cloak, C2)-hit-LA) 'when you hit it': masd. á-s-ra [intr.] 'to hit'. **3.** ø-na-w-xá-w-c'a-r ([it(the hat, C1)-]Par-your.M(Poss)-SV-you(C3)-put on-if) 'if you put on the hat': masd. a-xa-c'a-rá [tr.] 'to put on'.

(169) **1.** d-a-z-áa-[a]jgʷa-xa-jt': masd. a-záajgʷaxa-ra [intr.] 'to come near'.

(170) **1.** də-pšə́-n: masd. a-pš-rá [intr.] 'to look'. **2.** rə́-k'ʷ-ršа-nə (them(C2)-Prev-fence-Abs) 'fencing them': masd. á-k'ʷ-ršа-ra [tr.] 'to fence'. **3.** j-q'a-c'á-wp' (they(C1)-Prev-be done-Stat.Pres.Fin) 'they are done': masd. á-q'a-c'a-ra [tr.] 'to do'.

(171) **1.** ø-jʷa-j-xá-j-c'a-n ([it(C1)-]Par-his(Poss)-SV-he(C3)-put on-Past.Ind.Fin) 'he put it on ...': masd. a-xa-c'a-rá [tr.] 'to put on'. **2.** jə́-čʲčʲa-wa-z: masd. á-čʲčʲa-ra [intr.] 'to laugh'. **3.** j-č'ʷə́wa-wa-z: masd. a-č'ʷə́wa-ra [intr.] 'to cry'. **4.** ø-anə́-jʷa-[a]-xə-j-q'ʲa ([it(the whip, C1)]-when-Par-it(the felt cloak, C2)-Prev-he(C3)-lash-(Aor.NF)) 'when he lashed the felt cloak with the whip': masd. a-x-q'ʲa-rá [tr.] 'to lash'.

(172) **1.** ø-na-sə-ʒá-jt': masd. á-na-ʒa-ra [tr.] 'to carry out'.

(174) **1.** ak'agʲə́ ø-sə-z-ħʷa-wá-m ([it(C1)-]me(C2)-Pot-say-Dyn-Neg) 'I cannot say anything'.

(175) **1.** ø-r-wə́-n ([it]-they-do-Past.Ind.Fin) 'they did it': masd. a-w-rá [tr.] 'to do'.

(176) **1.** j-aa-j-xə́-j-ga-z (Rel-Par-his-SV-he-experience-Past.Ind.NF) 'that which he experienced': masd. a-x-ga-rá [tr.] 'to experience, to feel'. **2.** j-ajza-nə́: masd. ájza-ra [intr.] 'to gather'.

(177) **1.** ø-dʷə́kʷə-j-c'a-jt' ([it(C1)-]Prev-he(C3)-send-(Aor)-Fin) 'he sent it': masd. a-dʷə́kʷ-c'a-ra [tr.] 'to send'. **2.** d-jə́-ma-nə, lit. 'he, having her'. **3.** xʲə́ʒ-la-pšá-la 'с почетом'. **4.** d-wə-z-ná-j-wa-jt' (he(C1)-you.M(C2)-for-Prev-go thither-Dyn-Fin) 'he will go back to you'.

(178) **1.** j-pə́-la-jt': masd. a-pə́-la-ra [intr.] 'to meet'.

(179) **1.** ø-šʷ-zə́-q'a-la-ša ([they(C1)-]you.Pl(C2)-for-Prev-happen-Fut.II.NF) lit. 'may they happen for you!': masd. á-q'a-la-ra [intr.] 'to happen, to become'.

References

Allen, W. S. 1965. On One-Vowel Systems. In *Lingua* 13–2: 111–124.

Chirikba, V. A. 1996. *Common West Caucasian. The Reconstruction of its Phonological System and Parts of its Lexicon and Morphology*. Leiden: CNWS.

—— 2003a. *Abkhaz,* Languages of the World/Materials 119. Muenchen: Lincom Europa.

—— 2003b. Evidential category and evidential strategy in Abkhaz. In Alexandr Y. Aikhenvald & R. M. W. Dixon. (ed.) *Studies in Evidentiality*. Amsterdam: John Benjamin: 243–272.

Colarusso, J. 1988. *The Northwest Caucasian Languages: a Phonological Survey.* New York: Garland Publishing.

Dixon, R. M. W. 1994. *Ergativity*. Cambridge: Cambridge University Press.

—— 2010. *Basic Linguistic Theory*. Volum 1 Methodology. Oxford: Oxford University Press.

—— 2010. *Basic Linguistic Theory*. Volum 2 Grammatical Topics. Oxford: Oxford University Press.

—— and Alexandra Y. Aikhenvald. (ed.) 2000. *Changing Valency: Case Studies in Transitivity.* Cambridge: Cambridge University Press.

Dumézil, G. 1932. *Études comparatives sur les langues caucasiennes du Nord-Ouest* (*Morphologie*). Paris: Adrien-Maisonneuve.

—— 1967. *Documents anatoliens sur les langues et les traditions du Caucase. V. Études Abkhaz.* Paris: Adrien-Maisonneuve.

—— avec la collaboration de Tecfik Esenç. 1975. *Le verbe Oubykh. Études descriptives et comparatives.* Paris: Klincksieck.

Dzhanashia, B. 1954. *Apxazur-kartuli leksik'oni*. Tbilisi: Mecniereba.

Gamkrelidze, Thomas V. 1978. On the Correlation of Stops and Fricatives in a Phonological System. In Joseph H. Greenberg (ed.) *Universals of Human Language. Volume 2. Phonology.* Stanford. California: Stanford University Press.

Hewitt, B.G. 1979a. Aspects of Verbal Affixation in Abkhaz (Abzhui Dialect). In *Transactions of the Philologival Society 1979*: 211–238.

—— 1979b. The Relative Clause in Abkhaz (Abzhui Dialect). In *Lingua* 47: 151–188.

—— in collaboration with Z.K. Khiba. 1979c. *Lingua Descriptive Studies 2: Abkhaz.* Amsterdam: North-Holland.

—— 1982. 'Anti-Passive' and 'Labile' Constructions in North Caucasian. In *General Linguistics* 22: 158–171.

—— 1987. *The Typology of Subordination in Georgian and Abkhaz,* Empirical Approaches to Language Typology 5. Berlin: Mouton de Gruyter.

—— in collaboration with Z. K. Khiba. 1989a. *Abkhaz*[2]. Reprinted by Croom Helm and Routledge. [Hewitt, B. G. in collaboration with Z. K. Khiba. 1979. *Lingua Descriptive Studies 2: Abkhaz.* Amsterdam: North-Holland.]

—— 1989b. Abkhaz. In G. Hewitt (ed.) *The Indigenous Languages of the Caucasus 2: the North West Caucasian Languages*. Delmar. New York: Caravan Books. 37–88.

—— and Khiba, Z. 1998a. *Abkhaz Newspaper Reader (with supplements)*. Kensington: Dunwoody Press.

—— 1998b. *The Abkhazians: A Handbook.* New York: St. Martin's Press.

—— 1999. Morphology revisited: Some irregularities of the Abkhaz verb. In Berg, H. van den (ed.) *Studies in Caucasian Linguistics: Selected papers of the English Caucasian Colloquium*. Leiden: CNWS. 197–208.
—— 2004. *Introduction to the Study of the Languages of the Caucasus*. Muenchen: Lincom Europa.
—— 2005a. *Abkhazian Folktales (with grammatical introduction, translation, notes, and vocabulary)*, Languages of the World/Text Collections 22. Muenchen: Lincom Europa.
—— 2005b. North West Caucasian. In *Lingua* 115: 91–145.
—— 2005c. The Syntax of Complementation in Abkhaz. In *Iran and the Caucasus* 9–2: 331–379.
—— 2008a. Are Verbs Always What They Seem To Be? In *Iran and the Caucasus* 12: 57–73.
—— 2008b. Cases, arguments, verbs in Abkhaz, Georgian and Mingrelian. In G. G. Corbett and M. Noonan (ed.) *Case and Grammatical Relations. Studies in honor of Birnard Comrie*. Amsterdam: John Benjamin. 75–104.
—— 2010. *Abkhaz: a Comprehensive Self-Tutor.* Muenchen: Lincom Europa.
—— 2012. An Abkhaz Miscellany (with an Old Georgian Excursion). [Paper prepared for delivery at the Caucasian Linguistics Conference Istanbul, 29 Nov - 1 Dec 2012.]
Klimov, G. A. 1994. *Einführung in die kaukasische Sprachwissenschaft.* Aus dem Russischen übersetzt und bearbeitet von Jost Gippert. Hamburg: Buske.
Kuipers, A. H. 1960. *Phoneme and Morpheme in Kabardian.* 'S-Gravenhage: Mouton.
—— 1976. Typologically Salient Features of Some North-West Caucasian Languages. In *Studia Caucasica* 3: 101–127.
Nikolayev, S. L. & Starostin, S. A. 1994. *A North Caucasian Etymological Dictionary*. Moscow: Asterisk Publishers.
Spruit, A. 1983. Abkhaz Verbs of Local Reference. In *Studia Caucasica* 5: 55–75.
—— 1985. Stress in Abkhaz. In *Studia Caucasica* 6: 31–81.
—— 1987. Abkhaz Verb Morphology. In *Studia Caucasica* 7: 9–60.
Trigo, L. 1992. Abkhaz Stress Shift. In G. Hewitt (ed.) *Caucasian Perspectives*. Muenchen: Lincom Europa. 191–235.
Yanagisawa, T. 2004. *Studies in the Structure of the Abkhaz Verb*. 1–456. Results of a Research Project, Grant-in-Aid for Scientific Research, Nagoya University. (C)(2): No. 14510617.
—— 2005a. Schwa in Abkhaz. In *Japanese Slavic and East European Studies* 26: 23–36.
—— 2006. *Analysis of Texts and a Basic Lexicon of the Abkhaz Language*. 1–562. Results of a Research Project, Grant-in-Aid for Scientific Research, Nagoya University. (C)(2): No. 16520236.
—— 2010. *Analytic Dictionary of Abkhaz.* Tokyo: Hituzi Syobo.
—— (ed.) Forthcoming. *A Dictionary of the Bzyp Dialect.*
Аристава, Ш. К. 1960. *Деепричастие в абхазском языке.* Сухуми: Госиздат Абхазии.
—— и др. 1968. *Грамматика абхазского языка: фонетика и морфология.* Сухуми: Алашара.
Арстаа, Ш. Ҟ., Ҷкадуа, Л. П. 2002. *Аҧсуа литературатә бызшәа аграмматика.* Аҟәа.
Аршба, Н. В. 1992. Некоторые вопросы акцентологии абхазского языка. In G. B. Hewitt (ed.) *Caucasian Perspectives*. Muenchen: Lincom Europa. 236–239.
Бгажба, Х. С. (ed.) 1964. *Русско-абхазский словарь.* Сухуми: Алашара.
—— 1964a. *Бзыбский диалект абхазского языка (Исследование и тексты).* Тбилиси: Издательство академии наук грузинской ССР.

Гамкрелидзе, Т.В., Иванов, Вяч. Вс. 1984. *Индоевропейский язык и индоевропейцы. I.* Тбилиси: Издательство тбилисского университета.

Генко, А. Н. 1955. *Абазинский язык. Грамматический очерк наречия тапанта.* Москва: Издательство академии наук СССР.

—— 1998. *Абхазско-русский словарь.* Сухум: Алашапра.

Гецадзе, И. О. 1979. *Очерки по синтаксису абхазского языка (синхронно-диахронная характеристи-ка).* Ленинград: Наука.

Джонуа, Б. Г., Киут, А. Н. 2003. *Самоучитель абхазского языка. I.* Сухум.

Дыбо, В. А. 1981. *Славянская акцентология. Опыт реконструкции системы акцентных парадигм в праславянском.* Москва: Наука.

—— 1998. Балто-славянская акцентная система с типологической точки зрения и проблема реконструкции индоевропейского акцента. *Балто-славянские исследования. 1997.* Москва. 119–205.

—— 2000. *Морфонологизованные парадигматические акцентные системы: типология и генезис.* том I. Москва: Языки русской культуры.

Касландзия, В. А. (ed.) 2005. *Абхазско-русский словарь.* т. I, т. II. Сухум: ОЛМА-ПРЕСС.

Климов, Г. А. 1973. *Очерк общей теории эргативности.* Москва: Наука.

—— 1983. *Принципы контенсивной типологии.* Москва: Наука.

—— 1986. *Введение в кавказское языкознание.* Москва: Наука.

Клычев, Р. Н., Чкадуа, Л. П. 1999. Абхазский язык. In *Языки мира. Кавказские языки.* Москва: Academia. 113–131.

Ломтатидзе, К. В. 1942. Категория переходности в абхазском глаголе. Изв. ИЯИМК. т. XII. Тбилиси. (резюме, 27–29.)

—— 1967. Абхазский язык. In *Языки народов СССР. 4. Иберийско-кавказские языки.* Москва: Наука. 101–122.

—— 1976a. Категория потенциалиса (возможности) в картвельских и абхазско-адыгских языках. *Ежегодник иберийско-кавказского языкознания.* III.

—— 1976b. Категория версии в картвельских и абхазско-адыгских языках. *Ежегодник иберийско-кавказского языкознания.* III.

Марр. Н. 1926. *Абхазско-русский словарь. Пособие к лекциям и в исследовательской работе.* Ленинград: Издание академии абхазского языка и литературы.

Начḱьебиа-ҧха, С. М. 1988. *Аҧсуа бызшәа аомографқуа ржәар.* Аḱуа: Алашара.

Усларъ, П. К. 1887. *Этнографія Кавказа. Языкознаніе. Абхазскій языкъ.* Тифлисъ.

Цвенария-Абрамишвили, А., Члаидзе И. (ed.) 2003. *Фольклор народов кавказа. Абхазский фольклор.* 2003. Тбилиси: Кавказский дом.

Циколиа, М. М. 1974. *Порядок слов в абхазском языке.* Академия наук грузинской ССР. Тбилиси: Институт языкознания.

Чкадуа, Л. П. 1970. *Система времен и основных модальных образований в абхазско-абазинских диалектах.* Тбилиси: Мецниереба.

Шакрыл, К. С., Конджария, В. Х. (ed.) 1986. *Словарь абхазского языка. (Аҧсуа бызшәа ажәа).* т. 1. Сухуми: Алашара.

Шакрыл, К. С., Конджария, В. Х. Чкадуа, Л. П. (ed.) 1987. *Словарь абхазского языка. (Аҧсуа бызшәа ажәа).* т. 2. Сухуми: Алашара.

Шинкуба, А. Ш. 2003. *Интенсивный курс абхазского языка.* Сухум: Типография АГУ.

Яковлев, Н. Ф. 2006. *Грамматика абхазского литературного языка.* Сухум: Академия наук Абзазии Абхазский институт гуманитарных исследований им. Д. И. Гулиа.

Texts

Ашуба, Н. К., Ажиба, А. Ш. 1997. *Аҧсуа бызшәа тәым бызшәак еиҧш (апрограммеи арҵагеи).* Аҟәа: Алашара.

Зыхуба, С. (ed.) 1997. *Аҧсуа лакуқуа*. Аҟуа: Алашара.

Салаҟаиа, Ш. Хь. (ed.) 1975. *Аҧсуа жәлар рҿаҧыцтә рҿиамҭа. Ахрестоматиа.* Аҟуа: Қарҭ.

Index

【著者紹介】

柳沢 民雄（やなぎさわ たみお）

〈略歴〉
1953 年生まれ。長野県出身。
名古屋大学大学院博士後期課程退学。
名古屋大学大学院国際言語文化研究科教授。

〈主な著書〉
Analytic Dictionary of Abkhaz.（ひつじ書房、2010 年）

A Grammar of Abkhaz

発行	2013 年 2 月 14 日　初版 1 刷
定価	28000 円＋税
著者	© 柳沢民雄
発行者	松本 功
印刷所	株式会社 ディグ
製本所	株式会社 中條製本工場
発行所	株式会社 ひつじ書房
	〒 112-0011 東京都文京区千石 2-1-2　大和ビル 2F
	Tel.03-5319-4916 Fax.03-5319-4917
	郵便振替 00120-8-142852
	toiawase@hituzi.co.jp　http://www.hituzi.co.jp

ISBN 978-4-89476-635-8　C3087